The Old Latin Manuscripts of the Gospel of Luke

Arbeiten zur neutestamentlichen Textforschung

Herausgegeben im Auftrag des
Instituts für Neutestamentliche Textforschung
der Westfälischen Wilhelms-Universität Münster

von Holger Strutwolf und David C. Parker

Band 55

The Old Latin Manuscripts of the Gospel of Luke

A New Edition of the Codex Vercellensis Luke
Based on Multi-Spectral Images

Edited by
Annette Weissenrieder

in cooperation with
André Luiz Visinoni

DE GRUYTER

ISBN 978-3-11-113821-3
e-ISBN (PDF) 978-3-11-114253-1
ISSN 0570-5509

Library of Congress Control Number: 2023946999

Bibliographic information published by the Deutsche Nationalbibliothek
The Deutsche Nationalbibliothek lists this publication in the Deutsche Nationalbibliografie; detailed bibliographic data are available on the Internet at http://dnb.dnb.de.

Druck und Bindung: CPI books GmbH, Leck

www.degruyter.com

Dilectis collegis Almae Matris Hallensis
Stefan Schorch et Frank Ueberschaer

Acknowledgments

This volume could not have been completed so expeditiously without the help of many friends and colleagues. First and foremost, my heartfelt gratitude goes to André Luiz Visinoni, whose contributions to the edition (Chapter 7) were substantial and indispensable. Special thanks are also due to Prof. Dr. Gregory Heyworth, Rochester University, for the expert support he lent me in paleographic and codicological matters, which we discussed in numerous WebEx sessions. Dr. Timoty Leonardi, director of Biblioteca Capitolare di Verona, and Silvia Faccin, director of the Fondazione Museo del Tesoro del Duomo e Archivio Capitolare Vercelli, lent me their expertise on books and binding in antiquity, and Prof. Dr. Winfried Rudolf, Professor of Medieval English Language and Literature and founder of the Vercelli School of Medieval European Palaeography (VSMEP). Librarian Dr. Cornel Dora, Dr. Philip Lenz and Dr. Andreas Nievergelt of the Abbey Library of St. Gall critical appraised many aspects of the project and very helpfully responded to my questions concerning the *Fragmenta Sangallensia*. Dr. Georg Gäbel, Prof. Dr. Hugh Houghton, Prof. Dr. Matthias Perkams, Dr. David Trobisch, Prof. Dr. Beate Fricke, and Cornelius Volk (doctoral student, University of Vienna) gave me important advice during the early writing stages. In addition, I would like to thank the Working Group on the Vetus Latina Beuron, and especially Prof. Dr. Dr. Thomas J. Bauer, the Early Christian Workshop at the University of Chicago, especially Prof. Dr. Margaret Mitchell and Prof. Dr. David Martinez, as well as the Textual Criticism Section of SNTS 2021, where I was able to present and discuss our results with Prof. Dr. Brengt Nongbri, Prof. Dr. Martin Karrer, Prof. Dr. Christina Kreinecker, and Prof. Dr. Ferdinand Prostmeier, among others.

I am grateful to the Fondazione Museo del Tesoro del Duomo e Archivio Capitolare Vercelli and Silvia Faccin as well as to the Bischöfliche Archive in Chur (Switzerland) and Dr. Albert Fischer who granted permission to reproduce images of the Codex Vercellensis and the Fragmenta Curiensia in the book. This edition was made using the Classical Text Editor software developed by Stefan Hagel (Österreichische Akademie derWissenschaften, Vienna), who generously provided excellent support.

My heartfelt gratitude goes to Kosta Gligorijevic (doctoral student in philosophy, McGill University) for translating and proofreading the manuscript. I also thank Donate Wagner, Clarissa Patrizia Paul, and Lucas Froemberg (Halle) for their assistance in creating the index.

I sincerely thank the editors of this series, Prof. Dr. Strutwolf and Prof. Dr. David Parker, for their continued encouragement and inclusion in the series, as well as for the helpful suggestions we received while finalizing the book. I would also like to take this opportunity to thank Dr. Albrecht Döhnert, Florian Ruppen-

https://doi.org/10.1515/9783111142531-201

stein, and Antonia Pohl of the publishing house De Gruyter for supervising the publication of the volume with great reliability and kindness.

I owe the greatest thanks to my colleagues at the Department of Biblical Studies of the Martin Luther University Halle-Wittenberg, who have accompanied the transcription, edition, and commentary with great dedication over the past years, with special thanks due to my esteemed colleagues from the Department of Biblical Studies, Stefan Schorch and Frank Ueberschaer. This book is dedicated to them, in gratitude for the innumerable conversations concerning the multilingualism of ancient and early medieval textual cultures.

Annette Weissenrieder Halle/Saale, June 2023

Contents

Acknowledgments — VII

Index of Manuscripts — XIII

Abbreviations and Symbols — XXV

Preface — 1

1 The Manuscript of the *Codex Vercellensis* — 7
1.1 Introduction — **7**
1.2 Current State — **8**
1.3 Codicological Description — **9**
1.4 Paleographical Description — **12**
1.5 Paratextual Description — **17**

2 Previous Editions and New Insights on the *Codex Vercellensis* — 23
2.1 Giovanni Andrea Irico (1748) and Giuseppe Bianchini (1749/1845) — **23**
2.2 Johannes Belsheim (1894) — **27**
2.3 Francis Aidan Gasquet (1914) — **28**
2.4 Adolf Jülicher (1938), Walther Matzkow (1938–1954), and Kurt Aland (²1963–1971) — **34**
2.5 Corrections of Previous Editions — **37**
2.6 List of Readings in Previous Editions along with New Insights Gained from MSI-images — **51**

3 The Relation of the *Codex Vercellensis* Luke to the Greek Texts — 63
3.1 The Greek Layer of the *Codex Vercellensis* and the Papyri — **64**
3.1.1 Conflation of Greek Readings: Variation in Word Order in the *Codex Vercellensis* and the Papyri — **65**
3.1.2 Omissions in the *Codex Vercellensis* and the Papyri — **65**
3.1.3 Conflation of Syntax in the *Codex Vercellensis* and the Papyri — **67**
3.2 The Greek Layer of the *Codex Vercellensis* and the Majuscules — **68**
3.3 The Greek Layer of the *Codex Vercellensis* in Comparison with the *Codex Bezae* (D, 05) — **69**
3.3.1 Conflation of Greek Readings: Variation in Word Order in the *Codex Vercellensis* and the *Codex Bezae* (D, 05) — **73**
3.3.2 Omissions in the Text of *Bezae* Compared with the *Vercellensis* — **75**

3.3.3 Additions in the *Codex Bezae* and the *Codex Vercellensis* — **76**
3.3.4 Conflation of Syntax in the *Codex Bezae* (D, 05) and the *Codex Vercellensis* — **78**
3.3.5 Differences of Wording in the *Codex Bezae* and the *Codex Vercellensis* — **79**
3.4 The Old Latin Versions as a Source for the Text of the *Codex Corithedianus* (Θ, 038) — **81**
3.5 Conclusion: The Relation of the *Codex Vercellensis* to the Greek Texts — **86**

4 The Relation of the *Codex Vercellensis* Luke to the Latin Versions — 87
4.1 The Relationship between the *Codex Vercellensis* (VL3) and the *Codex Palatinus* (VL2) — **88**
4.1.1 Conflation of Phonetics and Syntax — **88**
4.1.2 Conflation of Semantics: A Christian Nomenclature? — **93**
4.2 The Relation of the *Codex Vercellensis* (VL3) to the *Fragmenta Curiensia* (VL16) — **116**
4.3 The Relation of the *Codex Vercellensis* (VL3) to the *Codex Bezae* (VL5) — **122**
4.3.1 Conflation of Greek Word Order — **124**
4.3.2 Conflation of the Syntax — **130**
4.3.3 Conflation of Semantics — **142**
4.4 The Relation of the *Codex Vercellensis* (VL3) to the *Codex Veronensis* (VL4) — **162**
4.4.1 Conflation with Greek — **164**
4.4.2 Conflation of Syntax — **166**
4.4.3 Conflation of Semantics — **170**
4.5 The Relation of the *Codex Vercellensis* (VL3) and the Codex Amiatinus (A) — **179**
4.5.1 Conflation of Greek Readings — **180**
4.5.2 Conflation of Semantics: A Christian Nomenclature? — **188**
4.6 Conclusion: The Relation of the *Codex Vercellensis* Luke to the Latin Versions — **193**

5 The Language of the *Codex Vercellensis* (VL3) Luke — 195
5.1 Phonetics and Orthography — **200**
5.1.1 Phoneme Inventory — **200**
5.1.2 Diphthongs — **203**
5.1.3 Consonants — **204**

5.1.4 Spelling of Hebrew and Greek Words — **209**
5.2 Morphology — **214**
5.2.1 Word Formation — **214**
5.2.2 Allocation to Noun Declension Classes — **215**
5.2.3 Verb Conjugation — **219**
5.3 Syntax — **224**
5.3.1 The Application of the Cases — **225**
5.3.2 The Use of Pronouns — **229**
5.3.3 Verbal Syntax in the *Codex Vercellensis* Luke — **241**
5.4 Latin Vocabulary Expansion: Semantics — **245**
5.4.1 Older Readings in the *Codex Vercellensis* — **245**
5.4.2 Contextual Sensitivity — **247**
5.4.3 Rare Terms and Poetical Expressions — **249**
5.4.4 Calques and Graecisms — **254**
5.4.5 Technical Vocabulary — **261**
5.4.6 Religious and Cultic Terms — **276**
5.5 Conclusion: The Translation Techniques of the *Codex Vercellensis* Luke — **281**

6 *Codex Vercellensis* Luke: Transcription — 307

7 *Codex Vercellensis* Luke: Edition — 507

Bibliography — 625

Index Locorum — 649

Index Rerum — 677

Index Verborum Latinorum — 683

Index of Manuscripts

We here discuss only the manuscripts of the Gospel of Luke central to this book; the texts of the Church Fathers are listed separately in the chapters.

Siglum	VL	
a	3	*Vercellensis*, 4th century Vercelli, Biblioteca e Archivio Capitolare, s. n. Order of the Gospels: Matthew, John, Luke, Mark lacunae: Luke 11:12–26; 12:37–59 The manuscript – probably the oldest surviving manuscript of the Latin Bible – has been traditionally attributed to Eusebius, the Bishop of Vercelli († 371). The state of preservation is very poor, to the point of fragmentary, since the codex was often used in swearing oaths. The literature usually posits proximity to the *Fragmenta Curiensia* (a[2], VL16) and the *Codex Sangallensis* (n, o, VL16).[1] In our view, the proximity to the *Codex Sangallensis* is of minor significance. G. A. Irico, Sacrosanctus Evangeliorum Codex Sancti Eusebii Vercellensis, Milano 1748; J. Belsheim, Codex Vercellensis, Christiana 1897 (not recommended); A. Gasquet, Codex Vercellensis, 2 vol. (Collectanea Biblica Latina 3), Rome 1914.
A		*Amiatinus*, around 700 Florence, BML, Amiatino 1 Order of the Gospels: Matthew, Mark, Luke, John The *Codex Amiatinus* was probably copied in Naples in the sixth century and is presumably later than the *Codex Sangallensis* (Σ 1395). Chapman[2] shows that Victor of Papua (around 546) used chapter titles found in the *Amiatinus*, though this thesis has been criticized.[3] The *Amiatinus* itself is characterized by *capitula* which precede each gospel. In addition, there is a list of liturgical commemorations, elaborated by texts from the respective biblical books. The readings of the *Codex Amiatinus* often do not coincide with the Vulgate. Thus, the list of special readings shared by the *Amiatinus* and the *Vercellensis*, found in chapter IV, is especially noteworthy. D. J. Chapman, Notes on the Early History of the Vulgate Gospels, Oxford 1908; B. Fischer, Codex Amiatinus and Cassiodor, BibZ 6 (1962), 57–79; idem, Die lateinischen Evangelien bis zum 10. Jahrhundert I. Varianten zu Matthäus, AGLB 15, Freiburg 1989; H.A.G. Houghton, Chapter Divisions, Capitula Lists, and the Old Latin

1 This thesis is espoused by the majority of researchers, including BAUER, Vetus Latina – Lukasevangelium, 1; BURTON, The Old Latin Gospels, 21; HOUGHTON, The Latin New Testament, 211; GAMPER ET AL., Die Vetus Latina-Fragmente, 28; GRYSON, Altlateinische Handschriften, 23 and more often.
2 CHAPMAN, Notes on the Early History of the Vulgate Gospels, 90–93.
3 HOUGHTON, "The Text of the Gospels on the Codex Amiatinus," 78.

https://doi.org/10.1515/9783111142531-202

Versions of John, RB 212 (2011), 316–356; idem, "The Text of the Gospels in the Codex Amiatinus," in: All Roads Lead to Rome. The Creation, Context and Transmission of the Codex Amiatinus, ed. J. Hawkes et al., Turnhout 2019.

ar 61 *Ardmachanus* (*Book of Armagh*), 9th century
Dublin, Trinity College Library, MS 52
Order of the Gospels: Matthew, Mark, Luke, John
Parchment manuscript with alternating white and purple pages. Gold, silver, black, and red letters, often illuminated; copied in Ireland.
Unlike in Acts, where the text contains echoes of Old Latin readings, the text of Luke is based on the Vulgate and offers a "Celtic mixed text" (shared with μ VL35; r^2 VL28; λ VL44)[4]; however, in some passages the manuscript exhibits peculiar spelling, such as *hyerusalem* for Jerusalem (13:22). In several passages, the codex shows proximity to VL35 and VL29 (*ipsi iudices uestri erunt* 11:19; *possedet* 11:21; *collegit* 13:23, 30), as well as to VL30 (*diuissum* 11:17; *belzebub* 11:15,18) and VL27 (13:25, 28). It is striking that Luke is preceded by a prologue along with a list of Hebrew names, while Matthew, described as a *novum opus*, is preceded by *capitula* for all the Gospels.

Th. J. Bauer, "Das fragmentum Rosenthal λ (44) als Zeuge der Vetus Latina des Lukasevangeliums. Edition, Rekonstruktion und Einordnung," in: Traditio et translatio, Freiburg 2016, 135–198; J. Gwynn, Liber Ardmachanus: The Book of Armagh, Dublin 1913; E. Gwynn, Book of Armagh. The Patrician Documents, Facsimiles in Collotype of Irish Manuscripts, Dublin 1937; M. McNamara, Studies on the Text of Early Irish Latin Gospels (A.D. 600–1200), Steenbrugge-Drodrecht 1990.

e-Codex: https://digitalcollections.tcd.ie/content/26/pdf/26.pdf

aur 15 *Aureus Holmiensis*, 8th century
Stockholm, Kungliga Biblioteket, A 135
Order of the Gospels: Matthew, Mark, Luke, John
lacuna: Luke 21:8–30
Parchment manuscript in uncial script with alternating white and purple pages; gold, silver, black, and red letters, often illuminated; copied in southern England, probably around 775[5] in the monastery of Echternach, founded in 698 by the English monk Willibrord, to which numerous copies of the Gospels can be traced.
In the first half of the Gospel of Luke, the codex transmits readings of the European text type; in the second half, however, the text approaches the Vulgate and also contains Jerome's preface to the Vulgate.
In addition to special readings, such as *belsebul* (11:19; 11:18: *belszebub*), *destribuet* (11:22), *quippent* (11:28) or *opportuit* (13:16), similarities with VL 15, 27, 29, 30, 51, 54 can be discerned (11:12: *porriget*; 11:13: *spiritum bonum*; 11:14: *et admiratae sunt*

4 More recently, Thomas Bauer, in his essay on the Rosenthal fragment, has argued against this attribution of λ 44 to the Celtic mixed text.
5 Houghton, The Latin New Testament, 80.

turbae), and also with VL10, 15, 27, 30 (11:27: *lactaverunt*). The latter should be interpreted as following the Vulgate text. Furthermore, there is a proximity to the *Codex Moliensis* (μ, VL35), such as the reading *de caelo querebant* (11:16), where classical and new spellings of Latin are juxtaposed.

J. Belsheim, Codex Aureus sive quattuor evangelia ante Hieronymum latine translata, Oslo 1878; R. Gameson, The Codex Aureus: An Eigth-Cenuty Gospel Book, Copenhagen 2002.

b 4 *Veronensis*, 5th century
Verona, Biblioteca Capitolare, VI
Order of the Gospels: Matthew, John, Luke, Mark
lacuna: Luke 19:26–21:9
The first page of each Gospel is written in golden letters, the rest in silver; the marginal apparatus of Eusebius is also written in silver and golden letters; some abbreviations are of interest, such as the letters "M" and "N" or *dix(it)*, written above the line, sometimes further marked by a dot below the letter.
The codex is considered the main witness for the Italian text of the Gospel of Luke, which Jerome used as his model in the revision of the Vulgate, and which probably used by Lucifer of Cagliari (no evidence for a^2,VL16; especially close relationship in the Gospel of Luke), Ambrose, and Ambrosiaster.[6] The *Codex Veronensis* is connected with the *Codex Corbeiensis* (ff^2, VL8), *Codex Vindobonensis* (i, VL17), *Codex Rehdigeranus* (l, VL11), *Codex Monacensis* (q, VL13) and the *Codex Usserianus* (r^1, VL14) by numerous common readings, such as *ipsi iudices erunt vestri* (11:19), *ea quae possidet* (11:21), *colligit* (11:23), *loca quae non habent aquam* (11:24). In 1:1 *conati sunt*; 1:6 *iustificationibus*; 1:15 *coram domino*; 1:17 *ante illum*; 1:22 *quod*; 1:27 *domino* instead of *deo*; 1:72 *ad faciendam*; 1:77 *plebi*; 2:3 *singuli*; 2:15 *transeamus*; 2:26 *nisi prius*; 3:14 *concutiatis*; 3:18 *cum corriperetur*; 4:6 *ait*; 4:14 *uniuersam*; 5:12 *procidens*; 5:18 *portantes*; 5:33 *obsecrationes*; 6:18 *sanarentur*; 12:32 *pusillus grex*; 22:2 *uero*; reads with VL8 and A. In 13:16 the *Codex Veronensis* (b, VL4) reads *inclinare*, together with the Vulgate, the verb used by Caelius Aurelianus and Cassius Dio in describing epileptic seizures. In a few passages, such as 13:33, VL3, 4, 5, and 16 attempt to imitate the δεῖ – ἐνδέχεται construction of the Greek text. The Gospel of Luke as a whole is thought to have some proximity to Jerome's Vulgate, but this is not the case in the parts of the text discussed here.

E. S. Buchanan, *The Four Gospels from the Codex Veronensis (b)* (Old Latin Biblical Texts 6), Oxford 1911.

c 6 *Colbertinus*, 12th century
Paris, Bibliothèque Nationale de France, latin 254 (Colb. 4051)
Order of the manuscript: Matthew, Mark, Luke, John

6 Gryson, Altlateinische Handschriften, 24.

Black ink with coloured ornaments and illustrations; each Gospel is introduced with a prologue and *capitula* and numbered in the marginalia based on the apparatus of Eusebius.
Numerous passages show older 'Afra' readings, such as in 11:14, where ἦν is translated with the perfect of the copula *esse* (also VL16). Some special readings found in c, VL6 are shared with a^2, VL16 such as *scitis* in 11:13 or *facultates eius* in 11:21. Particularly striking is 11:14; here only four Latin manuscripts (VL5, 6, 10, 16) attest to a longer version, extending the scenic introduction in v.14 and tracing the exposition of the exorcism from the parallel tradition. In a few places, moreover, a relationship with VL8 can be discerned, so that the European text is more prominent here, as can be seen in the resolution of the Latin diphthong in 11:14 *demonium* (VL6, 8, 13, 20, 45, 51, 61; see, for example 11:13: *bonum datum* VL4, 5, 6, 8). Additionally, according to Gryson, one finds a "gallische Deckschicht" shared with the *Codex Usserianus* (r^1,VL14), but this is not present in the *Vercellensis* Luke.[7]

J. Belsheim, Codex Colbertinus Parisiensis: Qvatuor Evangelia ante Hieronymum latine translata post editionem Petri Sabatier cum ipso códice collatam, Christiana, 1888; J. Vogels, Evangelium Colbertinum, 2Bde. (Bonner Biblische Beiträge 4-5), Bonn 1953.

e-Codex: Bibl. nat. de France, Dép. des manuscrits, Lat. 254

d 5 *Bezae Cantabrigiensis*, 4th–5th century
Cambridge, University Library, Nn. II. 41
Order of the Gospels: Matthew, John, Luke, Mark
The first three lines of each Gospel are written in red ink; copied about 400, possibly in Berytus.
The Latin text was initially corrected, resulting in bilingual additions; a later hand then adds entried in Greek only, such as content notes and liturgical references, including Eusebian section numbers. The codex closely resembles the *Codex Vercellensis* (a, VL3), the *Codex Palatinus* (e, VL2) and the *Fragmenta Curiensia.*

D.C. Parker, Codex Bezae. An Early Manuscript and its Text, Cambridge 1991; F. H. A. Scrivener, Bezae Codex Cantabrigiensis, Cambridge 1864; R.C. Stone, The Language of the Latin Text of Codex Bezae, Urbana, 2009; J.-M. Auwers, "Le Texte Latin des Évangiles dans le Codex de Bèze," in: D.C. Parker, C.B. Amphoux, Codex Bezae. Studies from the Lunel Colloquium, June 1994, Leiden 1996, 183–216.

e-Codex: Cambridge University Library, MS Nn.2.41

δ 27 *Sangallensis 48*, 9th century
St. Gall, Stiftsbibliothek, Cod. Sang. 48
Order of the Gospels: Matthew, Mark, Luke, John
Greek-Latin bilingual manuscript with interlinear Latin reading; parchment with black letters; the manuscript contains the name Godescalc in the marginalia, as

7 GRYSON, Altlateinische Handschriften, 27; see also FISCHER, Beiträge, 200f.

well as an abbreviation for Sedulius. The Latin text is based on the vg^{oe} (11:12: *porriget*; 11:19: *si autem*; 13:21: *sata tria*). In many places, the grammar conspicuously follows the Greek text because of the interlinear alignment. The Gospels are preceded by a poem by Hilary of Poitier on the Gospels, along with tables of contents of the Gospels, a preface, and *capitula* before Matthew (f. 15ff.). Most overlapping readings for the chapters examined here are shared with *Codex Colbertinus* (c, VL6), as for example *alii autem* (11:16), *ipse dixit* (11:28), with the *Codex Bezae* (d, VL5), such as *numquid* (11:12) and *similabo* (13:18). Some readings are encountered in South Umbria as well, such as *in se ipso* (11:17 aur, VL15) and also in Ireland, for example *belzebub* (11:19 ar, VL61), *contra* and *ubi* (11:23; 13:28 d, VL5).

H. C. M. Rettig, Antiquissimus quatuor evangeliorum canonicorum Codex Sangallensis, Graeco-Latinus interlinearis, Zürich 1836; J. R. Rendel, The Codex Sangallensis (Δ). A Study in the Text of the Old Latin Gospels, Cambridge, 1891; B. Bischoff, Zur Rekonstruktion des Sangallensis (Σ) und der Vorlage seiner Marginalien, *Biblica* 22 (1941) 147–158.

e 2 *Palatinus*, 4th century
Trient, Museo Nazionale (Castello del Buonconsiglio), 1589; a copy of the codex is preserved in the Bibliotheca Vallicelliana U. 66.
Order of the Gospels: Matthew, John, Luke, Mark
Purple parchment manuscript with silver and gold letters; of the Gospel of Luke, only 1:1–8:29; 8:49–11:3; 11:25–24:53 are extant. Houghton, referring to Augustine's *De doctrina*, points out that the highlighted first letters of each column are indicative of ancient book production.[8]
With regard to codicology, it appears that the manuscript is somewhat later than the *Codex Vercellensis* yet earlier than the *Fragmenta Curiensia*. The text is based on an 'Afra' base layer which shows proximity to Cyprian; proximity to the 'Afra' text type of the *Codex Colbertinus* (c, VL6) and *Fragmentum Carinthianum* (β, VL26) should also be emphasized. In addition to this 'Afra' basic layer, Thomas Bauer and Bonifatius Fischer posit a European layer assigned to the *Codex Corbeiensis secundus* (ff^2, VL8; especially 22:39–24:11);[9] this thesis, however, cannot be confirmed for the chapters studied in our edition of the Gospel of Luke.[10] Instead, readings shared with VL3, a and VL16, a^2 are found, especially in the common 13th chapter, such as *adsimilabo* (13:18, 20), *dixit* instead of *ait* (13:23), *operari* (13:26 VL5), *illic* (13:27), *oculorum* (13:28 VL16$^{corr.}$), *uulpi huic* (13:32). Some similarities with the *Codex Bezae* are also present (see, for example 13:17: *haec dicente eo* om.; 13:19:

8 Houghton, The Latin New Testament, 43–44.

9 Gryson, Altlateinische Handschriften, 21; Fischer, Beiträge, 198–201.

10 Bauer, Vetus Latina – Lukasevangelium – Literatur, 6; Fischer, Das Neue Testament in Lateinischer Sprache, 32–33; no classification offered in Houghton, The Latin New Testament, 210–211.

volatilia; 13:25: *ex quo*).[11] In the Synoptic Gospels, some readings agree with *De physicis* of Marius Victorinus.

C. Tischendorf, Evangelium Palatinum ineditum, Leipzig 1847; H. J. Vogels, Evangelium Palatinum: Studien zur ältesten Geschichte der lateinischen Evangelienübersetzungen, Münster 1926.

f 10 *Brixianus*, 6th century
Brescia, Biblioteca civica Queriniana, s. n. (‚Evangelario purpureo')
Order of the Gospels: Matthew, John, Luke, Mark
Manuscript from the sixth century on purple parchment with golden letters in the first three lines of each gospel, then followed by silver letters; the liturgical numberings of Eusebius are found in the left margin; the *praefatio Sanctus Petrus apostolus* precedes the gospels and discusses the translations of the biblical texts with examples from Greek, Latin and Gothic.
The manuscript is a Latin-Gothic bilingue, the text of which is most closely related to the Vulgate (such as in 11:12, 13, 14, 16, 17, 19).[12]

J. Wordsworth, H. J. White, Novum Testamentum Latine, Oxford 1889.

ff² 8 *Corbeiensis secundus*, 5th century
Paris, Bibliothèque Nationale de France, latin 17225 (Corb. 195)
Order of the gospels: Matthew, John, Luke, Mark
lacunae: Lk 9:48–10,20; 11:45–12:6.
A distinctive feature of the Gospel of is the anti-Marcionite preface that follows the *capitula*; the first line of each Gospel is written in red letters and numbered in the marginalia.[13]
The *Codex Corbeiensis secundus* is typically used in conjunction with the *Codex Veronensis* (b, VL4; here, for example 11:13: *bonum datum*; 11:15, 18, 19: *belzebul*; 11:20: *sed si* with VL8, 17; 11:24: *loca quae non habent aquam*; 11:25: *et ornatam* with VL4, 17; 11:26: *peior prioris* with VL4, 17; 11:28: *ad eos* with VL4, 17) and the *Codex Vindobonensis* (i, VL17; see here 11:14: *dum eicit*; 11:15, 18: *principem*; 11:20: *profecto prouenit*). Together, these are taken as representative of the Italian text, the main type of European text.[14] 8 17: 11:2 *pater sancte*; 13:27 *nescio unde sitis*; 18:8 *uicdictam*; 18:13 *propitiare*; 18:31 *iherosolima*; 22:6 *murmurauerunt;* 22:20 *reposita in sudario*; 19:29 *bethaniae*; 19:44 *super*; 22:7 *cum futura erunt*; 22:11 *et temptates*; 22:23 *quae ubera dant*; 22:25 *benigni*. Gryson also sees an "eindeutige" affinity with *Codex*

---

11 See already Mizzi, "The African Element in the Latin Text of Mt. XXIV of Cod. Cantabrigiensis," 33–66.

12 Gryson, Altlateinische Handschriften, 32; Fischer, Beiträge, 206.

13 Cf. Vezin, "Les divisions du texte dans les Évangiles," 53–68.

14 Cf. Bauer, "Vetus Latina – Lukasevangelium – Literatur," 7; Fischer, Das Neue Testament in Lateinischer Sprache, 34–36; Gryson, Altlateinische Handschriften, 31–32. Houghton, The Latin New Testament, 214 characterizes it as an Italian text of the late fourth century, which is quite close to the type of text on which Jerome based his revision.

Colbertinus (c, VL6), though this is not relevant to the present edition.[15] Vulgate readings are found throughout, but especially in 11:12, 13, 16, 21, 27.

J. Belsheim, Codex f^2 Corbeiensis siue quattuor euangelia ante Hieronymum latine translata, Christiana 1887; E. S. Buchanan, The Four Gospels from the Codex Corbeiensis (ff^2) (Old Latin Biblical Texts 5), Oxford 1907.

e-Codex: Bibliothèque nationale de France, Lat. 17225

g^1 7 *Sangermanensis primus*, 8th century
Paris, Bibliothèque Nationale de France, latin 11553
Order of the gospels: Matthew, Mark, Luke, John
The Gospel of Matthew offers an Old Latin base layer, the other Gospels likely followed the Vulgate, though admittedly also including Old Latin readings; *capitula* have survived for all four Gospels; the manuscript is written in a minuscule and was copied in the ninth century (probably 810) in St-Germain-des-Prés on parchment with black letters and a few ornaments. Especially in the marginalia we find abbreviations of letters such as ⁊, the so-called Tironian *et*, and ÷ for *est.*
Some Old Latin readings are found, especially in the Gospel of Luke, which should likely be attributed to the core group of the Italian text type, including the *Codex Veronensis* or the *Codex Corbeiensis secundus*. Some readings point to the Vulgate, admittedly with an impact on Old Latin manuscripts, such as *et admiratae sunt turbae* (11:14) or *ipsi iudices uestri erunt* (11:19).

Pierre Sabatier, Bibliorum Sacrorum Latinae Versiones Antiquae seu Vetus Italica. Tomus Tertius. Reims 1743 = Brepols 1976.

e-Codex: Bibl.nat. de France, Départ. des manuscrits, Lat. 11553.

g^2 29 *Sangermanensis secundus*, 10th century
Paris, Bibliothèque Nationale de France, latin 13169
Order of the Gospels: Matthew, Mark, Luke, John
Parchment with black letters and colorful illuminations; copied in Brittany in the 10th century. In a Carolingian minuscule script, but with capitals in Matt1:18 and Luke 1:5; the Gospels are preceded by *Novum opus, Sciendum etiam, Plures fuisse, argumentum* and *capitula* for the Gospel of Matthew. These are missing for the other Gospels, although space has been reserved for this purpose; chapter- and pericope-divisions and markings are present in the marginalia.
The text is often associated with a group of Gospels to which the Oxford Vulgate assigns the siglum DELQR: the *Liber Ardmachanus* (ar, 61), the Egerton Evangelien (vg^{oe}E; 609 British Library), the Liechfield Evangelien (vg^{oe}L), the *Cenannensis* (vg^{o}Q) and the Rushworth/Mac Regol Evangelien (vg^{Oe}R).[16] These share characteristics of Irish orthography, such as *bt* for *pt.* The text is mixed with insular characteristics. In addition, there are numerous Vulgate readings, such as *spiritum bonum*

15 GRYSON, Altlateinische Handschriften, 31.
16 HORTON, The earliest Gospels, 100; BERGER, Histoire de la Vulgate, 48.

(11:13), *beelzebub* (11:15, 18, 19), *erant* (13:30). Readings which first appear in the *Fragmenta Curiensia* and were then incorporated into the Vulgate from the early Italian text are also present, such as *daemonium* (11:14), *dicitis … eicere* (11:18).

Pierre Sabatier, Bibliorum Sacrorum Latinae Versiones Antiquae seu Vetus Italica. Tomus Tertius. Reims 1743 = Turnhout 1976.

e-Codex: Bibl.nat. de France, Départ. Des manuscrits, Lat. 13169.

gat 30 *Gatianus*, 8th century
Paris, Bibliothèque Nationale de France, nouv. Acq. Latin 1587
Order of the Gospels: Matthew, Mark, Luke, John
Copied in Brittany about 800 in a Celtic semi-uncial script on parchment with black letters and yellow and red ornamentation; the apparatus of Eusebius is found in the marginalia in red and white letters.
The text is mixed but clearly tends toward the Vulgate (see 11:14: *et admiratae sunt turbae*; 11:22: *aufert*). Nevertheless, some readings are shared with the *Codex Bezae*, such as 20:26 *responsione*; 22:22 *filius hominis traditur.*
The codex has some readings in common with the *Codex Ardmachanus* (ar, VL61) and the *Codex Aureus Holmiensis* (aur, VL15), as well as with the *Codex Amiatinus* (21:30 *similiter et secundus*; 22:8 *appropinquauit*). These commonalities may go back to the Egerton Gospels, but this cannot be proven (see 11:15: *belzebub*; 11:16: *diuissum*; 11:18, 19: *belzebub*; 13:18: *aestimabo*; 13,19: *missit*). Special readings can be found, including, for example, in 21:23 *praessura magna super terra*; 21:34 *grauetur cor uestrum*; 22:6 *paschae in quo necesse erat immolari pascha*; 22:31 *simoni petro*; 22:47 *appropinquauit*.
There are also two readings otherwise known from the *Fragmenta Curiensia*, as *in principe* (11:15), *aduersus* (11:23).

Pierre Sabatier, Bibliorum Sacrorum Latinae Versiones Antiquae seu Vetus Italica. Tomus Tertius. Reims 1743 = Turnhout 1976. J.M. Heer, Evanghelium Gatianum, Freiburg 1910.

e-Codex: Bibl.nat. de France, Départ. des manuscrits, NAL 1587.

gig 51 *Gigas*, 13th century
Stockholm, Kungliga Biblioteket, A 148
Order of the Gospels: Matthew, Mark, Luke, John
A large format manuscript in a Carolingian minuscule with numerous abbreviations and other decorative elements and illuminations; the codex has become famous because of an illustration of the devil on leaf 289r; copied probably in the Benedictine monastery of Podlažice in Bohemia. In addition to writings by Isidore of Seville and Flavius Josephus, the manuscript contains the entire text of the Bible, largely according to the Vulgate. Nevertheless, several variants typical of early Latin translations are found in Luke, such as *omnes turbe stupuerunt* (11:14; *admiratae sunt turbae* vg), *quidam autem ex phariseis dixerunt* (11:15; *ex eis* vg), *quod si ego in beelzebub eicio* (11:19; *si autem ego in beelzebub eicio* vg), *et qui non colligit mecum spargit* (11:23; *dispergit* vg), *ambulat per loca quae non habent aquam* (11:24; *perambulat per loca inaquosa* vg), *per angustum ostium* (13:24; per *angustam*

portam vg) or *recumbent in regno dei* (13:29; *accumbent in regno dei* vg). These variants show close correspondence with the late European text, such as with the *Codex Veronensis* (b, VL4), the *Codex Corbeiensis secundus* (ff^2, VL8) and the *Codex Vindobonensis* (i, VL17).

Acts and Revelation only: J. Belsheim, Apostlarnes Gjerninger og Aabenbaringen i gammel latinsk Oversættelse efter det store Haandskrift „Gigas librorum“ i det kgl. Bibliothek i Stockholm, Oslo 1879.

h 12 *Codex Claromontanus*, 7th century
Vatikan; Biblioteca Apostolica Vaticana, Vatic. Lat 7223
Order of the Gospels: Matthew, John, Mark, Luke
Uncial script on parchment with black letters; only the Gospel of Matthew is based on an Old Latin text belonging to the early Italian tradition and preceding the Vulgate[17]; the manuscript of the Gospel of Luke is based on a Vulgate text and is considered here only when the manuscript suggests a special reading which may be interpreted as an Old Latin reading.

J. Belsheim, Evangelium secundum Mattheum ante Hieronymum latine translatum e codice olim Claromontano nunc Vaticano, Christiana 1892. F. Crawford Burkitt, On Codex Claromontanus (h), JThS 4 (1903) 587–588.

i 17 *Vindobonensis*, 5th century
Naples, Biblioteca Nazionale, lat. 3
Probable order of the Gospels: Matthew, John, Luke, Mark
Purple parchment with silver letters and golden nomina sacra; copied at the end of the fifth century; of the Gospel of Luke, only 10:6–14:22; 14:29–16:4; 16:11–23:10 are preserved.
The text is old Latin and belongs to the core group of the Italian text type, along with the *Codex Veronensis* b, VL4 (see e.g. 10:20: *subiecti sunt*; 11:13: *bonum datum*; 11:18: *in principem*; 11:20: *sed si*; 11:26: *peior prioris*; 12:10 *eis*; 12:28 *modicae*; 13:17: *praeclariis*; 15:15 *uilla sua*; 17:2 *imponatur*; 19:7 *deuertit*) and the *Codex Corbeiensis secundus* ff^2, VL8 (10:31 *sacerdo autem*; 11:12: *porrigit*; 11:14: *dum eicit*; 11:15: *phariseis*; 11:18: *dicitis quoniam ... eicio*; 11:20: *profecto prouenit*; 19:6 *murmurauerunt*; 19:17: *serue bone*; 20:9 *hanc parabolam*; 21:6 *hic in parietem*; 21:7 *cum futura erunt*; 21:11: *et tempestas*; 22:25 *benigni*). Some of its readings are first attested in the *Fragmenta Curiensia* (11:14: *fuit*; 11:15.18.19: *beelzebul*; 11:19: *quod si* a^2 f ff^2 i q l r^1 gig: 11:24: *immundus*; 11:26: *inhabitant*; 13:24: *ostium*).

J. Belsheim, Codex Vindobonensis membraneus purpureus, Leipzig 1885; J. Bick, Wiener Palimpseste, I. Teil: Cod. Palat. Vindobonensis 16, olim Bobbiensis, Wien 1908.

l 11 *Rehdigeranus*, 8th century
Berlin, Staatsbibliothek Preußischer Kulturbesitz, Depot Breslau 5

---

17 Houghton, The Latin New Testament, 46.

Order of the Gospels: Matthew, Mark, Luke, John
Parchment with black letters; lacuna in Luke 11:28–37; copied in the early eighth century in northern Italy; chapter numbers throughout in the left margin; before the Gospel of Luke there is a prologue as well as *capitula*. The text is especially significant as a representative of the Old Latin text of Luke with an impact on the core group of Italian text manuscripts from the fourth century, but especially the *Codex Veronensis* (b, VL4; 11:15: *pharisaeis*; 11,18: *belzebul*; 11:26: *ingressus*) and the *Codex Corbeiensis secundus* (ff^{2}, VL8; 11:13: *bonum datum*; 11:19: *fili*; 11:19: *ipsi iudices erunt uestri*; 11:23: *spargit*; 11,24: *loca quae non habent aquam*). Bauer also suspects an influence of the *Codex Monacensis* (q, VL13; 13:17: *praeclaris quae uiderant fieri*), which can only be found once in the present text. In addition, here again we find readings that first appear in *Fragmenta Curiensia* (11:11: *piscem*; 11:12: *porrigit*; 11:14: *illut*; 11:14: *fuit*; 11:15: *beelzebul*; 11:23: *aduersus*; 13:24: *poterint*).

H. J. Vogels, Codex Rehdigeranus: Die vier Evangelien nach der lateinischen Handschrift R 169 der Stadtbibliothek Breslau (Collectanea Biblica Latina 2), Rome 1913.

μ 35 *Liber Moliensis* (*Book of Mulling*), 8th century
Dublin, Trinity College, MS 60
Order of the Gospels: Matthew, Mark, Luke, John
Parchment with black letters.
The text is based on an Irish text type, but it reveals an Old Latin base layer in Luke 4-9. A blueprint of Tech-Moling Abbey (St Mullin) is added at the end of the Gospels.
In addition to some Old Latin and European readings, for which the *Codex Veronensis* (b, VL4) and the *Codex Corbeiensis secundus* (ff^{2}, VL8) are basic (see, for example 11:14: *demonium*; 11:25: *et ornatam*; 11:28: *ad eos*; 13:18: *estimabo*), there are numerous Vulgate readings, as well as readings which connect the codex with the *Codex Aureus Holmiensis* (aur, VL15) and the *Codex Ardmachanus* (ar, VL61; 11:12: *porreget*; 11:13: *bona*; 11:15: *fariseis*; 11:20: *si autem*; 11:21: *possedet*; 11:23: *collegit*; 13,30: *erant*). These similarities may go back to the Egerton Gospels, but this cannot be proven.

P. Doyle, The Text of Luke's Gospel in the Book of Mulling, *PRIA 73* (1972): 177–200.

e-Codex: MS 40618 British Library; edition of some sections can be found in Hugh Jackson Lawlor, Chapters of the Book of Mulling, Edinburgh 1897.

p 54 *Perpinianensis*, 12th century
Paris, Bibliothèque nationale de France, latin 321
Order of the Gospels: Matthew, Mark, Luke, John
Minuscule manuscript copied in the second half of the 12th century on parchment with black letters. The text is mixed with close proximity to the Vulgate, but some readings date back to the fifth century (vg 11:15.18.19: *beelzebub*). A number of readings attest to the monophthongization of the classical diphthong, such as 11:13.16: *celo* or 11:14: *demonium*.
The manuscript is listed in the Vetus Latina catalog and is thus also included here.

e-Codex: Bibl. nat. de France, Dép. des manuscrits, Lat. 321.

q 13 *Monacensis*, 6th century
Munich, Bayerische Staatsbibliothek, Clm 6224
Order of the Gospels: Matthew, John, Luke, Mark
Parchment manuscript with black letters and colorful illuminations; two lacunae in Luke 23:23–35 and 24:11–39; presence of lectionaries in cursive script, only inserted in the seventh century in northern Italy.[18] The *Codex Monacensis* is based on an Old Latin text layer of the European type, resembling the *Codex Veronensis* (b, 4), as may be shown by numerous passages such as 11:18: *dicitis quoniam ... eicio*; 11:18: *in principem*; 11:25: *et ornatam*; 11,28: *ad eos* or also 13:25: *ex quo*. According to Fischer and Bauer, the manuscript is representative of the European text together with the *Codex Rehdigeranus* (l, VL11); some passages in chapters 11 and 13 may support this interpretation (11:15, 18, 19: *beelzebul*; 11:16: *alii autem*; 11:23: *aduersus*; 11:23: *spargit*; 13:17: *praeclaris quae uiderant fieri*; 13:25: *estis*). The manuscript also shows similarities with the *Codex Corbeiensis* (ff^2, VL8) and the *Codex Colbertinus* (c, VL6), as can be seen, for example, in the 11:16 reading *celo* and in the 11:16 reading *querebant*.

H. J. White, The Four Gospels from the Munich Ms. Q, now numbered Lat. 6224 in the Royal Library at Munich (Old Latin Biblical texts 3), Oxford 1888.

e-Codex: Evangeliar (Codex Valerianus) – BSB Clm 6224

r^1 14 *Usserianus primus*, 6th or 7th century
Dublin, Trinity College, MS 55
Order of the Gospels: Matthew, John, Luke, Mark
Parchment with black letters in an Irish semi-uncial script; characterized by the list of Hebrew names before the Gospel of Luke; the marginalia are not preserved, so that one cannot detect the Eusebian apparatus with certainty; the Gospels are subdivided according to chapters, and the first line is written, here as elsewhere, in colored letters; the Gospel of Luke begins with κατά and not secundum. The text is based on the Old Latin *Codex Veronensis* (b, VL4); shared readings are found, for example, in 11:11: *porrigit ei*; 11:13: *bonum datum*; 11:17: *cadit*; 11:18: *dicitis quoniam ... eicio*; 11:15, 18, 19: *belzebul*; 11:18: *in principem*; 11:24: *loca quae non habent aquam*.[19]
At the same time, in some special readings, the manuscript resembles the Gallo-Irish group. According to Bauer, the presence of a European text type cover layer comparable to the *Codex Carinthianum* (β, VL26) may be detected.
Moreover, the proximity to the text of the *Codex Vercellensis* and the *Fragmenta Curiensia* is remarkable; this is especially evident from readings that are preserved only in these two text types, such as 11:13: *cum eiceret*; 11:15: *illis*; 11:22: *illius*; 11:26:

18 Cf. Bruyne, Notes sur le manuscrit 6224 de Munich, 75–80.
19 Fischer, "Das Neue Testament in Lateinischer Sprache," 82; Gryson, Altlateinische Handschriften, 37.

intrantes.[20] Some readings also survive in other manuscripts with an Old Latin base layer, such as 11:12: *porrigit*; 11:13: *daemonium*; 11:21: *domum suam*; 13:24: *ostium*; 13:29: *discumbent* VL 3, 10, 14, 16. In addition, readings of the Vulgate text tradition are present, especially in chapter 11 (11:20: *profecto praeuenit*).[21]

T. K. Abbott, Evangeliorum versio antehieronymiana ex codice Usseriano (Dublinensi) adiecta collatione codicis Usseriani alterius, Dublin 1884.

e-Codex: Dublin, Trinity College – IE TCD MS 55

20 This observation is usually missing from survey works published thus far.
21 This pattern of resemblances has also gone unnoticed in the survey works.

Abbreviations and Symbols

]	single square bracket in the apparatus: separates the reading present in the text from the readings of other Old Latin manuscripts
< … >	*addendum*, encloses letters or words that have been added by the editors
{…}	*delendum*, encloses letters or words that should be deleted
[…]	encloses letters or words that have been lost through damage to the parchment
[[…]]	encloses letters or words that have been deleted by the ancient scribe
† … †	*locus sesperatus*, encloses words that are corrupt
ạ	a dot below a letter marks faint traces of ink whose reading is uncertain
ȧ	*expunctum* (dot above a letter) marks letters corrected by the scribe
a.r.	*ante rasuram* (written before an erasure)
lac.	marks a *lacuna* in the manuscript
ras.	*sub rasura*, marks text which has been scraped off in the manuscript
om.	*omittit*, marks letter, words or verses which are missing in the manuscript
VL	Vetus Latina

https://doi.org/10.1515/9783111142531-203

Abbreviations and Symbols

Preface

The present study has its origin in two kinds of intellectual curiosity.

One kind of curiosity concerned the possibility of reading a manuscript which has been multi-spectrally imaged and processed using Raman Spectrocopy. Dating most likely to the end of the first half of the fourth century, the *Codex Vercellensis* is a paginated (rather than foliated) manuscript consisting of 634 pages, with two columns to the page, preserved as disbound bifolia in the Archivio Capitolare di Vercelli. Many of the leaves have suffered irreparable damage ranging from the decay of the centers of the bifolia (leaving intact only the head and a corona of individual letters along parts of the margins) to the deterioration of the page as a whole, resulting in the fading of the text. In light of the state of the manuscript, one is justified in asking whether a fresh interpretation of its text is at all possible. This question is made all the more acute by the existence of 18th century editions made while the manuscript was still in a better condition.

In 2014, the *Codex Vercellensis* was imaged multi-spectrally in its entirety by the Lazarus Project with the collaboration of the early Manuscript Electronic Library (EMEL), a team of scientists and scholars headed by Prof. Dr. Gregory Heyworth of the University of Rochester. The team, consisting of imaging scientists Dr. Roger Easton (Rochester Institute of Technology), Dr. Keith Knox and Ken Boydston (Megavision Ltd.), as well as Michael Phelps (EMEL), Heyworth, and students from the University of Mississippi, deployed a portable MSI imaging system in the Archivio Capitolare di Vercelli. Functioning in three modes – reflectance, fluorescence, and transmission – the system was equipped with narrow-band sets of LEDs in 12 wavelengths ranging from the UV at 365nm to the near infrared at 940nm. Furthermore, the system incorporated the then-unique transmissive illuminating sheet designed to project light through the leaves from below and operating in four bands, green (535nm), red (635), and two varieties of infrared (870 and 940nm). All 318 bifolia were captured in a total of 30 bands (including fluorescence) per side, at a resolution of 700 ppi, producing a set of multispectral images along with highly accurate 8-band colour images. These were subsequently processed by Keith Knox and Roger Easton using deterministic and statistical algorithms.

We owe the new (special) readings of the manuscript almost entirely to these multi-spectral images. The findings may be illustrated using Luke 11:11–12 (420b) as an example:

https://doi.org/10.1515/9783111142531-001

Figure 1: UV-image

Figure 2: TX-image

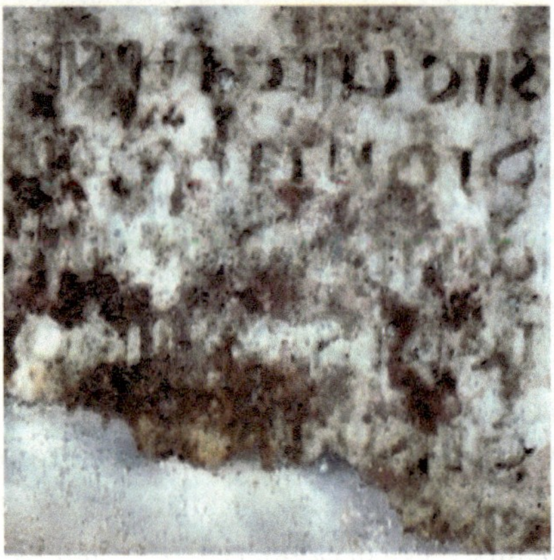

Figure 3: VIS-image

A visit to Vercelli also provided the opportunity to compare the manuscript with the existing MSI-images, which in turn allowed us to verify the results gained from new, multi-spectral images. In this context, we were also able to detect further readings. While this initial imaging, along with the autopsy of the handwriting, proved exceedingly helpful, a second round of investigations subsequently performed was less fruitful. In accessing manuscripts other than the *Codex Vercellensis*, we have relied on the digitized copies available to us. The one exception was the *Codex Veronensis* (b, VL4), whose digitized copies are not particularly useful; in this case, we resorted to the old edition by Edgar Simmons Buchanan, The Four Gospels from the *Codex Veronensis* (Oxford 1911).[1]

In 2007, a team of Italian scientists led by Maurizio Aceto of the University of Eastern Piedmont performed material analysis on the inks and pigments of the *Codex Vercellensis* using Raman Spectroscopy and X-ray fluorescence (XRF). The objective was to identify the type and number of inks and pigments used, which would in turn help verify the primary character of an earlier hand present in the majority of the manuscripts from what were suspected to be one or more later interpolations.

Raman Spectroscopy exploits the fact that light refracts off and is absorbed by various substances in a pattern of wavelengths chemically unique to that substance or compound. In this process, light emitted from a high intensity laser refracts off ink or pigment, a portion of which produces a spectral fingerprint measurable by a spectrophotometer, which in turn detects a chemical histogram that can be matched to histograms of known substances. This technique is used especially for organic compounds such as inks and dyes made from plants. The XRF technique, on the other hand, uses X-rays to cause materials to fluoresce in a unique pattern of wavelengths. Unlike Raman Spectoscropy, XRF is especially useful for measuring the amounts of various types of metals, including those occurring in ink (e.g., iron, copper, zinc), as well as those found in parchment (calcium). When used for material analysis, both methods measure individual points or a series of points. Having taken Raman and XRF measurements on several folios, Aceto confirmed that the primary ink of the *Codex Vercellensis* is iron gall; the ink used on pages 1–2 and 634–635, however, turned out to be different, namely iron gall mixed with carbon, and to resemble the marginalia found on several leaves. The red pigment, meanwhile, could be distinguished into two types, cinnabar and minium.[2] Unfortunately, the result is not very helpful, since the difference between the first and last pages from the rest of the manuscript is immediately visible based on the writing, which likely belongs to the fifth century. In this context, closer focus on the paratexts would certainly have been helpful, as would the study random samples taken from different places in the Gospels conducted to verify that the ink is indeed always of the same consistency.

At the same time, our study was equally driven by another kind of curiosity, namely the interest in investigating the character of the Latin used in the *Codex Vercellensis* Gospel of Luke. Already in our work on the *Fragmenta Curiensia*, we

1 The MSI-images to be produced under the direction of Winfried Rudolf and Alexander J. Zawacki and to be edited by Annette Weissenrieder are of great importance.

2 See Aceto et al., "The Vercelli Gospels laid open," 286–292.

were perplexed by the dissonance which emerged as we worked on the text: while the secondary literature unanimously and emphatically advances a particular theory of the textual history of the *Codex Vercellensis*, very little evidence in support of this theory is given, and the scholarship falls far short of that dedicated to, for instance, the *Codex Palatinus.* Again and again, one reads that the text of the *Codex Vercellensis* Gospel of Luke exhibits an "Italian influence" and that the Latin text of *Codex Bezae* may be classified as "zwischen dem *Codex Palatinus* und dem *Codex Vercellensis.*"[3] How should we imagine the process of translation into Latin? On the face of it, the first Latin Bible translations are found in references made by Tertullian and Cyprian, both from Carthage, in the Roman province of Africa. Others continued their work in the next two centuries, and numerous sources show that biblical books were already available in Latin at this time, being used in churches for worship or read in the houses of church members. As Christianity spread throughout the Roman Empire, translations into Latin gained more ground, first in North Africa and then in Italy, as it is evident from the works of Cyprian, who corresponded with Roman clergy, and especially with the presbyter Novatian, whose biblical references in turn resemble the *Codex Vercellensis.*[4] This project was also continued by Marius Victorinus, Fortunatianus, bishop of Aquileia, Hilary, bishop of Poitiers, and Augustine of Hippo, the author of *De doctrina Christiana*, which describes biblical texts in Latin using the term *Itala.*[5] Investigations of word use and method of translation conducted in the 19th century[6] were able to identify two primary groups of the Old Latin Bible texts, an 'African' or 'Afra' text type and an 'European' text type.[7] However, recent research has demonstrated that the period during which Latin translations began to spread around the Christian world was long enough to allow many mutual influences and various interactions between the different traditions, so that it is difficult to achieve a rigid classification of the text families. This is especially true when we consider some manuscripts, such as the *Codex Palatinus* (e, VL2), which follows the 'Afra' recension also discernible in John

3 BAUER, "Der Codex Bezae und der lateinische Text der lukanischen Cantica," 108; see also HOUGHTON, The Latin New Testament, 211; GRYSON, altlateinische Handschriften 1, 23.

4 MATTEI, "Recherches sur la Bible à Rome vers le milieu du IIIe siècle," 255–279.

5 Aug. *De doctrina Christiana* 2.15.22: *in ipsis autem interpretationibus, Itala ceteris praeferatur; nam est uerborum tenacior cum perspicuitate sententiae.* On the term *Itala*, see BURTON, "The Latin Version of the New Testament," 168; HOUGHTON, The Latin New Testament, 15.

6 VON SODEN, Das lateinische Neue Testament in Afrika zur Zeit Cyprians; SANDAY, Studia Biblica, 234–239.

7 The terms 'Afra' and 'European' text are very misleading but are still standard in the literature on the Old Latin Bible.

Cyprian,[8] or the *Codex Brixianus* (f, VL10) and *Monacensis* (q, VL13), which contain a mixed text often resembling the Vulgate.[9] Despite all this, in the ideal case, a direct comparison between the manuscripts on the one hand and Bible quotations found in the Church Fathers on the other allows us to try and determine the time and place of the translation. The 'Europeanisation' of the text of the Bible might have begun with Cyprian and continued with Hilary of Poitiers and Ambrose of Milan. In our view, whether variations in the texts of both types not attested in the Church Fathers should be taken into account is still an open question. The two textual layers are distinguished by the later use of specifically 'Christian' terms, such as *baptizare*, 'to dip in water' instead of *tingere*, 'to dye, make wet'.[10] The 'Afra' substrate cannot, however, be reconstructed mechanically. One approach to disentangling the 'Afra' from the 'European' text involves taking the Vulgate and other European text forms as the basis of comparison, since later manuscripts, mostly from the sixth century and from several geographic regions, exhibit an amalgam of the 'Afra' and 'European' traditions.[11]

The text of *Codex Vercellensis* itself – despite a few elements it has in common with later Italian texts –transmits several typical 'Afra' readings, that is, older variants reflecting the first attempts at translation. For instance, the manuscript often translates ὅτι with *quoniam* instead of with *quia* or *quod* (a total of 138 cases against 71 in the younger *Codex Veronensis*, normally regarded as a prototype of the "Itala" version). For the adverb ἐκεῖ, it tends to choose *illic* rather than *ibi* (Matt 25:30; Luke 13:2). It renders ἐπισυνάγειν as *colligere* rather than *congregare* (Mark 13:27), θλῖψις as *praessura* (sic) rather than *tribulatio* (Matt 13:24), and πονηρός (adjective) as *nequam* rather than *malus* (Luke 6:45). The list could be extended farther, but we must also note that these earlier, so-called 'Afra' readings coexist with the subsequent 'European' textual variants, and that they are especially frequent in the Gospel of Luke. However, independent of its assessment as 'Afra' or 'European' text, the *Codex Vercellensis* exhibits many peculiarities of spelling, morphology, and syntax which give it a special place in the tradition of early Latin translations of the Bible. Over the course of our study, we will show just how important the manuscript is both for textual criticism of the New Testament and for the history of the Latin language.

---

8 Houghton, The Latin New Testament, 211.

9 Houghton, The Latin New Testament, 211; 216; 218.

10 For further details, see the excellent book by Burton, The Old Latin Gospels.

11 For further examples, see Burton, The Old Latin Gospels.

1 The Manuscript of the *Codex Vercellensis*

1.1 Introduction

The *Codex Vercellensis* (a, VL3) is considered to be the oldest surviving manuscript of the Latin Gospels. Hagiographical accounts from the seventh and eighth century[1] credit its composition to Eusebius († 371), the first bishop of Vercelli in Northern Italy. However, this late tradition has raised some doubts: pious stories about saints tend to exaggerate biographical details, so that there is no factual basis to support the claim that the Gospels of Vercelli were in fact translated by Eusebius.[2] If, however, the translation was indeed made during Eusebius' tenure as bishop of Vercelli, this could have happened either before 355 – the year in which Eusebius was exiled by Emperor Constantius II after refusing to sign the synod of Milan condemnation of Athanasius – or after 361, when Emperor Julian's ascent to the throne allowed Eusebius to return to Vercelli.

The story is further complicated by the fact that we do not find indication of any other manuscripts, originating from Vercelli in this period, which suggests that the codex was not produced in Vercelli.[3] The *Fragmenta Curiensia* (a², VL16) is the only manuscript whose direct dependence to the *Codex Vercellensis* can be proven. Nonetheless, the manuscript is still traceable to the middle of the fourth century, a dating which is also plausible from a paleographical and codicological point of view. While we can be certain that both manuscripts were written in Italy, much else remains unclear. Paleographic and linguistic comparisons with other Old Latin manuscripts reveal a proximity to the *Codices Palatinus* (VL2) and *Bezae* (VL5), the details of which will be discussed in chapter 4.

---

1 Cf. Ughelli, Vita antiqua 4, 754: *Pugnabat autem contra immanissimas bestias Ariomanitas, qui eum expulerunt de ciuitate, persecutione populi contra eum excitata: at ille ne populus in eum peccaret, quos postea delectabatur habere filios, sciens scriptum: Si uos persecuti fuerint in una civitate, fugite in aliam; ultra flumen Padum transiit, et ad castrum quod dicitur Credonensium perveniens, ibi tribus mensibus degens, in honorem B. Dei genitricis construxit Oratorium; ubi etiam adhuc longius degens Euangelium Christi propria manu scripsit; cuius miraculum in eodem codice 4. Euangeliorum, non solum uerbis Christi, sed et eiusdem Patris tanta uirtus coruscat, ut si aliquis seductus a Diabolo, falsum super eum sacramentum fecerit, citius super eum plaga corporis ostenditur; ita ut aut morte mulctetur, aut perditis oculis spirituale, et corporale lumen amittat, aut ariditate membrorum mancus uel claudus efficiatur, aut inuasione Daemonum pene usque ad exitum dilanietur.*

2 For further discussion, see Levine, "Evidence for Calligraphic Activity in Vercelli," 564–567.

3 Cf. Levine, "Evidence for Calligraphic Activity in Vercelli," 561–581.

https://doi.org/10.1515/9783111142531-002

Figure 1.1: Purple blotches on a leave of the manuscript, indicating a fungal infection with aspergillus.

1.2 Current State

By any standards, the *Codex Vercellensis* is in poor condition. The writing is faded throughout, and in many places the iron gall ink has thinned the parchment and chemically degraded to the point of invisibility. On some folios, the vitriol in the ink has etched deeply enough into the substrate to leave a few letters visible in relief, but mostly it has caused parts of the pages to crumble away, leaving various lacunae. Furthermore, the parchment has decayed due to humidity, water stains, and mold, as well as one particularly interesting pathology represented by purple blotches frequently appearing in the margins as well as in the text block. These blemishes are namely indicative of a fungal infection with aspergillus, a fungus most likely transmitted to the parchment by liturgical use and in the swearing of oaths, when people affected by aspergillosis – a lung infection common in those suffering from tuberculosis – touched and kissed the manuscript, leaving traces of sputum which grew in the humid storage conditions;[4] this in turn provides evidence that the *Codex Vercellensis* had the status of a holy relic and was used accordingly.

4 For the pathological condition and its influence on old manuscripts, see POLACHECK ET AL., "Damage to an ancient parchment manuscript by *Aspergillus*," 89–93.

Moreover, there are several missing leaves, three of them from the Gospel of Luke: 11:14–26 (one leaf); 12:38–13:1 (two leaves). Since the page numbers added in the 18th century are continuous, this shows that the leaves were already missing at the time of pagination. It was probably one of these missing folios that Agostino Ferrero, Bishop of Vercelli, presented as a relic of Eusebius to some envoys from Switzerland in 1515.[5] The record mentions two *oratores*, D. Iacobus Cistercien and D. Petrus Ebult de Salus, from the diocese of Lausanne. The patron of the church in Salus was St. Eusebius, and the envoys accordingly expressed a great desire to take back with them one leaf of the Gospels believed to have been written by the saint.

In 1908, Franz Ehrle, the famed conservator at the Vatican Library, took steps to prevent the further decay, disbinding the manuscript and encasing the bifolia in clear gelatin which prevented bacterial and fungal growth and held the fragile leaves together.[6] In 2014, Gregory Heyworth of the Lazarus Project produced multi-spectral images of the complete manuscript, the processed versions of which form the basis of our study.[7] The method used to recover illegible text involves digital photography in multiple wavelengths of light (MSI), both visible and invisible, ranging from the ultraviolet to the infrared. In this case, imaging was conducted using 12 wavelengths, from ultraviolet at 365nm to infrared at 940nm, in three modes – reflectance, fluorescence, and transmission – yielding a set of raw images that enhanced the contrast between the faded text and the parchment. These raw images were then processed by Keith Knox using deterministic models to bring out both faded and invisible text. The result are pseudo-colour images which reveal details of codicological and paleographic interest and allow a new analysis of the manuscript's language and textual peculiarities.

1.3 Codicological Description

The manuscript consists of 634 extant pages, measuring 25.5 cm by 16 cm on average, with the writing occupying an average area of 19.5 by 12 cm. The text is divided into two parallel columns, each with 24 lines. This page layout shares significant similarities with that of the *Fragmenta Sangallensia* (n, o, VL16) and *Curiensia* (a^2,

5 Cf. GARLANDA, "Evangeliario eusebiano," 39. Therefore, not in 1575, as stated in GASQUET, Codex Vercellensis, xiv.

6 Cf. GARLANDA, "Il restauro del Codex Vercellensis Evangeliorum nel primo Novecento," 131–151. For the edition of the text by Gasquet based on the restored parchment, see chap. 2.3.

7 On multispectral imaging of ancient manuscripts, see DAVIES, ZAWACKI, "Making Light Work: Manuscripts and Multispectral Imaging," 183–199.

VL16) whose texts are – to a greater or lesser extent – related to the *Codex Vercellensis*.[8]

Figure 1.2: *Fragmenta Curiensia* (f. 1) and *Codex Vercellensis* (p. 342).

The four Gospels appear in the Western order (Matthew, John, Luke, and Mark), as in other Latin manuscripts of this period,[9] and their titles are written in smaller letters at the top of each page, centered between the columns: on the left-hand page, we read *secundum*, *secund.*, and, in the Gospel of Luke, *sec.*; on the right-hand page, *mattheum*, *iohannen* but also *iohannem*, *lucanum*, and *marcum*. There are a few pages on which the names of the evangelists were abbreviated: in the Gospel of Luke, we find *lucan·* for *lucanum* only on page 327. Another irregularity in the running titles can be observed on page 331, where the scribe wrote *mattheum* instead

8 For a detailed discussion on the relation between the three manuscripts, see WEISSENRIEDER, VISINONI, "Fragmenta Curiensia," 23–30.

9 For example, codices *Palatinus* (VL2), *Veronensis* (VL4) or *Bezae* (VL5).

of *lucanum*. The ink used is dark, though not black, as often claimed,[10] but rather brownish, apart from the first three lines and the excipits of each Gospel, which are written in red.

Figure 1.3: Running title *mattheum* instead of *lucanum* (p. 331).

There are not many corrections of any kind. Letters accidentally left out or insertions of longer text passages are found written in smaller uncials between the lines,[11] in rare instances at the lower margins, with the omission signs *hd* (*hic deorsum* for "here, look downwards") at the place of the missing passage and *hs* (*hic sursum* for "here, look upwards") above the addendum;[12] these signs are typical of early Italian manuscripts and can also be observed in the *Fragmenta Curiensia*. Minor scribal errors which may be ignored are marked by placing a common *expunctum* over the letters[13] or simply by crossing them out;[14] sometimes, both devices are used.[15] In addition, at least two errors were mechanically deleted by scraping the parchment (*rasura*).[16] An interesting indication of the work of later correctors is found at the bottom of page 65 in Matt, where the remark *usque hoc ego esemendaui*, "I have corrected up to here," is written in cursive letters.

10 Cf. HOUGHTON, The Latin New Testament, 211.

11 See, e. g., p. 376^{a}, l. 10–11: *(ec)ce in oculo tuo tra(bes)*.

12 See, e. g., p. 519^{b}: *ardens in uia cum adaperiebat nobis.* Cf. LOWE, "The Oldest Omission Signs in Latin Manuscripts," 36–79.

13 See, e. g., p. 388^{b}, l. 22–23: *interrogabatnt* to *interrogabant*.

14 See, e. g., p. 387^{b}, l. 13: *macdalelne* to *macdalene*.

15 See, e. g., p. 362^{b}, l. 4: *sociis* to *socii*.

16 See p. 456^{a}, l. 15–16: *qui di Dimissam* to *qui dimissam*; p. 453^{a}, l. 17: *amotuos* to *amotus*, even if the unnecessary *o* was also deleted through *expunctum*. In the case of p. 342^{b}, l. 16–17 (*praeprarasti* to *praeparasti*), the images are not clear enough, but the superfluous *r* seems to be a little blurry compared to the surrounding letters.

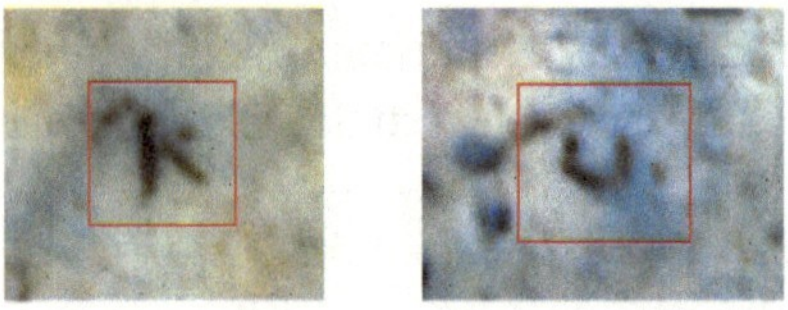

Figure 1.4: Letters for quire signatures in Luke (p. 478) and Mark (p. 632).

As observed by previous editors, the signature of some of the quaternions is still visible.[17] What has been overlooked so far, however, are the letters in front of the usual Roman numbering in the Gospels of Luke and Mark, which were revealed by the MSI-images. The order of these letters – from B (page 356) to M (page 510) in Luke, and from N (page 526) to U (page 632) in Mark – gives evidence for an additional numbering of the quaternions not present in Matt and John. This discovery is remarkable since scholarship on Latin manuscripts has so far assumed that the use of letters for quire signatures only emerged at the end of the fifth century;[18] with the *Codex Vercellensis*, however, we have much earlier evidence for this practice.

1.4 Paleographical Description

The *Codex Vercellensis* exhibits the main paleographic characteristics of Latin manuscripts from the fourth century. The text is written in very regular uncials, left-justified and continuous (*scriptio continua*), with no distinction between majuscules and minuscules; the letters measure 0.5 in breadth by 0.5 to 0.6 cm in height, depending on the extent to which they break the upper and bottom lines. Only a slight prominence of unabridged initials (*ekthesis* and *litterae notabiliores*) projecting into the margin is observed, indicating the beginning of each new sense unit. However, in the Gospel of Luke, we find these initials in the middle of a passage, sometimes even of a sentence, as on page 378[b] (*ipse Aedificabant nobis*), on page 450[a] (*proferte Stolam priorem*), on page 456[a] (*qui Dimissam*) and on page 518[a] (*dicentes Etiam uisionem*). These irregularities are certainly scribal errors, and, in the case of *qui Dimissam*, the mistake was corrected directly in the manuscript.[19] Also typical for Latin manuscripts from this period is the use of *spatia*, which, in the same way as *ekthesis* and *litterae notabiliores*, serve as punctuation marks, though separating

17 In the Gospel of Luke: XXIII, XXV, XXX and XXX[III]. Cf. GASQUET, Codex Vercellensis, xiii.
18 LOWE, "More Facts about Our Oldest Latin Manuscripts," 43–62.
19 Cf. chap. 2, p. 14.

shorter sense units, mostly sentences, from each other. However, the *Codex Vercellensis* exhibits a peculiarity in the use of *spatia*: they are often filled with a colon (:) in the manuscript,[20] and it is not obvious to what extent the colons differ from the regular *spatia*, found at other places in the manuscript.

Another typical feature of the oldest uncial manuscripts is the use of abbreviations and ligatures at the end of a line. In the *Codex Vercellensis*, the nasal consonants *m* and *n* are marked by a transversal stroke with a dot underneath (superline), the dative and ablative plural case marker *-bus* of is shortened to a dot (*notae communes*), whereas *-ae*, *-nt*, *-unt*, *-ur* and *-us* are written as nexus. In the Gospel of Luke, the only irregularity is found on page 389^{a} (8:9), where the ligature *-ae* appears in the middle of the pronoun *haec*.

The *Codex Vercellensis* exhibits an early system of *nomina sacra*, using DM̄S (*dominus*), DM̄I (*domini*), DŌM (*dominum*), DM̄O (*domino*), or DM̄E (*domine*) instead of DÑS, DÑI, DÑM, DÑO or DÑE, which are found in later manuscripts.[21] However, there are some exceptions, all in Matt and John, where the vocative DÑE instead of DM̄E is sometimes used, along with uncommon forms such as DÑUS (Matt 22:44, page 126^{a}) and DOM̄S (John 21:7, page 318^{a}) for the nominative, DÑUM (Matt 22:45, page 126^{a}) and DOÑM (John 21:7, page 318^{a}) for the accusative.

The details of the calligraphy of the *Codex Vercellensis* are currently subject of scientific investigations. While the allographs found in the codex are generally dated to the fifth century, together with the *Fragmenta Curiensia*, and paleographically comparable to the *Codex Veronensis* (VL4), the text of the *Codex Vercellensis* shows similarities with fourth-century manuscripts. In general, the form of the letters is representative of the most finely wrought and elegant uncials, with light weight, symmetrical balance, and artful transitions between hairline and flat-pen strokes. All these features together characterize the earliest form of the script, which in the late fourth century quickly gave way, as Edward Maunde Thompson has argued, to a heavier ductus.[22]

The columns are also exceedingly narrow, often accommodating scarcely more than a single word. As Franca Arduini, Guglielmo Cavallo,[23] and other scholars have shown, this is also a mark of earliest uncial *mise-en-page*. Finally, the *Codex Vercellensis* includes occasional dots between words or at the end of lines, which are

20 See, e. g., p. 379^{a}, l. 16: *et facit: his auditis.*

21 Traube, “Nomina sacra,” 167–193.

22 Thompson, Handbook of Greek and Latin Paleography, 192.

23 Arduini/Cavallo, The Shape of the Book; see also Bischoff and Maniaci, “Pergament – Handschriftenformate – Lagenkonstruktion,” 277–319.

typical of writings preceding the fourth century, and which had largely disappeared by the end of the third century.

Figure 1.5: Dots between words in p. 367b.

Generally speaking, a comparison of the form of the allographs with palimpsests and manuscripts from the fourth and fifth century is most instructive:

(1) The hasta on the "E" is distinctively high, being higher than that found in the fourth-century palimpsest from Cicero's *De re publica* (Cod. Vat. Lat. 5757).[24] Since the "E" descends to the middle of the line in manuscripts dating from the middle of the fifth century and thereafter,[25] this may be taken as a sign of a fourth-century manuscript:

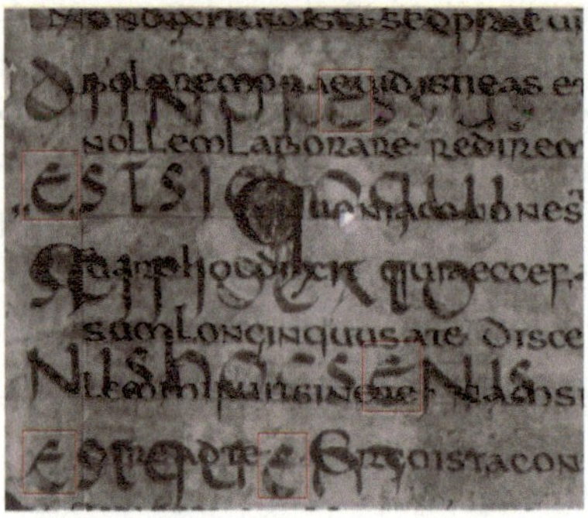

Figure 1.6: Hastas of "E" in Cod. Vat. Lat. 5757.

(2) The "M" consists of two-strokes, beginning with a curved upward stroke and a turning of the pen; this shape is found in the fourth-century Cicero palimpsest,

24 Thompson, "Handbook of Greek and Latin Paleography," 192.

25 See, e. g., the Viennese and Parisian Livius, fifth century, Z.W. Ex. 18,19; Bibli. Nat. lat . 5730; CLA V 562.

and also in North-African manuscripts, in which proto-uncial forms of various letters are seen to compete with each other:[26]

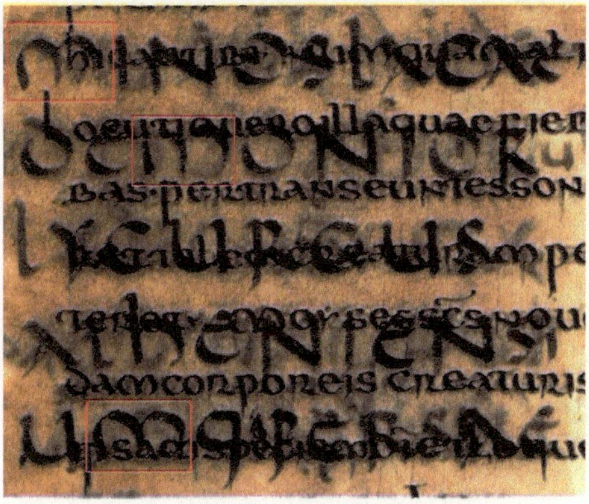

Figure 1.7: Two-stanza "M" in Cod. Vat. Lat. 5757.

(3) The "S" is of narrow girth, with symmetrical upper and lower bows resembling those found in earlier rustic capitals. This form differs from other early examples, including the Cicero palimpsest, and also from the seventh century *Codex Amiatinus*, which has the tendency to widen the letter, making either the upper or the lower bow asymmetrically wider.

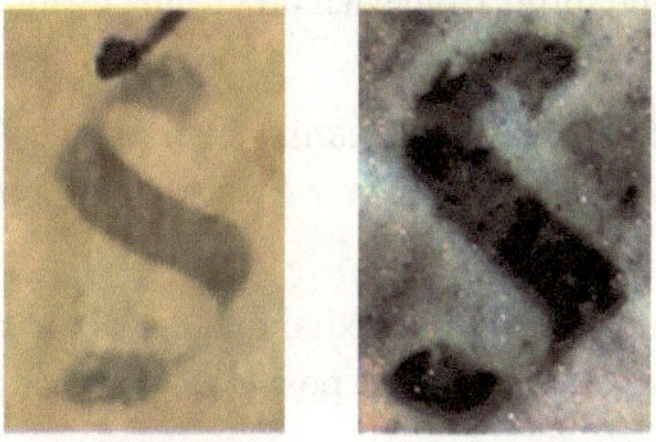

Figure 1.8: Comparison between the "S" in Cod. Vat. Lat. 5757 and in the *Codex Vercellensis.*

(4) The most convincing similarity is the "R", whose long vertical shaft runs far beyond the ligature, while its right shaft runs almost horizontally. This

26 HÜBNER, "Exempla Scripturae Epigraphicae Latinae," 1147f.; WEISSENRIEDER, VISINONI, Fragmenta Curiensia, 19; see also ULLMAN, "Ancient Writing and its Influence," 65.

allograph is an indication of a transitional stage between rustica small capitals and uncials, also seen in the "R" of the third century Latin proto-uncial *Oxyrhynchus 30*, which is morphologically closest to the oldest Latin proto-uncials.

Figure 1.9: P. Oxy. I 30, *De Bellis Macedonicis* by L. Arruntius.

A has an upright, triangular shape, but is distinguished by a loop for the left leg (a shadow stroke and a hair-stroke), which together form a prominent acute angle, not infrequently far below the base-line.

B, in contrast to older Roman cursive script, is two-storey: the upper belly is much smaller and less pronounced than the lower.

C, E and G have almost the same basic shape and differ from each other only by the additional hair-strokes of E and G.

D is round, similar to a cursive δ, but the ascender is straight, leaning over to the left and sometimes ending in a rounded tip; this "hook-like" form is characteristic of the manuscript's *manus prima*.

E consists of a curved stroke and resembles an uncial ε; the medial tongue, a hair-stroke frequently projecting beyond the base, is written in a very high position, an indication of the manuscript's early date.

F is narrow and projects over the base-line; the two horizontal lines are very short and hardly visible at the top.

G projects over the base-line with a long hair-stroke; this cauda is written so finely that it is often barely visible.

H projects over the head-line through the left shaft; the rounded bow on the right is half high and is connected with the vertical shaft by a hair-stroke.

I consists of a single vertical stroke and ends in a hair-stroke to the left; unlike F, the letter only occasionally projects over the base-line.

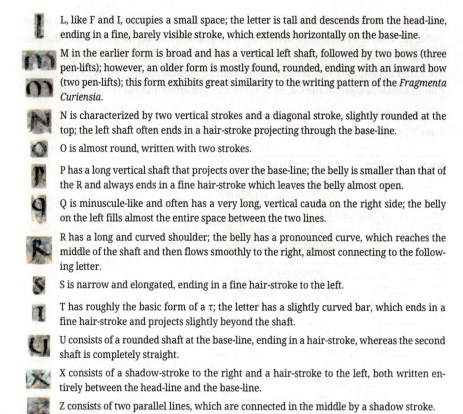

L, like F and I, occupies a small space; the letter is tall and descends from the head-line, ending in a fine, barely visible stroke, which extends horizontally on the base-line.

M in the earlier form is broad and has a vertical left shaft, followed by two bows (three pen-lifts); however, an older form is mostly found, rounded, ending with an inward bow (two pen-lifts); this form exhibits great similarity to the writing pattern of the *Fragmenta Curiensia.*

N is characterized by two vertical strokes and a diagonal stroke, slightly rounded at the top; the left shaft often ends in a hair-stroke projecting through the base-line.

O is almost round, written with two strokes.

P has a long vertical shaft that projects over the base-line; the belly is smaller than that of the R and always ends in a fine hair-stroke which leaves the belly almost open.

Q is minuscule-like and often has a very long, vertical cauda on the right side; the belly on the left fills almost the entire space between the two lines.

R has a long and curved shoulder; the belly has a pronounced curve, which reaches the middle of the shaft and then flows smoothly to the right, almost connecting to the following letter.

S is narrow and elongated, ending in a fine hair-stroke to the left.

T has roughly the basic form of a τ; the letter has a slightly curved bar, which ends in a fine hair-stroke and projects slightly beyond the shaft.

U consists of a rounded shaft at the base-line, ending in a hair-stroke, whereas the second shaft is completely straight.

X consists of a shadow-stroke to the right and a hair-stroke to the left, both written entirely between the head-line and the base-line.

Z consists of two parallel lines, which are connected in the middle by a shadow stroke.

The paleographic evidence, combined with historical and theological considerations, identify the period following Eusebius's accession to the episcopate of Vercelli, between 341 and 350, as the likely time of composition of the *Codex Vercellensis.*

1.5 Paratextual Description

While the *Codex Vercellensis* exhibits none of the characteristic paratexts of fifth century Latin manuscripts, such as chapter titles (*capitula*) or division according to the Eusebian canon, several liturgical notes and signs were added to the margins of the manuscript in the period following its composition. The paleographical character of these additions points to an eighth century Lombardic cursive,[27] which suggests the

27 Cf., e. g. the deed of Grimoaldus IV, Duke of Benevento, of the year 810.

use of the manuscript in church service or for the study of scripture. This date in turn coincides with the emergence of the first accounts attributing the creation of the manuscript to Eusebius. The still visible liturgical notes and signs in the Gospel of Luke are listed below; here it is important to observe that Gasquet's charts of the paratextual material present in the *Codex Vercellensis* are often inaccurate and incomplete:[28]

Table 1: Liturgical notes and signs in the Gospel of Luke.

page	verse	notes and signs
341	2:21	*kalend. i[a]nu[a]r[ii]*
347	3:2	*[do]minica ante natalem* d̅n̅i̅
352	3:38	⳨
372	6:23	⳨
379	7:11	⁜
384	7:36	⁜
388	8:5	*in sexagesima* ⁜
398	9:1	⁜[29]
403	9:23	⳨
410	10:1	⁜
418	11:1	⁜
427	12:4	*in* s̅c̅i̅ *systi*
439	14:1	⁜[30]
440	14:7	*domineca tertia*
446	14:35	*quarta* ⳨
448	15:11	⁜
452	16:1	⁜
456	16:19	*[do]menica secunda*
460	17:8	⳨
466	18:9, 10	*incipit* ⳨ ⁜
472	19:1	⳨
516	24:11	*tercia feria in albis*
516	24:13	⁜
520	24:36	*[se]xta feria in albis*

28 Cf. Gasquet, Codex Vercellensis, xvi–xix. For the other Gospels, see, e. g., the incorrect page references (p. 68 instead of p. 67 in Matt 13:24), the incorrect transcriptions (p. 64 in Matt 13:3: *in sexaghesima* instead of *in sexaginsima*), the questionable additions that are either no longer visible at all or were simply added by the editor (p. 148 in Matt 26:1 the manuscript lacks the ending [*domenica*] *secunda in advent. dni.*) and the omitted notes or attention signs (p. 46 in Matt 10:16: *in sancturum* followed by a cross, p. 49 at the end of Matt 10:33: *finit*, p. 234 in Joh 8:12: ⁜).

29 Overlooked by Gasquet.

30 Overlooked by Gasquet.

Two attention signs can be distinguished. The first one (⳨) is most likely the chi-rho siglum known as *chresimon*, a technical sign present both in ancient papyri and medieval manuscripts.[31] Its graphic form resembles that of *staurograms*, which are employed in the oldest witnesses of the Latin Gospels, such as in the *Codex Bobbiensis* (VL1) and in the *Codex Palatinus* (VL2), as an abbreviation for the various cases of Χριστός. In the Early Middle Ages, the two symbols were conflated, and this is also the case in the *Codex Vercellensis*. The result of this process was a convention in which the *chresima* pointed to passages of theological relevance. This analysis receives strong support from Cassiodorus' tables of technical signs, where *chresima* are used as indices for important doctrines.[32] In light of the list above, we can see which sections of the Gospel of Luke the manuscript readers regarded as especially significant, for instance, the Temptation narrative (Luke 4:1) and the Sermon on the Plain (Luke 6:24).

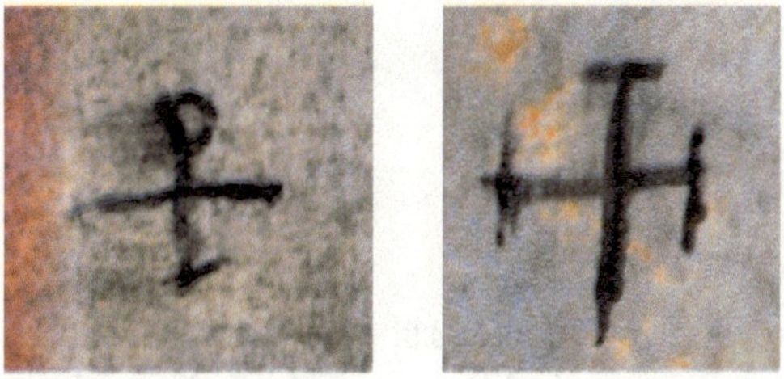

Figure 1.10: *chresimon* on page 472 and cross on page 448.

The second of these signs is the cross, a symbol associated with Christianity. Nevertheless, the origins of the cross as a technical sign are pre-Christian since it is found in first century Greek papyri from Egypt as well. But, just like with the *chresimon*, the Christian connotation certainly contributed to its dissemination in the Early Middle Ages, which lent it a variety of new purposes, for instance as an attention sign, dialogue marker or lesson sign, making it often difficult to determine the sign's exact function.[33] The list above, however, allows us to surmise the meaning of at

---

31 For further discussion on the origins and functions of *chresima*, see STEINOVÁ, "Notam Superponere Studui," 271–272.

32 Cf. CASSIODORUS, *In Psalterium Expositio* (BNF lat. 14491): *diuersas notas more maiorum certis locis aestimabimus effigiendas. has cum explanationibus suis subter adiuncximus. ut quicquid lector uoluerit inquirere per similitudines earum, sine aliqua difficultate debeat inuenire. ⳨ hoc in dogmatibus ualde necessariis.*

33 Cf. STEINOVÁ, "Notam Superponere Studui," 273.

least some of the crosses added to the *Codex Vercellensis* Gospel of Luke. It is noteworthy that many of these mark the beginning of a new chapter, as on pages 398 (9:1), 410 (10:1), 418 (11:1), 439 (14:1) and 452 (16:1), suggesting that the sign was here employed as a text-structuring instrument, and possibly as an alternative to the traditional text divisions, which would become common in later manuscripts. This is also a further indication that the manuscript was used for liturgical reading, as it will be discussed in other chapters.[34]

Figure 1.11: Pictorial formula for the Golgotha mounds (p. 466[a]).

The symbol appearing as a marginal postscript in Luke 18:9f. (466[a]) deserves special attention, especially in light of its potential liturgical function.[35] The Italian paleographers A. Felle and G. Cavallo have made the plausible suggestion that the three circles present a common pictorial formula for the Golgotha mounds and thus refer to the martyrdom of Jesus. We assume that this pictorial formula indicates the Easter Vigil lectionary, which is rightly made in connection with Luke 23:26–49, the execution of Jesus and the two criminals at the place of the skull. It is in this passage that the verb φοβεῖν occurs for the last time in the conversation of the crucified, in which the God-fearing criminal utters the fear in a negated rhetorical question, asking the unbelieving criminal if he does not fear God (οὐδὲ φοβῇ σὺ τὸν θεόν). Thus, the invective directed against Jesus is interpreted as an offense against God. Several Latin witnesses take up this aspect of the verse, translating the question as *non times tu dominum* (VL5, 8), thus departing from the more standard *nec times deum*. *Dominum* is the translation of Kyrios, the central Christological title in the Gospel of Luke, which Martin Buber already identified as a key term in the Gospel. While

34 Cf. chap. 4.1, p. 88.

35 Gamber, "Documenta Liturgiae Italiae," 89 assumes that these liturgical signs belong to the seventh century.

the Greek tradition is consistent in its usage, the *Codex Vercellensis* often alternates between *deus* and *dominus*. This may indicate that the Latin translators no longer saw a significant distinction between the two terms and therefore often chose arbitrarily between them. One also cannot exclude the possibility that the confusion was caused by the similarity of the abbreviations used for *nomina sacra*, e.g., DS (*dominus*), DM̄I (*domini*), DŌM (*dominum*), DM̄O (*domino*), or DM̄E (*domine*), a resemblance not present in the Greek text (e.g., between κς and θς).

Taken together, historical and paratextual evidence, reinforced by damage to the leaves likely due to the codex's use as a relic of St. Eusebius upon which people swore oaths by laying hands on particular passages between the 9th and 12th centuries – a practice that has left palm imprints on the manuscript in several places – makes it plausible that the manuscript was used for liturgical readings.

2 Previous Editions and New Insights on the *Codex Vercellensis*

In what follows, we will compare the previous editions of the manuscript with the new series of MSI-images. Our aim is to work out how the various editions available differ from each other and to identify the ways in which the present edition may offer improvements over its predecessors.

2.1 Giovanni Andrea Irico (1748) and Giuseppe Bianchini (1749/1845)

The first edition of the *Codex Vercellensis* was produced in 1748 by the Italian biblical scholar Giovanni Andrea Irico (*Sacrosanctus Evangeliorum Codex Sancti Eusebii Vercellensis*). This was followed, a year later, by Giuseppe Bianchini's work (*Evangeliarium Quadruplex Latinae Versionis Antiquae seu Veteris Italicae*) which, in addition to the text of the manuscript itself, also provided a transcription of the Old Latin Gospel codices *Veronensis* (VL4) on the facing pages, along with the *Corbeiensis secundus* (VL8) and *Brixianus* (VL10) in the bottom margins; more recently, Bianchini's edition was reproduced in the series *Patrologia Latina* 12.141–338 (*Sancti Eusebii Episcopi Vercellensis Opera Omnia*, 1845).

As stated above, the *Codex Vercellensis* is in poor condition, a fact which was ascertained before the publication of the first editions.[1] Considering that the parchment has deteriorated even further since then and that some passages are now irrecoverably lost, the editions of Irico and Bianchini are of indispensable value.[2] Irico's publication presents some advantages: alongside footnotes providing variants from the Vulgate, Irico offers a transcription of the manuscript, arranging the text line by line, column by column and page by page, and he makes use of majuscules exclusively, which allow for an accurate representation of the original uncial script. Likewise, he attempts to give information on the many paleographic features

1 Cf. 1.2, p. 8f. There are at least two early reports on the precarious conservation state of *Codex Vercellensis*, cf. MABILLON, "Iter Italicum," 9: *Certe membrana situ fere corrupta est, characteres pene fugientes ac semideleti*; MONTFAUCON, Diarium italicum, 444: *Codicem uetustissimum ibidem inspeximus, in charta membranacea tenuissima exaratum. Codex multis in partibus labefactatus putrefactusque est; quod casu, plusquam uetustate, euenisse dictitabant, narrabantque diu in flumine demersum.*

2 In Luke, especially in the first chapters, as in pp. 328–340.

https://doi.org/10.1515/9783111142531-003

of the manuscript, recording *litterae notabiliores*,[3] *ekthesis*[4] and blank spaces[5] within a line – which the scribe employed as punctuation marks – abbreviations, hanging lines and *nomina sacra*;[6] corrections are shown by equivalent *expuncta*, while textual additions are printed in smaller letters where necessary. The result is a layout close to that of the codex itself, which helps the reader localize any particular passage in the transcription and verify it in light of the manuscript. Bianchini, in turn, adds paratextual information, such as verse and chapter numbers, which is an improvement on Irico's edition. Bianchini follows the sequence of lines, but not that of columns and pages. In the same way, none of the various paleographic elements are marked, and abbreviations, hanging lines and *nomina sacra* are all spelled out. In addition, Bianchini uses minuscules throughout the transcription, reserving capital letters for the beginning of each verse and chapter and for the *nomina sacra*, so that it becomes difficult to identify where the scribe used *litterae notabiliores*.

Irico's transcription of the *Codex Vercellensis* had an impact on all subsequent investigations of the manuscript, and later editors were not seldom misguided by its inaccuracies, so that many mistakes found in Irico's transcription have been replicated in later editions. This is particularly true with regard to some scribal errors, such as *hac* instead of *haec* in Luke 7:12 (380[a]), the dittography *quod{d}* in Luke 7:43 (386[a]), and the haplography *pos<t> tertium* in Luke 9:22 (403[a]), just to name a few examples taken from the better-preserved pages. The propagation of such errors suggests that, in many cases, the parchment was not inspected diligently, and that scholars relied heavily on Irico's work instead.

Some of these mistakes reproduced in later editions are especially striking:

3 See, e. g., p. 325[a] (*Quoniam*), Irico, Sacrosanctus Evangeliorum, 630.

4 See, e. g., p. 450[a] (*Stolam*), Irico, Sacrosanctus Evangeliorum, 880.

5 See, e. g., p. 356[a] (*hic et*), Irico, Sacrosanctus Evangeliorum, 692.

6 See, e. g., p. 351[a] ($\overline{\text{sps}}$ for *spiritus*), Irico, Sacrosanctus Evangeliorum, 682; 355[b] (*uisu̅* for *uisum*), Irico, Sacrosanctus Evangeliorum, 691.

Figure 2.1: Luke 4:27 (357[a]).

In Luke 4:27 (357[a]), all editors follow Irico and read *set* (i. e. *sed*) *nullus*, where the manuscript in fact contains the conjunction *et*. It could be argued that the page is now visible only in the TX-images and that the text was probably not fully legible at the time when Irico was working on the parchment; however, *et* is not only the reading of all other manuscripts, but also found in all known Greek *Vorlagen* (καὶ οὐδείς). The Latin witnesses of Luke tend to be consistent in this respect since *sed* is usually the first translational choice to render ἀλλά and, to lesser degree, δέ, but not καί.[7] This means that previous editors made no effort to consult any other witness of the text while producing their transcription, and also that they had complete confidence in Irico's readings.

7 Cf., e. g., Luke 5:14; 6,27; 7,7; 8,16; 9:56; 11:4; 12:7; 13:5; 14:10; 16:21; 17:8; 18:13; 20:21; 21:9; 22:36; 23:55; 24:22 (ἀλλά) and 5:5; 6:44; 9:61; 14:12; 15:30 (δέ).

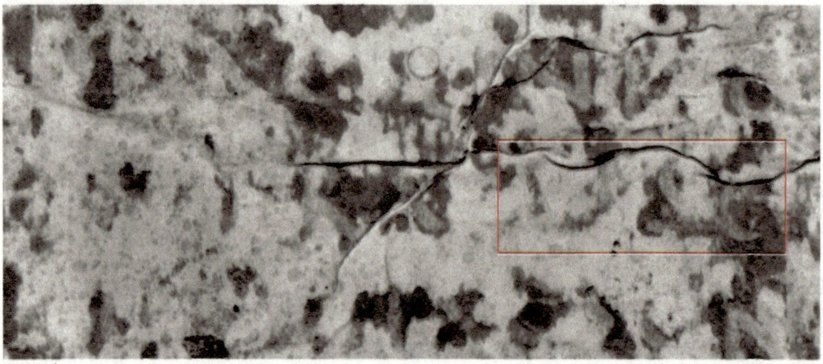

Figure 2.2: Luke 11:35 (423[a]).

A similar problem can be found in Luke 11:35 (423[a]) as well, where Irico offers the grammatically meaningless variant *tenebrae rese* [..]*atae*, later reproduced by all editors as *tenebrae rese* [*qua*]*ntae*. It is true that the passage is quite damaged and challenging to decipher even in the TX-images. However, a simple examination of the other witnesses together with a more careful understanding of the Latin text would have made the identification of the phrase *tenebrae ipse* [*qua*]*ntae* possible. The difficulty seems to have been the trivial orthographical irregularity contained in the manuscript, which has *ipse* for *ipsae*, a typical case of monophthongization.[8] Moreover, the variant agrees with all major Old Latin Gospels witnesses (*tenebrae quantae* VL5; *ipse tenebre quante* VL4) which, in turn, may derive from the text of D, 05 (τὸ σκότος πόσον).

8 Cf. below 5.1.2, p. 203.

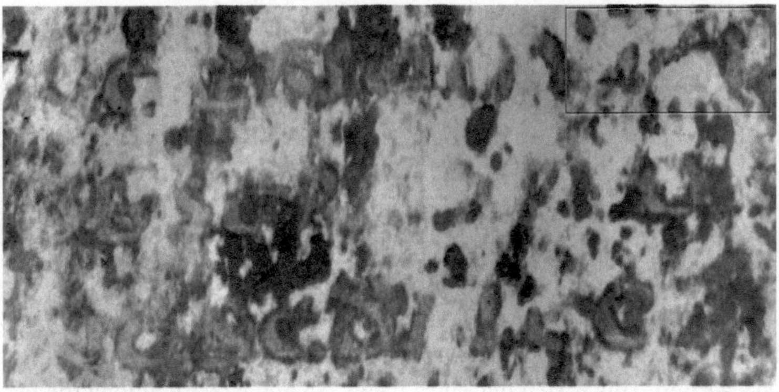

Figure 2.3: Luke 17:20 (462[a]).

One last example will make clear how decisive Irico's transcription was for later editions of the *Codex Vercellensis*. In Luke 17:20 (462[a]), all editors follow Irico's reading of the passage in printing *regnum cum obseruatione*. On this reading, the scribe would have skipped the genitive *dei* after *regnum*, present in all Latin and Greek witnesses (ἡ βασιλεία τοῦ θεοῦ μετὰ παρατηρήσεως). There is indeed an omission here, but the TX-image of the page reveals that what the scribe left out was in fact the preposition *cum*, and not the *nomen sacrum*. One cannot say with certainty if this is a scribal lapse or a kind of translation strategy: the Latin text can still be understood without the preposition since the phrase *regnum dei obseruatione* suggests the use of an instrumental ablative. This interpretation is further corroborated by the absence of any sign of correction or later addition in these lines.

Irico's edition formed the basis of all later editions. For one thing, the manuscript was in a better condition and remained legible in some places where we only have lacunae today. Moreover, the careful textual observation of the autographs preserved in the library of Vercelli makes his edition still worth consulting despite the errors contained therein.

2.2 Johannes Belsheim (1894)

The edition by the Norwegian teacher Johannes Belsheim, who transcribed and edited several Old Latin Gospels manuscripts in the 19th century, requires only brief treatment. As other scholars have observed, Belsheim's texts "have been found unreliable in many places,"[9] and this critical judgement also applies to his work on the *Codex Vercellensis* (*Quatuor Evangelia ante Hieronymum Latine Translata ex Reliquiis Codicis Vercellensis Saeculo ut videtur Quarto scripti et ex Editione Iriciana Principe*). Although Belsheim states that he inspected the manuscript in autumn of 1889, it seems obvious that he only copied Irico's transcription, simply turning it into continuous text and adding verse and chapter numbers, along with punctuation:[10] all imprecisions present in Irico's edition can be found here as well, including some additional blunders and curious oddities. For example, Belsheim incorporates the erroneous conjecture *caepit* instead of *coepit* in Luke 4:21 (355[b]), 18:43 (472[a]) and 20:9 (482[a]), which is certainly wrong and possibly due to a typographical error in Irico's edition. This is striking, since pages 355 and 472 are among the few pages which remain well-preserved even today and which allow a conclusive reading of the text, even with the naked eye. At any rate, Belsheim produced an edition of the *Codex Vercellensis* which omits the important paleographical features of the manuscript, just as Bianchini did before him.

2.3 Francis Aidan Gasquet (1914)

The most cited edition of the *Codex Vercellensis* so far was published at the beginning of the 20th century. It is the work of Francis Aidan Gasquet, an English Benedictine monk and scholar of (ancient) history, later elevated to Cardinal of the Roman Catholic Church (*Codex Vercellensis iamdudum from Irico et Bianchino bis Edutus Denuo cum Manuscripto*, 1914). He was appointed by Pius X[th] as president of the newly established Pontifical Commission for Revision of the Vulgate in 1907, which was entrusted with the task of producing a new edition.[11] It was in this context that Gasquet decided to re-examine the *Vercellensis*. To this end, several restoration measures were carried out on the parchment. The manuscript was sent to the laboratory of the Vatican Apostolic Library under the direction of Cardinal Franz Ehrle in 1908, where it was disbound, divided into bifolia, and mounted in clear gelatin. Each bifolium was then put in a cardboard folder and subsequently placed in three walnut wooden boxes. Furthermore, the guard paper inside the

9 Burton, The Old Latin Gospels, 9. See also Gasquet, Codex Vercellensis, XV, who describes Belsheim's edition of *Codex Vercellensis* as being "of not much value."

10 Except for some trivial modifications, e. g., in 14:4, where Irico misprints *adprhendens*, while Belsheim's edition offers the correct *adprehendens*.

11 Cf. Schelkens, Catholic Theology of Revelation on the Eve of Vatican II, 134.

folders was replaced with anti-acid paper and the folders were distributed among four new cypress wood containers, less subject to attack by parasites.[12]

Thanks to this meticulous restoration of the parchment, Gasquet was able to eliminate many inaccuracies contained in the previous editions. He also added some of the necessary paratextual information which enabled easier navigation of the manuscript, including pagination and divisions by chapter and verse. Gasquet's edition distinguishes between readings no longer visible but presented in the editions by Irico and Bianchini on the one hand and the text supplied by Gasquet himself on the other: the former is indicated by italics, while the latter is marked by italics within square brackets. Suspensions,[13] running titles,[14] and superlines for the nasal consonants "N" and "M" were also marked.[15] A convenient tool of Gasquet's edition is the annotation of the differences between Irico's and Bianchini's readings contained in the footnotes, even though the readings adopted are not always correct. For instance, in Luke 17:16 (461^{b}), Gasquet prints *samaritanus*, the same reading found in Irico's edition. Nonetheless, the manuscript has *samarites* instead, a reading already established by Bianchini. Gasquet seems to have overlooked the discrepancy, or, at least, there is no footnote showing that he was aware of it.[16] The same applies to *fulgul* in Luke 17:24 (462^{b}): Gasquet not only fails to notice the misspelling of the noun, which had been correctly identified by Irico and Bianchini, reading the standard form *fulgur* instead, but also claims in a footnote that Irico prints the same reading. Accordingly, we must note that Gasquet's edition unfortunately does not accurately reproduce the *Codex Vercellensis.*

Equally unfortunate are some careless replications of typographical errors from Irico's transcription. Two examples of these errors may suffice: in Luke 10:27 (415^{b}), Gasquet borrows from Irico the readings *totta* and *tottis* and, in Luke 16:23 (457^{a}), *occulos*. These spellings in fact do seem to have been widespread in Late Antiquity: gemination of consonants after stressed long vowels or diphthongs can be observed as early as the 5th century, when we see them explicitly rejected by the

12 For a detailed description of the restoration of the manuscript, see GARLANDA, "Il restauro del Codex Vercellensis," 132.

13 See, e. g., 377^{b} (*aurib·* for *auribus*), GASQUET, Codex Vercellensis, 41.

14 See, e. g., 326$^{a\text{-}b}$ (*secundum lucanum* for *sec lucanum*), GASQUET, Codex Vercellensis, 2–3. However, Gasquet did not take notice of the wrong running title on p. 331, where the scribe wrote *mattheum* instead of *lucanum.*

15 See, e. g., 445^{b} (*alioquin du̅* for *aliquion dum*), GASQUET, Codex Vercellensis, 94.

16 Cf. GASQUET, Codex Vercellensis, 106.

grammarian Consentius as barbarisms *per adiectionem litterae*;[17] many of these forms would eventually evolve to standard orthography in Romance languages, but, in the Old Latin Gospels witnesses, there is no sign of this development yet. Moreover, Bianchini read the more grammatical spellings *tota, totis* and *oculos* as they are found in the manuscript, a fact which shows the dependence of Gasquet's edition on Irico's transcription.[18]

Figure 2.4: Luke 10:27 (415[b]).

Another shortcoming concerns the recording of a considerable number of paleographical features of the *Vercellensis* Luke, such as *expuncta, rasurae* and additions. There are, for example, many instances where Gasquet's transcription of *litterae notabiliores* and *ekthesis* does not agree with the text of the manuscript: in Luke 7:45 (386[a]), Gasquet reads *osculum* for *Osculum*, in Luke 9:51 (408[b]), *Factum* for *factum*, in Luke 11:40 (423[b]), *nonne* for *Nonne*, in Luke 15:30 (451[b]), *cum* for *Cum*, in Luke 21:5 (489[a]), *et* for *Et*, in Luke 23:49 (513[a]), *stabant* for *Stabant*; in three instances (Luke 9:51; 15:30; 23:49), the error is found in Irico's transcription as well, showing, again, how Gasquet's edition is largely based on it.

17 Cf. Consentius, *Ars de barbarismis et metaplasmis*, 10: *per adiectionem litterae sic fit, ut si quis dicat coperit pro operit, gruit pro ruit, tottum pro toto, cottidie pro cotidie, quamdius pro quamdiu.* See also Väänänen, Introduction au latin vulgaire, 59–60.

18 Surprisingly, Gasquet adopts *oculos* in 6:20 (371[b]), even though Irico reads *occulos* (col. 723, l. 23) in this passage as well.

Figure 2.5: *litterae notabiliores* in Luke 7:45 (386[a]), in Luke 21:5 (489[a]), and in Luke 23:49 (513[a]).

In a similar vein, there is also no record of the scribal error in Luke 16:18 (456[a]), where the text reads *et qui{t} dimissam a marito ducit*. Initially, however, the scribe broke off in the middle of the sentence, after copying *qui*{t}, jumped to the following line, and resumed by writing the perfect participle *dimissam*, capitalizing the first syllable. The mistake seems to have been noted immediately, since *di* was erased, and the syllable, now correctly written in minuscules, was added into the previous line after *qui{t}*. None of this, however, is present in Gasquet's edition.

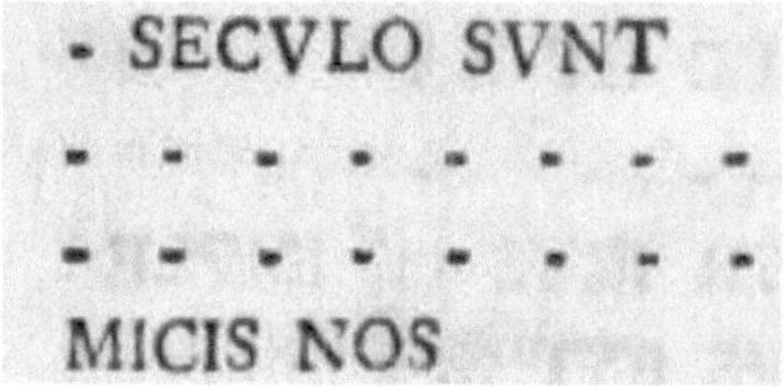

Gasquet's reconstruction	E	T	L	I	B	E	R	A
(based on b)	V	I	T	N	O	S	A	B
	M	I	C	I	S	N	O	S
	(No space for INI in the second line)							
Codex Palatinus (e)	S	A	L	U	T	E	M	A
	B	I	N	I	M	I	C	I
	S	N	O	S				
	(Too much space)							
We could conjecture	D	A	R	E	S	A	L	U
(based on f)	T	E	M	A	B	I	N	I
	M	I	C	I	S	N	O	S
	(This would fit better in the space.)							

Figure 2.6: Luke 1:71 (336[a]).

The most striking flaw in Gasquet's edition of the *Codex Vercellensis* can be seen in his reconstructions of the text. In Luke 1:71 (336[a]), he reconstructs [*et liberavit* | *nos ab ini*]*micis*, the reading transmitted in the *Codex Veronensis* (VL4), which is too long for the space available; on the other hand, the reading of the *Codex Palatinus* (VL2), [*salutem ab in*]*micis*, is too short. Thus, we may conjecture [*dare salu* | *tem* (*ex*) *ini*]*micis* instead, the reading found in *Codex Brixianus* (VL10). Of course, it is not possible to reconstruct the preposition with certainty since *ab* or *de* would fit the available space as well. In any case, this reconstruction takes up the variants found in the codices *Palatinus* (VL2) and *Bezae* (VL5), and the literal translation of the Greek σωτηρίαν ἐξ ἐχθρῶν.

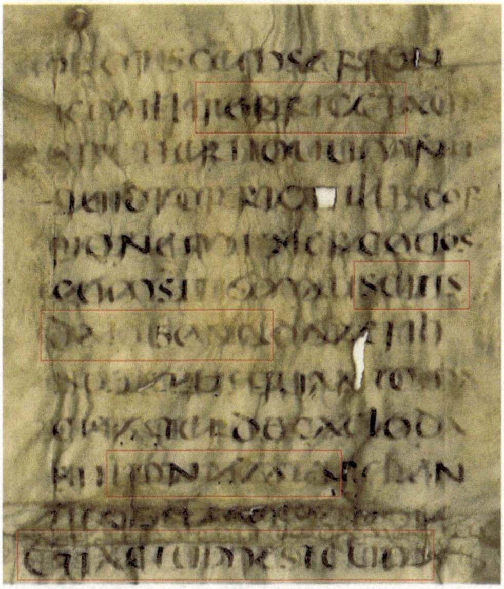

Figure 2.7: Luke 11:12–14 in the *Fragmenta Curiensia* (a², VL16).

Even more perplexing are Gasquet's text supplementations in Luke 11:12–14, where the text of the *Vercellensis* Luke is not extant due to two missing pages. Gasquet mentions in his introduction that he supplied long passages from *Fragmenta Curiensia* (VL16), which have been "recognized as practically the same version of the Vercelli Ms."[19] Yet, when it comes to the important reconstruction of chapter 11, Gasquet hesitates to use the fragments and again resorts to the text of *Codex Veronensis* (VL4). Accordingly, he completes the missing text with *porrigit* instead of *porriget* (Luke 11:12), *nostis* instead of *scitis, bonos datos* instead of *data bona, bonum datum* instead of *bona data* (Luke 11:13) and *et erat eiciens daemonium* instead of *et factum est cum eiceret* (Luke 11:14). The reconstructions *nostis* instead of *scitis* and *bonos datos* instead of *data bona* are especially debatable since *Fragmenta Curiensia* share this reading with the *Codex Bezae* (VL5), which suggests an older tradition for this passage in the *Codex Vercellensis*, differing from the other Italian manuscripts and the Vulgate.

To summarize this analysis of Gasquet's edition of the *Codex Vercellensis*, we may say that Gasquet deserves credit for eliminating several mistakes of previous transcriptions, the correction of which was mainly due to the restored parchment

19 Cf. GASQUET, Codex Vercellensis, XV.

available to him. Nevertheless, Gasquet handed down many of the imprecisions found in these earlier editions, and especially those in Irico's transcription. Furthermore, Gasquet did not always make accurate use of these earliest editions since he often failed to notice significant differences between them. Most importantly, however, Gasquet's reconstructions are based on later textual traditions, so that we may conclude that he clearly underestimated the relations between the *Vercellensis* Luke and the earlier witnesses of the Latin Gospels, such as codices *Palatinus* (e, VL2) and *Bezae* (d, VL5).

2.4 Adolf Jülicher (1938), Walther Matzkow (1938–1954), and Kurt Aland (^{2}1963–1971)

Another edition of the *Codex Vercellensis* which deserves attention is the *Itala* by the German scholar and biblical exegete Adolf Jülicher,[20] revised some years later by Walther Matzkow and Kurt Aland (1938–1954, ^{2}1963–1971). The *Itala* is not exactly a new edition of the manuscript but rather a collation of the most important Old Latin Gospels, including the *Codex Vercellensis*; for the text, Jülicher et al. rely – apart from some changes and corrections – on Gasquet's work. However, as other scholars have already noted,[21] the major deficiency of the *Itala* is the underlying concept adopted by its authors: they print an upper line of text giving a version designated as "Itala," and a lower line showing what is called "Afra." This format is problematic from two perspectives: it takes for granted both an absolute division between earlier and later textual traditions of the Old Latin Gospels and, most critically, a high degree of uniformity within them. This issue is further aggravated by the fact that Jülicher et al. do not follow any particular manuscript in the "Itala" line as they did in the "Afra," where they rely on the text of the codices *Bobbiensis* (VL1) and *Palatinus* (VL2); instead, they established a text based on various witnesses, giving no plausible justification for the reconstruction. Besides, in order to compress as many textual variants as possible into this format, Jülicher et al. were often forced to neglect details concerning abbreviations, *nomina sacra* and orthography, features of the individual manuscripts which uncover relevant information about the relationship between them. In this way, the editions of the individual

20 Jülicher et al., Itala: Das Neue Testament in altlateinischer Überlieferung.
21 Cf. Burton, The Old Latin Gospels, 9–10.

manuscripts often show spelling peculiarities, even though Jülicher et al. print the usual standard forms.[22]

Figure 2.8: Luke 24:39 (520^{b}).

Partly due to this lack of attention to orthographical deviations, the author was not able to avoid some curious blunders in his *Itala.* An example of this can be found in 24:39: Jülicher et al. consider that *Codex Vercellensis* omits the pronoun *ipse* in the sentence *quia ego sum ipse* (VL8, 4; *quoniam ego ipse sum* VL2; *quia ego ipse sum* VL5; *quia ipse ego sum* A) when, after the resurrection, Jesus reveals himself to two of his disciples while they are walking on the road to Emmaus. In fact, the text of the manuscript clearly transmits the pronoun *ipsi* instead of the *ipse* of the other witnesses, which Jülicher et al. inadvertently displaces into the next sentence since they conclude that *ipsi* is a nominative masculine plural and, therefore, stands in morpho-syntactical agreement with the imperative verbs *tractate et uidete* (*palpate et uidete* cet.). This, in turn, is taken to indicate an omission of *ipsi* in the other texts. However, given the typical confusion between *e* and *i* in the manuscript, there is no doubt that *ipsi* is merely a non-standard spelling of *ipse*. Thus, in contrast to what Jülicher's et al. collation indicate at first glance, the text of the *Codex Vercellensis* exhibits no textual difference in this verse but merely contains an orthographical irregularity.

22 This especially applies to the *Codex Corbeiensis secundus* (ff^{2}, VL8), whose scribe used very peculiar spelling. See, e. g., Luke 2:16 (*presipio* for *praesepio*), 6:45 (*densauro* for *thesauro*, corrected to *tensauro*), Luke 8:31 (*habissum* for *abyssum*) etc.

Another problem in Jülicher's et al. *Itala* relates to the text reconstructions in the *Codex Vercellensis*. In many passages,[23] the authors are excessively cautious and do not attempt any kind of conjecture, even if the missing texts leave little room for doubt. Two examples of this can be found in the account of Jesus's genealogy in Luke 3:23–38. In v. 28, Cosam's descendant is called *addi* in all Latin witnesses, with the exception of *Codex Palatinus* (e, VL2), which reads *abdi*; according to NA^{28}, the Greek text offers Ἀδδί to the exclusion of any variants. Moreover, both Irico and Bianchini indicate two missing letters after *ad-* (*ad*. .), so that there is no clear reason to hesitate in supplying *-di*, resulting in the reconstruction *addi*.

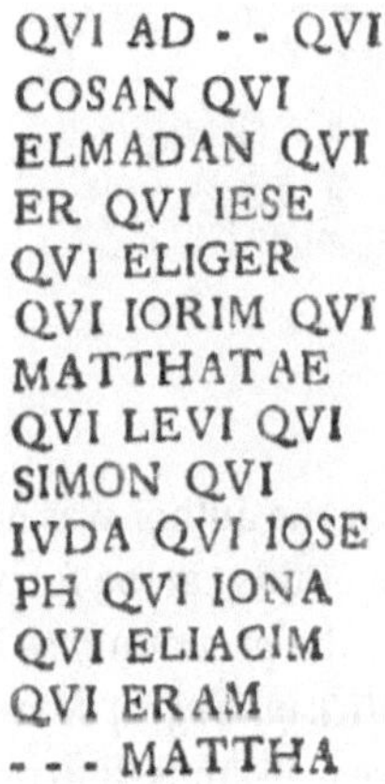
QVI AD . . QVI
COSAN QVI
ELMADAN QVI
ER QVI IESE
QVI ELIGER
QVI IORIM QVI
MATTHATAE
QVI LEVI QVI
SIMON QVI
IVDA QVI IOSE
PH QVI IONA
QVI ELIACIM
QVI ERAM
. . . MATTHA

Figure 2.9: The *lacunae* in Irico's transcription (Luke 3:28–31).

The *lacuna* in v. 31 is puzzling as well: in the whole passage, the scribe is consistent and writes *qui* followed by the name of Joseph's ancestor in the genitive, instead of *fili* (VL2), *qui fuit* (VL4 and A) or *filius* (VL8). Since Irico and Bianchini assume three missing letters in this line, it seems more than plausible to conjecture *qui* in this verse too. An identical objection applies to 4:2, in the temptation pericope. After *ed-*, there is space for two letters. All other Latin witnesses transmit *manducauit*, indicative perfect active of *manducare*, corresponding to the Greek aorist ἔφαγεν. We can thus supply, with a high degree of probability, the ending *-it*, resulting in the reconstruction *edit*, indicative perfect active of *edere*, a characteristic variant of

23 See pp. $351^{a\text{-}b}$ and $352^{a\text{-}b}$, Jülicher et al., Itala: Das Neue Testament in altlateinischer Überlieferung, 33–37.

manducare in older textual traditions of the Latin Gospels; however, following Gasquet, Jülicher et al. here again mark a lacuna.

Finally, Jülicher's et al. *Itala* volumes are now obsolete in one crucial respect. The text of the Vulgate cited is John Wordsworth and Henry Julian White's critical edition, the so-called "Oxford Vulgate," which was successively published between 1889 and 1954.[24] This has been supplanted by the "Stuttgart Vulgate", edited by Robert Weber and Roger Gryson from 1969 onwards. The *Itala* also has some inconsistencies in references to the textual variants of the Vulgate. In Luke 6:49, for instance, Jülicher et al. read the phrase *in quam inlisus est* from the Vulgate, recording no possible deviations, which are usually showed by brackets (vg). Yet, *Codex Amiatinus* clearly transmits *in qua inlisus est* instead: considering that Wordsworth and White do not report the variant in the *apparatus criticus* of their 1911 *editio minor*, it is even possible to deduce that Jülicher et al. used this publication as their source, and not the *editio critica maior*.

The *Itala* of Jülicher/ Matzkow/ Aland is the basis of numerous New Testament and early church studies and is therefore of central importance to biblical scholarship. The edition largely follows Gasquet's transcription. It is worth mentioning, however, that the edition of the *Itala* lacks numerous details, such as *nomina sacra* and important paratextual information including, for instance, the liturgical signs in the manuscript's margins.[25]

2.5 Corrections of Previous Editions

A comparison of these printed editions thus reveals a considerable number of verbal differences; determining which of these is the correct reading is of obvious importance, especially in light of the new multispectral images. In what follows, some important corrections made possible by the new images will be discussed:

24 All Gospels appeared in the first fascicle from 1889.

25 Cf. pp. 11–15.

1. Luke 2:21 (341[a]) and Luke 3:21 (350[b]): *cum* – *com*

Figure 2.10: Luke 3:21 (350[b]): *cum*, apparently corrected into *com.*

The orthographic interchangeability of *u* and *o* is a common feature of the text of Luke in the *Codex Vercellensis*, found, for instance, in Luke 10:21 (*paruolus* for *paruulus*), and in Luke 22:41 (*abolsus* for *auulsus*).[26] While previous editors were able to detect these two peculiar forms, they failed to identify the non-standard spellings of *lucrari* in 9:25 (403[b]) and, again, of *cum* in 20:16 (483[a]), where the MSI-images show *locrari* and *com* respectively. A further interesting case of such orthographic variation can be found in Luke 3:21 (350[b]), where the standard spelling of the conjunct-tion *cum* seems to have been corrected to *com*, probably by the scribe himself.

26 For a detailed discussion on the orthography of the *Codex Vercellensis*, see pp. 192ff.

2. Luke 2:48 (346[a]): *tristes* – *tristis*

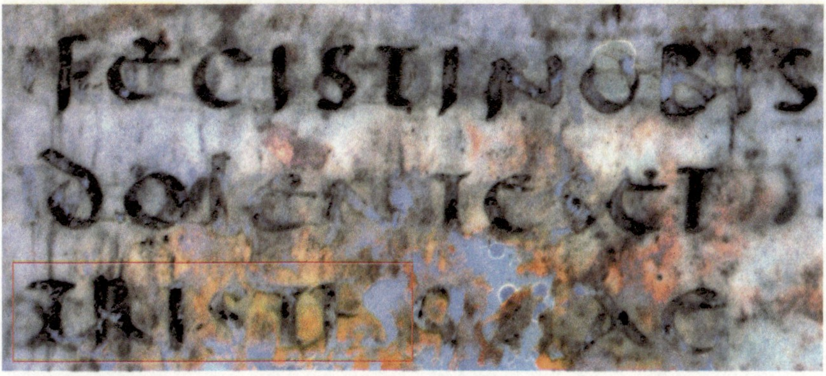

Figure 2.11: Luke 2:48 (346[a]): *tristis*, apparently corrected into *tristes*.

Orthographic confusion between *e* and *i* is a well-attested characteristic of most Latin manuscripts.[27] In this regard, the Gospel of Luke as transmitted in the *Codex Vercellensis* is no exception: there are numerous deviations from standard spelling involving the interchange of these vowels, some of which were not identified by any of the previous editors. Further examples are *pauperes* – *pauperis* in Luke 6:20 (372[a]), *dicentes* – *dicentis* in Luke 7:32 (383[b]), *ciuitates* – *ciuitatis* in Luke 8:1 (387[a]).

27 For a detailed discussion, see chap. 5.1.1, 192ff.

3. Luke 3:8 (348[a]): *uocabis* Irico; *uobis* Bianchini/ Gasquet/ Jülicher et al.; *uocabis*

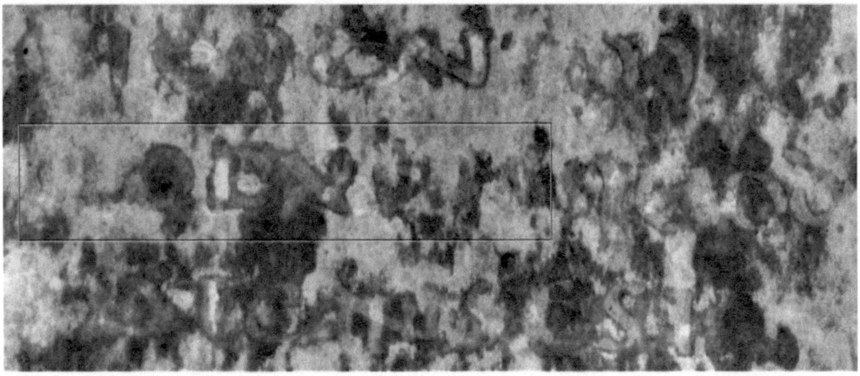

Figure 2.12: Luke 3:8 (348[a]).

This is obviously a scribal error resulting in the nonsensical reading *dico enim uo{ca}bis* for λέγω γὰρ ὑμῖν. The text of the manuscript was correctly identified and transcribed by Irico, but it was neglected by the following editors. There is no sign of any attempt at correction by the scribe or another hand in the manuscript.

4. Luke 4:23 (356[b]): *quaecumque* – *quaecumquae*

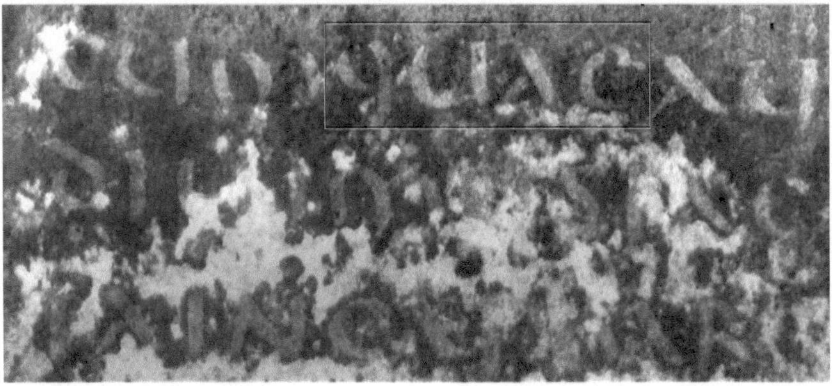

Figure 2.13: Luke 4:23 (356[b]).

Though the monophthongization of *ae* to *e* is not common in the *Codex Vercellensis*, some words written with *e* are spelt with *ae* instead, a phenomenon which may be considered an example of hypercorrection.[28] However, previous editors rarely took note of this major orthographic feature of the manuscript. Other examples which could be identified through the analysis of the MIS-images are found in Luke 7:23 (382[a]) and 11:28 (421[a]), where we read *baeatus* instead of *beatus* and *baeati* instead of *beati* respectively, or in Luke 22:22 (497[b]), which has *uaerum* instead of *uerum*.

5. Luke 4:28 (357[a]): *repleti* – *inpleti*

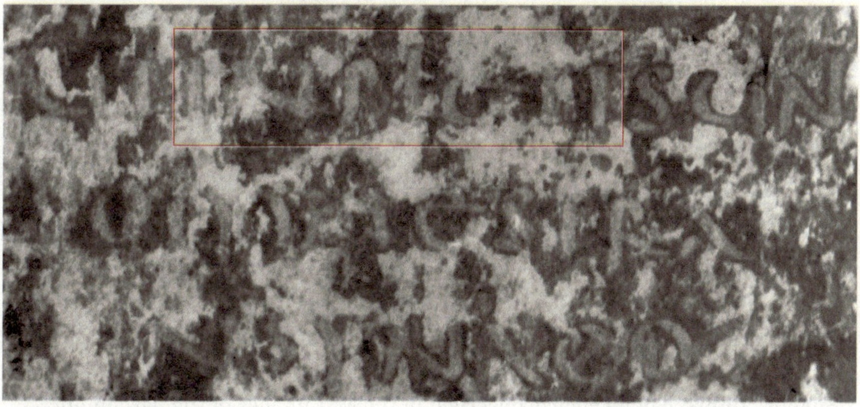

Figure 2.14: Luke 4:23 (356[b]).

Here, the manuscript reads *inpleti* with the codices *Palatinus* (VL2) and *Bezae* (VL5), and not *repleti* with later witnesses, such as the codices *Veronensis* (VL4) and *Corbeiensis secundus* (VL8). This variant, revealed only through the MSI-images, thus gives further evidence that the *Codex Vercellensis* resembles the older traditions of Luke more than hitherto supposed.[29] Here, too, we may conjecture that the reading *repleti* printed by earlier editors is the result of the mistaken conception of the manuscript as a later witness to the text.

28 See also chap. 5.1.1, 192ff.

29 For an in-depth discussion of the relations between the codices *Vercellensis, Palatinus* (VL2) and *Bezae* (VL5), see chap. 4.3.

6. Luke 5:33 (367[a]): *faciunt – faciant*

Figure 2.15: Luke 5:33 (367[a]).

It is difficult to determine precisely on what grammatical grounds the text has a present subjunctive (*faciant*) instead of the present indicative (*faciunt*) which is found in all Latin and Greek witnesses (ποιοῦνται). The scribe was very likely misled by the ending of the other verbs in the clause (*ieiunant* and *maducant*), inflecting *facere* in the same way. At any rate, the peculiar variant, which was ignored by all previous editors, can be clearly observed in the MSI-images of the parchment.

7. Luke 7:33 (384[a]): [*e*]*dere* Irico; *manducans* Bianchini; [*mandu*]*cans* Gasquet; *manducans* Jülicher et al.; [*e*]*dens*

Figure 2.16: Luke 7:33 (384[a]): The "D" of [*e*]*dens* is still visible.

Both the direct consultation of the manuscript and the MSI-images suggest that *-dens*, which may be reconstructed as *[e]dens*, originally stood in the passage. This finding partly confirms Irico's transcription *-dere* and invalidates Bianchini's and Gasquet's text *manducans*, which was later incorporated into Jülicher's et al. *Itala*. Since *edere* (instead of *manducare*) is considered a characteristic rendering of ἐσθίειν in the earlier traditions of the Latin Gospels, the restored text thus provides a further instance of an older variant in the *Vercellensis* Luke.[30]

8. Luke 8:16 (390[a]): *uase – uaso*

Figure 2.17: Luke 8:16 (390[a]).

The restored reading *uaso*, ablative singular of the masculine *uasus*, is one of the few examples of the reduction of gender classes in the *Codex Vercellensis*; in this case, variant in conformity with classical usage would be *uase*, ablative singular of the neuter *uas*.[31] This is noteworthy because *uaso* is found throughout the Old Latin tradition, with only the text of the Vulgate following the standard register. This passage thus poses another case in which the previous editors were misguided by the later witnesses.

30 For the earlier readings in the text, see chap. 5.4.1, p. 245f.

31 For a detailed discussion of the reduction of inflectional classes in the manuscript, see chap. 5.2.2, pp. 215ff.

9. Luke 8:23 (391[b]): *periculabantur – periclitabantur*

Figure 2.18: Luke 8:23 (391[b]).

In this verse, all previous editors took the variant *periculabantur* for a unique reading of the *Vercellensis* Luke. However, the MSI-images show that there is no deviation from the other Latin authorities, and that the textual transmission was consistent in this case. At the same time, the form *periculari* is attested only once in classical literature,[32] whereas *periclitari* is the most frequent term meaning "to be in danger."

32 Cf. Cato ap. *Fest.* 242.

10. Luke 9:14 (401[b]): *autem* – *enim*

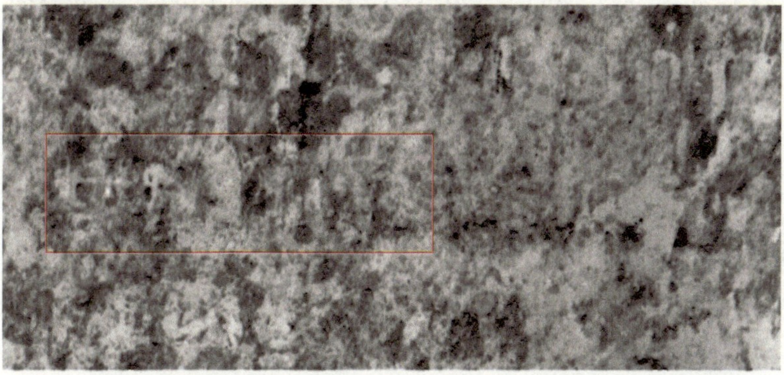

Figure 2.19: Luke 9:14 (401[b]).

The restored text follows the variant found in most Latin witnesses, as well as in the oldest Greek authorities (ℵ B C D). The reading *autem*, on the other hand, printed by all previous editors of the *Codex Vercellensis*, is widespread in the manuscripts of the Vulgate and in later Greek witnesses ($\aleph^{*,2b}$ L). In this way, our edition speaks in favor of positing γάρ instead of δέ as the original reading of the Gospel of Luke.

11. Luke 9:59 (410[a]): *illum* – *alium*

Figure 2.20: Luke 9:59 (410[a]).

Once more, the restored text shows that there is no deviation from the Greek text of the passage, which has ἕτερον. Most Latin witnesses here have *alterum*, with the exception of the *Codex Bezae* (VL5), which reads *alium* as well. In this way, the MSI-images give further evidence for the many similarities between the codices *Vercellensis* and *Bezae*.

12. Luke 11:28 (421[a]): *illi* – *illis*

Figure 2.21: Luke 11:28 (421[a]).

The restored plural *illis* shows that the manuscript partially follows the majority of Old Latin witnesses in this passage, which read *ad eos*. Noteworthy is the fact that older literature lists the reading *illi* printed by earlier editors as an important difference between the *Codex Vercellensis* and the *Fragmenta Curiensia* (VL16).[33] However, the MSI-images show that both manuscripts agree in this point in reading *illis*.

33 Cf. Wordsworth et al., Old Latin Biblical Texts, ccxiv.

13. Luke 13:22 (p. 437^{a}): *hierosolymis* Irico/ Bianchini; *hierusolymis* Gasquet; *hierosolymus* Jülicher; *hierosolymis*

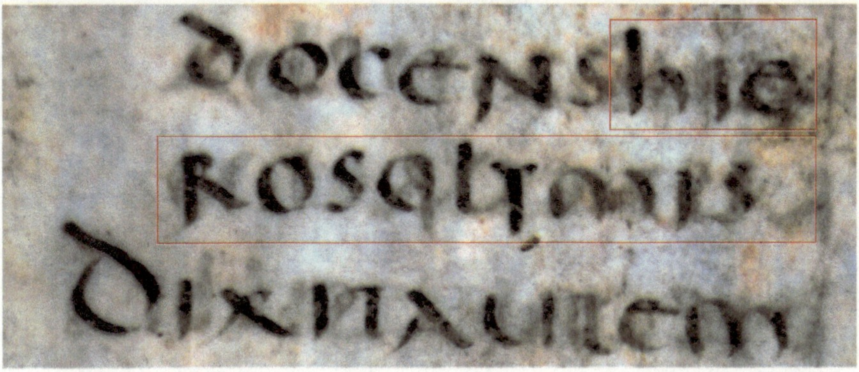

Figure 2.22: Luke 13:22 (p. 437^{a}).

The Hebrew form ירושלם was transliterated as either Ἱεροσόλυμα or Ἰερουσαλήμ in Greek. *Hierusolymis*, as proposed by Gasquet,[34] would be the fusion (conflation reading) of the two renderings of ירושלם which, however, does not appear in any witness of the Latin Bible from the first centuries of the textual transmission. At any rate, the MSI-images of the manuscript show *hierosolymis*. Moreover, in reading *hierusolymis* instead of *hierosolymis*, Gasquet cannot call on any earlier editions of *Vercellensis* Luke for support.

34 Cf. Gasquet, Codex Vercellensis, 87.

14. Luke 17:16 (461^{b}): *samaritanus* Irico; *samarites* Bianchini; *samaritanus* Gasquet and Jülicher et al.; *samarites*

Figure 2.23: Luke 17:16 (461^{b}).

Bianchini was able to identify the correct reading *samarites*, which was in turn disregarded by Gasquet. The restored text matches the older tradition of this passage, which is represented by the *Codex Palatinus* (e, VL2). The implications of the variant *samarites* instead of *samaritanus* are of such importance for the interpretation of the Gospel of Luke that they will be analyzed separately.[35]

35 See chap. 4.1.2.5, pp. 101f.

15. Luke 18:22 (468b): *da* Irico; *ea* Bianchini; $^{\textit{et da}}$ *ea* Gasquet; *dando ea* Jülicher et al.; $^{\textit{et diuide}}$ *ea*

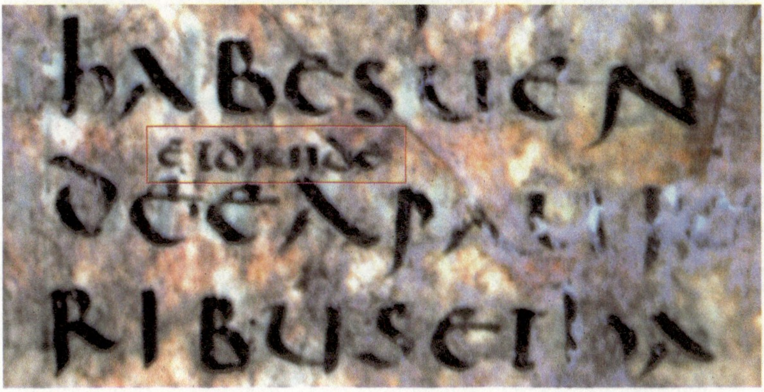

Figure 2.24: Luke 18:22 (468^{b}).

Gasquet identified the word insertion above the line but was unable to read it correctly.[36] Considering that *et da* is the variant of all other witnesses, we can assume that he was – again – misled by later Latin authorities in editing the passage. However, the MSI-image allows us to restore the original text of the manuscript with *diuidere* instead of *dare*, another unique reading of the *Codex Vercellensis*.

36 Cf. GASQUET, Codex Vercellensis, 111, fn. b.

16. Luke 19:33 (478ª): *illius* – *ipsius*

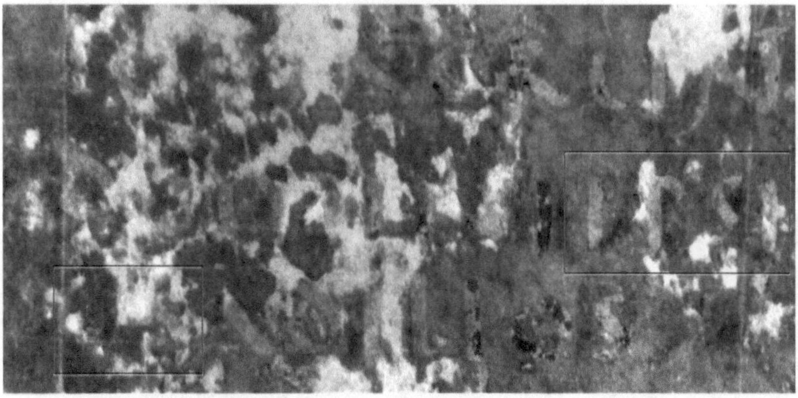

Figure 2.25: Luke 19:33 (478ª).

This is an uncharacteristic use of the personal pronouns in the *Codex Vercellensis*, which usually renders αὐτός with *ille*, less frequently with *is*, and only rarely with *ipse*.[37] It is possible that this fact, along with the poor preservation of the parchment, led the earlier editors to mistakenly read *illius* instead of the correct *ipsius*.

To summarize, our brief overview has shown the importance of revisiting the *Vercellensis* Luke, the oldest manuscript of the Latin Bible and removing the inaccuracies of the previous editions by means of MIS-imaging as well as of a different analytical translation theory concerning 'Afra'- and 'European' textual tradition. Gasquet, whose work is widely referred to in the literature – major examples being the *Itala* published by Jülicher et al. and the Vetus Latina Mark and John – reconstructs the text based on the later European textual tradition, to which the manuscript does not obviously belong. This editorial decision, however, has drastic implications since it suggests that the text of the *Codex Vercellensis* belongs to a later textual tradition. We will pursue this question in Chapter IV and V by analyzing the manuscript in more detail.

37 For a detailed discussion of the use of pronouns in the *Codex Vercellensis*, see chap. 5.3.2, pp. 229ff.

2.6 List of Readings in Previous Editions along with New Insights Gained from MSI-images

The table supplies the corrections made to previous editions of the *Codex Vercellensis* in light of the multispectral images examined in the present study:

<table>
<tr><th>Luke</th><th>Irico</th><th>Bianchini</th><th>Gasquet</th><th>Jülicher et al.</th><th>MSI-images/ New Readings</th></tr>
<tr><td>1:6 (326[a])</td><td>*iustificationis*</td><td>*iustificationibus*</td><td></td><td></td><td>*iustificationis*</td></tr>
<tr><td>1:18 (328[a])</td><td>*aud angelum*</td><td>*ad angelum*</td><td></td><td></td><td>*a{n}d angelum*</td></tr>
<tr><td>1:20 (328[b])</td><td>*Quae*</td><td></td><td></td><td></td><td>*qui*</td></tr>
<tr><td>1:23 (329[a])</td><td>*impleti*</td><td>*inpleti*</td><td>*impleti*</td><td></td><td>*inpleti*</td></tr>
<tr><td>1:45 (332[b])</td><td>*consumatio*</td><td>*-summatio*</td><td>*consumatio*</td><td></td><td>*consummatio*</td></tr>
<tr><td>2:4 (338[a])</td><td>*naza|ret*</td><td>*nazar|et*</td><td>*naza|ret*</td><td>---</td><td>*nazar|et*</td></tr>
<tr><td>2:10 (339[a])</td><td>*dixitquae*</td><td>*dixitque*</td><td>*dixitquae*</td><td></td><td>*dixitquae*</td></tr>
<tr><td>2:21 (341[a])</td><td>*cum*</td><td></td><td></td><td></td><td>*com*</td></tr>
<tr><td></td><td>*impleti*</td><td>*inpleti*</td><td></td><td>*impleti*</td><td>*inpleti*</td></tr>
<tr><td>2:22 (341[a])</td><td>*duxerunt*</td><td></td><td></td><td></td><td>*dixerunt*</td></tr>
<tr><td>2:23 (341[b])</td><td>*uoluam*</td><td></td><td></td><td>*uuluam*</td><td>*uoluam*</td></tr>
<tr><td>2:31 (342[b])</td><td>*praeparasti*</td><td></td><td></td><td></td><td>*praep{r}arasti*[38]</td></tr>
<tr><td>2:35 (343[b])</td><td>*uti reuelentur*</td><td></td><td></td><td></td><td>*uti {i} reuelentur*[39]</td></tr>
<tr><td>2:39 (344[a])</td><td>*quun*</td><td>*quem*</td><td></td><td></td><td>*quem*</td></tr>
<tr><td>2:39 (344[b])</td><td>*nazareus*</td><td>*nazoreus*</td><td></td><td></td><td>*nazoreus*</td></tr>
<tr><td>2:41 (344[b])</td><td>*pasche*</td><td>*paschae*</td><td>*pasche*</td><td>*paschae*</td><td>*pasche*</td></tr>
<tr><td>2:42 (345[a])</td><td>*sollemni*</td><td>*sollemnis*</td><td>*sollemni*</td><td></td><td>*sollemni*</td></tr>
<tr><td>2:48 (346[a])</td><td>*tristes*</td><td></td><td></td><td></td><td>*tristis*[40]</td></tr>
<tr><td>3:8 (348[a])</td><td>*uocabis*</td><td>*uobis*</td><td></td><td></td><td>*uocabis*</td></tr>
<tr><td></td><td>*quia*</td><td></td><td></td><td></td><td>*quod*</td></tr>
<tr><td>3:15 (349[b])</td><td>*in cordis*</td><td>*omnibus in cordis*</td><td></td><td></td><td>*omnibus in cordibus*</td></tr>
<tr><td></td><td>*iohannem*</td><td>*iohannen*</td><td></td><td></td><td>*iohannen*</td></tr>
<tr><td>3:17 (350[a])</td><td>*inexstintibili*</td><td>*inexstinguibili*</td><td></td><td>*inextinguibili*</td><td>*inextinctibili*</td></tr>
<tr><td>3:20 (350[b])</td><td>*iohannem*</td><td>*iohannen*</td><td></td><td></td><td>*iohannen*</td></tr>
<tr><td>3:21 (350[b])</td><td>*cum*</td><td></td><td></td><td></td><td>*com*[41]</td></tr>
<tr><td>4:7 (353[b])</td><td>*erint*</td><td>*erunt*</td><td>*erint*</td><td></td><td>*erint*</td></tr>
<tr><td>4:8 (353[b])</td><td>*soli*</td><td></td><td></td><td></td><td>*solo*</td></tr>
<tr><td>4:9 (354[a])</td><td>*es dei*</td><td>*dei es*</td><td>*es dei*</td><td></td><td>*es dei*</td></tr>
<tr><td>4:13 (354[b])</td><td>*consummata*</td><td></td><td>*comnsummata*</td><td>*consummata*</td><td>*comnsummata*[42]</td></tr>
<tr><td>4:17 (355[a])</td><td>*esaiae*</td><td>*eseiae*</td><td></td><td></td><td>*eseiae*</td></tr>
</table>

38 The error was probably corrected in the manuscript since the “R” appears to be slightly erased.
39 Just like above, the letter “I” appears slightly erased in the manuscript.
40 Apparent correction of tristis into tristes in the manuscript.
41 Apparent correction of *cum* to *com* in the manuscript.
42 The superfluous “M” was corrected through *expunctum* in the manuscript.

Luke	Irico	Bianchini	Gasquet	Jülicher et al.	MSI-images/ New Readings
4:18 (355^a)	*missit*	*misit*			*misit*
4:19 (355^b)	*deum*	*domini*			*domini*
4:21 (355^b)	*caepit*	*coepit*			*coepit*
4:21 (356^a)	*scripturam*	*scriptura*			*scripturam*
4:23 (356^b)	*quaecumque*				*quaecumquae*
4:26 (357^a)	*mearum*	*earum*	*mearum*		*mearum*
4:27 (357^a)	*set*				*et*
	sirus	*surus*			*surus*
4:28 (357^a)	*repleti*				*inpleti*
4:29 (357^b)	*supercilim*	*supercilium*			*supercilium*
4:30 (357^b)	*ibant*	*ibat*			*ibat*
4:32 (358^a)	*poteste*	*potestate*	*poteste*	*potestate*	*potes<ta>te*
4:35 (358^b)	*demonium*	*daemonium*	*demonium*	*daemonium*	*daemonium*
4:36 (358^b)	*uirtute*				*uirtutes*
4:39 (359^b)	*is*	*his*	*is*		*is*
4:43 (360^b)	*hab hoc*	*ob hoc*	*hob hoc*		*hob hoc*
5:3 (361^a)	*nauiculeam*	*nauiculam*			*nauiculam*
5:10 (362^b)	*sociis*	*socii*		*sociis*	*sociis*[43]
5:12 (363^a)	*potest*	*potes*			*potest*
5:15 (363^b)	*fama*				*eama*
5:17 (364^a)	*galilaee*	*galileae*		*galilaeae*	*galileae*
	hierusalem				*hierosalem*
5:19 (364^b)	*lectum*	*tectum*			*tectum*
5:33 (367^a)	*faciunt*				*faciant*
5:37 (368^a)	*effonditur*	*effunditur*			*effunditur*
6:10 (370^a)	*circunspiciens*	*circumspiciens*			*circumspiciens*
6:12 (370^b)	*erat*	*e|rat*		---	*e|rat*
6:16 (371^a)	*iudam*	*iudan*			*iudan*
	iudant	*iudan*	*iudant*		*iudant*
6:18 (371^b)	*immundis*	*inmundis*			*inmundis*
6:19 (371^b)	*omnes*	*om|nes*		---	*om|nes*
6:20 (371^b)	*occulos*	*oculos*			*oculos*
6:20 (372^a)	*pauperes*				*pauperis*
6:21 (372^a)	*ploratis*	*ploraratis*		*ploratis*	*plora{ra}tis*
	uidebitis	*ridebitis*			*ridebitis*
6:22 (372^a)	*eiecerint*				*eicerint*
6:24 (372^b)	*ueruntamen*	*uerumtamen*			*uerumtamen*
6:28 (373^b)	*eis*	*his*	*eis*		*is*
6:29 (373^b)	*autferet*	*auferet*			*autferet*
6:35 (374^b)	*ueruntamen*	*uerumtamen*			*uerumtamen*

43 The manuscript clearly reads *sociis*; the last "S" was corrected twice (*expunctum* and crossed out).

Luke	Irico	Bianchini	Gasquet	Jülicher et al.	MSI-images/ New Readings
6:37 (375[a])	*dimittitet*	*dimittite et*			*dimittite et*
6:39 (375[b])	*nunquid*	*numquid*			*numquid*
6:40 (375[b])	*consumatus*		*conssumatus*		*conssumatus*
6:42 (376[a])	*potest*	*potes*	*potest*		*potest*
6:45 (376[b])	*thesauro*	*thensauro*			*thensauro*
6:48 (377[b])	*supra*				*super*
	petram				*petraM*
6:49 (377[b])	*impulit*	*impulit*	*inpulit*	*impulit*	*impulit*
	domu	*domui*	*domu*	*domu*	*domu*
7:8 (379[a])	*potestatis*	*potestati*	*potestatis*		*potestatis*
7:10 (379[b])	*inuenerunt*	*et inuenerunt*		*inuenerunt*	*inuenerunt*
	seruum sanum	*seruum | sanum*		---	*seruum | sanum*
7:12 (380[a])	*haec*				*hac*
7:14 (380[a])	*locutum*	*loculum*			*loculum*
	steterunt	*steterunt et ait*			*steterunt et ait*
7:17 (380[b])	*in iudaea*	*iudaea*		*in iudaea*	*in iudaea*
7:18 (380[b])	*et*	---	*et*	---	*Et*
7:20 (381[a])	*et dixerunt*	*et | dixerunt*	*et dixerunt*	---	*et | dixerunt*
7:23 (382[a])	*beatus*				*baeatus*
7:26 (382[b])	*amplius*	*amplior*			*amplior*
7:32 (383[b])	*dicentes*				*dicentis*
7:33 (384[a])	[*e*]*dere*	*manducans*	[*mandu*]*cans*	*manducans*	[*e*]*dens*
7:38 (384[a])	*stas*	*stans*			*stans*
	irrigabat	*inrigabat*			*inrigabat*
	et ca|pillis	*et capillis*		---	{*et ca*} *et capillis*
7:38 (385[a])	*ungebat*			*unguebat*	*ungebat*
7:43 (386[a])	*quod*				*quod*{*d*}
7:44 (386[a])	*irrigauit*	*inrigauit*			*inrigauit*
7:45 (386[a])	*Osculum* (386[b])	---	*osculum* (386[a])	---	*Osculum* (386[a])
7:48 (386[b])	*illam ihs* (387[a])	*illam ihs*	*illam ihs* (386[b])	---	*illam ihs* (386[b])
8:1 (387[a])	*ciuitates*				*ciuitatis*
	adnuntians				*adnuntiasns*[44]
8:2 (387[b])	*s|piritibus*	*spiritibus*	*s|piritibus*	---	*s|piritibus*
	magdalene				*macdalelne*[45]
8:3 (387[b])	*chuse*	*chuza*	*chuze*	*chuza*	*chuza*
8:5 (388[a])	*qui seminat*				† *qui seannat* †
8:6 (388[a])	*aliud*				*aliut*
8:9 (388[b])	*interrogabant*				*interrogabatnt*[46]
8:10 (389[a])	*dicit*	*dixit*			*dixit*

44 Corrected to *adnuntians* in the manuscript.

45 Corrected to *macdalene* in the manuscript.

46 The superfluous "T" was corrected through *expunctum* in the manuscript.

<table>
<tr><th>Luke</th><th>Irico</th><th>Bianchini</th><th>Gasquet</th><th>Jülicher et al.</th><th>MSI-images/ New Readings</th></tr>
<tr><td>8:13 (389^{b})</td><td>temtationis</td><td>temptationis</td><td>temtationis</td><td>temptationis</td><td>temptationis</td></tr>
<tr><td>8:16 (390^{a})</td><td>uase</td><td></td><td></td><td></td><td>uaso</td></tr>
<tr><td></td><td>suptus</td><td></td><td></td><td>subtus</td><td>suptus</td></tr>
<tr><td>8:23 (391^{b})</td><td>periculabantur</td><td></td><td></td><td></td><td>periclitabantur</td></tr>
<tr><td>8:27 (392^{b})</td><td>neque domo</td><td>nec in domo</td><td></td><td></td><td>neque domo</td></tr>
<tr><td>8:28 (393^{a})</td><td>et et</td><td>et</td><td>et et</td><td>et et</td><td>et {et}</td></tr>
<tr><td>8:29 (393^{a})</td><td>praecipiebat</td><td>praecepiebat</td><td></td><td>praecipiebat</td><td>praecipiebat</td></tr>
<tr><td>8:33 (394^{a})</td><td>daemo|nia</td><td>dae|monia</td><td>daemo|nia</td><td>---</td><td>daemo|nia</td></tr>
<tr><td>8:38 (395^{a})</td><td>da|emonia</td><td>dae|monia</td><td>da|emonia</td><td>---</td><td>dae|monia</td></tr>
<tr><td>8:40 (395^{b})</td><td>exciper</td><td>excepit</td><td>excepit</td><td>excepit</td><td>excepet</td></tr>
<tr><td>8:43 (396^{a})</td><td>profluio</td><td>profluuio</td><td></td><td></td><td>profluuio</td></tr>
<tr><td>8:47 (397^{a})</td><td>statuise</td><td>latuisse</td><td></td><td></td><td>latuisse</td></tr>
<tr><td></td><td>ut</td><td>et</td><td></td><td></td><td>et</td></tr>
<tr><td></td><td>comfestim</td><td>confestim</td><td>comfestim</td><td>confestim</td><td>comfestim</td></tr>
<tr><td>8:48 (397^{a})</td><td>dicit</td><td></td><td></td><td>dixit</td><td>dixit</td></tr>
<tr><td>8:51 (398^{a})</td><td>iohannem</td><td>iohannen</td><td></td><td></td><td>iohannen</td></tr>
<tr><td>8:53 (398^{a})</td><td>sientes</td><td>scientes</td><td></td><td></td><td>scientes</td></tr>
<tr><td>8:54 (398^{a})</td><td>manum</td><td>manu</td><td>manum</td><td></td><td>manum</td></tr>
<tr><td>8:56 (398^{b})</td><td>obstupuerunt</td><td></td><td></td><td>obstipuerunt</td><td>Obstipuerunt</td></tr>
<tr><td>9:5 (399^{b})</td><td>illa</td><td></td><td></td><td></td><td>illam</td></tr>
<tr><td>9:7 (400^{a})</td><td>iohannes</td><td></td><td></td><td>iohanes</td><td>iohanes</td></tr>
<tr><td>9:10 (400^{b})</td><td>quaecumquae</td><td>quaecumque</td><td>quaecumquae</td><td>quaecumque</td><td>quaecumquae</td></tr>
<tr><td>9:13 (401^{a})</td><td>nisi si nos</td><td>nisi nos</td><td>nisi si nos</td><td></td><td>nisi si nos</td></tr>
<tr><td>9:14 (401^{b})</td><td>autem</td><td></td><td></td><td></td><td>enim</td></tr>
<tr><td>9:22 (403^{a})</td><td>post tertium</td><td></td><td></td><td></td><td>pos<t> tertium</td></tr>
<tr><td>9:24 (403^{b})</td><td>mea</td><td>mei</td><td>mea</td><td></td><td>mei</td></tr>
<tr><td>9:25 (403^{b})</td><td>omini</td><td>homini</td><td></td><td></td><td>homini</td></tr>
<tr><td></td><td>lucrari</td><td></td><td></td><td></td><td>locrari</td></tr>
<tr><td>9:29 (404^{b})</td><td>facies</td><td>efigies</td><td>facies</td><td>ficies</td><td>ficies</td></tr>
<tr><td></td><td>praesurgens</td><td>praefulgens</td><td>prefulgens</td><td>praefulgens</td><td>praefulgens</td></tr>
<tr><td>9:42 (407^{a})</td><td>reddet</td><td>reddidit</td><td></td><td></td><td>reddidit</td></tr>
<tr><td>9:45 (407^{b})</td><td>intelligerent</td><td>intellegerent</td><td></td><td></td><td>intellegerent</td></tr>
<tr><td></td><td>interrogare</td><td></td><td></td><td></td><td>intierrogare[47]</td></tr>
<tr><td>9:51 (408^{b})</td><td>Factum est</td><td>---</td><td>Factum est</td><td>---</td><td>factum est</td></tr>
<tr><td>9:54 (409^{a})</td><td>iohanes</td><td>iohannes</td><td></td><td></td><td>iohanes</td></tr>
<tr><td>9:59 (410^{a})</td><td>illum</td><td></td><td></td><td></td><td>alium</td></tr>
<tr><td>9:61 (410^{b})</td><td>nontiare</td><td>nuntiare</td><td></td><td></td><td>nuntiare</td></tr>
<tr><td>10:2 (411^{a})</td><td>operari</td><td>operarii</td><td>operari</td><td></td><td>operari</td></tr>
<tr><td>10:19 (414^{a})</td><td>scorp|iones</td><td>scor|piones</td><td></td><td>---</td><td>scor|piones</td></tr>
<tr><td>10:20 (414^{a})</td><td>abaudiunt</td><td>obaudiunt</td><td></td><td></td><td>obaudiunt</td></tr>
<tr><td>10:21 (414^{b})</td><td>reuelasti</td><td></td><td></td><td></td><td>reualasti</td></tr>
</table>

47 Corrected to *interrogare* in the manuscript.

<table>
<tr><th>Luke</th><th>Irico</th><th>Bianchini</th><th>Gasquet</th><th>Jülicher et al.</th><th>MSI-images/ New Readings</th></tr>
<tr><td></td><td>paruolis</td><td></td><td></td><td>paruulis</td><td>paruolis</td></tr>
<tr><td>10:22 (414^{b})</td><td>nobis</td><td>nobit</td><td></td><td>nouit</td><td>nobit</td></tr>
<tr><td>10:23 (415^{a})</td><td>uidetis</td><td></td><td></td><td>uidetis*</td><td>uidetis[48]</td></tr>
<tr><td>10:27 (415^{b})</td><td>totta</td><td>tota</td><td>totta</td><td>tota</td><td>tota</td></tr>
<tr><td></td><td>tottis</td><td>totis</td><td>tottis</td><td></td><td>totis</td></tr>
<tr><td>10:34 (416^{b})</td><td>colligauit</td><td>conligauit</td><td></td><td></td><td>conligauit</td></tr>
<tr><td>10:40 (418^{a})</td><td>sola</td><td>solam</td><td></td><td>sola</td><td>sola</td></tr>
<tr><td>11:11 (420^{b})</td><td>piscem</td><td>pisce</td><td>piscem</td><td></td><td>piscem</td></tr>
<tr><td>11:27 (421^{a})</td><td>cum</td><td></td><td>dum</td><td></td><td>dum</td></tr>
<tr><td>11:28 (421^{a})</td><td>illi</td><td></td><td></td><td></td><td>illis</td></tr>
<tr><td></td><td>beati</td><td></td><td></td><td></td><td>baeati</td></tr>
<tr><td>11:29 (421^{b})</td><td><em>nequaM</em></td><td><em>nequa</em></td><td></td><td></td><td><em>nequ</em>^{a}</td></tr>
<tr><td>11:32 (422^{b})</td><td>praedicationae</td><td>praedicatione</td><td></td><td></td><td>praedicationae</td></tr>
<tr><td>11:34 (423^{a})</td><td>tenebrosum</td><td></td><td></td><td></td><td>tenebrosum{sum}</td></tr>
<tr><td>11:35 (423^{a})</td><td><em>tenebrae</em></td><td></td><td></td><td></td><td>^{te}nebrae</td></tr>
<tr><td></td><td>tenebrae rese</td><td></td><td></td><td></td><td>tenebrae ipse</td></tr>
<tr><td>11:37 (423^{a})</td><td>loquentae</td><td>loquente</td><td></td><td></td><td>loquentae</td></tr>
<tr><td>11:40 (423^{b})</td><td>Nonne</td><td>---</td><td>nonne</td><td>---</td><td>Nonne</td></tr>
<tr><td></td><td>uerum interiora</td><td>interiora</td><td>uerum interiora</td><td></td><td>uerum interiora</td></tr>
<tr><td>11:44 (424^{b})</td><td>ignobilia</td><td></td><td></td><td>ingnobilia</td><td>ingnobilia</td></tr>
<tr><td>11:50 (425^{b})</td><td>et</td><td>est</td><td></td><td></td><td>e<s>t</td></tr>
<tr><td>11:54 (426^{b})</td><td>occasiuonem</td><td>occansonem</td><td>occasionem</td><td></td><td>occansionem</td></tr>
<tr><td>12:7 (428^{a})</td><td>dmi se|d</td><td>dei sed</td><td>dmi sed</td><td>---</td><td>dmi se|d</td></tr>
<tr><td>12:15 (429^{b})</td><td>superando</td><td></td><td>superrando</td><td></td><td>super{r}ando</td></tr>
<tr><td>12:16 (429^{b})</td><td>cui|iusdam</td><td>cu|iusdam</td><td></td><td>---</td><td>cu|iusdam</td></tr>
<tr><td>12:20 (430^{a})</td><td>erint</td><td>erunt</td><td></td><td></td><td>erint</td></tr>
<tr><td>12:33 (432^{a})</td><td>ueterascunt</td><td>ueterescunt</td><td>ueterascunt</td><td>ueterescunt</td><td>ueterescunt</td></tr>
<tr><td>13:7 (434^{a})</td><td>quaereus</td><td>quaerens</td><td></td><td></td><td>quaerens</td></tr>
<tr><td>13:22 (437^{a})</td><td>hierosolymis</td><td></td><td>hierusolymis</td><td>hierosolymus</td><td>hierosolymis</td></tr>
<tr><td>13:24 (437^{a})</td><td>poterint</td><td>poterunt</td><td>poterint</td><td></td><td>poterint</td></tr>
<tr><td>13:27 (438^{a})</td><td>operari</td><td>operarii</td><td>operari</td><td></td><td>operari</td></tr>
<tr><td>13:28 (438^{a})</td><td>fletus et</td><td>et stridor</td><td>fletus et et stridor</td><td></td><td>fletus et {et} stridor</td></tr>
<tr><td>14:4 (440^{a})</td><td>adprhendens</td><td>adprehendens</td><td></td><td></td><td>adprehendens</td></tr>
<tr><td>14:7 (440^{b})</td><td>quomodo quomodo</td><td>quomodo</td><td></td><td></td><td>quomodo</td></tr>
<tr><td>14:8 (441^{a})</td><td>aliquis inuitatus</td><td>aliquis sit inuitatus</td><td></td><td></td><td>aliquis ^{sit} inuitatus</td></tr>
<tr><td>14:10 (441^{a})</td><td>ut</td><td></td><td>et</td><td></td><td>ut</td></tr>
<tr><td>14:12 (442^{a})</td><td>reditio</td><td>redditio</td><td></td><td></td><td>redditio</td></tr>
<tr><td>14:23 (443^{a})</td><td>exi exi</td><td>exi</td><td>exi exi</td><td></td><td>exi {exi}</td></tr>
<tr><td></td><td>uia|s</td><td>uias</td><td>uia|s</td><td>---</td><td>uia|s</td></tr>
<tr><td>14:28 (445^{a})</td><td>com|putauit</td><td>compu|tauit</td><td></td><td>---</td><td>compu|tauit</td></tr>
</table>

48 Corrected to *uidet* through *expunctum* in the manuscript.

Luke	Irico	Bianchini	Gasquet	Jülicher et al.	MSI-images/ New Readings
14:35 (446^{a})	*in terra neque*		*in terram neque*	*in terram nec*	*in terra neque*
15:2 (446^{a})	*pharisaei et*	*pharisaei | et*		---	*pharisaei | et*
15:5 (447^{a})	*inponit*			*imponit*	*inpon^{i}et*
15:7 (447^{a})	*peccattorem*	*peccatorem*			*peccatorem*
15:8 (447^{b})	*perdederit*	*perdiderit*	*perdederit*	*perdiderit*	*perdederit*
15:9 (447^{b})	*eam uocat*				*conuocat*
15:9 (448^{a})	*dracmam*		*dracman*	*dragmam*	*dracman*
15:12 (448^{b})	*substantiam*				*sub<s>tantiam*
15:15 (449^{a})	*municipb*	*municipibus*	*municib*	*municipibus*	*municipib<us>*
15:17 (449^{a})	*mercenarii*		*mercennarii*		*mercennarii*
15:19 (449^{b})	*mercenariis*	*mercennariis*	*mercenariis*	*mercennariis*	*mercennariis*
15:20 (450^{a})	*pater pater*	*pater*	*pater pater*		*pater {pater}*
15:27 (451^{a})	*uitulum*				*{is} uitulum*
15:30 (451^{b})	*cum*	---	*cum*	---	*Cum*
15:32 (452^{a})	*aepula | ri*		*aepu | lari*	---	*aepu | lari*
16:4 (453^{a})	*amotus*				*amotuos*[49]
16:7 (454^{a})	*scribo*	*scribe*			*scribe*
16:14 (455^{a})	*irridebant*	*inridebant*			*inridebant*
16:17 (456^{a})	*facili | us*	*facilius*	*facili | us*	---	*facili | us*
16:18 (456^{a})	*qui dimissam*	*quit dimissam*			*quit di Dimissam*[50]
	moecatur	*moechatur*	*moecatur*	*moechatur*	*moecatur*
16:22 (457^{a})	*inferos*				*inferose*[51]
16:23 (457^{a})	*occulos*	*oculos*	*occulos*	*oculos*	*oculos*
	sinu				*sineu*[52]
16:24 (457^{a})	*abrhaham*	*abraham*			*abraham*
16:25 (457^{b})	*memor esto*			*memorrestotem*	*memor{r} estotem*[53]
16:29 (458^{b})	*habram*	*habraham*			*habraham*
17:8 (460^{a})	*praepara*				*praeparia*[54]
	succinttus	*succinctus*			*succinctus*
	bibet	*bibes*	*bibet*		*bibet*
17:12 (461^{a})	*s | teterunt*	*steterunt*		---	*s | teterunt*
17:13 (461^{a})	*iesum*	*iesu*			*iesu*
17:16 (461^{b})	*samaritanus*	*samarites*	*samaritanus*		*samarites*
17:20 (462^{a})	*cum*				*dei*
17:22 (462^{b})	*non uidebitis*	*et non uidebitis*			*^{et} non uidebitis*

49 Corrected to *amotus* twice in the manuscript (*expunctum* and *rasura*).
50 The dittography was corrected through *rasura* in the manuscript.
51 The superfluous letter "E" was crossed out in the manuscript.
52 Corrected to *sinu* in the manuscript.
53 The superfluous letters "TEM" were crossed out in the manuscript.
54 Corrected to *praepara* in the manuscript.

<table>
<tr><th>Luke</th><th>Irico</th><th>Bianchini</th><th>Gasquet</th><th>Jülicher et al.</th><th>MSI-images/ New Readings</th></tr>
<tr><td>17:24 (462^{b})</td><td>*fulgul*</td><td>*fulgul*</td><td>*fulgur*</td><td></td><td>*fulgul*[55]</td></tr>
<tr><td>17:25 (462^{b})</td><td>*prepobari*</td><td>*reprobari*</td><td>*prepobari*</td><td>*reprobari*</td><td>*prepobari*[56]</td></tr>
<tr><td>17:26 (463^{a})</td><td>*fili*</td><td>*filii*</td><td>*fili*</td><td></td><td>*fili*</td></tr>
<tr><td>17:29 (463^{a})</td><td>*lo|t*</td><td>*lot*</td><td>*lo|t*</td><td>---</td><td>*lo|t*</td></tr>
<tr><td>17:31 (463^{b})</td><td>*uase*</td><td>*uasa*</td><td></td><td></td><td>*uasa*</td></tr>
<tr><td>17:33 (463^{b})</td><td>*Quicunque*</td><td>*Quicumque*</td><td></td><td></td><td>*Quicumque*</td></tr>
<tr><td>17:34 (464^{a})</td><td>*nocte*</td><td></td><td></td><td>*noctu*</td><td>*noctu*</td></tr>
<tr><td></td><td>*erint*</td><td>*erunt*</td><td>*erint*</td><td></td><td>*erint*</td></tr>
<tr><td>17:35 (464^{a})</td><td>*erint*</td><td>*erunt*</td><td>*erint*</td><td></td><td>*erint*</td></tr>
<tr><td></td><td>*mollentes*</td><td>*molentes*</td><td></td><td></td><td>*mollentes*</td></tr>
<tr><td></td><td>*in | unum*</td><td>*in u|num*</td><td>*in | unum*</td><td>---</td><td>*in u|num*</td></tr>
<tr><td>17:35 (464^{b})</td><td>*adsumetur*</td><td></td><td></td><td></td><td>*adsumertur*[57]</td></tr>
<tr><td>17:37 (464^{b})</td><td>*ubicunque*</td><td>*ubicumque*</td><td>*ubicunque*</td><td>*ubicumque*</td><td>*ubicumque*</td></tr>
<tr><td>18:2 (465^{a})</td><td>*ciuitatate*</td><td>*ciuitate*</td><td></td><td></td><td>*ciuitate*</td></tr>
<tr><td></td><td>*timebat*</td><td></td><td></td><td>*timebant*</td><td>*timebant*[58]</td></tr>
<tr><td>18:3 (465^{a})</td><td>*ciuitatem*</td><td>*ciuitate*</td><td>*ciuitatem*</td><td></td><td>*ciuitatem*</td></tr>
<tr><td></td><td>*aduersaris meis*</td><td>*aduersario meo*</td><td></td><td></td><td>*aduersario meo*</td></tr>
<tr><td>18:4 (465^{a})</td><td>*reor*</td><td>*reuereor*</td><td>*reor*</td><td></td><td>*reor*</td></tr>
<tr><td>18:8 (465^{b})</td><td>*facet*</td><td>*faciet*</td><td></td><td></td><td>*facet*</td></tr>
<tr><td></td><td>*uindic*</td><td>*uindictam*</td><td>*uindic*</td><td></td><td>*uindic<tam>*</td></tr>
<tr><td>18:16 (467^{b})</td><td>*no|lite*</td><td>*noli|te*</td><td>*no|lite*</td><td>---</td><td>*no|lite*</td></tr>
<tr><td>18:22 (468^{b})</td><td>*da*</td><td>*ea*</td><td>$^{\textit{et da}}$ *ea*</td><td>*dando ea*</td><td>$^{\textit{et diuide}}$ *ea*</td></tr>
<tr><td>18:23 (469^{a})</td><td>*tristes*</td><td>*tristis*</td><td>*tristes*</td><td>*tristis*</td><td>*tristes*</td></tr>
<tr><td>18:25 (469^{a})</td><td>*forameM*</td><td>*forame*</td><td>*forame*</td><td>*foramen*</td><td>*forameM*</td></tr>
<tr><td></td><td>*acus*</td><td></td><td>*n acus*</td><td>*acus*</td><td>*namcus*[59]</td></tr>
<tr><td></td><td>*regum*</td><td>*regnum*</td><td></td><td></td><td>*regnum*</td></tr>
<tr><td>18:25 (469^{b})</td><td>*diuites*</td><td>*diuitem*</td><td>*diuite*</td><td>*diuite*</td><td>*diuite*</td></tr>
<tr><td>18:27 (469^{b})</td><td>*inposs|ibilia*</td><td>*inpos|sibilia*</td><td>*inposs|ibilia*</td><td>---</td><td>*inpos|sibilia*</td></tr>
<tr><td>18:30 (470^{a})</td><td>*posside|bit*</td><td></td><td>*possi|debit*</td><td>---</td><td>*possi|debit*</td></tr>
<tr><td>18:43 (472^{a})</td><td>*caepit*</td><td>*coepit*</td><td></td><td></td><td>*coepit*</td></tr>
<tr><td>19:5 (473^{a})</td><td>*zacchee*</td><td>*zacchaee*</td><td></td><td>*zacchee*</td><td>*zacchaee*</td></tr>
<tr><td>19:8 (473^{b})</td><td>*dm*</td><td>*dominum*</td><td>*dom*</td><td>*dominum*</td><td>*dom*</td></tr>
<tr><td>19:9 (473^{b})</td><td>*abrahe*</td><td>*abrahae*</td><td></td><td></td><td>*abrahae*</td></tr>
<tr><td>19:10 (474^{a})</td><td>*querere*</td><td>*quaerere*</td><td></td><td></td><td>*quaerere*</td></tr>
<tr><td>19:18 (475^{b})</td><td>*m|nas*</td><td>*mnas*</td><td>*m|nas*</td><td>---</td><td>*m|nas*</td></tr>
<tr><td>19:22 (476^{a})</td><td>*austerus*</td><td>*austeris*</td><td>*austerus*</td><td>*austerus*</td><td>*austeris*</td></tr>
</table>

55 Gasquet's observation is wrong (p. 107, fn. b) since both Irico and Bianchini read *fulgul*, not just Bianchini, as Gasquet claims.

56 Corrected to *reprobari* in the manuscript.

57 Corrected to *adsumetur* in the manuscript.

58 Corrected to *timebat* through *expunctum* in the manuscript.

59 Corrected to *acus* through *expunctum* in the manuscript.

Luke	Irico	Bianchini	Gasquet	Jülicher et al.	MSI-images/ New Readings
19:27 (476^{b})	*ueruntamen*	*uerumtamen*			*uerumtamen*
19:29 (477^{a})	*bethania*	*bethaniae*	*bethania*		*bethania*
	apellatur	*appellatur*			*appellatur*
19:31 (477^{b})	*solui|tis*	*sol|uitis*	*solui|tis*	---	*sol|uitis*
	dessiderat	*desiderat*			*desiderat*
19:32 (477^{b})	*sicut*	*et sicut*	^{et} *sicut*	*sicut*	*sicut*
19:33 (478^{a})	*illius*				*ipsius*
19:38 (479^{a})	*pacis*	*pax*			*pax*
19:43 (479^{b})	*sepem*	*saepem*			*saepem*
19:45 (480^{a})	*et uertit*	*euertit*	*etuertit*		*etuertit*[60]
20:1 (481^{a})	*adsteterunt*	*adstiterunt*			*adstiterunt*
20:2 (481^{a})	*potestate*				*potestatem*
	facis | et	*facis et*	*facis | et*	---	*facis | et*
20:3 (481^{a})	*respondete*	*respondite*			*respondite*
20:5 (481^{b})	*sed*	*ad*		*at*	*ad*
20:6 (481^{b})	*dixerimus*	*si dixerimus*			*si dixerimus*
20:6 (481^{b})	*iohannem*	*iohannen*	*iohannem*	*iohanen*	*iohanen*
20:9 (482^{a})	*caepit*	*coepit*			*coepit*
20:13 (482^{b})	*forsitan*			*forsitam*	*forsitam*
20:14 (483^{a})	*haeres*	*heres*	*haeres*	*heres*	*heres*
	occidamus				*oc{ca}cidamus*
20:16 (483^{a})	*com*	*cum*			*com*
20:20 (484^{a})	om.	*subor*			*subor<natos>*
	itaut	*se ut*			*se ut*
20:21 (484^{a})	*intero|gauerunt*	*inter|rog.*	*interro|gau-erunt*	---	*inter|rogauerunt*
	accipes	*accipis*	*accipes*		*accipes*
	personam			*persona*	*persona*
20:24 (485^{a})	*immaginem*	*imaginem*			*imaginem*
20:25 (485^{a})	*ut*	*et*			*et*
20:28 (485^{b})	*moyses*				*moises*
20:29 (486^{a})	*frares*	*fratres*			*fratres*
	accepit				*{a}accepit*
20:34 (486^{b})	*fili*	*filii*	*fili*		*fili*
	om.	*nubunt*			*nubunt*
20:35 (486^{b})	*atting|ere*	*attin|gere*	*atting|ere*	---	*attin|gere*
20:37 (487^{a})	*de|monstrauit*			---	*dem|onstrauit*
20:46 (488^{a})	*primos consessus*		*primo consessus*		*primos consessus*
20:47 (488^{a})	*paenae*	*poenae*			*poenae*
21:2 (488^{b})	*quemdam*	*quandam*	*quemdam*	*quendam*	*quendam*
21:4 (488^{b})	*domo*	*dona*			*dona*

60 Corrected to *euertit* through *expunctum* in the manuscript.

Luke	Irico	Bianchini	Gasquet	Jülicher et al.	MSI-images/ New Readings
21:5 (489[a])	*et*	---	*et*	---	*Et*
21:8 (489[b])	*nec*	*ne*			*ne*
21:11 (490[a])	*terrimotus*		*terremotus*		*terrimotus*
	-quae et	*-que de*			*-quae de*
21:14 (490[b])	*medetare*	*meditare*	*medetare*		*meletare*
21:15 (490[b])	*uobis*	*uobis os*	*uobis* [os]		*uobis* [os]
	poterint	*poterunt*	*poterint*		*poterint*
21:20 (491[a])	*circumdatam*				*circumdata{s}m*
21:23 (492[a])	*in in illis*	*in illis*	*in in illis*	*in illis*	*in {in} illis*
21:24 (492[a])	*uniuersa*	*uniuersas*	*uniuersa*		*uniuersa*
21:25 (492[a])	*erint*	*erunt*	*erint*		*erint*
	sole				*solet*[61]
	compressio	*conpressio*			*conpressio*
21:27 (492[b])	*potestate*				*potentia*
21:28 (493[a])	*adpropinquate*	*.propinquat*	*adpropinquate*		*adpropinquate*
21:31 (493[a])	*uideritis*			*uidebitis*	*uidebitis*
21:34 (493[b])	*sollicitudinibus*				*solligitudinibus*
21:35 (494[a])	*intrauit*	*intrabit*			*intrauit*
21:36 (494[a])	*futura sunt*				*futura*
	fifilium	*filium*			*fifilium*[62]
22:5 (495[a])	*se pecuniam*				*ei se pecuniam*
	daturos				*datiuros*[63]
22:15 (496[a])	*es est hora*	*est hora*			*est hora*
	cubuit	*discubuit*			*discubuit*
22:19 (497[a])	*dieccens*	*dicens*			*dieccens*[64]
22:22 (497[b])	*uerum*				*uaerum*
22:24 (497[b])	*esse*	*esset*			*esset*
	maior				*malior*[65]
22:31 (499[a])	*scribaret*	*scribraret*			*scribaret*
22:33 (499[b])	*et et in carcerem*	*et in carcerem*			*et in carcerem*
22:36 (499[b])	*simuliter*	*similiter*			*similiter*
22:42 (501[a])	*transfers*	*transfer*	*transfers*		*transfer{s}*
22:43 (501[a])	*conforti|ans*	*confor|tians*	*conforti|ans*	---	*conforti|ans*
22:47 (501[b])	*praecedebabat*	*praecedebat*			*praecedebat*
22:50 (502[a])	*dexteram*	*dextram*			*dextram*
22:53 (502[b])	*tenebrae*	*tenebrarum*			*a tenebrae*
22:54 (502[b])	*in domum*			*et in domum*	*et in domum*

61 The superfluous letter "T" was crossed out in the manuscript.

62 The dittography was corrected in the manuscript.

63 Corrected to *daturos* in the manuscript.

64 Corrected to *dicens*.

65 Corrected to *maior* in the manuscript.

Luke	Irico	Bianchini	Gasquet	Jülicher et al.	MSI-images/ New Readings
22:56 (503^{a})	*dixit et*	*dixit | et*	*dixit et*	---	*dixit et*
22:58 (503^{a})	*egressus in*	*egressum*			*egressu{s}m*
22:64 (504^{a})	*coperientes*	*cooperientes*	*coperientes*		*coperientes*
	percutebant	*percutiebant*			*percutebant*
	interrogaba…	*interrogabant*			*interrogabaM*
22:65 (504^{b})	*blasfemantes*				*blaspemantes*
23:2 (505^{b})	*esset*	*esse*	*esset*		*esse{t}*
23:4 (506^{a})	*pontificis*	*pontifices*	*pontificis*		*pontificis*
23:14 (507^{b})	*aduertentem*	*auertentem*	*aduertentem*		*aduertentem*
	uos	*uobis*		*uos*	*uos*
23:14 (508^{a})	*homine*				*homineM*
23:18 (508^{a})	*barabbant*	*barabban*	*barabbant*		*barabbant*
23:20 (508^{b})	*adlocuttus*	*adlocutus*			*adlocustus*[66]
23:23 (509^{a})	*inualescebant*	*et inualescebant*			*inualescebant*
23:30 (510^{b})	*nos*				*nors*[67]
23:31 (510^{b})	*in umido*	*si in umido*	^{si} *in umido*	*si in umido*	^{si} *in umido*
23:35 (511^{a})	*expectans*	*exspectans*			*exspectans*
	se faciat	*faciat*		*se faciat*	*se faciat*
23:39 (511^{b})	*eum*				*illum*
23:47 (513^{a})	*ui|disset*		*uidisset*	---	*ui|disset*
23:48 (513^{a})	*conuenerunt*	*conuenerant*			*conuenerant*
	ex ea	*ea*	*ex ea*		*ex ea*
	percutientes	*percutentes*	*percutientes*		*percutentes*
23:49 (513^{a})	*stabant*	---	*stabant*	---	*Stabant*
23:53 (514^{a})	*aliqui*	*aliquis*	*aliqui*^{s}		*aliqui*^{s}
23:54 (514^{a})	*cena*	*cenae*	*cena*		*cena*
	inlucescebat				*inlucecscebat*[68]
24:5 (515^{b})	*ad ad*	*ad*	*ad ad*		*ad {ad}*
24:8 (515^{b})	*maemoratae*	*memoratae*	*maemoratae*	*memoratae*	*maemoratae*
24:10 (516^{a})	*relique*	*reliquae*			*relique*
	que	*quae*			*que*
24:11 (516^{a})	*haec et*	*haec | et*	*haec et*	---	*haec et*
	delera	*delira*	*delera*		*delera*
24:13 (516^{b})	*ammaus|i*	*ammaus*	*ammau|s*	---	*ammaus|s*[69]
24:14 (516^{b})	*contegerant*	*contigerant*			*contegerant*
24:16 (516^{b})	*eorum eorum*	*eorum*	*eorum eorum*	*eorum*	*eorum eorum*[70]
24:17 (517^{a})	*est*	*et*	*est*		*e{s}t*

66 Corrected through *expunctum*.

67 Corrected to *nos* in the manuscript.

68 Corrected to *inlucescebat* in the manuscript.

69 The dittography was corrected through *expunctum* in the manuscript.

70 The dittography was corrected through *expunctum* in the manuscript.

Luke	Irico	Bianchini	Gasquet	Jülicher et al.	MSI-images/ New Readings
24:18 (517[a])	*nommen*	*nomen*			*nommen*
24:22 (518[a])	*nobis*	*nostris*	*nobis*		*nobis*
	nos				*hos*
24:24 (518[a])	*nobis*	*nostris*	*nobis*		*nobis*
24:25 (518[b])	*insensati*				*insentsati*[71]
	prophaetae	*prophetae*			*prophaetae*
24:33 (520[a])	*eas*	*eos*			*eos*
24:39 (521[a])	*uidebis*	*uidetis*		*uidetes*	*uidetes*
24:43 (521[a])	*cor|am*	*co|ram*	*cor|am*	---	*co|ram*
24:45 (521[b])	*intelligendum*	*intellegendum*	*intelligendum*	*intellegendum*	*intellegendum*
24:47 (522[a])	*om|nibus*		*omni|bus*	---	*om|nibus*
24:50 (522[a])	*seduxit*	*eduxit*			*eduxit*

71 Corrected to *insensati* in the manuscript.

3 The Relation of the *Codex Vercellensis* Luke to the Greek Texts

In Chapter 3, we turn to our second research question, namely that concerning the relationship of *Vercellensis* text to the Greek versions of the Gospel of Luke. We begin by comparing the text of the *Codex Vercellensis* to papyrological evidence (3.1) and to the oldest Majuscule witnesses of Luke (3.2). Then, we will turn our attention to the Greek texts of the codices *Bezae* (D, 05) and *Coridethianus* (Θ, 38), with which the *Vercellensis* shares significant similarities. In the following sections we concentrate on two kinds of evidence: first, cases of apparent conflation of Greek readings which the Vercellensis has in common with some Greek manuscripts (word for word translation; omissions and additions); and second, cases of apparent conflation of phonological, morphological, and syntactical readings. The focus of the discussion which follows is on the eventual influence of the Latin tradition on the Greek text as it is preserved in these two authorities.

It is often difficult to discern the precise interconnections between the Greek and Latin variants of a given passage. To take two examples: in Luke 5:2, during the calling of the first disciples, Jesus sees two boats while standing by the lake of Gennesaret. In most Latin texts, the reference to the boats is rendered as *duas naues*, a plain translation of the Greek reading δύο πλοῖα. However, there are two major exceptions: *Codex Palatinus* (VL2) reads *naues duas* (πλοῖα δύο), a variation in word order also attested by the *Vaticanus* (B, 03) and *Washingtonianus* (W, 032); *Codex Vercellensis* in turn employs the diminutive of *naues*, namely *nauiculas duas*. According to NA^{28}, the corresponding Greek diminutive of πλοῖον is transmitted in five Majuscules – *Alexandrinus* (A, 02), *Ephraemi Rescriptus* (C, 04: *manus prima*), *Regius* (L, 019), *Guelferbytanus B* (Q, 026) and *Athous Laurae* (Ψ, 044) – but always in the word order δύο πλοάρια. Given the reading of the *Vercellensis*, the following questions arise: does the rendering *nauiculas duas* come about through an internal process taking place in the Old Latin versions and reflecting a development of the Latin text without any reference to the Greek tradition? Alternatively, can the reading be traced back to an underlying Greek text with the variant πλοάρια δύο, for which no witnesses survive? In commenting on the *Vercellensis*, Jean-Claude Haelewyck describes its readings as deviating from all other Latin witnesses, noting that "[l]e libellé de D tranche sur les autres types de texte par un vocabulaire particulier."[1] The fundamental question, therefore, is: are all Latin 'translations' in the manuscript from Vercelli based on a Greek text unknown to us, or does the text reflect

1 HAELEWYCK, Evangelium secundum Marcum, 49f.

https://doi.org/10.1515/9783111142531-004

development of readings internal to the Latin tradition and thus based on earlier Latin versions?

The case of Luke 9:10 is also paradigmatic. There is no direct attestation for the Greek text used by any of the Latin manuscripts, except in case of the Latin *Codex Bezae* (VL5), which reads *in castellum, quod dicitur bedsaida*. The reading agrees – even orthographically (*bedsaida* with a *d*, not with the usual *t* or *th*) – with εἰς κώμην λεγομένην Βηδσαϊδά, found in the Greek column of the diglot manuscript. But the other witnesses, including the *Vercellensis*, transmit a combination of readings scattered throughout various Greek manuscripts, with the possibilities including: εἰς τόπον ἔρημον (א*,2b), εἰς κώμην καλουμένην Βηθσαιδαν εἰς τόπον ἔρημον (Θ), εἰς τόπον ἔρημον πολέως καλουμένης Βηθσαιδα (A C K N W Γ Δ Ξ, each with small modifications in word order or spelling), εἰς τόπον καλούμενον Βηθσαιδα (Ψ). None of these readings, however, matches the Latin readings *in locum desertum, qui* (A; *quod* VL2, 4, 8) *uocabatur* (*appelatur* VL2; *est* VL4, 8, A) *betsaida* (VL4; *bessaida* VL2, 8; *bethsaida* A).

Analyzing the transmission of the Old Latin Gospels in light of such passages gives rise to two questions: 1. To what extent is the text at hand dependent on the Greek tradition? 2. To what extent can the variants in the text instead be explained by a process of internal development in the Latin? In other words, it is essential to investigate whether the text of a certain manuscript is a direct translation from a Greek source or rather reproduces another Latin text, along with adjustments, corrections, and new translational choices. To answer these two questions with reference to the *Codex Vercellensis*, we must first clarify its relation to the known Greek witnesses.

3.1 The Greek Layer of the *Codex Vercellensis* and the Papyri

In general, papyri are considered to be the earliest sources containing the original text of the New Testament. At present, there are twelve known papyri with the Greek text of the Gospel of Luke ($\mathfrak{P}^{3}$, $\mathfrak{P}^{4}$, $\mathfrak{P}^{7}$, $\mathfrak{P}^{42}$, $\mathfrak{P}^{45}$, $\mathfrak{P}^{69}$, $\mathfrak{P}^{75}$, $\mathfrak{P}^{82}$, $\mathfrak{P}^{97}$, $\mathfrak{P}^{111}$ $\mathfrak{P}^{138}$ and $\mathfrak{P}^{141}$), most of them written between the second and third century.[2] Except for $\mathfrak{P}^{45}$ and $\mathfrak{P}^{75}$, which contain larger portions of the text, all these witnesses are fragmentary and not extensive. In the following tables, we list readings found in the *Codex Vercellensis* which are not attested in any other of the oldest Latin versions of Luke but are supported by papyrological evidence.

2 Cf. ALAND ET AL., "Kurzgefasste Liste," 3–17.

3.1.1 Conflation of Greek Readings: Variation in Word Order in the *Codex Vercellensis* and the Papyri

Table 1: Variation in word order in the *Codex Vercellensis* and the papyri

Verse	NA²⁸	Variant	Greek authorities	VL3
8:23	λαῖλαψ [...] λίμνην	λαῖλαψ [...] ἀνέμου	𝔓75 B	turbo [...] uenti
11:17	ἐφ' ἑαυτὴν διαμερισθεῖσα	διαμερισθεῖσα (μερισθεῖσα) ἐφ' ἑαυτήν	(𝔓45) ℵ A D L (Ψ)	diuisum super se
14:10	σοι δόξα	δόξα σοι	𝔓75	gloria tibi

Especially noteworthy is the different word order in Luke 14:10, not shown in the *apparatus criticus* of NA²⁸ but attested by the *Vercellensis* and 𝔓75. This papyrus, dated to the beginning of the fourth century, originally contained the complete Gospels of John and Luke.[3] For this reason, 𝔓75 has been said to be "the most significant" New Testament papyrus that has come to light in the twentieth century, an assessment also based on the manuscript's relatively good state of preservation.[4] For this reason, the common reading with 𝔓75 provides important evidence for the claim that the text of the *Vercellensis* belongs to an early stage of textual transmission.

3.1.2 Omissions in the *Codex Vercellensis* and the Papyri

Table 2: Omissions in the *Codex Vercellensis* and the papyri

Verse	NA²⁸	Variant	Greek authorities	VL3
23:17	ἀνάγκην [...] ἑορτὴν ἕνα	om.	𝔓75 A B K L T	om.
23:34	ὁ δὲ [...] ποιοῦσιν	om.	𝔓75 ℵ2a B D* W Θ	om.

3 Cf. Edwards, "P75 under the Magnifying Glass," 194–195.

4 Nongbri, "Reconsidering the Place of Papyrus Bodmer XIV–XV," 406. He argues considerable, that, if both Codex Vaticanus and 𝔓75 can be dated to the 4th century C.E., "then textual critics of the New Testament may need once again to entertain the idea that the 'B Text' is indeed the result of some sort of recensional activity in the fourth century" (p. 437). He also focuses on the shape of the codex page, giving attention to Eric G. Turner's proposal dating codices by shape (*The Typology of the Early Codex* ([University of Pennsylvania Press, 1977; reprint, Wipf & Stock, 2010], see especially pp. 20–23; the majority of Turner's material is Greek and papyrological). Nongbri compares 𝔓75 with "group 8" (14/ 12B – 30/ 25 H) noting that the shape is similar to codices dated to the 4th century.

Both omissions deserve attention. Luke 23:17 is not printed in the most recent editions of the Greek NT; however, this verse was the ***textus receptus*** up to the 19th century, losing this status only once the discovery of $\mathfrak{P}^{75}$ (along with support from B, 03 and A, 02) challenged the authenticity of this verse. In commenting on this passage, we may first remark that a verse of similar content is already found in Matt 27:15, Mark 15:6 as well as in John 18:39. For this reason, most scholars conclude that the verse was assimilated into Luke at a very early date. Its secondary character also becomes clear through its insertion, with minor variations, after v. 19, where it is found in the *Codex Bezae* (D, 05). Secondly, we may note that, even if the identical beginning of the words ἀνάγκην and ἀνέκραγον in v. 18 could have led a scribe to accidently exclude the verse (by homoeoarcton), this hypothesis does not explain its widespread omission and its transposition to a different place in the text.[5] Moreover, one must take into account the adversative δέ in verse 18, which can hardly refer to verse 17. Finally, the content of the verse may be taken to explain the sudden appearance of Barnabas in verse 18. However, the decisive consideration is the fact that the early $\mathfrak{P}^{75}$ and the majuscules A B K L, to name but a few, do not contain the verse, and that the *Codex Vercellensis* is the only Latin authority to also omit this verse.

The text critical problem in Luke 23:34, the prayer of Jesus asking his father to forgive his executioners, is even more difficult. The question who is to be forgiven – the local Jerusalem aristocracy or the Jerusalem Jews or the Roman soldiers carrying out the order – is already in itself controversial. The situation is made even more complex by the possibility that the prayer is perfectly general and in principle includes all groups. In any case, the external testimony on this matter is by no means clear. According to Metzger, the request was probably not part of the text of Luke; nevertheless, Metzger argues that this request goes back to Jesus and was accordingly inserted by copyists.[6] From the point of view of textual structure at least, it can be said that the vocabulary and style fit the Gospel of Luke, including for example the vocative πάτερ, which occurs in Luke 10:21 and Luke 11:2, and may as such be considered typical of the Lukan prayer. Bovon has also made it clear that this verse is in keeping with the demand of the Sermon of the Field, where Jesus first establishes prayer for enemies.[7] In any case, the external testimony of the

5 Cf. METZGER, A Textual Commentary," 179. For a divergent position, see JUDD, "A Case for the Authenticity of Luke 23:17," who argues that a closer examination of the passage shows that it is not a scribal harmonization but is thoroughly Lucan. According to his study, Luke 23:17 is authentic and was omitted by a scribe who wanted to emphasize the demand of the Jewish crowd and leaders that Jesus be crucified.

6 Cf. METZGER, A Textual Commentary, 99.

7 BOVON, Evangelium nach Lukas III/4, 461.

textual witnesses permits no certain solution, as Blum has made clear.[8] Accordingly, the textual tradition underlying the verse and the ambiguous status of the internal arguments favoring the logion have meant that the question of the verse's authenticity remains open. At any rate, the exclusion of this verse from 𝔓[75] and the *Codex Vercellensis* testifies to its absence in an early stage of textual transmission, in which the verse was not considered authentic.

3.1.3 Conflation of Syntax in the *Codex Vercellensis* and the Papyri

Table 3: Conflation of syntax in the *Codex Vercellensis* and the papyri

Verse	NA[28]	Variant	Greek authorities	VL3
7:43	ἀποκριθείς	ἀποκριθεὶς δέ	𝔓[3] A K P Γ Δ Θ Ψ	*respondens autem*
11:41	ἐστιν	ἔσται	𝔓[45] D Γ	*erunt*

The change in Luke 11:41, observed in 𝔓[45], is particularly significant. Tertullian also read a future tense (*erunt*) at the end of this verse instead of the present (*est*) attested by the majority of the manuscripts.[9] The sequence of tenses (δότε ἐλεημοσύνην – ἔσται) has been interpreted as a consecutive future, which can be regarded as an influence of the language of the Septuagint.[10] The fact that the reading appears not only in the *Vercellensis* and *Bezae*, but also in 𝔓[45], constitutes some evidence that it may offer the original text of Luke.

From this analysis, we observe that many of the readings of the *Vercellensis* not found in other Latin authorities are supported by papyrological evidence. Most impressive in this respect are the extensive omissions in Luke 23:17, 24, which have important theological implications. This reveals how the text of the *Vercellensis* preserved numerous readings which are not only very early but possibly also original. In this context, the importance of 𝔓[75] and the text of *Codex Vercellensis* becomes especially clear, since these witnesses attest to the oldest tradition, in Greek and Latin respectively.

8 Blum, "...denn sie wissen nicht, was sie tun," 17–21.

9 Cf. Tert. *adv. Marc*. 4.27.3.

10 Cf. Klinghardt, Das älteste Evangelium, 761.

3.2 The Greek Layer of the *Codex Vercellensis* and the Majuscules

The *Codex Vercellensis* transmits variant readings which, though encountered nowhere else in the oldest Latin tradition, are found in the earliest Greek Majuscules, and especially in the codices *Sinaiticus* (ℵ, 01), *Alexandrinus* (A, 02) and *Vaticanus* (B, 03). However, most of these variants concern minor changes in word order or in the use of conjunctions, prepositions, and particles. In the following tables, we list these common readings, comparing them with the mainstream Greek text:

Table 4: Conflation of Greek readings: variation in word order in the *Codex Vercellensis* and the Majuscules

Verse	NA^{28}	Variant	Greek authorities	VL3
3:14	τί […] καὶ ἡμεῖς	καὶ ἡμεῖς τί […]	A C^3 K N Γ Δ Θ Ψ	*et nos quid* […]
4:8	κύριον […] προσκυνήσεις	προσκυνήσεις κύριον	A K Γ Δ Θ	*diliges dominum*
20:6	ὁ λαὸς ἅπας	πᾶς ὁ λαός	A C K N Q W Γ Δ Θ Ψ	*omnis populus*
21:3	αὕτη ἡ πτωχή	ἡ πτωχὴ αὕτη	A K Q W Γ Δ Θ Ψ	*uidua paupera haec*

Table 5: Omissions in the *Codex Vercellensis* and the Majuscules

Verse	NA^{28}	Variant	Greek authorities	VL3
12:5	φοβήθητε	om.	ℵ D	om.

Table 6: Additions in the *Codex Vercellensis* and the Majuscules

Verse	NA^{28}	Variant	Greek authorities	VL3
6:20	om.	τῷ πνεύματι	$ℵ^{2a}$ Q Θ	*spiritu*
6:35	om.	ἐν τοῖς οὐρανοῖς	$ℵ^1$	*in caelo*

Table 7: Conflation of syntax in the *Codex Vercellensis* and the Majuscules

Verse	NA^{28}	Variant	Greek authorities	VL3
1:75	πάσαις ταῖς ἡμέραις	πάσας τὰς ἡμέρας	ℵ A C D K Γ Δ Θ Ψ	*omnes dies*
2:12	καὶ κείμενον	κείμενον	A K Γ Δ	*positum*
8:27	χρόνῳ ἱκανῷ	ἐκ χρόνων ἱκανῶν	$ℵ^{2a}$ A K W Γ Δ Θ Ψ	*ex temporibus multis*
10:12	λέγω ὑμῖν	λέγω δὲ ὑμῖν	ℵ D Θ Ξ	*dico autem uobis*
11:42	ταῦτα δὲ ἔδει	ταῦτα δεῖ	A	*haec oportet*
19:42	τὰ πρὸς εἰρήνην	τὰ πρὸς εἰρήνην σου	A K N W Γ Δ Ψ	*ad pacem tuam*
23:2	τὸ ἔθνος ἡμῶν	τὸ ἔθνος	A W Γ Δ Θ	*gentem*

Table 8: Differences of wording in the *Codex Vercellensis* and the Majuscules

Verse	NA²⁸	Variant	Greek authorities	VL3
3:35	Φάλεκ	Φάλεγ	A K Γ	*faleg*
4:16	Ναζαρά	Ναζαρέτ	B² K L	*nazaret*
8:13	οὗτοι	αὐτοί	B*	*ipsi*
8:29	δαιμονίου	δαίμονος	A C³ K L W Γ Δ Θ	*daemone*
20:27	ἐπηρώτησαν	ἐπηρώτων	B	*interrogabant*
24:28	προσεποιήσατο	προσεποιεῖτο	K P W Γ Δ Θ Ψ	*adfectabat*
24:49	ἀποστέλλω	ἐξαποστέλω	L	*mittam*

One change which deserves special attention is the addition of the dative of reference τῷ πνεύματι in Luke 6:20, found in the *Vercellensis* and in $\aleph^{2a}$ Q Θ. This is probably an attempt to harmonize the verse to the parallel in Matt 5:3. However, it is important to observe that, in the *Codex Sinaiticus*, the addition is a later correction whereas, in the *Vercellensis*, the phrase οἱ πτωχοὶ τῷ πνεύματι is the original reading of the manuscript. Also significant is the variation δαιμόνιον of the mainstream text, against δαίμων of the *Vercellensis* and A C^3 K L W Γ Δ Θ. This difference is remarkable, for it is the only place in the Gospels in which the singular δαίμων occurs, whereas the plural δαίμονες appears in Matt 8:31 and Mark 5:12 (only in A, 02).[11] The *Vercellensis* is thus one of the very few authorities to attest to this atypical reading.

3.3 The Greek Layer of the *Codex Vercellensis* in Comparison with the *Codex Bezae* (D, 05)

As an Old Latin Gospel, the *Codex Vercellensis* exhibits a series of features which are shared with the so-called D-text-type, traditionally designated in textual scholarship as the "Western text-type."

In order to account for the use of Greek originals, we must turn to the *Codex Bezae* (D, 05; VL5). The Greek text of the Gospel of Luke preserved in the manuscript contains some unique readings which distinguish it from other witnesses, such as

11 This is also the case in the LXX, where the term δαίμων appears only once, compared to the use of δαιμόνιον, which can be found up to 20 times. Cf. ANGELINI, "Δαίμονες and Demons," 3.

the Codices *Sinaticus* (ℵ, 01) and *Alexandrinus* (A, 02), including omissions (see e.g. Luke 22:20) and elaborations (see e.g. Luke 23:53).[12]

The *Codex Bezae* is a bilingual Greek-Latin manuscript whose Greek text is usually dated to the second century on the basis of references found in Irenaeus[13] and Justin.[14] Numerous comparisons have been made in order to establish this dating, but these parallels are not as clear as the scholars would have us believe. First of all, such correspondences (mostly word analogies) are quite coincidental in nature and also documented in numerous other Greek manuscripts; a similar overlap may be detected by applying this method to Ptolemy of Rome[15] or even Marcion.[16] In addition, we must note that, though the codex may refer to early writings, it was not itself written in this early period; instead, it seems equally possible that the author made the conscious effort to refer to these early writings. Focusing on the Gospel of Mark, Peter Lorenz[17] dates the manuscript to around 385 C.E., and indeed, the bilingual text can be well explained in the context of the rejection of Jerome's revision of the Vulgate. However, this explanation does not account for the existence of the common readings between *Bezae* D, 05 on the one hand and Justin Martyr or Ptolemy of Rome on the other, whose great number completely overshadows the numerous differences between these manuscripts.

---

12 This passage, and especially its Latin translation, are controversial: *imposuit in monumento lapidem quem uix uiginti mouerent*. The question is whether the translation may be traced back to a hexameter from Homer's Odyssey 9.240–242 (*imposuit lapidem quem uix uiginti mouerent*), which was only subsequently translated into Greek. See HARRIS, "Study of Codex Bezae," 48–52.

13 Admittedly, we must consider some readings found only in Irenaeus and *Codex Bezae* (D, 05), but which can ultimately be assigned to *adv. Haer*. 3.12,14; moreover, quotations from Irenaeus are also found in GA 1739. See GRYSON, "Répertoire général," 594 and PARKER, Bezae, 275–277; LORENZ, History of Codex Bezae's Text, 195ff.

14 See, e. g., KOESTER, Ancient Christian Gospels, 365, fn. 1; VAGANCY, AMPHOUX, "An Introduction to New Testament Textual Criticism," 96, who argue that "Justin and Irenaeus also use a text of the Gospels and Acts of the same type as Codex Bezae." For verbal parallels between Justin and Bezae (esp. in Acts), see BOUSSET, Evangeliencitate, esp. 104–109.

15 LORENZ, History of Codex Bezae's Text, 95–96, 104–110.

16 The more recent research question cannot be pursued here; on this, cf. SCHMID, Marcion und sein Apostolos, 40–58; ROTH, The Text of Marcion's Gospel, 78 and elsewhere; KLINGHARDT, Das älteste Evangelium. Vol. 1, 55, 68 and elsewhere; on Old Latin scholarship, see BAUER, "Das Evangelium des Markion und die Vetus Latina," 88, who argues as follows: "This picture is confirmed when one takes into account other places where the Codex Bezae and the witnesses of the 'Western text' offer a shorter text. [...] Where the text of Markion is ascertainable, it rarely offers the shorter variant." See also tables 1.12 and 1.13 in LORENZ, History of Codex Bezae's Text, 125f. and his further studies. We find the indiscriminate use of the Old Latin manuscripts claimed for the Marcionite text especially problematic.

17 LORENZ, History of Codex Bezae's Text, 181.

In view of numerous and often disparate exegetical judgments concerning the Greek and Latin texts of the *Codex Bezae* developed over the last three centuries, as well as the diversity of approaches taken to these texts, we will here limit ourselves to two basic interpretations which also touch on the understanding of the *Codex Vercellensis.* Over the last 50 years, research has especially focused on the question of the relationship between the Latin and Greek texts contained in the *Codex Bezae.* The Vercelli codex was usually consulted by researchers attempting to establish the proximity of *Codex Bezae* to the so-called *Itala*, the European or the Italian text.

Most exegetical studies have been based on the thesis of Johann Salomo Semler[18] and Johann Jacob Griesbach,[19] who posit that the great number (approximately 84%) of the readings[20] shared by Bezae D, 05 and Old Latin manuscripts are due to lost Greek manuscripts and expect that, sooner or later, such Greek manuscripts will be found. More recently, David Parker's important work has once again reinforced this thesis, speaking of an outdated "theory of Latinization" but at the same time conceding that "the fact remains that in a number of places Latinization remains the best explanation of the text."[21] Parker further argues, however, the number of parallels between the Greek *Bezae* and the Latin manuscripts is not sufficient to establish a Latin influence on the Greek *Bezae*, referring to Gospel of Luke 7:12; 21:7; 22:27; 23:14, 36, 40, 43; 24:31–32.[22] In addition, the Latin text of the *Codex Bezae* also contains numerous Greek glosses, which were presumably intended to replace the Greek D, 05 and thus lay claim to great authority. Especially numerous parallels have been identified between the Old Latin manuscripts and the Latin text contained in the *Codex Bezae*: Semler, Griesbach, Parker, and Metzger,[23] to name only a few, have based their analysis primarily on the Latin text contained in this bilingual manuscript.

However, the early research on the manuscripts undertaken by Johann Jakob Wettstein (1751)[24] and John Mill (1707)[25] already considered the possibility of ac-

18 Semler, "Apparatus ad liberalem Novi Testamenti," 45.

19 Griesbach, "Symbolicae criticae CXI writes: *Non e latinis sed e graecis libris recensionis occidentalis derivandae sunt ejusmodi lectiones.*"

20 We take this percentage from Aland et al, Text und Textwert, 57, although we note that determining individual readings can be problematic.

21 Parker, Codex Bezae, 256.

22 Parker, Codex Bezae, 188–190. A more nuanced view is also evident, however, in Parker's statement that "a more subtle reciprocal process was at work, in which each column molded the other. However, the chief influence was of the Greek on the Latin" (193).

23 Metzger, A Textual Commentary, 471.

24 Wettstein, Prolegomena ad Novi Testamenti, 30.

25 Mill, Prolegomena in Nouum Testamentum, CXXXIII–CXXXV.

counting for the Greek text of *Bezae* (D, 05) by reference to the Old Latin translations. Wettstein deserves special credit for noting the possibility that this Greek version appropriated Latin readings otherwise known only from the Latin tradition. This perspective was recently again taken up by Peter Lorenz,[26] who strengthens the argument by showing that, in the context of disputes between Jerome and Ambrosiaster concerning Greek originals,[27] the Greek originals were by no means assigned greater authority than the earliest Latin translations: *nam hodie quae in Latinis reprehenduntur codicibus, sic inveniuntur a ueteribus posita, Tertulliano et Uictorino et Cypriano.*[28] Lorenz also shows that the Greek *Bezae* does not consistently reflect Old Latin readings, and he argues that the resemblances may be due to a corrector who intervened in the text only at key passages, thus also creating a reading independent of the majority of Greek evidence.[29] The complex conceptions of original and translation which emerge from these works have guided the debates up until the present. The discussion which follows here and in Chapter 4.3 aims to contribute to the current renaissance of work on the *Codex Bezae* by helping determine the manuscript's relationship to Old Latin manuscripts, with a focus on the *Codex Vercellensis*. The following questions will serve as guiding threads in the discussion: first, can the relationship between the Latin translations of the codices *Vercellensis* and *Bezae* be described as one of translation and *Vorlage*, or is the situation more complex? Second, to what extent is it necessary to give a fresh account of the dependence of Old Latin translations on the Greek column of the *Codex Bezae*?

The D-text-type is most closely associated with the Greek text of the bilingual *Codex Bezae* (D, 05), even though comparable texts with comparable qualities may be observed in the Sinaitic and Curetonian manuscripts of the Old Syriac, as well as in early papyrus fragments from Egypt, and in some portions of the great uncials codices *Sinaiticus* (א, 01: John 1:1–8:38) and *Washingtonianus* (W, 032: Mark 1:1–5:30).[30]

In what follows, we will examine variants found in the *Codex Vercellesis* which parallel the Greek text of *Bezae*.

---

26 Lorenz, History of Codex Bezae's Text, esp. 228ff.; idem, "An examination of six objections to the theory of Latin influence on the Greek text of Codex Bezae," 173–187.

27 See also the numerous references to Ambrosiaster in Weissenrieder, Visinoni, "Fragmenta Curiensia".

28 Ambrst. Comm. Rome CSEL 81.1.177. Lorenz, "Ambrosiaster's Three Criteria of the True Text," esp. 139–141.

29 Lorenz, History of Codex Bezae's Text, esp. chap. IV.

30 Cf. Metzger, Ehrman, "The Text of the New Testament," 309.

3.3.1 Conflation of Greek Readings: Variation in Word Order in the *Codex Vercellensis* and the *Codex Bezae* (D, 05)

In describing his translation method in a letter to Pammachius, Jerome expressed the view that only a word-by-word translation is suitable for bible texts, "where even the order of the words is a mystery."[31] This suggests that Jerome has given the order of words serious consideration. For Augustine, minor grammatical categories are one of the convincing characteristics of a text, being referred to as "in the same order of the words," as he argues in his *De doctrina christiana*.[32] This points to the fact that parallels of word order in D, 05 and in the Old Latin manuscripts are significant: The Greek text of *Bezae* tends to deviate from other Greek authorities precisely in rearranging the word order of given phrases.[33] Accordingly, scholars have already attempted to identify possible directions of assimilation between D, 05 and the Latin versions by studying word transpositions which are not found in any other Greek witnesses.[34] The examination of such variants is difficult, considering that word order is relatively free in both languages. Nevertheless, there are some tendencies which must be considered in the analysis of the question. For instance, the variant reading in Luke 13:2 of *Bezae*, ἐγένοντο ἁμαρτωλοί instead of ἁμαρτωλοὶ [...] ἐγένοντο of the mainstream text, may suggest a Latinization of the column, if not a Latin *Vorlage*, since we find *fuerunt peccatores* (*peccatores fuerunt* A) transposed to the end of the verse in the Old Latin tradition. This contiguity of copula and predicate, also observed in the Greek text of *Bezae*, presents the most natural word order in Latin, but not in Greek. The reason for this is that Latin complements frequently adhere more closely to their verbs, especially in the case of the copula, which either immediately follows or precedes the predicative.[35] In this way, the variant reading ἐγένοντο ἁμαρτωλοί instead of ἁμαρτωλοὶ [...] ἐγένοντο may be taken either as an attempt to replicate the Latin word order in Greek or as evidence of a Latin source for the Greek text.

These impressions may be further elaborated by turning our attention to the variations in word order found only in the text of *Bezae* and the *Codex Vercellensis*:

31 Cf. Jer. *Epist.* 72: *ubi et uerborum ordo mysterium est.*
32 August. *Doctr. chr.* 2.22 (PL 34.46).
33 Cf. Yoder, "The Language of the Greek Variants of Codex Bezae," 246.
34 Cf. Harris, "Codex Bezae," 61; Jordaan, "The word-order differences," 103.
35 Cf. Leumann et al., "Lateinische Grammatik II," 405.

Table 9: Variation in word order in the *Codex Bezae* and the *Codex Vercellensis*

Verse	NA[28]	D, 05	VL5	VL3
2:51	πάντα τὰ ῥήματα	τὰ ῥήματα πάντα	*uerba omnia*	*uerba eius omnia*
7:20	πρὸς αὐτὸν οἱ ἄνδρες	οἱ ἄνδρες πρὸς αὐτόν	*uiri ad eum*	*uiri ad eum*
8:55	αὐτῇ δοθῆναι	δοθῆναι αὐτῇ	*dari ei*	*dari ei*
10:5	οἰκίαν πρῶτον	πρῶτον οἰκίαν*	*domum*	*primum domum*
15:32	καὶ χαρῆναι ἔδει	ἔδει καὶ χαρῆναι	*oportebat et gaudere*	*oportebat et gaudere*

In two cases, these variations show a clear tendency to depart from the majority of the Greek authorities when it comes to the position of the verb. Verbs come before the object (δοθῆναι αὐτῇ vs. αὐτῇ δοθῆναι in Luke 8:55) or the complementary infinitive (ἔδει καὶ χαρῆναι vs. καὶ χαρῆναι ἔδει in Luke 15:32). As with the position of the copula and the predicate, these examples may indicate Latinized word order. To be more precise, the rearrangement seen in the three manuscripts suggests the influence of colloquial forms of Latin, in which the word order verb–complement was widespread and preferred to complement–verb. This word order is attested in many inscriptions,[36] and it is widespread in late texts, such as the *Peregrinatio*.[37] Such considerations suggests that the variants here observed originated in a Latin version of the text and not in the Greek text of *Bezae*. Moreover, it is plausible that a Latin text similar to the *Vercellensis* may have served as the *Vorlage* for the Greek text of *Bezae*.

Returning to the table above, it is also noteworthy that, at Luke 10:5, the Latin column of *Bezae* contains a text which differs both from the *Vercellensis* and from the Greek *Bezae*: πρῶτον οἰκίαν* – *domum primum* – *domum*. Parker has interpreted the omission of πρῶτον in the Latin column as a case of harmonization with Matt 10:12, which was later corrected in the Greek text as part of the process of homogenizing the two columns.[38] Parker, however, does not consider the relation in which the original Greek stood to the reading found exclusively in the *Vercellensis*. Once again, this seems to provide further evidence that a Latin text similar to the *Vercellensis* may have served as a *Vorlage* to the Greek text of *Bezae*, which was then corrected to match the reading of its Latin column, which, in turn, derives from a different source.

36 Cf., e. g., CIL 1^2 3. For a detailed discussion, see VÄÄNÄNEN, Latin vulgaire, 153.

37 Cf., e. g., 5.4: *nos etiam, quemadmodum ibamus, de contra uidebamus summitatem montis, que inspiciebat super ipsa valle tota, de quo loco sanctus Moyses uidit filios Israel habentes choros his diebus, qua fecerant uitulum.*

38 PARKER, Codex Bezae, 210.

3.3.2 Omissions in the Text of *Bezae* Compared with the *Vercellensis*

Like variations in word order, omissions made by scribes give us a sense of the process of change a text undergoes in various translations. For instance, it is well known that the *Codex Bezae* and many Old Latin witnesses omit long passages in Luke[39] which are found in all other Greek authorities and in the Vulgate. However, other omissions seem to be products of scribal error having no significant theological consequence.[40] This observation also applies to the omissions found only in *Bezae* and *Vercellensis*, as the following table shows:

Table 10: Omissions in the *Codex Bezae* and the *Codex Vercellensis*

Verse	NA[28]	D, 05	VL5	VL3
8:10	γνῶναι τὰ μυστήρια		*mysterium*	*mysterium*
9:23	καὶ ἀράτω τὸν σταυρὸν αὐτοῦ	om.	om.	om.
15:31	τέκνον	om.	om.	om.
21:31	ὅταν ἴδητε ταῦτα γινόμενα	ὅταν ἴδητε ταῦτα	*cum uideritis haec*	*cum uidebitis haec*

Two such variations due to omission deserve special attention:

In the case of the variant reading in Luke 10:5 (οἰκίαν πρῶτον NA[28] πρῶτον οἰκίαν* 05; *domum* 5; *primum domum* 3), it is noteworthy that the Latin column of *Bezae* and the *Vercellensis* do not necessarily transmit the same Latin text, despite the fact that the Greek text of *Bezae* may be used to support both versions. This is the case due to various stages of translation and assimilation involved in the transmission of the text: in this process, the initial correspondence between πρῶτον οἰκίαν (D, 05) and *primum domum* (VL3), a word order not found elsewhere, is followed by the correction of the text in the *Bezae*'s Greek column (omission of πρῶτον), producing Greek which matches Latin version, which in turn has its own separate source. A similar situation arises in Luke 21:31, where the three texts omit γινόμενα after ταῦτα, possibly in an attempt to harmonize the passage with Matt 24:33, where the present participle is absent. But the Latin readings of *Bezae* and *Vercellensis* diverge from each other (*cum uidebitis haec* VL3; *cum uideritis haec* VL5), suggesting that their Latin texts do not necessarily derive from the same

---

39 Cf. Luke 11:36; 12:21; 22:19,20; 24:12,40, which are completely omitted, and 24:3,6,36,51,52, which are transmitted in shorter versions.

40 Cf., e. g., the omission of μηδὲ τοὺς συγγενεῖς σου (14:12) in *Bezae*, *Palatinus* and *Vercellensis*. Considering the polysyndetic construction of the sentence – μηδέ and *neque* are repeated up to four times, depending on the version –, the scribe would easily skip one of the coordinated elements.

source, even though the harmonization to the parallel in Matt is otherwise only found in the Greek text of *Bezae*.

The second of these variations – the extensive omission of καὶ ἀράτω τὸν σταυρὸν αὐτοῦ in Luke 9:23, which is translated in other Latin witnesses with *tollat crucem su equitulata cruce equituratur me* (VL4) – is more striking due to its potential theological implications. The shorter version, as found in the three manuscripts, may indicate that the redactors adhered to a different conception of discipleship. By leaving this phrase out, the text of the two manuscripts resists the literal interpretation of "denying oneself," ἀρνεῖσθαι ἑαυτόν (*abnegare se ipsum*), as a call to martyrdom, instead seemingly directing the readers toward a more ethical interpretation of the verse.[41] The omission accordingly indicates that some readers were inclined to take Jesus's words as calling for suffering and death, thus motivating the scribe of *Codex Bezae* (D, 05) and the translator/scribe of the *Codex Vercellensis* text to attempt to suppress such interpretations in their versions of the story.

3.3.3 Additions in the *Codex Bezae* and the *Codex Vercellensis*

The most important similarities between the texts of the *Vercellensis* and *Bezae* are the following textual additions of considerable extent:

Table 11: Additions in the *Codex Bezae* and the *Codex Vercellensis*

Verse	NA[28]	D, 05	VL5	VL3
2:39	om.	καθὼς ἐρρέθη διὰ τοῦ προφήτου ὅτι Ναζωραῖος κληθήσεται	*sicut dictum est per profetam quoniam nazoreus uocabitur*	*sicut dictum est per prophetam, quod nazoreus uocabitur*
7:26	om.	οὐδεὶς μείζων ἐν γεννητοῖς γυναικῶν προφήτης Ἰωάννου τοῦ βαπτιστοῦ (*post v.* 26)	*nemo maior in natis mulierum profeta iohanis baptiste* (*post v.* 26)	*nemo maior in natis mulierum amplior est iohannen baptista*
8:45	om.	ὁ δὲ Ἰησοῦς γνοὺς τὴν ἐξελθοῦσαν ἐξ αὐτοῦ δύναμιν ἐπηρώτα	*iesus autem sciens quae exiuit ab eo uirtus interrogabat*	*iesus autem sciens quod exierit ab illo uirtus dixit*
13:20	om.	καὶ τίνι ὁμοιώσω αὐτήν	*et cui similabo illut*	*et cui adsimilabo*
16:8	om.	λέγω ὑμῖν	*dico uobis*	*dico uobis*
21:2	om.	ὅ ἐστιν κοδράντης	*quod est codrantes*	*duos quadrantes*
21:6	om.	ἐν τοίχῳ ὧδε	*in pariete hic*	*in pariete hic*

41 Cf. Moss, "The Other Christs," 31.

The addition in Luke 2:39 may be explained by the attempt to harmonize the passage with Matt 2:23: ὅπως πληρωθῇ τὸ ῥηθὲν διὰ τῶν προφητῶν ὅτι Ναζωραῖος κληθήσεται. The origin and meaning of this Old Testament quotation is still disputed among scholars. A widespread view is that the gentilic Ναζωραῖος refers to the נצר, the "shoot," from the stump of Jesse in Isa 11:1.[42] The use of this word may have evoked analogous verses (Isa 4:2; Jer 23:5; 33:15; Zech 3:8; 6:12) which could, in turn, explain the use of the plural "prophets," as well as the other peculiarities of the introductory formula. However, it is important to note that the addition in the Gospel of Luke attested by the codices *Bezae* (D, 05) and *Vercellensis* mentions only one prophet, a discrepancy which poses difficulties for this hypothesis.

In both texts of the *Codex Bezae*, the addition in Luke 7:26 is rather an anticipation – with a different word order and along with the inclusion of the apposition τοῦ βαπτιστοῦ – of v. 28, where the mainstream Greek text reads μείζων ἐν γεννητοῖς γυναικῶν Ἰωάννου οὐδείς ἐστιν. But, in the *Vercellensis*, the reading appears again in v. 28, matching the mainstream Greek text and most other Latin authorities (*maior in natis mulierum iohannen baptista nemo est*). It is also interesting to note that, in v. 26, the comparative μείζων was translated twice, first with *maior*, then with *amplior*.

In Luke 8:45, instead of the simple καὶ εἶπεν ὁ Ἰησοῦς of the other Greek authorities, the *Codex Bezae* (D, 05) attempts to harmonize the text of Luke with Mark 5:30, adding the clause καὶ εὐθὺς ὁ Ἰησοῦς ἐπιγνοὺς ἐν ἑαυτῷ τὴν ἐξ αὐτοῦ δύναμιν ἐξελθοῦσαν ἐπιστραφεὶς ἐν τῷ ὄχλῳ ἔλεγεν. The Latin translation in *Codex Vercellensis* presents a small modification of the Greek text, considering that the verb ἐπηρώτα appears as *dixit*, the same reading found in Mark. Two explanations may be given for this change: first, the translator of the text in the *Codex Vercellensis* Luke may have aimed to expand the adjustment to the Gospel of Mark beyond the simple addition already contained in his Greek *Vorlage*. At the same time, we cannot exclude the possibility that the translator used an underlying Greek text with the addition to Luke also contained in the *Codex Bezae* (D, 05) in Luke, but with λέγει instead of ἐπηρώτα. Finally, the addition in Luke 13:20 is a word-for-word repetition of v. 18, whereas the other Greek witnesses have καὶ πάλιν εἶπεν· τίνι ὁμοιώσω τὴν βασιλείαν τοῦ θεοῦ. The Latin translation of the *Codex Vercellensis* shows a further textual difference: instead of being connected with the coordinating conjunction ἤ, as in the *Codex Bezae* (D, 05), the comparison between the kingdom of God and the leaven is here introduced by the clause *et iterum dixit*, found in all remaining Greek texts and Latin translations of the verse at hand. It is difficult to determine how this conflation reading emerged. As in 8:45, we can assume an

42 Cf. MENKEN, "The Sources of the Old Testament Quotation in Matthew 2:23," 456–457.

underlying Greek text close to *Codex Bezae* (D, 05) and with the same repetition of v. 18, but one which had καὶ πάλιν εἶπεν instead of ἤ. Alternatively, the use of more than one Greek *Vorlage* is also possible. A third possibility is an adjustment of the text in the *Codex Vercellensis* on the basis of other Latin translations.

3.3.4 Conflation of Syntax in the *Codex Bezae* (D, 05) and the *Codex Vercellensis*

Most examples of conflation of syntax and the changes in *verba minora*, such as prepositions, conjunctions, particles, or pronouns, found in the Greek text of *Bezae* and the Old Latin versions are traceable to attempts to harmonize the text to parallel passages in other Gospels.[43] The same applies to many textual differences between the Greek text of *Bezae* and the *Vercellensis* on one hand and the mainstream Greek text on the other, as the following table shows:

43 So, e.g., is the frequent omission of οὖν (Luke 20:44, 21:7, 22:70), which adjusts the verses with Mark. The first one in Luke 20:44 (Δαυίδ instead of Δαυὶδ οὖν) matches with the text in Mark 12:37, where the particle is missing in the *Sinaiticus* (א, 01), *Bezae* (D, 05), *Washingtonianus* (W, 32) and *Corithedianus* (Θ, 35); the distribution among the Old Latin versions is the same as the verse in Luke. We can observe a comparable pattern in Luke 21:7 (πότε instead of πότε οὖν) and 22:70 (σὺ εἶ instead of σὺ οὖν εἶ), where the omissions seem also to be a harmonization to Mark 13:4 and 14:61. But in these two last cases, the particle is missing, not only in all Greek authorities but also in the whole Latin tradition. For an in-depth discussion on the use and translation of οὖν, see PARKER, "The Translation of OYN in the Old Latin Gospels." However, a different case can be found in Luke 4:15, where the Greek *Bezae* and in Old Latin versions (VL3, 4, 5) omit the pronoun αὐτῶν in the phrase συναγωγαῖς αὐτῶν. On the one hand, the variant has theological relevance since it suggests an anti-Jewish bias: The use of the possessive may imply a schismatic interpretation of the passage, opposing Christians and Jews, who are then categorized in a homogenous group of "they" or "the others," whereas the reading of *Bezae* and the Old Latin versions without αὐτῶν seems to mitigate this contrast. Scholars have already argued that we cannot assume a general meaning of αὐτῶν in relation to synagogues since the term is sometimes used to indicate public institutions. In this case, synagogues would represent the inhabitants of a local community rather the specific place for worship, and their evaluation is neutral. On the other hand, if we discard any anti-Jewish tendency in this passage, a text critical question still remains. In this context, it is important to note that the phrase συναγωγαὶ αὐτῶν, "their synagogues," is characteristic of Matt but is used nowhere else in Luke. Therefore, it is somewhat surprising that the committee of the NA^{28} has chosen to ignore this significant omission, which has theological and/or stylistic consequences, or at least, not to resort to brackets, showing a degree of uncertainty in the use of αὐτῶν in this verse, since it is possible that the *Codex Bezae* with the support of the *Vercellensis* are witnesses to the original reading. For a detailed discussion, see RUNESSON, "Rethinking Early Jewish-Christian Relations," 112: "On the other hand, in the land of Israel synagogue terms could refer to a *public village* or *town assembly*, a kind of municipal institution, or the building in which the meetings of such an institution were held."

Table 12: Conflation of syntax in the *Codex Bezae* and the *Codex Vercellensis*

Verse	NA[28]	D, 05	VL5	VL3
3:12	τελῶναι	τελῶναι ὁμοίως	*publicani similiter*	*publicani similiter*
4:16	κατὰ τὸ εἰθὼς αὐτῷ	κατὰ τὸ εἰθὼς	*secundum consuetudinem*	*secundum consuetudinem*
6:43	οὐ γάρ ἐστιν δένδρον	οὐκ ἔστιν δένδρον	*non est arbor*	*non est arbor*
6:49	εὐθὺς συνέπεσεν	συνέπεσεν	*concidit*	*cecidit*
8:27	ὑπήντησεν ἀνήρ τις	ὑπήντησεν ἀνήρ	*obuiauit illi uir*	*occurrit illi uir*
10:12	λέγω ὑμῖν	λέγω δὲ ὑμῖν	*dico autem uobis*	*dico autem uobis*
11:28	αὐτὸς δὲ εἶπεν	ὁ δὲ εἶπεν	*ad ille dixit*	*qui ait*
12:2	οὐδὲν δέ	οὐδὲν γάρ	*nihil enim*	*nihil enim*
12:31	πλὴν ζητεῖτε	ζητεῖτε δέ	*quaerit autem*	*quaerite autem*
14:12	τοὺς φίλους σου	τοὺς φίλους	*amicos*	*amicos*
16:3	τὴν οἰκονομίαν	τὴν οἰκονομίαν μου	*uilicationem meam*	*uilicationem meam*
16:8	ὅτι	διὸ λέγω ὑμῖν	*propter quod dico uobis*	*dico uobis*
19:24	καὶ τοῖς παρεστῶσιν εἶπεν	εἶπεν δὲ τοῖς παρεστῶσι	*dixit autem his qui astabant*	*circumstantibus autem dixit*
24:15	καὶ αὐτὸς Ἰησοῦς	καὶ ὁ Ἰησοῦς	*et iesus*	*et iesus*

The most important of these changes concerns the use of αὐτός and ὁ in Luke 11:28 (αὐτὸς NA[28]; ὁ δὲ εἶπεν D,05; *ad ille dixit* VL5; *qui ait* VL3). It is striking that the text of the *Vercellensis* and the Greek column of *Bezae* share a reading against the Latin text of *Bezae*: whereas the *Vercellensis* introduces the main clause with a relative pronoun (*qui*), a construction morpho-syntactically corresponding to the Greek text of *Bezae* (ὁ), the Latin column has a demonstrative pronoun (*ille*), as do all other Old Latin versions. This clearly indicates a process of multiple translation and textual dependence.

3.3.5 Differences of Wording in the *Codex Bezae* and the *Codex Vercellensis*

Despite many similarities, codices *Bezae* and *Vercellensis* do not agree in every single respect. In Luke 4:19, for example, the *Codex Vercellensis* reads *praedicare annum acceptum domini et diem redemptionis*. The Latin variants of this passage all concern the last three words, rendered as *redditionis* in the *Codex Veronensis* (VL4) and *retribuitionis* in all other witnesses, except for the *Codex Bezae* (VL5), in which they are omitted. This corresponds to the Greek tradition, which is uniform in simply reading κηρύξαι ἐνιαυτὸν κυρίου δεκτόν, which is also the reading of the *Codex Bezae* (D, 05). The addition of *et diem redemptionis* (*redditionis* VL4; *retribui-*

tionis cet.; om. VL5) may thus point to the existence of a shared underlying Greek text since καὶ ἡμέραν ἀνταποδόσεως is a quotation from Isa 61:2, perhaps added to the Greek *Vorlage* used as the basis of most Latin witnesses, though nowhere directly attested.[44]

These differences can be observed when we compare the Latin text of *Bezae* and *Vercellensis* and the Greek text of *Bezae*. In the following table, we show how the Latin texts of the two manuscripts differ from each other, even though the Greek column of *Bezae* is the only witness to support the variants.

Table 13: Differences and similarities of wording in the *Codex Bezae* and the *Codex Vercellensis*

Verse	NA[28]	D, 05	VL5	VL3
5:5	ἐπιστάτα	διδάσκαλε	*magister*	*magister*
8:17	ὃ οὐ μή	ἀλλὰ ἵνα	*sed ut*	*nisi ut*
9:25	κερδήσας ἀπολέσας	κερδῆσαι ἀπολέσαι	*lucrari* *perdere*	*locrari* *perdere*
11:26	ἕτερα πνεύματα [...] ἑπτά	ἄλλα ἑπτὰ πνεύματα	*alios septem spiritus*	*alios septem spiritus*
11:51	τοῦ ἀπολομένου	ὃν ἐφόνευσαν	*quem occiderunt*	*quem occiderunt*
12:27	αὐξάνει οὐ κοπιᾷ οὐδὲ νήθει	οὔτε νήθει οὔτε ὑφαίνει	*neque neunt neque texunt*	*non texunt neque neunt*
13:20	τίνι ὁμοιώσω τὴν βασιλείαν τοῦ θεοῦ	ἢ τίνι ὁμοία ἐστὶν ἡ βασιλεία τοῦ θεοῦ	*aut cui simile est regnum dei*	*cui est simile regnum dei*
16:9	μαμωνᾶ τῆς ἀδικίας	ἀδίκου μαμωνᾶ	*iniquo mamona*	*iniquo mamona*
22:24	αὐτῶν δοκεῖ εἶναι	ἂν εἴη	*esset*	*esset*
23:3	ὁ δὲ ἀποκριθεὶς αὐτῷ	ὁ δὲ ἀποκρίθη αὐτῷ	*ille autem respondit illi*	*qui respondit illi*

To sum up: The (few) similarities between the Greek column of *Codex Bezae* and the text of Luke in *Vercellensis* are signs of a complex process of textual transmission. Frequently, word order, as in the case of verbs and complements, suggests that the Greek column of *Bezae* may have originated in a Latin version of the text. At the same time, there are many instances in which the text of *Vercellensis* replicates the Greek column of *Bezae* more closely than the Latin *Bezae* does. This is clearly seen in the use of relative pronouns at the beginning of clauses (*Vercellensis*) and of the demonstrative (*Bezae*) in the rendering of the set phrase ὁ δέ.

44 Cf. Burton, The Old Latin Gospels, 12.

3.4 The Old Latin Versions as a Source for the Text of the *Codex Corithedianus* (Θ, 038)

Along with its similarities to the *Codex Bezae* (D, 05), the *Codex Vercellensis* also exhibits some affinities to the *Codex Coridethianus* (Θ, 038), dated to the ninth century. The manuscript was found in the Caucasus and was apparently written by a scribe not fully familiar with Greek; the text is often interpreted as a witness of the Caesarean text. It is worth considering that, up to the fourth century, Caesarea was the spiritual and ecclesiastical stronghold of Christians, not Jerusalem, especially after the Bar Kokhba uprising, when a new Christian community formed. This only changed with the Constantine revolution. Georgia, where the *Codex Coridethianus* was discovered, is undoubtedly of central impotance; some features of this manuscript, more remote places, including especially an inscription on the book cover in Coptic and Georgian letters which "points to a connection with Egypt or with those districts immediately contiguous with it – Sinai and Palestine."[45] In this connection, Lake and Blake, note that the earliest evidence in Palestine is an Abbey in Jerusalem dated to the time of Justinian.

The codicology of the codex shows a text written in two columns, the size of which varies between 29 and 28 cm high and 24.1 and 23 cm wide. Even the Greek spelling shows numerous uncertainties on the part of the scribe, which is confirmed by six further correcting hands. Like the *Codex Vercellensis*, the Coridethianus is distinguished by a sliding element: The capitalisation and highlighting of new sections of text.

Many of the singular readings in the Lucan text of the *Codex Coridethianus* are transmitted by the entire Old Latin tradition. For instance, in Luke 9:55–56, when James and John ask Jesus if they ought to command fire to come down from heaven and consume the village of the Samaritans, all Old Latin witnesses – apart from the *Codex Bezae* (VL5) – give the answer *filius hominis non uenit animas hominum perdere, sed saluare*,[46] which corresponds to ὁ υἱὸς τοῦ ἀνθρώπου οὐκ ἦλθεν ψυχὰς ἀνθρώπων ἀπολέσαι ἀλλὰ σῶσαι, a textual addition otherwise attested only in the

45 LAKE and BLAKE, "The Text of the Gospels and the Koridethi Codex," 282, 280–284; ALAND, The Text of the New Testament, 76–77. In addition to the *Codex Coridethianus* (Θ, 038), the minuscules 565 and 700 are to be interpreted as the main text of the Caesarean text. But this text has not been attested either in Origen or in Eusebius, and the proximity to the Syrian-Palestinian versions is also disputed. For further details see BEERMANN and GEORGY, Die Koridethi Evangelien, 501–588; NICKLAS, "Eine Skizze zu Codex Coridethi (Θ 038)," 317; LORENZ, History of Codex Bezae's Text, 933f.

46 With minor changes in *Codex Veronensis* (VL4), which begins the sentence with the conjunction *quia*, and in the Vulgate, which omits *hominum* after *animas*.

manuscript;[47] most of the remaining Greek witnesses for this passage simply mention that Jesus rebuked them (ἐπετίμησεν αὐτούς). Passages where the codices *Bezae* (D, 05) and *Coridethianus* (Θ, 038), often along with the *Codex Washingtonianus* (W, 032), stand together against all other known authorities are of special interest in this context. For example, in Luke 20:20, the text of the two manuscripts differs from the other Greek witnesses in reading ἀποχωρήσαντες (ὑποχωρήσαντες W) instead of παρατηρήσαντες. The variant was incorporated into all Old Latin texts and translated with a compound of *cedere* (*secedere* VL2; *recedere* VL5, 8, 17), and in the *Codex Vercellensis* with *discedere*, a singular reading of the manuscript. At any rate, it is evident that the Old Latin variants found in this verse can be traced back to the reading of one of these three texts, whereas the Vulgate follows another Greek *Vorlage* since it has *obseruantes*, which corresponds to παρατηρήσαντες. In the following table, we show variant readings found in the *Codex Coridethianus* (Θ, 038) and in the Latin tradition of Luke. It will be noticed that many of these readings concern word order:

Table 14: The Old Latin versions and the *Codex Corithedianus* (Θ, 038)

Verse	NA[28]	Θ, 038	Latin rendering	Latin authorities
1:29	Ναζαρέθ	Ναζαρέτ	*Nazaret*	2 3 8
3:16	ὕδατι βαπτίζω ὑμᾶς	ὑμᾶς ὕδατι βαπτίζω	*uos aqua baptize(-abo)*	(3) 4 8
6:44	σταφυλὴν τρυγῶσιν	τρυγῶσιν σταφυλήν	*uidemiant uuam*	3 4 8 A
7:9	οὐδέ	ἐν οὐδενί	*in nullo*	3 4 8
9:55	om.	ὁ υἱὸς [...] ἀλλὰ σῶσαι	*filius* [...] *sed saluare*	2 3 4 A
12:35	ὑμῶν αἱ ὀσφύες	αἱ ὀσφύθες ὑμῶν	*lumbi uestri*	2 3 4 8 17 A
18:30	om.	Κληρονομήσει	*Possidebit*	3 4 8 17
18:31	Ἱερουσαλήμ	Ἱεροςόλυμα	*Hierosoluma*	3 4 8 17 A
23:37	εἰ σὺ εἶ	σὺ εἶ	*tu es*	3 4 8

Of special importance for our study are the readings which can be found only in the codices *Corithedianus* (Θ, 038) and *Vercellensis*:

47 The variant is similar to that found in codices *Cyprius* (K, 017) und *Tischendorfianus IV* (Γ, 036). The differences are that K adds γάρ between ὁ and υἱός, whereas Γ has ψυχήν instead of ψυχάς, and ἀποκτεῖναι for ἀπολέσαι.

Table 15: The *Codex Vercellensis* and the *Codex Corithedianus* (Θ, 038)

Verse	NA[28]	Θ, 038	VL3
3:15	λέγων πᾶσιν	πᾶσιν λέγων	*omnibus dicens*
7:11	om.	ὁ Ἰησοῦς[c]	*iesus*
8:14	οἱ ἀκούσαντες	οἱ τὸν λόγον ἀκούσαντες	*qui audiunt uerbum*
9:18	μαθηταί	μαθηταὶ αὐτοῦ	*discipuli sui*
11:13	πνεῦμα ἅγιον	δόματα ἀγαθά	*bona data*
19:2	καὶ αὐτὸς πλούσιος	καὶ αὐτὸς ἦν πλούσιος	*et ipse erat locuples*
19:14	om.	ὅτι	*quia*
21:1	εἰς τὸ γαζοφυλάκιον τὰ δῶρα	τὰ δῶρα εἰς τὸ γαζοφυλάκιον	*dona in altario*

Of all these readings, δόματα ἀγαθά in Luke 11:13 is especially striking. The variant is not attested in the *Codex Vercellesis* directly, though it is found in the *Fragmenta Curiensia.*[48] The numerous Latin variants for this verse correspond to the abundance of readings in the Greek tradition, which transmits the following possibilities: πνεῦμα ἅγιον (𝔓[75] ℵ A B C Marc. and others), πνεῦμα ἀγαθόν (𝔓[45] L),[49] ἀγαθὸν δόμα (D, 05) and δόματα ἀγαθά (Θ).[50]

The variant πνεῦμα ἀγαθόν (𝔓[45] L) is found in the Latin translations as *spiritum bonum*; this variant is also used in the writings of the Church Fathers, for instance in all manuscripts of Augustine's *Speculum.*[51] This reading found its ways into the Latin tradition through the Vulgate and texts dependent on it, such as the *Codex Aureus* (VL15), and was also later favored by Erasmus.[52] πνεῦμα ἀγαθόν is found in the marginalia of Thomas von Harkel as well, who wrote a review of the Syriac New Testament, likely based on Origen's *Hexapla*,[53] while living near Alexandria. This gives evidence against objections that the variant emerges due to erroneous

---

48 Cf. 4.2, pp. 116–122.

49 The reading in 𝔓[45] is based on a text reconstruction, whereas the *Codex Regius* (L, 019) is a 8th century gospel manuscript which, according to Scrivener, contains 138 common readings of the *Codex Vaticanus* (B, 02). Cf. SCRIVENER, "A Plain Introduction," 137–138. πνεῦμα ἀγαθόν can possibly be found in the tradition of Cyril of Alexandria (PG 72, col. 700A = TU 130, 124) as well as in the Syriac tradition CSCO 70, SS 27 hom. 79, 320, 322. For further references, see RÜCKERS, "The Luke Homilies," 11; 69.

50 For the following, cf. METZGER, Textual Commentary, 158; GRUNDMANN, Lukas, 235; PLUMMER, Luke, 300; NORTH, "Praying for a Good Spirit," 168–171; OTT, "Gebet," 107–109 and LAGRANGE, Évangile selon Saint Luc, 328.

51 Cf. Ps.-Aug. *Spec.* 27.

52 Eras. *Critici sacri* VI, 489, XI.13: *Magno consensu reclamantibus exemplaribus Latinis etiam vetustis, quibus ego sane magis assentior.*

53 Cf. JUCKEL, "Die Bedeutung des Ms. Vat. Syr. 268," 39–40.

transcription of ΑΓΙΟΝ as ΑΓΑΘΟΝ.[54] The reading can also be found in the Testament of Benjamin (4.5), where Benjamin as a good person has the grace of a "good spirit," although this attribution can be interpreted anthropologically and not theologically if we consider the parallelism of ἀγαθὴ διάνοια (4.1; 6.4.5); following this interpretation even further, the passage may be related to Empedocles, as stated by Aristotle in *Metaph.* 3.1000b (DK 31b109): ἡ δὲ γνῶσις τοῦ ὁμοίου τῷ ὁμοίῳ.[55] Philo may also have known this variant, who argues in a similar way in Prov. 2.23 (τὸ γὰρ ὅμοιον χαίρει τῷ ὁμοίῳ).[56] Thus, the "good spirit" is interpreted anthropologically.[57]

Two further examples from the LXX may also be central to this issue: 2Ezr 19:20 (Neh 9:20^{MT})[58] and Ps 142:10 (143:10^{MT}).[59] The evidence in Psalm 142 is an exhortation to do good, wherein God's spirit is contrasted with David's soul. The evidence in Ezra is part of a ceremony consisting of a prayer of covenant renewal which clearly names the dangers of idolatrous apostasy. The "good spirit" is found in the Torah, which can prevent this apostasy.[60] The term "good," mentioned several times in Neh 9:12–30, is always applied to the Torah. ἀγαθός qualifies πνεῦμα as well as ἐντολάς in both texts, which may have also been interpreted in this way by Didymus the Blind in his liturgical discussion of Luke 11:13 in light of Ps 142:10^{LXX}.[61] Thomas Harkel reinforces the relevance of Acts 2:9b by noting that this emphasis on πνεῦμα ἀγαθόν may be due to the fact that the verse concerns pilgrims from Cappadocia and Pontus, where Zoroastrianism was of central importance, as also reported by the geographer Strabo (11.8.4; 15.3.15). This is consideration may be elaborated by reference to the Greco-Egyptian diety Ἀγαθὸς Δαίμων, and also by taking account of Greek and Egyptian sources reporting snakes as household gods, which is significant in both Luke 10:19 and Acts 28:3–6. Furthermore, as J. Quaegebeur points out,

54 Cf. e. g., North, "Praying for a Good Spirit," 168.
55 Cf. North, "Praying for a Good Spirit," 187; Sext. *sent.* Text 61: ἀγαθὴ διάνοια χῶρος θεοῦ.
56 See Euseb. *Praep. evang.* 8.14.
57 See Phil. *Gig.* 9; North, "Praying for a Good Spirit," 172.
58 Cf. 2Ezr 19:20: καὶ τὸ πνεῦμά σου τὸ ἀγαθὸν ἔδωκας συνετίσαι αὐτοὺς καὶ τὸ μαννα σοῦ οὐκ ἀφυστέρησας ἀπὸ στόματος αὐτῶν καὶ ὕδωρ ἔδωκας αὐτοῖς τῷ δίψει αὐτῶν. Ezra takes up und deepens the notion that πνεῦμα can speak through a human being (such as David in Acts 1:16) or through the Scriptures, as here πνεῦμα speaks through the prophets.
59 See Ps 142:8c.10^{LXX}: γνώρισόν μοι, κύριε, ὁδὸν ἐν ᾗ πορεύσομαι, ὅτι πρὸς σὲ ἦρα τὴν ψυχήν μου; τὸ πνεῦμά σου τὸ ἀγαθὸν ὁδηγήσει με ἐν γῇ εὐθείᾳ.
60 Cf. Levison, The Spirit in First Century Judaism, 194–197; Koch, Geist und Messias, 61–62. Both argue that the phrase "good spirit" refers not only to God but also to Moses.
61 Did. *De spiritu sancto* PG 9, 1078A = 232 SC 386,352–354.

the title Ἀγαθὸς Δαίμων was attributed to Nero around 54.[62] The context of Luke 11:13 again gives room for interpretation: πνεῦμα ἀγαθόν poses the antonym to the πονηροί, the evil fathers in verse, and also to the seven unclean spirits in v. 26.[63] Nevertheless, it should be noted that ἀγαθόν is used only once in Luke; πνεῦμα ἅγιον, on the other hand, is used in various passages, and more frequently than in any other gospel.

The phrase δόματα ἀγαθά is found in the parallel Matt 7:11. George Howard traced the term back to the Hebrew term רוחו הטוב, an interpretation now followed by the majority of interpreters, even though Howard's feminine רוחו could easily be replaced by the masculine מתנה, "gift."[64] Apart from Matt 7:11, the wording may possibly refer to Sir 18:16, an admonition to self-critical way of life.[65] Here the emphasis becomes clear, since Luke 11:13 concludes with an instruction to pray. The request with which the disciples can approach God in hope of fulfillment, is not a request for the holy spirit, but a request for a self-critical way of life, which is grounded in prayer and humility before God. The resemblance to Eph 4:8 is also remarkable.[66] The passage from Ephesians can be read as a reference to Psalm 67:19 (*ascendisti in excelsum captiuam duxisti captiuitatem, accepisti dona in hominibus*). The verse speaks of Yahweh's triumphal march on Zion, during which he takes prisoners. In Eph 4:8, the ascent to Sinai is now related to Christ. A sermon by Augustine offers develops this interpretation and the statements made in Luke 11:9–13 by stating that Christ, after his ascent, desires to respond to our requests because of his mercy.[67] He interprets the snake and the scorpion as bad influences, while the bread represents love, the fish faith, and the egg hope. Augustine then continues this division into good and bad forces, in dialogue with Virgil's *Aeneid* and *Georgica*, by pointing out that Jupiter had already conjured up the downfall of the earthly empire with this Roman poet.[68] In this interpretation, Christ becomes the mediator of gifts; at the same time, the moral responsibility of those praying is emphasized.

62 Cf. QUAEGEBEUR, "Le dieu égyptien Shaï," 113, who refers to P.Oxy. 1021,8–10: Ἀγαθὸς Δαίμων δὲ τῆς οἰκουμένης. See also PGM 36 II 216–217; For further discussion, cf. NORTH, "Praying for a Good Spirit," 187, who draws attention to Suet. *Nero* 6, and Tac. *Ann.* 11.11.

63 Cf. Luke 11:26: παραλαμβάνει ἕτερα πνεύματα πονηρότερα ἑαυτοῦ ἑπτά.

64 Cf. HOWARD, The Gospel of Matthew, 59–61; 219–220.

65 Cf. Sir 18:16–17: οὐχὶ καύσωνα ἀναπαύσει δρόσος; οὕτως κρείσσων λόγος ἢ δόσις. οὐκ ἰδοὺ λόγος ὑπὲρ δόμα ἀγαθόν; καὶ ἀμφότερα παρὰ ἀνδρὶ κεχαριτωμένῳ.

66 Cf. Eph 4:8: Ἀναβὰς εἰς ὕψος ᾐχμαλώτευσεν αἰχμαλωσίαν, ἔδωκεν δόματα τοῖς ἀνθρώποις.

67 August. *Serm.* 105.6 (PL 38.620–621).

68 Cf. Verg. *Aen.* 1.278–279: *His ego nec metas rerum nec tempora pono, imperium sine fine dedi.* Verg. *georg.* 2.498: *Non res Romanae perituraque regna.*

At any rate, it is clear that the complex transmission of the Greek text of this passage resulted in many literal translations into Latin. The singular reading of the *Fragmenta Curiensia*, and consequently of the *Codex Vercellensis* must be considered in light of the Greek *Codex Coridethianus* (Θ, 38). However, since the origin of the *Coridethianus* is still rather unclear – though the manuscript is certainly later than our codex – and since its Greek is often faulty, the precise nature of the relationship between the Vercellensis to the Coridethianus cannot be specified without further ado.

3.5 Conclusion: The Relation of the *Codex Vercellensis* to the Greek Texts

Our analysis shows that, despite important textual similarities between the *Codex Vercellensis* and several Greek authorities, there is no single manuscript which can be considered the *Vorlage* of the text of Vercelli. It is clear that many readings of the text have an early character since they are also attested in Greek papyri, such as the extent omissions in Luke 23:17, 34, which are present in $\mathfrak{P}^{75}$ as well. The examination of the great uncial codices, in turn, reveals some minor affinities in word order, additions and wording. However, none of the Majuscules can be said to possess a text particularly close to the *Vercellensis*.

On the other hand, the relation to *Codex Bezae* is more complex and involves major textual expansions, such as those in Luke 2:39, 7:26, 8:45 and 13:20. But in most of these instances, the text of the *Codex Vercellensis* does not exactly reflect the Greek column of *Bezae*: we detect changes in wording or even in the position of one of these additions, as in the case of Luke 7:26. In regard to the *Codex Coridethianus*, we have observed that its text shares similarities with the whole Old Latin tradition, but especially noteworthy is the variant reading *bona data* instead of *spiritum bonum* in Luke 11:13 of the *Fragmenta Curiensia* which parallels δόματα ἀγαθά in the *Coridethianus*.

In conclusion, we can assume that the majority of the textual peculiarities found in the manuscript of Vercelli originated due to translational processes in the Old Latin tradition. In this way, they reflect developments of the Latin text not necessarily dependent on any Greek witness. Thus, it becomes clear that the singular character of the *Codex Vercellensis* should now be examined in light of the oldest witnesses of the Latin Luke.

4 The Relation of the *Codex Vercellensis* Luke to the Latin Versions

In Chapter 4, we turn once again to our second research question concerning the relation of the text of the Vercellensis and the Latin versions originating in the fourth century and thereafter. In doing so, we will identify a layer of readings in Vercellensis' text resembling other Latin versions, and even standing in a relation of dependency with them. The consensus view among scholars of the Vercellensis is that its text developed from later Old Latin versions. Failure to recognize the Vercellensis text as a product of the Vulgate led the first editor of the *Codex Vercellensis*, Irico,[1] to edit the text in his autograph kept at Vercelli in light of the *Codex Veronensis* (VL4) and the Vulgate, an error in which he was later followed by Gasquet and Jülicher et al. Bianchini relied on a collation with the codices *Veronensis* (VL4), *Corbeiensis secundus* (VL8), and *Brixianus* (VL10), assuming the Vercellensis to be a text of "early Italian" or "European" type.[2] However, we have reasons to suspect that the greater part of the distinctive Latin parallels in Vercellensis' text did not arise within the Latin tradition but were instead produced by translating an as yet unidentified Greek version, one which does not follow the text of a highly selective corrector.[3]

In the following, we firstly (4.1) present evidence suggesting that the unique readings shared with the *Codex Palatinus* originated either in the *Vercellensis* or in the *Palatinus*, and hence that the distinctive character of the Vercellensis text is due to influence exercised by the translation from Greek. We then (4.2) argue that the text of the *Fragmenta Curiensia* constitutes a revision of the *Vercellensis* exhibiting adaptations to Late Latin grammar. Some of the additions of the *Curiensia* seem to develop older readings otherwise called 'Afra,' thus aligning the fragments to texts such as those contained, for example, in the *Codex Palatinus* and the early Church Fathers. In comparison with the text from Vercelli and Chur, *Codex Bezae*'s Latin text (4.3) follows the pattern of a corrector whose phonological, syntactical and morphological readings are often consistent with classical Latin. A number of Bezan Latin readings can be explained as further developments of conjectures made in the Vercellensis and the Fragments from Chur. As a representative of the

1 Irico, *Sacrosanctus Evangeliorum*.

2 *Sancti Eusebii Episcopi Vercellensis Opera Omnia*. J. Belsheim [*Quatuor Evangelia ante Hieronymum Latine Translata ex Reliquiis Codicis Vercellensis*] also transcribed the manuscript, which is, however, not to be recommended; cf. chap. 2.

3 Cf. chap. 5, pp. 195–199 and more often.

https://doi.org/10.1515/9783111142531-005

so-called European text, the *Codex Veronensis* (4.4) may be analyzed on the basis of some unique readings which reveal aspects about the editorial process in Old Latin manuscripts from the fifth century onwards, and the *Codex Amiatinus* (4.5), as a representative of Vulgate, may possibly be best understood in light of the Vercellensis.

In the following sections we focus on three kinds of evidence: first, cases of apparent conflation of Greek readings which the Vercellensis has in common with some Latin manuscripts (word for word translation; omissions and additions); second, cases of apparent conflation of phonological, morphological, and syntactical readings, a significant quantity of which is trivial, concerns diction rather than meaning; and third, readings which are best explained as development in Latin semantics. Finally, we supply a list of unique readings comparing the Vercellensis with each of these Latin versions.

4.1 The Relationship between the *Codex Vercellensis* (VL3) and the *Codex Palatinus* (VL2)

In those passages in which Old Latin manuscripts differ conspicuously among themselves, the manuscripts from the surroundings of Vercelli show a strong tendency to agree with the *Codex Palatinus*, especially where this manuscript differs from the Vulgate. This confirms the assumption that the *Vercellensis* (VL3) is closer to the *Palatinus* (VL2) than to the early Italian and later European texts. The linguistic analysis of the two manuscripts reveals two tendencies: first, both manuscripts contain several simplified forms derived from spoken language, which in turn suggests reading conventions based on a phonographic writing system. Second, both manuscripts exhibit the semantic repertoire of Classical, non-Christian Latin, employing terms such as *discens, adnuntiare, benenuntiare, oratio*, and *orare*, a tendency that then becomes even more pronounced with the unique readings of the Vercellensis Luke (cf. Chap. 5).

4.1.1 Conflation of Phonetics and Syntax

The influence of the spoken language on the orthography, manifested in the interchangeability of */d/* and */t/* at the end of a word or the confusion between */b/* and */u/*, is a feature shared by many witnesses of the Latin Gospels. It is especially significant, however, that the texts of the *Vercellensis* and *Palatinus* contain such deviations in the same passages, as shown in the following table:

Table 1: Common orthographic variants in VL2 and VL3

Verse	VL2, 3	Other Latin authorities
6:23	*profetis*	*et prophetis* 4 *prophetis* cet.
8:6	*aliut*	*aliud* cet.
8:7	*aliut*	*aliud* cet.
10:28	*uibes*	*uiues* cet.
10:40	*reliquid*	*dereliquid* 5 *reliquit* cet.
	sola	*solam* cet.
11:42	*olus*	*holus* cet.
11:46	*honeratis*	*oneratis* cet.
18:7	*uindicta*	*uindictam* cet.
19:37	*discensum*	*descensum* cet.
20:21	*persona*	*personam* cet.
22:57	*ad*	*at* cet.
22:65	*blaspemantes*	*blasfemantes* 5 *blasphemiantes* 8 *blasphemantes* cet.
24:27	*interpraetans* 2c	*interpraetari* 5 *interpretabatur* A *interpretans* cet.

4.1.1.1 Phonetics: Aspirated and Non-Aspirated Consonants

The loss of the aspirate sound /h/ presents a development of later Latin, though the first signs of this phonetic change can already be traced back to the Republican *sermo rusticus*.[4] This change is especially significant insofar as it offers an example of spoken language exercising an influence on orthography. The *Appendix Probi*, one of the most important sources of information on Late Latin phonetic change, documents spelling errors due to this phenomenon in the word pairs *hostiae, non ostiae* and *adhuc, non aduc*. Since the work can probably be dated to the beginning of the fourth century, this process was likely already advanced by the time the first Bible translations into Latin were made in the middle of the fourth century. This phonetic development is recorded above all in doublets such as *harena/arena, hallec/allec, hircus/ircus* and *holus/olus*, all agricultural terms, to which we may also add *hortus/ortus*, occurring in Luke 13:19.[5] The impact of this development on the two codices is illustrated by a special orthographic reading involving a confusion

4 Cf. MÜLLER-LANCÉ, Latein für Romanisten, 92–93; cf. 5.1.3.3 in this volume.

5 Cf. in detail VÄÄNÄNEN, Introduction au latin vulgaire, 55.

between aspirated and non-aspirated vowels, namely the use of *honeratis* instead of *oneratis* in 11:46.

We should also note one more orthographic peculiarity:

Table 2: The orthographic variant *blaspemantes* in Luke 22:65

Verse	VL2, 3	Other Latin authorities
22:65	*blaspemantes*	*blasfemantes* 5 *blasphemiantes* 8 *blasphemantes* cet.

The cause of this orthographic variety is the Latin phonographic writing system. The Latin /*p*/ is not aspirated, while /p^h / is pronounced as an aspirate rather than as a fricative /*f*/, so that we can again suppose that we are dealing with an orthographical change produced by a phonetic peculiarity of spoken Latin. The fact that the two earliest manuscripts depart from the majority of witnesses in this way again suggests an interdependence of the two manuscripts.[6]

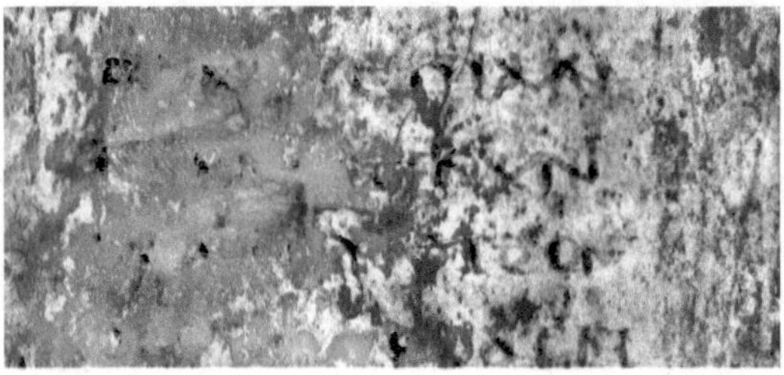

Figure 4.1: The reading *blaspemantes* in Luke 22:65 (504[b]).

4.1.1.2 Syntax: The Use of Demonstrative Pronouns

Latin does not have articles and third person pronouns, but it does have a variety of demonstrative pronouns, such as *ille*, *is*, and *hic*, which were functionally simplified in the transition from Classical to Late Latin. In the course of this transition, the demonstrative pronoun *ille* assumed two functions, coming to serve as the definite article when used before nouns, and as a personal pronoun when used independently. In Classical Latin, the demonstrative *is* and its oblique case forms played the role of the missing personal pronoun. *ille* served to designate that which is more

6 Cf. 5.1.4.2 (p. 210f.) in this volume.

distant from the speaker in time and space, and *hic, haec, hoc* designated everything that is close in space and time.[7] In Late and Vulgar Latin, the syntax of demonstrative pronouns was simplified insofar as *ille* came to assume the role *is* originally had.

Table 3: The use of *ille* in VL2 and VL3

Verse	VL2, 3	Other Latin authorities
4:23	*ad illos*	*ad eos* 5 *illis* 4 8 A
5:28	*illum*	*eum* cet.
5:33	*illum*	*eum* cet.
6:8	*illorum*	*eorum* cet.
6:18	*illum*	*eum* cet.
6:47	*illa*	*ea* 5 *eos* 4 A om. 8
7:3	*illum*	*eum* cet.
8:25	*Illi*	*imperio eius* 4 *ei* cet.
9:34	*illos*	*eos* cet.
9:49	*illum*	*eum* cet.
10:32	*illum*	*eum* cet.
15:5	*illam*	*eam* 4 17 om. cet.
22:10	*illum*	*eum* cet.
23:39	*illum*	*eum* cet. om. 8
24:18	*ad illum*	*ad eum* 5 *illi* 4 *ei* 8 A
24:31	*illum*	*eum* cet.

A few exceptions to this pattern may also be noted:

Table 4: The use of *is* in VL2 and VL3

Verse	VL2, 3	Other Latin authorities
2:20	*eos*	*illos* cet.
10:39	*eius*	*illius* cet. om. 5
10:41	*ei*	*illi* cet.

7 Cf. Müller-Lancé, Latein für Romanisten, 130; cf. also 5.3.2.1 (p. 207f.) in this volume.

The collated manuscripts reflect this process of simplification to various degrees. It is striking that the two oldest manuscripts of Luke, namely the codices *Vercellensis* and *Palatinus*, read *ille* instead of *is* against the majority of the other witnesses.[8] Yet the *Palatinus* is quite consistent in reading *ille* instead of *is*, which is not attested for the *Vercellensis*. At the same time, we observe exactly the opposite tendency in the *Codex Bezae*, where the scribe, in a uniform attempt to adhere to the conventions of Classical Latin, shows a preference for *is*; furthermore, it is perplexing that the *Vercellensis* sometimes simply reads *is* together with *Bezae*. The edition also shows that the Vulgate tradition resolutely avoids the use of *ille*, using the demonstrative only when *ille* occurs in the exemplar of the most important witnesses.[9] We can observe this loss of the pronouns' deictic function in the writings of Augustine who, in referring to the same passage, sometime uses *porriget ei* (*serm.* 105.4.6) and sometimes *illi porriget* (*symb.* 14). Another example is found in the ps.-Aug. *Speculum*, which has *porriget ei* in Matt 7:10 but *porriget illi* in Luke 11:11. The fact that codices *Vercellensis* and *Palatinus* tend to deviate from correct usage in the same way suggests that the two manuscripts are dependent on each other.

This assumption is supported by another linguistic peculiarity, namely the fact that, in the *Vercellensis*, the causal ὅτι is consistently translated using the conjunction *quoniam*, while the other witnesses mostly have *quia* (6:21, 7:39; 9:53; 11:44; 12:37; 13:33; 14:24; 24:39). Scholars here often speak of a characteristic 'Afra' reading,[10] a label which may be confirmed by the numerous correspondences between quotations from the writings of the Church Fathers and textual variants of the oldest Latin biblical manuscripts. For example, in the case of Luke 6:20, Tertullian writes *beati mendici, quoniam illorum est dei regnum*,[11] while most witnesses have *quia*; among the few exceptions are the *Codices Vercellensis, Palatinus*, and *Bezae*, which, like Tertullian, have *quoniam*.

8 There are admittedly a few exceptions: Luke 2:20, 44; 10:39, 44, where VL2 and 3 carry the special readings *is* instead of the *ille* of the other witnesses.

9 See also section 4.3 (p. 122ff.) on *Codex Bezae*.

10 See, among others, SITTL, Die lokalen Verschiedenheiten der lateinischen Sprache, 111; VON SODEN, Das lateinische Neue Testament in Afrika, 81; BURKITT, The Old Latin and the Itala, 40; HOUGHTON, The Latin New Testament, 10.

11 Cf. Tert. *adv. Marc.* 4.14.13. Textual variants for this passage include *regnum dei* and *regnum coelorum*, under obvious influence of the parallel tradition in Matthew 5:8.

Table 5: Common renderings of the conjunction ὅτι in VL2 and VL3

Verse	VL2, 3	Other Latin authorities
6:21	*quoniam*	*quia* cet.
7:39	*quoniam*	*quia* cet.
9:53	*quoniam*	*quia* cet.
10:23	*quia*	*quoniam* 5 *quod* cet.
11:44	*quoniam*	*quia* cet.
12:30	*quia*	*quoniam* cet.
12:37	*quoniam*	*quia* 5 *quod* cet.
13:33	*quoniam*	*quia* cet.
14:24	*quoniam*	*quia* 5 *quod* cet.
24:39	*quoniam*	*quia* cet.

4.1.2 Conflation of Semantics: A Christian Nomenclature?

As Christianity spread throughout the Roman Empire, translations into Latin established a new, distinctly Christian nomenclature. Among the most important semantic innovations introduced by Christians is the term *euangelizare*, a transliteration of the Greek εὐαγγελίζειν. According to Hugh Houghton, this translation is a later development; this observation has in turn motivated Burton to observe that "the translators (of Luke) show a certain amount of critical discretion in their choice."[12]

Table 6: Common renderings of Christian terms in VL2 and VL3

Verse	VL2, 3	Other Latin authorities
1:17	*populum*	*plebem* cet.
1:21	*populus*	*plebs* cet.
5:33	*orationes*	*praecationes* 5 *obsecrationes* cet.
6:20	*discentes suos*	*discipulos* 5 8 *discipulis suis* 4 *discipulos suos* A
6:35	*nequas*	*iniquos* 5 *malos* cet.

12 HOUGHTON, "Scripture and Latin Christian Manuscripts," 25; cf. Burton, The Old Latin Gospels, 54; cf. 5.2.1 "Word formation" (p. 214f.) in this volume.

6:45	*nequa*		*malus* 5 4
			malus homo cet.
8:1	*benenuntians*	*adnuntians*	*euangelizans* cet.
8:24	*magister*		*domine* 5
			praeceptor (*preceptor* 8) cet.
8:28	*oro*		*rogo* 5 *obsecro* cet.
9:26	*gloria sua*		*regno suo* 5
			maiestate sua cet.
9:38	*oro*		*rogo* 5 *obsecro* cet.
10:15	*inferos*		*infernum* cet.
11:1	*discentibus*		*discipulis* cet.
11:39	*niquitiae*	*nequitia*	*iniquitate* cet.
17:16	*samarites*		*samaritanus* cet.
19:47	*principes populi*		*primi populi* 5
			principales (*principes* A) *plebi* cet.
20:1	*benenuntiantem*	*adnuntiante*	*euangelizante* cet.
	pontifices		*principes sacerdotum* cet.
22:2	*pontifices*		*principes* (*principis* 8) *sacerdotum* cet.

4.1.2.1 *adnuntiare* and *benenuntiare* instead of *euangelizare*

The earlier translations of individual terms, found primarily in Luke,[13] include the calques *adnuntiare* and *benenuntiare*, avoiding the Greek loanword, as the following table shows:

Table 7: The readings *benenuntiare* and *adnuntiare* for εὐαγγελίζειν in VL2 and VL3

Verse	VL2, 3		Other Latin authorities
8:1	*benenuntians*	*adnuntians*	*euangelizans* cet.
20:1	*benenuntiatem*	*adnuntiatem*	*euangelizante* cet.

The fact that the two oldest and best manuscripts of Luke read *adnuntiare* and *benenuntiare* against the majority of 'European' manuscripts indicates that these manuscripts are to be taken as standing in a relationship of mutual dependence.

13 On these, see 1:19; 2:10 *adnuntio* VL2; 2:20; 3:18 in VL2; 4:18–19 *praedicare* VL3, *adnuntiare* VL5; 4:43; 4:18 in VL2; 4:42 in VL2; 7:18 *renuntiauerunt* VL3, *adnuntiauerunt* VL5; 7:22 in VL2; 8:1 *adnuntians* VL3; *benenuntians* VL2; 8:36 *adnuntiauerunt* VL3, VL5; 8:46 *adnuntiabit* VL5; 9:6; 13:1; 16:16; 20:1 *adnuntiante* VL3, *benenuntiantem* VL2 and elsewhere; the only departure is Matthew 11:5.

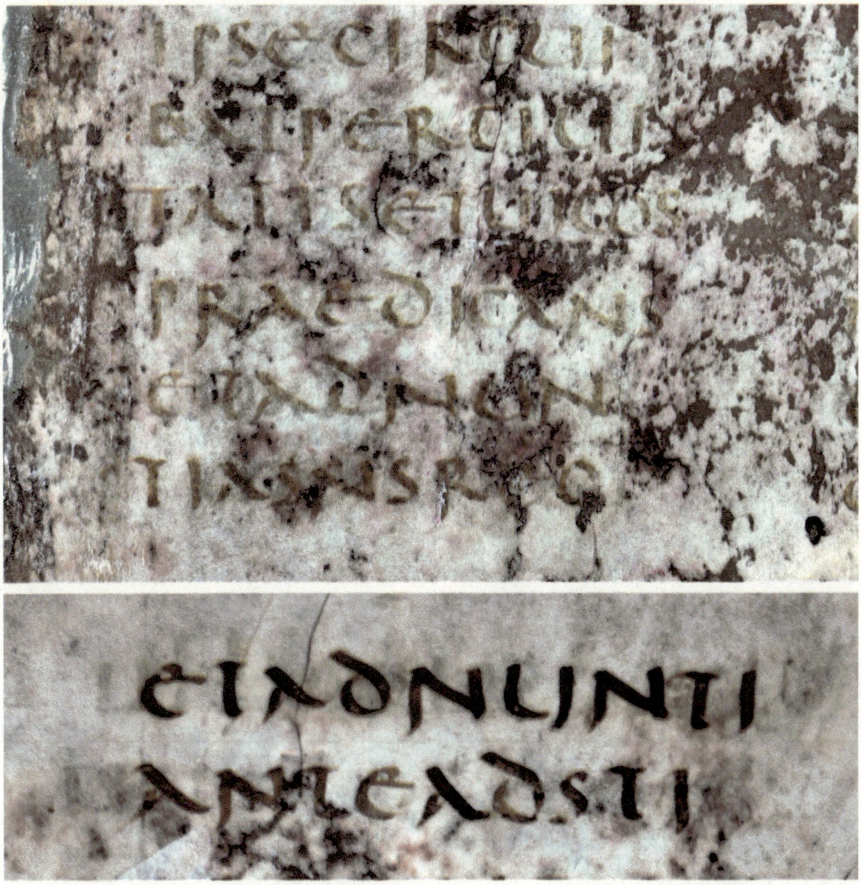

Figure 4.2: The readings *adnuntians* and *adnuntiantem* in Luke 8:1 (387[a]) and 20:1 (481[a]).

4.1.2.2 *discens* and *discipulus* for μαθητής

Moreover, in a detailed table included in his essay "Scripture and Latin Christian Manuscripts," Houghton[14] refers to two possible translations of μαθητής, namely *discens* and *discipulus*, arguing that the former is an earlier Afra term while the latter is distinctly European. In putting forward this argument, Houghton is taking

---

14 HOUGHTON, "Scripture and Latin Christian Manuscripts," 25.

up a thesis already discussed by Rendel Harris[15] and Carl Sittl,[16] to name but two authors. Etymologically, *discipulus* derives from *discere*, "to learn," *quia discunt*; in Latin, this was understood in the sense of *qui discit*, that is, the one who is taught. If we are to believe the lexicon Georges (I,1696), *discipulus* refers to an adult learner while *discens* is used for a school-aged child. Once we turn to ancient literature, however, it becomes clear that its authors do not adhere to this distinction, using both *discipulus* and *discens* side by side and even interchangeably, as in the case of Cicero.[17] The verb *discere* is used much more frequently in the OT than in the NT, being especially represented in the wisdom literature; the participle *discens*, however, is found only in the NT, usually with the meaning "disciple/the one who learns."[18] At first glance, this finding suggests that the differences in the choice of words are due to preferences expressed by individual translators. However, it is indeed striking that *discens* occurs as a unique reading only in the two oldest codices *Vercellensis* and *Palatinus*, where it appears in distinctly important passages. For example, at the beginning of the Sermon on the Plain, the disciples are addressed using *discens*, meaning that Jesus here refers not to those who already have the status of his disciples, but to all learners (Luke 6:20). Furthermore, in Luke 11:1, one of the disciples asks Jesus to teach them how to pray.

Table 8: The reading *discens* for μαθητής in VL2 and VL3

Verse	VL2, 3	Other Latin authorities
6:20	*discentes suos*	*discipulos* 5 8
		discipulis suis 4
		discipulos suos A
11:1	*discentibus*	*discipulis* cet.

15 Harris, A Study of the So-Called Western Text, 98; idem, The Codex Sangallensis, 5: "the old translation read *discens* where we read *discipulus*: and this reading was a frequent perplexity to later scribes when they found it surviving in their copies."

16 Sittl, Die lokalen Verschiedenheiten, 138.

17 See also Tert. *Apol.* 48 ; *Car. Chr.* 12 *nihil adhuc de deo discens; adv. Marc.* 4.12 *si discipulos sabbato ieiunare.*

18 For further examples, see Berndt, "Scientia" und "disciplina," 11–13.

Figure 4.3: The readings *discentes suos* and *discentibus* in Luke 6:20 (371ᵇ–372ᵃ) and Luke 11:1 (418ᵇ).

4.1.2.3 *oratio* and *orare* instead of *rogare*

In the Greek Gospels, two words are used for "prayer" or "praying," namely δέησις (Luke only) or δεῖσθαι on the one hand (only once in Matt, otherwise Luke) and προσευχή or προσεύχεσθαι on the other (used throughout). While the word pair προσευχή or προσεύχεσθαι seem general in terms of the content of the prayer, δέησις tends to designate a direct request; moreover, προσευχή is sacred in character, usually referring to a prayer to God; δέησις, on the other hand, can be used for a request addressed to a human being.[19]

The translation of προσευχή or προσεύχεσθαι in Latin Luke exhibits great regularity.[20] By far, the predominant reading is *oratio* or *orare*, the only variant (just

19 In documentary papyri, the word tends to occur in legal context, for instance in petitions. Cf. *SB* 5 8938, *P. Oxy*. 27 2479; cf. Fn 24 in this chapter.

20 προσευχή: 6:12 (*oratio* c. c.); 19:46 (*oratio* c. c.), 22:45 (*oratio* c. c.); προσεύχεσθαι: 1:10 (*orare, adhorare* VL2); 3:21 (*orare* c. c.); 5:16 (*orare* c. c.); 6:12 (*orare* c. c.); 6:28 (*orare* c. c.); 9:18 (*orare* c. c.); 9:28 (*orare* c. c.); 9:29 (*orare* c. c.); 11:1 (*orare* c. c.); 11:1 (*orare* c. c.); 11:2 (*orare* c. c.); 18:1 (*orare* c. c.); 18:10 (*orare* c. c.); 18:11 (*orare* c. c.); 20:47 (*orare, adhorare* VL2); 22:40 (*orare* c. c.); 22:41 (*orare* c. c.); 22:44 (*orare* c. c.); 22:46 (*orare* c. c.).

the verb) being *adhorare* (sic for *adorare*) in *Codex Palatinus* (VL2: 1:10; 20:47).[21] This is somewhat surprising when we consider that *oratio* and *orare* did not primarily have the sense of "prayer" or "praying" in classical Latin.[22] In any case, *orare* underwent two semantic developments: first, the transition from "to talk" to "to ask," which took place before the classical period; second, the transition from "to ask" to "to pray," which becomes more explicit only in Christian literature. In the sense of "to ask," the verb was in competition with other synonymous verbs, such as *rogare*, and already in the post-Augustan age it had lost ground to these other alternatives. For instance, in referring to asking, Petronius almost exclusively uses *rogare* (41-times) and only rarely *orare* (4-times).[23] It is equally important to note that no diachronic development is discernible: *orare* was clearly preferred since the beginning of Latin Christianity and retained this status in later times, being as frequent in Benedict's writing as it is in Cyprian's.

The situation is different in the case of δέησις and δεῖσθαι.[24] In the Latin witnesses, we find the nominal forms *oratio*, *obsecratio* and *deprecatio*; the verb exhibits other variants, such as *rogare*, *praecari* and *postulare* (VL2: 9:40; 10:2). Here it is significant to note that this variety occurs only in the Latin witnesses, whereas the Greek tradition is uniform. This fact may have led Augustine, for example, to observe: *orationes uero distinguere a precibus uel precationibus omnino difficile est* (*ep.* 149. 13.1.11–13); in Augustine, the terms are interchangeable to such an extent that he refers to the *pater noster* as *preces*, even though all Latin witnesses speak of it as an *oratio*: *Christus nobis preces dictauit* (*serm.* 58.1). For Ambrose, however, the different words denote a kind of spiritual progression.[25] The distribution of the Latin variants, however, shows a distinct pattern: the more recent texts, including the Vulgate, decidedly avoid *oratio* and *orare* as translations for δέησις and δεῖσθαι respectively – terms which occur only in 21:36 – preferring instead *obsecratio* and

---

21 For further details, see WEISSENRIEDER, "Die Vater-Anrede des Lukasevangeliums," 265.

22 See LÖFSTEDT, Late Latin, 72.

23 For further details, see GÓMEZ, La Petición Verbal en Latín, 164; BUSER, Die Bezeichnung für „Beten" und „Bitten" im christlichen Latein, 66.

24 δέησις: 1:13 (*oratio* with VL2, 5, 14, *obsecratio, deprecation* VL10, 15, vg); 2:37 (*oratio* with 2, 5, 13, 26, *obsecratio* cet.); 5:33 (*oratio* with VL2, 4, 14; *praecatio* VL5, *obsecratio* cet.) δεῖσθαι: 5:12 (*orare, deprecari* VL4, *rogare* cet.); 8:28 (*orare* with VL2, 4; *rogare* VL5; *obsecrare* cet.); 8:38 (*rogare* c. c.); 9:38 (*orare* with VL2, 4; *rogare* VL5, *obsecrare* cet.); 9:40 (*praecari* with VL5, *postulare* VL2, *rogare* cet.); 10:2 (*praecari* with VL5, *postulare* VL2, *rogare* cet.); 21:36 (*orare, depraecari* VL2, *rogare* VL5); 22:32 (*rogare, praecari* VL5); 22:32 (*rogare, orare* VL 11: no Greek equivalent)

25 Aug. *serm.* 58.1 *hactenus oratio, inde sequitur obsecratio, ut destruatur inimicus, postulatio, ut lunam et stellas uideat, lunam Ecclesiam, stellas filios Ecclesiae, caelestis gratiae luce fulgentes,* [...] *gratiarum actio, quod tuetur Dominus hominem* [...] *uel quod homini animantium genera uniuersa subiecit.* For further detials, cf. GIOANNI, "Apprendre à prier chez les Pères latins," 124.

obsecrare. Hofmann has observed that these two words belong to the vocabulary of an elevated literary register, since neither term is found in Petronius or in the later Romance languages.[26]

In the *Vercellensis*, however, it is precisely *oratio* and *orare* that are predominant; this tendency of the manuscript is exceptional among the Latin witnesses, associating it more closely to other old versions, such as the *Palatinus*. Of particular interest in this respect are three verses (5:12: 8:28; 9:38) in which the translation δεῖσθαι as *orare* may mark a transition between the senses "ask" and "pray." These verses always deal with healings (5:12: of the leper; 8:28: of the possessed Gerasene; 9:39: of the possessed boy); by contrast, passages in which the manuscript uses terms other than *orare* to translate δεῖσθαι (9:40; 10:2; 22:32) concern what one might call the non-miraculous requests made by Jesus. The passage 9:38–40 is particularly striking: at first, the possessed boy's father addresses Jesus with *oro te* (δέομαί σου, *rogo te* VL5 *obsecro te* cet.); once he has reported that the disciples have been unable to restore the child to health, he says *praecatus sum discipulos tuos* (ἐδεήθην τῶν μαθητῶν σου, *postulaui* VL2 *rogaui* cet.). The variation in the Latin translations of the same Greek verb suggest that the older manuscripts were already sensitive to the particularly religious character which *orare* had come to possess. This is visible, for instance, in the fact that *orare* is used not only for cultic prayer to God, but also in reference to requests made to Jesus. In other words, the use of *orare in* 9:38 may indicate an intensification of the request, which is elevated to the point of asking for a miraculous healing which can performed by Jesus alone. In the initial request made to the disciples, however, the translator chooses a term which has less of a religious connotation.

Table 9: The reading *orare* and *oratio* in VL2 and VL3

Verse	VL2, 3	Other Latin authorities
5:33	*orationes*	*praecationes* 5 *obsecrationes* 4 8 A
8:28	*oro*	*rogo* 5 *obsecro* cet.
9:38	*oro*	*rogo* 5 *obsecro* cet.

26 Hofmann, Lateinische Umgangssprache, 194.

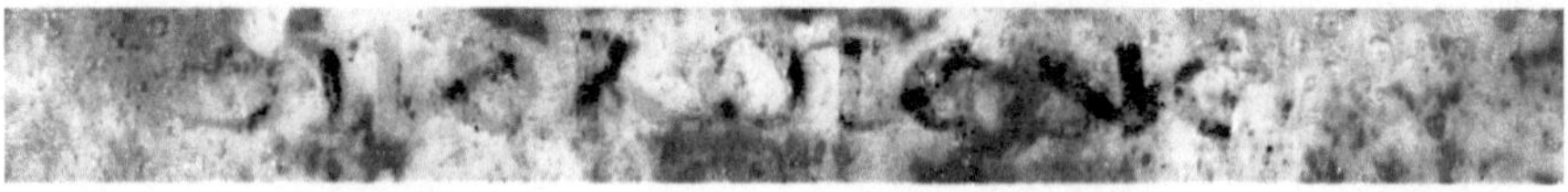

Figure 4.4: The reading *oro* in Luke 8:28 (393[a]).

4.1.2.4 The Translation of ὁ λαός with *plebs* and *populus*

In discussing the various translations of ὁ λαός, we may begin by observing that the Codices *Vercellensis* and *Palatinus* are very helpful for determining the extent to which the translation of the earliest Old Latin manuscripts reflects the demographic structures of the church. In this regard, Philip Burton has argued that the almost consistent translation of ὁ λαός with *plebs* in the *Codex Bobbiensis* (VL1), the oldest manuscript of Matthew, should be interpreted as an 'Afra' text (in 2:4 and 4:16, but not in 2:6; 2:21; 4:23 and 13:15, with *lacuna* for the other passages), unlike the rendering *populus* largely attested by the other manuscripts, with VL3 and VL5 having no consistent reading and VL2 leaning toward *populus.*[27]

In Luke, *populus* is especially frequent in the *Palatinus*, *Vercellensis* and *Bezae.*[28] Should we therefore take *plebs* as the reading characteristic of an early text traced to the "Roman province North Africa" and *populus* as its early European counterpart? Probably not. In his important study *Church, Cities, and People*, Alexander Evers[29] shows that Cyprian portrays the demographic structures of the nascent church as uniform, which in turn means that the terms were not in fact interchangeable. Rather, a study of the *sermones*, *epistulae*, and theological treatises shows that Cyprian, like Augustine of Hippo, uses *plebs* in speaking of particular local congregations. In particular, the term identifies the parts of the ecclesiastical groupings that were responsible for the election of bishops, thus paralleling the use

27 Burton, The Old Latin Gospels, 39–40; 51–52.

28 *Populus* is found in the Gospel of Luke in 1:68 (also VL2, 5); 1:77 (also VL2, 5); 2:10 (alsoVL2, 5); 2:31; 2:32 (with VL2, 5); but: 3:10 *turbae* (5 *populi*); 3:15 (VL2); 3:18; 3:21; but 5:1 *turba* (VL5 *populus*); 5:3 *turbas* (VL2 *populos);* 6:17 (VL2, 5); 6:18 *turba* (VL5 *populus);* 7:1 *populi* (VL2); 7:8 *turbae* (VL2, but VL5 *populo*); 7:12 *turba* (VL2 but VL5 *populus)*; 7:16 *populum;* 7:29 *populus*; 8:4 *turba* (but VL5 *populo*); 8:38 *turba* (but VL5 *populus); 8:*42 *turba* (but VL5 *populus)*; 8:47 *populo* (VL5 *populi);* 9:13 *populum* (VL5, 2); 8:16 *turbis* (but VL5 *populo*); 11:53 *populo* (VL2, 5); 13:14 *turbi* (but VL2 *populum* VL5 *populo*); 13:17 *populus;* 18:43 (VL2, 5); 19:47 *prinicipes populi* (2 *principes populi* 5); 19:48 (cet.); 20:1 *populum* (VL2 5 *populo* 17 A); 20:6 (VL2 5); 20:19 *populum (*cet.); 20:26 (VL2, 5); 20:45 *populo* (VL5, 8, 17, A; *populus* 2); 21:23 (cet.); 21:38 (cet.); 22:2 (VL2 5); 22:66 (VL5); 23:5 (cet.); 23:13 *populi* (but VL5 *plebem*); 23:14 *populum* (but VL5 *plebem); 23:*18 *populus (cet. turba); 23:*27 *populi* (cet.); 23:35 (cet.); 24:19 *populo* (A; *populi* VL2, 5).

29 Evers, Church, Cities, and People.

of *plebs* for political elections in the Roman Republic. *populus*, on the other hand, designated the Christian community as a whole, just as *populus* in Roman usage denoted not just the urban population but the entirety of the Roman Empire.

4.1.2.5 The Translation of Σαμαρίτης as *samarites* and *samaritanus*

In Luke 17:16, the Samaritan is introduced as a believer who follows the Torah and not as a "Gentile" Samaritan.[30] Here, the focus is not on the experience of difference in the sense of alienation from one's own (ritual) community. Again, the manuscripts here provide the unique reading of *samarites* instead of *samaritanus.*

Table 10: The reading *samarites* in Luke 17:16

Verse	VL2, 3	Other Latin authorities
17:16	*samarites*	*samaritanus* cet.

The use of the transliteration of Σαμαρίτης is a sign of a clear tendency on the part of the scribes or translators to closely follow the Greek text. The claim that the two scribes are guided by the earliest North African Latin interpretation receives further support from a comparison with Tertullian's work against Marcion, published around 207 C.E. Tertullian's argument concerning the Samaritans is complex and can only be understood in light of his Christology: a Samaritan is one who gives himself over to "idolatry, for he stigmatized idolatry under the name of Samaria, which was in disgrace because of the idolatry by which it had of old revolted from God under king Jerobeam."[31] Marcion's take changes in 4.35.9 in view of his interpretation of Luke 17:11–19, where he identifies the Samaritans as a party involved in the Northern schism between Ahijah and Jeroboam. More remarkable is Tertullian's interpretation of the one Samaritan who repents to give thanks to Jesus. Tertullian makes it clear – contrary to the text of the New Testament – that the Samaritan shows himself to the priests of the Jerusalem sanctuary, "for the whole of the promise made to the tribe of Judah was Christ himself (*tota enim promissio tribui Iudae Christus fuit*)." Tertullian subsequently asks to which god the healed one is returning. It is in this context that he calls the person *samarites* (*et tamen cui deo*

30 For a general introduction to literature on the Samaritans, see MONTGOMERY, The Samaritans: The earliest Jewish Sect; ZANGENBERG, Samareia: Antike Quellen zur Geschichte und Kultur der Samaritaner in deutscher Übersetzung, 180–229; CROWN, Samaritan Scribes and Manuscripts, 1–39; TSEDAKA, Samaritans.

31 Tert. *adv. Marc.* 3.13.8–10: *Idololatriam enim Samariae nomine notauit, ut ignominiosae ob idolatriam, qua des ciuerat tunc a Deo sub rege Hieroboam.* (Translation: Evans, 211).

gratiam reddidit samarites, quando nec Israhelites alium deum usque adhuc didicisset).[32] Against this background, it is clear that the texts of codices *Palatinus* and *Vercellensis* not only point to a common textual tradition, in which the Greek form of the noun is preferred, but possibly also to a distinction between believing Samaritans and "Gentile" Samaritans.

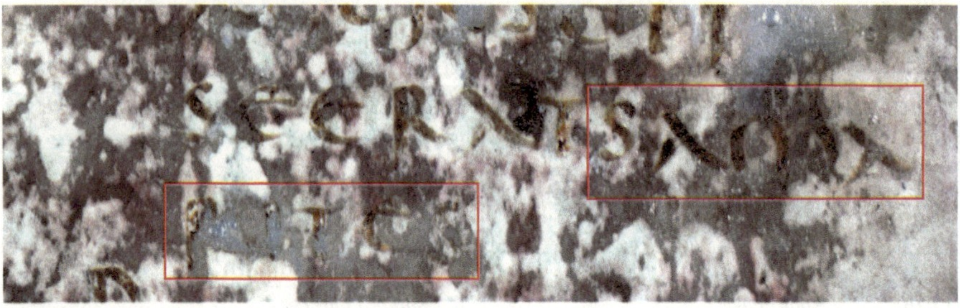

Figure 4.5: The reading *samarites* in Luke 17:16 (461^{b}).

4.1.2.6 Technical Vocabulary: The Translation of Medical Terms

Also of interest are the unique readings occurring in the context of healing stories, as shown in the following table:[33]

Table 11: Common renderings of medical terms in VL2 and VL3

Verse	VL2, 3	Other Latin authorities
4:38	*febre magna*	*febri magna* 5
		magnis febribus cet.
6:18	*curare*	*saluari* 5
		sanarentur cet.
16:21	*uulnera*	*ulcera* cet.
20:29	*decessit*	*mortuus est* cet.

One example, which foregrounds the designation of illnesses, is the story of the healing of Peter's mother-in-law in a private house. In Luke 4:38, the story follows Jesus's first programmatic speech and is often interpreted as an instance of exor-

32 Another angle on the *samarites* can be found in Hier. *ep*. 108.19.6, where we read: *Quem in euangelio et propinqui quasi mentis inpotem ligare cupiebant et aduersarii suggillabant dicentes: Daemonium habet et Samarites est et in Belzebul, principe daemoniorum, eicit daemonia.*
33 Cf. table 29 in chapter 5: Medical vocabulary in VL3 Luke.

cism. Luke here uses the phrase πυρεθῷ μεγάλῳ, "by a great fever," which almost all Latin manuscripts translate with *febre magna*,[34] a term often considered indicative of folk medicine and therefore taken as a sign that this illness may be outside the scope of rational medicine. In ancient Roman medicine, "fever" is commonly understood as synonymous with "illness,"[35] and Schulz has shown that the Latin distinction of *morbus* and *uitium* involves different kinds of fever.[36] While some manuscripts adhere to normal Latin usage by referring to fever in the plural (VL4, 8, A), we also see the Latin term used in the singular in the Palatinus (VL2) and the Vercellensis (VL3), πυρεθῷ μεγάλῳ. This non-standard preservation of the singular could be characterized as a Graecism, also seen in Bezae (VL5), though with the non-standard orthography *febri* instead of *febre*.

Table 12: The renderings of πυρεθῷ μεγάλῳ in Luke 4:38

Verse	VL2, 3	Other Latin authorities
4:38	*febre magna*	*febri magna* 5
		magnis febribus 4 8 A

However, Pliny the Younger[37] and Scribius Largus[38] usually do discuss fever in the singular. In the writings of Alexander of Tralles, we find mention of *cotidiana febris* ("daily or quotidian fever")[39] and *febris chronica*. This is different in the case of Celsus, a Latin-speaking author. Celsus was not a medical professional, but he may have had medical experience, and he acknowledged the Greek sources used in his writings; his preferred terms include *febris acuta* "an acute fever"[40] and *febris ardens*.[41] In discussing the intensification of fever, he speaks of *in recenti uehemetique praecipueque ardente febre* (5.28.18b).[42] Fever is often regarded as lethal; the *febris chronica* or *tertianae* is considered especially dangerous, since the frequent attacks

34 With the exception of the codices *Palatinus* (VL2), *Vercellensis* (VL3) and *Bezae* (VL5) which follow the Greek text in using the singular form *febre magna*.

35 Information on the ancient conception of fever is given by Diogenes Laërtius 9.49 who refers to Democritus, in Celsus *De medicina* 3.3–17 and 4.14, Alexander Aphrodisias *De febris libellus*.

36 See SCHULZE, *Celsus*, 45.

37 See Plin. *nat. hist.* 7.170ff.; 22.115; 26.17

38 See Sribonius Largus, *comp.* 97.1; *ep.* 7.19.2–3.

39 Alex. Tralles *therap.* 6.1.407.1–10.

40 Cels. 3.5.3.

41 In Celsus, this is a pathological term (2.15.1; 5.28.18b); Cassius mentions *febris incendiosa* (Felix Cass. 142.15; 149.9). See also Seneca *ep.* 14.6 *febrem viscera*.

42 For further discussion see LANGSLAW, Medical Latin, 260.

make the prediction of the fever cycle difficult. Therefore, "great care is required to avoid a mistake [...]. Many die suddenly due to the error made by the practitioner in one way or the other (*plurimique sub alterutro curantis errore subito moriuntur*)."[43] The peril posed by fevers is also evident in Ammanius, who has Julian express his fear of losing his life even to a *febricula*.[44] The term *febre magna* may thus be regarded as a compound which is not unusual for Roman medicine. We may thus suspect, with all due caution, that medical interpretation also played a role in the translation of the Greek text in the Codices *Vercellensis* and *Palatinus*. The very next verse, however, seems to question this evaluation by saying: *et stans super illam imperauit febri et dimissit illam* (Luke 4:39). Jesus is here described as exercising authority over the fever (*imperauit*) and casting it out (*dimissit* or *remisit*). The only exception to this characterization is the variant in *Codex Vercellensis* (VL3), which uses an intransitive verb, "and it (sc. the fever) left (*reliquid* sic)." In a similar vein, the medical historian D.R. Langslow refers to a disease "approaching or more aggressively attacking the patient, seizing the patient, letting him go, and departing."[45]

4.1.2.7 Female and Male Prostitutes: *fornicariis*

In addition to the healing stories, readings unique to *Palatinus* and *Vercellensis* are also found in the parable narratives. Particularly striking is a semantic innovation in Luke 15:30. The verse is part of the response of the elder son who refuses to "go in," which here picks up on the admonition in 13:24 to enter through the narrow door. In v. 30, the elder son contrasts his own good behavior (Deut 26:13) with his brother's misbehavior. The Greek text refers to the younger son squandering his part of the inheritance on prostitutes, using the feminine πόρνη for this purpose.

Most manuscripts use *meretricibus*, a feminine noun derived from *mereor*, "to earn" or "to gain" (act.) and "to deserve" (dep.),[46] and *-trīx*, agent suffix (feminine),[47] and usually translated "harlot," "public prostitute," or "courtesan." The two codices under consideration, however, translate *fornicariis* instead which, due to its inflection in the ablative plural, is gender-neutral. In the Vulgate, the noun is attested in both the masculine *fornicarius* (1 Cor 6:9) and the feminine *fornicaria* (Acts 17:16).

43 Cel. 3.8. It is interesting that Celsus uses *curans* rather than *medicus*.

44 Amm. Marc. 24.3.7; for further examples, see HORN, "Fieber," *RAC* 7 (1969): 877–909.

45 LANGSLAW, Medical Latin, 196. On what follows, see ANDRE, "Remarques sur la traduction des mots grecs dans le textes médicaux du Ve. Siècle," 47–67 and Langslaw, Medical Latin, 196.

46 De Vaan, Etymological Dictionary, 374–375.

47 It is disputed whether the /t/ of the PPP belongs to the stem, which means that the suffix may be *-rīx* or *-trīx*. For our purposes, this makes no difference.

In the Gospels, *fornicaria/-us* is found only three times, in Matthew 21:31, 32 and in the passage at hand. Thus, the two manuscripts deepen the criticism of the younger brother by at least hinting at the possibility that he spent his time with female *and* male prostitutes.

Figure 4.6: The reading *fornicariis* in Luke 15:30 (452[a]).

4.1.2.8 Geographical Understanding and Theological Interpretation in Luke 17:11–12

Of special interest is also the healing story in Luke 17:11–12 recounting a meeting between Jesus and the ten lepers which, in the Greek texts, takes place in a strangely vague geographical location. Both the description of Jesus's route as "between Samaria and Galilee" and the location of his meeting with the "lepers" are unclear. The first point of uncertainty in Greek concerns Jesus's route "between Samaria and Galilee." In the Gospel of Luke, his journey brings him through Samaria and not – as in Mark – through Judea and Peraea.[48] The road which led through Samaria was the shortest route between Galilee and Judea. If we can trust Josephus's records, then Jesus takes a route used by pilgrims and travelers.[49] We are told that pilgrims would have been able to complete this journey in three days.[50] Studies[51] have

48 Jos. *Ant.* 20.118; *Bell.* 2.232; *Vit.* 241.145.268–270. 317ff; Judges 21:19; 1 Kings 12; 2 Kings 10; Jer 41:4–6; see also BEITZEL, "Art. Roads and Highways-Peroman," *ABD* 5: 780.

49 The parallels and differences between Jos. *Antiquitates* and *De Bellum Judaicum* are important for the study of the conflict between Jews and Samaritans. It is uncertain whether Josephus had access to more information when he wrote the *Antiquitates*. HJELM, *The Samaritans and Early Judaism*, 223 doubts that this was the case; see also EGGER, *Josephus Flavius*, 247–250, and SAFRAI, Wallfahrt, 137–140.

50 MASON, *Josephus. Jewish War*, 189.

51 BÖHM, Samarien und die Samaritai bei Lukas, 273f. says: "In der Lage des unbekannten Dorfes in der 'großen Ebene' wird wohl auch der Schlüssel für die Ortsbestimmung bei Lukas liegen. Diese Ebene bildet einen weiten Zwischenraum zwischen Galiläa und Samaria, der auch durch Bergland

shown that the text probably refers to the special region of Jezreel Valley. When we are told that Jesus returns to Jerusalem via a region between Samaria and Galilee, this is certainly not a merely geographic statement, but rather a reference to the differences between: Jerusalem, the heir of Davidic traditions; Samaria, the heir of the Mosaic tradition; and finally, Galilee, the place where these traditions received a new meaning. To further specify the proximity of the itinerary to Gerizim and Ebal, a pair of hills located 2,5 km east of Jericho which served as Samaritan places of prayer and worship, even the earliest witnesses insert a reference to the city of Jericho.[52]

Table 13: The renderings of Ἱεριχώ in Luke 17:11

Verse	VL2, 3	Other Latin authorities
17:11	*iericho*	*hiericho* cet.
		om. 5 A

The codices *Vercellensis* and *Palatinus* expand the two regions of Samaria and Galilee by adding a reference to the city of *iericho*. In Roman times, Jericho was located in the Wādī Qelt, about 35 km from Jerusalem. Though the name *iericho* is based on the Hebrew forms יְרִחוֹ, יְרֵחוֹ or יְרִחֹה, other manuscripts use *hiericho*, the inflected form found in the Septuagint, Josephus (e.g. in *A.J.* 18.6.3) and Eusebius of Caesarea (*Onomasticon* 64.9–20). Accordingly, the aspirate /h/ in later Latin Bible manuscripts is probably best explained by the influence of the Septuagint.[53] But why was Jericho added in the first place? There was a wide debate among the Church Fathers about the location of this city: in antiquity, Eusebius is often cited on this matter

auf beiden Seiten umgrenzt ist. Wenn Jesus in der Richtung nach Jerusalem auf ihr wanderte, konnte das ein 'Durchziehen mitten zwischen Samarien und Galiläa' heißen. "

52 Many church authors have a decidedly negative view of Jericho, which may be illustrated by Epiphanius of Salamis's statement on the subject: "And yet this sect, which denies resurrection but rejects idolatry, is continually idolatrous in itself with knowing it, because the idols of the four nations are hidden in the mountain they quibblingly call Gerizim." (pan. 2.4; translation: Williams).

53 In *doctr. chr.* 2.16.23, Augustine remarks on the availability of expert translations of Hebrew terms occuring in Latin Bible translations: *sic etiam multa, quae ab auctoribus eorundem librorum interpretata non sunt, nomina Hebraea non est dubitandum habere non parvam vim atque adiutorium ad solvenda aenigmata scripturarum, si quis ea possit interpretari. Quod obnonnulli eiusdem linguae periti viri non sane parvum beneficium posteris contulerunt, qui separata de scripturis eadem omnia verba interpretati sunt: et quid sit Adam, quid Eva, quid Abraham, quid Moyses; sive etiam locorum nomina, quid sit Hierusalem vel Sion vel Hiericho vel Sina vel Libanus vel Iordanis et quaecumque alia in illa lingua nobis sunt incognita nomina, quibus apertis et interpretatis multae in scripturis figuratae locutiones manifestantur.*

(*Onomasticon* 64.9–20), who insists that Jericho should be located near the Mountains Gerizim and Ebal, a hypothesis that is also repeated by Jerome. In his work *Theophania* 4.23 (after 323) Eusebius claims that "the Temple near the city of Neapolis was sullied and soiled by indecent pictures, idols, sacrifices and the spilling of blood."[54] Even though this account is historically unreliable, several Church Fathers do refer to a location near the city of Neapolis.

Figure 4.7: The reading *iericho* in Luke 17:11–12 (461[a]).

To sum up: the variety of unique readings shared by the codices *Vercellensis* and *Palatinus* is indicative of two distinct textual strains, both of which contain a number of significant readings belonging to the early Latin text type. The consensus among scholars of Old Latin versions is that the *Vercellensis* builds upon and develops the *Palatinus*, which itself represents the earlier stage. However, the conflation of Greek phonology and semantics shared by the two manuscripts suggests that both occupy a similar stage in the history of Old Latin versions; this is especially evident in the use of renderings produced under the influence of Classical Latin usage, for example, *orare* and *oratio* (Luke 1:13; 2:37; 9:38 for *obsecrare* and *obsecratio*), *benedicere* (Luke 1:28 instead of *euangelizare*), *aeternum* (Luke 1:55 for *saecula*) or *curare* (Luke 6:18; 14:4 instead of *sanare*). In later translations, these readings come to be increasingly abandoned in favour of more Christianised language.

However, a different pattern is revealed by the comparison of the *Codex Vercellensis* with the *Veronensis*, where important theological terms are used quite differently, for example, in Luke 2:25 (*exortatio* VL3; *consolatio* VL4); 2:47 (*sapientia* VL3; *prudentia* VL4); 4:27; 5:14; 7:22 (*purgare*/*purgatio* VL3; *mundare*/*mundatio* VL4). In addition to having the typical marks of an "Afra" text (shared with Church Fathers) and of Classical Latin, the codices *Palatinus* and *Vercellensis* also exhibit characteristics of Late Latin, for example in using *ille* instead of *is*. However,

54 The English translation: PLUMMER, Early Christian Authors, 91.

whereas the *Codex Palatinus* conveys rather uniform syntax and morphology, the inconsistencies in syntax and morphology present in the *Vercellensis* are more heterogeneous and may represent an earlier stage of translation from Greek. Confirming this suspicioun, however, would require a fuller understanding of the Greek tradition.

It is also noteworthy that both manuscripts share common readings involving orthographic variants which point to the influence of the spoken language. The translation of the *Vercellensis* text may thus be explained without resorting to the assumption that its text contains more 'Italian' type readings than the *Palatinus*.

Table 14: Unique readings of VL2 and VL3 compared to the other Latin authorities

Verse	VL2, 3		Other Latin authorities
1:15	*impleuitur*	*inplebitur*	*replebitur* cet.
1:17	*populum*		*plebem* 5 4 8 A
1:21	*populus*		*plebs* 5 4 8 A
1:24	*istos autem dies*		*dies istos* 5
			hos autem dies 4 8 A
1:35	*ex te*		om. 5 4 8 A
1:39	*et*		om. 5 4 8 A
1:45	*es*		om. 5 4 8 A
1:61	*isto nomine*	*nomine isto*	*nomen hoc* 5
			hoc nomine cet.
1:66	*quidnam*		*quid utique* 5 4 8
			quid putas A
2:1	*illis diebus*		*diebus illis* 5 4 8 A
2:4	*nazaret*		*nazared* 5
			nazareth 4 A
			nazareht 8
2:15	*sicut*		*quod sic* 4
			quod 5 8 A
2:20	*eos*		*illos cet.*
2:21	*erat*		*est* 5 4 8 A
2:22	*essent*		*sunt* 5 4 8 A
2:40	*euper*		*cum* 5 4 in 8 A
2:43	*iesus*		*puer iesus* 5 A
			iesus puer 4 8
2:44	*esse eum*		*eum esse* 5 *illum esse* 4 A *illum* 8
2:45	*quaerentes*		*requirentes* 5 4 8 A
2:48	*ad illum mater eius*		*ad eum mater eius* 5
			mater eius ad illum 4 8 A
2:51	*subiectus*		*subdictus* 5 4 8 A
3:17	*sua*		*eius* 5 4 8 A
4:13	*discessit*		*recessit* 5 4 8 A

Verse	VL2, 3		Other Latin authorities
4:14	*reuersus*		*conuersus* 5
			egressus 4 A
			regressus 8
4:23	*ad illos*		*ad eos* 5
			illis 4 8 A
4:25	*quomodo*		*sicut* 5
			cum 4 8 A
4:36	*super*		*in* 5 4 8 A
4:38	*febre magna*		*febri magna* 5
			magnis febribus 4 8 A
4:40	*eorum*		om. 5 4 8 A
4:41	*christum illum esse*		*eum christum esse* 5
			ipsum esse christum 4 8 A
5:1	*gennesaret*		*gennesared* 5
			gennesar 4 8
			gennesareth A
5:2	*uidit*		*et uidit* 5 4 8 A
5:7	*annuebant*	*adnuebant*	*innuebant* 5
			adnuerunt 4 8
			annuerunt A
5:15	*diuulgabatur*		*transiebat* 5
			perambulabat 4 8 A
5:19	*cum non inuenissent*		*non inuenientes* 5 4 8 A
5:25	*grabattum suum*		*grabattum* 5
			lectum 4 om. 8 A
5:28	*illum*		*eum* cet.
5:33	*illum*		*eum* cet.
	orationes		*praecationes* 5
			obsecrationes 4 8 A
6:4	*accepit*		*sumpsit* 4 8 A
			om. 5
6:7	*et accusarent illum*		*accusare eum* 5
			quemadmodum accusarent illum 4
			unde accusarentur illum 8
			accusare illum A
6:8	*illorum*		*eorum* cet.
6:17	*iudea*		*iudaea* 5 4 8 A |
6:18	*illum*		*eum* cet.
	curari		*saluari* 5
			sanarentur 4 8 A
6:20	*discentes suos*		*discipulos* 5 8
			discipulis suis 4
			discipulos suos A
6:21	*quoniam*		*quia* cet.
6:22	*segregauerint*		*exprobabunt* 5
			separabunt 4 8
			separauerint A

Verse	VL2, 3		Other Latin authorities
6:23	*profetis*		*et prophetis* 4
	illorum		*prophetis* 5 8 A
			eorum cet.
6:35	*nequas*		*iniquos* 5 *malos* cet.
6:45	*nequa*		*malus* 5 4
			malus homo cet.
6:47	*illa*		*ea* 5
			eos 4 A
			om. 8
	sit similis		*est similis* 5
			simile est 4
			similis est 8
			similis sit A
7:2	*carus*		*honoratus* 5
			praetiosus (*pretiosus* A) cet.
7:3	*illum*		*eum* cet.
7:11	*comitabantur*		*ibant* cet.
	magna		*multa* 5
			copiosa cet.
7:12	*adpropinquaret*		*appropinquaret* A
			adpropiaret cet.
7:17	*tota*		*totam* 5
			uniuersa (*uniuersam* A) cet.
7:29	*cum audissent*		*audiens* cet.
7:32	*qui adclamant*	*qui clamant*	*et adloquentibus* 5
			et loquentibus cet.
7:38	*flens*		*plorans* 5
			om. 4 8 A
7:39	*quoniam*		*quia* cet.
8:1	*benenuntians*	*adnuntians*	*euangelizans* cet.
8:6	*aliut*		*aliud* cet.
8:7	*aliut*		*aliud* cet.
8:8	*bonam et optimam*	*optimam et bonam*	*bonam et uberam* 5
			bonam cet.
8:17	*nihil*		*non* cet.
8:24	*magister*		*domine domine* 5
			praeceptor (*preceptor* 8) cet.
8:25	*illi*		*imperio eius* 4
			ei cet.
8:28	*oro*		*rogo* 5
			obsecro cet.
8:37	*in naue*		*nauem* 4 A
			in nauiculam 8
			om. 5
8:49	*loquente eo*		*eo loquente* 5
			illo loquente cet.

Verse	VL2, 3	Other Latin authorities
9:8	*de antiquis*	*anticus* 5
		unus de antiquis cet.
9:11	*excipiens*	*suscipiens* 5
		excepit cet. |
9:16	*rescipiens*	*ascipiens* 5
		respexit cet.
	benedixit	*orauit et benedixit* 5
	et confregit	*et benedixit* cet.
		et fregit cet.
		om. 5
9:22	*interfici*	*occidi* cet.
9:26	*gloria sua*	*regno suo* 5
		maiestate sua cet.
9:34	*illos*	*eos* cet.
9:37	*turba magna*	*turbam multam* 5
		turba multa cet.
9:38	*oro*	*rogo* 5
		obsecro cet.
9:41	*incredibilis*	*incredula et peruersa* 5
		infidelis et peruesa cet.
9:43	*de*	*in* 5 A
		super 4 8
9:48	*qui enim*	*qui autem* 5
		nam qui cet.
9:49	*illum*	*eum* cet.
9:53	*quoniam*	*quia* cet.
10:3	*mitto*	*ego mitto* cet.
10:7	*migrare*	*transire* cet.
10:8	*quacumque*	*quamcumque* cet.
	receperint	*susceperint* A
		acceperint cet.
10:15	*inferos*	*infernum* cet.
10:19	*nihil*	*et nihil* cet.
10:20	*uerum*	*uerumtamen* cet.
10:21	*illa*	*ipsa* cet.
10:23	*quia*	*quoniam* 5
		quod cet.
10:27	*tanquam*	*sicut* cet.
10:28	*uibes*	*uiues* cet.
10:32	*uidisset*	*uidens* 5
		uideret cet.
	illum	*eum* cet.
10:36	*inciderat*	*incidit* (*incidet* 17) cet.
10:38	*domo sua*	*domum suam* cet.
10:39	*eius*	*illius* cet. om. 5
10:40	*reliquid*	*dereliquid* 5
		reliquit cet.

Verse	VL2, 3	Other Latin authorities
	sola	*solam* cet.
10:41	*ei*	*illi* cet.
11:1	*discentibus*	*discipulis* cet.
11:26	*tunc*	*et tunc* cet.
		om. 5 |
11:35	*est in te*	*in te est* cet.
11:39	*niquitiae* *nequitia*	*iniquitate* cet.
11:42	*olus*	*holus* cet.
11:44	*quoniam*	*quia* cet.
11:46	*legis doctoribus uae*	*uae legis doctoribus* 5
	honeratis	*legis peritis uae* cet.
		oneratis cet.
12:2	*cognoscatur*	*scietur* 5
		sciatur cet.
12:15	*alicui*	*cuiquam* 5
		cuiusquam cet.
	uita ipsius est	*est uita* 5
		uita (uitae 8)
		eius est cet.
12:30	*quia*	*quoniam* cet.
12:36	*expectantibus*	*exspectantibus* cet.
	et	*ut* cet.
12:37	*quoniam*	*quia* 5 *quod* cet.
13:5	*nisi*	*sin* 5
		si non cet.
13:7	*triennium est*	*anni tres sunt* (om. 5) cet.
	excide	*praecide* 5
		succide cet.
13:15	*ducit et adaquat*	*ducens adquat* 5
		ducit adaquare cet.
13:16	*cum sit filia*	*filiam* cet.
13:18	*adsimilabo illud*	*et similabo illud* 5
		et simile illud esse existimabo 4
		et simile illud estimabo 8
		simile illud existimabo 17
		et simile esse existimabo illud A
13:23	*dixit autem quidam illi*	*dixit autem ei quidam* 5
		et ait illi quidam 4 8 17
		ait autem illi quidam A
13:28	*illic*	*ibi* cet.
13:33	*quoniam*	*quia* cet.
13:35	*enim*	*autem* 5 A
14:5	*si*	om. cet.
	non	*et non* cet.
	in die sabbati	*die sabbati* cet.
		om. 5 17

Verse	VL2, 3		Other Latin authorities
14:10	*inuitatus fueris*		*inuitaris* 5
			uocatus fueris cet.
			add. *in nuptias* 2
14:12	*facies*		*facis* cet.
14:13	*prandium*		*aepulationem* 5
	inuita		*conuiuium* cet.
			uoca cet.
14:15	*manducauerit*		*manducauit* (*maducabit* 4 8) cet.
14:16	*inuitauit*		*uocauit* cet.
14:21	*hoc*		*hic* 5
			huc cet.
14:24	*quoniam*		*quia* 5
			quod cet.
14:25	*comitabantur*[c]	*comitabatur*	*ibant* cet.
15:2	*uescitur*		*manducat* 5 A
			manducaret cet.
15:4	*oues centum*		*centum oues* cet.
	reliquit	*relinquet*	*dismittit* 5
			dimittet 4 8
			dimittit 17 A
	quaerens		om. cet.
15:5	*cum inuenerit*		*inueniens* 5
			cum inuenerit (*inueniet* 17) *eam* cet.
	inponit		*imponet* 17
			imponit (*inponit* 5) cet.
	illam		*eam* 4 17 om. cet.
15:6	*et cum uenerit*		*ueniens autem* 5
			et ueniens cet.
15:7	*unum peccatorem*		*uno peccatore* cet.
	iustos		*iustis* cet.
15:10	*unum peccatorem*		*uno* (om. 4 17) *peccatore* (*peccatori* 5) cet.
15:15	*agro suo*		*agro* 5
			uilla sua 4 17
			uillam suam 8 A
15:17	*panem*	*pane*	*panibus* cet.
15:25	*et*		om. cet.
15:26	*quidnam*		*quid* 5
			quaenam 4
			quae cet.
15:30	*fornicariis*		*meretricibus* cet.
16:1	*dissiparet*		*dissipans* 5
			dissipauit 8
			dissipasset cet.
16:9	*uobis*		om. cet.
16:17	*transire*		*praeterire* cet.
16:21	*uulnera*		*ulcera* cet.

Verse	VL2, 3		Other Latin authorities
17:3	*corripe*		*emenda* 5
			increpa cet.
	remitte		*dimitte* cet.
17:6	*plantare*		*transfretare* 8
			transportare 17
			transplatare (*transplantari* 5) cet.
17:8	*postea*		*sic* 4
			post haec cet.
17:11	*iericho*		*hiericho* cet.
			om. 5 A
17:16	*samarites*		*samaritanus* cet.
17:22	*dixit autem*		*dixit ergo* 5
			et ait cet.
17:31	*reuertatur*		*conuertatur* 5
			redeat cet.
18:7	*uindicta*		*uindictam* cet.
18:19	*est*		om. cet.
18:24	*contristatum*		*tristem factum* cet.
18:26	*dixerunt autem*		*dixerunt ergo* 5
			et dixerunt cet.
18:43	*cum uidisset*		*uidens* 5
			ut uidit cet.
19:4	*transiturus erat*		*habebat transire* 5
			erat transiturus cet.
19:7	*et cum uidissent*		*uidentes* 5
			et cum uiderent (*eum* 8) cet.
	apud	*aput*	*ad* cet.
19:18	*et uenit alius*		*et alter uenit* (*ueniens* 5) cet.
19:22	*ex*		*de* cet.
19:23	*exegissem*		*exigebam* 5
			utique exegissem cet.
19:30	*super quem*		*cui* A
			in quo cet.
19:35	*adduxerunt*		*adducentes* 5
			duxerunt cet.
19:37	*discensum*		*descensum* cet.
19:42	*absconsa essent*		*nunc autem absconsum est* 5
			nunc uero abscondita sunt 8
			abscondita sunt 17
			nunc autem abscondita sunt A
19:47	*principes populi*		*primi populi* 5
			principales (*principes* A) *plebi* cet.
19:48	*facerent*		*facerent ei* 5
			facerent illi cet.
20:1	*benenuntiantem*	*adnuntiante*	*euangelizante* cet.
	pontifices		*principes sacerdotum* cet.

Verse	VL2, 3		Other Latin authorities
20:9	*illam*		*eam* cet.
	temporibus multis		*tempora multa* 5
			multis temporibus cet.
20:19	*quaesierunt*		*tempora multa* 5
			multis temporibus cet.
	inice	*inicere*	*mittere* cet.
	illi		*super eum* 5
			in illum cet.
20:21	*persona*		*personam* cet.
20:23	*ad illos*		*eis* 8 *ad* (om. A) *eos* cet.
20:29	*decessit*		*mortuus est* cet.
20:31	*filium*		*semen* A
			filios cet.
20:34	*generant et generantur*		*pariuntur et pariunt* 5
			generantur et generant 8 17
			om. A
20:35	*in resurrectione*	*in resurrectionem*	*et resurectione* A
			et resurrectionis cet.
	a		*ex* cet.
	non		*neque* cet.
20:46	*cauete*		*attendite* (*adtendite* A) cet. add. *uobis* 8
21:2	*quendam*		*quandam* cet.
21:4	*dona*		*munera* cet.
21:9	*bella*		*pugnas* 5
			proelia cet.
21:10	*super*		*contra* cet.
	super		*contra* 5
			aduersus cet.
21:21	*secedant*		*non exeant* 5
			discedant (*disced*at 8) cet.
21:31	*in proximo*		*prope* cet.
21:32	*transiet*		*praeteriet* 4
			preteriit 8
			praeteribit (*praeteriuit* 17) cet.
21:34	*sollicitudinibus*	*solligitudinibus*	*soniis* 5
			curis A
			cogitationibus cet.
21:35	*totius terrae*		*omnis* (om. 8) *terrae* cet.
22:2	*pontifices*		*principes* (*principis* 8) *sacerdotum* cet.
22:10	*illum*		*eum* cet.
22:22	*uerum*	*uaerum*	*uerumtamen* cet.
22:23	*quisnam*		*quis* cet.
22:31	*postulauit*		*expetiuit* cet.
22:32	*ne*		*ut non* cet.
22:57	*ad*		*at* cet.

Verse	VL2, 3	Other Latin authorities
22:65	*blaspemantes*	*blasfemantes* 5
		blasphemiantes 8
		blasphemantes cet.
22:69	*ad dextram*	*ad dexteram* 5
		ad dextris 8 17
		a dextris 4 A
23:39	*illum*	*eum* cet.
		om. 8
24:18	*ad illum*	*ad eum* 5
		illi 4
		ei 8 A
24:22	*ex nobis*	*ex nostris* cet.
		om. 5
24:23	*se*	om. cet.
24:24	*nobis*	*his qui erant nobiscum* 5
		nostris cet.
24:27	*interpraetans* 2[c]	*interpraetari* 5
		interpretabatur A
		interpretans cet.
24:31	*illum*	*eum* cet.
24:33	*collectos*	*congregatos* cet.
24:39	*quoniam*	*quia* cet.
24:46	*tertia die*	*die tertia* 5 A
		om. 4 8
24:47	*incipiens*	*incipientium* 5
		incipientibus cet.
24:50	*manus suas*	*manus* 5
		manibus suis (om. 8) cet.

4.2 The Relation of the *Codex Vercellensis* (VL3) to the *Fragmenta Curiensia* (VL16)

The *Fragmenta Curiensia* were discovered in 1872 inside a book cover in the Episcopal Archives in Chur (*thecae cuiusdam scriptoriae operculis adhaerentes*)[55] by Basilius Hidber (1817–1901), a historian and later professor and librarian of the Historical Research Society.[56] The fragments of the Gospel of Luke are named after the parish of Chur, a name in turn derived from the Latin *curia* (town hall, senate,

55 RANKE, *Fragmenta antiquissimae evangelii Lucani*, 1.

56 Basilius Hidber published, among other things, “Schweizer Geschichte für Schule und Volk” and was the editor of the Swiss Register of Deeds.

assembly) or the Celtic *coria* (clan, tribe). *Fragmenta Curiensia* (catalogue number Ms 041.0.1) thus designates two fragments containing Latin text from parts of chapter 11 and 13 of the Gospel of Luke. Shortly after the discovery, a first edition of the *Fragmenta Curiensia* was published by Ernst Ranke, professor of theology in Marburg.[57] In this paper, Ranke compared the fragments with the *Codex Vercellensis* and found significant textual consistency between them. Consequently, he assumed that the new manuscript also originated from the surroundings of Vercelli, and the fragments were eventually marked as siglum a^2.[58] In addition, the palaeographic analysis of the *Fragmenta Curiensia* suggested a dating around the beginning of the fifth century, which made them one of the oldest witnesses of the Latin Bible. For comparison, the *Codex Vercellensis*, following our assessment in Chap. 1 and that of the *Codices Latini Antiquiores*, should be dated to the second half of the fourth century.[59] The fragments consist of two parchment double-leaves, divided horizontally by a fold along the middle line.

In comparing VL3 and VL16, we must take into account the fact that the *Codex Vercellensis* – incidentally a very comprehensive witness of the Gospels – is missing an entire folio precisely in Chapter 11, where a^2 begins (11:11b), which in turn means that the text runs from 11:26 onwards, and Chapter 13. Nevertheless, the close relationship between the two manuscripts is evident.

The table below lists all the differences between the manuscripts.[60] A cursory inspection suggests that these differences are insignificant and primarily limited to phonetic and orthographic phenomena, along with minor discrepancies in the use of grammatical cases. This impression is further reinforced by the fact that the sentence structure and word order of VL3 and VL16 are precisely the same. In the following table, the smaller superscript represents additions by later correctors:

57 Ranke, Curiensia Evangelii Lucani fragmenta = Fragmenta antiquissimae evangelii Lucani (1873); see also idem, "Ein kleiner Italafund," 505–520.

58 Ranke, "Ein kleiner Italafund," 514–516; idem, Curiensia evangelii Lucani fragmenta = Fragmenta antiquissimae evangelii Lucani, 8. The Vetus Latina Institute marked them – together with the Codex Sangallensis n – with the number 16, which indicates that these pages belong to one gospel book.

59 Cf. Houghton, The Latin New Testament, 211; Burton, The Old Latin Gospels, 21.

60 Cf. Wordsworth et al., Portions of the Gospel according to St. Mark and St. Matthew, CCXIV–CCXV. In conformity with Ranke's work on the *Codex Vercellensis*, Sanday lists one more difference for 11:27: *dum* a^2 versus *cum* a. However, the inspection of a shows clearly that there is no divergence between the manuscripts and that both read *dum*, unlike all other Latin witnesses of this passage. Gasquet, Codex Vercellensis, 75 prints the correct reading.

Table 15: Differences between VL 16 and VL3

Verse	VL16	VL3
11:26	*nouissima*	*nobissima*
11:28	*dī*	*dei*[61]
	beati	*baeati*
13:16	*iam*	om.
	annis	*anni*
13:17	*aduersantur*	*aduersabantur*
13:18	*illut*	*Illud*
13:19	*quod*	*Quo*
13:20	*illut*	om.
13:21	*farina* [*mensuras tres*]	*farina*
	fermentaretur [*totum*]	*fermentaretur*
13:22	*docens* [*et iter faciens in*] *hyerosolymis*	*docens hierosolymis*
13:28	*fletus* [*oculorum*]	*fletus*
	regnum	*regno*[62]

The list shows that the differences are largely insignificant. For example, the confusion between /u/ and /b/ in 11:26 – arising due to the coincidence of /w/ and /b/ in vulgar language – is a feature of many early Latin biblical texts.[63] These observations may be corroborated by observing that word order and sentence structure in the *Fragmenta Curiensia* and the *Codex Vercellensis* are always exactly the same. In addition, the deviation *aduersantur* and *aduersabantur* in Luke 13:17 can likely be explained by a haplographic transcription error on the part of the copyist, since the use of the present tense in a narrative otherwise largely set in the imperfect is rather atypical.[64]

This list could be extended by taking into account the word order, sentence structure, pronoun usage, and other subtleties of the *Curiensia* and the *Vercellensis*. For example, both manuscripts read *dum diceret haec ipse in* Luke 11:27, for which the majority of the other witnesses have *cum haec diceret*. In addition, in Luke 13:23, both manuscripts contain the unusual *qui dixit* with a connecting relative instead of the more common variant employing the personal pronoun *ille* (VL2, 5) or *ipse* (cet.). Furthermore, in 13:32, both manuscripts transmit *tertia*, while the other manuscripts either vacillate between *tertia die* (VL4, 10, 13, 14, 20, 15, 61, 30), *sequenti die*

61 Same as 13:28, 29.

62 Same as 13:29.

63 E.g., Luke 11:12 (*obum* VL15; *ouum* cet.), 11:27 (*ueatus* VL5; *beatus* cet.), and 13:26 (*uiuimus* VL8; *bibimus* cet.). Cf. Väänänen, Introduction au latin vulgaire, 57–58 and Müller-Lancé, Latein für Romanisten, 98–99.

64 Ranke, "Ein kleiner Italafund," 514.

(VL6), and *tertio die* (VL2, 7) or simply omit the noun (VL5, 8, 17, 11, 27). These matters are discussed at further length in the commentary below in 4.3 and Chapter 5.

The close relationship between the *Fragmenta Curiensia* and the *Codex Vercellensis* becomes even more evident once we consider the respects in which the text of these two manuscripts departs from the majority of other witnesses, Greek tradition included. For the time being, then, we may say that the fragments provide otherwise neglected means of studying the *Codex Vercellensis*. The additions *totum* and *et iter faciens in* (13:21,22) should be interpreted in a similar manner.

The omission of ἀγωνίζεσθε in 13:24 is also noteworthy (NA28: ἀγωνίζεσθε εἰσελθεῖν διὰ τῆς στενῆς θύρας; VL3: *intrate per angustum ostium*), since the *Fragmenta Curiensia* and the *Codex Vercellensis* here have the mere imperative *intrate*, which again presents a unique reading of the passage. By contrast, all other Latin witnesses translate both Greek verbs (*elaborate* VL2; *certamini* VL5; *contendite* cet.; add. *certate uel* VL27). The omission of ἀγωνίζεσθε, a term usually interpreted in light of Hellenistic agonistics, is striking (see Plato, *Gorg*. 526d–e; Epictetus, *Diatr.* 1.24.1f.; but also, Matt 11:12) and thus reinforces the close relationship between the texts of the manuscripts. The translators and correctors may have considered this term negligible, thus rendering it with a final infinitive. According to Michael Wolter, this translation removes the the agonal connotations, which are also absent from the synoptic parallels, thus achieving alignment with Matt 7:13 (the *Codex Vercellensis* and the Vulgate translate *intrate per angustam portam*). [65]

These similarities suggest that the manuscripts are either derived from a single exemplar or that the Fragmenta are a copy of the Vercellensis. In their edition of the *Fragmenta Curiensia*, Weissenrieder and Visinoni interpret the presence of several grammatical innovations as a sign that the latter is the case. If these observations are correct, this means that the text of the *Codex Vercellensis* may be used to supplement the damaged passages of the Fragmenta and, conversely, that the Fragmenta may be used to fill large gaps in the *Codex Vercellensis*, and especially the missing folium that contained 11:11–26. A comparison of the two manuscripts shows that they are almost identical, as shown in the following overview:

65 WOLTER, Lukasevangelium, 490–496.

Table 16: Unique readings in VL 16

Verse	Unique readings in VL16 11:11–26 (likely also in VL3)	Other Latin authorities
11:13	*bona data*	*bona* 35 61 *bonum datum* 4 5 6 8 11 14 17 *spiritum sanctum* 10 13 *spiritum sanctum uel bonum* 48 *spiritum bonum* cet.
11:14	*et factum est*	*et erat* cet.
11:18	*super satanan*	*super se* 4 *aduersus se ipsum* 14 *in semet ipsum* 13 15 *in se ipsum* cet.
	quoniam	*quia* cet.
11:20	*certe anticipauit*	*forsitam adproprinquauit* 4 *profecto praeuenit* 10 14 35 61 *praeuenit* 4 *utique praeuenit* 13 *profecto prouenit* 8 17 *profecto peruenit* cet.
11:21	*cum quis fortis et armatus*	*quando fortis armatus* 5 6 *et cum fortis armatus* 11 *cum autem fortis armatus* 30 *cum fortis armatus* cet.
	tueatur	*fuerit custodire* 6 *custodiat* 14 *custodit* cet.
11:22	*quod si*	*si autem* cet.
11:24	*circuit*	*uadit* 5 *ambulat* 4 19 61 *perambulat* cet.
	arida loca quae aquam non habent	*arida loca* 5 *loca arida* 6 10 13 *loca quae non habent aquam* 4 8 11 14 *loca ubi non habent aquam* 17 *inaquosa loca* 48 *loca inaquosa* cet.
11:25	*commundatam et ornatam*	*emundatam et conpositam* 2 *mundatum adornatum* 5 *scopis mundatam et compositam* 6 *scopis mundatam et ornatam* 4 8 10 13 14 17 29 30 35 48 *scopis mundatam* cet.

Table 17: Unique Readings of VL16 and VL3

Verse	Unique readings in VL16 and VL3	Other Latin authorities
11:26	*peiora priorum*	*deteriora prioribus* 2
		peior peioris 13
		peior prioris 4 8 17
		peius priori 11
		peiora prioribus cet.
11:27	*leuata uoce*	*leuauit uocem* 2 6
		eleuans uocem 5
		extollens uocem cet.
11:28	*qui ait*	*ipse dixit* 2 6 48
		ille dixit cet.
11:29	*turba conueniente*	*et cum turbae colligerentur* 2
		turbis congregatis 5 6
		turbis conuenientibus 14
		turbis concurrentibus cet.
13:17	*mirificis quae fiebant ab illo*	*quae uidebant praeclara fieri ab illo* 2
		quibus uidebant mirabilibus ab eo fieri 5
		praeclaris quae uiderant fieri ab eo 6
		praeclaris quae uiderant fieri ab ipso 4 8 11 13 17
		praeclaris quae uidebant ab ipso fieri 14
		praeclaris uirtutibus quae uidebantur fieri ab eo 10
		virtutibus quae viderant fieri ab eo 35
		quae fiebant ab eo 29
		quae gloriose fiebant ab eo cet.
13:19	*orto suo*	*hortum suum* cet.
13:22	*ciuitates et uicos*	*ciuitates et castella* cet.
13:23	*salui futuri sunt*	*saluentur* 2 15
		salui fiunt 4 6 10 11 13 14
		salui fiant 8 17
		saluantur cet.
13:24	*nec poterint*	*et non inuenient* 5
		et non potuerunt 6 13 15 61
		et non poterint 11
		et non poterunt cet.
13:28	*proici foris*	*excludimini foras* 2
		eici foras 5
		excludi foris 14
		expelli uel expulsandos foras 48
		expelli foras cet.
13:30	*fuerunt nouissimi*	*erant nouissimi* 2 15 29 35 54 61
		erunt nouissimi cet.
13:31	*eadem die*	*ipsa die* 11
		in ipsa hora 5
		in illa die 30

Verse	Unique readings in VL16 and VL3	Other Latin authorities
		in ipsa die cet.
	discede et uade	*exi et uade* cet.
	quoniam	*quia* cet.
13:32	*ipse autem dixit eis*	*ille autem dixit illis* 2 *et dixit illis* 5 *et ait illis* cet.
	euntes indicate	*euntes dicite* 48 *abeuntes dicite* 5 *ite et dicite* 2 10 14 17 29 30 35 *ite dicite* cet.
13:33	*sed oportet*	*uerumtamen oportet* cet.
	in futurum	*uentura* 5 *sequenti* cet.

These tables show the proximity between the *Fragmenta Curiensia* and the *Codex Vercellensis*, which is evident not only from the choice of words and the identical sentence structure, but also, critically, in the omission of several readings otherwise handed down by all other witnesses of the early Latin Gospels. The few differences here observed, which are usually limited to variations in orthography and case, are either insignificant or may be attributed to possible copying errors. This not only confirms the early stage of transmission preserved in the *Curiensia* and in the *Vercellensis* but could also suggest that the correctors of the fragments were fully aware of this fact and attempted to revise the text accordingly.

4.3 The Relation of the *Codex Vercellensis* (VL3) to the *Codex Bezae* (VL5)

In Chapter 3, we examined the Codex Vercellensis in light of Bezae's Greek text and encountered evidence against the widespread view that the Greek Bezae might be the *Vorlage* of the *Vercellensis* translation. The claim that the *Vercellensis* developed its readings from this Greek tradition faces several problems, one of which is the presence of word for word translations in the Greek Bezae which sometimes seem to follow an Old Latin version. We have already argued that the Latin Bezae does not substantially align with the Greek Bezae text, and we will continue to do so in this chapter. Here, however, we turn to discuss the possibility that the *Vercellensis* may depend on the Latin *Bezae* or vice versa. These two manuscripts have already been the subject of several studies pursuing various questions, and a considerable number of these studies has posited some proximity between them. In his article, "The Translation of OYN in the Old Latin Gospels," David Parker takes the Latin column of Bezae as a translation of a Greek text, pointing to a consistency in rendering οὖν as *ergo* and saying that the "translator chose *ergo* to translate ουν, and then stuck to it with remarkable fidelity. This method was preserved in the subsequent transmission of the version."[66] Parker then concludes: "The possibility that such consistency has been achieved by a process of revision is ruled out by two facts. The first is that the age of the text is well attested by many other features of it. The second, that other revised texts, including the Vulgate, seem to retain some evidence of their earlier nature."[67] In his monograph *Codex Bezae*, Parker builds on this argument in proposing that the Latin column depends on two stages of the Greek column. He suggests that the existing text depends on both stages, but predominantly on the later stage and that "it seems possible that these Greek texts also had undergone some change and augmentation since the Latin translation based on it had been made."[68] While Parker argues that Bezae's Latin column may be reconstructed on the basis of the Greek text, Lorenz in his *History of Codex Bezae's Text* reflects the common view that there was one single Latin translation, with *Bezae* VL5 being influenced by an early 'European' text-type which "appear to have come about through internal processes taking place within the version, such as the preference for particular synonyms, stylistic refinements of Latin diction, and harmonization to other Latin texts, rather than dependence on Greek texts."[69]

Yet the question remains open whether or not the *Vercellensis* is based on the Old Latin version of *Bezae* or vice versa. In Chapter 3 we already suggested that, in a few passages, the Greek *Bezae* could be better explained as a translation from a Latin text, our manuscript from Vercelli being one possibility. In the case of Luke, however, a few distinctive features suggest that the the *Bezae* and the *Vercellensis* originate from a common source manuscript. In what follows, we build on Parker's observation regarding the consistency of the *Bezae* and the *Vercellensis*, including, for example, the tendency to use *is* consistently rather than alternating between *ille* and *is*. At the same time, in addition to the consistency in translation, we find: that both manuscripts follow the Greek word order; that they bear some syntactical resemblance to each other; that their unique readings employ identical renderings,

---

66 PARKER, "The Translation of OYN in the Old Latin Gospels," 264.

67 PARKER, "The Translation of OYN in the Old Latin Gospels," 268.

68 PARKER, Codex Bezae, 249; in this book he deepens his reconstruction in duplicating the number of translations underlying the Latin column.

69 LORENZ, The History of Codex Bezae's Text, 342.

which we observe in comparing the unique readings of the *Vercellensis* with the Old Latin version of *Bezae.* It is also noteworthy that, in some passages, we find harmonization between the *Codex Bezae* VL5 and the fragments from Chur VL16, which can in turn be explained by reference to the *Vercellensis.* However, we cannot say with certainty, if the Vercellensis and the fragment from Chur were sources of Bezae's text, since the stylistic enhancements Bezae exhibits are closer to later text-stages:

Table 18: Unique readings of the VL16 (VL3) and VL5

Verse	VL3, 16	VL5
11:13	*scitis*	
11:17	*deseretur*	
	super se	
11:18	*super satanan*	*super se*
11:19	*eicient*	
	ipsi uestri iudices erunt	
11:22	*illum*	
	armaturam	
	tollit	
11:25	*commundatam et ornatam*	*mudatum adornatum*
11:26	*intrantes* (with VL14)	*intrant*
13:16	*oportebat*	
	hoc	
13:17	*confundebantur*	
13:19	*quo accepto* (VL3)	
13:22	*Circuibat*	
13:27	*operari* (with VL2)	
13:32	*vulpi huic* (with VL2)	
13:33	*oportet* (with VL4)	

4.3.1 Conflation of Greek Word Order

The proximity of the codices *Vercellensis* and *Bezae* may be observed in *the literal translation* of the Greek, and especially in the characteristically Greek word order of the Latin. These observations may be verified by reference to the Majority Text:

Table 19: Common word order in VL3 and VL5 against other Latin authorities

Verse	VL3, 5	Other Latin authorities
4:9	*es dei*	*dei es* cet.
6:32	*uobis gratia est*	*est uobis gratia* 2 *uobis gratia* 4 *erit uobis gratia* 8 *uobis est gratia* A
6:48	*mouere illam*	*illam mouere* 2 *eam mouere* cet.
7:31	*et cui sunt similes*	*et cui similes sint* 2* *et cui similes sunt* 2[c] A *et cui similes est* 8 om. 4
8:38	*exierant daemonia*	*daemonia* (*demonia* 8) *exierant* cet.
8:46	*ego enim*	*nam et* (om. A[c]) *ego* cet.
8:52	*enim mortua est*	*non est* (add. *enim* 8) *mortua* cet.
8:55	*dari ei*	*illi dari* (*dare* 8) cet.
9:25	*mundum totum*	*totum mundum* 2 *uniuersum mundum* cet.
10:16	*spernit uos*	*uos spernit* cet.
10:31	*uiam illam*	*illam uiam* 2 *eadem uia* (*uiam* 8) cet.
11:5	*inducas nos*	*nos induca* cet.
11:19	*uestri iudices erunt*	*iudices uestri erunt* A *iudices erunt uestri* cet.
19:22	*iudicabo te*	*te condemno* 2 *te iudico* cet.
20:25	*quae sunt caesaris*	*quae caesaris sunt* cet.
21:26	*quae sun in caelo*	*quae in caelo sunt* 8 *in caelo* (*caelorum* A) cet.
21:37	*in templo docens*	*docens in templo* cet.
23:9	*respondebat illi*	*respondebat* 2 *ei respondebat* 4 *illi respondebat* cet.
24:6	*esset in galilaea*	*in galilaea esset* cet.
24:17	*uerba ista* (*ista uerba*)	*ista uerba* 5 *hi* (*hii* 2 isti 8) *sermones* cet.
24:18	*diebus istis*	*istis diebus* 2 *his diebus* cet.

The Vercellensis/ Curiensia and the Latin Bezae VL5 have common readings based on word order, as e.g. in Luke 11. Indeed, Luke 11:19 puts the notion that the Greek text of Bezae D, 05 obviously served as the exemplar for Bezae d, 5 and the Vercellensis / Curiensia into question. In this verse, we find the reading *ipsi uestri iudices erunt* in VL5 and 16, with a correspondence in VL6 (*ipse uobis iudices erunt*), whereas the other authorities transpose the possessive pronoun, placing it either after the predicate (*ipsi iudices erunt uestri* VL4, 10, 8, 17, 13, 11, 14, 30, 51) or directly after the noun *iudices* (*ipsi iudices uestri erunt* VL20, 15, 7, 29, 77; *iudices uestri ipsi erunt* 48). In the case of this verse, the large number of Latin textual variants (differing only in word order) reflects the state of the Greek tradition. The text of the *Curiensia* and *Bezae* (VL5) *ipsi uestri iudices erunt* corresponds to the reading of *Codex Vaticanus* (B), one of the oldest uncial manuscripts of the New Testament. By contrast, the reading of the main European text-type VL4, 10, 8, 17, 13, 11, 14, 30, 51, *ipsi iudices erunt uestri*, corresponds to the reading of the *Sinaiticus* (01, א). Finally, the Vulgate reading (VL7, 15, 20, 29, 77) *ipsi iudices uestri erunt* matches the *Alexandrinus* (A).

4.3.1.1 Additions in Vercellensis', Curiensia's and Bezae's Base Layer

The central aspects of the conflation of Greek may be further explored on the basis of insights gained from research on the early Fragmenta Curiensia VL16. Paleographic observations of Codex Bezae have revealed the phenomenon of textual expansion by many primae based on Bezae VL5.

The first textual expansion is found in Luke 11:14, on folio 1ra, line 11:[70]

Figure 4.8: The textual expansion in Luke 11:14 *Fragmenta Curiensia*, on folio 1ra, line 11.

Table 20: Textual expansion in VL16 of Luke 11:14, 1ra, l. 11

VL3	*deest usque ad v. 26*							
VL2	*deest usque ad v. 24*							
VL5			haec	autem	dicente eo		offertur	illi
VL16			haec		cum	dixisset	offerebant	illi
VL4			haec		cum	dixisset	offerunt	illi
VL10	cum	autem	haec			dixisset	adduxerunt	ad eum

VL3	*deest usque ad v. 26*				
VL2	*deest usque ad v. 24*				
VL5		daemoniosus	surdus		
VL16	unum	daemoniacum			
VL4	unum	demoniacum	surdum	et	mutum
VL10	unum	daemoniacum			

70 Synoptic parallels: Matt 9:32; 12:22 | Mark 7:32.

The healing of the mute and – depending on the tradition – deaf man introduces Jesus's defense speech against the Pharisees, who accuse him of allying with Satan. Four Latin translations (VL16, 5, 6,[71] 10) attest to a longer version of this episode, expanding the scenic introduction in v.14 and filling out the exposition of the exorcism with material from the parallel tradition.[72]

The *Fragmenta Curiensia* exhibit numerous similarities with the version in Matthew (Matt 12:22: προσήνεγκαν αὐτῷ δαιμονιζόμενον B, 03), which are especially evident in insertions from the parallel tradition made by a different hand. The exegetical literature assumes that the text of Luke heavily borrows from the Q version,[73] and the *Curiensia* confirm this impression.

Bezae contains a unique reading which is significant since this bilingual manuscript provides the only Greek transmission of the passage, which it also renders in a literal Latin translation: ταῦτα δὲ εἰπόντος αὐτοῦ προσφέρεται αὐτῷ δαιμονιζόμενος κωφός (D, 05). While the dependency between the different readings is evident (cf. Table 20), they differ in a few respects: instead of the participial construction and the adjective *daemoniosus* of the *Codex Bezae* (VL5), the other witnesses prefer a temporal clause introduced with *cum* and *d(a)emoniacum*; for *adduxerunt ad eum* in *Codex Brixianus* (VL10), a form of *offerre* in various tenses (present: VL5, 6; imperfect: VL16) and diatheses (passive: VL5; active: VL16, 6) with the dative object *illi*. The omissions and additions are perhaps even more important: the *Codex Bezae* (VL5) speaks of a man described as *surdus* ("dark, deaf"); in the *Codex Colbertinus* (VL6), the man is *surdus et mutus* ("deaf and mute").[74] The

71 At this point, it also appears that the *Codex Veronensis* shows awareness of this addition, which is probably to be assumed on the basis of the Bezae.

72 v.22 *scribae et ceteri dicebant enim quoniam belsebul habet principem daemoniorum et expellit per ipsum daemonia* (here according to the *Codex Palatinus*; lacuna in the *Vercellensis*), v.23 *et convocans eos dicebat illis in parabolis dominus iesus: quomodo potest satanas satanam expellere*, v.24 *regnum in se dividatur, non potest stare regia illa*, v.25 *et si domus super se divisa fuerit, non poterit stare domus illa*, v.26 *et si satanas satanan eicit, dispertitus super se, non potest stare regnum eius, sed finem habet*, v.27 *nemo autem potest vasa fortis intrare in domum et diripere, nisi prius fortem alliget, et tunc domus illius diripiet.*

73 FLEDDERMANN, Mark and Q, 41–44; WOLTER, Lukasevangelium, 415–416; LAUFEN, Doppelüberlieferung, 126–130.

74 See Dig. 5.1.12.2: "Not everybody may be appointed a judge by those with the right to appoint judges. For some are prevented by statute (*lex*) from becoming judges, some by nature (*natura*), and some by custom (*mores*). For example, the deaf and the dumb (*surdus mutus*) [...]." See also Digest 45.1. See LAES, "Disabilities and the Disabled in the Roman World. A Social and Cultural History," 192–214. See Hier. PL 1065 cc 305: *Cur caecus et surdus et mutus ita create sunt?*; Bed. *hom. T.* VII c. 65–66 1.22; cf. also. Ambr. *Vid.* 10.63: *simul enim praeceptum dederit, caecus videt, paralyticcus ambulat, mutus loquitur, surdus audit, febriens ministrat, lunaticus liberator.*

Curiensia and the *Codex Brixianus* describe the man's suffering in further detail in the continuation of the verse. In the fragments, the text is expanded by a gloss between lines 11 and 12; this correction also turns out to be a unique reading.

It seems clear that the copyist of the fragments is working with a longer beginning of v.14 (though one which does not list the symptoms of the disease), but also with a shorter ending, which does not mention the healed man again (VL16, 4, 5 om. *locutus est mutus*); in this way, the text of the fragments agrees with the codices *Bezae* and *Veronensis*. The difference, however, is that, according to the *Curiensia*, the sick man is not mute due to his illness (for the fragments omit any mention of the illness), but because he is prevented from speaking by a mute demon.

Table 21: Further textual expansion in VL5, 16 of Luke 11:15, 1ra, lower margin

VL 3	*deest usque ad v. 26*							
VL2	*deest usque ad v. 24*							
VL5	ad	ille		respondens				Dixit
VL16		ille	Autem	respondit			et	Dixit
VL14	et			respondens	eis	iesus		Dixit
//								
VL3	*deest usque ad v. 26*							
VL2	*deest usque ad v. 24*							
VL5	quodo	potest	satanas	satanan	eicere			
VL16	quomodo	potest	satanas	satanan	expellere			
VL14	quomodo	potest	satanas	satanan	eic[ere]			

Figure 4.9: The textual expansion in VL16 of Luke 11:15, 1ra, lower margin.

Three Latin translations attest to a longer version of Luke 11:15, which forms a kind of anticipation of Jesus's question in v. 18;[75] in the *Curiensia*, this version is found as a gloss. Here we again observe an interaction between the fragments and the Greek *Bezae* (D, 05), which contains a Greek textual variant. Must we then assume that the Codex Bezae D, 05 was the template for this Latin variant? Not necessarily, since we also find the variant in the *Codex Alexandrinus* (A): ὁ δὲ ἀποκριθεὶς εἶπεν· πῶς δύναται σατανᾶς σατανᾶν ἐκβάλλειν.[76] The version of *Codex Usserianus primus* (VL14), which instead of the adversative conjunction (*autem* VL16; *ad* VL5) prefers an additive connector (*et*),[77] essentially preserves the wording of the *Codex Cyprius* (K), which inserts καὶ ἀποκριθεὶς; indeed, the parallel tradition in Mark attests to a different introductory phrase.[78] It is evident that the insertion, together with the textual material in v. 18, has the function of clarifying the untenable character of the accusations made against Jesus's exorcisms, which ultimately imply that Satan proceeds against himself. Furthermore, it becomes clear that the statements about the *omnem regnum* in v.17 would also apply to Satan's kingdom.

In two respects, however, the reading of the fragments from Chur differs from that of the *Codex Bezae*: one central difference between the two manuscripts is the choice of *expellere* in the *Fragmenta Curiensia*, in contrast to the majority of Latin witnesses, which transmit *eicere*. In Mark 3:23, we find the verb *expellere* in the codices *Palatinus*, *Vercellensis*, and *Veronensis*, whose earliest surviving support is found in texts of the 'Afra' type.[79] *Bezae* paraphrases the participial construction (*respondens dixit*) instead of using a coordinate clause (*respondet et dixit*; VL16); this correction can be compared with the readings in v.14, where the text of the fragments replaces the ablative absolute of the *Bezae* with a temporal clause introduced with *cum*.

Even outside the glosses, we find a considerable number of readings shared by the Fragmenta and Latin Bezae. Thus, the Latin manuscripts exhibit a number of textual variants for the translation of ἄνυδρος in Luke 11:24, which may be classified into two groups: in the first group, the Greek is rendered literally using a cor-

---

75 *Si et satanas super satanan divisus est, quomodo stabit regnum eis?*

76 D, 05: σαναν εκβαλειν.

77 On *at* and *autem* as discourse markers, see Kroon, "Discourse markers," 25: "*At* is primarily a marker of protests and objections, that is, of challenging or problematising reactive moves. [...] *autem*, on the other hand, functions primarily as a marker of thematical (or topical) discontinuity [...]."

78 Καὶ προσκαλεσάμενος αὐτοὺς ἐν παραβολαῖς ἔλεγεν αὐτοῖς.

79 Cf. Wordsworth et al, Portions of the Gospels, CXXVI; also Vogels, Evangelium Palatinum, 123; see also Tert. *adv. Marc.* 4.26.11: *Quodsi ego in digito dei expello daemonia, ergone adpropinquavit in vos regnum dei?*

responding adjective in Latin, either *arida* (*arida loca quae aquam non habent* VL16, *arida loca* VL5; in reverse word order: *loca arida* VL6, 10, 13) or *inaquosa* (VL27, 29, 30, 61), a neologism encountered only in Christian literature whose formation is obviously due to an attempt to etymologically reconstruct and translate the Greek term; in the second ground, ἄνυδρος is paraphrased with a relative clause *quae* (*ubi* VL17) *non habent aquam* (VL4, 8, 11, 14). The strikingly pleonastic unique reading of the *Fragmenta Curiensia* – *arida loca quae aquam non habent* – turns out to be a combination of these two variants. It is precisely this redundant formulation – with only a slightly changed word order, *loca arida* instead of *arida loca* – that is handed down by some of the oldest manuscripts of Ambrose's *Expositio evangelii Lucae* (A α C). Moreover, the complex transmission of this passage is made all the more vivid by comparing the passage to Matt 12:43, where *arida* is found in the majority of manuscripts, including the Vulgate, while the *Codex Bezae* (VL5) and the *Codex Bobbiensis* (VL1) offer the adjective *inaquosa.*

These additions conflate several well-attested Greek readings, which first appear in Latin in either the Latin Bezae or the Fragments from Chur, depending on the final verdict on the dating of these texts. Readings suffice to emphasize the hitherto neglected importance of the *Fragmenta Curiensia* for the study of the *Codex Bezae*, especially when it comes to chapters 11 and 13. The European text-type in turn presumably assimilated these distinct renderings from Bezae.

4.3.2 Conflation of the Syntax

4.3.2.1 The Use of Pronouns

To begin with, we may observe that both the manuscripts and the testimonia of Church Fathers exhibit the indiscriminate use of the demonstrative in lieu of the third person pronoun; this lack of differentiation presents a grammatical phenomenon characterizing all Latin translations of the Bible.[80] The use of pronouns in the codices *Vercellensis* and *Bezae* can also shed light on the relation between these manuscripts. The following table illustrates a tendency toward classical Latin, in which the functions of the missing third person pronouns were often taken over by the demonstrative *is*, a tendency which is found in almost all passages in the Bezae. By contrast, in section 4.1, which was dedicated to the common readings of the Vercellensis and Palatinus, we saw the opposite pattern: the investigation undertaken there showed that the two oldest Latin Bible translations depart from classical Latin precisely on this point of translation.

---

80 Cf. Müller-Lancé, Latein für Romanisten, 130.

Table 22: The use of *is* in VL3 and VL5

Verse	VL3, 5		Other Latin authorities
1:32	*ei*		*illi* cet.
1:36	*ei*		*illi* 2 4 8^{c} A
			illis 8*
1:51	*eorum*		*illorum* 2
			ipsorum 4 8
			sui A
1:58	*ea*		*eo* 2
			illa 4 8 A
2:22	*eum*		*illum* 2 4 8 A
2:40	*eum*	*eo*	*illo* 4 8 A
3:12	*ad eum*		*illi* 2
			ad illum 4 8 A
3:19	*eo*		*illo* 2 4 8 A
3:22	*eum*		*illum* 2
			ipsum 4 8 A
4:5	*eum*		*illum* 2 4 8 A
4:26	*earum*	*eorum*	*illarum* cet.
4:29	*eum*		*illum* 2 4 8 A
4:39	*eam*		*illam* 2 4 8 A
	eam		*illam* 2 4 8 A
4:42	*eum*		*illum* 2
			ipsum 4 8 A
8:38	*eum*		*illum* cet.
8:52	*eam*		*illam* cet.
9:10	*eos*		*illos* 2
			illis cet. add. *iesus* 8
9:18	*eos*		*illos* cet.
9:45	*ab eis*		*ab illis* 2
			inter ipsos 4
			inter ipsis 8
			ante eos A
10:34	*eum*		*illum* cet.
			om. 2
19:5	*ei*		*illi* 2 *ad eum* cet.
19:13	*ad eos*		*illis* 2 *ad illos* cet.
20:41	*eos*		*illos* cet.
22:15	*ad eos*		*ad illos* 2 *illis* cet.
22:56	*eum*		*illum* cet.
	eo		*ipso* cet.

Some of the few exceptions from this pattern are found in *Bezae* and the Fragmenta, which use *ille* instead of *is* for the demonstrative:

Table 23: The use of *ille* in VL16 and VL5

Verse	VL5, 16	Other Latin authorities
11:22	*illum*	*eum* cet.

In the *Codex Palatinus* and the *Fragmenta*, we see a uniform use *ille* as a demonstrative, while the *Bezae* (VL5) exhibits a nearly consistent use of *is*, in what seems like a clear case of imitation of classical Latin. Once we turn to the Vercellensis, we find that the pronouns have lost their original deictic function of indicating distance from the speaker, and that the scribe – like Augustine – uses the demonstratives interchangeably. This usage may possibly be due to the influence of contemporary *spoken* Latin.

Another instance of post-classical usage is found in the use of the preposition *super* to express antagonism and hostile opposition in 5:18 (*super lectum* instead of *portantes*); 5:19; 8:8; 11:18; 15:20; 20:18; 22:44. So we see VL5 and VL3[81] opting for the preposition *super* instead of *in* in the parable of the sower (Luke 8:8) in order to express the contrast between the seed falling on barren and fertile ground. This reading is also found in Ambrose (Ps 36.12.2; written c. 395 CE),[82] Anonymus comm. Prud. (1023 *supra petram, aliud in terram bonam*) and the *Opus imperfectum in Matthaeum.* [83]

Table 24: The use of *super* in VL16 and VL5

Verse	VL16, 5	Other Latin authorities
11:18	*super satanan* 16 | *super se* 5	*aduersus se ipsum* 14 *in semet ipsum* 13 15 *in se ipsum* cet.

The translation of the preposition ἐπί as *super* also occurs in the *Curiensia* (Luke 11:18), serving as indication of post-classical Latin. At the same time, this translation presents another literal imitation of the Greek text. In this case, the other witnesses read *in* or *aduersus*.

81 Matt 13:7–8, on the other hand, has *in terram bonam* throughout.

82 Frede, Kirchenschriftsteller, 107.

83 J. van Banning, Opus imperfectum in Matthaeum, *CC* 87B (1988); The *Opus imperfectum* is a commentary based on Origen and written by an Arian bishop versed in Greek and Latin culture.

Table 25: The use of *hic* in VL3 and VL5

Verse	NA[28]	VL3, 5, 16	Other Latin authorities
8:41	οὗτος	*hic*	*ipse* cet.
9:44	τοὺς λόγους τούτους	*uerba haec*	*uerba ista* 5
			sermones istos (*hos* 8) cet. om. 4
9:45	τὸ ῥῆμα τοῦτο	*uerbum hoc*	*uerbum illud* 2
			uerbum istud cet.
13:16	οὗτος	*hoc*	| *istis* 10 | *isto* rell. | om. 2, 4
13:32		*hic*	*ille*
19:9	αὐτός	*hic*	*ipse* cet.
20:19	ταύτην	*hanc*	*istam* cet.
23:5		*hic*	*huc* 8 A
			hoc cet.
23:22		*hic*	*iste* cet.
24:11		*haec*	*ista* cet.

Early Latin translations of the Bible depart from classical usage not only with respect to the pronoun *ille*, but also in the way they employ the various forms of *hic*. Like *ille*, the pronoun *hic* too seems to have lost its function of designating temporal or spatial proximity, providing another sign of the dissolution of classical Latin's deictic system. Classical Latin employed a three-tiered system for demonstratives, corresponding to the three personal pronouns: *hic* for *ego* (the person speaking), *iste* for *tu* (the one addressed), and *ille* for the third person (the one discussed).[84] An example of the looseness of usage present in the Biblical translations occurs in Luke 13:32, where the *Fragmenta Curiensia* and the codices *Vercellensis*, *Palatinus*, and *Bezae* have the demonstrative pronoun *hic* instead of the *ille* used in all other witnesses. Here we should note that *hic* is admittedly used interchangeably with *iste* as a translation of οὗτος; furthermore, *hic* is retained especially in set phrases, such as after *omnia* and *verba*. Compared to ancient Latin texts, however, we observe a considerable increase in the use of *iste* in the biblical writings, as illustrated by the passages under consideration. At the same time, we should note that the reading *hoc* present in the Fragmenta departs from the majority of Latin witnesses, thereby both following the general use of the pronoun *hic*, and also faithfully rendering the Greek original.

As already discussed above, the causal ὅτι is consistently translated with the conjunction *quoniam* in the *Codex Vercellensis* and the *Fragmenta*, while the other witnesses mostly have *quia*. Against this background, it is significant that *Bezae* sides with the *Vercellensis* and the *Fragmenta* in 13:24 (*quoniam* VL3, 5, 16, *quia* rell.;

84 Cf. ABEL, "Die Ausbildung des bestimmten Artikels," 230.

for the *Vercellensis* and *Bezae* see also: 4:32; 4:43; 7:4; 15:7; 15:24; 16:24; 17:19; 19:21; 19:43; 21:22; 23:31; 23:40; 24:6; 24:34; 24:39; but see 13:31: *quoniam* VL3, 16, *quia* cet.; 13:33: *quoniam* VL2, 3, 16, *quia* cet.). In only one passage do the two manuscripts have *quia* (5:8) against the majority reading.[85] Scholars commonly refer to this as a characteristic 'Afra' reading,[86] an assessment confirmed by the numerous correspondences between the writings of the Church Fathers and textual variants of the oldest Latin biblical manuscripts: for example, Tertullian writes *beati mendici, quoniam illorum est dei regnum*[87] (Luke 6:20), where the majority of witnesses have *quia*. The 'Afra' reading *quoniam* is thus an important linguistic phenomenon shared by the *Vercellensis* and the *Fragmenta*. The same reading is found in the Latin Bezae, occurring with great frequency within only a few chapters, including the passion narrative as well as chapters 4, 15, and 16; to this we might contrast the omission of the term in chapter 13, where VL3 and VL16 both again have *quoniam*.

4.3.2.2 Verbal Syntax in the Vercellensis and Bezae: The Tenses

In addition to demonstratives and prepositions, the *verbal morphology* of Latin also underwent changes. The uncertainty of translation is especially striking in the case of some verbs. For example, in Luke 7:2, we find two Latin translations of the Greek construction μέλλειν with the infinitive, with VL2 and 5 preferring a paraphrase with the verb *incipere* plus infinitive, and the other manuscripts largely using the copula with the future participle (as found, for instance, in the Vulgate).[88]

---

85 See also 10:20 (only in VL2).

86 See, among others, SITTL, Die lokalen Verschiedenheiten der lateinischen Sprache, 111; VON SODEN, Das lateinische Neue Testament in Afrika, 81; BURKITT, The Old Latin and the Itala, 40; HOUGHTON, The Latin New Testament, 10.

87 Cf. Tert. *adv. Marc.* 4.14.13. Textual variants for this passage include *regnum dei* and *regnum coelorum*, under obvious influence of the parallel tradition in Matt 5:8.

88 Cf. Luke 9:31: *inpleturus erat* (ἤμελλεν πληροῦν)
incipiebat implere 2
incipit conplere 5
conpleturus (*completurus* A) *erat* cet.;
Luke 9:44: *incipit tradi* (μέλλει παραδίδοσθαι)] 2
incipiet tradi 5
tradetur 4 8
futurus est ut tradatur A;
Luke 22:23: *hoc facturus esset* (μέλλων πράσσειν)] 2 A
incipiet hoc agere 5
hoc facturus 4 8 17;
Luke 24:21: *redempturus esset istrahel* (μέλλων λυτροῦσθαι)] 4
redempturus erat isdrahel 2

The periphrastic tenses offer examples of analytic tense structure, which had already been used in Classical Latin (especially for the future tense), but which became much more widespread in later times. An example of a periphrastic conjugation is found in 4:31 (ἦν διδάσκων), where VL3 and 5 have a verbatim rendering of the Greek form. Among the Latin translations of the Gospels, the *Codex Vercellensis* especially prefers the periphrastic construction to the simple imperfect.[89] A linguistic peculiarity is also present in the use of the participle in Luke 2:9, which describes the glory of the Lord shining around the shepherds. This combination of an angelophany with the presence of the glory of the Lord is exceptional in the NT.

Figure 4.10: *circumluxit* in Luke 2:9 (339^{a}).

A similar event is mentioned only in connection with the transfiguration of Jesus (Luke 9:31–32), but there, we find a different formulation. In the OT, the glory of God is still described as visible in Exod 16:7,10 and 24:16–17. The verbs used to describe this event are *videre*, *apparere*, or even *fulgere*, which lends plausibility to the reading *circumfulgere*, used by all other witnesses. Except for a small number of passages in Classical Latin (see Plin. nat. hist. 2.101), the verb *circumfulgere* (to shine or radiate around) is found exclusively in the Christian tradition, as in Augustine, *Ennarationes in Psalmos* 75.14, and in Isidore's *Liber quaestionem* (30.24).[90] The

---

incipebat saluare israhel 5
incipit liberare istrahel 8
esset redempturus israhel A.

89 Cf. 4:44: *erat praedicans* (ἦν κηρύσσων)] *praedicabat* VL2; 5:16: *erat secedens* (ἦν ὑποχωρῶν)] *recedens* VL2 *erat subtrahens se* VL5 *secedebat* VL4 Ac *sedebat* VL8, A*; 6:12: *erat pernoctans* (ἦν διανυκτερεύων)] c.c.; 9:53: *erat tendens* (ἦν πορευμένον)] *erat euntibus* VL2 *erat iens* VL5 *erat euntis* VL4, A (the genitive *euntis* here seems to be influenced by the faulty reading of $\mathfrak{P}^{45}$ πορευομένου); 19:47: *erat docens* (ἦν διδάσκων)] *fuit docens* VL2; 23,8: *erat cupiens* (ἦν θέλων)] *erat uolens* 5.

90 See Heine, Bibliotheca Anecdotorum, 96–99.

participle *circumlucens* used by codices *Vercellensis and Bezae* is, to our knowledge, otherwise attested only in Seneca.[91] It thus seems possible that the reading of the two manuscripts is derived from the participle used by Seneca, presenting a hapax legomenon in all of Latin literature. In any case, this reading shows that a clear relationship of dependence exists between the two manuscripts.

We also find parallels to the Greek Bezae D, 05: in particular, the participles κερδήσας and ἀπολέσας in the conditional relative clause in 9:25 also occur in NA 28, where they are found in a sentence dealing with the relativization of wealth and the question of saving life. In Greek Bezae D, 05, the verbs are taken as instances of *accusativus cum infinitivo* and transmitted as two infinitives, κερδῆσαι and ἀπό-λεσαι. In this passage and elsewhere, the infinitive construction has the function of conveying the central message that possessions cannot outweigh the loss of one's own life.

Table 26: The use of infinitive construction in VL3 and VL5

Verse	NA[28]	VL3, 5	Other Latin authorities
9:25	κερδήσας τὸν κόσμον ὅλον ἑαυτὸν δὲ ἀπολέσας	*mundum totum locrari* (*lucrari*) *perdere*	*totum mundum* 2 *uniuersum mundum* cet. *si lucrum fecerit* 2 *si lucretur* cet. *perdat* cet.

The Latin Codices Vercellensis and *Bezae* also agree in using infinitives *locrari* (*lucrari*) and *perdere* in this passage, which are not found in the majority of the Latin and Greek witnesses. A direct dependence of the Latin witnesses on the Greek Bezae D, 05 is not as obvious as Klinghardt suggests,[92] because we already find two versions of Luke 9:25 in Cyprian's second century *Ad Quirinum*, namely *lucrare* and *perdere* but also *lucretur* and *perdat* (*te* 3.61; p. 165.5). We cannot rule out the possibility that this older Latin tradition cited in VL3, which uses infinitives instead of participles, influenced the reading of the Greek text, but we also cannot establish this point with any certainty.

91 *A sollemnibus officiis seducta et ipsam magnitudinis fraternae nimis circumlucentem fortunam exosa defodit se et abdidit. Adsidentibus liberis, nepotibus lugubrem vestem non deposuit, non sine contumelia omnium suorum, quibus saluis orba sibi uidebatur.* "Surrounded by children and grand-children, she would not lay aside her garb of mourning, and, putting a slight on all her nearest, accounted herself utterly bereft though they still lived." Here Seneca sharply attacks Octavia's way of mourning, which is inconsistent with the honor in fact due to Marcellus.

92 KLINGHARDT, Das älteste Evangelium. *Vol. 2*, 657.

The imperfect *oportebat* in the codices *Vercellensis* and *Bezae* translation of Luke 13:16 – also found in the *Fragmenta Curiensia*, as well as in Cassiodor's *Expositio in Psalterium*[93] – may again be a sign of a translation strategy which linguistically imitates the syntactic structures and the diastratic variety of the Greek original (*oportebat* VL2, 16, 5; *opportuit* VL15; *potuit* VL29; *oportuit* rell.). In Greek, impersonal expressions of unfulfilled demands such as ἔδει occur predominantly in the indicative imperfect and only rarely in the aorist.[94] By contrast, Latin shows a rather undifferentiated use of the perfect and the imperfect, which is also evident in the Latin witnesses of the Gospels, where occasionally variants in the present tense (*oportet*)[95] and even in the past perfect (*oportuerat*) also occur.[96] An analysis of the occurrence of these two forms suggests that the perfect *oportuit* only gradually became established as a rendering of the Greek verb: the Codices *Palatinus* (in the present passage) and *Bezae* (Matt 23:23) each contain only one example of the perfect; otherwise, the imperfect *oportebat* is predominant in these older manuscripts. It is also significant that the Codices *Palatinus* and *Bezae* translate Luke 22:7 ἔδει with *oportebat* (see also VL10, 14), while the other manuscripts have *necesse erat*.

Another passage which illuminates the relationship between VL3 and VL5 is also noteworthy: in Luke 2:17, it is the shepherds who report the appearance of the angels to other figures in the narrative, while Zechariah and Mary keep quiet on their visions.

---

93 But cf. the Latin translation of Irenaeus' *Adversus haereses*.

94 Cf. KÜHNER, Ausführliche Grammatik, 391.

95 E.g. Matt 23:23 (VL2) or Luke 15:32 (it).

96 E.g. Matt 18:33 (VL2) or Matthew 23:23 (VL8, 12, 14). The present tense δεῖ is again regularly translated *oportet*, except for a few passages with indirect speech, for which the appropriate sequence of the tenses is observed in many manuscripts. Cf. e.g. John 20:9.

Figure 4.11: *quod eis dictum erat* in Luke 2:17 (340^{b}).

In this context, central importance may be assigned to the lexeme τοῦ λαληθέντος αὐτοῖς, which the Vercellensis translates literally as *quod eis dictum erat*. The Latin Bezae takes the aorist passive of λαλέω as a coniugatio periphrastica of εἶναι, and accordingly translates *quod factum est ad eos*. H.W. Smyth refers to the use of εἶναι with the present participle or perfect as a way "to form a periphrasis, especially when the participle has an adjectival character."[97] The Hebrew text often has a היה with a participle,[98] which in Hebrew either links two texts or introduces a new section. This Hebrew construction is subsequently translated as a periphrastic imperfect, which, according to Evans, is an indication of "independent Greek usage and Hebrew interference."[99] No Greek original which may account for this construction is known to us. It is, however, clear that Bezae D, 05 cannot serve this function.

And finally, we refer to Luke 11:11,12 (*porrigit* versus *porriget*), 11:17 (*cadit* versus *cadet*), and also Luke 11:18 (*eicient* VL5, 16 vs. *eicie*^{u} nt VL11; *ieciunt* VL61; *eicieuntur* VL51; *eieciunt* VL30; *eiciunt* rell.). The loosening of the conjugation classes typical of Vulgar Latin at times makes it unclear whether the manuscripts have a verb in the present tense, erroneously formed in the second conjugation, or in a future tense. This phenomenon is especially relevant to Luke 11:18, where the

97 LAGRANGE, Évangile selon Saint Luc, cv–cvi; SMYTH, Greek Grammar, 437, § 1961.
98 Cf. EVERSON, "An Examination of Synoptic Portions," 183–186.
99 EVANS, Verbal Syntax in the Greek Pentateuch, 256; see also VERBOOMEN, L'imparfait périphrastique, esp. 25–71.

correction in *Codex Rehdigeranus* (from *eicient* in *eiciunt*) is indicative of the copyists' uncertainty concerning conjugation classes.

Table 27: The loosening of the conjugation classes in VL3 and VL5

Verse	VL3, 5	Other Latin authorities
2:20	*audierunt*	*audiuerant* 8
		audierant cet.
	uiderunt	*uiderant* cet.
3:23	*incipiens*	om. 2 4 8 A
4:17	*reuoluens*	*cum reuoluissit* 2
		ut reuoluit cet.
4:20	*reddens*	*reddidit* 2 4 8 A
4:25	*errant*	*fuerunt* 2 4 8
4:29	*surgentes*	*exsurrexerunt* 2
		surrexerunt cet.
4:31	*erat docens*	*docebat* cet.
4:40	*occidente sole*	*cum occidisset sol* 2 8
		cum sol occidisset 4 A
5:28	*sequebatur*	*et secutus* 2 *secutus est* cet.
6:10	*circumspiciens*	*circuminspexit* 2 *circumspectis* cet.
6:13	*eligens*	*elegit* cet.
6:19	*quaerebat*	*quaerebant* cet.
6:22	*estis*	*eritis* cet.
7:2	*incipiebat mori*	*moriturus erat* 2
		erat moriturus cet.
7:14	*accedens tetigit*	*accessit et tetigit* cet.
8:28	*uidens*	*cum uidisset* 2
		ut uidit cet.
8:41	*rogabat*	*rogans* cet.
8:44	*accendens*	*accessit* cet.
8:47	*procidens*	*procidit* cet.
	tetigit	*tetigerit* cet.
9:30	*erat*	*erant* cet.
9:54	*uidentes*	*cum uidissent* cet.
11:19	*eicient*	*eiciunt* cet.
13:16	*oportebat*	*oportuit* cet.
14:4	*adprehendens*	*adpraehendit* 2
		adprehensum cet.
14:15	*audiens*	*cum audisset* cet.
15:11	*habebat*	*habuit* cet.
15:18	*surgens*	*surgam* cet.
16:21	*uenientes*	*ueniebant* cet.
17:2	*proiectus esset*	*proiectus sit* 2
		proiciatur cet.
17:31	*erit*	*fuerit* cet.

Verse	VL3, 5	Other Latin authorities
18:10	*orare*	*ut orarent* cet.
18:15	*uidentes*	*cum uidessent* 2
		cum uiderent 17
		cum uiderent cet.
18:30	*accipiet*	*recipias* 2 *recipiat* cet.
19:20	*habebam*	*habui* cet.
20:27	*accedentes*	*accesserunt* cet.
22:13	*dixerat*	*dixit* cet.
22:45	*surgens*	*cum surrexit* cet.
23:13	*conuocans*	*conuocatis* cet.
23:18	*dicentes*	*dicens* cet.
23:23	*crucifige* (*crucifigi*)	*ut crucifigeretur* cet.
23:25	*erat*	*fuerat* cet.
23:32	*interfici*	*ut interficerentur* A
		ut crucifigerentur cet.
23:48	*uidentes*	*et uidebant* A
		qui uidebant cet.
23:56	*reuersae autem*	*et reuertentes* cet.
24:5	*uiuum*	*uiuentem* cet.
24:21	*sperauimus*	*speramus* 2 8 *sperabamus* 4 A
24:43	*accipiens*	*accepit* 2 om. cet.

4.3.2.3 Syntactic Function: The Substantivized Adjective

In Luke 7:15, the manuscripts VL3 and VL5 do not expand the substantivized Greek adjective ὁ νεκρός using a relative clause (*qui erat mortuus*) but instead render the construction directly into Latin. This translation is also found in Irenaeus (4.13.1) and has its parallel in the translation of 1 Kgdms 3:17–23b and in Valentinus' version of the present passage (4; *Acta Sanctorum* II 757E).

Table 28: The use of the substantivized adjective ὁ νεκρός to *mortuus* in VL3 and VL5

Verse	NA[28]	VL3, 5	Other Latin authorities
7:15	ὁ νεκρός	*mortuus*	*ille mortuus* 2
			qui erat mortuus cet.

Only the Palatinus VL2 additionally renders the Greek article using a demonstrative, resulting in a translation which also found its way into Augustine (Ps 97.1.17; PL 1372; 354.3).

A further example is offered by Luke 9:30, where the codex Bezae D, 05 has ἄνδρες δύο, which in the Vercellensis is rendered as *uiri duo*, following the Greek wording, while the Latin *Bezae*, along with numerous other witnesses, reads *duo uiri.* The latter formulation is more in keeping with the usage of Classical Latin since "adjectives indicating a distinguishing property, as well as measures, degrees (comparatives and superlatives), and numerals [usually] precede the word to which they refer."[100] Thus it is clear that the writer is concerned to give an exact rendering of the Greek, even where the translation produced may seem awkward in Latin. Finally, we see a similar situation in Luke 12:12, where the majority of Greek manuscripts have τὸ γὰρ ἅγιον πνεῦμα, which the Vercellensis instead translates literally as *sanctus enim spiritus*. This is all the more remarkable since VL3 usually opts for *spiritus sanctus* (see 1:35; 2:25; 3:22). Even on this point, however, we should not hastily conclude that the reading of the manuscript is due to the Greek Bezae, since Tertullian already translates the lexeme in this way (*sanctus enim, inquit, spiritus docebit*),[101] thus clearly following the Lucan tradition. This is not so in the case of the VL5: there, the scribe resorts to the parallel traditions of Matt 12:32b and Mark 3:29 and writes *spiritus sanctus* together with the other witnesses.

Table 29: The use of the substantivized adjectives in VL3 and VL5

Verse	VL3, 5	Other Latin authorities
1:15	*in conspectu domini*	*ante dominum* 2
		coram domino cet.
1:17	*ad*	*in* cet.
1:19	*in conspectu dei*	*ante faciem dei* 2
		ante dominum 4
		dominum 8
		ante deum A
1:20	*qui*	*quae* cet.
1:22	*quia*	*quoniam* 2
		quod cet.
2:26	*priusquam*	*quoadusque* 2
		nisi prius cet.
2:33	*in*	*de* 2 *super* cet.
2:46	*dies tres*	*diem tertium* 2
		triduo 4 8
		triduum A
4:32	*quoniam*	*quia* cet.
4:43	*quoniam*	*quia* 4 8 A om. 2
5:12	*dum*	*cum* cet.
5:19	*super*	*in* 2
		supra cet.
	in conspectu iesu	*ante iesum* cet.

100 Rubenbauer § 267.
101 Tert. *adv. haer.* 4.28.7; this is striking since Tertullian writes in 4.28.6: *in spiritum sanctum*.

Verse	VL3, 5	Other Latin authorities
6:33	*etenim*	*nam et* 2 4
		cum et 8
		si quidem et A
6:34	*etenim peccatores*	*et peccatores enim* 2
		nonne et peccatores 4
		nam et peccatores 8 A
6:48	*mouere illam*	*illam mouere* 2
		eam mouere cet.
7:4	*quoniam*	*quia* cet.
8:6	*propter quod*	*propterea quod* 2
		quia cet.
8:8	*super*	*in* cet.
8:13	*qui autem*	*quod autem* 2
		nam qui cet.
8:19	*propter turbam*	*per turbas* 2
		prae (*pre* 8) *turba* cet.
8:27	*domo*	*in domo* cet.
8:35	*et*	*ac* cet.
8:46	*ego enim*	*nam et* (om. A^{c}) *ego* cet.
8:52	*enim mortua est*	*non est* (add. *enim* 8) *mortua* cet.
8:55	*dari ei*	*illi dari* (*dare* 8) cet.
9:12	*quoniam*	*quia* cet.
10:15	*ad*	*in* cet.
10:20	*quia*	*quoniam* 2 *quod* cet.
11:17	*super*	*supra* cet.
16:24	*quoniam*	*quia* cet.

4.3.3 Conflation of Semantics

4.3.3.1 The Translation of διδάσκαλε and ἐπιστάτα as *magister*

At first glance, the reading *magister* in the Codices *Vercellensis* and *Bezae* Luke 5:5 seems to be due to influence of the Greek D, 05, since this manuscript has διδάσκαλε instead of ἐπιστάτα.

Table 30: The translation of διδάσκαλε and ἐπιστάτα in VL3 and VL5

Verse	NA^{28}	VL3, 5	Other Latin authorities
5:5	διδάσκαλε D, 05	*magister*	*praeceptor* (*preceptor* 8) cet.
	ἐπιστάτα NA^{28}		
8:45	ἐπιστάτα	*magister*	*praeceptor* (*preceptor* 8) cet.
17:13	ἐπιστάτα	*magister*	*praeceptor* (*preceptor* 8) cet.

Figure 4:12: The translation of ἐπιστάτα in Luke 17:13 (461[a]).

Again, however, the Greek text of the bilingual manuscript need not have served as the original, for the two Latin manuscripts consistently use *magister* even where the Greek manuscripts have ἐπιστάτα in 8:45[102] and 17:13.[103] Accordingly, this reasoning is no more plausible in the case of the *Bezae* D, 05.

4.3.3.2 The Translation of περιβλεψάμενος

Even in 6:10, where the Greek text has the aorist participle περιβλεψάμενος, the Latin translations in VL3 and VL5 do not have D, 05 as their Greek *Vorlage* but read *circumspeciens omnes illos* (*eos* VL5) instead.

Table 31: The translation of σπλαγχνίζειν in VL3 and VL5

Verse	VL3, 5	Other Latin authorities
6:10	*circumspiciens*	*circuminspexit* 2 *circumspectis* 4 8 A

4.3.3.3 The Translation of σπλαγχνίζειν as *misertus est*, *commotus* or *contristatus esse*

In Luke, a key term used to capture the bodily effect of mercy is the verb σπλαγχνίζειν (7:13; 10:33; 15:20), which literally means "to be touched in the internal organs."

---

102 Cf. also VL14; Ambrose *Expositio Evangelii secundum Lucam* 8.60; 320.703.

103 Cf. VL14; see also Sedulius *paschale opus* 4; 266.13; around 431 C.E. (ed. Dreves) from Spain, southern Gaul, or Italy, see FREDE, Kirchenschriftsteller, 749.

Table 32: The translation of σπλαγχνίζειν in VL3 and VL5

Verse	NA[28]	VL3, 5	Other Latin authorities
7:13	ἐσπλαγχνίσθη	*misertus est* VL3	*commotus est super eam* 2
		misertus est ei VL5	*misertus est super eam* 4
			misericordiam (*misericordia**) *motus* 8
			misericordia motus super ea A
10:33	ἐσπλαγχνίσθη	*misertus est*	*commotus est* 2
			misericordia motus est cet.
15:20	ἐσπλαγχνίσθη	*et misericordia motus est* VL3	*et contristatus est* 2
		et misertus est 5	om. 8

Since the verb is not very common, it comes as no surprise that the Old Latin translations offer several different renderings of it: the codices Vercellensis (in 7:13; 10:33) and Bezae have *misertus est*, also found in Classical Latin, meaning both "to feel compassion" and "to be pitied." The Palatinus has *commotus esse* (7:13; 10:33) – which equally emphasizes the senses of "to move with compassion" and "to motivate participation"[104] – as well as *contristatus esse* (15:20). In contrast, the Vulgate consistently reads *misericordia motus esse*, referring both to mercy and to pious works.

104 Georges I, 1025.

Figure 4.13: The translation of σπλαγχνίζειν in Luke 7:13 (380[a]), 10:33 (416[b]), and 15:20 (450[a]).

4.3.3.4 The Translation of κλαίειν as *plorare*

The codices *Vercellensis* and *Bezae* also agree in translating κλαίειν as *plorare*, "to howl, cry, weep," which is more common in spoken language and would be replaced in Late Latin by *flere* "to weep" (8:52). *plorare* is the most common translation for κλαίειν in 2 and 5 and may therefore be considered the reading typical of older text types. The verb is attested in Classical literature, but the fact that it was replaced by *flere* in Romance languages suggests that, in Classical times, *plorare* was predominantly used in spoken language.

Table 33: The translation of κλαίειν as *plorare* in VL3 and VL5

Verse	NA^{28}	VL3, 5	Other Latin authorities
8:52	ἔκλαιον	<u>*plorabant*</u>	<u>*flebant*</u> cet.

4.3.3.5 Knowlegde of God and Self-Knowledge

Moreover, in several passages, the relationship between corporeality and *ratio* is discussed in the context of the themes of self-knowledge and knowledge of God.

In the Greek tradition, these topics are expressed in the formulas τὰς ἐνθυμήσεις αὐτῶν (Matt 12:25), τοὺς διαλογισμοὺς αὐτῶν (Luke 5:22; 6:8), τὸν διαλογισμὸν τῆς καρδίας αὐτῶν (Luke 9:47), or αὐτῶν τὰ διανοήματα (Luke 11:17). In Matt, *cogitatio* is used as the translation of all three nouns (ἐνθύμησις, διαλογισμός, διανόημα) in all Latin witnesses except for the *Codex Bobbiensis* (k,1), which has *praesumptio* instead. Several variants of the verb are found: εἰδώς and ἰδών for Matt 12:25; ἐπιγνούς for Luke 5:22; ᾔδει and γινώσκων for Luke 6:8; εἰδώς, ἰδών and γνούς for Luke 9:47; εἰδώς for Luke 11:17. We may suppose that the great variety of Latin translations is due to various overlapping attempts at alignment with the respective parallel traditions, with εἰδέναι, ἰδεῖν, and (ἐπι)γιγνώσκειν being translated with *scire* (Matt 12:25; Luke 5:22; 6:8; 11:17), *videre* (Matt 12:25; Luke 9:47; 11:17), and *cognoscere* (Luke 5:22). In the Latin witnesses, the participle is also often replaced by a subordinate clause (Matt 12:25 VL1; Luke 5:22 VL2; 9:47 VL2). While translations of the verb vacillate between *scire* (2 4 5 13 14) and *cognoscere* (VL3 cet.), the *Codex Usserianus primus* (VL14) includes the additional accusative *cogitationes eorum*, which should be interpreted as clear contamination from the Synoptic Gospels. Such a combination of textual variants is present in Luke 11:17 (αὐτὸς δὲ εἰδὼς αὐτῶν τὰ διανοήματα εἶπεν; *ipse aute[m sci]ens cogotatio[nes] illorum dix[it]* VL16): on the one hand, the reading of the *Fragmenta Curiensia* and the *Codex Bezae* (VL5), *sciens*, is also found in the Vulgate (Matt 12:25); on the other hand, the Vulgate's subordination *ut vidit* has a parallel only in Luke 5:22, but there the verb is *cognoscere* (i.e. *ut cognovit*), not *videre*. It is noteworthy that the *Codex*

Vercellensis (VL3), which has a lacuna here, also read *sciens* in Matt 12:25, so that we would expect a reading similar to that of the Fragmenta. Whereas the introduction of the Greek text is modelled on 5:22 and 6:8, where the hidden intentions of the opponents (scribes and Pharisees) are made public, the *Curiensia* might be picking up on verse 6:8 of the *Codex Bezae* (VL5), whose reading may in turn have been later taken up by the codices *Veronensis* (VL4) and *Brixianus* (VL10).

4.3.3.6 The Embodied State of Spiritual Confusion: *confundere*

Another passage discussing the embodied state of spiritual confusion is Luke 13:17, where we read *confundebantur* in the codices *Vercellensis* (VL3) and *Bezae* (VL5), while VL2 has *confusi sunt*, and the majority of the manuscripts have *erubescebant*.

Table 34: The translation of καταισχύνεσθαι as *confundere* in VL3 and VL5

Verse	NA[28]	VL3, 5	Other Latin authorities
9:26	ἐπαισχυνθῇ	*confusus fuerit me*	*confessus fuerit me* 2 *me erubuerit* 4 A
	ἐπαισχυνθήσεται	*confondet* VL3 *confundetur* VL5	*erubuerit me* 8 *confitebitur* 2 *erubescet* (*erubescit* A) cet.
13:17	κατῃσχύνοντο	*confundebantur*	*confusi sunt* 2 *erubescebant* cet.

Apart from a few passages in the Pauline and Catholic epistles, the verb καταισχύνεσθαι is found exclusively in the present verse;[105] the base form αἰσχύνεσθαι ("to be ashamed") is used in the Vercellensis and the Bezae (Luke 16:3),[106] while the compound ἐπαισχύνεσθαι occurs in the synoptic parallel passage Mark 8:38 and Luke 9:26.[107] Two Latin translations of these three verbs exist; of these, the reading *confundi* ("to confuse, to cause *consternation*") found in VL3, 5, and 16 may be considered early, as confirmed by its agreement with Cyprian's wording.[108] Moreover, this

---

105 Rom 5:5; 9:33; 10:11; 1Cor 1:27; 11:4, 5, 22; 2Cor 7:14; 9:4; 1Pet 2:6; 3:16.

106 Cf. Luke 16:3: σκάπτειν οὐκ ἰσχύω, ἐπαιτεῖν αἰσχύνομαι.

107 Cf. Mark 8:38: ὃς γὰρ ἐὰν ἐπαισχυνθῇ με καὶ τοὺς ἐμοὺς λόγους ἐν τῇ γενεᾷ ταύτῃ τῇ μοιχαλίδι καὶ ἁμαρτωλῷ, καὶ ὁ υἱὸς τοῦ ἀνθρώπου ἐπαισχυνθήσεται αὐτὸν ὅταν ἔλθῃ ἐν τῇ δόξῃ τοῦ πατρὸς αὐτοῦ μετὰ τῶν ἀγγέλων τῶν ἁγίων; Luke 9:26: ὃς γὰρ ἂν ἐπαισχυνθῇ με καὶ τοὺς ἐμοὺς λόγους, τοῦτον ὁ υἱὸς τοῦ ἀνθρώπου ἐπαισχυνθήσεται, ὅταν ἔλθῃ ἐν τῇ δόξῃ αὐτοῦ καὶ τοῦ πατρὸς καὶ τῶν ἁγίων ἀγγέλων.

108 Cf. Cyp. *ep.* 63.15: *porro autem dominus in evangelio dicit: qui confusus me fuerit, confundetur eum filius hominis.*

term is also attested several times in Augustine, as in *Ennarationes in Psalmos* 48, 1.12.9: *quid facio? Fodere non possum, mendicare confundor.*[109] On a basic level, the verb *confundere* means "to make the body's main features fluid," such as by disfigurement due to injury (Plin. *nat. hist.* 2.94), "to disturb the body or the mind" (Cels. 3.5), "to make someone's features flush with shame" (Ov. *Trist.* 3.1), or "to put someone in a state of consternation" (Liv. 34.50.1). The sense thus includes not only embarrassment but also confusion of the mind, and it is thus more comprehensive than the likely more recent reading *erubescere* ("to become red with shame, to be ashamed"), which is predominant only in late European texts. It is possible that the early manuscripts took their cue from Mark 8:38, which has *confundi* in all Latin manuscripts.[110]

The feeling of deep sadness, also manifested physically, is expressed by the adjective περίλυπος, which is used in the Gospel of Luke description of the rich man who ought to leave his wealth to the poor. Now, whereas the codices *Vercellensis* and *Bezae* render the adjective with *tristes factus*, thus emphasizing sadness, which may also manifest visually,[111] the majority of witnesses offer a moral term, *contristatus*. While this term can likewise mean "gloomy, sad," it has a decidedly negative connotation.

To sum up: we have seen that producing a literal translation of the Greek original was the scribe's priority in VL3 and 5. This is evident, for example, in the decision to retain Greek participles rather than replace them with subordinate clauses (11:14,17; 13:17), thus preserving the Lucan preference for participial constructions. Other examples included: the use of the adjective *mortuus* for ὁ νεκρός (7:15) instead of a relative clause; the translation of κερδήσας and ἀπολέσας (9:25) as *locrari* and *perdere*, set in an accusative and infinitive construction rather than as participles; the use of the imperfect *oportebat* instead of *opportuit* for impersonal expressions of unfulfilled demands such as ἔδει (13:16); the interchanges between verb classes typical of Vulgar Latin such as *porrigit* versus *porriget* (Luke 11:11,12) or the use of *intrare* rather than *ingredi* as a translation of εἰσέρχεσθαι (11:26). Also striking is the consistent rendering, typical of the Vercellensis, of διδάσκαλε and ἐπιστάτα as *magister* (5:5; 8:45; 17:13), σπλαγχνίζειν as *misertus est* (7:13; 10:33), and (κατ)αισχύνεσθαι as *confundebantur* (13:17; 16:3), also used in the Latin *Bezae*. An

---

109 Cf. Aug. *serm.* 359A9; op. monach. 16 (ed. Zycha); serm. (Lambrecht ed.) 4. 265; for further commentary, see VINCENT, Continuity and Change from Latin to Romance, 259–260.

110 For a detailed discussion of the forms of *confiteri* as textual variants for ἐπαισχύνεσθαι in Mark 8:38 and Luke 9:26, see MERX, Die Evangelien des Markus und Lukas, 264.

111 The adjective *contristatum* is nevertheless used in v. 24; see Georges II, 4825.

inspection of passages shared by the codices *Vercellensis* and *Bezae* reveals a preference for Classical Latin usage. This is the case: in the use of the demonstrative *is* for the missing personal pronoun; in the use of *hic* instead of *ille*, against all other witnesses; in the translation of the causative ὅτι with the conjunction *quoniam*. We do also find some features of Late Latin throughout the Vercellensis, such as the use of *super* instead of *in*, and the translation of ἐπί as *supra* (11:17).

Table 35: Unique readings shared by the *Vercellensis*, *Bezae* and Old Latin Versions

Unique readings of the *Codex Vercellensis*, the *Fragmenta Curiensia*, and the *Codex Bezae*			**Other Latin authorities**
	VL3,16	**VL5**	
1:15	*in conspectu domini*		*ante dominum* 2
			coram domino 4 8 A
1:17	*ad*		*in* 2 4 8 A
1:19	*in conspectu dei*		*ante faciem dei* 2
			ante dominum 4
			dominum 8
			ante deum A
1:20	*qui*		*quae* 2 4 8 A
1:22	*quia*		*quoniam* 2
			quod 4 8 A
1:32	*ei*		*illi* 2 4 8 A
1:33	*saecula*		*aeternum* 2 4 A
			eternum 8
1:36	*ei*		*illi* 2 4 8c A
			illis 8*
1:39	*montanam*		*montuosa* 2
			montana 4 8 A
1:51	*eorum*		*illorum* 2
			ipsorum 4 8
			sui A
1:58	*ea*		*eo* 2
			illa 4 8 A
2:9	*circumluxit*		*circumfulsit* cet.
2:15	*pertranseamus*		*eamus* 2
			transeamus 4 8 A
2:19	*committens*		*conferens* 2 4 8 A
2:20	*audierunt*		*audierant* 2 4 A
			audiuerant 8
	uiderunt		*uiderant* 2 4 8 A
2:22	*eum*		*illum* 2 4 8 A
2:26	*priusquam*		*quoadusque* 2
			nisi prius 4 8 A
2:31	*praep<r>arasti*	*praeparasti*	*parasti* 2 4 8 A

2:33	*In*		*de* 2
			super 4 8 A
2:38	*deum*	*deo*	*ad dominum* 2
			dominum 4
			domino 8 A
2:40	*eum*	*eo*	*illo* 4 8 A
2:43	*nescierunt*		*non cognouerunt* 2 A
			non cognouit 4 8
2:46	*dies tres*		*diem tertium* 2
			triduo 4 8
			triduum A
3:12	*similiter*		om. 2 4 8 A
	ad eum		*illi* 2
			ad illum 4 8 A
3:14	*sufficientes*		*contenti* 2 4 8 A
3:19	*cum argueretur*		*correptus* 2
			cum corriperetur 4 8 A
	eo		*illo* 2 4 8 A
3:22	*eum*		*illum* 2
			ipsum 4 8 A
3:23	*incipiens*		om. 2 4 8 A
4:5	*eum*		*illum* 2 4 8 A
4:6	*illam*		*illa* 2 4 8 A
4:8	*ipsi*		*illi* 2 4 8 A
4:9	*es dei*		*dei es* 2 4 8 A
4:10	*custodiun te*		*te conseruent* 2
			conseruent te 4 8 A
4:14	*omnem*		*totam* 2
			uniuersam 4 8 A
4:16	*secundum consuetudinem*		*secundum consuetudinem suam* 4 A
			secundum consuetudinem tuam 8
			om. 2
4:17	*reuoluens*		*cum reuoluissit* 2
			ut reuoluit 4 8 A
4:20	*reddens*		*reddidit* 2 4 8 A
4:21	*scripturam haec*	*scriptura haec*	*scriptura ista* 2
			scriptura haec 5
			haec scriptura cet.
4:23	*dixit*		*ait* 2 4 8 A
	parabola hanc		*similitudinem istam* 2
			hanc similitudinem 4 8 A
4:24	*dixit autem*		*ille autem dixit illis* 2
			dixit autem iesus 4
			ait autem iesus 8
			ait autem A
4:25	*erant*		*fuerunt* 2 4 8 add. *in strahel* 8
4:26	*earum*	*eorum*	*illarum* cet.

4:29	*surgentes*	*exsurrexerunt* 2
		surrexerunt 4 8 A
	eum	*illum* 2 4 8 A
4:31	*erat docens*	*docebat* cet.
4:32	*quoniam*	*quia* 2 4 8 A
4:39	*eam*	*illam* 2 4 8 A
	eam	*illam* 2 4 8 A add. *febris* 2 *continuo* 5
4:40	*occidente autem sole*	*cum occidisset autem sol* 2 8
		cum sol autem occidisset 4 A
4:42	*abiit*	*et abiit* 2
		ibat 4 8 A
	eum	*illum* 2
		ipsum 4 8 A
4:43	*quoniam*	*quia* 4 8 A
		om. 2
5:4	*retias uestras*	*retia uestra* 2 A *retiam uestram* 4 8
5:5	*magister*	*praeceptor* 2 4 A *preceptor* 8
5:8	*quia uir peccator sum domine*	*quoniam homo peccator* sum 2
		domine quia homo peccator sum 4 8
		quia homo peccator sum domine A
5:12	*dum*	*cum* 2 4 8 A
5:16	*desertis*	*solitudine* 2
		deserto 4 8 A
5:18	*adferentes*	ferentes 2
	super lectum	*portantes* 4 8 A
5:19	*super*	*in* 2
		supra 4 8 A
	in conspectu iesu	*ante iesum* 2 4 8 A
5:25	*honorificans*	*clarificans* 2
		magnificans cet.
5:26	*inpleti*	*impleti* 2
		repleti 4 8 A
5:28	*sequebatur*	*et secutus* 2
		secutus est 4 8 A
5:29	*cenam magnam*	*epulum magnum* 2
		cenam illi magna 5
		conuiuium magnum cet:
5:36	*parabolam*	*similitudinem* 2 4 8 A
	tunicae rudis	*a uestimento nouo* 2 4 8 A
	scindet	*conscindet* 2
		rumpit 4 8 A
5:37	*ipse*	*uinum* 2
		ipsum 4 A
		ipsud 8
6:10	*circumspiciens*	*circuminspexit* 2
		circumspectis 4 8 A
6:13	*eligens*	*elegit* 2 4 8 A

6:19	*quaerebat*	*quaerebant* 2 4 8 A
6:22	*estis*	*eritis* 2 4 8 A
	odierint uos	*oderint uos* 2
		uos oderint 4 A
		uos odierint 8
6:32	*uobis gratia est*	*est uobis gratia* 2
		uobis gratia 4
		erit uobis gratia 8
		uobis est gratia A
6:33	*etenim*	*nam et* 2 4
		cum et 8
		si quidem et A
6:34	*etenim peccatores*	*et peccatores enim* 2
		nonne et peccatores 4
		nam et peccatores 8 A
6:39	*incident*	*cadunt* 2
		cadent 4 8 A
6:43	*est*	*est enim* 2 4 8 A
6:48	*mouere illam*	*illam mouere* 2
		eam mouere 4 8 A
6:49	*et*	*et continuo* 2 4 8 A
7:2	*incipiebat mori*	*moriturus erat* 2
		erat moriturus cet.
7:4	*quoniam*	*quia* cet.
7:14	*accedens tetigit*	*accessit et tetigit* cet.
7:15	*mortuus*	*Ille mortuus* 2
	eum … suae	*qui erat mortuus* cet.
7:16	*timor omnes*	*timor magnus omnes* 4
		omnes timor cet.
	honorificabant	*clarificabant* 2
		magnificabant cet.
7:27	*uiam tuam*	add. *ante te* 2 4 8 A
7:31	*et cui sunt similes*	A *et cui similes sint* 2*
		et cui similes sunt 2[c] A
		et cui similes est 8 om. 4
7:32	*infantibus*	*pueris* cet.
7:33	*edens*	*manducans* cet.
7:41	*denarius*	om. 2 4 8 A
8:1	*circuibat*	*perambulabat* 2
		iter faciebat cet.
8:4	*parabolam*	*per similitudinem* A
		similitudinem cet.
8:6	*propter quod*	*propterea quod* 2
		quia cet.
8:8	*super*	*in* cet.
8:13	*qui autem*	*quod autem* 2
		nam qui cet.

8:19	*propter turbam*	*per turbas* 2
		prae (*pre* 8) *turba* cet.
8:23	*et conplebantur*	*et implebatur a fructibus nauicula* 4
		et conplebatur fructibus nauiculam 8
		et complebatur A om. 2
8:27	*uir*	*uir quidam* cet. add. *de ciuitatem* 2
		de ciuitate 5 4
	domo	*in domo* cet.
8:28	*uidens autem iesum*	*cum uidisset autem iesum* 2
		is (*his* 4) *ut uidit iesum* cet.
8:34	*agros*	*uillas* cet.
8:35	*et*	*ac* cet.
	iesu	*eius* cet.
8:36	*adnuntiauerunt*	*nuntiauerunt* cet.
8:37	*eis*	*ipsis* cet.
8:38	*eum*	*illum* cet.
	exierant daemonia	*daemonia* (*demonia* 8) *exierant* cet.
8:40	*reuerteretur*	*redisset* cet.
8:41	*hic*	*ipse* cet.
	rogabat	*rogans* cet.
8:42	*et factum est*	*et contingit* (*contingint* 8) cet.
8:43	*quae*	*quaedam* (*quedam* 8) cet.
8:44	*accendens*	*accessit* cet.
	tetigit	*et tetigit* cet.
8:45	*magister*	*praeceptor* (*preceptor* 8) cet.
8:46	*ego enim*	*nam et* (om. Ac) *ego* cet.
8:47	*procidens*	*procidit* cet.
	tetigit	*tetigerit* cet.
8:52	*plorabant*	*flebant* cet.
	eam	*illam* cet.
	enim mortua est	*non est* (add. *enim* 8) *mortua* cet.
8:55	*dari ei*	*illi dari* (*dare* 8) cet.
9:6	*exeuntes autem*	*et exeuntes autem* 2
		egressi autem cet.
9:10	*eos*	*illos* 2
		illis cet. add. *iesus* 8
9:12	*autem*	om. cet. add. *illi* 2
		ad eum 4
	quoniam	*quia* cet.
9:13	*populum hunc*	*populum istum* 2 *hanc turbam* cet.
9:16	*turbis*	*populo* 2
		ante turbas (*turbam* 8) cet.
9:18	*eos*	*illos* cet.
	turbae esse	*homines esse* 2
		esse turbae cet.
9:20	*autem*	om. cet.

9:23	*sequatur me*	*sublata cruce sua sequatur me* 4
		tollat crucem suam (add. *cotidie* A) *et sequatur me* cet.
9:25	*mundum totum*	*totum mundum* 2
	locrari (*lucrari*)	*uniuersum mundum* cet.
	perdere	*si lucrum fecerit* 2 *si lucretur* cet.
		perdat cet.
9:28	*ascendit*	*et ascendit* cet.
9:30	*erat*	*erant* cet.
9:34	*eo dicente*	*cum ille diceret* 2
		illo loquente cet.
	timuerunt	
	autem	*et timuerunt* cet.
		om. cet. add. *in eo* 2 5
9:40	*praecatus sum*	*postulaui* 2
		rogaui cet.
9:42	*adlisit*	*conlisit* 2 et (om. 4 A) *elisit* cet.
	imperauit autem	*corripuit autem* 2
		et increpauit cet.
9:44	*uerba haec*	*uerba ista* 5
		sermones istos (*hos* 8) cet. om. 4
9:45	*uerbum hoc*	*uerbum illud* 2
		uerbum istud cet.
	ab eis	*ab illis* 2
		inter ipsos 4
	uerbo hoc	*inter ipsis* 8
		ante eos A
		uerbo illo 2
		hoc uerbo cet.
9:47	*Infantem*	*eum* 4* 8 *puerum* cet.
9:54	*uidentes autem*	*cum uidissent autem* cet.
9:59	*alium*	*alterum* cet.
10:12	*autem*	om. cet.
10:13	*bedsaida*	*bethsaida* A
		betsaida cet
10:15	*ad*	*in* cet.
	exaltaueris	*exaltaberis* 4
		exaltata es (om. A) cet.
10:16	*spernit uos*	*uos spernit* cet.
10:20	*quia*	*quoniam* 2
		quod cet.
10:31	*uiam illam*	*illam uiam* 2
		eadem uia (*uiam* 8) cet. *et*] om. 2
10:33	*misertus est*	*commotus est* 2 *misericordia motus est* cet.
10:34	*conligauit*	*alligauit* cet.
	eum	*illum* cet.
		om. 2

10:37	*ad ille dixit*		*ille autem dixit* 2 *at ille dixit* cet.
11:5	*inducas nos*		*nos induca* cet.
11:6	*adponam*		*ponam* cet.
	illi		*ante illum* (*eum* 8) cet.
11:13	*scitis* (mit c)		*nostis* cet.
11:17	*deseretur*		*desolatur* cet.
	super se		*supra* cet.
11:18	*super satanan*	*super se*	super se diuisus est 5 in se ipsum diuisus est 4 A satanam (*sanatam**) *eicit in se ipsum diuisum est* 8* *satanas satanan eicit in se ipsum diuisus est* 17
11:19	*eicient*		*eiciunt* cet.
	vestri iudices erunt		*erunt uestri* 4 8 17 *iudices uestri erunt* A
11:20	*certe anticipavit*	*forsitam adpropinquavit*	*praeuenit* 4 A *prouenit* 8 17
11:21	*facultates eius* (mit c)	*substantia eius*	*sunt ea quae possidet* cet.
11:22	*illum*		
	armaturam		*uniuersa arma* cet.
	tollit		*auferet* cet.
11:24	*circuit*	*vadit*	ambulat 4 perambulat 8 A peram 17
	arida	*arida loca*	
	loca quae aquam non habent		om. cet.
11:25	*commundatam et ornatam*	*mudatum adornatum*	*eam* (om. A) *scopis mundatam* cet.
11:26	*intrantes* (mit r^1)	*intrant*	*introiit et* 2 *ingressus* 4 *regressi* 8 *ingressi* 17 A
11:29	*turba autem conveniente*	*turbis autem congregatis* (mit c)	*et cum turbae colligerentur* 2 *turbis autem concurrentibus* cet.
12:22	*edatis*		*manducetis* cet.
13:13	*honorificabat*		*clarificabat* 2 *magnificabant* 4 8 17 *glorificabat* A
13:16	*oportebat*		*oportuit* cet.
	hoc		*isto* 8 17 A om. 2 4
13:17	*confundebantur*		*confusi sunt* 2 *erubescebant* cet.
	omnibus mirificis quae fiebant	*omnibus quibus videbant mirabilibus*	*mirificis praeclaris* 4 8 17 om. 2 5 A

13:19	*quod accepto* (5,13)	*quo* (5)	*cum accepisset* 2
			acceptum cet.
13:22	*circuibat*		*perambulabat* 2
			ibat cet. add. *iesus* 8
13:32	*euntes*	*abeuntes*	*Ite* cet.
14:4	*adprehendens*		*adpraehendit* 2
			adprehensum cet.
14:7	*dicens ad eos*		*dicens* (*et dicebat* 17) *ad illos* cet.
			om. 2
14:9	*confusione*		*rubore* cet.
14:12	*amicos*		*amicos tuos* cet.
	fratres tuos		*fratres* 4 add. *cognatos tuos* 8 A
			cognatos 17
14:15	*audiens autem*		*haec* (*hic* 17) *cum audisset* cet.
14:22	*praecipisti*		*iussisti* 2
			imperasti cet.
15:7	*quoniam*		*quod* cet.
			om. 2
15:8	*drachmas*		*denarius*
15:11	*habebat*		*habuit* cet.
15:14	*egeri*		*indigere uictum* 2
			esurire et necessitatem habere 4*
			egere (add. uictum 4c) cet.
15:16	*porci edebant* (*edebant porci*)		*manducabant porci* 2
			porci manducabant cet.
15:18	*surgens*		*surgam et* cet.
15:20	*incubuit*		*superiecit se* 2
			cecidit cet.
	super		*in* 2
			supra cet.
15:24	*quoniam*		*quia* cet.
15:26	*unum de pueris*		*uno ex pueris* 2
			unum de seruis cet.
15:27	*quoniam*		*quia* 4
			om. cet.
15:30	*occidist*		*laniasti* 2
			occidisti illi cet.
15:31	*tu*		*filii* 17 A
			fili cet.
16:2	*eum*		*illum* cet. add. *ad se* 4
16:4	*de uilicatione*		*ab actu* 2
			a uilicatione cet.
	domus		*domos* cet.
16:9	*iniquo mamona*		*mamona iniquitatis* cet.
	defecerit		*defecerint* 2
			defeceritis cet.

16:15	*et dixit eis*	*ille autem dixit ad illos* 2
		et ait illis cet.
16:20	*pauper autem quidam*	*egens autem quidam* 2
		pauper autem quidam erat 17
		et erat (*erat autem* 4) *quidam mendicus* cet.
16:21	*et*	om. cet.
	uenientes	*ueniebant* cet.
16:22	*ut moreretur pauper*	*mori inopem illum* 2
		ut moreretur lazarus (om. A) *mendicus* (*pauper* 17) cet.
16:24	*quoniam*	*quia* cet.
16:26	*confirmatus*	*stabilitus* 4
		firmatum cet.
		om. 2
16:29	*dixit autem*	*dicit* 2
		et ait cet.
16:31	*nec*	*neque* cet.
17:2	*proiectus esset*	*proiectus sit* 2
		proiciatur cet.
17:6	*obaudisset uobis*	*exaudiet uos* 2
		oboediret uobis A
		utique obaudisset uobis (*uos* 17) cet.
17:9	*praecepta sunt ei*	*sibi inperauerat* 8
		sibi imperauerat A
		sibi (om. 2) *imperata sunt* cet. add. *non puto* cet.
17:13	*magister*	*praeceptor* cet.
17:14	*illis*	om. cet.
17:15	*eis*	*illis* cet.
	reuersus est	*rediuit* 2
		regressus est cet.
17:19	*dixit*	*dicit* 2
		ait cet.
	quoniam	*quia* cet. om. 17
17:23	*aut*	*et* cet.
		om. 2 A
17:24	*sicut enim*	*quomodo enim* 2
		nam sicut cet.
17:31	*erit super tectum*	*qui fuerit in tecto* cet.
18:1	*quod*	*quia* 2
		quoniam cet.
18:10	*orare*	*ut orarent* cet.
18:15	*uidentes autem*	*cum uidessent autem* 2
		quod cum uiderent (*uiderunt* 17) cet.
18:17	*infans* (*infantem*)	*puer* (add. *iste* 17) cet.

18:23	*tristes factus*	*ristis factus* 5	*contristatus* cet.
18:30	*accipiet*		*recipias* 2 *recipiat* cet.
18:31	*dixit*		*et ait* (*dixit* 2) cet.
	in		om. cet.
18:36	*quidnam*		*quid* cet.
18:39	*ad ille*		*ille autem* 2 *ipse uero* cet.
19:2	*locuples*		*diues* cet. add. *erat* 8
19:5	*ei*		*illi* 2 *ad eum* cet
19:9	*hic*		*ipse* cet.
19:13	*ad eos*		*illis* 2 *ad illos* cet
19:15	*suos*		om. cet.
19:20	*habebam*		*habui* cet.
19:21	*quoniam timebant te*		*quia timebam te* 2 *timui enim te* A *quia timui te* cet.
19:22	*iudicabo te*		*te condemno* 2 *te iudico* cet.
	quia		*quoniam* 2 *quod* cet.
19:28	*ibat*		*ambulabat* 2 *praecedebat* A *abiit* 8 17
19:31	*quoniam*		*quia* cet.
19:37	*omnis multitudo*		*omnis turba* 2 *omnes turbae* cet.
19:41	*eam*		*illum* 8 *illam* cet.
19:43	*quoniam*		*quia* cet.
19:46	*eis*		*illis* 8 17 A om. 2
20:8	*nec*		*neque* cet.
20:10	*dimiserunt uacuum*		et dimiserunt inanem 2 *dimiserunt inanem* 8 17 *dimiserunt eum inanem* A
20:11	*uacuum*		*inanem* cet. om. 2
20:18	*super*		*in* 2 *supra* cet.
20:19	*scierunt*		*intellexerunt* 2 *cognouerunt* cet. *eos* 2
	illos		*ipsos* cet.
	hanc		*istam* cet.
20:20	*ut*		*et* cet.
	VL3 *illum*	VL5*eum*	om. cet.
20:25	*quae sunt caesaris*		*quae caesaris sunt* cet.
20:27	*accedentes*		*accesserunt* cet.

20:28	*eius*		om. cet.
20:31	*et septem*		*septimum omnes* 2
			omnes (*omnis* 8) *septem* cet.
20:34	*nubunt et nubuntur*		*nubunt et traduntur ad nuptias* A
			om. cet.
20:36	*nec*		*neque* cet.
20:38	*illi uiuent*		*illi uiuunt* 2
			illi uiuent ei 8
			illi uiunt 17
			uiuunt ei A
20:41	*eos*		*illos* cet. add. *iesus* 8 17
			add. *quid uobis uidetur de christo cuius filius est* 2
20:44	*illius*		*eius* cet.
21:8	*ad ille dixit*		*ille autem dixit* 2
			qui autem (om. A) *dixit* cet.
21:12	*ante haec autem*		*ante haec* 2
			sed ante haec cet.
	VL 3 *carceribus*	VL5 *carcares*	*custodias* cet.
21:18	*periet*		*periuit* 2
			peribit cet.
21:22	*quoniam*		*quia* cet.
	inpleantur		*impleantur* cet.
21:26	*a*		*prae* (*pre* 8) cet.
	orbi terrarium		*orbi terrae* 2 *uniuerso orbi* cet.
	quae … caelo		*quae in caelo sunt* 8
			in caelo (*caelorum* A) cet.
21:27	*gloria*		*claritates* 2 *maiestate* cet.
21:28	*liberatio uestra*		*redemptio uestra* cet.
21:29	*parabolam illis*		*illis similitudinem* (*similitudinem illis* 2) cet.
21:31	*sic*		*ita* cet.
21:34	*quando*		*forte* cet.
21:37	*in templo docens*		*docens in templo* cet.
22:11	*edam*		*manducem* cet.
22:13	*dixerat*		*dixit* cet.
22:15	*ad eos*		*ad illos* 2
			illis cet.
22:17	*partimini*		*uiuite* 2
			diuidite cet.
22:18	*uineae*		*uitis huius* 4
			uitis cet.
22:31	*dixit autem dominus*		*ille autem dixit* 2
			ait autem dominus cet.
22:40	*loco*		*locum* cet.
22:43	*confortians*		*conforstans* 2
			confortans cet.

22:44	*super*		*in* cet.
22:45	*surgens*		*cum surrexit* cet.
	a		*prae* cet.
22:46	*dixit*		*ait* cet.
22:47	*accedens*		*adpropians* 2 4 8
			appropians 17
			appropinquauit A
22:49	*qui*		*hi qui* cet.
22:54	*adduxerunt*		*duxerunt* cet.
	autem		*uero* cet. |
22:55	*igne*	VL5 *ignem*	*igni* cet.
22:56	*eum*		*illum* cet. om. A
	eo		*illo* A
			ipso cet.
22:60	*dixit autem*		*et ait* (*at* 2) cet.
22:63	*continebant*		tenebant cet.
22:66	*populi*		plebis cet.
22:70	*tu es filius*		*ergo tu es filius* 8
			tu ergo es filius cet.
23:1	*adduxerunt*		*duxerunt* cet.
23:5	*hic*		*huc* 8 A
			hoc cet.
			add. *et filios nostros et uxores auertit a nobis non enim baptizantur sicut et nos nec se mundant* 2
23:9	*respondebat illi*		*respondebat* 2
			ei respondebat 4
			illi respondebat cet.
23:11	*et*		*om.* cet.
23:13	*conuocans*		*conuocatis* cet.
	principes		*senioribus* 8
			magistratibus cet.
23:14	*mihi hominem hunc*		*hunc hominem mihi* 8
			mihi hominem hunc cet.
23:15	*nec*		*neque* cet.
23:18	*dicentes*		*dicens* cet.
	dimitte autem		*et dimitte* (*demitte* 2) cet.
23:22	*hic*		*iste* cet.
23:23	*crucifige* (*crucifigi*)		*crucifigi* 5
			ut crucifigeretur cet.
23:25	*erat*		*fuerat* cet.
	autem		*uero* cet.
23:26	*inposuerunt*		*eum et inposuerunt* 2 8
			et inposuerunt 4 A
23:28	*uos*		*super uos ipsas* A
			uos ipsas cet.
23:30	*tegite*		*operite* cet.

23:31	*quoniam*		*qua* 2 *quia* cet.
23:32	*interfici*		*ut interficerentur* A
			ut crucifigerentur cet.
23:33	VL3 *cum*[2.]	*cum*	*postquam* cet.
23:35	*subsannabant autem; sannor*		et deridebant cet
23:36	*acetum*		*et acetum* cet.
	ei		*illi* cet.
23:38	*inscriptio*		*superscriptio* cet.
23:40	*alius*		*alter* cet.
	eum		*illum* cet.
	quoniam		*quid* 2
			quod 4 8
			qui A
23:41	*autem*		*uero* cet.
23:47	*honorificauit* (*honorificabat*)		*magnificabant* 2 8
			magnificat 4
			glorificauit A
23:48	*omnes*		*omnis turba eorum* A
	uidentes		*omnis turba* cet.
			et uidebant A
			qui uidebant cet.
23:49	*uidentes haec*		*haec uidentes* cet.
23:51	*iudaeorum*		*iudeae* cet.
23:53	*ubi*		*in quo* cet.
23:56	*reuersae autem*		*et reuertentes* cet.
24:1	*adferentes*		*portantes* cet.
24:5	*uiuum*		*uiuentem* cet.
24:6	*esset in galilaea*		*in galilaea esset* cet.
24:7	*quoniam*		*quia* cet.
24:9	*reuersae*		*egresse* 8
			regressae cet.
			add. *a monumento* A
24:10	*cum eis*		*uae cum ipsis* (*eis* A) *fuerant* (*erant* A) cet.
24:11	*haec*		*ista* cet.
24:17	*quae*		*qui* cet.
	uerba ista (*ista uerba*)		*ista uerba* 5
			hi (*hii* 2 isti 8) *sermones* cet.
24:18	*respondens autem unus ex eis*		*respondit autem unus ad eum* 2
			respondit unus ex ipsis 4
			et respondens unus ex ipsis 8
	diebus istis		*et respondens unus* A
			istis diebus 2
			his diebus cet.
24:21	*sperauimus*		*speramus* 2 8
			sperabamus 4 A
24:25	*quibus*		*quae* cet.

24:30	*benedixit*	*et benedixit* cet.
24:33	*xi*	in unum 2
		undecim cet.
24:34	*quoniam*	*quia* 2
		quod cet.
24:37	*putabant*	*putauerunt* 2
		existimabant cet.
24:39	*quoniam*	*qua* 8
		quia cet.
24:41	*aliquid*	*aliquid hic* 4
		hic aliquid cet.
	hic	om. cet.
24:43	*accipiens*	*accepit* 2
		om. cet.
24:44	*et dixit eis*	*et dixit illis* 2
		(add. *et* A) *dixit ad eos* cet
24:50	*ad*	*quasi* 2
		in cet.

4.4 The Relation of the *Codex Vercellensis* (VL3) to the *Codex Veronensis* (VL4)

The Codex *Veronensis* VI (VL4, b), preserved in the Fondazione Biblioteca di Capitolare Verona, contains the text of the four Gospels (with lacunae in Matt 1:1–11; 15:12–22; 23:18–27; John 7:44–8:12; Luke 19:26–21:29; Mark 14:61–16:8); it is one of the most influential testimonies to the linguistic, philological, and liturgical history of the 5th and 6th century. As such, this manuscript has often been copied, giving rise to further textual witnesses produced from the 5th to the 8th century [Codices *Corbeiensis secundus* (ff2; VL8), *Colbertinus* (c, VL6), *Rehdigeranus* (l,VL11), *Monacensis* (q,VL13), *Usserianus primus* (r1, VL14), and *Vindobonensis* (i,VL17)]. Written in ink of gold, silver, and red hues, the Codex has been described as a valuable 'purple' manuscript and an introduction to Christianity for elites. A note on the manuscript's 8th century cover reinforces this impression by stating that King Pipin presented this Codex to the Bishop of Verona. The most recent analysis of various purple parchments has shown that, in many cases, the parchment was dyed not with Tyrian purple derived from the murex snail but rather using less expensive, plant-based alternatives: this is the case, for instance, with the Old Latin Codices Aureus and Brixianus, which were dyed using orchil. An XRF-analysis of a fragment from the Biblioteca Capitolare suggests a similar result for the Codex Veronensis.

The translation technique employed in the codex came to be questioned over time, resulting in a number of corrections, as modern imaging techniques have revealed. In particular, the MSI-images available at the moment show several uncial correctors changing the manuscript at different times. Of these, the hitherto completely unknown corrector b1 has made numerous additions to the manuscript (at least in Matthew) by glossing between the lines in smaller uncials. Previously, it had been assumed that the manuscript was based on the Vulgate, but these newly discovered corrections can be attributed to the Codex *Bezae*, revising the former communis opinio. A second corrector (b2), mostly focusing on Luke, relied on the Vulgate/Amiatinus instead. A third corrector (b3), probably active in the 6th century, mostly focused on Mark, again changing the text in line with the Vulgate. A fourth corrector (b4) marked sections of the text with circumflex and golden ink for use in church services. The fifth corrector (b5) entered Ammonian sections in very tiny Roman numerals in the marginalia, though initial analysis shows that these do not necessarily correspond to the Eusebian Canon. Taken together, these changes show that the initial translation of the *Veronensis* was found to be in need of correction. It was adapted not only for liturgical purposes (as many other manuscripts) but also out of linguistic and theological considerations.

In Chapter 1, we argued that earlier editions of the Vercellensis (Irico, Belsheim, Gasquet, Jülicher et al.) are largely based on later Italian manuscripts, especially on the codices *Veronensis* and *Corbeiensis secundus*, and sometimes simply on the Vulgate. In text-critical research, these similarities have been taken primarily as a reason to assign both manuscripts to a single branch. Belsheim expressed his support of this analysis by editing the *Veronensis* along with the *Vercellensis*, and Irico (especially the autograph) and Gasquet made extensive use of the manuscript from Verona in their editions of the *Vercellensis*. Other scholars differ in their assessment: Burton lists, among the core group of manuscripts bearing the European text, the codices *Veronensis* VL4, *Vindobonensis* VL17, *Corbeiensis* VL8 and *Sarzanensis* VL22, while associating our codex with the *Fragmenta Curiensia* and the *Fragmenta Sangallensia* n and o. Let us begin with the former, single-branch thesis, whose proponents rely on Westcott and Hort's division of manuscripts,[112] in which the *Codex Palatinus* – taken as the representative of the 'Afra' text – is contrasted with manuscripts containing the European text, including VL3, 16, 4, 6, 8, and 17. In addition to these two poles, Westcott and Hort recognize a group of mixed-text manuscripts consisting of VL7, 11, 15, and so on. If one studies the manuscripts from Vercelli and Verona against the background of this division, it comes as no surprise that these manuscripts often share their "significant readings" with other European text manuscripts. If, on the other hand, we adopt the division favoured by Burton, the two manuscripts turn out to share virtually no significant common readings in the Gos-

112 Westcott/Hort, The New Testament in the Original Greek I, 81–82.

pel of Luke, except for *elisabet* instead of *maria* or *fuit propheta* for *fuit uir propheta*. In our view, the latter division sheds a better light on the readings the manuscript has in common with VL2 and 5. We therefore present evidence suggesting that the common readings originated in the Vercellensis, and we analyze the resulting readings in light of editorial processes by which the Veronensis appears to have come about, focusing especially on conflations with Greek and conflations of semantics.

4.4.1 Conflation with Greek

4.4.1.1 Conflation with the Word Order

Let us begin by discussing word order. It is striking that both manuscripts frequently agree in reproducing the word order of the Greek, as for example in 4:33, where both codices offer *et erat in synagoga homo*, thus literally rendering the Greek text as attested in NA[28] (Καὶ ἐν τῇ συναγωγῇ ἦν ἄνθρωπος). Likewise, in 23:47, *homo hic iustus* again translates the Greek ἄνθρωπος οὗτος δίκαιος literally, while the other witnesses present variations.[113] 15:17 also contains a faithful rendering of the Greek word order in the two sets of prepositions. Noteworthy here is the reading of *Codex Palatinus*, which has "to retire to," and also that of the Codex *Bezae*, which opts for *uenire*.

Table 36: Conflation of Greek word order

Verse	NA[28]	VL3, 4	Other Latin authorities
4:33	Καὶ ἐν τῇ συναγωγῇ ἦν ἄνθρωπος	*et erat in synagoga homo*	*erat autem in synagoga homo* 2 5 *et erat homo in synagoga* 8 *et in synagoga erat homo* A
4:36	τοῖς καθάρτοις πνεύμασιν	*immundis spiritibus*	*spiritibus immundis* 2 *inmundis spiritibus* 5 *spiritibus inmundis* 8 A
15:17	εἰς ἑαυτὸν δὲ ἐλθὼν ἔφη·	*in se autem conuersus*	*conuersus autem ad se* 2 *in semetipsum autem ueniens* 5 *in se autem reuersus* rell.
23:47	ἄνθρωπος οὗτος δίκαιος	*homo hic iustus*	*iustus erat hic homo* 5 *hic homo iustus* cet.

113 See also 4:36, where *immundis spiritibus* directly translates the Greek τοῖς καθάρτοις πνεύμασιν. The Latin manuscripts of Luke sometimes have the expression in the plural, *immundis spiritibus*, and sometimes in the singular as *daemonio immundo, spiritus habens infirmatis* (Luke 8:29, 30). In some cases, the notion of "uncleanness" is not made explicit at all. Thus, only *spiritus* is found (VL3, 6, 5, 11 in Luke 9:39).

Figure 4.14: Conflation of Greek word order in Luke 4:33 (358^a) and 4:36 (358^b).

In a few passages, the two manuscripts do depart from the Greek text. Particularly striking is the confusion of cases, for example in 9:44, where the majority of manuscripts render the Greek εἰς χεῖρας with an accusative, while the two codices have the ablative *manibus*.

4.4.2 Conflation of Syntax

There are only a few unique examples of conflation of syntax and the changes in *verba minora*, such as prepositions, conjunctions, particles, or pronouns, found in the Vercellensis and the Veronensis:

Table 37: The use of *ille* in VL 3 and VL4

Verse	VL3, 4	Other Latin authorities
8:32	*illum*	*eum* cet.
12:8	*eum*	*illum* 2
		in eo 5
		in illo cet.
17:2	*illius*	*eius* cet.

Table 38: The use of possessive pronouns

Verse	VL3, 4	NA[28]	Other Latin authorities
10:23	*discipulos*	πρὸς τοὺς μαθητὰς	*discentes* 2
			discipulos suos cet.

Table 39: The use of the preposition *in* and *super*

22:30	*in*	*super* cet.

Table 40: Common renderings of the conjunction *ipse*, *quia*, *quoniam*

Verse	VL3, 4	Other Latin authorities
24:21	*ipsum esse*	*quia ipse fuit* 2
		quoniam ipse erat 5
		quia ipse 8 A

Table 41: Common orthographic peculiarities

Verse	VL3, 4	Other Latin authorities
3:3	*paenitentiae*	*penitentiae* 8
		add. *in remissionem (remissa) peccatorum* 2 5 A
4:13	*omni temptatione*	*omnem temptationem* 2 5
		omni temptationem 8
		omni temtatione A
5:10	*filii*	*fili* 2 5 8
		filios A

8:51	*iohannen*	*iohanen* 5
		iohannem rell.
16:13	*unum patietur*	*unum adprehendet* 5
		uni adhaerebit (*adherebit* 2) cet.
13:4	*siloa*	*siloam* cet.
16:23	*sinu*	*sinus* 2 5
		sinum cet.
24:19	*fuit propheta*	*fuit propheta uir* 8
		fuit uir propheta (*profeta* 2) cet.
24:21	*uero*	*autem* rell.
	ipsum esse	*quia ipse fuit* 2
		quoniam ipse erat 5
	qui redempturus esset istrahel	*quia ipse* 8 A
		qui redempturus erat isdrahel 2
		qui incipebat saluare israhel 5
		incipit liberare istrahel 8
		esset redempturus israhel A

In 4:36, the two manuscripts Vercellensis and Veronensis contain examples of consonantal assimilation (n > m) within groups of consonants created by the addition of prefixes, with the *Codex Palatinus* translating τοῖς καθάρτοις πνεύμασιν with *immundis spiritibus* and the Codex Bezae correctly reading *inmundis spiritibus.* Such assimilation phenomena are due to phonetic change expressed graphically in the spelling of words. For this reason, the variation observed may again reflect the influence of oral usage on the codices. Moreover, an emulation of the Greek text is found in 24:21, where we read *uero* for ἀλλά γε, usually rendered *autem* (which in fact corresponds more to the Greek δέ). The rendering *vero* here takes on the sense of "truly, verily." In 13:4, both manuscripts have the locative *siloa* (ablative without a preposition) instead of the Greek Σιλωάμ.

Figure 4.15: The locative *siloa* instead of the Greek Σιλωάμ in Luke 13:4 (433[b]).

Another concession to the Greek text, admittedly found only in the Codex *Coridethianus*, is also worth mentioning.[114] The relevant passage is 8:14, which uses a predicative participle in discussing the correct way to hear the word (ἀκούσαντες τὸν λογόν). Now, while the majority of Latin textual witnesses correctly translate the aorist participle using the perfect tense, our two manuscripts render the aorist in the present tense.

Table 42: The loosening of the conjugation classes in VL3 and VL4

Verse	VL3, 4	Other Latin authorities
5:20	*remissa sunt*	*dimittentur* 2
		homo dimittentur 5
		homo remissa sunt 8
		homo remittuntur A
6:22	*eicerint*	*maledixerint* 2
		eicient 5 A
		eicent 8
		exprobauerunt A
6:38	*qua metitis*	*mensuraueritis* 2
		metieritis 5
		quam metitis 8
		qua mensi fueritis A
8:14	*audiunt*	*audierunt* cet.

114 On the importance of Coridethianus for the text of the Vercellensis, see under Chap 3.

8:18	*audiatis*	*audistis* 2 *auditis* cet.
14:9	*incipies*	*eris* 2 incipiens 5 8 *incipias* A
15:25	*audiit*	*audisset* 2 *uidet* 17 *audiuit* rell.
16:8	*fecerit*	*fecisset* A *fecit* cet.
16:11	*dabit uobis*	*crederit uobis* 2 *credet* (*credit* 8 A) *uobis* cet.
23:49	*fuerant*	*sunt* 5 *erant* cet.
24:21	*qui redempturus esset istrahel*	*qui redempturus erat isdrahel* 2 *qui incipebat saluare israhel* 5 *incipit liberare istrahel* 8 *esset redempturus israhel* A

The majority of Latin manuscripts do not translate κατασκηνώσεις in Luke 9:58. The conspicuously pleonastic reading of codices *Vercellensis* and *Veronensis* turns out to be an attempt to reconstruct the Greek word etymologically (κατασκηνώσεις from κατα / σκηνή or σκηνόω), resulting in a redundant formulation. Comparable phrases are found in the parallel passage in Matt 8:20 *nidos ubi requiescant* (at 2 4 u.ö.), and also in the writings of Ambrose,[115] Jerome,[116] and Tertullian.[117] Although the pleonastic reading is unusual, it may nevertheless be traced to North African translations.

Table 43: The translation of κατασκηνώσεις

Verse	NA[28]	VL3, 4	Other Latin authorities
9:58	κατασκηνώσεις	*ubi requiescant*	*om.* rell.

115 Luke 7:22, CC 14.222.

116 Hieron. *adv. Pel.* 2.12, PL 23.547; *Comm. In Is* 9:28, CC 73.360; *Hom in Ps.* CC 78.275.

117 Tert. *Id.* 185, CC 2.1119

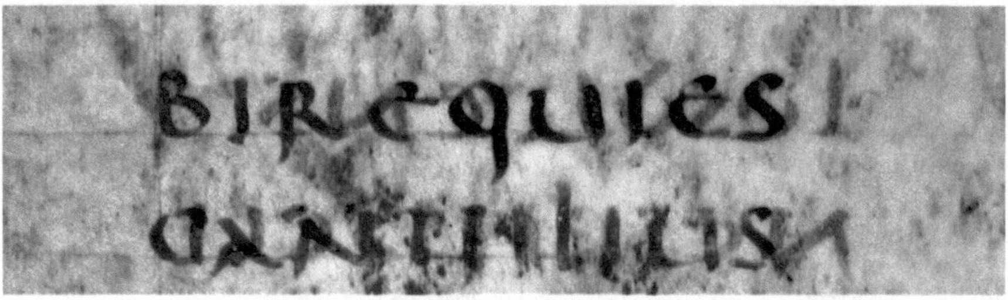

Figure 4.16: The translation of κατασκηνώσεις into *(u)bi requiescant* in Luke 9:58 (409^b–410^a).

4.4.3 Conflation of Semantics

Another perspective on the manuscripts is that achieved via *semantics*. An example of semantic variation is the use of the adjective *copiosus* instead of *multus* to translate the recurring phrases μισθὸς πολύς and ὄχλος πολύς (6:23; 10:2, concerning the superabundance of rewards in heaven). Burton finds this word choice "rather odd"[118] and suggests that it could be explained by the fact that the translators learned Greek only through a Greek-Latin glossary. Indeed, one characteristic of the term *copiosus* is its ability to express magnitude in the singular as well as quantity in the plural. However, Burton failed to notice that *copiosus* is also often attested in the writings of Tertullian and Cyprian in such contexts, so that the word choice may be traced back to choices made by translators from North Africa rather than to the translators' limited knowledge of Greek.

4.4.3.1 Internal Textual Criteria: Readings Shaped by Christology

The weightiest significant reading of the two manuscripts is found in Luke 24:19c, in the dialogue between Jesus and the disciples on the road to Emmaus. In this episode, the disciples emphasize Jesus's prophetic ministry as the substance and outcome of Jesus's life; in this context, v. 19c concerns Jesus's death and its repercussions without, of course, referring to the resurrection. The disciples here primarily see Jesus as a historical figure to whom they have directed their messianic hopes, thus addressing the theme of Jesus's humanity. In the Greek, two disciples stress Jesus's Nazarene origin in the words τὰ περὶ Ἰησοῦ τοῦ Ναζαρηνοῦ (4:16, 34; 22:56;

118 BURTON, The Old Latin Gospels, 118.

see also Mark 10:47; 14:67),[119] and they subsequently characterize Jesus as a prophet who acted powerfully in word and deed (ὅς ἐγένετο ἀνὴρ προφήτης δυνατὸς ἐν ἔργῳ καὶ λόγῳ). The Greek, possibly following the Septuagint (see, for example, Judg 6:8; 1 Kgs 18:4 אִישׁ נָבִיא / 3 Kgdms 18:4 ἀνὴρ προφήτης), uses the apposition "a man, a prophet." The scholarship has, following Siebenthal, pointed out that the apposition is optional in this passage, with the formulation being comparable to other passages in which a person's origin or profession is emphasized.[120] In our view, the apposition here again emphasizes Jesus's humanity, which is contrasted with ὁ χριστός in v. 26, and it is this contrast that is omitted in the two manuscripts Vercellensis and Veronensis:

Table 44: The translation of ἀνὴρ προφήτης

Verse	VL3, 4	Other Latin authorities	NA^{28}
24:19	*fuit propheta*	*fuit propheta uir* 8 *fuit uir propheta* (*profeta* 2) cet.	ἀνὴρ προφήτης

Figure 4.17: The translation of ἀνὴρ προφήτης into *fuit propheta* in Luke 24:19 (517^{a}).

The scribes are thus very concerned to downplay the explicit emphasis on Christ's humanity, so that we might, with all due caution, detect the presence of a change

119 Klinghardt's claim that this reading remained in the text via Mcn due to an editorial oversight does not seem likely to us, since the reading is universally transmitted.
120 SIEBENTHAL, Griechische Grammatik, 260j.

made on Christological grounds. The codices *Vercellensis* and *Veronensis* thus omit this emphasis of Jesus's humanity, an omission also found in Ps.-Cyprian and in some *sermones of* Augustine. [121]

4.4.3.2 Internal Textual Criteria: Readings Concerning the Role of Mary, Elizabeth, and Mary Magdalene

Perhaps the best-known reading shared by the codices *Vercellensis* and *Veronensis* on the one hand and the first hand of the *Rhedigerianus* VL11 on the other is found in 1:46, in which *elisabet* or *elisabel* speaks the Magnificat.

Table 45: The Magnificat put in the mouth of Mary or Elizabeth

Verse	NA^{28}	VL3, 4,11		Other Latin authorities
1:46	Μαριάμ	*elisabet*	*elisabel* 4	*maria* cet.

While the majority of Greek manuscripts here put the Magnificat in the mouth of Mary, the first reference to Elizabeth is already found in Origen and Irenaeus, though with some variation in the manuscripts.[122] In the Lucan textual tradition, the fact that Elizabeth is "filled with the holy spirit" in v. 41 supports the notion that she is speaking not only in vv. 42–45, but also in v. 46. Furthermore, since the Greek text continues with καὶ εἶπεν and not with δέ, it inevitably follows that it is still Elizabeth who is speaking. This interpretation is further supported by the fact that, after v. 56, Mary is said to remain with her (αὐτῇ), which shows that no change of subject is intended. Still, we ought not simply dismiss the reading which identifies Mary as the speaker of the Magnificat. In favor of this reading, one could argue that the phrase "lowliness of his slave" cannot refer to Elizabeth, because δούλη is used of Mary in v. 38 and 48. Accordingly, both sides are supported by arguments which make it clear that the translations were not made schematically but rather in response to the context; on this point, we must agree with Benko, who writes that "the two sides just about balance each other out."[123]

121 Ps.-Cyp. Reb. 9; Aug. *serm.* 111.2; *serm.* 232 (Migne 5.1); *serm.* 236 (Migne 5.1).
122 Orig. *in Luc. Hom.* 7 preserved only in Jerome PL 26.233: *Non enim ignoramus, quod secundum alios codices et haec Elisabeth vaticinetur* "her words are placed in Elisabeth's mouth." The two extant manuscripts of Iren. *adv. haer.* 4.7.1 do not read consistently, although there is a second reference to Mary in 3.10.2. For further discussion, see DURAND, L'origine du Magnificat, 74–77 and especially BARDENHEWER, "Ist Elisabeth eine Sängerin?," 192–194,199–200.
123 BENKO, History of the Controversy, 271.

Moreover, the alteration of speaker based on internal textual criteria such as *elisabet* in 1:46, is not unique to the Vercellensis. It is well known that, in Luke 23:55, the Latin tradition departs from the majority of Greek witnesses in mentioning two nameless women (*duae mulieres*) at the cross.

At 24:10, however, three women are mentioned. Two women can be identified in light of D, 05 Mark 15:47, as recorded also in the *Codex Bobbiensis*, which states: *maria autem magdalene et maria iosetis uiderunt ubi positus est.*

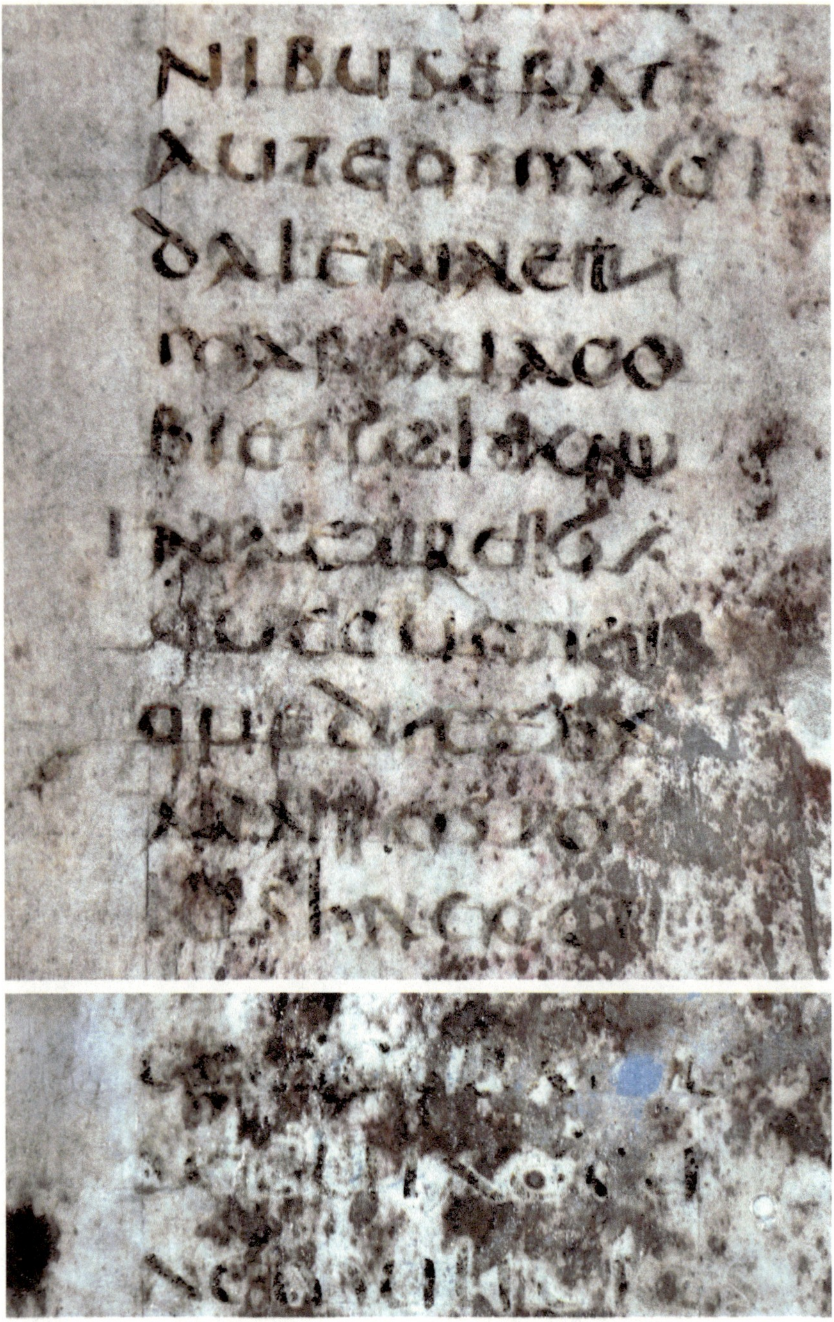

Figure 4.18: Three women in Luke 24:10 (516[a]) and two women in Luke 23:55 (514[a]).

This inconsistency of the number of women present is corrected by some scribes only in Mark 16:1, as in the *Codex Colbertinus*, which is consistent in listing only two women; other manuscripts, however, add *et maria iacobi* (VL30) or *salomae* (VL15) in Mark 15:47. Matt 27:61; 28:1 introduces only two women, whom the manuscripts also consistently identify as *maria magdalene et altera maria.* Luke, at any rate, gives the names of the women at the cross at 24:10: while the Greek text and the Latin witnesses explicitly name Mary Magdalene, Joanna, and Mary, mother of James (ἡ Μαγδαληνὴ Μαρία καὶ Ἰωάννα καὶ Μαρία ἡ Ἰακώβου), the *Vercellensis* changes the order of the names (*maria iacobi et iohanna*) and thus places "Mary, [sc. mother] of James" (Mark 16:1) between Magdalene and Joanna. In doing so, the translator makes it difficult for readers to immediately identify two of the women present at the tomb with the women healed from evil spirits in 8:2–3. Unlike the Greek witnesses, our translator has also varied the first woman's name. In 8:2, against the majority of Latin witnesses, the scribe writes *macdalene* instead of *magdalenae* or *magdalene.*

Figure 4.19: The devoicing of */g/* to */c/* in Luke 8:2 (387[b]): *macdalene.*

The devoicing of */g/* to */c/* may be considered a scribal error, though it may also be due to partial assimilation dating to sometime between the second and fifth century. This reading is indeed also found in the *Liber Commicus*, a lectionary with readings from the Vulgate and Old Latin manuscripts dated to 1067.[124] The *-e* ending is certainly indicative of a Graecism (Μαγδαληνή). At the same time, our writer also distinguished between the *macdalene* in Luke 8:2 and *magdalena* in Luke 24:10 by omitting 'Mary' from the name and thus referring only to the woman only as "the one from Magdala." Whether this confusion of names in Luke 24:11 and Luke 8:2[125] is also due to an attempt to avoid the association of *tanquam delera uerba* (like

124 Liber Commicus ed. Morin, 169.12. Of course, the question of whether the Lectionary here draws on the Vercellensis must remain open.

125 *ex qua daemonia septem exierant* 3 *exierant daemonia septe* 2 *uii daemonia exierant* 5 *daemonia uii exierant* 4 *daemonia exierunt septem* 8 *daemonia septem exierant* A.

crazy/ moronic/ insane chatter 24:11)[126] and *ex qua daemonia septem exierant* (from which seven demons had gone out) is not entirely clear.

To sum up: one limitation of Westcott and Hort's approach is the failure to distinguish between readings which belong to the Vercelli manuscript, but which cannot be explained by reference to Greek due to the lack of any corresponding Greek testimony on the one hand, and Latin versions which are likely to have developed their readings based on the *Vercellensis* on the other. These readings are supposed to have a genealogical explanation in the *Vercellensis*, though they also find considerable support in some Greek manuscripts. Burton describes this text as offering "numerous peculiarities of rendering, apparently motivated mainly by linguistic purism."[127] But it is uncertain whether a Greek text is really the basis of these changes. Recently, Lorenz argued that these parallels must be explained independently of any Greek text by saying that "it is not necessary to consult Greek texts to achieve linguistic purism in Latin."[128] Benedict Fischer observes a homogeneous background in the Old Latin translation of Paul, where the stage between the third century K-text-type and the Italian text-types is characterized by word choice and alternating use of synonyms.[129] According to Lorenz, the state of the *Vercellensis* text may be due to similar developments, and it may have arisen without the consultation of Greek texts.[130] The notion that the Latin version developed without reference to any Greek tradition is, however, put into question by the examples given above, such as the use of *elisabet* instead of *maria* in Luke 1:46, the omission of *uir* and the accompanying emphasis on Jesus's humanity in 24:19, and the omission of Mary Magdalene in *maria iacobi et iohann* in Luke 24:10. In fact, many variations in the *Vercellensis* Luke can be attributed to the translation technique used in rendering the Greek text, and also to the scribe's employment of a large and sophisticated vocabulary, including many terms which are hapax legomena in the Old Latin Bible and rare in Classical and Late Latin. While we have emphasized the theological and semantic features of the two manuscripts, it should by now be clear that the literal and erroneous translations of the Greek text account for the majority of shared passages under consideration. Earlier, we stated that these two features are among the hallmarks of the translation technique employed in the *Vercellensis*.

---

126 See the medical discussion in Soran. *Gyn.* 90.17; Cael. Aur. *acut.* 1 praef. See also Serv.Aen. 8,187*: Superstitio est timor superfluus et delirus,aut ab aniculis dicta superstitio, quae multis superstites per aetatem delirant, et, stultae sunt.*
127 Burton, The Old Latin Gospels, 21.
128 Lorenz, A History of Codex Bezae's Text, 906.
129 Fischer, "Lateinische Sprache," 24f. with focus on the Pauline letters.
130 Lorenz, A History of Codex Bezae's Text, 272f.

Table 46: Unique readings common to the Vercellensis, the Veronensis, and Old Latin Versions

Verse	VL3, 4	Other Latin authorities
1:46	*elisabet* *elisabel* 4	*maria* cet.
2:21	*Iesum*	*iesus* 2 5 8 A
3:3	*paenitentiae*	*penitentiae* 8 add. *in remissionem (remissa) peccatorum* 2 5 A
4:13	*omni temptatione*	*omnem temptationem* 2 5 *omni temptationem* 8 *omni temtatione* A
4:33	*et erat in synagoga homo* Καὶ ἐν τῇ συναγωγῇ ἦν ἄνθρωπος	*erat autem in synagoga homo* 2 5 *et erat homo in synagoga* 8 *et in synagoga erat homo* A
4:36	*immundis spiritibus* τοῖς καθάρτοις πνεύμασιν	*spiritibus immundis* 2 *inmundis spiritibus* 5 *spiritibus inmundis* 8 A
4:38	*intrauit* εἰσῆλθεν	*uenit* 5 *introiuit* 8 A *om.* 2
5:10	*filii*	*fili* 2 5 8 *filios* A
5:20	*remissa sunt*	*dimittentur* 2 *homo dimittentur* 5 *homo remissa sunt* 8 *homo remittuntur* A
6:22	*eicerint*	*maledixerint* 2 *eicient* 5 A *eicent* 8 *exprobauerunt* A
6:23	*copiosa*	*multa* 5 8 A *om.* 2
6:36	*miseretur*	*beniuolus est* 5 *misericors est* 2 8 A
6:38	*qua metitis*	*mensuraueritis* 2 *metieritis* 5 *quam metitis* 8 *qua mensi fueritis* A
6:45	*enim*	*om.* 2 5 8 A
8:14	*audiunt*	*audierunt* cet.
8:18	*audiatis*	*audistis* 2 *auditis* cet.
8:32	*illum*	*eum* rell.
8:34	*renuntiauerunt*	*nuntiauerunt* cet.
8:51	*iohannen*	iohanen 5 iohannem cet.
9:44	*in minibus*	*manus* cet.
9:58	*ubi requiescant*	*om.* cet.

10:23	*discipulos*	*discentes* 2
		discipulos suos cet.
12:8	*eum*	*illum* 2
		in eo 5
		in illo cet.
13:4	*siloa*	*siloam* cet.
14:9	*incipies*	*eris* 2
		incipiens 5 8
		incipias A
14:14	*reddere*	*retribuere* cet.
15:17	*in se autem conuersus*	*conuersus autem ad se* 2
		in semetipsum autem ueniens 5
		in se autem reuersus cet.
15:25	*audiit*	*audisset* 2
		uidet 17
		audiuit cet.
15:28	*intrare*	*introire* cet.
16:8	*fecerit*	*fecisset* A
		fecit cet.
	dixit autem ad discipulos suos	*dixit autem ad discentes suos* 2
		dixit autem 8
		om. 5 A
16:11	*dabit uobis*	*crederit uobis* 2
		credet (*credit* 8 A) *uobis* cet.
16:13	*unum patietur*	*unum adprehendet* 5
	ἀνθέξεται	*uni adhaerebit* (*adherebit* 2) cet.
16:23	*sinu*	sinus 2 5
		sinum cet.
17:2	*illius*	*eius* cet.
18:16	*caelorum*	*dei* cet.
22:26	*ut*	*quasi* 2
		sicut 5 8 17 A
22:30	*in*	*super* cet.
23:47	*homo hic iustus*	*iustus erat hic homo* 5
	ἄνθρωπος οὗτος δίκαιος	*hic homo iustus* cet.
23:49	*fuerant*	*sunt* 5
		erant cet.
24:19	*fuit propheta*	*fuit propheta uir* 8
		fuit uir propheta (*profeta* 2) cet.
24:21	*uero*	*autem* cet.
	ipsum esse	*quia ipse fuit* 2
		quoniam ipse erat 5
	qui redempturus esset istrahel	*quia ipse* 8 A
		qui redempturus erat isdrahel 2
		qui incipebat saluare israhel 5
		incipit liberare istrahel 8
		esset redempturus israhel A

4.5 The Relation of the *Codex Vercellensis* (VL3) and the Codex Amiatinus (A)

The Codex Amiatinus is the oldest surviving complete manuscript of the Vulgate which Pope Damasus I commissioned from Jerome (Florence, Biblioteca Medica Laurenziana, Cod. Amiat. 1). Named after the Abbaia di San Salvatore on Mount Amiata, the codex was possibly intended as a gift from the abbot Ceolfrith to Pope Gregory II (ca. 716).[131]

This of course does not yet constitute an assessment of the textual value of the Amiatinus. Already in the 19th century, A. Souter showed, on the basis of Luke 15:11–32 and Jerome's letter to Pope Damasus I (*ep.* 21.4f.), that what Jerome presented was surprisingly not his own translation, but rather the text of the *Codex Vercellensis* which, except for a few changes, closely resembles the text of the Vulgate. In light of this finding, Souter asks "if, then, St. Jerome regularly used this type of text, and chose it to comment on in a letter to Pope Damasus at the very time when the preparation of the revision we know as the Vulgate was in hand, may it not be, is it not in fact probable, that this was the type of text he used, in St. Luke's Gospel at least, as the basis of his revision?" What, then, was the purpose of this new translation? Calling on Cicero, the most famous ancient translator of biblical writings writes that the sense of translation is "not [to express] one word by another," but rather to give highest priority to the meaning (*sensum exprimere de sensu*).[132] Jerome characterizes the translation process using the term *interpretari*, which he associates with the *hyperbatorum amfractus* and the *varietas figurarum.*[133] Jerome never tires of emphasizing that his tasks consists in elucidating unclear passages of previous translations. So, in the *praefatio* to his 380 C.E. translation of the *Chronicon* of Eusebius of Caesarea,[134] Jerome speaks of the difficulties of following another's reasoning and also of adequately rendering the complex phrases, elegance (*decor*), and stylistic figures (*hyperbatorum amfractus, varietas figurarum*), and he ultimately asks whether translation is possible at all.[135] Jerome explains that

---

131 On what follows, see *All Roads Lead to Rome. The Creation, Context and Transmission of the Codex Amiatinus* by J. Hawkes and M. Boulton with collected essays on the Amiatinus, and especially H.A.G. Houghton, "The Text of the Gospels in the Codex Amiatinus," 77–88.

132 Cic. *opt. gen.* 14: *In quibus non verbum pro verbo necesse habui reddere, sed genus omne verborum vimque servavi. Non enim ea me adnumerare lectori putavi oportere, sed tamquam appendere.*

133 Hier. *chron. praef.* 2.

134 Hier. *chron. praef.* 2. *Difficile est enim alienas lineas insequentem non alicubi excedere, arduum, ut quae in alia lingua bene dicta sunt eundem decorem in translatione conservent.*

135 Hier. *chron. praef.* 2: *Significatum est aliquid unius verbi proprietate: non habeo meum, quo id efferam, et dum quaero implere sententiam, longo ambitu vix brevis viae spatia consummo. Accedunt*

there are "untranslatable terms" (*unius verbi proprietate*), which can only be reproduced using laborious descriptions (*quaero implere sententiam*) and that "every language has a peculiar, so to speak native idiom."[136] Translation thus always involves an intervention into the original text, as Jerome notes in response to Marcella's question concerning why he merely transcribed terms such as *alleluia* instead of translating them. Every language has its own untranslatable characteristics, which justifies the introduction of new foreign words. [137]

Things are somewhat different in the Gospel revision of 383, whose approach Jerome justifies in his *praefatio* by the fact that this work was commissioned by Pope Damasus I in order to put an end to the sloppiness of earlier manuscripts (i.e. of the Old Latin manuscripts).[138] It is, of course, remarkable that the prefaces to the Gospels and the books of the Old Testament include an apologia for his work but do not elaborate on his theory of translation. Here, as in the quotation from the 57th Letter presented above, Jerome defends his translation, which aims to follow the *genus omne verborum vimque servavi* while respecting the *mos* of the target language. In light of all this, how does the Amiatinus compare to the Codex Vercellensis Gospel of Luke?

4.5.1 Conflation of Greek Readings

The genetic relationship between the two manuscripts is evident in those places in which they depart from the other witnesses in the same way. In both manuscripts, such departures are due to their shared commitment to closely adhering to the Greek.

---

hyperbatorum amfractus, dissimilitudines casuum, varietas figurarum, ipsum postremo suum et, ut dicam, vernaculum linguae genus.

136 *ipsum postremo suum et, ut dicam, vernaculum linguae genus.*

137 Cf. Hier. *ep.* 27. He, in a state of great agitation, that Marcella has slandered him: *adversus auctoritatem veterum et totius mundi.*

138 Vulg. *ev. praef.* 6–10.13–16: *Sin autem veritas est quaerenda de pluribus, cur non ad Graecam originem revertentes ea quae vel a vitiosis interpretibus male edita vel a praesumptoribus imperitis emendata perversius vel a librariis dormitantibus aut addita sunt aut mutata corrigimus?* [...] *Hoc certe cum in nostro sermone discordat et diversos rivulorum tramites ducit: uno de fonte quaerendum est.*

Table 47: Common orthographic peculiarities

Verse	VL3, A	Other Latin authorities
16:11	*fideles*	*fidelis* cet.
22:55	*Petrus*	*et petrus* cet.

4.5.1.1 Conflation of Greek Cases

At the same time, however, the manuscripts do exhibit numerous differences, which may be accounted for in the following way: many of these differences namely appear to be due to attempts to improve the text – for instance, by intervening in the use of the cases – made by the scribe of the Codex Amiatinus. Many variations in the use of cases consist of non-standard constructions with the accusative, which repeatedly show the early translators' attempts to adapt the Latin text to Greek syntax. For this reason, phrases such as *benedicere aliquem* (εὐλογεῖν τινα) instead of *benedicere alicui*, "to bless someone," are found in Latin translations, *nocere aliquem* (βλάπτειν τινά) for *nocere alicui*, "to harm someone," *petere aliquem* (αἰτεῖν τινα) instead of *petere ab aliquo*, "to ask someone about something." In such passages, ms. A usually provides a "corrective" reading that corresponds to classical usage. Thus, in 2:34 Amiatinus has *et benedixit illis symeon* (καὶ εὐλόγησεν αὐτοὺς Συμεών) instead of the syntactically literal rendering *et benedixit illos symeon* of the *Codex Vercellensis*.

Figure 4.20: *et benedixit illos symeon* in Luke 2:34 (343[a]).

The scribes seem to have accepted the fact that this approach also results in erroneous translations, for example in 1:35, where the angel explains to Mary that the "power of the Most High will overshadow you."

Table 48: Translating the Greek personal pronoun σοι

Verse	VL3, A	Other Latin authorities
1:35	*tibi*	*te* 2 5 4
		me 8

Here, the Vercellensis VL3 and Amiatinus both translate the Greek personal pronoun σοί (in the dative) using the dative *tibi*, where the Latin normally requires an accusative, namely *te*, which is in fact found in the majority of the manuscripts.[139] It is striking that the majority of Vulgate manuscripts imitate the Greek by using the linguistically unusual dative. Here we can also detect a change motivated by the fact that the verb "to overshadow" is often taken as a euphemism for sexual intercourse. Accordingly, in choosing the unusual verb *inumbrare*, the Latin tradition of the Vercellensis refers to Num 9:18 (Cod. Ludg., 262), where we read: *et per praeceptum Domini promouebunt per omnes dies in quibus inumbrat nubs per tabernaculum.*[140] Moreover, it is striking that Cyprian also uses this poetic expression in his translation of Num 10:36 in writing: *discentem nubs clara tegit agmenque refertum inmensasque acies obtentu uestis inumbrat* (Cyp *hept.* 4.239–240).

4.5.1.2 Conflation of Syntax

The conflation of syntax focuses on the changes in *verba minora*, such as prepositions, conjunctions, particles, or pronouns, found in the Vercellensis and the Amiatinus versions:

This is the case with pronoun usage. For example, we see the demonstrative *is* used instead of *ille.* Strictly speaking, in classical Latin, the demonstrative *is* performed the function of the missing personal pronoun, while *ille* and *hic* respectively served to denote that which is spatially or temporally distant from or close to the speaker.[141]

---

139 The *me* transmitted in 8 ("overshadow me") is certainly wrong.

140 In contrast, Augustine in his commentary on Numbers (241.276; see also 242.309; 242.325) lists *obumbrat* and thus refers to Jerome's rendering. See, moreover, SapSal 19:7 vg; Ps 90:4 in b,4 (*obumbrabit tibi*); see also Ambros. Ps 102; Ps 139:8 VL4: *obumbrasti super caput me.*

141 Cf. MÜLLER-LANCÉ, Latein für Romanisten, 130.

Table 49: Renderings of the demonstrative pronouns *is, ea, id –ille, illa,illud*

Verse	VL3, A	Other Latin authorities
10:30	*eum*	*illum* cet. *om.* 5
18:22	*ei*	*illi* 2 5 *om.* cet.
22:54	*sequebatur*	add. *eum* 5 17 *illum* 2 4 8
23:1	*eorum*	*illorum* cet. *om.* 2 5

Table 50: Common renderings of the conjunctions *quoniam* and *quia*

Verse	VL3, A	Other Latin authorities
12:27	*nec*	*quoniam* (*quia* 2) *nec* (*neque* 5) cet.
19:34	*quia*	*quoniam* 5 *om.* cet.
22:70	*quia*	*quoniam* 5 *quod* cet.

Table 51: Renderings of the conjunction *et*

Verse	VL3, A	Other Latin authorities
19:35	*inposuerunt*	*et inposuerunt* cet.
20:31	*et*	*om.* cet.
20:44	*et*	*om.* cet.
22:55	*petrus*	*et petrus* cet.

A similar situation occurs with prepositions governing more than one case, especially those used with both the accusative and the ablative. With such prepositions, the accusative was usually preferred to describe direction of motion (lative), while the ablative described the location (locative). This distinction was almost completely lost in Late Latin, a development which may be seen in many manuscripts of the Latin Gospel, *Codex Vercellensis* being no exception. Thus, in 7:11, the text transmits *ibat Iesus in ciuitatem* (ἐπορεύθη εἰς πόλιν), but in 9:52 we read *intrauerunt in ciuitate* (εἰσῆλθον εἰς κώμην); in 8:22, we find *ascendit in nauiculam* (ἐνέβη εἰς πλοῖον), but 8:37 has *ascendens in naue* (ἐμβὰς εἰς πλοῖον). Codex A, on the other hand, has the classical accusative in all these places (*in ciuitatem*, *in nauiculam*, and *in nauem*).

The classical usage of Latin is found in the case of *ciuitatum* (5:12), where the Palatinus has a hypercorrection (*ex ciuitatibus*) and the majority of manuscripts has the Vulgar Latin *ciuitatium*.

Table 52: Differences in case in VL3 and A

Verse	VL3, A	Other Latin authorities
2:13	*caelestis*	*caelestium* 2 4
		caeli
		celestis 8
5:12	*ciuitatum*	*ex ciuitatibus* 2
		ciuitatium 5 4 8
24:19	*populo*	*populi* 2 5
		plebe 4 8

"Corrective" readings of A are also seen in the use of reflexive pronouns. In 2:26, for example, in translating μὴ ἰδεῖν θάνατον, "that he would not see death," ms. A retains classical syntax by giving *non uisurum se mortem*; in this sentence, the subject of the infinitive construction is Simeon, a righteous and pious man from Jerusalem to whom the holy spirit had revealed that he would meet *christum domini* before he died. The *Codex Vercellensis*, however, reads *non uisurum eum mortem*, using a demonstrative pronoun instead of the expected reflexive, with the result that the reflexive relation is no longer expressed syntactically ("that he himself (and not someone else) would not see death").

Table 53: Conflation of Syntax in VL3 and A

Verse	VL3, A	Other Latin authorities
2:46	*interrogantem*	*interrogantem illos* 2
		interrogantem eos 5 4 8
6:11	*facerent iesu*	*illi facerent* 2
		perderent eum 5
		facerent de iesum 4
		facerent de iesu 8
7:24	*coepit dicere de iohannen ad turbas coepit*	*dicere ad tubas de iohannem* 2
		dicere de iohane turbis 5
		dicere ad turbas de iohanne 4
		de iohannem dicere ad tubas 8
7:41	*Duo*	*et iesus ait duo* 2
		ad ille dixit duo 5
		dixit ergo iesus erant duo 4
		et ait duo 8

17:10	*sic et uos*	*sic itaque et uos* 2 *ita et uos* 5 *et uos* cet.
18:24	*iesus* *dixit*	*om.* cet. *dixit illi (ill*) iesus* 2 *dixit iesus* cet.
19:13	*uocatis autem decem seruis suis*	*et uocitis autem decem seruis suis* 2 *uocans autem decem seruos suos* 5 *et uocauit decem seruos* cet.
19:35	*inposuerunt*	*et inposuerunt* cet.
20:39	*respondentes autem quidam*	*responderunt autem quidam* 2 *respondens autem quidam* cet.
22:52	*dixit autem iesus ad eos, qui uenerant ad se*	*dixit autem ad eos qui aduenerant ad eum* 5 *et ad eos qui ad se uenerant* (*uerant* 2) *dixit* cet.
22:56	*quem ... uidisset*	*uidens autem eum* 5 *quem* (om. 17) *ut uidit* (*cum uidibit* 4) cet.
23:36	*offerentes*	*offerebant* cet.

4.5.1.3 Greek Tenses

Other passages also show close adherence to the Greek text, as in 2:46, where the majority of the Latin witnesses render the Greek text (ἐπερωτῶντα αὐτούς) with *interrogantem* and the personal pronoun *illos* (VL2) or *eos* (VL4, 5, 8).

Another example is 3:10, where the imperfect *interrogabant* translates the imperfect ἐπηρώτων (instead of the perfect *interrogauerunt* in VL2, 5, 4, 8).[142]

Figure 4.21: The imperfect *interrogabant* in Luke 3:10 (348^{b}).

142 On the interpretation of the Greek participle, see also 23:36.

Comparable translations of the Greek tenses are also found in 4:25, where ἐκλείσθη (aorist passive) is suitably translated as *clausum*, while VL5, 4 and 8 render the verb using the Vulgar Latin form *clusum*;[143] in 5:35, Vercellensis and Amiatinus render the prospective subjunctive ὅταν ἀπαρθῇ using the subjunctive perfect, while the majority of manuscripts give the subjunctive imperfect *auferetur*.

The sequence of the tenses is also ably reproduced by the translators: in 14:7, the imperfect *eligerent* can be taken as a literal rendering of the Greek, in contrast to the *eligebant* of the majority of the other manuscripts. In 15:2, the translation of the present tense verb προσδέχεται as *recipit* shows that the sequence is not observed in the case of the present tense, where it is grammatically optional. Also noteworthy is the translation of the subjunctive aorist οὐ μὴ ἀποκριθῆτε in 22:68 using the future *respondebitis*, which emphasizes the futural sense of the subjunctive.[144]

Also striking is the verb *adpropinquauerunt*, which introduces onomatopoeic *adfectabat* and *ad uesperum*, emphasizing the nearby village boundary (24:28). The kinship between the two codices is likewise evident from the sentence structure, which often imitates Greek, as in 17:10, where *sic et uos* literally renders the Greek phrase οὕτως καὶ ὑμεῖς (instead of *sic itaque et uos* 2, *ita et uos* 5, *et uos* rell.).[145]

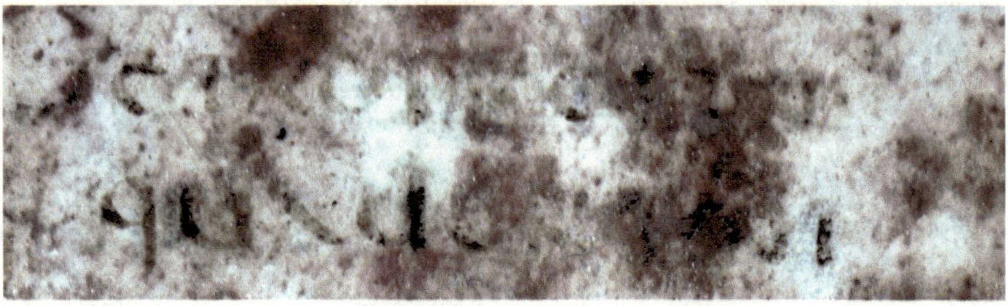

Figure 4.22: *adpropinquauerunt* in Luke 24:28 (519[a])

Table 54: Verb conjugation (tenses, modes, diathesis)

Verse	VL3, A	Other Latin authorities
2:49	*me quaerebatis*	*quaerebatis me* 2 5 8 *me quaeretis* 4

143 See Georges I, 926.940. The translation of 2 with *conclusum* is imprecise since the Greek lacks the prefix σύν-.

144 See likewise 6:45 *profert*, which better captures the Greek.

145 See also 7:24; 18:33; 19:13; 19:35; 20:39; 22:52 et al.

3:10	*interrogabant*	*interrogauerunt* 2 5 4 8
		om. 2 5 4 8
5:35	*ablatus fuerit*	*auferetur* 2 4 8
		sublatus fuerit 5
6:45	*profert,*	*proferet* 2 5 4 8
7:23	*non scandalizabitur in me*	*non scandalizatus fuerit in me* 2
		non fuerit scandalizatus in me 5
		in me non fuerit scandalizatus 4
		non fuerit in me scandalizatus 8
7:42	*diligent*	*amat* 2
		diligit 5 8
		dilexit 4
7:48	*remittuntur*	*mulier remissa sunt*
		dimissa sunt 5
		mulier remissa sunt 4
		remissa sunt 8
11:38	*baptizatus esset*	*baptizauit* 2
		baptizatus est cet.
		add. ante prandium 2 A
		priusquam (*antequam* 5 17) *manducaret* (*pranderet* 5) cet.
14:7	*eligerent*	*eligebant cet.*
15:2	*recipit*	*suscipit* 2
		adsumit 5
		reciperet cet.
17:30	*reuelabitur*	*uenerit* 2
		qua (*qui* 5 *quia* 4 *que* 8) *reuelabitur* cet.
18:32	*conspuetur*	*sputis agitur* 2
		expuent in eum 5 8
		inspuetur 4
		spuerunt 17
21:5	*esset*	*est* cet.
		om. 5
22:66	*conuenerunt*	*congregati sunt* 5
		conuenit cet.
22:68	*respondebitis*	*respondetis* cet. *add. mihi* cet.
		om. 2

Table 55: Verb forms (different prefixion, substitution)

Verse	VL3, A	Other Latin authorities
4:25	*clausum*	*conclusum* 2
		clusum 5 4 8
5:35	*ablatus fuerit*	*auferetur* 2 4 8
		sublatus fuerit 5
7:42	*diligent*	*amat* 2

		diligit 5 8
		dilexit 4
7:48	*remittuntur*	*mulier remissa sunt*
		dimissa sunt 5
		mulier remissa sunt 4
		remissa sunt 8
15:2	*recipit*	*suscipit* 2
		adsumit 5
		reciperet cet.
20:20	*caperent*	*repraehenderent* 2
		adprehenderent cet.
22:31	*scribaret* (*cribaret*)	*cerneret* 5
		cribraret A
		uentilet cet.
22:66	*conuenerunt*	*congregati sunt* 5
		conuenit cet.
23:7	*remisit*	*misit* cet.
24:18	*peregrinus es*	*peregrinaris* 2
		aduena es 5
		pelegrinus es 4 pelegrinus
		pelegrinus 8
24:28	*adpropinquauerunt*	*propinquauerunt* 2

4.5.2 Conflation of Semantics: A Christian Nomenclature?

The decisive evidence for the early dating of the Vercellensis Luke lies in the text's lexical peculiarities.

Table 56: Lexical peculiarities

Verse	VL3, A	Other Latin authorities
6:29	*uestimentum*	*palleum* 2
		tunicam 5 4 8
8:15	*in patientia*	*in sufferentia* 5
		per patientiam cet.
16:6	*cautionem tuam*	*chirografum tuum* 2
		tuas litteras 5
		litteras tuas 4 8
24:19	*populo*	*populi* 2 5
		plebe 4 8

One significant reading is found in the parable of the debtor, where Jesus asks the Pharisee: τίς οὖν αὐτῶν πλεῖον ἀγαπήσει αὐτόν. While the *Palatinus* renders the verb ἀγαπήσει as *amat*, suggesting passionate (erotic) love, 3 and A give the more appropriate *diligent* instead, with the sense of "to esteem, to value highly."[146] A further semantic feature is evident in the avoidance of "Christian" terms, as shown, for example, by the literal translation of ἐν ὑπομονῇ as *in patientia.*

Figure 4.23: ἐν ὑπομονῇ as *in patientia* in Luke 8:15 (390[a]).

By contrast, the Bezae translation *in sufferentia* ("in endurance" or "patience") uses Christian vocabulary also found in Tertullian.[147] Another striking feature is the choice of *conspuetur*, which is Jerome's preferred word and occurs again in the

146 *diligite* in VL5 and 8 shows vowel reduction typical of Late Latin.
147 See Tert. *De or.* 4 and *adv. Marc.* 4.15; for other passages, see Georges II, 4580.

Vulgate translations of the Book of Job.[148] A further special reading found in both manuscripts concerns 4:38, where Jesus goes to the house of Simon (*in domum simonis*), instead of to the house of Simon and Andrew (see *in domum simonis et andreae* 5 4 8). In this way, the Amiatinus may be adopting a peculiarity of the Codex Vercellensis, for it is only there that the Latin Acts of Peter (also preserved in Vercelli) have come down to us.

While Souter comes to the conclusion that "[t]he two texts [...] are clearly the same," we add that the Codex Amiatinus derives from the Codex Vercellensis. This conclusion is primarily based on the fact that both manuscripts try to reproduce the Greek text, often literally, even where this results in morphological and syntactical errors in the Latin. We consider it likely that either Jerome or a scribe belonging to Jerome's circle had access to the *Codex Vercellensis*, and that the syntax of this manuscript was subsequently smoothed over, resulting in the text of the *Codex Amiatinus*.

Table 57: Unique Readings shared by the Vercellensis, the Amiatinus and Old Latin Versions

Verse	VL3, A	Other Latin authorities
1:28	*gratia plena*	*gratificata* 2
		benedicta 5
		gratiam plena 8
		om. 4
1:32	*dominus*	*dominus deus* 2 5 4 8
1:35	*tibi*	*te* 2 5 4
		me 8
2:13	*caelestis*	*caelestium* 2 4
		caeli
		celestis 8
2:34	*israhel*	*isdrahel* 2 5*
		istrahel 5c 4 8
2:36	*phanuel*	*fanuel* 2 5 4 8
2:42	*duodecim*	*xii* 2 5 4 8
2:46	*interrogantem*	*interrogantem illos* 2
		interrogantem eos 5 4 8
2:49	*me quaerebatis*	*quaerebatis me* 2 5 8
		me quaeretis 4
3:10	*interrogabant*	*interrogauerunt* 2 5 4 8
		om. 2 5 4 8
4:25	*clausum*	*conclusum* 2
		clusum 5 4 8

148 See Georges I, 1197.

4:38	*in domum simonis*	*andreae socrus autem simonis* 2 *in domum simonis et andreae* 5 4 8
5:12	*ciuitatum*	*ex ciuitatibus* 2 *ciuitatium* 5 4 8
5:35	*ablatus fuerit*	*auferetur* 2 4 8 *sublatus fuerit* 5
6:11	*facerent iesu*	*illi facerent* 2 *perderent eum* 5 *facerent de iesum* 4 *facerent de iesu* 8
6:29	*uestimentum*	*palleum* 2 *tunicam* 5 4 8
6:45	*profert*	*proferet* 2 5 4 8
7:23	*non scandalizabitur in me*	*non scandalizatus fuerit in me* 2 *non fuerit scandalizatus in me* 5 *in me non fuerit scandalizatus* 4 *non fuerit in me scandalizatus* 8
7:24	*coepit dicere de iohannen ad turbas coepit*	*dicere ad tubas de iohannem* 2 *dicere de iohane turbis* 5 *dicere ad turbas de iohanne* 4 *de iohannem dicere ad tubas* 8
7:41	*duo*	*et iesus ait duo* 2 *ad ille dixit duo* 5 *dixit ergo iesus erant duo* 4 *et ait duo* 8
7:42	*diligent*	*amat* 2 *diligit* 5 8 *dilexit* 4
7:48	*remittuntur*	*mulier remissa sunt* *dimissa sunt* 5 *mulier remissa sunt* 4 *remissa sunt* 8
8:15	*in patientia*	*in sufferentia* 5 *per patientiam* cet.
9:10	*qui*	*quod* cet.
9:33	*dum*	*cum* cet.
10:30	*eum*	*illum* cet. *om.* 5
11:38	*baptizatus esset*	*baptizauit* 2 *baptizatus est* cet. *add. ante prandium* 2 A *priusquam* (*antequam* 5 17) *manducaret* (*pranderet* 5)
12:27	*nec*	*quoniam* (*quia* 2) *nec* (*neque* 5) cet.
14:7	*eligerent*	*eligebant cet.*
14:14	*quia*	*quod* 4^{c} *quoniam* cet. om. 4*

15:2	*recipit*	*suscipit* 2
		adsumit 5
		reciperet cet.
16:6	*cautionem tuam*	*chirografum tuum* 2
		tuas litteras 5
		litteras tuas 4 8
16:11	*fideles*	*fidelis* cet.
17:10	*sic et uos*	*sic itaque et uos* 2
		ita et uos 5
		et uos cet.
17:30	*reuelabitur*	*uenerit* 2
		qua (*qui* 5 *quia* 4 *que* 8) *reuelabitur* cet.
17:33	*animam suam saluam*	*biuicare animam suam* 5
		animam suam (*anima sua* 2) *liberare*
		(*saluare* 2 8) cet.
18:22	*ei*	*illi* 2 5
		om. cet.
18:24	*iesus*	*om.* cet.
	dixit	*dixit illi (ill**) *iesus* 2
		dixit iesus cet.
18:32	*conspuetur*	*sputis agitur* 2
		expuent in eum 5 8
		inspuetur 4
		spuerunt 17
18:33	*die tertia*	*deteriores* 2
		tertia die rell.
18:37	*nazarenus*	*nazorenus* 2 17
		nazoreus cet.
19:13	*uocatis autem decem seruis suis*	*et uocitis autem decem seruis suis* 2
		uocans autem decem seruos suos 5
		et uocauit decem seruos cet.
19:31	*quare soluitis*	*ut quid soluitis* 17
		om. cet.
19:34	*quia*	*quoniam* 5
		om. cet.
19:35	*inposuerunt*	*et inposuerunt* cet.
20:20	*caperent*	*repraehenderent* 2
		adprehenderent cet.
20:31	*et*	*om.* cet.
20:39	*respondentes autem quidam*	*responderunt autem quidam* 2
		respondens autem quidam cet.
20:44	*et*	*om.* cet.
21:5	*esset consecutio temporis*	*est* cet.
		om. 5
22:31	*scribaret* (*cribaret*)	*cerneret* 5
		cribraret A
		uentilet cet

22:47	*adhuc*	*adhuc autem* cwet.
22:52	*dixit autem iesus ad eos, qui uenerant*	*dixit autem ad eos qui aduenerant ad eum* 5
		et ad eos qui ad se uenerant (*uerant* 2) *dixit* cet.
22:54	*sequebatur*	add. *eum* 5 17
		illum 2 4 8
22:55	*petrus*	*et petrus* cet.
22:56	*quem … uidisset*	*uidens autem eum* 5
		quem (om. 17) *ut uidit* (*cum uidibit* 4) cet.
22:66	*conuenerunt*	*congregati sunt* 5
		conuenit cet.
22:68	*respondebitis*	*respondetis* cet. *add. mihi* cet.
		om. 2
22:70	*quia*	*quoniam* 5
		quod cet.
23:1	*eorum*	*illorum* rell.
		om. 2 5
23:7	*remisit*	*misit* rell.
23:36	*offerentes*	*offerebant* rell.
24:10	*que*	*om.* 5
		haec rell.
24:18	*peregrinus*	*peregrinaris* 2
		aduena es 5
		pelegrinus es 4
		pelegrinus 8
24:19	*populo*	*populi* 2 5
		plebe 4 8
24:28	*adpropinquauerunt*	*propinquauerunt* 2

4.6 Conclusion: The Relation of the *Codex Vercellensis* Luke to the Latin Versions

The *Codex Vercellensis* is often classified as belonging to the 'early European' (or 'Italian') text-type and also as characterized by distinctive word choices which separate it from the majority of Old Latin translations. Burton describes the text as presenting "numerous peculiarities of rendering, apparently motivated by linguistic purism."[149] However, we have found little evidence to support the notion that the *Vercellensis* is exceptional from the point of view of vocabulary and grammar, at least compared to the Old Latin manuscripts discussed so far. In Chapter V, we will go on to develop this point further in Chapter V where we discuss unique readings of the Vercelli manuscript. While it is not clear whether the *Palatinus* served as the

149 BURTON, The Old Latin Gospels, 21.

Vorlage of the Vercelli manuscript, the *Curiensia*, the *Veronensis* and the *Amiatinus* do exhibit certain similarities of style and semantic affinity with the *Vercellensis*. The manuscript certainly resembles the *Fragmenta Curiensia*, the *Palatinus* and *Bezae* in exhibiting many features of Classical Latin along with later development of Latin which already began in the first centuries of the common era. While the *Bezae* imitates early Classical Latin especially in its structure and word order, and while the *Palatinus* is largely consistent in employing morphological and phonological innovations (some already attested in Classical Latin), the *Vercellensis* vacillates between these two alternatives and thus conveys the impression of a text that is rooted in oral rather than written transmission. One noteworthy feature of the *Vercellensis* is the use of a literal, word-for-word translation technique which results in Latin which, though at times morphologically and syntactically somewhat unusual, does have near parallels in the *Palatinus* as well as in the *Bezae*. Another feature which deserves attention is the presence of word choices unlike those otherwise found in the Old Latin texts. As we have shown in Tables 6, 9, 10, 11, 12, 13, 16, 30–34, 44, and 56 above, these terms and semantic word fields may be considered: very early renderings of non-Christian nomenclature (see 4.1), often referred to as 'Afra' text-type; technical vocabulary reflecting the interest of an educated scribe or translator (4.1; 4.3); attempts to maintain and interpret rare Greek terms using similar Latin words. We next turned to a comparison with *Codex Bezae*, which showed that fragments from Chur have an especially strong tendency to reproduce certain readings from Greek codices and Bezae. We saw that these readings have been consistently homogenized in terms of their content, but not their wording, and that we hence cannot conclude with certainty that these readings in chapter 11 and 13 depend on either the Latin or the Greek column of the *Bezae*. Presenting a further stage, the *Codex Veronensis* shows some renderings which depend on textual interpretation as e.g. the use of *elisabet* instead of *maria* in Luke 1:46. Finally, the *Amiatinus* Vulgate manuscript does not have as many distinctive parallels with the *Vercellensis* as some scholars would have us believe, and its grammar and vocabulary exhibit a number of innovations not found in the *Vercellensis*.

5 The Language of the *Codex Vercellensis* (VL3) Luke

On the whole, we have no reliable information on when and where the translation of biblical writings from Greek into Latin began, nor do we know who assumed responsibility for the translation and how the work proceeded.[1] Congregations in Rome are often thought to be responsible for these translations, but this assumption ignores the fact that Romans retained Greek as their *lingua franca* until the third century. Clement of Rome, Ignatius of Ephesus, and Justin, for example, wrote in Greek. The earliest extant Latin translations are found in North Africa, and the first potential reference to the Old Latin translation occurs in the *Acts of the Scillian Martyrs*: even though the precise date of the composition of this work is unknown, the trial of the martyrs described in it took place in 180. The *Acts* mention the *libri et epistulae Pauli viri iusti* (12),[2] presumably the collected books and letters of Paul in Latin, which one of the defendants claims to own. As Christianity spread across the Roman Empire, Latin replaced Greek as the universal language of the church. There are two current views on how this process unfolded. One possibility is that an array of Latin Bible translations emerged simultaneously, usually uncontrolled by any church authority and frequently containing inaccuracies. However, since the mid-20th century, scholars have come to consider the possibility that there was a single initial translation rather than a multiplicity of versions.[3]

In any case, the Old Latin Bible text is transmitted in two ways, namely directly and indirectly. The *direct tradition* of the Old Latin Bible text of the Hebrew Bible and New Testament consists of 495 manuscripts designated in the current version of the Beuron list,[4] including the 49 known manuscripts of the Gospels and several fragments. The Gospel of Luke is preserved in 11 Old Latin manuscripts (VL2, 3, 4, 5, 6, 8, 10, 11, 13, 14, 17) and 10 mixed-text manuscripts (VL7, 9A, 11A, 12, 15, 27, 28, 29, 30, 35, 48) as well as 6 fragments (VL16, 21, 22, 36, 44).

---

1 It is not clear whether Tertullian's treatises can help us gain access to the text of the Old Latin Bible; see STUMMER, Einführung in die lateinische Bibel, 11–14.

2 RUGGIERO, Atti dei martiri scilitani; however, the meaning of "books and letters" is not entirely clear. One can also refer to Tertullian, though his references to biblical texts are inconsistent, and he may not have been working with a Latin Bible at all; for further details, see ROTH, "Did Tertullian possess a Greek copy or a Latin translation of Marcion's Gospel?," 429–467.

3 HOUGHTON, The Latin New Testament, 156.

4 GRYSON, Altlateinische Handschriften/Manuscrits Vieux Latins, 1–275 (vol. 1.1 Vetus Latina: Die Reste der lateinischen Bibel); IDEM, Altlateinische Handschriften/Manuscrits Vieux Latins, 300–485 (vol. 1.2 Vetus Latina. Reste der lateinischen Bibel).

https://doi.org/10.1515/9783111142531-006

The *indirect tradition* of the text of the Old Latin Bible includes quotations and allusions to the Latin Bible authors, which can be compared with texts from the Church Fathers. This indirect tradition is of particular interest in cases where correspondence between a church author's Bible quotation and the text transmitted in a manuscript of the Old Latin Bible can be identified. In this context, the most essential citations come from Cyprian, Bishop of Carthage († 258), whose letters and tracts (*testimonia, Ad Quirinum; Ad Fortunatum*) usually contain the first indication of the existence of Latin translations. In addition, Cyprians works also employ consistent biblical citation which very closely corresponds, for example, to the Gospel text found in the *Codex Bobbiensis* (VL1; not preserved for Luke).[5] Although there is no evidence that Cyprian himself was responsible for these early versions of the Latin Bible – he probably had little acquaintance with the Greek language[6] – the quotations nevertheless exhibit an attempt to render the original through word-by-word translation. However, like all writings in the Old Latin traditions, Cyprian's text was not standardised and was, therefore, subject to numerous modifications. Cyprian's vocabulary and translation techniques distinctly differ from those used in later versions of the translations. Nonetheless, the temporal and geographic classification of the texts often remains difficult. Even in cases in which we know when and where a manuscript originated, the question of its content's origin remains open.

By focusing on word analysis and the method of translation, investigations made in the 19th century[7] were able to identify two primary groups of Old Latin Bible texts, an 'African' or 'Afra' text type and a 'European' text type.[8] However, it is frequently difficult to achieve a rigid classification of the text families since the period during which Latin translations began to spread across the Christian world was long enough to allow for many mutual influences and diverse interactions between the different traditions, as seen in *Codex Palatinus* (VL2), *Codex Brixianus* (VL10) and *Codex Monacensis* (VL13), which offers a mixed text often resembling the Vulgate.[9] At any rate, the 'Europeanisation', might have begun with Cyprian of Carthage and continued with Hilary of Poitiers and Ambrose of Milan.

5 Cf. GRYSON, Répertoire general.

6 Cf. MICHAELIS, Introduction to the New Testament, 426.

7 VON SODEN, Das lateinische Neue Testament in Afrika; SANDAY, Studia Biblica, 234–239.

8 The terms 'Afra' and 'European' are very misleading but remain standard in the literature on the Old Latin Bible. A new set of labels is yet to be introduced. In any case, these terms should be taken as diachronic indications for the development of the Old Latin Bible translations rather than as merely geographical or dialectal distinction.

9 HOUGHTON, The Latin New Testament, 211; 216; 218.

We have already mentioned that the first Latin translations appear in the works of Cyprian of Carthage. Cyprian in turn inspired other Christian writers, such as the Christian poet Lactantius, born in Africa, and Juvencus, who produced a versified form of the Gospels. In this way, Cyprian's efforts were built upon by others in the fourth century. Numerous sources show that biblical books were available for use in churches as a part of worship and also for study in the houses of church members. As Christian centres became established throughout the Roman Empire, translations into Latin gained ground in North Africa and Italy. This occurred not only through the agency of Cyprian who corresponded with Roman clergy, and especially with the presbyter Novatian whose biblical references are close to the *Codex Vercellensis*,[10] but also through Marius Victorinus, Fortunatianus, bishop of Aquileia, Hilary, bishop of Poitiers, and Augustine of Hippo, whose *De doctrina Christiana* describes the biblical texts in Latin using the term Itala: in ipsis autem interpretationibus, *Itala ceteris praeferatur; nam est uerborum tenacior cum perspicuitate sententiae.*[11]

In examining Old Latin translations of the Bible,[12] one is faced with a complex of questions concerning the appreciation and classification of the linguistic features of these texts, both in relation to the social history of early Christianity and with respect to the post-classical development of Latin itself. In particular, one prominent question is: Does the Latin of the Latin Bible represent a 'special Christian language', or may it be described simply as 'Vulgar Latin'? If the latter is the case, what is the significance of this classification? Is Vulgar Latin merely a variety of Late Latin?

One of the central theses of 19th century research on the Old Latin Bible was that, from the very beginning, Christian communities developed a 'special Christian language', also termed 'translationese', characterised largely by its concern with lexical matters. This, for instance, was the view developed by Joseph Schrijnen and Christine Mohrmann.[13] According to this school of thought, the differences between the pagan and Christian worldviews required a major, lasting transformation of the language on the part of the converts.[14] Moreover, this new special form of Latin was neither literary nor vernacular, because it approached both registers at the same

10 MATTAI, "Recherches sur la Bible à Rome vers le milieu du IIIe siècle," 255–279.

11 August., *Doctr. chr.* 2.15.22; on the term Itala, see BURTON, The Latin Version, 168; HOUGHTON, The Latin New Testament, 15.

12 VINCENT, "Continuity and Change from Latin to Romance," 4 refers to the "periodization paradox" meaning that "the Latin usage seems to depart from classical usage."

13 Cf. MOHRMANN, Die altchristliche Sondersprache; SCHRIJNEN, Charakteristik des altchristlichen Latein; MOHRMANN, Études sur le latin des Chrétiens; IDEM, Collectanea Schrijnen, 335–336.

14 MOHRMANN, Die altchristliche Sondersprache, 18.

time. Despite harsh criticism from various sides, this thesis has endured for an astonishingly long time. By contrast, recent studies by Robert Coleman and David Langslow, to name but two scholars, have emphasised that scholarship on the Latin Bible ought to be based on a conception of the biblical text as an instance of "Bible Latin" and not of "Christian Latin."[15] However, apart from transliterations from Hebrew such as *satan* or *beelzebul*,[16] the *Codex Vercellensis* (VL3) and the *Fragmenta Curiensia* (VL16) (which are derived from the *Vercellensis*) contain only a few terms which may be considered characteristic of a special Christian language, however conceived. An example may help illustrate this point: although the *Codex Bezae* (VL5) uses the verbum *congregare*, which had come to assume a Christian sense in Late Latin, the *Codex Vercellensis* – as well as the majority of Old Latin witnesses – pointedly avoid this verb.[17] The most common loan-translations in Vetus Latina of this sort are probably *baptizare* (βαπτίζειν) or *euangelizare* (εὐαγγελίζειν). These terms are genuine neologisms which do not occur in classical literature. The term "Bible Latin" or 'special Christian language' applies only to such transliterated terms, but certainly not to the Old Latin Bible translations as such.

Recent studies have emphasised the proximity of the language of early Latin Bible translations to Vulgar Latin (*sermo plebeius*; *sermo vulgaris*),[18] an intermedi-

15 See for further details COLEMAN, "Vulgar Latin and the Diversity of Christian Latin," 37–52; IDEM, "The Formation of Specialized Vocabularies in Philosophy, Grammar, and Rhetoric: Winners and Losers," 77–89; Wright, ed., *Latin vulgaire – latin tardif VIII*.

16 In Luke 11:15, a passage located on a page missing in the *Codex Vercellensis*, Latin Bible translations attest to several possible transcription for the Hebrew name בַּעַל זְבוּב. In the Old Testament, this is primarily the name of a local deity of the Philistines which gave oracular sayings. The *Fragmenta Curiensia* do not give the transliteration *beelzebub* (so e.g. VL 6, 20, 27, 29, 51, vg.) but rather read *beelzebul* along with the *Codex Bezae* VL5 (see also VL7, 10, 11, 13, 17). Since the page containing Luke 11:15 is missing, the lexeme *satan* is also not found in the *Vercellensis*; however, the *Fragmenta Curiensia* offer a text close to the *Vercellensis*. The lexeme *satan* has a Semitic background (Hebrew: סָטָן; Aramaic סָטָנָא), where a transliteration of the Aramaic term should in fact read σατανᾶ. The lexeme *satan* is very rare in the Septuagint, which instead has διάβολος (see, for example, Zech 3:1–2; Iob 1:6–8, 12; 2:2–4; 2:6–6; 1 Chr 21:1) or διαβολή (Num 22:32); διάβολος is also preferred in Luke 4:2 and 8:12. Satan differs from *beelzebul* in that, in addition to "embodying" states of the soul, he also acts as an enemy of God or of human beings. The character of Satan furthers the dualism of the world; while elsewhere, Satan, like Beelzebub, acts demonically in human beings, in Luke, 'Satan' stands for any person through whom Satan exercises his power and his role as God's adversary. One thing is evident: along with the textual material in v.18, the reference to Satan is intended to disarm the accusations made against Jesus's exorcisms, which are shown to ultimately imply that Satan would act against himself by making such exorcisms possible. For further considerations on this point, see WEISSENRIEDER and VISINONI, *Fragmenta Curiensia*, chap. IV.

17 Cf. Preface, p. 5.

18 Cic. *Fam.* 9.21; *Epp. ad famm.* 9.

ate language spoken by the "middle classes."[19] On account of its diversity and even confusion, Vulgar Latin has sometimes been called a "shimmering mirage" concealing a submerged variety of language in "seismic areas where occasional eruptions reveal the intense subterranean activity."[20] A debate persists in the literature concerning whether Vulgar Latin always existed along with Classical Latin, as Roger Schöntag seemed to argue; following the theories of Roger Bruni (1435), Schöntag made a distinction between primary Latin learned from parents and secondary, formalized Latin learned in school.[21] Alternatively, varieties of Vulgar Latin may have undergone gradual changes in successive stages of language development occurring in various social layers, as James Adams argues.[22] Burton acknowledges the variations in the Old Latin Bible by noting that "the translators employ constructions which may be influenced by the Greek, but which are in accord with known tendencies in Vulgar Latin."[23] Recently, however, Kees Versteegh has argued in favour of discarding the term Vulgar Latin, referring instead to a variety of Latin used by a "population at large with varying proficiency in reduced forms of Latin, with children in mixed marriages growing up speaking a creolized variety of Latin. Only a select group of children from a small elite were granted access to Latin grammar and literature in formal education."[24]

Recent times have seen the development of terms 'Late Latin' and 'Later Latin'.[25] Late Latin is shaped by Christian literature coming from the East, which is in turn characterised by (lexical) Grecisms originating in the Greek-speaking world. In addition to such lexical innovations, Late Latin also underwent considerable morphological and syntactic changes, with usage of cases and moods not being (or no longer being) mastered by all speakers of Latin. In addition to the writers already mentioned, Boethius (ca. 480 – ca. 525), who built a bridge between Greco-Roman education and the Christian faith, as well as the grammarians Donatus and Priscian,

---

19 GRANDGENT, Introduction to Vulgar Latin, 3 makes a distinction between the language of the cultural elite, the rustic natives of the countryside and the lowest economic classes.

20 PALMER, The Latin Language, 149.

21 SCHÖNTAG, "Il dibattito intorno al volgare antico tra Leonardo Bruni," 553–572; IDEM, "Das Verständnis von Vulgärlatein," 117.

22 Cf. also ADAMS, Social Variation and the Latin Languages, 234; VÄÄNÄNEN, Introduction au latin vulgaire, 4, and HELMUT LÜDTKE, Der Ursprung der romanischen Sprachen, 401–402, who claims that "[d]er Sprachwechsel war abgeschlossen, als die letzten älteren, auf dem Lande ansässigen Unterschichtssprecher der betreffenden vorrömischen Sprache gestorben waren."

23 BURTON, Old Latin Gospels, 187.

24 VERSTEEGH, "The Ghost of Vulgar Latin," 218; Versteegh also refers to the role Roman soldiers played in transmitting Latin throughout the Roman empire.

25 WRIGHT, A Sociophilological Study of Late Latin; cf. MÜLLER-LANCÉ, Latein für Romanisten, 46 and throughout.

are of central importance in this respect. The majority of scholarly approaches to Late Latin tend to follow the *Comité International pour l'Étude du Latin Vulgaire et Tardif*, which is in turn substantially based on Wright's division of the development of Latin into two stages of Late spoken Latin, spanning the 3rd–5th and 6th–7th centuries. However, such registers of spoken language ranging across social classes and covering large geographic areas are more or less hypothesised on the basis of reconstructions, resulting in labels which designate language which may have been taught in monasteries and elite circles, though not spoken in the everyday domestic context.[26] In their influential contribution, Baldi and Cuzzolin narrowed down the era of Classical Latin to the period from 90 B.C. to the death of Augustus in 14 C.E., subsequently introducing further categories, namely "silver Latin" used in the period between 14 C.E. to 200 C.E. and "late Latin" used up to the year 600; the last category is in turn divided into three distinct phases corresponding to the third and fourth, fifth and sixth, and sixth and seventh centuries.

Even so, the central question of the date at which one may legitimately speak of an Old Latin Bible remains open. Our thesis is that the *Codex Vercellensis* provides a text which, rather than creating new words, represents tradition of using the existing lexical register while exhibiting only a minor degree of lexical and syntactical shift. In implementing this translation strategy, the *Codex Vercellensis* often strives to translate the Greek text as literally as possible and even attempts to imitate the Greek sentence structure. Nevertheless, we find some signs of Late Latin and a few terms which may be attributed to Vulgar Latin, i.e. the spoken language.

5.1 Phonetics and Orthography

The investigation of the phoneme inventory is central from the standpoint of linguistic development. The basic assumption involved in this investigation is that sounds used in a language system become codified over time. Thus, the phoneme inventory of a text can be taken as a rough approximation of the time when a text was written, except in cases where the writer attempted to emulate a classical style.

5.1.1 Phoneme Inventory

Classical Latin had five basic vowels, each of which existed in a short or long variant; these variants changed the meaning of the terms. In this way, several pairs of

26 LÖFSTEDT, Syntactica 1, 61ff.

words were identical except for the length of a single vowel. Examples include *lĕuis* ("light") and *lēuis* ("smooth"), *ŏs* ("bone") and *ōs* ("mouth"), and *sŏlum* ("ground") and *sōlum* ("only"). As the language developed, it experienced numerous changes in its vowel inventory, the most important of which was the loss of vowel quantity, a change which took place all over the Roman Empire.[27] Eventually, this quantitative opposition would disappear in the Romance languages, and it would be replaced by a qualitative distinction between open and closed vowels, producing a vowel system which distinguishes between four degrees of aperture:[28]

Table 1: Phonological differences between Classical Latin and the Romance languages

Classical	Ī	Ĭ	Ē	ĕ	ă	Ā	ŏ	Ō	ŭ	Ū
Romance	i	e /e/		e /ɛ/	A		o /ɔ/	o /o/		U

This phonological transformation is well attested in most Old Latin Bible manuscripts, since it is namely this change that is responsible for the typical orthographic confusion between *e* and *i* and *o* and *u*. In addition, in unstressed syllables, the change of *i* to *e* and of *u* to *o* can be traced back to the further mechanism of vowel reduction, a radical modification of the acoustic quality of the vowel. Thus, in many witnesses, especially in codices *Palatinus* (VL2) and *Bezae* (VL5), we find the spellings *disponsatam* for *desponsatam* (Luke 1:27), *pugillaris* for *pugillares* (Luke 1:63), *iohannis* for *iohannes* (Luke 1:64) etc.[29]

The Gospel of Luke as transmitted in the *Codex Vercellensis* offers some examples of these vowel changes, and especially of the confusion between *e* and *i*. It is important to note that previous editors disregarded many of these non-standard spellings, losing an assignment to the classification of Latin, Classical Latin – Vulgar Latin – Late Latin:

Table 2: Confusion between *e* and *i* in VL3 Luke

i instead of *e*	*e* instead of *i*
tristis for *tristes* (2:48, 18:23)	*palleum* for *pallium* (6:29)
pauperes for *pauperis* (6:20)	*diligites* for *diligitis* (6:32)
dicentis for *dicentes* (7:32)	*excepet* for *excepit* (8:40)

27 Cf. SPENCE, "Quantity and Quality in the Vowel-System of Vulgar Latin," 1.
28 Cf. VÄÄNÄNEN, Introduction au latin vulgaire, 30.
29 Cf. STONE, The Language of the Latin Text of Codex Bezae, 18.

ciuitatis for *ciuitates* (8:1)	*stetet* for *stetit* (8:44)
discensum for *descensum* (9:37)	*depondio* for *dipondio* (12:6)
	perdederit for *perdiderit* (15:8)
	saturare for *saturari* (15:16)
	contegerant for *contigerant* (24:14)
	ipsi for *ipse* (24:30)
	uidetes for *uidetis* (24:40)

Furthermore, we can detect the following instances of confusion between *o* and *u*:

Table 3: Confusion between the *o* and *u* in VL3 Luke

o instead of u:	*u* instead of *o*
com for *cum* (2:21, 3:18; 20:16)	*diabulo* for *diabolo* (4:1)
locrari for *lucrari* (9:25)	*muro* for *moro* (17:6)
paruolus for *paruulus* (10:21)	
abolsus for *auulsus* (22:41)	

An interesting case involving confusion between vowels is the reading *dixerunt* for *duxerunt* in Luke 2:22, which was not noted by the previous editors. The interchangeability of *i* and *u* is a not uncommon feature of Latin in all its historical periods and, in some cases, forms with both *i* and *u* are considered standard, so that *lubet* and *libet*, *optumus* and *optimus* are equally widespread in inscriptions. An instance of this phenomenon in the Latin Gospels is Luke 23:55, where both forms *monimentum* and *monumentum* are transmitted. Still, the orthographical confusion between *i* and *u* does not seem to be very frequent in the *Codex Vercellensis*, so that, in the case of *dixerunt* and *duxerunt*, this could simply be a matter of scribal error.

Figure 5.1: *dixerunt* for *duxerunt* in Luke 2:22 (341ª).

5.1.2 Diphthongs

A central aspect of the Latin phoneme inventory is monophthongization, that is, the transformation of diphthongs such as /oi/ or /ei/ into monophthongs like /u/. Originally, Latin had five diphthongs, *ou*, *oi*, *ei*, *ai* and *au*. The first three, which were monophthongized (*ou* and *oi* > *u*, *ei* > *i*) as early as around the third century B.C., survive only in archaic inscriptions.[30] At the same time, *ai* changed to *ae*, only to be later also monophthongized, resulting in *e*. This phonological evolution, which, according to the Roman polymath Varro (first century B.C.), commenced in the more rural areas of the Roman Empire,[31] was still ongoing when the first Latin Bible translations emerged. As a consequence, a certain degree of confusion between */ae/* and */e/* is a characteristic of all manuscripts of the Latin Bible.

In this respect, the orthography of *Codex Vercellensis* is oriented towards classical conventions, especially in comparison to other contemporary witnesses.[32] The monophthongization of */ae/* to */e/* is not yet common in the manuscript, so that we mostly find the regular spellings *daemonium* or *caelum* instead of the later forms

30 Cf. VÄÄNÄNEN, Introduction au latin vulgaire, 38.

31 Varro, *l.l.* 7.96: *obscaenum dictum ab scaena. eam, ut Graeci, et Accius scribit scenam. in pluribus uerbis a ante e alii ponunt, alii non, ut quod partim dicunt scaeptrum, partim sceptrum, alii Plauti Faeneratricem, alii Feneratricem. sic faenisicia ac fenisicia, ac rustici pappum Mesium, non Maesium, a quo Lucilius scribit Cecilius pretor ne rusticus fiat.*

32 So, to pick an example, in *Codex Bezae* (d, VL5), the interchangeability between *ae* and *e* is usual to such an extent that *ille* and *iste* serve as regular forms of the feminine plural. Cf. STONE, The Language of the Latin Text of Codex Bezae, 19.

demonium or *celum*. However, some words which should be written with /*e*/ are spelt with /*ae*/ instead, a phenomenon which may be considered a case of hypercorrection.[33] This last point is important because the oldest witnesses of the Gospels exhibit the same tendency: *Codex Bobbiensis* (VL1) transmits *baetus* for *beatus* in Matt 5:5–10, which establishes a relationship of *Codex Vercellensis* (*baeatus*) with the oldest witnesses of the Latin Bible, at least from the point of view of scribal habits. The translation with *beatus* became established only late in the Latin manuscripts of the Gospels, as Cyprian generally uses *felix*.[34] In any case, the orthographical peculiarities involving the confusion between *ae* and *e* in the Gospel of Luke are listed below:

Table 4: Confusion between *ae* and *e* in VL3 Luke

e instead of *ae*:	*ae* instead of *e*
bone for *bonae* (2:14)	*prophaeta* for *propheta* (3:4; 4:17; 16:16; 24:25)
pasche for *paschae* (2:41)	*-quae* for *-que* (2:10; 4:23; 9:10; 21:11)
galileae for *galilaeae* (5:17)	*baeatus* for *beatus* (7:23; 11:28)
preue for *praebe* (6:29)	*praecari* for *precari* (10:2)
relique for *reliquae* (24:10)	*loquentae* for *loquente* (11:37)
que for *quae* (ebenda)	*aepulari* for *epulari* (12:19; 15:24,29,32; 16:19)
	maedianum for *medianum* (22:12)
	uacrum for *uerum* (22:22)
	maemoratae for *memoratae* (24:8)

5.1.3 Consonants

Classical Latin employs 13 consonant phonemes, such as voiceless (p), voiced (b), and even nasal (m, n). In addition, there was an aspirated sound /h/ before /f/, /p/ or /t/. However, as Latin developed, its consonantal inventory underwent numerous sound changes. Many of them can be observed in characteristic orthographical confusions found in the manuscripts of the Latin Gospels. In what follows, we will analyze the changes which are most important for the Lucan text of the *Codex Vercellensis*.

33 Cf. Müller-Lancé, Latein für Romanisten, 89.

34 Cf. Cypr. *ad Quir.* 1.22: *beatus* A M *felix* W L Bv; 2.6: *beati* A *felices* W L M Bv; but 9.95: *felix* codicum consensus.

5.1.3.1 Confusion between *b* and *u* (*merger* of /b/ and /w/)

It is well established that the semivowel *u* was pronounced as [w] in Classical Latin (i.e., as *w* in 'wine'). Nevertheless, there is enough evidence that *u* was pronounced as a voiced bilabial fricative [β] even as early as the middle of the 1st century. In a receipt written on a wax tablet dating from 39 C.E. and recording a transaction undertaken by the grain merchant Gaius Nouius Eunus, we read the prepositional phrase *per iobe* [...] *et nume dibi* instead of *per iouem* [...] *et numen diui*.[35] These non-standard spellings suggest that original intervocalic [w] was already changing its character during the first years of the Empire.

This phonetic development is a common feature of Old Latin Bible manuscripts, in which we frequently find non-standard spellings such as *diauolus*, *parauola* and *uethleem* (*u* instead of *b*), or *bentilabrum*, *labare* and *oblibio* (*b* instead of *u*). Luke as transmitted in the *Codex Vercellensis* offers a few examples of this phonetic development:[36]

Table 5: Confusion between *b* and *u* in VL3 Luke

u instead of *b*	*b* instead of *u*
preue for *praebe* (6:29)	*nobit* for *nouit* (10:22)
	uibes for *uiues* (10:28)
	nobissimus for *nouissimus* (11:26; 14:9)
	dilubium for *diluuium* (17:27)
	abolsus for *auulsus* (22:41)

5.1.3.2 Confusion between *d* and *t* (Allography of Dental Occlusives at the End of Syllables)

In Latin, final consonants had a weak articulation and were thus subject to sandhi phenomena, that is, phonological changes at the end of syllables depending on the initial sound of the following word. This is particularly true for monosyllabic words, such as *ad* or *quod*, in which *-d* or *-t* were most likely devoiced before voiceless consonant. For this reason, inscriptions in Pompeii read *at quem* and *quot scripsi* instead of the more standard *ad quem* and *quod scripsi*.[37] At some point, *-t* began being written in other phonetical environments, even before vowels, as in

35 TPsulp 18.2.12–13. For further discussion, see ADAMS, "The Latinity of C. Novius Eunus," 231, and CLACKSON, HORROCKS, The Blackwell History of the Latin Language, 239.

36 For the future tense of verbs of the 1st and 2nd conjugation classes formed with *u* instead of *b*, cf. below, p. 221ff.

37 CIL 4.1860; 1880.

quit ego for *quid ego* or *set intra* for *sed intra.*[38] The same applies to the pair *apud* and *aput*, the second form being frequent, for instance, in the bronze law tablets from Heraclea Lucania (*Tabulae Heracleenses*, 45 B.C.), where we read *aput forum* or *aput exercitum* instead of *apud forum* or *apud exercitum.*[39] Quintilian's remarks on this matter suggest that the doublets *ad* vs. *at* and *apud* vs. *aput* coexisted since very ancient times, so that it is impossible to detect a strict distribution from the point of view of syntactic phonetics.[40] Several inscriptions confirm the phenomenon: in Pompeian testimonies, for example, QVOTSCRIPSI[41] stands instead of QVODSCRIPSI, ATQVEM[42] for ADQVEM, or ATPORTA[43] instead of ADPORTA.

The confusion between *-d* and *-t* caused by this phonological phenomenon can be seen in all witnesses of the Old Latin Bible as well. However, the text of the *Codex Vercellensis* Luke is again rather conservative in this respect. In the Gospel of Luke, we find only the examples listed below:

Table 6: Confusion between *d* and *t* in VL3 Luke

d instead of *t*	*t* instead of *d*
ed for *et* (2:46)	*aliut* for *aliud* (8:7)
capud for *caput* (9:58)	*aput* for *apud* (8:39; 9:57; 16:1; 19:7)
ad for *at* (10:34; 20:5; 22:25; 23:5)	*at* for *ad* (17:4)

Very similar is the allography of the bilabial consonants at the end of a syllable, which is not as common as the allography of dental occlusives. This phenomenon is also described by Quintilian,[44] and has led, in some manuscripts, to a certain degree of interchangeability between *b* and *p*, as seen, for instance, in the *Codex Bezae* (VL5), where we find *expropari* for *exprobari* (9:22), in the *Codex Palatinus* (VL2), where we read *lebra* for *lepra* (5:12), and in the *Codex Sangallensis 1395* (Σ), a Vulgate manuscript, in which *scriptus* is often spelt *scribtus*. In the *Codex Vercellensis*

38 CIL 4.1824; 2400.

39 CIL 1^2.593.

40 Quint. *inst.* 1.7.5: *illa quoque seruata est a multis differentia, ut ad, cum esset praepositio, d litteram, cum autem coniunctio, t acciperet.* Cf. VÄÄNÄNEN, Introduction au latin vulgaire, 69.

41 CIL 4.1860.

42 CIL 4.1880.

43 CIL 4.2013.

44 Quint. *inst.* 1.7.7–8: *quaeri solet, in scribendo praepositiones sonum quem iunctae efficiunt, an quem separatae, observare conveniat. ut, cum dico optinuit, secundam enim b litteram ratio poscit, aures magis audiunt p.*

Gospel of Luke, we find a rare example of such a change in 8:16, where the reading *suptus* stands for *subtus*. There is no case of the reverse change, i. e., of *p* into *b*.

Figure 5.2: *suptus* for *subtus* in 8:16 (390[a]).

5.1.3.3 Confusion between Aspirate and Non-Aspirate (Loss of Aspirates)

The non-articulation of *h* ([h]), described as vulgar, undoubtedly originated in rustic setting, as indicated by the doublets *harena* – *arena*, "sand," *hallec* – *allec*, "pickle," *hircus* – *ircus*, "buck," *holus* – *olus*, "vegetable," all terms from agricultural language. Throughout the Late Republic, there was already a general trend towards the dropping of *h* in spoken Latin, as the growing uncertainty about the standard forms testifies. Varro, for instance, despite his undeniable erudition, tried to derive *umor* from *humus*, even though the words are not connected etymologically.[45] The omissions and misplacing of the *h* are also attested in the inscriptions in Pompeii and elsewhere.

This phonetic development is a common feature of Old Latin Bible manuscripts as well, where we frequently find non-standard spellings, such as *abere*, *ora* and *ypocrita* (omission of *h*), or *habire*, *exhortare* and *hopus* (addition of *h*). Here, Luke as transmitted in the *Codex Vercellensis* offers only a few examples for this orthographical confusion, suggesting, once more, a carefully cultivated use of the language:

45 Varro, *l.l.* 5.23–24: *et dicitur humilior, qui ad humum, demissior, infimus humillimus, quod in mundo infima humus. humor hinc.* Cf. COLEMAN, "Dialectal Variation in Republican Latin," 15.

Table 7: Confusion between *h* and vowels in VL3 Luke

h instead of vowel	vowel instead of *h*
hob hoc for *ob hoc* (4:43)*	*ortus* for *hortus* (13:19)
horta for *orta* (6:13.48, 22:66)	
honeratis for *oneratis* (11:46)	
habraham for *abraham* (16:29)	

* But *ob hoc* in 19:44.

5.1.3.4 Assimilation and Dissimilation

In Latin, there is a general tendency to assimilate the consonant clusters arising from prefixation in prepositional compounds, as seen, for instance, in the reconstructions **disferre* > *differe* or **transdare* > *tradere*; in most cases, the posterior consonant exerts an influence on the preceding consonant. Nevertheless, the evidence found in ancient grammar works shows that the spelling and pronunciation of these words were relatively free.[46] By contrast, towards the Middle Ages, we detect a prescriptive tendency to assimilation, probably under the influence of Jerome's language.[47]

Accordingly, previous scholars of Latin Bible manuscripts have correctly observed the general rule that the earlier texts exhibit more dissimilated forms,[48] and this statement certainly also applies to the *Codex Vercellensis*. In Luke, most prepositional compounds are spelt in the dissimilated form, as shown in the following chart:

Table 8: Dissimilation and assimilation of prefixes in VL3 Luke

Prefix	Dissimilation	Dissimilation and Assimilation	Assimilation
ad-	*adclaudere* *adferre* *adficere* *adnuntiare* *adponere*		*accendere* *accipere* *apparere* *appellere*

46 Velius Longus, *De orthographia*, 61.16–62.2: *itaque Lucilius atque accurrere scribas d ne an c, non est quod quaeras atque labores.*

47 Beda, *De orthographia*, I (Giles, The Complete Works of Venerable Bede, 19): *imputribile per m scribendum, non per n, impono similiter et huiusmodi similia immitto, non inmitto, irrigo, non inrigo, impleo, non inpleo, immundus, non inmundus.* Cf. Turner, The oldest manuscript of the Vulgate Gospels, xliv.

48 Cf. Plater, White, A Grammar of the Vulgate, 44.

	adprehendere *adpropinquare* *adstare* *adsumere*			
con-	*conlaudare* *conligare* *conlocare* *conloqui* *conparere* *conplere* *conplures* *conprimere*			*committere* *comminuere* *commundare* *computare*
in-	*inpendia* *inponere* *inportabilis* *inpossibilis* *inridere*	*inmundus* (4:33, 6:18) *inplere* (2:21, 4:28, 7:1, 22:16.37)	*immundus* (4:36, 8:29) *implere* (1:20, 14:23)	*impellere*
ob-				*ommutescere*

5.1.4 Spelling of Hebrew and Greek Words

5.1.4.1 Confusion between *i* and *y*

A common confusion in Old Latin Bible manuscripts concerns the letters *y* and *i*. *y* was not an original member of the classical writing system, having been introduced in the post-Republican period in order to represent the Greek closed front rounded vowel υ (/y/) in loanwords; before that time, υ had been rendered by *u*.[49] The use of *y* in both spelling and pronunciation was thus disseminated among the most educated circles, but the sound apparently did not exist in colloquial registers, in which υ continued to be pronounced as /u/ or changed to /i/. As one might expect, this led to numerous cases of hypercorrection, so that Flavius Caper finds it necessary to censure the mistaken spelling of *gula* as *gyla*,[50] while the *Appendix Probi* insists on *crista, non crysta*. This explains non-standard spellings of Greek loanwords in several manuscripts of the Latin Bible, such as *elemosina* for *elemosyna* (VL2: Luke

49 This is attested by some early borrowings, e. g., *bursa* ("animal skin") from βύρσα, *buxus* ("boxwood") from πύξος, or *trutina* ("balance") from τρυτάνη. For further discussion, see ALLEN, Vox Latina, 52.

50 Cf. Flavius Caper, *De orthographia* 105.17–18: *y litteram nulla vox nostra adsciscit. ideo insultabis gylam dicentibus.*

12:33), *simphonia* for *symphonia* (VL2: Luke 15:25), or *gazophilacium* for *gazophylacium* (VL2: Luke 21:1).

In this respect, Luke in *Codex Vercellensis* again shows almost complete adherence to the more scholarly registers and exhibits a cultivated use of the language, containing only one example of a word spelled with of *i* instead of *y*, namely *sinagoga* for *synagoga* (Luke 8:49).

5.1.4.2 Confusion between *f* and *ph*, *k* and *ch*, *t* and *th* (Aspirated and Unaspirated Consonants)

In Classical Latin phonology, the digraphs *ph*, *ch* and *th* represented aspirated voiceless plosives, which were initially foreign to the language. These digraphs occupy a peculiar place in the orthographic system since they are not seen in the earliest inscriptions, making their first appearance only in the second century B.C. These digraphs subsequently came into widespread use and became a standard part of Latin orthography, primarily used in transcribing the Greek letters φ, χ and θ in loanwords containing those sounds: *p^{h}aretra* (φαρέτρα), *machina* (μηχανή, from the Doric form μαχανά), *cithara* (κιθάρα), etc.; before this time, the aspirates were normally transcribed using *p*, *c*, and *t*.[51] It is likely that educated Romans tried to reproduce these Greek consonants with more or less accuracy. Later, the Greek pronunciation of φ itself changed to /f/, causing much orthographic confusion between aspirated plosives and fricatives, as seen in most witnesses of the Old Latin Bible, for instance, *aphoteca* for *apotheca* (VL2: Luke 12:18), *cofinus* for *cophinus* (VL17: Luke 13:8), or *phascha* and *phasca* for *pascha* (VL8: Luke 22:1,11).

The text of the *Codex Vercellensis* is, once again, oriented towards classical conventions in this regard. In the Gospel of Luke, we find only the examples listed below:

Table 9: Confusion between aspirated and unaspirated consonants in VL3 Luke

f instead of *ph*	*p* instead of *ph*	*th* instead of *t*
profeta for *propheta* (6:23; 9:19)	*ampora* for *amphora* (22:10)	*theloneum* for *teloneum* (5:27)
profetizare for *prophetizare* (22:64)		
blaspemare for *blasphemare* (22:65)*		

* See the in-depth discussion in IV 3.

51 This is attested again by some early borrowings, e. g., *purpura* ("purple") from πορφύρα, *calx* ("limestone") from χάλιξ, or *tus* ("incense") from θύος.

5.1.4.3 Insertion of Euphonic Consonants

The early translators of the Latin Bible rendered foreign words from Greek and Hebrew according to their sense of the language, and in particular of the language as it was spoken in the less literary circles, where the Latin Gospels presumably first gained their currency. Therefore, many words in the New Testament could not be transliterated without some concession which would them conform to the Latin phonological system. In this context, translators commonly added consonants to make the sequence of sounds more tolerable for Latin ears (euphony).

One prominent example of such changes is the use of *thensaurus* for *thesaurus* (θησαυρός), found in almost all manuscripts. In the *Codex Vercellensis, thensaurus* is the regular spelling of the word (Luke 6:45; 12:33, 34; 18:22). Interestingly, the spelling with *n* after the first syllable is not limited to the textual tradition of the Latin Bible: in fact, this euphonic device is found much earlier, being very well attested also in epigraphic evidence from all periods.[52] Despite the wide diffusion of this form, the spelling was not accepted by most grammarians. The second century C.E. grammarian Flavius Caper, for instance, warns that *thesaurum sine n scribendum, non thensaurum et cetera.*[53]

5.1.4.4 Rendering of Proper Names

The transliteration of place and personal names presented a challenging task for Latin Bible translators and scribes, especially since the ancient Hebrew writing system lacked any kind of marking for vocalization and accents.[54] As a result, a

52 Cf., e. g., CIL 14.3679.

53 Cf. *De orthographia* 93.6. *n* before *f* or *s* seems to have become a mere nasal, lengthening the preceding vowel. Cicero speaks of this as justified by the ear and by custom, rather than by reason. Cf. Cic. *orat.* 48.159: *quid uero hoc elegantius, quod non fit natura, sed quodam institute? indoctus dicimus brevi prima littera, insanis producta. inhumanus breui, infelix longa. et, ne multis, quibus in uerbis eae primae litterae sunt quae in sapiente atque felice, producte dicitur; in ceteris omnibus breuiter. itemque composuit, consueuit, concrepit, confecit. consule ueritatem, reprehended. refer ad aures, probabunt. quaere, cur? ita se dicent iuuari. uoluptati autem aurium morigerari debet oratio.* Thus, many words were spelt with or without *n* before *f* or *s*, such as *frons* or *fros*, "foliage," or *quotiens* or *quoties*, "as often as."

54 The signs that were developed in the Middle Ages reflect three major vocalization traditions, which are usually referred to as Tiberian, Babylonian, and Palestinian. Each tradition had a distinctive vowel system: the Tiberian tradition distinguished the vowels /a/ (*pataḥ*), /ɔ/ (*qameṣ*), /e/ (*ṣere*) and /ɛ/ (*segol*); the Babylonian lacked a sign for *segol* and generally used a *pataḥ* sign where Tiberian had *segol*, suggesting that the Babylonian tradition did not distinguish between /a/ and /ɛ/, but only had the /a/; the Palestinian tradition did not distinguish between *pataḥ* and *qameṣ*, on the one hand, and between *ṣere* and *segol*, on the other, but rather had only /a/ and /e/ as vowel sounds. Cf. KHAN, The Tiberian Pronunciation of Biblical Hebrew, 12–13. At any rate, the translators of the

comparison of Latin Bible manuscripts reveals that translators and scribes frequently rendered the same proper names in a variety of forms. Furthermore, the transliteration into Latin was influenced by earlier transliteration into Greek, and also by the particular forms found in the source texts. For instance, in Luke 4:16, there are several Greek variant readings for the name of Nazareth, including Ναζαρεδ, Ναζαρετ and Ναζαρα, each with the corresponding renderings *Nazared* (VL5), *Nazaret* (VL3) and *Nazara* (VL2) in the oldest Latin witnesses. Finally, the transliteration process was also shaped by numerous attempts to make Hebrew names more acceptable for Latin language habits, which in turn depended on the above-mentioned phonological features of Late and Vulgar Latin. This process naturally engendered many irregularities, non-standard spellings, and orthographical inconsistencies among the scribes. For instance, two consecutive vowels in Greek transliterations of Hebrew names, and especially the repetition of the same vowel, seemed to be unbearable to Roman ears. Consequently, names such as Ἀαρών (אַהֲרֹן), Ἀβραάμ (אַבְרָהָם), Βηθλεέμ (בֵּית לֶחֶם) or Ἰσαάκ (יִצְחָק) were, at first, latinized either by dropping one of the repeated vowels or by inserting an *h* between them; the latter strategy suggests an awareness of the original Hebrew forms, since it preserves the letter *he* /h/ (ה) of the Semitic abjad. In this way, *Aron* and *Aharon*, *Isac* and *Isahac*, *Bethleem* and *Bethlehem* came to be found in all textual traditions of the Latin Bible.[55] However, where the successive vowels were different, as in Ἰωάννης (יוֹחָנָן; *Yo'chah'nahn*), the insertion of *h* was the only possible expedient, preserving the voiceless rough breathing letter ח /ħ/, creating the transliteration *Iohannes*, even though older witnesses, such as *Codex Palatinus* (VL2), also attest the reading *Ioannes*. In this context, an important case of consonantal euphony is the intrusion of *d* or *t* in the name *Israel* (יִשְׂרָאֵל), with *Isdrahel* or *Istrahel* being the spellings characteristic of the oldest manuscripts of the Latin Bible.[56] In Luke, the *Codex Palatinus* always reads *Isdrahel*, while the *Codex Vercellensis* varies between the older reading *Istrahel* (Luke 1:16,54; 2:25,38; 7:9; 24:21) and the newer *Israhel* (Luke 2:32,34; 4:27) or *Israel* (22:30).

Another observation is perhaps more obvious. The consistent hyphenation according to the rules of Classical Latin is remarkable and suggests that the scribe was proficient in Latin. An exception, however, occurs in a striking passage in Luke 2:4,

LXX, the Vetus Latina, and the Vulgate used Hebrew source texts which antedate the creation of these vocalization systems by many centuries.

55 Note that *Abram* was an impossible reading, for it would have invalidated the distinction between Ἀβραάμ (אַבְרָהָם) and Ἀβράμ (אַבְרָם), so that *Abraham* was the necessary alternative. Cf. TURNER, The oldest manuscript of the Vulgate Gospels, xxxviii.

56 Cf. RÖNSCH, "Worauf beruht die Italaform Istrahel?," 499.

where the scribe hyphenates the place name Nazareth as Nazar-eth rather than the expected Naza-reth. What seems like an error in light of Latin hyphenation in fact follows the rules of Hebrew syllabification: the toponym Nazareth may be etymologically traced to the Hebrew root נצר (*nṣr*) "to shepherd, to watch out for something," so that the hyphenation Nazar-eth at this point possibly follows the Hebrew.

Figure 5.3: Hyphenation Luke 2:4 (338[a]).

The following table shows a comparison of some proper names found in the Gospel of Luke:

Table 10: Proper names in different Latin authorities for Luke

Verse	VL2	VL3	VL16	VL5	VL4	A
1:13	*Elisabet*	*Elisabet*	---	*Elisabed*	*Elisabel*	*Elisabet*
1:24	*Elisabet*	*Elisabet*	---	*Elisabed*	*Elisabel*	*Elisabet*
1:36	*Elisabet*	*Elisabet*	---	*Elisabet*	*Elisabeth*	*Elisabet*
3:1	*Herodes*	*Herodes*	---	*Herodes*	*Herodes*	*Herodes*
3:19	*Herodes*	*Erodes*	---	*Herodes*	*Herodes*	*Herodes*
8:3	*Herodes*	*Erodes*	---	*Herodes*	*Herodes*	*Herodes*
13:28	*Isac*	*Isac*	*Isac*	*Isac*	*Isac*	*Isaac*
20:37	*Isac*	*Isac*	---	*Isac*	Deest	*Isaac*
3:9	*Abraham*	*Abraham*	---	*Abraham*	*Abraham*	*Abraham*
13:28	*Habraham*	*Abraham*	*Abraham*	*Abraham*	*Abraham*	*Abraham*
16:29	omisit	*Habraham*	---	*Abraham*	*Abraham*	*Abraham*

The text of *Codex Vercellensis* exhibits a certain consistency in the rendering of these names. The reason for the variation between names such as *Herodes* and *Erodes*, or *Abraham* and *Habraham*, is the confusion between aspirate and non-aspirate sounds (loss of aspirates), a development of the Latin sound inventory, rather than the variable rendering of Hebrew names. At the same time, it is possible to observe the typical spelling found in Old Latin Gospel texts, in which the repetition of the same vowel, as in *Isaac*, is not tolerated. In this way, the *Vercellensis* exhibits the typical feature of an Old Latin authority in the transliteration of Hebrew proper names.

5.2 Morphology

Some corrections contained in the manuscripts suggest that the translations from Greek use a Latin that conveys higher social prestige. Whether these corrections occur equally in all Gospels and in all witnesses is a subject for further comparative investigation. To date, there has been a lack of preliminary research in this regard.

5.2.1 Word Formation

When it comes to form, in Vulgar Latin, there is a tendency to prefer accented suffixes to unaccented suffixes.[57] Therefore, diminutives such as *anellus* or *uitellus* prevail over the classical variants *anulus* or *uitulus*. However, this process had not advanced very far in the Latin witnesses of the Gospels, so that we still observe the use of the more standard forms. For instance, in the Lucan text of the *Codex Vercellesis*, we find *nauicula* for πλοιάριον (Luke 5:3,7), *lectulus* for κλινίδιον (Luke 5:19), *uitulus* for μόσχος (Luke 15:23, 27, 30), *paupercula* for πενιχρά (Luke 21:2), or *auricula* for ὠτίον (Luke 22:49).[58]

At the same time, suffixation gave rise to terms which, though characteristic of the Latin Bible, were unknown in classical literature. The main example of a nominal derivation produced in this way is probably *peccator*, "male sinner,"[59] or *peccatrix*, "female sinner," both terms found in the *Vercellensis* Luke.[60] In the same way, verbs frequently used in the Latin Gospels are derived by adding the suffix *-izare*. The suffix itself is not native to Latin and has a Greek origin (-ιζειν), so that most examples are calques coined to render the specific religious vocabulary

57 Cf. VÄÄNÄNEN, Introduction au latin vulgaire, 84.
58 From the examples, the translators mostly used diminutives in an attempt to reproduce the Greek original. A major exception is παιδίον, always rendered with *puer* or *infans*, despite the alternative *puerculus*, found, e. g., in Apul. *Herb*. 25.3.
59 Cf. e. g. Luke 13:2; 15:1, 2, 7.
60 Cf. e. g. Luke 7:37, 39.

of the texts.[61] The most common of these loan-translations are probably *baptizare* (βαπτίζειν), *euangelizare* (εὐαγγελίζειν), *prophetizare* (προφητίζειν), or *scandalizare* (σκανδαλίζειν). These are genuine neologisms, and none of these terms are found in classical literature.

5.2.2 Allocation to Noun Declension Classes

One of the most noteworthy differences between Classical and Late Latin concerns the changes in noun inflection. Above all, a clear tendency towards the reduction in the number of declension paradigms can be observed: nouns of the consonant-declension, the *u*-declension and *e*-declension were especially affected and, in the course of time, came to be absorbed into the formally more predictable *a*- and *o*-declension. So, for instance, *nurus* and *socrus*, "daughter-in-law" and "mother-in-law," with their abnormal feminine ending in *-us*, were regularized into *nura* and *socra* (*a* instead of *u*) already around the first half of the fourth century C.E., as attested by the *Appendix Probi*. The same applies to many adjectives with two endings, which started being inflected as regular adjectives with three endings, as in *acrus, -a, -um*, "sharp," or *tristus, -a, -um*, "sad," instead of the more classical variants *acer*, *-e* or *tristis, -e*. Obviously, this kind of morphological reassignment was not instantaneous, and different forms could coexist side by side in a single text; further evidence for the transmission of older and newer inflections can also be found in the Romance languages, which often possess doublets deriving from both language registers.[62]

Moreover, confusion of grammatical gender emerged with the gradual disappearance of the classical neuter and the ensuing tendency to treat neuter nouns of the *a*-declension as masculine. Thus, in Petronius' *Satyricon* one can find forms such as *balneus* for *balneum* (bath), *fatus* for *fatum* (fate), *caelus* for *caelum* (heaven), *uinus* for *uinum* (wine), and so on. Most of these forms occur in the speech of Trimalchio, an uneducated and ostentatious former slave, and therefore function as satirical characterizations of a vulgar register of the language.[63] This development is also confirmed by Pompeian graffiti, which contain phrases such as *cadauer mortuus* for *cadauer mortuum* or *hoc locum* for *hunc locum.*[64] At the same time, due to the plural ending in *-a*, neuter nouns were frequently reanalyzed as feminine

61 Cf. p. 198f. and more often.

62 Cf., e. g., Spanish "acre" (from *acer*, -e) and "agro" (from *acrus, -a, -um*).

63 Cf., e. g., Petr. 39.5–6. For further discussion, see BOYCE, The Language of the Freedmen, 46–53.

64 Cf. CIL 4.3129, 6641.

nouns of the *a*- declension: in Classical Latin, for instance, *folia* was the regular plural to *folium* (leaf), but a synonymous form *folia*, generating a full *a*-declension paradigm (*foliae*, *foliarum*, etc.), is documented in Isidore's *Etymologiae*.[65]

In the Lucan text of *Codex Vercellensis*, these morphological changes are not yet dominant, and the system inherited from Classical Latin is very well preserved, especially in comparison with other contemporaneous witnesses, such as *Codex Bezae* (VL5). For instance, there is no single case of the variant reading *spirito* or *spiritos* for *spiritu* or *spiritus* (*o*-declension instead of *u*-declension), a common non-classical inflection in many Latin Bible manuscripts.[66] Nevertheless, a few morphological peculiarities are evident in the text:

Table 11: Allocation to noun declension classes in VL3 Luke

a-declension instead of consonant	*o*-declension instead of consonant	consonant-declension instead of *a* and *o*
iustificationis for *iustificationibus* (1:6)	*praesepio* for *praesepe* (2:12)	*austeris* for *austerus* (19:22)*
retia for *rete* (5:2.5)	*uaso* for *uase* (8:16)	
paupera for *pauper* (21:3)		

* But *austerus* in 19:21.

Moreover, in the case of Latin translations of the Gospels, we have to consider the influence of the Greek text on the reanalysis of noun genders. Two interesting examples may be found in the Gospel of Luke as transmitted in the *Codex Vercellensis* (1:20): in the sentence *non credidisti* (*credisti* VL8) *uerbis meis, qui* (VL5 *quae* cet.) *implebuntur* (VL4, A; *supplebuntur* VL2; *conplebuntur* VL5; *inplebuntur* VL8), the relative pronoun *qui* refers to *uerbis*, dative plural of *uerbum*, a neuter noun. From the perspective of classical Latin, however, we would here expect to find *quae* as the correct morpho-syntactical concordance, which is in fact found in most texts of this passage. But the manuscript has *qui*,[67] a plural masculine, the same reading found in *Codex Bezae* (VL5). In this case, the variant shows the reanalysis of *uerbum* as masculine (*uerbus*), clearly under the influence of the Greek text and the gender of the Greek terms (λόγος and οἵτινες, both masculine). The same applies to Luke 5:37:

65 Cf. 17.9.105: *denique ex una uirgula altitudine cubitali una scissa folia gignitur, res inplicata uelut pinna.*

66 Cf. *Codex Palatinus* (VL2), 11:26: *alios septe spiritos nequiores*; *Codex Bezae* (VL5), 2:27: *et uenit in spirito in templo.*

67 None of the previous editors took notice of this variant, reading *quae* instead.

again, codices *Vercellensis* and *Bezae* (VL5) use the pronoun *ipse* to refer to *uinum nouum*, in an agreement with οἶνος (masculine), not *uinum* (neuter); the other Latin authorities have the expected neuter (*ipsum* VL4, A; *ipsud* VL8).

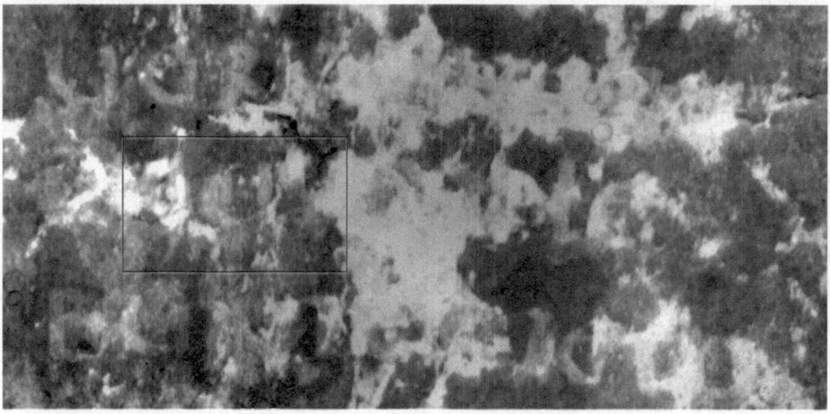

Figure 5.4: The variant *qui* instead of *quae* in Luke 1:20 (328[b]).

At any rate, non-standard gender agreements are not as common in the Lucan text of the *Codex Vercellensis* as they are, for instance, in the *Codex Bezae* (VL5).[68] Some instances in which the scribe of the *Codex Bezae* confounded noun genders in Latin, mostly under the influence of the Greek grammar, include *puer meum* (neuter) instead of *puer meus* (masculine) in Luke 7:7, *in quemcumque domum* (masculine) instead of *in quamcumque domum* (feminine) in Luke 9:4, and *castellus* (masculine) for *castellum* (neuter) in Luke 19:30. Therefore, the comparison of the two witnesses clearly shows that the scribe of the *Codex Vercellensis* Gospel of Luke had better knowledge of the gender system of Classical Latin.

The reduction of the ending *-ii* to a simple *-i* in the nominative plural and genitive singular of the nouns ending in *-ius* and *-ium* may also be considered a common orthographic peculiarity of the oldest witnesses of the Latin Bible. The shortening seems to be a feature of the vulgar language since it is condemned by the grammarian Velius Longus.[69] Further evidence that the reduction of *-ii* to *-i* was frequent in

---

68 Cf. Stone, The language of the Latin Text of Codex Bezae, 27.

69 Cf. *De orthographia* 57.6–8: *quaeritur item, Iulii et Claudii et Cornelii utrum per unum i productum an per duo debeant scribi. et ratio exigit ut huius Iulii per duo i scribamus, tam hercule quam huius pallii et huius graphii. non enim tantum in masculinis hoc quaeritur, sed etiam in neutris, quoniam id postulat ratio. nam quaecumque datiuo singulari o littera terminantur, o in i mutant*

colloquial registers can also be found in epigraphical sources, for instance, in several electoral endorsements (*programmata*), graffiti urging people to vote for a certain candidate, found scattered around Pompeii. The sponsors of these political posters were often referred to by their professions, so that one often reads *quactiliari*, "felt makers,"[70] *lignari*, "carpenters,"[71] or *pomari*, "greengrocers,"[72] instead of the expected forms *quactiliarii, lignarii, pomarii.*

The Gospel of Luke, as transmitted in *Codex Vercellensis*, displays many examples of the shortening of the nominative plural and genitive singular of the nouns in *-ius* and *-ium*. In this way, *fili* (Luke 2:48; 5:34; 6:22,35; 8:28; 16:8,25; 17:26; 18:38, 39; 20:34, 36) is much more common than its variant *filii* (Luke 5:10; 17:22), while *operari* (Luke 10:2; 13:27) is the regular form for *operarii*. It is important to note that these readings are often shared with *Codex Palatinus* (VL2) and *Codex Bezae* (VL5), which indicates the prevalence of non-standard inflections in older text types. At any rate, *Codex Bezae* (VL5) goes one step further and prefers shortened forms even for the dative and ablative plural. So, in Luke 7:35 and 11:13, we find *filis* instead of *filiis*.[73]

Another feature of Latin Bible manuscripts is the hypercorrection of the final *-m*, a phenomenon on the boundary between phonetics and morphology. It is not completely clear when the sound ceased to be pronounced as a bilabial nasal in this position, or even if it was ever pronounced at all. The grapheme itself does not appear in many of the earliest surviving Latin inscriptions: for instance, fragments of the sarcophagus of Lucius Cornelius Scipio's sarcophagus,[74] consul in 259 B.C., read *duonoro optumo fuise uiro* instead of the later *bonorum optimum fuisse uirum* and show, therefore, that a phonetic change may have been in progress already since the pre-classical times. The same is seen in inscriptions from the Republican and Imperial era, in which the final *-m* is also frequently omitted.[75] Moreover, the weak pronunciation of the final *-m* is confirmed by grammarians: both Quintilian and

manentibus ceteris litteris et sic genetiuum faciunt, ut maximo maximi, candido candidi. sic ergo in Iulio nihil aliud quam o debet mutari et in pallio, atque ut fiat Iulii et pallii. aeque hanc eandem rationem seruare debemus in nominatiuis pluralibus, etiamsi pauciores habeant syllabas in nominatiuo singulari. sed quoniam inuenimus et nominatiuum pluralem et datiuum eiusdem numeri esse, ut i littera terminatus nominatiuus adsumpta s faciat datiuum, detracta redeat rursus ad nominatiuum, ut in eo quod est boni bonis, mali malis, docti doctis, sic rursus e contrario, Iuliis et Claudiis si detraxeris s, relinquetur Iulii et Claudii.

70 CIL 4.7838.

71 CIL 4.960.

72 CIL 4.202.

73 For further discussion, see Stone, The Language of the Latin Text of Codex Bezae, 25.

74 CIL 6.1287.

75 Cf. CIL 1.168; 10.8249.

Velius Longus state that, although the letter is written at the end of a word, it is pronounced so faintly that it may be regarded as producing the sound of an entirely new letter, different from the *m* in other positions.[76]

At any rate, the omission of final *-m* blurred the distinction between the nominative, ablative and accusative singulars of nouns of the *a-* and *e*-declensions, and between the accusative and ablative singular of nouns of the consonantal and *u*-declension. This led to several hypercorrections in most Latin Bible manuscripts, for which the Lucan text of the *Codex Vercellensis* offers the following examples:

Table 12: Confusion of final *-m* in VL3 Luke

accusative instead of nominative	accusative instead of ablative
columbam for *columba* (3:22)	*causam fili* for *causa filii* (5:22)
est scripturam for *est scriptura* (4:21)	*eadem mensuram* for *eadem mensura* (6:38)
	uisam eam for *uisa ea* (7:13)
	adprehensa manum for *adprehensa manu* (8:54)
	ciuitatem illam for *ciuitate illa* (9:5)
	eadem ciuitatem for *eadem ciuitate* (18:3)

5.2.3 Verb Conjugation

Even though the tenses and modes of Classical Latin are preserved in the witnesses of the Latin Gospels, we can still observe some features of verbal morphology of Vulgar and Late Latin in these texts. These include the reduction of conjugation classes, the alignment of irregular forms, and the change of forms in the passive, all of which will be discussed in what follows.

76 Cf. Quint. *inst.* 9.4.40: *atqui eadem illa littera, quotiens ultima est et uocalem uerbi sequentis ita contingit, ut in eam transire possit, etiamsi scribitur, tamen parum exprimitur, ut multum ille et quantum erat, adeo ut paene cuiusdam nouae litterae sonum reddat. neque enim eximitur, sed obscuratur et tantum ut hoc aliqua inter duas uocales uelut nota est, ne ipsae coeant*; Velius Longus, *De orthographia* 54.1–5: *ingredienti mihi rationem scribendi occurrit statim ita quosdam censuisse esse scribendum, ut loquimur et audimus. nam ita sane se habet non numquam forma enuntiandi, ut litterae in ipsa scriptione positae non audiantur enuntiatae. sic enim cum dicitur illum ego et omnium optimum, illum et omnium aeque m terminat nec tamen in enuntiatione apparet.* For further discussion, see ALLEN, Vox Latina, 30–32.

5.2.3.1 Reduction of Conjugation Classes

On the whole, Classical and Vulgar Latin differ less in their verbal than in their nominal systems. Most tenses, moods and their functions are preserved, with only the synthetic passive being abandoned in favor of periphrases or reflexive constructions. Since this transformation took place from the sixth to the eighth century, it apparently did not affect the early Christian literature to a considerable state.[77] Nevertheless, other important changes occurred, many of which can be observed in Latin Bible manuscripts of all text traditions.

On the one hand, when the Gospels were being translated from Greek into Latin, the morphological changes in the verbal system had not evolved to the point at which the loss of postvocalic *-t* in the endings of the 3rd person can be detected; this is in contrast, for instance, to Pompeian graffiti, where we find phrases such as *quisquis ama ualia peria qui nosci amare*, for *quisquis amat ualeat periat qui nescit amare* ("whoever loves, may he be well, may he be lost, who ignores love").[78] The Lucan text of the *Codex Vercellensis*, however, transmits at least two examples of how this crucial development in the verbal system of the Romance languages was already in progress when the first Latin Bible translations were produced: in Luke 5:12 and 6:42, one reads *si uis, potest me mundare* ("if you want, you can cleanse me") for *potes me mundare* and *quomodo potest dicere fratri tuo* ("how can you tell your brother") for *potes dicere* – doubtlessly two cases of hypercorrection due to the progressive loss of *-t* in verbal forms, leading to a confusion between the 2nd and 3rd person singular of *posse*.

On the other hand, the vowel shift in Late Antiquity – particularly, the merging of short *i* with long *ē* – caused many spelling mistakes and non-standard variants in verb forms. Above all, there is much confusion between the endings *-es*, *-et* and *-is*, *-it*, giving rise to a number of ungrammatical forms in virtually every witness of the Latin Bible. For instance, the *Codex Vercellensis* renders ἀγαπᾶτε in Luke 6:32 with *diligites*, clearly an orthographic error for *diligitis* found in the other manuscripts. In this context, some morphological phenomena are difficult to categorize: for example, *sedet* for *sedit* (cet.), translating the Greek ἐκάθισεν in Luke 4:20, may be taken as a regular historical present used to render the Greek aorist; as an intended perfect, simply misspelled with *-et* because of the relative interchangeability between *-et* and *-it*; or even as an indication of a Greek original which had the

---

77 Cf. MÜLLER, A Chronology of Vulgar Latin, 74. For further discussion, see BURTON, The Old Latin Gospels, 180.

78 CIL 4.1173. Cf. HERMAN, Vulgar Latin, 41. Only a few traces of final *-t* remain in the Romance languages, notably in French, but not elsewhere. So, e. g., *venit*, "he comes" changes into "il vient" (French) against "viene" (Italian), "viene" (Spanish), "vem" (Portuguese), "vine" (Romanian).

present (καθίζει) instead of the aorist, but which has not survived.[79] The same applies to the translation of λαμβάνεις in Luke 20:21: whereas most witnesses seem to follow the Greek text and render the verb as *accipis*, the *Codex Vercellensis* reads *accipes* instead, and the *Codex Palatinus* (VL2) has *accipies*, the regular future form. Thus, *accipes* can be seen as an intended present, misspelled with *-es* for *-is*, or as an ungrammatical future instead of the correct *accipies*.

Figure 5.5: The variant *accipes* in Luke 20:21 (484[b]).

Furthermore, the progressive collapse of phonemic vowel length made the distinctions between conjugation paradigms almost impossible to sustain, causing the *e*- and the consonantal conjugations to grow closer together. For this reason, in some verses, it is not always easy to tell whether a verb is being used in the present or the future indicative. An example of this can be found in Luke 5:37, in the parable of the new wine in old wineskins. The Greek text tradition is uniform and offers three future forms in a row: ῥήξει, ἐκχυθήσεται, and ἀπολοῦνται. In the *Codex Vercellensis*, these are rendered with *rumpet* (VL2, 5, 8, A; *rumpit* cet.), *effunditur* (*effundetur* cet.) and, finally, *peribunt* (c. c.), where *peribunt* is the only form which can be unmistakably taken as future tense, since *rumpet* und *effunditur* may be taken for misspellings for *rumpit* and *effundetur*.

Despite these many inconsistencies, we may note that this kind of confusion between conjugations is not as prominent in the *Codex Vercellensis* as, for example, in the *Codex Bezae* (VL5): the *a*-conjugation, the most regular one, holds its own, and its forms are never mixed up with forms of other conjugations. Therefore, in

79 The last of these hypotheses is unlikely since Luke rarely uses the historical present.

the majority of cases, when confusions do occur, verbs of the consonantal conjugation tend to change to the *e*-conjugation:

Table 13: Allocation to verb conjugation classes in VL3 Luke

e-conjugation instead of consonantal	*i*-conjugation instead of *e*
resurgent for *resurgunt* (7:22)	*respondite* for *respondete* (20:3)
tollet for *tollit* (8:12)	*florient* for *florebunt* (21:31)
recipient for *recipiunt* (8:13)	
dicet for *dicit* (18:6)	
accipes for *accipis* (20:21)	
uiuent for *uiuunt* (20:38)	
percutebant for *percutiebant* (20:64)	
percutentes for *percutientes* (23:48)	

5.2.3.2 Forms of the *i*-Conjugation

Solecistic forms in the *i*-conjugation are quite characteristic of the *Codex Vercellensis* Luke. This includes readings such as *operiet* for *operit* (Luke 8:16, gr. καλύπτει), *facet* for *faciet* (Luke 18:8, gr. ποιήσει) or *inuenibant* for *inueniebant* (Luke 19:48, gr. εὕρισκον). Equally characteristic are compounds of *ire* conjugated as verbs of the *i*-class in indicative imperfect and future. Their tense indicator is often *-ie-* instead of the regular *-b*, even though they seem to be interchangeable with the more classical conjugation patterns. In this way, one can find in the same sentence both forms, for instance in Luke 21:33, where *caelum et terra transiet, uerba autem mea non praeteribunt* is found. These non-standard forms are not restricted to any particular text tradition, but they are certainly more frequent in older witnesses, such as in codices *Palatinus* (VL2) and *Bezae* (VL5). The following examples may be found in Luke: *transiebat* for *transibat* (Luke 17:11, gr. διήρχετο), *perietis* for *peribitis* (Luke 13:3, 5, gr. ἀπολεῖσθε), *periet* for *peribit* (Luke 21:18, gr. ἀπόληται), *transiet* for *transibunt* (Luke 21:32, 33, gr. παρελεύσονται).

Figure 5.6: Different future conjugation forms for the compounds of *ire* in the same sentence in Luke 21:33 (494[a]).

5.2.3.3 Forms of the Future of *esse* and *posse*

The use of the third person plural of *esse* and *posse* ending in *-erint* instead of *-erunt* are very typical for the Lucan text in the *Codex Vercellensis* as well. These new constructions are analogous to the future perfective and can be found sporadically in later inscriptions.[80] The *Codex Vercellensis* transmits many examples of this irregularity, though interestingly only in Luke (4:7; 13:24; 17:34; 21:25) and Mark (10:31; 11:24; 13:8,19,25), the last two Gospels contained in the manuscript. This text variant is rather unusual in Latin witnesses of the New Testament: *poterint* instead of *poterunt* is found, for example, in the *Codex Amiatinus* (Luke 20:36: *neque enim mori poterint**) and *Bezae* (Luke 21:15: *et sapientiam ad quam non poterint contradicere*, with A).

80 Cf. CIL 13.1668: *Sed ne provinciales quidem, si modo ornare curiam poterint, reiciendos puto.*

Figure 5.7: Forms of *erint* in Luke (17:34 [464[a]]) and Mark (11:24 [602[b]]).

From the examples given above, it becomes clear that the verbal morphology in the *Codex Vercellensis* Luke resembles the other Latin authorities. However, two aspects may be emphasized: first, the innovative verb forms of the *i*-conjugation are more common in the earlier text traditions, a fact which reinforces the relation between the text of the manuscript and witnesses such as the codices *Palatinus* (VL2) and *Bezae* (VL5). Moreover, the fact that the third person plurals of *esse* and *posse* ending in *-erint* instead of *-erunt* are only found in Luke and Mark suggests that the composition of these Gospels differs from that of Matt and John. This hypothesis will be reinforced by some further evidence when we come to analyze the semantic peculiarities of the text.[81]

Our analysis of the morphological peculiarities of the text reveals that the *Codex Vercellensis* contains numerous innovations indicative of later stages of Latin language development. When it comes to the morphology of nouns, this process is not yet very far advanced, with the system inherited from Classical Latin still being well preserved, especially in comparison with other authorities, such as *Codex Bezae* (VL5). Nevertheless, the verbal morphology demonstrates some important innovations, in particular the emergence of new forms for the verbs of the *i*-conjugation on the one hand and of new forms for the future tense of *esse* und *posse* on the other.

5.3 Syntax

So far, we have seen that Classical Latin underwent changes in its pronunciation and in the decay of its word endings. This made it more difficult to identify the relations between elements of a sentence, which in turn lead to the establishment of a standard word order, subject – predicate – object, as well as to changes in pro-

81 Cf. 5.4, pp. 245–275.

nouns. We have already noticed that the *Codex Vercellensis* more often follows the Greek wording, while at the same time emphasizing the orality of the language. In what follows, we will attempt to understand the relation in which the Codex stands with respect to changes of Latin.

5.3.1 The Application of the Cases

As stated above, the vowel shifts occurring in the vulgar language caused the merger of case endings in nominal declensions.[82] Thus, around the fifth century, the number of cases had already been dramatically reduced, a development which explains most inconsistencies in the use of cases in textual sources. The case system collapsed at last, and Latin gained the main features of an analytic language, depending more and more on particles, prepositions, and word order to convey the different relationships that had been previously marked through the wide range of morphosyntactic inflections.

Many of these changes can be traced back to as early as the second century B.C., and evidence notably abounds in the Roman Comedy. The frequency of prepositional phrases in the plays of Plautus and Terence suggests that the transformations in the case system, which would eventually prevail in Late Latin, are related to colloquial registers of the language. In this way, the genitive and all its functions began to be supplanted by periphrases with *de* and the ablative.[83] Genitive forms continued to be used in a few exceptional cases, including some pronouns, certain fossilized expressions, and proper names, for instance, the French "jeudi," derived from Vulgar Latin *iouis die*, "Jupiter's day." The same applies to the dative case, which continued to be used longer than the genitive but would also be substituted by prepositional phrases with *ad* and the accusative.[84] Since ancient times, the accusative had alternated with other cases, especially with the ablative, to express distance, duration, price, or place. In this way, Caesar writes *milia passuum ab ipsius castris octo*,[85] "eight thousand paces away from his own camp," but some lines later *milibus passuum sex a Caesaris castris*,[86] "six thousand paces away from Caesar's camp,"

82 Cf. above, 5.2.2, pp. 214–223.

83 Plaut. *Persa* 4.3: *iam hodie alienum cenabit, nil gustabit de meo* for *nil gustabit mei*; Ter. *Heaut.* 4.1.39: *si moreretur, ne expers partis esset de nostris bonis* for *ne expers partis esset nostrorum bonorum.*

84 Plaut. *Capt.* 1019: *ego hunc ob furtum ad carnuficem dabo*; Plaut. *Truc.* 4.1.4: *ita ad me magna nuntiauit Cyamus hodie gaudia.*

85 Caes. *B. G.* 1.21.1.

86 Caes. *B. G.* 1.48.1.

without any difference in meaning. Towards the end of the imperial period, because of the loss of final *-m* and the merger of *ō* and *ŭ*,[87] the morphological differences between the accusative and the ablative disappeared altogether, generating the two-case-system typical of modern Romance languages (*casus rectus* and *casus obliquus*). Finally, the vocative, which was identical with the nominative for most words in Classical Latin, was entirely abandoned, except perhaps in a few set phrases, such as *mi domine*. Words which had a separate vocative form tended to lose it, and we see vocatives in *-us* instead of *-e* occur in Plautus, Horace, and Livy;[88] *meus* instead of *mi* is very common as well, for instance, in Matt 27:46, where Jesus's exclamation on the cross θεέ μου, θεέ μου, ἵνα τί με ἐγκατέλιπες is typically rendered into Latin with the phrase *deus meus, deus meus, ut quid me dereliquisti* (my God, my God, why have you forsaken me?).[89]

These syntactical developments had not advanced very far in the witnesses of the Latin Gospels, and the main functions of the classical case system are overall well preserved in the texts transmitted by the surviving manuscripts. The employment of prepositional phrases with *ad* with the accusative rather than an indirect object in the dative is probably the most common innovation found after *uerba dicendi*. Therefore, the recurrence of variant readings such as *haec illo loquente ad eos* instead of *haec illo loquente eis* (Matt 9:18), *dicunt ad Iesum* instead of *dicunt Iesu* (Mark 11:33), *et respondit ad illum* instead of *et respondit illi* (Luke 4:4), and *quem locutus sum ad uos* instead of *quem locutus sum uobis* (John 15:3) is a pattern observed in every manuscript of the Latin Gospels and cannot be considered a feature of any single text tradition. It is also important to note that these variants occur independently from the underlining Greek text. In the examples mentioned above, only Luke has a prepositional object (καὶ ἀπεκρίθη πρὸς αὐτὸν ὁ Ἰησοῦς). At the same time, there seem to be no instance of the periphrastic construction with *ad* and the accusative taking the place of the classical dative after *uerba dandi* in the Latin tradition. For example, no prepositional alternative to the indirect object has been transmitted for readings such as *da nobis hodie* (Matt 6:11), *et dedit illis potestatem curandi* (Mark 3:15), *porrexerunt ei partem piscis* (Luke 24:42), or *quae*

---

87 Cf. above, 5.2.2; Table 12.

88 Cf. Grandgent, An Introduction to Vulgar Latin, 43. For further discussion, see Rauk, "The Vocative of Deus and its Problems," 138–149.

89 Most Gospel manuscripts do not use a *nomen sacrum* (θ̅ε̅) for θεέ here, only א, A, D, L, Δ, and 69. In Mark 15:34, one finds θεός μου, θεός μου: the nominative functions as a vocative and is always written as *nomen sacrum* (θ̅ς̅). Latin witnesses, such as *Codex Vercellensis* and *Codex Bezae*, also have the *nomen sacrum* (d̅s̅) in both Gospels. For further discussion, see Prior, "The use and nonuse of *nomina sacra*," 161–165.

dedit mihi pater (John 5:36), where later formulations would read *ad nos*, *ad illos*, *ad eum* or *ad meum*.

Nevertheless, several deviations from classical syntax may be detected in the use of cases as verbal complements. The most frequent is the use of the genitive instead of the ablative, probably under the influence of the Greek text; it is noteworthy that this is a major feature of the Old Latin Gospels, since the Vulgate prefers to use the genitive rather than the ablative, according to a more classical usage. For instance, Matt 6:32 has χρῄζετε τούτων ἁπάντων ("you have need of all these things"). In Old Latin manuscripts, the phrase is typically rendered with *horum omnium indigetis*, whereas the Vulgate reads *his omnibus*. However, it should be clear that this is not a mechanical process: in Matt 20:25, Mark 10:42 and Luke 22:25, *dominari*, normally followed either by the preposition *in* and the ablative or simply the ablative, takes a genitive in almost every manuscript of the Old Latin tradition. The resulting variant, *dominantur eorum* ("they rule over them"), for (κατα)κυριεύουσιν αὐτῶν,[90] is retained by the Vulgate text, except in Mark, where one finds *eis* instead of *eorum*.

Further examples of such deviations in the use of cases as verbal complements include many non-standard constructions with the accusative, which demonstrate the early translators' repeated attempt to align the Latin text to Greek syntax. In this way, one will often come across renderings such as *benedicere aliquem* (εὐλογεῖν τινα) instead of *benedicere alicui* ("to bless someone"),[91] *nocere aliquem* (βλάπτειν τινά) for *nocere alicui* ("to harm someone"),[92] *petere aliquem* (αἰτεῖν τινα) instead of *petere ab aliquo* ("to ask someone").[93] Once again, such agreements were not completely unknown in Latin and may be observed in the Roman Comedy: Plautus, for instance, writes *uos amo, uos uolo, uos peto atque obsecro* ("I love you, I want you, I ask you and implore") instead of *ab uobis peto*.[94] But this kind of formulation is meant to be mimetic, reproducing low-register varieties of conversational

90 The text of Luke has the simplex. In the same way, Tert. *Cult. Fem.* 1.1: *ille dominabitur tui* (in reference to Gen. 3:16; *ipse dominabitur tui* vg *tibi* vg^{O}, αὐτός σου κυριεύσει); Tert. *De pud.* 17: *mors non iam dominetur eius* (in reference to Rom 6:9; *mors illi ultra non dominabitur* vg, θάνατος αὐτοῦ οὐκέτι κυριεύσει).

91 Cf., e. g., Luke 1:64, *benedicens deum* (*dominum* VL2, 14^{1}, εὐλογῶν τὸν θεόν); Luke 2:28, *benedixit deum* (*dominum* VL3, εὐλόγησεν τὸν θεόν), Luke 2:34, *benedixit illos* (*eos* VL2, 5, 13, 14, 26; *illis* VL15 vg, εὐλόγησεν αὐτόυς).

92 Cf. Mark 16:18, *non illos nocebit* (*illis* VL13, *eos* VL15 vg, *eis* VL11 vg^{Φ} vg^{c}, οὐ μὴ αὐτοὺς βλάψῃ), Luke 4:35, *illum nocuit* (*eum* VL2, 5, 14, *illi* VL13 vg^{C}, βλάψαν αὐτόν).

93 Cf. e. g., Matt 6:8, *petatis eum* (*illum* VL2; *ab eo* VL3, 4, 6, 7, 15, τοῦ ὑμᾶς αἰτῆσαι αὐτόν), John 16:23, *si quid petieritis patrem* (*a patre* VL 4, 6, 8, 15, ἄν τι αἰτήσητε τὸν πατέρα).

94 Plaut. *Curc.* 1.2.55.

Latin, and it is rarely found in the standard literary language of the writers of the late Republic and early Empire. At any rate, when it comes to the Latin Gospels, the more authoritative constructions with dative or ablative are sometimes transmitted as variant readings. This is the case especially in later manuscripts or in Vulgate witnesses, which seems to indicate a subsequent effort to improve the text in a more classicizing and erudite manner. This tendency may be illustrated by an exceptional variant reading found in the *Codex Vercellensis*, namely *solo* in Luke 4:8 (353^b):

The correct reading of the manuscript was only possible through the TX-images of the passage. This special reading can be interpreted as one of two forms: one possibility is that the ablative *solo* stands here for the more grammatical dative *soli*. Another hypothesis is that *solo* is the result of influence of non-standard registers since the form *solo* for the dative instead of *soli* is found in some Classical inscriptions.[95]

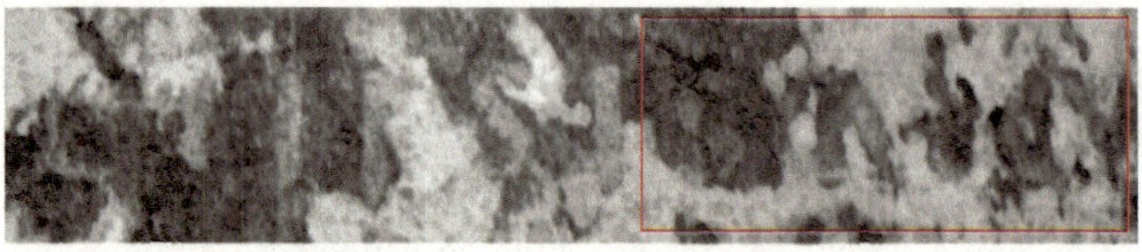

Figure 5.8: The reading *et ipsi solo* instead of *et ipsi soli* in Luke 4:8 (353^b).

While these phenomena can all be taken for common features of the Latin Gospels, the text of Luke in *Codex Vercellensis* exhibits a peculiarity in case syntax, namely the use of genitives instead of ablatives after comparative adjectives. The two instances where this occurs are unique readings, that is, they are not found in other witnesses of these verses. Again, the construction suggests an attempt to adjust the Latin wording to the Greek original, despite the fact that this entails rendering the phrase using the *genitivus comparationis*, a syntactical relation unusual for Classical Latin: Luke 11:26 has *peiora priorum* (χείρονα τῶν πρώτων) instead of *peiora prioribus* ("worse than the first"), and 21:3 reads *plus omnium* (πλεῖον πάντων) for *plus omnibus* ("more than all of them"). It is true that the use of the genitive instead of the ablative after comparative adjectives is not entirely absent from ancient Roman literature. Plautus writes *non ego nunc parasitus sum, sed regum rex regalior* ("I am no parasite now, but a king kinglier than kings"),[96] Ennius formulates *mater*

95 Cf. CIL 14.2977 and Inscr. Orell. 2627.
96 Plaut. *Capt.* 825.

optumarum multo mulier melior mulierum ("the mother, a woman better than the best of women").[97] These examples are, however, exceptions, and the *genitivus comparationis* becomes more frequent in Latin Bible translations, so that one may assume that the language of the Gospels decidedly favored this grammatical construction.[98] Consequently, it is not surprising that the new function of the Latin genitive is so commonly found in the bilingual *Codex Bezae* (VL5) which, in contrast to the other manuscripts, reads *et ecce plus ionae hic* ("someone greater than Jonah is here") for *quam iona* (*ionas* VL3, 4, 12, καὶ ἰδοὺ πλεῖον Ἰωνᾶ ὧδε) in Matt 12:41, *plura signa faciet quorum* ("he will do more signs than those") instead of *faciet quam quae* (πλείονα σημεῖα ποιήσει ὧν) in John 7:31, and *omnium maior est* for *maius omnibus est* (*maius est omnibus* VL2, 3, 14, πάντων μεῖζόν ἐστιν) in John 10:29.[99] In the case of Luke 11:26, the *genitivus comparationis* proves to be of particular interest, especially in reference to the synoptic passage in Matt 12:45, where all Latin manuscripts, including the *Codex Veronensis* (VL4) and the *Codex Vercellensis* itself, have either *peiora prioribus* or *peiora magis quam priora*. This means that the reading *peiora priorum* in Luke 11:26, shared exclusively with the *Fragmenta Curiensia* (VL16), not only represents a singular variant in the whole Latin tradition, but also indicates that the *Codex Vercellensis* translation of Luke is more literal than that of Matt.

5.3.2 The Use of Pronouns

5.3.2.1 The Use of Personal and Demonstrative Pronouns

There is a notorious looseness and variety in the rendering of pronouns, and especially of demonstratives, throughout all manuscripts of the Latin Gospels, including the Vulgate text. Many instances show that *hic* – *iste* – *ille* – *is* and their forms were often employed in the same context to refer to the same person without any distinction in meaning, a clear indication of the weakening of demonstratives and of radical departure from their classical use. So, in Luke 4:9, the Vulgate offers *et duxit illum in Hierusalem et statuit eum supra pinnam templi et dixit illi* ("and he brought him to Jerusalem, and set him on the pinnacle of the temple, and said to him"), where *illum* – *eum* – *illi* all refer to Jesus, who is being tempted by the Devil. This kind of variation seems to be even more impressive if one considers that the two demonstratives used here, *ille* and *is*, are the equivalents of a single Greek pronoun,

97 Enn. *Trag.* 41 R^{2-3}.

98 Cf. WÖLFFLIN, "Der Genetivus comparationis und die präpositionalen Umschreibungen," 120.

99 For more on these and other examples, cf. STONE, The Language of the Latin Text of Codex Bezae, 35.

αὐτός. Furthermore, one finds a considerable number of corrections of these demonstratives in the manuscripts, which serves as evidence of the difficulties translators, scribes and revisors had in rendering them properly. A few examples from the Gospel of Luke will suffice to illustrate the point: Luke 20:16, ἐλεύσεται καὶ ἀπολέσει τοὺς γεωργοὺς τούτους, *ueniet et perdet colonos illos* ("he will come and destroy these farmers") *istos* VL2 corr. 15; Luke 22:63, ἐνέπαιζον αὐτῷ, *inludebant illum* ("they mocked him") *eum* VL2 corr. 17; Luke 24:17, εἶπεν πρὸς αὐτούς, *ille autem dixit ad eos* ("but he said to them") *illos* VL2 corr. 2. Several manuscripts also commonly mark alternative readings by means of *uel* (or), for example the *Codex Gatianus* (VL30), Luke 13:23, where the variant reading *ait autem ei uel illi* is found.

The confusion is mainly due to the complete disruption of the three-fold deictic system of Classical Latin, based on the contrast between *hic* – *iste* – *ille* and anaphoric *is*. Roughly speaking, the Classical system posited a spatial and temporal correlation between *hic* and the first person (close to the speaker, proximal, "here"),[100] *iste* and the second person (close to the person spoken to, medial, "there"),[101] *ille* and the third person (close to the person or thing spoken about, distal, "over there").[102] The pronoun *is*, on the other hand, had a non-specific use and could assume the functions of the missing third person pronoun.[103] Therefore, contrast was an important factor in maintaining the force of these demonstratives. Furthermore, it is significant that, in situations requiring sharp spatial or temporal distinctions, the classical language had recourse to the two extremes *hic* and *ille*. Hence, Cicero writes: *sed hoc commune uitium, illae Epicuri propriae ruinae*[104] ("this error is common to them, these are the ones which do ill to Epicurus"), where *hoc* refers to the errors which have just been pointed out and *illae* to the errors which are yet to be stated. Moreover, we may add two pronouns which are also frequently confused with *hic* – *iste* – *ille* – *is* in manuscripts of the Latin Gospels: *idem*, the identity pronoun, meaning "the same,"[105] and *ipse*, an emphatic or intensifier demonstrative, meaning "he, not anyone else."[106]

---

100 Cf. Ter. *An.* 2.1.10: *tu si hic sis, aliter sentias.*

101 Cf. Ter. *Heaut.* 4.1.36–37: *at istos rastros interea tamen adpone.*

102 Cf. Cic. *Brut.* 132: *iam Q. Catulus non antiquo illo more, sed hoc nostro, nisi quid fieri potest perfectius, eruditus.*

103 Cf. Caes. *B. C.* 3.39.1: *oppido Caninus legatus praeerat, is naues nostras reduxit.*

104 Cic. *fin.* 1.18.

105 Cf. Cic. *off.* 1.19.1: *alterum est uitium, quod quidam nimis magnum studium multamque operam in res obscuras atque difficiles conferunt easdemque non necessarias.*

106 Cf. Cic. *Att.* 9.6.3: *de hac re litterae L. Metello tribuno pl. Capuam adlatae sunt a Clodia socru quae ipsa transiit.*

It is likely that these distinctions disappeared from spoken language very early, as may be seen, for instance, in Pompeian inscriptions from the first century.[107] *is* clearly loses ground before *hic*, and even Cicero prefers *hoc est* to *id est*.[108] At the same time, *hic* was replaced by *iste* as the demonstrative of the first person,[109] and would subsequently be completely lost, surviving in Romance languages only as the neuter *hoc* grammaticalized to adverbs or conjunctions.[110] *ille*, in turn, inherited most of the functions of *is* and came to be used as a non-specific demonstrative. This process resulted in the emergence of the personal pronouns of the third person, while adjectival forms produced the definite articles of Romance languages.[111]

The weakening of the deictic force of demonstratives may also be inferred from the fact that many texts composed at this time exhibit an exaggerated use of participles such as *praedictus*, *supradictus* (all meaning, essentially, "aforesaid"), which mean little more than "this" or "that" and function as substitutes for the demonstratives. In the sixth century, Gregory of Tours, for instance, writes *erat autem beatissimus Anianus in supradicta urbe episcopus*[112] ("blessed Anianus was bishop in that city"), where one might have simply expected *in illa urbe*. Such formulations show that the former demonstrative adjectives were felt to be no longer specific enough and hence required paraphrase. Reconstructed forms also suggest that the inherited Latin demonstratives were made more forceful only by being compounded with *ecce*, originally an interjection, or *eccum*; these compound forms are the ancestors of the demonstrative pronouns in most Romance languages.[113]

Despite the confusion and the lax usage of demonstrative pronouns in nonclassical sources, it is still possible to identify some tendencies in the witnesses of the Latin Gospels. In this way, *hic* is usually employed to render οὗτος, especially in neuter accusative for phrases such as *haec omnia* (πάντα ταῦτα). When variant readings do occur, *hic* is almost always replaced by *iste*, mirroring the changes described above.[114] This trend is especially clear in derogatory contexts: in Luke 4:3, for instance, the devil tells Jesus to transform a stone into bread, εἰπὲ τῷ λίθῳ τούτῳ

---

107 Cf. CIL 4.3702: *Bruttium Balbum īiuir(um). hic* (= *is*) *aerarium conseruabit.*

108 Cf. Ernout, Thomas, Syntaxe latine, 190.

109 So, e. g. Iuv. 1.4.66–67: *genialis agatur iste dies* (= *hic dies*); CIL 1^2.1012: *mortuos qui istic sepultus est* (= *hic sepultus est*).

110 Cf. Italian "però," derived from *per hoc*.

111 Cf. Italian "egli," "ella," "il," "la," Spanish "ello," "ella," "el," "la," all derived from forms of *ille*.

112 Greg. Tur. *Franc.* 2.7.

113 Cf. French "ce" (from *ecce hoc*), Spanish and Portuguese "aquel" and "aquele" (from *ecce ille*), Italian "questo" (from *ecce istum*) etc.

114 Cyprian, e. g., has *omnia ista* for πάντα ταῦτα as well. Cf. Soden, Das Lateinische Neue Testament in Afrika, 84.

ἵνα γένηται ἄρτος. For τῷ λιθῷ τούτῳ, the majority of the authorities has *lapidi huic* (*lapidibus his* in the *Codex Vercellensis*); the *Codex Bezae* (VL5), however, has *lapides isti*, emphasizing the insignificance and worthlessness of the stones.[115] Similar is Luke 22:42: Jesus's prayer to "remove this cup from me" (παρένεγκε τοῦτο τὸ ποτήριον ἀπ' ἐμοῦ) reads *transfer calicem istum a me* in most Latin manuscripts, though codices *Vercellensis* and *Bezae* (VL5) have *hunc* instead, possibly reflecting an effort to provide a more consistent rendering of οὗτος. For the adverbial phrase διὰ τοῦτο, however, *propterea* or *ideo* are the prevailing choices; *propter hoc* sometimes appears as a variant, again in *Bezae*.[116] The witnesses of all text types exhibit a surprising regularity in using *ille* to render ἐκεῖνος, especially in recurring phrases such as ἐν ἐκείνῳ τῷ καιρῷ or ἐν ἐκείναις ταῖς ἡμέραις, which are translated with *in illo tempore* and *in illis diebus* respectively.

The by far most frequent variation in the Latin Gospels concerns the demonstratives *is* and *ille*, both standard renderings of αὐτός. These pronouns rarely suggest any spatial or temporal relation and are seemingly interchangeable without any difference in meaning. Confusion occurs only when the Greek pronoun is a verbal or prepositional complement (*casus obliquus*); when it comes to the nominative (*casus rectus*), on the other hand – which, contrary to Classical Greek usage, stands for a simple personal pronoun of the third person with no particular emphasis (especially in the text of Luke) – there is noticeable consistency in the manuscripts, with αὐτός commonly rendered by *ipse*. In the very few exceptions where no variant such as οὗτος or ὁ δέ has been transmitted in the Greek text itself, the alternative is almost always *ille*, but never *is*.[117] At the same time, certain text traditions favor one of the two demonstratives in oblique cases. This phenomenon can be observed, for instance, in the *Codex Bobbiensis* (VL1), a chief witness for the oldest text of the Latin Gospels. There are approximately 60 instances of the pronominal variation *is* – *ille* in the Gospel of Matthew (extant only up to 15:36) where the text of *Codex Bobbiensis* diverges from the main stem of later traditions, prototypically represented by Codices *Veronensis* (VL4) and *Corbeiensis secundus* (VL8). Only

---

115 For a detailed discussion of the derogatory use of *hic* and *iste*, see AGHABABIAN, Translating the Gospel of Matthew, 18.

116 Cf. e. g. Luke 11:19, 49; 12:22.

117 Cf. Matt 1:21 (*hic* VL1 *ipse* cet.), 12:50 (*hic* 1 9 *ille* 2 *ipse* cet.), 14:2 (*hic* VL5 *ipse* cet.), 16:20 (*hic* VL5, 13 *ipse* cet.), Mark 1:8 (*ipse* VL3, 5, 6, 8; *ille* cet.), 7:36 (*ille*), Luke 2:50 (*ille* VL2 *ipse* cet.), 6:11 (*ille* VL2, 6, 8; *ipse* cet.), 11:28 (*ipse* VL2, 6; *ille* cet.), 11:48 (*ille* VL3, 4, 10, 13; *ipse* cet.), 14:12 (*ille* VL2, 5; *ipse* cet.), 15:14 (*ille* VL6; *ipse* cet.), 17:16 (*ipse* VL2, 5; *hic* cet.), 18:34 (*ille* VL2, 14; *ipse* cet.), 18:39 (*ille* 2 3 5 *ipse* cet.), 19:2 (*iste* VL10; *ipse* cet.), 19:9 (*hic* VL3, 5, 21; *iste* VL11; *ipse* cet.), 22:23 (*ille* VL2, 10 ; *ipse* cet.), 23:9 (*ille* VL5 ; *ipse* cet.), 24:25 (*ille* VL2, 5, 6 ; *ipse* cet.), John 17:8 (*ille* VL13 ; *ipse* cet.), 17:21 (*ille* VL3, 13 ; *ipse* cet.).

in 15 instances does the *Codex Bobbiensis* have *is* for αὐτός in oblique cases,[118] which unmistakably demonstrates a preference for *ille* (about 75% of the occurrences). Similar numbers can be found in the Gospel of Mark (extant only from 8:22 onwards), where only 30 of circa 90 instances have *is* instead of *ille*,[119] showing again a clear predilection of the translators for the latter (about 65%). These findings confirm that rendering αὐτός in oblique cases with *ille* rather than *is* is an important feature of older text types, so that one may postulate the frequency of *ille* as a criterion for dating translations of the Latin Gospels.

The same applies to the *Codex Vercellensis* Luke. Here, one finds a clear tendency towards using *ille* instead of *is*. So, for instance, Luke 12:36, ἵνα ἀνοίξωσιν αὐτῷ, is rendered with *ut aperiant ei*, "so that they may open to him," in most Latin witnesses; but, in *Codex Vercellensis* (with VL2, 5 as well), the translation is *aperiant illi* instead. Likewise, where most witnesses translate Luke 17:16, παρὰ τοὺς πόδας αὐτοῦ as *ante pedes eius* ("at his feet"), the *Codex Vercellensis* has *illius* (singular reading). Finally, Luke 20:9, ἐξέδετο αὐτὸν γεωργοῖς reads *locauit eam colonis* ("he rented it out to farmers") in most witnesses but *illam* in *Codex Vercellensis* (singular reading). This implies that the Lucan text of the *Codex Vercellensis* shares a crucial feature with older translations when it comes to the use of *is* and *ille*. Limitations of space do not allow the analysis of all the many relevant passages, but an analysis of a single chapter may suffice to demonstrate this aspect. In Luke 6, one finds about 20 passages with a possible change of *is* to *ille* or vice-versa. In nine of these, *Codex Vercellensis* transmits *ille* rather than the *is* of other witnesses; in six instances, the reading is shared with *Codex Palatinus* (VL2), also a central witness of the oldest text of the Latin Gospels.[120]

We have already argued that the use of *is* and *ille* depends primarily on the language register of the text in question, so that variation of these terms reflects not only diachronic but also diastratic variations of Latin.[121] Augustine's writings are paradigmatic in this respect. As an author, Augustine holds a special within Latin literature since his education included rhetoric and philosophy, and since he had an affection for the conservative style of Classical Latin, in particular, for the

118 Matt 3:6; 4:16; 5:25.41; 6:26; 8:4; 9:15, 30, 36; 12:29; 13:19, 44, 58; 14:5, 14.

119 Mark 8:22, 23, 31; 9:2, 7, 14, 16, 19, 20, 22, 25, 34, 36, 43, 45, 47; 10:14, 35, 42; 11:2, 3, 6, 7, 18; 12:15; 14:11, 43, 59, 67; 15:20.

120 6:1: *illius* (with VL2, *eius* cet.); 6:8: *illorum* (with VL2, *eorum* cet.); 6:10: *illius* (*eius* cet.); 6:18: *illum* (with VL2, *eum* cet.); 6:23: *illorum* (with VL2, 6 ; *eorum* cet.); 6:40: *illius* (*eius* cet.); 6:45: *illius* (*eius* cet.); 6:47: *illa uerba* (with VL2 ; *eos sermones* cet.); 6:48: *illam* (with VL2, 5, *eam* cet.).

121 Cf. ANDRE, "La concurrence entre *is* et *ille* dans l'évolution de la langue latine," 322.

language of Cicero;[122] at the same time, however, Augustine also advocated forms of expressions closer to the way of speaking employed by common people. In his own words, *melius est reprehendant nos grammatici quam non intelligant populi* (it is better that grammarians reprove us than that the people do not understand us).[123] This attitude is explored in a variety of ways in Augustine's works. So, for instance, the *De ciuitate Dei* tends to exhibit a complex language use, while the *Sermones* are evidence of a language register close to that of colloquial Latin. In fact, *is* appears 28 times in the *Sermones*, *ille* 61 times; in the *De ciuitate Dei*, the distribution of these demonstratives is exactly the opposite: *is* is used 59 times, but *ille* only 26 times. In this context, it is also important to note that *ille* is rarer in the Vulgate than in the manuscripts of the Old Latin Gospels. In the examples given above, all manuscripts of the Vulgate have *is* instead of *ille*. Moreover, *ille* never appears as a reading unique to the Vulgate, which arguably means that the revisors working on the text never introduced it into the text, instead frequently removing the *ille* found in older translations. Furthermore, in cases where *ille* is retained, it is for the most part attested in many Old Latin witnesses.[124]

Two conclusions may be drawn from these observations: the oldest texts of the Latin Gospels reflect, at least in their use of demonstratives, a language closer to a colloquial register, where *ille* would have been more frequent than *is*. This assumption is supported by the fact that *ille*, not *is*, evolved into the personal pronouns and articles of the Romance languages. In addition, it seems clear that the Vulgate, by replacing *ille* with *is*, aims at a more cultivated revision of the older translations, adopting several forms of expression of Classical Latin as a model.

5.3.2.2 The Use of Reflexive Pronouns

Classical Latin possessed an unambiguous differentiation between reflexive and non-reflexive use of object pronouns (*casus obliquus*) in the third person singular and plural. *se* and its corresponding possessive *suus* are always preferred in the predicate when they refer to the subject of the clause. Hence, in a sentence such as *cum aut suis finibus eos prohibent aut ipsi in eorum finibus bellum gerunt*[125] ("by either repelling them from their frontiers, or waging war in their territories"), the frontiers of the Helvetians (who are the subject of the sentence) are precisely

122 Cf. Aug. *conf.* 3.4.7: *inter hos ego inbecilla tunc aetate discebam libros eloquentiae, in qua eminere cupiebam fine damnabili et uentoso per gaudia uanitatis humanae. et usitato iam discendi ordine perueneram in librum cuiusdam Ciceronis, cuius linguam fere omnes mirantur, pectus non ita.*

123 Aug. *in Ps.* 138.20.

124 Cf. ABEL, "Die Ausbildung des bestimmten Artikels," 247.

125 Caes. *B. G.* 1.1.4.

distinguished from the territories of their foes, the Germans, using the pronominal morphosyntax captured in the phrases *suis finibus* and *eorum finibus* respectively.[126] In the Romance languages, however, the situation is remarkably different, since the old distinction between reflexive and non-reflexive use of object pronouns in the third person has been lost altogether. Consequently, in Italian, for instance, "ama suo padre" can be considered the translation of two Latin sentences, *amat suum patrem* or *amat eius patrem*, and one is forced to find alternative strategies to remove this ambiguity.[127]

Several manuscripts of the Latin Gospels attest to this syntactical development, showing that the differentiation between reflexive and non-reflexive use of pronouns was already less marked in Late Antiquity. For instance, instead of the expected *se* or *suus*, one sometimes comes across an ordinary demonstrative form, generally *is* or *ille*. It is true that this confusion seems not to have become widespread before the seventh century, and classical usage is still almost untouched in the writings of Gregory of Tours;[128] nevertheless, the misuse of reflexive pronouns is an important cause for the emergence of variant readings in many witnesses of the Latin Gospels. For instance, Matt 3:12, τὸ πτύον ἐν τῇ χειρὶ αὐτοῦ, is typically translated with *habens uentilabrum in manu sua* ("having the winnowing fork in his hand"), even though *Codex Bezae* (VL5) has *eius* for *sua*. But the opposite process is not uncommon either: Mark 7:2, ἰδόντες τινὰς τῶν μαθητῶν αὐτοῦ, is rendered in most texts with *cum uidissent quosdam ex discipulis eius* ("when they saw some of his disciples"), whereas *Codex Bezae* reads *discipulorum suorum* instead of *ex discipulis eius*. If interpreted strictly in accordance with the standard language register, the phrase would mean not that the Pharisees and scribes saw Jesus's disciples eating bread with unwashed hands, but rather that they saw *their own* disciples doing so.

The same unpredictable use of reflexive pronouns can be observed in the *Codex Vercellensis* Gospel of Luke. On the one hand, in Luke 2:26, for instance, μὴ ἰδεῖν θάνατον ("that he would not see death") is – according to classical syntax – mostly rendered with *non uisurum se mortem*; the subject of the infinitive construction is Simeon, righteous and devout man from Jerusalem, to whom the holy spirit had been revealed that he would encounter the Christ of God before passing away. The *Codex Vercellensis*, however, here reads *non uisurum eum mortem* (with VL14), with

126 It is worth noting that, even in classical authors, a reflexive pronoun can occasionally refer to the more prominent entity in a sentence, even if it is not the subject. Cf. Cic. *Sest.* 68: *hunc sui ciues a ciuitate eiecerunt*.

127 Cf. Mari, "Third person possessives from early Latin to late Latin and Romance," 47.

128 Cf. Stone, The Language of the Latin Text of Codex Bezae, 39.

a demonstrative pronoun instead of the expected reflexive. On the other hand, in Luke 8:41, παρεκάλει αὐτὸν εἰσελθεῖν εἰς τὸν οἶκον αὐτοῦ ("he implored him to come to his house") is translated with *rogans eum, ut intraret in domum eius* in almost all witnesses to this verse. But *Codex Vercellensis* transmits *rogans illum, ut intraret in domum suam* (again with VL14), marking, through classical morphosyntax, the difference between Jesus (*illum*), who is asked to enter the house, and Jaïrus (*suam*), the owner of the house.

5.3.2.3 The Use of Reciprocal Pronouns

Lacking a reciprocal pronoun like the Greek ἀλλήλων, Latin had to make use of several syntactic devices to express mutuality. It is well-known that the reflexive pronoun *se* could also serve as a reciprocal pronoun,[129] but, since this usage was ambiguous in some contexts, other means of conveying the idea of two parties doing some single thing to each other were developed in Latin. This peculiarity had already been noticed by the grammarian Priscian, the author of the *Institutiones Grammaticae*, the standard textbook for the study of Latin during the Middle Ages. He observes: *dubitatio fit, utrum per sui passionem singulae in se agant, an altera in alteram, si dicam iste et ille se amant, dubium enim fit, utrum* ἑαυτοὺς ἢ ἀλλήλους *significet* ("it raises a doubt, whether the individual persons acting affect themselves or each other, if I say *iste et ille se amant*, for it is unclear whether it means ἑαυτοὺς [themselves] ἢ ἀλλήλους [each other]").[130] Therefore, the oldest way of eliminating this ambiguity was by means of prepositional phrases consisting of *inter* along with *nos*, *uos* and *se*. These constructions are found among the earlier writers and were the most important device to unequivocally express reciprocity in the classical language.[131] In addition, polytoptonic constructions with the repetition of *alter* (for two persons) or *alius* (for more than two) were also common.[132]

A later way of expressing mutuality in Latin is by means of *inuicem*, an adverb which shows a very interesting semantic development. It has been postulated that

129 Cf., e. g., Caes. *B. G.* 2.18.6: *ut intra siluas aciem ordinesque constituerant atque ipsi sese confirmauerant*; Liv. 6.28.1: *nam cum esset Praenestinis nuntiatum nullum exercitum conscriptum Romae, nullum ducem certum esse, patres ac plebem in semet ipsos uersos, occasionem rati duces eorum raptim agmine acto peruastatis protinus agris ad portam Collinam signa intulere.*

130 Prisc. *inst. gramm.* 17.141.

131 Cf., e. g., Caes. *B. G.* 1.3.7: *hac oratione adducti inter se fidem et iusiurandum dant*; Verg. *Aen.* 11.120: *conuersique oculos inter se atque ora tenebant.* For further discussion, see BALDI, "A Structural Ambiguity in Latin," 51.

132 Cf., e. g., Caes. *B. G.* 5.44.14: *sic fortuna in contentione et certamine utrumque uersauit, ut alter alteri inimicus auxilio salutique esset*; Liv. 2.10.9: *cunctati aliquamdiu sunt, dum alius alium, ut proelium incipiant, circumspectant.*

the original sense of this term was "changing or taking place of," as suggested by fixed expressions or nominal derivatives such as *uice uersa* ("the other way around") or *uicequaestor* ("one who will serve in place of the main *quaestor*").[133] At first, *inuicem* was employed in hypercharacterized constructions together with *inter se*, reinforcing the aspect of reciprocity of the prepositional phrase pleonastic-cally.[134] In a subsequent stage, this term appears with *se* only, which is in turn usually modified by *ipsi* or some other intensifier.[135] Finally, *inuicem* takes on the meaning of *se* itself: once the semantic development has reached this point, even the reflexive pronoun can be eliminated as unnecessary and redundant.[136]

Another noteworthy means of conveying mutuality emerged in the form of the compound *alterutrum* or, alternatively, *alterutro*. The earliest evidence for the usage of this term usage can be found in the introduction to a dialogue entitled *Virgilius orator an poeta*, commonly attributed to the 2nd-century rhetorician Publius Annius Florus.[137] Considering that the author himself states that he comes from Africa, it has been proposed that *alterutrum* is characteristic of the language spoken in the province of that time, one of "the first traces of African Latin."[138] But the exact source of this new term is not yet certain: scholars assume that it arose in colloquial registers, derived, through contamination, from *alteruter alterum* ("one of the two").[139]

This abundance of forms expressing reciprocity resulted in many variants in the manuscripts of the Latin Gospels. Nevertheless, some tendencies can still be detected: *inuicem* is by far the most frequent rendering of Greek ἀλλήλων and is often the reading preferred by the Vulgate.[140] Next comes *alterutrum*, which the Vulgate surprisingly retains only in Mark (4:41; 8:16; 15:31); by contrast, this later form is a distinctive variant of codices *Vercellensis* and *Bezae* (VL5), especially in Luke,[141]

133 For further discussion, see Baldi, "Latin *invicem*," 300–302.

134 Cf., e. g., Liv. 9.43.17: *iam triginta milibus hostium caesis signum receptui consules dederant colligebantque in unum copias inuicem inter se gratantes, cum repente uisae procul hostium nouae cohortes, quae in supplementum scriptae fuerant, integrauere caedem.*

135 Cf., e. g., Tac. *Agr.* 6.1: *uixeruntque mira concordia, per mutuam caritatem et inuicem se anteponendo.*

136 Cf., e. g., Lucan. 7.177: *inque uicem uultus tenebris mirantur opertos.*

137 Flor. *Verg.* 1.5: *manu alterutrum tenentes*. For further discussion, see Wackernagel, Lectures on Syntax, 523.

138 Thielmann, "Der Ersatz des Reciprocums im Lateinischen," 373.

139 Cf. Hofmann, Szantyr, Lateinische Syntax und Stilistik 2, 178.

140 Cf., e. g., Matt 24:10, 25:32, Luke 2:15, 4:36, 6:11, 7:32, 8:25, 12:1 (with pleonastic *se*), 23:12, 24:14.17.32, John 4:33, 5:44, 6:43.53, 11:56, 13:22, 34, 35, 15:12, 17, 16:17, 16:24.

141 Luke 2:15 (VL5), 4:36 (VL3), 7:32 (VL3), 12:1 (VL5), 24:17 (VL3), 24:32 (VL3).

even though singular readings are found in Matt and John as well.[142] But the surviving manuscripts of the Latin Gospels give no support for the possible African origin of *alterutrum* posited by some researchers, especially since the word does not occur in the witnesses commonly associated with the writings of Tertullian and Cyprian, *Bobbiensis* (VL1) and *Palatinus* (VL2). Finally, of particular interest are the variants *alis alium* and *alius alium*, which present unique readings contained in the *Codex Vercellensis* Luke (8:25; 12:1): the use of the invariable fossilized form *alis* – also found in inscriptions – instead of the inflected *alius* suggest a strong influence of colloquial registers of the language.[143]

5.3.2.4 The Use of the Relative Pronouns

While Classical Latin has a pronominal system which includes a complete set of inflected modifying pronouns, the Romance languages have evolved in such a way that they no longer mark any agreement of the modifying pronouns, using only a single invariable element to introduce adjective clauses instead.[144] This is likely a consequence of thorough levelling of the relative pronouns in colloquial registers. The first stage of this development consisted in the replacement of the interrogative *quis* and the feminine relative *quae* in all its forms with the masculine relatives *qui* and *quem*, as observed in epigraphic sources from the late Empire;[145] later, the same process would be extended even to the neuter, thus displacing *quod*.[146]

The Latin Gospels, however, do not exhibit any of these innovations, and the syntax of relative pronouns is pretty much consistent with classical usage. The only important deviation can apparently be traced back to the influence of Hebrew, namely the pleonastic use of personal (demonstrative) pronouns after relativizers (*pronomen abundans*).[147] One instance of this phenomenon is encountered in Mark

---

142 Matt 24:10 (VL5); John 13:14 (VL3).

143 Cf. CIL 2.2633: *renouauerunt eique alis alium.*

144 "che" in Italian and "que" in the other Romance languages both derive from the classical accusative singular *quem*. For further discussion, see POLETTO/ SANFELICI, "Relative clauses," 806.

145 Cf., e. g., IPOstie A20 = ISIS 321: *Restutus Piscinesis et Prima Restuta Primae Florentiae filiae carissimae fecerunt qui (= quae) ab Orfeu maritu in Tiberi decepta est.*

146 Cf., e. g., *Mul. Chir.* 416: *intestinum, qui (= quod) uocatur monenteron.*

147 The redundant use of demonstratives in relative clauses is not entirely absent from Classical Greek and Latin. Cf., e. g., Hdt. 4.44.1: τῆς δὲ Ἀσίης τὰ πολλὰ ὑπὸ Δαρείου ἐξευρέθη, ὃς βουλόμενος Ἰνδὸν ποταμόν, **ὃς** κροκοδείλους δεύτερος **οὗτος** ποταμῶν πάντων παρέχεται, τοῦτον τὸν ποταμὸν εἰδέναι τῇ ἐς θάλασσαν ἐκδιδοῖ, πέμπει πλοίοισι ἄλλους τε, τοῖσι ἐπίστευε τὴν ἀληθείην ἐρέειν, καὶ δὴ καὶ Σκύλακα ἄνδρα Καρυανδέα; Xen. *rep. Lac.* 10.4: τόδε γε μὴν τοῦ Λυκούργου πῶς οὐ μεγάλως ἄξιον ἀγασθῆναι; **ὃς** ἐπειδὴ κατέμαθεν ὅτι ὅπου οἱ βουλόμενοι ἐπιμελοῦνται τῆς ἀρετῆς οὐχ ἱκανοί εἰσι τὰς πατρίδας αὔξειν, **ἐκεῖνος** ἐν τῇ Σπάρτῃ ἠνάγκασε δημοσίᾳ πάντας πάσας ἀσκεῖν τὰς ἀρετάς;

1:7, where **οὗ** οὐκ εἰμὶ ἱκανὸς λῦσαι τὸν ἱμάντα τῶν ὑποδημάτων **αὐτοῦ** ("the strap of **whose** sandals **of his** I am not worthy to untie") is typically rendered with ***cuius*** *non sum dignus soluere corrigiam calciamentorum* ***eius***. The root of this phenomenon seems to lie in the fact that the Hebrew relative pronoun אשר is, properly speaking, a particle undefined with respect to case, number, and gender. For this reason, the exact syntactical function of אשר must be marked through the employment of a resumptive (independent or suffixed) pronoun within the relative clause which in turn unambiguously identifies the referent of אשר.[148]

A peculiarity of *Vercellensis* Luke is the frequent employment of the relative *qui* as a link between two main clauses (Relativischer Satzanschluss), a very common construction in Latin.[149] But, contrary to classical use, in the text of the manuscript, *qui* often renders only the ὁ δέ in formulaic expressions introducing direct speech, especially ὁ δὲ εἶπεν, whereas other witnesses prefer the demonstrative *ille* or even *ipse* in this context. Thus, for instance, Luke 8:48 reads ὁ δὲ εἶπεν αὐτῇ ("and he said to her"), which is translated as *qui dixit ei* in the *Codex Vercellensis*, rather than as the *at ipse dixit illi* of the Vulgate. Such formulations may be seen as indications of an attempt to produce a Gospel text according to Greek syntax; in some cases, this project has been taken so far that eccentric, wholly ungrammatical readings occur, as in 8:46. Here, the manuscript renders ὁ δὲ Ἰησοῦς εἶπεν as *qui dixit iesus*, showing that the translator ignored the other function of ὁ as an article in this verse.

Plat. *Phaid.* 99b: τὸ γὰρ μὴ διελέσθαι οἷόν τ' εἶναι ὅτι ἄλλο μέν τί ἐστι τὸ αἴτιον τῷ ὄντι, ἄλλο δὲ ἐκεῖνο ἄνευ οὗ τὸ αἴτιον οὐκ ἄν ποτ' εἴη αἴτιον· **ὃ** δή μοι φαίνονται ψηλαφῶντες οἱ πολλοὶ ὥσπερ ἐν σκότει, ἀλλοτρίῳ ὀνόματι προσχρώμενοι, ὡς αἴτιον **αὐτὸ** προσαγορεύειν.

148 Cf., e. g., Gen 1:11: וַיֹּאמֶר אֱלֹהִים תַּדְשֵׁא הָאָרֶץ דֶּשֶׁא עֵשֶׂב מַזְרִיעַ זֶרַע עֵץ פְּרִי עֹשֶׂה פְּרִי לְמִינוֹ אֲשֶׁר זַרְעוֹ־בוֹ. Considering that the relative particle אשר is not marked for case, number, or gender, the subsequent noun זרע, "seed," contains the 3rd person masculine pronoun ו, "its," as a reference back to עץ פרי, "fruit tree." Accordingly, there would be no need to translate the Hebrew pronoun ו into Greek, since the relative pronoun οὗ corresponds to the gender and number of ξύλον κάρπιμον, "fruit tree." Yet, instead of leaving it untranslated, the Septuagint follows the wording of the Hebrew text and renders the – in Greek – unnecessary pronoun: καὶ εἶπεν ὁ θεὸς βλαστησάτω ἡ γῆ βοτάνην χόρτου, σπεῖρον σπέρμα κατὰ γένος καὶ καθ' ὁμοιότητα, καὶ ξύλον κάρπιμον ποιοῦν καρπόν, οὗ τὸ σπέρμα αὐτοῦ ἐν αὐτῷ κατὰ γένος, providing τὸ σπέρμα αὐτοῦ, "its seed," as the translation of זַרְעוֹ. For further discussion, see Rubio, "Semitic influence," 212.

149 Typical, e. g., for Caesar's narrative style, where this kind of construction abounds. Cf., e. g., *B. G.* 3.14: *Caesar statuit exspectandam classem. quae ubi conuenit ac primum ab hostibus uisa est circiter CCXX naues eorum paratissimae atque omni genere armorum ornatissimae profectae ex portu nostris aduersae constiterunt.*

Figure 5.9: The reading *qui dixit iesus* in Luke 8:46 (397^{a}).

5.3.2.5 The Use of the Prepositions

As stated above, Late Latin texts display a more extensive use of prepositions than texts of classical literature, a phenomenon likely due to the intrusion of popular means of expression into more scholarly registers and their subsequent acceptance.[150] In Late Latin, we see the use of prepositional phrases in lieu of oblique cases, along with a certain looseness in case agreement. This variation in prepositional government certainly poses one of the most striking phenomena of Vulgar Latin and a widespread feature of several manuscripts of the Latin Gospels. Especially noticeable in this context is a confusion between the accusative and the ablative, caused by the dropping of the final *-m* and the loss of vowel quantity, which often made the phonetic distinction between the two cases impossible.[151] This in turn gradually resulted in the breakdown of case distinctions, so that ablatives were generally used as accusatives and vice-versa.

Contrary to this general tendency, the *Codex Vercellensis* Luke exhibits a surprising consistency in the case agreement of the most frequent prepositions. For instance, the use of *a* (*ab*), *ad*, *cum*, *de*, *ex* and *per* shows no significant departure from the standards of the classical language. In the case of the sociative *cum*, only one deviation may be observed, namely in 19:30, where one reads *asinam cum*

150 Cf. above, 4.4.2; 5.3.1 and more often.
151 Cf. above, 5.3.1, pp. 225–228.

pullum instead of *cum pullo*.[152] Directly influenced by Greek syntax, *ex* takes a genitive in Luke 14:28 (*ex uestrum* for *ex uobis*, gr. ἀπὸ ὑμῶν)[153] and in Luke 20:10 (*ex fructuum* for *ex fructibus*, gr. ἀπὸ τοῦ καρποῦ). *per* is twice followed by an ablative, in Luke 18:5 (*per tempore* instead of *per tempus*) and Luke 19:4 (*per illa parte* instead of *per illam partem*).

Nevertheless, confusions do occur with prepositions which governed either an accusative or an ablative in Classical Latin, and especially with the preposition *in*. In these cases, the accusative was usually preferred to describe movement towards something (lative), whereas the ablative was used to describe the position of something (locative). There is evidence of the confusion of the accusative and the ablative as early as the first century, though it was probably not very common before the third century. It was precisely this distinction that was almost completely lost in Late Latin, a development that can be seen in many manuscripts of the Latin Gospel, the *Codex Vercellensis* being no exception. Thus, Luke 8:22 reads *ascendit in nauiculam* (ἐνέβη εἰς πλοῖον), but Luke 8:37 has *ascendens in naue* (ἐμβὰς εἰς πλοῖον), Luke 7:11 reads *ibat Iesus in ciuitatem* (ἐπορεύθη εἰς πόλιν), but Luke 9:52 has *intrauerunt in ciuitate* (εἰσῆλθον εἰς κώμην).

5.3.3 Verbal Syntax in the *Codex Vercellensis* Luke

5.3.3.1 The Usage of the Tenses

In general, the functions of the six tenses of Classical Latin (present, imperfect, future, perfect, pluperfect, and future perfect) are very well preserved in the manuscripts of the Latin Gospels, reflecting the character of the Romance languages in this respect. The substitution of the present for the future is characteristic of popular speech, as seen, once more, in Roman comedy, especially in dialogue passages and with *verba mouendi*.[154] In this way, Plautus writes *sed ad prandium uxor me vocat, redeo domum* ("but my wife is calling me to lunch, I am going home") instead of *redibo*,[155] and even Caesar, whose style and diction served as undisputed models of classical prose, has *ego reliquas portas circumeo et castrorum praesidia confirmo* ("I will surround the other gates, and encourage the guards of the camp") instead

152 *cum* with the accusative is very frequent in inscriptions. Cf., e. g., CIL 1.170: *fecit cum sodales*; CIL 4.275: *Saturninus cum suos discentes, cum sodales*.

153 Cf. 15:4, where ἐξ ὑμῶν is rendered with *ex uestris* instead of *ex uobis*.

154 Cf. SJÖRGEN, Zum Gebrauch des Futurums im Altlateinischen, 6–38.

155 Plaut. *Rud.* 904.

of *circumibo* and *confirmabo*.[156] Nevertheless, textual evidence mostly comes from later periods, where it points to a development towards the well-established interchangeability between present and future tenses in the Romance languages. In the *Peregrinatio Aetheriae*, for instance, constructions such as *attendite et uidete, et dicimus uobis singula* ("wait and see, and we will tell you everything") or *nam si uis, ecce modo pedibus duco uos ibi* ("for if you wish, behold, I will straightaway lead you on foot there") are commonplace.[157] By contrast, there are not many instances in the manuscripts of the Latin Gospels where this syntactical development can be detected. In the *Codex Vercellensis*, they are restricted to Luke 11:5 (ἕξει φίλον, *habet amicum* for *habebit amicum*) and John 7:36 (ζητήσετέ με, *quaeritis me* for *quaeretis me*).

One characteristic of the manuscript is the use of *incipere* with an infinitive to render the Greek verb μέλλειν and express futurity without resorting to the participle future (Luke 7:2, *incipiebat mori* a d for *erat moriturus* cet., Luke 21:7, *haec incipient fieri* a e for *erunt futura* cet.). The future is sometimes given the force of the imperative, a common usage in Greek as well. In this way, Luke 4:4, οὐκ ἐπ' ἄρτῳ μόνῳ ζήσεται ὁ ἄνθρωπος is typically rendered with *non in pane solo uiuet homo*. Nevertheless, it is important to note that this use of the future tense is not exclusively found in Latin translations of the Bible. Terence, for instance, writes *assimulabis tuam amicam huius* (*Heaut.* 2.2). Just as here the future tense expresses advice or a wish, it can also, depending on the circumstances, express an energetic order, and thus serve as the equivalent of the Latin future imperative. The Vulgate also uses this tense to render the Ten Commandments: *non habebis deos alienos coram me* (Ex 20:2; Deut 5:6: *in conspectu meo*) etc.[158]

In the same vein, we find the future tense used as an imperative in the Lucan text of the *Codex Vercellensis*. In Luke 18:20, Jesus quotes the Ten Commandments, given in Greek in the subjunctive (*prohibitivus*), whereas the majority of the Latin witnesses, including the *Codex Vercellensis*, uses the future in this verse: *non adulterabis* (μὴ μοιχεύσῃς), *non homicidium facies* (μὴ φονεύσῃς), *non furtum facies* (μὴ κλέψῃς), *non falsum testimonium dices* (μὴ ψευδομαρτυρήσῃς). The only exception is the *Codex Palatinus* (VL2), which morpho-syntactically follows the Greek text and has the perfect subjunctive: *ne adulterium admiseris, ne furtum feceris, ne falsum testimonium dixeris*.

---

156 Caes. *B. C.* 3.94.5.

157 For more on these and other examples, cf. Löfstedt, Philologischer Kommentar zur *Peregrinatio Aetheriae*, 212–213.

158 The Hebrew text has a Qal imperfect: לֹא יִהְיֶה־לְךָ

5.3.3.2 Nominal Forms of Verbs

The use of nominal forms of verbs (gerunds and gerundives) in Latin Bible translations is of particular interest since these constructions have no direct equivalent in Greek syntax. In this way, they are employed to translate several idiomatic features of Greek, such as the aorist active participle or prepositional phrases involving the articular infinitive, which cannot be reproduced verbatim in Latin.[159] Unsurprisingly, the rendering of these structures into Latin is responsible for the emergence of many variant readings, not only in individual manuscripts but also across different text traditions.

Gerund and gerundive constructions may be taken as characteristic of more formal registers of the language and were, therefore, almost absent from colloquial Latin. This becomes clear when the text of Vegetius' guide to veterinary medicine is compared to its source, the *Mulomedicina Chironis*, both written during the fourth century. As Vegetius himself states, *Chiron uero et Apsyrtus diligentius cuncta rimati eloquentiae inopia ac sermonis ipsius vilitate sordescunt*[160] ("in spite of the detailed research, Chiron and Apsyrtus are unrefined due to the poorness of their language and helplessness of their expression"). Thus, in his version of the treatise, Vegetius made several attempts to improve the original text, very often replacing phrases with modal verbs, imperatives, or other similar constructions used in lieu of the classical nominal forms of verbs.[161]

The only exception to this trend is the Vulgar Latin usage of the ablative gerund as an equivalent of present participles, a later syntactical innovation which survived in many Romance languages. The phenomenon certainly has its roots in the construction's old modal function, which is almost indistinguishable from the plain instrumental-causal sense. Once more, the use of the ablative gerund in Roman Comedy shows that it had a popular character: for instance, Plautus writes *ita miser cubando in lecto hic expectando obdurui*[162] ("lying unhappy like this and waiting here upon the couch, I'm grown numbed"), with *cubando* and *expectando* instead of *cubans* and *expectans* respectively. In later periods, the construction would eventually gain ground as the normal substitute for present participles, as seen in the

159 Cf. MALTBY, "Gerunds, Gerundives and their Greek Equivalents in Latin Bible Translations," 425.

160 Veg. *mulom.* 1.3–4.

161 Cf. e. g., *asino sanguis detrahi numquam debet de matrice* (*Mul. Chir.* 9.3) vs. *asinis de matrice numquam detrahendus est sanguis* (Veg. *mulom.* 48.9); *sollicite ualde percuti debent* (*Mul. Chir.* 10.10) vs. *cum summa cautela tangendae sunt* (Veg. *mulom.* 49.19). For further discussion, see LÖFSTEDT, Philologischer kommentar zur *Peregrinatio Aetheriae*, 156–158; GREVANDER, Untersuchungen zur Sprache der *Mulomedicina Chironis*, 78–79.

162 Plaut. *Truc.* 5.24.

commentaries on the Spanish War, *ita erumpendo nauis, quae ad Baetim flumen fuissent, incendunt*[163] ("so, in this sally, they set the ships that were in the river Baetis on fire"), with *erumpendo* instead of *erumpentes*, a phrase which Caesar would probably not have allowed himself. Similarly, in Livy, we read *noui consules populando usque ad moenia peruenerunt*[164] ("the new consuls, carrying on their depredations, arrived at the walls"), with *populando* instead of *populantes*. Later yet, in the *Peregrinatio Aetheriae* we find *omnia loca, quae filii Israhel tetigerant eundo uel redeundo ad montem Dei*[165] ("all the places which the children of Israel had touched, when they were going to or from the mount of God"), with *eundo uel redeundo* instead of *euntes uel redeuntes*.

Ablative gerunds appear in the Latin Gospels as well, but their distribution varies widely among the different text families, with the Vulgate employing them more extensively than the oldest translations, such as those found in the *Bobbiensis* (VL1) and *Palatinus* (VL2). So, for instance, in Luke 10:25, τί ποιήσας ζωὴν αἰώνιον κληρονομήσω ("what shall I do to inherit eternal life"), and 15:13, διεσκόρπισεν τὴν οὐσίαν αὐτοῦ ζῶν ἀσώτως ("he wasted his property in reckless living"), the Greek aorist active participles are translated with an ablative gerund in later texts and in the Vulgate (*faciendo* and *uiuendo*), whereas Codices *Palatinus* and *Bezae* give present participles for both verses (*faciens* and *uiuens*), following the Greek syntax more closely. The same applies to the *Codex Vercellensis*, which has the same readings *faciens* and *uiuens*. But in these two cases, it seems that the translators strictly adhere to classical usage since the ablative gerund occurs in contexts where a modal or instrumental-causal sense "by doing" and "by living" is conveyed. For this reason, scholars have usually stated that the Latin Gospels do not reflect vulgar usage, which employs the ablative gerund in lieu of a participle.[166]

An important and hitherto neglected deviation from this tendency may be found in Luke 7:45. The Greek texts reads οὐ διέλιπεν καταφιλοῦσά μου τοὺς πόδας ("she has not ceased to kiss my feet"). The typical rendering of this verse into Latin is *non cessauit osculari pedes meos*; *Codex Bezae* (VL5) imitates the Greek construction with the present participle *osculans* instead of the expected infinitive, which normally follows the verb *cessare*. An older tradition, however, represented by the *Codex Palatinus* (VL2) and continued by the *Codex Vercellensis*, transmits the ablative gerund *osculando*, without any modal or instrumental-causal sense.

163 *Bell. Hisp.* 36.2.
164 Liv. 8.17.1.
165 *Per. Aeth.* 5.11.
166 Cf. BURTON, The Old Latin Gospels, 187.

The by far most common usage of nominal forms of verbs in the Latin Gospels is in the construction *ad* plus gerund or gerundive expressing purpose and consistently rendering the Greek πρός or εἰς with the articular infinitive. The usual variant readings are final clauses introduced with *ut* and the subjunctive. In the *Codex Vercellensis* Luke, we find the following unique readings:

Table 14: Nominal forms of verbs in VL3 Luke

Verse	VL3	Other Latin authorities	NA[28]
3:17	*ad purgandam*	*ut emundet* 2 *et purgabit* (*purgauit* 4) cet.	διακαθᾶραι
5:24	*potestatem remittendi*	*potestatem dimittere* cet.	ἐξουσίαν ἀφιέναι
9:1	*curandi*	*ut curent* cet.	θεραπεύειν
12:5	*potestatem mittendi*	*potestatem mittere* cet.	ἐξουσίαν ἐμβαλεῖν
12:15	*in superrando*	*in abundantia* cet.	ἐν τῷ περισσεύειν
22:6	*Tradendi*	*ut traderet* cet.	τοῦ παραδοῦναι
24:45	*ad intellegendum*	*ut intellegerent* cet.	τοῦ συνιέναι

Our analysis and examples demonstrate that the Lucan text of the *Codex Vercellensis* does not differ in its syntactical character from other witnesses of the Latin Gospels. However, there are a few general differences. Distinctive is the use of the variants *alterutrum* and *alius alium* as reciprocal pronouns, which are not commonly found in other texts. But the most important peculiarity is probably the employment of the relative *qui* to link two main clauses in the rendering of Greek ὁ δέ, where other authorities have the demonstratives *ille* or *ipse*.

5.4 Latin Vocabulary Expansion: Semantics

5.4.1 Older Readings in the *Codex Vercellensis*

As stated above,[167] scholarship on the Latin Gospels distinguishes two textual traditions. The main witness of the older tradition is the *Codex Bobbiensis* (VL1), whose text is dated to the first half of the third century in light of the many correspondences between its text and patristic citations from the same period. However, some features of this oldest tradition can also be detected in later texts, and in particular in the form of characteristic readings such as *similitudo* instead of *parabola* for

167 Cf. Preface, pp. 1–6; Chapter 5, pp. 195–199.

παραβολή, *sermo* instead of *uerbum* for λόγος, *felix* instead of *beatus* for μακάριος, or *discens* instead of *discipulus* for μαθητής.[168]

This applies to *Codex Vercellensis* Luke as well, in which many of these earlier word choices are present, such as *edere* instead of *manducare* for ἐσθίειν (a unique reading in Luke 4:2, 6:1,4, 12:29),[169] *infans* instead of *puer* for παιδίον (Luke 9:47, 18:16, 17),[170] *nequam* instead of *malus* for πονηρός (a unique reading in 6:22,45), possibly *cruciatus* instead of *tormentum* for βάσανος in 16:28, a rendering otherwise only found in the *Codex Bobbiensis* (VL1) in Matt 4:24. Also noteworthy is the fact that this older textual tradition retained in the *Codex Vercellensis* avoids Greek loan-words, preferring native Latin equivalents, such as *adulterare* instead of *moechari* for μοιχεύειν (18:20) or *tanto melior* instead of *euge* for εὖγε (unique reading in Luke 19:17). In some cases, these earlier characteristic readings are shared with the *Palatinus* (VL2) and *Bezae* (VL5), such as *doctors legis* instead of *peritus* for νομικός (Luke 7:30, 10:25, 11:45, 46, 14:3).[171]

In what follows, we will analyze the *Codex Vercellensis* Gospel of Luke based on readings which are predominantly found in its text. It will be argued that, from a semantic point of view, the translation: (1) captures nuances of Greek terms depending on the context in which they appear; (2) is often based on a vast knowledge of Latin classical literature since it uses uncommon terms, poetic expressions and a broader vocabulary compared to the majority of the Latin authorities; (3) focuses on the emulation of morphological characteristics of the language of the original text. Furthermore, we will (4) discuss variant readings found in the technical vocabulary, before (5) engaging in the renderings of religious terms and their particular meanings for the interpretation of the *Codex Vercellensis* Luke.

---

168 Cf. BURTON, The Old Latin Gospels, 18–19.

169 For the complete list, see BURTON, The Old Latin Gospels, 51: *edere* makes up approximately 1/3 of the renderings of ἐσθίειν in the Gospel of Luke in the *Codex Vercellensis*, whereas, in the later text of the *Codex Veronensis* (VL4), it makes up only 1/6. Besides, it is necessary to correct Burton's list in 7:33, where *manducare* is given as the reading in the *Codex Vercellensis*. The consultation of the manuscript and the MSI-images, however, show that [*e*]*dens* stood in the manuscript instead. The reconstruction confirms Irico's reading *.dere* and refutes Bianchini's and Gasquet's reading [*mandu*]*cans*.

170 *infans* predominates in the codices *Palatinus* (VL2) and *Bezae* (VL5), e. g., in 1:59, 66, 79; 2:17, 21, 27, 40. Since the *Codex Bobbiensis* (VL1) often transmits *infans* instead of the *puer* of the other authorities, e. g., in Matt 2:8 or 18:2–5, *infans* can be considered the older variant.

171 For a detailed discussion of the relation among these three texts, see ch. IV.

5.4.2 Contextual Sensitivity

In many passages of the Latin Gospels, we see translators render the same Greek words differently when this is required by the context. This tells us a great deal about the translators' level of understanding of the original text, indicating that they were not only conscious of the polysemy of Greek words, but also took stylistic aspects of various constructions and expressions into consideration. In recent scholarship on the Latin Bible, the capacity of Latin translators to vary their word choices to render the same Greek term in various contexts has been named "contextual sensitivity."[172] The list below provides unique readings in the *Codex Vercellensis* Luke which demonstrate how the text distinguishes the various connotations of the same Greek words, frequently doing so in a more suitable way than other Latin witnesses.

Two unique readings deserve a detailed analysis:

Table 15: The rendering of ἀνέβλεψεν in 18:43

Verse	NA^{28}	VL3	Other Latin authorities
18:43	ἀνέβλεψεν	*uidere coepit*	*respexit* 5 *uidit* cet.

Erasmus had already noticed, with some astonishment, that the Latin Gospels do not possess any translation for ἀναβλέπειν in the sense of recovering the ability to see.[173] In the phraseology of narratives concerning the healing of the blind, ἀναβλέπειν is simply translated with *uidere* or *respicere*,[174] even though neither term precisely covers the sense of the Greek verb. Lucan text in *Codex Vercellensis*, however, provides an alternative and renders ἀνέβλεψεν with *uidere coepit*, "began to see." It is noteworthy that the *Codex Vercellensis* offers the same singular reading, *uidere coepit*, in the pericope in Mark 10:52.

172 Burton, The Old Latin Gospels, 86–87.
173 Cf. Erasmus, In Nouum Testamentum Annotationes, 216: *idem uerbum est Graecis, quod significat recipere uisum.*
174 Cf. for the semantic and stylistic properties of *coepi* with infinitive Galdi, "On *coepi/incipio* + infinitive: some new remarks," 258f.

Figure 5.10: The reading *uidere coepit* in Luke 18:43 (472[a]) and Mark 10:52 (597[b]).

Table 16: The rendering of γενήματος in 22:18

Verse	NA[28]	VL3	Other Latin authorities
22:18	γενήματος	*fructu*	*potione* 2 *creatura* 5 *generatione* cet.

The same observation applies to the verse at hand. After taking the cup of wine, Jesus says to his disciples that, until the kingdom of God comes, he will not drink "of the fruit of the wine," ἀπὸ τοῦ γενήματος τῆς ἀμπέλου. In most Latin witnesses, the phrase is rendered as *de generatione uitis*. However, *generatio* is not only the rendering of γένημα, which can mean either "offspring" or "the fruits of earth," but also of γενεά, "race," "family" or "generation." The words are similar, but there is clearly a difference between them. Nonetheless, with the translation *de generatione uitis*, the majority of the Latin authorities does not capture the nuance of the Greek text: *Codex Veronensis* (VL4), for instance, has the same terms in Luke 9:41 (*generatio infidelis* for γενεὰ ἄπιστος) and in the verse at hand (*de generatione uitis* for ἀπὸ τοῦ γενήματος τῆς ἀμπέλου). In this context, the text of *Codex Vercellensis* makes an appropriate distinction by using the special reading *fructu uineae*. Once more, it is important to mention that the *Codex Vercellensis* has the same reading, *fructu uineae*, in Mark 14:25, whereas, in the pericope in Matt 26:29, the reading is *creatura uitis*.

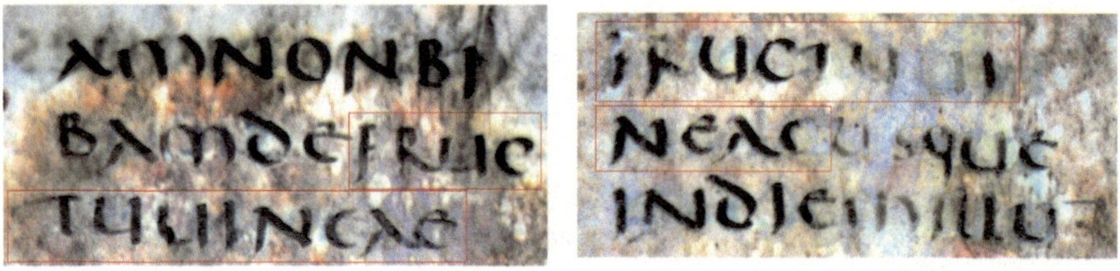

Figure 5.11: The reading *de fructu uinae* in Luke 22:18 (497[a]) and Mark 14:25 (625[a]).

From these two examples, we can observe how the Lucan text of the *Codex Vercellensis* shows a great sensitivity for the polysemy of Greek words. Moreover, the translation of these terms suggests a certain degree of inner coherence between Luke and Mark contained in the manuscript, or at least some efforts to homogenize common readings. This hypothesis may be further reinforced in light of the remarkable form *inextinctibilis* instead of the more standard *inextinguibilis* for ἄσβεστος in Luke 3:17 and Mark 9:43.[175] The correct reading of the manuscript, *inextinctibili*, was only made possible by the new MIS-images. No previous editor proposed this reading, each giving a slightly different form of the adjective instead (*inexstintibili* Irico; *inexstinguibili* Bianchini; *inextinguibili* Gasquet and Jülicher).

Figure 5.12: The reading *inextinctibili* in Luke 3:17 (350[a]) and Mark 9:43 (587[a]).

5.4.3 Rare Terms and Poetical Expressions

Many semantic particularities of the *Codex Vercellensis* Luke consist in terms and words not frequently found in other Latin witnesses or in other Gospels. This indicates that such terms may have already become obsolete outside literary usage during the first centuries C.E., that is, at the time when the Greek text began to be translated into Latin. To name two examples: the noun ἀγκάλη, "the inner angle of the arm," in Luke 2:28 is a hapax legomenon in the NT. Whereas the other authorities render this word with *manus*, a loose translation, in codices *Vercellensis* and *Amiatinus* (A), we observe an effort to translate the uncommon term in a way closer to the Greek: *ulna* of the Vulgate means "elbow," a word which captures the sense of the original, while *amplexus*, derived from the deponent *amplecti*, "to surround," or "to encompass," has the poetical connotation of "embrace," which emphasizes the Simeon's tenderness in taking the child Jesus up in his arms. The same applies to the reading *maerore* in 22:45: the Greek term used is λύπη, "grief" or "sorrow," otherwise only found in the Gospel of John and always rendered with the straightforward noun *tristitia*.[176] *Maeror*, on the other hand, is rare and occurs, for instance,

175 For a detailed discussion of previous editions, see chap. 2, pp. 23–62.

176 16:6, 20, 21, 22.

in Horace's *Ars Poetica* (110), where it appears in his discussion on the character of tragedy.[177] The noun was apparently avoided by the Augustans, suggesting that it was already archaic in the last years of the Republic, but enjoyed a new vogue in Neronian literature.[178] At any rate, the word was incorporated into Christian literature and enjoyed popularity with the Church Fathers, which testifies to its erudite tone.[179]

In this section, we will demonstrate that, in order to capture the connotation of uncommon Greek words, the translation of the *Codex Vercellensis* Luke frequently draws on the vocabulary of Latin classical literature. The following table provides an overview of the terms borrowed from cultivated language registers, and rarely found in other witnesses of the Latin Gospels.

Table 17: Rare and poetical terms in VL3 Luke

Verse	NA^{28}	VL3	Other Latin authorities
2:28	ἀγκάλας	*amplexum*	*manus* 2 *alas* 5 *manibus* 4 *ulnas* A om. 8
8:23	λαῖλαψ	*turbo*	*procella* cet.
15:27	ὑγιαίνοντα	*incolume*	*saluum* cet.
19:27	κατασφάξατε	*iugulate*	*occidite* 5 *interficite* cet.
21:11	φόβητρα	*formidines*	*timores* 2 5 *terrores* cet.
22:45	λύπης	*maerore*	*tristitia* cet.
23:10	εὐτόνως	*uehementer*	*fortiter* 5 *constanter* cet.
23:45	ἐσκοτίσθη*	*intenebricatus*	*obscuratus* cet.
24:11	λῆρος	*delera*	*derisus* 5 *delibramentum* 4 *deliramentum* (*deleramentum* 2) cet.

* A C^{3} D K Q W Γ Δ Θ Ψ.

Three of these renderings may be analyzed in further detail:

Table 18: The rendering of ὑγιαίνοντα in 15:27

Verse	NA^{28}	VL3	Other Latin authorities
15:27	ὑγιαίνοντα	*incolume*	*saluum* cet.

177 Cf. Hor. *Ars P.* 108: *format enim natura prius nos intus ad omnem fortunarum habitum, iuuat, aut impellit ad iram, aut ad humum maerore graui deducit, et angit.*
178 Cf. TARRANT, "The Authenticity of the Letter of Sappho to Phaon," 140.
179 Cf., e. g., August. *De civ. D.* 21.9: *sicut tinea uestimentum et uermis lignum, sic maeror excruciat cor uiri.*

In Luke 15:27, the father celebrates the return of his repentant son because he came back "sane and sound," ὑγιαίνοντα αὐτὸν ἀπέλαβεν. The Greek word is a present participle of ὑγιαίνειν, a verb only found in Luke. The typical Latin translation is the adjective *saluus*, "sound" or "safe," but *Codex Vercellensis* has *incolumis*, "unharmed" or "still alive," a word well-attested in classical literature, but rare in the Latin Gospels.[180] With the exception of this passage, *incolumis* appears only in Matt 15:31 in the text of *Codex Bezae* (VL5), where it serves as a translation of ὑγιής and is associated with κυλλός, "crooked" or "deformed." In this case, it is possible that *incolumis* was employed because of its etymology: the word is namely derived from *columna*, "column" or "pillar," so that the adjective originally referred to an erect column, and later to anything stable or strong.[181] One might of course object that *saluus* and *incolumis* are to a certain extent synonymous;[182] however, the Lucan text of the *Codex Vercellensis* reserves *saluus* as a translation of the Greek verb σῴζειν, mostly in the phrase *saluum facere*, which – in contrast to ὑγιαίνειν in Luke 15:27 – has theological implications as well.[183] At any rate, in the other passages in which ὑγιαίνειν is used, the translator still avoids the rendering *saluus*, preferring *sanus* instead, as opposed to sick, as in Luke 5:31 (οὐ χρείαν ἔχουσιν οἱ ὑγιαίνοντες ἰατροῦ – *non egent sani medico*) or in Luke 7:10 (εὗρον τὸν δοῦλον ὑγιαίνοντα – *inuenerunt seruum sanum*).

180 Cf., e. g., Caes. *B. Gall.* 1.53, Cic. *Cat.* 3.10.

181 Cf. Isid. *Etym.* 10.55: *a columna uocatus, eo quod erecto et firmissimus sit.*

182 Cf. Caes. *B. Civ.* 2.5: *an poenitet uos, quod saluum atque incolumem exercitum nulla omnino naue desiderata traduxerim.* See also DOEDERLEIN, Lateinische Synonyme und Etymologien, 34.

183 Cf., e. g., 17:19: ἀναστὰς πορεύου ἡ πίστις σου σέσωκεν σε (*surge et uade, quoniam fides tua te saluum fecit*), 18:42: ἀνάβλεψον· ἡ πίστις σου σέσωκεν σε (*respice, fides tua te saluum fecit*), 19:10: ἦλθεν γὰρ ὁ υἱὸς τοῦ ἀνθρώπου ζητῆσαι καὶ σῶσαι τὸ ἀπολωλός (*uenit enim filius hominis saluum facere et quaerere perditum*).

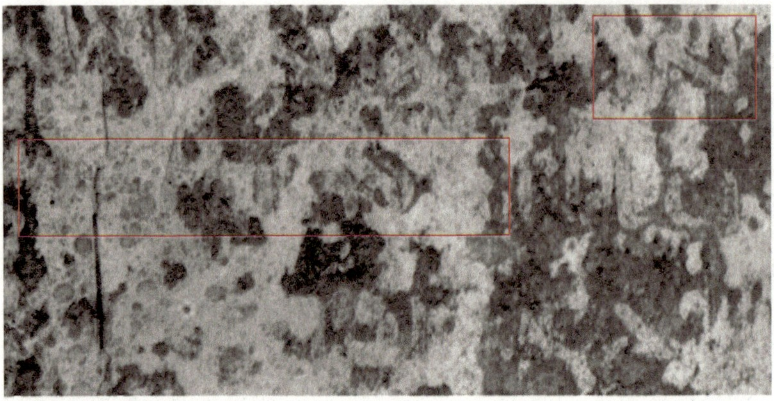

Figure 5.13: The reading *incolume* in Luke 15:27 (451[a]).

Table 19: The rendering of κατασφάξατε in Luke 19:27

Verse	NA[28]	VL3	Other Latin authorities
19:27	κατασφάξατε	*iugulate*	*occidite* 5 *interficite* cet.

The translator's effort to capture these variations of the Greek can be detected here as well. At the end of the Parable of the Ten Minas, the nobleman demands that his enemies be brought before him and slain. The Greek text has κατασφάζειν, "to kill" or "murder," a verb and a hapax legomenon in the NT. This verb is translated as *interficere* in the majority of the Latin authorities, with the exception of the *Codex Bezae* (VL5), which has *occidere*, both verbs being customary expressions for putting somebody to death.[184] In contrast, the *Codex Vercellensis* translation *iugulare* conveys a nuance of the Greek: *iugulum* literally means "collarbone" and hence the hollow part of the neck above it, where a cut is made, especially when slaughtering animals.[185] In this way, *iugulare* means not only "to kill" but specifies that the killing is performed by a cut to the throat. This corresponds to the Greek wording since the

184 *interficere* and *occidere* are the usual renderings of ἀποκτείνειν (11:47, 13:31,34), and to a lesser extent of ἀναιρεῖν, as in Luke 22:2.

185 Cf. Fronto, *De differentiis vocabulorum* 523: *interficere et perimere prisca sunt, occidere ob caedem dictum est, iugulare ob iugulum, necare a nece, interficere a facto.*

substantive σφαγή primarily means “slaughter,” but metonymically also “throat,” that is, the spot where the victim is struck.[186]

Figure 5.14: The reading *iugulate* in 19:27 (476[b]).

Table 20: The rendering of φόβητρα in 21:11

Verse	NA[28]	VL3	Other Latin authorities
21:11	φόβητρα	*formidines*	*timores* 2 5 *terrores* cet.

The *plurale tantum* φόβητρα, “something that strikes terror” or “the cause of fright,” is another hapax legomenon in the NT, presenting a Lucan addition to the eschatology of the synoptic parallels in Matt and Mark. In avoiding the alternatives *timor* and *terror*, the *Codex Vercellesis* rendering *formido* seems designed to capture the oddness of the Greek noun, which emerges especially if we consider the variant reading *timor* – the typical translation for φόβος – contained in codices *Palatinus* (VL2) and *Bezae* (VL5). At the same time, *formido* is also the word choice of Tertullian in his rendition of the verse, an agreement that sheds light on the relation of the *Codex Vercellensis* Luke with the earliest witnesses of the Latin Bible.[187]

186 A possible parallel is Isa 22:13, where the LXX reads σφάζοντες μόσχους καὶ θύοντες πρόβατα, rendered in the Vulgate with *occidere uitulos et iugulare arietes*.

187 Cf. Tert. *adv. Marc.* 4.39.3: *uideamus et quae signa temporibus imponat, bella, opinor, et regnum super regnum, et gentem super gentem, et pestem, et fames, terraeque motus, et formidines, et prodigia de caelo, quae omnia seuero et atroci deo congruent. haec cum adiicit etiam oportere fieri, quem*

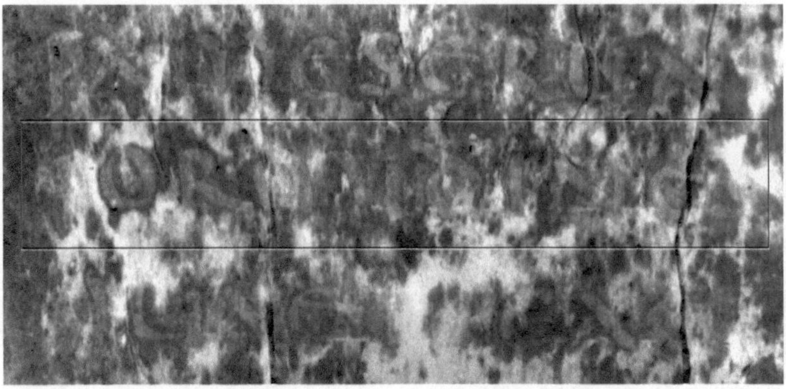

Figure 5.15: The reading *formidines* in 21:11 (490^{a}).

To sum up: many of the unique readings considered in this section are words not commonly found in other Latin authorities of the Gospels but come from classical literature instead. Therefore, they demonstrate how the Lucan text of the *Codex Vercellensis* employs a vocabulary that might have already become archaic at the time when the first Latin translations of the Greek Gospels appeared. At the same time, the parallels to Tertullian, give evidence of the age of these readings, which are seemingly older than even those found in the *Codex Palatinus* (VL2), often considered the representative par excellence of the earlier text traditions.

5.4.4 Calques and Graecisms

Calques are produced by morphologically translating expressions using combinations of native elements which match the meaning and structure of the original and of its component parts.[188] This translation technique is extensively used in the *Codex Vercellensis* Luke, and it can indeed be seen as a central feature of its text. Many such readings present true lexicographical innovations because they are not attested in classical literature and almost exclusively appear in Christian texts.

se praestat, destructorem an probatorem creatoris? See also Job^{vg} 18:11: *undique terrebunt eum formidines et inuoluent pedes eius.*

188 Cf. BURTON, The Old Latin Gospels, 129.

Table 21: Calques and Graecisms in VL3 Luke

Verse	NA[28]	VL3	Other Latin authorities
8:6	ἐξηράνθη	*exaruit*	*aridum factum est* 5
			aruit cet.
11:44	ἄδηλα	*ignobilia*	*sine specie* 5
			quae non parent (*apparent* 17) cet.
11:46	δυσβάστακτα	*inportabiles*	*grauibus* 2
			quae non possunt portari 5
			quae non possunt portare 4
			quae portari non possunt 17 A
14:12	ἀνταπόδομα	*redditio*	*retributio* cet.
16:14	φιλάργυροι	*amatores pecuniae*	*cupidissmi* 2
			cupidi 5
			auari cet.
17:18	δοῦναι δόξαν	*honorem dare*	*claritatem dare* 2
			gloriam dare 5 A
			gratias ageret (*agaret* 4 *agere* 8) cet.
19:14	ἐδαφίζειν	*pauimentabunt*	*ad solum deponent* 2
			ad nihilum deducent 5
			ad terram (add. et 17) *prosternent* cet.
21:14	προμελετᾶν	*prius meletare*	*promeletantes* 5
			praemeditari (*prameditari* 2) cet.
21:26	ἀποψυχόντων	*arefrigescentibus*	*deficientium* 5
			arescentibus cet.
22:53	τοῦ σκότος	*a tenebrae*	*tenebrae* 5
			tenebrarum cet.
23:29	κακούργων	*malefici*	*malignis* 5
			latronibus cet.
23:52	λαξευτῷ	*sculptili*	*sculpto* 5
			exciso cet.

Some of these word formations will be discussed separately, since they are rare in non-Christian literature:

Table 22: The rendering of δυσβάστακτα in 11:46

Verse	NA[28]	VL3	Other Latin authorities
11:46	δυσβάστακτα	*inportabiles*	*grauibus* 2
			quae non possunt portari 5
			quae non possunt portare 4
			quae portari non possunt 17 A

The rendering *inportabilis* stands for the Greek verbal adjective δυσβάστακτα, "hard to bear," whereas most other witnesses simply paraphrase the term using a whole relative clause: *quae portari non possunt*. The calque *inportabilis* is exclusively in Christian literature and was apparently coined to render the Greek term, being first attested in Tertullian.[189]

Figure 5.16: The reading *inportabiles* in Luke 11:46 (425ª).

Table 23: The rendering of ἀνταπόδομα in Luke 14:12

Verse	NA²⁸	VL3	Other Latin authorities
14:12	ἀνταπόδομα	*redditio*	*retribution* cet.

redditio is almost unknown in classical literature, occurring only in Quintilian's *Institutio Oratoria* to designate the consequent in a conditional clause.[190] The components of the Latin noun match the Greek since *dare* corresponds to διδόναι, while the suffix *-ditio* translates -δομα. Strikingly, the text of the *Codex Vercellensis* is so consistent in rendering this term, that, in Luke 14:14, where the verb ἀνταποδιδοναι occurs twice, the text has *reddere*, while the other witnesses read *retribuere*.

189 Cf. Tert. *adv. Marc.* 427.

190 Quint. 8.3.77–80.

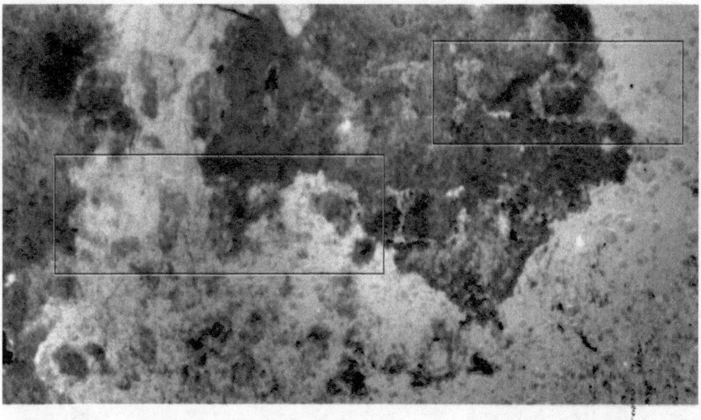

Figure 5.17: The reading *redditio* in 14:12 (441[b]).

Table 24: The rendering of ἐδαφίζειν in 19:44

Verse	NA[28]	VL3	Other Latin authorities
19:44	ἐδαφίζειν	*pauimentabunt*	*ad solum deponent* 2
			ad nihilum deducent 5
			ad terram (add. et 17) *prosternent* cet.

The verb *pauimentare* is rarely attested, even in classical literature. The wording in the *Codex Vercellensis* clearly tries to capture the etymology of the Greek original: *pauimentare* derives from *pauimentum*, "ground-floor," in the same way as ἐδαφίζειν derives from ἔδαφος, with the identical meaning. In this context, the Greek verb clearly has the metaphorical sense "to raze to the ground," applying, in Jesus's predictions of the future destruction of Jerusalem, both to the houses, which will be destroyed, and the inhabitants, who will be slain; the Latin equivalent *pauimentare*, however, was employed in classical literature only in its concrete sense, "to cover with pavement," in reference to cities or buildings etc., so that it is not surprising that the verb is found several times in the writings of Vitruvius.[191] There is apparently no other case of the verb being used in the sense it has in the *Codex Ver-*

191 Cf. e. g., Vitr. 6.5.3: *earum autem rerum non solum erunt in urbe aedificiorum rationes, sed etiam ruri, praeterquam quod in urbe atria proxima ianuis solent esse, ruri ab pseudourbanis statim peristylia, deinde tunc atria habentia circum porticus pauimentatas spectantes ad palaestras et ambulationes.*

cellensis. It is true that *pauimentare* occurs in two of Augustine's sermons, but there it is used in a sense closer to its classical meaning.[192]

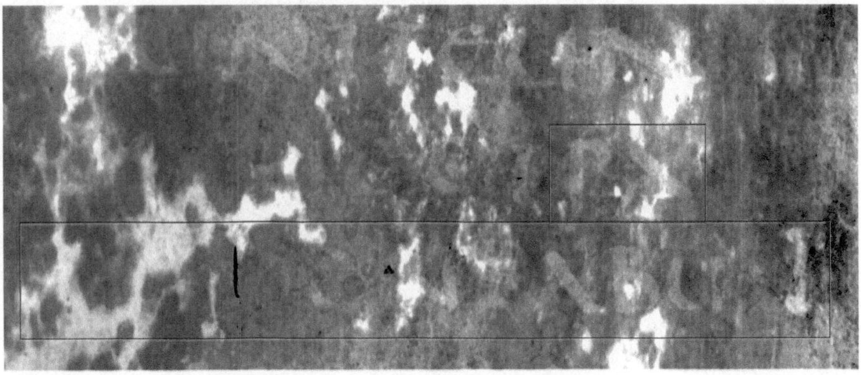

Figure 5.18: The reading *pauimentabunt* in Luke 19:44 (479b).

Table 25: The rendering of ἀποψυχόντων in Luke 21:26

Verse	NA28	VL3	Other Latin authorities
21:26	ἀποψυχόντων	*arefrigescentibus*	*deficientium* 5
			arescentibus cet.

Earlier scholarship has already argued that the intended reading of the manuscript in this verse was not *arefrigescentibus*:[193] the scribe found *refrigescentibus* in his copy but made a mistake in writing under the influence of *arescentibus* of the other witnesses. This argument is certainly plausible, especially considering that the reading *refrigescentibus* is also supported by Tertullian's rendering of this passage in *De resurrectione carnis*.[194] However, this account neglects the possibility that the letter *a*- may have already been in the scribe's copy, where it was intentionally included to reconstruct the Greek verb ἀποψύχειν in the form of the Latin calque

192 Cf. August. *sermo* 82.14: *sed malam conscientiam pugnis pauimentare, solidiorem reddere, non correctiorem*; In this passage, Augustine states that the purpose of penance is not to beat a bad conscience, ram it down into concrete and make it harder and more solid than ever, but to correct it. See also *sermo* 332.4: *nihil est aliud quam peccata pauimentare.*

193 Cf. AALDERS, "Tertullian's quotations from ST Luke," 275; HIGGINS, "The Latin Text of Luke in Marcion and Tertullian," 12.

194 Cf. Tert. *Res.* 22.5–6: *cum stupore sonitus maris et motus refrigescentium hominum prae metu et expectatione eorum, quae immineant orbi terrae.*

arefrigescere, with the prefix *a*- morpho-syntactically matching ἀπο-. This hypothesis receives further support by the reading *refrigescet* (c. c.) in Matt 24:12, which there serves as the rendering of the simplex ψύχειν.

Figure 5.19: The reading *arefrigescentibus* in Luke 21:26 (492[b]).

Table 26: The rendering of προμελετᾶν in Luke 21:14

Verse	NA[28]	VL3	Other Latin authorities
21:14	προμελετᾶν	*prius meletare*	*promeletantes* 5 *praemeditari* (*prameditari* 2) cet.

The previous editors offer a variety of readings on page 490[b] of the *Codex Vercellensis*.[195] However, the MSI-images of the page are clear and distinctly show an *l* instead of a *d*, resulting in the variant reading *meletare*, a Latinized form of the Greek verb προμελετᾶν. The Graecism is also supported by the reading *promeletantes* of the *Codex Bezae* (VL5), although the prefix προ- was not incorporated into the verb in the *Codex Vercellensis*, but rather rendered separately with the adverb *prius*.

195 *medetare* Irico, Gasquet and Jülicher; *meditare* Bianchini.

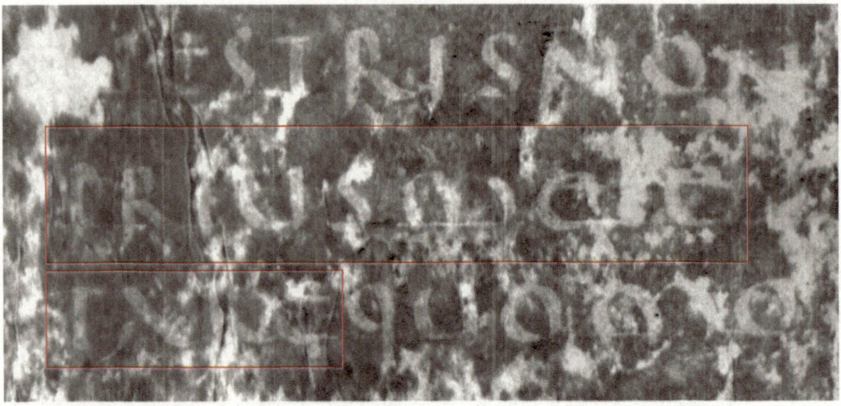

Figure 5.20: The Graecism *prius meletare* in Luke 21:14 (490[b]).

Table 27: The rendering of τοῦ σκότος in Luke 22:53

Verse	NA[28]	VL3	Other Latin authorities
22:53	τοῦ σκότος	*a tenebrae*	*tenebrae* 5 *tenebrarum* cet.

As in the example above, the reading on page 502[b] of the manuscript could only be deciphered by means of MSI-images. Here, Irico made the better suggestion with the reading *tenebrae*, whereas the other editors simply followed the majority of the authorities, which have *tenebrarum*. However, Irico was not able to identify the preposition *a* before the noun. The correct reading *a tenebrae* is striking from several perspectives. First, as we can see in the other witnesses, *tenebra* is almost always used in the plural, whereas the *Codex Vercellensis* offers a singular. Moreover, the reading *a tenebrae* results in the non-standard case agreement *a tenebrae* (genitive) instead of *a tenebra* (ablative), clearly a Graecism in case agreement due the influence of ἀπό, what suggests an underlying Greek text which read ἀπὸ τοῦ σκότος instead of the well-known τοῦ σκότος.

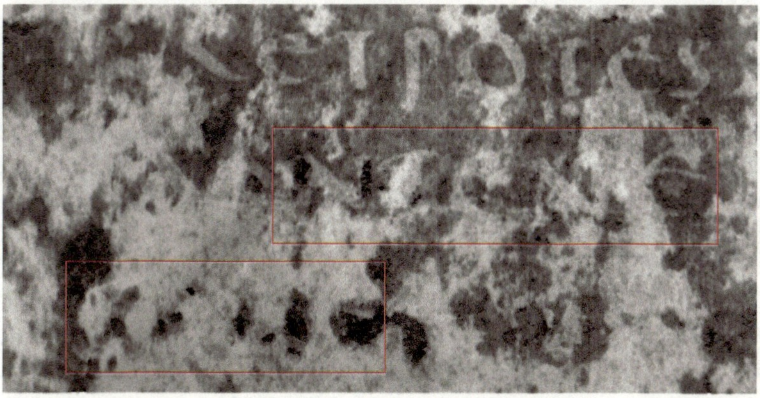

Figure 5.21: The reading *potestas a tenebrae* in Luke 22:53 (502^{b}).

From the examples given above, we may attribute an attempt to render Greek words and expressions morpho-syntactically by using combinations of native Latin elements to the Lucan text in the *Codex Vercellensis*. As already stated,[196] this translation strategy is not uncommon for the oldest textual traditions; accordingly, our investigation of calques and Graecisms in the text gives further evidence for identifying the *Codex Vercellensis* as one of the oldest witnesses of the Latin Gospels.

5.4.5 Technical Vocabulary

An important aspect of translations concerns the rendering of technical vocabulary. Since all texts are anchored in a culture to a certain degree, we can state that culturally specific terms present in the source text – such as those designating buildings, trade, public administration, currency etc. – can present problems for translators, especially if there are notable differences between source and target languages. In many instances, Latin translators had to employ various strategies (paraphrase, transliteration, loanwords etc.) to find a suitable rendering for the technical terms, expressions, and concepts they encountered in the Greek Gospels. In what follows, we will discuss variant readings which concern architecture (4.1), medicine (4.2), and realia (4.3) in order to better understand the differences between the translation of the *Codex Vercellensis* Luke and other Latin witnesses.

196 Cf. 5.3.3 p. 241ff., and more often.

5.4.5.1 Architecture

Architectural terminology was a challenge for translators of the Gospels since the appropriate rendering of architectural terms requires an in-depth understanding of their specialized (and often historical) meanings. The difficulty becomes evident when we take into consideration the number of transliterations, neologisms, and calques which the translators used for terms which had no precise equivalent in the target language. For instance, in the OT accounts of Solomon's Temple, the LXX transliterates the most important Hebrew technical terms (גלה Pl.: גלות – γωλάθ, אולם – αἰλάμ, דביר – δαβίρ etc.). However, the Vulgate prefers to translate them all, either adopting Greek words, like *epistylia* for γωλάθ, or Latin ones, such as *uestibulum* for αἰλάμ, often with a meaning completely different from the classical sense of the term, as in the case of *oraculum* for δαβίρ.[197] The same reasoning applies to neologisms and calques of all sorts, as we can also see in non-biblical Christian literature: for example, in Juvencus' epic *Euangeliorum libri*, a description of Jesus Christ's life in dactylic hexameters, *conuerticulum* is used to refer to a synagogue, thus avoiding the Greek loanword *synagoga* and latinizing the emerging Christian vocabulary.[198]

In what follows, we will analyse some unique readings taken from the *Codex Vercellensis* Luke which provide an outline of the variety of translation strategies used to represent spaces, building elements, their interiors, and partitions.

Table 28: Architectural vocabulary in VL3 Luke

Verse	NA[28]	VL3	Other Latin authorities
11:43	πρωτοκαθεδρίαν	*consessus*	*sessiones* 2 5 *cathedras* cet.
12:18	οἰκοδομήσω	*aedificabam*	*faciam* cet.
20:46	πρωτοκαθεδρίας	*consessus*	*praesidere* 2 *cathedras* cet.
21:1	γαζοφυλάκιον	*altario*	*gazophilacium* 2 *zaiophylacium* 8 *gazophylacium* cet.
21:5	ἀναθήμασιν	*bonis*	*depositionibus* 5 *donis* cet.

197 Cf. O'Hare, 'Have you seen, Son of Man?,' 63: "Of the nineteen total transliterations that occur in LXX Ezek 40–48, eight are unique to the translator of this corpus, and the rest are known outside Ezekiel. Of these eight unique transliterations, six are architectural terms."

198 Cf. Dijkstra, "Epic Architecture," 158. In this way, VL3 Luke exhibits several readings which represent a variety of translation strategies used in depicting spaces and their objects.

	κεκόσμηται	*extructum*	*exornatum* 2 *ornata* 5 *ornatum* cet.
22:12	ἀνάγαιον	*maedianum*	*superiorem* 5 *pede plano* 4 *caenaculum* A *in superioribus* cet.

Luke 21:5 is especially noteworthy since here, the *Codex Vercellensis* transmits a singular reading for λίθοις καλοῖς καὶ ἀναθήμασιν κεκόσμηται, 'it was adorned with noble stones and offerings.' Instead of the usual *lapidibus bonis et donis ornatum*, contained in most other witnesses, the *Codex Vercellensis* reads *lapidibus optimis et bonis* [*ex*]*tructum*, 'it was constructed with excellent and noble stones.' This variant is striking for several reasons. The participle *ex(s)tructus* is an inflected form of *ex(s)truere*, a verb commonly linked to the construction of buildings.[199] The reading suggests an emphasis on the temple's basic structural characteristics, with a focus on the reliability of its engineering, not on the artistry of its ornaments, which is described by the more usual variant *ornatum*. This view is reinforced by the exclusion of the Greek ἀναθήμασιν in the text of our manuscript, which is replaced by *bonis* instead of *donis*. What is stressed in the translation of this passage is the value of the stones and their quality as stabilizers of the solid construction, rather than the non-essential decoration of the temple façades. Moreover, the variant in the *Codex Vercellensis* seems to highlight the reply of Jesus, who does not mention the ornaments, but only the stones, in saying οὐκ ἀφεθήσεται λίθος ἐπὶ λίθῳ ὧδε ὃς οὐ καταλυθήσεται, "there will be no stone left upon stone here that will not be pulled down." However, the Latin textual tradition goes even further in this architectural interpretation of the verse, emphasizing the structural aspects of the construction by the addition of *hic in parietem* (*in pariete hic* a d), 'here in the wall,' after *lapis super lapidem*. This addition is common to most Old Latin witnesses, but it is not attested in the earlier text forms, such as the *Codex Palatinus*. Thus, *Codex Vercellensis* is the oldest manuscript – including the Greek witnesses – to record this emphasis on the stability of the construction in Luke 21:5. On the other hand, one certainly finds many opulent objects among the ἀναθήματα.[200] ἀνάθημα is a hapax

199 Cf. Tac. *Ann.* 3.72: *at Pompei theatrum igne fortuito haustum Caesar extructurum pollicitus est eo quod nemo e familia restaurando sufficeret*; Caes. *Gall.* 6.17.4: *multis in civitatibus harum rerum exstructos tumulos locis consecratis conspicari licet.*

200 Josephus mentions, e.g., offerings and gifts to the temple in Jerusalem made by the kings Xerxes and Ptolemy. Cf. Josephus *A.J.* 11.120: Δαρείου δὲ τελευτήσαντος παραλαβὼν τὴν βασιλείαν ὁ παῖς αὐτοῦ Χέρξης ἐκληρονόμησεν αὐτοῦ καὶ τὴν πρὸς τὸν θεὸν εὐσέβειάν τε καὶ τιμήν: ἅπαντα

legomenon in the Gospels and was used intentionally. We might suspect that, in using this term, Luke wanted to contrast the poor widow putting all her living in the treasury of the temple (v. 1) not only with the other, much richer donors, but also with the rich votive offerings themselves,[201] which decorated the temple complex and to which Jesus's attention was drawn by his interlocutors. Therefore, the omission of any rendering for ἀναθήμασιν in the *Codex Vercellensis* makes the transition between the two narrative moments – the widow and the future destruction of the temple – more surprising.

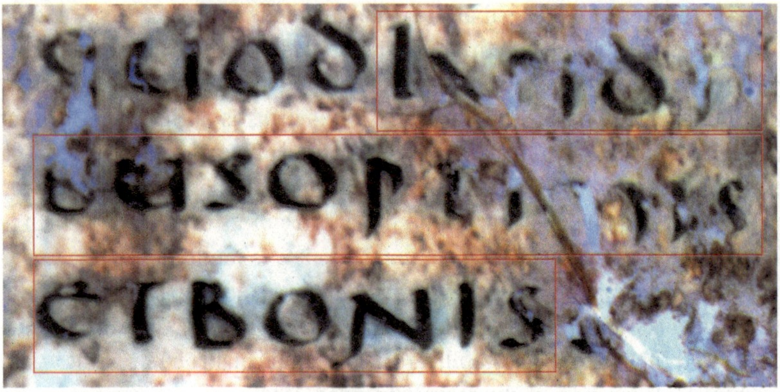

Figure 5.22: The reading *lapidibus optimis et bonis* in Luke 21:5 (489[a]).

But also Luke 21:1 reveals a further interesting aspect in *Codex Vercellensis* concerning architectonic terminology. Usually, the Latin textual tradition employs the loanword *gazophylacium* for the Hellenistic Jewish term γαζοφυλάκιον, with minor orthographical variation.[202] This term designates a repository ('treasury') where offerings and things needed for the temple service were kept, but especially the

γὰρ ἀκολούθως τῷ πατρὶ τὰ πρὸς τὴν θρεσκείαν ἐποίησεν καὶ πρὸς τοὺς Ἰουδαίους ἔσχεν φιλοτιμότατα; 12.58: τὴν μέντοι γε τῶν ἀναθημάτων πολυτέλειαν καὶ κατασκευήν, ἣν ἀπέστειλεν ὁ βασιλεὺς τῷ θεῷ, οὐκ ἀνεπιτήδειον ἡγησάμην διελθεῖν, ὅπως ἅπασιν ἡ τοῦ βασιλέως περὶ τὸν θεὸν φιλοτιμία φανερὰ γένηται. Cf. FELDMAN, Josephus' Interpretation of the Bible, 602.

201 See Josephus *A.J.* 18.1 (εἰς δὲ τὸ ἱερὸν ἀναθήματα στέλλοντες), 18.312–313 (πεπιστευκότες τό τε δίδραχμον [...] καὶ ὁπόσα δὲ ἄλλα ἀναθήματα), *B.J.* 2.413 (ἀλλὰ καὶ τὰ βλεπόμενα καὶ τὰ παραμένοντα τοσοῦτον χρόνον ἀναθήματα περὶ τῷ ἱερῷ καθιδρυκέναι). The only passage in which he goes into any detail on this topic is in *A.J.* 12.78, where he mentions two golden jars, thirty golden bowls, all gifts adorned with precious stones, etc.

202 For example, *gazophilacium* e *gazofilacium* VL11, 13, 14.

property of widows and orphans. *Codex Vercellensis*, however, reads *altarium*, a later form for the classical *altar*, which was mostly used in the plural, *altaria*.[203] The variant *altarium* is found only in the text of Luke, while the other books have the expected reading *gazophylacium*.[204] Hence, the Lucan text of our manuscript seems to suggest that the place where the offerings were placed (*mittebant dona*) was the temple's altar, not the treasury. There is only one other passage in the Gospels where offerings on the altar are mentioned, namely Matt 5:23–24.[205] In this case, it is not very clear what kind of offerings the author had in mind, since the Greek term δῶρον may apply to all kinds of sacrifices, including domestic animals, grain, incense, or silverware,[206] which could not be placed in the *gazophylacium*.

203 Originally, the word meant that which was properly placed upon the altar, called *ara*, for the burning of the victim. *altarium* is also used in Luke 11:51 (μεταξὺ τοῦ θυσιαστηρίου καὶ τοῦ οἴκου), while all other witnesses transmit the classical form *altar*.

204 Mark 12:41, 43; John 8:20.

205 Cf.: ἐὰν οὖν προσφέρῃς τὸ δῶρόν σου ἐπὶ τὸ θυσιαστήριον κἀκεῖ μνησθῇς ὅτι ὁ ἀδελφός σου ἔχει τι κατὰ σοῦ, ἄφες ἐκεῖ τὸ δῶρόν σου ἔμπροσθεν τοῦ θυσιαστηρίου, καὶ ὕπαγε πρῶτον διαλλάγηθι τῷ ἀδελφῷ σου, καὶ τότε ἐλθὼν πρόσφερε τὸ δῶρόν σου. In Acts 4:34–35, the author depicts how the believers sold their properties, brought the money to the apostles, and put it at their feet. Subsequently, it was distributed to anyone who had need: ὅσοι γὰρ κτήτορες χωρίων ἢ οἰκιῶν ὑπῆρχον, πωλοῦντες ἔφερον τὰς τιμὰς τῶν πιπρασκομένων καὶ ἐτίθουν παρὰ τοὺς πόδας τῶν ἀποστόλων: διεδίδετο δὲ ἑκάστῳ καθότι ἄν τις χρείαν εἶχεν. An altar is not explicitly mentioned, though.

206 This is clear in many LXX-passages. Cf. Lev 2:1 for flour: Εàν δὲ ψυχὴ προσφέρῃ δῶρον θυσίαν τῷ κυρίῳ, σεμίδαλις ἔσται τὸ δῶρον αὐτοῦ, καὶ ἐπιχεεῖ ἐπ᾽ αὐτὸ ἔλαιον καὶ ἐπιθήσει ἐπ᾽ αὐτὸ λίβανον· θυσία ἐστίν; Num 7:49 for silverware: τὸ δῶρον αὐτοῦ τρύβλιον ἀργυροῦν ἕν, τριάκοντα καὶ ἑκατὸν ὁλκὴ αὐτοῦ, φιάλην μίαν ἀργυρᾶν ἑβδομήκοντα σίκλων κατὰ τὸν σίκλον τὸν ἅγιον, ἀμφότερα πλήρη σεμιδάλεως ἀναπεποιημένης ἐν ἐλαίῳ, εἰς θυσίαν·

Figure 5.23: The reading *altario* instead of *gazophylacium* in Luke 21:1 (488[b]).

Another aspect concerning architecture in the text is the importance of the Temple in Jerusalem, which is emphasized in the *Codex Vercellensis* in a striking way. In the second temptation (Luke 4:5–8), Jesus is taken up by the devil and is shown all the kingdoms of the world. The devil promises him authority and glory if Jesus worships him. In the Lucan tradition, this space above is not specified at all, except in some witnesses (A K Γ Δ Θ Ψ it vg[cl]), in which Jesus is taken to a high mountain (εἰς ὄρος ὑψηλόν, *in montem excelsum*). This should be considered as an attempt to adjust the text to the synoptic passage in Matt, where the textual transmission is homogenous, and all witnesses mention this high mountain. However, in the Vercellensis, the Lucan text states that Jesus is taken to the same pinnacle of the Temple in Jerusalem (*adduxit eum Hierusalem et statuit eum supra pinnam templi*), from which he would later be asked to leap off (vv. 9–11: *et adduxit illum in Hierusalem et statuit illum super pinnam templi*). This singular reading has many exegetical implications since it underlines the centrality of Jerusalem and of its most sacred spot. Furthermore, it follows OT conceptions, as seen, for instance, in the book of Ezekiel,[207] or in Josephus' writings,[208] where the city is called the "navel of the country." Thus, in the *Codex Vercellensis*, *pinna templi* is not merely an architectural

207 Ezek 38:12: καὶ ἐπ' ἔθνος συνηγμένον ἀπὸ ἐθνῶν πολλῶν πεποιηκότας κτήσεις κατοικοῦντας ἐπὶ τὸν ὀμφαλὸν τῆς γῆς.

208 Jos. *B.J.* 3.52: μεσαιτάτη δ' αὐτῆς πόλις τὰ Ἱεροσόλυμα κεῖται, παρ' ὃ καί τινες οὐκ ἀσκόπως ὀμφαλὸν τὸ ἄστυ τῆς χώρας ἐκάλεσαν.

component of the sanctuary in Jerusalem but is seen as the centre of the world itself, a place from which all power emanates and can be exerted.[209]

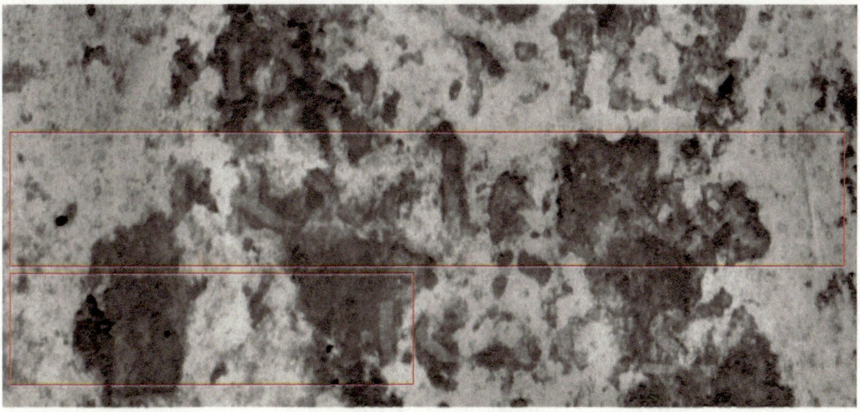

Figure 5.24: The reading *supra pinnam templi* in 4:5 (353[a]).

5.4.5.2 Medicine

It is well-known that, while Greek texts use few terms to designate illness in general, such as νόσος, ἀσθένεια, βάσανος, μαλακία and μάστιξ, their Latin translations employ a variety of terms and concepts, which are – at first sight – difficult to distinguish.[210] A simple example may be found in Jesus's answer to the disciples of John the Baptist in Luke 7:21, where we read that Jesus "healed many people of diseases and plagues and evil spirits, and he gave sight to many who were blind." The Greek has no variants and reads ἐθεράπευσεν πολλοὺς ἀπὸ νόσων καὶ μαστίγων καὶ πνευμάτων πονηρῶν, καὶ τυφλοῖς πολλοῖς ἐχαρίσατο βλέπειν, whereas the typical Latin translation of the verse is *curabat multos a languoribus et plagis et spiritibus inmundis et caecis donauit uisum.* However, each affliction term used here has a variant reading in the Latin authorities: *Codex Bezae* (VL5) reads *infirmitatibus* instead of *languoribus*; *Palatinus* (VL2) has *flagellis*, while *Vercellensis* has *uerberis*

209 For a detailed discussion on the architectonic concept of pinnacle in the Latin tradition of the Gospels, see WEISSENRIEDER, "Die Versuchung Jesu und die Übersetzungen von πτερύγιον"; WEISSENRIEDER, VISINONI, "Archi*texture*: Sacred Spaces in the *Codex Vercellensis* (a, 3) Gospel of Luke."

210 Cf. WEISSENRIEDER, "'Medical' Vocabulary," 43–60; WEISSENRIEDER, "'Medical Vocabulary' and the Women with the Issue of Blood," 270–285; WEISSENRIEDER, VISINONI, "Illness, Suffering and Treatment in a Changing World," 321.

instead of *plagis*.[211] In the table below, we list all the unique readings relating to illnesses and their treatments in the *Codex Vercellensis* Luke:

Table 29: Medical vocabulary in VL3 Luke

Verse	NA[28]	VL3	Other Latin authorities
4:27	ἐκαθαρίσθη	*purgatus*	*emundatus* 2 *mundatus* cet.
4:40	ἀσθενοῦντας	*aegros*	*languentes* 2 *infirmantes* 5 *infirmos* cet.
5:14	καθαρισμοῦ	*purgatione*	*purificatione* 5 *emundatione* (*emundationem* 8) cet.
5:15	ἀσθενῶν	*languoribus*	*infirmitatibus* cet.
7:21	μαστίγων	*uerberibus*	*flagellis* 2 *plagis* cet.
7:22	καθαρίζονται	*purgantur*	*emundantur* 2 *mundantur* cet.
9:2	ἀσθενεῖς	*aegros*	*infirmos* cet.
9:39	ῥήσσει*	*concidit*	*collidit* 2 *adlidit* 5 *elidit* cet
	σπαράσσει	*discarpit*	*disrumpit* 5 *dissipat* cet.
9:42	συνεσπάραξεν	*concarpsit*	*conturbabit* 5 *dissipauit* cet.
13:11	ἀσθενείας	*languoribus*	*in infirmitate* 5 *infirmitatis* cet.
17:14	ἐκαθαρίσθησαν	*emundati*	*purgati* 2 *mundati* cet.
17:15	ἰάθη	*sanus*	*curatus* 2 *sanatus* 8 17 *mundatus* cet.
21:11	λοιμοί	*pestes*	*lues* 2 *morbi* 5 *pestilentiae* (*pestilentia* 8) cet.

* א D Θ

In what follows, we will discuss two of these terms at further length.

211 Cf. WEISSENRIEDER, "'Medical' Vocabulary," 43–60.

Table 30: The rendering of σπαράσσει and συνεσπάραξεν in 9:39,42

Verse	NA[28]	VL3	Other Latin authorities
9:39	σπαράσσει	*discarpit*	*disrumpit* 5 *dissipat* cet.
9:42	συνεσπάραξεν	*concarpsit*	*conturbabit* 5 *dissipauit* cet.

The first example is found in Luke 9:39,42, in the account of the epileptic boy. At first, the boy is described by his father as experiencing seizures and convulsing. The Greek term used to characterize this set of symptoms is the verb σπαράσσειν, "to rend asunder," or "to pull to pieces," also attested in medical writings.[212] In Luke 15:13 and 16:1, the Latin tradition has *dissipare,* which is employed in all texts – including the *Codex Vercellensis* – to render διασκορπίζειν in the sense of "to squander" or "to waste" someone's property. In Luke 9:39, however, the *Codex Vercellensis* has *discarpere,* a secondary form (without vowel reduction through prefixation) of the more standard *discerpere,*[213] "to tear" or "to mutilate," as found, for instance, in Mark 1:26, and in the pericope in Mark 9:26 in most Latin authorities. Later, however, when the boy is brought to Jesus in v. 42 and suffers from a seizure anew, the narrator does not repeat the verb σπαράσσειν, but uses its compound συσπαράσσειν. The majority of Latin witnesses does not record this lexical variation in the Greek text and insists on using *dissipare,* as in v. 39, whereas the *Codex Vercellensis* has *concarpere,* an obvious attempt to reproduce the subtlety of the original in its morphological features by precisely matching the prefixes, *con-* and συν-.[214] *Concerpere* is an uncommon verb, even in classical literature,[215] and a hapax legomenon in the Latin Gospels; however, the archaism can be considered a justifiable rendering of the original, and the word choice captures a nuance of the Greek text which other Latin texts simply ignore.

212 Cf., e. g., Gal. *Ad Glauconem de Methodo Medendi* 11.57: τρίβων τὸ στόμα τῆς κοιλίας καὶ σπαράττων. For a detailed discussion of the medical background of this passage, see WEISSENRIEDER, Images of Illness in the Gospel of Luke, 267–282.

213 Cf. SCHUCHARDT, Der Vokalismus des Vulgärlatein, 36.

214 Something similar applies to *Codex Bezae* (VL5), in which the reading varies from *disrumpit* to *conturbabit*. But, considering that the simplexes are not the same in the two verses (*rumpere* vs. *turbare*), it seems that the text of *Codex Vercellensis* is more accurate in following this detail of a Greek *Vorlage*. For the influence of Greek wording on the Latin text of *Codex Vercellensis,* cf. 5.4.3.

215 Cf., e. g., Liv. 38.55.11: *in senatu tradunt librumque rationis eius cum Lucium fratrem adferre iussisset, inspectante senatu suis ipsum manibus concerpsisse.*

5.4.5.3 Material World

Realia are words and expressions used for culturally specific material elements of everyday life, such as public administration, farming, measures, currency, trading, craftsmanship, and food. Such terms often carry a local overtone, posing another challenge for translators, since they refer to things having no precise native equivalent. Therefore, it is clear that translators of the Latin Gospels had to rely on a number of borrowings from Greek, many of which were in turn Semiticisms such as *batus*, *corus* or *satum*. This is evident in the sphere of public administration, where we can even speak of cultural borrowings:[216] for instance, it seems that Latin-speaking officials preferred to retain local terms for institutions, such as *tetrarcha* or *teloneum*, which were then also incorporated in the lexicon of the Latin Gospels.

However, in many cases, we see the translators attempting to find native Latin terms to convey these objects and concepts of daily life. In 15:8, the *Codex Vercellensis* retains the Greek term δραχμή, spelling the name of the coin in a way close to the original, *drachmas*, whereas later texts have the variant *dragma*. Of interest also is the reading *denarius* in the *Codex Palatinus* (VL2), designating a Roman coin which had the same value as the Greek δραχμή.

Frequently, the Latin word choice emphasizes various aspects of the Greek text, as in Luke 5:29, where the Greek text speaks of δοχή μεγάλη,[217] rendered as *epulum* in the *Codex Palatinus* (VL2), *cena* in the codices *Vercellensis* and *Bezae* (VL5) and *couiuium* in the later witnesses. With *cena*, the emphasis lies on the meal itself, whereas, with *conuiuium*, it is rather the meeting that is emphasized. A similar example is found in 11:22, where the *Fragmenta Curiensia* (VL16) and *Bezae* (VL5) translate πανοπλία with *armaturam* rather than with the *universa arma* of the other witnesses. In contrast to its frequency in the LXX, Greek term occurs only twice in the NT, in the verse at hand and in Eph 6:11, 13. In Eph, the author describes the struggle of the Christian community against darkness and therefore discusses in detail what he takes to be the necessary equipment in this fight: the believers should gird their hips (περιζωσάμενοι τὴν ὀσφύν), put on a breastplate (ἐνδυσάμενοι τὸν θώρακα), shoes (ὑποδησάμενοι τοὺς πόδας), the shield of faith (τὸν θυρεόν τῆς πίστεως), the helmet of salvation (τὴν περικεφαλαν τοῦ σωτηρίου) and the sword of the spirit (τὴν μάχαιραν τοῦ πνεύματος). Significantly, the reading of the *Fragmenta Curiensia* and the *Codex Bezae* is the only variant also found in the Vulgate translation of the OT (Wis 5:18), since πανοπλία, in the sense of armament

216 Burton, The Old Latin Gospels, 142.

217 Scholarship often refers on the Hebrew background of this passage, see מִשְׁתֶּה m.n pl. מִשְׁתָּאוֹת, also מִשְׁתִּים: 1. drinking, drink; 2. banquet, feast, formed from שׁתה (= to drink), with pref. מִ.

or heavily armed guards, is otherwise rendered differently: translations with *arma*, or also metonymically with *lucusta* and *potentia* are found most frequently, whereas the translation with *uniuersa arma* is unusual. Therefore, we can assume that these more common textual variants found their way into the tradition of Latin Bible translations on the basis of the letter to the Ephesians. For example, in writing about the passage Cyprian already testifies to a very similar reading.[218]

The following list provides unique readings of realia as found in the *Codex Vercellensis* Gospel of Luke; some of these deserve detailed commentary:

Table 31: Realia in VL3 Luke

Verse	NA[28]	VL3	Other Latin authorities
5:17	κώμης	*municipio*	*castello* cet.
5:19	κλινιδίῳ	*lectulo*	*grabattum* 2 5 *lecto* cet.
7:37	ἀλάβαστρον	*ampullam*	*uas* 2 *alabastrum* cet.
8:1	κώμην	*uicos*	*castellum* 5 A *castella* cet.
9:6	κώμας	*municipia*	*castella* 2 *ciuitates* 5 *castella et ciuitates* 4 8 *castella* A
9:12	κώμας ἀγρούς	*uicos* *agros*	*castella* cet. *uillas* cet.
10:4	ὑποδήματα	*calciamentum*	*calciamenta* cet.
10:38	κώμην	*uicum*	*castellum* (*castello* 4) cet.
11:46	φορτία	*sarcinas*	*honeribus* 2 *honera* 5 *oneribus* cet.
12:15	ὑπαρχόντων	*facultates*	*substantia* 5 *quae possidet* cet.
13:22	κώμας	*uicos*	*castella* cet.
14:28	δαπάνην	*inpendia*	*erogationem* 5 *sumptus* (*sumptum* 2) cet.
14:33	ὑπάρχουσιν	*facultatibus*	*substantiae suae 5* *quae possidet* cet.

218 Cf. *Propter quod induite tota arma, ut possitis resistere in die nequissimo, ut cum omnia perfeceritis, stetis accincti lumbos vestros in veritate, induti loricam iustitiae, et calciati pedes in praeparatione evangelii pacis, assumentes scutum fidei, in quo possitis omnia ignita iacula nequissimi extinguere, et galeam salutis, et gladium spiritus, qui est sermo Dei.*

15:15	πολίτων	*municipibus*	*ex ciuibus* 2 *ex ciuium* 17 *ciuium* cet. om. 4*
15:30	βίον	*facultatem*	*omnia tua* 2 *omnia* 5 *substantiam suam* (*tuam* 8 om. 4) cet.
16:6	βάτους	*uatos*	*cados* 2 A *siclos* 5 *bathos* 4 *batis* 8
16:7	γράμματα	*cautionem*	*cirografum* 2 *litteras* cet.
17:12	κώμην	*uico*	*castello* 4 *castellum cet.*
19:30	κώμην	*uicum*	*castellus* 5 *castellum* cet.
20:10	γεωργούς	*colonos*	*agricolas* 2 5 *cultores* cet.
21:4	βίον	*facultatem*	*substantiam* 5 *uictum* cet.
22:11	κατάλυμα	*refectio*	*hospitium* 2 *diuersorium* cet.
24:13	κώμην	*municipium*	*castellum* cet.
24:28	κώμην	*uicum*	*castello* 4 A *castellum* cet.

The translation of the word κώμη in the text is especially striking and involves the following set of variants:

Table 32: Renderings of κώμη in VL3 Luke

Verse	NA^{28}	VL3	Other Latin authorities
5:17	κώμης	*municipio*	*castello* cet.
8:1	κώμην	*uicos*	*castellum* 5 A *castella* cet.
9:6	κώμας	*municipia*	*castella* 2 *ciuitates* 5 *castella et ciuitates* 4 8 *castella* A
9:12	κώμας	*uicos*	*castella* cet.
10:38	κώμην	*uicum*	*castellum* (*castello* 4) cet.
13:22	κώμας	*uicos*	*castella* cet.
17:12	κώμην	*uico*	*castello* 4 *castellum cet.*

19:30	κώμην	*uicum*	*castellus* 5 *castellum* cet.
24:13	κώμην	*municipium*	*castellum* cet.
24:28	κώμην	*uicum*	*castello* 4 A *castellum* cet.

It is assumed that *uicus* originally designated a quarter or a precinct and, by extension, the chief street of a neighborhood, as, for instance, in the name of the ancient Roman street *Uicus Tuscus*; side streets and blind alleys, on the other hand, were called *semitae* and *angiporta* respectively.[219] In the *Peregrinatio Aetheriae*, composed at the end of the fifth century, *uicus* is defined as a "village," and we can find the noun in the Latin Gospels in this sense as well.[220] The distribution of this word is interesting. On the one hand, *uicus* is not used in any other gospel in the *Codex Vercellensis*: in Matt and John, *castellum* appears in all passages, whereas in Mark we only find the rendering *municipium*. On the other hand, *uicus* turns out to be the preferred reading in *Bezae* (VL5) Mark; otherwise, the text always has *castellum*. It is important to consider the political implications of the terms in considering such differences in translation. In particular, we should note that both *uicus* and *castellum* may denote a small town since both lack the *dignitas ciuitatis*.[221] Thus, there was no difference in political status between the two, despite the fact that *castellum* is more properly a fortified place, whereas *uicus* is a town or a military station without walls.[222] The rendering of κώμη by *municipium*, found only in the *Codex Vercellesis*, is more difficult to explain. *municipium* named an urban agglomeration whose people were mainly Roman citizens and governed by their own laws and magistrates. In the second and third centuries, however, groups of several com-

219 Cf. CIL 6.975; Suet. *Aug.* 30; Vitr. 1.6.1; 1.6.8; 1.6.12. For a further discussion, see HARSH, "'Angiportum,' 'Platea,' and 'Vicus'," 50–54.

220 Cf. *Aetheria* 7.7: *Heroum autem ciuitas, quae fuit illo tempore, id est ubi occurrit Ioseph patri suo Iacob uenienti, sicut scriptum est in libro Genesis, nunc est come, sed grandis, quod nos dicimus uicus.*

221 Isid. *Etym.* 15.2.11: *uici et castella et pagi hi sunt qui nulla dignitate ciuitatis ornantur, sed uulgari hominum conuentu incoluntur, et propter paruitatem sui maioribus ciuitatibus adtribuuntur.*

222 Cf. WORDSWORTH, SANDAY, WHITE, Portions of the Gospels, 137–138: "We consequently find castella predominating in wild hilly districts, or on the frontiers, or where Roman posts had been established among barbarian tribes. In the African provinces all these conditions were present, and it is in these that the 'castella' appear most frequently. Some of them would seem to have been of the same type as those already referred to in North Italy, many however were, to start with, Roman military stations, or at least connected with the numerous settlements of Roman veterans planted under the rule of the emperors in the African provinces. But whatever their origin 'castella' are unusually frequent in Africa."

munities, such as *uici* or *castella*, were elevated to the rank of *municipia*. At the same time, individual cities, *urbes*, were elevated to a metropolitan position, and claimed supremacy over the *municipia* around them, a process which took place, for instance, in Carthage and Milan. It is therefore conceivable that a writer or scribe might have identified the relation between *municipium* and *urbs* with that between κώμη and πόλις, especially if he was familiar with the recent administrative change, which promoted *municipia* from the lower status of *uici*.[223]

Table 33: Renderings of ὑπάρχοντα and βίος in VL3 Luke

Verse	NA[28]	VL3	Other Latin authorities
11:21	ὑπάρχοντα	*facultates*	*substantia* 5 *quae possidet* cet.
12:15	ὑπαρχόντων	*facultate*	*substantia* 5 *quae possidet* cet.
14:33	ὑπάρχουσιν	*facultatibus*	*substantiae 5* *quae possidet* cet.
15:30	βίον	*facultatem*	*omnia* 2 5 *substantiam* cet.
21:4	βίον	*facultatem*	*substantiam* 5 *uictum* cet.

Also striking are the numerous variants for the nominalized participle τὰ ὑπάρχοντα. This is a recurring phrase in Luke,[224] but appearing in three passages of Matthew.[225] In Latin, the variants include *substantia, quae possidet, quae habet, omnia* or simply *res*.[226] The reading *facultates* in *Codex Vercellensis* can be seen as exceptional, considering that it appears in other authorities (VL2 and VL4) only in 8:3. The preference for this rendering of τὰ ὑπάρχοντα is so prevailing in the text, that it is even employed to translated the similar term βίος in the sense of "wealth" or "means to live" in 15:30 and 21:4, where the majority of the witnesses vary between *substantia* and *uictum*. However, the origin of the reading remains unclear: It has already been observed that the appearance of *facultates* in a paraphrastic allusion by Tertullian to 8:3 is rather remarkable, suggesting that the reading should be

223 For further discussion, see ARTHUR, "From Vicus to Village," 103–134.

224 Cf. 8:3, 9:21, 12:15.33.44, 14:33, 16:1, 19:8.

225 Cf. 19:21, 24:47, 25:14.

226 For a complete overview of these renderings, see WORDSWORTH, SANDAY, WHITE, Portions of the Gospels, 135.

counted among one of oldest renderings of τὰ ὑπάρχοντα.[227] In this case, the reading gives further evidence of an early layer of the Lucan text in *Codex Vercellensis* and, regarding the different renderings of the Greek expression, even older than *Palatinus* (VL2). At any rate, *facultates* can be a borrowing from the juridical language, as attested in many passages of the *Corpus Iuris Ciuilis*, and clearly has the character of a technical term.[228]

Table 34: The rendering of κατάλυμα in 22:11

Verse	NA[28]	VL3	Other Latin authorities
22:11	κατάλυμα	*refectio*	*hospitium* 2 *diuersorium* cet.

In Luke 22:11, Jesus gives the disciples instructions on how to find a proper place to celebrate Passover. When they enter the city, they are supposed to ask a man carrying a jar of water, "where is the guest room where I may eat the Passover with my disciples," in Greek, ποῦ ἐστὶν τὸ κατάλυμα ὅπου τὸ πάσχα μετὰ τῶν μαθητῶν φάγω. The word κατάλυμα was rendered in three different ways in this verse, *hospitium* in *Codex Palatinus* (e, 2), *diuersorium* in the other texts, and *refectio*, a special reading in the *Codex Vercellensis*. *refectio* designates a meal, but also, by extension, the room where the meal is served, whereas *hospitium* and *diuersiorium* are generic terms for a lodging, not necessarily in reference to a meal. κατάλυμα had already appeared in the beginning of Luke, in the account of Jesus's birth, where it is stated, in Luke 2:7, that Mary had to lay the child in a manger, since "there was no place for them in the inn," διότι οὐκ ἦν αὐτοῖς τόπος ἐν τῷ καταλύματι. In this case, κατάλυμα was translated with two different nouns, *stabu<lo>* in *Codex Palatinus* (VL2) and *diuersorium* in all other witnesses, including *Codex Vercellensis*. Therefore, it seems that the translator differentiates between κατάλυμα as lodging in Luke 2:7 and as a dining room in Luke 22:11, using *diuersorium* as an acceptable rendering for the former, but varying the word choice in 22:11, where τὸ πάσχα is explicitly mentioned. Again, in Mark 14:14, *Vercellensis* also has *refectio*, this time agreeing with the majority of Latin witnesses, with the exceptions of *Bobbiensis*

227 Cf. Tert. *adv. Marc.* 4.19.1: *quod diuites Christo mulieres adhaerebant, quae et de facultatibus suis ministrabant ei.* For further discussion, see Wordsworth, Sanday, White, Portions of the Gospels, 136.

228 Cf, e. g., *CIC* 1.20.4: *in prouinciis autem praesides, ex inquisitione tutores crearent, uel magistratus, iussu praesidum, si non sint magnae pupilli facultates*; *CIC* 4.6.37: *Item si de dote iudicio mulier agat, placet eatenus maritum condemnari debere, quatenus facere possit, id est quatenus facultates eius patiuntur.*

(VL1), which has *hospitium*, and *Codex Corbeiensis secundus* (VL 8), which has *refectorium.*

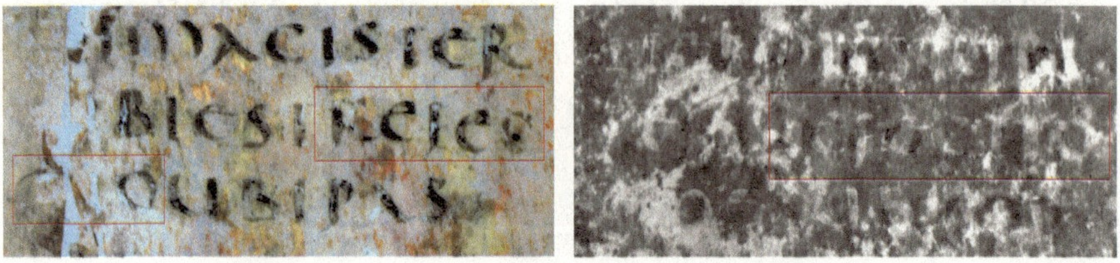

Figure 5.25: The readings *refectio* in Luke 22:11 (496[a]) and Mark 14:14 (621[a]).

5.4.6 Religious and Cultic Terms

We can observe considerable fluctuation in the use of religious terms in the various witnesses of the Gospel of Luke. For example, we find four variant readings for δοξάζειν, "to praise" or "to extol." The earliest tradition, represented by the *Codex Palatinus* (VL2), has *clarificare* practically throughout; later authorities, such as the codices *Veronensis* (VL4), *Corbeiensis secundus* (VL8) and *Vindobonensis* (VL17) prefer the rendering *magnificare* instead; by contrast, the *Codex Amiatinus* (A), a Vulgate manuscript, has *glorificare*, a term not found in any other authority. The codices *Vercellensis* and *Bezae* (VL 5), in turn, are the only texts to use *honorificare* (7:16; 13:13; 23:47), even though the *Codex Bezae* often reads *honorare* instead, possibly due to a confusion between the verbs δοξάζειν and τιμᾶν.[229]

Similar distributions apply to nearly all important theological terms within the different traditions. An examination of the renderings of παραβολή is instructive as well in this context. The *Palatinus* (VL2) has only *similitudo*, a native Latin term characteristic of earlier textual traditions.[230] The codices *Vercellensis* and *Bezae* (VL5) exhibit affinities also in this respect and always have *parabola*. This is surprising since, as stated above,[231] the *Codex Vercellensis* Luke avoids the use of Greek borrowings, preferring calques or archaic terms for words which have no direct equivalent in Latin. In all other texts, the two renderings coexist side by side, even though, in the Vulgate, the older variant *similitudo* is strikingly widespread.

229 Cf., e. g., 17:15 and 18:43.
230 Cf. 5.4.1, pp. 245–247.
231 Cf. 5.1.4.1, pp. 209f. and more often.

The fluctuations in the rendering of religious terms in Luke can be seen in the following list:

Table 35: Religious vocabulary in VL3 Luke

Verse	NA28	VL3	Other Latin authorities
1:23	λειτουργίας	*sacerdotii*	*ministerii* 5 *officii* cet.
1:51	κράτος	*potestatem*	*fortitudinem* 2 *uirtutem* 5 *potentiam* cet.
1:75	ὁσιότητι	*castitate*	*ueritate* 2 *sanctitate* cet.
2:24	θυσίαν	*hostias*	*sacrificium* 2 5 *hostiam* cet.
2:25	παράκλησιν	*exortationem*	*praecem* 2 *consolationem* (*consulatione* 8) cet.
3:18	παρακαλῶν	*hortatus*	*consolans* 5 *exhortans* cet.
4:15	δοξαζόμενος	*honorem accipiens*	*gloriam accipiens* 5 *magnificabatur* (*magnificabantur* 8) cet.
4:19	om.	*redemptionis*	*redditionis* 4 *retributionis* cet. om. 5
5:12	ἐδεήθη	*orabat*	*rogabat* 4 8 *rogauit* A om. 2 5
5:26	παραδόξα	*mirifica*	*praeclara* 2 *mirabilia* cet.
6:22	πονηρόν	*nequam*	*malum* cet.
6:35	ὑψίστου	*excelsi*	*altissimi* cet.
6:45	πονηρός	*nequa*	*malus* cet.
8:14	βίου	*saeculi*	*uitae* cet.
8:28	ὑψίστου	*summi*	*altissimi* cet.
8:50	σωθήσεται	*uiuet*	*saluabitur* 2 5 *salua erit* cet.
9:22	ἀρχιερέων	*ponticifibus*	*principibus sacerdotum* cet.
9:43	μεγαλειότητι	*magnalia*	*magnificentiam* 2 *magnitudine* (*magnitudinem* 8) cet.
12:30	κόσμου	*saeculi*	*mundi* (*modi* 4) cet.
13:17	ἐνδόξοις	*mirificis*	*praeclaris* 4 8 17 om. cet.
17:15	δοξάζων	*honorificans*	*clarificans* 2 *honorans* 5 *magnificauit* 17 *magnificans* cet.
18:43	δοξάζων	*honorificans*	*clarificans* 2 *honorans* 5 *magnificans* cet.
19:37	αἰνεῖν	*conlaudare*	*laudare* cet.
19:37	ἐν ὑψίστοις	om.	*in excelsi* 2 *altissimis* 5 *in excelsis* cet.
19:47	ἀρχιερεῖς	*pontifices*	*pontificis sacerdotum* 2 *principes sacerdotum* cet.
21:19	ὑπομόνῃ	*tolerantia*	*sufferentia* 5 *patientia* cet.
22:4	ἀρχιερεῦσιν	*ponticifibus*	*principibus* (*principes* 17) *sacerdotum* cet.
22:50	ἀρχιερέως	*pontificis*	*principis* (*principes* 2) *sacerdotum* cet.
22:52	ἀρχιερεῖς	*ponticifes*	*principes sacerdotum* 5 A *principibus sacerdotum* cet.
22:52	στρατηγούς	*antistites*	*praepositos* 5 *magistratus* A *magistratibus* cet.
22:54	ἀρχιερέως	*pontificis*	*principis sacerdotum* cet.

22:66	ἀρχιερεῖς	*pontifices*	*principes* (*principis* 8) *sacerdotum* cet.
23:4	ἀρχιερεῖς	*pontificis*	*principes* (*principis* 2) *sacerdotum* cet.
23:10	ἀρχιερεῖς	*pontifices*	*principes sacerdotum* cet.
23:13	ἀρχιερεῖς	*pontifices*	*principibus* (*principes* 5) *sacerdotum* cet.
24:20	ἀρχιερεῖς	*pontifices*	*sacerdotes* 2 *summi sacerdotes* A *principes sacerdotum* cet.
24:49	ἐπαγγελίαν ὕψους	*repromissionem summo*	*promissionem* 2 5 *promissa* 4 8 *promissum* A *alto* cet.
24:53	αἰνοῦντες*	*conlaudentes*	*laudentes* cet.

* Reading of the *Codex Bezae* (D, 05).

This list shows that one of the consistent special readings in the Lucan text of the *Codex Vercellensis* is the rendering of ἀρχιερεύς as *pontifex*. The other authorities often refer to a *princeps sacerdotum* as well as to *sacerdos*.[232] In any case, the lexeme *pontifex* is not an exclusively Christian term, since the *pontifices* counted among the most distinguished priestly colleges in Rome.[233] Etymologically, the term derives from *pons*, "way" or "path," and may be literally translated as "way-maker." There are, of course, other etymologies that may explain the term even better, such as the derivation from the Latin *posse* and *facere*: "those who have power to act."[234] The tasks of this priestly college are well attested in Dionysius of Halicarnassus, who describes the *pontifices* as holding a monopoly over cult language and cult actions.

232 *Codex Bobbiensis* (VL1) has *pontifex* in Mark, except for 14:47, 15:10.31; when it comes to Matthew, there is no evidence for this term in any of the witnesses; in John, *Codex Vercellensis* always reads *sacerdos*, however, in John 11:57, 15:21, 18:3, 15; 16:22 and 19:6, the Vulgate uses *pontifex*. See also Cf. BURTON, The Old Latin Gospels, 46: "At this point it is appropriate to introduce the second criterion for discerning the primal unity of the Old Latin versions, namely the variation in rendering between the Gospels. It was pointed out by Eberhard Nestle (1907) that παρακαλέω was regularly rendered *deprecari* in the Vulgate Mark but *rogare* in Matthew and Luke, that ἐπιτιμάω was usually *comminari* in Mark but *increpare* (or *compere*) in Matthew and Luke, and that ὁ ἀρχιερεύς was often *summus sacerdos* in Mark and usually *pontifex* in John, but almost always *princeps sacerdotum* in Matthew and Luke. Nestle supposed this reflected a time when the Gospels were circulated separately in Latin translation. Burkitt (1908) acknowledged the variation, traced it back to the Old Latin, and added that in Mark παρά plus accusative of place is often rendered *circa* or *ad*, whereas in Matthew and Luke it was usually *secus*; but he supposed this was due to a later revision of the versions of Mark. These articles have been curiously neglected by subsequent scholarship, but I believe the method proposed has considerable value for our investigation of the textual origins of the OLG."

233 Cf. Livy 1.20.5–7.

234 Cf. Varro, *Ling*. 5.83. Even though this etymology is wrong, it explains the Roman conception of these terms; see SZEMLER, "Art. Pontifex," 332–396; SCOTT, "Art. Regia," 189–192; GORDON, "Pontifex, Pontifices," NP 2006 (online access 2022). Cf. for the following: WEISSENRIEDER, "Pater sancte."

Accordingly, we can assume that *pontifices* were indispensable for the correct execution of cult practices. Jörg Rüpke was also able to show that the *pontifices* promulgated legal acts and civil law,[235] as legal speech formulas show clear similarities to sacral cultic formulas.[236] Thus, *pontifices* assumed responsibility for cultic, civil and profane law.[237]

The reading *pontifex* is also found in the Latin translation of OT, where the term high priest, ἀρχιερεύς, occurs only a few times in the canonical books of the LXX.[238] Nevertheless, the translation of ἀρχιερεύς as *pontifex* is found only twice in the Vulgate. An exception may be detected in Lev 21:10, where the Vulgate reads *pontifex id es, sacerdotes maximus inter fratres suos*, which is translated similarly by Hesychius of Jerusalem[239] and is again similarly worded by Isidore.[240] Cyprian Gallus,[241] on the other hand, translates this term as *purus sacerdos* and Augustine as *sacerdos magnus.*[242]

Already Tertullian links the lexeme *pontifex* with the aforementioned cult language of the Romans: on the one hand, he calls pagans priests *pontifex*,[243] but on the other, he of course leaves no doubt that for him there is only one true *pontifex*, and that is Christ.[244] This point becomes even clearer in light of the translations of Josephus's works into Latin, which Prof. Geil kindy made available to us. With the exception of *A.J.* 20.15, where ἀρχιερεύς is translated with *sacerdos* and *A.J.* 7.56, where the term is translated with *princeps sacerdotum*, in Josephus we consistently find the translation *pontifex.*[245] This evidence of course does not allow us to straight-

---

235 See especially the comparison with the *tabulae duodecim*; Dig. 1.2.2.35–53.

236 RÜPKE, Fasti Sacerdotum, 4, 19ff.

237 BLEICKEN, "Kollisionen zwischen Sacrum und Publicum," 446–480.

238 Cf. 2Kings 12:9 (*sacerdos* vg), 2Kings 22:8 (*Helcias pontifex* vg, but VL *sacerdos*), 2Chronicle 26:20 (*pontifex* vg), Lev 21:10, Num 35:25ff. (*sacerdos maximus* vg), Neh 13:4–9.28 (*Eliasib sacerdos* vg).

239 Cf. PG 93.1058c–d, 1059b.

240 Isid. *Quaestiones in Leviticum* 12.1; PL 83.330a.

241 *Heptateuchos* 3.203–205.

242 *Quaestiones in Leviticum* 79; PL 34.710.

243 Tert. *Praescr.* 40.5; *Exh. cast.* 13.1; *Mon.* 17.3; *Apol.* 26.2.

244 Tert. *adv. Marc.* 4.35.11: *Et ideo, ut vidit agnovisse legem illos Hierosolymis expungendam, ex fide iam iustificandos sine legis ordine remediavit. Unde et unum illum solutum ex decem memorem divinae gratiae Samariten miratus, non mandat offerre munus ex lege, quia satis iam obtulerat gloriam deo reddens, hoc et domino volente interpretari legem. Et tamen cui deo gratiam reddidit Samarites, quando nec Israelites alium deum usque adhuc didicisset? Cui alii quam cui omnes remediati retro a Christo? Et ideo, Fides tua te salvum fecit, audiit, quia intellexerat veram se deo omnipotenti oblationem, gratiarum scilicet actionem, apud verum templum et verum pontificem eius Christum facere debere.*

245 Cf. Josephus, *A.J.* 7.56, 72, 110 (ἀρχιερεύς, *princeps sacerdotum*); 20.15 (ἀρχιερεύς, *sacerdos*; otherwise, *sacerdos* is the rendering of ἱερεύς). For the translation of ἀρχιερεύς as *pontifex*, see *B.J.*

forwardly identify the origin of the use of *pontifex* in the *Codex Vercellensis*, but it remains clear that the term is used with striking consistency, and that, despite its rarity, the term cannot be considered neither typically Christian nor a later European invention.

Worthy of note is also the translation of προσευχή, "prayer," as *oratio* and προσεύχεσθαι as *orare* (Luke 6:12; 19:46; 22:45). *oratio* and *orare* have the basic meaning of "speech," "language," "expression," and, in the second and third century, they refer especially to the "imperial decree" or the "public speech of a Caesar." The verbal form *orare* has at least the connotation of "addressing (the Caesar) and asking for help in the solution of any problem." In Virgil's *Aeneid*, we find the expression *talibus orabat dictis* (6.124), in Plautus, *ne oderim item ut alias, quando orasti* (*mil.* 1269), *nisi quod orasseis* (*epid.* 728), and Seneca uses *deinde oro atque obsecro, ne te difficilem amicis et intractabilem praestes* (*cons. Marc.* 6.5.1), which refers to prayers. A much more straight-forward derivation would have produced *precatio*, "prayer" and "plea-request" on the one hand and *precor*, "begging with prayer," "to address," or "praying" on the other. This is the word often found in classical Latin, as in Cicero (e.g., *Mur.* 1.1.).

Noteworthy is also *pater sancte* in 11:2, a reading for which the *Codex Vercellensis* provides the oldest attestation,[246] but which is shared with other Latin authorities, such as the codices *Corbeiensis secundus* (VL8) and *Vindobonensis* (VL17). *sanctus* is derived from Latin *sac-*, which signifies that something is removed from human influence and accordingly reserved for God or – in ancient pagan religion – for any deity. *Sanctus* is the perfect passive participle of *sancire*, "consecrate, make inviolable," and is very similar to *sacer*. *Sanctus* connotes being "hallowed, pertaining to God," and it also has the connotation of increased legal protection for sanctified objects or people. According to E. Dickey, the lexeme *sanctus* is used only for emperors, while the superlative *sanctissimus* could again be applied to normal citizens. Even the mere basic meaning complicates an identification of *sanctus* with *pater noster*.[247]

1.26, 31, 33, 53, 68, 109, 152–153, 562, 573; *A.J.* 6.11,359; 7.382, 393; 20.6, 131, 162, 181, 194, 198, 205, 207, 208, 224, 227, 231.

246 Cf. for the following: WEISSENRIEDER, "Pater sancte."

247 DICKEY, "*sanctus*," DNP (2011): 31–32.

Figure 5.26: The reading *pater sancte* in 11:2 (418b).

5.5 Conclusion: The Translation Techniques of the *Codex Vercellensis* Luke

In considering the translation techniques of Vercellensis' Latin text with other Old Latin versions, two aspects must be taken into account: the influence of Greek *Vorlage*, and the innovations which characterize the development of Latin in the first centuries C.E. These two aspects contributed to the formation of the heterogeneous material of the Latin Gospels, in which different traditions conflate and produce a range of idioms and expressions, ranging from colloquial diction to rhetorical stylization at the highest level. Certainly, some features can be considered more or less classical, post-classical or 'silver', late, or medieval. Nevertheless, the coexistence of these forms suggests that, from the point of view of the translators and scribes, there was no disruption in the use of the language, but rather a continuity in which new modes of expression are created and old forms are integrated to cope with the necessities of the emerging social, religious, and cultural reality. Therefore, the simplifying modern labels such as 'literal,' 'vulgar,' or 'late' can hardly grasp the linguistic fluidity and variety of translation strategies which characterize the texts.

Attesting to these practices, the *Codex Vercellensis* Luke exhibits several vulgarisms, post-classical usages, hypercorrections, and innovations that are associated with the later developments of Latin. Most of these irregularities are of orthographical nature, as seen in the blurring of some phonemic differences. However, such orthographical irregularities are relatively rare in comparison with other authorities, for instance, the *Codex Corbeiensis secundus* (VL8), which abounds with non-standard spellings, such as those produced by the monophthongization of *ae* to *e*; in the *Codex Vercellensis*, this is a secondary phenomenon and mostly involves hypercorrections, such as *baetus* for *beatus*, or *prophaeta* for *propheta*, but we do not find any post-classical forms whose dissemination shows the influence of oral registers in the literary production, such as *celum* for *caelum* or *demonium* for *daemonium*. With respect to nominal morphology, we can observe the reanalysis of the gender of a few nouns and the progressive disappearance of the neuter, such as in the case of the replacement of *rete* (neuter) with *retia* (feminine) in Luke 5:2, 5, or the substitution of *uinum* (neuter) with *uinus* (masculine) in Luke 5:37. When it comes to verbal morphology, we can detect the appearance of new conjugation patterns, especially for verbs of the *i*-class and the compounds of *ire*, developments which correlate with the simplifications of Latin grammar in late antiquity. Nevertheless, the most important differences in the verbal system between Latin and the Romance languages – the loss of the synthetic passive and the rise of the periphrastic future and perfect tenses using the auxiliary *habere* – are absent in the Lucan text of the *Vercellensis* as well as in all other witnesses, which in turn serves as evidence for the use of classical forms in the Latin Gospels.

In this sense, the main peculiarities of the text are of semantic character. First, we observe an attempt to render the Greek as closely as possible. The strategy is demonstrated either by the usage of loan-translations, which reproduce the Greek terms by coining concepts with native Latin morpho-syntactical elements, or by the adoption of words which were before restricted to poetical or technical contexts. The use of *amplexus* (Luke 2:28), *concarpere* (Luke 9:42), *pauimentare* (Luke 19:44), and *redditio* (Luke 14:12) are some examples discussed in our study of how the translation of the *Vercellensis* Luke incorporates rare terms in order to remain faithful to the Greek text, while *arefrigescere* (Luke 21:26), *inportabiles* (Luke 11:46), or *prius meletare* (Luke 21:14) are lexical innovations which possibly distort natural Latin idiom, but which were chosen out of respect for the Greek original. At the same time, as a representative of the oldest tradition of the Gospel of Luke, we can notice that the text avoids the use of loan-words, such as *moechari* (Luke 18:20) or *euge* (Luke 19:17), which are found in all other authorities, preferring instead Latin alternatives such as *adulterium facere* or *tanto melior*. The only exception is the use of the central concept of *parabola* for παραβολή, a translational feature also found in the *Codex Bezae* (VL5); other authorities use the loan-word *parabola* and its Latin equivalent *similitudo* without any distinction. In other passages, it is clear that the translator tried to capture the exact nuance of the Greek term by drawing on vocabulary not found in any textual tradition of the Latin Gospels: *maeror* (Luke 22:45) or *formido* (Luke 21:11) are poetical equivalents of *tristitia* and *terror* and may be considered uncommon even in classical literature. This suggests that many passages in the text were translated based on more cultivated registers of Latin, and that the translator and scribe did not have a merely average knowledge of the language.

To conclude, these observations make it clear that the *Vercellensis* Luke is one of the oldest witnesses of the Latin Bible. The text exhibits a variety of linguistic forms that defy any simple categorization as 'vulgar', 'post-classical' or 'Christian', but which demonstrate an in-depth understanding of the Greek and Latin. The result is one of the most interesting witnesses of the Old Latin Gospels and a fine example of the achievements of ancient translation practices.

Table 36: Singular readings in VL3 Luke compared to the oldest Latin witnesses:

Verse	VL3	Other Latin authorities
1:21	*moram faceret*	*tardaret* cet.
1:23	*sacerdotii*	*ministerii* 5 *officii* cet.
1:51	*potestatem*	*fortitudinem* 2 *uirtutem* 5 *potentiam* cet.
	dissipauit	*dispersit* 2 A *disparsit* cet.
1:54	*recordatus*	*commemoratus est* 2 *memorari* (*memorare* 5) cet.
1:75	*castitate*	*ueritate* 2 *sanctitate* cet.
1:80	*confirmabatur*	*corroborabatur* 2 *inbaliscebat* 5 *confortabatur* cet.
2:7	*conlocauit*	*collauerunt* 2 *reclinauit* 5 A *posuit* 4 8
2:22	*expleti*	*suppleti* 2 *consummati* 5 *impleti* 4 A *inpleti* 8
2:24	*hostias*	*pro eo sacrificium* 2 *sacrificium* 5 *hostiam* cet.
2:25	*exortationem*	*praecem* 2 *consolationem* (*consulatione* 8) cet.
2:28	*in amplexum*	*in manus suas* 2 *in alas suas* 5 *in manibus* 4 *in ulnas suas* A om. 8
	dominum	*deum* cet.
2:38	*istrahel*	*hierusalem* cet.
2:39	*quemadmodum*	*secundum* cet.
	reuersi	*regressi* cet.
	nazaret	*nazarath* 2 *nazared* 5 *nazareth* cet.
2:40	*repletus*	*et implebat* 2 *adinplebatur* 5 *et implebatur* 4 *et inplebatur* 8 *plenus* A
2:42	*sollemni*	*festum* 2 *festi* cet.
2:46	*docentium*	*magistrorum* 2 5 *doctorum* cet.
2:47	*sapientia*	*intellecto* 5 *prudentiam* (*prudentia* A) cet.
2:51	*nazaret*	*in nazaret* 5 *nazareht* 8 *nazareth* cet.
3:3	*totam*	*omnem* cet.
3:8	*uellitis*	*incipiatis* 5 *coeperitis* cet.
3:13	*plus*	*amplius* cet.
3:15	*arbitrante*	*cum speraret* 2 *expectantes* 5 *existimante* cet.
3:18	*hortatus*	*consolans* 5 *exhortans* cet.
4:1	*ferebatur*	*ducebatur* 2 5 *agebatur* cet.
4:2	*edit*	*manducauit* cet.
4:5	*adduxit*	*et inposuit* 2 *et adsumens* 5 *et duxit* cet.

Verse	VL3	Other Latin authorities
	supra pinnam templi	*supra montem* 2 *in montem altum ualde* 5 *in montem altum* 8 om. 4 A
	orbis terrarum	*mundi* 5 *orbis terrae* cet.
4:14	*finitimam*	*circumadiacente* 2 om. cet.
4:15	*honorem accipiens*	*gloriam accipiens* 5 *et magnificabatur (magnificabantur* 8) cet.
4:16	*nazaret*	*nazara* 2 *nazared* 5 *nazareth* cet.
4:18	*humilibus*	*pauperibus* cet.
4:19	*redemptionis*	*redditionis* 4 *retributionis* cet. om. 5
4:20	*reuoluens*	*uoluens* 5 *cum plicuisset* (*plicuissit* 2) cet.
	intuentes	*intenti* 2 *intendentes* cet.
4:22	*prodibant*	*exiebant* 5 *procedebant* cet.
4:24	*nullus propheta*	*nemo propheta* cet.
4:25	*per triennium*	*annis tribus* cet.
4:27	*nullus*	*nemo* cet.
	purgatus	*emundatus* 2 *mundatus* cet.
	ineman	*naemas* 5 *neman* cet.
	surus	*syrus* cet.
4:30	*praeteriens*	*ueniens* 2 *transies* 5 A *transiit* 4 om. 8
4:31	*deuenit*	*discendit* 2 4 *descendit* cet.
4:35	*obiurgauit*	*corripuit* 2 *increpauit* cet.
4:36	*ad alterutrum*	*apud semetipsos* 2 *ad inuicem* cet.
4:37	*exibat*	*facta est* 2 *exiuit* 5 *diuulgabatur* cet.
	finitimam regionem	*locum regionis* cet.
4:38	*detinebatur*	*erat conprehensa* 5 *tenebatur* cet.
4:39	*adstans*	*astitit* 2 *instans* 5 *stans* cet.
	reliquid	*demisit* 2 *dimisit* 5 A *remisit* 4 8
	confestim autem	*continuo et* 2 *ut etiam continuo* 5 *et continuo* cet.
4:40	*aegros*	*languentes* 2 *infirmantes* 5 *infirmos* cet.
4:41	*exclamantia*	*clamantia* cet.
	obiurgans	*corripiens ea* 2 *increpans* cet.
4:42	*orta autem die*	*cum factus autem esset dies* 2 *facta autem die* cet.
5:1	*turba*	*populus* 5 *turbae* cet.
	incumbit ei	*super eum esset* 5 *inruerent in* (*super* 2) *eum* cet.
	iuxta	*ad* 2 5 *secus* cet.
5:2	*nauiculas duas*	*naues duas* 2 *duas naues* cet.
	litus	*stagnum* cet.
	egressi	*ab eis exientes* 5 *descenderant* cet. om. 2
5:3	*nauiculam*	*naues* cet.
	producerent	*exaltaretur* 2 *inducere* 5 *inducerent* 4 *duceret* 8 *reducere* A
5:4	*desiit*	*cessaret* 2 *cessasset* 5 *cessauit* cet.

Verse	VL3	Other Latin authorities
	leua	*recede* 2 *adduc* 5 *duc* cet.
	expandite	*summitite* 2 *mittite* 5 *laxa* A* *laxate* cet.
5:5	*expandam retiam*	*non intermittimus* 2 *non praeteribo* 5 *laxabo retiam* (*rete* A) cet.
5:6	*magnam*	*multam* 5 *copiosam* cet. om. 2
5:7	*nauicula*	*naue* 5 *naui* cet.
5:9	*pauor*	*timor* 5 *miratio* 4 *stupor* cet.
5:12	*prostratus*	*caecidit* 2 *cecidit* 5 *procidens* cet.
	orabat	*rogabat* 4 8 *rogauit* A om. 2 5
5:13	*protinus*	*continuo* 2 *confestim* cet.
5:14	*purgatione*	*purificatione* 5 *emundatione* (*emundationem* 8) cet.
5:15	*eama* (sic for *fama*)	*sermone* 2 *uerbum* 5 *sermo* cet.
	languoribus	*infirmitatibus* cet.
5:17	*conuenerant*	*erant aduenientes* 2 *erant congregati* 5 *uenerant* cet.
	municipio	*castello* cet.
5:19	*dimiserunt*	*deposuerunt* 2 5 *et summiserunt* 4 *summiserunt* 8 A
	lectulo	*grabattum* 2 5 *lecto* cet.
5:24	*remittendi*	*dismittere* 2 *dimittendi* 8 *dimittere* cet.
5:25	*omnibus*	*eorum* 2 5 *illis* 4 A *ipsis* 8
	sustulit	*et tulit* 2 *tollens* 5 *tulit* cet.
5:26	*pauor*	*stupor* cet. om. 2 5
	mirifica	*praeclara* 2 *mirabilia* cet.
5:27	*intuitus est*	*uidit* cet.
5:29	*ingens*	*magna* 2 *multa* cet.
5:33	*manducant*	*edunt* cet. om. 2 5
5:36	*insumentum*	*inmissuram* 5 *commissuram* cet.
	adsuit	*addit* 2 *scindens inmittit* 5 *inmittit* 8 A om. 4
	panno	*tunicam* 5 *uestimento* 4 *uestimentum* cet.
	insumentum	*additamentum* 2 *a rude inmissura* 5 *commissura* cet.
6:1	*conterentes*	*fricantes* 5 *confricantes* cet.
	edebant	*manducarent* 4 *manducabant* cet.
6:4	*edere*	*manducare* cet.
6:11	*stupore*	*ira* 2 *insipientia* 5 A *iniquitate* 4 8
6:15	*appellatur*	*uocabatur* 2 4 *uocatur* cet.
6:17	*campense*	*campestri* (*canpestri* 2) cet.
	ingens	*magna* 2 *multa* 5 *copiosa* cet.
6:20	*adleuans*	*leuauit* 2 *eleuans* 5 *eleuatis* 4 A *leuatis* cet.
	spiritu	om. cet.
6:22	*nequam*	*malum* cet.
	causam fili	*propter filium* cet.
6:30	*poscenti*	*qui petit* 2 *potenti* 8 *petenti* cet.

Verse	VL3	Other Latin authorities
6:35	*excelsi*	*altissimi* cet.
6:38	*agitatam cumulatam*	*commota* 2 *conquassatam inpletam* 5 *confersam commotam* 4 *conmodatam* *confersam* 8 *confertam et coagitatam* A
6:39	*utrique*	*ambo* cet.
6:40	*cons{s}umatus*	*confectus* 5 *perfectus* cet.
6:44	*dinoscitur*	*cognoscetur* 4 *cognoscitur* cet.
	sed nec	*neque* cet.
6:45	*nequa*	*malus* cet.
6:47	*demonstrabo*	*ostendam* cet.
6:48	*tempestate horta*	*inundatio autem facta* 2* *inundantia autem facta* 4 *inundatione autem facta* cet.
	impulit	*impegit* 2 *allisit* 5 4 *inlisit* 8 *inlisum est* A
	nec ualuit	*et non potuit* cet.
6:49	*inpulit*	*impegit* 2 *in qua inlisus est* A *allisit* cet.
7:8	*potestatis subiectus*	*sub potestate constitutus* cet.
7:11	*iesus*	om. cet.
	appellatur	*dicitur* 5 *uocatur* cet.
7:15	*consedit*	*sedit* 2 *resedit* cet.
7:16	*adprehendit*	*inuasit* 2 *accepit* cet.
	populum	*plebem* cet.
7:17	*finitima regione*	*regione* 5 *confinio regionis* 4 *confini regione* 8 *circa regionem* A om. 2
7:18	*renuntiauerunt*	*adnuntiauerunt* 2 *nuntiauerunt* cet. om. 5
7:21	*uerberibus*	*flagellis* 2 *plagis* cet.
	malignis	*iniquorum* 5 *inmundis* 4 *malis* cet.
7:22	*purgantur*	*emundantur 2 mundantur cet.*
7:31	*gentis*	*saeculi* 2 *generationis* 5 A *generationes* 4 8
7:32	*alterutrum*	*inuicem* 5 *ad inuicem* cet.
	planxistis	*lamentastis* 2 *plorastis* cet.
7:36	*eum*	*illum* cet.
	cibum caperet	*manducaret* cet.
7:37	*accumbere*	*recumbet* 5 *recumbit* cet.
	ampullam	*uas* 2 *alabastrum* cet.
7:38	*inrigabat*	*lababat* 2 *inpleuit* 5 *rigabat* 4 8 *coepit rigare* A add. *pedes eius* cet.
7:39	*inuitauerat*	*uocauerat* cet. om. 2 5
7:40	*dic magister*	*magister dic* cet.
7:42	*illum*	*eum* cet.
	amplius	*plus* cet.
7:43	*amplius redonauit*	*plus donauit* cet.
7:45	*desiit*	*intermisit* 2 *cessauit* cet.

Verse	VL3	Other Latin authorities
7:47	*qua ex causa tibi dico*	*propter quod dico tibi* (*uobis* 8) cet.
	remittuntur	*remittentur* 2 *dimittentur* 5 *remissa sunt* 4 8 *remittentur* A
	ei	*tibi* 4 *illi* cet.
7:49	*qui discumbebant pariter*	*conrecumbentes* 2 *qui simul recumbebant* 5 4 *qui simul recumbebant* (*recumbebat**) 8 *qui simul discumbebant* A
8:1	*uicos*	*castellum* 5 A *castella* cet.
8:2	*cognominatur*	*uocatur* 8 A *uocabatur* cet.
	macdalene	*magdalenae* 8 *magdalene* cet.
8:3	*erodis*	*herodis* cet.
	conplures	*multae* cet.
8:5	*qui seannat*	*seminans* 2 *seminator* 5 *qui seminat* cet.
	quoddam	*aliut* 4 *aliud* cet.
	iuxta	*ad* 2 5 *secus* cet.
8:6	*enatum*	*cum fructificasset* 2 *cum creuisset* 5 *natum cet.*
	exaruit	*aridum factum est* 5 *aruit* cet.
8:7	*creuerunt*	*simul natae sunt* 2 *cum germinassent* 5 *simul exortae* 4 A *simul exhorta est* 8
8:8	*optimam et bonam*	*bonam et optimam* 2 *bonam et uberam* 5 *bonam* cet.
	centies tantum	*centuplum* cet.
8:9	*quidnam*	*quae* cet.
8:10	*qui dixit*	*ille autem dixit illis* 2 *ad ille dixit* 5 *quibus ipse dixit* cet.
	traditum est	*datum est* cet.
8:13	*recipient*	*percipiunt* 2 *accipiunt* 5 8 *recipiunt* 4 *suscipiunt* A
	discedunt	*recedunt* cet.
8:14	*luxuriis*	*uoluntates* 2 *suabitati* 5 *uoluptatibus cet.*
	saeculi	*uitae* cet.
	ingredientes	*abientes* 5 *euntes* cet. om. 2
	dant fructum	*fecundantur* 2 *adferent fructum* 5 *referunt fructum* cet.
8:15	*fructum dant*	*fructiuicant* 5 *fructum adferent* (*afferet* 8 *afferunt* A) cet.
8:16	*operiet*	*coperit* 5 *et ponit* 4 *et* (om. 8 A) *operit* cet.
8:17	*palam fiat*	*manifestabitur* 2 *in palam uenit* 5 *manifestetur* cet.
8:18	*quisque*	*qui* cet.
	habuerit	*habet* cet.
8:19	*set*	*et* cet.
	conloqui ei	*contingere ei* 5 *adire ad* (om. 8) *eum* cet.
8:21	*ad illos*	*illis* 2 *eis* 5 *illum* 4* *ad eos* cet.
	illi	*hi* 5 4^{c} A *hii* cet.
8:22	*stagnum*	*contra hoc stagnum* 2 *in contra stagnum* 5 *trans stagnum* cet.
	et sustulerunt	*et nauigauerunt* 5 *et leuauerunt* 4 8 *et ascenderunt* A om. 2
8:23	*condormiit*	*obdormiuit* 5 A *obdormiit* cet.
	turbo	*procella* cet.

Verse	VL3	Other Latin authorities
8:24	*discipuli*	om. cet.
	illum	*eum* cet.
	destiterunt	*cessauit* 8 A *cessauerunt* cet.
8:26	*trans fretum*	*trans contra* 8 *contra* cet.
8:27	*daemonem*	*daemonia* 2 5 *daemonium* cet.
8:28	*summi*	*altissimi* cet.
8:29	*erumpens uincula*	*disrumpebat uincula* 2 5 *ruptis uinculis* cet.
	fugabatur	*agitabatur enim* 2 *ducebatur* (*ducebantur**) *enim* 5 *agebatur* cet.
	daemone	*daemonio* cet. om. 8
	desertis	*loca deserta* 2 4 *desertum* 5 *loco deserto* 8 *deserta* A
8:31	*illis*	*eis* cet.
8:32	*magna*	*multorum* cet. om. 5
	quae pascebatur	*pascentium* cet.
8:33	*mare*	*stagnum* cet.
8:35	*constantem mentem*	*uestitum sedentem* 5 *sanae mentis* 4 *sana mente* 8 A
	ante	*ad* cet.
8:37	*detinebantur*	*conpraehensi* 5 *tenebantur* (*tenebatur* 8) cet.
8:38	*iesus*	om. cet.
8:39	*reuertere*	*uade* 5 *redi* cet.
	totam	*uniuersam* cet.
8:40	*dum*	*cum* cet.
8:41	*prostratus*	*cadens* 5 *cecidit* cet.
	illum	*eum* cet.
	suam	*eius* cet.
8:43	*consumpserat*	*erogauerat* cet. om. 5
8:44	*protinus*	*confestim* cet.
8:45	*dixit*	*interrogabat* 5 *et ait iesus* cet.
8:48	*qui dixit*	*ad ille dixit* 5 8 *ad ipse dixit* 4 *at ipse dixit* A
8:50	*uiuet*	*saluabitur* 2 5 *salua erit* cet.
8:51	*est passus*	*admisit* 5 *permisit* cet.
8:54	*adpraehensa*	*tenens* cet.
	exclamauit	*clamauit* cet.
8:55	*statim*	*confestim* 5 *continuo* cet.
8:56	*obstipuerunt*	*admirati sunt* 2 *expauerunt* 5 *stupuerunt* cet.
9:1	*languores curandi*	*langores curare* 2 *infirmitates curare* 5 *ut languores curarent* cet.
	aegros	*infirmos* cet.
9:6	*municipia*	*castella* 2 *ciuitates* 5 *castella et ciuitates* 4 8 *castella* A
9:7	*stupebant*	*hesitabant* 2* *hesitabat* 2^c^ A *confundebatur* 5 *constenebatur* 4 *consternabatur* 8
9:10	*nontiauerunt*	*narrauerunt* cet.

Verse	VL3	Other Latin authorities
	uocabatur	*appelatur* 2 *dicitur* 5 *est* cet.
9:11	*necesse habebant curari*	*necessariam habebant curam* 2 *opus habebant sanitatis eius* 5 *cura* (*curam* 4) *indigebant* (*indigebat* 8*) cet.
9:12	*uicos*	*castella* cet.
	agros	*uillas* cet.
9:16	*ut adponerent*	*adponere* 2 5 *ut ponerent* cet.
9:17	*satiati sunt*	*saturati sunt* cet.
9:18	*esset in secreto*	*esset ipse singularis* 2 *essent soli* 5 *solus esset orans cet.*
9:20	*christum*	*christum filium dei* 2 5 *christum dei* cet.
9:21	*obiurgasset*	*increpauit* 5 *increpans* cet.
9:22	*ponticifibus*	*principibus sacerdotum* cet.
	post tertium diem	*post triduum* 2 *post tres dies* 5 8 *post dies tres* 4 *tertia die* A
9:24	*causa mei*	*propter me* cet.
9:25	*iacturam*	*damnum* 2 *iactum* 5 *detrimentum* cet.
9:28	*circiter*	*quasi* 2 5 *fere* cet.
9:29	*ficies*	*figura* 2 *species* cet.
	candida	*alba* 5 *albus* cet.
	praefulgens	*ut nix* 2 *scoruscantia* 5 *refulgens* cet.
9:31	*apparentes*	*uisi* cet.
9:32	*adsistentes ei*	*qui cum eo stabant* 2 *qui simul stabant cum eo* 5 *qui stabant cum illo* cet.
9:36	*indicauerunt*	*renuntiauerunt* 2 *dixerunt* cet.
9:38	*magna*	*multa* cet.
9:39	*concidit*	*collidit* 2 *adlidit* 5 *elidit* cet
	discarpit	*disrumpit* 5 *dissipat* cet.
9:41	*quousque*	*usquequo* cet.
	sufferam	*sustineo* 2 *patiar* cet.
9:42	*spiritus malus*	*daemonium cet.*
	concarpsit	*conturbabit* 5 *dissipauit cet.*
9:43	*magnalia.*	*magnificentiam* 2 *magnitudine* (*magnitudinem* 8) cet.
9:49	*quoniam*	*quia* cet.
9:50	*sinite illum et*	om. cet.
9:51	*receptionis*	*adsumptionis* (*assumptionis* A) cet.
9:53	*illius*	*eius* cet.
	tendens	*euntibus* 2 *iens* 5 *euntis* 4 A
9:55	*obiurgauit*	*corripuit* 2 *increpauit* cet.
9:57	*eum*	*illum* cet.
9:59	*prius*	*primo* 2 *primum* cet.
9:61	*prius*	*primo* 2 *primum* cet.
10:1	*intraturus erat*	*introiturus erat* 2 *habebat uenire* 5 *erat uenturus* 4 *erat ipse uenturus* A

Verse	VL3	Other Latin authorities
10:4	*nec*	*non* 2 5 *neque* 4 A
	calciamentum	*calciamenta* cet.
	circa	*in* 5 *per* cet.
	primum	*autem* 2 5 om. 4 A
10:6	*super*	*ad* 2 A *in* 5 *supra* 17
10:7	*apponuntur*	*sunt* cet.
10:11	*excutimus*	*extergimus* cet.
	adtamen	*uerum* 2 *uerumtamen* 5 *tamen* cet.
10:13	*fors*	*forte* 2 *iam* 5 *om.* cet.
10:17	*daemones*	*daemonia* cet.
10:18	*tamquam*	*quasi* 2 *sicut* cet.
10:19	*uiperas*	*serpentes* cet.
10:20	*obaudiunt*	*subiecta sunt* 2 *subdita sunt* 5 *subiecti sunt* 4 17 *subiciuntur* A
10:21	*sensatis*	*sapientibus* 5 *et prudentibus* cet. om. 2
10:35	*in crastinum diem*	*in crastinum* 5 *altera die* cet.
	diligenter	om. cet.
	amplius erogaueris	*supererogaueris* cet.
10:38	*uicum*	*castellum* (*castello* 4) cet.
10:39	*quae uocabatur*	*nomine* cet. om. 2
	cum consedisset	*sedebat* 2 *adsidens* 5 *etiam sedens* cet.
10:40	*turbabatur*	*auocabatur* 2 *abalienabatur* 5 *satagebat cet.*
	plurimum	*multum* 2 5 *frequens* A om. cet.
	adtinet	*pertinet* 2 *cura est* cet.
11:1	*quieuit*	*cessauit* cet.
11:20	*anticipauit*	*adpropinquauit* 5 *praeuenit* 4 A *prouenit* 8 17
11:21	*tueatur*	*custodit* cet.
	domum	*aulam* 5 *atrium* cet.
	facultates	*substantia* 5 *quae possidet* cet.
11:22	*illius*	*eius* cet.
11:23	*aduersus*	*contra* 5 *aduersum* cet.
	colligit	*congregat* cet.
11:24	*circuit*	*uadit* 5 *ambulat* 4 *perambulat* 8 A *peram* 17
11:25	*communddatam*	*emundatam* 2 *mundatum* 5 *eam* (om. A) *scopis mundatam* cet.
11:26	*peiora priorum*	*deteriora prioribus* 2 *peiora prioribus* 5 A *multo peior prioris* cet.
11:28	*qui ait*	*ipse autem dixit* 2 *at* (ad 5 4) *ille dixit* cet.
	illis	*ad eos* 4 8 17 om. 2 5 A
11:29	*conueniente*	*colligerentur* 2 *congregatis* 5 *concurrentibus* cet.
	gens	*generatio* cet.
11:31	*quoniam*	*quia* cet.
11:32	*eam*	*illam* cet.

Verse	VL3	Other Latin authorities
11:33	*intrantes*	*introeuntes* 2 5 *qui ingrediuntur* cet.
11:38	*quod*	*quare* cet.
11:39	*exteriorem partem*	*a foris* 2 5 *de foris* cet.
11:40	*interiora et exteriora*	*intus et foris* cet.
11:43	*quoniam*	*qui* 17 A *quia* cet.
	consessus	*sessiones* 2 5 *cathedras* cet.
11:44	*ignobilia*	*sine specie* 5 *quae non parent* (*apparent* 17) cet.
	ignorant	*nesciunt* cet.
11:45	*ei*	*illi* cet.
11:46	*sarcinas inportabiles*	*honeribus grauibus* 2 *honera quae non possunt portari* 5 *oneribus quae non possunt portare* 4 *oneribus quae portari non possunt* 17 A
	ea	*ipsas sarcinas* 2 *sarcinas ipsas* 17 *sarcinas* A om. 5 4
11:47	*quoniam*	*quia* 2 A *qui* 4 17
11:50	*ab origine mundi*	*a mundi constitutionem* 2 *a constitutione mundi* cet.
11:52	*intratis*	*introitis* 2 4 *introistis* cet.
11:53	*comminare*	*conferre* 2 *opprimere* A *committere* cet.
12:1	*se continentium*	*circumdedissit* 2 *adstantium* 5 *circumstantibus* cet.
	discentes	*discipulos* 5 17 *discipulos suos* cet.
	cauete	*adtendite* 2 A *attendite* cet.
12:3	*supra*	*in* A *super* cet.
12:5	*demonstrabo*	*ostendam* cet.
12:11	*rationem reddatis*	*excusetis* 2 *respondeatis* cet.
12:12	*eadem hora*	*in ipsa* (*illa* 8) *hora* cet.
12:15	*super{r}ando*	*omni abundantiam* 8 *abundatia* cet.
	facultate	*substantia* 5 *quae possidet* cet.
12:17	*recogitabat*	*cogitabat* 5 A *cogitauit* cet.
	congeram	*colligam* 2 *non congregem* 8 *congregrem* cet.
12:18	*cogitans*	om. cet.
	aedificabo	*faciam* cet.
	congeram	*colligam* 2 *non congregem* 8 *congregrem* cet.
12:20	*reposcunt*	*auferetur* 2 *petunt* 5 *repetunt* cet.
12:28	*paruae*	*modice* 2 *pusillae* 5 A *modicae* 4 17 *minime* 8
12:29	*edatis*	*manducetis* cet.
12:30	*saeculi*	*mundi* (*modi* 4) cet.
12:31	*minima*	*pusillus* cet.
12:32	*placuit*	*in quo bene sensit* 2 *in eo beneplacitum est* 5 *complacuit* cet.
12:33	*consumit*	*corrumpit* cet.
12:35	*succincti*	*praecinti* 2* *cinctus* 5 *adcincti* 8 *praecincti* cet.
13:1	*eodem*	*illo* 2 *in ipso* cet.
	uictimis	*sacrificiis* cet.

Verse	VL3	Other Latin authorities
13:2	*perpessi*	*passi* cet.
13:7	*quod*	*quid* cet.
13:8	*qui*	*ille* cet.
	eam	*illam* cet.
	donec	*quoadusque* 2 *usque dum* (*quo* 4) cet.
13:9	*ceteroquin*	*si quominus* 2 5 *sin autem* cet.
13:11	*languoribus*	*in infirmitate* 5 *infirmitatis* cet.
13:12	*ei*	*illi* cet. om. 2
	absoluta	*liberata* 2 *dimissa* cet.
13:13	*subito*	*continuo* 2 *confestim* cet.
13:17	*mirificis*	*praeclaris* 4 8 17 om. cet.
13:22	*uicos*	*castella* cet.
13:22	*qui*	*ille* 2 5 *ipse* cet.
13:25	*adcluserit*	*cludere* 2 *cluserit* cet.
13:28	*proici*	*excludimini* 2 *eici* 5 *expelli* cet.
	foris	*foras* cet.
13:29	*discumbent*	*accumbent* A *recumbent* cet.
13:30	*fuerunt*	*erant* 2 *erunt* cet.
13:31	*eadem*	*in ipsa* cet.
	discede	*exi* cet.
	quoniam	*quia* cet.
13:32	*ipse*	*ille* 2 *iesus* 4 om. cet.
	euntes	*abeuntes* 5 *ite* cet.
	indicate	*et dicite* 2 17 *dicite* cet.
14:1	*illum*	*eum* cet.
14:4	*manum illius*	*illum* 2 *eum* cet. om. A
14:7	*denotans eos*	*notans sibi* 2 *uidens* 5 *intendens* cet.
14:9	*detinere*	*tenere* cet.
14:10	*discumbe*	*recumbe* cet.
14:12	*et*	*aut* cet.
	sed nec	*neque* cet.
	nec	*neque* cet. om. A
	redditio	*retributio* cet.
14:16	*qui*	*dominus* 2 *ille* 5 *ipse* cet.
14:17	*praeparata*	*parata* 2 5 A *paratum* cet.
14:18	*prior*	*primus* cet.
	ait	*dixit* cet.
14:19	*conparaui*	*emi* cet.
	uado	*eo* cet.
	experimentum accipere	*probare* cet.

Verse	VL3	Other Latin authorities
	propter hoc	*propter quod* 5 *ideo* cet. om. 2 A
14:21	*alacriter*	*celerius* 5 *cito* cet.
14:23	*circa*	*in* cet.
14:24	*nullus*	*nemo* cet.
14:26	*aut* (3x)	*et* cet.
	insuper et	*adhuc* (om. 4) *etiam* (om. 2 *autem* A) *et* (om. 8) cet.
14:27	*portat*	*tulerit* 2 *tollit* 8 *baiulat* cet.
14:28	*ex uestrum*	*ex uobis* cet.
	inpendia	*erogationem* 5 *sumptus* (*sumptum* 2) cet.
	opus sunt	*necessarii sunt* cet. om. 2 5
14:29	*ne si*	*ne forte cum* 2 *ut ne forte cum* 5 *ne posteaquam* (*postea cum* 8) cet.
	ualuerit	*possit* 2 *potuerit* cet.
14:30	*nec ualuit*	*et non potuit* cet.
14:31	*uenturus est*	*uenit cet.*
	ad illum	*super eum obuiari* 5 *aduersus se* 4 *aduersum se* 8 17 *ad se* A om. 2
14:33	*facultatibus suis*	*substantiae suae* 5 *quae possidet* cet.
14:35	*nisi ut*	*sed* cet. om. 5
	proiciatur	*iactant illud* 2 *mittent illud* 5 *mittent eum* 4 *mittetur* cet.
15:1	*accedentes*	*adpropinquantes* 2 *adpropiant* 5 *appropinquantes* A *adpliciti* cet.
	quare	*quia* 2 A *quoniam* 5 *quod* cet.
	eis	*illis* cet.
15:4	*perierit*	*errauerit* 4 8 *perdiderit* cet. om. 17
15:9	*quoniam*	*quia* 2 5 A *quod* 4 8 17
15:13	*collectis omnibus*	*congregauit omnia* 2 *congregans omnia* 5 *congregatis omnibus* cet.
15:15	*coniunxit se*	*adplicuit se* 2 4[c] *adhaesit ibi* 5 *proiecit se ante* 4* *adhesit* 8 A *hesit* 17
	de municipibus	*ex ciuibus* 2 *ex ciuium* 17 *ciuium* cet. om. 4*
	qui	*et his* 2 *et* 5 A *et is* 4 *et ille* 8 17
15:20	*usque*	om. cet.
	procurrens	*cucurrit et* 2 *currens* 5 *acurrens* cet.
	ipsius	*eius* cet.
15:21	*illi*	*ei* cet. om. 2 5
15:22	*pueros*	*seruos* cet.
	celerius	*cito* cet.
	priorem	*primam* cet.
	illius	*eius* cet.
15:25	*illius*	*eius* cet.
15:27	*qui ait*	*ille autem dixit* 2 *isque dixit* 4 A *ad ille dixit* cet.
	incolume	*saluum* cet.
15:29	*ipse*	*ille* cet. om. 2
15:30	*omnem facultatem suam*	*omnia tua* 2 *omnia* 5 *substantiam suam* (*tuam* 8 om. 4) cet.

Verse	VL3	Other Latin authorities
	uiuens	om. cet.
15:32	*quoniam*	*quod* 4 *quia* cet.
16:1	*fuerat*	*est* 2 5 A *erat* 4 8 17
	tanquam	*quod* 8 *quasi* cet.
16:2	*dominus suus*	om. cet.
	amplius	*adhuc* 5 om. cet.
16:3	*quoniam*	*quia* cet.
16:5	*priori*	*ad primum* 2 *primo* cet.
	qui	*ille* cet.
16:6	*uatos*	*cados* 2 A *siclos* 5 *bathos* 4 *batis* 8
	celerius	*cito* cet. om. 2 5
16:7	*domino meo*	om. cet.
	cautionem	*cirografum* 2 *litteras* cet.
16:8	*gente*	*saeculum* 2 *generationem* 5 *generatione* cet.
16:10	*minimo*	*modico* cet.
	magno	*multo* 2 5 *maius* 4 8 *maiori* A
	uobiscum	*uerum* cet.
16:12	*credet*	*dabit* cet.
16:13	*alium*	*unum* 5 *alterum* cet.
16:14	*amatores pecuniae*	*cupidissmi* 2 *cupidi* 5 *auari* cet.
16:15	*scit*	*dinoscit* 2 *nouit* cet.
	quoniam	*quia* cet.
	aput homines	*in hominibus* 2 5 4 *hominibus* 8 17 A
	ante conspectum	*in conspectu* 5 *ante* cet.
16:16	*euangelizantur*	*adnuntiatur* 2 *euangelizat* 5 *euangelizatur* cet.
16:17	*illum*	*eum* 2 *eam* 5 *illud* cet.
	festinant	*conatur* 2 5 *uim facit* (*faciunt* 17) cet.
	excedere	*capere* 2 *cadere* cet.
16:18	*adulterium facit*	*moechatur* (*moecatur* 2) cet.
16:19	*uestiebatur*	*induebatur* cet.
	aepulabantur	*iucundabatur* 2 *aepulans* 5 *epulatur* 17 *epulabatur* cet.
16:20	*diuitis*	om. cet.
	illius	*huius* 2 *eius* cet.
16:21	*satiari*	*saturari* cet.
	lambebant	*et ablingebant* 2 *elingebant* 5 *et lingebant* (*lingebat* 8) cet.
16:23	*de inferno*	*in inferno* 5 4 17 om. 2 8 A
16:25	*memor{r} esto*	*memento* 2 5 *recordare* cet.
16:26	*hiatus terrae*	*chaus* 2 *chaum* 8 *chaos* cet.
16:27	*illi*	om. cet.
16:28	*cruciatus*	*tormenti* 5 *tormentorum* cet.

Verse	VL3	Other Latin authorities
16:30	*qui*	*ille* cet.
17:1	*difficile*	*impossibile* 4 17 *inpossibile* cet.
17:2	*collo*	*super collum* 17 *circa collum* cet.
17:4	*septiens*	*septies* cet.
17:6	*quibus*	*illis* cet. om. A
17:7	*statim*	om. cet.
17:8	*praepara*	*para* cet.
	succinctus	*accingere* 2 *cinge te* 5 *procinge te* 17 *praecinge te* cet.
	bibet	*bibis* 8 *bibes* cet.
17:9	*quoniam*	*quia* 2 5 A *quod* 4 8 17
17:12	*uico*	*castello* 4 *castellum* cet.
17:14	*audisset*	*uidisset* 2 *uidens* 5 *uidit* cet.
	euntes	*curati estis ite* 5 *ite* cet.
	emundati	*purgati* 2 *mundati* cet.
17:15	*sanus*	*curatus* 2 *sanatus* 8 17 *mundatus* cet.
	honorificans	*clarificans* 2 *honorans* 5 *magnificauit* 17 *magnificans* cet.
17:16	*procidit*	*cecidit* (*caecidit* 2) cet.
17:18	*honorem dare*	*claritatem dare* 2 *gloriam dare* 5 A *gratias ageret* (*agaret* 4 *agere* 8) cet.
17:20	*uenturus esset*	*ueniret* 2 *uenit* cet.
17:21	*sed nec*	*neque* cet.
17:23	*nec sequi*	*ne secuti fueritis* 2 *neque persequemini* 5 *neque sectemini* cet.
17:25	*prius*	*primum* cet.
17:30	*similiter*	*secundum haec* cet.
	qua	om. cet.
17:31	*illius*	*eius* cet.
	ea	*illa* (*illam* 8) cet.
17:37	*conueniuunt*	*colliguntur* 2 *congregabuntur cet.*
18:1	*ob hoc*	*ad huc* 2 om. cet.
	deberent	*oportet* cet.
18:2	*sed nec*	*nec* 4 om. cet.
18:4	*per tempus*	*longo tempore* 2 *in aliqod temporis* 5 *per tempore multo* 4* *per multum tempus* cet.
18:5	*per tempore*	*usque ad finem* 2 *in tempus* 5 *in nouissimo* cet.
18:8	*celeriter*	*cito* 2 *confestim* 5 *om. cet.*
	attamen	*uerum* 2 *uerumputat* 5 *uerumtamen* A *tamen* cet.
18:9	*fidentes sibi*	*qui sibi placebant* 2 *qui confidens super se* 5 *qui sibi* (*in se* A) *confidebant* cet.
	quasi	*quia* 2 *quoniam* 5 *tamquam* cet.
18:12	*dono*	*do* cet. om. 5 17
18:13	*quidem*	om. cet.

Verse	VL3	Other Latin authorities
	adleuare	*leuare* cet.
18:14	*prae illum*	*praeter illum* 5 *ab illo* A *magis* (om. 4) *quam ille* cet.
18:15	*ei*	*illi* 2 5 *ad illum* cet.
	illos	*eos* cet.
	obiurgabant	*corripuerunt* 2 *increpabant* cet.
	imperauit eis	*ad se uocabat ea* 5 *conuocans illos* (*eos* 2) cet.
18:17	*quisque*	*quicumque* cet.
	tamquam	*quasi* 2 *sicut* cet.
18:20	*non homicidium facies*	*non moechabis* 5 *non occides* cet. om. 2
	non adulterabis	*ne admiseris* 2 *non occides* 5 *non adulterium admittes* 4 *non adulterium comittes* 8 *non moechaueris* 17 *non moechaberis* A
18:22	*diuide*	*da* cet.
18:24	*quem*	*illum* cet.
18:31	*conuocatis*	*sumpsit* 2 *adsumens* 5 *adsumpsit* 4 8 *assumpsit* 17 A
18:37	*indicauerunt*	*renuntiauerunt* 2 *dixerunt* cet.
18:39	*praeteribant*	*praecedebant autem* 2 *at illi antecedebant* 5 *et* (om. 17) *qui praeibant* cet.
18:41	*qui*	*ille* cet.
18:43	*uidere coepit*	*respexit* 5 *uidit* cet.
	honorificans	*clarificans* 2 *honorans* 5 *magnificans* cet.
19:1	*circuibat*	*pertransiebat* 2 5 *perambulabat* cet.
19:2	*erat*	om. cet.
19:3	*quis*	*qui* cet.
	quoniam	*quia* cet.
	breui	*pusillus* cet.
19:4	*procurrens*	*praecessit in priore* 2 *antecedens ab ante* 5 *praecurrens* cet.
	quoniam	*quia* cet.
	per illa parte	*illic* 2 *inde* 5 A *illa parte* cet.
19:5	*quoniam*	*quia* cet.
19:6	*uirum*	*hominem* cet.
19:8	*dimidiam partem*	*dimidium* cet.
19:9	*quidem*	om. cet.
19:10	*perditum*	*quod perierat* cet.
19:11	*addidit*	*aiecit* 2 *adiciens* cet.
	quod	*quia* cet. om. 2 5
19:12	*profectus est*	*abiit* (*habit* 8) cet.
19:13	*donec*	*dum* cet.
19:14	*illius*	*eius* 2 17 A om. cet.
	quia	om. cet.
19:16	*prior*	*primus* cet.
19:17	*tanto melior*	*euge* cet.

Verse	VL3	Other Latin authorities
	minimo	*modico* cet.
19:19	*potestatem habens*	om. cet.
19:22	*ait*	*dixit* cet.
	et male	om. cet.
19:23	*eam*	*illud* 2 5 A *illum* 4 *illam* 8 17
19:24	*circumstantibus*	*adsistentibus* 2 *qui astabant* 5 *adstantibus* cet.
	ei	*illi* cet. om. 5
19:25	*illi*	*ei* 17 A om. cet.
19:26	*qui habuerit*	*habenti* cet.
	illi	om. cet.
19:27	*iugulate*	*occidite* 5 *interficite* cet.
19:28	*hierosolymis*	*hierusalem* 2 *in hierusalem* 5 *in* (om. 17 A) *hierosolyma* (*iherosolima* 8 *hierosolymam* 17) cet.
19:29	*appellatur*	*uocatur* cet. om. 2
19:30	*uicum*	*castellus* 5 *castellum* cet.
	ingredientes	*introieritis* 2 *introeuntes* cet.
	nullus	*nemo hominum* 2 5 *nemo* 8 17 *nemo umquam hominum* A
	illam	*illum* cet. om. 5
19:31	*illi*	*ei* A om. cet.
19:34	*qui*	*illi* cet. om. 2 5
19:35	*supersternentes*	*superiecerunt* 2 *supermiserunt* 5 *iactauerunt* 8 17 *iactantes* A
19:37	*conlaudare*	*laudare* cet.
19:38	*gloria*	*in excelsi* 2 *altissimis* 5 *in excelsis* cet.
19:39	*obiurga*	*corripe* 2 *increpa* cet.
19:40	*qui*	*ipse* cet. om. 2 5
19:42	*quamquam*	*equidem* 17 *et quidem* 8 A om. 2 5
	tuam	*tibi* cet.
19:43	*inicient saepem*	*circumfodient fossam* 2 *mittent saepem* 5 *circumdabut uallo* cet.
	continebunt	*conpraehendent* 5 *obsidebunt* 8 *coangustabunt* A om. 2 17
19:44	*pauimentabunt*	*ad solum deponent* 2 *ad nihilum deducent* 5 *ad terram* (add. *et* 17) *prosternent* cet.
	natos	*filios* cet.
	ob hoc	*pro eo* 2 *propter* 5 *eo* cet.
	ignorasti	*non cognouisti* 5 *non cognoueritis* 17 *non cognoueris* cet.
19:45	*uertit*	*effundebat* 2 *et fudit* 5 *effudit* 8 om. 17 A
19:47	*pontifices*	*pontificis sacerdotum* 2 *principes sacerdotum* cet.
20:5	*intra se*	*apud se* 2 *ad semetipsos* 5 *inter se* cet.
	nobis	om. cet.
20:10	*illos*	om. cet.
	colonos	*agricolas* 2 5 *cultores* cet.
20:11	*quoque*	*illi autem* cet.

Verse	VL3	Other Latin authorities
20:12	*proiecerunt*	*expulerunt* 2 *dimiserunt uacuum* 5 *eiecerunt* cet.
20:14	*eum*	*illum* cet.
20:16	*tradet*	*dabit* (*dauit* 2) cet.
	qui	*illi* 2 5 om. cet.
20:17	*qui*	*ipse* 17 *ille* cet.
20:18	*offendiderit*	*ceciderit* (*caeciderit* 2) cet.
20:19	*eadem hora*	*ipsa* (*illa* A) *hora* cet. om. 2
20:20	*discessissent*	*secesserunt* 2 *recedentes* 5 *cum recessissent* 8 17 *obseruantes* A
	subor<natos>	*unum adque alterum* 2 *obsiduanos* 5 *insidiatores* A om. 8 17
	fingentes se	*qui simularent se iustos* 2 *in dolo loquentes esse se iustos* 5 *qui se iustos esse* (om. A) *simularent* cet.
	illius	*eius* cet. om. A
	illum	*eum* 5 om. cet.
20:21	*uera*	*recte* cet.
	hominum	om. cet.
20:25	*qui*	*ille* 2 5 *iesus* 8 om. cet.
20:26	*capere*	*repraehendere* 2 *adpraehendere* 5 *reprehendere* cet.
20:28	*unius*	*cuius* 2 5 *alicui* cet.
	illius	*eius* cet.
20:29	*prior*	*primum* cet.
20:31	*defuncti sunt*	*mortui sunt* 2 5 A om. 8 17
20:32	*sed*	*nouissime* 5 8 *nouissima* A om. 2 17
20:35	*attingere*	*habituri* 2 *obtinere* 5 om. cet.
20:36	*morituri sunt*	*incipient mori* 2 *mori possunt* 5 *morientur* 8 17 *mori poterunt* (*poterint**) A
20:37	*demonstrabit*	*significauit* 2 5 *ostendit* cet.
20:38	*uiuentium*	*uiuorum* cet.
20:46	*consessus*	*praesidere* 2 *cathedras* cet.
20:47	*amplius poenae*	*abuntius iudicium* 2 *amplius iudicium* 5 *damnationem maiorem* cet.
21:1	*altario*	*gazophilacium* 2 *zaiophylacium* 8 *gazophylacium* cet.
21:4	*super illius fuit*	*superfuit illis* 2 *abundantia sua* 5 *abundanti sibi* (om. 8) cet.
	exiguitate sua	*inopia sua* 2 *minimo suo* 5 *eo quod deest illi* cet.
	facultatem	*substantiam* 5 *uictum* cet.
21:5	*optimis*	*bonis* cet.
	et bonis extructum	*et donis exornatum* 2 *ornata est et depositionibus* 5 *et donis ornatum* cet.
21:7	*eum*	*discipuli* 5 *illum* cet.
21:8	*sequi*	*abieritis* 5 *ire* cet.
21:9	*separationes*	*turbationis* 2 *dissensiones* 5 *seditiones* cet.
	nundum	*non continuo* 2 5 *non statim* cet.
	erit	om. cet.

Verse	VL3	Other Latin authorities
21:11	*pestes*	*lues* 2 *morbi* 5 *pestilentiae* (*pestilentia* 8) cet.
	formidines	*timores* 2 5 *terrores cet.*
	hiemes	*tempestates* 8 17 om. cet.
21:12	*inmittent*	*mittent* 5 *inicient* cet.
	uos	om. cet.
	causa	*propter* cet.
21:13	*sit*	*obtinget* 5 *continget* (*contingent* 8) cet.
21:14	*quomodo*	*quae* 2 *quemadmodum* cet. om. 5
	prius meletare	*promeletantes* 5 *praemeditari* (*prameditari* 2) cet.
	rationem reddatis	*respondere* 5 *respondeatis* (*respondatis* 2) cet.
21:17	*causa*	*propter* cet.
21:19	*tolerantia*	*sufferentia* 5 *patientia* cet.
21:20	*exercitibus*	*exercitu* (*excitu* 2 *exercitum* 8) cet.
21:22	*iudicii*	*uindictae* 2 *uindictae* 5 *ultionis* cet.
21:24	*gentes uniuersa*	*omnibus gentis* 8 17 *omnes gentes* cet.
	erit in concultationem	*erit inculcata* 2 *erit calcata* 5 *calcabitur* cet.
21:25	*repleantur*	*adimpleantur* 2 *inpleantur* 5 8 *impleantur* 17 A
	conpressio	*conclusio* 2 *conflictio* 5 *pressura* (*praessura* 17) cet.
	stupore	*confessione* 2 *aporia* 5 *confusione* cet.
	sonus maris	*sonante mare* 5 *sonitus maris* (*mares* 2) cet.
	undis	*inundationes* 2 *salo* 5 *fluctuum* (*fluctum* 8) cet.
21:26	*arefrigescentibus*	*deficientium* 5 *arescentibus* cet.
	superuenientium	*quae superueniunt* 2 *quae uentura sunt quae superuenient* (*superueniet* 17) cet.
21:27	*potentia*	*potentatu* 2 *uirtute* 5 *potestate* cet.
21:29	*ficum*	*ab arbore fici* 2 *ficulneam* cet.
21:30	*florient*	*coeperint mittere* 2 *produxerint* 5 *producant* 4 *producunt* cet.
	a se	*fructus suos* 2 *fructum suum* 5 *iam fructus* 17 *iam ex se fructum* cet.
21:32	*gens*	*caelum* 2 *generatio* (*generatione* 17) cet.
21:34	*gratulatione*	*crapula* (*crepula* 5) cet.
	instet	*adsistet* 2 *superueniat* cet.
	repentaneus	*subitaneus* 2 *subitanus* 5 *repentina* cet.
21:37	*egrediebatur*	*exiebat* 2 *exiens* cet. om. 5
	demorabatur	*manebat* 2 *habitabat* 5 *morabatur* A *auocabatur* cet.
	dicitur	*uocabatur* 4 *uocatur* cet.
22:4	*ponticifibus*	*principibus* (*principes* 17) *sacerdotum* cet.
22:5	*polliciti sunt*	*constituerunt* 2 5 *pacti sunt* cet.
22:9	*qui*	*illi* cet.
22:10	*intrantibus*	*introeuntibus* cet.
	ingreditur	*introiit* 2 *introierit* 5 *intrant* 8 *intrat* cet.

Verse	VL3	Other Latin authorities
22:11	*refectio*	*hospitium* 2 *diuersorium* cet.
22:12	*maedianum*	*superiorem* 5 *pede plano* 4 *caenaculum* A *in superioribus* cet.
22:16	*quoniam*	*quia* cet. om. 5
	edam	*manducabo* cet.
22:17	*sumite*	*accipite* cet.
	in uobis	*uobis* 5 *inter uos* cet.
22:18	*quoniam*	*amodo* 2 5 *quod* cet.
	fructu	*potione* 2 *creatura* 5 *generatione* cet.
22:19	*confregit*	*fregit* cet.
22:21	*attamen*	*uerum* 2 *uerumtamen* cet.
	proditoris mei	*eius qui me tradat* 2 *qui tradet me* 5 *tradentes me* 4 8 *tradentis me* cet.
22:23	*inquirebant*	*coeperunt conquire* 2 5 *coeperunt quaerere* A *conquirebant* cet.
22:31	*tamquam*	*sicut* cet.
22:32	*tandem*	*aliquando* cet. om. 2 5
22:34	*qui*	*iesus* 8 *ille* cet.
	ait	*dicit* 2 *dixit* cet.
	tu	om. cet.
22:39	*abiit*	*ibat* cet.
22:40	*esset*	*fuisset* 5 *peruenisset* cet.
	in	*ad* 8 17 A om. 2 5 4
22:41	*tanquam*	*quasi* 5 *quantum* cet.
	ictus	*remissionem* 5 *iactus* 17 A *iactum* cet.
22:44	*illius*	*eius* cet.
	quasi	*tamquam* 8 *sicut* cet.
22:45	*maerore*	*tristia* cet.
22:46	*eis*	*illis* cet. om. 8
22:47	*praecedebat*	*antecedebat* cet.
	illos	*eos* cet.
22:49	*illum*	*eum* 5 *ipsum* cet.
	illi	*domino* 5 *ei* cet.
22:50	*quidam*	om. cet.
	pontificis	*principis* (*principes* 2) *sacerdotum* cet.
	abscindit	*abstulit* 5 *amputauit* cet.
	illius	*eius* cet.
22:52	*ponticifes*	*principes sacerdotum* 5 A *principibus sacerdotum* cet.
	antistites	*praepositos* 5 *magistratus* A *magistratibus* cet.
	tamquam	*sicut* 5 *quasi* cet.
22:53	*a tenebrae*	*tenebrae* 5 *tenebrarum* cet.
22:54	*et*	om. cet.

Verse	VL3	Other Latin authorities
	pontificis	*principis sacerdotum* cet.
22:55	*illorum*	*eis* 5 *eorum* cet.
22:56	*illis*	*eis* cet. om. 5 A
22:57	*eum*	*illum* cet.
22:59	*paulo*	*intercesso* 5 *interuallo facto* cet.
22:60	*protinus*	*continuo* cet.
22:61	*antequam*	*priusquam* cet.
	te scire	*nosse* 4 om. cet.
22:63	*deridebant*	*inludebant* cet. om. 8
22:64	*illius*	*eius* 5 eum *cet. om. 2 4*
	illum	*eum* cet. om. 5 4
22:66	*horta est*	*factus est* cet.
	pontifices	*principes* (*principis* 8) *sacerdotum* cet.
	deduxerunt	*adduxerunt* 5 *duxerunt* cet.
22:70	*ei*	om. cet.
22:71	*qui*	*illi* cet.
	egemus	*opus habemus* 5 *desideramus* cet.
	illius	*eius* 5 A *ipsius* cet.
23:1	*uniuersa*	*omnes* (*omnis* 2) cet.
23:2	*euertentem*	*subuertentem* cet.
	tributum	*tributam* 8 *tributa* cet.
23:3	*qui*	*ille* cet. om. 5
23:4	*pontificis*	*principes* (*principis* 2) *sacerdotum* cet.
	nullam	*nihil* cet.
	culpam	*causa* 8 *causae* cet.
23:5	*totam*	*omnem* 5 *uniuersam* (*uniuersa* 8) cet.
	inchoans	*incipiens* cet.
23:6	*an*	*si* cet.
23:7	*his*	*illis* cet.
23:8	*propterea quod*	*propter quod* 5 *eo quod* cet.
	frequenter	*multa* cet. om. 5
	illo	*eo* cet.
23:9	*uero*	*autem* 5 17 *at* (*ad* 2) cet.
23:10	*pontifices*	*principes sacerdotum* cet.
	uehementer	*fortiter* 5 *constanter* cet.
23:11	*delusum*	*inludens* 5 *inlusit* cet.
23:12	*in amicitiam*	*in lite* 5 *amici* cet.
	eadem	*ipso* 5 *ipsa* cet.
	hora	*die* cet.
	praeerant	*antea fuerant* cet.

Verse	VL3	Other Latin authorities
23:13	*pontifices*	*principibus* (*principes* 5) *sacerdotum* cet.
	populi	*plebem* 5 *plebe* A *plebis* cet.
23:14	*detulistis*	*obtulistis* 2 *adduxistis* 5 *optulistis* cet.
	tanquam	*sicut* 5 *quasi* cet.
	dignum	om. cet.
	iis	*his* cet.
23:15	*gestum*	*actum* cet.
23:16	*castigatum*	*emendans* 5 *emendabo* 4 *emendatum* cet.
23:18	*totus populus*	*uniuersi* 5 *uniuersa turba* cet.
23:19	*coniectus*	*missus* cet.
	quia homicidium fecerat	om. cet.
23:20	*rursus*	*iterum* cet.
	adlocutus	*aduocauit* 5 *locutus* cet.
23:21	*qui*	*illi* cet.
	proclamabant	*clamauerunt* 5 *succlamabant* cet.
23:22	*qui*	*ille* cet.
	nihil	*ullam* 5 *nullam* cet.
	dignum	*causam* cet.
	castigatum	*emendans* 5 *corripiam* cet.
23:23	*qui*	*illi* cet.
	imminebant	*incumbebant* 5 *instabant* cet.
	illorum	*eorum* cet.
23:24	*decreuit*	*adiutauit* 2 *iudicauit* 5 *adiudicauit* cet.
	illorum	*eorum* 5 A *ipsorum* cet.
23:25	*coniectus*	*missus* cet.
	ipsorum	*eorum* cet.
23:26	*deducerent*	*duxerunt* 5 *ducerent* cet.
	cyreneum	*cyrenensem* cet.
	ferre	*ut adferret* 5 *portare* cet.
23:27	*eum*	*illum* cet.
	ingens	*multa* A om. cet.
	se	*eum* 5 om. cet.
23:28	*quas*	*eas* 5 *illas* cet.
	uero	*autem* cet.
	natos	*super filios* A *filios* cet.
23:29	*felices*	*beata* 2 *beatae* cet.
	educauerunt	*enutrierunt* 5 *lactauerunt* A *nutrierunt* cet.
23:33	*appellatur*	*uocabatur* 2 *dicitur* 8 *uocatur* cet.
	quidem	om. cet.
23:34	*ipsius*	*eius* cet.

Verse	VL3	Other Latin authorities
23:35	*intra se*	*cum eis* om. cet.
	se	om. cet.
23:36	*inridebant*	*dulebant* 8 *inludebant* A *deludebant* cet.
23:37	*salua te ipsum*	*saluum te fac* A *libera te* cet. om. 5
23:39	*iis*	*his* A om. cet.
	qui suspensi erant	*qui pendebant* A *pendentibus* cet.
	malefici	*malignis* 5 *latronibus* cet.
23:40	*obiurgabat*	*increpabat* cet.
23:41	*gessimus*	*egimus* 5 *factis* cet.
	fecit	*egit* 5 *gessit* cet.
23:44	*circiter*	*sicut* 5 *fere* cet.
	super	*in* cet.
23:45	*intenebricatus*	*obscuratus* cet.
23:46	*exclamans*	*clamans* cet.
23:48	*conuenerant*	*simul erat* 2 8 *simul uenerant* 5 *simul aderant* 4 A
	hoc	*istud* cet.
	ex ea	om. cet.
23:49	*illius*	*eius* cet.
23:51	*opere*	*actioni* 5 *actionibus* cet.
	illorum	*eorum* cet.
23:52	*eum*	*corpus iesu* 5 *illum* 4* *illut* 4[c] *om. cet.*
	illum	*eum* cet.
	sculptili	*sculpto* 5 *exciso* cet.
	aliquis	*nemo* 5 *quisquam* cet.
23:55	*consecutae*	*secutae* 5 *subsecutae* (*subsaecutae* 2) cet.
	secutae	*errant uenientes* 5 *uenerant* cet.
	illum	*ipso* cet. om. 5
	quomodo	*quaeadmodum* 4 *quemadmodum* cet.
	est	*erat* cet.
	illius	*eius* cet.
23:56	*quieuerunt*	*requieuerunt* 5 *siluerunt* cet.
24:1	*prima*	*una* cet.
	die sabbatorum	*sabbati* cet.
	ante lucem	*diluculo* 5 A *deluculo* 8 *tempore* cet.
24:4	*stuperent*	*aporiarentur* 5 *contristarentur* 8 *mente consternatae essent* (*sunt* 2) cet.
	hoc	*eo* 5 *facto* 4 *isto* cet.
	adstiterunt	*adsisterunt* 5 *steterunt* cet.
	iuxta	*sicut* 8 *secus* cet. om. 5
24:5	*timore adprehensae*	*in timore factae* 5 *cum timerent* cet.

Verse	VL3	Other Latin authorities
	faciem	*uultos suos* 5 *uultum* cet.
24:6	*memoramini*	*mementote* 5 *recordamini* A *rememoramini* cet.
	sicut	*quanta* 5 *qualiter* cet.
	dum	*cum* cet.
24:10	*magdalena*	*maria magdalena* 5 *maria magdalene* cet.
	relique	*ceterae* cet.
24:11	*tanquam*	*quasi* 5 *sicut* cet.
	delera	*derisus* 5 *delibramentum* 4 *deliramentum* (*deleramentum* 2) cet.
24:13	*municipium*	*castellum* cet.
	cui	om. cet.
24:14	*tractabant*	*loquebantur* A *fabulantur* cet.
24:15	*tractarent*	*fabulantur* 2 4 *fabulari* 5 *fabularentur* 8 A
	ascendens	*adpropinquauit* 2 *adpropians* 5 *superuenit* 4 8 *appropinquans* A
24:17	*tractatis*	*referitis* 2 *conferitis* 5 *confertis* cet.
	ad alterutrum	*uos* 5 *ad inuicem* cet.
24:18	*gesta*	*facta* cet.
24:19	*qui*	*ille* cet.
	ipsi	*illi* cet. om. 5 4
24:20	*pontifices*	*sacerdotes* 2 *summi sacerdotes* A *principes sacerdotum* cet.
	nostri	*magistratus nostri* 2 *potentes nostri* 5 *omnes populus* 4 *principes nostri* A om. 8
	illum	*eum* cet.
24:22	*exterruerunt*	*commemorauerunt* 2 *seduxerunt* 5 *terruerunt* cet.
	mane	*ante lucana* 2 *matutinae* 5 *ante lucem* cet.
24:24	*ut*	*sicut* cet.
24:25	*graues*	*tardi* cet.
24:27	*inchoans*	*incipiens* cet.
	eis	*illis* cet.
	se	*eo* 2 5 *ipso* cet.
24:28	*uicum*	*castello* 4 A *castellum* cet.
	quem	*ubi* 5 *quo* cet.
	adfectabat	*similauit* 2 *fecit* 5 *finxit* cet.
24:29	*eis*	*illis* cet.
24:30	*discumbuisset*	*recumberet* 2 A *recubuisset* 5 *recumbit* 4 8
24:31	*adaperti*	*aperti* cet.
	illis	*eorum* A *eis* cet.
24:32	*alterutrum*	*semetipsos* 5 *inuicem* cet.
	adaperiebat	*aperiebat* 2 5 *aperiret* cet.
24:33	*eadem*	*ipsa* cet.
24:35	*enarrabant*	*exponebat* 2 *narrabant* cet.

Verse	VL3	Other Latin authorities
	sicut	*quoniam* 2 *quia* 5 *quomodo* cet
24:37	*exterriti*	*turbati* 2 *pauerunt* 5 *conturbati* cet.
	timore adprehensi	*in timorem missi* 2 *timore tacti* 5 *conterriti* cet.
24:38	*qui*	*ille* 2 5 om. cet.
24:39	*tractate*	*palpate* cet.
24:41	*stupentibus*	*cum admirarentur* 2 *mirantium* 5 *mirantibus* cet.
	edamus	*manducem* 4 *manducetur* A *manducare* cet.
24:42	*qui*	*illi* cet. om. 2 5
24:47	*illius*	*eius* cet.
24:49	*repromissionem*	*promissionem* 2 5 *promissa* 4 8 *promissum* A
	donec	*usque dum* 5 *quoadusque* cet.
	summo	*alto* cet.
24:50	*usque*	*foras* 5 A *foris* 4 8 om. 2
	extollens	*lebabit* 2 *lebans* 5 *eleuatis* cet.
24:53	*conlaudentes*	*laudentes* cet.

6 *Codex Vercellensis* Luke: Transcription

325 LUCANUM

1:1 QUONIAM QUI
DEM MU[L]TI
TEM[PTAUERUNT]
– – –
– – –
– – –
– – –
– – –
– – –
– – –
– – –
– – –
– – –
– – –
– – –
– – –
– – –
– – –
– – –
– – –
– – –
– – –
– – –
– – –

1:4 NOSCAS EORU∸
SEṚṂỌNEM
[DE QUIBUS
ERUDITUS
ES] – –
– – –
– – –
– – –
– – –
– – –
– – –
– – –
– – –
– – –
– – –
– – –
– – –
– – –
– – –
– – –
– – –
– – –
– – –
1:6 – – [MAN]

https://doi.org/10.1515/9783111142531-007

326 SEC·

DATIS EṬ IUSTI
FICATIONIS
DM̄I Ṣ[INE QUE]
Ṛ[ELLA]
– – –
– – –
– – –
– – –
– – –
– – –
– – –
– – –
– – –
– – –
– – –
– – –
– – –
– – –
– – –
– – –
– – –
– – –
– – –
1:9 – – [IN]

CENSUM PO
NEṚET INGRES
ṢỤṢ [IN] TEM
[PLUM]
– – –
– – –
– – –
– – –
– – –
– – –
– – –
– – –
– – –
– – –
– – –
– – –
– – –
– – –
– – –
– – –
– – –
– – –
– – –
1:13 – – [QUO]

327 LUCAN·

NIAM ECCE
EXAUDITA EST
OṚẠTỊỌ TUA
ET UX[O]R TUA
ELISA[B]ET PA
RIET Ṭ[IBI] ḶFILI
ỤṂ ẸT [UOCA
RIS NOMEN
EIUS IOHAN
1:14 NEM ERITQUE
GAUDIUM TI
BI ET EXULTA
TIO ET MULTI
IN NATIUITA
TE EIUS GAUDE
1:15 BUNT ERIT
ENIM MAG
NUS IN CONS
PECTU DM̄I
ET UINUM ET
SICERA NON
BIBET ET SP̄U
SANCTO IN
PLEBITUR AD]

HUC EX UTE
RO MATRIS
1:16 SUAE ET MUL
TOS FỊḶỊORUM
ISṬR[AHE]Ḷ ÇỌ[¯̇]
Ụ[ERTET AD]
DŌ[M· D̄M̄· IP
SORUM ET
1:17 IPSE PRAEIBIT
IN CONSPEC
TU EIUS IN SP̄U
ET UIRTUTE
HELIAE AD CO¯
UERTENDA
CORDA PATRU¯
AD FILIOS ET IN
CREDIBILES
AD PRUDEN
TIAM IUSTO
RUM PARA
RE DM̄O PO
PULUM PER
FECTUM
1:18 ET AIT ZACHARI]

328 SEC·

AS AN[D A]NGE
LỤṂ U[N]DE ḤOC
SCỊẠM EG̣O
ẸN[I]Ṃ ṢẸNEX
[SUM E]T ỤXOR
[MEA PROCES
SIT IN DIEBUS
SUIS
1:19 ET RESPONDENS
ANGELUS DI
XIT EI EGO SUM
GABRIEL QUI
ADSISTO IN
CONSPECTU
DĒI ET MISSUS
SUM LOQUI
AD TE ET UENI N
UNTIARE TIBI
1:20 HAEC ET ECCE
ERIS TACENS
ET NON POTE
RIS LOQUI US
QUE IN DIEM
QUO FIANT HAEC]

QUỌNIAM NO¯
CREDIDIṢTI
UER[BIS ME
IS] Q̣ỤỊ ỊṂP̣LE
BUNT[UR] TEM
[PORE SUO
1:21 ET ERAT POPU
LUS EXPECTANS
ZACHARIAM
ET MIRABAN
TUR QUOD MO
RAM FACERET
IN TEMPLO
1:22 EGRESSUS AU
TEM NON PO
TERAT LOQUI
AD EOS ET COG
NOUERUNT
QUIA UISIONE¯
UIDIT IN TEM
PLO ET IPSE ERAT
[[AD]]NUENS IL
LIS ET PERMA¯
SIT MUTUS]

329 LUCANUM

1:23 ET ḌACTUM EST
ỤṬ Ị[NPLE]TI SUNT
[DIES SACE]RḌO
[TII EIUS ABIIT
IN DOMUM
1:24 SUAM POST IS
TOS AUTEM DI
ES CONCEPIT
ELISABET UXOR
EIUS ET OCCUL
TABAT SE MEN
SIBUS QUIN
QUE DICENS
1:25 QUID ITA MIHI
FECIT DM̅S· IN
DIEBUS QUIBUS
RESPEXIT AU
FERRE OBPRO
BRIUM MEUM
INTER HOMI
1:26 NES EODE¯
AUTEM TEMPO
RE MISSUS EST
ANGELUS]

GABRỊEL Ạ D̅Ọ̅
IṆ CIỤI[TATEM]
G̣Ạ[LILAEAE CUI
NOMEN NA
1:27 ZARE[[T]] AD UIR
GINEM
– – –
– – –
– – –
DE DOMO DA
UID ET NOMEN
UIRGINIS MA
1:28 RIA ET INGRES
SUS ANGELUS
BENEDIXIT
EAM DICENS
HABE GRATIA
PLENA [[DM̅S EST]]
TECUM BENE
DICTA TU IN
TER MULIERES
1:29 IPSA AUTEM
UT UIDIT [[EUM MO]]
TA EST IN INTRO]

330 SEC·

ỊTU EIUṢ ET ERAT
[COGI]Ṭ[A]ṆṢ QỤOD
[. . . . . BEN]Ẹ
1:30 [. . . . . . ET
. . . . . ANGE
LUS . NE TIME
[[AS]] – –
– – –
– – –
1:31 – – [ECCE
[. . . . . .]CIP
IES IN UTERO
ET PARIES FIL
IUM ET UOCA
BIS NOMEN
1:32 EIUS IH̄M HIC
ERIT MAGNUS
ET FILIUS ALTIS
SIMI UOCA
BITUR ET DA
BIT EI DM̄S
SEDEM DA
UID PATRIS
1:33 EIUS ET REG]

NAUIT IN DO
ṂỤṂ IACOB
IN SAEC̣ỤLẠ
ẸṬ ṚEG̣NI EỊỤS
[NON ERIT FI
1:34 NIS ET AIT
ILLI MARIA
QUOMODO
ERIT HOC QUO
NIAM NON
NOUI UIRUM
1:35 ET RESPON
DENS ANGE
LUS DIXIT EI
SP̄S SANCTUS
SUPERUENI
ET IN TE ET UIR
TUS ALTISSI
MI INUMBRA
UIT TIBI IDEO
1:36 QUE QUOD NAS
CETUR EX TE SANC
TUM UOCA
UITUR FILIUS]

331 MATTHEUM

DĒI· ET ECCE
ELIṢẠBET COG
Ṇ[A]TẠ TUA ET
IP̣SA COṆCEPIT
[FI]LIUM IN SE
ṆECTA SUA
ẸṬ Ḥ̣IÇ MEṆ
[SIS SEXTUS EST
EI QUAE UOCA
TUR STERILIS
1:37 QUIA NON EST
IMPOSSIBILE
APUT DŌM
OMNE UER
1:38 BUM ET DIXIT
MARIA ECCE
ANCILLA D[[M̄I]]
FIAT MIHI] –
– – –
– – –
– – –
– – –
– – –
– – –

1:39 MARIẠ [IN]
DIEB[US IL]
LIS [ET ABIIT]
I[N MONTA
NAM CUM
FESTINATIO
NE IN CIUITA
TEM IU. . .]
– – –
– – –
– – –
– – –
– – –
– – –
– – –
– – –
– – –
– – –
– – –
– – –
– – –
– – –
– – –

332 SEC·

1:42 [ET EX]CLAMA
[UIT UO]C̣Ẹ ṂAG
[NA ET A]IT
[BENEDICT]Ạ TỤ
[INTER MULI
ERES ET BE
NEDICTUS
FRUCTUS UE⁻
TRIS TUI]
– – –
– – –
– – –
– – –
– – –
– – –
– – –
– – –
– – –
– – –
– – –
– – –
– – –
– – –
1:45 – [ET BEA]

TA ES QUAE [C]ṚẸ
DIDISTI QỤOD
ẸRỊṬ [CONSUM]
MAT[IO] EO[R]U[⁻]
[QUAE] TIBI Ḍ[IC
T]A S[U]NT Ạ DM̄[O]
1:46 [E]Ṭ ẠỊṬ ELISAB[ET
MAGNIFICAT
ANIMA MEA
1:47 DŌM· ET EXUL
TAUIT SP̄S ME
US IN D[[ĒO SA]]
LUTARE MEO
1:48 QUIA RESPE
XIT HUMILI
TATEM ANCIL
LAE SUAE]
– – –
– – –
– – –
– – –
– – –
– – –
– – –

333 LUCANUM

1:49 POTENS EST ET
SA[NCT]UṂ EST
Ṇ[OMEN EIUS]
1:50 EṬ [MISERICO]R
Ḍ[IA EIUS IN SA]E
[CULA SAECULO
RUM SAECU
LA TIMEˉ
TIBUS EUM
1:51 FECIT POTES
TATEM IN BRA
CHIO SUO DIS
SIPAUIT SUPER
BOS MENTE
ET CORDA EO
1:52 RUM DEPOSU
IT POTENTES
DE SEDE ET
EXALTAUIT]
– – –
– – –
– – –
1:53 [DIUITES DIMI
SIT INANES]

1:54 SUSCEPI[T IS]
T[RAHEL PUE
RUM SUUM
RECORDATUS
MISERICOR
1:55 DIAE SICUT LO
CUTUS EST AD
PATRES NOS
TROS ABRAHAˉ
ET SEMINI
EIUS IN AE
TERNUM
1:56 MANSIT AUTEM
MARIA CUM
EA MENSIBUS
TRIBUS ET RE
UERSA EST] –
– – –
– – –
– – –
– – –
– – –
– – –
1:57 – – [PE]

[P]ẸRIT FILIU‾
1:58 [ET A]UḌỊ[ER]ỤN̄
[UICINI ET
COGNATI] EIUS
[QUIA MAG
NIFICAUIT
DM̄S MISE
RICORDIAM
SUAM CUM
EA ET CONGRA
TULABANTUR
1:59 EI ET FAC
TUM EST [[DIE]]
OCTAUO
UENERUNT
CIRCUMCI
DERE PUE
RUM] –
– – –
– – –
– – –
– – –
– – –
1:60 [ET RESPON]

DENS MATER
IP̣SIUS D[I]X̣[I]T
Ṇ[O]Ṇ ṢẸḌ ỤO
CABIṬU[R] ỊỌ
1:61 ḤẠN[NES ET
DIXERUNT
AD EAM NE
MO EST IN COG
NATIONE TUA
QUI UOCETUR
NOMINE IS
TO
1:62 ADNUEBANT
ETIAM PATRI
EIUS QUEM
UELLET UO
1:63 CARI EUM ET
ACCEPTO PU
GILLARE] –
– – –
– – –
– – –
– – –
– – –

335 SEC·

1:64 SOLUTA EST LIN
GUA ẸIUS ET
MI[RATI SU]NT
[OMNES
APERTUM EST
AUTEM OS EIUS
ET LOQUEBA
TUR BENEDI
1:65 CENS D̅M̅· ET
FACTUS EST SU
PER OMNES
TIMOR QUI CIR
CUM ILLOS HA
BITABANT
IN OMNI
MONTANA IU
DEAE DIUULGA
BANTUR OM
NIA HAEC UER
1:66 BA ET POSUE
RUNT OMNES
QUI AUDIE
RANT IN COR
DE SUO DICEN]

TES QUIDNAM
PUẸ[R ISTE] ERIT
[ETENIM MA
NUS DM̅I ERAT CU̅
1:67 ILLO ET ZA
CHARIAS PA
TER EIUS IMPLE
TUS EST SP̅U
SANCTO ET PRO
PHETAUIT DI
CENS
1:68 BENEDICTUS
D̅S̅ ISTRAHEL
QUIA UISITA
UIT ET FECIT
REDEMPTIO
NEM POPU
1:69 LO . . . . . COR
NUM SALU
TIS NOBIS IN
DOMO DAUID]
– – –
– – –
1:70 – – [LOCU]

TUS EST PER
OṢ [SANCTORU̅
PROPHETARU̅
SUORUM QUI
A SECULO SUNT]
– – –
1:71 – – [INI
MICIS NOS
TRIS ET DE MA
NU OMNIU̅
QUI NOS ODE
1:72 RUNT FACERE
MISERICOR
DIAM CUM
PATRIBUS NOS
TRIS ET MEMO
RARI] –
– – –
– – –
– – –
– – –
– – –
– – –
1:73 – – [NOS]
1:74 TṚUṂ DẠṚE
NOBI[S UT S]Ị
[NE TIMORE
DE MANU INI
MICORUM
NOSTRORUM
LIBERATOS
SERUIRE IPSI
1:75 IN CASTITATE
ET IUSTITIA
IN CONSPEC
TU EIUS OM
NES DIES NOS
TROS
1:76 ET TU PUER PRO
PHETA ALTIS
SIMI UOCA
BERIS PRAE
IBIS ENIM AN
TE FACIEM
DM̅I PARARE
1:77 UIAS EIUS AD
DANDAM SCI
ENTIAM SA]

337 SEC·

LUTIS POPULO
EIỤṢ ỊN RE
Ṃ[ISSIO]NE [⁻]
[PECCATO]ṚUM
1:78 [IPSORU]M PER
[UISCER]Ạ [MI
SERICORDI
AE D̅E̅I̅· NOS
TRI IN QUIBUS
UISITAUIT NOS
ORIENS EX AL
1:79 TO INLUMINA
RE I IN TENE
BRIS ET UM
BRA MORTIS
SEDENTES AD
DIRIGENDOS
PEDES NOS
TROS IN UIAM
1:80 PACIS PUER
AUTEM CRES
CEBAT ET CON
FIRMABATUR
IN SP̄U ET ERAT]

IN DESERTIS
USQUE IN [DI]
EM ỌṢTE[NSIO]
ṆIṢ [SUAE AD
ISTRAHEL
2:1 FACTUM EST AU
TEM IN ILLIS
DIEBUS EXIIT
EDICTUM
A CAESARE AU
GUSTO UT PRO
FITERETUR
PER UNIUER
SUM ORBEM
2:2 HAEC PRIMA
FACTA EST PRO
FESSIO PRAESIDE
SYRIAE CYRI
2:3 NO ET IBANT
OMNES PRO
FITERI UNUS
QUISQUE IN
SUAM CIUI
TATEM]

2:4 ASCENDIT AUTĒ·
ET IOṢEPH A GA
ḶỊ[LA]ẸẠ DE CI
[UITAT]E NAZAR
[ET IN TE]RRAM
[IUDEAM IN
CIUITATEM
DAUID QUAE
UOCATUR BE
THLEM EO QUOD
ESSET DE DO
MO ET PATRIA
2:5 DAUID PROFI
TERI CUM MA
RIA DESPON
SATA SIBI PREG
NANTE
2:6 FACTUM EST AU
TEM CUM IBI
ESSENT IN
PLETI SUNT
DIES UT PARE
RET ET PEPE
RIT FILIUM]

2:7 SUUM PRI
MOGENITU⁻
EṬ PAṆṆIS
EUṂ [INUOL]
ỤỊṬ Ẹ[T CONLO]
CAU[IT EUM
IN PRAESEPIO
QUONIAM
NON ERAT LO
CUS IN DIUER
SORIO
2:8 PASTORES AU
TEM ERANT
IN ILLA REGIO
NE UIGILAN
TES ET CUSTO
DIENTES UIGI
LIAS NOCTIS
SUPER GRE
2:9 GEM SUUM ET
ECCE ANGE
LUS DM̄I· STE
TIT SUPER EOS
ET MAIESTAS]

339 SEC·

DM̄I CIRCUM
LUXIT EOS ET TI
MUERUNT
TIMORE MAG
2:10 NO DIXIT
Q[U]AE EIS AN
GELUS NOLITE
TIMERE ECCE
ENIM EUAN
GELIZO UOBIS
GAUDIUM
MAGNUṂ
[QUOD E]RỊ[T OM
2:11 NI POPULO QUIA
NATUS EST UO
BIS HODIE SAL
UATOR QUI EST
XP̄S· DM̄S· IN
CIUITATE DA
2:12 UID ET HUIUS
HOC UOBIS
SIGNUM IS
TUT INUE
NIETIS INFAN]

TEM PANNIS
INUOLUTUM
POSITUṂ [IN]
PRAEṢ[EPIO]
2:13 ET SUBI[TO FAC]
TA ES[T CUM]
ILLIS Ạ[NGELO]
Ṛ[UM MULTI]
Ṭ[UDO EXER
CITUS CAELES
TIS LAUDAN
TIUM D̄M̄· ET
DICENTIUM
2:14 GLORIA IN EX
CELSIS DĒO
ET SUPER TER
RAM PAX HO
MINIBUS BO
NE UOLUNTA
2:15 TIS ET FAC
TUM EST UT
ABIERUNT
[[AB EIS]] IN CAE
LUM ANGELI]

PAS[TO]ṚES LO
QỤẸ[BA]ṆTUR
[AD I]NUICEṂ
[ET DIX]EṚỤṆṬ
[PERT]RANSẸẠ
[MUS US]QUE
BETHLEṂ ẸṬ
[UIDEAMUS]
[HOC UERBU]M
[QUOD FACTUM
EST SICUT DM̄S
OSTENDIT NO
2:16 BIS ET UENE
RUNT FESTI
NANTES ET IN
UENERUNT
MARIAM ET
IOSEF ET INFA¯
TEM POSITUM
IN PRAESEPIO
2:17 UIDENTES AU
TEM ET COG
NOUERUNT
DE UERBO]
QUOD EIS DIC
TUM ERAT DE
2:18 PUERO ET OṂ
NES QUI AUDIE
RUNT MIRA
TI SUNT DE [II]Ṣ
QUAE AD EOS
LOCUTI SUNṬ
PASTORES
2:19 MARIA Ụ[E]RỌ
CONSERUABẠ[T]
[O]MNỊA UEṚ
[BA I]S[TA COM
MITTENS IN
CORDE SUO
2:20 ET REUERSI SUNT
PASTORES MAG
NIFICANTES
ET LAUDANTES
D̄M̄ IN OMNI
BUS QUAE AU
DIERUNT ET
UIDERUNT SI
CUT DICTA SUNT]

341 LUCANUM

kalend. i[a]nu [a]r[ii] AD EOS
ET COM INPLETI
SUNT DIES OC
TO UT EUM CIR
CUMCIDEREN
[U]OCATUM EST
NOMEN EIUS
IH̄M QUOD UO
CATUM ERAT
AB ANGELO PRI
USQUAM CON
CIPERETUR
2:22 IN UTERO ET
CUM EXPḶE[TI]
ESSENT DIES
PURGATIO
NIS EIUS SE
CUNDUM LE
GEM MOYSI
DIXERUNṬ
EUM IN H[IE]
RUSALEM
UT OFFẸRREN
EUM DM̄O·

2:23 SICUT SCRIP
TUṂ EST IN
[LE]G̣E DṂ̄I
Q̣ỤỊ[A OM]NE
MASC̣[ULI]NU¯
QUỌ[D APER]IT
UOLỤ[AM S]ẠNC
TUM [D]Ṃ̄[O]
UOC̣[ABITU]Ṛ
2:24 ET UṬ DAREN
HOSTIAS SE
CUNDỤM
QUOD DICTU¯
EST IN LEGE
ḌM̄I PAR TUR
TURUM UEL
DUOS PULLOS
COLUMBA
RUM
2:25 ET ECCE [E]RAT
HOMO IN HIE
RỤSALẸM
C[UI NO]MEN
S[YM]EON ET

342 SEC·

HOMO ISTE I^{U}S
TUS ET TIMORA
TUS EXPECTANS
EXORTATIO
NEM ISTRAHEL
ET SP̄S· SANC
TUS EṚẠT SUPER
2:26 EUM ET ERAT
EI RESPONSU¯
A SP̄U· SANCTO
NON UISURU¯
EUM MORTE¯
PRIUSQUAM
UIDERET ·XP̄M·
DM̄I·
2:27 ET UENIT IN ·SP̄U·
IN TEMPLUM
ET CUM INDU
CERENT PA
RENTES PUE
RUM ·IH̄M·
UT FAC̣ERENT
DE ILLO SECU¯
DUM COṆṢUE
TUDINEM LE
2:28 GIS ET IPSE AC
CEPIT EUM
IN AMPLEXU¯
ET BENEDIXIT
DŌM· ET AIT
2:29 NUNC DIMIT
TIS SERUUM
TUUM ·DM̄E·
SECUNDUM
UERBUM TU
UM IN PACE
2:30 QUIA UIDERUNT
OCULI MEI SA
LUTARE TUU¯
2:31 QUOD PRAE
PRARASTI SE
CUNDUM O¯
NIUM FACI
EM POPULO
2:32 RUM LUME¯
REUELATIO
NE GENTIUM
ET GLORIAM

343 LUCANUM

POPULI TUI IS
RAHEL
2:33 ET ERAT IOSEPH
ET MATER EIUS
MIRANTES
IN HIS QUAE
DICEBANTUR
2:34 DE EO ET BENE
DIXIT ILLOS SY
MEON ET AIT
AD MARIAM
MATREM EIUS
ECCE HIC POSI
TUS EST IN RUI
NAM ET RESUR
RECTIONEM
MULTORUM
IN ISRAHEL ET
IN SIGNUM
QUOD CONTRA
2:35 DICITUR ET
TUAM UERO IP
SIUS ANIMA‾
PERTRANS

IT GLADIUS UTI
IREUELENT^{U}R
MULTORUM
CORDIUM CO
GITATỊO[N]ES
2:36 ET ERẠ[T ANN]A
PR[OPHETISS]Ạ
FIḶ[IA] P̣[HAN]Ụ
EL DE [TRIBU] Ạ
SERI [HAEC P]ṚO
CESS[ERAT] IN
DIEBU[S] ṂUL
TIS QUAE UI
XERAT CUM
UIRO ANNIS
UII· A UIRGI
NITATE SUA
2:37 ET HAEC UIDUA
ANNORUM
L·XXX·IIII QUǢ
NON DESCEN
[DEBAT] DE TEM
[PLO IN] IEIU
[NIIS E]Ṭ ORA

344 SEC·

TIONIBUS SER
UIENS [NOC]
2:38 TẸ AC DI[E] ẸT HAEÇ
SṬAN[S] ỊP̣ṢA HỌ
R[A] [CO]N[F]ITE
B[ATUR D̅M̅]
ET [LOQUEBA]
T[UR DE EO] ỌṂ
N[IBUS] ẸX̣P̣ẸC
TẠ[NTIB]ỤS RE
DẸ[MPTI]OṆE[̄]
IṢṬ[RAHEL]
2:39 ẸṬ ỤṬ [P]Ẹ[RFECE]
RUṆ[T OMNIA]
Q̣ỤẸ[MA]Ḍ[MO]
DỤṂ [LE]Ģ[E]Ṃ
DM̅I· Ṛ[E]ĢṚẸS
SI SUNṬ [IN GA]
LILEAṂ [I]Ṇ [CI]
ỤITATẸM [S]Ụ
AM NẠ[ZAR]ET
ṢỊÇỤṬ [DICTU]̄
ẸṢṬ [PER PRO]
P̣HẸṬẠ[M QUOD]

NAZOREUS
UOCẠBỊTUR
2:40 P̣UER AUTẸM
CRẸṢÇ[EB]ẠT
E[T] ÇỌNF̣Ọ[R]ṬẠ
ḄAṬ[UR R]ẸP̣Ḷ[E]
TUS [I]Ṇ ṢẠP̣[I]Ẹ[N]
Ṭ[IA ET GRA]Ṭ[IA]
Ḍ[Ē]Ị [ERAT] SỤP̣[ER]
2:41 E[U]Ṃ EṬ ỊḄ[A]N
IOSEPH EṬ [M]Ạ
RỊA PEṚ [OM]
NES ANṆỌS IṆ
HIERUṢA[LEM]
DIE S[O]LḶEṂ
NI PAṢ[C]HẸ
2:42 ET CỤṂ EṢṢEN[T]
ILḶỊ [A]Ṇ[NI] ḌỤ[O]
DEÇ[IM ET] A[S]
CEN[DERU]ṆT
IN [HIEROSO]
LYṂ[A] SECUN
ḌỤṂ Ç[O]NSUE
[TUDIN]ẸṂ DI

345 LUCANUM

EI SOLLEMNI
AZYMORUṂ
2:43 ET CUM CON
SUMṂẠṢṢẸN̄
DIEṢ [REUER
TENTIBUS IL
LIS REMANSIT
IH̄S· IN HIERU
SALEM ET NES
CIERUNT PA
RENTES EIUS
2:44 ARBITRATI ENI¯
ESSE EUM IN
COMITATU UE
NERUNT ITER
DIEI ET QUAE
REBANT EUM
INTER COG
NATOS ET NO
2:45 TOS ET NON IN
UENIENTES
EUM REUER
SI SUNT HIE
RUSALEM QUAE]

RENTES EUM
2:46 ET FẠCTUM EST
POṢ[T DI]ẸS ṬRES
ỊN[UENE]RUN̄
ẸỤ[M ET IN
TEMPLO SEDE¯
TEM IN ME
DIO DOCENTI
UM AUDIEN
TEM ILLOS ED
INTERROGAN
2:47 TEM STUPE
BANT AUTEM
OMNES QUI
AUDIEBANT
EUM SUPER
SAPIENTIA
ET RESPON
2:48 SIS EIUS ET UI
DENTES EUM
EXPAUERUNT
ET AIT AD ILLU¯
MATER EIUS
FILI QUID ITA]

346 SEC·

FECISTI NOBIS
DOLENTES ET
TRISTIS QUAE
REBẠ[MU]Ṣ TE
2:49 EṬ Ạ[IT AD I]ḶLOS
Q[UID EST QUOD
ME QUAERE
BATIS NESCI
TIS QUIA IN
PATRIS MEI
OPORTET ME
2:50 ESSE ET IPSI
NON INTEL
LEXERUNT
UERBUM
QUOD LOCU
TUS EST ILLIS
2:51 ET DESCEN
DIT CUM ILLIS
ET UENIT NA
ZARET ET ERAT
SUBIECTUS
ILLIS ET MA
TER EIUS CON]

SERUABAT UER
BA EIUS OM
NIA IN COR
DE S[U]Ọ
2:52 ET IH̅[S· PR]OFI
C̣Ị[EBAT AETA
TE ET SAPIEN
TIA ET GRATIA
APUT ·D̅M̅· ET
HOMINES
3:1 IN ANNO AU
TEM QUINTO
DECIMO IM
PERII TIBERI
CAESARIS PRO
CURANTE
PONTIO PILA
TO IUDAEAE TE
TRARCHA AU
TEM GALILAE
AE HERODE
PHILIPPO AU
TEM FRATRE
EIUS TETRAR]

347 LUCANUM

CHA ITURE ET
DRACHONI
TIDIS REGIO
NIBUS ET LY
SANIAE ABI
LIANAE TETRAR
3:2 CHA SUB PRI¯
CIPIBUS SACER
DOTUM AN
NA ET CAIPHA
[do]min ica ante natalem dn̄i FACTUM EST
UERBUM ·DĒI·
SUPER IOHA¯
NEM FILIUM
ZACHARIAE
IN DESERTO
3:3 ET UENIT IN
TOTAM REGIO
NEM IORDA
NIS PRAEDI
CANS BAPTIS
MUM PAENI
3:4 TENTIAE SI
CUT SCRIPTU¯

ET IN LIBRO
SERMỌNUM
ESẠ[EIA]E PRO
PH[ETA]Ẹ UOX
CLẠ[MANT]IS
IN D[ESE]ṚṬO
PARAṬ[E] UIAM
DM̄O ṚẸÇTAS
FACITẸ ṢEMI
3:5 TAS Ẹ[IU]S OM
NIS [U]ALLIS IN
PLEḄITUR ET
OMNIS MONS
ET Ç[O]LLIS HU
MILỊABITUR
ET ERUNT PRA
UA IN DIREC
TA ET ASPERA
IN UIAS PLA
3:6 NAS ET UIDE
BỊT OMNIS
CARO SALUT[A]
REM ḌĒI·
3:7 Ḍ[ICE]ḄAT ERGO

348 SEC·

PROCEDENTI
BUṢ [T]ỤṚḄ[I]S UṬ
[AB EO BAPTIZA]
RE[NTUR PR]O
G̣Ẹ[NIES UIP]E
ṚẠ[RUM] Q̣UIS
OSTE[NDIT] UO
BIṢ [FUG]EṚẸ
AḄ ỊRẠ [UE]NTỤ
3:8 ṚA FAC̣[ITE IT]A
QUẸ [FRU]C̣TU[S]
DIGNỌ[S P]AE
NITENT[I]AE
NE UELL[I]TIS
DIC̣EṚ[E] P̣ẠṬRE[¯]
HABEṂỤS
AB[R]AHAM
Ḍ̣ICỌ ENỊM
ỤOC̣ABỊS QUOD
P̣OTENS EST
$\overline{\text{D[S]}}$ DE LAPIDI
[B]US ISTIS SUS
[CI]ṬARẸ F̣ILIỌṢ
ABRAḤ[AE]

3:9 IAM QUID ENIṂ
SECURIS AD
RADICEM ẠR
BORUM PỌṢI
ṬA EST OMNIS
ỊṬAQUE ARBỌṚ
NON FACIENS
FRUCTUM EX
CIDETUR ET
IN ỊGNEM MỊṬ
TETUR
3:10 ET INTERRO
GABANT EUM
TURBAE DICE¯
TES QUID ERGO
FACIEMUS
3:11 RESPONDENS
AUTEM DIXIT
ILLIS QUI HABE[T]
DUAS TUNICAS
DET NON HA
BENTI ET QUI
HABENT ES
C̣AṢ SIMILITẸR

349 LUCANUM

FACIANT
3:12 UENERUNT AỤ
TE[M] ET PUBLI
CANI SIMILI
TER UT BAPTI
ZARENTUR
ET DIXERUNT
AD EUM MA
GISTER QUID
3:13 FACIEMUS QUI
BUS IPSE AIT NI
HIL PLUS EXE
GERITIS QUAM
QUOD CONSTI
TUTUM EST UỌ
3:14 BIṢ INTER
ROGABANT AU
TEM EUṂ ET
MILITES DICE[¯]
TES ET NOS QUID
FACIEMUS ET
AIT ILLIS NEMI
NEM CONCUS
ṢERITIS NEQỤẸ

CALUMNIAM
F̣EC̣[ER]ỊTIS ET
SỤF̣F̣ỊC̣[IEN]TES
Ẹ[STOTE STI]PE¯
ḌỊỊS [UES]ṬṚIS
3:15 ẠṚḄỊ[TRA]ṆṬẸ
AUṬẸṂ P̣OPU
[LO] ẸṬ COG̣[ITA]N
TIBỤ[S] ỌMNI
BUṢ IṆ CORDI
BUS ṢUỊṢ DE
IOHANNEN
NE FORTE IP
ṢE E[S]ṢẸṬ X̣P̄S
3:16 RESPỌṆḌ[I]T
OMNIBUS DỊ
CENS
EGO QUIDẸṂ
UOS AQUA B[AP]
TIZABO IN P̣[AE]
NITẸNTIAṂ
UENỊṬ ẠUṬ[E¯]
F̣ỌṚ[TI]OR ME
[CUIU]S NON

350 SEC·

SUM DIGNUS
CALCIAMEN
TA PỌṚṬAṚẸ
IPSE UOS B[AP]
TIẒẠ[BI]Ṭ ỊN SP̄Ụ
SANC̣Ṭ[Ọ] ET IG
3:17 NI H[A]BENS
UENTIḶẠBRU̅
IN MAṆU SUA
AD PURGAN
DAM AREAM
SUAM ET CON
GREGAT TRI
TICỤM ỊN HỌṚ
REUM SUUM
PALEAS UERO
COMBURET
[I]GNI INEXTINC
TIBILI
3:18 MULTA QUI
DEM EṬ ALIA
[H]ORTATUS PO
P̣ỤḶỤṂ ẸUAN
GELIZ[ABAT]
3:19 ERODES AUTE̅
TETRARCHAS
CUM ARGUE
RETUR AB EO
DE HERODIA
DE UXORE FRA
TRIS SUI ET DE
OMNIBUS
MALIS QUAE
FECIT HERODES
3:20 ADIECIT HOC
SUPER OMNIA
ET INCLUSIT
IOHANNEN
IN CARCERE̅
3:21 FACTUM EST
AUTEM COM
BAPTIZATUS
ESSET OMNIS
POPULUS ET
IH̄U BAPTIZA
TO ET ỌRANTE
. APẸR TU̅
[E]ST CAELUM

351 LUCANUM

3:22 ET DESCENDIT
SP̄S· SANCTUS
[CORP]ORALI SPE
[CIE SICUT CO
LUMBAM IN
EUM ET UOX
DE CAELO FAC
TA EST FILIUS
MEUS ES TU
EGO HODIE GE
NUI TE
3:23 ET IPSE IH̄S ERAT
FERE ANNO
RUM XXX· IN
CIPIENS FILI
US UT EXISTI
MABATUR IO
SEPH
QUI FUIT HELI
QUI FUIT MAT
3:24 THAE QUI LE
UI QUIBUS
MELCHI QUI
ANNE QUI IO]

3:25 SEPH QUI NA
UM QUI SED
DI QUI NAN
3:26 CE QUI MẠTTA
ṬHỊẠE [Q]ỤI SE
[MEIA Q]UI IO
[SEPH Q]UI IỤ
3:27 [DA QUI I]ỌHAN
[NA QUI RESAE
3:28 RI QUI MELCHI
QUI AD[[DI]] QUI
COSAN QUI
ELMADAN QUI
3:29 ER QUI IESE
QUI ELIGER
QUI IORIM QUI
MATTHATAE
QUI LEUI QUI
3:30 SIMON QUI
IUDA QUI IOSE
PH QUI IONA
QUI ELIACIM
3:31 QUI ERAM
[[QUI]] MATTHA]

352 SEC·

THA QUI NATHA¯
3:32 QUI DAUỊD QUI
IẸ[S]ṢẠẸ QUI Ọ
BEṬ[H] Q[UI] ḄỌỌS
QỤI [SAL]MON
QUI [NAASON]
3:33 QUI [AMINA]
DAB [QUI ARAM
QUI ESROM
QUI FARES QUI
3:34 IUDAE QUI IA
COB QUI ISAC
QUI ABRAHA¯
QUI THARA QUI
3:35 NACHOR QUI
SERUCH QUI
REGAU QUI
FALEG QUI EBER
QUI SALE QUI
3:36 CAINAN QUI ARFA
XAD QUI SEM
QUI NOE QUI
LAMECI QUI
MATHUS...]

3:37 QUI ENOC QUI
ỊẠREṬ QỤỊ ṂA
LEEḶ QỤ[I CAIN
☧ 3:38 AN QUI ENOS
QUI SET QUI A
DAM QUI DEI
4:1 IH̄S AUTEM PLE
NUS SP̄U· SANC
TO REUERSUS
EST AB IORDA
NEN ET FERE
BATUR A SP̄U·
IN DESERTO
4:2 DIEBUS XXXX
CUM TEMPTA
RETUR A DIA
BULO ET NON
ED[[IT]] QUICQUA¯
IN DIEBUS ILLIS
ET CONSUM
MATIS EIS ESU
RIIT
4:3 DIXIT AUTEM IL
LI DIABOLUS]

353 LUCANUM

SI FILIUS ·DĒI·
ẸṢ DIC ḶAPIDỊ
[B]Ụ[S HIS UT] F̣ỊAṆṬ
[PANES]
4:4 [ET R]ẸṢP̣ỌNDIṬ
[AD] ILḶUM ·IH̄S·
[ET D]ỊX[IT] SCRI[P]
[TU]Ṃ EST QUIẠ
[NO]N IN P̣AN[E
SOLO] ỤIỤET Ḥ[O]
ṂO SED IN OṂ
[NI U]ERḄO ḌEỊ
4:5 [A]ḌDỤXIṬ EỤ¯
[HI]Ẹ[RUS]ẠLEM
[ET] STAṬ[UI]T ẸỤ¯
SUPRA P̣ỊNNẠ[¯]
[T]ẸṂP̣ḶI EṬ ỌS
[T]ẸṆḌỊT Ị[LLI] OM
NỊ[A] ṚẸG̣NA OR
B[IS T]ẸṚṚARU¯
[IN] MỌṂ[E]N
[TO] ṬEṂ[P]ỌṚIS
4:6 [ET DI]XIT AD IL
[LU]Ṃ Ḍ[I]ẠB[OLUS]

TIBI DABO PO
TESTATEM HANC
OMNEM ET
G̣LOR[I]Ạ[M] IP
ṢỌṚ[UM QU]Ọ
ṆỊ[AM MIH]Ị
ṬṚẠ[DITA E]ST
EṬ [CUICU]Ṃ
QUẸ ỤỌḶỌ [D]O I
4:7 [LLAM TU ERG]O
[S]Ị PRỌC̣[IDE]ṆṢ
ADORẠỤẸṚIS
ANTE ME ERIN
[TU]A OMNIA
4:8 EṬ ṚẸṢPONḌENS
DIX[I]T ILLI IH̄S·
SCRIPṬUM EST
DILIG̣ES DŌM
D̄M̄· TUUṂ
ET IP̣SI SOLO
SERUIES
4:9 [ET A]DDUXI[T] IL
[LU]Ṃ IN HIE
[RUS]ẠLEM ET

354 SEC·

STATUIT ILLUM
SUPER PINNA¯
TEMPLI ET DI
XIT ILLI SI FILI
US ES DĪ MITTE
4:10 TE Ḥ[IN]C SCRIP
TỤM [E]ṢṬ ENIM
QỤỌṆỊẠM AN
GẸ[L]ỊS SUIS MA¯
D[AUIT] DE TE
Ụ[T CU]STODI
4:11 A[N]T TE SUPER
MANUS TOL
LENT TE NE [F]ỌṚ
TE OFFENDAS
AD LAPIDEM
PEDEM TUU¯
4:12 ET RESPON
DENS DIXIṬ
ILLI IH̄S· QUIA
SCRIPTUM
EST NON TE[MP]
TABIS DŌṂ
D̄M̄ TU[UM]
4:13 ET COṀNSU¯
MATA OMNI
TEMPTATIO
NE DIABOLUS
DISCESSIT AB EO
USQUE IN TE¯
PORE
4:14 ET REUERSUS
EST ·IH̄S[·] IN UIR
TUTE SP̄S· IN
GALILAEAM
ET FAMA EXI
IT PER OMNE¯
FINITIMAM
REGIONEM
4:15 DE ILLO ET IPSE
DOCEBAT IN
SYNAGOGIS
HONOREM
ACCIPIENS
AB OMNIBUS
4:16 ET UENIT IN
NAZARET U
BI ERAT NU

355 LUCANUM

TRITUS
ET INTRAUIT
SECUNDUM
CONSUETU
DINEM DIE
SABBATO IN SY
NAGOGA ET SUR
REXIT LEGERE
4:17 ET PORRECTUS
EST ILLI LIBER
PROPHAETAE
ESEIAE ET RE
UOLUENS LI
BRUM INUE
NIT LOCUM U
BI ERAT SCRIP
TUM
4:18 SP̅S̅· DM̅I̅· SUPER
ME PROPTER
QUOD UNXIT
ME EUANGE
LIZARE HU
MILIBUS MI
SIT ME PRAE

4:19 DICARE CAP
TIUIS REMIS
SIONEM ET
CAECIS UISU̅
DIMITTERE
CONFRACTOS
IN REQUIEM
PRAEDICARE
ANNUM DM̅I̅·
ACCEPTUM
ET DIEM RE
DEMPTIONIS
4:20 ET REUOLUENS
LIBRUM ET
REDDENS MI
NISTRO SEDET
ET OMNIUM
IN SYNAGOGA
OCULI ERANT
INTUENTES
4:21 IN EUM COE
PIT AUTEM
DICERE AD
ILLOS QUONI

356 SEC·

AM HODIE IN
[P]LETẠ EST SCRIP
TURAM HAEC
IN AURIBUS
ỤESTRIS
4:22 ET OMNẸṢ TES
TIMONIUM
DABAN[T] ILLI
ET MIRẠBAN
TUR IN UER
BIS GRATIAE
QUAE PRODI
BANT DE ỌRE
ILLIỤS ET DICE
BANT NONNE
FILIUS IOSEPH
4:23 HIC ET DI
XIT AD ILLOṢ
FORSITAM [DI]
CETIS M[I]ḤỊ
PARABỌḶ[A]Ṃ
HANC Ṃ[E]ḌỊ
CE CUṚ[A] Ṭ[E]
IP[S]ỤṂ QỤ[AE]

CUMQUAE AU
DIUIMỤS FAC
TA IN CAPHAR
NAUM FAC ET
[HI]C IN PATRIA
ṬUA
4:24 DIXIT AUTEM
AMEN DICO UO
BIS QUIA NUL
LUS PROPHE
TA ACCEPTUS
EST IN ṚATRIA
4:25 SUA IN UERI
TATE DICO UO
BIS MULTAE
UIDUAE ERANT
[I]Ṇ DỊẸBUS HE
LIAE QUANDO
CLAUSUM ES[T]
CAELUM PER
TRIENNIUM
ET MENSES
SEX QỤOMO
[DO FACT]A EST

BXX̣[III]

357 LUCANUM

FAMIS MAG
NA SUPER OM
NEM TERRA¯
4:26 ET AD NULLAM
MEARUM MỊṢ
SUS EST HELI
AS NISI IN SA
REPTA SIDONIA
AD MULIERE¯
UIDUAM
4:27 ET MULTI LE
PROSI ERANT
IN ISRAHEL
SUB HELISEO
PROPHETA ET
NULLUS EORU¯
PURGATUS EST
NISI INEMA¯
SURUS
4:28 ET INPLETI SUN
OMNES IRA
IN SYNAGO
[G]A AU[D]IEN
[TE]S [HAEC ET]

4:29 SURGENTES
EICIEBANT
ILLUM EXTRA
CIUITATEM
ET ADDUXE
RUNT EUM
USQUE AD SU
PERCILIUM
MONTIS SU
PER QUEM CI
UITAS AEDIFI
CATA ERAT IP
4:30 SỌRUM ET PRǢ
T[E]RIEN[S] P̣ER
MEDIO ILḶO
RUM IBAT
4:31 ET DEUENIT IN
ÇAPHARNA
ỤM CIUIṬA
ṬẸM GẠLILAE
AẸ [E]Ṭ ẸRAṬ DO
[C]ẸṆṢ ỊḶLOṢ SAB
4:32 [BATIS] ẸṬ ṢTU
[PEB]ANT IN

358 SEC·

DOCTRINA
EIUS QUONI
AM IN POTES
TE ERAT UER
BUM ILLIUS
4:33 ET ERAT IN SY
NAGOGA HO
MO HABENS
DAEMONI
UM INMUN
DUM ET EX
CLAMAUIT UO
CE MAGNA
4:34 DICENS QUID
NOBIS EST ET
TIBI IH̅U· NA
ZARENE UE
NISTI PERDE
RE NOS SCIO
TE QUI SIS SANC
TUS ·DĒI
4:35 ET OBIURGA
UIT ILLUM
IH̅S· DICENS
OMMUTES
CE ET EXI AB IL
LO ET CUM PRO
IECISSET ILLU̅
DAEMONI
UM EXIIT AB
ILLO NIHIL NO
CENS ILLUM
4:36 ET FACTUS EST
PAUOR SUPER
OMNES ET
CONLOQUE
BANTUR AD
ALTERUTRU̅
DICENTES
QUOD EST HOC
UERBUM
QUIA IN PO
TESTATE ET UIR
TUTES IM
PERAT IMMU̅
DIS SPIRITI
BUS ET EXE
4:37 UNṬ ẸṬ EXỊ[B]ẠṬ

359 LUCANUM

FAMA DE EO
IN OMNEM
FINITIMAM
REGIONEM
4:38 SURGENS AU
[T]EṂ ḌE SYNA
[GOGA] [INTR]A
[UIT IN DOMU¯
SIMONIS
SOCRUS AUTE¯
SIMONIS DE
TINEBATUR
FEBRE MAG
NA ET ROGA
UERUNT IL
LUM PRO EA
4:39 ET ADSTANS
SUPER EAM
IMPERAUIT
FEBRI ET RE
LIQUID EAM
CONFESTIM
AUTEM SUR
GENS MINIS]

TRABAT IS
4:40 OCCIDEN[TE]
AUTEM [SOLE]
OMNE[S QUOD]
QUOD HA[BE
[B][ANT AEGROS
LANGUORI
BUS UARIIS
ADDUCEBANT
ILLOS AD EUM
QUI UNICUI
QUE EORUM
MANIBUS IN
POSITIS CURA
BAT ILLOS
4:41 EXIBANT AU
TEM ET DAE
MONIA A
MULTIS EX
CLAMANTIA
ET DICENTIA
TU ES FILIUS
DEI ET OBIUR
GANS NON SI]

360 SEC·

[NE]ḄẠT EA LOQUI
[QUO]ṆIAM
[SCIEB]ANT ·XP̄M[·]
[ILLU]Ṃ ESSE
4:42 [ORTA A]ỤṬEM
[DIE EGRESSUS
ABIIT IN DE
SERTUM LO
CUM ET TUR
BAE REQUIRE
BANT ILLUM
ET UENERUNT
USQUE AD EU̅
ET DETINE
BANT ILLUM
NE DISCEDE
RET AB IPSIS
4:43 QUI DIXIT AD
ILLOS QUONI
AM ET ALIIS
CIUITATIBUS
OPORTET ME
EUANGELI
ZARE REGNU̅]

DEI QUIA ḤOB
HOC MIS[S]ỤS
4:44 [SU]Ṃ [ET] ẸṚẠT
P̣ṚAEDỊCAṆṢ
[I]Ṇ ṢỴNA[G]ỌG̣[I]Ṣ
G̣ẠḶỊḶẠ[EAE
5:1 FACTUM EST AU
TEM DUM TUR
BA INCUM
BIT EI AD AU
DIENDUM
UERBUM DEI
ET IPSE ERAT
STANS IUXTA
STAGNUM
GENNESARET
5:2 UIDIT NAUI
CULAS DUAS
STANTES AD
LITUS DE QUI
BUS PISCATO
RES EGRES
SI LABABANT
RETIAS SUAS]

361 LUCANUM

5:3 ASCENDENS
AU[T]ẸM IN U
[NA]Ṃ ṆAỤ[I]
Ç̣ỤLAM QUẠẸ
Ẹ̣R[AT S]IMO
[NI]Ṣ [R]Ọ̣GAỤỊṬ
EUṂ ỤṬ PRO
Ḍ̣UÇ̣EREN
[TERRA QUAN
TULUMCUM
QUE
SEDENS AUTEM
DOCEBAT
DE NAUICU
LA TURBAS CU¯
5:4 QUE DESIIT LO
QUI DIXIT AD
SIMONEM
LEUA IN ALTO
ET EXPANDI
TE RETIAS UES
TRAS AD CAPI
ENDUM
5:5 ET RESPONDENS]

SIMON DI
XIT ILLI MA
G[ISTE]R PEṚ
T[OTAM NOC]
Ṭ[EM LABORA¯
TES NIHIL CE
PIMUS SED
IN UERBO TUO
EXPANDAM
RETIAM
5:6 ET CUM HOC
FECISSENT
CONCLUSE
RUNT PISCI
UM MULTI
TUDINEM
MAGNAM
RUMPEBAN
TUR AUTEM
RETIAE EORUM
5:7 ET ADNUEBANT
SOCIOS IN ALIA
NAUICULA UT
UENIRENT]

362 SEC·

ET ADIUUAREN
EOS ET UENE
[R]ỤNT Ẹ[T IMPLE
UERUNT A]Ṃ
[BAS NAUES IT]A
[UT MEṚGER]E¯
5:8 [TUR HOC
UISO SIMON
PROCIDIT GE
NIBUS IH̄U
DICENS EXI A
ME QUIA UIR
PECCATOR SU¯
DM̄E
5:9 PAUOR ENIM
ADPREHEN
DERAT EUM
ET OMNES
QUI CUM IL
LO ERANT IN
CAPTURA PIS
CIUM QUAE
CEPERANT SI
5:10 MILITEṚ IA]
COBUS ET IOHA¯
NES FILII ZE
BEDEI QUI Ẹ
RANT SOCIIṠ
SIMONIS
ET DIXIT AD SI
MONEM ·IH̄S·
NOLI TIME
[R]Ẹ ỊẠṂ ẠṂỌ
[DO ERIS UIUI
FICANS HOMI
5:11 NES ET DEDUC
TIS NAUICU
LIS AD TERRA¯
RELICTIS OM
NIBUS SECU
TI SUNT EUM
5:12 ET FACTUM EST
DUM ESSET
IPSE IN UNA
CIUITATUM
ET ECCE UIR
PLENUS LE
PRA ET IPSE]

363 LUCANUM

PROSTRATUS
IṆ [F]ẠÇỊEM ORA
BẠṬ ILLUM DI
CENS QUONI
AM SI UIS PO
TEST ME MUN
DARE
5:13 [ET] ẸXTENDENṢ
[M]ẠNUM Ṭ[E
TIG]IT ILLU[M
DIC]E[NS UOLO
ET PROTINUS
LEPRA DISCES
5:14 SIT AB ILLO ET IP
SE PRAECE
PIT EI NEMI
NI DICERET
SED UADE ET
OSTENDE TE
SACERDOTI
ET OFFERS PRO
PURGATIONE
TUA SICUT PRAE
CEPIT MOYSES]

UT SIT IN TES
TỊṂỌNIUM
HOC UOBIS
5:15 DIỤULGABATUR
ẠU[T]ẸM MẠ
GIS EAMA DE
EO EṬ CONUẸ
[NIE]BAṆ[T TUR
BAE MULTAE
AUDIRE ET CU
RARI A LAN
GUORIBUS
5:16 SUIS IPSE AU
TEM ERAT SE
CEDENS IN
DESERTIS ET
ORABAT
5:17 ET FACTUM EST
IN UNA DIE
RUM ET IPSE
ERAT DOCENS
ET ERANT PHA
RISAEI SEDE¯
TES ET LEGIS]

364 SEC·

ḌOC̣ṬỌṚẸṢ QUI
CONỤẸ[NER]ẠN
ẸX̣ OMN[I MU]
NICIPIỌ G̣[A]ḶỊ
LEAE EṬ ḌẸ ỊỤ
DEA ẸṬ Ḥ[I]ẸṚỌ
ṢẠḶẸM ẸṬ ỤỊṚ
[TUS ER]Ạ[T] Ḍ[M̅I
AD SANAN
DUM EOS
5:18 ET ECCE UIRI
ADFERENTES
SUPER LECTUM
HOMINEM
QUI ERAT PARA
LYTICUS ET QUAE
REBANT IN
FERRE ILLUM
ET PONERE AN
TE EUM
5:19 ET CUM NON
[[INUEN]]ISSENT
[[QUA INFE]]R
RE[[NT EUM]]
PRỌPṬER TUR
ḄAM ẠṢC̣[EN]
DERU[NT SU]P̣ER
TECTUṂ [ET] PẸ[R]
TEGULAṢ [DI]MI
SERUNṬ ẸỤṂ
C̣ỤṂ LEC̣[TU]
LO IN C[ONSPEC
TU] IH̅U
5:20 [ET UI]ṢA F̣ỊḌẸ [IL
LORUM] Ḍ[IXIT
HOMINI RE
MISSA SUNT
TIBI PECCATA
5:21 TUA ET COEPE
RUNT COGITA
RE SCRIBAE
ET PHARISAEI
DICENTES QUIS
EST QUI LOQUI
TUR BLASPHE
MIAS QUIS PO
TERIT DIMIT
TERE PECCA]

365 LUCANUM

TA NISI U[N]ỤṢ
5:22 D̅S̅ C̣ỌG̣NI
TIṢ [AUTEM IH̄S
COGITATIO
NIBUS EORUM
DIXIT AD ILLOS
QUID COGITA
TIS IN CORDIBUS
5:23 UESTRIS QUI
EST FACILIUS
DICERE REMIT
TUNTUR TIBI
PECCATA TUA
AUT DICERE
SURGE ET AM
BULA
5:24 UT SCIATIS AU
TEM QUIA PO
TESTATEM HA
BET FILIUS HO
MINIS IN TER
RA REMITTEN
DI PECCATA AIT
PARALYTICO TI]

ḄI ḌICO ṢỤ[RGE]
ẸṬ ṬỌḶḶẸ ḶẸC̣ṬỤ¯
[TUUM ET
UADE IN DOMU¯
TUAM
5:25 ET CONFESTIM
SURGENS CO
RAM OMNI
BUS SUSTULIT
GRABATTUM
SUUM IN QUO
IACEBAT ET ABIIT
IN DOMUM
SUAM HONO
RIFICANS D̅M̅·
5:26 ET PAUOR AD
PREHENDIT
OMNES ET IN
PLETI SUNT TI
MORE DICEN
TES QUONIAM
UIDIMUS [[MI
RIFICA HODIE]]
5:27 ET POST HAEC]

366 SEC·

[E]X̣IIT ET Ị Ṇ TỤ
[I]TUS EST̩ [PU]Ḅ[LI]
Ç[A]ṆUṂ [NOMI
NE L]EỤI [SEDEN
TEM] AD Ṭ[HELO
NEUM ET DI
XIT ILLI SEQUE
5:28 RE ME ET RE
LICTIS OMNI
BUS SURGENS
SEQUEBATUR
ILLUM
5:29 ET FECIT ILLI CE
NAM MAGNA‾
LEUI IN DO
MO SUA ET E
RAT TURBA IN
GENS PUBLI
CANORUM
ET ALIORUM
QUI ERANT CU‾
ILLIS DISCOM
5:30 BENTES ET
MURMURA]

UẸṚUNT PHA
Ṛ[I]ṢẠ[EI E]Ṭ ṢCRI
Ḅ[A]E [EORU]M
Ḍ[ICENTES AD]
Ḍ[ISCIPULOS]
Ị[LLIUS QUARE
CUM PUBLICA
NIS ET PECCA
TORIBUS MAN
DUCAT ET BIBET
5:31 ET RESPONDENS
IH̅S· DIXIT AD
ILLOS NON E
GENT SANI ME
DICO SED QUI SE
MALE HABENT
5:32 NON UENI
UOCARE IUS
TOS SED PECCA
TORES IN PAE
NITENTIAM
5:33 QUI DIXERUNT
AD ILLUM QUA
RE DISCIPULI]

367 LUCANUM

IOHAN^{N}IS IE
IUNẠNT F̣[R]E
QUE[NTE]Ṛ
ET PHARISAEO
RUM ET ORA
TIONES FACỊ
ẠNT [T]ỤI AUTE[¯]
[MANDU]CAN̄
[ET BIBENT
5:34 QUI DIXIT AD IL
LOS NUMQUID
POSSUNT FILI
SPONSI QUA¯
DIU SPONSUS
CUM ILLIS CU¯
ILLIS EST IEIU
5:35 NARE UENI
ENT DIES ET
CUM ABLA
TUS FUERIT
AB ILLIS SPON
SUS TUNC IE
IUNABUNT
IN ILLIS DIE]

5:36 BUS : DIXIT
AUTEM ET PA
RAḄ[O]LAM ẠḌ
Ẹ[OS QUIA NE]
Ṃ[O INSUME¯]
Ṭ[UM TUNI
CAE RUDIS
ADSUIT PAN
NO UETERI
ALIOQUIN ET
NOUUM SCI¯
DET ET UETE
RI NON CON
UENIET IN
SUMENTUM
A NOUO
5:37 ET NEMO MIT
TIT UINUM
NOUUM IN
UTRES UETE
RES ALIOQUIN
RUMPET UI
NUM NOUU¯
UTRES ET IPSE]

368 SEC·

ẸF̣F̣UNḌỊTUR
ET UTREṢ P̣ERI
5:38 [B]ỤNṬ SẸ[D] UI
[NUM IN UT]ṚẸṢ
[NOUOS MIT
TUNT ET AM
BO SERUAN
6:1 TUR ET FACT
TUM EST IN
SABBATO SE
CUNDO PRI
MO CUM TRA¯
SIRET PER SA
TA ET UELLE
RENT DISCI
PULI ILLIUS
SPICAS MANIBUS
CONTERE¯
TES ET EDEBANT
6:2 QUIDAM AU
TEM PHARI
SAEORUM
DICEBANT
QUID FACITIS]
SABBATIS QUOD
NỌṆ [LICET]
6:3 [ET] ṚẸ[SPON]ḌENS
ḌIXỊṬ ILLIS
IH̄S NEC̣ HOC̣
LEGISTIS QỤ[O]Ḍ
FEC̣ỊṬ D[A]UID
CUṂ [ESURIIT
IPSE ET QUI CU¯
6:4 EO ERANT QUO
MODO INTRA
UIT IN DOMU¯
DEI ET PANES
PROPOSITIO
NIS ACCEPIT
ET MANDU
CAUIT ET DE
DIT EIS QUI
SECUM ERANT
QUOS NON LI
CET EDERE NI
SI SOLIS SACER
6:5 DOTIBUS ET
DICEBAT ILLIS]

369 LUCANUM

QUONỊAM
DM̄S[·] EṢT F̣ỊḶ[I]
UṢ HOMỊNIS
ETIAM SẠB
BATI
6:6 FACTUM EST
AUTEM IṆ ẠLI
[O] SABBẠṬỌ ỊṆ
[TR]ẠRE ILLỤṂ
[IN SYNAGO
GA ET DOCE
RE ET ERAT
IBI HOMO ET
MANUS ILLI
US DEXTRA
ERAT ARIDA
6:7 OBSERUABANT
AUTEM SCRI
BAE ET PHARI
SAEI SI SAB
BATO CURA
RET UT INUE
NIRENT ET
ACCUSARENT]

6:8 ILLUM IPSE
AUṬEM SCIE
BAṬ COGỊTA
TIOṆ[ES ILLO]
ṚỤṂ
[DIXIT AUTEM
HOMINI QUI
HABEBAT MA
NUM ARIDA¯
SURGE ET STA
IN MEDIO ET
SURGENS STE
6:9 TIT DIXIT
AUTEM IH̄S
AD ILLOS IN
TERROGABO
UOS SI LICET
SABBATIS BE
NEFACERE
AN MALE
ANIMAM
SALUAM FA
CERE AN
PERDERE ET]

370 SEC·

6:10 CIRCUMSPI
CIENS OMNES
ILLOS ESSE IN
ỊṚA [DI]XIT HO
[MINI E]ẊTEN
[DE MANU]Ṃ
[TUAM ET EX
TENDIT ET RES
TITUTA EST MA
NUS ILLIUS
6:11 IPSI AUTEM
IMPLETI SUNT
STUPORE ET
CONLOQUE
BANTUR AD
INUICEM
QUIDNAM
FACERENT
IH̄U
6:12 FACTUM EST
AUTEM IN ILLIS
DIEBUS EXIIT
IN MONTEM
ORARE ET E]

RAT PERNOC
TANS IN ORA
6:13 TIONE DEI ET
CUM DIES HOR
TA EST UOCA
UIT DISCIPU
LOS SUOS ET E[LI]
GENS EX EIS
DUODECỊ[M
QUOS ET APOS
TOLOS NOMI
NAUIT
6:14 SIMONEM QUE̅
ET COGNOMI
NAUIT PETRU̅
ET ANDREAM
FRATREM EIUS
ET IACOBUM
ET IOHANNE̅
ET PHILIPPUM
ET BARTHOLO
6:15 MEUM ET
MATTHEUM
ET THOMAM]

371 LUCANUM

ET IACOBUM
ALPHEI ET SI
MONEM QUI
APPELLATUR
6:16 ZELOTES ~~T~~ ET
IUDAN IACO
BI ET IUDANT
QUI ERAT PRO
DITOR
6:17 ET DESCENDENS
CUM ILLIS STE
TIT IN LOCO
CAMPENS^{E} ET
TURBA DISCI
PULORUM EIUS
ET MULTITU
DO INGENS
POPULI AB OM
NI IUDEA ET
HIERUSALEM
ET TRANS FRE
TUM ET MA
RITIMA TY
RI ET SIDONIS

6:18 QUI UENE
RANT AUDI
RE ILLUM
ET CURARI
A LANGUORI
BUS SUIS ET
QUI UEXA
BANTUR AB ~~S~~
^{S}PIRITIBUS
INMUNDIS
~~CURABANTUR~~
~~REBANTUR~~
6:19 ET OMNIS TUR
BA QUAERE
BAT TANGERE
EUM QUO
NIAM UIR
TUS AB ILLO
EXIBAT ET SA
NABAT OM
6:20 NES ET IPSE
ADLEUANS
OCULOS IN
DISCENTES

372 SEC·

SUOS DICEBAT
BEATI PAUPE
RIS ·SP̄U· QUO
NIAM UES
TRUM EST̩ REG̣
NUM̩ DĒI·
6:21 BEATI QUI̩ ESU
RIT̩I̩S NUNC̣
ET SITITIS QUO
NIAM SATU
RI ERIT̩I̩S
BEATI QUI PLORA
RATIS NUNC
QUONIAM RI
DEBITIS
6:22 BEATI ESTIS CU¯
ODIERINT UOS
HOMINES
ET CUM SEGRE
G̣AUERINT
Ụ OS ET CUM
EICERINT
UOS ET CỤM
EX̣P̣RỌḄRAUE

RINT NOME¯
UESTRUM
TAMQUAM NE
QUAM CAU
SAM FILI HO
6:23 MINIS GAUDE
TE IN ILLA HO
RA ET EXULTA
MINI ECCE E
NIM MERCES
UESTRA COPIO
☧ SA EST IN CAE
LO SIMILITER
FACIEBANT
PROFETIS PA
TRES ILLORU¯
6:24 UERUMTAMẸ[¯]
UAE UOBIS DI
UITIBUS QUỌ
NIAM HABE
TIS CONSOLA
TIONEM UES
6:25 TRAM UAẸ UO
BIS SATURIS

C XXI̩Ṿ

373 LUCANUM

QUIA ESURIE
TIS UAE UOBIṢ
QUI RIDETỊS
NUNC QUỊẠ
LUGEBITIS E[T]
6:26 FLEBITIS UAE
CUM ḄẸNE
UOBIS DIXE
RINT OMNES
HOMINES SI
MILITER FACI
EBANT PSEU
DOPROPHETIS
PATRES EORU̅
6:27 SED UOBIS DICO
AUDIẸNTIBUS
DILIGITE INI
MICOS UES
TROS BENEFA
CITE EIS QUI
ODERUNT UOS
6:28 BENEDICITE
MALEDICEN
TES UOS ORA

TE PRO IS QUI
CAḶUMNIAN
6:29 TUR UOS PER
CUTỊẸNTI ṬE
ỊN MAXILLA
P̣ṚEUẸ ẸI AL
TẸRAM ET
AB EO QUI AUT
FEREṬ UESTI
MENTUM
ṬUỤṂ ET PẠL
LEUṂ UETẠ
6:30 RE NOLI OM
NI AUTEM
P̣O[S]C̣ENTI TE
DA ET AB EO
QUI TOLLIT TUA
REPEPERE
6:31 NOLI ET QUEM
ADMODUM
ỤULTỊS UT FA
CIANT UOBIS
HOṂINEṢ
SIC̣ F̣ẠC̣Ị[TE] EỊ[S]

374 SEC·

6:32 ET SI DỊLIGI
TES EOS QUI
UOS DILIGUN̄
QUAE UOBIS
GRATIA EST
NAM ET PEC
CATORES EOS
QUI SE DILI
GENT DỊLIGUN̄
6:33 ET SI BENEFE
CERITIS QUI
BENEFACI
UNT UOBIS
QUAE GRATIA
EST UOBIS ET
ENIM PEC
CATORES HOC
6:34 FACIUNT ET
SI FENERE
TIS EIS A QUIBỤṢ
SPERATIS RE
CIPERE QUAE
GRATIA EST
UOBỊS ẸTENI̅
PECCATORES
PECCATORIBUS
FENERANT UT
RECIPIANT
6:35 UERUMTAME̅
DILIGITE INI
MICOS UES
TROS ET BENE
FACITE ET FE
NERATE NIHIL
DESPERAN
TES ET ERIT MER
CES UESTRA
MULTA IN CAE
LO ET ERITIS
FILI EXCELSI
QUONIAM
IPSE SUAUIS
EST SUPER IN
GRATOS ET NE
QUAS
6:36 ESTOTE MISE
RICORDES SI
CUT ET PATER

375 LUCANUM

UESTER MISE
6:37 RETUR NOLI
TE IUDICARE
NE IUDICEMI
NI NOLITE CO¯
DEMNARE
UT NON CON
DEMNEMI
NI DIMITTI
TE ET DIMITTE
6:38 MINI DATE ET
DABITUR UO
BIS MENSU
RAM BONAM
AGITATAM
CUMULATAM
SUPERFLUEN
TEM DABUNT
IN SINU UES
TRO EADEM
MENSURAM
QUA METITIS
REMETIETUR
UOBIS

6:39 DICEBAT AU
TEM ET PARA
BOLAM ILLIS
NUMQUID
POTEST CAE
CUS CAECUM
DUCERE NO¯
NE UTRIQUE
IN FOUEAM
6:40 INCIDENT NO¯
EST DISCENS
SUPER MA
GISTRUM
CONSSUMA
TUS AUTEM
OMNIS ERIT
SI SIT SICUT
MAGISTER
ILLIUS
6:41 QUID AUTEM
UIDES FESTU
CAM IN OCU
LO FRATRIS
TUI TRABEM

376 SEC·

AUTEM QUAE
IN OCULO TUO
EST NON CON
6:42 SIDERẠṢ ẠUT
QUOMOḌỌ PO
TEST DICERE
FRATRI TUO SI
NE EICIAM
FESTUCAM DE
OCULO TUO ET EC
CE IN OCULO TUO TRA
BES SUBIACET
HỴPOC̣RITA
EICE PRIMU¯
ṬRABEM DE
OCUḶO TUO ET
TUNC PERSPI
CIES EICERE
FESTUCAM
DE OCULO FRA
6:43 TRIS TUI NON
EST ARBOR
BONA FACIENS
FRU[C]TUS MA
LOS NEC AR
BOR MALA FA
CIENS FRUC
TUS BONOS U
6:44 NAQUAEQUẸ
ARBOR EX FRUC
ṬU SUO DINỌS
CITUR NEQ̣UẸ
LEGUNT DẸ
SPINIS FICUS
SED NEC DE
RUBO UINDẸ
MIANT UUA¯
6:45 BONUS ẸNỊM
HOMO DE BO
NO THENṢAỤ
RO CORDIS SUỊ
PROFERT BO
NUM ET NE
QUA DE MAḶỌ
PROFERT ṂẠ
LUM ẸX ABỤN
DANTIA COR
DIS OS ILLIUS
LOQUITUR

377 LUCANUM

6:46 QUID AUTEM ME
UOCATIS ·DM̄Ẹ
·DM̄E ET NON
F̣AC̣IṬIS QUAE
6:47 DICO OMNIṢ
QUI UENỊT Ạ[D]
[M]Ẹ ET AUDIT
ỤẸṚḄA MEẠ
ẸṬ F̣ACIT ILLA
ḌẸMONSTRA
[B]Ọ UOBIS CUI
ṢỊṬ SIMILIS
6:48 ṢỊMILIS EST HO
Ṃ[I]NI AEDIFỊ
[CA]NTI DOMU̅
[Q]ỤỊ FỌDIT IN
[ALT]ỤM ET PO
SỤIT FUNDA
ṂENTA SUPER
[P]ẸṬRAM TEM
PESTATE HOR
TA IMPULIT FLU
MEN DOMUI
ILLI NEC UALU
IT MOUERE
ILLẠ[M] F̣UNDA
TA Ẹ[NI]Ṃ ERAT
ṢỤP̣ẸṚ [PE]ṬRA
6:49 Q̣[UI A]ỤṬẸṂ
ẠỤḌỊṬ EṬ NON
F̣ẠC̣ỊṬ SIMILIS
ESṬ HOMINI
AEDIFICANTI
DOMUM SU
PRA TERRAM
SINE FUNDA
MENTO IMPU
LIT FLUMEN
DOMU ILLI ET
CECIDIT ET
FACTA EST RUI
NA DOMUS IL
LIUS MAGNA
7:1 FACTUM EST
AUTEM CUM
INPLESSET
OMNIA UER
BA IN AURIB·

378 SEC·

POPULI INTRA
UIT IN CAPHAR
7:2 NAUṂ CEN
TUR[I]ONIS AU
TEM CUỊ[US]
DAM SERỤUS
MALE HAḄENS
INCIPIEBAT
MORI QUI E
RAT EI CARUS
7:3 AUDIENS AUTE¯
DE ·IH̄U· MISIT
SENIORES IU
DAEORUM
ROGANS ILLU¯
UT UENIRET
ET SANARET
SERUUM IL
LIUS
7:4 QUI CUM UENIS
SENT ROGA
BANT ·IH̄M·
SOLLICITE DI
CENTES QUO

NIAM DIG
NUS EST UT IL
LI PRAESTES
7:5 HOC DILIGIT
ENIM GENTE¯
NOSTRAM ET
SYNAGOGA¯
IPSE
AEDIFICAUIT
7:6 NOBIS: IBAT
AUTEM CUM
ILLIS ·IH̄S· CUM
QUE IAM NO¯
LONGE ABES
SET A DOMO
MISIT AD ILLU¯
CENTURIO
AMICOS DI
CENS EI
DM̄E· NOLI UE
XARE TE NO¯
SUM ENIM
DIGNUS UT
SUB TECTUM

379 LUCANUM

MEUM INTRES
7:7 SED DIC UER
BO ET SANABI
TUR PUER ME
7:8 US NAM ET
EGO HOMO SU¯
POTESTATIS
SUBIECTUS
HABEO SUB ME
MILITES DICO
HUIC UADE ET
UADIT ET ALIO
UENI ET ET
SERUO MEO
FAC HOC ET FA
7:9 CIT : HIS AU
DITIS ·IH̄S· MI
RATUS EST ET
CONUERSUS
SEQUENTI SE
TURBAE DIXIT
AMEN DICO
UOBIS IN NUL
LO TANTAM

FIDEM INUE
NI IN ISTRA
7:10 HEL ET RE
UERSI SUNT
DOMUM QUI
MISSI ERANT
INUENERUN
SERUUM SA
NUM
☩ 7:11 ET FACTUM EST
DEINCEPS
IBAT ·IH̄S· IN
CIUITATEM
QUAE APPEL
LATUR NAIN
ET COMITA
BANTUR CU¯
ILLO DISCIPU
LI SUI ET TUR
BA MAGNA
7:12 FACTUM EST
AUTEM CUM
ADPROPIN
QUARET POR

380 SEC·

TAE CIUITATIS
ET ECCE EFFE
REBATUR MOR
TUUS FILIUS
UNICUS MA
TRIS S^UAE ET HAC
ERAT UIDUA
ET TURBA CIUI
TATIS MAGNA
7:13 CUM ILLA ET
UISAM EAM
DM̄S MISER
ET DIXIT EI
TUS EST EI NO
LI ΓLERE
7:14 ET ACCEDENS
TETIGIT LOCU
LUM ET QUI
PORTABANT
STETERUNT EṬ ẠỊṬ
ADULESCENS
ADULESCENS
TIBI DICO SUR
7:15 GE ET CONSE
DIT MORTU
US ET COEPIT
LOQUI ET DEDIT
EUM MATRI
SUAE
7:16 ADPREHENDIT
AUTEM TIMOR
OMNES ET HO
NORIFICA
BANT ·D̅M̅ DI
CENTES QUO
NIAM PROPHE
TA MAGNUS
SURREXIT IN
NOBIS ET QUIA
UISITAUIT ·D̅S̅·
POPULUM SU
UM IN BONO
7:17 ET EXIBIT UER
BUM HOC IN
TOTA IN IUDẠEA
DE ILLO ET IN
OMNI FINITI
MA REGIONE
7:18 ET RENUNTIA

381 LUCANUM

UERUNT IO
HANNI DISCI
7:19 PULI SUI ET CO̅
UOCATIS DUO
BUS QUIBUS
DAM EX DISCI
PULIS SUIS IO
HANNEṢ MI
SIT AD DŌM
DICENS
TU ES QUI UEN
TURUS ES AN A
LIUM EXPEC
7:20 TAMUS ET UE
NERUNT UỊ
RI AD EUM ET
DIXERUNT
IOHANNES
BAPTISTA MI
SIT NOS DICẸNS
TU ES QUI UEN
TURUS ES AN
ALIUM EXPEC
7:21 TAMUS EADEM

HORA CURA
BAṬ MULTOS
A Ḷ[A]ṆGUORI
BUS ẸṬ UER
BERIBUS ET
SPIRITIBUS
MALIGNIS
ET CAECIS MUL
TIS DONAUIT
7:22 UISUM ET RES
PONDENS DI
XIT ILLIS EUN
TES RENUN
TIATE IOHAṆ
NI QUAE UIDIS
TIS ET AUDIS
TỊS CAECI UI
DENT CLODI
AMBULANT
LEPROSI P̣UṚ
GANTUR SUṚ
DI AUDIUNT
MORTUI RE
SURGENT PAU

382 SEC·

PERES EUAN
GELIZANTUR
7:23 ET BAEATUS
ERIT QUICU¯
QUE NON SCA¯
DALIZABITUR
IN ME
7:24 CUMQUE DIS
CESSISSENT
NUNTII IOHA¯
NIS COEPIT
DICERE DE
IOHANNEN
AD TURBAS
QUID EXISTIS
IN DESERTO
UIDERE HA
RUNDINEM
A UENTO ~~N~~MO (M written above)
7:25 UERI SED QUID
EXISTIS UIDE
RE HOMINE¯
MOLLIBUS UES
TIMENTIS IN
DUTUM EC
CE QUI IN UES
TE PRAETIOSA
ET IN DELICI
IS SUPERABU¯
DANT IN DO
MIBUS REGU¯
SUNT
7:26 SED QUID EXIS
TIS UIDERE
PROPHETAM
ETIAM DICO
UOBIS NEMO
MAIOR IN NA
TIS MULIERU¯
AMPLIOR EST
IOHANNEN
BAPTISTA ET
AMPLIUS QUA¯
PROPHETA
7:27 HIC EST DE QUO
SCRIPTUM
EST ECCE MIT
TO ANGELUM

383 LUCANUM

MEUM ANTE
FACIEM TU
AM QUI PRAE
PARAUIT UỊ
AM TUAM
7:28 DICO AUTEM ỤỌ
BIS MAIOR IN
NATIS MULIE
RUM IOHAN
NEN BAPṬỊṢ
TA NEMO EST
ET QUI MINI
ṂUS EST IN
REGNO DĒI·
MẠIOR ILLO
7:29 EST : E^{T} OMNIS
POPULUS CUˉ
AUDISSENT
ET PUBLICANI
IUSTIFICAUE
RUNT D̄M̄·
BAPTIZATI BAP
TISMUM IO
7:30 HANNIS PHA

RISAEI AUTEˉ
ET LEGIS DOC
TỌṚ[ES CO]NSI
Ḷ[IUM DEI] ṢPRE
[UER]ỤNṬ IN
Ṣ[E CU]M NON
[ESSE]ṆT BAP
ṬỊ[ZA]TI
7:31 Ç[UI E]ṚGO ADSI
[MILI]ABO HỌ
MỊṆES GEN
TIS HUIUS ET
CUI SUNT SI
7:32 MILES SIMI
LES SUNT IN
FANTIBUS IN
FORO SEDEN
TIBUS QUI CLA
MANT AD AL
TERUTRUM
DICENTIS
CANTAUIMUS
UOBIS ET NON
SALTASTIS LA

384

MENTAUIMUS
UOBỊṢ [ET] NO¯
PLẠ[NXISTIS]
7:33 UEN[IT]
IOḤ[A]Ṇ[NIS BAP]
ṬỊṢ[TA NEQUE E]
DENS [NEQUE]
ḄIBENṢ [ET DI]
CIṬIS DẠ[EMO]
Ṇ[I]ỤM HẠ[BET]
7:34 UẸNỊT FỊ[LI]ỤṢ
ḤOṂINIṢ MẠ[¯]
DUCANS ET ḄỊ
BEṆṢ ET DICI
TIS ECCE ḤỌ
MO DEUORA
TOR ET BIBENS
UINUM AMI
CUS PUBLICA
7:35 NORUM ET
IUSTIFICATA
EST SAPIENTIA
AB OMNIBUS
FILIIS SUIS

SEC·

⳨ 7:36 ROGAUIT AU
T[E]Ṃ Ẹ[U]Ṃ QUI
[DAM PH]ARI
[SAEUS U]Ṭ CIḄỤ[¯
CAPE]RET ṢẸCU¯
ẸṬ ỊṆGṚ[ESS]US
[IN DO]Ṃ[U]M
PHẠṚỊṢAEI DIS
[CUB]ỤỊṬ
7:37 ẸṬ [EC]Ç[E M]UḶ[I]
ẸṚ ỊN C[I]Ụ[ITA]
ṬẸ [QUAE] ẸṚ[AT]
P̣Ẹ[CCAT]Ṛ[IX]
ÇOG̣ṆỊṬ[O E]O
ẠCCUMḄẸṚE
IN DOMO PHA
RISAEI AD[F]Ẹ
RE[BA]T AMPUḶ
ḶẠM ỤNG̣Ụ
7:38 ENṬI ẸT STANṢ
A REṬRO PE
DES IḶḶIUṢ F̣ḶẸNṢ
LACRIMIS IN
RIG̣ABAT ET CA

385 LUCANUM

ET CAPILLIS CA
PITIS SUI EXTER
GEBAT ET ỌSCU
LABATUR P̣E
DES ILLIUS EṬ
UNGẸBAT UN
G̣UENTO
7:39 UIDENS AUTEM
P̣HARISAEỤS
QUI INỤITA
UERAṬ EUM
[DI]XỊT ỊNTRA
SẸ [D]IÇẸNS HIC
SI ERAT PRO
PHETA SCIRET
UTIQUE QUAE
ET QUALIS EST
MULIER QUÆ
TANGIT ILLUM
QUONIAM PEC
CATRIX EST
7:40 EṬ RESPONDEṆS
IH̅S· DIXIT AD
ILLUM SIMO⁻
HABEO TIBI
ALIQUID DICE
RE QUI AIT DIÇ
MAG̣IṢTER
7:41 DUO DEBITORES
ERẠNT CUI
ḌAM FENERA
Ṭ[O]RI UNUS DE
BEBAT DENA
RIOS QUINGE⁻
TOS ET ALIUS
DENARIOS
QUINQUAGIN
7:42 TA NON HABE⁻
TIBUS ILLIS UN
DE REDDEREN
UTRISQUE DO
NAUIT QUIS
ERGO ILLUM
AMPLIUS DI
LIGET
7:43 RESPONDENS
AUTEM SIMO⁻
DIXIT AESTI

386 SEC·

MO QUODD IS
CUI AMPLIUS
REDONAUIT
QUI DIXIT EI
RECTE IUDI
CASTI
7:44 ET CONUER
SUS AD MULI
EREM DIXIT
SIMONI UI
DES HANC MU
LIEREṂ IN
TRAUI IN DO
MUM TUAM
AQUAM IN PE
DIBUS MIHI
NON DEDIS
TI HAEC AUTEˉ
LACRIMIS IN
RIGAUIT MI
HI PEDES ET
CAP̣ILLIS SUI[S]
EXTERSIT
7:45 OSẠCULUM MI
HI NON DEDIS
TI HAEC AUTEˉ
EX QUO INTRA
UIT NON DESI
IT OSCULANDO
PEDES MEOS
7:46 OLEO NON Uˉ
XISTI PEDES
MEOS HAEC
AUTEM UN
GUENTO UN
7:47 XIT QUA EX CAU
SA TIBI DICO
REMITTUN
TUR EI PECCA
TA MULTA QUO
NIAM DILE
XIT MULTUM
CUI AUTEM
MINUS DI
MITTITUR
MINUS DILI
7:48 GIT ET AIT AD
ILLAM IH̄S

387 LUCANUM

REMITTUN
TUR TIBI PEC
CATA
7:49 ET COEPERUNT
QUI DISCUM
BEBANT PARI
TER DICERE
INTRA SE QUIS
EST HIC QUI PEC
CATA REMIT
7:50 TIT DIXIT AU
TEM AD MU
LIEREM FI
DES TUA TE SAL
UAM FECIT UA
DE IN PACE
8:1 ET FACTUM EST
DEINCEPS ET
IPSE CIRCUI
BAT PER CIUI
TATIS ET UICOS
PRAEDICANS
ET ADNUN
TIA~~S~~NS REG

NUM DĒI ET
DUODECIM
DISCIPULI CU¯
ILLO
8:2 ET MULIERES
QUAEDAM
QUAE ERANT
CURATAE AB S
PIRITIBUS IN
MUNDIS MA
RIA QUAE COG
NOMINATUR
MACDALE~~L~~NE
EX QUA DAE
MONIA SEP
TEM EXIE
8:3 RANT ET IOHA¯
NA UXOR CHU
ZA PROCURA
TORIS ERO
DIS ET SUSAN
NA ET ALIAE
CONPLURES
QUAE ET MI

388 SEC·

NISTRABANT
ILLI DE FACUL
TATIBUS SỤỊṢ
8:4 CONỤEṆIEN
TE AUṬẸM TỤṚ
BA MA[G]NA ET
EORUM QUI
EX CIUITA[T]I
BUS ADỤẸNI
EBANT DIXIT
PARABỌLAṂ
8:5 ECCE EXIIT
in se☩*xagesima* QUI SEANNAT
SEMINARE
SEMEN SUU¯
(DUM SEMINAT QUODDAM CECIDIT)
IUXTA UIAM
EṬ CONCULÇA
TUṂ EST ET UO
ḶUÇRES COME
DERUNT IL
8:6 LUD ET ALIUT
CECIDIT SU
PER PẸTRẠM
ẸṬ ẸNATUM

EXARUIT PROP
TER QUOD NON
ḤẠBERET UMO
ṚẸM
8:7 EṬ AḶ[I]U[T] CEÇI
DIT INTER ṢP̣Ị
NAS ET CṚẸUẸ
RUNT SPINAẸ
ET SUṬFỌÇẠUẸ
8:8 ṚUNT ỊḶḶỤḌ ẸṬ
ALIUD Ç[E]CID[IT]
SUPER TẸ[R]RA¯
O[P]TIMẠM ET
BONAṂ [ET] OR
TUṂ ṬẸÇIT ṬRỤ[C]
ṬUM ÇENṬỊẸS
TANTUM
ET HAEC DICENS
CLAMABAT QUỊ
HABET AURES
AUDIENDI AU
8:9 DIAT INTERRO
GABAṫNT AU
TEM ILLUM

D X[XU]

389 LUCANUM

DỊSCIPULI QUỊḌ
NAM ESSET HÆC
8:10 PARABOLA QUI
DIXIT UOBIS
TRADITUM EṢṬ
ṂYSTERIUM
RẸ[G]NI D̅I̅ CE
T[E]ṚIS AUTEM
[IN] PARABOLIS
ỤṬ ỤIDENTES
ṆỌN ỤIDEAN̍
[ET] AUDIEN
[T]ẸS NON INTEL
ḶẸG̣ẠN[T]
8:11 ẸST ẠUṬ[E]Ṃ HAEC
P̣Ạ[R]Ạ[BOL]Ạ SE
MEN EST UER
8:12 ḄỤM DĒI QUI
AUTEM SECUS
ỤỊẠM HI SUN̍
QỤ[I] AUDIUNT
[UE]NIT AUTEM
[DI]ẠBỌLUS ET
TỌ[L]ḶET DE COR
DE EORUM
UẸRBUM NE
CREDENTES
ṢALU[I F]IANT
8:13 Q̣UI [AUT]ẸṂ
SUP[E]Ṛ PETRA¯
ḤỊ SỤṆṬ QUI
CỤM AUDIE
RỊṆT CUM GAU
ḌIO RECIPIEN̍
UERBUM ET
IPSI RADICES
NON HABENT
QUI AD TEM
PUS CREDUNT
ET IN TEMPO
RE TEṂPTA
TIONỊ[S] ḌI[S]C̣Ẹ
8:14 DUNT Q̣[UO]D
AUṬE[M I]N S[P]I
NẠṢ C̣ECIDIT
HI SUNṬ QUI
AUDIUNT UER
BUM ^{ET} A SOLLICI

390 SEC·

TUDINIBUS ET
DIUITIIS ET LU
XURIIS SAECU
LI INGREDIEN
TES SỤF̣F̣Ọ̣CAN
TUR ET NỌN
DANT FRUC
TUM
8:15 QUOD AUTEM
IN TERRAM
BONAM HI SUN
QUI IN CORDE BO
NO AUDIENTES
UERBUM RE
TINENT ET FRUC
TUM DANT IN
PATIENTIA
8:16 NEMO AUTEM
LUCERNAM
ACC[E]ṆSAM
OPERIET ILLA¯
UASO AUT SUP
TUS LECTUM
PONIT SED SU
PRA CANDELA
BRUM PONIT
UT OMNES IN
TRANTES UI
DEANT LUME¯
8:17 NIHIL ENIM
EST OCCULTU¯
QUOD NON PA
LAM FIAT SEḌ
NEC ABSCON
SUM NISI U[T]
COGNOSCATUR
ET IN PALAM
UẸNIẠT
8:18 UIDETẸ QUOMO
DO AUḌIẠṬIṢ
QUISQUE ENI¯
HABUERIT D[A]
BITUR ỊLLI ET
QUI NON HA
BUERIT ET QUO[D]
PUTAT SE HA
BERE AUFE
RETUR ẠB EO

391 LUCANUM

8:19 UENERUNT
AUTEM AD ILLU¯
MATER ET FRA
TRES ILLIUS
SET NON POTE
RANT CONLO
QUI EI PROPTER
8:20 TURBAM NUN
TIATUM EST AU
TEM ILLI QUO
NIAM MATER
TỤẠ ẸṬ F̣RẠṬṚES
TUI [STANT] F̣O
RIS ỤOLENTES
TE UIDERẸ
8:21 QUI RESPON
ḌENS DIXIT
AD ILLOS MA
TER MEA ET
F̣[R]ATRES MEI
ILḶỊ SUNT QUI
[UER]ḄUM DĒI
[AUD]ỊUNT ET
F[A]C̣IUNT

8:22 FACTUM EST
AUTEM IN UNA
DIERỤM ET
IPSE AS[C]EN
DIT IN NAUI
CULAM ET DIS
CIPULI EIUS
ET DIXIT AD
ILLOS TRANS
FRETEṂUS
STAG̣NUM
EṬ SU[S]ṬỤLE
RỤ[NT]
8:23 NAỤ[IGANT]I
BUṢ A[UT]EM
EIS C̣Ọ[N]DOR
MIIṬ [ET] ḌES
CEN[DIT T]ỤR
BO ỊN Ṣ[T]ẠG̣
NUM UEN
TI ET CONP̣LE
BANTUR ET
PERICLITA
8:24 BANTUR Ạ[C]

392 SEC·

CIDENTES AỤ
TEM ḌỊṢCIPU
ḶI SUSCITAUE
RUṆṬ ILLUM
DICẸṆṬES MA
GISṬẸR [P]ERI
ṂỤS ṬUṆC
[SUR]ĢE[NS IM]
Ṗ[E]RAỤỊṬ ỤE[̄]
Ṭ[O ET TE]M[P]E[S]
ṬẠṬỊ AQUAE
ẸT ḌẸ[STITERU]ṆṬ
Ẹ[T FACTA E]ṢṬ
Ṭ[RANQUI]ḶḶỊ
8:25 ṬAṢ [DIXI]Ṭ ẠỤ
ṬEṂ Ị[LL]ỊṢ ỤḄỊ
ESṬ [FIDE]Ṣ UES
ṬRẠ [TIM]ẸN
ṬES AỤṬEM
ṂỊṚATI SỤNṬ
AD ẠḶỊS ALIUM
DIÇENTES QUIS
NAM ỤT HIC
ẸṢṬ QUI ET UẸ ̄

TIS IMPERAT
ET AQUAE ET OB
AUDIUNT ILLI
8:26 ENAUIGAUE
RUNT AUTEM
IN REGIONE ̄
GERASENO
RUM QUAE
EST TRANS FRE
TUM GALILAE
8:27 AE ĢṚ[E]SSO AU
TEṂ [ILLO OC]
ÇỤ[RRIT IL]
LI ỤIR QUI DA[E]
MONEM HA
BEBAT ẸX [TEM]
ṖO[R]IBỤ[S MUL]
ṬIS ET U[ESTI]
MENTUM
NON INDỤẸ
BATUR NEQỤẸ
DOMO M[ANE]
BAT SED [IN MO]
NUMENṬ[IS]

393 LUCANUM

8:28 UIDENS AUTEM
IH̄M· PROSTRA
UIT SE ET EṬ EX
CLAMANS UO
CE MAGNA DI
XIT QUID MIḤỊ
EST TECUM ·IH̄U·
F̣ILI DEI SUM
MI ORO TE NE
ME TỌRQUEAS
8:29 PRAECIP̣IEBAT
EN[IM] Ṣ[PI]RITỤỊ
[IMM]ỤṆḌ[O EXI
RE DE HOMINE
MULTIS ENIM TEMPO
RIBUS ARRIPU
ERAT ILLUM AL
LIGABATUR
ENIM CATENIS
ET CONPEDI
BUS UT CUSTO
DIRETUR ET
ET ERUMPENS
UINCULA FU]

GABATỤR A DÆ
MONẸ IN DE
SERTIS
8:30 INTERROGAUI[T]
AUTEM ILLUṂ
IH̄S· QUOD TỊ
BI NOME[N EST]
QỤ[I] ḌỊXỊ[T LE]
GIO QUOṆ[IAM]
ḌAEM[ONIA]
MULT[A ERANT]
8:31 Ị̣N [EO ET ROGA]
ḄAṆ[T ILLUM]
Ṇ[E IMPERA
RET EIS IN ABY
SUM IRE
8:32 ERAT AUTEM
IBI GREX POR
CORUM MAG
NA QUAE PAS
CEBATUR ET
ROGAUERUNT
ILLUM UT IN
EIS INTRARENT]

394 SEC·

ET PERMISIT
ILLIS
8:33 ET CUM EXIS
SENT DAEMO
NIA AB HOMI
NE INTRAUE
[RU]NT IN POR
[COS] ẸT IN[P]Ẹ
[TUM] ̣FECIṬ GREX
[PER P]ṚAECEPS
[IN MAR]E ET SUF
[FOCATA EST] ỤỊ
8:34 [DENTES A]ỤTE[‾
PASTORES FU
GERUNT ET RE
NUNTIAUE
RUNT QUOD
FACTUM EST
IN CIUITATEM
ET IN AGROS
8:35 EXIERUNT AU
TEM UIDERE
QUOD FACTUM
EST ET UENE]
RUNT AD ·IH̄M·
ET INUENE
RUNT SEDEN
TEM HOMINE‾
Ạ QUO DAEMO
NIA EXIERAN̄
UESTITUM ET
CONSTANTEM
MENTE ANTE
PEDES ·IH̄U·
ET TIMUERUN
8:36 ẠDṆ[U]Ṇ[T]ỊA
[UERU]ṆṬ A[U
TEM ILLIS QUI
UIDERANT
QUOMODO
SANATUS EST IS
QUI A DAEMO
NIIS ERAT UE
XATUS
8:37 ROGAUIT AUTEM
ILLUM OMNIS
MULTITUDO
REGIONIS GE]

395 LUCANUM

RASENORUM
UT DISCEDE
RET AB EIS QUO
NIAM TIMỌ
RE MAGNO
DETINEBAN
TUR IPSE AU
TEM ASCEN
DENS IN NA
UE REUERSUS
8:38 EST ROGABAT
AUTEM EUM
ILLE UIR A QUO
EXIERANT DÆ
MONIA UT ES
SẸ[T] SECUM
DIMISIT AU
[T]EM IH̅S· IL
LUM DICENS
8:39 REUERTERE
DOMI APUT
TE ET ENARRA
QUANTA TIBI
FECERIT DE̅U̅S̅·

ET ABIIT PER
TOTAM CIUI
TATEM PRAE
DICANS QUA¯
TA ·IH̅S· FECIS
SET ILLI
8:40 [F]ACTUM EṢT [AU]
TẸ[M] Ḍ̣U[M RE]
ṲẸṚTEREẸ[TUR]
Ị̣H̅Ṣ· ET [EXCE]
PE[T ILLUM]
T[URBA ERANT]
EN[IM OM]ṆẸṢ
EX[P]Ẹ[CTAN]ṬẸ[S]
EUM
8:41 ET ECCE ṲEN[I]T
UIR NOMỊNE
IAIRUS ET
HIC ERAT PRINCEPS
SYNAGOGAE
ET PROSTṚ[A]
TUS AD PEDES
IH̅U· ROGA
BAT ILLUM UT I¯

396 SEC·

TRARET IN
DOṂUM SUA⁻
8:42 QUIA FILIA UNI
CA ERAT ILLI FE
RE ANṆORUM
DUODECIM
[ET] ḤẠẸÇ ṂỌR[I]
[EBAT]Ụ[R]
[ET FAC]T[U]Ṃ ẸṢṬ
[DUM IRET TU]R
Ḅ[A [URGEB]A]Ṭ ẸṬ
[CONPRIME
BAT EUM] ỊTẠ
ỤṬ [SUFFOCA]RE[NT]
8:43 Ẹ[UM ET] ṂULỊ
[E]Ṛ QỤẠE ERAT
Ị[N P]ṚOFLUUIỌ
SAN[G]UINIS AB
ANṆỊS DỤO
D[E]Ç[I]Ṃ QUAE
I[N] MEDỊCIS
CONSUMP̣SE
RAT OMNEM
SUḄSTAṆTIAM

SUAM NEC [PO]
TUIT AB ALIQUO
8:44 CURARI ACCE⁻
DENS DE RE
TRO TETIGIT
ỤE[S]TIMENTU⁻
EIUS ET PRO
TINUS STETIT
FLUXUS SAN
GUINIṢ EIUS
8:45 IH̄S· AUTEM SCI
EN[S] QỤOD EXI
ẸṚỊṬ [AB] ẸỌ ỤIR
ṬỤṢ [D]IXIT QUI
TETIGIT ME ṆẸ
GANTIBU[S]
ẠUTEM OM
NIBUS AIT P̣Ẹ
TRUS ET QUI ÇỤ[⁻]
ILLO ERANT MA
GISTER TURBǢ
TAM MAGNǢ
CONPRIMỤN
TE ET DICIS QUIS

397 LUCANUM

TETIGIT ME
8:46 QUI DIXIT IH̄ƗS
TETIGIT ME
ALIQUIS EGO
ENIM COGNO
UI UIRTUTEṂ
EXISSE A ME
8:47 UT UIDIT AUTE[̅]
MULIER SE NỌ̅
LATUISSE Ụ[E]
NIT TRẸṂENS
ET PRỌ[CID]ẸNS
ANTE PEDEṢ IḶ
LIUS EṬ OB QUA̅
CAUSAM TETỊ
GỊṬ EUM IN
DI[C]ẠUIT CORẠ[̅]
ỌMNI POPU
[L]O ET QUOMO
ḌO SANATA EṢṬ
COMFESTIM
8:48 QUI DIXIT EI
FILIA FIDES ṬUA
TE SALUAM FẸ
CIT UADE IN
PẠ[CE]
8:49 ADHUC Ḷ[OQ]ỤẸ̅
TE EO Ụ[E]ṆỊṬ
A PRIN[CI]PE
SINAGOGẠẸ
DICEN[S EI MOR]
Ṭ[U]Ạ [E]Ṣ[T FILIA
TUA NOLI UE
XARE ILLUM
8:50 IH̄S· AUTEM
CUM AUDIS
SET UERBUM]
DỊ[XIT PATRI]
PUẸ[LLAE NO]
LI T[I]Ṃ[ERE]
TANTUM [CRE]
DE ET UIỤ[ET]
8:51 CUMQUẸ [UE]
ṆỊṢSET DỌ[M]I
ṆỌN ESṬ [PAS]
SUS INṬ[R]A[R]Ẹ
SECUṂ QUẸ[̅]
QUAM NỊ[SI PE]

398 SEC·

TRUM ET IO
HAṆṆEN ET
ỊẠC̣[OB]UM ET
PATṚEM ET
MA[T]REM PU
ELḶẠE
8:52 [PLO]ṚẠBANT AU
[TE]Ṃ Ọ̣ṂṆẸṢ
[ET PLANGE]BẠ[NT
EAM QUI DI
XIT NOḶIT]E F̣LE
Ṛ[E NON ENIM]
Ṃ[ORTUA E]ṢṬ
ṢẸ[D DOR]ṂIT
8:53 Ẹ[T DERID]ẸḄAN̄
[EUM S]CIEN
Ṭ[ES] ẸAM MOR
Ṭ[UA]M ESSE
8:54 Ị̣P[SE A]UTEM AD
P̣ṚẠEHẸNSA
ṂẠNUM EIUS
EXCLAMAUIT
DICENS PUEL
8:55 LA SURGE ET RE
UERSUS EST
SP̄S· EIUS ET
SURREXIT STA
TIM ET IUSSIT
DARI EI MAN
DUCARE
8:56 OBSTIPUERUN̄
AUTEM PAREM
TES EIUS PRAE
[CE]P̣ITQUE IL
LIS ỤṬ NEMI
NI Ḍ̣ICERENT
QUOD FACTUM
9:1 EST ☩ CON
UOCATIS AU
TEM DUODE
CIM APOSTO
LIS DEDIT ILL[IS]
UIRTUTEM
ET POTESTA
TEM SUPER
OMNIA DAE
MONIA ET LAN
GUORES CURA̅

399 LUCANUM

9:2 DI ET MISIT ILLOS
PRAEDICARE
REGNUM ·D̅I̅·
ET SANARE
9:3 AEGROS ET DI
XIT AD ILLOS
NIHIL TOLLATIS
IN UIA NEQUE
ỤIRGAM ṆẸ
QUE PERA[¯]
NEQU[E CALCE]
ẠMẸṆTA [NE
QUE PANEM
NEQUE PECU
NIAM NEQUE
DUAS TUNICAS
HABEATIS
9:4 IN QUAMCUM
QUE DOMUM
INTRAUERI
TIS IBI MANE
TE ET INDE EXI
9:5 TE ET QUICUM
QUE NON RE]

CEPERINT UOS
EXẸỤ[NT]ẸS
DE CIỤ[ITAT]Ẹ[¯]
ILLAM P̣[ULU]Ẹ
REM UEṢ[TR]Ụ¯
DE PEDIB[US]
EXCUTIṬ[E IN]
TE[STI]MỌ[NI]
U[M I]LLIṢ
9:6 [EXEUN]T[ES AU
TEM CIRCUI
BANT PER MU
NICIPIA EUA¯
GELIZANTES
ET CURANTES
UBIQUE
9:7 AUDIIT AUTEM
HERODES TE
TRARCHA OM
NIA QUAE FIE
BANT ET STU
PEBAT EO QUOD
DICERETUR
A QUIBUSDAM]

400 SEC·

QUIẠ IOHANES
SUR[RE]XỊṬ A
9:8 [MORT]ỤỊ[S] Ạ QUI
[BUS]ḌẠṂ AỤ
[TE]Ṃ QUIA HẸ
[LIAS] ẠP̣P̣ARU
[IT A]Ḅ ALỊIS AU
[TEM] Q[UIA P]ṚỌ
[PHET]Ạ [DE AN
TIQUIS SURRE
9:9 XIT DIXIT
AUTEM]
– – –
– – –
– [DECOLLA
UI QUIS AUTE‾
EST HIC DE QUO
AUDIO EGO
TALIA ET QUAE
REBAT UIDE
RE ILLUM
9:10 ET REUERSI
APOSTOLI NON
TIAUERUNT]

ILLI QUAECU‾
CUMQUAE FE
C̣ERUNT ET AD
SUMENS ẸOS
SECESSIT SẸ
ỌṚSUM IN LỌ
CUM DESER
TUM QUI ỤO
C̣ẠBATUR ḄẸ
9:11 [TSA]ỊDA TURBÆ
[AUTE]M CUM
[COGNO]ỤIS[SENT
SECUTAE SUNT
EUM ET EXCI
PIENS ILLOS
LOQUEBATUR
ILLIS DE REG
NO DEI EOS QUI
NECESSE HA
BEBANT CU
RARI SANA
9:12 BAT DIES AU
TEM COEPE
RAT DECLINARE]

401

LUCANUM

ACCEDENTES
AUTEM DUO
DECIM DIX̣Ẹ
RUNT ILLI Ḍ[I]
ṂITTE TURBẠ[¯]
UT EUNTES ẠḌIA
[C]ẸNTES UICOS
ẸṬ ẠG̣ROS RE
F̣ỊC̣ỊANT$^{\text{S[E]}}$ ẸṬ IN
UẸNỊẠNṬ [ES
C]ẠṢ QỤ[O]ṆỊ[AM
HIC] ỊṆ [DESER]
TỌ ḶỌC̣Ọ Ṣ[UMUS]
9:13 ḌỊXỊṬ AUṬẸ[M]
AD [I]ḶLOṢ Ḍ[ATE]
Ẹ[IS M]ẠṆ[DU
C]Ạ[RE] QUỊ Ḍ[I
X]ẸRỤNṬ ṆO[¯]
ṢỤṆṬ ṆỌḄIS
[PL]ỤṢ [QU]ẠM
Q̣ỤỊṆ[QUE] P̣Ạ
NẸ[S ET] P̣IṢC̣Ẹ[S]
DỤỌ [NISI] SỊ
[NOS E]ỤṆṬẸ[S]

EMAMUS IN
OM[NEM] PO
P̣U[LUM] ḤỤṆC
9:14 EṢCAS EṚẠṆT
ENỊM [UIRI]
F̣ẸṚẸ QUỊṆ
QỤẸ ṂỊḶỊ[A]
ḌỊX[IT A]ỤṬ[EM]
AD D[I]SCỊP̣Ụ
LOṢ SỤ[OS FACI]
ṬẸ ỊḶḶ[OS RECU¯
BERE PER]
– – –
– – –
9:15 – – –
[R]EC[UBUERUNT
OM]Ṇ[ES]
9:16 [AC]C̣EPṬỊS [AUTEM]
Q̣UINQ̣[UE PA]
NIBUṢ [ET] ḌỤO
BUS P̣ISC[IB]ỤS
[RE]SP̣ỊC̣ỊẸṆṢ
ỊṆ CAẸḶỤṂ
ḄENEDIXIT

402 SEC·

SUPER ILLOS
ET CONFREGIT
ET DABAT DIS
CIPULIS UT AD
PONERENT TUR
9:17 ḄỊṢ ET MANDU
CAUERUNT
ET SATIATI SUN̄
ET SUBLATUM
EST QUOD SU
PEṚ[F]UIT ILLIS
FRAGMENTO
RUM COPḤI
[NOS DUO]ḌECI¯
9:18 Ẹ[T FACTU]Ṃ EST
[CUM E]SSET IN
[SEC]ṚẸTO ADE
[RA]ṆT ILLI DIS
C̣ỊP̣[UL]I SUI ET
INṬERROGA
UIṬ EOS DICENS
QUEM ME DI
CUNT TURBÆ
9:19 ESSE QUI RES
PONDENTES
DIXERUNT IO
HANNEM BAP
TISTAM ALII AU
TEM HELIAM
ALIQUI UERO
QUIA PROFE
TA UNUS DE
PRIORIBUS
9:20 SỤRREXIT DI
X̣ỊṬ AUTEM
ILLIS UOS AU
ṬEM ~~ILLIS UOS~~
~~AUTEM~~ QUE¯
ME DICITIS
ESSE RESPON
DENS AU[T]E¯
PETRUS ḌIX̣[I]Ṭ
9:21 XP̄M QUI CUM
OBIURGASSET
ILLOS PRAECE
PIT NẸ C̣ỤỊ DI
CERENT HOC
9:22 DICENS QUỌ

403 LUCANUM

NIAM OPORTET
FILIUM HOMI
NIS MULTA PA
TI ET REPROBA
RI A SENIORI
BUS ET PONTI
FICIBUS ET SCRI
BIS ET INTER
FICI ET POS TER
TIUM DIEM RE
⳨ SURGERE DI
CEBAT AUTEM
AD OMNES
SI QUIS UULT
P̣OST ME UENI
[R]E ẠḄN[EGET
SE IPSUM ET
SEQUATUR ME
9:24 QUISQUE ENI̅
UOLUERIT ANI
MAM SUAM
SALUAM FACE
RE PERDET IL
LAM ET QUI PER]

DIDERIT ANI
MAM SUAM
CAUSA MEỊ
SALUABIṬ [IL]
9:25 LAM [Q]Ụ[ID]
ENIM PRO[DEST]
HOMINI ḶO
CRARI M[UN]
DUM TO[TUM]
SE AUTEṂ [IP]
SUM PE[RDE]
RE AUT I[AC]
TURẠ[M FA]
9:26 Ç[IAT QUISQUIS
ENIM CON
FUSUS FUERIT
ME ET MEOS
HUNC FILIUS
HOMINIS CON
FONDET
CUM UENE
RIT IN GLO
RIA SUA ET PA
TRIS ET SANC]

404 SEC·

TORUM ANGE
LORUM
9:27 [DI]ÇỌ ẠUTEM UO
[BIS U]ERE SUN
[QUI]ḌẠM HIC
[STA]ṆṬES QUI
[N]ỌN ĢUSTA
[BUN]Ṭ MORTE¯
[DON]EC UIDE
[ANT] ṚEGNUM
9:28 [DĒ]Ị : FAC
[TUM] EST AUTE¯
[POST HAE]Ç UER
[BA CIRCITER
POST DIES OC
TO ADSUMPTIS
SECUM PETRO
ET IOHANE ET
IACOBO ASCE¯
DIT IN MON
TEM UT ORA
9:29 RET ET FACTU¯
EST DUM O
RABAT IPSE ET FAC]

TA EST FICIES
UULTUS EIUṢ
ALIA ET UES
TIS EIUS CAN
DIDA PRAEFUL
9:30 GENS ET ECCE
UIRI DUO CON
LOQUEBANTUR
EI ERAT AUTẸ¯
MOYSES ET HE
9:31 LIAS APPAREN
TES IN GLORIẠ[¯]
[D]ICEBANṬ CỌ[¯]
SUṂṂẠTIO
NEṂ ILLỊỤṢ
[QUAM IMPLE
TURUS ERAT IN
HIERUSALEM
9:32 PETRUS AUTE¯
ET QUI CUM
EO ERANT GRA
UATI SUNT SO¯
NO EUIGILAN
TES AUTEM UI]

405 LUCANUM

DERUNT GLO
RIAM EIUS ET
DUOS UIROS AD
SISTENTES EI
9:33 ET FACTUM EST
DUM DISCERENN̄
AB ILLO DIXIT
PETRUS MAGỊṢ
[TER BONUM
EST NOS HIC ES
SE ET FACIAMUS
TABERNACU
LA TRIA UNUM
TIBI ET UNUM
MOYSI ET UNU¯
HELIAE NESCI
ENS QUID DI
9:34 CERET HAEC
AUTEM EO DI
CENTE FACTA
EST NUBS ET OB
UMBRABAT IL
LOS TIMUERUNT
AUTEM DUM]

ILLI INTRAREN̄
9:35 IN NUBẸM ET
UOX FAÇṬ[A] ẸST
DE NU[BE DI]
CENS [HIC EST]
FILIU[S MEUS
ELECTUS IPSUM
AUDITE
9:36 ET CUM FACTA
EST UOX IN
UENTUS EST
IH̄S SOLUS ET
IPSI TACUERUNT
ET NEMINI
INDICAUERUNT
IN ILLIS DIEB·
QUIDQUAM
EX IIS QUAE UI
DERANT
9:37 FACTUM EST AU
TEM PER DIE¯
DESCENDEN
TIBUS EIS DE
MONTE OC]

406 SEC·

CURRIT ILLIS
TURBA MAG
9:38 NẠ [E]T ECCE UIR
[D]E [TU]ṚBA EX
[CLAM]ẠUIT DI
[CENS M]AGIS
[TER ORO TE RES
PICIAS IN FILI
UM MEUM
QUIA UNICUS
9:39 MIHI EST ET
ECCE SP̄S AR
RIPIT ILLUM
SUBITO ET CO̅
CIDIT ET DIS
CARPIT ILLUM
CUM SPUMA
ET UIX RECE
DIT AB ILLO CO̅
TRIBULANS
9:40 EUM ET PRAE
CATUS SUM
DISCIPULOS
TUOS UT EICE]

RENT ILLUM EṬ
NON POTUE
RUNT
9:41 RESPONDENS
AUTEM IH̄S·
DIXIT O GENE
RATIO INCRE
ḌIBILIS QUỌ
[US]Ọ[UE ERO
APUT UOS
ET SUFFERAM
UOS ADDUC
HOC FILIUM
9:42 TUUM ADHUC
AUTEM ACCE
DENTE ILLO
ADLISIT ILLUM
ILLE SP̄S MA
LUS ET CONCARP
SIT IMPERAUIT
AUTEM IH̄S·
SPIRITUI IMMU̅
DO ET SANAUIT
PUERUM ET]

407 LUCANUM

REDDIDIT IL
LUM PATRI SUO
9:43 STUPEBANT AU
TEM OMNES
IN MAGNALIA
DĒI· OMNIB·
AUTEM MIRA‾
TIBUS DE OM
NIBUS QUAE
FACIEBAT DI
XIT AD DISCI
9:44 PULOS PONITE
UO[S] IN AURI
BUS UESTRIS
UERBA HAEC̣
FILIUS ENIM
[H]ỌMINIS IN
[CI]P̣IT TRADI IN
MANIBUS HO
9:45 MINUM AD
ILLI IGNORA
BANT UERBU‾
HOC̣ ET ERAT
OCCULTUM
AB EIS NE IN
TELLEGEREṄ
ET TIMEBANT
INTƗERṚOGA
RE EUM ḌẸ UER
9:46 BO HỌC̣ [IN]ṬRA
UIT AUTEM
COGITATỊỌ IN
EIS QUISNAM
ESSET MAIOR
ILLORUM
9:47 IH̄S· AUTEM UI
SA COGITATIO
NE CORDIS
ILLORUM AD
PREHENSUM
INFANTEM
STATUIT APUD
9:48 SE ET DIXIT QUI
CUMQUE ME
RECIPIT NON
ME RECIPIT
SED EUM QUI
ME MISIT QUI

408 SEC·

ENIM MINI
MUṢ IN OMNI
BUS UOBIS EST
HIC̣ [ES]T MAG
NỤ[S]
9:49 [RESPON]ḌENS
AU[T]ẸM IOHA[‾]
NEṢ ḌIXIT MA
GỊṢṬER UIDI
MUṢ QUENDA[‾]
IN NOMINE
TUO EỊCIEN
TEM DAẸMO
NIA EṬ PROHI
BEBAMUS IL
LỤM QUONI
AM NON SEQUI
TUṚ NOBISC̣U‾
9:50 DIXIT AUTEM
AD ILLUM IH̄S
SINITE ILLUM
ET NOLITE PRO
HIBERE QỤI
ENIM NON
EST ADUERSUS
UOS PRO UOBIS
EST NEMO EST
ENIM QUI NO‾
FACIAT UIRTU
TEM IN ṆOMI
NE MEỌ ẸT [PO]
ṬẸṚIT MALE
LOQUI ḌE MẸ
9:51 FAC̣TUṂ ẸṢṬ
AUTEṂ DUM
CONPLEṚEN
ṬỤṚ ḌỊẸṢ ṚEC̣[EP]
TỊỌṆỊṢ ẸỊỤṢ
ET IP̣[SE DI]ṚẸ
[XIT] ḞACIEM
SUAM IRẸ [IN]
ḤỊERUSAḶ[EM]
9:52 ET MIṢIT N[U]Ṇ
TIOS ẠṆṬẸ C̣ONṢ
PECTUM [SU]
ỤM EṬ [EUN]
ṬES Ị N[TRAU]E
ṚỤNT IN CIU[I]

409 LUCANUM

TATE SAMARI
TANORUM TA¯
QUAM PARA
9:53 TURI ILLI ET
NON RECEPE
RUNT EUM
QUONIAM FA
CIES ILLIUS ERAT
ṬENDENS IN
HIERUSALẸṂ
9:54 ỤIDENTES AỤ[T]E¯
ḌIṢÇ[IP]ỤLI E[I]US
ỊACỌ[BU]Ṣ ẸT [IO]
HẠṆEṢ DỊXE
ṚUNT DM̄[E]
ỤIS DICIṂ[U]Ṣ
[UT I]GNIS ḌẸ
[CAE]ḶO DESCEṆ
[DAT SUP]ER IḶ
ḶOS Ẹ[T C]ỌṆṢỤ
ṂẠT EOS SICUṬ
[HELI]ẠṢ ḞẸÇIṬ
9:55 [ET] ÇỌṆỤẸṚSU[S]
ỌBIUṚGAỤỊṬ IḶ

LOS DICENS
NESCITIS CỤ
IUS [·]SP̄S[·] ẸṢṬỊṢ
9:56 FILIUS HỌMỊ
NIS NON [U]Ẹ
NIT ANỊṂAS
HOMINỤṂ
PERDẸRE SẸḌ
SẠLUARE
ẸT ABIERUNṬ
IN ALỊUṬ CAS
9:57 TELLUM ET
FAC[T]Ụ[M] EST
EUNTIḄUS IḶ
LIS IN UỊA DI
XIT QUIDAṂ
ẠD EUM SEQUAR
TẸ QUỌCỤṂ
9:58 QUE ỊERIS EṬ
DIXIT EI ·IH̄[S]·
UỤLPES CUBI
LIA ḤABENT
ET UỌḶUÇRES
CAEL[I N]IDOS Ụ

410 SEC·

BI REQUIES
CANT FILIUS
AUTEM HOMI
NIS NON HA
BẸ[T] UBI CAPUD
9:59 RECLINET DI
XIT AUTEM
AD ALIUM SE
QUERE ME
QUI DIXIT ·DM̄E·
PERMITTE
MIHI PRIUS
IRE ET SEPELI
RE PATREM
9:60 MEUM DIXIT
AUTEM ILLI SI
NE MORTUOS
SEPELIRE MOR
TUOS SUOS TU
AUTEM UADE
ADNUNTIA
REGNUM DĒI·
9:61 DIXIT AUTEM
ET ALỊUS SEQUAR TE
DM̄E· PRIUS AUTE¯ PERMITT[E]

MIHI IRE ET NU¯
TIARE EIS QUI
IN DOMO SUN
9:62 DIXIT AUTEM
AD ILLUM ·IH̄S·
NEMO RETRO
RESPICIENS
ET EXTENDENS
MANUM SU
PER ARATRUM
APTUS EST REG
10:1 NO DĒI ELE
GIT AUTEM ET
ALIOS ·LXXII·
ET MISIT ILLOS
BINOS ANTE
FACIEM SUAM
IN OMNEM
LOCUM ET CI
UITATEM UBI
INTRATURUS
10:2 ERAT DICE
BAT AUTEM IL
LIS MESSIS CO

411 LUCANUM

PIOSA OPERA
RI AUTEM PAU
CI PRAECAMỊ
NI ERGO ·D̄ŌM̄
MESSIS UT MIT
TAT OPERARI
OS IN MESSEṂ
SUAM
10:3 ECCE MITTɄO
UOS TAMQUA[̄]
AGNOS IN ME
DIO ḶUPORU ̄
10:4 NOLITE POR
TARE SACCU
LUM NON PE
[RA]Ṃ NE[C] CAL
[CIAMENT]ỤM
[ET NEMINE ̄
CIRCA UIAM
SALUTAUE
10:5 RITIS IN QUAM
CUMQUE PRI
MUM DOMU ̄
INTRAUERI]

TIS DICITE PAX
HUIC DOMUI
10:6 SI IBI F̣UERIT
FILIUS PẠCỊS
REQUIE[SCE]Ṭ ·hd·
[S]UPER U[OS] ṚE
[UE]RTE[TU]Ṛ
10:7 [IN EAD]ẸṂ ḌO
[MO MA]NE
Ṭ[E] Ẹ[D]ẸNṬ[E]S
ẸṬ BIBENṬES
Q̣UAẸ [AB I]ḶLIS
APP̣ỌNỤN
TUR [U]OBIS
DIGNUS EST
EN[IM] ỌPERA
RIỤ[S M]ERCE
DEṂ SUAṂ
ṆOLITE MIG̣RA
RE [DE D]ỌMO
[I]N D[OM]UM
10:8 ẸṬ [IN QUA]ÇUṂ
QUE CIUIT]Ạ
[TE INTRAUE]

412 SEC·

RITIS Ẹ[T] ṚẸC̣E
PEṚ[INT] ỤOS
MẠND[UCA]TE
QỤ[A]Ẹ AḌP̣[O]
Ṇ[UNTUR U]Ọ
10:9 Ḅ[IS E]Ṭ [C]Ụ[RA]
Ṭ[E QUI IN EA]
ṢỤN[T INFIR]
ṂỌṢ [ET DICI]
ṬẸ [IL]ḶỊṢ [ADPRO]
P̣ỊṆQỤ[AUIT]
ỊN Ụ[OS REG]
NỤṂ ḌĒỊ
10:10 ỊN QUẠC̣ỤṂQỤ[E]
ẠỤTEṂ C̣[I]ỤỊ
ṬẠṬẸ [INTRA
ỤẸṚỊ[TIS ET]
N[ON] ṚẸC̣[EP]Ẹ
Ṛ[INT U]ỌS ẸX̣
[EU]Ṇ[TES IN]
PḶẠṬ[EA EIUS]
10:11 DIC̣[ITE ETIA]Ṃ
P̣[ULUEREM
QUI ADHAESIT]

NOBIS ḌẸ CI
UỊṬATE UESTRA
ỊN P̣EḌẸS ẸX̣
C̣ỤṬỊṂỤS SU
P̣[E]R U[OS]
[A]DTAM[E]N SCI
T[O]T[E] ẠḌP̣ṚỌP̣Ị[¯
QUASS]Ẹ Ṛ[E]G̣
10:12 [NUM DĒI] DI
C[O A]U[TE]Ṃ ỤỌ
Ḅ[IS SODO]MI[S]
ỊṆ ṚẸ[G]ṆỌ Ṛ[E]
Ṃ[ISSIU]Ṣ EṚ[IT]
QỤẠṂ C̣ỊU[ITA
[TI] ỊḶḶ[I]
10:13 UẠẸ [T]ỊḄỊ [CORO]
Z]Ạ[IN ET BEDSAI]
Ḍ[A QUIA SI IN
TYRO ET SIDO
NE FACTAE
FUISSENT UIR
TUTES QUAE
FACTAE SUNT
IN UOBIS OLIM]

413 LUCANUM

FORS IN CINE
RE ET CILIÇỌ
ṢEDẸ[NT]ẸṢ PAẸ
NIṬẸ[N]TIAṂ
10:14 ẸGỊ[SSE]ṆT [UE]
ṚUMṬAMEṆ
[T]ỴRO E[T SI]D[O]
NI IN I[UDICI]
O ṚẸṂ[ISSI]
ỤṢ EṚ[IT] QỤẠṂ
UOḄỊṢ
10:15 ẸṬ TU Ç[A]P[H]ẠṚ
NAUM ṆỤM
QUIṬ ỤṢ[Q]UE
AD ÇẠẸḶỤM
[EXALTAUERIS]
– [USQUE
AD INFEROS
DEMERGE
10:16 RIS QUI AU
DIT UOS ME
AUDIT ET QUI S
PERNIT UOS
ME SPERNIT]

ET EUM QUI
ME MISIT QUI
AUTEM ṂẸ
AỤḌỊṬ [AUDIT]
EUM QỤ[I]
ṂE MISỊ[T]
10:17 ṚẸỤERSI Ṣ[U]ṆT
[AUTEM ·]LXX·
ẸṬ [D]UỌ CUM
[G]Ạ[UDI]O D[I]CE¯
[T]ẸṢ ·ḌM̄Ẹ· ET[I]
ẠṂ ḌẠEMỌ
[NES S]ỤḄỊẠ
C[EN]T NOBIS
[IN] ṆỌṂỊṆẸ
10:18 [TUO DIX]ỊṬ ẠU
[TEM ILLIS UI
[DEBAM S]AṬ[A
NAM TAM
QUAM F]ỤḶG̣Ụ[R
DE CAELO] ÇA
10:19 [DENTEM EC
CE] – [UO
BIS POTESTA]

414 SEC·

TEM CALCAN
DI SUPẸR UI
PERAS EṬ ^{S}COR
PIỌNES ET SU
PER [O]MNEM
UỊẠM INIṂI
CI NIHIL UỌṢ
NOCEBIT
10:20 UERUM IN HOC̣
N[O]LITE GAU
DERE QUOD
SP̄S· UOBIṢ ỌB
AUDỊ[UNT GAU]
DETE [AUTEM]
QUIA ṆỌṂ[I]
NA Ụ[ESTRA]
SC̣[RIPTA SUNT]
ỊṆ [CAELO]
10:21 IN [ILLA HORA]
ẸX̣ỤḶ[TAUIT]
IN Ṣ[P̄U SANC]
TO [ET DIXIT CO̅
FITEOR TIBI
DM̄E] –
ET TERRAE
QUONIAM ABS
COND[IS]TI HAEC
A SAPIENTIB·
[ET] SEṆSATIS
EṬ REUALAS
TI EA [P]ẠRUO
Ḷ[I]S ỊṬA PATER
QUIA SIC PLA
CUIT AṆTE TE
10:22 OMNIA MIHI
TR[A]DITA SUNT
A PA[T]ṚE ET NE
MO NOBIṬ Q̣UIS
EST PATER NỊ
[S]Ị [FILIUS ET
CUICUNQUE
UOLUERIT FI
LIUS REUELA
UIT
10:23 ET CONUERSUS
AD DISCIPU
LOS DIXIT BE
ATI OCULI QUI]

415 LUCANUM

UIDE^{N}TİṠ QUÆ
UOS UIDETIS
10:24 DICO ENIM
UOBIS QUIA
MULTI PROPHE
TAE UOLUERUN
UIDERE QUAE
UOS UIDETIS
ET NON UIDE
RUNT
10:25 ET ECCE QUIDA¯
LEGIS DOCTOR
SURREXIT TEMP
TANS ILLUM
DICENS MA
GISTER QUID
FACIENS UI
TAM AETER
NAM POSSIDE
10:26 [B]Ọ ET DIXIT
AD ILLUM
IN LEGE QUID
SCRIPTUM
EST QUOMO

10:27 DO LEGIS QUI
RESPONDENS
DIXIT DILIGES
DŌM· D̅M̅ TU
UM IN TOTO
CORDE TUO
ET IN TOTA ANI
MA TUA ET EX
TOTIS UIRIB·
TUIS ET DILI
GES PROXIMU¯
TUUM TAN
QUAM TE IP
10:28 SUM DIXIT AU
TEM ILLI REC
TE RESPONDIS
TI HOC FAC ET
UIBES
10:29 QUI CUM SE UEL
LET IUSTIFI
CARE DIXIT
AD IH̄M ET
QUIS EST MI
[HI P]ṚOXIMUS

416 SEC·

10:30 SUSCIPIENS
AUTEM ·IH̄S·
DIXIT HOMO
QUIDAM DES
CENDEBAT AB
HIERUSALEM
IN HIERICO
ET HIC ỊNCIDIT
IN ḶATRONES
QUI EXPOLIA¯
ṬES EUM ET PLA
GIS INPOSITIS
ABIERUNT SE
MIUIUO EO
10:31 RELICTO FOR
TUITO SACER
DOS QUIDAM
DESCENDE
BAT PER UIAM
ILLAM ET UI
SO ILLO PRAE
TERIIT
10:32 SIMILITER [AU]
TEṂ ET Ḷ[EUI]
TES CUM TRAN
SIRET PER EO
DEM LOCO ET
UIDISSET ILLU¯
PERTRANSIIT
10:33 SAMARITANUS
AUTEM QUI
^{D}ƗAM ITER FA
CIENS UENIT
PER EUM ET UI
DENS EUM
MISERTUS EST
10:34 ET CONLIGA
UIT UULNERA
EIUS INFUN
DENS OLEUM
ADQUE UINU[¯]
ET INPOSITUM
EUM IN SUỌ
IUMENṬỌ
DUXIT ỊN ṢṬ[A]
BULO EṬ [CURA¯]
HABUIT EIUS
10:35 ET IN ÇRASṬỊ

417 LUCANUM

NUM DIEM
PROTULIT DUOS
DENARIOS ET
DEDIT STABULA
RIO ET DIXIT IL
LI DILIGENTER
CURAM ILLIUS
HABE EṬ QUODcumque [amplius erogaueris ego]
REUERTENS
REDDAM TIBI
10:36 QUIS HỌṚUM UI
DETUR PRỌXI
MUS FUISSE
EIUS QUI INCI
DERAT IN LA
10:37 TRONES AD IL
LE DIXIT QUI
ḌECIṬ MISEṚI
CORDIAM IN IL
ḶỤṂ DIXIT
[AU]ṬẸṂ ILLI [·]IH̄Ṣ[·]
[RECT]Ẹ ṚESPON
[DIST]Ị UADE ET
[TU FAC] ṢỊMILITER

10:38 FACTUM EST AU
TEM DUM IREN
IPSE INTRAUIT
IN UICUM
QUENDAM MULIER
AUTEM QUAE
DAM NOMI
NE MAṚTHA
EXCEPIT ILLUM
IN DOMO ṢUA
10:39 ET HUIC ERAṬ
SOROR QUAE
UOCABATUR
MARIA QUAE
CUM CONSE
DISSET AD PE
DES ·DM̄I· AU
DIEBAT UER
10:40 BUM EIUS MAR
THA AUTEM
TURBABATUR
CIRCA PLURI
MUM MINIS
TE[R]ỊUM

418 SEC·

ADSTANS AUTE¯
·DM̄E·
DIXIT NON AD
TINET AT TE QUOD
SOROR ṂẸA
RELIQUID ME
SOLA MIṆISTRA
RE DIC ERGO
EI UT ADIUUET
10:41 ME RESPON
DENS ẠUTEM
DỊXIT EI ·DM̄S·
MARTHA MAR
10:42 THA MARIA
OPTIMAM PAR
TEM SIBI ~~L~~ELE
GIT QUAE NON
AUFERETUR
11:1 EỊ ✠ ET FAC
TUM EST CUM
ESSET IPSE IN
QUODAM LO
CO ORANS ET
UT QUIEUIT
DIXIT QUIDA¯
EX DISCENTI
BUS EIUS ·DM̄E·
DOCE NOS ORA
RE SICUT IOHA¯
NES DOCUIT
DISCIPULOS
SUOS
11:2 DIXIT AUTEM
ILLIS CUM ORA
BITIS DICITE
PATER SANCTE
QUI ES IN CAE
LIS SANCTIFI
CETUR NOME¯
TUUM ADUE
NIAT REGNU¯
TUUM FIAT UO
11:3 LUNTAS TUA PA
NEM NOSTṚ[UM]
COTIDIAṆ[UM]
DA NOBIṢ [HO]
11:4 DIE EṬ D[IMIT]
TE NOBIṢ [PEC]
CATA N[OSTRA]

419 LUCANUM

SICUT ET IPSI
DIMITTIMUS
OMNI DEBI
TORI NOSTRO
ET NE IND[U]
CAS [NOS]
– – –
– – –
– – –
– – –
– – –
– – –
– – –
– – –
– – –
– – –
– – –
– – –
– – –
– – –
– – –
– – –
– – –
– – –

ADPONAM IL
11:7 LI ET ILLE DE Ị[N]
TRO RẸ[SPON]
DEN[S DI]–
– – –
– – –
– – –
– – –
– – –
– – –
– – –
– – –
– – –
– – –
– – –
– – –
– – –
– – –
– – –
– – –
– – –
– – –
– – –
– – [SUR]

420 SEC·

[G]ENS DABIT IL
[LI] QỤẠṆṬOS DE
[SIDERA]Ṭ
11:9 [ET EGO U]ỌBIS
[DICO] –
– – –
– – –
– – –
– – –
– – –
– – –
– – –
– – –
– – –
– – –
– – –
– – –
– – –
– – –
– – –
– – –
– – –
– – –
– – –

SI PETIERIT PIS
CEM NUM
QUID PRO PIS
CEM SERPEN
[TE]M ỊḶỊ POR
11:12 [RIGET AUT] SI PE
[TIERIT OUUM]
– – –
– – –
– – –
– – –
– – –
– – –
– – –
– – –
– – –
– – –
– – –
– – –
– – –
– – –
– – –
– – –
– – –

421 LUCANUM

11:26 ET ADSUMIT
ADHUC ALIOS
SEPTEM SPIRI
TUS NEQUIOR
ES SE ET INTRA¯
TES INHABITAN
ET FIUNT NOBIS
SIMA HOMI
NIS ILLIUS PE
IORA PRIORU¯
11:27 FACTUM EST AU
TEM DUM DI
CERET HAEC
IPSE LEUATA
UOCE QUAE
DAM MULI
ER DIXIT ILLI
BEATUS UEN
TER QUI TE POR
TAUIT ET UBE
RA QUAE SU
11:28 XISTI QUI Ạ[IT]
ILLIṢ BAEATI
QUI AUDIUNT
UERBUM ·DĒI·
ET CUSTODI
UNT
11:29 TURBA AUTEM
CONUENIEN
TE COEPIT DI
CERE GENS
HAEC GENS
NEQU^{A} EST SIG
NUM QUAE
RIT ET NON
DABITUR [E]I
NISI SIGNUM
IONAE
11:30 SICUT ENIM
FUIT IONAS
SIGNUM NI
NEUITIS SIC
ERIT ET FILI
US HOMINIS
HUIC GENE
RATIONI ET
SICUT IONAS
IN UENTRE

422 SEC·

COETI FUIT SIC
ERIT FILIUS HO
MINIS IN TER
11:31 ṚAM REGINA
AUṢ[T]ṚI SUR
GET IN IUDICI
O CUṂ UIRIS
GENẸRATIO
NIS HUIUS ET
CONDEMNA
ṾỊṬ ẸOS QUO
N[I]AM UENIṬ
DE FỊNIBUS
TERRAE AUDI
RE SAPIENTIA¯
SOLOMONIS
ET ECCE HIC
PLUS SOLOMO
11:32 NE : UIRI
NINEỤITAE
SURGENṬ IN
IỤD[I]Ç[IO C]ỤṂ
G̣Ẹ[NTE] ḤẠÇ
EṬ COṆḌ[EM]

NABUNT EAM
QUȦIA PAENI
TENTIAM EGE
RUNT ỊN PRÆ
DICATIONAE
IONAE ET EC
CE HIC PLUS
QUAM IONA
11:33 NEMO LUCER
NAM ACÇEN
ṢẠM IN OCCUL
ṬỌ PONỊT NE
QUE SUB ṂỌ
DIUM SẸ[D] ṢỤ
PER Ç̣Ạ[N]DẸḶẠ
ḄṚUṂ ỤṬ ỊN
ṬṚ[A]ṆṬẸṢ ḶỤ
MEN UIDE
11:34 ANṬ ḶỤÇ̣ẸṚ
NẠ CỌ[RP]ỌRIṢ
[TUI ES]Ṭ ỌÇ̣U
[LUS] ṬUỤS SI
ỌÇ̣U[L]Ụ[S TU]ỤS
ṢIMP̣ḶẸX ƑUE

423 LUCANUM

RIT TOTUM COR
PUS TUUM LU
CIDUM EST SI
UERO OCULUS
TUUS NEQUA
FUẸRIT ET COR
PU[S T]UUM ṬE
ṆE[BR]OSUM
11:35 SUM [ERI]Ṭ SI ER
G̣Ọ [L]ỤṂEN QUOD
[ES]Ṭ IN ṬE [TE]NẸ
ḄṚẠE [S]ỤNT [T]Ẹ
Ṇ[E]ḄRA[E IP]SE
[Q]Ụ[ANṬAE] SỤN
11:37 LỌQ̣[UE]ṆTAẸ
AỤṬE[M E]Ọ RỌ
G̣ẠỤỊṬ ẸỤṂ
Q̣Ụ[IDAM] P̣Ḥ
ṚỊṢẠ[E]ỤṢ ỤT
P̣ṚẠṆ[D]EṚEṬ
Ṣ[E]C̣ỤṂ IN
[G]ṚEṢ[SUS] ẠỤ
ṬẸṂ [R]ẸC̣Ụ
11:38 [B]ỤỊṬ PHAṚỊSÆ

US AUTEM COE
PIT RECOGITANS
INTRA SE DI
CERE QUOD
ṆỌṆ P̣RIUS
ḄẠ[PTI]ZATUS
EṢ[S]ET
11:39 DIX̣ỊT AỤṬEM
DM̅S· AD ILLUM
NUNC UOS
PHARISAEI
UTRUMṆE
EXTERIORE¯
PARTEM CALI
CIS EṬ CATINI
MỤNDAṬIS
QUOD AUṬEM
INTUS EST ỤES
T[R]UM PLENU¯
EST RAPIṆA
EṬ NEQUIṬIA
11:40 STUL[TI]
NỌ[N]Ṇ[E Q]ỤI
F̣EC̣ỊṬ UERU¯

424 SEC·

INTERIORA
ET EXTERIO
11:41 RA FECIT UE
RUM QUOD SU
PEREST ḌAṬ[E]
ELEMOSỴNA¯
ET ECCE OM
NIA MUNDA
UOBIS ERUN
11:42 SED UAE UO
BIS PHARISAE
IS QUONIAM
DECIMATIS
MENTAM ET
RUTAM ET OM
NEM OLUS
ET PRAETER
ISTIS IUDICI
UM ET CARI
TATEM DĒI·
HAEC OPOR
TET ḞIEṚI ET IL
LA NON RELIN
QUERE

11:43 UAE UOBIS PHA
RISAEI QUO
NIAM DILIGI
TIS PRIMOS
CONSESSUS
IN SYNAGOGIS
ET SALUTAṬIO
NES IN FORO
11:44 UAE UOBIS QUO
NIAM ESTIS
MONUMEN
TA INGNOBI
LIA ET HOMI
NES AMBULA¯
TES SUPRA IG
NORANT
11:45 RESPON[DEN]S AUTE¯
QUIDAM EX
LEGIS DOCTO
RIBUS DIXIT
EI MAGISTER
HAEC DICENS
ET NOBIS [C]ON
TUMELIAM

425 LUCANUM

11:46 FACIS QUI DI
XIT ET UOBIS
LEGIS DOCTO
RIBUS UAE QUI
A HONERATIS
HOMINES SAR
CIṆAS INPOR
TABILES ET IP
SI UNO DIGITO
RUM UESTRO
RUM NON AT
[T]INGITIS EA
11:47 UAE UOBIS QUO
NIAM AEDI
FICATIS MO
NUMENTA
PROPHETA
RUM NAM PA
TRES UESTRI
OCCIDERUNT
11:48 ILLOS ERGO
T[E]STIMONIU¯
PERHIBETIS
NON CONSE¯
TIENTES OPE
RIBUS PATRU¯
UESTRORUM
QUONIAM IL
LI QUIDEM OC
[C]IDERUNT
EOS UOS AUTE¯
AEDIFICATIS
11:49 IDEO ET SAPIEN
TIA ·DĒI· DICIT
MITTAM ỊṆ
ILLIS PROPHE
TAS ET APOSTO
LOS
E^{TE}X ILLIS OCCI
DENT ET PER
SEQUENTUR
11:50 UT EXQUIRA
TUR SANGUIS
OMNIUM
PROPHETARU¯
QUI EFFUSUS
ET AB ORIGI
NE MUNDI

426 SEC·

USQUE IN GEN
TE HAC
11:51 A SANGUINE A
ḄẸḶ UṢ[QUE AD]
ṢA[NGUINEM]
ZAC̣ḤẠ[RIAE]
QUEM OCC̣[I]
DẸRUNT IṆ
TER AL[T]ARIUṂ
ET AEDEM ỊṬ
A ḌỊC̣Ọ UOBIS
EXQUIRETUR
A GENTE HAC
11:52 UAE UOBIS LE
GIS DOCTORỊ
BỤṢ Q̣UONIAṂ
Ạ[BSC]ONDISTIS
C̣ḶAỤẸM ṢC̣[I]
ENṬIAẸ ẸṬ ỊP̣
SI NỌṆ INṬṚẠ
TIS ET INTRO
ẸUṆṬẸṢ [P]ṚO
HIBUISTIS
11:53 DICENT[E] ẠỤṬẸṂ
ILLO HAEC CO
RAM OMNI PO
PULO COEPE
ṚỤNṬ TAM SCRI
BAE Q̣UẠṂ ET
LEGIS DOCTO
RES ṂẠḶẸ ṢE
HABEṚ[E] ẸT CO¯
MIṆ[AR]Ẹ ỊḶḶ[I]
DE P̣ḶỤṚIBỤS
11:54 QUAẸṚẸNTES
OCC̣ẠṆṢỊỌṆẸ[M]
[ALIQU]ẠṂ [IN
U]ẸṆỊṚẸ AB ỊḶ
[LO] UṬ [ACCUS]A
R[E]N[T EU]Ṃ
12:1 ṂỤḶṬẠ [AUTE]Ṃ
ṬỤṚ[BA SE CON]
TINẸN[TI]U¯
IN . . . . . Ṭ
ITẠ Ụ[T ALIUS A]ḶỊ
ỤM Ṣ[E CON
CUL]C̣Ạ[RENT
COEPIT] ḌỊC̣Ẹ

427 LUCANUM

RE AD DISCEN
TES PRIMUM
CAUETE A FER
MENTO PHẠṚỊ
SAEỌṚỤ[M] QUOD
EST ADFE[C]ṬA
12:2 TIỌ ṆIH[IL] ENI¯
OPERTUM EST
QUỌḌ N[ON] RE
ỤELA[BI]ṬUR ET
ỌCCỤ[L]ṬUM
QUỌḌ [NON]
Ç[OGNOSCA]ṬỤ[R]
12:3 Q̣[UAE IN] ṬẸṆẸ
B[RIS DIXERITI]Ṣ
IṆ ḶỤ[CE] .... [R]ẠẸ
T .... ṬỤR ẸṬ
Q̣ỤỌ[D AD AU]ṚẸṂ
ḶỌ[CUTI] F̣Ụ[ERI]
TỊṢ [IN] Ç̣Ụ[BI]Ç̣Ụ
L]IS [PRA]ẸḌ[I]Ç̣Ạ
[BI]Ṭ[UR S]ỤPR[A]
12:4 Ṭ[EC]ṬA ḌỊ[CO] Ụ[O]
In s͞c͞i systi ḄỊṢ Q̣Ụ[A]ṢỊ AṂỊÇ̣IS

NOLITE TERRE
RI A[B] HIS QU[I]
OCCIDUNT
ẸṬ P̣ỌṢṬ ḤẠẸÇ̣
[NON] ḤẠḄẸṆṬ
[A]ṂP̣ḶỊUS [QU]ỌD
[FA]CIANṬ
12:5 Ḍ[E]MOṆṢT[RA]
BỌ AU[T]EM UO
BIS QUEM ṬỊ
MEATI[S] E[U]Ṃ
Q[U]I POSTQ̣UA[¯]
OCCIDEṚỊT HA
BET POTESTA
TEM MITTEN
DI IN GEHEN
NAM DỊ[C]Ọ UO
BIS HUNC ṬI
ṂẸTE
12:6 NONN[E] Q̣[U]ỊN
QUE PASSERES
ḌẸP̣[O]N[D]IO UE
NIUNT ET U
NUS E[O]ṚUM

428 SEC·

NON EST IN OBLI
UIONE IN CONS
12:7 PECTU ·DM̄I· SE
D ET CAP̣ILLI CẠ
PITIS UESTRI
OMNES NUME
RATI SUNT NO
LITẸ TIMERE
MULTO UOS PAS
SERIBUS DIF
FERTIS
12:8 DICO UOBIS OM
NIS QUICUM
QUE CONFES
SUS FUERIT ME
CORAM HOMI
NIBUS ET FILI
US HOMINIS
CONFITEBITUR
EUM CORAM
ANGELIS ·DĒI·
12:9 QUI AUTEM
NEGAUERIT
ME CORAM HO

MINIBUS AB
NEGABITUR
CORAM ANGE
12:10 LIS ·DĒI· ET OM
NIS QUI DIXE
RIT UERBUM
IN FILIUM HO
MINIS REMIT
TETUR ILLI QUI
AUTEM BLAS
PHEMAUERIT
SP̄M· SANCTU¯
NON REM[I]T
TETUR ILḶI
12:11 CUM AUṬEM
ADDUCENT
UOS AD SYNA
GOGAS ẸT PRIṆ
CIPES ET PO
TESTATEṢ Ṇ[O]
LITE SOLLICIT[I]
ESSE QUOMO
DO RATION[E]M
REDDATIS AUT

429 LUCANUM

QUID DICATIS
12:12 SANCTUS ENI⨪
SP̄S· DOCEBIT
UOS EADEM
HỌRA QUAE
OPO[R]TEẠT Ḍ[I]
CE[R]E
12:13 DỊXIT AUTEM
[IL]LI QUIDAM
[DE TU]ṚBA MA
[GISTER] ḌỊÇ
[FRATRI MEO
UT PARTIATUR
MECUM HE
REDITATEM
12:14 QUI DIXIT EI
HOMO QUIS]
– – –
– – –
– – –
– – –
– – –
12:15 – CAU[E]
T[E AB] OMNI

AUARITIA QUIA
NỌN IN SUPER
RANDO ALICUI
UITA [I]P̣SIUS
EST DE FACUL
12:16 ṬAṬE SUA DI
XIT AUTEM
PARABỌḶAM
AD ILLOS DICENS
HOMINIS CU
[IU]ṢDAM DIUI
[TIS] UBERES
[FR]UCTUS ATTU
12:17 [LI]T AGER ET RE
[C]OGITABAT IN
[T]ṚA SE DICENS
[Q]ỤID FACIAM
[QU]OD NON HA
[BE]O UBI CON
[GE]RAM FRUC
12:18 [T]ỤṢ MEOS ET
CO[GI]ṬANS DI
XIT HOC FACI
AM DEPONA⨪

430 SEC·

HORREA ET MA
IORA AEDI[FIC]A
BO ẸṬ ỊBỊ CON
G̣[E]ṚẠṂ [OM]
N[ES] F̣ṚỤ[CTUS]
12:19 MEOS E[T DICAM]
ẠṆỊM[AE M]ẸẠẸ
ḤẠBẸ[S] MUḶṬẠ
BỌNA ẠẸP̣ỤḶ[A
12:20 RE] DỊX̣ỊṬ [AUTE̅]
ỊḶ[LI ·D̅S̅· STULTE]
ḤẠÇ̣ [NOCTE ANI]
ṂẠM ṬỤẠ[M]
REPOṢ[CUNT]
Ạ TẸ [QUAE ER]
G̣O P̣Ạ[RASTI CU]
IUS ẸṚỊṆṬ
12:22 DIXIṬ A[UTEM]
AD DIṢÇ̣I[P]UḶO[S]
SUỌS [PROPTE]
ṚẸẠ [UOBIS DI]
CO Ṇ[OLITE SOL]
LIÇ̣[ITI ESSE DE]
ANỊṂẠ ỤẸṢṬṚẠ

QUID EDATIS
NẸQUẸ ḌẸ Ç̣ỌR
[P]ỌṚ[E] UẸṢ[T]ṚO
Q̣ỤỊḌ [INDU]ẠMỊ
12:23 [NI ANIMA P]ḶỤ
[RIS EST QUA]Ṃ ES
[C]Ạ [ET CORPUS
PL]ỤS Q̣ỤẠṂ [UE]Ṣ
ṬỊ[TUS
12:24 CONSIDERATE
CORUOS QUIA]
– – –
– – –
– – –
– – –
– – –
– – –
– – –
– – –
– – –
– – –
– – –
12:25 – – Ạ[DI]
Ç̣ẸṚẸ ṢṬẠ[TURAE]

431 LUCANUM

SUAE CUBITU¯
12:26 UṆUṂ ẸT DẸ
CẸṬẸṚỊ[S] QUID
ṢOLḶỊCITI ẸṢṬỊṢ
12:27 ÇỌṆṢIDERẠ
ṬE LIḶIA AGṚỊ
QỤỌṂỌḌỌ
ṆON TEẊỤṆṬ
ṆẸQUẸ ṆẸỤ[NT
DI]ÇO ỤỌ[BIS] ṆẸ[C
SOLO]MỌṆ IN
[O]ṂṆI GḶỌṚỊẠ
ẠṂỊÇṬỤṢ ẸṚẠ[T]
Ṭ[AN]QỤẠṂ U
NU[M] Ẹ[X] Ị[STIS]
12:28 QUỌḌ ṢỊ [FAE]
ṆỤṂ – –
ḤỌḌ[IE] – –
– – –
– – –
– – –
– – [UESTIT]
QỤẠṆṬỌ ṂẠ
ĢỊṢ ỤOS PAṚỤÆ

12:29 FIDEI ET UOS
NOḶITE QUAE
RERE QUID E
DATIS ẠUT QUID
[BI]ḄATIS NOḶỊ
ṬẸ ṢOLḶỊCITI EṢ
12:30 ṢẸ HAEC ENIM
OMNIA GEN
ṬẸS SAECULI
QUAERUNT
ṢÇỊT ẸNIM PẠ
ṬẸṚ UESTẸR
QỤỊA HAEC OM
ṆỊẠ ỌPUS SUNT
12:31 ỤỌBIṢ QỤAE
ṚỊTE ẠỤṬẸṂ
REGNỤM EIUS
EṬ HAEC ẠḌỊCỊ
ẸNTUR ỤỌ
12:32 ḄỊṢ NỌḶỊ
ṬE ṬỊṂẸṚẸ MI
NIM[A GR]EX
QUON[IA]Ṃ PLA
CUIṬ PẠTRI UES

432 SEC·

TRO DARE UO
BIS REGNUM
12:33 UENDITE BO
NA UESTRA ET
DATE ELEMO
SYNAM FACI
TE UOBIS SAC
CULOS QUI NO‾
UETERESCUN
THENSAURUM
NON DEFICI
ENTEM IN
CAELIS UBI FUR
NON ACCEDIT
NEC TINEA CO‾
12:34 SUMIT UBI ENI‾
FUERIT THEN
SAURUS UES
TER IBI ERIT
ET COR UESTRU‾
12:35 ET SINT LUMBI
UESTRI SUC
CINCTI ET LU
CERNAE AR

12:36 DENTES ET UOS
SIMILES HOMI
NIBUS EXPEC
TANTIBUS ·DŌM·
SUUM QUAN
DO REUERTA
TUR A NUPTI
IS ET CUM UE
NERIT ET PUL
SAUERIT CON
FESTIM APE
RIANT ILLI
12:37 BEATI SERUI IL
LI QUOS CUM
UENERIT ·DM̄S·
INUENERIT
UIGILANTES
AMEN DICO
UOBIS QUỌ[NI]
AM SỤ[CCIN]
GET SE EṬ [DIS]
CUMBER[E]
FACIET ILLOS
ET TRANSIENS

433 LUCANUM

13:1 UENERUNT AU
TEM QUIDAM
[EOD]EM TEM
[PORE] ṆUNTI
[A]Ṇ[TES EI] DE
[GA]ḶỊLAEIṢ Q̣UO
[RUM S]ẠNGUI
[NEM PIL]ATUS
[MISCU]ỊT CU¯
[UICTI]MIS
13:2 [SUIS ET RE]S
[PONDENS
DIXIT ILLIS
PUTATIS QUO
NIAM ISTI GA
LILAEI PRAE
OMNIBUS
GALILAEIS FUE
RUNT PECCA
TORES QUONI
AM PERPESSI
SUNT TALIA
13:3 NON DICO UO
BIS NISI PAE]
NITENTIAM
EGERITIS OM
Ṇ[ES SIM]ỊLI
[TER PERIET]IS
13:4 SIC̣[UT ET ILL]Ị DECE¯
ET OC̣[TO SUP]ER
QUOS [CEC]IDIT
TURRIS IN SI
LOA ET OCCI
DIT EOS PUTA
TIS QUIA IPSI
DEBITORES
FUERUNT
PRAE OMNI
BUS HOMI
NIBUS INHA
BITANTIBUS
IN HIERUSA
LEM
13:5 NON DICO UO
BIS SED NISI
PAENITEN
TIAM EGERI
TIS OMNES

434 SEC·

SIMILITER PE
13:6 RIEṬỊṢ [DICE]
BẠṬ [AUTEM PARA]
B[OLAM ILLIS]
A[R]Ḅ[OREM FI]
C̣[US HABEBAT]
QỤ[ID]ẠM
P̣ḶẠ[NTATAM]
IN UI]ṆẸẠ [SUA]
ẸṬ ỤẸṆỊṬ QỤA[E]
RENS FṚỤC̣
TUM IN EA EṬ
NỌN ỊṆUE
13:7 NỊṬ : DIXỊ[T]
AUTEṂ [A]Ḍ C̣ỤḶ
TORE[Ṃ] UỊ
NEAE EC̣C̣Ẹ
TRỊẸṆṆỊỤ[̄]
ESṬ EX QUO UE
NIO QỤAE
RENS FRUCTU[̄]
IN [FI]CU ḤẠC̣
ET NOṆ [INUE]
NIO EX̣CIDẸ

ERGO ILLAU̶M
UṬ Q̣[UOD] ẸṬ TER
ṚẠṂ Ọ[CCUPET
13:8 QUI] – –
– – [DI
XIT DM̄E SINE]
ẸẠṂ [ET HUNC
ANNUM DO
NEC FODIAM
CIRCA ILLAM
ET MITTAM
COPHINUM
STERCORIS
13:9 ET SI QUIDEM
FECERIT FRUC
TUM CETER
OQUIN IN FU
TURUM EX
CIDES
13:10 ERAT AUTEM
DOCENS IN SY
NAGOGA SAB
13:11 BATIS ET EC
CE MULIER]

435

LUCANUM

QUAE SP̄M HA
ḄỤỊṬ [L]ẠṆG̣ỤO
[RIS] – –
– – –
– – –
– – –
– – [RUM
13:12 QUAM CUM
UIDISSET IH̄S
UOCAUIT EAM
ET DIXIT EI MU
LIER ABSOLU
TA ES AB INFIR
MITATE TUA
13:13 ET INPOSUIT
ILLI MANUS ET
SUBITO EREC
TA EST ET HONO
RIFICABAT D̄M̄
13:14 RESPONDENS
AUTEM ARCHI
SYNAGOGUS
INDI]G̣NA[NS]
DICEBAT ṬUR

BAE QUOD SAB
BATO C̣ỤṚA
[RET IH̄S S]EX̣
Ḍ[IES SU]Ṇ[T] [I]N
[QUIBUS O]P̣OR
[TET OPERA]ṚỊ
[IN HIS ERGO
UENIENTES
CURAMINI
ET NON DIE
SABBATI
13:15 RESPONDE]ṆS
[AUTEM] ẠḌ ỊḶ
[LUM ·DŌM·
DIXIT HY]PO
[CRITAE U]NUS
[QUISQUE] ỤẸṢ
[TRUM SA]BBA
[TO NON S]OL
[UET BOU]EM
[SUUM A]ỤṬ
[ASINUM A P]ṚAẸ
[SEP]IO ET DU
C̣ỊṬ ẸṬ ADAQUẠṬ

436 SEC·

13:16 HANC AUTEM
CUM SIT FILIA
ABRAHAE QUA¯
ALLIG̣AUIT SA
TAN[AS ECCE]
X̣ỤỊ[II ANNI]
NỌ[N OPORTE]
BAṬ [SOLUI A UI¯]
CUḶ[O HOC DIE]
SAḄ[BATI]
13:17 HAE[C̣ DICENTE]
EO C̣[ONFUN]
DEḄ[ANTUR]
OM[NES QUI]
ADỤ[ERSABA¯]
TUR [EI ET OM]
NIS P̣[OPULUS]
GAU[DEBAT IN]
OM[NIBUS]
MI[RIFICIS]
QUA[E FIEBANT]
AB [ILLO]
13:18 DICEBAT ERG̣O
ĊU̇İ CUI SIMI
LE EST REGNU¯
DĒI· ET CUI AD
SIMILABO IL
13:19 Ḷ[U]D SIMILE EST
[GRANO] SINA
[PIS QUOD ACC]ẸP
[TO HOMO MISIT
IN ORTO SUO
ET CREUIT ET
FACTA EST AR
BOR ET UOLU
CRES CAELI RE
QUIEUERUNT
IN RAMIS EIUS
13:20 ET ITERUM
DIXIT
CUI EST SIMILE
REGNUM DEI
ET CUI ADSI
MILABO
13:21 SIMILE EST]
F̣ẸṚ[MENTO]
QUOD ACCẸ[P]
TUM

437 LUCANUM

MULIER ABSCO¯
DIT IN FARINA
DONEC FERME¯
TARETUR
13:22 ET C~~U~~IRCUIBAT
PER CIUITA
TES ET UICOS
DOCENS HIE
ROSOLYMIS
13:23 DIXIT AUTEM
QUIDAM ILLI
DM̄E SI PAU
CI SUNT QUI
SALUI FUTU
RI SUNT
QUI DIXIT AD IL
13:24 LOS INTRATẸ
PER ANGUS
TUM OSTIUM
QUONIAM M^{U}L
TI DICO UOBIS
QUAERENT
NEC POTERIN̄
INTROIRE

13:25 CUM AUTEM
INTRAUERIT
PATER FAMI
LIAS ET ADCLU
SERIT OSTIUM
ET INCIPIETIS
FORIS STARE
DICENTES ·DM̄E·
APERI NOBIS
ET RESPON
DENS DICET
NESCIO UOS
UNDE SITIS
13:26 TUNC INCIPIE
TIS DICERE
MANDUCA
UIMUS CORA¯
TE ET BIBIMUS
ET IN PLATAEIS
NOSTRIS DO
13:27 CUISTI ET DI
CET UOBIS NES
CIO UOS UNDE
SITIS DISCEDI

438 SEC·

TE A ME OMNES
OPERARI INI
13:28 QUITATIS ILLIC
ERIT FLETUS ET
ET STRIDOR DE¯
TIUM
CUM UIDERITIS
ABRAHAM ET
ISAC ET IACOB
ET OMNES PRO
PHETAS DĒI· IN
TROEUNTES
IN REGNO DĒI·
UOS AUTEM
PROICI FORIS
13:29 ET UENIENT
AB ORIENTE
ET OCCIDEN
TE ET AB AQUI
LONE ET AUS
TRO ET DISCU¯
BENT IN REG
13:30 NO DĒI· ET EC
CE SUNT NO
UISSIMI QUI
ERUNT PRIMỊ
ET SUNT PRIMI
QUI FUERUN̄
NOUISSIMI
13:31 EADEM DIE AC
CESSERUNT
QUIDAM PHA
RISAEORUM
DICENTES ILLI
DISCEDE ET UA
DE HINC QUO
NIAM HERO
DES UULT TE
13:32 OCCIDERE IP
SE AUTEM DI
XIT EIS EUN
TES INDICATE
UULPI HUIC
ECCE EICIO DÆ
MONIA ET SA
NITATES PER
FICIO HODIE
ET CRAS ET DIE

439 LUCANUM

TERTIA CONSU‾
13:33 MOR SED OPOR
TET ME HODIE
ET CRAS ET IN FU^{TU}
RUM
QUONIAM NO‾
OPORTET PRO
PHETAM PERI
RE EXTRA HIE
RUSALEM
13:34 HIERUSALEM
HIERUSALEM
QUAE OCCIDIS
PROPHETAS
ET LAPIDAS EOS
QUI MISSI SUNT
AT TE SAEPIUS
UOLUI CON
GREGARE FILI
OS TUOS QUEM
ADMODUM
GALLINA NI
DUM SUUM
SUB ALAS SUAS
ET NOLUISTIS

13:35 ECCE RELIN
QUITUR UO
BIS DOMUS UES
TRA DESERTA
DICO ENIM UO
BIS QUIA NON
UIDEBITIS ME
DONEC UENI
AT DIES QUAN
DO DICATIS BE
NEDICTUS QUI
UENIT IN NO
MINE ·DM̄I·
✠ 14:1 ET FACTUM EST
CUM INTRAS
SET IN DOMU‾
CUIUSDAM
PRINCIPIS PHA
RISAEORUM
SABBATO MAN
DUCARE PA
NEM ET IBI
ERANT OBSER
UANTES ILLU‾

440 SEC·

14:2 ET ECCE HOMO
QUIDAM HY
DROPICUS ERAT
ANTE ILLUM
14:3 ET RESPONDENS
DIXIT ·IH̄S· ȦḊ
L̇ĖĠİṠ AD LEGIS
DOCTORES ET
PHARISAEOS
SI LICET SAB
BATIS CURA
14:4 RE AD ILLI TA
CUERUNT IP
SE ITAQUE AD
PREHENDENS
MANUM IL
LIUS CURATU¯
EUM DIMISIT
14:5 ET DIXIT ɨ AD
ILLOS CUIUS
UESTRUM ASI
NUS AUT BOS
SI CECIDERIT
IN PUTEUM

domineca tertia

SABBATO NON
CONTINUO
EXTRAHET IL
LUM IN DIE
14:6 SABBATI ET NO¯
POTERANT EI
RESPONDERE
AD HAEC
14:7 DICEBAT AUTE¯
ET AD INUITA
TOS PARABO
LAM DENO
TANS EOS QUO
MODO PRI
MOS DISCU
BITOS ELIGE
RENT DICENS
AD EOS
14:8 CUM INUITA
TUS FUERIT
ALIQUIS AD
NUPTIAS NO¯
DISCUMBAT
IN PRIMO LO

441 LUCANUM

CO NE FORTE
HONOṚATIOR
TE ALIQUIS ^{SIT} IN
14:9 UITATUS ET
UENIENS QUI
TE ET ILLUM
INUITAUIT
DICAT TIBI DA
HUIC LOCUM
ET TUNC INCI
PIES CUM CO⁻̇
ḌỤSIONE NO
BISSIMUM
LOCUM DETI
NERE
14:10 ṢED CUM INUI
TATUS FUERIS
ỤADE ET DIS
[CU]ṂBE IN
[NOU]ISṢIMO
[LOCO] ỤT CUM
UENERIT QUI
TE Q̶U̇İ INUI
TAUIT DICAT

AMICE ACCE
DE SUPERIUS
TUNC ERIT
GLORIA TIBI
C[O]RAM DIS
C[U]MBENTI
14:11 Ḅ[US] QUONI
[AM O]ṂNIS
[QUI EXA]ḶṬAT
[SE HU]MI
LI[ABITUR] ET
QU[I S]E Ḥ[U]ṂI
LIABERIT EXAL
TABIṬUR
14:12 DICEBAT AU
ṬEM ET INUI
TATORI CUM
FACIES PRAN
DIUM ET CE
ṆẠM NOLI IN
UIṬARE AMI
COS NEQUE
FRATRES TU
OS SED NEC UI

442 SEC·

CINOS NEC DI
UIT[ES NE FO]R
ṬẸ [ET IPSI TE]
IṆ[U]ỊTEṆ[T]
EṬ FIAT RE[D]
ḌỊṬỊỌ TIḄỊ
14:13 SẸ[D] C̣UM [FACI]
ES P[R]A[NDIUM IN]
ỤỊṬẠ P̣[AUPE]
ṚẸṢ D[EBI]
ḶẸṢ [CLOD]ỌṢ
14:14 E[T] [CAEC]OS [ET] BEA
T[U]S [ER]IS [QUIA]
Ṇ[ON HABENT]
U[NDE] ṚẸḌ[DE]
R[E] T[I]B[I] [RED]
DET[U]R ẸṆỊ[¯]
TỊḄ[I] ỊN [RESUR]
ṚẸC̣Ṭ[IONE
Ị[US]ṬỌ[RUM]
14:15 AU[DIE]N[S AU]
TẸṂ QỤ[I]DAM
EX DỊṢ[CUM]
BEṆṬIBUS

HAEC DIXIT IL
L[I BEATU]Ṣ Q̣UI
[MANDUCAUE
RIT P̣ẠNEṂ
[I]Ṇ [R]ẸGNỌ [D̅I̅·
14:16 Q]ỤỊ ḌIXIṬ
[HO]ṂỌ QỤỊDẠ[M]
F̣ẸC̣ỊT C̣ẸṆẠ[M]
ṂẠG̣ṆẠ[M ET]
ỊNUITA^{ỤIT} MU[L]
14:17 TOS ET MISI[T]
SERỤỤM [SU]
ỤM HOṚẠ C̣[E]
[NAE] DIC[E]Ṛ[E]
[INU]ỊTATIS ỤẸ
[NITE QUONI]
AM ỌṂṆỊẠ
P̣ṚẠẸP̣ẠṚẠ
14:18 [TA] ṢỤ[NT ET COE]
P̣Ẹ[RUNT OM]
ṆẸ[S SIMUL
EXCUSARE]
ṢE [PR]ỊOR
AIT UI[LL]AM

443 LUCANUM

EMI ET NECES
SE ḤẠ[BEO EXI]
Ṛ[E ET UIDERE
ILLAM ROGO
TE HABE ME
EXCUSATUM
14:19 ET ALIUS DIXIT]
I]UGẠ [BOUUM
C]ONPARAỤ[I]
ṖARIA QUIN
Q̣UE ET UADỌ
[EXPERI]ṂE[N
TUM] ACCI[PE
RE I]ḶḶỌ[R]Ụ[M
ET] ṖṚỌṖ[TER
HOC UENIRE
NON POSSUM
14:20 ET ALIUS D]IXIT
[UXOREM DU
XI ET NON POS
SUM UENI
14:21 RE ET REUER
SUS SERUUS
RENUN]TIA

UIT DM̄O· SUO
ḤẠẸ[C TU]ṆC
[IRATUS PAT]ẸR
[FAMILIAS] ḌỊ
[XIT SERUO
SUO EXI ALA
CRITER IN PLA
TEAS ET UICOS
CIUITATIS ET
PAUPERES
ET DEBILES ET
CAECOS ET CLO
DOS INTRO
DUC HOC
14:22 ET AIT SERUUS
DOMINO SUO
DOMI
NE FACTUM
EST SICUT PRAE
CEPISTI
ET ADHUC LO
14:23 CUTUS E]ṢT [ET
DIXIT DM̄S
SERU]Ọ SỤO ẸX̣I

444 SEC·

EXI CIRCA UIA
S ET SAEP̣ES ET
COG̣Ẹ [INTR]A
RẸ [QUOSCU]Ṃ
Q̣[UE INUE]NẸ
Ṛ[IS UT IMPLEA]
Ṭ[UR DOMUS]
14:24 Ṃ[EA DICO]
E[NIM UOBIS]
Q̣[UONIAM]
Ṇ[ULLUS UIRO]
R[UM ILLOR]ỤṂ
Q[UI UOCAT]I
SỤ[NT ET NO]N
Ụ[ENERUNT]
G̣[USTABUNT]
D[E CENA MEA]
14:25 COṂ[ITABATUR]
AỤ[TEM CU]Ṃ
EỌ T[URBA ET]
CỌṆỤẸṚṢỤS
D[I]X̣IT A[D] ILLOS
14:26 SI QUIṢ ỤENIT
AD ME ET NO¯
ODIT PATREM
SUỤM AUT
Ṃ[ATREM] AUT
[UXOREM A]UT
[FILIOS AUT FRA
TRES ET SORO
RES INSUPER
ET ANIM]AṂ
[S]UAM NON
POTEST MEU[S]
DISṖCIPULUṢ
14:27 ESSE ET QUI
NON PORTA[T]
CRUCEM SỤ
AM ET UEN[I]Ṭ
POST ME NỌ[¯]
POTEST DISCI
PULUS MEUS
ESSE
14:28 QUIS EX̣ UEṢ
TṚUM UOLẸṆṢ
ṬURREM AE
DIFICARE NO¯
NE PRIUS SE

445 LUCANUM

DENS COMPU
TAUIT INPEN
DIA SI HABE
AT QUAE OPUS
SUNT AD CON
SUMMAN
DUM EAM
14:29 NE SI POSITO
FUNDAMEN
TO NON UALU
ERIT CONSUˉ
MARE OM
NES QUI UI
14:30 DENT DICEN
HIC HOMO
COEPIT AEDI
FICARE NEC
UALUIT CON
SUMMARE
14:31 AUT QUIS REX
ITURUS COM
MITTERE
CUM ALIO RE
GE BELLUM

NONNE SE
DENS PRIUS
COGITAUIT
SI POTENS EST
CUM DECEM
MILIBUS OB
UIARE EI QUI
CUM UIGIN
TI MILIBUS
UENTURUS
EST AD ILLUM
14:32 ALIOQUIN DUˉ
ADHUC CUM
LONGE EST LE
GATIONEM
MITTENS RO
GAT PACEM
14:33 SIC ERGO OM
NIS EX UOBIS
QUI NON RE
NUNTIAT OM
NIBUS FACUL
TATIBUS SU
IS NON POTEST

446 SEC·

ESSE MEUS
DISCIPULUS
14:34 BONUM EST SAL
QUOD SI ET SAL
INFATUATUM
FUERIT IN QUO
14:35 CONDIETUR NEQUE IN TERRA NE
QUE IN STER
CORE UTILE
EST NISI UT FO
RIS PROICIA
TUR
☧ QUI HABET AU
RES AUDIEN
15:1 DI AUDIAT E
quarta RANT AUTEM
ACCEDENTES
AD EUM OM
NES PUBLICA
NI ET PECCA
TORES AUDI
15:2 RE EUM ET MUR
MURATI SUN
PHARISAEI
ET SCRIBAE
DICENTES QUA
RE HIC PECCA
TORES RECI
PIT ET UESCI
TUR CUM EIS
15:3 DIXIT AUTEM
AD EOS PARA
BOLAM HANC
DICENS
15:4 QUIS EX UESTRIS
HOMO QUI HA
BET OUES CEN
TUM ET PE
RIERIT UNA
EX EIS NON
NE RELINQUIT
XCUIIII IN DE
SERTO ET UA
DIT AD ILLAM
QUAE PERIT
QUAERENS
DONEC INU[E]
NIAT ILLAM
15:5 ET CUM INUE

H XXIX

447 LUCANUM

NERIT INPO
NIɆT ILLA^{M} SUPER
ỤMEROS SU
OS GAUDENS
15:6 ẸṬ C̣UM UẸṆẸ
ṚIṬ DỌMUM
C̣ONUOCẠT
AMICOS EṬ ỤI
CINOS DICENS
ỊLLIS CONGRA
ṬULAMINI MI
HI QUONIAM
Ị[N]UENI OUE¯
Ṃ[EA]Ṃ Q̣ỤAE
P̣ẸṚỊẸṚẠṬ
15:7 Ḍ[I]CO UOḄỊS [Q]UỌ
ṆIAM ṢIC̣ G̣ẠỤ
DIUM ERIT ỊN
CAELO ṢUPER
UNUM [PEC]
CATOṚ[EM PAE]
ṆITEṆṬ[IA]M
AG̣ENṬEM
QUAM SUPER
XCUIIII· IUS
TOS QUIḄUS
NON EST NE
C̣ESSARIA PAE
NITENTIA
15:8 AUT QUAE MU
LIER HABENS
DRAC̣ḤMAS
X ET SI PERDE
DERIT UNAM
EX ILLIS NON
NE ACCENDIT
LUCERNAM
ET SCOPIS COM
MUNDAT ḌO
MUM ET QUǼ
RIT ḌILỊG̣EN
TER QUOẠḌUS
QUE INUẸNI
15:9 AT ET CUM IṆ
UENERIT CO¯
UOCAT AMI
CAS SUAS ET UI
CINAS DICENS

448 SEC·

CONGRATULA
MINI MIHI
QUONIAM IN
UENI DRAC
MAN QUAM
PERDIDERAM
15:10 SIC DICO UO
BIS GAUDIUM
ERIT CORAM
ANGELOS DĒI
SUPER UNUM
PECCATOREM
PAENITENTI
AM AGENTE¯
15:11 DIXIT ERGO
☩ HOMO QUIDAM
HABEBAT DU
15:12 OS FILIOS ET
DIXIT ILLI ADU
LESCENTIOR
PATER DA MI
HI PORTIONE¯
SUBSTANTIAE
QUAE ME CO¯

TINGIT ET DI
UISIT ILLIS SUB
TANTIAM
15:13 ET NON POST
MULTOS DIES
COLLECTIS OM
NIBUS ADU
LESCENTIOR
FILIUS PERE
GRE PROFEC
TUS EST IN RE
GIONEM LON
GINQUAM
ET IBI DISSIPA
UIT SUBSTAN
TIAM SUAM
UIUENS LUXU
RIOSE
15:14 CUMQUE CON
SUMPSISSET
OMNIA FACTA
EST FAMIS UA
LIDA PER RE
GIONEM ILLA¯

449 LUCANUM

ET IPSE COEPIT
15:15 EGERI ET ABIIT
ET CONIUN
XIT SE UNI DE
MUNICIPIB
REGIONIS IL
LIUS QUI MISIT
ILLUM IN AGRO
SUO UT PASCE
RET PORCOS
15:16 ET CUPIEBAT
SATURARE
UENTREM
SUUM DE SILI
QUIS QUAS POR
CI EDEBANT
NEC QUISQUA¯
15:17 DABAT ILLI IN
SE AUTEM CO¯
ỤERSUS DIXIT
QUANTI MER
CENNARII
PATRIS MEI
ABUNDANT

PANE EGO AU
TEM HIC FAME
15:18 PEREO SUR
GENS IBO AD
P̣ATREM ME
UM ET DICAM
ILLI PATER PEC
CAUI IN CAE
LUM ET CORA¯
15:19 TE IAM NON
SUM DIGNUS
UOCARI FILI
US TUUS FAC
ME SICUT U
NUM EX MER
CENNARIIS
15:20 TUIS ET SUR
GENS UENIT
USQUE AD PA
TREM SUUM
CUMQUE AD
HUC LONGE
ESSET UIDIT
ILLUM PATER

450 SEC·

PATER IPSIUS
ET ṂISERỊC̣OR
DIA ṂOṬ[US]
ESṬ [E]Ṭ PRO[CUR]
R[EN]Ṣ [INCU]
ḄỤỊṬ ṢỤP̣ẸṚ
C̣ỌḶḶỤM ỊP̣ṢỊ
US ẸṬ [OSCULA]
ṬỤṢ [EST EUM]
15:21 DIXIT AỤ[TEM]
ỊḶḶỊ F̣[ILIUS PA]
TẸṚ P̣Ẹ[CC]ẠUỊ
IṆ C̣ẠẸḶỤṂ
EṬ [CORA]Ṃ [TE]
IAṂ Ṇ[ON SUM]
DIG̣ṆỤṢ [UO]
CẠ[RI FILIUS TU]
15:22 U[S] DỊXỊṬ
AỤṬẸṂ P̣Ạ[TER]
AḌ P̣ỤẸṚ[OS] ṢỤ
OS C̣ẸḶẸṚỊỤṢ
PRỌF̣[ERTE]
STOLAM [PRIO]
REM ET INDU
ITE ILLUM ET
DATE ẠṆỤḶỤṂ
ỊṆ Ṃ[ANU] ỊḶLI
[US ET C]ẠḶC̣ỊA
[MEN]TA ỊṆ P̣E
15:23 ḌỊḄỤ[S EIUS] E[T]
ADDUCỊṬẸ ỤỊ
[TULUM] ỊḶḶUM
SAGIṆẠṬUM
ẸṬ OCCIDITE
ẸṬ M[ANDUCE]
MỤṢ EṬ [AEPU]
15:24 ḶẸMUṚ [Q]ỤỌ
N[I]AM HIC̣ F[I]Ḷ[I]
US MEUS MỌR
TUUS F̣UERAT
ET REUIXIT [P]E
R[I]EṚAT EṬ [IN]
UEṆṬU[S EST]
ET COEPẸṚỤ[NT]
AẸP̣[U]LẠṚ[E]
15:25 ERAT [A]Ụ[TEM]
FILIỤ[S] ILL[I]ỤṢ
SENIOR IṆ A

451 LUCANUM

GRO ET C̣UM
UENỊRET AD
P̣Ṛ[OPINQUA]
ỤỊṬ ḌỌṂỤỊ [ET]
ẠỤḌỊỊṬ Ṣ[YM
PH]ỌṆ[IAS] ẸṬ
15:26 C̣ḤỌ[RU]M ẸṬ
[UOCA]ỤỊṬ U[NU¯
DE PUERIS ET
INT]ERRỌG̣[A
UIT QU]ỊḌṆA[M]
ẸS[SE]ṆṬ ḤẠẸ[C
15:27 QUI AI]Ṭ ỊḶḶỊ Q̣ỤỌ
[NIAM] F̣RATE[R]
ṬỤỤṢ ỤENỊT
ẸṬ OCCIḌIT P̣Ạ
Ṭ[ER] ṬỤUS IS UỊ
ṬỤḶỤṂ ỊḶLUM
ṢẠG̣ỊṆẠṬỤM
Q̣ỤONIAM ỊN
[CO]ḶUMẸ ILLU[¯
15:28 RECEP]ỊṬ ỊRA
ṬỤS ẸSṬ [AU]TEM
EṬ ṆỌḶỤỊṬ ỊN

TRARE
EG̣[RE]SSUS AỤ
[TE]Ṃ P̣ẠṬẸṚ ỊḶ
[LIU]S COẸ[PIT
ROG]AṚẸ ẸỤ¯
15:29 [IPSE A]ỤṬẸṂ
[RE]ṢP̣ỌṆḌẸṆṢ
Ạ[IT PATRI SU]O
[ECCE TOT A]Ṇ
[NIS SERUIO
TIBI ET NUM
QUAM] MẠN
[DATUM] TỤ
[UM PRA]ETER
ỊBỊ [E]Ṭ ṆỤṂ
Q̣ỤẠṂ Ḍ[EDIS]
ṬỊ ṂỊḤ[I HA]E
DỤM ỤṬ CỤṂ
AMỊC̣ỊS ṂE
ỊS ẠẸP̣ỤḶẠṚER
15:30 CỤM AỤṬẸṂ
F̣ILIUS TUUS
ḤỊC̣ QỤỊ COMẸ
DIT OMNEM

452 SEC·

FACULTATEM
SUAM UIUENS
CUM FORNI
CARIIS UENIT
ET OCCIDISTI
UITULUM ILLỤ¯
SAGINATUM
15:31 IPSE AUTEM
DIXIT ILLI TU
MECUM FU
ISTI SEMPER
ET ES ET OM
NIA MEA TUA
15:32 SUN[T] AEPU
LARI AUTEM
NOS OPORTE
BAT ET GAUDE
RE QUONIAM
HIC FRATER
TUUS MORTU
US FUERAT ET
REUIXIT PE
RIERAT ET IN
UENTUS EST

16:1 DICEBAT AU
TEM ET AD DIS
CIPỤLOS SUOS
☩ HOMO QUIDAM
ERAT DIUES
QUI HABEBAT
UILICUM ET
HIC DIFFAMA
TUS FUERAT
APUT ILLUM
TANQUAM DIS
SIPARET BO
NA IPSIUS
16:2 ET UOCABIT EU¯
DOMINUS SU
US ET AIT ILLI
QUID HOC AU
DIO DE TE RED
DE RATIONE¯
UILICATIONIS
TUAE IAM ENI¯
NON POTERIS
AMPLIUS AC
TUM MEUM

453 LUCANUM

ADMINISTRA
16:3 RE DIXIT
AUṬ[E]Ṃ ILLE
UILICUS IN
TRA SE QUID FA
CIAM QUONI
AM DOMINUS
MEUS AUFE
RET UILICATIO
NE^{M} MEAM
A ME FODERE
NON UALEO
MENDICARE
CONFUNDOR
16:4 COGNOUI QUID
FACIAM UT CU¯
AMOTUȮS ḞUE
RO DE UILICA
TIONE RECI
PIANT ME IN
DOMUS SUAS
16:5 ET CONUOCATO
UNOQUOQUE
EX DEBITORI

BUS ·DM̄I· SUI
DICEBAT PRI
ORI QUANTU¯
DEBES DOMI
16:6 NỌ MEO QỤI
DIXIT CẸN[T]U¯
ỤẠṬOS Ọ[LEI D]I
XIṬ AUT[EM]
ILLI ACCI[PE C]AU
TIONEṂ [TU]
AM ET S[ED]ENS
CELER[IUS] SCRI
BE QU[INQU]A
GINTẠ
16:7 DEINDE [ALI]I
DIXIT TU [A]U
TEM QUAṆ
TUM DEBES
DM̄O MEO
QUI DIXIT ÇEN
TUM COṚOS
ṬRITICI DIXIT
AUṬẸM ET
HUIC ACCIPE

454 SEC·

CAUTIONEM
TUẠṂ [ET SCRI]
BẸ [OCTOGIN]
16:8 TẠ [ET] ḶẠỤḌ[AUIT]
DM̄[S UILICU‾]
I[NIQUIATIS
QUIA PRUDE‾]
T[ER FECERIT]
DI[XIT AUTEM]
A[D DISCIPUL]O[S]
S[UOS D]ICO UO
[BIS] [FI]LI HU
[IUS S]ẸCỤḶỊ
P̣[RUDE]ṆṬỊỌ
[RES SU]NT SU
[PER] F̣IḶỊỌṢ ḶỤ
[CIS I]N G̣ENTẸ
ḤẠC
16:9 ET [EGO DICO UO]
B[IS FACITE UO]
B[IS AMICOS]
DE [INIQUO]
MAṂ[ONA]
UT CUM ḌEFE

CERIT UOBIS
R[ECIPI]AṆṬ
[UOS IN AE]ṬER
[N]A [TABE]ṚṆẠ
[CULA
16:10 QUI FIDE]ḶỊṢ
Ẹ[S]T [I]N MỊṆỊ
M[O] ẸṬ [IN MUL]
ṬỌ [FIDELIS EST]
ET QUI IN MINI]
[M]O IN[IQUUS
E]ṢṬ [ET IN MAG
NO [INIQUUS
ES]T
16:11 [SI E]RGO Ị[N INI]
QUO Ṃ[AMO
NA] FID[ELES
NO]N F̣[UISTIS
QUOD UOBISCU‾
EST QUIS DABIT
UOBIS ET SI IN
ALIENO FIDE
LES NON FU]
ỊṢṬỊṢ QỤỌḌ

455 LUCANUM

UESTRUM EST
QUIS ÇṚẸ[D]ẸT
UỌḄ[IS]
16:13 NẸMỌ [PO]ṬẸṢ[T]
ṢẸṚỤ[US DUO]
ḄỤS ḌỌM[INIS
SERUIRE AUT]
ẸṆỊṂ UṆ[UM
ODI]EṬ [ET ALI
UM DILIGET]
ẠỤṬ ỤNỤṂ
[P]ẠṬỊẸṬUṚ ẸṬ
ẠḶỊỤṂ ÇỌ[N
TEM]NET N[ON]
ṔỌṬẸSTIS D[Ē̄O]
Ṣ[ERUI]ṚE EṬ
[MAM]ONẠ[E
16:14 HAEC O]ṂṆ[IA
CUM AUDIS
SENT PHARI
SAEI QUI E
RANT AMA
TORES] P̣ẸÇỤ
ṆỊẠẸ ỊṆṚỊDẸ

BANT EUM
16:15 ET ḌỊX̣ỊṬ [EIS
UOS ESTIS
QUI IUSTIFI
CATIS UOS CO
RAM HOMI
NIBUS D̄S̄ AU
TEM SCIT CO]R
[D]Ạ ỤẸ[STRA
QUONIAM
QUOD APUT]
Ḥ̣OM[INES SU]B
LIME [EST AB]O
MINẠ[TIO E]ṢT
ẠNTE CO[NS]
PECTUM ḌĒ̄Ị[·]
16:16 [L]EX ET PRỌ[PH]Æ
Ṭ[A]E USQUE
Ạ[D I]OHAN[NE]Ṃ
EX̣ QỤỌ [RE]G̣
NỤM [DĒI E]ỤA⁻
G̣ẸL[I]ẒẠNTUR
ẸṬ ỌṂNES IN
ILLUM FESTI

456 SEC·

16:17 NANT FACILI
US EST AUTEM
CAẸ[L]UM ET
TERRAM TṚ[A¯]
SỊRE QUA[M]
DE LEGE U[N]U[¯]
Ạ P[I]CEM EX
CEDERE
16:18 OMNỊS QUI DỊ
[M]ỊTṬIT UXO
REM ṢUAM
ET ṆUBIT ALI
AṂ [A]ḌULTE
R[I]ỤM FACIT
ET [Q]ỤIT Ḋİ
DIMISSAM A MA
RITO DUCIT
MOECATUR
16:19 HOMO QUIDAM
[do]menica secunda ERAT DIUES
QUI UESTI^{E}BA
TUR PURPU
RAM ET BYS
SUM ET AE
PULABANTUR
COTIDIE SPLE¯
DIDE
16:20 PAUPER AUTE¯
QUIDAM NO
MINE LAZA
RUS IACEBAT
AD IANUAM
DIUITIS ILLI
US ULCERI
BUS PLENUS
16:21 ET CUPIEBAT
SATIARI DẸ
MICIS QUAE
CADEBANT
DE MENSA
DIUITIS SED ET
CẠNES UENI
ENTES LAM
BẸḶANT UUL
NERA EIUS
16:22 FACTUM EST AU
TEM UT MO
RERETUR PAU

457 LUCANUM

PER ET PORTA
RETUR AB AN
GELIS IN SINU
ABRAHAE
MORTUUS EST
AUTEM ET DI
UES ET SEPUL
TUS EST APUT
INFEROS~~E~~
16:23 ET DE INFERNO
ELEUANS OCU
LOS SUOS CUM
ESSET IN TOR
MENTIS UIDET
ABRAHAM
A LONGE ET LA
ZARUM IN
SIN~~E~~U EIUS
16:24 ET IPSE EXCLA
MANS DIXIT
PATER ABRA
HAM MISE
RERE MIHI
ET MITTE LA

ZARUM UT
INTINGAT EX
TREMUM
DIGITI SUI IN
AQUAM ET
REFRIGERET
LINGUAM
MEAM QUO
NIAM CRU
CIOR IN HAC
16:25 FLAMMA DI
XIT AUTE[M]
ILLI ABRAḤẠ¯
FILI MEMOR
R ESTO~~TEM~~
QUONIAM RECE
PISTI BONA
IN UITA TUA
ET LAZARUS
SIMILITER
MALA
NUNC AUTEM
HIC CONSO
LATUR TU AU

458 SEC·

TEM CRUC̣IA
16:26 RIṢ [ET] ṢỤP̣ẸṚ
OMṆ[IBUS IS]
TIṢ ỊṆṬẸṚ ṆO[S]
ET [UOS HIAT]ỤS
ṬẸ[RRAE MAG]
NỤṢ [CONFIR]
Ṃ[ATUS] ẸṢṬ ỤṬ
ḤỊ Q̣[UI UE]NI
ỤṆṬ [ḤOC] ṬṚẠ¯
Ṣ[IRE NON P]ỌṢ
[SINT] Ạ[D UOS]
Ṇ[EQ]UE [IN]DE
ḤỌC̣ [T]ṚẠṆṢ
MẸẠRE
16:27 DI[X]IT AUTEṂ
IḶLI ROGO EṚ
GO TẸ PATEṚ
ỤṬ MIṬTAṢ IN
ḌỌṂỤṂ P̣Ạ
16:28 ṬṚỊṢ [MEI] ḤẠ
BE[O EN]I[M]
QUI[NQUE] FRA
TRES ỤT TESTI
FICETUR ILLIS
N[E] Ẹ[T IP]ṢỊ UE
Ṇ[IANT IN] ḤUNC
LỌC̣[UM] C̣RU
C̣IA[TUS]
16:29 DIXIT ẠỤṬẸṂ IḶ
[LI] HAḄṚẠ[H]ẠM
ḤAḄẸṆṬ Ṃ[O]Ỵ
[S]Ẹ[N] ẸT P̣[R]OPḤ[E]
TAṢ A[U]DIAN[T]
16:30 ILLOṢ Q̣UỊ D[I]XỊ[T]
NON PATEṚ
ABRAHAM Ṣ[ED]
SI QUIṢ ẸX̣ MỌ[R]
TUIS SỤ[RRE]
XERIT P̣Ạ[ENI]
TENTIAM [A]
GENT
16:31 DIXIT AUTEṂ
ILLI SI MOYṢẸ[¯]
ET PROPḤ[ETAS]
NON AU[DIU]Ṇ[T]
ṆEC̣ SỊ Q̣Ụ[IS]
EX MORTUIS

459

LUCANUM

AD ILLOS IERIT
CREDẸNT
17:1 DIXIṬ AUTEṂ
AD DISCIPỤLOṢ
ṢỤỌ[S] DỊF̣F̣ỊC̣Ị
ḶẸ ESṬ ỤṬ NON
ỤẸṆỊẠṆṬ SC̣Ạˉ
ḌAḶA UẸṚỤM
ṬẠM[EM U]ẠẸ
ỊḶḶỊ PẸR [QUE]M
17:2 ỤẸṆỊỤṆṬ UṬỊ
[LIU]S ESṬ AUTEˉ
[ILLI] ṆẸ ṆẠSC̣Ẹ
ṚẸṬỤṚ ẠUT
[L]Ạ[PIS M]ỌLAṚỊṢ
[I]ṆP̣ỌṢITUS
F̣ỤỊṢṢẸṬ COLLO
ỊḶḶỊỤṢ [E]T PRO
[I]ẸC̣ṬỤṢ ESSET
[I]Ṇ MẠREM
[QU]Ạ[M] UT SCAˉ
Ḍ[ALIZ]ẸT UNUˉ
ḌE P̣ỤSILLIS
ISTIS

17:3 ATTENDITE UO
BIS ṢỊ P̣ẸC̣C̣ẠỤE
[RIT FRATER] T[U]
[US CORRIPE] IL
LUM [ET SI PAE]
[NITENTIAM]
[EGERIT] RẸMỊṬ
17:4 TE ỊḶḶỊ ẸṬ ṢỊ ṢẸP̣
ṬỊẸṆṢ [PEC]C̣Ạ
ỤE[RIT IN D]ỊẸ
ỊN TẸ ẸṬ ṢẸP̣Ṭ[I]
ẸṢ C̣ỌṆỤẸ[R]
SU[S] F̣ỤẸṚ[IT AT]
TE DIC̣EN[S] ẠG̣Ọ
P̣ẠENỊTẸṆṬỊẠˉ
RẸMITTE IḶḶỊ
17:5 ẸT DIXERUṆṬ
APOSTOLI DM̄O·
A[UG]E NOBIS
17:6 FIDEṂ QUIB·
ILLẸ ḌỊX̣ỊṬ S[I] ḤA
BUẸṚỊṬ[IS F]Ị
DEM ṬẠNQUAˉ
GRANUM SI

460 SEC·

NAPIS DICETIS
MURO HỤIC
ERADICARE
ET PLANTARE
IN MARE ET
ỌBAUDISṢET
UOBIS
17:7 QUIS AUTEM UES
TRUM HABENS
SEṚUUM ARA‾
TEM AUT PAS
CENTEM OUES
QUI REGRES
SO EO DE AGRO
STATIM DICET
ILLI TRANSI ET
17:8 RECUMBE SED
DICET ILLI PRǢ
PARƗA MIHI ⳨
QUOD CENEM
ET SUCCINC
TUS MINISTRA
MIHI DONEC
MANDUCEM

ET BIBAM ET
POSTEA TU MA‾
DUCABIS ET
17:9 BIBET NUM
QUID AGET GRA
TIAS SERUO
QUONIAM FE
CIT QUAE PRAE
CEPTA SUNT
17:10 EỊ : SIC ET
UOS CUM FECE
RITIS QUAE
PRAECEPTA
SUNT DICITIS
SERUI INUTI
LES SUMUS
FACERE FECI
MUS
17:11 ET FACTUM EST
DUM IRET IN
HIERUSALEM
ET IPSE TRAN
SIEBAT PER
MEDIAM SA

461 LUCANUM

MARIAM ET GA
LILAEAM ET IE
17:12 RICHO INGRE
DIENS AUTEM
IN QUENDAM
UICUM ET EC
CE DECEM UI
RI LEPROSI S
TETERUNT
17:13 A LONGE ET LE
UAUERUNT
UOCEM SUAM
DICENTES IH̄U·
MAGISTER
MISERERE NO
17:14 BIS ET CUM
AUDISSET IL
LOS DIXIT ILLIS
EUNTES OSTE¯
DITE UOS SACER
DOTIBUS
ET FACTUM EST
DUM IRENT
EMUNDATI

17:15 SUNT UNUS
AUṬEM EX E
Ị[S] CUM ỤIDỊS
SẸṬ QUIA Ṣ[AN]US
EST REUẸṚ
SUS EST CUM
UOCE MAG
NẠ HỌNORI
FICANS ·D̄M̄·
17:16 ET PROÇIDIT
IN FAC[I]EṂ
AḌ P̣ẸDEṢ [IL]LI
US GRATI[AS]
AGENS ET Ị[P]
SE ERAT SAMA
RITES
17:17 RESPONDENS
AUTEM ·IH̄S·
DIXIT HI DE
CEM MUNDA
TI SUNT NO
UEM UBI SUN
17:18 EX HIS NOṆ
EST INUEN

462 SEC·

TUS QUI REUER
SUS Ḥ[ONORE]Ṃ
ḌA[RET] Ḍ[ĒO NI]
Ṣ[I HIC] ẠḶỊẸ[NIGE]
17:19 NẠ ET DIXI[T] ỊḶ
ḶỊ SURGE ẸṬ
ỤADE QUONỊẠ[¯
F]IDE[S T]ỤẠ [TE] SAL
UUM FECIṬ
17:20 INTEṚṚỌGATỤ[S]
AỤ[T]EṂ A PHA
RỊ[S]ẠEIS Q̣[U]ẠN
[DO] ỤENṬỤ[R]Ụ[¯
ESSE]T ṚẸG̣ṆỤṂ
ḌĒỊ DIXIT E[I]Ṣ
ṆON U[E]ṆỊ[T]
ṚEGNUM ḌĒỊ
OBSER[U]AṬỊO
17:21 ṆE SED NEC̣
[DI]CENT ECCE
ḤIC AUT ECC̣[E]
ỊḶ[LIC] ECC̣[E ENI¯]
REG̣NUM DĒỊ·
INTRA UOS EST

17:22 DIXIT AUTEM
AD DISCỊPULOS
SUOS UENIEN
DIES UT CONCU
PISCATIS UIDE
ṚE UNUM DI
EM FILII HOMI
Ṇ[I]S [E]T NON UIDẸ
17:23 [BITI]Ṣ EṬ DICẸN
UOBIS ECCE
ḤIC AUT EC̣C̣Ẹ
ILLIC̣ NOLITE
IRE NEC SEQUI
17:24 [SIC]ỤT ENIM FUḶ
G̣ỤḶ CORUS
CANS SỊC̣ ERIT
FILIUS HOMI
17:25 NIS PRIUS ẠU
TEM OPORTET
Ị[L]LUM MULTA
PATI ET ꝐREPRO
[B]ARI A GENE
RATIOṆẸ HAC
17:26 ET SIC[UT] ḤACTU¯

Ị [XXX]

463 LUCANUM

EST IN DIEBUS
NOE SIC̣ ERIT
ET IN DIEBUS
F̣ILI ḤOMINIS
17:27 EDEBANT BI
BẸBANT NUBẸ
ḄANT NUBẸBẠ[¯]
TUR USQUE IN
ḌIEM QỤỌ ỊṆ
ṬRỌỊRẸ[T] ṆỌẸ
[I]N ARCAM ET
UENIT DILU
BIUM ET PER
DIDIT OMNEṢ
17:28 SIMILITER ET
F̣ACTUM EST
ẸṬ IN DIEBUS
ḶỌṬ ẸḌEBANT
ḄỊBEBANT EME
ḄANT ỤẸ[NDE]
BA[N]Ṭ PLANTA
BANṬ AEDỊFỊ
17:29 CA[BA]ṆṬ QUA
DIE [EXIIT LO]

T A SODOMIS
P̣Ḷ[UIT] IGNEM
ḌẸ C̣ẠẸḶỌ ẸṬ P̣ẸR
D[ID]ỊṬ OṂ[N]ES
17:30 SIMILITER E
ṚỊṬ IN DIE QUA
FILIUS HOM[I]
N[IS] ṚEUELA
ḄỊṬUR
17:31 IN ILLẠ ḤORA
QUI Ẹ[R]ỊṬ SU
P̣[ER] ṬEC[T]ỤM
[ET U]ẠSA Ị[LL]ỊUS
ỊṆ Ḍ[O]ṂỌ N[O]¯
DESCENDAṬ
[T]ỌḶ[L]ẸRE EA
Ẹ[T] QUI IN AGRO
SIṂILITER
NON REUEṚ
[T]ẠṬUR RETRỌ
17:32 ṂẸṂORES
[E]ṢTOTE UXO
RIS LOT
17:33 QUICUMQUE

464 SEC·

ERGO QUAE
SIERIT ANI
MAM SUAM
SALUAM FACE
RE PERDET IL
LAM ET QUI
PERDIDERIT
SALUAM EAM
17:34 FACIET DICO
ENIM UOBIS
HAC NOCTU
ERINT DUO
IN LECTO UNO
UNUS ADSU
METUR ET ALI
US RELINQUE
17:35 TUR ERINT
DUAE MOL
LENTES IN U
NUM UNA
RELINQUE
TUR ET ALIA
ADSUMETUR
DUO IN AGRO

UNUS ADSU
MERTUR ET
ALIUS RELIN
QUETUR
17:36 ET RESPONDE¯
TES DIXERUN
ILLI UBI ·DM̄E·
17:37 QUI DIXIT ILLIS
UBICUMQUE
FUERIT COR
PUS ILLUC CO¯
UENIUNT
AQUILAE
18:1 DICEBAT AUTE¯
PARABOLAM
ILLIS OB HOC
QUOD DEBE
RENT SEMPER
ORARE ET NO¯
18:2 DEFICERE DI
CENS
IUDEX QUIDAM
ERAT IN QUA
DAM CIUITA

465 LUCANUM

TE QUI ·D̅M̅·
NON TIME
BAṄT SED NEC
HOMINEM
REUEREBA
18:3 TUR UIDUA AU
TEM QUAEDAˉ
ERAT IN EA
DEM CIUITA
TEM ET UENIE
BAT AD ILLUM
DICENS UIN
DICA ME DE
ADUERSARIO
18:4 MEO ET NO
LEBAT PER TEˉ
PUS
POST HAEC AU
TEM DIXIT IN
TRA SE SI ·D̅M̅·
NON TIMEO
NEC HOMI
NEM REOR
18:5 ATTAMEN QUIA

MOLESTA EST
MIHI UIDUA
HAEC UINDI
CABO ILLAM
NE PER TEM
PORE UENI
ENS SUGGIL
LET ME
18:6 DIXIT AUTEM
DM̄S AUDITE
QUID IỤDẸX̣
INIQUIṬATIS
18:7 DICET ·D̅S̅· AU
TEM NOṆ F̣Ạ
CIET UINḌIC
TA ELECṬORUˉ
SUORUM
CLAMANTIUˉ
DIE AC NOC
TE PATIENTI
AM HABENS
18:8 IN ILLIS DICO
UOBIS QUIA
FACET UINDIC

466 SEC·

ILLORUM CE
LEṚỊTER AṬTA
MEN [FIL]IUS
HỌ[MINIS U]Ẹ
N[IENS INUE]
N[IET PUTAS]
F̣I[DE]Ṃ SỤ[PER]
TEṚ[RAM]
18:9 DIẊ[IT AUTEM]
incipit ET [AD QUOS
DAM FIDEN
TES SIBI QUA
SI SINT IUSTI
ET SPERNEN
TES CETEROS
PARABOLAM
HANC]
18:10 DU[O HOMINES]
AṢ[CENDE]
RUṆṬ ỊṆ Ṭ[EM]
PLỌ [ORARE]
UN[US PUBL]I
CANUS ET A
LIUS PHARI
18:11 SAEUS STANṢ
ITAQUE PHA
RIṢ[AE]ỤṢ ỊṆ
T[RA SE] Ḥ[AE]Ç
ỌṚẠ[BAT ·D̅S̅·]
G̣Ṛ[ATIAS] ẠG̣Ọ
ṬỊḄỊ QỤỊẠ ṆỌ[¯
SU]M Ṣ[ICU]Ṭ
[CETERI HOMI
NUM RAPTO
RES INIUSTI]
ẠḌỤ[LTER]Ị ỤẸḶ
ỤṬ ḤỊ[C] P̣ỤḄḶỊ
18:12 [CA]ṆỤṢ ỊẸỊỤ
NỌ ḄỊṢ ỊṆ [S]ẠḄ
ḄẠṬỌ ḌẸÇỊ
ṂẠ[S] ḌỌṆỌ
OṂṆỊỤṂ
[QUAEC]ỤM
[QUE] P̣OSS[IDEO]
18:13 ẸṬ P̣ỤḄḶỊÇẠṆỤ[S]
A ḶỌṆG̣Ẹ ṢṬẠ[NS]
NOḶẸḄẠṬ ṆEC
QUIDEM OÇỤ

467 LUCANUM

LOS SUOS IN
CAELUM AD
ḶẸỤẠṚẸ ṢẸṬ
P̣ẸṚC̣ỤṬỊẸḄẠṬ
P̣ẸC̣ṬỤṢ ṢUU̅
DIC̣ẸṆṢ [·D̅S̅·]
P̣ROPITIỤS ẸṢ
[T]O MỊHI PEC̣
C̣ATOṚỊ
18:14 ḌỊC̣Ọ ỤỌḄỊṢ [QUI]Ạ
DESC̣ẸṆ[DIT]
ḤỊC̣ [IU]ṢṬỊF̣Ị
C̣ẠṬUS ỊṆ DO
ṂỌ SUA PR[AE]
ỊḶḶỤṂ PHA
ṚỊSAEUM QUO
[NIA]Ṃ ỌṂNIS
[Q]ỤỊ ṢE EXẠḶ
ṬẠṬ ḤỤṂỊḶ[IA
BI]TUR ET QUI
SE HỤṂILIAT
ẸX̣ẠḶṬẠBIT^{U}R
18:15 O[FFERE]BAN
AUTEM EI IN
FANTES UT IL
LOS TANGE
RET ỤỊD[E]Ṇ
ṬEṢ [AUTE]Ṃ
ḌỊṢC̣ỊP̣ỤḶỊ ỌB
ỊUṚG̣ABẠN
[EOS
IH̄S· AUTEM
IMPERAUIT
EIS DICE]ṆS
[SINITE INFA̅]
ṬẸṢ Ụ[E]ṆỊṚẸ
AD ṂE ẸṬ NO
ḶỊṬẸ [PROHI]Ḅ[E]
ṚẸ [ILLOS TALI
UM EST] ẸNIM
[REGNUM CAE]
ḶỌṚỤṂ
18:17 AM[E]N DỊ[CO]
UỌBIS Q̣ỤỊS
Q̣UE ṆỌN AC
CEP[E]R[I]Ṭ REG̣
NUṂ ·DĒỊ· TA̅
QUAM INFANS

468 SEC·

NON INTRA
BIT IN ILLUT
18:18 INTERROGA
UIT AUTEM
EUM QUIDA¯
DICENS MA
GISTER BONE
QUID FACIENS
UITAM AETER
NAM POSSI
DEBO
18:19 DIXIT AUTEM
ILLI ·I̅H̅S̅· QUID
MẸ ḌICIṢ BO
NUM NEMO
EST BONUS
NISI UNUS
18:20 D̅S̅· MANDA
TA NOSTI AIṬ
QUAE NON
HOMICIDI
UM FACIES
NON ADUL
TERABIS NO¯
FURTUM FA
CIES NON
FALSUM TES
TIMONIUM
DICES HONO
RA PATREM
TUUM ET MA
TREM TUAM
18:21 QUI DIXIT
HAEC OMNI
A CUSTODIUI
A IUUENTU
TE MEA
18:22 QUOD CUM AU
DISSET ·I̅H̅S̅·
DIXIT EI AD
HUC UNUM
TIBI DEEST
OMNIA QUÆ
CUMQUAE
HABES UEN
ET DIUIDE
DE EA PAUPE
RIBUS ET HA
BEBIS THEN

469 LUCANUM

SAURUM IN
CAELIS ET UE
NI SEQUERE
18:23 ME : QUI
CUM AUDIS
SET HAEC TRIS
TES FACTUS EST
ERAT ENIM
DIUES UALDE
18:24 QUEM CUM
UIDISSET ·IH̄S·
CONTRISTA
TUM DIXIT
QUAM DIFFI
CILE QUI PECU
NIAS HABEN
IN REGNO
DEI INTRA
18:25 BUNT FACILI
US EST ENIM
CAMELLUM
PER FORAME¯
ṄAṀCUS
TRANSIRE

QUAM DIUI
TE IN REGNU¯
DĒI·
18:26 DIXERUNT AU
TEM QUI AU
DIEBANT ET
QUIS POTE
RIT SALUUS
18:27 FIERI DIXIT
AUTEM ILLIS
QUAE INPOS
SIBILIA SUNT
APUT HOMI
NES POSSIBI
LIA UERO APUT
D̄M̄· SUNT
18:28 DIXIT AUTEM
PETRUS EC
CE NOS RELIC
TIS OMNIB·
NOSTRIS SE
CUTI SUMUS
18:29 TE QUI DIXIT
EIS AMEN DI

470 SEC·

CO UOBIS NE
MO EST QUI
RELIQỤERỊT
DOṂ[UM] AỤṬ
PARẸ[N]ṬES
AỤṬ ḶṚẠṬṚẸṢ
Ạ[U]Ṭ ỤXỌRẸṂ
A[UT FILIO]S
P̣ṚỌP̣ṬẸṚ REG
18:30 Ṇ[U]Ṃ [DĒI] QỤ[I]
Ṇ[O]Ṇ ẠÇ[CIPI]
EṬ ṢẸP̣[TIES]
TẠ[N]ṬỤṂ [IN]
TE[MPORE ISTO]
ET [IN FUTURO]
SẠẸ[CULO UI]
TAṂ [AET]E[R]
NẠ[M P]ỌSS[I]
DE[BIT]
18:31 CON[UOCATIS]
AUṬ[EM DUO]
DE[CIM DIS]
CIPỤḶỊṢ [DIXIT]
AD ILLOS ECCE

ASCENDIMUS
IN HIERỌSO
LỴ[MA ET CON]
ṢỤṂ[MABU̅]
ṬỤṚ ỌṂ[NI]Ạ
Q[UA]Ẹ S[C]RIP
TA ṢỤṆṬ P̣ẸR
[PR]ỌP̣ḤẸṬẠṢ
ḌẸ ḶIL[IO HO
MINIS]
18:32 [TRADETUR ENI̅
GENTIBUS ET
INLUDETUR]
ẸT ÇỌNSP[UE]
18:33 TUR ET F[LAGEL]
ḶATUM ỌÇ[CI
DE]ṆṬ [ILLUM
ET DIE TE]R[TIA]
18:34 ṚẸṢỤṚ[G]ET ẸṬ
[IPSI NIHI]L H[O
RUM INTEL
LEXERUNT]
SẸḌ [ERAT UER]
BỤṂ [AB]ṢCOṆ

471 LUCANUM

SUM AB EIS ET
NON INTELLE
X̣EṚ[UNT QU]Æ
Ḍ[ICEBANTU]R
A[D EOS]
18:35 [F]ẠCṬU[M] EST [AU]
ṬEM Ḍ[UM] ẠḌ
PROP̣ỊṆQUA
[R]EṬ [IN I]ERI[CHO]
QU[IDAM CAE]
C̣ỤṢ [SEDEBAT
SECUS UIAM]
MẸ[NDICANS
18:36 QU]I C̣ỤM [AU
DISS]ET TUR
[B]AṂ P̣RAETEṚ
[EUN]ṬẸṂ IṆ
[T]ẸRRỌG̣ẠḄẠṬ
Q̣UIDNAM
18:37 [H]OC ESSET IN
DICAUERUNT
AUTEM EI
QUIA IH̄S· NA]
ZARENUS

18:38 TRANSIT ET
EXCLAMAUIT
DICE[N]S
IH̄U· F̣[ILI D]AỤID
ṂỊS[ER]EṚẸ
18:39 [M]EI ẸṬ QUI
[P]RAEṬ[ERIBA]N
[I]NC̣ṚẸ[PAB]AN
ẸỤM [UT TACE
RET AD ILLE
MULTO MA
GIS CL]Ạ[MA
BAT FILI DA]ỤID
[MISERER]E
[M]Ẹ[I]
18:40 [STANS AUTE]M
IH̄[S· IUSSIT] IL
ḶỤM [ADD]Ụ
[CI CUMQ]ỤE
[ADPROP]IN
[QUASSET I]N
[TERROGA]UIT
18:41 [IL]ḶỤṂ ḌICENS
QUID TIBI UIS

472 SEC·

FACIAM QUI
DIXIT UT UI
DEAM
18:42 ET RESPONDENS
DIXIT ILLI ·IH̄S·
RESPICE FI
DES TUA TE
SALUUM FE
18:43 CIT ET CONFES
TIM UIDERE
COEPIT ET SE
QUEBATUR
EUM HONO
RIFICANS ·D̄M̄·
ET OMNIS PO
PULUS CUM
UIDISSET DE
DERUNT LAU
DEM DĒO·
⳨ 19:1 ET INGRESSUS
CIRCUIBAT
19:2 HIERICHO ET
ECCE UIR NO
MINE ZACCHE
US ET HIC ERAT
PRINCEPS PU
BLICANORUM
ET IPSE ERAT
19:3 LOCUPLES ET
QUAEREBAT
UIDERE ·IH̄M·
QUI ESSET ET
NON POTERAT
PRAE TURBA
QUONIAM
STATURA BRE
19:4 UI ERAT ET PRO
CURRENS AS
CENDIT IN AR
BOREM SYCO
MORI UT UI
DERET ILLUM
QUONIAM
PER ILLA PAR
TE TRANSITU
RUS ERAT
19:5 ET FACTUM EST
DUM TRANSI

473 LUCANUM

RET ·IH̄S· UIDIT
ILLUM ET RES
PICIENS DIXIT
EI ZACCHAEE
FESTINANS
DESCENDE
QUONIAM
HODIE IN DO
MO TUA OPOR
TET ME MA
NERE
19:6 ET FESTINANS
DESCENDIT
ET EXCEPIT IL
LUM GAUDENS
19:7 ET CUM UIDIS
SENT OMNES
MURMURA
TI SUNT QUOD
APUT UIRUM
PECCATOREM
INTROISSET
MANERE
19:8 STANS AUTEM
ZACCHEUS DI
XIT AD ·DŌM·
ECCE DIMI
DIAM PARTE¯
BONORUM
MEORUM
DM̄E· DO PAU
PERIBUS ET
SI CUI QUID
FRAUDAUI
QUADRUPLU¯
REDDAM
19:9 DIXIT AUTEM
IH̄S· AD ILLOS
QUIA HODIE
SALUS DOMUI
HUIC FACTA
EST QUONIA¯
QUIDEM ET
HIC FILIUS EST
19:10 ABRAHAE UE
NIT ENIM FI
LIUS HOMI
NIS SALUUM

474 SEC·

FACERE ET QUÆ
RERE P̣ERDI
TUM
19:11 AUDỊENTIBUS
AUṬEM HAEC
I[LLI]S ẠDDIDIT
Ḍ I[C]Ẹ[NS] PAR[A]
BOḶẠ[M E]O QỤ[OD]
ẸṢṢẸṬ IU[X]ṬẠ
HIERUS[ALEM]
ẸṬ [QU]OḌ [PU]Ṭ[A]
ḄẠNṬ QUIA
Ç ỌṆ[FES]ṬỊṂ
REG̣[NUM] DẸỊ[·]
MANỊ[FESTA]
ṚẸṬỤ[R]
19:12 DỊXIT ẸṚGO Ḥ O
Ṃ[O] QUIDAM
PATERFAMI
LIAS PROF̣ẸÇ
TUS EST IN RE
GIONẸṂ [LON]
GINQUAM AC
CIPERE REG
NUM ET REUER
19:13 TI UOCATIS AU
ṬẸ[M DECE]M
[SERUIS S]ỤIS
ḌẸ[DIT ILLI]S
D[ECEM] ṂṆẠS
[ET DIXIT AḌ] Ẹ[OS
NEGOTIA]MỊ
[NI DONEC UE
19:14 NIO CIUES] ẠỤ
[TE]M [ILLIUS ODIE
BANT EUM]
ẸṬ [MISER]ỤNT
ḶẸG̣ẠṬỊỌṆEM
PỌṢṬ ỊḶLUM
DICENTES QUIA
NOḶỤMUṢ
HUNC REGNA
RẸ [SU]PER NO[S]
19:15 EṬ [FA]CTUṂ
[ES]T REỤE[R]
ṬẸNTẸ ILLỌ
Ạ[C]CEP̣TO REG̣
NO IUSSIT UO

475 LUCANUM

CARI SERUOS
SUOS QUIBUṢ
Ḍ[EDERA]T [P]Ẹ
Ç̣ỤṆIAM [UT]
ṢÇ̣[IRET QUIS
QUID NEGO
TIATUS FUIS
SET
UENIT AUTEM]
P̣ṚỊỌṚ Ḍ[IC]ẸṆṢ
ḌM̄Ẹ ṂṆ[A]
ṬỤẠ [DECEM
ADQUISIUIT]
19:17 MṆ[AS ET DI]
X̣IT ỊḶḶ[I T]ẠṆ
ṬO MẸḶỊỌṚ
ḄỌNẸ ṢERUẸ
[Q]ỤIA ỊṆ MỊ
NỊMO [FID]E
[LI]S F̣ỤỊṢṬỊ ẸṚỊṢ
P̣ỌṬẸṢṬẠṬẸṂ
[HA]ḄẸNS Ṣ[U]
PRA DE[C]ẸM
CIUITATES

19:18 ET UENIT ALI
UṢ DICENS
DM̄E ṂNA
[TU]Ạ F̣[ECIT ALI]AS
QUINQUE M
19:19 ṆẠṢ ḌỊX̣ỊṬ ẸT
[H]UIC ET TỤ
ẸṢṬỌ ṢỤP̣ṚA
[QUINQUE CI
UITATES PO
TESTATEM HA]ḄẸṆṢ
19:20 EṬ Ạ[LIUS UENI]Ṭ
[DICENS DM̄E
ECCE MNA
TUA QUAM HA]
ḄẸ[BAM RE]
POṢ[ITA]M ỊṆ
SUDAṚ[IO Q]UO
19:21 N[IAM T]ỊṂE
[BAM TE] Q̣ỤIA
[HOMO] ẠUS
Ṭ[ER]ỤS ẸS TỌL
LIS QUOD NO‾

476 SEC·

POSUISTI ET
METES QUOD
NON SEMINAS
19:22 TI : AIT IL
LI EX ORE TUO
IUDICABO TE
IN[F]IDELIS SER
UE ET MALE
SCIEBAS ME
QUIA HOMO
AỤ[S]ṬERIS SU¯
TOLLO QUOD
NON POSUI
ET METỌ QUOD
NON SEMI
19:23 NAUI ET QUA
RE NON DE
DISTI PECU
NIAM MEA¯
AD MENSAM
ET EGO CUM
UENISSEM
CUM USURIS
EXEGISSEM

EAM
19:24 CIRCUMSTA¯
TIBUS AUTE¯
DIXIT AUFER
TE AB ILLO ET
DATE EI QUI
DECEM MNAS
19:25 HABET ET DI
XERUNT ILLI
DM̅E· HABET
DECEM MNAS
19:26 DICO UOBIS
OMNI QUI HA
BUERIT DABI
TUR ILLI AB EO
AUTEM QUI
NON HABET
ET QUOD HA
BET AUFERE
TUR AB EO
19:27 UERUMTA
MEN INIMI
COS MEOS IL
LOS QUI NOLUE

477 LUCANUM

RUNT ME REG
NARE SUPER
SE ADDUCITE
HOC ET IUGU
LATE IN CONS
PECTU MEO
19:28 ET HIS DICTIS
IBAT HIERO
SOLYMIS AS
CENDENS
19:29 ET FACTUM EST
CUM ADPRO
PINQUASSET
BETPHAGE ET
BETHANIA
AD MONTEM
QUI APPELLA
TUR OLIUETI
MISIT DUOS
EX DISCIPU
19:30 LIS SUIS DI
CENS
ITE IN UICUM
CONTRA IN

QUO INGRE
DIENTES IN
UENIETIS
ASINAM CU̅
PULLUM AL
LIGATUM SU
PER QUEM
NULLUS SEDIT
SOLUITE ILLA̅
ET ADDUCI
19:31 TE ET SI QUIS
UOS INTER
ROGAUERIT
QUARE SOL
UITIS DICE
TIS ILLI QUO
NIAM ·D̅M̅S
OPERAM
EIUS DESI
DERAT
19:32 ABIERUNT
AUTEM QUI
MISSI ERAN
SICUT DIXE

478 SEC·

RAT ILLIS IN
UENERUNT
ASINAM STA¯
19:33 TEM ET SOLUE¯
T[I]BUS EIS ASI
NẠM ÇUM P̣ỤḶ
ḶỌ [D]ỊXERUNT
DOMINI IPSI ~~AD~~
ỤS AD ILLOS
QỤ[I]D SOLUITIS
19:34 PULLUM QUI
DIXERUNT
QUIẠ DM̄O
SUO NECES
SARIỤS Ẹ S[T]
19:35 ET ADDUXE
ṚUNT ILLUṂ
AD IH̄Ṃ Ẹ T
SUḄṢṬẸṚNE[¯]
TES UESTIME[¯]
TẠ SUA SUPER
P̣ULḶỤM [I]N
P̣[OS]U[E]ṚUNT
[I]H̄M·

19:36 EUNTEM AU
TEM ILLO SUBS
TERNEBANT
EI UESTIṂE¯
TA SUA ỊN [U]IA
19:37 ADPROPIN
QUANṬẸ ẠỤ
TEM Ẹ Ọ AD D[IS]
ÇENSỤ[M MO¯]
ṬỊṢ ỌḶỊUEṬỊ
COEPIT OṂN[IS]
MULTITUḌỌ
GAUDEṆṢ CO¯
LAUDARE D̄M̄
UOCE MAG
NA DE QUIBUṢ
UIDEBANT O¯
NIBUS ỤIR
19:38 TUTIBUṢ DI
CENTES BE
NEDICTỤ[S]
QUI UENIT IN
NOMINẸ [D]M̄Ị
BENEDICTUS

K [XXXI]

479 LUCANUM

REX PAX IN
CAELO ET GLO
19:39 RIA ET
QUIDẠM PHA
RIṢẠẸORUM
DE TỤṚḄẠ DI
X̣ẸRUṆṬ AD
[ILLUM] ṂẠ[GIS]
ṬẸṚ [OBIURGA]
19:40 ỊḶ[LOS QUI] DI
XỊ[T] EIS DIC[O]
ỤOḄIS SI ISTI
ṬACUERINT
ḶAP̣IDES [CLA]
M[ABUNT]
19:41 [E]Ṭ C̣Ụ[M] ADP̣Ṛ[O]
P̣ỊṆ[QU]ASSẸ[T]
UIṢẠ C̣IUIṬ[A]
ṬẸ F̣Ḷ[E]ỤIT SU
19:42 P̣ER ẸAM D[I]
C̣[ENS] QUONI
AM SI SCIRES
TỤ QUAMQUA¯
IN HAC TUA DIE
QUAE AD PACE¯
TUAṂ ABSCO¯
ṢA ẸSSENT AB
19:43 OCULIS QUO
NIAM UENI
ENT ḌIES ṢỤ
P̣ẸR ṬE ẸṬ ỊṆỊ
CIENT INIMI
CI TUỊ ṢẠEPE¯
ET CIRCUM
[D]ABUNT TE
ẸṬ C̣ONTINE
[B]UNT [T]E UN
19:44 DI[QUE] ET PA
[UIMEN]ṬABUNT
ṬE ET NATOS
[T]UOS QUI IN
TE SUNT ET NO¯
RẸ[LI]NQUENT
LAP[I]DẸM SU
P̣RA LAPIDEM
IN TE OB HOC
QỤỌD IGNO
ṚASTI TEṂ

480 SEC·

PUS UISITATI
ONIS TUAE
19:45 ET INGRESSUS
IN TEMPLO
COEPIT EICE
RE UENDEN
TES IN ILLO ET
EMENTES ET
MENSAS NU¯
MULARIORU¯
E~~F~~UERTIT ET
CATHEDRAS
UENDENTI
UM COLUM
19:46 BAS DICENS
EIS
SCRIPTUM EST
DOMUS MEA
DOMUS ORA
TIONIS EST UOS
AUTEM ILLAM
FECISTIS SPE
LUNCAM LA
TRONUM

19:47 ET ERAT DO
CENS COTTI
DIE IN TEM
PLO PONTIFI
CES AUTEM
ET SCRIBAE
ET PRINCIPES
POPULI QUAE
REBANT ILLU¯
19:48 PERDERE ET
NON INUENIẸ
BANT QUID
FACERENT
POPULUS ENI¯
OMNIS SUS
PENSUS ERAT
A~~D~~UDIENS
EUM
20:1 ET FACTUM EST
AUTEM IN
UNA DIERU¯
DOCENTE IL
LO POPULUM
IN TEMPLO

481 LUCANUM

ET ADNUNTI
ANTE ADSTI
TERUNT PON
TIFỊ[C]ES ET SCRI
BAE CUM SE
20:2 NIORIBUS DI
CENTES DIC
NOBIS IN QUA
POTESTATEM
HAEC FACIS
ET QUIS EST
QUI DEDIT TI
BI HANC PO
TESTATEM
20:3 RESPONDENS
AUTEM DIXIT
AD ILLOS IN
TERROGABO
UOS ET EGO
ET RESPON
DITE MIHI
20:4 BAPTISMU
IOHANNIS
DE CAELO E

RAT AN EX HO
MINIBUS
20:5 AD ILLI COGITA
BANT INTRA
SE DICENTES
QUIA SI DIXE
RIMUS DE
CAELO DICET
NOBIS QUA
RE ERGO NON
CREDIDISTIS
20:6 ILLI ET SI DI
XERIMUS
AB HOMINI
BUS OMNIS
POPULUS LA
PIDABIT NOS
SCIUNT ENIM
IOHANEN
PROPHẸṬAM
20:7 FUISSE [E]T RES
PONDERUN
SE NESCIRE
20:8 UNDE ET DI

482 SEC·

XIT ILLIS ·IH̄S·
NEC EG̣Ọ DICO
UOBIS IN QUA
POT[EST]ATE HẠẸC
20:9 FAC̣[IO C]ỌEPIT
AUT[E]Ṃ ḌIC̣Ẹ
RE [P]ẠRABỌ
LAṂ [HANC] ỤI
NEẠM P̣[L]ẠN
TAUIṬ [HO]M[O]
ET LOCẠỤIT
ILLA[M] C̣OLO
NIṢ [ET IP]SE
P̣Ẹ[R]ẸG̣[RI]NA
ṬỤṢ Ẹ[ST TE]M
P̣ỌṚ[IBU]Ṣ MỤ[L]
20:10 ṬỊṢ [EṬ TE]Ṃ[PO]
ṚE QỤ[ODAM]
MỊSIṬ AḌ ỊḶḶ[OS]
COḶỌṆỌṢ [S]EṚ
ỤU[M] ỤṬ ẸX
F̣ṚỤC̣ṬỤỤṂ
ỤỊNẸẠẸ [DA]
ṚENT ILLI ET
CAESUM ILLU¯
DIMISẸṚUNT
20:11 ỤACUỤṂ ET
AD[POSUIT ALI
ỤM ṂỊTTE
RE S[ERU]ỤM
[QUOQ]ỤẸ ẸṬ
[ILLUM] C̣Ạ[E]
ṢỤM ḌỊṂỊṢ[E
RUNT UACU
20:12 UM ET ADPO]
ṢUIT ṬERTỊU[¯]
ṂIṬ[T]ERE ẸṬ
ỊḶḶỤM UUL
NEṚ[A]TỤṂ
[PROIECERUNT]
20:13 ḌỊ[XIT A]U[TEM
DOMINUS
UINEAE QUID
FACIAM MIT
TAM FILIUM
MEUM CARIS
SIMUM] F̣ỌṚ
SITAM HUNC

483 LUCANUM

REUEREBUN
20:14 TUṚ QUEM UT
UIḌEṚUNT
Ç̣ỌḶ[ON]Ị COGI
Ṭ̣AUẸ[R]ỤNT
INTẸ[R] ṢẸ DI
[C]EṆTES Ḥ[IC]
[E]ṢṬ ḤEṚẸ[S OC]
Ç̣ACIDAMỤ[S]
EUM ỤṬ NỌ[S]
TṚẠ F[I]ẠT ḤẸṚẸ[DI
20:15 TAS] ET PROIECTU̅
ILLUM EXTRA
UINEAM OC
CIDERUNT
QUID ERGO FA
[CIE]Ṭ [D]ỌM[INUS· UI]
20:16 ṆEẠẸ [U]ẸṆI
ẸT ET P̣E[R]DE[T]
COLON[OS] ỊS
TOS ET TRA
[DE]T UINEẠṂ
ẠLIIS QUI CO[̅]
AUDISSENT

DIXERUNT
ABSIT
20:17 QUIỌỤE ỊNTU
ẸNS [EOS] DIXIT
QUIḌ Ẹ[RG]Ọ
ṢÇ̣R[IPTU]Ṃ
ẸṢṬ L[APIDE]M
Ọ[UEM REPRO
BAUERUNT
AEDIFI]Ç̣AṆ
ṬEṢ [HIC] FAÇ̣
ṬỤS EṢ[T I]N CA
PITE ẠṆG̣U
20:18 LI ỌṂṆIS
QỤỊ ỌF̣F̣ẸN
ḌỊD[E]ṚỊṬ ṢU
P̣ẸṚ ỊḶḶUM
[LAP]IḌEM CO̅
QUASSABITUR
[S]UP̣Ẹ[R Q]UEM
CECIDERIT
AUTEM COM
MINUET [I]L
20:19 LUM ET QUAẸ

484 SEC·

SIERUNT PO¯
TIFICES ET SCRI
BAE INICERE
ILLI MANUS
EADEM HO
RA ET TIMUE
R[UN]T POPU
LUM SCIEṚUNT
EṆỊM QUOD
AD ILLOS DI
XISSET PARA
BOLAM HANC
20:20 ET CUM DIS
CESSISSENT
SUBMISE
RUNT SUBOR
FINGENTES
SE UT CAPE
RENT SERMO
NES ILLIUS
UT TRADEREN
EUM POTES
TATI PRAESI
20:21 DIS ET INTER
ROGAUERUN
ILLUM DICEN
TES MAGISTER
SCIMUS QUO
NIAM DICIS
UERA ET NO¯
ACCIPES PER
SONA HOMI
NUM SED IN
UERITATE
UIAM ·DĒI·
20:22 DOCES LICET
NOBIS TRI
BUTUM DA
RE CAESARI
AUT NON
20:23 QUORUM UI
SA NẸQUITIA
DIXIT AD ILLOS
QUID ME TEM[P]
20:24 TATIS OSTEN
DITE MIHI
DENARIUM
CUIUS HABET

485 LUCANUM

IMAGINEM
ET INSCRIP
TIONEM RES
POṆDENTES
DIXERUNT
20:25 CAESARIS QUI
DIXIT REDDI
TE CAESARI
QUAE SUNT
CAESARIS CÆ
SARI ET QUAE
DĒI· SUNT ·DĒO
20:26 ET NON POTU
ERUNT SER
MONEM EIUS
CAPERE CORA÷
POPULO ET MI
RATI IN RES
PONSO EIUS
TACUERUNT
20:27 ACCEDENTES
AUTEM QUI
DAM SADDU
CEORUM QUI

CONTRADI
CUNT RESUR
RECTIONEM
NON ESSE IN
TERROGABAN
20:28 ILLUM DICEN
TES
MAGISTE[R MO]Ị
SES SCR[IPS]ỊṬ
NOBIS SI [U]Ṇ
IUS FRATEṚ
MORTUUS
FUERIT HABENS
UXOREM ET
HIC FILIOS
NON HABUE
RIT UT ACCI
PIAT FRATER
ILLIUS UXO
REM EIUS
ET RESUSCI
TET FRATRI
SUO SEMEN
20:29 SEPTEM FRA

486 SEC·

TRES ERANT
ET PṚIỌṚ A AC
CEP[IT UX]ỌRE¯
ET DEÇ[ESS]ỊṬ Ṣ[I]
20:30 ṆẸ [FILIIS ET SE]
QỤ[ENS ACCE
PIT EA]Ṃ [ET IP
SE DECESSIT SI
20:31 NE FILIIS TER
TIUS SIMILI
TER AUTEM ET]
SE[PTEM ET NO¯]
RẸ[LIQ]ỤERUNT
FILIUM ET DE
FUNCTI SỤNṬ
20:32 SED EṬ MỤḶỊ
20:33 ER ỊṆ RESUR
RECṬỊỌNE CU
IUS ẸORUM
ERIT UXỌR
SEPTEM ENI[¯]
HABỤ[E]RUNT
ILLAM UXO
REM

20:34 DIXIT ILLIS IH̄S·
FILI HUIUS SAE
CULI GẸNẸ
RANṬ Ẹ[T GENE]
RANṬ[UR] NỤ
BUNT ET NỤ[BU¯]
20:35 ṬỤṚ [QUI A]UṬẸ[¯]
[DIGNI] F̣ỤER[IN]Ṭ
[SAECU]ḶỤM
[ILL]Ụ[M] ẠṬṬIN
G̣Ẹ[RE] IN RE
SỤṚṚẸCTIO
NEṂ A MOR
[TU]IṢ NON NU
[B]UNT NEC NU
20:36 [B]UNṬUR NEC
ẸṆỊṂ [IAM]
MORITURI
ṢUNT AEQUA
ḶẸṢ ẸNỊṂ AN
GELIS SUNT DĒI
RẸṢURRẸÇ
T[I]ONIS F̣Ị[LI CU¯]
SINT

487 LUCANUM

20:37 QUIA AUTEM SUR
GUNT MORTUI
MOYSES DEM
[ON]STRAUIT
ỤỌḄỊ[S] ḌỊC̣IT DE
RUḄ[O D̅M̅·]
ABRAHẠ[M D̅M̅·]
ISAC Ẹ[T D̅M̅· I]Ạ
20:38 COB N[ON EST]
D̅S̅· MỌRTỤ[O]
RUM SEḌ Ụ[I]
UENTIUM O¯
NES ENIM [ILLI]
UIUENT
20:39 RESPONDEN
TES AUTEM
QUIḌ[A]M DE
SCRIBIS DIXE
RUNT MẠ[GIS]
TER Ḅ[EN]Ẹ Ḍ[I]
20:40 XISTI ṆEC̣ [A]M
P̣Ḷ[IUS A]UḌẸ
Ḅ[AN]Ṭ INTẸ[R]
ROG̣[A]RE EUM

QUICQUAM
20:41 DIXIT AUTEM
AD Ẹ[OS] Q̣UO
MỌ[DO] DICUN
[XP̅]M· F̣[ILIU]M
ḌẠ[UID ESS]E
20:42 [ET IPSE DA]ỤID
[DICIT IN LIB]ṚO
[SALMORU]M
[DICIT DM̅S
DM̅O MEO
S]ẸDE ẠḌ ḌEX̣
[TERA]Ṃ ṂẸ
20:43 ẠṂ D[ON]ẸC̣ PO
NAM ỊṆỊMỊ
[CO]Ṣ TUOS SUB
PEDỊBUS ṬỤIS
20:44 [D]AUID DO̅M· ỊL
LUM UO[C]AT ET
[Q]UOMODO
FILIỤ[S I]LLIUS
20:45 EST AUDI
ẸNTE AUTEM
Ọ[M]NI POPU

488 SEC·

LO DIXIT AD DIS
CIPULOS SUOS
20:46 CAUETE A SCRI
BIS QUI UOLUN
AMBULARE I¯
STOLIS ET AMAN
SALUTATIO
NES IN FORO
ET PRIMOS CO¯
SESSUS IN SY
NAGOGIS ET
PRIMOS DIS
CUBITOS IN
CONUIUIIS
20:47 QUI COME
DUNT DOMOS
UIDUARUM
FINGENTES
LONGAM ORA
TIONEM HI
ACCIPIENT
AMPLIUS POE
NAE
21:1 RESPICIENS AU
TEM ·IH̅S· UIDIT
MITTENTES
DONA IN ALTA
RIO DIUITES
21:2 UIDIT ETIAM
QUENDAM UI
DUAM PAUPER
CULAM MIT
TENTEM DU
OS QUADRAN
21:3 TES ET DIXIT UE
RE DICO UO
BIS QUIA UIDUA
PAUPERA HAEC
PLUS OMNIU¯
21:4 MISIT OMNES
ENIM ISTI DE
QUO SUPER IL
LIS FUIT MISE
RUNT IN DO
NA DE̅I· HAEC
AUTEM DE EXI
GUITATE SUA
OMNEM FA

489 LUCANUM

CULTATEM SU
AM QUAM HA
BEBAT MISIT
21:5 ET QUIBUSDAM
ḌỊCENTIBUS
DE TEMPLO
QUOD LAPIDI
BUS OPTIMIS
ET BONIS Ẹ[X]
TRUCTUM
ESSET DIXIT
21:6 HAEC UIDE
TIS UENIENT
DIES IN QUI
BUS NON RE
LINQUETUR
LAPIS SUPER
ḶAPIDEM IN
PARIETE HIC
QUI NON DES
TRUATUR
21:7 ỊNTERROGA
UERUNT AU
TEM EUM DI

CENTES MA
GISTER QUAN
DO HAEC ERUN
ET QUO[D S]ỊG
NU[M] CUM
HA[EC] INCIPI
21:8 ENT Ṭ FIERI AD
ILLE DIXIT UI
DETE NE SE
DUCAMINI
MULTI ENIM
UENIENT IN
NOMINE MEO
DICENTES QUIA
EGO SUM ET
TEMPUS AD
PROPINQUA
UIT NOLITE SE
QUI POST ILLOS
21:9 CUM AUTEM
AUDIERITIS
BELLA ET SEPA
RATIONES
NOLITE TER

490 SEC·

RERI OPORTET
Ẹ̣Ṇ̣Ị̣M HAEC
FIEṚỊ [PRI]MU¯
SẸḌ [NUN]DUM
ẸṚỊ[T FINIS] ỊN
21:10 ILLIS SỤṚ[G]ẸT
ENỊṂ G̣[EN]S
ṢỤP̣ẸṚ G̣Ẹ[N]ṬE[¯]
ET ṚẸG̣ṆỤ[M]
SỤP̣Ẹ[R REGNUM]
21:11 TERRIMOTỤṢ
QUOQ̣UE MAG
NI P̣ER ḶỌÇ̣Ạ
ET PESTES ET
FAMES ERUNT
FORMIDINES
QUAE ḌẸ CAE
ḶO EṬ SIGNẠ
MAGNA ERUNT
21:12 ET HIẸMES ẠN
TE HAEC AUTEM
OMN[I]A [I]N
MITTENT ṢỤ
PER UOS MA

NUS SUAS ET
PERSEQUEN
ṬUR ET ṬR[AD]ENT
ỤỌS IṆ [SY]NA
G̣OG̣[IS ET CAR]
Ç̣[E]ṚỊBUS ET DU
Ç̣EMINI AD RE
G̣[ES C]ẠUSA NO
21:13 [MI]NIS MEI UT
ṢỊT IN TESTI
ṂONIO UOBIS
21:14 PONITE ERGO
IN CORDIBUS
UESTRIS NON
PRIUS MEḶE
TARE QUOMO
DO RATIONE¯
21:15 REDDATIS EG̣Ọ
ENIM DABO
UOBIS ^{OS} ET SA
PIEN[T]IAM Ç̣Ụ[I]
ṆOṆ POTERIN[T]
RESISTER[E]
QUI ADUEṚ

491 LUCANUM

SANTUR ỤO
21:16 ḄỊS TRADEMI
[NI] ẠỤṬẸṂ ẸṬ
[A PARENTIBUS]
ẸṬ [COGNA]ṬIS
ẸṬ ẠṂỊÇ[IS] ẸṬ
ṂỌṚṬỊ [ADFI]
ÇỊENṬ [EX UO]
21:17 ḄỊṢ ET ER[ITI]Ṣ
ODIỌ OMṆ[I]
ḄUS ÇAUṢẠ [N]Ọ
ṂINIS MEỊ
21:18 ET ÇAPILLỤS
DE CAPITE ỤEṢ
ṬṚỌ NON PER[I]
21:19 ẸṬ ỊṆ ṬOḶERA¯
TỊẠ ỤẸṢṬṚẠ
[P]Ọ[S]SỊDEBITIS
ANIMAS UES
[T]ṚAS
21:20 [CUM] AU[T]EM [UI
DER]ỊṬỊṢ ÇỊṚ
[CU]ṂDAṬASM
ẠB EXERCITI
BUS HIERUSA
LEṂ T[UN]C ṢÇỊ
TOṬẸ [QU]ỌNI
AṂ ẠḌ[PROPI¯]
QỤẠỤ[IT DES]Ọ
21:21 [LAT]ỊO EI[US T]ỤNC
QUỊ [SU]ṆṬ ỊṆ
IUD[AE]Ạ [FU]ĢỊ
ẠṆ[T] ỊṆ [MON
ṬỊḄỤṢ Ẹ[T QU]I
ỊṆ ṂẸḌỊỌ EIUS
SECẸDAṆṬ ET
QUI ỊṆ ṚẸĢỊỌ
ṆỊḄỤṢ ṆẸ ỊṆ
TRENT ỊṆ EẠM
21:22 QUONIAM ḌI
ẸṢ ỊỤḌỊCII HỊ
SUNT UṬ IN
PLEANTUR O¯
NIA QUAE SCRIP
ṬA SUNT
21:23 UAE PRAEGNA¯
TIBUS ET LAC
TAṆṬỊBUS IN

492 SEC·

IN ILLIS DIEB·
ERIT NECESSI
TAS MAGNA
SUPER TERRA¯
ET IRA POPU
21:24 LO HUIC ET CA
DENT IN ORE
GLADII ET CAP
TIUI DUCEN
TUR IN GEN
TES UNIUER
SA ET HIERU
SALEM ERIT
IN CONCULCA
TIONEM NA
TIONUM DO
NEC REPLEAN
TUR TEMPO
RA GENTIUM
21:25 ET ERINT SIG
NA IN SOLEǂ
ET LUNA ET STEL
LIS SUPER TER
RAM CONPRES
SIO GENTIUM
IN STUPORE
SONUS MARIS
21:26 ET UNDIS ARE
FRIGESCEN
TIBUS HOMI
NIBUS A TI
MORE ET EX
PECTATIONE
SUPERUENI
ENTIUM OR
BI TERRARU¯
UIRTUTES ENI¯
QUAE SUNT
IN CAELO MO
UEBUNTUR
21:27 TUNC UIDEBUN
FILIUM HOMI
NIS UENIEN
TEM IN NU
BE CUM PỌ[TEN]
TIA MAGN[A]
ET GLORIA
21:28 INCIPIENTIB·

493 LUCANUM

AUTEM HIS FIE
RI RESPICITE
ET LEUATE CA
PITA UESTRA
QUONIAM
ADPROPINQUA
TE LIBERATIO
UESTRA
21:29 ET DIXIT PARA
BOLAM ILLIS
UIDETE FICU¯
ET OMNES AR
21:30 BORES CUM
FLORIENT A SE
SCITIS IN PRO
XIMO ESSE AES
21:31 TATEM SIC ET
UOS CUM UIDE
BITIS HAEC
SCITOTE QUO
NIAM IN PRO
XIMO EST REG
NUM DI·
21:32 AMEN DICO UO
BIS QUIA NON
TRANSIET GENS
ILLA DONEC O¯
21:33 NIA FIANT CÆ
LUM ET TER
RA TRANSIET
UERBA AUTE¯
MEA NON PRÆ
TERIBUNT
21:34 ATTENDITE AU
TEM UOBIS
NE QUANDO
GRAUENTUR
CORDA UES
TRA GRATULA
TIONE ET EBRI
ETATIBUS ET
SOLLIGITUDI
NIBUS SAECU
LARIBUS ET
INSTET SUPER
UOS REPEN
TANEUS DIES
ILLE TANQUA¯

494 SEC·

21:35 LAQUEUS IN
TRAỤỊṬ ẸNIM
SU[PER OM]
ṆẸṢ Ọ[UI SE]
ḌẸṆṬ ṢỤP̣ER
F̣ẠÇ[I]ẸṂ ṬỌṬỊ
ỤṢ ṬẸṚṚẠE
21:36 UIGIḶ[A]TẸ ẠỤTE‾
ỊṆ ỌṂṆỊ [TE]Ṃ
P̣ỌṚẸ ỌṚẠN
TES ỤṬ DIGṆỊ
ḤABEAMỊNI
ẸF̣F̣UGERE OM
NIA HAEÇ QUǢ
F̣UTURA ET STA
B[I]TIS ANTE F̶H̶
FỊLIUM HOMI
21:37 NIS ERAT AU
TEM PER DIES
IN TEMPLO DO
CENS NOCTI
ḄUS UERO E
GREDIEBATUR
EṬ DEMORA
BATUR IN MOM
ṬẸ [QUI] ḌỊÇỊṬỤR
[OL]I[UE]Ṭ[UM]
21:38 EṬ ỌṂ[NIS POP]U
LUS DE LUC]Ẹ ỤỊ
[GILA]ḄẠṆṬ AD E
ỤṂ [IN] ṬẸM
P̣ḶỌ Ạ[UD]ỊṚẸ IL
[LUM
22:1 ADPROPINQUA
BAT] ẠỤTEM
DIES FẸṢTUS
ADZYMORUM
QUI DICITUR
22:2 PASCHA ET
QUAEREBAN̄
PONTỊFICES
ET SCRIBAE
QUOMODO
INTẸRFICE
RENT ILLUM
TIMEBANT
ẸNIM POP[U]
LUM

[L XXXII]

495 LUCANUM

22:3 INTRAUIT AU
TEM ṢATANAS
IN [I]ỤDAM
QỤỊ Ç[O]GNO
Ṃ[INAT]UR IṢ
CAṚIỌTH ỤṆ[U⁻]
ḌẸ NUME[RO]
22:4 XII· ET ABII[T]
ET CONLOC[U]
TUS EST PỌ[N]
TIFICIBUṢ ẸṬ
ṢÇṚỊBIS QUẸ⁻
ADMODUM
TRADERET IL
22:5 LUM ET GAUI
SI SUNT ET ṖỌḶ
ḶỊÇỊṬI SUNT
EI SE PECUNI
AM DATꝈUROS
22:6 ẸT QUAERE
BAT OPPORṬU
NITATEM ṬRA
ḌENDI ILLUM
[SI]ṆE TURBA

22:7 UENIT AUTEM
DIES PASCHAE
22:8 ET MISIT PE
ṬRUM [ET] IO
HAN[NEM] ḌỊ
ÇẸṆ[S] ẸỤṆ[T]ES
[PARATE] NỌ
BỊṢ [PASCHA
MA]ṆDỤ[CA
22:9 ṚE [QUI
DIXERUNT EI
UBI U]ỊṢ PA
22:10 REMỤṢ DIẊỊT
AUTEM AD E
OS ECCE IN
TRANTIBUS
UỌBIS CI
UITATEM OC
CURRET UO
BIS HOMO A⁻
ṖORAM AQUÆ
PORTANS SE
QUIMINI IL
LUM IN DOMO

496 SEC·

QUA INGRE
22:11 DITUR ET DI
CETIS PATRI
FAMILIAE DO
MUI DICIT TI
[B]I MAGISTER
UBI EST REFEC
TIO UBI PAS
ÇHA CUM DIS
CIPULIS MEIS
22:12 EDẠM ET ILLE
UOBIS OSTEN
DET MAEDIA
NUM STRA
TUM MAGNU̅
IBI PARATE
22:13 EUNTES AUTE̅
INUENERUN
SICUT DIXE
RAT ILLIS ET PA
RAUERUNT
PASCHA
22:14 ET CUM FACTA
EST HORA DIS
CUBUIT ET A
POSTOLI CUM
22:15 ILLO ET DIXIT
AD EOS DESI
DERIO CUPI
UI HOC PASCHA
MANDUCA
[RE] UOBISCU̅
[A]NTEQUAM
22:16 [P]ATIAR DICO
ENIM UOBIS
QUONIAM
NON EDAM
ILLUD DONEC
INPLEATUR
IN REGNO DĒI
22:17 ET ACCEPTO CA
LICE GRATIAS
EGIT DICENS
SUMITE HOC
ET PARTIMI
NI IN UOBIS
22:18 DICO ENIM
UOBIS QUONI

497 LUCANUM

AM NON BI
BAM DE FRUC
TU UINEAE
DONEC REG
NUM DĒI·
UENIAT
22:19 ET ACCEPTO PA
NE GRATIAS
EGIT ET CON
FREGIT ET DE
DIT ILLIS DI~~EC~~
CENS HOC EST
CORPUS ME
22:21 UM ATTAMEN
ECCE MANUS
PRODITORIS
MEI MECUM
SUPER MEN
SAM
22:22 FILIUS QUIDEˉ
HOMINIS SE
CUNDUM
QUOD DEFI
NITUM EST

UADIT
UẠERUM UAE
HOMINI ILLI
PER QUEM
22:23 TRADITUR ET
IPSI INQUỊRE
BANT INTER
SE QUIS NAM
ESSET QUI HOC
FACTURUS
ESSET
22:24 FACTA EST AUTEˉ
CONTENTIO
INTER ILLOS
QUIS NAM
ESSET MAŁIOR
22:25 AD ILLE DIXIT
EIS REGES
GENTIUM
DOMINAN
TUR EORUM
ET QUI POTES
TATEM IN EOS
EXERCUNT

498 SEC·

BENEFICI[O]
RUṂ [LARGI]
TỌ[RES DICUN]
TỤ[R]
22:26 UỌṢ ẠU[TE]Ṃ NO[¯]
IṬẠ ṢẸḌ [QUI]
MẠIOR ẸṢṬ ỊṆ
UOBIS ṆIẠṬ ṢỊ
ÇỤṬ MINOR
ẸṬ [QUI] PRAE
ẸṢṬ [UT] QUI MI
22:27 [NIS]ṬṚẠṬ QỤỊṢ
ENIṂ MAIỌṚ
ESṬ QUI RECU¯
BIT AUT QUI
MINISṬR[AT]
IN GENTIBUS
QỤIDEM QUI
RECUMBỊ[T]
IN UOBIṢ AU
TEM NON ṢỊÇ
SED QUI MI
NISTRAṬ EGO
AUTEM SUM

IN MEDIO UES
T[RU]M SIÇUT
[QUI] MINIṢ
22:28 Ṭ[RA]Ṭ UOS AU
ṬEM EST[I]S QUI
[PER]MANSỊS
[T]ỊṢ MẸÇỤM
ỊṆ ṬẸMP[T]A
ṬỊỌṆỊBUS MẸ
22:29 [IS] ẸṬ ẸGỌ ḌỊṢPỌ
ṆỌ ỤỌḄỊṢ [SI]
CUT DISPỌSU
[I]T ṂỊ[HI] PAT[ER]
MEUS REGNU¯
22:30 ỤT EDATIS ET
BIBATIS SUPER
ṂENṢAM
ṂẸAṂ IN REG
NỌ ṂẸỌ ET ṢẸ
Ḍ[E]ẠṬỊṢ IN XII·
ṢẸ[DI]ḄỤṢ IU
[DIC]ẠNṬẸṢ X̣I[I·]
TṚỊḄỤṢ [I]SRA
22:31 EḶ DIXIT

499 LUCANUM

AUTEM ·DM̄S·
PETRO SIṂ[Oˉ]
SIMON Ẹ[CCE]
SATANAS POS
ṬULAUIT UOS
UT SCRIBẠR
ET TAMQUẠˉ
TRITICUM
22:32 EGO AUTEM
ROGAUI [PRO]
TẸ ṆẸ DẸF̣ỊCẸ
[RET F]IDES TUA
[ET T]Ụ TANDEˉ
CONUERSUS
CONFIRMA
FRATRES TUOS
ET ROGATE NE
INTRETIS IN
TEMPTATIO
22:33 NE : DIXIT
ẠUTEM EI PE
[TR]US ·DM̄E·
TECUM PARA
TUS SUM ET

IN CARCEREˉ
ET IṆ [MORT]Eˉ
22:34 IRE [QUI AIT] ḌI
CO TIḄ[I PET]ṚE
NON CAṆ[T]A
BIT HOD[I]Ẹ GAL
LUS DONEC̣
ṬU ME TER AḄ
[N]EGES
22:35 ET DIX̣IT EIS Q̣[U]Ạˉ
DO MI[SI] UOS
SIN[E] SACCU
LO ET PERA ET
CALCIAMEN
TIS NUMQUID
ALIQUID DEFU
22:36 IT UOBIS AD IL
LI DIXERUNT
NIHIL DIXIT
ERGO SED NUNC
QUI HABET SAC
CULUM TOL
LAT SIMILITER
ET PERAM ET

500 SEC·

QUI ṆỌN HA
BET [UEND]ẠṬ
Ṭ[UNICA]Ṃ ṢỤ
ẠṂ [ET E]ṂẠṬ
G̣[L]ẠḌỊỤṂ
22:37 DI[CO] ẸṆỊ[M UO
Ḅ[IS QUONIAM]
ẠḌ[HUC HOC
QUOD] S[CRIB]
TỤṂ [EST OPOR]
Ṭ[ET INPLERI]
ỊṆ Ṃ[E QUOD]
ẸṬ C̣ỤṂ ỊṆ
ỊỤṢṬIS DEPU
TATUS [ES]Ṭ
ET DE ME QUÆ
SUNT FINEṂ
22:38 HABENT AḌ IL
LE DIXIT DM̄E·
ECCE GLADII
DUO HIC̣ QUI
DIXIT EI SAT
22:39 EST ET E
GREṢṢỤS ABI

IT SECUNDUM
[CONS]UEṬUDI
[NEM] IN MON
ṬẸṂ ỌḶỊUẸṬI
SEC̣UṬỊ SUNT
[AU]ṬEM ILLỤ[M]
[ET] ḌISCIP̣U
22:40 [LI EIUS] ET CU¯
[ESSET] ỊṆ ẸỌ
[LOCO DIX]ỊṬ ỊḶ
[LIS] OR[ATE NE]
[I]ṆṬṚẸ[TIS IN]
ṬẸ[MPTATIO]
ṆẸ[M]
22:41 ET IPSE ẠBOLSUS
EST ẠḄ ILLIS ṬA¯
QỤAM LAPIDIS
ICTUS ET POSI
ṬIS GENIBUS
22:42 ỌṚ[AB]AT DICEN[S]
[P]ATẸR NON
UOLỤNT[A]S
MẸA SED TUA
[F]ỊAT TRẠṆ[S]

501 LUCANUM

FERS CALICEM
HUNC A MẸ
22:43 APPARUIT Ạ[U]
TEM ILLI AN
GELUS DE CAE
LO CONFORṬỊ
ANS EUM
ET FACTUS IN
AGONIA ET
PROLIXIUS
22:44 ỌṚABAT ET FAC
T[US E]ST SUDOR
I[LLI]US QUASI
GUTTAE SAN
GUINIS DECUR
RENTIS SU
PER TERRAM
22:45 ET SURGENS
AB ORATIO
NE UENIT AD
DISCIPULOS
ET INUENIT ILLOS
SUOS DORMI
ENTES A MAE
22:46 RORE ET DIXIT

EIS QUID DOR
MITIS SURGI
TE ORATE ṆE
INTRETIS IN
TEMPTATIO
22:47 NEM ET AD
HUC EO LOQUE¯
TE ECCE TUR
BA ET QUI UO
CABATUR IU
DAS UNUS
DE DUODECIM
PRAECEDE
BAT ILLOS ET AC
CEDENS OS
CULATUS EST
22:48 IH̄M DIXIT
AUTEM ·IH̄S·
IUDA OSCULO
FILIUM HOMI
NIS TRADIS
22:49 UIDENTES AU
TEM QUI ERANT
CIRCA ILLUM

502 SEC·

QUOD FUTURU̅
ESSET DIXERUN̄
IL[LI] Ḍ[M̄]Ẹ· ṢỊ PER
CỤṬ[I]EṂỤṢ [I̅]
22:50 GL[A]DIO ET PER
CỤṢṢỊṬ UNUS
QUIDAM E[X] IL
LIS SẸRUUM
PỌNTIFICIS
ẸṬ AḄṢCIDIT
AUREM Ị[LLIUS]
22:51 DEX̣TRAṂ DỊ
XỊṬ ẠUṬẸṂ
ILḶỊ ·ỊH̄Ṣ· [S]ỊṆE
USQUE HỌÇ
ET EXTẸNDEṆ[S]
MAṆỤM SU
AM TEṬỊ[GIT]
EUM ET R[E]
INTEGRA[TA]
EST AURỊṢ ẸỊỤṢ
22:52 DIXIT AUTEM
IH̄S AD EOS QUI
UENERANT
AD SE PONTI
Ḟ[ICES ET A]NTIS
Ṭ[ITES TE]Ṃ[P]LI
Ẹ[T SE]NIỌṚ[E]S
ṬẠṂQUAṂ A[D]
[LATR]ỌNEM
[EXIST]ỊS CUM
[GLADII]S ET ḞUS
22:53 [TIBUS] ÇUM
[COTTIDIE] ES
[SEM] ỤỌ[BIS]
CỤM IN [TEM]
PLO NON [EX]
TENDEBATIS
MANUS SU
PER ME SED HÆC
EST UESTRA HO
RA ET POTES
ṬẠṢ A TENE
ḄṚẠẸ
22:54 C[O]ṆP̣ṚEHEṆ
ṢỤM AỤṬẸM
EUM ADDUXE
RUNT ET IN DO

503 LUCANUM

MUM PONTI
FICIṢ P̣ẸṬṚỤṢ
AUTEM ṢẸ[QUE]
ḄA[T]ỤR [A LON
22:55 GE INÇẸṆ[SO]
AUTEM [IGNE]
IN MEḌ[IO ATRI]
O ET ÇỌṆ[SEDEN]
TIBỤṢ [SEDEBAT]
PEṬṚỤ[S IN ME]
DỊỌ [ILLORUM]
22:56 QU[E]Ṃ ÇUM U[I]
DISSET QUAE
DAM ANCIL
LA INTUENS
EUM DIXIT ET
HIC EX ILLIS ẸṢṬ
QUICUM EO
22:57 ERANT AD ILLẸ
NEGAUI[T] ḌI
CENS [MULIER]
NON ṆỌUI
22:58 EUM ET EGRES
SUSM ILLUM

AD IANUAM
[UIDIT ALIA] ẸṬ
[AIT ET ... IBI
ERANT ET HIC
FUIT CUM ·IH̄U·
NAZARENO
ET RURSUS
NEGAUIT CU¯
22:59 IURE IURAN
DO] Q̣UEM [PAU
LO POST CUM
UIDISSET QUI
DAM DIXIT
UERE ET HIC
CUM ·IH̄U· E]
ṚAT ṆẠM [ET
G]ẠḶỊḶẠ[EUS
EST]
22:60 Ḍ[IXIT] AUTEM
P̣ẸṬṚỤṢ HO
MO NESCIO
QUIḌ [D]ỊÇỊṢ
ET PRỌṬỊṆUS
ADHUC LỌQUE¯

504 SEC·

TE ILLO GALLUS
CẠNṬẠUIT
22:61 E[T CONU]ER
[SUS ·D]M̄S· REṢ
P̣[EXIT PET]ṚU¯
Ẹ[T RE]MEMO
ṚATUS EST PE
T[R]US UERBU¯
DM̄I· SICUT
ḌIXIT ILLI AN
[T]E QUAM GAḶ
[L]ỤS CANTET
T[ER] ME NEGA
[BIS T]Ẹ ṢC̣IRE
22:63 ET [UIRI QUI] C̣O¯
T[I]ṆEBANT
ILLUM DERI
DEBANT EUM
22:64 ET COPERIEN
TES FACIEM
ILLIUS PERCU
TEBANT ET IN
TERROGABA¯
ILLUM DICEN
TES PROFETI
ZA QUIS EST
QUI PERCUS
SIṬ TE
22:65 ET ALIA MULTA
BLASPEMAN
TES DI[C]EBAN
22:66 AD EUM ET CU¯
DIEṢ ḤỌRTA EST
C[O]NỤENE
[R]UNṬ SENIO
RES POPULI
PONTIFICES
ET SCRIBAE
ET DEDUXE
RUNT ILLUM
IN CONCILI
UM SUUM
22:67 ET INTERRỌ
GẠ[B]ẠNT EUM
DI[CE]NTES
SI TU ES ·XP̄S·
DIC NOBIS
DIXIT AUTEM

505 LUCANUM

ILLIS SI UOBIS
DIXERO NỌN
22:68 CRẸDIṬIS [SI IN
TE[R]ROGẠ[UE]
[R]O NON RẸṢ
[PON]ḌẸ[BITIS]
SED [NEC DIMIT]
22:69 TETỊ[S ME AMO]
DỌ [AUTEM]
E[RIT FILIUS HO
MINIS SEDENS]
ẠḌ [DEXTRAM
UIRTUTIS DĒI
22:70 DIXERUN]Ṭ ẠỤ
TEM] ẸI ỌM
NẸṢ TU EṢ [FILI
US DĒI Ḍ[IXIT]
AỤṬẸṂ [ILLIS
UOS DICITIS]
QỤỊẠ [EGO SU⁻]
22:71 Q̣ỤI D[IXERUNT]
QUID ẠḌ[HUC]
EGEMỤṢ TEṢ
TIMONIO AỤ

DIUIMUS ENI⁻
DE ỌRẸ [ILL]IUS
23:1 ET [S]ỤṚG[ENS]
[U]NI[UERSA]
ṂULTITUḌ[O]
ẸỌṚỤṂ [AD]ḌU
[XERUN]Ṭ ILLU⁻
ẠḌ P̣ỊḶẠṬỤṂ
23:2 [CO]ẸP̣ẸṚỤṆṬ
[AUTE]Ṃ ẠC̣C̣Ụ
[SARE] ỊḶḶ[UM]
[DICENT]ẸṢ
[HUNC IN]ỤE
[NIMUS EUE]R
[TENTEM G]ẸN
[TEM TRIBU
TUM DARE CA]Ẹ
[SA]RI D[I]CEN
[TEM SE ·]XP̄M·
ṚẸ[GEM] ẸṢ
23:3 ṢẸṬ [PILATUS]
AỤṬẸṂ ỊN
TERRỌGAUIT
EUM DICEṆS

506 SEC·

TU ES REX IU
DAEORUM QUI
R[ES] P̣ONDIT
IḶḶ[I T]U DICIS
23:4 PILATUS AU
TEM AIT AD PO¯
TIFICIS ET TUR
BAM NULLAM
INUENIO C̣Ụ[L]
PAM IN HO
MINE HOC̣
23:5 AD ILLỊ IṆ[UALES]
C̣ẸḄẠṆ[T DICE¯]
TEṢ [CO]Ṃ[MO]
ỤẸṬ [POPULUM]
DỌC̣[ENS PER]
TỌṬ[AM] ỊỤ[DAE]
AM INCḤỌ
ANS A GAL[IL]Ạ[E]
A USQUE H[I]C
23:6 PILATUS AUTE¯
UT AUḌIIṬ GA
LILAEAM IN
TERROGAUIT

AN A GALILAE
A HOMO ISTE
23:7 ESSET ET CUM
COGNOUIS
SEṬ EUM DE
HEṚODIS PO
TES[T]ẠTEM ES
SE [R]ẸMISIT
[ILLU]Ṃ ẠḌ ḤE
[RODEM] QỤỊ
[ERAT ET IPSE]
HIEROS[OLY]
MIS IN Ḥ[IS
D]IEBUS
23:8 [HE]RODES AU
ṬẸM UISO ·IH̄U·
GAUISUS EST
UALDE ERAT
ẸNIM CUPI
[E]NS UIDERE
ILLUM PROP
TEREA QUOD
AUDIRET FRE
QUENTER DE

507 LUCANUM

ILLO ET SPERA
BAT ALIQ̣ỤỌD
SIGNUM ỤỊ
ḌE[R]E AB ILLỌ
[FI]ERI
23:9 [IN]TERROGAḄẠṬ
AUTEM ILLUṂ
UERḄIS P̣ḶỤṚỊ
ḄỤS ỊP̣ṢẸ ỤẸṚỌ
NI[HIL RESP]O¯
23:10 Ḍ[EBAT ILLI STA]
[BAN]Ṭ AUTEM
[PON]ṬIF[I]CES
[U]E[H]EMENTE[R]
ACCUSANṬẸṢ
23:11 EUM SPER
NENS AUTEM
ILLUM ET HE
[R]ODES CUM
ẸX̣ERCITU SUO
ET DELUSUṂ
ỊṆDUENS UES
TẸ CANDIDA
REMISIT PILA
23:12 TO : FACTI
SUṆṬ A[UT]EM
ỊN ẠṂ[I]C̣[ITI]A¯
HEROḌẸṢ ET
[P]ỊLATUṢ EẠ
ḌEM HỌṚẠ
PRAEERANT
ẸNIṂ ỊN ỊṆỊ
ṂỊC̣ỊTIAṂ
23:13 [P]ILATUS AUTEM
[CO]NỤ[O]CẠNS
[PONTI]F̣ICES
ẸṬ P̣ṚỊṆC̣Ị
23:14 P̣ES P̣ỌP̣ỤḶỊ [DI
XIT] AḌ ỊḶḶỌṢ
[DE]ṬỤḶỊṢṬỊṢ
ṂỊḤỊ ḤỌṂỊ
[N]ẸṂ [HU]ṆC
[TANQ]ỤAM AD
ỤẸṚṬẸṆṬEM
P̣ỌP̣ỤḶỤM ET
ECCE ẸGO CO
RAM UOS IN
TERROGANS

508 SEC·

NIHIL INUE
NI DIGNUM
IN HOMINE¯
HOC DE IIS QUǼ
ACCUSATIS
23:15 EUM SED NEC
HERODES RE
MISI ENIM
UOS AD ILLUM
ET ECCE NIHIL
DIGNUM MOR
TE GESTUM
23:16 EST ILLI CASTI
GATUM ERGO
ILLUM DIMIT
TAM
23:18 EXCLAMABẠNT
AUTEM TO
TUS POPULUS
DICENTES TOL
LE HUNC DI
MITTE AUTE¯
NOBIS BARAB
23:19 BANT QUI E

RAT PROPTER
SEDITIONEM
QUANDAM
FACTAM IN
CIUITATEM
CONIECTUS
IN CARCERE¯
QUIA HOMICI
DIUM FECE
RAT
23:20 RURSUS AUTE[M]
PILATUS [AD]
LOCUṠTUS ẸṢT
EIS UOLENS
DIMITTERE
23:21 IH̄M· QUI PRO
CLAMABANT
DICENTES
CRUCIFIGE
23:22 ILLUM QUI TER
TIO DIXIT AD
ILLOS QUID
ENIM MALI
FECIT HIC NI

509 LUCANUM

HIL DIGNUM
MORTIS IN
UENI IN ILLO
CASTIGATŪ
ERGO ILLUM
DIMITTAM
23:23 QUI IMMI
NEBANT UO
CIBUS MAG
NIS POSTULĀ
TES XFIGE IL
LUM INUA
ḶESCEBANT
UOCES ILLO
RUM
23:24 ET PILATUS DE
CREUIT FIE
RI PETITIONĒ
23:25 ILLORUM DI
MISIT AUTĒ
EUM QUI PROP
TER HOMICI
DIUM ET SE
DITIONEM

CONIECTUS
ERAT IN CAR
CEREM ·IH̄M·
AUTEM TRA
DIDIT UOLUN
TATI IPSORUM
23:26 ET CUM DEDU
CERENT EUM
SIMONEM
QUENDAM
CYRENEUM
UENIENTĒ
A UILLA ADPRE
HENDENTES
INPOSUERUN
ILLI CRUCEM
FERRE POST
23:27 IH̄M· SEQUE
BATUR AUTĒ
EUM MUL
TITUDO IN
GENS POPU
LI ET MULIE
RUM QUAE

510 SEC·

PLANG̣ẸḄANT
SẸ EṬ LA[M]EN
TABAN[T]
23:28 AD QUAS Ç̣ON
UERSUS ·IH̄S·
DIXIT FILỊAE
HIERUSALEM
NOLITE FLERE
ME UERUM
UOS FLETE ET
NATOS UES
23:29 TROS QUOṆỊ
AM UENIẸ[NT]
DIES IN QỤ[I]
BUṢ [DI]CENT
FẸLICES STERI
LES ET UENṬ
RES QUI NON
GENUERUN̄
ET UBERA QUÆ
NON EDỤÇ̣Ạ
UERỤNT
23:30 TUNC INCIPI
ENT DICERE

MONTIBUS
CADITE SU
PER NOS ET COL
LIBUṢ TEGITE
23:31 NO~~R~~S QUONI
AM [SI] ỊṆ UM[I]
DO LIGNO HAEC
FACIUNT IN
ARIDO QUID
FIET
23:32 DỤCEBANTUR
AUTEM ET ALI
I DUO LATRO
NES CUM IL
LO INTERFICI
23:33 ET CUM UE
NISSENT AD
LOCUM QUI
APPELLATUR
CALUARIAE
CRUCIFIXE
RUNT EUM ET
LATRONES
UNUM QUI

M XX̣XI[III]

511 LUCANUM

DEM AD DEX
TRAM ET ALIUˉ
AD SINISTRAM
23:34 ET DIUIDEN
TES UESTIMEˉ
TA IPSIUS MIT
TEBANT SOR
23:35 TES ET STABAT
POPULUS EX
SPECTANS SUB
SANNABANT
AUTEM EUM
PRINCIPES
INTRA SE DI
CENTES ALIOS
SALUOS FE
CIT SE SALUUˉ
SE FACIAT SI
HIC EST XP̄S
DĒI ELECTUS
23:36 INRIDEBANT
AUTEM EUM
EỊ MILITES
ACCEDEN
TES ACETUM
OFFERENTES
23:37 EI ET DICEN
TES TU ES REX
IUDAEORUˉ
SALUA TE IP
23:38 SUM ERAT
AUTEM ET
INSCRIPTIO
SCRIPTA SU
PER EUM REX
IUDAEORUˉ
HIC
23:39 UNUS AUTEM
EX IIS QUI
SUSPENSI
ERANT MA
LEFICỊI BLAS
PHEMABAT
ILLUM DICENS
NONNE TU
ES XP̄S LIBE
RA TE ET NOS
23:40 RESPONDENS

512 SEC·

AUTEM ALI
US OBIURGA
BAT EUM DI
CENS NEC TI
MES ·D̅M̅ QUO
NIAM IN EO
DEM IUDICI
23:41 O ES ET NOS
QUIDEM
IUSTE DIGNA
ENIM QUO
RUM GESSI
MUS RECE
PIMUS
HIC AUTEM NI
HIL MALI FE
23:42 CIT ET DICE
BAT AD ·IH̄M·
MEMENTO
MEI CUM
UENERIS IN
REGNO TUO
23:43 ET DIXIT ILLI
IH̄S· AMEN

DICO TIBI HO
DIE MECU¯
ERIS IN PA
23:44 RADISO ET
ERAT CIRCI
TER HORA SEX
TA ET TENE
BRAE FACTǢ
SUNT SUPER
OMNEM
TERRAM ET
USQUE HO
RAM NONA¯
23:45 INTENEBRI
CATUS EṢṬ
SOLỤ ET UELU¯
TEMPLI SCIS
SUM EST ME
23:46 DIUM ET EX
CLAMANS
UOCE MAG
NA IH̄S·
PATER IN MA
NIBUS TUIS

513 LUCANUM

COMMENDO
SP̄M· MEUM
ET EMỊSIT ·SP̄M·
23:47 QUOD CUM UI
DISSET CEN
TURIO HONO
RIFICAUIT
D̅M̅· DICENS
UERE HOMO
HIC [I]USTUS
23:48 ERẠṬ ET OM
NẸS QUAE CO⁻
ỤENERANT
TURBAE AD
SPECTACULU⁻
HOC UIDEN
TES EX EA QUÆ
FIEBANT PER
CUTENTES
PECTORA SUA
REUERTEBA⁻
23:49 TUR STA
BANT AUTEM
OMNES NO

TI ILLIUS A LO⁻
GE ET MULIE
RES QUAE SE
CUTAE FUE
RANT ILLUM
A GALILAEA
UIDENTES
HAEC
23:50 ET ECCE UIR
NOMINE IO
SEPH QUI E
RAT DECURIO
BONUS ET IUS
23:51 TUS HIC NON
CONSENSE
RAT CONSILIO
ET OPERE IL
L[O]RUM AB A
RIMATHIA
CIUITATE IU
DAEORUM
QUI EXPECTA
BAT REGNU⁻
23:52 DĒI· : HIC

514 SEC·

ACCESSIT AD
PILATUM ET
PETIT CORPUS
23:53 IH̄U· ET DEPO
SITUM INUOL
UIT EUM IN
SINDONEM
ET POSUIT IL
LUM IN MO
NUMENTO
SCULPTILI Ụ
BI NONDUṂ
ALIQUI^S ERẠṬ
23:54 POSITUS ET DI
ES ERAT CENA
PURAE ET SAB
BATUM INḶỤ
23:55 CEЄSCEBAT Ç̣Ọ[N]
SECUTAE [D]U
AE MULIERES
QUAE SECU
TAE F̣UERAN̄
ILLUM DE GA
LILAEA UIDE

RUNT MONỊ
MẸNTUM
ET QUOṂ[O]DO
POSITUM EST
[C]OR[P]US ỊḶḶỊ
23:56 [US R]ẸUER
[SA]Ẹ AUTEM
[PARA]UERUN̄
AROṂATA ET
UNG̣U[E]NTA
ẸṬ [SABBATO]
QUID[E]Ṃ [QUI]
[E]UERUNT Ṣ[E]
CUNḌUṂ MA¯
DATUM
24:1 P̣RIMA AUTEM
DIE SABBATO
RUM UENE
RUNT ANTE
LUCEM ỤẠḶ
DE AD MONỤ
MENTUṂ
ADFERENTE[S]
QUAE PARA

515 LUCANUM

24:2 UERUNT IN
UENERUNT
AU[T]EṂ ḶAP̣Ị
DEM [REU]OḶỤ
TUM Ạ [M]ONU
24:3 MEṆ[TO IN
[GRE]SṢ[A]E [AU
TEM NON IN
[UENERU]NT
C̣OṚ[PUS]
24:4 [ET FACT]ỤṂ EST
[DUM S]TUPE
[RE]NṬ [DE] HOC
ECC̣[E UI]ṚỊ DU
O ADSTITERUN
IUXTA ILLAS
IN UESTE FUL
24:5 GENTI TIMO
RẸ AỤTEM
ADPREHEN
ṢAE INCLINA¯
[T]ẸS FẠCIEM
AD TERRAM
DIXERUNT AD

AD ILLAS QUID
QUAERITIS
UIUUM CU¯
MORTUIS
24:6 MEMORAMI
NI SICUT LO
CUTUS EST
UOBIS DUM
ADHUC ESSET
IN GALILAEA
24:7 DICENS QUO
ṆIAM FILIU¯
HOMINIS
ỌPORTET TRA
DI ET TERTIA
DIE RESUR
24:8 GERE ET MAE
MOṚATAE
SUNT UER
BOṚUM HO
ṚUM
24:9 ET REUERSÆ
RENUNTIA
UERUNT HAEC

516 SEC·

OMNIA ILLIS
UNDECIM
ET CETERIS O̅
24:10 NIBUS ERAT
AUTEM MAG
DALENA ET
MARIA IACO
BI ET IOHAN
NA ET RELI
QUE CUM EIS
QUE DICEBAN
AD APOSTO
24:11 LOS HAEC ET
UISA SUNT
ILLIS TANQUA̅
DELERA UER
tercia feria in albis BA HAEC ET
NON CREDE
BANT EIS
✠ 24:13 ET ECCE DUO
ERANT EX IL
LIS EUNTES
IN MUNICI
PIUM STADI

OS HABENTE̅
LX· AB HIERU
SALEM CUI NO
MEN AMMAUṢ
24:14 Ṡ ET IPSI TRAC
TAḄẠṆT DE O̅
N[I]BUS QUA[E]
HIS CONTEGE
24:15 RAN[T] ET FAC
TUM E[ST] DU[̅]
TRAÇṬẠ[RENT]
IPSI ET [IH̅S· AS]
CENDENS [CO]
MITẠḄẠTUR
24:16 CUM ILLIS O
CULI AUTEM
ĖȮṘU̇Ṁ EO
RUM TENE
BANTUR NE
AGNOSCERE[NT]
ILLUM
24:17 DIXIT AUTEM
AD EOS QUAE
SUNT UERBA

517 LUCANUM

ISTA QUAE TRAC
TATIS AD ALTER
UTRUM EST
ESTIS TRISTES
24:18 RESPONDENS
AUTEM UNUS
EX EIS CUI NŌ
MEN EST CLEO
PHAS DIXIT
AD ILLUM
TU SOLUS PERE
GRINUS ES Ī
HIERUSALEM
NESCIS QUAE
GESTA SUNT
IN ILLA IN DI
EBUS ISTIS
24:19 QUI AIT ILLIS
QUAE ET IPSI
DIXERUNT
DE ·IH̄U· NA
ZARENO QUI
FUIT PROPHE
TA POTENS IN

OPERE ET UER
BO CORAM
DEO ET OM
NI POPULO
24:20 QUOMODO
HUNC TRA
DIDERUNT
PONTIFICES
NOSTRI IN
IUDICIO MOR
TIS ET CRUCI
FIXERUNT
24:21 ILLUM NOS
UERO SPERA
UIMUS IPSŪ
ESSE QUI RE
DEMPTURUS
ESSET ISTRA
HEL NUNC
TERTIA DIES
EST HODIE
EX QUO FAC
TA SUNT HAEC
24:22 ET SUPER HIS

518 SEC·

OMNIBUS
MULIERES
QUAEDAM EX
NOBIS EXTER
RUERUNT HOS
QUAE FUERUN̄
MANE AD
MONUMEN
24:23 TUM ET CUM
NON INUE
NISSENT COR
PUS EIUS UE
NERUN̄ DỊ
CENTES
ETIAM UISIO
NEM ANGE
LORUM SE UI
DISSE QUI DI
CUNT ẸUM
UIUERE
24:24 ET ABIERUNT
QUIDAM EX
NOBIS AD MO
NUMENTỤ⁻

ET INUENE
RUNT ITA UT
MULIERES DI
XẸ[R]ỤNT IPSU⁻
A[UTE]M NON
UIDERUNT
24:25 ET IPSE ḌIXIT AD ILḶOṢ
INSENŦSATI
ET ḌṚẠUES COṚ
DẸ ỊṆ ÇREDE⁻
DO OMNIḄUS
QUIBUS LO
CUTI SUNT
P̣ṚỌPHAETAE
24:26 NONNE HAEC
OPORTEBAT PA
TI ·XP̄M· ET IN
TRARE IN GLO
RIAM SỤAM
24:27 ET ERAṬ INCHO
ANS A MOY
SEN ET OMNI
BỤ[S] PROPHE
TIṢ INTERPRǢ

519 LUCANUM

TANS EIS IN O¯
NIBUS SCRIP
TURIS DE SẸ
24:28 ẸṬ ADPROPỊN
QUAUERỤNT
IN UICUM
QUEM ỊḄẠṆṬ
ET IPSE ẠḌF̣Ẹ[C]
TABAT SE LON
24:29 GIUS IRE ẸṬ
COEGERỤN
ILLUM DICEN
TES MANE NO
BISCUM QUO
NIAM AD UES
PERUM IAM
DECLINAUIT
DIES
ET INTRAUIT
UT C̣UM EIS
MANERET
24:30 ET FACTUM
EST CUM ḌỊṢ
CUBUISSET

CUM ILLIS AC
CEPTUM PA
NEM BENE
DIXIT ET FRA¯
GENS PORRI
GEBAT ILLIS
24:31 ET ADAPERTI
SUNT OCULI
EORUM ET
COGNOUE
RUNT ILLUM
ET IPSE NUS
QUẠM CON
PARỤIT AB IL
24:32 LIS ET DI
XERUNT AD
ALTERUTRU¯
NONNE COR
[N]OS[T]RUM
ERAT IN NO
BIS [hd] SCRIPTU
24:33 RAS ET SUR
GENTES EA
DEM HORA

ARDENS IN UIA CUM AD
APERIEBAT NOBIS

520 SEC·

REUERSI SUN
IN HIERUSA
LEM ET INUE
NERUNT COL
LECTOS ·XI· ET
EOS QUI CUM
ILLIS ERANT
24:34 DICENTES
QUONIAM
UERE RESUR
REXIT ·DM̄S·
ET UISUS EST
SIMONI
24:35 ET IPSI ENARRA
BANT QUAE
IN UIA GES
TA ERANT ET
SICUT AGNI
TUS EST ILLIS
IN FRACTIO
24:36 NE PANIS ET
DUM HAEC
[se]xta feria in albis LOQUUNTUR
IPSE STETIT

IN MEDIO EO
24:37 RUM EXTER
RITI AUTEM
ET TIMORE
ADPREHEN
SI PUTABANT
SE ·SP̄M· UIDE
24:38 RE : QUI DI
XIT ILLIS QUID
TURBATI ESTIS
ET QUARE CO
GITATIONES
ASCENDUNT
IN CORDE UES
24:39 TRO UIDETE
MANUS ME
AS ET PEDES
MEOS QUONI
AM EGO SUM
IPSI TRACTA
TE ET UIDETE
QUONIAM
SP̄S· CARNE¯
ET OSSUM NO¯

521 LUCANUM

HABET SICUT
ME UIDETES
HABENTEM
24:41 ADHUC AUTE¯
NON CREDEN
TIBUS ILLIS ET
STUPENTIBUS
PRAE GAUDIO
DIXIT HABE
TIS ALIQUID
QUOD EDAM[U]S
24:42 HIC Q̣UI P[O]R
REXẸṚỤṆṬ
ILLỊ [PISCE]Ṣ ẠSSI
PART[EM] ET FA
24:43 UUM ET ACCI
PIENS MAN
DUCAUIT CO
24:44 RAM ILLIS ET
DIXIT EIS HÆC
UERBA QUAE
LOCUTUS SUM
APUT UOS CU¯
ADHUC ESSEM

UOBISCUM
QUONIAM
OPORTET IN
PLERI OMNIA
QUAE SCRIP
TA SUNT IN LE
GE MOYSI ET
PROPHETIS ET
PSALMIS DE
24:45 ME ṬUNC
APERUIT SE¯
SUM [I]ḶLORU¯
AD INTELLE
GENḌUM
SCRIPTURAS
24:46 ET DIXIT EIS
QUONIAM
SIC SCRIPTU¯
EST ·XP̄M· PA
TI ET RESUR
GERE A MOR
TUIS TERTIA
24:47 DIE ET PRAEDI
CARI IN NO

522 SEC·

MINE ILLIUS
PAENITENTIA¯
ET REMISSIO
NEM PECCATO
RUM IN OM
NIḄUS GENTI
BUS INCIPIEṆS
AB HIERUSA
24:48 LEM [UO]S AU
TEM [ES]TIS TE
STES HOṚUṂ
24:49 ET [E]GO [MITTA¯]
REP̣ṚỌṂỊṢ[SI]
ONẸM [PA]ṬṚ[IS]
SUP̣EṚ ỤỌṢ
UOS AỤṬẸ[M]
SEDẸTE ỊṆ [CI]
UIT[ATE]Ṃ ḌỌ
NẸC ỊṆ[DUA]
MINI ỤI[RT]U
TEM A SUM
24:50 MO EDU
XIT AUTEM
ILLOS USQUE
AD BETHANI
AM ET EXTOL
LENS MANUS
SUẠṢ BENEDI
X[IT] EOS
24:51 ẸṬ F̣ẠÇṬUM EST
Ḍ[UM] ḄENE
[DICERE]T ILLOS
[DISCE]ṢṢỊṬ AB
24:52 [EIS] ẸṬ IPSI RE
[U]Ẹ[R]SI SUNT
I[N H]IER[U]ṢA
LẸM [CUM GAU]
DI[O MAGNO]
24:53 ET E[RAN]T SEṂ
PER IN TEM
PLO CONLAU
[DA]NTES ·$\overline{\text{DM}}$·

523 LUCANUM

EUANG. SECUN.

LUCANUM

EXP. INC.

SECUNDUM

MARCUM

7 *Codex Vercellensis* Luke: Edition

1 Quoniam quidem multi temptauerunt [– – –] **4** noscas eorum sermonem, de quibus eruditus es [– – –] **6** mandatis et iustificationis domini sine querella [– – –]

1:1 temptauerunt] 2 5 conati sunt cet. | deest usque v. 4: disponere narrationem de his rebus quae impletae sunt in nobis sicut tradiderunt nobis qui a principio contemplatores et ministri fuerunt uerbi placuit et mihi ad initio diligenter omnia adsecuto secundum ordinem scribere tibi optime o theofile ut 2 conscribere narrationem de his quibus conpleta sunt in nobis rebus sicut tradiderunt nobis qui ab initio ipsi uiderunt et ministri fuerunt uerbi uisum est et mihi adsecuto desusum omnibus diligenter ex ordine tibi scribere optime theofile uti 5 ordinare narrationem (narrationem rerum 4 rerum narrationem 8) quae in nobis completae (complete 8) sunt rerum (om. 4 8) sicut tradiderunt nobis qui ab initio ipsi uiderunt et ministri fuerunt sermonis (sermones 4) uisum est (placuit 4) et mihi (add. et spirituo sancto 4) assecuto (adsecuto 4 8) a principio omnia (omnibus 4) diligenter ex ordine tibi scribere optime theofile (theophile 4 theopile 8) ut cet. **4** noscas] agnoscas 2 cognoscas cet. | eorum sermonem de quibus eruditus es] de quibus edoctus sis sermonibus 2 de quibus structus es uerborum 5 eorum uerborum de quibus eruditus es cet. deest usque v. 6: firmitatem fuit in diebus herodes reges iudae sacerdos quidam nomine zacharias de uice abiam et uxor illius de filiabus aron et nomen eius elisabet fuerunt autem iusti ambo ante faciem dei ambulantes in omnibus 2 ueritatem fuit in diebus hierodis regis iudaeae sacerdos quidam nomine zacharias de uice abia et uxor illi de filiabus aaron et nomen eius elisabet erant autem iusti ambo in conspectu dei ambulantes in omnibus 5 ueritatem fuit in diebus herodis (herodes 4) regis iudaeae (iudeae 4 8) sacerdos quidam nomine zacharias (zaccharias 4 8) de uice abia (auia 4 8) et uxor illi (illius 4) de filiabus aaron et nomen eius (om. 8) elisabet (elisabel 4) erant autem ambo iusti (iusti ambo 4) ante deum (dominum 4) incedentes (incidentes 8) in omnibus cet. | **6** mandatis] praeceptis 2 | iustificationis] iustiis 2 iustitiis 5 iustificationibus cet. querella] 8 A quaerella 2 4 macula 5 | deest usque v. 9: et non erat illis filius quoniam erat elisabet steriles et ambo erant progressi in diebus suis factum est autem cum sacerdotium administraret in ordine uicis suae ante dominum secundum consuetudinem sacerdotii sors illi exiuit ut 2 et non erat illis filius quoniam erat elisabed sterilis et ambo erant seniores in diebus suis factum est autem dum sacerdotio fungeretur in ordine sacerdotii sui in conspectu dei secundum consuetudinem sacrificii forte accidit 5 et non erat illis filius eo quod (qod A*) esset elisabet (elisabel 4 elisabeht 8) sterelis (sterilis 4) et ambo processissent (processi erant 4 8) in diebus suis factum est autem cum sacerdotio fungeretur (add. zaccharias 4 zaccarias 8) in ordine (ordinem 4) uicis suae ante deum (dominum deum 8) secundum consuetudinem sacerdotii (sacerdoti 8) sorte exiit ut cet.

https://doi.org/10.1515/9783111142531-008

9 incensum poneret ingressus in templum [– – –] **13** quoniam ecce exaudita est
oratio tua, et uxor tua elisabet pariet tibi filium, et uocaris nomen eius iohannem.
14 eritque gaudium tibi et exultatio, et multi in natiuitate eius gaudebunt. **15** erit
enim magnus in conspectu domini, et uinum et sicera non bibet, et spiritu sancto
inplebitur adhuc ex utero matris suae, **16** et multos filiorum istrahel conuertet ad
dominum deum ipsorum, **17** et ipse praeibit in conspectu eius in spiritu et uirtute
heliae ad conuertenda corda patrum ad filios et incredibiles ad prudentiam
iustorum parare domino populum perfectum. **18** Et ait zacharias a{n}d angelum:
unde hoc sciam? ego enim senex sum, et uxor mea processit in diebus suis. **19** Et
respondens angelus dixit ei: ego sum gabriel, qui adsisto in conspectu dei, et
missus sum loqui ad te et ueni nuntiare tibi haec. **20** et ecce eris tacens et non

---

9 incensum poneret] sacrificare 5 | ingressus] 4 A et ingressus 2 8 intrantem 5 | deest usque v. 13: domini et omnes turba populi fuit adhorans illa hora supplicationis eius uisus est autem illi angelus domini stans in medio altaris supplicationis et turbatus est zacharias cum uidisset et timor inuasit illum et dixit ad illum angelus noli timere zacharia 2 domini et omnis multitudo populi erat orans forans hora incensi uisus est autem illi angelus domini stans a dextris altari incensi et conturbatus est zacharias uidens et timor incidit super eum et dixit ad eum angelus ne timueris zacharia 5 domini et (om. 8) omnis multitudo erat populi orans (multitudo orabat 4 multitudo populi orabat 8) foris (om. 4) hora (ora 4 8) incensi apparuit autem illi angelus domini (om. 4) stans a dextris altaris (altarii 4) incensi et zacharias turbatus est uidens (et uidens zacharias turbatus est 4 et uidens zaccharuas turbatus est 8) et timor inruit (cecidit 4 8) super eum (illum 4 8) ait autem (et ait 4 8) ad illum angelus (add. domini 8) dicens (om. A) ne timeas zacharia (zaccharias 8) cet. | **13** quoniam] quia 5 | ecce] 8 om. cet. | exaudita est oratio tua] 2 5 obsecratio tua exaudita est 4 obsecratio tua audita est 8 exaudita est deprecatio tua A | elisabet] 2 A elisabed 5 elisabel 4 elisabeth 8 | uocaris] uocauis 2 uocabis cet. | iohannem] 8 A ioannem 2 iohannen 5 4 | **14** eritque] et erit cet. | gaudium tibi] tibi gaudium 2 5 | exultatio] laetitia 2 exaltatio 5 | in] super 5 | **15** in conspectu domini] 5 ante dominum 2 coram domino cet. sicera] siceram 4 | bibet] uiuet 2 | inplebitur] impleuitur 2 replebitur cet. | adhuc] om. 4 ex] in 2 de 5 | utero] uentre 2 5 | **16** filiorum] filios 4 | istrahel] isdrahel 2 israhel A | ipsorum] eorum 5 | **17** praeibit] prodiet 2 antecedet 5 praecedet (precedet 8) cet. | in conspectu eius] 5 ante faciem eius 2 ante illum cet. | heliae] heliae autem 8 | ad conuertenda] conuertere 2 5 ut conuertat cet. | ad[2]] 5 in cet. | incredibiles] contumaces 2 non consentientes 5 | ad prudentiam] in sensum 2 in sapientia 5 | parare] conparare 2 praeparare 5 | populum] 2 plebem cet. | perfectum] conpositum 2 consummatam 5 perfectam cet. | **18** ait] dixit cet. | zacharias] zaccharias 4 8 | unde] per quid 2 quomodo 5 | hoc sciam] cognoscam hoc 2 5 | senex sum] 4 sum senior 5 sum senex cet. | processit] 8 A progressa 2 praecedens 5 processior 4 **19** respondens] respondit 2 8 | dixit] et dixit 2 8 | ei] illi 2 | ego] ego enim 2 | sum[1]] sunt 8 gabriel] 5 4 grabriel 2 grabiel 8 gabrihel A | adsisto] adsto 8 A | in conspectu dei] 5 ante faciem dei 2 ante dominum 4 dominum 8 ante deum A | missus sum] missum 4 | ueni] om. cet. nuntiare tibi haec] benenuntiare tibi haec 2 euangelizare tibi haec 5 haec tibi euangelizare cet. **20** et[2]] ut 2

poteris loqui usque in diem, quo fiant haec, quoniam non credidisti uerbis meis, qui implebuntur tempore suo. **21** Et erat populus expectans zachariam et mirabantur, quod moram faceret in templo. **22** Egressus autem non poterat loqui ad eos, et cognouerunt, quia uisionem uidit in templo. et ipse erat adnuens illis et permansit mutus. **23** Et factum est, ut inpleti sunt dies sacerdotii eius, abiit in domum suam. **24** post istos autem dies concepit elisabet uxor eius et occultabat se mensibus quinque dicens, **25** quid ita mihi fecit dominus in diebus, quibus respexit auferre obprobrium meum inter homines? **26** eodem autem tempore missus est angelus gabriel a deo in ciuitatem galilaeae, cui nomen nazaret, **27** ad uirginem [– – –] de domo dauid, et nomen uirginis maria. **28** et ingressus angelus benedixit eam dicens: habe gratia plena, dominus est tecum, benedicta tu inter mulieres. **29** ipsa autem, ut uidit eum, mota est in introitu eius et erat cogitans, quod [...] bene[...] **30** [...] angelus [...] ne timeas [– – –] **31** ecce [...]cipies in utero et

poteris] possis 2 potens 5 | in diem] in illum diem 2 | fiant haec] 2 5 haec fiant 4 A haec fiat 8 quoniam] pro eo quod 2 A quia 5 propter hoc quia 4 propter hoc 8 | credidisti] credisti 8 | qui] 5 quae cet. | implebuntur] 4 A supplebuntur 2 conplebuntur 5 inplebuntur 8 | tempore suo] in tempore suo cet. | **21** populus] 2 plebs cet. | zachariam] zacchariam 4 8 | mirabantur] admirabantur 2 add. in eo 5 eo 4 | moram faceret] tardaret cet. add. ille 2 ipse 8 A | **22** Egressus] ubi prodiuit 2 exiens 5 | non] ille non 8 | poterat] potuit 8 | ad eos] illis 5 ad illos cet. | cognouerunt] intellexerunt 2 | quia] 5 quoniam 2 quod cet. | uisionem] uisione 8 | uidit] 2 5 uiderit 4 uidisset 8 A | erat] fuit 2 | adnuens] innuens A | illis] eis 5 | permansit] permanebat 5 mutus] surdus 5 | **23** ut] quomodo 2 | inpleti] 4 A repleti 2 conpleti 5 inpleti 8 | dies] dies illi 8 sacerdotii] ministerii 5 officii cet. | eius] om. 8 | abiit] tunc abiit 5 | **24** post] et post 5 | istos autem dies] 2 dies istos 5 hos autem dies cet. | elisabet] 2 A elisabed 5 elisabel 4 elisabeht 8 occultabat] celabat 2 abscondebat 5 | mensibus] menses 5 | **25** quid] quia 2 A quoniam 5 | ita mihi fecit] sic mihi fecit 2 5 mihi sic fecit 4 8 sic fecit mihi A | respexit] aspexit 2 | inter homines] in hominibus 5 | **26** eodem autem tempore] 4 8 in sexto autem mense 2 in mense autem sexto 5 A | angelus gabriel] 5 4 grabriel angelus 2 angelus grabiel 8 angelus gabrihel A | deo] domino 4 8 | galilaeae] galileae 2 galiaeam 5 | cui nomen] quae uocatur 2 om. 5 | nazaret] nazareth 4 om. 5 | **27** (add. maria 4) desponsatam (disponsatam 2) uiro cui nomen erat ioseph (iosef 2) cet. | **28** et ingressus] et cum introisset 2 et introiens 5 | angelus] 4 angelus ad illam 2 angelus ad eam 5 A ad eam angelus 8 | benedixit eam dicens] benedixit illam et dixit 2 dixit 5 A euangelizauit eam et dixit illi 4 benedixit eam et dixit illi 8 | habe] haue A om. 4 | gratia plena] A gratificata 2 benedicta 5 gratiam plena 8 om. 4 | est] om. cet. | inter mulieres] in mulieribus A **29** ipsa autem] 4 8 illa autem 2 5 quae A | ut uidit eum] 4 8 cum uidisset angelum 2 cum uidisset A om. 5 | mota est in introitu eius] 4 8 admirata est ad introitum 2 super uerbo conturbata est 5 turbata est sermone eius A | et erat cogitans] 4 8 recogitans 2 et recogitabat in semetipsa 5 et recogitabat A | quod bene] quia sic benedixit eam 2 qualis sit salutatio haec 5 quod sic benedixisset eam 4 8 qualis esset ista salutatio A | **30** angelus²] et dixit angelus ad illam 2 et dixit ei angelus 5 et ait ei angelus domini 4 8 et ait angelus ei A | deest: maria inuentisti enim (om. 8) gratiam (gratia 2) apud deum cet. | **31** ecce] 2 A et ecce cet. | cipies] concipiens 5 concipies cet.

paries filium et uocabis nomen eius iesum. **32** hic erit magnus et filius altissimi
uocabitur et dabit ei dominus sedem dauid patris eius. **33** et regnauit in domum
iacob in saecula. et regni eius non erit finis. **34** et ait illi maria: quomodo erit hoc,
quoniam non noui uirum. **35** et respondens angelus dixit ei: spiritus sanctus
superueniet in te et uirtus altissimi inumbrauit tibi. ideoque, quod nascetur ex te
sanctum uocauitur filius dei. **36** et ecce elisabet, cognata tua, et ipsa concepit
filium in senecta sua. et hic mensis sextus est ei, quae uocatur sterilis, **37** quia non
est impossibile aput dominum omne uerbum. **38** et dixit maria: ecce ancilla
domini, fiat mihi [– – –] **39** maria in diebus illis et abiit in montanam cum
festinatione in ciuitatem iu[...] [– – –] **42** et exclamauit uoce magna et ait:

---

uocabis] uocauis 2 | **32** ei] 5 illi cet. | dominus] A dominus deus cet. | sedem] thronum 2 5 eius] sui 2 | **33** regnauit] regnabit 4 A | in[1]] super 5 | domum] 5 8 domo cet. | saecula] 5 aeternum (eternum 8) cet. | **34** et ait illi maria] et dixit maria ad angelum 5 dixit autem maria ad angelum (om. 4) cet. | quomodo erit hoc quoniam non noui uirum] quomodo erit hoc cum uirum nesciam 2 quomodo erit hoc quia uirum non noui 5 ecce ancilla domini contigat mihi secudum ucrbum tuum 4 quomodo fiet istud ego enim nescio uirum 8 quomodo fiet istud quoniam uirum non cognosco A | **35** respondens] respondit 8 | dixit] et dixit 8 | ei] ad illam 2 illi 4 | superueniet] ueniet 8 | in te] 2 A super te 5 8 te 4 | uirtus] potentia 2 | inumbrauit] obumbrauit (obumbrabit 8) cet. | tibi] A me 8 te cet. | ideoque] quia propter 2 propter quod 5 quod] et quod 5 A | nascetur] nacetur 2 nascitur 5 | ex te] 2 om. cet. | sanctum] sanctus 4 **36** elisabet] elisabeth 4 8 | cognata] propinqua 2 | concepit] concipit 2 | filium in senecta sua] filium in senectute sua 5 in senectutem suam filium 8 | hic mensis] his menses 2 | sextus est] 2 5 est sextus 4 A est xestus est 8 | ei] 5 illi 2 4 8[c] A illis 8* | quae] que 8 | uocatur] uocabatur 4 8 sterilis] steriles 2 sterelis 8 | **37** est] erit A | impossibile] 8 difficile 5 inpossibile cet. | aput dominum omne uerbum] deo omnem uerbum 2 omne uerbum apud deum 5 deo omne uerbum 4 8 apud deum omne uerbum A | **38** et dixit maria ecce ancilla domini fiat mihi] dixit autem (et dixit 5) maria ecce ancilla domini contingat (fiat A) mihi cet. om. 2 4 | deest: secundum uerbum tuum cet. om. 2 4 | et discessit (recessit 5) ab illa (ea 5) angelus cet. | exsurrexit autem 2 surgens autem 5 exsurgens autem cet. | **39** illis] istis 5 | et] 2 om. cet. | montanam] 5 montuosa 2 montana cet. | cum festinatione] 4 A instanter 2 cum festinationem 5 8 | ciuitatem] ciuitate 5 4 iu] iudeae 2 4 iuda 5 A iudaeae 8 | deest usque v. 42: et introiuit in domum zachariae et salutauit elisabet et factum est quomodo audiuit salutationem mariae elisabet exultauit infans in utero eius et impleta est spiritu sancto 2 et introibit in domum zachariae et salutabit elisabet et factum est ut audiuit salutationem mariae elisabet exultauit in utero elisabet infans eius et inpleta est spiritu sancto elisabet 5 et intrauit (introiuit 8) in domum zachariae (zaccariae 8) et salutauit (salutabit 4 8) elisabet (elisabel 4 elisabeth 8) et factum est ut audiuit salutationem mariae elisabet (elisabel 4 elisabeht 8) exultauit infans in utero eius et repleta est spiritu sancto elisabet (elisabel 4 om. exultauit . . . elisabet 8) cet. | **42** exclamauit] clamauit 2 | et ait] dicens 4 8 et dixit cet.

Benedicta tu inter mulieres et benedictus fructus uentris tui. [– – –] **45** et beata es, quae credidisti, quod erit consummatio eorum, quae tibi dicta sunt a domino. **46** Et ait elisabet: magnificat anima mea dominum, **47** et exultauit spiritus meus in deo, salutare meo, **48** quia respexit humilitatem ancillae suae [– – –] **49** potens est et sanctum est nomen eius **50** et misericordia eius in saecula saeculorum {saecula} timentibus eum. **51** fecit potestatem in brachio suo, dissipauit superbos mente et corda eorum. **52** deposuit potentes de sede et exaltauit [– – –] **53** diuites dimisit inanes. **54** suscepit istrahel puerum suum recordatus misericordiae. **55** sicut locutus est ad patres nostros abraham et semini eius in aeternum. **56** Mansit autem maria cum ea mensibus tribus et reuersa est [– – –] **57** peperit filium. **58** et audierunt uicini et cognati eius, quia magnificauit dominus misericordiam suam

---

deest usque v. 45: et unde hoc mihi contigit ut ueniat mater domini mei ad me ecce enim quomodo facta est uox salutationis tuae in aures meas exultauit infans in laetitia in utero meo 2 et unde mihi hoc ut ueniat mater domini mei ad me ecce enim ut facta est uox salutationis tuae in aures meas exultauit in laetitia infans in utero meo 5 et unde hoc mihi ut ueniat mater domini (add. mei 4 dei 8) ad me ecce enim ut facta est uox salutationis tuae in auribus meis exultauit (exultabit 8) in gaudio infans in utero meo cet. | **45** es] 2 om. cet. | quae credidisti] 4 credens 2 quae crediderit 5 qui credidisti 8 quae credidit A | quod] quia 2 5 quoniam cet. | erit consummatio eorum] erit perfectio de his 2 erit consummatio 5 perficientur ea (omnia 8) cet. | tibi dicta sunt] dicta sunt tibi (illi 5 ei A) cet. | **46** ait] dixit 2 5 | elisabet] elisabel 4 maria cet. | mea] meam 8 dominum] dominus 2 | **47** exultauit] laetatus est 2 | in] super 2 | salutare] saluatori 5 salutari cet. | **48** quia] quoniam 5 | respexit] inspexit 2 respexit dominus 5 | humilitatem] super humilitatem 5 | deest usque v. 49: ecce enim enim ex hoc beata me dicunt omnes nationes quoniam fecit mihi magnalia ille 2 ecce enim amodo beatam me dicent omnes generationes quoniam fecit mihi magna deus qui 5 ecce enim ex hoc beatam (beata 8) me dicent omnes generationes quia fecit mihi magna qui cet. | **49** est[1]] om. 2 | est[2]] om. cet. | **50** misericordia] misericordiam 8 | saecula saeculorum saecula] saecula eius 2 generationes et generationes 5 saecula saeculorum 4 progeniem et progeniem 8 progenies et progenies A | timentibus eum] qui eum metuunt 2 | **51** potestatem] fortitudinem 2 uirtutem 5 potentiam cet. | brachio] braccio 2 bracchio cet. | dissipauit] dispersit 2 A disparsit cet. | superbos] superuo 2 | mente] sensu 2 cogitatione 5 | et] om. cet. | corda] 2 corde 4 cordis cet. | eorum] 5 illorum 2 ipsorum 4 8 sui A **52** deposuit] destruxit 2 | de] a 2 5 | sede] sedibus 2 5 | deest: humiles esurientes impleuit bonis (bonorum 5) et cet. | **53** diuites] locupletes 5 | dimisit] dismist 5 | **54** suscepit] adsumpsit 2 adiubauit 5 | istrahel] 4 8 isdrahel 2 sdrahel 5* israhel A | puerum suum] pueri sui 5 recordatus] commemoratus est 2 memorari (memorare 5) cet. | misericordiae] misericordiam 5 **55** abraham] abrahae 2 4 | aeternum] 2 5 saecula 4 A secula 8 | **56** Mansit] remansit 2 | cum] apud 2 | ea] 5 illam 2 illa cet. | mensibus tribus] menses tres 5 quasi mensibus tribus A | et] et tunc 2 | deest usque v. 57: in domum suam elisabet autem templus impletum est ut pariret et 2 in domum suam elisabet autem conpletum est tempus ut pariret et 5 in domum suam (domi suae 4) elisabeth (elisabel 4) autem impletum (inpletum 8) est tempus pariendi et cet. | **57** peperit] genuit 4 | **58** uicini] circumhabitantes 2 | cognati] propinqui 2 | quia] quoniam 2 5 | dominus] deus 2

cum ea, et congratulabantur ei. **59** et factum est die octauo uenerunt circumcidere
puerum [– – –] **60** et respondens mater ipsius dixit: non, sed uocabitur iohannes.
61 et dixerunt ad eam: nemo est in cognatione tua, qui uocetur nomine isto. **62**
Adnuebant etiam patri eius, quem uellet uocari eum. **63** et accepto pugillare
[– – –] **64** soluta est lingua eius, et mirati sunt omnes. Apertum est autem os eius,
et loquebatur benedicens deum. **65** et factus est super omnes timor, qui circum
illos habitabant, in omni montana iudeae diuulgabantur omnia haec uerba. **66** et
posuerunt omnes, qui audierant, in corde suo dicentes: quidnam puer iste erit?
etenim manus domini erat cum illo. **67** et zacharias pater eius impletus est spiritu
sancto et prophetauit dicens: **68** benedictus deus istrahel, quia uisitauit et fecit
redemptionem populo [...] **69** cornum salutis nobis in domo dauid [– – –] **70**

ea] 5 eo 2 illa cet. | congratulabantur] 4 A gratulabantur 2 congaudebant 5 congratulabuntur 8 ei] illi 2 | **59** die] 2 5 in die cet. | octauo] octaba 2 octaua 4 | uenerunt circumcidere] ut uenirent et circumderent 4 ut uenirent et circumderet 8 | puerum] infantem 2 5 | deest usque v. 60: et uocabant eum nomine patris eius zacharia 2 et uocabant eum in nomine patris sui zacharian 5 et uocant (uocauerunt 4 8) eum in (om. A) nomine patris eius zachariam (zacchariam 8) A **60** respondens] respondit 2 | ipsius] eius cet. | dixit] et dixit 2 | non] nequaquam A | uocabitur iohannes] iohannes nomen eius 5 | **61** eam] 5 illam cet. | nemo] quia nemo A | in cognatione tua] in propinquitate tua 2 om. 8 | uocetur] uocatur 2 5 | nomine isto] isto nomine 2 nomen hoc 5 hoc nomine cet. | **62** Adnuebant] innuebant 5 A | etiam] autem cet. | quem] quid 2 5 | uellet uocari eum] eum uellet uocari 2 uult uocari eum 5 | **63** et accepto pugillare] ille autem petit pugillaris 2 et cum petisset tabulam 5 et accepit pugillarem 4 et adcepit pugillares 8 et postulans pugillarem A | deest usque v. 64: et scripsit iohannis est nomen eus 2 scripsit iohanes est nomen eius 5 et (om. A) scripsit dicens iohannes est nomen eius cet. add. et mirati sunt omnes 8 | **64** soluta est lingua eius] 5 resoluta est lingua eius 4 8 om. 2 A | et mirati sunt omnes] 5 et admirati sunt omnes 2 et omnes mirati sunt 4 et mirati sunt uniuersi A om. 8 Apertum] et apertum 2 8 | autem] 5 4 autem ilico A om. 2 8 | os eius] os eius et lingua 2 os eius et lingua eius A | deum] dominum 2 | **65** factus] factum 2* 5 | super omnes timor] est timor (add. magnus 5 4) super omnes cet. | qui circum illos habitabant] circumhabitantes 2 uicinos eorum (eius 5) cet. | in omni montana] et in tota montuosa 2 et in tota montana 5 et in uniuersa montana 4 et super omnia montana 8 A | iudeae] iudaeae 5 8 | diuulgabantur] 8 A et diuulgabantur 2 4 loquebantur 5 | omnia haec uerba] omnia uerba ista 2 omnia uerba haec 5 A haec omnia uerba 4 uerba haec omnia 8 | **66** qui audierant] 4 A qui audierunt 5 qui audiebat omnia uerba haec 8 om. 2 | corde suo] cordibus suis 2 5 | quidnam] 2 quid putas A quid utique cet. puer iste erit] A erit infans iste 2 erit infans hic 5 erit puer iste 4 8 | etenim] nam 2 | erat cum illo] erat cum ipso 2 cum illo est 4 cum illo cet. | **67** zacharias] zaccharias 8 | eius] om. 4 impletus] repletus 8 | spiritu sancto] sancto spiritu 2 spirito sancto 5 | prophetauit] 8 A prophetabat 2 4 om. 5 | dicens] dixit 5 | **68** deus] 4 8 dominus deus cet. | istrahel] 4 8 isdrahel 2 sdrahel 5* israhel 5^c A | quia] qui 2 | uisitauit] prospexit 2 | et fecit] om. 2 | redemptionem] salutem 5 | populo^2] populo suo et excitauit 2 populo suo et eleuabit 5 plebis suae et erexit 4 8 plebi suae et erexit A | **69** cornum] cornu A | domo] domum 8 | deest usque v. 70: pueri sui sicut cet.

locutus es per os sanctorum prophetarum suorum, qui a seculo sunt **71** [– – –]
inimicis nostris et de manu omnium, qui nos oderunt, **72** facere misericordiam
cum patribus nostris et memorari [– – –] **73** nostrum, **74** dare nobis, ut sine timore
de manu inimicorum nostrorum liberatos seruire ipsi **75** in castitate et iustitia in
conspectu eius omnes dies nostros. **76** Et tu puer propheta altissimi uocaberis.
praeibis enim ante faciem domini parare uias eius **77** ad dandam scientiam salutis
populo eius in remissionem peccatorum ipsorum, **78** per uiscera misericordiae dei
nostri, in quibus uisitauit nos oriens ex alto, **79** inluminare {i} in tenebris et
umbra mortis sedentes ad dirigendos pedes nostros in uiam pacis. **80** puer autem
crescebat et confirmabatur in spiritu et erat in desertis usque in diem ostensionis
suae ad istrahel.

---

70 locutus] locus 2 | os] ore 2 | prophetarum suorum qui a seculo sunt] suorum prophetarum qui a principio temporis sunt 2 profetarum eius qui a saeculo 5 suorum prophetarum qui ab aeuo sunt 4 prophetauerunt qui ab aeuo sunt 8 qui a saeculo sunt prophetarum eius A | **71** inimicis nostris et de manu omnium qui nos oderunt] salutem ab inimicis nostris et manus omnium qui nos oderunt 2 salutem de manu inimicorum nostrorum et omnium qui oderunt nos 5 et liberauit nos ab inimicis nostris et de manus omnium qui nos oderunt 4 et liberauit nos ab inimicis nostris et de manu omnium qui oderunt nos 8 salutem ex inimicis nostris et de manu omnium qui nos oderunt A | **72** facere] 2 5 ad faciendam cet. | cum] suam 8 | et] om. 5 | memorari] commemorari 2 rememorari 8 | deest usque v. 73: testamenti sancti sui quod iurauit abrahae patri 2 testamenti sancti eius iuramentum quod iurauit ad abraham patrem 5 testamenti sui sancti iusiurandum (iusiurandi 8) quod iurauit ad abraham patrem cet. | **73** nostrum] nostro 2 **74** dare] ut det 2 ut daret 5 daturum cet. | nobis] se nobis 4 A nobis se nobis 8 | ut] om. 2 5 timore] metu 2 | de manu] de manus 4 om. 2 | nostrorum] om. 2 | liberatos seruire] seruire 2 liberati seruiamus cet. | ipsi] ei 5 illi cet. | **75** castitate] ueritate 2 sanctitate cet. | in conspectu eius] 2 5 coram ipso cet. | omnes dies nostros] 5 omnibus diebus nostris cet. | **76** tu puer] tu autem infans 5 | propheta] profeta 2 | uocaberis] uocaueris 2 | praeibis] antecedes 5 | faciem] facie 8 | parare] praparare 2 | uias] uiam 8 | **77** ad dandam] ad mandandam 2 dare 5 scientiam] agnitionem 2 intellectum 5 | salutis] om. 8 | populo] 2 populi 5 plebi cet. | eius] suo 2 | remissionem] A remissa 2 remissione cet. | ipsorum] suorum 2 eorum cet. | **78** per] propter 2 5 | misericordiae] sericordiae 2 | **79** inluminare] praelucere 2 inluminare lumen 5 | i in] his (eis 2 iis 4) qui in cet. | tenebris] tenebris sunt 2 | et] 5 A et in 2 4 et qui in 8 | sedentes] sedentibus 2 5 sedent cet. | ad dirigendos] ut prospere faciat 5 | in[2]] ad 2 | **80** confirmabatur] corroborabatur 2 inbaliscebat 5 confortabatur cet. | in[1]] 4 8 om. cet. | desertis] 5 8 solitudinibus 2 deserto 4 A | ostensionis] progressionis 2 om. 4 | suae] eius 5 suum 4 | istrahel] 4 8 isdrahel 2 sdrahel 5* israhel A

2 Factum est autem in illis diebus, exiit edictum a caesare augusto, ut
profiteretur per uniuersum orbem. **2** haec prima facta est professio praeside
syriae cyrino. **3** et ibant omnes profiteri unusquisque in suam ciuitatem. **4**
Ascendit autem et ioseph a galilaea de ciuitate nazaret in terram iudeam in
ciuitatem dauid, quae uocatur bethlem, eo quod esset de domo et patria dauid, **5**
profiteri cum maria desponsata sibi pregnante. **6** Factum est autem, cum ibi
essent, inpleti sunt dies, ut pareret. **7** et peperit filium suum primogenitum et
pannis eum inuoluit et conlocauit eum in praesepio, quoniam non erat locus in
diuersorio. **8** Pastores autem erant in illa regione uigilantes et custodientes
uigilias noctis super gregem suum. **9** et ecce angelus domini stetit super eos, et
maiestas domini circumluxit eos, et timuerunt timore magno. **10** dixitquae eis
angelus: nolite timere, ecce enim euangelizo uobis gaudium magnum, quod erit

2:1 illis diebus] 2 diebus illis cet. | exiit] exiuit 2 5 | ut profiteretur] profeteri 2 profiteri 5 ut proficeretur 4* 8 ut describeretur A | per uniuersum orbem] omnem orbem 5 uniuersus orbis terrarum 4 uniuersus orbis terrae 8 uniuersus orbis A om. 2 | **2** haec prima facta est professio] haec fuit professio prima ducatum 5 haec professio prima 4 haec professio prima facta est 8 haec descriptio prima facta est A om. 2 | praeside syriae cyrino] agente syriae cyrenio 5 praeside syrio cyrino 4 preside syrio cyrino 8 praeside syriae cyrino A om. 2 | **3** et ibant omnes] om. 2 profiteri] 5 ut proficerentur 4* 8 ut profiterentur 4[c] A om. 2 | unusquisque] 2 5 singuli cet. suam ciuitatem] suam patriam 5 ciuitate suam 8 | **4** et[1]] om. 2 | ioseph] iosef 2 | a] de 2 5 galilaea] galilea 8 | nazaret] 2 nazared 5 nazareth 4 A nazareht 8 | terram] 2 5 om. cet. iudeam] 4 8 iuda 2 5 iudaeam A | in[2]] om. A | ciuitatem] ciuitate 2 5 | bethlem] 8 uethlem 2 uethleem 5* bethleem cet. | eo quod esset de domo et patria dauid] 4 8 propterea quod essent de domo et patria dauid 2 profiteri cum maria disponsata ei praegnanti 5 eo quod esset de domo e familia dauid A | **5** profiteri cum maria desponsata sibi pregnante] profiteri cum maria sponsa sua cum esset praegnas 2 propter quod esset de domo et patria dauid 5 ut proficeretur (profitere-tur[c]) cum maria uxore sua praegnate 4 ut proficeretur cum maria desponsata sibi uxore cum esset in utero habens 8 ut profiteretur cum maria desponsata sibi uxore praegnante A | **6** Factum est autem] factum autem est 8 om. 5 | cum ibi essent] 8 cum esset illic 2 cum autem aduenirent 5 cum esset ibi 4 cum essent ibi A | inpleti sunt] 8 consummati sunt 5 impleti sunt cet. dies] illi dies 2 | pareret] paraeret 2 pariret 5 | **7** peperit] peperet 2* | suum] om. 4 8 | primogenitum] primitiuum 2 | pannis] om. 2 | eum inuoluit] obuoluerunt illum 2 inuoluit eum 5 eum inuoluit cet. | conlocauit] collauerunt 2 reclinauit 5 A posuit 4 8 | eum[2]] illum 2 om. 4 | quoniam] quia cet. | non erat locus] 2 8 non erat illis locus 5 locus non erat 4 non erat eis locus A diuersorio] stabu 2 | **8** Pastores autem] et pastores A | illa regione] 4 8 regione illa 2 5 regione eadem A | uigilantes] pernoctantes 2 cantantes 5 | uigilias noctis] nocturnas uigilias 2 custodias noctis 5 | super] supra 4 A | gregem suum] gregem suam 2 pascua sua 5 | **9** et ecce angelus] angelus autem 2 | domini[1]] om. 2 | stetit] adstitit 5 | super eos] eis 5 iuxta illos cet. om. 2 | et[2]] om. 8 | maiestas] 8 gloria 5 claritas cet. | domini[2]] dei 2 A om. cet. | circumluxit] 5 circumfulsit cet. | eos[2]] eis 5 illum 8 illos cet. | timore magno] timorem magnum 5 | **10** dixitquae] et ait 2 et dixit cet. | eis] illis cet. | angelus] om. 4 | nolite timere] ne timueritis 2 | euangelizo] adnuntio 2 euangeliio 8 | quod] quae 5 | erit] est 2 omni populo, **11** quia natus est uobis hodie saluator, qui est christus dominus in ciuitate dauid. **12** et huius hoc uobis signum istut: inuenietis infantem pannis inuolutum positum in praesepio. **13** Et subito facta est cum illis angelorum multitudo exercitus caelestis laudantium deum et dicentium: **14** gloria in excelsis deo et super terram pax hominibus bone uoluntatis. **15** et factum est, ut abierunt ab eis in caelum angeli, pastores loquebantur ad inuicem et dixerunt: pertranseamus usque bethlem et uideamus hoc uerbum, quod factum est, sicut dominus ostendit nobis. **16** et uenerunt festinantes et inuenerunt mariam et iosef et infantem positum in praesepio. **17** uidentes autem et cognouerunt de uerbo, quod eis dictum erat de puero. **18** et omnes, qui audierunt, mirati sunt de iis, quae ad eos locuti sunt pastores. **19** Maria uero conseruabat omnia uerba ista committens in corde suo. **20** Et reuersi sunt pastores magnificantes et laudantes deum in omnibus, quae audierunt et uiderunt, sicut dicta sunt ad eos. **21** Et com

---

omni] et omni 5 | populo] plebi 4 8 | **11** quia] quoniam 2 | uobis hodie] hodie uobis 8 christus] christus iesus 2 5 | dominus] om. 5 | **12** huius] 4 8 om. cet. | uobis signum] signum uobis 8 | istut] om. cet. add. sit 5 | pannis] in pannis 4 om. 2 | positum] et positum cet. om. 5 praesepio] presipio 8 | **13** et subito] subito autem 2 et continuo 5 | cum illis angelorum multitudo] multitudo cum angelo 5 multitudo 4 cum angelo multitudo cet. | exercitus] militiae 5 A caelestis] A caelestium 2 4 caeli 5 celestis 8 | laudantium] laudantes 5 | **14** in] om. 2 | excelsis] altis 5 altissimis cet. | super terram pax] pax in terra 2 super terra pax 5 in terra pax cet. hominibus] in hominibus 5 A | bone] bonae cet. om. 5 8 | uoluntatis] consolationis 5 | **15** ut] quomodo 2 | abierunt ab eis in caelum angeli] discessit ab ipsis angelus in caelum 2 abierunt angeli ab eis in caelum 5 discessit ab illis angelus in caelum 4 discesserunt ab illis angelus in celum 8 discesserunt ab eis angeli in caelum A | pastores] et homines pastores 5 | loquebantur] dixerunt 2 5 | inuicem] alterutrum 5 | et dixerunt] 4 8 om. cet. | pertranseamus] 5 eamus 2 transeamus cet. | usque] om. 2 | bethlem] 2 A bethleem cet. | hoc uerbum] sermonem istum 2 uerbum hoc 5 | quod factum] qui factus 2 | sicut] 2 quod sic 4 quod cet. | dominus ostendit nobis] 4 8 dominus notum nobis fecit 2 dominus demonstrauit nobis 5 fecit dominus et ostendit nobis A | **16** festinantes] festinanter 2 | inuenerunt] uiderunt 2 | mariam] maria 8 | et^{3}] om. 8 | iosef] 2 5 ioseph cet. | praesepio] praesepium 2 presipio 8 | **17** uidentes autem] 5 A cum uidissent autem 2 om. 4 8 | et] 4 8 om. cet. | cognouerunt] retulerunt 2 | uerbo] uerbum 2 eis dictum erat] dictum est ad illos 2 factum est ad eos 5 dictum est illis 4 dictum es illis 8 dictum erat illis A | puero] infantem 2 infante 5 puero hoc cet. | **18** audierunt] audiebant 2 5 | mirati sunt] admirabantur 2 | de iis] de eis 2 et de his A de his cet. | ad eos locuti sunt pastores] dicta sunt a pastoribus ad se 2 dicta sunt pastoribus ad eos 5 dicta erant a pastoribus ad ipsos cet. **19** uero] autem cet. | conseruabat] obseruabat 2 | omnia uerba ista] omnes sermones istos 2 omnia uerba haec cet. | committens] 5 conferens cet. | corde suo] cor suum 2 | **20** reuersi sunt] reuertebantur 2 | magnificantes] honorificantes 5 glorificantes A add. deum 8 | deum] dominum 2 om. 8 | in] de 2 | quae] quibus 5 | audierunt] 5 audiuerant 8 audierant cet. uiderunt] 5 uiderant cet. | dicta sunt] 4 8 dictum est cet. | eos] 2 illos cet. | **21** com] cum 2 5 postquam cet.

inpleti sunt dies octo, ut eum circumciderent, uocatum est nomen eius iesum, quod uocatum erat ab angelo, priusquam conciperetur in utero. **22** et cum expleti essent dies purgationis eius secundum legem moysi, dixerunt eum in hierusalem, ut offerrent eum domino. **23** Sicut scriptum est in lege domini, quia omne masculinum, quod aperit, uoluam sanctum domino uocabitur, **24** et ut darent hostias secundum, quod dictum est in lege domini, par turturum uel duos pullos columbarum. **25** Et ecce erat homo in hierusalem, cui nomen symeon, et homo iste iustus et timoratus expectans exortationem istrahel, et spiritus sanctus erat super eum. **26** et erat ei responsum a spiritu sancto non uisurum eum mortem, priusquam uideret christum domini. **27** Et uenit in spiritu in templum, et cum inducerent parentes puerum iesum, ut facerent de illo secundum consuetudinem legis, **28** et ipse accepit eum in amplexum et benedixit dominum et ait: **29** Nunc dimittis seruum tuum, domine, secundum uerbum tuum in pace, **30** quia uiderunt

---

inpleti] perfecti 2 consummati cet. | sunt] essent 2 | ut eum circumciderent] ad circumcidendum infantem 2 ut circumciderent infantem 5 ut circumcideretur cet. | uocatum¹] et uocatum 2 nominatum 5 | iesum] 4 iesus cet. | uocatum²] dictum 2 | erat] 2 est cet. | priusquam] antequam 5 | conciperetur in utero] conciperet in utero 2 conciperetur in uentre matris 5 in utero conciperetur cet. | **22** cum] 2 5 postquam cet. | expleti] suppleti 2 consummati 5 impleti 4 A inpleti 8 | essent] 2 sunt cet. | purgationis] purificationes 4 | moysi] mosı A | dixerunt] inposuerunt 2 adduxerunt 5 tulerunt cet. | eum¹] 5 illum cet. | in] om. 2 | hierusalem] hierosolyma 5 iherusalem 8 | ut offerrent eum] ostendere illum 2 adsistere 5 uti sisterent eum 4 ut eum statuerent 8 ut sisterent eum A | domino] ante dominum 2 | **23** lege] legem 8 | omne] omnis 2 omnes 8 | masculinum] masculus 2 masculum 4 8 | quod aperit] aperiens 2 5 adaperiens cet. uoluam] uulbam 2 uuluam cet. | sanctum] sanctus 2 | **24** hostias] pro eo sacrificium 2 sacrificium 5 hostiam cet. | secundum] om. 2 | turturum] turtures 4 | uel] et 4 8 aut cet. | pullos] nidos 5 | columbarum] columbinos 2 conlumbarum 8 | **25** ecce] om. 5 | erat homo] 2 5 homo erat cet. | in] om. 2 | hierusalem] iherusalem 8 | nomen] nomen erat 4 | symeon] symaeon 4 et¹] om. 2 | iste] hic 5 om. 2 | iustus] iustus erat 8 | timoratus] 8 A timens 2 metuens 5 timoratus erat 4 | exortationem] praecem 2 consolationem (consulatione 8) cet. | istrahel] 4 8 isdrahel 2 5* israhel A | sanctus erat super eum] 5 erat in eo sanctus 2 sanctus erat in ipso 4 sanctus erat in eo 8 A | **26** et erat ei responsum] responsum enim 2 et responsum A responsum autem cet. a spiritu sancto] acceperat ab spiritu sancto 2 fuerat super eum a spiritu sancto 5 accepit ab spiritu sancto 4 adceperat a spiritu sancto 8 acceperat ab spiritu sancto A | non uisurum eum] ne uideret 2 non uidere 5 non uisurum 4 non uisurum se 8 A | priusquam] 5 quoadusque 2 nisi prius cet. | uideret] uideat 5 | domini] dominum 4 deum 8 | **27** Et uenit] uenit autem 2 spiritu] spirito 5 | templum] templo 4 | parentes puerum iesum] parentes iesum 2 parentes infantem iesum 5 puerum iesum parentes eius 4 A puerum iesum in templum parentes eius 8 de illo] om. cet. | legis] legem 2 add. de eo 5 pro eo cet. | **28** in amplexum] in manus suas 2 in alas suas 5 in manibus 4 in ulnas suas A om. 8 | dominum] deum cet. | ait] locutus est 2 dixit cet. | **29** dimittis] 8 A dismitte 2 dismittis 5 dimitte 4 | **30** quia] quoniam 8

oculi mei salutare tuum, **31** quod praeparasti secundum omnium faciem
populorum **32** lumem reuelatione gentium et gloriam populi tui israhel. **33** Et erat
ioseph et mater eius mirantes in his, quae dicebantur de eo. **34** et benedixit illos
symeon et ait ad mariam matrem eius: ecce hic positus est in ruinam et
resurrectionem multorum in israhel et in signum, quod contradicitur. **35** et tuam
uero ipsius animam pertransit gladius, uti reuelentur multorum cordium
cogitationes. **36** Et erat anna prophetissa, filia phanuel de tribu aseri, haec
processerat in diebus multis, quae uixerat cum uiro annis uii a uirginitate sua. **37**
et haec uidua annorum lxxxiiii, quae non descendebat de templo in ieiuniis et
orationibus seruiens nocte ac die. **38** et haec stans ipsa hora confitebatur deum et
loquebatur de eo omnibus expectantibus redemptionem istrahel. **39** Et ut
perfecerunt omnia quemadmodum legem domini, regressi sunt in galileam in
ciuitatem suam nazaret, sicut dictum est per prophetam, quod nazoreus

---

salutare] salutarem 4 8 | **31** praeparasti] 5 parasti cet. | secundum omnium faciem populorum] in conspectu omnium populorum 5 ante faciem omnium populorum cet. | **32** reuelatione] in reuelationem 2 5 ad reuelationem cet. | gentium] 8 A oculorum 2 4 om. 5 | et] sed 2 | populi tui] 2 5 plebis tuae cet. | israhel] A isdrahel 2 5* istrahel cet. | **33** ioseph] 4 8 iosef 2 pater eius 5 A | eius] om. 5 A | mirantes] admirantes 2 | in] 5 de 2 super cet. | his] omnibus 2 | eo] 2 5 illo cet. | **34** illos] 4 8 eos 2 5 illis A | symeon] symaeon 4 | ait] dixit cet. | hic positus est] positus est hic 8 A | ruinam] casum 4 | resurrectionem] resurrexionem 2 in resurrectionem 5 israhel] A isdrahel 2 5* istrahel cet. | quod contradicitur] cui contradicitur 2 contradicentem 5 quod contradicetur 4 8 cui contradicetur A | **35** uero ipsius] autem 2 ipsius autem 5 ipsius cet. pertransit] pertransibit A pertransiet cet. | gladius] famea 2 | uti] ut cet. | reuelentur] denudentur 2 | multorum cordium] de multis cordibus 2 ex multis cordibus A | cogitationes] consilia 5 | **36** erat] 8 A fuit 2 om. 5 4 | prophetissa] 4 A profetis 2 prophetis 5 profetissa 8 | phanuel] A fanuel cet. | aseri] aser cet. | haec] et haec 5 | processerat] progressa 2 | in diebus multis] multis diebus 2 | quae] et 4 A que 8 | uixerat] 4 A uixit cet. | cum uiro annis uii] cum uiro suo annis septe 2 annos septem cum uiro 5 annos cum uiro suo uii 4 annos cum uiro suo septe 8 cum uiro suo annis septem A | **37** haec] ipsa 2 | annorum] usque ad annos A | lxxxiiii] octoginta quattuor A | descendebat] recedebat 2 5 discedebat cet. | de] a 2 | in] om. cet. orationibus] 2 5 obseruationibus 4 obsecrationibus 8 A | seruiens] seruiens domino 2 | ac] et 2 5 die] diem 8 | **38** haec stans ipsa hora] ipsa illa hora adsit eis 2 in ipsa hora instans 5 haec ipsa hora stans 4 8 haec ipsa hora superueniens A | confitebatur] confitebantur 2* depraecabatur 5 deum] ad dominum 2 deo 5 dominum 4 domino 8 A | loquebatur] dicebat 5 | eo] 2 5 illo cet. expectantibus] 2 qui spectabant 5 qui expectabant cet. | redemptionem] saluationem 5 | istrahel] in hierusalem 5 hierusalem cet. | **39** ut] cum 2 5 | perfecerunt] perfecissent 2 consummauerunt 5 | quemadmodum] secundum cet. | regressi] reuersi cet. | galileam] 8 galilaeam cet. suam] om. 2 | nazaret] nazarath 2 nazared 5 nazareth cet. | sicut dictum est per prophetam quod nazoreus uocabitur] sicut dictum est per profetam quoniam nazoreus uocabitur 5 om. cet.

uocabitur. **40** Puer autem crescebat et confortabatur repletus in sapientia, et gratia dei erat super eum. **41** et ibant ioseph et maria per omnes annos in hierusalem die sollemni pasche. **42** Et cum essent illi anni duodecim, et ascenderunt in hierosolyma secundum consuetudinem diei sollemni azymorum, **43** et cum consummassent dies reuertentibus illis, remansit iesus in hierusalem, et nescierunt parentes eius. **44** arbitrati enim esse eum in comitatu uenerunt iter diei et quaerebant eum inter cognatos et notos. **45** et non inuenientes eum reuersi sunt hierusalem quaerentes eum. **46** Et factum est, post dies tres inuenerunt eum et in templo sedentem in medio docentium audientem illos ed interrogantem. **47** stupebant autem omnes, qui audiebant eum, super sapientia et responsis eius. **48** et uidentes eum expauerunt. Et ait ad illum mater eius: fili, quid ita fecisti nobis?

---

40 Puer autem] infans autem iesus 5 | crescebat et confortabatur] A corroborabatur et adcrescebat 2 conualescebat et crescebat 5 confortabatur et crescebat 4 8 | repletus] et implebat 2 adinplebatur 5 et implebatur 4 et inplebatur 8 plenus A | in] om. cet. | sapientia] sapientiam 8 super] 2 cum 5 4 in 8 A | eum] illum 2 eo 5 illo cet. | **41** et ibant] ibant autem et 5 | ioseph et maria] 4 ioseph et maria mater eius 8 parentes eius cet. | per omnes annos] quodquod annis 2 secundum tempus 5 | in] om. 2 | hierusalem] iherusalem 8 | die sollemni pasche] ad dies solomni paschae 2 in die (diem 4) sollemni (festo 5) paschae cet. | **42** cum essent illi anni] factus esset annorum 2 A facti sunt ei anni 5 facti essent illi anni 4 factus esset iesus annorum 8 duodecim] A xii cet. | et ascenderunt] ascenderunt parentes eius 2 5 et ascendissent 4 8 ascendentibus illis A | in hierosolyma] 4 hierosolema habentes illum 2 habentes eum 5 in iherusalem 8 in hierosolymam A | secundum] secumdum 2* | consuetudinem] morem 2 | diei] per diem 2 sollemni] festum 2 festi cet. | azymorum] 2 5 om. cet. | **43** et cum consummassent dies] et cum fecissent dies 2 et consummatis diebus 5 consummatisque diebus cet. | reuertentibus illis] et reuerterunt 2 cum reuerterentur 5 cum redirent cet. | iesus] 2 puer iesus 5 A iesus puer 4 8 | in] om. 2 | hierusalem] iherusalem 8 | nescierunt] 5 non cognouerunt 2 A non cognouit 4 8 parentes eius] ioseph et mater eius 4 iesus et mater eius 8 | **44** arbitrati] arbitrantes 2 et putantes 5 existimantes cet. | enim] autem A om. cet. | esse eum] 2 eum esse 5 illum esse 4 A illum 8 in comitatu] in comitatum 2 secum comitari 8 | uenerunt] uenerunt autem 2 et uenerunt 8 iter diei] domi 2 uiam diei unius 5 | quaerebant] quaesierunt 2 requirebant cet. | eum[2]] eos 2* inter] in 5 | cognatos] propinquos 2 cognatis 5 | notos] inter notos 5 | **45** et] om. 2 | eum[1]] 4 8 om. cet. | reuersi] 2 5 regressi cet. | hierusalem] hierosolyma 2 in hierusalem (iherusalem 8) cet. | quaerentes] 2 requirentes cet. | **46** dies tres] 2 5 diem tertium 2 triduo 4 8 triduum A eum] 5 8 illum cet. | et] om. cet. | in templo sedentem] sedentem in templo 5 | docentium] magistrorum 2 5 doctorum cet. | illos] 8 A eos 5 illum 4 om. 2 | ed] et cet. | interrogantem] A interrogantem illos 2 interrogantem eos cet. | **47** stupebant autem omnes qui audiebant eum] 8 et omnes qui audiebant admirabantur 2 expauescebant autem omnes qui audiebant eum 5 stupebant autem omnes qui eum audiebant 4 A | super] in 5 om. 2 | sapientia] intellecto 5 prudentiam (prudentia A) cet. | et] om. 8 | responsis eius] 4 A os et responsa 2 responsionibus eius 5 responsi eius 8 | **48** et uidentes eum] 5 et cum uiderent eum 2 et uiso illo 4 8 et uidentes A expauerunt] 4 8 admirati sunt 2 de mente facti sunt 5 ammirati sunt A | ait] dixit cet. | ad illum mater eius] 2 ad eum mater eius 5 mater eius ad illum cet. | ita fecisti nobis] fecisti nobis A fecisti nobis sic cet.

dolentes et tristis quaerebamus te. **49** et ait ad illos: Quid est, quod me quaerebatis? nescitis, quia in patris mei oportet me esse? **50** et ipsi non intellexerunt uerbum, quod locutus est illis. **51** et descendit cum illis et uenit nazaret et erat subiectus illis. et mater eius conseruabat uerba eius omnia in corde suo. **52** Et iesus proficiebat aetate et sapientia et gratia aput deum et homines.

3 In anno autem quinto decimo imperii tiberi caesaris procurante pontio pilato iudaeae tetrarcha autem galilaeae herode, philippo autem fratre eius tetrarcha iture et drachonitidis regionibus et lysaniae abilianae tetrarcha **2** sub principibus sacerdotum anna et caipha. Factum est uerbum dei super iohannem, filium zachariae, in deserto. **3** et uenit in totam regionem iordanis praedicans baptismum paenitentiae, **4** sicut scriptum e<s>t in libro sermonum esaeiae prophetae: uox clamantis in deserto: parate uiam domino, rectas facite semitas eius. **5** omnis uallis inplebitur et omnis mons et collis humiliabitur et erunt praua

---

dolentes] 4 8 nam et propinqui et ego dolentes 2 ecce pater tuus et ego dolentes 5 A | et tristis] et tristes cet. om. 4 A | quaerebamus] quaesiuimus 2 | **49** ait] dixit 2 5 | illos] eos 5 | Quid est] quid utique 2 quid 5 | quod] om. 2 | me quaerebatis] A quaerebatis me 2 5 8 me quaeretis 4 nescitis] non scitis ipsi 2 nesciebatis A | quia] quoniam 5 | patris mei] 8 re patris mei 2 his quae sunt patris mei 5 propria patris mei 4 his quae patris mei sunt A | esse] esset 8 | **50** et ipsi] illi autem 2 ipsi autem 5 | locutus est illis] illis locutus est 2 dixit illis 5 locutus est ad illos cet. **51** et descendit cum illis] 8 et cum discendisset cum illis 2 et descendit cum eis 5 A om. 4 | et[2]] om. 2 5 | uenit] om. 5 | nazaret] in nazaret 5 nazareht 8 nazareth cet. | erat] fuit 2 | subiectus] 2 subditus cet. | et mater] mater autem 2 5 | uerba eius omnia] uerba omnia 5 uerba omnia haec cet. | **52** Et iesus] iesus autem 2 | aetate et sapientia] 2 5 aetate et sapientiam 4 8 sapientia et aetate A | aput] 2 ad 5 apud cet. | homines] ad hominibus 5 | **3:1** In] 2 5 om. cet. | imperii] imperi 2 ducatus 5 | tiberi] tiberii 8 A | caesaris] cesaris 8 | iudaeae] iudeae 2 iudaeam A tetrarcha[1]] quattuoruiratum habentem 2 quaterducatus 5 | autem[2]] om. 2 5 | galilaeae herode] herodem galileae 2 galileae herode 8 | philippo autem fratre eius tetrarcha] fratre eius philippo quatuoruiratum habientem 2 philippi autem fratris eius quaterducatus 5 | iture] ityreae 2 itureae cet. | drachonitidis] tetrachontidis 2 trachonitidis 5 A traconidis 4 traconitidis 8 regionibus] regionis cet. | lysaniae] lysitania 2 lysanio 8 lysania A | abilianae] 4 abilianeae 2 abillianetis 5 ablianae 8 abilinae A | tetrarcha[3]] quattuor 2 quaterducatus 5 | **2** sub principibus sacerdotum] 8 A pontifice 2 sub (su*) principe sacerdotum 5 e sub sacerdotum principe 4 caipha] capha 2 caiapha A | dei] domini 5 8 | super] ad 5 | iohannem] iohanen 5 iahannen 4 iohannen A | filium zachariae] filium zacchariae 8 zachariae filium cet. | **3** et uenit] cum uenisset autem 2 | totam] omnem cet. | iordanis] iordanes 4 | praedicans] praedicabat 2 baptismum] baptisma 5 | paenitentiae] penitentiae 8 add. in remissionem (remissa) peccatorum cet. | **4** sicut] sicuti 2 | sermonum] uerborum 5 8 | esaeiae] eseiae 2 8 esaiae cet. | prophetae] profetae 2 | domino] domini cet. | **5** inplebitur] 8 impleuitur 2 adinpleuitur 5 implebitur 4 A mons et] om. 4 | praua] tortuosa 2 in directa et aspera in uias planas. **6** et uidebit omnis caro salutarem dei. 7 Dicebat ergo procedentibus turbis, ut ab eo baptizarentur: progenies uiperarum, quis ostendit uobis fugere ab ira uentura? **8** facite itaque fructus dignos paenitentiae, ne uellitis dicere: patrem habemus abraham. dico enim uo{ca}bis, quod potens est deus de lapidibus istis suscitare filios abrahae. **9** Iam quid enim securis ad radicem arborum posita est. omnis itaque arbor non faciens fructum excidetur et in ignem mittetur. **10** Et interrogabant eum turbae dicentes: quid ergo faciemus? **11** respondens autem dixit illis: qui habet duas tunicas, det non habenti, et qui habent escas, similiter faciant. **12** Uenerunt autem et publicani similiter, ut baptizarentur, et dixerunt ad eum: magister, quid faciemus? **13** quibus ipse ait: nihil plus exegeritis, quam quod constitutum est uobis. **14** interrogabant autem eum et milites dicentes: et nos, quid faciemus? et ait illis: neminem concusseritis neque calumniam feceritis et sufficientes estote stipendiis uestris. **15** Arbitrante autem populo et cogitantibus omnibus in cordibus suis de iohannen, ne forte ipse

---

directa] directum 2 5 | aspera] asperas 4 8 | planas] lenes 5 | **6** salutarem] salutare A | dei] domini 5 | 7 ergo] autem 2 5 add. iohannes 8 | procedentibus turbis] prodeuntibus turbis 2 qui egrediebantur populi 5 ad turbas quae (que 8) exiebant cet. | ut ab eo baptizarentur] cum baptizarentur in conspectu eius 2 baptizari in conspectu eius 5 ut baptizarentur coram ipso 4 ut baptizarentur ab illo 8 ut baptizarentur ab ipso A | progenies] generatio 4 8 genimina A | ostendit uobis] uobis ostendit 5 | ab ira uentura] 4 8 a uentura ira cet. | **8** itaque] ergo cet. | fructus] uobis fructum 2 fructos 4 | dignos] 4 A dignum 2 5 dignus 8 | paenitentiae] penitentiae 8 | ne] et ne cet. | uellitis] incipiatis 5 coeperitis cet. | dicere] dicere in semetipsis 5 | abraham] habraham 8 | dico] amen amen dico 2 | enim] 5 A autem 4 om. 2 8 | quod] quoniam 5 quia cet. potens est] potest 4 A | lapidibus istis] istis lapidibus 2 | suscitare] excitare 2 | abrahae] istrahel 8 | **9** quid] om. cet. | enim] autem 5 4 | radicem] radices 2 | itaque] ergo 2 5 A om. 4 8 | fructum] 8 A fructum bonum cet. | excidetur] exciditur 5 A | in] om. 4 A | ignem] igne 2 8 mittetur] mittitur 5 A | **10** interrogabant] A interrogauerunt cet. | eum] 8 A illum cet. | turbae] populi 5 | dicentes] et dixerunt ei 4 | ergo] A om. cet. | faciemus] faciemus ut salbi simus 5 faciemus ut uiuamus 4 | **11** respondens autem dixit] 5 4 ille autem dixit 2 respondens autem dicebat 8 A | det] communicet 2 | non habenti] cum non habente 2 | habent] habet cet. escas] bonas escas 8 | similiter faciant] similiter 2 faciat similiter 8 similiter faciat cet. | **12** similiter] 5 om. cet. | ut baptizarentur] baptizari 2 5 | ad eum] 5 illi 2 ad illum cet. | quid] nos quid 2 et nos quid 4 | faciemus] faciamus ut salbi simus 5 | **13** quibus ipse ait] ille autem dixit illis 2 at ille dixit ad eos A ad ille dixit (add. ad eos 5) cet. | plus] amplius cet. add. quod 8 exegeritis] egeritis 2 exigatis cet. om. A | quam quod constitutum est uobis] 4 8 quam quod praeceptum est uobis 2 aduersus quod praeceptum uobis est agere 5 quam constitutum esti uobis faciatis A | **14** interrogabant] 2 A interrogauerunt cet. | eum] illum 4 om. 5 | et nos quid faciemus] quid faciemus et nos add. ut salbi simus 5 | et ait] 8 A ille autem dixit 2 ad ille dixit 5 ait 4 | concusseritis] 2 5 concutiatis 4 8 A | calumniam feceritis] calumniaueritis 2 5 calumniam faciatis cet. | sufficientes] 5 contenti cet. | **15** Arbitrante] cum speraret 2 expectantes 5 existimante cet. | populo] populus 2 | cogitantibus omnibus] cogitarent omnes (omnibus*) 2 cogitatium omnium 5 | iohannen] 2 4 iohanne cet.

esset christus, **16** respondit omnibus dicens: Ego quidem uos aqua baptizabo in paenitentiam. uenit autem fortior me, cuius non sum dignus calciamenta portare, ipse uos baptizabit in spiritu sancto et igni **17** habens uentilabrum in manu sua ad purgandam aream suam et congregat triticum in horreum suum, paleas uero comburet igni inextinctibili. **18** Multa quidem et alia hortatus populum euangelizabat. **19** erodes autem tetrarchas cum argueretur ab eo de herodiade uxore fratris sui et de omnibus malis, quae fecit herodes, **20** adiecit hoc super omnia, et inclusit iohannen in carcerem. **21** Factum est autem, com baptizatus esset omnis populus, et iesu baptizato et orante, † [.] aper tum † est caelum, **22** et descendit spiritus sanctus corporali specie sicut columbam in eum, et uox de caelo facta est: filius meus es tu. ego hodie genui te. **23** Et ipse iesus erat fere annorum

---

esset] est 8 | **16** respondit omnibus dicens] respondit dicens omnibus iohannes 2 cognoscens (conoscens*) intellectum eorum dixit 5 respondens ait omnibus 4 respondit dicens omnibus 8 respondit iohannes dicens omnibus A | quidem] om. 5 | uos aqua baptizabo] uos baptizo in aquam 2 uos baptizo in aqua 5 uos aqua baptizo 4 8 aqua baptizo uos A | in paenitentiam] paenitentiae 2 om. A | uenit autem fortior me] qui autem uenit fortior me est 5 ueniet autem fortior me 4 | calciamenta portare] 4 8 soluere coregiam calciamentorum 2 solbere corregiam calciamenti 5 soluere corrigiam calciamentorum eius A | baptizabit] baptizauit 2 4[c] | spiritu] spirito 5 | **17** habens] 2 4 cuius 5 A et 8 | uentilabrum] bentilabrem 2 | sua] 2 eius cet. | ad purgandam] ut emundet 2 et purgabit (purgauit 4) cet. | aream] haream 8 | suam] om. 5 | et] et quidem 5 | congregat triticum] colligat frumentum 2 triticum congregabit 5 congregabit (congregauit 4) triticum cet. | horreum] horreo 2 repositionem 5 | suum] om. 2 5 | paleas] paleam 5 | uero] autem cet. | comburet] exuret 2 | inextinctibili] inextintibili 5 inextinguibili cet. | **18** hortatus] consolans 5 exhortans cet. | populum euangelizabat] benenuntiabat ad populum 2 euangelizabat populum cet. | **19** erodes] herodes cet. | tetrarchas] quaterducatus 5 tetrarcha cet. om. 2 | cum argueretur] 5 correptus 2 cum corriperetur cet. | eo] 5 illo 2 4 8 A de[1]] saepe propter 2 | herodiade uxore] erodiadem uxorem 2 | de omnibus] propter omnia 2 malis quae fecit] quae fecit nequissima 2 quibus fecit malis 5 | herodes] om. 2 | **20** adiecit] et adiecit 8 | hoc] et hoc (oc*) 2 et hoc 5 A | super omnia] in omnibus 5 supra omnia cet. | et] 8 A om. 2 5 4 | iohannen] iohannem 8 | carcerem] 2 8 carcere cet. | **21** com] cum cet. | baptizatus esset] baptizaretur 2 A | omnis] om. 2 | iesu] iesum 2 | baptizato] baptizante 4* 8 | orante] orantem 8 | aper tum est caelum[1]] aperti sunt caeli 2 aperiri caelum 5 apertum est caelum cet. **22** descendit] discendit 2 descendere 5 | spiritus sanctus] spiritum sanctum 5 | specie] forma 2 figura 5 | sicut] quasi 2 5 | columbam] 2 5 columba cet. | eum] 5 illum 2 ipsum cet. | uox] uocem 5 | facta est] factam 5 add. dicens 8 | filius meus es tu] 5 8 tu es filius meus dilectus 2 A filius meus tu 4 | ego hodie genui te] in te bene sensi 2 in te complacuit mihi A | **23** Et ipse iesus erat] erat autem iesus 5 et ipse erat iesus 8 | fere] quasi 2 5 incipiens fere (quasi A) cet.

xxx incipiens, filius ut existimabatur ioseph. Qui fuit heli, **24** qui fuit matthae, qui
leui, quibus melchi, qui anne, qui ioseph, **25** qui naum, qui seddi, qui nance, **26** qui
mattathiae, qui semeia, qui ioseph, qui iuda, **27** qui iohanna, qui resae, <qui † [...
.]a † zorobabel, qui salatiel, qui ne>ri, **28** qui melchi, qui addi, qui cosan, qui
elmadan, qui er, **29** qui iese, qui eliger, qui iorim, qui matthatae, qui leui, **30** qui
simon, qui iuda, qui ioseph, qui iona, qui eliacim, **31** qui eram, qui matthatha, qui
nathan, qui dauid, **32** qui iessae, qui obeth, qui boos, qui salmon, qui naason, **33**

---

xxx] triginta 2 A | incipiens] 5 om. cet. | filius ut existimabatur ioseph] sicut putabatur esse filius iosef 2 ut uidebatur esse filius ioseph 5 quod uidebatur et dicebatur esse filius ioseph 4 quod putabatur esse filius ioseph 8 ut putaretur esse filius ioseph A add. qui fuit matthan qui fuit eleazar qui fuit eliud qui fuit lachin qui fuit sadoc qui fuit azor qui fuit eliacim qui fuit abiud qui fuit zorobabel qui fuit salathiel qui fuit iechoniae qui fuit ioacim qui fuit eliacim qui fuit iosia qui fuit amos qui fuit manasse qui fuit ezecia qui fuit achas qui fuit ioathan qui fuit ezecia qui fuit amasiu qui fuit ioas qui fuit ochoziae qui fuit ioram qui fuit iusafad qui fuit asaph qui fuit abiud qui fuit roboam qui fuit solomon qui fuit dauid 5 et om. v. 24-31 | Qui fuit] filius 2 8 | heli] elii 2 eli 4 heliae 8 | **24** qui fuit] filius 2 8 | matthae] matthei 2 4 matthiae 8 mattat A | qui^{2}] fili 2 qui fuit 4 A filius 8 | leui] leuui 4 8 | quibus] fili 2 qui fuit 4 A filius 8 | qui^{3}] fili 2 qui fuit 4 A filius 8 | anne] annae 2 iannae cet. | qui^{4}] fili 2 qui fuit 4 A filius 8 | ioseph] add. fili matthiae filius amos 8 qui fuit matthathiae qui fuit amos A | **25** qui^{1}] fili 2 qui fuit 4 A filius 8 | naum] natum 2 anum 8 | qui^{2}] fili 2 qui fuit 4 A filius 8 | seddi] aedi 2 sedi 4 8 esli A | qui^{3}] fili 2 qui fuit 4 A filius 8 | nance] naggae cet. add. fili maaht 8 | **26** qui^{1}] fili 2 qui fuit 4 A filius 8 | mattathiae] mattatiae 2 matthiani 8 matthathiae A | qui^{2}] fili 2 qui fuit 4 A filius 8 | semeia] semein 2 4 semei 8 A | qui^{3}] fili 2 qui fuit 4 A filius 8 | ioseph] iosec 2 A osec 4 osehc 8 | qui^{4}] fili 2 qui fuit 4 A filius 8 | iuda] iudae 2 4 8 ioda A | **27** qui^{1}] fili 2 qui fuit 4 A filius 8 | iohanna] ioannae 2 ioanae 4 iohannae 8 | qui^{2}] fili 2 qui fuit 4 A filius 8 | resae] sarec 2 resa A | qui^{3}] fili 2 qui fuit 4 A filius 8 | zorobabel] zorababel 8 | qui^{4}] fili 2 qui fuit 4 A filius 8 | salatiel] salathiel 8 A qui^{5}] fili 2 qui fuit 4 A filius 8 | **28** qui^{1}] fili 2 qui fuit 4 A filius 8 | qui^{2}] fili 2 qui fuit 4 A (om.*) filius 8 | addi] abdi 2 om. A* | qui^{3}] fili 2 qui fuit 4 A filius 8 | cosan] caese 2 cosae 4 cosam 8 A qui^{4}] fili 2 qui fuit 4 A filius 8 | elmadan] eimadam 2 hermadam 4 helmadam A | qui^{5}] fili 2 qui fuit 4 A filius 8 | er] ier 2 add. filius zoses 8 her A | **29** qui^{1}] fili 2 qui fuit 4 A filius 8 | iese] ihesu A iesu cet. | qui^{2}] fili 2 qui fuit 4 A filius 8 | eliger] eliazar 2* eliazer 2^{c} eliezer cet. | qui^{3}] fili 2 qui fuit 4 A filius 8 | qui^{4}] fili 2 qui fuit 4 A filius 8 | matthatae] matal 2 mattha 4 matthim 8 matthad A | qui^{5}] fili 2 qui fuit A filius 8 om. 4 | leui] leuui 8 om. 4 | **30** qui^{1}] fili 2 qui fuit 4 A filius 8 | simon] simeon 2 symae 4 symeon 8 A | qui^{2}] fili 2 qui fuit 4 A filius 8 | iuda] iudeae 2 iudae 4 8 | qui^{3}] fili 2 qui fuit 4 A filius 8 | ioseph] iosefh 2 | qui^{4}] fili 2 qui fuit 4 A filius 8 iona] ionam 2 ionae 4 8 | qui^{5}] fili 2 qui fuit 4 A filius 8 | eliacim] eliachim 4 8 A | **31** qui^{1}] fili 2 qui fuit 4 A filius 8 | eram] enam 2 4 aenam 8 melea A add. qui fuit menna A | qui^{2}] fili 2 qui fuit 4 A filius 8 | matthatha] mattatiae 2 mattatha 4 mhattata 8 matthata A | qui^{3}] fili 2 qui fuit 4 A filius 8 | nathan] natam 2 4 natham 8 | qui^{4}] fili 2 qui fuit 4 A filius 8 | **32** qui^{1}] fili 2 filius 8 qui fuit cet. | iessae] 4 8 eseiae 2 iesse 5 A | qui^{2}] fili 2 filius 8 qui fuit cet. | obeth] 2 4 obed 5 A obeht 8 | qui^{3}] fili 2 filius 8 qui fuit cet. | boos] booz A | qui^{4}] fili 2 filius 8 qui fuit cet. salmon] salomon 5 | qui^{5}] fili 2 filius 8 qui fuit cet. | naason] nassem 2 naasson cet.

qui aminadab, qui aram, qui esrom, qui fares, qui iudae, **34** qui iacob, qui isac, qui
abraham, qui thara, qui nachor, **35** qui seruch, qui regau, qui faleg, qui eber, qui
sale, **36** qui cainan, qui arfaxad, qui sem, qui noe, qui lameci, qui mathus[...], **37**
qui enoc, qui iaret, qui maleel, qui cainan, **38** qui enos, qui set, qui adam, qui dei.

4 Iesus autem plenus spiritu sancto reuersus est ab iordanen et ferebatur a
spiritu in deserto. **2** diebus xxxx cum temptaretur a diabulo et non edit quicquam
in diebus illis et consummatis eis esuriit. **3** Dixit autem illi diabolus: si filius dei es,
dic lapidibus his, ut fiant panes. **4** Et respondit ad illum iesus et dixit: scriptum est,
quia non in pane solo uiuet homo, sed in omni uerbo dei. **5** Adduxit eum
hierusalem et statuit eum supra pinnam templi et ostendit illi omnia regna orbis

---

33 qui^{1}] fili 2 filius 8 qui fuit cet. | qui^{2}] fili 2 filius 8 qui fuit cet. | aram] aran A add. qui fuit ioaram 4 | qui^{3}] fili 2 filius 8 qui fuit cet. | esrom] asron 5 esron 8 | qui^{4}] fili 2 filius 8 qui fuit cet. | fares] 5 4 phares 2 8 A | qui^{5}] fili 2 filius 8 qui fuit cet. | iudae] iuda 5 | **34** qui^{1}] fili 2 filius 8 qui fuit cet. | qui^{2}] fili 2 filius 8 qui fuit cet. | isac] isach 8 isaac A | qui^{3}] fili 2 filius 8 qui fuit cet. | qui^{4}] fili 2 filius 8 qui fuit cet. | thara] 5 4 tarae 2 tharae 8 A | qui^{5}] fili 2 filius 8 qui fuit cet. | nachor] nacor 2 | **35** qui^{1}] fili 2 filius 8 qui fuit cet. | seruch] 8 A seruth 2 seruc 5 4 qui^{2}] fili 2 filius 8 qui fuit cet. | regau] ragau cet. | qui^{3}] fili 2 filius 8 qui fuit cet. | faleg] falec 2 phalec cet. | qui^{4}] fili 2 filius 8 qui fuit cet. | qui^{5}] fili 2 filius 8 qui fuit cet. | sale] A salae 2 8 sala 5 salec 4 | **36** qui^{1}] fili 2 filius 8 qui fuit 4 A om. 5 | cainan] thamon 2 chainan A om. 5 qui^{2}] fili 2 filius 8 qui fuit cet. | arfaxad] arfaxa 2 arphaxad 5 arfaxat cet. | qui^{3}] fili 2 filius 8 qui fuit cet. | sem] seth 2 | qui^{4}] fili 2 filius 8 qui fuit cet. | qui^{5}] fili 2 filius 8 qui fuit cet. | lameci] lameth 2 lamech cet. | qui^{6}] fili 2 filius 8 qui fuit cet. | mathus] matusalae 2 mathusala 5 mattusale 4 mattusalam 8 matthusale A | **37** qui^{1}] fili 2 filius 8 qui fuit cet. | enoc] aenox 5 enoch A qui^{2}] fili 2 filius 8 qui fuit cet. | iaret] alet 2 iared 5 A iareth 4 zareth 8 | qui^{3}] om. 2 filius 8 qui fuit cet. | maleel] maleleel 5 4 malelel 8 malelehel A om. 2 | qui^{4}] fili 2 filius 8 qui fuit cet. cainan] ainan 5 aenam 4 cainam 8 | **38** qui^{1}] fili 2 filius 8 qui fuit cet. | enos] aenos 5 | qui^{2}] fili 2 filius 8 qui fuit cet. | set] seth cet. | qui^{3}] fili 2 filius 8 qui fuit cet. | qui^{4}] filius 8 qui fuit filius 4 qui fuit cet. | **4:1** plenus spiritu sancto] spiritu sancto plenus 2 | reuersus] regressus 8 A ab] ad 2 | iordanen] iordane 2 A iordanem 8 | ferebatur] ducebatur 2 5 agebatur cet. | a spiritu] in spiritu cet. om. 4 | deserto] eremum 2 desertum A | **2** diebus^{1}] per dies 2 | xxxx] xl 4 8 quadraginta cet. | cum temptaretur a diabulo] temptante eum satana 2 temptatus a satana 5 temptabatur a diabulo 4 8 et temtabatur a diabolo A | non edit quicquam] non maducauit quicquam 2 nihil maducauit cet. | in diebus illis] in illis diebus 2 8 diebus illis 4 | eis] illis diebus 4 illis cet. | esuriit] postea esuriit 8 | **3** Dixit autem] et dixit 2 | illi] illis 5* | diabolus] satanas 2 | dei es] es dei 5 dei est 8 | lapidibus his ut fiant panes] lapidi huic et fiant panis 2 ut lapides isti panes fiant 5 lapidi huic ut fiat panis 4 8 lapidi huic ut panis fiat A | **4** respondit] respondens 5 | ad illum] om. 5 | et] 4 8 om. cet. | dixit] dicens 2 om. A | quia] qui 4 om. 5 pane solo] solo pane 8 | uiuet] uiuit 2 | **5** Adduxit] et inposuit 2 et adsumens 5 et duxit cet. eum^{1}] 5 illum cet. | hierusalem et statuit eum] secundo 2 diabolus cet. om. 5 | supra pinnam templi] supra montem 2 in montem altum ualde 5 in montem altum 8 om. 4 A | et^{2}] om. 5 orbis terrarum] mundi 5 orbis terrae cet.

terrarum in momento temporis. **6** et dixit ad illum diabolus: tibi dabo potestatem
hanc omnem et gloriam ipsorum, quoniam mihi tradita est, et cuicumque uolo, do
illam. 7 tu ergo si procidens adoraueris ante me, erint tua omnia. **8** Et respondens
dixit illi iesus: scriptum est: diliges dominum deum tuum et ipsi solo seruies. **9** Et
adduxit illum in hierusalem et statuit illum super pinnam templi et dixit illi: si
filius es dei, mitte te hinc. **10** scriptum est enim, quoniam angelis suis mandauit de
te, ut custodiant te, **11** super manus tollent te, ne forte offendas ad lapidem pedem
tuum. **12** Et respondens dixit illi iesus, quia scriptum est: non temptabis dominum
deum tuum. **13** et consummata omni temptatione diabolus discessit ab eo usque in
tempore. **14** Et reuersus est iesus in uirtute spiritus in galilaeam. et fama exiit per
omnem finitimam regionem de illo. **15** et ipse docebat in synagogis honorem
accipiens ab omnibus. **16** et uenit in nazaret, ubi erat nutritus. Et intrauit
secundum consuetudinem die sabbato in synagoga et surrexit legere. **17** et

---

momento] puncto 2 | **6** dixit] 2 5 ait cet. | ad illum] 2 4 ad eum 5 illum 8 ei A | diabolus] 5 8 diauolus 2 om. 4 A | potestatem hanc omnem] potestatem istorum omnium 2 hanc potestatem omnem 5 potestatem hanc uniuersam cet. | gloriam] claritatem 2 | ipsorum] eorum 5 illorum cet. | quoniam] quia cet. | est] 2 5 sunt cet. | cuicumque] cui cet. | uolo] uoluero 4 | illam] 5 illa cet. | 7 ergo] uero 8 | procidens] prostatus 2 om. 5 A | ante me] in conspectu meo 2 in conspecto meo 5 coram me A | erint] erit 2 erunt cet. | tua omnia] tua omnes 2 omnia tua haec 4 | **8** dixit illi iesus] 4 8 iesus dixit 2 illi iesus dixit 5 iesus dixit illi A add. uado retro satanans 2 uade post me satanas 4 | est] est enim 4 | diliges dominum deum tuum] dominum deum tuum adorabis (adorauis 2) cet. | ipsi] 5 illi cet. | solo] soli cet. | seruies] deseruies 5 | **9** Et] iterum 2 | adduxit] 2 5 duxit cet. | illum[1]] eum 5 | in] om. 2 | hierusalem] iherusalem 8 | illum[2]] 4 8 eum 5 A om. 2 | super] 5 4 in 2 supra 8 A | pinnam] fastigio 2 | illi] om. 2 | es dei] 5 dei es cet. hinc] hinc deorsum cet. | **10** quoniam] quia 2 5 quod cet. | mandauit] 2 8 demandabit 5 mandabit 4 A | custodiant te] 5 te conseruent 2 conseruent te cet. | **11** super manus] quia in manibus 2 et in manus 5 et in manibus 4 et quia in manibus 8 A | tollent te] te ferent 2 tollant te 4 | offendas] perdas 8 | **12** respondens] respondit 2 | dixit illi iesus] 4 8 et dixit illi iesus 2 iesus dixit illi 5 iesus ait illi A | quia] et 8 om. cet. | scriptum] dictum A | temptabis] temptauis 2 temptabis A **13** consummata] cum perfecisset 2 | omni temptatione] 4 omnem temptationem 2 5 omni temptationem 8 omni temtatione A | discessit] 2 recessit cet. | eo] 2 5 illo cet. | in tempore] ad tempus cet. | **14** reuersus] 2 conuersus 5 egressus 4 A regressus 8 | galilaeam] galileam 8 fama] fama eius 4 | exiit] exiuit 2 5 add. de illo 8 | omnem] 5 totam 2 uniuersam cet. | finitimam] circumadiacente 2 om. cet. | de illo] de eo 2 om. 8 | **15** ipse] om. 2 | synagogis] 5 4 synagogis eorum cet. | honorem accipiens] gloriam accipiens 5 et magnificabatur (magnificabantur 8) cet. | omnibus] hominibus 8 | **16** et uenit] cum uenisset autem 2 ueniens autem 5 in[1]] 2 5 om. cet. | nazaret] nazara 2 nazared 5 nazareth cet. | erat] fuit 2 | nutritus] nutricatus 5 | intrauit] introiuit 2 8 introibit 5 | secundum consuetudinem] 5 secundum consuetudinem suam 4 A secundum consuetudinem tuam 8 om. 2 | die sabbato] sabbato 2 in sabbato 5 die sabbati cet. | synagoga] 8 synagogam cet.

porrectus est illi liber prophaetae eseiae. et reuoluens librum inuenit locum, ubi erat scriptum: **18** Spiritus domini super me, propter quod unxit me euangelizare humilibus, misit me praedicare captiuis remissionem et caecis uisum, dimittere confractos in requiem, **19** praedicare annum domini acceptum et diem redemptionis. **20** et reuoluens librum et reddens ministro sedet. Et omnium in synagoga oculi erant intuentes in eum. **21** coepit autem dicere ad illos, quoniam hodie inpleta est scripturam haec in auribus uestris. **22** Et omnes testimonium dabant illi et mirabantur in uerbis gratiae, quae prodibant de ore illius, et dicebant: nonne filius ioseph hic? **23** et dixit ad illos: forsitam dicetis mihi parabolam hanc: medice, cura te ipsum. quaecumquae audiuimus facta in capharnaum, fac et hic in patria tua. **24** Dixit autem: amen dico uobis, quia nullus propheta acceptus est in patria sua. **25** in ueritate dico uobis, multae uiduae erant in diebus heliae, quando clausum est caelum per triennium et menses sex, quomodo facta est famis magna super omnem terram. **26** et ad nullam {m}earum

---

17 porrectus] 2 5 traditus cet. | liber] om. 5 | prophaetae eseiae] eseie profetae 2 profeta esaias 5 prophetae eseiae 4 eseiae prophetae 8 prophetae esaiae A | reuoluens] 5 cum reuoluissit 2 ut reuoluit cet. | librum] om. 5 | locum] om. 2 | erat scriptum] 2 5 scriptum erat cet. | **18** propter quod] propterea 4 | euangelizare] benenuntiare 2 | humilibus] pauperibus cet. | praedicare] adnuntiare 5 | uisum] uisum restituere 2 | dimittere] demittere 5 remittere 4 | confractos] quassatos 2 conquassatos 8 | requiem] 2 8 remissione 5 remissionem 4 A | **19** praedicare] adnuntiare 5 | acceptum] acceptabilem 2 | et diem redemptionis] et diem redditionis 4 et diem retributionis cet. om. 5 | **20** reuoluens] uoluens 5 cum plicuisset (plicuissit 2) cet. | et[2]] om. cet. reddens] 5 reddidit cet. | ministro] ministros 8* | sedet] deinde sedit 2 sedit 5 et sedit cet. | in synagoga] qui in synagoga erant 2 | oculi erant] erant oculi 4 oculi 8 | intuentes] intenti 2 intendentes cet. | in eum] in illum 2 ei 5 | **21** illos] eos 5 | quoniam] quia cet. om. 5 | inpleta] adimpleta 2 repleta 5 impleta cet. | scripturam haec] scriptura ista 2 scriptura haec 5 haec scriptura cet. | **22** omnes] cum uiderent 2 | testimonium dabant illi] testimonium illis reddebat 2 testabantur ei 5 testimonium illi reddebant 4 8 testimonium illi dabant A | mirabantur] admirati sunt 2 | in uerbis] super sermonem 2 | quae] qui 5 | prodibant] exiebant 5 procedebant cet. | ore] core 2 | illius] eius 2 5 ipsius cet. | filius ioseph hic] filius ioseph est iste 2 filius ioseph est hic 5 hic est filius ioseph 4 hic est filius ioseph fabri 8 hic est filius ioseph A | **23** dixit] 5 ait cet. | ad illos] 2 ad eos 5 illis cet. | forsitam] utique cet. | dicetis] dicitis 2 | parabolam hanc] 5 similitudinem istam 2 hanc similitudinem cet. | quaecumquae] quacumque 5 quanta cet. in[1]] 5 A om. cet. | capharnaum] cafarnaum 5 4 | patria tua] patriam tuam 2 | **24** Dixit autem] 5 ille autem dixit illis 2 dixit autem iesus 4 ait autem iesus 8 ait autem A | amen dico uobis] 4 A amen amen dico uobis 5 8 om. 2 | quia nullus propheta acceptus est in patria sua] quod (quia 5 A) nemo propheta acceptus est in patria sua (patriam suam 8) cet. om. 2 | **25** in ueritate dico uobis] amen dico uobis 2 | multae] quia multae 2 | erant] 5 A fuerunt cet. add. in strahel 8 heliae] eliae 4 add. isdrahel 2 5* istrahel 5[c] 4 israhel A | clausum] A conclusum 2 clusum cet. per triennium] annis tribus cet. | menses sex] men 5 mensibus sex cet. | quomodo] 2 sicut 5 cum cet. | famis] fames A | magna] grandis 5 om. 2 | super] 8 in cet. | omnem terram] omni terra 4 A | **26** nullam] neminem 5 | mearum] eorum 5 illarum cet.

missus est helias nisi in sarepta sidonia ad mulierem uiduam. **27** Et multi leprosi
erant in israhel sub heliseo propheta. et nullus eorum purgatus est nisi ineman
surus. **28** Et inpleti sunt omnes ira in synagoga audientes haec. **29** et surgentes
eiciebant illum extra ciuitatem et adduxerunt eum usque ad supercilium montis,
super quem ciuitas aedificata erat ipsorum. **30** et praeteriens per medio illorum
ibat. **31** Et deuenit in capharnaum ciuitatem galilaeae et erat docens illos sabbatis.
32 et stupebant in doctrina eius, quoniam in potes<ta>te erat uerbum illius. **33** Et
erat in synagoga homo habens daemonium inmundum et exclamauit uoce magna
34 dicens: quid nobis est et tibi, iesu nazarene? uenisti perdere nos? scio te, qui sis
sanctus dei. **35** Et obiurgauit illum iesus dicens: ommutesce et exi ab illo. et cum
proiecisset illum daemonium, exiit ab illo nihil nocens illum. **36** Et factus est
pauor super omnes et conloquebantur ad alterutrum dicentes: quod est hoc

---

helias] elias 2 4 | in] om. 4 | sarepta] sarapta 4 sareptha A | sidonia] sidonae 2 sidoniae (sidonie 8) cet. | **27** israhel] A isdrahel 2 5* istrahel 5^c 4 | sub] tempore 2 | heliseo] 8 elie 2 eliseo 5 elisaeo 4 helisaeo A | propheta] profetae 2 profeta 5 | nullus] nemo cet. | eorum] ex eis 2 purgatus] emundatus 2 mundatus cet. | ineman] naemas 5 neman cet. | surus] syrus cet.
28 et inpleti] illi autem impleti 2 illi autem inpleti 5 et repleti cet. | omnes] om. 2 | ira in synagoga audientes haec] ira cum haec audissent in synagogam 2 furore in synagoga audientes haec 5 in synagoga ira haec audientes cet. | **29** et^{1}] om. 2 | surgentes] 5 exsurrexerunt 2 surrexerunt cet. | eiciebant] et expulerunt 2 et (om. 5) eiecerunt cet. | illum] eum 5 | adduxerunt] 2 5 deduxerunt 4 duxerunt 8 A | eum] 5 illum cet. | supercilium] supercliuum 8 | super quem] ubi 5 supra quem A | aedificata erat ipsorum] aedificata erat illorum 2 aedificata est eorum 5 eorum erat aedificata 4 ipsorum erat aedificata 8 illorum erat aedificata A add. ut praecipitarent (precipitarent 8) eum (illum 2) cet. | **30** et praeteriens per medio illorum] ipse autem per medios illos ueniens 2 ipse autem transiens per medium eorum 5 ipse autem transiit per medium illorum 4 ipse autem per medium illorum 8 ipse autem transiens per medium illorum A | ibat] A ambulabat 2 abiit 5 et abiit 4 et ibat 8 | **31** deuenit] discendit 2 4 descendit cet. | in] om. 2 | capharnaum] cafarnaum 5 4 | galilaeae] galieae 2 8 add. ad maritimam in finibus zabulon et nepthalim 5 | et] 2 5 ibique cet. | erat docens] 5 docebat cet. | illos] eos 5 | sabbatis] in sabbatis 5
32 et stupebant] 4 A et admirabantur 2 et mirabantur 5 stupebant autem 8 | in doctrina] super doctrinam 2 8 | quoniam] 5 quia cet. | uerbum] uerbus 5 sermo cet. | illius] ipsius A eius cet.
33 Et erat in synagoga homo] 4 erat autem in synagoga homo 2 5 et erat homo in synagoga 8 et in synagoga erat homo A | daemonium] demonium 8 | inmundum] immundum 2 | **34** quid] sine quid A | est] om. cet. | iesu] iesum 2 | nazarene] nazorene 2 8 | uenisti] 8 A uenisti ante tempus 2 uenisti nos hic 5 quid ante tempus uenisti 4 | nos] om. 5 | scio] scito 8 | qui sis] 4 A quis es cet. add. tu 2 tu es 4 8 | **35** obiurgauit] corripuit 2 increpauit cet. | illum^{1}] illi 5 A iesus] dominus 8 | ommutesce] obmutesce 8 | illo^{1}] eo 5 | cum proiecisset] cum deiecisset 2 proiciens 5 | illum^{2}] eum 2 5 | daemonium] demonium 8 add. in medium 2 A in medio exclamans 5 | exiit] exiuit 2 exibit 5 | illo^{2}] eo 5 | nihil nocens illum] et nihil eum nocuit 2 nihil nocens eum 5 nihilque illum nocuit (nocens 4) cet. | **36** factus] facta 2 | pauor] admiratio 2 pauor magnus 5 4 | super] 2 in cet. | omnes] 2 5 omnibus cet. | ad alterutrum] apud semetipsos 2 ad inuicem cet. | quod] quid 2 quis 5 | hoc] iste 2 hic 5

uerbum, quia in potestate et uirtute{s} imperat immundis spiritibus, et exeunt? **37**
et exibat fama de eo in omnem finitimam regionem. **38** Surgens autem de
synagoga intrauit in domum simonis. Socrus autem simonis detinebatur febre
magna, et rogauerunt illum pro ea. **39** et adstans super eam imperauit febri et
reliquid eam. confestim autem surgens ministrabat is. **40** Occidente autem sole
omnes quodquod habebant aegros languoribus uariis adducebant illos ad eum.
qui unicuique eorum manibus inpositis curabat illos. **41** Exibant autem et
daemonia a multis exclamantia et dicentia: tu es filius dei. et obiurgans non
sinebat ea loqui, quoniam sciebant christum illum esse. **42** Orta autem die
egressus abiit in desertum locum, et turbae requirebant illum. et uenerunt usque
ad eum et detinebant illum, ne discederet ab ipsis. **43** qui dixit ad illos, quoniam et
aliis ciuitatibus oportet me euangelizare regnum dei, quia hob hoc missus sum. **44**
et erat praedicans in synagogis galilaeae.

---

uerbum] sermo 2 5 | quia] 5 A quoniam 2 quod 4 8 | immundis spiritibus] 4 spiritibus immundis 2 inmundis spiritibus 5 spiritibus inmundis 8 A | exeunt] eiciuntur 2 | **37** et] cum prodiret autem 2 | exibat] facta est 2 exiuit 5 diuulgabatur cet. | eo] 2 5 illo cet. | finitimam regionem] locum regionis cet. add. illius 4 | **38** Surgens autem de synagoga] om. 2 | intrauit] uenit 5 introiuit 8 A om. 2 | in domum simonis] A andreae 2 in domum simonis et andreae cet. | detinebatur] erat conprehensa 5 tenebatur cet. | febre magna] 2 febri magna 5 magnis febribus cet. illum] eum 5 | pro] de 5 | **39** adstans] astitit 2 instans 5 stans cet. | eam[1]] 5 illam cet. | imperauit] et corripuit 2 increpauit 5 | febri] febrem 2 | reliquid] demisit 2 dimisit 5 A remisit 4 8 eam[2]] 5 illam cet. add. febris 2 continuo 5 | confestim autem] continuo et 2 ut etiam continuo 5 et continuo cet. | surgens] surgentem eam 5 | ministrabat] ministraret 5 | is] illi 2 eis 5 8 illis 4 A **40** Occidente autem sole] 5 cum occidisset autem sol 2 8 cum sol autem occidisset 4 A | quodquod] 2 5 qui cet. | aegros] languentes 2 infirmantes 5 infirmos cet. | languoribus uariis] infirmitatibus uariis 2 uariis languoribus cet. | adducebant] adduxerunt 2 adferebant 5 ducebant cet. | illos[1]] 4 A eos cet. | eum] illum 2 8 | qui] ille autem 2 5 ad (at A) ille cet. | unicuique] 2 5 singulis cet. | eorum] 2 om. cet. | manibus inpositis] manus (manum 4) inponens (imponens 4 A) cet. | curabat] sanabat 5 | illos[2]] eos cet. | **41** Exibant] exiebant (exiebat 8*) cet. | autem] om. A | et[1]] etiam A om. 4 | daemonia] demonia 8 | a multis] multa 4 | exclamantia] clamantia cet. | tu] quia tu 5 A | obiurgans] corripiens ea 2 increpans cet. | sinebat] patiebatur 2 permittebat 5 | ea] et 8 | quoniam] 2 5 quia cet. | sciebant] sciebant iesum 8 | christum illum esse] 2 eum christum esse 5 ipsum esse christum cet. | **42** Orta autem die] cum factus autem esset dies 2 facta autem die cet. | egressus] exiit 2 exiens 5 | abiit] 5 et abiit 2 ibat cet. | turbae] turbae multae 2 turbe 8 | requirebant] inquirebant 2 quaerebant 5 | illum[1]] eum cet. | eum] 5 illum 2 ipsum cet. | detinebant] retinebant 4 | illum[2]] eum 2 5 | ne discederet ab ipsis] ne discederet ab his 2 ut non abiret ab eis 5 ut ab ipsis non discederet 4 ne ab ipsis discederet 8 ne discederet ab eis A | **43** qui dixit ad illos] ille autem dixit ad illos 2 ad ille dixit ad eos 5 quibus ille (ipse 8) ait cet. | quoniam] 5 quia cet. om. 2 | et aliis ciuitatibus oportet me] oportet me et in alias ciuitates 2 5 | euangelizare] benenuntiare 2 | quia hob hoc] in hoc enim 2 5 quia ideo cet. missus sum] sum missus 2 | **44** erat praedicans] praedicabat 2 | galilaeae] galilea 2 8

5 factum est autem, dum turba incumbit ei ad audiendum uerbum dei, et ipse
erat stans iuxta stagnum gennesaret. **2** uidit nauiculas duas stantes ad litus, de
quibus piscatores egressi lababant retias suas. **3** Ascendens autem in unam
nauiculam, quae erat simonis, rogauit eum, ut producerent terra
quantulumcumque. Sedens autem docebat de nauicula turbas. **4** cumque desiit
loqui, dixit ad simonem: leua in alto et expandite retias uestras ad capiendum. **5**
Et respondens simon dixit illi: magister, per totam noctem laborantes nihil
cepimus, sed in uerbo tuo expandam retiam. **6** Et cum hoc fecissent, concluserunt
piscium multitudinem magnam. rumpebantur autem retiae eorum. **7** et
adnuebant socios in alia nauicula, ut uenirent et adiuuarent eos. et uenerunt et
impleuerunt ambas naues, ita ut mergerentur. **8** hoc uiso simon procidit genibus

---

5:1 factum est autem] factum est autem in eo 2 5 | dum] 2 5 cum cet. | turba] populus 5 turbae cet. | incumbit ei] super eum esset 5 inruerent in (super 2) eum cet. | ad audiendum] ut audirent (audiret 5) cet. | et ipse erat stans] cum staret ipse 2 stante illo 5 et ipse stabat cet. | iuxta] ad 2 5 secus cet. | gennesaret] 2 gennesared 5 gennesar 4 8 gennesareth A | **2** uidit] 2 et uidit cet. | nauiculas duas] naues duas 2 duas naues cet. | stantes] stare 4 8 | ad] 2 5 secus cet. litus] stagnum cet. | de quibus piscatores] et piscatores 2 piscatores autem cet. | egressi] ab eis exientes 5 descenderant cet. om. 2 | lababant retias suas] retia lauabant 2 lauabant retiam 5 et lauabant retia cet. | **3** Ascendens autem] et ascendit 2 | unam] om. 2 | nauiculam] nauem cet. erat] fuit 2 | rogauit eum] et desiderabat ab eo 2 | ut producerent terra] ut exaltaretur a terra 2 inducere a terra 5 ut inducerent ad terram 4 ut duceret a terra 8 a terra reducere A | quantulumcumque] quantum quantum 5 pusillum A aliquantulum cet. | Sedens autem] et sedens cet. docebat de nauicula turbas] in naui docebat populos 2 in naue turbas docebat 5 | **4** cumque desiit loqui] cum cessaret autem loquendo 2 cum autem cessasset loquens 5 ut cessauit autem loqui cet. | leua] recede 2 adduc 5 duc cet. | alto] altum cet. | expandite] summitite 2 mittite 5 laxa A* laxate cet. | retias uestras] 5 retia uestra 2 A retiam uestram 4 8 | ad capiendum] ad piscandum 2 in capturam cet. | **5** Et respondens simon dixit] 4 A simon autem dixit 2 simon autem respondens dixit 5 et respondit simon dixit 8 | illi] om. 2 | magister] 5 praeceptor (preceptor 8) cet. | laborantes] lauorauomis 2 | nihil] et nihil 2 | cepimus] profecimus 2 accepimus 5 | sed in uerbo tuo] super uerbo autem tuo 2 in tuo autem uerbo 5 in uerbo autem tuo A expandam retiam] non intermittimus 2 non praeteribo 5 laxabo retiam (rete A) cet. | **6** Et cum hoc fecissent] et continuo miserunt retia 2 et confestim mittentes retias 5 et cum hoc fecisset 8 concluserunt] et concluserunt 2 | magnam] multam 5 copiosam cet. om. 2 | rumpebantur autem retiae] ut retia dirumperetur 2 ut etiam retiae rumperentur 5 rumpebatur autem retia 4 rumpebantur autem retia 8 rumpebatur autem rete A | eorum] om. 5 | **7** adnuebant] annuebant 2 innuebant 5 adnuerunt 4 8 annuerunt A | socios] sociis cet. | in alia nauicula] qui erant in alia naui 2 qui erant in (de 8) alia naui (naue 5) cet. | uenirent] uenientes 5 | et[2]] om. 5 | eos] illos 2 | et uenerunt] cum uenissent itaque 2 uenientes ergo 5 om. 4 | et[4]] om. 2 5 | ambas] utrasque 5 | naues] 2 5 nauiculas cet. | ita ut] ut etiam 5 | mergerentur] pene mergerentur 2 paene mergerent 5 | **8** hoc uiso simon] simon autem cum uidisset 2 simon autem 5 quod cum uideret simon petrus (om. 4) cet. | procidit] concidit 2 | genibus] ad pedes 2 5 ad genua cet.

iesu dicens: exi a me, quia uir peccator sum, domine. **9** Pauor enim adprehenderat eum et omnes, qui cum illo erant in captura piscium, quae ceperant. **10** similiter iacobus et iohannes, filii zebedei, qui erant socii simonis. Et dixit ad simonem iesus: noli timere. iam amodo eris uiuificans homines. **11** et deductis nauiculis ad terram relictis omnibus secuti sunt eum. **12** Et factum est, dum esset ipse in una ciuitatum, et ecce uir plenus lepra. et ipse prostratus in faciem orabat illum dicens, quoniam si uis, potes{t} me mundare. **13** Et extendens manum tetigit illum dicens: uolo. et protinus lepra discessit ab illo. **14** et ipse praecepit ei, nemini diceret, sed uade et ostende te sacerdoti et offers pro purgatione tua, sicut praecepit moyses, ut sit in testimonium hoc uobis. **15** Diuulgabatur autem magis {e}<f>ama de eo, et conueniebant turbae multae audire et curari a languoribus

---

iesu] eius 2 5 | dicens] dicens ad iesum 2 | exi] oro te exi 2 rogo exi 5 | quia uir peccator sum domine] 5 quoniam homo peccator sum 2 domine quia homo peccator sum 4 8 quia homo peccator sum domine A | **9** Pauor] timor 5 miratio 4 stupor cet. | adprehenderat] adpraehendit 5 circumdederat A habebat cet. | eum] illum 2 8 | et omnes qui cum illo erant] om. 5 add. in miratione ab eo 2 | in] super 2 | captura] capturam istam 2 | quae] quam cet. | ceperant] ceperat 2 8 | **10** similiter] similiter fuerunt socii 2 erant autem socii eius 5 similiter autem cet. iacobus et iohannes] iacobum et iohannem A | filii] 4 filios A fili cet. | zebedei] 2 8 zebedaei cet. qui erant socii simonis] om. 2 5 | Et dixit ad simonem iesus] qui ait ad simonem iesus 2 ille autem dixit illis 5 et ait ad simonem iesus cet. | noli timere] nolite esse piscatores piscium 2 uenite et nolite fieri piscatores piscium 5 | iam amodo eris uiuificans homines] faciam enim uos piscatores hominum 2 5 ex hoc iam eris homines uiuificans 4 ex hoc iam eris hominis uiuificans 8 ex hoc iam eris homines capiens A | **11** et deductis nauiculis ad terram relictis omnibus] illi autem cum audissent omnia dimiserunt super terram 2 ad illi audientes omnia dereliquerunt super terra 5 et subductis ad (a 8) terram nauiculis (nauibus A) relictis omnibus cet. | secuti sunt] et secuti sunt 2 5 | eum] illum A | **12** Et factum est] factum est autem 2 | dum] 5 cum cet. ipse[1]] om. cet. | ciuitatum] A ex ciuitatibus 2 ciuitatium cet. | et[1]] om. 4 | ecce] ecce illic 2 ecce in qua erat 5 | plenus lepra] plenus lebra 2 leprosus 5 add. cum uidisset autem iesum 2 et uidens iesum 5 A | et ipse] om. cet. | prostratus] caecidit 2 cecidit 5 procidens cet. | faciem] faciem suam 2 | orabat illum] rogabat eum 4 8 et rogauit eum A om. 2 5 | quoniam] domine cet. | uis] uolueris 2 | mundare] emundare 2 | **13** Et extendens manum] et extendit manum 2 extendens autem manum 5 | tetigit] et tetigit 2 | illum] eum 5 | uolo] add. emundare 2 mundari 5 mundare cet. | protinus] continuo 2 confestim cet. | lepra discessit ab illo] emundatus est 2 mundatus est 5 lepra eius discessit ab illo 4 8 | **14** ei] illi cet. add. dicens 2 | nemini] ut nemini 8 A diceret] dixeris 2 dicere 5 | sed uade] uade autem 5 | et[2]] 2 5 om. cet. | te] te ipsum 5 | sacerdoti] sacerdotibus 4 8 | offers] offert illi 2 offer A add. munus 4 | purgatione] purificatione 5 emundatione (emundationem 8) cet. | tua] tuam 8 | sicut] quod 2 | moyses] moses A | ut sit] ut 2 om. A | testimonium] testimonio 2 | hoc uobis] 4 8 sit illis 2 uobis hoc 5 illis A add. ille autem exiens coepit praedicare et diuulgare uerbum ut non amplius posse eum palam in ciuitatem introire sed foris erat in desertis locis et conueniebant ad eum et uenit iterum in cafarnaum 5 **15** Diuulgabatur] 2 transiebat 5 perambulabat cet. | magis efama de eo] magis deo sermone 2 uerbum magis de eo 5 magis sermo de illo cet. | audire] 2 5 ut audirent cet. add. eum 8 | curari] 2 5 curarentur cet. | languoribus] infimitatibus cet.

suis. **16** ipse autem erat secedens in desertis et orabat. **17** Et factum est in una dierum, et ipse erat docens, et erant pharisaei sedentes et legis doctores, qui conuenerant ex omni municipio galileae et de iudea et hierosalem, et uirtus erat domini ad sanandum eos. **18** Et ecce uiri adferentes super lectum hominem, qui erat paralyticus, et quaerebant inferre illum et ponere ante eum. **19** Et cum non inuenissent, qua inferrent eum propter turbam, ascenderunt super tectum et per tegulas dimiserunt eum cum lectulo in conspectu iesu. **20** Et uisa fide illorum dixit homini: remissa sunt tibi peccata tua. **21** et coeperunt cogitare scribae et pharisaei dicentes: quis est, qui loquitur blasphemias? quis poterit dimittere peccata nisi unus deus? **22** cognitis autem iesus cogitationibus eorum dixit ad illos: quid cogitatis in cordibus uestris? **23** qui est facilius dicere: remittuntur tibi peccata tua, aut dicere: surge et ambula? **24** Ut sciatis autem, quia potestatem habet filius

---

suis] eorum 5 | **16** erat secedens] recedens 2 erat subtrahens se 5 secedebat 4 A^c sedebat 8 A* desertis] 5 solitudine 2 deserto cet. | orabat] orant 5 | **17** dierum] die 2 | et ipse erat docens] 4 ipso loquente 2 ipso docente 5 et ipse sedebat docens 8 A | et erant pharisaei sedentes] 4 A conuenire pharisaeos 2 5 et erant pharisei docentes 8 | qui conuenerant] erant autem aduenientes 2 erant autem congregati 5 qui uenerant cet. | ex] de 2 | municipio] castello cet. | galileae] galilaeae 5 A | de] om. cet. | iudea] iudeae 2 4 iudaeae cet. | et^5] om. 5 | hierosalem] iherusalem 8 hierusalem cet. om. 5 | et uirtus erat domini] om. 5 | ad sanandum] 4 A ut curaret 2 ut salbaret 5 ad sanandos 8 | **18** uiri] homines 2 | adferentes] 5 ferentes 2 portantes cet. | super lectum] 5 in lecto cet. | quaerebant] querebant 8 | inferre illum] inferre eum 2 inducere eum 5 eum inferre cet. | ponere] deponere 2 | ante eum] in conspectu eius 2 5 | **19** cum non inuenissent] 2 non inuenientes cet. | qua] 2 5 qua parte cet. | inferrent eum] eum inferrent 2 8 inducerent eum 5 illum inferrent 4 A | propter turbam] 2 5 prae turba 4 A pre turbas 8 | super] 5 in 2 supra cet. | et] om. A | per tegulas] 8 A per tegulatum 2 detegentes inbrices ubi erat 5 discoperuerunt tectum 4 | dimiserunt] deposuerunt 2 5 et summiserunt 4 summiserunt 8 A | eum cum lectulo] illum in medio cum grabattum 2 grabattum cum paralytico in medio 5 illum cum lecto in medio (medium A) cet. | in conspectu iesu] 5 ante iesum cet. | **20** Et uisa fide illorum] ille autem cum uidisset fidem illorum 2 uidens autem iesus fidem eorum 5 quorum ut uidit fidem 4 quorum fidem ut uidit iesus 8 quorum fidem ut uidit A | dixit] dicit 5 | homini] 4 illi homni 2 paralytico 5 om. 8 A | remissa sunt] 4 dimittentur 2 homo dimittentur 5 homo remissa sunt 8 homo remittuntur A | **21** pharisaei] phrisaei 2 pharisei 8 | dicentes] 2 A in cordibus suis dicentes cet. | quis^1] qui 2 quid 5 | est] hic 5 est hic cet. | qui] om. 5 | blasphemias] blasphemia 2 poterit] potest cet. | dimittere peccata] 4 A peccata dismittere 2 peccata dimittere 5 dimittere peccatum 8 | unus] solus cet. | **22** cognitis] ubi cognouit 2 cognoscens 5 ut cognouit cet. cogitationibus] cogitationes cet. | dixit] 4 8 respondens dixit 2 A dicit 5 | ad illos] ad eos 2 eis 5 in cordibus uestris] mala in cordibus uestris 2 in cordibus uestris iniqua 5 | **23** remittuntur] mittuntur 2 dimittentur 5 dimissa sunt 4 remissa sunt 8 dimittuntur A | peccata] pecca 2 | tua] 4 8 om. cet. | aut] an A | **24** Ut sciatis autem] 4 8 ut autem sciatis cet. | quia] quoniam 2 potestatem habet filius hominis] 2 5 filius hominis potestatem habet 4 A filius hominis habet potestatem 8

hominis in terra remittendi peccata, ait paralytico: tibi dico: surge et tolle lectum tuum et uade in domum tuam. **25** Et confestim surgens coram omnibus sustulit grabattum suum, in quo iacebat, et abiit in domum suam honorificans deum. **26** et pauor adprehendit omnes, et inpleti sunt timore dicentes, quoniam uidimus mirifica hodie. **27** et post haec exiit et intuitus est publicanum nomine leui sedentem ad theloneum et dixit illi: sequere me. **28** et relictis omnibus surgens sequebatur illum. **29** Et fecit illi cenam magnam leui in domo sua. et erat turba ingens publicanorum et aliorum, qui erant cum illis discombentes. **30** et murmurauerunt pharisaei et scribae eorum dicentes ad discipulos illius: quare cum publicanis et peccatoribus manducat et bibet? **31** Et respondens iesus dixit ad illos: non egent sani medico, sed qui se male habent. **32** non ueni uocare iustos, sed peccatores in paenitentiam. **33** Qui dixerunt ad illum: quare discipuli iohannis

---

in[1]] super 5 4 | terra] 5 A terram cet. | remittendi] dismittere 2 dimittendi 8 dimittere cet. | ait] dicit 5 | tibi dico] om. 2 | et[1]] 5 4 om. cet. | tolle lectum tuum] tolle grabattum tuum 5 om. 2 **25** confestim] continuo 2 | surgens] surrexit 2 | coram] in conspectu 2 5 | omnibus] eorum 2 5 illis 4 A ipsis 8 | sustulit] et tulit 2 tollens 5 tulit cet. | grabattum suum] grabattum 5 lectum 4 om. 8 A | in quo iacebat] om. 2 5 | et] om. 5 | honorificans] 5 clarificans 2 magnificans cet. **26** et pauor adprehendit omnes] et stupor adprehendit omnes cet. om. 2 5 add. et magnificabant deum cet. | inpleti] 5 impleti 2 repleti cet. | dicentes] omnes dicentes 5 | quoniam] quia cet. om. 5 | uidimus] uidemus 5 | mirifica] praeclara 2 mirabilia cet. add. et uenit iterum ad mare qui autem sequebatur eum populus docebat 5 | **27** et post haec] postea autem 2 om. 5 | exiit] exiuit 2 transiens 5 add. iesus 4 | et[2]] om. 5 | intuitus est] uidit cet. | publicanum nomine] om. 5 | leui] 4 A leuin 2 leui alphaei 5 leuui 8 | ad] super 5 | **28** theloneum] toloneum 2 teloneum cet.et dixit illi] cui dixit 2 dicit illi 5 ait illi cet.relictis omnibus] dismissis omnibus 2 relinques omnia 5 | surgens] surrexit 2 | sequebatur] 5 et secutus 2 secutus est cet. | **29** illum] 2 eum cet.illi] ei A om. 2 5 add. leui 5 | cenam magnam] epulum magnum 2 cenam illi magna 5 conuiuium magnum cet. | leui] A leuui 8 om. cet. | domo sua] domum suam 4* | ingens] magna 2 multa cet. | qui erant cum illis] qui cum illis erant cet. om. 2 5 | **30** discombentes] recumbentium 2 5 dicumbentes cet.et murmurauerunt pharisaei et scribae eorum dicentes ad discipulos illius] pharisaei autem et scribae mormuraverunt ad discentes eius dicentes 2 et pharisaei et scribae murmurabant ad discipulos eius dicentes 5 et murmurauerunt pharisaei et scribae eorum dicentes ad discipulos eius 4 A et murmurauerunt pharisaei et scribe dicentes ad discipulus eius 8 et peccatoribus] om. 5 | **31** manducat et bibet] 4 8 manducat et uibit 2 edit et bibit 5 manducatis et bibitis AEt respondens iesus] iesus autem respondit 2 respondens autem iesus 5 | dixit] et dixit 2 | illos] eos 5 | egent] opus est 2 habent opus 5 | sani] sanis 2 salui 5 qui sani sunt cet. medico] medicus 2 medicum 4 8 | **33** qui se male habent] male habentibus 2 qui male habent cet.Qui] illi autem 2 ad (at A) illi cet. | illum] 2 eum cet. | iohannis] iohannes 4

ieiunant frequenter et pharisaeorum et orationes faciant, tui autem manducant et bibent? **34** Qui dixit ad illos: numquid possunt fili sponsi, quamdiu sponsus cum illis {cum illis} est, ieiunare? **35** uenient dies, et cum ablatus fuerit ab illis sponsus, tunc ieiunabunt in illis diebus. **36** dixit autem et parabolam ad eos: quia nemo insumentum tunicae rudis adsuit panno ueteri. alioquin et nouum scindet et ueteri non conueniet insumentum a nouo. **37** Et nemo mittit uinum nouum in utres ueteres. alioquin rumpet uinum nouum utres, et ipse effunditur et utres peribunt. **38** sed uinum in utres nouos mittunt et ambo seruantur.

6 et factum est in sabbato secundo primo, cum transiret per sata, et uellerent discipuli illius spicas manibus conterentes et edebant. **2** quidam autem pharisaeorum dicebant: quid facitis sabbatis, quod non licet? **3** Et respondens

---

ieiunant frequenter et pharisaeorum] 8 ieiunant frequenter 2 et discipuli pharisaeorum ieiunant frequenter 5 iaiunant frequenter et pharisaeorum 4 ieiunant frequenter A | et[2]] om. 4 | orationes] 2 praecationes 5 obsecrationes cet. | faciant] faciunt similiter et pharisaeorum 2 A faciunt cet. | tui autem manducant et bibent] tui autem discentes nihil horum faciunt 2 tu autem discipuli nihil horum faciunt 5 tui autem discipuli edunt et bibunt 4 discipuli autem tui edunt et bibunt 8 tui autem edunt et bibunt A | **34** Qui dixit ad illos] ille autem dixit ad illos 2 iesus autem dixit ad eos 5 quibus ipse ait cet.numquid] non 2 | possunt] possum 8 potestis A | fili] filii 4 filios A | sponsi] sponsi ieiunare 4 | quamdiu] 2 4 cum 5 dum 8 A | sponsus cum illis cum illis est] habent sponsum secum 2 habeant sponsum secum 5 cum illis est sponsus (add. facere A) cet. | **35** ieiunare] om. 4 uenient] ueniet 2 8 add. autem cet. | et] 5 A om. cet. | ablatus fuerit] A auferetur 2 4 8 sublatus fuerit 5 | illis[1]] 4 A eis cet. | **36** tunc] 5 A et tunc cet.dixit] 4 8 dicebat 2 A dicebant 5 | et[1]] om. 2 | parabolam] 5 similitudinem cet. | eos] 2 5 illos cet. add. talem 4 | quia] quoniam 2 5 | insumentum[1]] inmissuram 5 commissuram cet. | tunicae rudis] 5 a uestimento nouo cet. | adsuit] addit 2 scindens inmittit 5 inmittit 8 A om. 4 | panno ueteri] in tunicam ueterem 5 in uestimento ueteri 4 in uestimentum uetus cet. | alioquin] si quominus 2 5 | nouum] rudem 5 | scindet] 5 conscindet 2 rumpit cet. | ueteri[2]] ueterem 8 | conueniet] 2 5 conuenit cet. | insumentum[2]] additamentum 2 a rude inmissura 5 commissura cet. | **37** a nouo] quod est a nouo 2 om. 5ueteres] ueteris 8 | alioquin] si quominus 2 5 | rumpet] rumpit 4 utres[2]] utres ueteres 5 | ipse] 5 uinum 2 ipsum 4 A ipsud 8 | effunditur] periet 2 effundetur cet. peribunt] om. 2 | **38** uinum in utres nouos mittunt] mittunt uinum nouum in utres nouos 2 uinum nouum in utres nouos mittunt (mittent 5 mittendum est A) cet. | ambo] 2 5 utrique 4 utraque 8 A | seruantur] serbantur 2 conseruantur cet. add. et nemo bibens uetus statim uult nouum dicit enim uetus melius est A | **6:1** et[1]] 2 5 om. cet. | factum est in sabbato] sabbato mane factum est 2 factum est (add. eum 5) in sabbato cet. | secundo primo] 5 A secundo primum 8 om. 2 4 | cum] ut 2 om. 5 | transiret] 4 8 perambularent 2 abire 5 transirent A | sata] A segetem 2 segetes 5 4 seminata 8 | et uellerent discipuli illius] discentes autem illius uellebant 2 discipuli autem illius coeperunt uellere 5 coepissent discipuli eius uellere 4 uellebant discipuli eius 8 A | manibus conterentes et edebant] et confricantes illas manibus suis manducabant 2 et fricantes manibus manducabant 5 et manducarent confricantes ea manibus suis 4 et manducabant confricantes manibus 8 A | **2** quidam autem pharisaeorum] A pharisaei autem 2 quidam autem de farisaeis 5 aliqui autem ex pharisaeorum 4 aliqui autem pharisaeorum 8

dixit illis iesus: nec hoc legistis, quod fecit dauid, cum esuriit ipse et qui cum eo
erant? **4** quomodo intrauit in domum dei et panes propositionis accepit et
manducauit et dedit eis, qui secum erant, quos non licet edere nisi solis
sacerdotibus. **5** et dicebat illis, quoniam dominus est filius hominis etiam sabbati.
6 Factum est autem in alio sabbato intrare illum in synagoga et docere. et erat ibi
homo, et manus illius dextra erat arida. **7** obseruabant autem scribae et pharisaei,
si sabbato curaret, ut inuenirent et accusarent illum. **8** ipse autem sciebat
cogitationes illorum. Dixit autem homini, qui habebat manum aridam: surge et sta
in medio. et surgens stetit. **9** dixit autem iesus ad illos: interrogabo uos, si licet
sabbatis benefacere an male, animam saluam facere an perdere. **10** et
circumspiciens omnes illos esse in ira dixit homini: extende manum tuam. et
extendit et restituta est manus illius. **11** ipsi autem impleti sunt stupore et

---

3 dicebant] add. ei 5 ad eos 4 illis 8 Afacitis] facietes 2 faciunt discipuli tui 5sabbatis quod non licet] sabbatis non licet 8 quod non licet in sabbatis AEt respondens dixit illis iesus] et respondens dixit ad illos 2 respondens autem iesus dixit ad eos 5 et respondens iesus dixit illis 8 et respondens iesus ad eos dixit Anec] numquam 5 | quod] quid 4 8 | fecit] fecerit 4 | cum[1]] quando 2 5 esuriit] 5 8 esuriuit 2 esuriret 4 esurisset A | erant] erat 5 | **4** quomodo] om. 5 | intrauit] introiuit 2 5 | propositionis] propositiones 4 | accepit] 2 sumpsit cet. om. 5 | et[2]] om. 5 | dedit eis qui secum erant quos non licet edere nisi solis sacerdotibus] eis qui secum erant dedit quos non licebat manducare nisi solis sacerdotibus 2 et dedit et qui cum erant quibus non licebat manducare si non solis sacerdotibus 5 his qui cum ipso (secum 4) erant quos non licet (licebat 4) manducare nisi solis (tantum A) sacerdotibus cet. add. eodem die uidens quendam operantem sabbato et dixit illi homo si quidem scis quod facis beatus es si autem nescis maledictus et trabaricator legis 5 | **5** (p. v. 10 5) dicebat] dicit 2 | illis] eis 5 | quoniam] 5 quia cet. | dominus est filius hominis] filius dominus hominis est 8 | etiam sabbati] et sabbati ipsius 2 | **6** Factum est autem in alio sabbato intrare illum in synagoga et docere] et factum est in alio sabbato cum introisset in synagogam docere 2 et cum introisset iterum in synagogam sabbato 5 factum est autem (add. et A) in (om. 4) alio sabbato ut intraret in synagogam (synagoga 8) et doceret cet. | et erat] erat autem 2 in qua erat 5 | ibi] 8 A illic 2 om. 5 4 | et manus illius dextra erat arida] manum habens aridam 2 aridam habens manum 5 manum habens aridam dexteram 4 et manus eius dextra erat arida 8 A | **7** obseruabant] obseruabant eum 5 | autem] om. 5 | pharisaei] farisaei 4 | et accusarent illum] 2 accusare eum 5 quemadmodum accusarent illum 4 unde accusarentur illum 8 accusare illum A | **8** autem[1]] uero 8 A | sciebat] sciens 4 | illorum] 2 eorum cet. | dixit autem] et dicit 2 dicit 5 ait 4 et ait 8 A | homini] illi homini 2 illi 5 homini illi 4 habebat manum aridam] manum aridam habibat 5 | medio] medium 2 A | surgens] surrexit 2 stetit] et stetit 2 | **9** dixit autem iesus ad illos] dixit autem iesus ad eos 5 ait autem ad illos iesus cet. | interrogabo] interrogo 2 A | sabbatis] sabbato cet. | an[1]] aut 2 5 | male] 4 A malefacere cet. | saluam facere] saluare 2 5 | an[2]] aut 2 5 | perdere] occidere 2 add. ad illi tacuerunt 5 **10** circumspiciens] 5 circuminspexit 2 circumspectis cet. | omnes illos] illos omnes 2 eos omnes 5 illis omnibus 4 8 omnibus A | esse in ira] et uidit et uiliabundus 2 in ira cet. om. A | dixit] dicit 5 homini] illi homini 2 | illius] eius cet. add. sicut et alia 5 sicut alia 4 | **11** ipsi] illi 2 8 | impleti] 2 repleti cet. lac. 4 | stupore] ira 2 insipientia 5 A iniquitate 4 8

conloquebantur ad inuicem, quidnam facerent iesu. **12** factum est autem in illis diebus exiit in montem orare. et erat pernoctans in oratione dei. **13** et cum dies horta est, uocauit discipulos suos et eligens ex eis duodecim, quos et apostolos nominauit, **14** simonem, quem et cognominauit petrum, et andream fratrem eius et iacobum et iohannem et philippum et bartholomeum **15** et mattheum et thomam et iacobum alphei et simonem, qui appellatur zelotes, **16** et iudan iacobi et iudan{t}, qui erat proditor. **17** Et descendens cum illis stetit in loco campense et turba discipulorum eius et multitudo ingens populi ab omni iudea et hierusalem et trans fretum et maritima tyri et sidonis. **18** qui uenerant audire illum et curari a languoribus suis. et qui uexabantur ab spiritibus inmundis. **19** Et omnis turba quaerebat tangere eum, quoniam uirtus ab illo exibat, et sanabat omnes. **20** et ipse adleuans oculos in discentes suos dicebat: Beati pauperis spiritu, quoniam

conloquebantur] colloquebantur 2 cogitabant 5 | quidnam] quomodo 5 quid 8 | facerent iesu] A illi facerent 2 perderent eum 5 facerent de iesum 4 facerent de iesu 8 | **12** illis diebus] diebus illis 5 | exiit] exire illum 2 exire eum 5 | montem] monte 4 | orare] et orare 5 | oratione] orationem 8 | dei] om. 5 | **13** dies horta est] factus esset dies 2 facta est dies 5 dies factus est (esset A) cet. | uocauit] uocauit ad se 4 8 | eligens] 5 elegit cet. | ex eis duodecim] ex eis xii 2 ab eis duodecim 5 duodecim (xii 4) ex ipsis A | apostolos] apostolus 8 | nominauit] uocauit 5 **14** simonem] primum simonem 5 | quem et cognominauit petrum] quem et petrum cognominauit 5 petrum quem cognominauit 8 quem petrum cognominauit cet. | et[3]] 5 4 om. cet. | iacobum] iohannem 4 add. zebedei 8 | et[4]] om. 2 | iohannem] 8 A ioannem 2 iohannen 5 iacobum 4 add. fratrem eius quos cognominauit boanerges quod est fili tonitrui 5 fratrem eius 8 | et[5]] 5 4 om. cet. | bartholomeum] bartolomeum 2 | **15** et[1]] om. 2 A | mattheum] matthaeum 5 thomam] thoman 2 add. qui cognominatus est didymus 5 | et[3]] om. 2 A | alphei] alfei 8 appellatur] uocabatur 2 4 uocatur cet. | **16** et[1]] om. 2 A | iudan] 5 iudam cet. | iudant] iuda 2* iudam cet. add. scarioth 2 8 A inscarioth 5 | qui erat proditor] qui tradidit illum 2 qui etiam et tradidit eum 5 qui fuit proditor eius 4 qui factus est traditor 8 qui fuit proditor A | **17** descendens] 5 A discendit 2 4 descendit 8 | illis] eis 5 | stetit] 5 A et stetit cet. | campense] campestri (canpestri 2) cet. | turba] turbae 5 | discipulorum] discentium 2 | ingens] magna 2 multa 5 copiosa cet. | populi] 2 5 plebis cet. | ab] de 2 ex 5 | omni] tota 2 | iudea] 2 iudaea cet. | et hierusalem] et iherusalem 8 | et trans fretum et maritima tyri et sidonis] 8 et de trans marinis tyro et sidone et aliorum ciuitatium 2 et aliarum ciuitatium 5 et trans fretum et maritima tyrii et sidonis 4 et maritima tyri et sidonis A | **18** qui uenerant] 2 4 uenentium 5 qui uenerunt 8 A audire] 2 5 ut audirent cet. | illum] 2 eum cet. | curari] 2 saluari 5 sanarentur cet. | a languoribus] ab omne infirmitate 5 | suis] eorum 5 | uexabantur] uexebantur 8 | ab] a A om. 5 inmundis] immundis 2 add. curabantur (curarentur 4) cet. | **19** omnis] omnes 2 4 | turba] populus 5 | quaerebat] 5 quaerebant cet. | tangere eum] tangere illum 2 tangere eius 5 eum tangere cet. | quoniam uirtus] uirtus enim 2 quia uirtus (uir 5) cet. | ab] 2 5 de cet. | illo] eo 2 5 exibat] proficiscebatur 2 exiebat cet. | sanabat] curabat 2 | **20** ipse] om. 2 5 | adleuans oculos] leuauit oculos 2 eleuans oculos suos 5 eleuatis (leuatis 8) oculis cet. | in] ad 2 | discentes suos] 2 discipulos 5 8 discipulis suis 4 discipulos suos A | dicebat] et dixit 2 | pauperis] egeni 2 spiritu] om. cet. | quoniam] 5 8 quia cet.

uestrum est regnum dei. **21** Beati, qui esuritis nunc et sititis, quoniam saturi eritis.
Beati, qui plora{ra}tis nunc, quoniam ridebitis. **22** Beati estis, cum odierint uos
homines et cum segregauerint uos et cum eicerint uos et cum exprobrauerint
nomen uestrum tamquam nequam causa<m> fili hominis. **23** gaudete in illa hora
et exultamini. ecce enim merces uestra copiosa est in caelo. similiter faciebant
profetis patres illorum. **24** Uerumtamem uae uobis diuitibus, quoniam habetis
consolationem uestram. **25** uae uobis saturis, quia esurietis. uae uobis, qui ridetis
nunc, quia lugebitis et flebitis. **26** uae, cum bene uobis dixerint omnes homines.
similiter faciebant pseudoprophetis patres eorum. **27** Sed uobis dico audientibus:
diligite inimicos uestros, benefacite eis, qui oderunt uos, **28** benedicite
maledicentes uos, orate pro is, qui calumniantur uos. **29** percutienti te in maxilla,
preue ei alteram, et ab eo, qui au{t}feret uestimentum tuum, et palleum uetare

---

uestrum] ipsorum 8 | **21** esuritis nunc] esuriunt nunc 5 nunc esuritis A nunc esuriunt cet. | et sititis] et sitiunt cet. om. 5 A add. iustitiam 2 | quoniam[1]] 2 quia cet. | saturi eritis] ipsi satiabuntur 2 saturamini 5 ipsi saturabuntur 4 saturabuntur 8 saturabimini A | Beati qui ploraratis nunc quoniam ridebitis] beati qui nunc plorant quoniam ridebunt 2 beati qui nunc fletis quia (quoniam 4) ridebitis cet. om. 5 | **22** estis] 5 eritis cet. | cum[1]] quando 5 | odierint uos] 5 oderint uos 2 uos oderint 4 A uos odierint 8 | cum[2]] quando 2 | segregauerint] 2 exprobabunt 5 separabunt 4 8 separauerint A | uos[2]] om. 5 | cum[3]] 4 8 om. cet. | eicerint] maledixerint 2 eicient 5 4 eicent 8 exprobauerint A | uos[3]] om. cet. | cum[4]] om. cet. | exprobrauerint] expellent 2 reprobent 5 exprobabunt 4 8 eiecerint A | tamquam] quasi 2 sicut 5 | nequam] malum cet. | causam fili] propter filium cet. | **23** in illa hora] illum diem 2 illo die 5 illa die cet. | exultamini] exultate cet. | ecce enim] quoniam 5 | copiosa] 4 multa cet. om. 2 | est] 4 8 om. cet. | caelo] caelis est 2 similiter] per eadem enim 2 sic enim 5 secundum haec enim (om. 8) cet. | profetis] 2 et prophetis 4 prophetis cet. | illorum] 2 eorum cet. | **24** Uerumtamem] uerum 2 5 | quoniam] 2 5 quia cet. habetis] consecuti estis 2 | consolationem] postulationem 2 | **25** saturis] saturati 2 qui saturati (repleti 5) estis cet. | quia[1]] quoniam 2 5 | ridetis nunc] nunc ridetis 2 deridetis 4 | quia[2]] quoniam 5 | lugebitis] plangetis 2 plorabitis 5 | flebitis] plorabitis 2 lugetis 5 | **26** uae] uae uobis 5 4 | cum bene uobis dixerint] A cum uobis benedixerint 2 quando bene uobis dixerint 5 cum benedixerint 4 cum benedixerim uobis 8 | omnes homines] homines 5 omnis hominis 8 similiter] per eadem 2 secundum haec cet. | faciebant] faciebat 8 | pseudoprophetis] 5 4 pseudoprofetis 2 8 prophetis A | **27** dico audientibus] qui nunc auditis dico 2 dico qui auditis cet. eis qui oderunt uos] eis qui uos oderunt 2 odientibus uos 5 his qui odiunt uos 4 his qui oderunt uos 8 his qui uos oderunt A | **28** maledicentes] maledicentibus A | uos[1]] uobis A | is qui calumniantur uos] eis qui uobis iniuria faciunt 2 calumniantibus uos cet. | **29** percutienti te] et (om. 5) qui te percutit (percusserit 2 4) cet. | maxilla] maxillam cet. | preue] praebe cet. | ei] illi 5 om. A | alteram] 2 et aliam 5 et alteram cet. | ab eo] ei 2 eum 4 8 | autferet] a te auferet 2 tollit 5 auferet (aufert A) tibi cet. | uestimentum] A palleum 2 tunicam cet. | tuum] tuum 2 tuam 5 om. cet. | et[2]] etiam 8 A om. 2 | palleum uetare noli] remitte tunicam 2 pallium ne uetueris 5 pallium (tunicam A) noli prohibere cet.

noli. **30** omni autem poscenti te da. et ab eo, qui tollit tua, repetere noli. **31** et quemadmodum uultis, ut faciant uobis homines, sic facite eis. **32** et si diligites eos, qui uos diligunt, quae uobis gratia est? nam et peccatores eos, qui se diligent, diligunt. **33** et si benefeceritis, qui benefaciunt uobis, quae gratia est uobis? etenim peccatores hoc faciunt. **34** et si feneretis eis, a quibus speratis recipere, quae gratia est uobis? etenim peccatores peccatoribus fenerant, ut recipiant. **35** Uerumtamem diligite inimicos uestros et benefacite et fenerate nihil desperantes. et erit merces uestra multa in caelo et eritis fili excelsi, quoniam ipse suauis est super ingratos et nequas. **36** Estote misericordes, sicut et pater uester miseretur. **37** nolite iudicare, ne iudicemini. nolite condemnare, ut non condemnemini. dimittite et dimittemini. **38** date et dabitur uobis. mensuram bonam, agitatam cumulatam, superfluentem dabunt in sinu uestro. eadem mensuram, qua metitis,

30 autem] om. 4 8 | poscenti] qui petit 2 potenti 8 petenti cet. | te] om. 2 | da] 2 5 tribue cet. ab eo] 2 5 om. cet. | tollit] tollet 5 aufert A auferet a te (om. 2) cet. | tua] 2 5 quae tua sunt cet. repetere noli] noli deposcere 2 ne repetieris 5 noli prohibere 4 8 ne repetas A | **31** quemadmodum] quomodo 2 sicut 5 prout cet. | faciant uobis] uobis faciant 2 faciam uobis 5 | sic facite eis] uos illis facite 2 et uos facite illis 5 facite illis et uos similiter 4 facitis illis similiter 8 et uos facite illis similiter A | **32** et si] nam si 2 | diligites] diligitis 2 | eos[1]] om. 2 5 | qui uos diligunt] diligentes uos 5 | uobis gratia est] 5 est uobis gratia 2 uobis gratia 4 erit uobis gratia 8 uobis est gratia A | nam et peccatores] et peccatores enim 2 etenim peccatores 5 | eos[2]... diligunt[2]] diligunt eos qui se diligunt 2 hoc faciunt diligentes illos diligunt 5 diligentes se diligunt 4 A diligunt diligentes se 8 | **33** et si benefeceritis qui benefaciunt uobis] et si benefacitis benefacientibus uobis 5 et si benefeceritis his qui uobis benefaciunt cet. om. 2 | gratia est uobis] est uobis gratia 2 gratia uobis est 5 uobis erit gratia 4 8 uobis est gratia A | etenim] 5 nam et 2 4 cum et 8 si quidem et A | hoc faciunt] 5 A id ipsud faciunt 2 haec faciunt 4 hoc faciant 8 | **34** et] sed 2 | feneretis eis] feneraueris eis 2 feneratis 5 mutuum (mutum 4) dederitis his cet. | speratis] speratis uos 4 gratia est uobis] uobis gratia 2 gratia uobis est 5 | etenim peccatores] 5 et peccatores enim 2 nonne et peccatores 4 nam et peccatores 8 A | fenerant] fenerantur A | recipiant] recipiant aequalia A | **35** Uerumtamem] uerum dico 2 | diligite] amate 4 8 | benefacite] benefacite his 2 fenerate] 2 5 mutum date 4 8 mutuum date A | desperantes] disperantes 2 inde desperantes A merces] mercis 2 | multa] magna 2 | in caelo] om. cet. | fili] filii A | excelsi] altissimi cet. add. dei 2 | quoniam] 2 5 quia 4 8 A | suauis] bonus 2 suabis 5 benignus cet. | ingratos] gratos 4 nequas] 2 iniquos 5 malos cet. | **36** Estote] estote ergo A | misericordes] beneuolentes 5 | et] om. 5 | miseretur] 4 beniuolus est 5 misericors est cet. | **37** ne iudicemini] ne iudicetur de uobis 2 ut non iudicemini 5 et de uobis non iudicabitur 4 8 et non iudicabimini A | ut non condemnemini] ne condemnemini 2 et non condemnamini 4 A | dimittite] dimitte 5 | dimittemini] 4 8 dimittitur uobis 2 demittemini 5 dimittimini A | **38** dabitur] dauitur 2 | mensuram bonam] mensura bona 2 | agitatam cumulatam] commota 2 conquassatam inpletam 5 confersam commotam 4 conmodatam confersam 8 confertam et coagitatam A | superfluentem dabunt] superfundens dabitur 2 supereffundentem dabunt 5 supereffluentem dabunt 4 dabunt supereffundentem 8 et supereffluentem dabunt A | sinu uestro] sinos uestros 2 sinus uestros 5 sinum uestrum cet. | eadem] quae enim (enm*) 2 in qua enim 5 eadem quippe A | mensuram[2]] 4 8 mensura cet. | qua metitis] 4 mensuraueritis 2 metieritis 5 quam metitis 8 qua mensi fueritis A

remetietur uobis. **39** dicebat autem et parabolam illis: numquid potest caecus
caecum ducere? nonne utrique in foueam incident? **40** non est discens super
magistrum. cons{s}umatus autem omnis erit, si sit sicut magister illius. **41** Quid
autem uides festucam in oculo fratris tui, trabem autem, quae in oculo tuo est,
non consideras? **42** aut quomodo potest dicere fratri tuo: sine eiciam festucam de
oculo tuo, et ecce in oculo tuo trabes subiacet? hypocrita, eice primum trabem de
oculo tuo, et tunc perspicies eicere festucam de oculo fratris tui. **43** non est arbor
bona faciens fructus malos nec arbor mala faciens fructus bonos. **44** unaquaeque
arbor ex fructu suo dinoscitur. neque legunt de spinis ficus, sed nec de rubo
uindemiant uuam. **45** Bonus enim homo de bono thensauro cordis sui profert
bonum, et nequa de malo profert malum. ex abundantia cordis os illius loquitur.
46 Quid autem me uocatis: domine, domine. et non facitis, quae dico? **47** omnis,
qui uenit ad me et audit uerba mea et facit illa, demonstrabo uobis, cui sit similis.
48 Similis est homini aedificanti domum, qui fodit in altum et posuit fundamenta

---

remetietur] eadem et metietur 2 metietur 4 | **39** dicebat autem et parabolam illis] et similitudinem dicebat illis 2 dicebant autem et parabolam illis 5 dicebat autem illis et similitudinem istam 4 dicebat autem et similitudinem 8 dicebat autem illis et similitudinem A | ducere] deducere 2 ducatum praebere 4 | utrique] ambo cet. | foueam] fouea 8 | incident] 5 cadunt 2 cadent cet. **40** discens] disces 2 discipulus cet. | conssumatus] confectus 5 perfectus cet. | omnis] omnes 2 om. 4 | erit] erits 2 | si sit] ut sit 4 8 om. cet. | illius] eius cet. | **41** Quid] qui 2 | festucam] stipulam 2 | in oculo[1]] quae est in oculo 2 in oculum 8 | trabem] trauem 2 | quae in oculo tuo est] in oculo tuo 2 5 | consideras] uidis 2 inspicis 5 | **42** aut] et A om. 2 8 | potest] 4 8 potes cet. sine] frater sine A | festucam[1]] stipulam 2 festucum 8 | et ecce in oculo tuo trabes subiacet] et ecce in oculo tuo trabis est 2 et ecce trabis in tuo oculo est 5 et ecce in oculo tuo trabis subiacet 4 ipse in oculo tuo trabem non uidens A | hypocrita] ypocrite 2 | eice] ecice 2 | trabem] trauem 2 | perspicies] uidebis 2 5 respicies 4 A perspiciis 8 | eicere] 2 5 ut educas cet. | festucam[2]] stipulam 2 festucum 8 | **43** est] 5 est enim cet. | faciens[1]] 2 5 quae facit cet. | fructus[1]] fructos 2 5 | nec] neque cet. add. iterum 4 | fructus[2]] fructum 8 A fructos cet. | bonos] bonum 8 A **44** unaquaeque] unaqueque 2 unaquaequae 8 unaquaeque enim A | ex] a 2 de 5 A | fructu] 4 A fructos 2 fructo 5 8 | suo] suos 2 | dinoscitur] cognoscetur 4 cognoscitur cet. | neque legunt de spinis ficus] 8 de spinis enim ficus non leguntur 2 non enim legunt de spinis ficus 5 neque legunt de spinis uuas 4 neque enim de spinis colligunt ficus A | sed nec] neque cet. | uindemiant uuam] uendeamiantur ubae 2 ubam uindemiant 5 | **45** enim] 4 om. cet. | thensauro] tensauro (densauro*) 8 thesauro A | cordis sui] suo 8 | profert[1]] A proferet cet. | bonum] bona 2 nequa] malus 5 4 malus homo cet. | malo] malo thensauro cordis sui 2 malo thensauro 4 profert malum] A malum proferet 2 proferet malum 5 8 proferet mala 4 | ex abundantia] de abundantia 2 de enim abundantia 5 ex abundantia enim cet. | os illius loquitur] loquitur malum 2 loquitur os eius 5 os (hos 8) eius (om. A) loquitur cet. | **46** me uocatis] mihi dicitis 5 uocatis me cet. | quae] quod 2 | **47** ad me] et ad me 4 | uerba mea] 2 mea berba 5 sermones meos (add. hos 4) cet. | illa] 2 ea 5 eos 4 A om. 8 | demonstrabo] ostendam cet. | sit similis] 2 est similis 5 simile est 4 similis est 8 similis sit A | **48** in altum] et exaltauit 2 et altum fecit 5 | fundamenta] fundamentum 2 5

super petram. tempestate horta impulit flumen domui illi, nec ualuit mouere
illam. fundata enim erat super petra. **49** qui autem audit et non facit, similis est
homini aedificanti domum supra terram sine fundamento. impulit flumen domu
illi et cecidit et facta est ruina domus illius magna.

7 Factum est autem, cum inplesset omnia uerba in auribus populi, intrauit in
capharnaum. **2** centurionis autem cuiusdam seruus male habens incipiebat mori,
qui erat ei carus. **3** Audiens autem de iesu misit seniores iudaeorum rogans illum,
ut ueniret et sanaret seruum illius. **4** Qui cum uenissent, rogabant iesum sollicite
dicentes, quoniam dignus est, ut illi praestes hoc. **5** diligit enim gentem nostram et
synagogam ipse Aedificauit nobis. **6** ibat autem cum illis iesus. cumque iam non
longe abesset a domo, misit ad illum centurio amicos dicens ei: Domine, noli
uexare te. non sum enim dignus, ut sub tectum meum intres. **7** sed dic uerbo et

---

super[1]] 2 5 supra cet. | tempestate horta] inundatio autem facta 2* inundantia autem facta 4 inundatione autem facta cet. | impulit] impegit 2 allisit 5 4 inlisit 8 inlisum est A | flumen] fluuius 2 | domui illi] in domum illam 2 | nec ualuit] et non potuit cet. | mouere illam] 5 illam mouere 2 eam mouere cet. | enim erat] est enim 2 | super[2]] supra A | petra] petram cet. **49** qui autem] nam qui 4 8 | audit] audiuit 5 A | facit] fecit 5 A | domum] 2 5 domum suam cet. supra] 4 A super cet. | terram] harenam 2 4 | impulit] impegit 2 in qua inlisus est A allisit cet. flumen] fluuius 2 A | domu illi] 8 domui illi 4 om. cet. | et[2]] 5 et continuo cet. | cecidit] concidit 4 | **7:1** Factum est autem] et factum est cet. om. 2 A | cum] cum autem 2 A | inplesset] 8 perfecisset 2 consummasset 5 implesset 4 A | omnia] om. 2 | uerba] uerba sua A | in auribus populi] quae loquebatur ad populum 2 loquens 5 in aures plebis cet. | intrauit] introiret 2 uenit 5 in[2]] om. cet. | capharnaum] cafarnaum 5 4 | **2** centurionis autem cuiusdam] et seruus centuriones 2 | seruus male habens] puer male habens 5 om. 2 | incipiebat mori] 5 moriturus erat 2 erat moriturus cet. | erat ei] erat illi 2 5 illi erat cet. | carus] 2 honoratus 5 praetiosus (pretiosus A) cet. | **3** Audiens autem de iesu] et audiens de iesus 5 et cum audisset de iesus (iesum 2) cet. misit] misit ad eum A | seniores] maiores natu 2 | iudaeorum] iudeorum 8 | illum] 2 eum cet. ueniret et] 2 A ueniens 5 4 uenirent et 8 | sanaret] liberaret 2 saluet 5 saluaret 4 A liberarent 8 illius] eius cet. | **4** Qui] illi autem 2 ad (at A) illi cet. | cum uenissent] cum aduenissent 2 aduenientes 5 uenientes 4 uenerunt 8 add. ad iesum 4 A | rogabant] et rogabant 8 | iesum] 2 8 eum cet. | sollicite] instanter 2 festinanter 5 | dicentes] dicentes ei A | quoniam] 5 quia cet. | ut illi praestes hoc] cui praestes istut 2 cui hoc praestes 5 ut hoc illi praestes (prestes 8) cet. | **5** synagogam] synagoga 8 | Aedificauit] aedificabit 5 4 | **6** ibat autem cum illis iesus] 8 abiit itaque cum illis iesus 2 ibat autem cum eis iesus 5 iesus autem abiit cum eis 4 iesus autem ibat cum illis A cumque iam non longe abesset] iam autem non longe cum essed 5 et cum iam non longe esset cet. a] de 5 | illum] eum 5 A | centurio amicos] amicos centurio 2 centurio amicos suos 4 | ei] 5 8 illi 2 om. 4 A | uexare te] uexari A te uexare cet. | sum enim dignus] enim sum dignus 2 5 enim dignus sum cet. | tectum meum] tecto meo 4 8 | intres] introeas 2 | **7** sed dic uerbo] propter quod et me ipsum non sum dignum arbitratus ut uenirem ad te sed dic uerbo A sanabitur puer meus. **8** nam et ego homo sum potestatis subiectus. habeo sub me milites, dico huic: uade, et uadit. et alio: ueni, et <uenit>. et seruo meo: fac hoc, et facit. **9** his auditis iesus miratus est et conuersus sequenti se turbae dixit: amen dico uobis: in nullo tantam fidem inueni in istrahel. **10** et reuersi sunt domum, qui missi erant, inuenerunt seruum sanum. **11** Et factum est, deinceps ibat iesus in ciuitatem, quae appellatur nain, et comitabantur cum illo discipuli sui et turba magna. **12** Factum est autem, cum adpropinquaret portae ciuitatis, et ecce efferebatur mortuus filius unicus matris suae. et hac erat uidua, et turba ciuitatis magna cum illa. **13** et uisam eam dominus misertus est ei et dixit ei: noli flere. **14** Et accedens tetigit loculum, et qui portabant, steterunt. et ait: adulescens, adulescens, tibi dico: surge. **15** et consedit mortuus et coepit loqui. et dedit eum matri suae. **16** Adprehendit autem timor omnes et honorificabant deum dicentes, quoniam propheta magnus surrexit in nobis et quia uisitauit deus populum suum

---

sanabitur] 8 A curabitur 2 salbabitur 5 salbitur 4 | meus] meum 5 | **8** nam et ego] et enim ego 5 nam ego 8 | sum] om. 5 | potestatis subiectus] sub potestate constitutus cet. | habeo] habens cet. | milites] lites 4 | dico] et dico cet. | alio] ali 2 alii 5 | **9** his auditis] cum audisset autem ista 2 audiens autem haec 5 4 quo audito 8 A | miratus] admiratus 2 | sequenti se turbae dixit] dixit sequenti se turbae 2 dixit sequenti populo 5 sequentibus se (add. turbis A) dixit cet. | amen] amen amen 8 om. 4 | in nullo tantam fidem inueni in istrahel] 4 non inueni talem fidem in isdrahel 2 numquam tantam fidem inueni in istrahel 5 in nullo tantam fidem inueni in israhel 8 nec in israhel tantam fidem inueni A | **10** reuersi sunt domum qui missi erant] reuersi domum illi qui missi erant 2 conuersi in domum qui missi erant 5 reuersi domum qui missi fuerant 4 reuersi domum qui missi erant 8 reuersi qui missi fuerant domum A | inuenerunt] serui inuenerunt 5 | seruum] aegrum 5 seruum qui languerat A | sanum] saluum 2 | **11** Et factum est] et 2 5 | deinceps] sequenti die 2 alia die 5 | iesus] om. cet. | ciuitatem] ciuitate 2 | appellatur] dicitur 5 uocatur cet. | nain] 5 8 capharnaum 2 naim 4 A | comitabantur] 2 ibant cet. | illo] eo 5 | discipuli] discentes 2 | sui] illius 2 eius cet. add. multi 4 | magna] 2 multa 5 copiosa cet. **12** Factum est autem] 2 5 et factum est 4 8 om. A | cum[1]] ut 5 | adpropinquaret] 2 appropinquaret A adpropiaret cet. | portae] porta 2 | ecce] om. 5 | efferebatur mortuus] ferebatur mortuus 2 efferebatur mortuum 5 efferebatur defunctus 4 8 defunctus efferebatur A | matris] matri 5 A et hac erat uidua] quae erat uidua 2 cum esset uidua 5 haec uidua erat cet. | turba ciuitatis magna] multa turba 2 multus populus 5 turba (add. ciuitatis A) multa cet. | cum illa] consequebatur illam 2 cum ea erat 5 | **13** et uisam eam] cum uidisset autem illam 2 uidens autem 5 quam (quem 4) cum uideret (uidisset A) cet. | dominus] iesus 5 | misertus est] commotus est super eam 2 misertus est ei 5 misertus est super eam 4 misericordiam (misericordia*) motus 8 misericordia motus super ea A | et[2]] om. 8 A | ei[2]] illi cet. | flere] plorare 5 | **14** accedens tetigit] 5 accessit et tetigit cet. | loculum] sartofagum 5 locum 8 | et qui] illi autem 2 qui autem 5 hi autem cet. | ait] dixit 2 5 add. iesus 8 | adulescens[1]] iuuenis 2 5 | adulescens[2]] 8 iuuenis 5 om. cet. | **15** consedit] sedit 2 resedit cet. | mortuus] 5 ille mortuus 2 qui erat mortuus cet. | eum matri suae] 5 ad matrem suam 2 illum matri suae (eius 4) cet. | **16** Adprehendit] inuasit 2 accepit cet. | timor omnes] 5 timor magnus omnes 4 omnes timor cet. | honorificabant] 5 clarificabant 2 magnificabant cet. | quoniam] 5 quia 2 A quod 4 8 | propheta] 4 A profeta cet. | quia] quoniam 5 | uisitauit deus] deus uisitauit A | populum suum] plebem suam cet.

in bono. **17** et exibit uerbum hoc in tota in iudaea de illo et in omni finitima regione. **18** Et renuntiauerunt iohanni discipuli sui. **19** et conuocatis duobus quibusdam ex discipulis suis iohannes misit ad dominum dicens: Tu es, qui uenturus es, an alium expectamus? **20** et uenerunt uiri ad eum et dixerunt: iohannes baptista misit nos dicens: tu es, qui uenturus es, an alium expectamus? **21** eadem hora curabat multos a languoribus et uerberibus et spiritibus malignis et caecis multis donauit uisum. **22** et respondens dixit illis: euntes renuntiate iohanni, quae uidistis et audistis, caeci uident, clodi ambulant, leprosi purgantur, surdi audiunt, mortui resurgent, pauperes euangelizantur. **23** et baeatus erit, quicumque non scandalizabitur in me. **24** Cumque discessissent nuntii iohannis, coepit dicere de iohannen ad turbas: quid existis in deserto uidere? harundinem a

---

in bono] 4 8 in bonum 2 om. 5 A | **17** exibit] exiuit 2 5 8 exiit 4 A | uerbum hoc] iste sermo 2 hoc uerbum 5 hic sermo cet. | tota] 2 totam 5 uniuersa (uniuersam A) cet. | in[2]] om. cet. | iudaea] 4 8 iudea 2 iudaeam 5 A | de illo] 5 ea deo 2 de eo A om. 4 8 | et in omni finitima regione] in quibus 2 et in omni regione et in quibus 5 et omni confinio regionis illius de eo 4 et in omni confini regione 8 et omnem circa regionem A | **18** Et renuntiauerunt iohanni discipuli sui] adnuntiauerunt ad iohannen baptistam 2 usque ad iohanen baptistam 5 et nuntiauerunt iohanni discipuli eius de omnibus his cet. | **19** et conuocatis duobus quibusdam ex discipulis suis iohannes] qui etiam conuocatis quibusdam de discentibus suis 2 qui et aduocans duos ciscipulorum suorum 5 et conuocauit duos iohannes de discipulis suis 4 et conuocatis duobus discipulis suis iohannes 8 et conuocauit duos de discipulis suis iohannes A | misit ad dominum] et misit ad dominum (iesum 4) cet. om. 2 5 | dicens] dixit euntes inquirite dicentes 2 euntes dicite ei 5 | Tu es] tu es tu es 2* | uenturus es] uenis 2 uenturus est 8 | an] aut 2 | **20** et uenerunt uiri ad eum] et cum aduenissent ad eum illi uiri 2 et aduenientes uiri ad eum 5 aduenientes autem ad eum uiri 4 8 cum autem uenissent ad eum uiri A | et dixerunt] dixerunt cet. | iohannes] iohannis 2 baptista misit nos] misit nos baptista 4 add. ad te cet. | uenturus es] uenis 2 uenturus est 8 | an] aut 2 | **21** eadem] in illa 2 in ipsa cet. add. autem cet. | curabat multos] 4 8 multos curauit 2 curauit multos 5 A | a languoribus] a langoribus 2 ab infirmitatibus 5 | uerberibus] flagellis 2 plagis cet. | spiritibus malignis] malis spiritibus 2 iniquorum spirituum 5 spiritibus inmundis 4 spiritibus malis 8 A | caecis multis donauit uisum] caecos faciebat uidere 2 5 | **22** respondens] respondit iesus 8 | euntes] ite 4 8 | renuntiate] 2 dicite 5 nuntiate cet. | uidistis] uiderunt oculi uestri 2 5 | et[2]] et quae 5 | audistis] audierunt aures uestrae 2 audierunt aures uestre 5 | caeci uident] 4 8 quia caeci uident cet. | clodi] 5 4 et clodi 2 claudi 8 A | leprosi] et lebrosi 2 | purgantur] emundantur 2 mundantur cet. | surdi audiunt mortui resurgent] 8 A mortui resurgunt surdi audiunt 2 et surdi audiunt mortui resurgunt 5 mortui resurgunt 4 | pauperes] et egenis 2 euangelizantur] benenuntiatur 2 | **23** erit] 2 5 est cet. | quicumque] qui 5 4 | non scandalizabitur in me] non scandalizatus fuerit in me 2 non fuerit scandalizatus in me 5 A in me non fuerit scandalizatus 4 non fuerit in me scandalizatus 8 | **24** Cumque discessissent nuntii] euntibus autem nuntiis 5 et cum discessissent nuntii (add. illi 4) cet. | iohannis] iohanni 5 iohannes 4 coepit dicere de iohannen ad turbas] dicere ad turbas de iohannem 2 dicere de iohane turbis 5 dicere ad turbas de iohanne 4 de iohannem dicere ad turbas 8 coepit dicere de iohanne ad turbas A | deserto] 8 deserta 2 desertum cet. | a] om. 2

uento moueri? **25** sed quid existis uidere? hominem mollibus uestimentis
indutum? ecce, qui in ueste praetiosa et in deliciis superabundant, in domibus
regum sunt. **26** Sed quid existis uidere? prophetam? etiam dico uobis: nemo maior
in natis mulierum amplior est iohannen baptista. et amplius quam propheta. **27**
Hic est, de quo scriptum est: ecce mitto angelum meum ante faciem tuam, qui
praeparauit uiam tuam. **28** Dico autem uobis: maior in natis mulierum iohannen
baptista nemo est. et qui minimus est in regno dei, maior illo est. **29** et omnis
populus cum audissent et publicani iustificauerunt deum baptizati baptismum
iohannis. **30** pharisaei autem et legis doctores consilium dei spreuerunt in se, cum
non essent baptizati. **31** Cui ergo adsimiliabo homines gentis huius et cui sunt
similes? **32** similes sunt infantibus in foro sedentibus, qui clamant ad alterutrum,
dicentis: cantauimus uobis et non saltastis, lamentauimus uobis et non planxistis.
33 Uenit iohannis baptista neque edens neque bibens, et dicitis: daemonium
habet. **34** uenit filius hominis manducans et bibens, et dicitis: ecce homo

---

moueri] agitari 2 | **25** mollibus] in mollibus 5 | uestimentis] om. 2 | indutum] uestitum 2 5 ueste] uestimentis 5 | praetiosa] clara 2 gloriosis 5 | et in deliciis] 4 8 et diliciis 2 et deliciis A om. 5 | superabundant] sunt 2 et aepulatione agent 5 superabundat 8* om. 4 A | domibus regum] domo regis 2 regibus 5 | sunt] sum 8* | **26** prophetam] profetam 2 5 | etiam dico uobis] 5 ita dico uobis 2 utique dico uobis 4 A om. 8 | nemo maior in natis mulierum amplior est iohannen baptista] om. cet. | et amplius quam propheta] et abundantius profetam 2 et amplius profeta 5 et plus quam prophetam 4 A om. 8 add. quoniam nemo maior in natis mulierum profeta iohanis baptiste 5 | **27** Hic est de quo scriptum est] de eo enim scriptum est 2 hic est enim de quo scriptum est 4 | praeparauit] 5 4 parauit 2 prepararet 8 praeparabit A | uiam tuam] 5 uiam tuam ante te cet. | **28** autem] enim A | maior in natis mulierum iohannen baptista nemo est] quia nemo in natis mulierum maior iohannes baptista est 2 maior inter natos mulierum (add. propheta A) iohanne baptista nemo est cet. om. 5 | et qui minimus est] qui minimus autem est 2 quoniam qui minor est eius 5 nam qui minor est 4 8 qui autem minor est A | dei] caelorum 5 maior illo est] 2 5 maior est illo cet. | **29** omnis populus] omnes turba 2 | cum audissent] 2 audiens cet. | iustificauerunt] iustificabit 5 | deum] dominum 5 | baptismum] baptisma 5 baptismo A | iohannis] iohannes 2 | **30** doctores] 2 5 periti cet. | spreuerunt] reprobauerunt 2 abusi sunt 5 | in se] 2 8 semetipsos 4 A om. 5 | cum non essent baptizati] quod non sint baptizati 2 non baptizati (add. ab eo 5 A) cet. | **31** ergo adsimiliabo] ergo similabo 2 5 similes ergo dicam 4 ergo similes dicam 8 A | homines] hominem 2 | gentis huius] saeculi huius 2 generationis huius 5 A huius generationes 4 generationes huius 8 | et cui sunt similes] A et cui similes sint 2* et cui similes sunt 2[c] A et cui similes est 8 om. 4 | **32** similes sunt] adsimilabo illos 2 similis sunt 8 infantibus] 5 pueris cet. | in foro sedentibus] qui in foro (firo*) sunt 2 qui in foro sedentibus 5 sedentibus in foro cet. | qui clamant] qui adclamant 2 et adloquentibus 5 et loquentibus cet. alterutrum] inuicem 5 ad inuicem cet. | dicentis] et dicentibus 5 A dicentes cet. | cantauimus] tiuiam cantauimus 2 cantabimus 5 add. tibiis A | saltastis] saltastes 2 | lamentauimus] plaximus 2 | uobis[2]] 4 8 om. cet. | planxistis] lamentastis 2 plorastis cet. | **33** Uenit] uenit enim cet. iohannis] 4 8 iohannes cet. | edens] 5 manducans panem A manducans cet. | bibens] bibens uinum A | dicitis] dicites 2 | **34** manducans] edens 5 | dicitis] dicites 2

deuorator et bibens uinum, amicus publicanorum. **35** et iustificata est sapientia ab omnibus filiis suis. **36** Rogauit autem eum quidam pharisaeus, ut cibum caperet secum. Et ingressus in domum pharisaei discubuit. **37** Et ecce mulier in ciuitate, quae erat peccatrix, cognito eo accumbere in domo pharisaei, adferebat ampullam unguenti. **38** et stans a retro pedes illius flens lacrimis inrigabat {et ca} et capillis capitis sui extergebat et osculabatur pedes illius et ungebat unguento. **39** Uidens autem pharisaeus, qui inuitauerat eum, dixit intra se dicens: hic si erat propheta, sciret utique, quae et qualis est mulier, quae tangit illum, quoniam peccatrix est. **40** Et respondens iesus dixit ad illum: simon, habeo tibi aliquid dicere. qui ait: dic, magister. **41** Duo debitores erant cuidam feneratori, unus debebat denarios quingentos et alius denarios quinquaginta. **42** non habentibus illis, unde redderent, utrisque donauit. quis ergo illum amplius diliget? **43** Respondens autem simon dixit: aestimo, quod{d} is, cui amplius redonauit. qui

---

deuorator] uorax 2 manducator 5 | bibens uinum] uinarius 2 uinipotator 5 | amicus publicanorum] publicanorum et peccatorum amicus 4 amicus publicanorum et peccatorum cet. | **35** ab omnibus filiis] a filis 5 | **36** Rogauit] rogabat A | eum] illum cet. | pharisaeus] 4 ex pharisaeis 2 pharisaeorum 5 phariseus 8 de pharisaeis A | cibum caperet secum] manducaret cum illo (eo 5) cet. | ingressus] cum introisset 2 intrans 5 | in] om. 2 A | discubuit] recubuit 2 5 | **37** in ciuitate quae erat] quae erat 5 que erat in ciuitatem 8 quae erat in ciuitate A | cognito eo] sciens 5 ut (postquam 2) cognouit cet. | accumbere in domo pharisaei] quoniam in domo pharisaei recumbit 2 quoniam in domo pharisaei recumbet 5 quod recumbit in domo pharisaei cet. adferebat ampullam unguenti] adtulit uas unguenti 2 accipiens unguenti alabastrum 5 attulit alabastrum unguenti cet. | **38** a] om. cet. | pedes[1]] ad pedes 2 5 secus pedes cet. | illius[1]] eius cet. | flens] 2 plorans 5 om. cet. | lacrimis] et lacrimis suis 2 | inrigabat] lababat 2 inpleuit 5 rigabat 4 8 coepit rigare A add. pedes eius cet. | et capillis capitis sui extergebat et osculabatur pedes illius] et capillis capitis sui tergebat (extersit 5) et osculabatur pedes eius cet. om. 2 ungebat unguento] ungento ungebat A unguebat unguento cet. | **39** Uidens autem pharisaeus] cum uideret pharisaeus 2 | qui inuitauerat eum] aput quem recumbebat 2 ad quem recumbebat 5 qui uocauerat eum cet. | dixit] 2 5 ait cet. | intra se] apud semetipsum 2 | dicens] om. 2 5 erat propheta] esset propheta (profeta 2 8) cet. | sciret] cognouisset 2 sciebat 5 | utique] om. 2 quae et qualis est mulier] quae mulier et quales est 2 quis et qualis mulier 5 quae et qualis mulier est (om. 8) cet. | tangit illum] eum tanget 2 tangit eum cet. | quoniam] 2 quia cet. | **40** respondens] respondit 2 8 | dixit ad illum] ad petrum dixit illi 2 dixit ad eum 5 | aliquid dicere] dicere aliquid 2 quod dicere 5 | qui ait] ille autem ait 2 ad ille dixit 5 8 at ille ait 4 A | dic magister] magister dic cet. | **41** Duo] A et iesus ait duo 2 ad ille dixit duo 5 dixit ergo iesus erant duo 4 et ait duo 8 | erant] om. 4 | unus] et unus quidem 2 | quingentos] d 4 | et] 8 om. cet. | alius] alius autem 2 5 | denarios[2]] 5 om. cet. | quinquaginta] l 4 | **42** non habentibus illis] et cum non haberent 2 non habentibus autem illis 4 | redderent] soluerent 2 | utrisque donauit] ambobus donauit 2 donauit utrisque (add. eorum 8) cet. | ergo] om. 2 | illum] eum cet. amplius] plus cet. | diliget] A amat 2 diligit 5 8 dilexit 4 | **43** Respondens] respondit 2 | autem] om. cet. | dixit[1]] et dixit illi 2 | aestimo] puto 2 suspicor 5 extimo 8 | quodd] quoniam 5 quia cet. om. 2 | is] om. 2 5 | amplius redonauit] plus donauit cet. | qui dixit] ille autem dixit 2 at (ad 5) ille (iesus) 8 dixit cet.

dixit ei: recte iudicasti. **44** Et conuersus ad mulierem dixit simoni: uides hanc
mulierem? intraui in domum tuam, aquam in pedibus mihi non dedisti. haec
autem lacrimis inrigauit mihi pedes et capillis suis extersit. **45** Osculum mihi non
dedisti, haec autem, ex quo intrauit, non desiit osculando pedes meos. **46** oleo non
unxisti pedes meos, haec autem unguento unxit. **47** qua ex causa tibi dico:
remittuntur ei peccata multa, quoniam dilexit multum. cui autem minus
dimittitur, minus diligit. **48** et ait ad illam iesus: remittuntur tibi peccata. **49** et
coeperunt, qui discumbebant pariter, dicere intra se: quis est hic, qui peccata
remittit? **50** dixit autem ad mulierem: fides tua te saluam fecit. uade in pace.

8 Et factum est deinceps, et ipse circuibat per ciuitatis et uicos praedicans et
adnuntians regnum dei et duodecim discipuli cum illo. **2** Et mulieres quaedam,
quae erant curatae ab spiritibus inmundis, maria, quae cognominatur macdalene,
ex qua daemonia septem exierant, **3** et iohanna, uxor chuza procuratoris erodis,

---

ei] illi 5 om. 2 | **44** simoni] ad simonem 2 | hanc] istam 2 | mulierem²] mulierem plorantem 2 intraui] introiui 2 5 | aquam] et aquam 2 5 | in pedibus mihi] mihi ad pedes 2 in pedes mihi 5 in pedibus meis 4 pedibus meis A | lacrimis] 5 A lacrimis suis cet. | inrigauit mihi pedes] 5 lauit mihi pedes 2 rigauit pedes meos 4 A pedes meos rigauit 8 | extersit] 2 5 tersit cet. | **45** intrauit] 8 A introiuit 2 introiui 5 intraui 4 | desiit] intermisit 2 cessauit cet. | osculando pedes meos] pedes meos osculando 2 osculans mihi pedes 5 osculari pedes meos cet. | **46** non unxisti pedes meos] 8 pedes meos non unxisti 2 caput meum non unxisti 5 A non unxisti caput meum 4 unxit] unxit pedes meos A | **47** qua ex causa tibi dico] propter quod dico tibi (uobis 8) cet. remittuntur] remittentur 2 dimittentur 5 remissa sunt 4 8 remittentur A | ei] tibi 4 illi cet. peccata] om. 5 8 | multa] om. 2 | quoniam dilexit multum] 8 A quia dilexit multum 4 om. 2 5 cui autem minus dimittitur minus diligit] cui autem pusillum dimittuntur diligit modicum 2 om. 5 **48** et ait] 8 dixit autem cet. | ad illam] 2 A ei 5 illi 8 om. 4 | iesus] 4 8 om. 2 5 A add. ad eam 4 remittuntur] A mulier remissa sunt 2 dimissa sunt 5 mulier remissa sunt 4 remissa sunt 8 peccata] peccata tua 8 | **49** coeperunt qui discumbebant pariter] coeperunt conrecumbentes 2 coeperunt qui simul recumbebant 5 4 qui simul recumbebant (recumbebat*) coeperunt 8 coeperunt qui simul discumbebant A | dicere] dicerent 4* | intra se] apud seipsos 2 | hic] om. 4 peccata] et peccata 2 5 etiam peccata cet. | remittit] 4 8 demittet 2 dimittit 5 A | **50** dixit autem] dixit autem iesus 2 dixit iesus 4 | fides] mulier fides 5 | saluam fecit] salbabit 2 saluum fecit 4 uade] ambula 2 | **8:1** deinceps] in sequenti 2 in continenti 5 | et ipse] om. 2 | circuibat] 5 perambulabat 2 iter faciebat cet. | per] circa 5 | ciuitatis] ciuitatem 5 A ciuitates cet. | uicos] castellum 5 A castella cet. | adnuntians] benenuntians 2 euangelizans cet. | duodecim] 8 A illi duodecim 2 xii 5 4 | discipuli] 2 4 om. cet. | **2** quaedam] 2 5 aliquae A om. 4 8 | ab] a 5 spiritibus] ispiritibus 4 8 | inmundis] 5 malis 2 immundis 4 malignis 8 A add. et infirmitatibus cet. | cognominatur] uocatur 8 A uocabatur cet. | macdalene] magdalenae 8 magdalene cet. ex] 2 de 5 A a 4 8 | daemonia septem exierant] exierant daemonia septe 2 uii daemonia exierant 5 daemonia uii exierant 4 daemonia exierunt septem 8 daemonia septem exierant A | **3** chuza] 5 A cusae 2 chuzae 4 8 | erodis] herodis cet.

et susanna et aliae conplures, quae et ministrabant illi de facultatibus suis. **4**
Conueniente autem turba magna et eorum, qui ex ciuitatibus adueniebant, dixit
parabolam: **5** ecce exiit, qui † seannat †, seminare semen suum. dum seminat,
quoddam cecidit iuxta uiam et conculcatum est, et uolucres comederunt illud. **6** Et
aliut cecidit super petram et enatum exaruit, propter quod non haberet umorem.
7 et aliut cecidit inter spinas, et creuerunt spinae et suffocauerunt illud. **8** et aliud
cecidit super terram optimam et bonam. et ortum fecit fructum centies tantum. Et
haec dicens clamabat: qui habet aures audiendi, audiat. **9** interrogabant autem
illum discipuli, quidnam esset haec parabola. **10** qui dixit: uobis traditum est
mysterium regni dei. ceteris autem in parabolis, ut uidentes non uideant et
audientes non intellegant. **11** Est autem haec parabola: semen est uerbum dei. **12**
qui autem secus uiam, hi sunt, qui audiunt. uenit autem diabolus et tollet de corde

---

susanna] susannae 2 susannam 4 | conplures] multae cet. | et[4]] om. 2 A | ministrabant illi] eis ministrabant 2 ministrabant (ministrabat 8*) illi 5 8 ministrabant ei 4 ministrabant eis A facultatibus suis] substantia sua 5 | **4** Conueniente autem turba magna] cum uenisset autem turba magna 2 congregato autem populo multo 5 cum ergo turba conuenisset 4 cum ergo tur conuenisset 8 cum autem turba plurima conueniret A | et] om. A* | eorum qui ex ciuitatibus adueniebant] hii qui de ciuitatibus aduenerant 2 qui ad ciuitatem iter faciebant ad eum 5 de ciuitatibus aduenirent 4 de ciuitatibus aduenirent (adueniret*) multi 8 de ciuitatibus properarent ad eum A | parabolam] similitudinem talem 2 parabolam talem ad eos 5 similitudinem ad illos talem 4 similitudinem 8 per similitudinem A | **5** ecce] om. 5 A | exiit] exiuit 2 5 | qui seannat[2]] seminans 2 seminator 5 qui seminat cet. | dum seminat] et in seminando 2 et in quo seminat 5 et dum seminat cet. | quoddam] aliut 4 aliud cet. add. quidem 5 | cecidit] caecidit 2 | iuxta] ad 2 5 secus cet. | uolucres] uolatilia 5 uolucres caeli A | comederunt illud] 5 A consumpserunt illud 2 illud comederunt 4 8 | **6** aliut] 2 aliud cet. | cecidit] om. 2 | super] in 2 supra 4 | petram] terram 4 | enatum] cum fructificasset 2 cum creuisset 5 natum cet. | exaruit] aridum factum est 5 aruit cet. | propter quod] 5 propterea quod 2 quia cet. | haberet] 2 5 habebat 4 A habuit 8 umorem] humorem 5 8 | **7** aliut] 2 aliud cet. | cecidit] om. 2 | inter spinas] in medio spinarum 2 5 | creuerunt] simul natae sunt 2 cum germinassent 5 simul exortae 4 A simul exhorta est 8 et[3]] 2 8 om. cet. | illud] illut 4 8 | **8** aliud] aliut 2 | cecidit] caecidit 2 | super] 5 in cet. optimam et bonam] bonam et optimam 2 bonam et uberam 5 bonam cet. | ortum] A fructificauit 2 cum germinasset 5 natum 4 exortum 8 | fecit] et fecit 2 | centies tantum] centuplum cet. | Et] om. cet. | **9** interrogabant] interrogauerunt 4 8 | illum] 2 5 eum cet. | discipuli] 4 8 discentes eius 2 discipuli eius 5 A | quidnam] quae cet. | esset] essent 5* | haec parabola] similitudo ista 2 parabola haec 5 | **10** qui dixit] ille autem dixit illis 2 ad ille dixit 5 quibus ipse dixit cet. traditum est] datum est cet. add. cognoscere 2 nosse 4 A scire 8 | mysterium] sacramentum 2 regni] om. 8 | dei] dei scire 5 | ceteris] reliquis 5 | in parabolis] non est datum nisi in similitudinem 2 in parabolis loquor 4 | intellegant] audiant 5 | **11** haec parabola] similitudo haec 2 haec parabola talis 4 | **12** qui[1]] quod 2 | secus] ad 2 5 | uiam] uiam seminatum est 2 uiam seminati 4 uiam sunt cet. | hi] om. 5 A* hii cet. | sunt] om. A | audiunt] audiunt uerbum 2 audiunt uerbum dei 4 | uenit autem] quorum uenit 5 deinde uenit A | tollet] tollit cet. | de corde eorum uerbum] de cordibus eorum uerbum 2 a corde eorum uerbum 5 de corde illorum uerbum 4 8 uerbum de corde eorum A

eorum uerbum, ne credentes salui fiant. **13** qui autem super petram, hi sunt, qui
cum audierint, cum gaudio recipient uerbum, et ipsi radices non habent, qui ad
tempus credunt et in tempore temptationis discedunt. **14** quod autem in spinas
cecidit, hi sunt, qui audiunt uerbum et a sollicitudinibus et diuitiis et luxuriis
saeculi ingredientes suffocantur et non dant fructum. **15** Quod autem in terram
bonam, hi sunt, qui in corde bono audientes uerbum retinent et fructum dant in
patientia. **16** Nemo autem lucernam accensam operiet illam uaso aut suptus
lectum ponit, sed supra candelabrum ponit, ut omnes intrantes uideant lumen. **17**
nihil enim est occultum, quod non palam fiat, sed nec absconsum, nisi ut
cognoscatur et in palam ueniat. **18** Uidete, quomodo audiatis. quisque enim
habuerit, dabitur illi. et qui non habuerit, et quod putat se habere, auferetur ab
eo. **19** uenerunt autem ad illum mater et fratres illius, set non poterant conloqui ei
propter turbam. **20** nuntiatum est autem illi, quoniam mater tua et fratres tui

---

ne] ut non 5 | salui fiant] saluentur 2 | **13** qui autem] 5 quod autem 2 nam qui cet. | super] supra 4 8 | hi sunt] hii sunt 4 8 om. cet. | audierint] 8 A audierunt 2 5 audierint uerbum 4 recipient] percipiunt 2 accipiunt 5 8 recipiunt 4 suscipiunt A | uerbum] illud 4 | ipsi] hi cet. om. 2 5 | radices] 4 8 radicem cet. | qui[3]] 5 A illi 2 quia 4 8 | tempus] oram 2 | tempore] die 2 discedunt] recedunt cet. | **14** spinas] 5 8 spinis cet. | cecidit] caecidit 2 | hi] 5 A hii cet. audiunt] 4 audierunt cet. | uerbum] om. cet. | a sollicitudinibus] per sollicitudinis 2 | et[2]] om. 2 5 | diuitiis] diuitiarum 2 5 | luxuriis] uoluntates 2 suabitati 5 uoluptatibus cet. | saeculi] uitae cet. om. 5 | ingredientes] abientes 5 euntes cet. om. 2 | suffocantur] simul suffocantur 4 8 dant fructum] fecundantur 2 adferent fructum 5 referunt fructum cet. | **15** terram bonam] 5 8 bonam terram cet. | hi] hii 4* 8 om. 2 | sunt] om. 2 | in[2]] om. 8 | bono] bono et optimo A audientes] audiunt 2 | uerbum] uerbum dei 5 | retinent] et tenent 2 continent 5 | fructum dant] fructiuicant 5 fructum adferent (afferet 8 afferunt A) cet. | in patientia] A in sufferentia 5 per patientiam cet. | **16** lucernam accensam] lucernam accendit 2 lucernam accendens 5 A accendit lucernam 4 lucernam adcensam 8 | operiet] coperit 5 et ponit 4 et (om. 8 A) operit cet. illam] 2 eam 5 A om. 4 8 | uaso] sub modio 4 uase A om. 2 | suptus lectum ponit] neque sub lecto ponit illam 2 subtus (sub 8) lectum ponit cet. om. 4 | supra candelabrum ponit] 4 A super candelabrum 2 super candelabrum ponit 5 ponit eam super candelabrum 8 | omnes intrantes uideant lumen] omnibus luceat 2 omnibus qui intrant uideant lumen 5 ut intrantes uideant lumen cet. | **17** nihil] 2 non cet. | enim est] est enim 2 5 | occultum] absconsum 2 5 | palam fiat] manifestabitur 2 in palam uenit 5 manifestetur cet. | sed] om. cet. | nec] neque 2 | absconsum] 4 8 celatum 2 occultum 5 absconditum A | nisi ut] quod non 2 A sed ut 5 nisi 4 8 cognoscatur] sciatur 5 | palam[2]] medium 2 | ueniat] ueniet 5 | **18** Uidete] 4 8 uidete ergo cet. audiatis] 4 audistis 2 auditis cet. | quisque] qui cet. | habuerit[1]] habet cet. | illi] ei 5 | qui] 2 5 quicumque cet. | habuerit[2]] habet cet. | et quod putat se habere auferetur ab eo] auferetur ab eo quod uidetur habere 2 tolletur ab eo et quod putat se habere 5 etiam quod putat se habere auferetur ab illo cet. | **19** uenerunt] aduenerunt 2 aduenit 5 | illum] eum 2 5 | mater] mater eius 2 5 | illius] eius cet. om. 2 | set] et cet. | conloqui ei] contingere ei 5 adire ad (om. 8) eum cet. | propter turbam] 5 per turbas 2 prae (pre 8) turba cet. | **20** nuntiatum est autem] et nuntiatum est 2 A | illi] ei 5 | quoniam] qui 5 quia cet. om. A | mater] materter 5 | tua] eius 2 tui] om. 2

stant foris uolentes te uidere. **21** Qui respondens dixit ad illos: mater mea et fratres mei illi sunt, qui uerbum dei audiunt et faciunt. **22** Factum est autem in una dierum, et ipse ascendit in nauiculam et discipuli eius. et dixit ad illos: transfretemus stagnum. et sustulerunt. **23** Nauigantibus autem eis condormiit, et descendit turbo in stagnum uenti et conplebantur et periclitabantur. **24** accidentes autem discipuli suscitauerunt illum dicentes: magister, perimus. tunc surgens imperauit uento et tempestati aquae et destiterunt. et facta est tranquillitas. **25** dixit autem illis: ubi est fides uestra? timentes autem mirati sunt ad alis alium dicentes: quisnam, ut hic est, qui et uentis imperat et aquae, et obaudiunt illi? **26** enauigauerunt autem in regionem gerasenorum, quae est trans fretum galilaeae. **27** <e>gresso autem illo occurrit illi uir, qui daemonem habebat ex temporibus multis et uestimentum non induebatur neque domo manebat, sed in monumentis.

---

stant foris] foris stant 2 foras stant 5 | uolentes te uidere] uolentes teum (eum[c]) uidere 2 quaerentes te 5 | **21** Qui respondens] A ille autem respondit 2 ad ille respondens 5 qui respondit 4* 8 dixit] et dixit 2 | ad illos] illis 2 eis 5 illum 4* ad eos cet. | mater mea et fratres] fratres et mater 4* mater et fratres 4[c] 8 | illi] hi 5 4[c] A hii cet. | **22** dierum] ex diebus 2 | et[1]] ut 2 om. 5 | ipse ascendit] ascenderent 2 ascenderunt eum 5 | nauiculam] nauem 2 5 | discipuli] discentes 2 dixit] 2 5 ait cet. | illos] eos 5 | transfretemus] pertranseamus 5 | stagnum] contra hoc stagnum 2 in contra stagnum 5 trans stagnum cet. | et sustulerunt] et nauigauerunt 5 et leuauerunt 4 8 et ascenderunt A om. 2 | **23** Nauigantibus autem eis] et cum nauigaret 2 nauigantibus autem illis cet. | condormiit] obdormiuit 5 A obdormiit cet. | descendit] discendit 4 | turbo in stagnum uenti] procella uenti 2 procella uenti multa in stagnum 5 procella uenti 4 8 procella uenti in stagnum A | et conplebantur] 5 et implebatur a fructibus nauicula 4 et conplebatur fructibus nauiculam 8 et complebatur A om. 2 | **24** accidentes] accesserunt 2 accedentes cet. | discipuli] om. cet. | suscitauerunt] et excitauerunt 2 excitauerunt 5 | illum] eum cet. add. discentes 2 discipuli 8 | magister] 2 domine domine 5 praeceptor (preceptor 8) cet. | tunc surgens] ille autem surrexit 2 ad ille (at ille A) surgens cet. | imperauit uento] 4 et corripuit uentum 2 inperauit uento 5 increpauit uentum 8 A | tempestati] 4 inundationem 2 tempestatem 8 A om. 5 aquae] undae 5 | destiterunt] cessauit 8 A cessauerunt cet. | tranquillitas] malacia 2 tranquilitas magna 4 | **25** illis] illis iesus 2 | timentes autem] 5 et timuerunt 2 et timentes 4 8 qui timentes A | mirati sunt] et admirabantur 2 mirabantur 5 | ad alis alium dicentes] dicentes ad inuicem 5 A ad inuicem dicentes cet. | quisnam] quis 4 quis putas A | ut hic est] hic est 5 A est hic (his 8*) cet. | qui] 8 quod 2[c] 4 quoniam 5 quia A | et[1]] om. 4 8 | uentis imperat et aquae] 2 uentis inperat et aquae 5 mari et uentis imperat 4 uentis imperat et mari 8 A | et[3]] om. 2 obaudiunt] oboediunt A | illi] 2 imperio eius 4 ei cet. | **26** enauigauerunt autem] 8 A et accesserunt 2 deuenerunt autem 5 et nauigauerunt 4 | in] 2 5 ad cet. | trans fretum] trans contra 8 contra cet. | galilaeae] galilaeam (galileam 8) cet. | **27** egresso autem illo] et cum egressus est (exisset 2 exierunt 5) ad terram (in terram 5 om. 8) cet. | occurrit] orcurrit 2* et obuiauit 5 | uir] 5 uir quidam cet. add. de ciuitatem 2 de ciuitate 5 4 | daemonem habebat] habuit daemonia 2 habebat daemonium (daemonia 5) cet. | ex temporibus multis] temporibus conpluribus 2 a temporibus multis 5 temporibus multis 4 iam temporibus multis 8 A | et] qui 2 5 | uestimentum] tunicam 5 uestimento A | induebatur] uestibatur 2 | neque] et 2 5 | domo] 5 in domo cet. manebat] non manebat 2 5

28 Uidens autem iesum prostrauit se et {et} exclamans uoce magna dixit: quid
mihi est tecum, iesu, fili dei summi? oro te, ne me torqueas. **29** praecipiebat enim
spiritui immundo exire de homine. multis enim temporibus arripuerat illum.
alligabatur enim catenis et conpedibus, ut custodiretur. et {et} erumpens uincula
fugabatur a daemone in desertis. **30** Interrogauit autem illum iesus: quod tibi
nomen est? qui dixit: legio, quoniam daemonia multa erant in eo. **31** et rogabant
illum, ne imperaret eis in abysum ire. **32** Erat autem ibi grex porcorum magna,
quae pascebatur. et rogauerunt illum, ut in eis intrarent, et permisit illis. **33** Et
cum exissent daemonia ab homine, intrauerunt in porcos. et inpetum fecit grex
per praeceps in mare et suffocata est. **34** uidentes autem pastores fugerunt et
renuntiauerunt, quod factum est, in ciuitatem et in agros. **35** Exierunt autem
uidere, quod factum est, et uenerunt ad iesum. et inuenerunt sedentem hominem,

---

28 Uidens autem iesum] 5 cum uidisset autem iesum 2 is (his 4) ut uidit iesum cet. | prostrauit se] procidit ante illum cet. om. 2 5 | et[1]] om. 2 5 | exclamans] exclamauit 2 5 | dixit] et prostatus est dicens 2 | est tecum] et tibi (add. est 8 A) cet. | iesu] om. 2 5 | fili] filii A | dei] om. 5 summi] altissimi cet. | oro] 2 rogo 5 obsecro cet. | **29** praecipiebat] 4 A dicebat 2 5 precipiebat 8 enim[1]] autem 8 | spiritui] daemonio 2 5 | immundo] inmundo 5 8 | exire] exi 2 5 ut exiret cet. de] ab cet. | arripuerat] inuaserat 2 abripiebat 5 ruperat 4 adripuerat 8 arripiebat A | illum] eum 5 | alligabatur enim] 2 ligabatur enim 5 nam uinctus 4 8 et uinciebatur A | conpedibus] compedibus 2 A | ut custodiretur] detinebatur 2 et custodiabatur 5 custodiebatur 4 8 custoditus A | erumpens uincula] disrumpebat uincula 2 5 ruptis uinculis cet. | fugabatur] agitabatur enim 2 ducebatur (ducebantur*) enim 5 agebatur cet. | a daemone] a daemonio cet. om. 8 desertis] loca deserta 2 4 desertum 5 loco deserto 8 deserta A | **30** autem] om. 8 | illum] eum 5 iesus] iesus dicens 5 A | quod] quid 5 | qui dixit] ad (at A) ille (add. respondens 8) dixit cet. legio] legio nomen mihi 5 | quoniam daemonia multa erant in eo] 2 multa enim erant daemonia 5 quia multi sumus 4 qui multi daemonia (demonia*) erant 8 quia intraueunt daemonia multa in eum A | **31** et rogabant] rogabant autem 5 et rogabant autem 8 | illum] eum A om. 5 | ne imperaret] ut non praeciperet 5 | eis] illis cet. | in abysum ire] in abyssum abire 5 ut in abyssum (habissum 8) irent cet. | **32** magna] multorum cet. om. 5 | quae pascebatur] pascentium cet. add. in montem 5 in monte A | et rogauerunt] rogabant autem 5 et rogabant A | illum] 4 eum cet. | in eis intrarent] in porcos introirent 5 in illos irent 4 in illis irent 8 permitteret eis in illos ingredi A | et permisit illis] ad ille praecepit eos 5 | **33** Et cum exissent] cum exissent autem 5 exierunt ergo cet. | daemonia] demonia 8 | intrauerunt] abierunt 5 et intrauerunt cet. in[1]] ad 8 | et inpetum fecit grex] abiit autem grex 5 et impetu (inpetum 8) abiit grex cet. praeceps] praecipitium 5 | mare] stagnum cet. | suffocata est] 5 suffocati sunt 4 8 suffocatus est A | **34** uidentes autem pastores] uidentes autem qui pascebant quod factum est 5 4 quod ut factum uiderunt qui eos pascebant (pascebat*) 8 quod ut uiderunt factum qui pascebant A fugerunt] fugierunt 4 A* | renuntiauerunt] 4 nuntiauerunt cet. | quod factum est] om. cet. agros] 5 uillas cet. | **35** Exierunt autem uidere] aduenientes autem de ciuitate 5 | quod factum est et uenerunt ad iesum] quid factum est et uenerunt ad iesum 8 om. 5 | inuenerunt] uidentes 5 sedentem hominem] sedentem 5 hominem sedentem cet.

a quo daemonia exierant, uestitum et constantem mente ante pedes iesu. Et
timuerunt. **36** adnuntiauerunt autem illis, qui uiderant, quomodo sanatus est is,
qui a daemoniis erat uexatus. **37** Rogauit autem illum omnis multitudo regionis
gerasenorum, ut discederet ab eis, quoniam timore magno detinebantur. ipse
autem ascendens in naue reuersus est. **38** rogabat autem eum ille uir, a quo
exierant daemonia, ut esset secum. dimisit autem iesus illum dicens: **39** reuertere
domi aput te et enarra, quanta tibi fecerit deus. et abiit per totam ciuitatem
praedicans, quanta iesus fecisset illi. **40** Factum est autem, dum reuerteretur
iesus, et excepet illum turba. erant enim omnes expectantes eum. **41** Et ecce uenit
uir nomine iairus, et hic erat princeps synagogae. et prostratus ad pedes iesu
rogabat illum, ut intraret in domum suam, **42** quia filia unica erat illi fere
annorum duodecim, et haec moriebatur. et factum est, dum iret, turba urgebat et
conprimebat eum ita, ut suffocarent eum. **43** et mulier, quae erat in profluuio
sanguinis ab annis duodecim, quae in medicis consumpserat omnem substantiam

---

a quo daemonia exierant] qui habuerat daemonium 5 | uestitum] sobrium 5 | et[3]] 5 ac cet. constantem mente] uestitum sedentem 5 sanae mentis 4 sana mente 8 A | ante] ad cet. | iesu] 5 eius cet. | Et] om. 5 | timuerunt] timuerunt ualde 4 | **36** adnuntiauerunt] 5 nuntiauerunt cet. autem] enim 5 | illis] illi 4 | sanatus est] salbatus est 5 saluus factus est 4 8 sanus factus esset A is qui a daemoniis erat uexatus] legion 5 qui a daemoniis uexabatur 4 a legione 8 A | **37** Rogauit autem] rogauerunt autem 5 et rogauerunt cet. | illum] iesum 5 | omnis multitudo regionis] omnes et regio 5 | ut discederet] abire 5 | eis] 5 ipsis cet. | quoniam timore magno detinebantur] timore enim magnum conpraehensi erant 5 quia timore magno tenebantur (tenebatur 8) cet. ipse autem ascendens] ascendens autem 5 ipse autem ascendit 8 | in naue] nauem 4 A in nauiculam 8 om. 5 | reuersus est] et reuersus est 8 | **38** rogabat autem] 5 et rogabat 4 A et rogauit 8 eum] 5 illum cet. | ille] om. cet. | exierant daemonia] 5 daemonia (demonia 8) exierant cet. esset secum] esset cum eo 5 cum ipso esset 4 cum ipso esset (essent*) 8 cum eo esset A | dimisit] dismisit 5* | iesus] om. cet. | illum] eum A | **39** reuertere] uade 5 redi cet. | domi aput te] in (om. 4 A) domum tuam (om. 4) cet. | et enarra] narrans 5 et narra cet. | fecerit deus] deus fecit 5 dominus fecerit 4 fecit deus 8 A | abiit] uadens 5 | per] in 5 | totam] uniuersam cet. om. 5 praedicans] et nuntiabat 5 | fecisset illi] illi fecit iesus 5 iesus fecit illi 4 8 illi fecisset iesus A **40** dum] cum cet. | reuerteretur] 5 redisset cet. | et] om. cet. | excepet] excipet cet. | illum] eum 5 | turba] populus 5 | eum] illum 4 | **41** Et ecce uenit] et ueniens 5 | nomine] cui nomen cet. | iairus] iarus 8* | hic] 5 ipse cet. | erat princeps synagogae] 8 princeps synagogae 5 princeps synagogae erat 4 A | et[2]] om. 5 | prostratus] cadens 5 cecidit cet. | ad] sub 5 | rogabat] 5 rogans cet. | illum] eum cet. | ut intraret] introire 5 | suam] eius cet. | **42** quia filia unica erat illi] erat enim filia illi unica 5 quia filia unica erat ei 8 | fere] om. 5 | duodecim] xii 5 4 | et haec moriebatur] moriens 5 | et factum est] 5 et contingit (contingint 8) cet. | dum iret] cum iter faceret 5 dum iret iesus 4 | turba urgebat et conprimebat eum ita ut suffocarent eum] turbae suffocabant eum 5 praemebat eum populus 4 a turbis sic conprimebatur ut suffocarent eum 8 a turba comprimebatur A | **43** quae[1]] 5 quaedam (quedam 8) cet. | profluuio] fluxu 4 A duodecim] xii 5 4 | quae in medicis consumpserat omnem substantiam suam] quae in medicos erogauerat omnem substantiam suam cet. om. 5

suam nec potuit ab aliquo curari, **44** accendens de retro tetigit uestimentum eius et protinus stetit fluxus sanguinis eius. **45** iesus autem sciens, quod exierit ab eo uirtus, dixit: qui tetigit me? negantibus autem omnibus ait petrus et qui cum illo erant: magister, turbae tam magnae conprimunt te, et dicis: quis tetigit me? **46** Qui dixit iesus: tetigit me aliquis. ego enim cognoui uirtutem exisse a me. **47** ut uidit autem mulier se non latuisse, uenit tremens et procidens ante pedes illius et ob quam causam tetigit eum, indicauit coram omni populo et quomodo sanata est comfestim. **48** qui dixit ei: filia, fides tua te saluam fecit. uade in pace. **49** Adhuc loquente eo uenit a principe sinagogae dicens ei: mortua est filia tua. noli uexare illum. **50** iesus autem cum audisset uerbum, dixit patri puellae: noli timere, tantum crede, et uiuet. **51** Cumque uenisset domi, non est passus intrare secum quemquam nisi petrum et iohannen et iacobum et patrem et matrem puellae. **52** plorabant autem omnes et plangebant eam. qui dixit: nolite flere, non enim

---

nec potuit ab aliquo curari] quem nemo poterat curare 5 nec ab ullo potuit curari cet. | **44** accendens] 5 accessit cet. | de retro] retro cet. om. 5 | tetigit] 5 et tetigit cet. | uestimentum eius] 8 tunicam eius 5 uestimentum eius fimbriam 4 fimbriam uestimenti eius A | protinus] confestim cet. | fluxus] profluuius 5 fluxum 8 | eius[2]] ipsius 8 | **45** iesus autem sciens quod exierit ab eo uirtus] iesus autem sciens quae exiuit ab eo uirtus 5 om. cet. | dixit] interrogabat 5 et ait iesus cet. | qui[1]] quis 5 quis est qui cet. | tetigit me[1]] me tetigit cet. | ait] dixit cet. | illo] eo 5 magister] 5 praeceptor (preceptor 8) cet. | turbae tam magnae conprimunt te] turbae te conprimunt et contribulant 5 turbae te conpriment tam magnae 4 turbae te conpremunt tam magnae 8 turbae te comprimunt et affligunt A | dicis] dicit 8* | tetigit me[2]] me tetigit cet. | **46** Qui dixit iesus] ad ille dixit 5 ad iesus dixit 4 et dixit iesus 8 A | aliquis] quis 5 | ego enim] 5 nam et (om. A[c]) ego cet. | cognoui] sciui 5 cognobi 4 noui A | exisse a me] 5 de me exisse 4 A exisse de me 8 **47** ut uidit] uidens cet. | se non latuisse] quia non latuit illum (om. d A) cet. | uenit tremens] tremibunda uenit 5 uenit timens 4 uenit tremes 8* tremens uenit A | procidens] 5 procidit cet. ante] ad 5 | pedes illius] eum 5 pedes eius 8 | et ob] propter 5 | tetigit] 5 tetigerit cet. | eum] illum 4 | indicauit] adnuntiabit 5 | coram] in conspectu 5 | omni populo] omnis populi 5 omnibus 4 | quomodo] quia 5 quemadmodum cet. | sanata est comfestim] sanata est confestim 5 confestim sanata est (sit A) cet. | **48** qui dixit] ad ille dixit 5 8 ad ipse dixit 4 at ipse dixit A ei] illi 4 A | pace] pacem 5 8 | **49** loquente eo] 2 eo loquente 5 illo loquente cet. | uenit] uenit quidam 2 8 ueniunt 5 | a principe sinagogae] 4 A princeps synagogae 2 ab archisynagogo 5 ad principem synagogae 8 | dicens ei] dicens 2 dicentes illi 5 add. domine ueni ut filia mea salues loquente eo uenit puer principis dicens 2 | mortua est filia tua] quoniam mortua est filia tua iam 5 quia mortua est filia tua cet. | illum] magistratum 5 | **50** cum audisset uerbum] audiens sermonem 2 audiens uerbum 5 audito hoc uerbo cet. | dixit] 2 respondit 5 A ait 4 8 | patri puellae] illi dicens 5 | tantum crede] 2 5 crede tantum cet. | uiuet] saluabitur 2 5 salua erit cet. **51** Cumque uenisset] uenies autem 2 intrans autem 5 et cum uenisset cet. | domi] domum 4 A in domum cet. | est passus] admisit 5 permisit cet. | intrare secum] 4 A introire secum 2 5 secum intrare 8 | quemquam] alios 2 | iohannen] 4 iohanen 5 iohannem cet. | patrem et matrem puellae] patrem puellae et matrem 2 5 | **52** plorabant] 5 flebant cet. | eam] 5 illam cet. | qui] ille autem 2 ad (at A) ille cet. | dixit] dixit illis 2 | flere] plorare 2 5 | enim mortua est] 5 non est (add. enim 8) mortua cet.

mortua est, sed dormit. **53** et deridebant eum scientes eam mortuam esse. **54** Ipse autem adpraehensa manum eius exclamauit dicens: puella, surge. **55** et reuersus est spiritus eius et surrexit statim, et iussit dari ei manducare. **56** Obstipuerunt autem parentes eius, praecepitque illis, ut nemini dicerent, quod factum est.

9 conuocatis autem duodecim apostolis dedit illis uirtutem et potestatem super omnia daemonia et languores curandi. **2** et misit illos praedicare regnum dei et sanare aegros. **3** et dixit ad illos: Nihil tollatis in uia, neque uirgam neque peram neque calceamenta neque panem neque pecuniam neque duas tunicas habeatis. **4** in quamcumque domum intraueritis, ibi manete et inde exite. **5** et quicumque non receperint uos, exeuntes de ciuitatem illam, puluerem uestrum de pedibus excutite in testimonium illis. **6** exeuntes autem circuibant per municipia euangelizantes et curantes ubique. 7 audiit autem herodes tetrarcha omnia, quae

---

dormit] dormiit 4* | **53** deridebant] inridebant 2 | eum] illum 2 | eam mortuam esse] 8 quia (quoniam 5 quod 4) mortua est cet. | **54** adpraehensa] tenens cet. | exclamauit] clamauit cet. **55** reuersus est spiritus] 2 A conuersus est spiritus 5 conuertit spiritum 4 8 | statim] confestim 5 continuo cet. | iussit] praecepit 5 | dari ei] 5 illi dari (dare 8) cet. | **56** Obstipuerunt autem parentes eius] admirati sunt autem parentes 2 parentes autem eius uidentes expauerunt 5 et stupuerunt parentes eius cet. | praecepitque illis] qui autem praecepit illis 2 praecepit autem illis 5 quibus praecepit (precepit 8) cet. | ut nemini dicerent] nemini dicere 2 5 ne alicui dicerent cet. | factum est] 5 4 est factum 2 factum es 8 factum erat A | **9:1** conuocatis] conuocans 2 5 duodecim] xii 5 4 | apostolis] A apostolos 2 discipulis suis 4 8 om. 5 | dedit] et dedit 2 | illis] eis 5 | super] in 2 | omnia daemonia] omne daemonium 5 | languores curandi] langores curare 2 infirmitates curare 5 ut languores curarent cet. | **2** illos] eos 5 | sanare] curare 2 | aegros] infirmos cet. | **3** dixit] 2 5 ait cet. | ad illos] ad eos 5 illis 8 | tollatis] tuleritis cet. | uia] 4 A uiam cet. | neque[1]] non 2 5 | neque[2]] non 2 | peram] petram 2 8 | neque[3]] 4 8 non 2 om. 5 A calceamenta] calciamenta 2 4 calciamentum 8 om. 5 A | neque[4]] non 2 | panem] pane 2* neque[5]] non 2 | neque[6]] non 2 | duas tunicas] ana duas tunicas 5 | habeatis] habueritis 2 habere 5 | **4** in] 8 et in cet. | quamcumque] 4 A quacumque 2 8 quemcumque 5 | intraueritis] introieritis 2 intraberitis 4 | ibi] illic 2 | manete] manate 8 | exite] 2 5 proficiscimini 4 8 ne exeatis A | **5** quicumque] quodquod 2 quecumque 5 | receperint] acceperint 5 | ciuitatem] ciuitate cet. | illam] 8 illa cet. | puluerem uestrum de pedibus excutite] etiam puluerem uestrum a pedidus uestris excutite 2 excutite puluerem pedum uestrorum 5 etiam puluerem uestrum de pedidus excutite 4 etiam puluerem de pedibus uestris excutite 8 etiam puluerem pedum uestrorum excutite A | illis] super eos 2 super (supra 4 A) illos cet. | **6** exeuntes autem] 5 et exeuntes autem 2 egressi autem cet. | circuibant per municipia] per castella pertransiebant 2 circa ciuitates transibant 5 ibant per castella et ciuitates 4 circumibant ciuitates et castella 8 circumibant per castella A | euangelizantes] benenuntiantes 2 | ubique] om. 4 | **7** audiit] audiens 5 audiuit cet. | tetrarcha] quattuoruir 2 | omnia] om. 5 | quae] quaecumque 4

fiebant, et stupebat eo, quod diceretur a quibusdam, quia iohanes surrexit a
mortuis, **8** a quibusdam autem, quia helias apparuit, ab aliis autem, quia propheta
de antiquis surrexit **9** dixit autem [...] decollaui. quis autem est hic, de quo audio
ego talia? et quaerebat uidere illum. **10** Et reuersi apostoli nontiauerunt illi,
quaecum{cum}quae fecerunt, et adsumens eos secessit seorsum in locum
desertum, qui uocabatur betsaida. **11** turbae autem, cum cognouissent, secutae
sunt eum. et excipiens illos loquebatur illis de regno dei, eos, qui necesse
habebant curari, sanabat. **12** dies autem coeperat declinare. Accedentes autem
duodecim dixerunt illi: dimitte turbam, ut euntes adiacentes uicos et agros
reficiant se et inueniant escas, quoniam hic in deserto loco sumus. **13** Dixit autem
ad illos: date eis manducare. qui dixerunt: non sunt nobis plus quam quinque
panes et pisces duo, nisi si nos euntes emamus in omnem populum hunc escas.

---

fiebant] 5 A faciebant 2 erant facta 4 8 add. ab eo A | et] om. 5 | stupebat] hesitabant 2* hesitabat 2[c] A confundebatur 5 consternebatur 4 consternabatur 8 | eo] propterea 2 propter 5 | quia] quod 4 | iohanes] iohannis 2 8 iohannes cet. | surrexit a mortuis] a mortuis resurrexit 2 a mortuis surrexit 5 | **8** a quibusdam] ab alios 5 | autem[1]] uero A | quia[1]] A quoniam 5 quod 4 8 om. 2 | apparuit] uisus est 5 | ab aliis] alii 2 5 | quia[2]] quod 4 8 | propheta] 4 A profeta cet. de antiquis] 2 anticus 5 unus de antiquis cet. | **9** dixit autem] 2 5 ait autem 4 8 et ait A | quis autem est hic] quis est hic 2 qui est autem hic 5 hic quis est b hic qui est 8 quis autem est iste A audio ego talia] A audio ista 2 ego haec audio 5 ego audio talia 4 8 | quaerebat] querebat 8 uidere illum] illum uidere 4 8 uidere eum cet. | **10** nontiauerunt] narrauerunt cet. | illi] ei 5 quaecumcumquae] quanta 2 5 quaecumque cet. | fecerunt] fecerant 4 | adsumens] 2 5 adsumptis (assumptis A) cet. | eos] 5 illos 2 illis cet. add. iesus 8 | secessit seorsum] secessit singulariter 2 recessit seorsum 5 | locum desertum] castellum 5 | qui] A quod cet. | uocabatur] appelatur 2 dicitur 5 est cet. | betsaida] 4 bessaida 2 8 bedsaida 5 bethsaida A | **11** turbae autem cum cognouissent] turbae autem cognoscentes 2 5 quod cum (ut 8) cognouissent turbae cet. | secutae] secuti 4 | eum] 2 5 illum cet. | excipiens] 2 suscipiens 5 excepit cet. | illos] eos 2 5 | loquebatur] 2 5 et loquebatur cet. | illis] eis 2 | eos] et 5 et eos cet. | necesse habebant curari] necessariam habebant curam 2 opus habebant sanitatis eius 5 cura (curam 4) indigebant (indigebat 8*) cet. | sanabat] curabat 2 omnes curabat 5 | **12** dies autem] iam ubi dies 2 | coeperat] coepit 5 coeperunt 8 | Accedentes] 2 5 et accesserunt 4 et adcesserunt 8 et accedentes A | autem[2]] 5 om. cet. add. illi 2 ad eum 4 | duodecim] xii discipuli 4 duodecim discipuli eius 8 | dixerunt] et dixerunt 4 8 | illi] ad eum 5 | dimitte] dismitte 5 | turbam] 2 4 turbas cet. | euntes] eant 4 8 adiacentes uicos] in proxima castella 5 circa (in A) castella cet. | et agros] uillasque A et uillas cet. add. quae circa sunt A | reficiant se] deuertant 2 A maneant 5 et reficiant se 4 8 | et inueniant escas] aut inueniant sibi escas 2 om. 5 | quoniam] 5 quia cet. | deserto loco] 2 5 loco deserto cet. | **13** Dixit autem] 2 5 ait autem cet. | illos] eos 5 add. iesus 8 | date eis manducare] uos date illis manducare A date illis uos manducare (manducare uos 4*) cet. | qui dixerunt] ille autem dixerunt 2 at (ad 5 8) illi dixerunt cet. | sunt] sum 8 | pisces duo] duos pisces 2 8 A[c] duo pisces cet. | nisi si nos euntes emamus] nisi si forte euntes nos ememus (emamus[c]) 2 nisi forte nos euntes emamus 5 nisi nos eamus et emamus 4 nisi si nos eamus et eamus (emamus[c]) 8 nisi forte nos eamus et emamus A | populum hunc] 5 populum istum 2 hanc turbam cet.

14 erant enim uiri fere quinque milia. Dixit autem ad discipulos suos: facite illos
recumbere per [...] **15** recubuerunt omnes. **16** Acceptis autem quinque panibus et
duobus piscibus respiciens in caelum benedixit super illos et confregit et dabat
discipulis, ut adponerent turbis. **17** et manducauerunt et satiati sunt et sublatum
est, quod superfuit illis, fragmentorum cophinos duodecim. **18** Et factum est, cum
esset in secreto, aderant illi discipuli sui. et interrogauit eos dicens: quem me
dicunt turbae esse? **19** qui respondentes dixerunt: iohannem baptistam, alii autem
heliam, aliqui uero, quia profeta unus de prioribus surrexit. **20** dixit autem illis:
uos autem quem me dicitis esse? respondens autem petrus dixit: christum. **21** qui,
cum obiurgasset illos, praecepit, ne cui dicerent hoc, dicens, **22** quoniam oportet
filium hominis multa pati et reprobari a senioribus et pontificibus et scribis et
interfici et pos<t> tertium diem resurgere. **23** dicebat autem ad omnes: Si quis uult

---

14 enim] autem 2 A | uiri fere] 8 uiri quasi 2 uiri ut 5 fere uiri 4 A | Dixit] 2 5 ait cet. | discipulos] discipulus 8 | suos] om. 2 4 | facite illos recumbere] facite eos recumbere 2 reclinate eos discubitiones 5 facite illos discumbere cet. | per] om. 2 5 | **15** recubuerunt omnes] recumbere fecerunt omnes 2 discubuerunt omnes 4 8 discumbere fecerunt omnes A om. 5 | **16** Acceptis] accipiens 2 5 | autem] autem iesus 4 8 | panibus] panes 2 5 | duobus piscibus] pisces duo 2 duos pisces 5 | respiciens] 2 ascipiens 5 respexit cet. | in] ad 2 | benedixit] 2 orauit et benedixit 5 et benedixit cet. | super illos] 4 8 eos 2 5 illis A | et confregit] 2 et fregit cet. om. 5 | dabat] 2 5 distribuit cet. | discipulis] discipulis suis 2 A | ut adponerent] adponere 2 5 ut ponerent cet. turbis] 5 populo 2 ante turbas (turbam 8) cet. | **17** et manducauerunt] et manducauerunt omnes A om. 2 | satiati sunt] saturati sunt cet. add. omnes 2 5 | quod] om. 2 | superfuit] reliqum 2 superauit 5 | illis] om. 2 5 | fragmentorum] fracturarum 2 fractamentorum 5 | cophinos] 4 8 cophini cet. | duodecim] xii 4 8 | **18** esset in secreto] esset ipse singularis 2 essent soli 5 solus esset orans cet. | aderant illi discipuli sui] cum illo fuerunt discipuli 2 erant (add. autem 4) cum illo (eo 5) et (om. 5) discipuli cet. | eos] 5 illos cet. | turbae esse] 5 homines esse 2 esse turbae cet. | **19** qui respondentes dixerunt] ille autem responderunt 2 ad illi respondentes dixerunt 5 ad (at A) illi responderunt et dixerunt cet. | iohannem] 8 A iohannen 2 5 iohanne 4 | heliam] helian 5 4 | aliqui uero] aut 2 5 alii uero 8 alii 4 A | quia] om. 2 5 | profeta unus de prioribus surrexit] unum profetarum 2 unum ex profetis 5 propheta (profeta 8) unus de prioribus surrexit (resurrexit 4) cet. | **20** autem[1]] om. 8 | quem me] me quem 4 | dicitis esse] esse dicitis 8 A respondens] respondit 8 | autem[3]] 5 om. cet. | petrus dixit] 2 5 ait simon petrus 4 simon petrus dixit 8 simon petrus dixit A | christum] christum filium dei 2 5 christum dei cet. | **21** qui cum obiurgasset illos] ille autem increpans illos 2 ad ille increpauit eis et 5 et ille increpans illos 4 ad ille increpans eos 8 at ille increpans illos A | praecepit] precepit 8 praecipit A | ne cui dicerent hoc] A nemini dicere istut 2 nemini dicere hoc 5 ne cui haec dicerent 4 ne cui hoc dicerent (diceret*) 8 | **22** quoniam] 2 5 quod 4 8 quia A | reprobari] exproprari 5 | senioribus et pontificibus] senioribus et principibus sacerdotum 2 A presbyteris et a principibus sacerdotum 5 princibipus sacerdotum 4 principibus sacerdotum et senioribus 8 | scribis] scribas 4 | interfici] 2 occidi cet. | post tertium diem] post triduum 2 post tres dies 5 8 post dies tres 4 tertia die A | **23** dicebat autem ad omnes] ait autem ad omnes 2 et dixit iesus eis 4* | Si quis uult] si quis uoluerit 2 omnis qui uult ad uitam 4* post me uenire, abneget se ipsum et sequatur me. **24** quisque enim uoluerit animam suam saluam facere, perdet illam. et qui perdiderit animam suam causa mei, saluabit illam. **25** quid enim prodest homini locrari mundum totum, se autem ipsum perdere aut iacturam faciat? **26** quisquis enim confusus fuerit me et meos, hunc filius hominis confondet, cum uenerit in gloria sua et patris et sanctorum angelorum. **27** Dico autem uobis: uere sunt quidam hic stantes, qui non gustabunt mortem, donec uideant regnum dei. **28** factum est autem post haec uerba circiter post dies octo, adsumptis secum petro et iohane et iacobo, ascendit in montem ut oraret. **29** et factum est, dum orabat ipse, et facta est ficies uultus eius alia et uestis eius candida praefulgens. **30** et ecce uiri duo conloquebantur ei. erat autem moyses et helias **31** apparentes in gloriam. dicebant consummationem illius, quam impleturus erat in hierusalem. **32** Petrus autem et qui cum eo erant grauati sunt

---

post] ad 4[c] | abneget] neget 2 | se ipsum] se 2 semetipsum 5 | sequatur me] 5 sublata cruce sua sequatur me 4 tollat crucem suam (add. cotidie A) et sequatur me cet. | **24** quisque] qui cet. saluam facere] salbare 2 saluare 5 | illam[1]] eam 5 8 | et qui] qui autem 2 5 nam qui cet. animam suam[2]] illam 2 | causa mei] propter me cet. | saluabit illam] hic saluauit illam 2 hic salbabit eam 5 hic saluabit eam in uitam aeternam 4 saluabit eam 8 saluam faciet illam A **25** prodest homini] 5 4 prodeest homini 2 proficit homo 8 A | locrari] si lucrum fecerit 2 lucrari 5 si lucretur cet. | mundum totum] 5 totum mundum 2 uniuersum mundum cet. | se autem ipsum] A se ipsum autem 2 semetipsum autem 5 se autem 4 8 | perdere] 5 perdat cet. | aut] et 4 A | iacturam faciat] damnum faciat 2 iactum pati 5 detrimentum (add. sui A) faciat cet. **26** quisquis enim] qui enim 2 5 nam qui cet. | confusus fuerit me] 5 confessus fuerit me 2 me erubuerit 4 A erubuerit me 8 | meos] 2 5 meos sermones cet. | filius hominis] hominis filius 2 confondet] confitebitur 2 confundetur 5 erubescet (erubescit A) cet. | gloria sua] 2 regno suo 5 maiestate sua cet. | patris] patris sui 5 | **27** Dico autem uobis] ueritatem autem dico uobis 2 uere sunt quidam hic stantes] sunt quidam eorum qui hic stant 2 quoniam uere sunt quidam qui hic stant 5 uere aliqui sunt hic stantes 4 uere sunt aliqui hic stantes 8 A | donec] quousque 2 usque cum 5 | regnum dei] filium hominis uenientem in gloria sua 5 | **28** haec uerba] istos sermones 2 | circiter] quasi 2 5 fere cet. | post[2]] om. 2 5 A | adsumptis] et adsumens 5 et (om. 4 8) adsumpsit (assumpsit A) cet. | secum petro et iohane et iacobo] petrum et iohannem (iohannen 4 iacobum 5 A) et iacobum (iohanen 5 iohannen A) cet. | ascendit] 5 et ascendit cet. montem] monte 4 | ut oraret] orare 2 5 | **29** et factum est] 5 A et cet. | dum orabat ipse] in orando 2 dum (cum 5) orat (oraret 5 A) cet. | et[2]] om. cet. | facta est] om. 5 A | ficies] figura 2 species cet. | uultus] aspectus 4 8 | eius[1]] ipsius 2 | alia et uestis eius candida] commutata alia et uestitus albus 2 mutata est et uestimenta eius alba 5 albus 4 altera et uestitus eius albus 8 A praefulgens] ut nix 2 scoruscantia 5 refulgens cet. | **30** uiri duo] duo uiri cet. | conloquebantur ei] conloquebantur illi 2 conloquebantur cum eo 5 loquebantur cum illo (eo A) cet. | erat] 5 erant cet. | moyses] moysi 2 moses A | helias] elias 2 | **31** apparentes in gloriam] uisi in gloriam 2 uisi in gloria 5 uisi in maiestate 4 A in maiestate uisi 8 | dicebant] dicebant autem 2 5 et dicebant cet. | consummationem] exitum 2 5 excessum cet. | illius] eius cet. | quam] quem cet. impleturus erat] incipiebat implere 2 incipit conplere 5 conpleturus (completurus A) erat cet. in hierusalem] in iherusalem 8 om. 2 | **32** autem[1]] 2 5 uero cet. | eo] 2 5 illo cet. | erant] om. A grauati sunt] 8 grauati erant 2 A erant grauati 5 erant grabati 4

somno. euigilantes autem uiderunt gloriam eius et duos uiros adsistentes ei. **33** Et
factum est, dum discerent ab illo, dixit petrus: magister, bonum est nos hic esse, et
faciamus tabernacula tria, unum tibi et unum moysi et unum heliae, nesciens
quid diceret. **34** haec autem eo dicente facta est nubs et obumbrabat illos.
timuerunt autem, dum illi intrarent in nubem. **35** et uox facta est de nube dicens:
hic est filius meus electus, ipsum audite. **36** Et cum facta est uox, inuentus est iesus
solus. et ipsi tacuerunt et nemini indicauerunt in illis diebus quidquam ex iis,
quae uiderant. **37** Factum est autem per diem descendentibus eis de monte
occurrit illis turba magna. **38** et ecce uir de turba exclamauit dicens: magister, oro
te, respicias in filium meum, quia unicus mihi est. **39** et ecce spiritus arripit illum
subito et concidit et discarpit illum cum spuma, et uix recedit ab illo contribulans
eum. **40** et praecatus sum discipulos tuos, ut eicerent illum, et non potuerunt. **41**
Respondens autem iesus dixit: o generatio incredibilis, quousque ero aput uos et

---

somno] a somno 4 | euigilantes autem] 5 cum euigilassent autem 2 et euigilantes 4 A et uigilantes 8 | gloriam] 2 5 maiestatem cet. | duos] duo 2 | adsistentes ei] qui cum eo stabant 2 qui simul stabant cum eo 5 qui stabant cum illo cet. | **33** Et] om. 2 | dum] A cum cet. | discerent] separarentur 5 disceret 8 discederent cet. | illo] eo 5 | dixit] 2 5 ait cet. | petrus] 4 8 petrus ad iesum cet. | magister] 5 4 praeceptor cet. | nos] nobis 5 | et faciamus] uis facio hic 5 si uis faciamus 8 tabernacula tria] 4 tria tabernacula cet. | unum moysi] moysi unum 8 unum mosi A | unum heliae] heliae unum 8 | nesciens] non sciens 2 | diceret] dicit 5 | **34** eo dicente] 5 cum ille diceret 2 illo loquente cet. | nubs] nubis 2 A | et] om. 2 | obumbrabat] adumbrauit 2 inumbrauit 4 obumbrauit cet. | illos] 2 eos cet. | timuerunt] 5 et timuerunt cet. | autem[2]] 5 om. cet. add. in eo 2 5 | dum illi intrarent] cum illi introirent 2 cum illi introierunt 5 et intrantibus illis cet. **35** et] om. 4 8 | facta est] uenit 5 | dicens] om. 4 | electus] 8 dilectus cet. add. in quo bene sensi 5 | ipsum audite] audite illum 2 audite eum 5 | **36** cum] 2 5 dum cet. | facta est] facta esset 2 facta fuisset 5 fit 4 8 fieret A | uox] uos 8 om. 2 | et ipsi] hii autem 2 ipsi autem 5 | nemini] 2 A nulli 5 nemini nihil 4 8 | indicauerunt] renuntiauerunt 2 dixerunt cet. | quidquam] quicquam 2 A om. cet. | ex iis] ex hiis cet. om. 5 | uiderant] uiderunt 2 5 | **37** per diem] in sequenti die A descendentibus eis] descendente eo 5 descendentibus (discendentibus 2) illis cet. | occurrit] conuersa est 2 conuenire 5 | illis] ad illum 2 ei 5 illi cet. | turba magna] 2 turbam multam 5 turba multa cet. | **38** uir] unus 2 | turba] turbais 2* turbis 2[c] | oro] 2 rogo 5 obsecro cet. respicias] adtende 2 respice cet. | in] ad 2 super 5 | quia] quoniam 5 | mihi est] 2 5 est mihi cet. **39** et ecce] om. 2 5 | spiritus arripit illum subito] arripit enim illum spiritus immundus subito 2 accipit enim illum desubito spiritus 5 spiritus adprehendit (apprehendit A) illum et (om. 8) subito clamat (om.8) cet. | concidit] collidit 2 adlidit 5 elidit cet. | discarpit] disrumpit 5 dissipat cet. illum[2]] eum 4 A om. cet. | cum spuma] et spumat 2 cum spumam 8 | et uix recedit ab illo] et uix recedet ab eo 5 et uix discedit 4 A et uix discedit ab illo 8 om. 2 | contribulans] et confringit 2 et contribulat 5 dilanians cet. | eum] illum 2 8 | **40** praecatus sum] 5 postulaui 2 rogaui cet. discipulos tuos] a discipulis tuis 2 | eicerent] liuerarent 2 dimittant 5 | illum] eum 5 | **41** Respondens autem iesus dixit] respondit iesus et dixit 2 | incredibilis] 2 incredula et peruersa 5 infidelis et peruesa cet. | quousque] usquequo cet. | aput] ad 5 add. usquequo ero uobiscum 4 et sufferam uos] et usquequo uos sustineo 2 et patiar uos cet.

sufferam uos? adduc hoc filium tuum. **42** adhuc autem accedente illo adlisit illum ille spiritus malus et concarpsit. imperauit autem iesus spiritui immundo et sanauit puerum et reddidit illum patri suo. **43** Stupebant autem omnes in magnalia dei. omnibus autem mirantibus de omnibus, quae faciebat, dixit ad discipulos: **44** ponite uos in auribus uestris uerba haec. filius enim hominis incipit tradi in manibus hominum. **45** ad illi ignorabant uerbum hoc et erat occultum ab eis, ne intellegerent, et timebant interrogare eum de uerbo hoc. **46** intrauit autem cogitatio in eis, quisnam esset maior illorum. **47** Iesus autem uisa cogitatione cordis illorum adprehensum infantem statuit apud se. **48** et dixit: quicumque me recipit, non me recipit, sed eum, qui me misit. qui enim minimus in omnibus uobis est, hic est magnus. **49** Respondens autem iohannes dixit: magister, uidimus

---

hoc] huc 4 8 om. 5 A | **42** adhuc autem accedente illo] cum accederet autem ille 2 adhuc autem accedente eo 5 et cum accessit (adcessitset 8 accederet A) cet. | adlisit] 5 conlisit 2 et (om. 4 A) elisit cet. | illum[1]] eum 5 | ille spiritus malus] daemonium cet. | concarpsit] conturbabit 5 dissipauit cet. | imperauit autem] 5 corripuit autem 2 et increpauit cet. | spiritui immundo] 4 immundum spiritum 2 inmundo spiritui 5 spiritum immundum 8 A | sanauit puerum] dimisit illum 2 dimisit eum 5 | reddidit] restituit 8 | illum[2]] puerum 5 eum 8 | suo] eius 8 A | **43** Stupebant autem omnes] omnes autem admirabantur 2 omnes autem stupuebant 5 | in] super 2 magnalia] magnificentiam 2 magnitudine (magnitudinem 8) cet. | omnibus autem mirantibus] omnibus autem admirantibus 2 omnium autem mirantium 5 omnibusque mirantibus cet. | de] 2 in 5 A super 4 8 | omnibus[2]] omnia 8 | faciebat] add. dixit petrus domine quare nos non potuimus eicere illum quibus dixit quoniam huiusmodi orationibus et ieiuniis eicitur 2 dixit ei petrus domine quare nos non potuimus eicere illum quibus dixit quoniam eiusmodi oratione eiciuntur et ieiunio 8 | dixit ad discipulos] dixit autem et discentibus suis 2 dixit autem (om. 5 A add. iesus 4) ad discipulos suos cet. | **44** uos] sermones hos 4 | auribus uestris] aures uestras 5 cordibus uestris A | uerba haec] uerba ista 5 sermones istos (hos 8) cet. om. 4 | filius enim] nam filius 4 8 incipit tradi] 2 incipiet tradi 5 tradetur 4 8 futurus est ut tradatur A | manibus] 4 manus cet. **45** ad illi] ille autem 2 5 | uerbum hoc] 5 uerbum illud 2 uerbum istud cet. | occultum] 4 8 absconsum 2 coopertum 5 uelatum A | ab eis] 5 ab illis 2 inter ipsos 4 inter ipsis 8 ante eos A ne intellegerent] ut non sentirent cet. add. illud 2 5 A | eum] A illum 4 8 om. 2 5 | uerbo hoc] 5 uerbo illo 2 hoc uerbo cet. | **46** intrauit autem cogitatio in eis] introiuit autem cogitatio in illis 2 intrauit atem cogitatio in eos A | quisnam] 2 5 quis cet. | esset maior illorum] esset maior eorum 5 eorum maior esset cet. | **47** Iesus autem uisa] iesus autem cum uidisset 2 iesus autem uidens 5 ad (at A) iesus uidens cet. | cogitatione] cogitationem 5 cogitationes cet. | cordis illorum] eorum cordis 5 | adprehensum] adpraehendit 2 adprehendit 4* adprehendens cet. infantem] 5 eum 4* 8 puerum cet. | statuit] et statuit 2 4* add. eum 4* A | apud] ante 2 ad 5 secus cet. | **48** dixit] 2 5 ait cet. add. illis A add. quicumque acceperit (receperit 2 susceperit A) puerum istum (infantem hunc 5) in nomine meo me recipit (accipit 5 recepit 8) cet. | quicumque me recipit non me recipit] qui me recipit recipit 2 A om. 5 | sed] 4 8 et 5 om. 2 A | qui enim] 2 qui autem 5 nam qui cet. | minimus] minimus fuerit 2 minor est cet. | in] 2 5 inter cet. | omnibus uobis] 2 5 omnes uos cet. | est[1]] om. cet. | est magnus] erit magnus 2 5 | **49** Respondens] respondit 2 | dixit] et dixit 2 | magister] 2 5 praeceptor cet.

quendam in nomine tuo eicientem daemonia et prohibebamus illum, quoniam non sequitur nobiscum. **50** Dixit autem ad illum iesus: sinite illum et nolite prohibere. qui enim non est aduersus uos, pro uobis est. nemo est enim, qui non faciat uirtutem in nomine meo et poterit male loqui de me. **51** factum est autem, dum conplerentur dies receptionis eius, et ipse direxit faciem suam ire in hierusalem. **52** Et misit nuntios ante conspectum suum et euntes intrauerunt in ciuitate samaritanorum tamquam paraturi illi. **53** et non receperunt eum, quoniam facies illius erat tendens in hierusalem. **54** Uidentes autem discipuli eius iacobus et iohanes dixerunt: domine, uis dicimus, ut ignis de caelo descendat super illos et consumat eos, sicut helias fecit? **55** et conuersus obiurgauit illos dicens: nescitis, cuius spiritus estis? **56** filius hominis non uenit animas hominum perdere, sed saluare. Et abierunt in aliut castellum. **57** et factum est euntibus illis in uia dixit quidam ad eum: sequar te, quocumque ieris. **58** et dixit ei iesus: uulpes cubilia habent et uolucres caeli nidos, ubi requiescant. filius autem hominis non

---

eicientem] expellentem 2 | prohibebamus] 4 uetabamus 2 prohibus 5 prohibuimus A | illum] 2 eum cet. | quoniam] quia cet. | sequitur] sequitur te 4 | **50** Dixit autem] 2 5 et ait cet. | ad illum] A ad illos 4 om. 2 5 | sinite illum et] om. cet. | prohibere] uetare 2 prohibere eum 5 est[1]] es 5 | aduersus] aduersum 2 contra 5 | nemo est enim qui non faciat uirtutem in nomine meo et poterit male loqui de me] 4 nemo enim est qui non faciat uirtutem in nomine meo 2 om. 5 A | **51** factum est autem] factum est autem in eo 2 | dum] ut 2 5 | conplerentur] supplerentur 2 complerentur A | receptionis] adsumptionis (assumptionis A) cet. | ipse direxit faciem suam] ipse faciam suam (uultum suum 5) firmauit (confirmauit 2) cet. | ire in hierusalem] ad hierusalem 2 ut iret (abiret 5) in (om. 4) hierusalem cet. | **52** misit] praemisit 2 | conspectum suum] eos 2 faciam suam 5 | et euntes intrauerunt in ciuitate] et euntes intrauerunt in castellum 5 et euntes intraberunt in ciuitatem 4 et euntes intrauerunt in ciuitatem A om. 2 | samaritanorum] om. 2 | tamquam paraturi] quasi praepararent 2 ut praeparent 5 quasi paraturi 4 ut pararent A illi] ei 5 | **53** receperunt] susceperunt 5 | eum] illum 2 4 | quoniam] 2 quia cet. | facies] uultus 5 | illius] eius cet. | tendens] euntibus 2 iens 5 euntis 4 A | in] om. 4 A | **54** Uidentes autem] 5 cum uidissent autem cet. | ut ignis de caelo descendat] ignem descendere de caelo 5 ut ignis descendat (discendat 2 4) de caelo cet. | super illos] ad illos 2 om. 5 A | consumat] consumere 5 | eos] illos 4 A | sicut helias fecit] sicut et helias fecit 5 om. 2 A | **55** et conuersus] conuersus autem 2 5 | obiurgauit] corripuit 2 increpauit cet. | illos] eos 5 | dicens] et dixit cet. add. illis 2 | cuius spiritus estis] A cuius spiritui estis cet. | **56** filius hominis non uenit animas hominum perdere sed saluare] 2 quia filius hominis non uenit animas hominum perdere sed saluare 4 quia filius hominis non uenit animas perdere sed saluare om. 5 | abierunt] abiit 2 habierunt 4 | aliut castellum] aliud castellum 2 A alium castellum 5 aliam ciuitatem 4 | **57** et factum est] factum est autem 4 A | euntibus illis] cum ambularent 2 ambulantibus illis A | uia] uiam 2 | eum] illum cet. | sequar] domine sequar 4 | **58** et[1]] om. 2 | dixit] ait 4 A | ei] illis 2 illi cet. | cubilia] 5 receptacula 2 foueas 4 A | habent] habeant 4 | uolucres] uolatilia 2 5 nidos] habitacula 5 | ubi requiescant] 4 om. cet. | filius autem hominis] nam ego sum homo qui 4* nam filius 4[c]

habet, ubi capud reclinet. **59** dixit autem ad alium: sequere me. qui dixit: domine,
permitte mihi prius ire et sepelire patrem meum. **60** dixit autem illi: sine mortuos
sepelire mortuos suos. tu autem uade, adnuntia regnum dei. **61** Dixit autem et
alius: sequar te, domine, prius autem permitte mihi ire et nuntiare eis, qui in
domo sunt. **62** dixit autem ad illum iesus: nemo retro respiciens et extendens
manum super aratrum aptus est regno dei.

10 elegit autem et alios lxxii et misit illos binos ante faciem suam in omnem
locum et ciuitatem, ubi intraturus erat. **2** dicebat autem illis: messis copiosa,
operari autem pauci. praecamini ergo dominum messis, ut mittat operarios in
messem suam. **3** Ecce mitto uos tamquam agnos in medio luporum. **4** nolite
portare sacculum non peram nec calciamentum et neminem circa uiam
salutaueritis. **5** in quamcumque primum domum intraueritis, dicite: pax huic

---

habet] habet domum 4* | capud] capud suum 2 caput cet. | reclinet] declinet 4 | **59** dixit autem] et ait 4 ait autem A | alium] 5 alterum cet. | sequere me] ut sequerer se 2 | qui dixit] ad ille dixit 5 ille autem dixit cet. | domine] om. 5 | mihi] me 2 | prius] primo 2 primum cet. ire et sepelire] ire et sepilire 2 ut eam et sepeliam 5 | **60** dixit autem illi] et dixit illi iesus 2 ad ille dixit illi iesus 5 dixit autem ei iesus 4 dixitque iesus A | mortuos sepelire] mortui sepelliant 2 ut mortui sepeliant A | adnuntia] et adnuntia 2 et praedica 5 nuntia 4 | **61** Dixit autem et alius] et ait alter 4 A | prius autem permitte mihi] primo autem mihi permitte 2 permitte autem mihi primum 5 sed primum permitte mihi 4 A | ire et] om. cet. | nuntiare] abrenuntiare 5 renuntiare A | eis] 2 his 4 A om. 5 | in domo sunt] domo sunt 2 sunt in domum meam 5 domi sunt 4 A **62** dixit autem ad illum iesus] iesus autem dixit illi 2 iesus autem dixit illis 5 ait ad illum iesus 4 A retro respiciens et extendens manum super aratrum] retro adtendens et superponens manum suam super aratrum 2 retro aspiciens et inmittens manum suam in aratrum 5 respiciens retro mittit manum in aratrum 4 mittens manum suam in aratrum et aspiciens retro A | regno] in regnum 5 | **10:1** elegit autem] 2 ostendit autem 5 designauit autem iesus 4 post haec autem designauit autem dominus A | lxxii] septuaginta duos A | misit] praemisit 2 | illos] eos 5 om. 2 locum et ciuitatem] ciuitatem et locum A | ubi] 5 quocumque 2 quo 4 A | intraturus erat] introiturus erat 2 habebat uenire 5 erat uenturus 4 erat ipse uenturus A | **2** dicebat autem] et dicebat 4 A | illis] et ad illos 2 ad eos 5 | messis[1]] 5 messes 2 messis quidem 4 A | copiosa] multa et 2 multa 5 A copiosa est 4 | operari] 2 operarii 5 4 A | praecamini] 5 postulate 2 rogate 4 A | ergo] om. 2 | dominum] a domino 2 | mittat operarios] operarios mittat 2 | in] ad 2 **3** Ecce] ite ecce cet. | mitto] 2 ego mitto cet. | tamquam agnos] ad messem quomodo agnos 2 sicut agnos cet. | in medio luporum] inter lupos A | **4** portare] baiolare 5 | sacculum] saccellum 2 sacellu 5 | non] neque 4 A | nec] non 2 5 neque 4 A | calciamentum] calciamenta cet. circa] in 5 per cet. | salutaueritis] salataueritis 2* | **5** quamcumque] 5 A quacumque 2 4 primum] autem 2 5 om. 4 A | domum intraueritis] introieritis domum 2 intraueritis domum 5 domum primum intraueritis 4 domum intraueritis A | dicite] primum dicite 2 A | huic domui] domui huic 2 5

domui. **6** si ibi fuerit filius pacis, requiescet † super uos † reuertetur. **7** in eadem
domo manete edentes et bibentes, quae ab illis apponuntur uobis. dignus est enim
operarius mercedem suam. Nolite migrare de domo in domum. **8** et in quacumque
ciuitate intraueritis et receperint uos, manducate, quae adponuntur uobis. **9** et
curate, qui in ea sunt infirmos, et dicite illis: adpropinquauit in uos regnum dei. **10**
In quacumque autem ciuitate intraueritis et non receperint uos, exeuntes in
platea eius dicite: **11** etiam puluerem, qui adhaesit nobis de ciuitate uestra in
pedes, excutimus super uos. Adtamen scitote adpropinquasse regnum dei. **12** dico
autem uobis: sodomis in regno remissius erit quam ciuitati illi. **13** Uae tibi,
corozain et bedsaida, quia si in tyro et sidone factae fuissent uirtutes, quae factae
sunt in uobis, olim fors in cinere et cilicio sedentes paenitentiam egissent. **14**
uerumtamen tyro et sidoni in iudicio remissius erit quam uobis. **15** Et tu

---

6 si] et si cet. | ibi fuerit] fuerit illic 2 fuerit ibi 5 | requiescet] requiescet super (in 5) illam (eam 2 eum 5) pax uestra sin autem (si quominus 2 5) cet. | super] ad 2 A in 5 supra 17 | reuertetur] reuertetur pax uestra 5 | **7** eadem] ipsa 2 5 eadem autem cet. | edentes] manducantes 2 | ab illis apponuntur uobis] ab eis sunt 2 sunt ab eis 5 apud illos sunt cet. | est enim] enim 17 enim est A | operarius] operaraus 2* | mercedem suam] mercede sua 4 A | migrare] 2 transire cet. domum] domo 2 | **8** quacumque] 2 quamcumque cet. | ciuitate] ciuitatem cet. | intraueritis] introieritis 2 17 | receperint] 2 susceperint A acceperint cet. | manducate] edite 5 | quae] quaecumque 2 ea quae 4 | adponuntur uobis] 5 uobis adponuntur 2 aput uos ponuntur 4 ante uos ponuntur 17 apponuntur A | **9** qui in ea sunt infirmos] eos qui in illam infirmantur 2 qui sunt in ea infirmi 5 infirmos qui (quae 4) in illa sunt cet. | dicite] dicetis 17 | adpropinquauit] adpropiauit 5 adpropiauit (adpropiabit*) 4 appropiauit 17 appropinquauit A | in uos regnum dei] aduentus regni dei 2 super uos regnum dei 5 | **10** quacumque] quamcumque 17 A | autem] om. A | ciuitate intraueritis] 5 4 introieritis ciuitatem 2 ciuitatem intraueritis 17 A | receperint] accipient 5 | uos] om. 2 | platea] plateas 2 A plateis cet. | **11** etiam] ecce 2 et 5 | adhaesit nobis] nobis adhesit 2 adhesit nobis A | in pedes] in pedibus cet. om. A | excutimus] extergimus cet. | super uos] nobis 2 uobis 5 in uos cet. | Adtamen] uerum 2 uerumtamen 5 tamen cet. scitote] istut scitote 2 hoc scitote cet. | adpropinquasse] quia (quoniam 2 5) adpropinquauit (adpropiabit 4* adpropiauit 4^{c} appropiauit 17 appropinquauit A) cet. | **12** autem] 5 om. cet. sodomis in regno remissius erit quam ciuitati illi] quia tolerabilius erit sodomis in regno dei quam ciuitati illi 2 quoniam sodomis tolerabilius erit in regno dei quam ciuitati illi 5 sodomis in regno tolerabilius erit quam ciuitati illi 4 sodomis in die illa tolerabilius erit quam illi ciuitati 17 quia sodomis in die illa remissius erit quam illi ciuitati A | **13** corozain] 4 capharnaum 2 chorozain 5 corazain 17 A | et[1]] uae tibi A | bedsaida] 5 bethsaida A betsaida cet. | quia] quoniam 2 in[1]] 17 A om. cet. | tyro] tyru 5 | sidone] sidoni 5 | factae[1]] facta 2 | fuissent] essent 2 5 uirtutes] om. 4 | factae sunt in uobis] 2 5 in uobis factae sunt cet. | fors] forte 2 iam 5 om. cet. cinere et cilicio] sacco et in cinere 2 sacco et sidone 5 cilicio (cilio 4) et cinere cet. | sedentes] resedentes 5 om. 2 | paenitentiam egissent] 5 4 paeniterent 2 A paeniterentur 17 | **14** uerumtamen] uerum 5 | sidoni] sidone 2 | in iudicio remissius erit] tolerabilis erit 2 tolerabilius erit 5 in iudico tolerabilius erit 4 tolerabilius in iudico erit 17 remissius erit in iudicio A | **15** tu] tu autem 2

capharnaum, numquit usque ad caelum exaltaueris [...] usque ad inferos demergeris? **16** qui audit uos, me audit, et qui spernit uos, me spernit et eum, qui me misit. qui autem me audit, audit eum, qui me misit. **17** Reuersi sunt autem lxx et duo cum gaudio dicentes: domine, etiam daemones subiacent nobis in nomine tuo. **18** dixit autem illis: uidebam satanam tamquam fulgur de caelo cadentem. **19** ecce [...] uobis potestatem calcandi super uiperas et scorpiones et super omnem uiam inimici, nihil uos nocebit. **20** Uerum in hoc nolite gaudere, quod spiritus uobis obaudiunt. gaudete autem, quia nomina uestra scripta sunt in caelo. **21** In illa hora exultauit in spiritu sancto et dixit: confiteor tibi, domine [...] et terrae, quoniam abscondisti haec a sapientibus et sensatis et reualasti ea paruolis. ita, pater, quia sic placuit ante te. **22** Omnia mihi tradita sunt a patre. et nemo nobit, quis est pater, nisi filius et cuicumque uoluerit filius reuelauit. **23** Et conuersus ad discipulos dixit: beati oculi qui uident, quae uos uidetis. **24** dico enim uobis, quia

---

capharnaum] cafarnaum 5 4 | numquit] nedum 2 numquid cet. om. A | ad[1]] 5 in cet. | exaltaueris] 5 exaltaberis 4 exaltata es (om. A) cet. | ad[2]] in 4 | inferos] 2 infernum cet. | demergeris] deprimaris 2 descendet 5 | **16** audit uos] 2 5 uos audit cet. | et[1]] om. 4 | spernit uos] 5 uos spernit cet. | et eum qui me misit] 2 5 om. cet. | qui autem me audit] qui me audit 17 qui me spernit A om. 2 | audit eum qui me misit] spernit meum qui me misit A om. 2 | **17** reuersi sunt] redierunt 2 | lxx et duo] lxx 17 septuaginta duo A lxxii cet. | etiam] et 2 5 | daemones] daemonia cet. | subiacent nobis in nomine tuo] nobis subiecta sunt in nomine tuo 2 subdita sunt nobis in nomine tuo 5 in nomine tuo nos audiunt 4 subiecta sunt nobis in nomine tuo 17 subiciuntur nobis in nomine tuo A | **18** dixit autem] 2 5 et ait 4 A ait autem 17 | illis] ad eos 5 om. 2 satanam] satanan cet. | tamquam] quasi 2 sicut cet. | fulgur] fulgor 2 | de caelo cadentem] descendentem de caelo 2 | **19** ecce] et ecce 4 | calcandi] ut calcetis 2 5 | super[1]] supra 4 A uiperas] serpentes cet. | scorpiones] super scorpiones 2 | super[2]] 2 5 supra cet. | uiam] uirtutem (uirtut 2) cet. | nihil] 2 et nihil cet. | uos] uobis A | nocebit] noceuit 2 | **20** Uerum] 2 uerumtamen cet. | hoc] isto 2 | quod] quoniam 2 5 quia cet. | spiritus] daemoniam 2 daemonia 5 spiritus maligni 4 | obaudiunt] subiecta sunt 2 subdita sunt 5 subiecti sunt 4 17 subiciuntur A quia] 5 quoniam 2 quod cet. | caelo] caelis 5 A celo 8* | **21** illa] 2 ipsa cet. add. autem 5 | hora] die 2 | exultauit] exhilaratus est iesus 2 | in] om. A | spiritu sancto] sancto spiritu 2 | confiteor] confiter 5 confitebor 8 | domine] domine pater 2 8 17 pater domine 5 4 A | et[2]] ac 17 quoniam] 5 qui 2 quia 8 quod cet. | haec a sapientibus] ista a sapientibus 2 haec ab intellegentibus 4 a sapientinus haec 5 | et sensatis] et sapientibus 5 et prudentibus cet. om. 2 | paruolis] 2 8 paruulis cet. add. tuis 17 | ita] etiam 5 A | quia] quoniam 2 5 | placuit] A placitum factum est 2 beneplacitum 5 bona uoluntas fuit 4 8 fuit bona uoluntas 17 | ante te] coram te 2 in conspectu tuo 5 | **22** Omnia] omnia enim 2 dixit omnia 8 17 | patre] 5 A patre meo cet. | nobit] cognoscit 2 5 nouit 4 scit cet. | quis est pater nisi filius] quis est filius nisi pater et qui est pater nisi filius 2 17 qui est filius nisi pater et quis est pater nisi filius 5 patrem nisi filius et quis est qui nobit filium nisi pater 4 quis est filius nisi pater et quis est pater nisi filius 8 qui sit filius nisi pater et qui sit pater nisi filius A | cuicumque] quibus 2 cui cet. | uoluerit] uult 2 | reuelauit] reuelare cet. **23** Et conuersus] conuersus autem 2 5 | discipulos] 4 discentes 2 discipulos suos cet. | dixit] dixit illis 2 dixit eis 5 | beati] beati itaque 4 | qui] quia 8 | uos] 2 8 om. cet. | uidetis] add. et aures quae audiunt 2 et audientes quae auditis 5 | **24** quia] 2 quoniam 5 quod cet.

multi prophetae uoluerunt uidere, quae uos uidetis, et non uiderunt. **25** Et ecce
quidam legis doctor surrexit temptans illum dicens: magister, quid faciens uitam
aeternam possidebo? **26** et dixit ad illum: In lege quid scriptum est? quomodo
legis? **27** qui respondens dixit: diliges dominum deum tuum in toto corde tuo et in
tota anima tua et ex totis uiribus tuis et diliges proximum tuum tanquam te
ipsum. **28** dixit autem illi: recte respondisti. hoc fac et uibes. **29** Qui cum se uellet
iustificare, dixit ad iesum: et quis est mihi proximus? **30** suscipiens autem iesus
dixit: homo quidam descendebat ab hierusalem in hierico et hic incidit in
latrones, qui expoliantes eum et plagis inpositis abierunt semiuiuo eo relicto. **31**
fortuito sacerdos quidam descendebat per uiam illam et uiso illo praeteriit. **32**
Similiter autem et leuites, cum transiret per eodem loco et uidisset illum,
pertransiit. **33** Samaritanus autem quidam iter faciens uenit per eum. et uidens
eum misertus est. **34** et conligauit uulnera eius infundens oleum adque uinum et

---

prophetae] profetae 2 5 8 add. et iusti 4 et reges A | uidetis] uidistis 2 | uiderunt] 17 add. et audire quae uos (om. 2 8 A) auditis (audistis 4) et non audierunt (audirunt 2*) cet. | **25** Et] 17 A om. cet. | ecce] A haec eo dicente ecce 4 8 17 om. 2 5 | quidam legis doctor surrexit] exsurrexit autem quidam legis doctor 2 surrexit autem quidam legis doctor 5 quidam legis peritus (peritor 8) surrexit cet. | illum] eum 5 A | dicens] et dicens 5 4 A | magister] om. 5 | faciens] 2 5 faciendo cet. | possidebo] hereditabo 2 5 | **26** et dixit] ille autem dixit 2 at (ad 5) ille dixit cet. | ad illum] ad eum cet. om. 2 | **27** qui respondens dixit] ille autem respondit et dixit 2 ille respondens dixit 4 A at (ad 5) ille respondens dixit cet. | diliges[1]] diligis 8 | in[1]] ex 2 A | in[2]] ex 2 A | ex] 2 A in cet. totis uiribus tuis] totis uisceribus tuis 2 tota uirtute tua 5 17 omnibus uiribus tuis 4 8 A add. et ex tota mente tua e et ex omni mente tua A | diliges[2]] om. cet. | tuum[2]] tibi 2 | tanquam] 2 sicut cet. | **28** dixit autem] dixitque 8 17 A add. iesus 8 | uibes] 2 uiues cet. | **29** Qui cum se uellet iustificare] ille autem (ad ille 5) uolens iustificare se ipsum (se iustificare 2 5) cet. | ad iesum] om. 17 | mihi] 2 5 meus cet. | **30** suscipiens] 5 8 subiciens 2 suspiciens cet. | dixit] dixit ei 5 descendebat] ascendebat 2 | hierusalem] hierusale 4 iherusalem 8 | hierico] ierico 2 5 iherico 8 hic] om. cet. | qui] qui et 2 ad illi 5 qui etiam cet. | expoliantes] spoliauerunt 2 dispoliantes 5 despoliauerunt cet. | eum] A illum cet. om. 5 | plagis inpositis] uulnerauerunt 2 plagas inponentes 5 | abierunt semiuiuo eo relicto] 17 et demiserunt semiuiuum 2 abierunt demittentes semiuiuum 5 semiuiuo relicto abierunt 4 abierunt semiuiuo relicto 8 A | **31** fortuito] de repente autem 2 forte autem 5 accidit autem ut A om. cet. | sacerdos quidam] sacerdos autem 8 17 | descendebat] discendens 2 descendens 5 | per] om. 8 17 A | uiam illam] 5 illam uiam 2 eadem uia (uiam 8) cet. | et] om. 2 | uiso illo] cum uidisset illum 2 uidens eum 5 | praeteriit] praeteriuit 2 A pertransiuit 5 | **32** autem] 2 5 om. cet. | leuites] leuitis 2 leuuita 5 | cum transiret per eodem loco] factus ad locum 5 cum esset secus locum (locus 8 locum ipsum 17) cet. | et[2]] om. 2 | uidisset] 2 uidens 5 uideret cet. | illum] 2 eum cet. | pertransiit] praeteriuit 2 pertransiuit 5 | **33** Samaritanus] samarites 2 sammaritanus 8 | iter] om. 5 | faciens] agens 2 transiens A | per] secundum 2 ad 5 secus cet. | eum[1]] illum 2 | uidens] cum uidisset 2 | eum[2]] illum 2 om. 4 17 misertus est] 5 commotus est 2 misericordia motus est cet. | **34** et[1]] et accessit et 2 et accedens 5 et appropians A | conligauit] 5 alligauit cet. | infundens] et infundens 4 | adque] et cet.

inpositum eum in suo iumento duxit in stabulo et curam habuit eius. **35** et in crastinum diem protulit duos denarios et dedit stabulario et dixit illi: diligenter curam illius habe, et quodcumque amplius erogaueris, ego reuertens reddam tibi. **36** Quis horum uidetur proximus fuisse eius, qui inciderat in latrones? **37** ad ille dixit: qui fecit misericordiam in illum. dixit autem illi iesus: recte respondisti. uade et tu fac similiter. **38** Factum est autem, dum irent, ipse intrauit in uicum quendam. mulier autem quaedam nomine martha excepit illum in domo sua. **39** et huic erat soror, quae uocabatur maria, quae cum consedisset ad pedes domini, audiebat uerbum eius. **40** martha autem turbabatur circa plurimum ministerium. Adstans autem dixit: domine, non adtinet at te, quod soror mea reliquid me sola ministrare? dic ergo ei, ut adiuuet me. **41** respondens autem dixit ei dominus: martha, martha, **42** maria optimam partem sibi elegit, quae non auferetur ei.

---

inpositum] inposuit 2 imponens cet. | eum] 5 illum cet. om. 2 | in[1]] super 2 5 | suo iumento] suum iumentum 2 suum pecus 5 iumento suo 4 17 iumentum suum 8 A | duxit in stabulo] et in stabulum deduxit 2 adduxit eum in diuersorium 5 duxit ad (in A) stabulum cet. | habuit eius] 5 eius habuit 2 eius egit cet. | **35** in crastinum diem] in crastinum 5 altera die cet. | protulit] eiciens 5 | duos denarios] denarios duos 2 5 | et[2]] om. 5 | dixit] 2 5 ait cet. | illi] om. cet. diligenter] om. cet. | curam illius habe] adtende illi 2 curam habeto eius 5 curam eius habe 4 quodcumque] quidquid 2 5 8 | amplius erogaueris] supererogaueris cet. | ego reuertens] in redeundo ego 2 cum reuertor ego 5 ego cum rediero A | reddam tibi] tibi reddam 2 restituam 5 **36** Quis] quem ergo 2 5 | horum] om. 2 5 | uidetur proximus fuisse eius] putas ex his duobus proximum 2 putas proximum fuisse 5 trium uidetur tibi (om. 17) proximus fuisse illi (eis 4) cet. inciderat] 2 incidit (incidet 17) cet. | **37** ad ille dixit] 5 ille autem dixit 2 at ille dixit cet. | in illum] cum eo 2 5 in eum 4 | dixit autem] 2 5 et ait cet. | illi] om. 5 | recte respondisti] om. cet. **38** dum] 8 A ut 17 cum cet. | irent] iter faceret 5 | ipse] et ipse cet. om. 5 | intrauit] introiuit 2 5 in[1]] om. 17* | uicum quendam] castellum quoddam 5 quoddam (quendam 2) castellum (castello 4) cet. | mulier autem] 2 5 et mulier cet. | quaedam] quedam 2 om. 5 | nomine martha] cui nomen erat martha 2 martha nomine 4 A | excepit] suscepit 5 | illum] eum 5 | domo sua] 2 domum suam cet. | **39** et] om. 2 5 | huic] cuius 2 cui 5 | erat] fuit 2 | quae uocabatur] nomine cet. om. 2 | cum consedisset] sedebat 2 adsidens 5 etiam sedens cet. | ad] 2 5 secus cet. | audiebat] et audiebat 2 | uerbum] sermones 2 | eius] 2 illius cet. om. 5 | **40** turbabatur] auocabatur 2 abalienabatur 5 satagebat cet. | circa] in 5 | plurimum] multum 2 5 frequens A om. cet. Adstans autem dixit] adstitit autem et dixit 2 instans autem dixit 5 quae stetit et ait cet. | domine] ad domine 5 | non adtinet at te] pertinet ad te 2 tibi cura est 5 est tibi cura (curae A) cet. quod] 8 A quia 2 5 eo quod 4 17 | reliquid] 2 dereliquid 5 reliquit cet. | sola] 2 solam cet. | ei] illi cet. | adiuuet me] 17 A me adiuuet cet. | **41** respondens autem dixit ei dominus] respondit autem et dixit illi iesus 2 respondens autem iesus dixit ei 5 et respondens dixit illi dominus (iesus 4) cet. | martha[2]] add. turbas te 5 sollicita es et turbaris circa plurrima A | **42** maria] porro unum est necessarium maria A | optimam] bonam 2 5 | sibi elegit] elegit sibi 4 17 elegit cet. ei] 2 ab ea 5 A illi cet.

11 et factum est, cum esset ipse in quodam loco orans, et ut quieuit, dixit quidam ex discentibus eius: domine, doce nos orare, sicut iohannes docuit discipulos suos. **2** Dixit autem illis: cum orabitis, dicite: Pater sancte, qui es in caelis, sanctificetur nomen tuum, adueniat regnum tuum, fiat uoluntas tua. **3** panem nostrum cotidianum da nobis hodie **4** et dimitte nobis peccata nostra, sicut et ipsi dimittimus omni debitori nostro. et ne inducas nos [...] **5** *deest* **6** [...] adponam illi, **7** et ille de intro respondens di[...] **8** surgens dabit illi, quantos desiderat. **9** et ego uobis dico [...] **10** *deest* **11** si petierit piscem, numquid pro piscem serpentem illi porriget? **12** aut si petierit ouum, numquid porrigit illi scorpionem? **13** si ergo uos, cum sitis mali, scitis data bona dare filiis uestris, quanto magis pater de caelo dabit bona data petentibus se? **14** Et factum est, cum eiceret daemonium, et illut fuit mutum. eiciente autem illo mutum daemonium omnes turbae stupebant. **15**

11:1 et factum est] factum est autem 2 | cum esset] om. 8 | ipse] 2 4 om. cet. | in quodam loco] in loco quodam 2 5 A | orans] orantem 5 | et[2]] om. A | ut] quomodo 2 cum 5 | quieuit] cessauit cet. | quidam] 2 5 unus cet. | ex] de 5 | discentibus] 2 discipulis cet. | eius] eius ad eum cet. | sicut] sicut et 2 5 A | iohannes] iohannis 8 | discipulos suos] discentes suos 2 nos 5* **2** Dixit autem] ille autem dixit 2 ad ille dixit 5 et ait cet. | illis] om. 5 | orabitis] oratis (orates 2) cet. add. nolite multum loqui sicut et ceteri putant enim quidam quia in multiloquentia sua exaudientur sed orantes 5 | sancte] 8 17 noster cet. om. A | qui es in caelis] qui in caelis es 5 17 qui in celis est 8 om. A | adueniat] 2 A super nos ueniat 5 ueniat cet. | fiat uoluntas tua] fiat uoluntas tua sicut (om. 2 4) in caelo (caelis 5 caelos 4 celis 8) et in terra cet. om. A | **3** cotidianum] cottidianum 5 4 8 | hodie] cotidie A | **4** dimitte] demitte 2* remitte 2[c] | peccata] 17 A debita et peccata 2 debita cet. | sicut] quomodo 17 siquidem A | ipsi] 17 A nos cet. | omni debitori nostro] omni debenti nobis 17 A debitoribus nostris cet. | inducas nos] 5 nos induca cet. **6** adponam] 5 ponam cet. | illi] 5 ante illum (eum 8) cet. | **7** et] ad 5 | de intro respondens] respondens de intus 8 de intus respondens (om. A) cet. | **8** surgens dabit illi] 17 surgens dabite 5 surget et dabit illi cet. | quantos desiderat] 4 17 quantum opus habet 5 quantus desiderat 8 quot habet necessarios A | **9** et ego] om. 8 | uobis dico] dico uobis 5 8 | **11** si petierit piscem] aut piscem petierit 5 aut si piscem petit 4 petet filius eius piscem 8 petet filius piscem 17 aut si piscem A | piscem[2]] 4 8 pisce cet. | illi porriget] ei dabit 5 porrigit ei 4 dabit illi cet. | **12** aut] et 5 petierit ouum] ouum petierit 5 | v. 12b–25 ex cod. 16 (a[2]) suppletum | porrigit illi scorpionem] 8 A scorpionem ei dabit 5 scorpionem porrigit illi 4 porrigit ei scorpionem 17 | **13** uos] om. 17 mali] iniqui 5 | scitis] 5 nostis cet. | data bona] 5 bonos datos 4 bona data cet. | filiis uestris] uestris filiis 4 | pater] 5 pater uester cet. | de caelo] om. 17 | bona data] spiritum bonum A bonum datum cet. | se] eum 5 | **14** Et factum est] haec autem dicente eo offertur illi daemoniosus surdus 5 et erat cet. | cum eiceret daemonium] eiciens 4 A dum eicit demonium 8 dum eicit daemonium 17 om. 5 | et illut fuit mutum] et illud erat mutum 4 A et illud fuit mutum 8 17 om. 5 eiciente autem illo] et eiecto eo 5 et cum eiecisset (eiceret 4) cet. | mutum daemonium] mutum demonium 8 daemonium A om. 5 4 add. locutus est mutus 8 17 A | omnes turbae stupebant] 4 omnes mirabantur 5 et omnes turbae stupuerunt 8 et omnes turbae stupebant 17 et ammiratae sunt turbae A

quidam autem ex illis dixerunt: in beelzebul, principe daemoniorum, eicit
daemonia. **16** alii autem temptantes signum quaerebant de caelo ab illo. **17** ipse
autem sciens cogitationes illorum dixit: Omnem regnum diuisum super se
deseretur, et domus super domum cadet. **18** si et satanas super satanan diuisus
est, quomodo stabit regnum eius? quoniam dicitis in beelzebul, principe
daemoniorum, eicere me daemonia. **19** quod si ego in beelzebul eicio, filii uestri in
quo eicient? ideo ipsi uestri iudices erunt. **20** Si autem in digito dei eicio
daemonia, certe anticipauit in uos regnum dei. **21** Cum quis fortis et armatus
tueatur domum suam, in pace sunt facultates eius. **22** quod si fortior illo
superueniens uicerit illum, armaturam illius tollit, in qua confidebat, et spolia
illius diuidet. **23** qui non est mecum, aduersus me est, et qui non colligit mecum,
dispargit. **24** Cum immundus spiritus exierit de homine, circuit per arida loca,
quae aquam non habent, quaerens requiem et non inueniens dicit: reuertar in

---

15 quidam autem] et quidam 5 | illis] eis 5 A pharisaeis 4 phariseis 8 17 | beelzebul] 5 17 belzebul 4 8 belzebub A | principe] 5 principem cet. | daemoniorum] demoniorum 8 | eicit daemonia] demonia eicit 8 add. ad ille respondens dixit quodo potest satanas satanan eicere 5 | **16** alii autem] 5 et alii cet. | quaerebant de caelo ab illo] de caelo quaerebant ab eo 5 17 A ab eo quaerebant de caelo 4 de celo querebant ab eo 8 | **17** sciens] 5 uidens 8 ut uidit cet. | cogitationes illorum] eorum cogitationes 5 cogitationes eorum cet. | dixit] dixit illis 5 dixit eis A | diuisum super se] 5 in se diuisum 4 in se ipsum diuisum 8 17 in se ipso diuisum A | deseretur] 5 desolatur cet. | super[2]] 5 supra cet. | domum] domum posita 4 | cadet] cadit 4 | **18** si et] si autem et 5 A sic et 4 si et 8 et si 17 | satanas] sanatas 8* | super satanan diuisus est] super se diuisus est 5 in se ipsum diuisus est 4 A satanam (sanatam*) eicit in se ipsum diuisum est 8* satanas satanan eicit in se ipsum diuisus est 17 | quomodo] non 5 | eius] ipsius 8 A | quoniam] quia cet. | dicitis] 5 A dicitis quoniam ego 4 dicitis quoniam 8 17 | beelzebul] 5 17 belzebul 4 8 belzebub A | principe daemoniorum] 17 principem daemoniorum 4 8 om. 5 A | eicere me daemonia] 5 A eicio daemonia 4 17 eicio demonia 8 | **19** quod si] si autem 5 A si 4 | beelzebul] 5 17 belzebul 4 8 belzebub A eicio] eicio daemonia 4 A | filii] fili 5 8 | eicient] 5 eiciunt cet. | ideo] propter hoc 5 | uestri iudices erunt] 5 iudices erunt uestri 4 8 17 iudices uestri erunt A | **20** Si autem] si autem ego 5 porro si A sed si cet. | eicio] ego eicio 8 | daemonia] demonia 8 | certe] forsitam 5 profecto cet. om. 4 | anticipauit] adpropinquauit 5 praeuenit 4 A prouenit 8 17 | **21** Cum quis] quando 5 cum cet. | et] om. cet. | tueatur] custodit cet. | domum suam] aulam suam 5 atrium suum cet. sunt facultates eius] est substantia eius 5 sunt ea quae possidet cet. | **22** quod si] si autem cet. illo] om. 5 | superueniens uicerit illum] superuenerit 5 superueniens uicerit eum cet. | armaturam] 5 uniuersa arma cet. | illius[1]] eius cet. | tollit] 5 auferet cet. | qua] 5 quibus cet. | confidebat] confidet 5 | illius[2]] om. 4 | diuidet] 5 distribuet (distribuit A) cet. | **23** qui[1]] et qui 17 aduersus] contra 5 aduersum cet. | colligit] congregat cet. | dispargit] 5 4 spargit 8 sparget 17 dispergit A | **24** Cum] 8 A cum autem 5 4 et cum 17 | immundus] inmundus 8 | de] ab 5 4 circuit] uadit 5 ambulat 4 perambulat 8 A peram 17 | per] de 8 | arida] 5 om. cet. | quae aquam non habent] loca quae non habent aquam 4 8 loca ubi non habent aquam 17 loca inaquosa A om. 5 | non inueniens] cum non inuenerit 17 | dicit] dicet 4

domum meam, unde exiui. **25** et cum uenerit, inuenit commundatam et ornatam.
26 tunc uadit et adsumit adhuc alios septem spiritus nequiores se et intrantes
inhabitant et fiunt nobissima hominis illius peiora priorum. **27** Factum est autem,
dum diceret haec ipse, leuata uoce quaedam mulier dixit illi: beatus uenter, qui te
portauit, et ubera, quae suxisti. **28** qui ait illis: baeati, qui audiunt uerbum dei et
custodiunt. **29** Turba autem conueniente coepit dicere: gens haec gens nequa est,
signum quaerit et non dabitur ei nisi signum ionae. **30** Sicut enim fuit ionas
signum nineuitis, sic erit et filius hominis huic generationi. et sicut ionas in uentre
coeti fuit, sic erit filius hominis in terram. **31** regina austri surget in iudicio cum
uiris generationis huius et condemnauit eos, quoniam uenit de finibus terrae
audire sapientiam solomonis. et ecce hic plus solomone. **32** uiri nineuitae surgent
in iudicio cum gente hac et condemnabunt eam, quia paenitentiam egerunt in

---

meam] om. 4 | **25** cum uenerit] ueniens 5 | inuenit] inuenerit 4 inueniet 17 | commundatam] emundatam 2 mundatum 5 eam (om. A) scopis mundatam cet. | et ornatam] et conpositam 2 adornatum 5 om. A | **26** tunc] 2 et tunc cet. om. 5 | et¹] om. 8 | adsumit] assumit A | adhuc] 8 om. cet. | alios septem spiritus] 5 ille nequa alios septe spiritos 2 septem alios spiritus cet. | se] om. 8 | et²] om. 17 | intrantes] introiit et 2 intrant et 5 ingressus 4 regressi 8 ingressi 17 A inhabitant] 8 17 habitant 5 habitat 4 habitant ibi A | fiunt] 2 5 sunt A fit cet. | nobissima] nouissima 2 A om. cet. | hominis illius] hominis huius 2 eiusmodi hominis 4 huiusmodi hominis 8 17 om. 5 add. uita 4 8 17 | peiora priorum] deteriora prioribus 2 peiora prioribus 5 A multo peior prioris cet. | **27** autem] om. 8 | dum diceret haec ipse] in eo cum diceret haec 5 cum haec (ista 2) diceret cet. | leuata uoce quaedam mulier] mulier quaedam leuauit uocem (uoce*) de turbis et 2 mulier quaedam eleuans uocem de pleue 5 extollens uocem quaedam (quedam 8) mulier de turba (om. 4) cet. | portauit] sustulit 2 baiolauit 5 | ubera] mammae 2 mamillae 5 | quae suxisti] qui te lactauerunt 2 quas suxisti 5 | **28** qui ait] ipse autem dixit 2 at (ad 5 4) ille dixit cet. illis] ad eos 4 8 17 om. 2 5 A | baeati] beati cet. | dei] domini 5 | **29** Turba autem conueniente] et cum turbae colligerentur 2 turbis autem concurrentibus (congregatis 5) cet. | gens¹] generatio cet. | haec] ista 2 | gens²] generatio cet. | nequa] 17 pessima 2 4 iniqua 5 nequam 8 A | est] om. 4 | quaerit] add. de caelo 17 | et] et signum cet. | ei] 5 illi cet. | ionae] ionae profetae 2 **30** Sicut enim] nam sicut 4 8 A | signum nineuitis] signum in nineuitis 5 om. 2 | sic erit et filius hominis] 5 ita erit et filius hominis cet. om. 2 | huic generationi] generationi huic 5 4 in generatione hac 8 in corde terrae 17 generatioini isti A om. 2 | et sicut ionas in uentre coeti fuit] in uentre coeti tribus diebus et tribus noctibus 2 et sicut ionas in uentre ceti fuit tribus diebus et tribus noctibus 5 et sicut ionas in utero coeti fuit 8 om. 4 17 A | sic erit filius hominis in terram] sic erit et (om.*) filius hominis in cor terrae 2 sic et filius hominibus in terra 5 sic et filius hominis in corde terrae 8 om. 4 17 A | **31** austri] ab austro 4 | surget] 4 A resurget 2 8 exsurget 5 surgit 17 | in iudicio] om. 5 | condemnauit] condemnabit 4 A | eos] eam 5 illos cet. | quoniam] quia cet. | de] 5 a cet. | solomonis] salomonis 4* 17 A | hic plus solomone] plus salomone hic 2 plus quam solomon hic 5 plus hic quam solomon (salomon*) 4 solomone plus hic 8 plus salomone hic 17 A | **32** nineuitae] ninaeuitae 2 | surgent] resurgunt 2 resurgent 8 | gente hac] ista generatione 2 uiris generationis huius 17 generatione hac cet. | condemnabunt] damnabunt 2 | eam] illam cet. | paenitentiam egerunt] ipsi paenitentiam gesserunt 2 | in²] ad A praedicationae ionae. et ecce hic plus quam iona. **33** Nemo lucernam accensam in occulto ponit neque sub modium, sed super candelabrum, ut intrantes lumen uideant. **34** lucerna corporis tui est oculus tuus. si oculus tuus simplex fuerit, totum corpus tuum lucidum est. si uero oculus tuus nequa fuerit, et corpus tuum tenebrosum{sum} erit. **35** si ergo lumen, quod est in te, tenebrae sunt, tenebrae ipse quantae sunt. **36** *omissum* **37** loquentae autem eo rogauit eum quidam pharisaeus, ut pranderet secum. ingressus autem recubuit. **38** pharisaeus autem coepit recogitans intra se dicere, quod non prius baptizatus esset. **39** Dixit autem dominus ad illum: nunc uos pharisaei, utrumne exteriorem partem calicis et catini, mundatis, quod autem intus est uestrum, plenum est rapina et nequitia. **40** stulti, Nonne qui fecit, uerum interiora et exteriora fecit? **41** uerum quod superest,

---

praedicationae] praedicatione (praedicationem 2 17 A) cet. | hic plus quam iona] plus iona hic est 2 plus hic quam ionas 4 plus iona hic cet. | **33** Nemo] nemo autem 4 8 | lucernam] lucerna 4 accensam] accendens 5 accendit et cet. | in occulto ponit] ponit sub absconso 2 in occultum ponit 5 in absconso (abscondito A) ponit cet. | modium] 5 modio cet. | super] supra 4 17 A | intrantes] introeuntes 2 5 qui ingrediuntur cet. | **34** lucerna] lucerna enim 2 | tui] om. 17 | si oculus tuus simplex fuerit] si fuerit oculus tuus simplex 2 cum est oculus tuus simplex 5 cum fuerit oculus tuus simplex 4 cum fuerit oculus tuus sinplex 8 princeps 17 si oculus tuus fuerit simplex A totum] et totum 2 | est[2]] erit 2 4 A | si[2]] A cum cet. | uero] autem cet. | oculus tuus[3]] om. cet. nequa] excaecatum 2 malus 5 nequam A | et] 2 5 etiam cet. | tenebrosumsum erit] teneborsum est 2 est tenebrosum est 5 obscurum erit 4 | **35** si ergo lumen] uide ergo ne lumen A | est in te] 2 in te est cet. | sunt[1]] sint A | tenebrae ipse quantae sunt] tenebrae tuae quantae sunt 2 tenebrae quantae 5 ipse tenebre quante sunt 4 tenebre tuae quante sunt 8 tenebrae in te quantae sunt 17 om. A | **37** loquentae autem eo] in eo autem cum loqueretur ipse 4 et cum (add. iesus 8) loqueretur haec (om. A) cet. om. 5 | rogauit eum quidam pharisaeus] petit ab eo pharisaeus quidam 2 pharisaeus quidam rogabit illum 4 rogauit (add. autem 5) illum (eum 5) quidam phariseus (pharisaeum 5 phariseis A) cet. | ut pranderet secum] ut pranderet aput ipsum 2 ut pranderet cum eo 5 ut cum eo pranderet 4 ut cum illo pranderet 8 17 ut pranderet apud se A | ingressus autem] abiit autem et 2 intrans autem 5 et ingressus cet. | **38** recogitans intra se dicere] apud se reputans dicere 2 cogitare in semetipso dicens 5 intra se (add. dicere 4) reputans (cogitans 8 putans 17) dicere cet. | quod] quare cet. | prius] 8 primo 2 primum cet. om. A | baptizatus esset] A baptizauit 2 baptizatus est cet. add. ante prandium 2 A priusquam (antequam 5 17) manducaret (pranderet 5) cet. | **39** Dixit autem dominus] 5 dixit autem iesus 2 et ait dominus cet. illum] eum 5 | nunc] om. 17 | pharisaei] farisae 5 pharisei 8 17 add. ypocritae 5 hypocritae 4 utrumne exteriorem partem calicis] prius est a foris calicis 2 prius (om. 5 A) quod de (a 5) foris est calicis cet. | catini] catilli 5 | mundatis] commundatis 2 | quod autem intus est uestrum] quod autem intrinsecus est uobis 2 abintus autem uestrum 5 | plenum] plena 17 | rapina] rapinae 2 rapinam 8* | nequitia] niquitiae 2 iniquitate cet. | **40** uerum interiora et exteriora fecit] quod est intus fecit et quod foris est 2 quod intus est et quod a foris est fecit 5 quod de foris est etiam id (om. 17) quod de intus est fecit cet. | **41** uerum] 2 uerumtamen 5 A tamen cet. | quod superest] quae sunt 5 4 om. 2

date elemosynam, et ecce omnia munda uobis erunt. **42** sed uae uobis, pharisaeis, quoniam decimatis mentam et rutam et omnem olus et praeteristis iudicium et caritatem dei. haec oportet fieri et illa non relinquere. **43** Uae uobis, pharisaei, quoniam diligitis primos consessus in synagogis et salutationes in foro. **44** Uae uobis, quoniam estis monumenta i{n}gnobilia, et homines ambulantes supra ignorant. **45** Respondens autem quidam ex legis doctoribus dixit ei: magister, haec dicens et nobis contumeliam facis. **46** qui dixit: et uobis, legis doctoribus, uae, quia honeratis homines sarcinas inportabiles, et ipsi uno digitorum uestrorum non attingitis ea. **47** Uae uobis, quoniam aedificatis monumenta prophetarum, nam patres uestri occiderunt illos. **48** ergo testimonium perhibetis non consentientes operibus patrum uestrorum, quoniam illi quidem occiderunt eos, uos autem aedificatis. **49** Ideo et sapientia dei dicit: mittam in illis prophetas et apostolos. Et ex illis occident et persequentur, **50** ut exquiratur sanguis omnium prophetarum,

---

date] datae 2 | elemosynam] misericordiam 5 om. 2 | omnia munda uobis erunt] uobis munda omnia 2 omnia munda et erunt uobis 5 omnia munda (mundata 17) sunt uobis cet. | **42** pharisaeis] phariseis 8 pharisei 17 pharisaei cet. | quoniam] 5 quia 2 A qui cet. | mentam] menta 5 rutam] anetum 2 | omnem] 2 8 omne cet. | olus] 2 holus cet. | praeteristis] transitis 2 praeteritis cet. | caritatem] dilectum 2 | haec oportet fieri et illa non relinquere] haec enim oportebat facere et illa non pratermittere 2 haec (add. autem A) oportuit facere et illa non omittere cet. om. 5 | **43** pharisaei] pharisaeis A | quoniam] qui 17 A quia cet. | primos consessus] primas sessiones 2 5 primas cathedras cet. | foro] add. et primos adcubitos in cenis 5 et primos discubitos in conuiuiis 4 | **44** Uae uobis] uae uobis scribae et pharisaei 5 4 17 add. hypocritae 4 | quoniam] 2 quia cet. | estis monumenta] 2 5 estis ut monumenta A monumenta estis cet. | ingnobilia] sine specie 5 quae non parent (apparent 17) cet. | ambulantes supra] A ambulantes super illa 2 17 supra ambulantes 5 ambulantes supra illa 4 8 | ignorant] nesciunt cet. | **45** ex] de 5 | doctoribus] 2 5 peritis cet. | dixit] dicit 2 5 ait cet. | ei] illi cet. | et] 5 etiam cet. om. 2 | contumeliam] iniuriam 2 5 | **46** qui dixit] ille autem dixit 2 ad ille dixit 5 at ipse (ille A) ait cet. | legis doctoribus uae] 2 uae legis doctoribus 5 legis peritis uae cet. | quia] qui 2* quoniam 5 | honeratis] 2 oneratis cet. | homines] hominis 2 | sarcinas inportabiles] honeribus grauibus 2 honera quae non possunt portari 5 oneribus quae non possunt portare 4 oneribus quae portari non possunt 17 A | digitorum uestrorum] 5 ex digitis 2 digito uestro cet. | attingitis] 5 tangitis cet. | ea] ipsas sarcinas 2 sarcinas ipsas 17 sarcinas A om. 5 4 | **47** quoniam] quia 2 A qui 4 17 | prophetarum] profetarum 2 5 | nam patres] patres autem cet. | occiderunt illos] eos occiderunt 2 occiderunt eos 5 | **48** ergo] nempe 2 profecto A | testimonium perhibetis] 4 consentitis 2 testificatis 5 testificamini 17 A | non consentientes operibus] 4 non placere uobis facta 2 non consentire 5 consentiere 17 quod consentitis A | quoniam] quia 2 5 | illi quidem] 4 ipsi 2 ipsi quidem 5 17 quidem ipsi A | occiderunt eos] eos occiderunt 2 A | aedificatis] gloriamini 2 aedificatis eorum sepulcra A | **49** Ideo] 4 propterea 2 17 A propter hoc 5 | et sapientia dei] om. 5 4 | dicit] dixit 2 17 A om. 5 4 | mittam] mitto 5 4 | in illis] in illos 2 4 17 in eos 5 ad illos A | prophetas] profetas 2 5 | Et ex illis] et ex ipsos 2 ex eis 5 | occident] interficient 5 | **50** exquiratur] 2 exquirat 5 inquiratur cet. | sanguis] sangues 2 | prophetarum] profetarum 2 5 qui effusus e<s>t ab origine mundi usque in gente hac. **51** A sanguine abel usque ad sanguinem zachariae, quem occiderunt inter altarium et aedem. ita dico uobis: exquiretur a gente hac. **52** uae uobis, legis doctoribus, quoniam abscondistis clauem scientiae et ipsi non intratis et introeuntes prohibuistis. **53** Dicente autem illo haec coram omni populo coeperunt tam scribae quam et legis doctores male se habere et comminare illi de pluribus, **54** quaerentes occa{n}sionem aliquam inuenire ab illo, ut accusarent eum.

12 Multa autem turba se continentium in [...]t ita, ut alius alium se conculcarent, coepit dicere ad discentes: primum cauete a fermento pharisaeorum, quod est adfectatio. **2** nihil enim opertum est, quod non reuelabitur, et occultum, quod non cognoscatur. **3** quae in tenebris dixeritis in

---

qui effusus est] quod effunditur 5 | ab origine mundi] a mundi constitutionem 2 a constitutione mundi cet. | usque in gente hac] usque ad generationem hanc 5 usque ad generationem istam 4 17 a generatione ista A om. 2 | **51** abel] abel iusti 2 17 | sanguinem] sanguine 5 | zachariae] 5 zacariae 2 zacchariae 4 17 add. fili barachiae 5 | quem occiderunt] 5 qui perit (periit A) cet. inter altarium et aedem] inter altare et templum 2 inter medium altaris et templi 5 inter altare et aedem 4 17 A | ita] etiam 5 | dico uobis] dico uobis quia 2 | exquiretur] 5 inquitur 2 requiretur cet. | a gente hac] a saeculo isto 2 a generatione hac 5 ad hac generatione cet. | **52** doctoribus] 2 5 peritis cet. | quoniam] 2 5 quia 4 A qui 17 | abscondistis] abstulistis 17 tulistis A | et[1]] aut A om. 2 | ipsi] uos 2 | intratis] introitis 2 4 introistis cet. | introeuntes] eos qui introibant 4 eos qui introiebant A | prohibuistis] uetastes introire 2 uetastis 5 perhibuistis 17 | **53** Dicente autem illo haec] cum haec autem diceret ad eos 2 dicente autem haec ad eos 5 cum ad illos diceret 4 cum haec ad illos diceret et 17 cum haec ad illos diceret A | coram omni populo] in conspectu totius populi 2 in conspectu omnis populi 5 coram omni plebe 4 17 om. A | tam scribae quam et legis doctores] pharisaei et legis doctores 2 5 pharisaei et legis periti 4 A legis periti et pharisaei 17 male se habere] grauiter habere 2 17 male habere 5 4 grauiter insistere A | comminare illi de pluribus] conferre illi de pluribus 2 committere illi de plurimis 5 committere cum illo 4 committere cum illo de multis 17 os eius opprimere de multis A | **54** quaerentes] insidiantes et quaerentes A add. de multis 4 | occansionem aliquam inuenire ab illo] occasionem aliquam accipere eius 5 capere aliquid ex ore eius A occansionem (occasionem 17) aliquam inuenire de illo (in illo 17 om. 2) cet. | ut accusarent eum] ut inuenirent accusare eum 5 ut eum accusarent cet. | **12:1** Multa autem turba] cum multa autem turba 2 multis autem turbis cet. | se continentium] circumdedissit 2 adstantium 5 circumstantibus cet. | in t] eum undique 2 circa 5 om. cet. | ita] om. 2 5 alius alium se conculcarent] inuicem se conculcarent 2 alterutros esuffocarent 5 se inuicem conculcarent cet. | coepit] ita coepit 4 | discentes] discipulos 5 17 discipulos suos cet. primum] 5 17 primo 2 om. 4 A | cauete] adtendite uobis 2 attendite uobis 5 attendite uobis 4 attendite 17 A pharisaeorum] om. 2 | quod] 17 A quid 5* quae cet. | adfectatio] fictio pharisaeorum 2 hypocrisis cet. | **2** enim] 5 autem cet. | opertum] tectum 2 coopertum 5 | reuelabitur] 5 retegatur 2 reueletur cet. | et] 2 5 neque cet. | occultum] 4 absconsum 5 absconditum cet. | cognoscatur] 2 scietur 5 sciatur cet. | **3** quae] propter quod quaecumque 2 uerum quae 5 quoniam quae cet. dixeritis] locuti estis 2

luce [...]rae t[...]tur. et quod ad aurem locuti fueritis in cubiculis, praedicabitur supra tecta. **4** dico uobis quasi amicis: nolite terreri ab his, qui occidunt et post haec non habent amplius, quod faciant. **5** Demonstrabo autem uobis, quem timeatis, eum, qui postquam occiderit, habet potestatem mittendi in gehennam. dico uobis: hunc timete. **6** Nonne quinque passeres depondio ueniunt? et unus eorum non est in obliuione in conspectu domini. **7** sed et capilli capitis uestri omnes numerati sunt. nolite timere. multo uos passeribus differtis. **8** Dico uobis: omnis, quicumque confessus fuerit me coram hominibus, et filius hominis confitebitur eum coram angelis dei. **9** qui autem negauerit me coram hominibus, abnegabitur coram angelis dei. **10** et omnis, qui dixerit uerbum in filium hominis, remittetur illi. qui autem blasphemauerit spiritum sanctum, non remittetur illi. **11** Cum autem adducent uos ad synagogas et principes et potestates, nolite solliciti

luce] 2 17 lumine cet. | ad] 5 in cet. | aurem] 5 A aure cet. | locuti fueritis] dixistis 5 locuti estis cet. | in cubiculis] A in promptuariis 2 in promptalibus 5 in cellaris 17 om. 4 | supra] in A super cet. | tecta] tectis A | **4** dico] dico autem cet. | quasi amicis] amicis meis cet. add. uidete 4 nolite terreri] noli metuere 2* nolite metuere 2ᶜ non timere 5 ne terreamini cet. | his] eis 2 17 occidunt] occidunt corpus cet. | et post haec non habent amplius quod faciant] 4 A et postea non habet amplius aliquid facere 2 animam autem non possunt occidere nequa habentium amplius quid facere 5 et post haec amplius non habent quod faciant 17 | **5** Demonstrabo] ostendam cet. timeatis] metuatis 2 | eum] metuite eum 2 timete eum cet. om. 5 | qui] quem 5 | postquam] posteaquam 2 post 5 | occiderit] 5 A occidit cet. | habet] habentem 5 | mittendi in gehennam] in gehenam mittere 5 mittere in gehennam cet. | dico] etiam dico 5 4 ita dico cet. | **6** quinque] duo 4 | passeres] passares 5 | depondio ueniunt] ueniunt dipundio 2 ueniunt dipundis duobus 5 asse ueniunt 4 ueniunt dipundio 17 ueniunt depundio A | unus] unum 5 4 | eorum] ex eis 5 ex illis cet. | est in obliuione in conspectu domini] est in oblibione in conspectu domini 2 est oblitum in conspectu dei 5 cadit sine uoluntate dei 4 in obliuione coram domino (deo A) cet. | **7** capitis] om. 5 17 | omnes] omnes de capite 5 | numerati] numeratae 5 | nolite timere] nolite itaque timere 2 ne ergo timueritis 5 nolite ergo timere A | multo uos passeribus] multis (add. enim 5) passeribus cet. | differtis] differitis 5 pluris (plures 2 4 A) estis (add. uos 2) cet. | **8** Dico uobis] dico autem uobis 2 5 A | omnis] 8 A omnes 2 4 quia omnes 5 om. 17 | quicumque] qui 2 5 confessus fuerit me] 8 me confessus fuerit 2 4 confessus fuerit in me cet. | coram hominibus] in conspectu hominum 5 | eum] 4 illum 2 in eo 5 in illo cet. | coram angelis dei] in conspectu angelorum dei 5 cum angelis dei 8 | **9** qui autem negauerit me] om. 2 | coram hominibus] in conspectu hominum 5 om. 2 | abnegabitur] 5 negabo et ego eum 4 denegabitur et ipse 8 negabitur ipse 17 denegabitur A om. 2 | coram angelis dei] in conspectu angelorum dei 5 coram patre meo qui est in caelis 4 | **10** omnis] omnes 2 4 | dixerit] 2 5 dicit cet. | uerbum] sermonem 2 remittetur¹] remittitur 2 dimittetur 5 | illi¹] ei 4 illis 17 | qui autem blasphemauerit spiritum sanctum] qui autem dixerit in spiritu sancto 2 in spiritum autem sanctum 5 qui autem in spiritu sancto dixerit 4 in spiritu autem sancto qui dixerit 8 17 ei autem qui in spiritum sanctum blasphemauerit A | non] tunc non 2 | remittetur²] remittitur 2 demittetur 5 | illi²] 2 5 ei 4 17 eis 8 om. A add. neque in isto saeculo neque in futuro 2 neque in saeculo hoc neque in futuro 5 | **11** adducent] 5 ducent 4 inducent cet. | ad synagogas] in synagogis (synagogas 2 4) cet. om. 17 | principes] principatus 5 ad magistratus cet. | et²] om. 5 | potestates] ad potestates 2 5

esse, quomodo rationem reddatis aut quid dicatis. **12** sanctus enim spiritus docebit uos eadem hora, quae oporteat dicere. **13** dixit autem illi quidam de turba: magister, dic fratri meo, ut partiatur mecum hereditatem. **14** qui dixit ei: homo, quis [...] **15** cauete ab omni auaritia, quia non in super{r}ando alicui uita ipsius est de facultate sua. **16** dixit autem parabolam ad illos dicens: Hominis cuiusdam diuitis uberes fructus attulit ager. **17** et recogitabat intra se dicens: quid faciam, quod non habeo, ubi congeram fructus meos? **18** et cogitans dixit: hoc faciam: deponam horrea et maiora aedificabo. et ibi congeram omnes fructus meos. **19** et dicam animae meae: habes multa bona aepulare. **20** dixit autem illi deus: stulte, hac nocte animam tuam reposcunt a te. quae ergo parasti, cuius erint? **21** *omissum* **22** Dixit autem ad discipulos suos: propterea uobis dico: nolite solliciti esse de anima uestra, quid edatis, neque de corpore uestro, quid induamini. **23** anima pluris est quam esca, et corpus plus quam uestitus. **24** Considerate coruos, quia [...] **25**

---

quomodo] 2 5 qualiter cet. add. aut quid A | rationem reddatis] excusetis 2 respondeatis cet. quid] 5 A om. cet. | dicatis] loquamini 2 dicetis 5 | **12** sanctus enim spiritus] spiritus enim sanctus cet. | docebit] docet 2 | eadem hora] in ipsa (illa 8) hora cet. | quae] quid 8 | oporteat] oportet 5 | **13** dixit autem illi quidam] 2 dixit autem quidam ad illum 5 et ait quidam 4 8 17 ait autem ei quidam A | ut partiatur] partiri 5 ut diuidat cet. | **14** qui dixit] ille autem dixit 2 et ille (iesus 8) dixit cet. | ei] illi 2 5 | homo] homo quis es 2 o homo 4 | quis] quis enim 2 **15** cauete] obserbate 5 | auaritia] cupiditate 2 5 | quia] quoniam 5 | superrando] omni abundantiam 8 abundatia cet. | alicui] 2 cuiquam 5 cuiusquam cet. | uita ipsius est] 2 est uita 5 uita (uitae 8) eius est cet. | de facultate sua] de substantia eius 5 ex his quae possidet (habet 2) cet. **16** parabolam ad illos] ad eos parabolam 5 similitudinem ad illos cet. | attulit ager] adtulit possessio 2 attulit regio 5 attulit possessio 4 8 possessio attulit 17 ager attulit A | **17** recogitabat] cogitabat 5 A cogitauit cet. | intra] apud 2 | quod] quoniam 2 5 | habeo] habeam 17 | ubi] 5 17 quo cet. | congeram] colligam 2 non congregem 8 congregrem cet. | fructus] fructos 5 4 meos] meus 2 8 | **18** cogitans] om. cet. | deponam] 5 destruam cet. | horrea] 17 aphotecas meas 2 apothecas 5 horrea mea 4 A horream 8 | maiora aedificabo] faciam illas maiores 2 faciam eas maiores 5 maiora faciam cet. | ibi] illuc 4 8 A | congeram] colligam 2 congregabo cet. omnes fructus meos] omnis fructus meus 2 omnes fructos meos 5 omnia quae nata sunt mihi cet. add. et bona mea A | **19** animae] anime 8* | habes] anima habes 5 A | bona] mala 8* bona posita A | aepulare] 5 4 iucundare 2 epulare in annos multos 8 in annos multos aepulare 17 in annos plurimos requiesce comede bibe epulare A | **20** hac] ac 5 | animam tuam reposcunt a te] anima tua auferetur a te 2 petunt animam tuam a te 5 animam tuam repetunt a te 4 A repetunt animam tuam a te 8 repetunt a te animam tuam 17 | ergo] autem 4 8 A | cuius] cui 8 17 | erint] erunt cet. | **22** Dixit autem] et dixit 8 dixitque 17 A | discipulos] discentes 2 | suos] om. 2 propterea] 4 propter hoc 2 5 ideo 8 A om. 17 | uobis dico] 2 4 dico uobis 5 8 A om. 17 | de anima uestra] animae uestrae 2 animae cet. | edatis] 5 manducetis cet. | de corpore uestro] corpori cet. | induamini] 5 4 induatis 17 uestiamini cet. | **23** anima] anima enim 2 5 4 | pluris] plus cet. quam esca] cibo 2 | corpus] corbus 2 | plus quam] 4 8 quam cet. om. 5 | uestitus] uestimento 5 uestimentum cet. | **24** Considerate] aspicite 2 intuemini 5 | coruos] uolatia caeli 2 5 | quia] quoniam 5

adicere staturae suae cubitum unum? **26** et de ceteris, quid solliciti estis? **27** considerate lilia agri, quomodo non texunt neque neunt. dico uobis: nec solomon in omni gloria amictus erat tanquam unum ex istis. **28** quod si faenum [...] hodie [...] uestit, quanto magis uos paruae fidei? **29** et uos nolite quaerere, quid edatis aut quid bibatis, nolite solliciti esse. **30** haec enim omnia gentes saeculi quaerunt. scit enim pater uester, quia haec omnia opus sunt uobis. **31** quaerite autem regnum eius et haec adicientur uobis. **32** nolite timere, minima grex, quoniam placuit patri uestro dare uobis regnum. **33** uendite bona uestra et date elemosynam. facite uobis sacculos, qui non ueterescunt, thensaurum non deficientem in caelis, ubi fur non accedit nec tinea consumit. **34** ubi enim fuerit thensaurus uester, ibi erit et cor uestrum. **35** Et sint lumbi uestri succincti et

---

25 staturae suae] ad statum aetatis suae 2 in aetatem suam 5 ad staturam suam (statum suum 4) cet. | cubitum] gubitum 2 5 4 | unum] om. 5 8 17 | **26** et de ceteris quid solliciti estis] et de ceteris cogitatis 2 et de ceteris utquid 5 solliciti estis 4 si ergo neque quod minimum est potestis quid de ceteris solliciti estis A | **27** considerate] aspicite 2 intuemini 5 | agri] om. 5 8 A quomodo] om. 17 | non texunt neque neunt] crescunt et florescunt neque laborant neque neunt 2 neque neunt neque texunt 5 crescunt non laborant neque neunt neque texunt 4 crescunt non laborant non neunt neque texunt 8 non crescunt non laborant neque neunt neque texunt 17 crescunt non laborant non neunt A | dico uobis] 8 17 dico autem uobis cet. | nec] A quoniam (quia 2) nec (neque 5) cet. | solomon] salomon 4 17 A | gloria] illa gloria 4 gloria sua cet. amictus erat] ita amictus est 2 indutus est 5 uestiebatur 4 A sic uestiebatut 8 17 | tanquam] quomodo 2 sicut cet. | unum] unus 2 4 | istis] his 5 | **28** quod si] si enim 2 si autem 5 17 A aut uidete 4 si ergo 8 | faenum] faenum agri 2 5 | paruae] modice 2 pusillae 5 A modicae 4 17 minime 8 | **29** edatis] manducetis cet. | aut] et 2 | bibatis] bibetis 5 | nolite solliciti esse] 8 17 et solliciti estis 2 et non abalienetis uos 5 et nolite solliciti esse 4 et nolite in sublime tolli A **30** omnia[1]] om. 4 8 17 | saeculi] huis (om. 5 A) mundi (modi 4) cet. | quaerunt] faciunt 2 inquirunt 8 | scit enim pater uester] 2 5 pater autem uester scit A scit autem pater uester cet. | quia] 2 quoniam cet. | haec omnia opus sunt uobis] necessaria sunt uobis ista 2 opus habetis horum 5 horum omnium indigetis 4 his indigetis cet. | **31** quaerite autem] uerum quaerite 2 quaerit autem 5 uerumtamen quaerite (add. primum 17) cet. | eius] dei cet. | haec] haec omnia cet. **32** timere] metuere 2 | minima grex] pusillum gregem 2 5 17 pusillus grex 4 8 A | quoniam] 5 quia cet. om. 2 | placuit] in quo bene sensit 2 in eo beneplacitum est 5 complacuit cet. | patri uestro] pater uester 2 | **33** uendite bona uestra] res uestras uendite 2 uendite substantiam uestram 5 uendite quae possidetis cet. | et] om. 17 | elemosynam] elemosinam 2 | facite] et facite 4 | sacculos] saccellus 2 sacculum 8 | qui non ueterescunt] 8 A non ueterescentes 2 5 qui non ueterescant 4 qui non ueterescent 17 | thensaurum] thesaurum A | non deficientem] indeficientem 4 | ubi] 2 5 quo cet. | accedit] 2 5 adpropiat (appropiat A) cet. | nec] 5 neque cet. consumit] corrumpit cet. add. et ubi fures non effodiunt et furantur 4 | **34** ubi enim] nam ubi 4 8 | fuerit thensaurus uester] fuerit thensaurus tuus 2 est thensaurus uester 5 8 thensaurus uester est 4 17 thesaurus uester est A | ibi] illic 2 | erit et cor uestrum] erit et cor tuum 2 et cor uestrum erit 17 A | **35** Et sint] sit 5 sint autem (om. A) cet. | lumbi uestri] lumbus uester 5 succincti] praecinti 2* cinctus 5 adcincti 8 praecincti cet.

lucernae ardentes. **36** et uos similes hominibus expectantibus dominum suum, quando reuertatur a nuptiis et, cum uenerit et pulsauerit, confestim aperiant illi. **37** Beati serui illi, quos, cum uenerit dominus, inuenerit uigilantes. amen dico uobis, quoniam succinget se et discumbere faciet illos et transiens [...] **38–59** *deest*

13 Uenerunt autem quidam eodem tempore nuntiantes ei de galilaeis, quorum sanguinem pilatus miscuit cum uictimis suis. **2** et respondens dixit illis: putatis, quoniam isti galilaei prae omnibus galilaeis fuerunt peccatores, quoniam perpessi sunt talia? **3** non, dico uobis: nisi paenitentiam egeritis, omnes similiter perietis. **4** sicut et illi decem et octo, super quos cecidit turris in siloa et occidit eos, putatis, quia ipsi debitores fuerunt prae omnibus hominibus inhabitantibus in hierusalem? **5** Non, dico uobis, sed nisi paenitentiam egeritis, omnes similiter perietis. **6** dicebat autem parabolam illis: Arborem ficus habebat quidam

---

ardentes] ardentis in manibus uestris 8 | **36** similes] similis 2 5 8 | expectantibus] 2 exspectantibus cet. | reuertatur] 4 A uenit 2 ueniet 5 reuertetur 8 reuertitur 17 | a nuptiis] ad nuptias 2 a nuptias 5 | et[2]] 2 ut cet. | cum uenerit et pulsauerit] uenienti et pulsanti 5 | confestim] om. 2 aperiant] aperiatis 8 | illi] 2 5 ei cet. | **37** cum uenerit] adueniens 2 ueniens 5 | inuenerit] inueniet 5 | quoniam] 2 quia 5 quod cet. | succinget] 2 5 praecinget cet. | se] uos 17 | discumbere faciet illos] recumbere eos faciet 2 reclinauit eos 5 iubet illos discumbere 4 17 iubebit illos discumbere 8 faciet illos discumbere A | transiens] 5 A transiet et cet. | **13:1** Uenerunt] aduenerunt 2 aderant A | quidam eodem tempore] 5 quidam illo tempore 2 in ipso tempore quidam 8 quidam ipso in tempore cet. | nuntiantes] adnuntiantes 2 5 | ei] 5 inde illi 17 illi cet. | sanguinem] sanguem 2 | pilatus miscuit] pilatus commiscuit 2 miscuit pilatus 17 | uictimis suis] sacrificiis eorum (ipsorum 2) cet. | **2** respondens] respondens iesus 5 8 | illis] eis 5 | quoniam[1]] quia 2 5 quod cet. om. 4 | isti] 2 5 hii 4* hi cet. | prae] super 2 | omnibus galilaeis] omnes galilaeos 2 5 | fuerunt peccatores] peccatores fuerunt A | quoniam[2]] 2 5 qui 4 17 quia 8 A perpessi sunt talia] passi sunt haec 2 talia (haec 5) passi sunt cet. | **3** dico uobis] dico autem uobis 2 | nisi] sed si non 5 sed nisi A | egeritis] 2 5 habueritis cet. | omnes similiter perietis] omnes sic perietis 2 similiter peribis 8 similiter omnes peribitis cet. | **4** sicut] aut 2 5 | et[1]] 8 om. cet. | decem et octo] xuiii milia 2 xuiii 4 8 | super] supra 8 17 A | cecidit] caecidit 2 | turris] turres 2 8 | siloa] 4 siloam cet. | putatis] speratis 4 | quia] quoniam 5 4 quod 8 | ipsi] 4 et ipsi 17 A soli ipsi 8 om. 2 5 | prae] 5 super 2 4 praeter cet. | omnibus hominibus inhabitantibus] omnes homines qui habitant 2 omnes homines qui inhabitant 5 omnes homines qui sedebant 4 omnes homines habitantes 8 17 A | in[2]] om. 2 5 17 | hierusalem] iherusalem 8 | **5** dico uobis] dico enim uobis 2 dico autem uobis 5 | sed] 4 A quod 5 om. cet. | nisi] 2 sin 5 si non cet. paenitentiam egeritis] 2 A penitueritis 5 8 credideritis 4 potueritis 17 | omnes similiter perietis] omnes sic peritis 2 omnis similier peribitis 5 omnes homines peribitis 4 similiter peribitis 8 similiter perietis 17 omnes similiter peribitis A | **6** parabolam] istam similitudinem 2 hanc parabolam 5 hanc similitudinem cet. | illis] om. cet. | Arborem ficus] arborem fici 2 A ficulneam 5 habebat quidam] A quidam habuit 2 quidam habebat 5 habuit quidam cet.

plantatam in uinea sua et uenit quaerens fructum in ea et non inuenit. **7** dixit autem ad cultorem uineae: ecce triennium est, ex quo uenio quaerens fructum in ficu hac et non inuenio. excide ergo illam, ut quod et terram occupet? **8** Qui [...] dixit: domine, sine eam et hunc annum, donec fodiam circa illam et mittam cophinum stercoris, **9** et si quidem fecerit fructum, ceteroquin in futurum excides. **10** Erat autem docens in synagoga sabbatis. **11** et ecce mulier, quae spiritum habuit languoris [...]rum **12** quam cum uidisset iesus, uocauit eam et dixit ei: mulier, absoluta es ab infirmitate tua. **13** et inposuit illi manus, et subito erecta est et honorificabat deum. **14** respondens autem archisynagogus indignans dicebat turbae, quod sabbato curaret iesus: sex dies sunt, in quibus oportet operari, in his ergo uenientes curamini et non die sabbati. **15** Respondens autem ad illum dominum dixit: hypocritae, unusquisque uestrum sabbato non soluet bouem suum aut asinum a praesepio et ducit et adaquat? **16** hanc autem, cum sit filia

---

plantatam] nouellatam 2 | uinea sua] 5 A uineam suam (om. 4) cet. | quaerens fructum] quarens fructum 2 fructum quaerens 8 17 | ea] 5 illa 2 4 A illam 8 17 | non inuenit] cum non inuenisset 2 non inueniens 5 | **7** autem] om. 2 5 | cultorem uineae] uineae cultorem 5 | triennium est] 2 anni tres sunt (om. 5) cet. | ficu hac] ista arbore fici 2 ficulnea (ficulneam 8 17) hac cet. excide] 2 praecide 5 succide cet. | ergo] om. 2 5 | illam] eam 5 | quod] quid cet. | et²] 5 enim et 2 etiam cet. | terram occupet] terram intricat 2 terram occupat 5 A terram euacuat 4 8 detinet terram 17 | **8** Qui] ille autem 2 at ille cet. | dixit] 8 ait illi 4 dixit illi cet. | sine] 2 dimitte 5 A remitte 4 8 remittam 17 | eam] illam cet. | et hunc annum] adhuc hunc annum 5 et hoc anno cet. | donec] quoadusque 2 usque dum (quo 4) cet. | fodiam circa illam] circumfodiam eam 2 cophinum] 4 8 qualum 5 cofinum 17 om. 2 A | stercoris] stercus 2 stercora A | **9** quidem] om. 2 ceteroquin] si quominus 2 5 sin autem cet. | futurum] futuro 2 | excides] excidetur 2 euellis eam 5 succides eam (illam 4) cet. | **10** synagoga] 17 synagogis 2* una ex synagogis 2ᶜ una de synagogis 5 una synagogarum 4 8 synagoga eorum A | sabbatis] sabbato 5 17 | **11** quae spiritum habuit languoris] erat spiritum habens infirmitatis 2 in infirmitate erat spiritus 5 quae habebat spiritum (spiritus 17) infirmitatis cet. | **12** quam cum uidisset] A cum uidisset autem illam 2 uidens autem eam 5 quam cum uideret cet. | iesus] om. 4 17 | uocauit eam et] uocauit eam ad se et 4 8 uocauit ad se et 17 A om. 2 5 | dixit] 2 5 ait cet. | ei] illi cet. om. 2 | absoluta] liberata 2 dimissa cet. | es] est 8 | ab] ex 17 | **13** inposuit] cum inposuisset 2 imposuit cet. | illi manus] manus ei 5 illi manum 4 8 | et²] om. 2 | subito] continuo 2 confestim cet. | honorificabat] 5 clarificabat 2 glorificabat A magnificabant cet. | deum] dominum 2 | **14** dicebat turbae] dicebat ad populum 2 dicebat populo 5 om. cet. | quod] quia 2 5 A | curaret] curauit 5 curasset A add. (et 17) dicebat turbae 4 8 17 A | operari] curari 5 | ergo] igitur 2 | uenientes] 5 uenite et (om. 8) cet. | die sabbati] 2 4 die sabbat 5 in die sabbati cet. | **15** Respondens] respondit 5 4 A | ad illum] ad illam 2* ad illos 2ᶜ ei 5 | dominum] dominus cet. | dixit] et dixit 5 4 A | hypocritae] hypocrite 2 hypocrita 5 | unusquisque] unusunusquisque 2 | sabbato] die sabbati 5 | soluet] soluit 4 8 A | bouem] uobem 2 | praesepio] praesepe 17 | ducit et adaquat] 2 ducens adquat 5 ducit adaquare cet. | **16** cum sit filia] 2 filiam cet.

abrahae, quam alligauit satanas ecce xuiii anni, non oportebat solui a uinculo hoc die sabbati? **17** Haec dicente eo confundebantur omnes, qui aduersabantur ei, et omnis populus gaudebat in omnibus mirificis, quae fiebant ab illo. **18** Dicebat ergo: cui simile est regnum dei et cui adsimilabo illud? **19** simile est grano sinapis, quod accepto homo misit in orto suo, et creuit et facta est arbor, et uolucres caeli requieuerunt in ramis eius. **20** et iterum dixit: cui est simile regnum dei et cui adsimilabo? **21** simile est fermento, quod acceptum Mulier abscondit in farina, donec fermentaretur. **22** Et circuibat per ciuitates et uicos docens hierosolymis. **23** Dixit autem quidam illi: domine, si pauci sunt, qui salui futuri sunt? Qui dixit ad illos: **24** intrate per angustum ostium, quoniam multi, dico uobis, quaerent nec poterint introire. **25** cum autem intrauerit pater familias et adcluserit ostium, et

abrahae] habrahae 2 add. cum esset d | quam] qua 4 | alligauit] A alligauerat 2 8c ligauit 5 17 adligauerat 8* | ecce] om. 2 | xuiii anni] annis xuiii 2 anni xuiii 5 x et uiii annis 4 decem et octos annos 8 xuiii annos 17 decem et octo annis A | oportebat] 5 oportuit cet. | hoc] 5 isto 8 17 A om. 2 4 | **17** Haec dicente eo] et 2 5 et cum haec diceret cet. | confundebantur] 5 confusi sunt 2 erubescebant cet. | omnes] A om. cet. | qui aduersabantur ei] qui ei aduersabantur 2 aduersarii eius cet. | omnis] omnes 4 | omnibus] 2 5 uniuersis A om. cet. | mirificis] praeclaris 4 8 17 om. cet. | quae fiebant ab illo] quae uidebant praeclara fieri ab illo 2 quibus uidebant mirabilibus ab eo fieri 5 quae gloriose fiebant ab eo A quae uiderant fieri ab ipso cet. | **18** cui simile est regnum dei] cui similis est regnum dei 8 om. 17 | et cui adsimilabo illud] 2 et similabo illud 5 et simile illud esse existimabo 4 et simile illud estimabo 8 simile illud existimabo 17 et simile esse existimabo illud A | **19** quod] quo 5 | accepto] 5 cum accepisset 2 acceptum cet. | orto suo] hortum suum cet. | facta] factum 2 A | arbor] in arborem 2 in arborem magnam A | et[3]] ita ut 4 uolucres] uolatilia 2 5 | requieuerunt] habitabant 2 habitauerunt 5 requiescerent 4 | in[2]] sub 5 subtus 17 | ramis] ramos 5 | eius] om. 17 | **20** et iterum dixit] et iterum dixit illis 2 om. 5 | cui est simile] cui adsimilabo 2 aut cui simile est 5 cui simile aestimabo (aestimabitur 8) cet. | et cui adsimilabo] et cui similabo illut 5 om. cet. | **21** acceptum] cum accepit 2 accipiens 5 | farina] farinae mensuras 2 farinae mensuras tris 5 farinae sata tria A farinam cet. | donec] quousque 2 usque quo 5 | fermentaretur] A fermentetur totum 2 fermentatum est totum cet. | **22** circuibat] 5 perambulabat 2 ibat cet. add. iesus 8 | uicos] castella cet. | hierosolymis] et iter faciens in (om. 17) hierusalem (iherusalem 8) cet. | **23** Dixit autem quidam illi] 2 dixit autem ei quidam 5 ait autem illi quidam A et ait illi quidam cet. | si] om. 2 8 | qui salui futuri sunt] saluentur 2 qui saluantur 5 A qui salui fiunt 17c qui salui fiant cet. | Qui dixit] ille autem dixit 2 ad ille respondens dixit 5 ipse autem dixit cet. | ad illos] illis 2 ad eos 17 om. 5 | **24** intrate] elaborate introire 2 certamini introire 5 contendite intrare cet. | angustum ostium] angustum osteum 2 angustam ianuam 5 angustam portam 4 A angunstum hostium 8 angustium ostium 17 | quoniam] 5 quia cet. | multi dico uobis] 5 A dico uobis multi cet. | quaerent] quaerunt 8 17 A | nec poterint introire] introire et non inuenient 5 intrare (om. 4) et non poterunt cet. | **25** cum autem] ex quo 2 5 4 | intrauerit pater familias] incipiet pater familias surgere 2 pater familias introierit 5 surrexerit pater familias 4 | adcluserit] cludere 2 cluserit cet. | ostium] osteum 2

incipietis foris stare dicentes: domine, aperi nobis. et respondens dicet: nescio uos,
unde sitis. **26** Tunc incipietis dicere: manducauimus coram te et bibimus et in
plataeis nostris docuisti. **27** et dicet uobis: nescio uos, unde sitis. discedite a me
omnes operari iniquitatis. **28** illic erit fletus et {et} stridor dentium. Cum uideritis
abraham et isac et iacob et omnes prophetas dei introeuntes in regno dei, uos
autem proici foris. **29** et uenient ab oriente et occidente et ab aquilone et austro et
discumbent in regno dei. **30** et ecce sunt nouissimi, qui erunt primi, et sunt primi,
qui fuerunt nouissimi. **31** eadem die accesserunt quidam pharisaeorum dicentes
illi: discede et uade hinc, quoniam herodes uult te occidere. **32** ipse autem dixit
eis: euntes indicate uulpi huic: ecce eicio daemonia et sanitates perficio hodie et
cras et die tertia consummor. **33** sed oportet me hodie et cras et in futurum,
quoniam non oportet prophetam perire extra hierusalem. **34** Hierusalem,
hierusalem, quae occidis prophetas et lapidas eos, qui missi sunt at te, saepius
uolui congregare filios tuos quemadmodum gallina nidum suum sub alas suas, et
noluistis. **35** ecce relinquitur uobis domus uestra deserta. dico enim uobis, quia

---

incipietis] incipientis 5 | stare] stare et pulsare ostium (osteum 2 om. 5 4) cet. | domine] 2 A domine domine cet. | respondens] respondes 8 | dicet] 4 17 dicet nobis 2* dicet uobis 2[c] dicet uobis 5 A dicens 8 | nescio] non noui 2 | sitis] estis 5 | **26** manducauimus] domine manducauimus 5 | coram te] in conspectu 2 in conspecto tuo 5 | et[1]] om. 8 | bibimus] uiuimus 8 | **27** et] sed 8 | uobis] dico uobis 5 | nescio uos unde sitis] A numquam uos uidi 2 numquam uidi uos 5 nescio unde estis 4 nescio unde sitis 8 17 | discedite] recedite 5 recide 8 | operari iniquitatis] operarii iniquitatis 4 qui operamini iniquitatem 17 | **28** illic] 2 ibi cet. | fletus] fletus oculorum 2 ploratus 5 | abraham] habraham 2 | isac] isaac A | prophetas] profetas 2 8 | dei[1]] om. cet. introeuntes] om. 2 5 A | regno] regnum 8 | proici] excludimini 2 eici 5 expelli cet. | foris] foras cet. | **29** occidente] occidentem 5 8 | ab[2]] 5 om. cet. | discumbent] accumbent A recumbent cet. | **30** erunt] erant 2 | fuerunt] erant 2 erunt cet. | **31** eadem] in ipsa cet. add. autem 4 die] hora 5 | accesserunt] accesserunt ad eum 2 accesserunt illi 5 | pharisaeorum] ex pharisaeis 2 om. 17 | illi] om. 5 | discede] exi cet. | et] om. 8 | quoniam] quia cet. | uult] quaeret 5 **32** ipse autem dixit eis] ille autem dixit eis 2 et dixit illis 5 et ait illis iesus 4 et ait illis cet. euntes] abeuntes 5 ite cet. | indicate] et dicite 2 17 dicite cet. | huic] 2 5 illi cet. | eicio] expello 2 sanitates] curas 2 | die tertia consummor] tertio die consummabor 2 tertia (sequenti 8 17) die (om. 5 A) consummor (perficior 5 consummabor 8) cet. | **33** sed] uerumtamen 2 5 A | oportet me hodie et cras et in futurum] oportet me hodie et crastino sequenti abire 2 oportet me hodie et cras et uentura abire 5 abite 4 ite 8 oportet me hodie et cras et sequenti ambulare A om. 17 quoniam] 2 quia cet. | oportet[2]] 5 4 est possibile 2 capit cet. | prophetam perire] propheta perire 2 perire prophetam 5 | hierusalem] iherusalem 8 | **34** occidis] interfices 2 | prophetas] profetas 2 | eos] om. 2 5 | qui missi sunt at te] missus ad te 2 missos ad te 5 qui ad te mittuntur 4 17 qui mittuntur ad te 8 A | saepius] saepe 8 17 quotiens cet. | quemadmodum] quomodo 2 gallina] gallinas 8 auis A | nidum suum] 4 A pullos suos cet. | alas] pinnis 4 A | suas] om. 4 8 A noluistis] noluisti 4 17 A | **35** relinquitur] A remittetur 2 dimittetur 5 relinquetur cet. | uestra] uos 5 | deserta] om. 8 17 A | enim] 2 autem 5 A | quia] A om. cet.

non uidebitis me, donec ueniat dies, quando dicatis benedictus, qui uenit in nomine domini.

14 Et factum est, cum intrasset in domum cuiusdam principis pharisaeorum sabbato manducare panem, et ibi erant obseruantes illum. **2** Et ecce homo quidam hydropicus erat ante illum, **3** et respondens dixit iesus ad legis doctores et pharisaeos: si licet sabbatis curare? **4** ad illi tacuerunt. ipse itaque adprehendens manum illius curatum eum dimisit. **5** et dixit ad illos: cuius uestrum asinus aut bos, si ceciderit in puteum sabbato, non continuo extrahet illum in die sabbati? **6** et non poterant ei respondere ad haec. **7** Dicebat autem et ad inuitatos parabolam, denotans eos, quomodo primos discubitos eligerent, dicens ad eos: **8** Cum inuitatus fuerit aliquis ad nuptias, non discumbat in primo loco, ne forte honoratior te aliquis sit inuitatus **9** et ueniens, qui te et illum inuitauit, dicat tibi:

---

uidebitis me] me uidebitis 2 5 4 | donec] quoadusque 2 | ueniat dies quando] ueniat ut 5 ueniat dies cum 4 uenia cum 8 ueniat cum A om. 2 17 | dicatis] dicetis 4 8 A | **14:1** factum] factus 5 cum] ut 4 8 17 | intrasset] introiret ipse 2 introiret 5 intraret cet. | principis] ex principibus 2 principum 5 | sabbato] in sabbato 2 | manducare] ad edendum 2 | panem] manem 5 | ibi] ipsi cet. | erant obseruantes] 2 5 obseruabant cet. | illum] eum cet. | **2** quidam] 2 A om. cet. hydropicus erat] erat hydropicus 5 | ante illum] apud ipsum 2 in conspectu eius 5 | **3** dixit iesus] 8 17 dominus dixit 2 iesus dixit (om. 4) cet. | doctores] 2 5 peritos cet. | et pharisaeos] 5 4 et pharisaeos dicens cet. om. 2 | si] om. 5 | sabbatis] sabbato cet. | curare] curare aut non 2 5 4 **4** ad illi] illi autem 2 at illi cet. | ipse itaque] ille autem 2 et 5 ipse uero cet. | adprehendens] 5 adpraehendit 2 adprehensum cet. | manum illius] illum 2 eum cet. om. A | curatum] et curauit 2 et sanans 5 sanauit cet. | eum dimisit] et dimisit 2 dimisit 5 ac dimisit illum (om. 4 A) cet. **5** et] et respondens A | dixit ad illos] dixit ad eos 5 ad illos dixit A | uestrum] ex uobis 5 asinus] filius 2 ouis 5 | bos] bus 2 bobis 5 | si] 2 om. cet. | ceciderit in puteum] in puteum (puteo 8) cadit (caeciderit 2 incidet 5 cadens 4 cadet A) cet. | sabbato] die sabbati 2 5 om. cet. non] 2 et non cet. | continuo] confestim 5 | extrahet] 17 A extrah 2* leuabit 5 extrahit cet. illum] eum 5 | in die sabbati] 2 die sabbati cet. om. 5 17 | **6** et non poterant ei respondere ad haec] illi autem nihil potuerunt respondere ad ista 2 ad illi non responderunt ad haec 5 et non poterant ad haec respondere illi cet. | **7** Dicebat] dicebant 8 | et] 8 A om. cet. | ad inuitatos] ad eos qui inuitati fuerant 2 | parabolam] similitudinem 2 om. 4 | denotans eos] notans sibi 2 uidens 5 intendens cet. | primos discubitos] primum locum 2 primus dicubitos 8 primos accubitus (accubitos 5 recubitos 4) cet. | eligerent] A eligebant cet. | dicens ad eos] 5 dicens (et dicebat 17) ad illos cet. om. 2 | **8** inuitatus fuerit aliquis] inuitati fueritis 2 inuitaris 5 inuitatus (add. quis 8) fueris (fuerit 8 17) cet. add. ab aliquo 4 | ad nuptias] in nuptias 5 om. 4 | non discumbat] 17 nolite recumbere 2 noli recumbere 5 noli discumbere 4 non discunbat 8 non dicumbas A | primo loco] locum primum 2 primum adcubitum 5 primo in loco 8 | honoratior] honorificentior 5 | te aliquis sit inuitatus] sit uobis inuitatus illo 2 te ueniet 5 te sit inuitatus ab eo A te sit uocatus cet. **9** ueniens] 5 A adcedens 8 ueniat cet. | qui] is qui A | te] uos 2 | inuitauit] 2 5 uocauit cet. om. 17 | dicat] dicet 5 et (om. 8 A) dicat cet.

da huic locum. et tunc incipies cum confusione nobissimum locum detinere. **10**
Sed cum inuitatus fueris, uade et discumbe in nouissimo loco, ut cum uenerit, qui
te inuitauit, dicat: amice, accede superius. tunc erit gloria tibi coram
discumbentibus, **11** quoniam omnis, qui exaltat se, humiliabitur, et qui se
humiliaberit, exaltabitur. **12** Dicebat autem et inuitatori: cum facies prandium et
cenam, noli inuitare amicos neque fratres tuos, sed nec uicinos nec diuites, ne
forte et ipsi te inuitent, et fiat redditio tibi. **13** Sed cum facies prandium, inuita
pauperes, debiles, clodos et caecos. **14** et beatus eris, quia non habent unde
reddere tibi. reddetur enim tibi in resurrectione iustorum. **15** Audiens autem
quidam ex discumbentibus haec dixit illi: beatus, qui manducauerit panem in
regno dei. **16** qui dixit: Homo quidam fecit cenam magnam et inuitauit multos. **17**
et misit seruum suum hora cenae dicere inuitatis: uenite, quoniam omnia
praeparata sunt. **18** et coeperunt omnes simul excusare se. prior ait: uillam emi et
necesse habeo exire et uidere illam. rogo te, habe me excusatum. **19** et alius dixit:

---

tunc] om. 4 8 17 | incipies] 4 eris 2 incipiens 5 8 incipias A | confusione] 5 rubore cet. | detinere] tenere cet. | **10** inuitatus fueris] 2 inuitaris 5 uocatus fueris cet. add. in nuptias 2 | uade] om. 5 | et] om. cet. | discumbe in nouissimo loco] in nouissimum locum recumbe 2 5 recumbe in nouissimo loco cet. | qui te] qui te et illum 2 | dicat] 17 dicat tibi cet. | accede] ascende 5 4 A tunc] hoc enim 2 et tunc 5 | gloria tibi] tibi gloria (gloriae 17) cet. | coram discumbentibus] in conspectu qui simul recumbunt 5 cum simul recumbentibus 4 coram simul discumbentibus cet. **11** quoniam] 2 5 quia cet. | omnis] om. 2 | exaltat se humiliabitur] se humiliauerit exaltauitur 2 se exaltat humiliabitur cet. | se humiliaberit exaltabitur] exaltat se humiliabitur 2 se humiliat (humiliat se 5) exaltabitur cet. | **12** inuitatori] qui se inuitauerat 2 ad eum qui inuitauerat eum 5 ei qui se inuitauerat A | facies] 2 facis cet. | et^{2}] aut cet. | inuitare] 2 4 uocare cet. | amicos] 5 amicos tuos cet. | fratres tuos] 5 fratres 4 add. cognatos tuos 8 A cognatos 17 | sed nec] neque cet. | nec^{2}] neque cet. om. A | ne forte] om. 2 | ipsi] illi 2 5 | te inuitent] reinuitent te 2 5 te reinuitent cet. | fiat] 5 A fiet 2 erit cet. | redditio tibi] retributio tibi 2 5 tibi retributio cet. **13** facies] feceris 2 facis cet. | prandium] 2 aepulationem 5 conuiuium cet. | inuita] 2 uoca cet. pauperes] mendicos 2 egenos 5 | clodos et caecos] caecos clodos 2 17 clodos caecos cet. | **14** et beatus eris] ita multa erit merces tua 4* | quia] A quod 4^{c} quoniam cet. om. 4* | unde] om. 2 5 17 | reddere] 4* retribuere cet. | reddetur enim] tamen reddetur 4* retribuetur (restituetur 2) autem (enim 5 A) cet. | resurrectione] resurrectionem 8^{c} | **15** Audiens autem] 5 haec (hic 17) cum audisset cet. | quidam ex discumbentibus haec] quidam ex conrecumbentibus 2 quis haec qui simul recumbebant 5 quidam de simul discumbentibus cet. | dixit] dixerunt 4 | illi] ei 5 om. 17 | manducauerit] 2 manducauit (maducabit 4 8) cet. | **16** qui dixit] et dixit dominus 2 ad ille dixit 5 at ipse dixit ei (om. 4) cet. | inuitauit] 2 uocauit cet. | **17** suum] om. 2 | dicere] ut diceret 4 8 17 | uenite] ut uenirent A | quoniam] 2 5 quia A om. cet. | omnia praeparata sunt] omnia parata sunt 2 iam parata sunt omnia 5 A iam paratum est cet. | **18** et^{1}] om. 2 | omnes simul] 8 singuli 2 ab una omnes 5 simul omnes cet. | excusare se] 4 8 se excusare 5 excusare cet. | prior ait] et primus dixit 2 primus dixit ei A primus dixit cet. | uillam] agrum 5 | necesse] necessem 2 exire et] exiens 5 ire 17 | illam] eum 5 | habe] habeto 5 | **19** alius] 2 5 alter cet.

iuga bouum conparaui paria quinque et uado experimentum accipere illorum et propter hoc uenire non possum. **20** et alius dixit: uxorem duxi et non possum uenire. **21** et reuersus seruus renuntiauit domino suo haec. tunc iratus pater familias dixit seruo suo: exi alacriter in plateas et uicos ciuitatis et pauperes et debiles et caecos et clodos introduc hoc. **22** et ait seruus domino suo: domine, factum est, sicut praecepisti et adhuc locutus est. **23** et dixit dominus seruo suo: exi {exi} circa uias et saepes et coge intrare quoscumque inueneris, ut impleatur domus mea. **24** dico enim uobis, quoniam nullus uirorum illorum, qui uocati sunt et non uenerunt, gustabunt de cena mea. **25** Comitabatur autem cum eo turba, et conuersus dixit ad illos: **26** si quis uenit ad me et non odit patrem suum aut matrem aut uxorem aut filios aut fratres et sorores, insuper et animam suam, non potest meus discipulus esse. **27** et qui non portat crucem suam et uenit post me, non potest discipulus meus esse. **28** Quis ex uestrum uolens turrem aedificare nonne prius sedens computauit inpendia, si habeat, quae opus sunt ad

---

bouum] uoum 2 boum cet. | conparaui] emi cet. | paria] om. cet. | uado] eo cet. | experimentum accipere illorum] probare illa cet. | et propter hoc] propter quod 5 et ideo cet. om. 2 A uenire non possum] habe me excusatum 2 non possum uenire 5 rogo te habe me excusatum A **20** et[2]] propter quod 5 et ideo 8 A | **21** reuersus] uenit 2 adueniens 5 | renuntiauit] et renuntiauit 2 adnuntiauit 5 nuntiauit cet. | domino suo haec] domino suo 2 domino suo omnia haec 5 domino suo 4 haec domino suo cet. | tunc] et 2 5 | dixit seruo suo] seruo suo dixit 5 | alacriter] celerius 5 cito cet. | plateas et uicos] plateis et uicis 4 plateis et in uicis 8 | ciuitatis] ciuitas 17 pauperes] mendicos 2 egenos 5 | et[4]] ac 4 8 A | et[5]] om. 8 | caecos et clodos] clodos et caecos 2 introduc] perduc 2 adduc 5 | hoc] 2 hic 5 huc cet. | **22** ait seruus] seruus dixit 2 5 | domino suo] om. cet. | domine factum est] A factum est 2 5 factum est domine 4 8 | sicut] quod 2 5 ut A praecepisti] 5 iussisti 2 imperasti cet. | locutus] locus 5 A | **23** dixit] 2 5 ait cet. | seruo suo] 4 ad seruum suum 2 ad serbum suum 5 seruo 8 A | circa] in cet. | uias] uia 4 | saepes] in saepes 5 circa saepes 4 8 | coge] compelle 4 A conpellere 8 | intrare] introeuntes 2 introire 5 intrent 4 quoscumque inueneris] om. cet. | domus mea] mihi domus 2 | **24** enim] 2 5 autem cet. quoniam] 2 quia 5 quod cet. | nullus] nemo cet. | uirorum illorum] ex hominibus illis 2 illorum hominorum 5 | qui uocati sunt] inuitatis 2 qui inuitati sunt 5 | et non uenerunt] om. cet. gustabunt] gustauit 2 gustabit 5 A | de cena mea] 2 5 cenam meam cet. | **25** Comitabatur] 2* comitabantur 2[c] ibant cet. | cum eo turba] cum illum turbae 2 turbae multae cum eo A cum illo turbae cet. | ad illos] illis 5 | **26** quis] qui 2 | ad me] om. 8 | odit] odiit 2 | suum] om. 2 aut[1]] et cet. | matrem] matrem suam 5 | aut[2]] et cet. | aut[3]] et cet. | insuper et] adhuc (om. 4) etiam (om. 2 autem A) et (om. 8) cet. | animam suam] suam animam 5 | meus discipulus esse] discens meus esse 2 meus esse discipulus A | **27** qui] si qui 2 | portat] tulerit 2 tollit 8 baiulat cet. | uenit] uenerit 2 | post] retro 5 | discipulus meus esse] meus discipulus esse 5 meus esse discipulus A* esse meus discipulus cet. | **28** Quis] quis autem 2 5 quis enim A | ex uestrum] ex uobis cet. | nonne] non 2 4 A[c] | prius] primo 2 primum 5 | sedens] sedet et 2 sedes 8* | computauit] 4 conputat 2 5 conputauit 8 computat A | inpendia] erogationem 5 sumptus (sumptum 2) cet. | si habeat quae opus sunt] si habet 2 5 qui necessarii sunt si habet cet.

consummandum eam, **29** ne si posito fundamento non ualuerit consummare, omnes, qui uident, **30** dicent: hic homo coepit aedificare nec ualuit consummare. **31** Aut quis rex iturus committere cum alio rege bellum nonne sedens prius cogitauit, si potens est cum decem milibus obuiare ei, qui cum uiginti milibus uenturus est ad illum? **32** alioquin, dum adhuc cum longe est, legationem mittens rogat pacem. **33** sic ergo omnis ex uobis, qui non renuntiat omnibus facultatibus suis, non potest esse meus discipulus. **34** Bonum est sal. quod si et sal infatuatum fuerit, in quo condietur? **35** neque in terra neque in stercore utile est, nisi ut foris proiciatur. Qui habet aures audiendi, audiat.

15 erant autem accedentes ad eum omnes publicani et peccatores audire eum. **2** et murmurati sunt pharisaei et scribae dicentes, quare hic peccatores recipit et uescitur cum eis. **3** Dixit autem ad eos parabolam hanc dicens: **4** Quis ex

---

consummandum] consummationem 2 perfectum 5 perficiendum A | eam] om. cet. | **29** ne si] ne forte cum 2 ut ne forte cum 5 ne posteaquam (postea cum 8) cet. | posito fundamento] posuerit fundamentum cet. | non] 2 5 et non cet. | ualuerit] possit 2 potuerit cet. | consummare] 4 aedificare 2 5 explicare 8 17 perficere A | omnes] et omnes 2 5 | uident] uidebunt 4 8 17 add. incipient 2 5 incipiant inludere ei A | **30** dicent] dicere 2 5 dicentes quia A | nec ualuit] et non potuit cet. | consummare] perficere 2 5 | **31** quis] qui 2 A | iturus] uadens 2 abiens 5 | committere cum alio rege bellum] comittere ali regi ad bellum 2 alio regi comittere in pugnam 5 comittere bellum aduersus alium regem cet. | nonne] non 2 4 A | sedens prius] 8 A primum sedet et 2 continuo sedens primo 5 prius sedens 4 17 | cogitauit] 8 17 computat 2 cogitat 5 A cogitabit 4 | potens est] 2 5 possit A potuerit cet. | cum[2]] in 5 | decem] x 2 4 | milibus[1]] milia militibus 2 militibus 8 | obuiare] occurrere 2 A om. 5 | ei] illi 5 | uiginti] xx 2 5 | milibus[2]] milia militibus 2 militibus 8 | uenturus est] uenit cet. | ad illum] super eum obuiari 5 aduersus se 4 aduersum se 8 17 ad se A om. 2 | **32** alioquin] ceterum 2 si quominus 5 | dum adhuc cum longe est] cum adhuc longe est 2 adhuc eo longe constituto 5 adhuc illo longe agente cet. | legationem mittens] mittet rogationem 2 mittens legatos 5 legationem mittet 4 mittet legationem 8 legationem mittit 17 | rogat pacem] rogat quae ad pacem 5 rogat ea quae pacis sunt A rogans pacem cet. | **33** omnis ex uobis] 2 A et ex uobis omnis 5 ex uobis cet. | renuntiat] abrenuntiat 5 renuntiauerit 17 | omnibus] om. 5 | facultatibus suis] substantiae suae 5 quae possidet cet. esse meus discipulus] meus esse discipulus A meus discipulus esse cet. | **34** quod si] 8 17 sed si 2 4 etsi autem 5 si autem A | et] om. cet. | sal[2]] sal quoque 4 A | infatuatum fuerit] 2 5 euanuerit cet. | condietur] salietur 5 | **35** neque[1]] neque enim 2 | terra] 8 terram cet. | stercore] 2 5 sterculinum A sterculino cet. | utile] aptum 2 | nisi ut] sed cet. om. 5 | foris] 4 8 foras cet. proiciatur] iactant illud 2 mittent illud 5 mittent eum 4 mittetur cet. | habet] habent 4 **15:1** erant] erat 2* | accedentes ad eum] adpropinquantes illi 2 adpropiant ei 5 appropinquantes ei A adpliciti illi cet. | omnes] om. 4 A | audire] 2 5 ut audirent cet. | eum[2]] 2 5 illum cet. **2** murmurati sunt] murmurabant cet. | dicentes] om. 4 8 17 | quare] quia 2 A quoniam 5 quod cet. | recipit] A suscipit 2 adsumit 5 reciperet cet. | uescitur] 2 manducat 5 A manducaret cet. eis] illis cet. | **3** Dixit autem] 2 5 et ait cet. | eos] 2 5 illos cet. add. iesus 8 | parabolam] 5 A similitudinem cet. | hanc] istam 2 A | dicens] om. 2 5 4 | **4** ex uestris homo] hominum ex uobis 2 ex uobis homo cet.

uestris homo, qui habet oues centum, et perierit una ex eis, nonne relinquit xcuiiii in deserto et uadit ad illam, quae perit, quaerens, donec inueniat illam? **5** et cum inuenerit, inponit illam super umeros suos gaudens. **6** Et cum uenerit domum, conuocat amicos et uicinos dicens illis: congratulamini mihi, quoniam inueni ouem meam, quae perierat. 7 Dico uobis, quoniam sic gaudium erit in caelo super unum peccatorem paenitentiam agentem quam super xcuiiii iustos, quibus non est necessaria paenitentia. **8** Aut quae mulier habens drachmas x, et si perdederit unam ex illis, nonne accendit lucernam et scopis commundat domum et quaerit diligenter, quoadusque inueniat? **9** et cum inuenerit, conuocat amicas suas et uicinas dicens: congratulamini mihi, quoniam inueni dracman, quam perdideram. **10** sic, dico uobis, gaudium erit coram angelos dei super unum peccatorem paenitentiam agentem. **11** dixit ergo: homo quidam habebat duos

---

qui habet] habiens 2 | oues centum] 2 centum oues cet. | et perierit una ex eis] et cum perdiderit ex illis unam 2 et perdiderit unum ex eis 5 et si errauerit una ex eis 4 et si errauerit una ex illis 8 et si perdiderit unam ex illis A om. 17 | nonne] non 4 | relinquit] relinquet 2 dismittit 5 dimittet 4 8 dimittit 17 A | xcuiiii] 2 4 nonaginta (add et 8) nouem cet. | deserto] 17 A solitudine 2 desertum 5 4 montibus in deserto 8 | uadit] uadit et quaerit 5 abit 4 ibit 8 17 | ad illam] om. 5 quae] quod 5 | perit] perierat 2 5 A errauit 4 8 17 | quaerens] 2 om. cet. | donec] usquem dum 5 | illam^{2}] 2 A illud 5 eam cet. | **5** cum inuenerit] 2 inueniens 5 cum inuenerit (inueniet 17) eam cet. | inponit] 5 inponet 2 imponet 17 imponit cet. | illam] 2 eam 4 17 om. cet. | super] 5 17 in cet. | gaudens] om. 4 8 17 | **6** Et cum uenerit] 2 ueniens autem 5 et ueniens cet. | domum] in domum 5 | conuocat] conuocans 2 | amicos] amicos suos 2 | illis] eis 5 | congratulamini] gratulamini 2 cumgaudete 5 | mihi] 5 A mecum cet. | quoniam] 2 5 quia cet. | inueni ouem meam] 5 A inuenta est ouis (oues 2) mea cet. | **7** Dico uobis] dico ergo uobis 2 dico autem uobis 5 quoniam] 5 quod cet. om. 2 | sic] 2 5 ita cet. | gaudium erit] erit gaudium 2 | in caelo] ante deum 4* | super^{1}] in 4 8 17 | unum peccatorem] 2 uno peccatore cet. | agentem] 2 8^{c} agenti 5 habenti (habente A) cet. | super^{2}] in 4 8 17 | xcuiiii] 2 4 nonaginta (xc 5 add. et 8) nouem cet. iustos] 2 iustis cet. | quibus non est necessaria paenitentia] quibus non est paenitentia necessaria 2 qui non habent opus paenitentiae 5 qui non indigent paenitentiam (paenitentia A) cet. **8** drachmas] 5 denarios 2 dragmas cet. | x] decem cet. | et^{1}] 2 5 om. cet. | perdederit] perdiderit cet. | unam] unum 2 dragmam unam A | ex illis] om. cet. | nonne] non 2 | accendit] accendet 8 17 | scopis commundat] emundat 2 scopis mundat 5 euertit A mundauit (mundabit 17) cet. | domum] domum suam 8 | quoadusque] usque quo 5 donec cet. | **9** amicas suas et uicinas] amicos et uicinos 2 uicinas et amicas 5 amicas et uicinas cet. | congratulamini] gratulamini 2 congaudete 5 | quoniam] quia 2 5 A quod 4 8 17 | dracman quam perdideram] quem perdideram denarium 2 quam perdideram drachmam 5 dragman 4 draghman 17 dragmam quam perdideram 8 A | **10** sic] 2 5 ita cet. | gaudium] sic gaudium 4 8 17 | erit] erit uobis 17 | coram angelos] in conspectu angelorum 2 5 coram angelus 8 coram angelis cet. | super] in 4 8 17 unum peccatorem] 2 uno (om. 4 17) peccatore (peccatori 5) cet. | paenitentiam] paenitentia 2 5 agentem] 8 agente 2 A agenti 5 4 habente 17 | **11** dixit ergo] dixit autem 2 5 et ait 4 ait autem cet. habebat] 5 habuit cet.

filios. **12** et dixit illi adulescentior: pater, da mihi portionem substantiae, quae me contingit. et diuisit illis sub<s>tantiam. **13** Et non post multos dies collectis omnibus adulescentior filius peregre profectus est in regionem longinquam et ibi dissipauit substantiam suam uiuens luxuriose. **14** Cumque consumpsisset omnia, facta est famis ualida per regionem illam, et ipse coepit egeri. **15** et abiit et coniunxit se uni de municipib<us> regionis illius. qui misit illum in agro suo, ut pasceret porcos. **16** et cupiebat saturare uentrem suum de siliquis, quas porci edebant, nec quisquam dabat illi. **17** in se autem conuersus dixit: quanti mercennarii patris mei abundant pane, ego autem hic fame pereo. **18** surgens ibo ad patrem meum et dicam illi: pater, peccaui in caelum et coram te. **19** iam non sum dignus uocari filius tuus. fac me sicut unum ex mercennariis tuis. **20** et surgens uenit usque ad patrem suum. Cumque adhuc longe esset, uidit illum pater {pater} ipsius et misericordia motus est, et procurrens incubuit super collum

---

12 illi adulescentior] 4 8 iunior patri 2 adulescentior eorum patri 5 adulescentior patri 17 adulescentior ex illis patri A | portionem substantiae quae me contingit] partem patrimonii mei quae me tangit 2 quod me tanget partem substantiae 5 portionem substantiae meae quae me contingit 17 | illis] eis 5 | substantiam] substantiam suam 2 substantiae quae me contingit 8 | **13** non post] post non 2 | collectis omnibus] congregauit omnia 2 congregans omnia 5 congregatis omnibus cet. | adulescentior] iunior 2 | peregre profectus est] 17 A et peregrinatus est 2 peregrinatus est 5 pelegre profectus est 4* 8 | regionem longinquam] regione longinqua 2 17 | ibi] illic 2 | dissipauit] disparsit 5 | substantiam] omnem substantiam 2 | uiuens] 2 5 uiuendo cet. luxuriose] luxuriosae 2 8 | **14** Cumque consumpsisset omnia] et cum consumpsisset omnia 2 cum erogasset autem omnia 5 et postquam omnia consumpsit (consummasset A) cet. | famis] fames 4 17 A | ualida] 2 A magna 5 om. cet. | per regionem illam] in illa regione 2 in regione illa A | ipse coepit] coepit 4* coepit et ille 4^c 8 | egeri] 5 indigere uictum 2 esurire et necessitatem habere 4* egere (add. uictum 4^c) cet. | **15** abiit] habiit 8 | coniunxit se] adplicuit se 2 4^c adhaesit ibi 5 proiecit se ante 4* adhesit 8 A hesit 17 | uni] unum 4* cuidam 4^c | de municipibus] ex ciuibus 2 ex ciuium 17 ciuium (om. 4*) cet. | regionis] regioni 5 | qui] et his 2 et 5 A et is 4 et ille 8 17 | illum] eum 2 5 | agro suo] 2 agro 5 uilla sua 4 17 uillam suam 8 A | ut pasceret] pascere 5 porcos] porcos eius 17 | **16** cupiebat] concupiscebat 2 | saturare] saturari 2 5 implere cet. uentrem suum] om. 2 5 | quas] quae 4 | porci edebant] manducabant porci 2 edebant porci 5 porci manducabant cet. | nec quisquam] et nemo cet. | dabat illi] 5 illi dabat cet. | **17** in se autem conuersus] 4 conuersus autem ad se 2 in semetipsum autem ueniens 5 in se autem reuersus cet. | dixit] ait 17 | mercennarii] mercinnari 2 | pane] panem 2 panibus cet. | hic fame] fame hic 2 8 | **18** surgens] 5 surgam et cet. | caelum] celo 8 | coram te] in conspectum tuum 2 in conspecto tuo 5 | **19** iam] et iam A | uocari filius tuus] filius tuus uocari 2 | fac] sed fac 4 sicut unum] unum quasi 2 | ex mercennariis tuis] 8 ex mercinnaris tuis 2 de mercennariis tuis A mercennariorum tuorum cet. | **20** surgens uenit] surrexit et abiit 2 | usque] om. cet. | Cumque adhuc longe esset] et cum adhuc longe abesset 2 adhuc autem eo longe iter habentes 5 cum autem (dum 17) adhuc longe esset (abesset 4) cet. | illum] eum 5 | ipsius[1]] eius 5 illius 17 om. 2 et misericordia motus est] et contristatus est 2 et misertus est 5 om. 8 | procurrens] cucurrit et 2 currens 5 acurrens cet. | incubuit] 5 superiecit se 2 cecidit cet. | super] 5 in 2 supra cet.

ipsius et osculatus est eum. **21** Dixit autem illi filius: pater, peccaui in caelum et coram te. iam non sum dignus uocari filius tuus. **22** dixit autem pater ad pueros suos: celerius proferte stolam priorem et induite illum et date anulum in manu illius et calciamenta in pedibus eius. **23** et adducite uitulum illum saginatum et occidite. et manducemus et aepulemur, **24** quoniam hic filius meus mortuus fuerat et reuixit, perierat et inuentus est. et coeperunt aepulare. **25** Erat autem filius illius senior in agro. et cum ueniret, adpropinquauit domui et audiit symphonias et chorum **26** et uocauit unum de pueris et interrogauit, quidnam essent haec. **27** qui ait illi: quoniam frater tuus uenit et occidit pater tuus {is} uitulum illum saginatum, quoniam incolume illum recepit. **28** iratus est autem et noluit intrare. Egressus autem pater illius coepit rogare eum. **29** ipse autem respondens ait patri suo: ecce tot annis seruio tibi et numquam mandatum tuum praeteribi, et numquam dedisti mihi haedum, ut cum amicis meis aepularer. **30**

---

ipsius^{2}] eius cet. | eum] illum 4 8 | **21** Dixit autem] 4 5 ille autem dixit 2 dixitque cet. | illi filius] filius eius 5 ei filius eius 4 ei filius cet. om. 2 | coram te] 8 A in conspectum tuum 2 in conspecto tuo 5 in te 4 17 | iam] om. 17 | non sum dignus uocari filius tuus] add. fac me sicut unum mercennariorum tuorum 5 | **22** pater] pater eius 4 8 | pueros] seruos cet. | celerius] cito cet. | proferte] proferite 2 adferte 5 proferte mihi 4 | stolam] stolam illam 4 8 17 | priorem] primam cet. | et induite illum] et induite eum 5 om. 2 | manu] 4 17 manum cet. | illius] eius cet. | et calciamenta in pedibus eius] 4 8 et calciamenta in pedes eius 5 17 et calciamenta in pedes A om. 2 | **23** uitulum illum saginatum] saginatum illum uitulum 2 saginatum uitulum 5 uitulum saginatum A | occidite] laniate 2 | manducemus et] manducantes 2 | aepulemur] iucundemur 2 epulemur cet. | **24** quoniam] 5 quia cet. | fuerat] 4 8 erat cet. | inuentus] modo inuentus 5 | aepulare] iucundari 2 epulari cet. | **25** erat autem filius] cum maior autem filius 2 illius] eius cet. | senior in agro] qui in uilla erat 2 senior in uilla 5 iunior in agro 8 | et cum ueniret] uenisset 2 ueniens autem 5 et factum est cum ueniret 4 | adpropinquauit] et adpropiasset 2 et proximans 5 et appropinquaret A et adpropiaret cet. | domui] ad domum 2 | et^{2}] 2 om. cet. | audiit] 4 audisset 2 uidet 17 audiuit cet. | symphonias] simponia 2* simphonia 2^{c} symfoniam 8 symphoniam cet. | chorum] choros 2 4 chori 5 | **26** et uocauit] aduocato ad se 2 aduocans 5 | unum de pueris] 5 uno ex pueris 2 unum de seruis cet. | et^{2}] om. 2 5 | interrogauit] quaerebat 2 interrogabat 5 | quidnam] 2 quid 5 quaenam 4 quae cet. | essent haec] esset 2 uellet hoc esse 5 haec (om. 8) essent cet. | **27** qui ait] ille autem dixit 2 isque dixit 4 A ad ille dixit cet. | illi] ei 4 17 om. 5 | quoniam^{1}] 5 quia 4 om. cet. | uitulum illum saginatum] saginatum uitulum illi 5 uitulum saginatum 17 A | quoniam^{2}] 17 quia cet. | incolume] saluum cet. illum^{2}] eum 2 5 | **28** iratus] 2 5 indignatus cet. | noluit] 8 17 nolebat cet. | intrare] 4 introire cet. | Egressus autem pater illius] pater autem eius exiuit 2 pater autem eius exiens 5 pater uero (ergo A) illius egressus cet. | coepit rogare eum] et rogabat illum 2 rogabat eum 5 coepit illum rogare 8 coepit rogare illum cet. | **29** ipse autem respondens] respondens autem 2 at ille respondens cet. | ait] dixit cet. | tot] quot 8 17 | annis] annos 5 | mandatum tuum praeteribi] praeceptum tuum egressus sum 2 praeteriui mandatum tuum 5 mandatum tuum praeterii (praeteriui 4) cet. | numquam^{2}] non 17 | dedisti mihi] mihi dedisti 2 | haedum] hedum 2 haedum de capris 5 | aepularer] iucundarer 2 prandeam 5 epularer cet.

Cum autem filius tuus hic, qui comedit omnem facultatem suam uiuens cum
fornicariis, uenit, et occidisti uitulum illum saginatum. **31** Ipse autem dixit illi: tu
mecum fuisti semper et es et omnia mea tua sunt. **32** aepulari autem nos
oportebat et gaudere, quoniam hic frater tuus mortuus fuerat et reuixit, perierat
et inuentus est.

16 dicebat autem et ad discipulos suos: Homo quidam erat diues, qui habebat
uilicum, et hic diffamatus fuerat aput illum, tanquam dissiparet bona ipsius. **2** Et
uocabit eum dominus suus et ait illi: quid hoc audio de te? redde rationem
uilicationis tuae. iam enim non poteris amplius actum meum administrare. **3** dixit
autem ille uilicus intra se: quid faciam, quoniam dominus meus auferet
uilicationem meam a me? fodere non ualeo, mendicare confundor. **4** cognoui,
quid faciam, ut, cum amotus fuero de uilicatione, recipiant me in domus suas. **5** Et
conuocato unoquoque ex debitoribus domini sui dicebat priori: quantum debes
domino meo? **6** qui dixit: centum uatos olei. dixit autem illi: accipe cautionem

---

30 Cum autem filius tuus hic] filio autem tuo 2 5 sed postquam filius tuus hic cet. | comedit] 2 5 deuorauit cet. | omnem facultatem suam] omnia tua 2 omnia 5 substantiam tuam (suam A om. 4) cet. | uiuens] om. cet. | fornicariis] 2 meretricibus cet. | uenit] aduentiente 2 et uenienti 5 | et] om. 5 Λ | occidisti] 5 laniasti 2 occidisti illi cet. | uitulum illum saginatum] 4 17 saginatum uitulum 2 5 uitulum saginatum 8 A | **31** Ipse autem] ille autem 2 at ille 5 at (et 4) ipse cet. | tu] 5 filii 17 A fili cet. | mecum fuisti semper et es] 4 mecum es 2 semper mecum es cet. | **32** aepulari autem nos oportebat et gaudere] iucundatus sum autem et gauisus sum 2 aepulari autem oportebat et gaudere 5 epulari autem nos et gaudere oportet 4 aepulare autem nos et gaudere oportet 8 epulari autem et gaudere oportet nos 17 epulari autem et gaudere oportebat A | quoniam] quod 4 quia cet. | hic frater tuus] frater tuus hic (om. 17) cet. | fuerat] 4 8 erat 2 17^{c} A est 5 17*
16:1 et^{1}] om. 2 5 4 | suos] om. 2 5 | diues] honestus 2 | habebat] habuit 2 | uilicum] despensatorem 2 | et^{2}] om. 17 | diffamatus] diffatus 8 delatus 17 | fuerat] est 2 5 A erat 4 8 17 | aput] apud cet. om. 5 | illum] ei 5 | tanquam] quod 8 quasi cet. | dissiparet] 2 dissipans 5 dissipauit 8 dissipasset cet. | bona] substantiam 2 5 | ipsius] 17 A eius cet. | **2** Et] om.17 | uocabit] clamauit 2 uocans 5 | eum] 5 illum cet. add. ad se 4 | dominus suus] om. cet. | ait] dixit 2 5 | uilicationis] actus 2 uilicationes 4 | tuae] tui 2 om. 5 | iam] om. 2 5 | enim non] non enim 2 5 poteris] potes 2 5 potest 8 | amplius] adhuc 5 om. cet. | actum meum administrare] actum administrare 2 uilicare cet. | **3** dixit] 2 5 ait cet. | ille uilicus intra se] sibi actor ille 2 intra se uilicus 5 uilicus intra se cet. | quoniam] quia cet. | auferet] aufert 2 5 | uilicationem meam a me] actum 2 uilicationem meam 5 a me uilicationem cet. | confundor] 2 5 erubesco cet. | **4** cognoui] 4 8 cogitaui 2 17 scio 5 A | ut] et 5 | cum amotus] quando motus 2 | de uilicatione] 5 ab actu 2 a uilicatione cet. | recipiant] accipiant 5 | domus] 5 domos cet. | **5** Et] 2 5 om. cet. conuocato unoquoque ex debitoribus] conuocauit singulos debitores 2 aduocans unumquemque debitorum 5 conuocatis itaque singulis debitoribus cet. | dicebat] et dicebat 2 | priori] ad primum 2 primo cet. | **6** qui dixit] ille autem dixit 2 at ille dixit cet. | uatos] cados 2 A siclos 5 bathos 4 batis 8 | dixit autem] dixitque 8 A | cautionem tuam] A chirografum tuum 2 tuas litteras 5 litteras tuas 4 8

tuam et sedens celerius scribe quinquaginta. **7** Deinde alii dixit: tu autem quantum debes domino meo? qui dixit: centum coros tritici. dixit autem et huic: accipe cautionem tuam et scribe octoginta. **8** et laudauit dominus uilicum iniquiatis, quia prudenter fecerit. Dixit autem ad discipulos suos: dico uobis, fili huius saeculi prudentiores sunt super filios lucis in gente hac. **9** Et ego dico uobis: facite uobis amicos de iniquo mamona. Ut, cum defecerit uobis, recipiant uos in aeterna tabernacula. **10** qui fidelis est in minimo, et in multo fidelis est, et qui in minimo iniquus est, et in magno iniquus est. **11** Si ergo in iniquo mamona fideles non fuistis, quod uobiscum est, quis dabit uobis? **12** et si in alieno fideles non fuistis, quod uestrum est, quis credet uobis? **13** Nemo potest seruus duobus dominis seruire. aut enim unum odiet et alium diliget, aut unum patietur et alium contemnet. non potestis deo seruire et mamonae. **14** haec omnia cum audissent pharisaei, qui erant amatores pecuniae, inridebant eum. **15** Et dixit eis: uos estis, qui iustificatis uos coram hominibus, deus autem scit corda uestra, quoniam quod

---

sedens celerius] sede 2 sede cito cet. om. 5 | scribe] et scribe cito 2 | **7** Deinde alii dixit] dixit autem altero 2 deinde alio dixit cet. | autem[1]] 2 5 uero A om. 4 8 | domino meo] om. cet. | qui dixit] et dixit 2 ad ille dixit 5 ait 4 8 qui ait A | coros] mensuras 5 | dixit autem et huic] ad ille dixit illi 5 ait et illi 4 ait illi cet. | cautionem tuam] cirografum tuum 2 tuas litteras 5 litteras tuas cet. | et[2]] om. 8 | octoginta] lxxx 4 | **8** et laudauit dominus] dominus autem laudauit 2 et laudabit dominus 8 | uilicum iniquiatis] actorem iniustitiae 2 | quia] A quoniam 2 5 eo quod 4 quod 8 | prudenter] sapienter 5 | fecerit] 4 fecisset A fecit cet. | Dixit autem ad discipulos suos] 4 dixit autem ad discentes suos 2 dixit autem 8 om. 5 A | dico uobis] propter quod dico uobis 5 quia A om. cet. | fili] filii 2 A | huius saeculi] saeculi huius 2 5 | prudentiores] sapientiores 5 | sunt] om. 2 5 A | super filios] quam fili 4 quam filii 8 filiis A | gente hac] saeculum istut sunt 2 generationem suam sunt 5 hac generatione 4 8 generatione sua sunt A | **9** dico uobis] uobis dico 2 4 A | iniquo mamona] 5 mamona iniquitatis cet. | defecerit] 5 defecerint 2 defeceritis cet. | uobis[3]] 2 om. cet. | recipiant] accipiant 5 excipiant 4* | tabernacula] tabernacula sua 4 | **10** minimo[1]] modico 2 5 | multo] 2 5 maius 4 8 maiori A | minimo[2]] modico cet. iniquus[1]] inustus 2 fidelis 8 | magno] multo 2 5 maius 4 8 maiori A | iniquus[2]] iniustus 2 | est[4]] fit 5 | **11** iniquo] iniusto 2 | fideles] A fidelis cet. | fuistis] fuisti 2 | uobiscum] uerum cet. dabit uobis] 4 crederit uobis 2 credet (credit 8 A) uobis cet. | **12** fideles] fidelis 2 5 8 | quod] om. 5 | uestrum] meum 2 17 | est] om. 5 | credet] dabit cet. | **13** potest seruus] seruus potest cet. enim] om. 4 | odiet] odit 2 | alium[1]] unum 5 alterum cet. | diliget] amabit 4 | unum patietur] 4 unum adprehendet 5 uni adhaerebit (adherebit 2) cet. | alium[2]] 5 alterum cet. | potestis] potestes 2 | **14** haec omnia cum audissent] audiebant autem omnia haec A audiebant autem haec omnia (om. 5 17) cet. | qui erant amatores pecuniae] qui erant cupidissimi 2 cum essent cupidi 5 qui erant auari cet. | inridebant] et inridebant 2 et subsannabant 5 et deridebant cet. eum] 2 5 illum cet. | **15** Et dixit eis] 5 ille autem dixit ad illos 2 et ait illis cet. | coram hominibus] in conspectu hominum 2 5 | scit] dinoscit 2 nouit cet. | quoniam] quia cet.

aput homines sublime est, abominatio est ante conspectum dei. **16** Lex et prophaetae usque ad iohannem, ex quo regnum dei euangelizantur et omnes in illum festinant. **17** facilius est autem caelum et terram transire, quam de lege unum apicem excedere. **18** Omnis, qui dimittit uxorem suam et nubit aliam, adulterium facit. et qui{t} dimissam a marito ducit, moecatur. **19** Homo quidam erat diues, qui uestiebatur purpuram et byssum et aepulabantur cotidie splendide. **20** Pauper autem quidam nomine lazarus iacebat ad ianuam diuitis illius ulceribus plenus. **21** et cupiebat satiari de micis, quae cadebant de mensa diuitis, sed et canes uenientes lambebant uulnera eius. **22** Factum est autem, ut moreretur pauper et portaretur ab angelis in sinu abrahae. mortuus est autem et diues et sepultus est aput inferos. **23** Et de inferno eleuans oculos suos, cum esset in tormentis, uidet abraham a longe et lazarum in sinu eius. **24** et ipse exclamans dixit: pater abraham, miserere mihi et mitte lazarum, ut intingat extremum digiti

---

aput homines sublime est] excelsum est in hominibus 2 in hominibus sublime 5 in hominibus sublime est 4 hominibus altum est cet. | abominatio] execratio 2 | est[2]] om. 5 | ante conspectum dei] in conspectu dei 5 ante deum cet. | **16** prophaetae] profetae 2 prophetae cet. | iohannem] iohanen prophetarunt 5 iohannen 4 A | ex quo] ex inde 2 a quo 5 ex eo A | euangelizantur] adnuntiatur 2 euangelizat 5 euangelizatur cet. | omnes] omnis 4 A omnies 8 | illum] eum 2 eam 5 illud cet. | festinant] conatur 2 5 uim facit (faciunt 17) cet. | **17** est autem] autem est 5 transire] 2 praeterire cet. | de lege] legis 2 | apicem] apice 4 | excedere] capere 2 cadere cet. **18** dimittit] remittit 2 | nubit aliam] nubens aliam 5 duxerit aliam 17 ducit alteram (aliam 2) cet. adulterium facit] moechatur (moecatur 2) cet. | et quit dimissam a marito ducit moecatur] et qui dimissam nubit moechatur 5 et qui dimissam (quae dimissa 4) a uiro ducit moechatur cet. **19** Homo] 2 A dixit autem et aliam parabolam homo 5 homo autem cet. | erat] fuit 2 | diues] honestus 2 | qui uestiebatur purpuram] et (qui 2 4 17) induebatur purpuram (purpura A) cet. et byssum] et bysso A om. 4 | et[2]] om. 5 | aepulabantur] iucundabatur 2 aepulans 5 epulatur 17 epulabatur cet. | cotidie] cottidie cet. | splendide] splendebat 8* | **20** Pauper autem quidam] 5 egens autem quidam 2 pauper autem quidam erat 17 et erat (erat autem 4) quidam mendicus cet. lazarus] eleazarus 2 | iacebat] proiectus erat 2 missus erat 5 qui iacebat cet. | ad] in ad 17* diuitis] om. cet. | illius] huius 2 eius cet. | **21** et[1]] 5 om. cet. | cupiebat] concupiscens 2 cupiens cet. | satiari] saturari cet. | de micis] 5 A ab eis 2 ex his cet. | cadebant] cadebat 8 | mensa] mensam 2 | uenientes] 5 ueniebant cet. | lambebant] et ablingebant 2 elingebant 5 et lingebant (lingebat 8) cet. | uulnera] 2 ulcera cet. | **22** ut moreretur pauper] 5 mori inopem illum 2 ut moreretur lazarus (om. A) mendicus (pauper 17) cet. | portaretur] tolli 2 ductus est 5 | ab angelis in sinu abrahae] in sinus abrahae ab angelis 5 ab angelis in sinum (sinus 2) abrahae cet. et[2]] om. 4 | diues] diues ille 2 | aput inferos] 17 in inferno cet. om. 5 4 | **23** Et de inferno] et in inferno 5 4 in inferno 17 om. cet. | eleuans] leuans autem 2 leuans 5 eleuans autem A | uidet] uidit 4 17 uidebat A | a longe] de longinquo 2 longe 17 | lazarum] elearum 2* eleazarum 2[c] sinu] 4 sinus 2 5 sinum cet. | eius] eius requiescentem 2 5 4 | **24** et ipse exclamans dixit] 5 4 exclamauit autem et dixit 2 et ipse clamans dixit cet. | pater] o pater 4* | mihi] mei 2 4 A lazarum] eleazarum 2 | intingat] intinguat A | extremum digiti sui] summum digiti sui 2 extremo digito suo 8

sui in aquam et refrigeret linguam meam, quoniam crucior in hac flamma. **25**
dixit autem illi abraham: fili, memor{r} esto, quoniam recepisti bona in uita tua et
lazarus similiter mala. Nunc autem hic consolatur, tu autem cruciaris. **26** et super
omnibus istis inter nos et uos hiatus terrae magnus confirmatus est, ut hi, qui
ueniunt hoc, transire non possint ad uos neque inde hoc transmeare. **27** Dixit
autem illi: rogo ergo te, pater, ut mittas in domum patris mei. **28** habeo enim
quinque fratres, ut testificetur illis, ne et ipsi ueniant in hunc locum cruciatus. **29**
Dixit autem illi habraham: habent moysen et prophetas, audiant illos. **30** qui dixit:
non, pater abraham, sed si quis ex mortuis surrexerit, paenitentiam agent. **31**
Dixit autem illi: si moysen et prophetas non audiunt, nec, si quis ex mortuis ad
illos ierit, credent.

17 Dixit autem ad discipulos suos: difficile est, ut non ueniant scandala.
uerumtamem uae illi, per quem ueniunt. **2** utilius est autem illi, ne nasceretur aut

---

in[1]] om. 5 | et[3]] ut 2 17 A | quoniam] 5 quia cet. | crucior in hac flamma] uror in flamma ista 2 adfligor in ustione ignis huius 5 | **25** dixit autem illi abraham] abraham autem dixit 2 dixit autem abraham 5 et dixit illi abraham cet. | memorr esto] memento 2 5 recordare cet. | quoniam] quia 4 A om. 8* | recepisti] percepisti 2 recepisti tu 4 cipisti 8 | bona] bona tua 5 | et lazarus] eleazar autem 2 | similiter] om. 2 | consolatur] consolabitur 2 | autem[3]] 2 5 uero cet. cruciaris] ureris 2 adfligeris 5 | **26** super omnibus istis] super ista omnia 2 in omnibus his 5 in his omnibus cet. | inter nos et uos] 5 17 inter et nos et uos 8 inter uos et nos cet. | hiatus terrae] chaus 2 chaum 8 chaos cet. | magnus] 2 4 magnum cet. | confirmatus] 5 stabilitus 4 firmatum cet. om. 2 | ut] et 4 | hi] om. 2 5 | ueniunt hoc transire] 4 17 uolunt transgredi ad uos 2 uolunt transire ad uos 5 ueniunt hinc transire 8 uolunt hinc transire ad uos A | possint] possunt 2[c] possent 5 possum 8 | ad uos] om. 2 5 A | hoc transmeare] 4 17 transire hoc 2 hic transmeare 5 huc transmeare 8 A | **27** Dixit autem] et ait 8 17 A | illi] om. cet. | rogo ergo te] rogo te 2 rogo te ergo 5 rogo ergo 17 | pater] pater abraam 5 om. 2* | mittas] mittas eum 5 A | **28** testificetur] 2 5 testetur cet. | ne] ut ne 8 | et] om. 17 | ipsi] illi 2 | hunc locum] locum hunc 4 17 A cruciatus] tormenti 5 tormentorum cet. | **29** Dixit autem] 5 dicit 2 et ait cet. | illi] om. 5 habraham] abraham cet. | moysen] mosen A | prophetas] profetas 2 8 | illos] eos 5 | **30** qui dixit] ille autem dixit 2 at ille dixit cet. | quis] qui 2 | ex] a 2 de 5 | surrexerit] abierit ad illos 2 ierit ad eos 5 A resurrexerit 4 surrexit 8 | paenitentiam agent] 2 A paenitebuntur 5 persuadebit eis (illis 4) cet. | **31** Dixit] 2 5 ait cet. | illi] ad eum 5 | moysen] mosen A | prophetas] profetas 2 | nec] 5 neque cet. | quis ex mortuis ad illos ierit] qui abierit a mortuis 2 quis ex mortuis surrexerit et ierit ad eos 5 quis ex mortuis ad illos abierint 4 quis ex mortuis ad illo ierit 8 quis ex mortuis ad illos ierint 17 quis ex mortuis surrexerit A | credent] persuadebuntur 2 credent ei 17 **17:1** Dixit autem ad discipulos suos] 5 4 dixit autem ad discentes 2 et ad discipulos suos ait 8 A ait autem ad discipulos suos 17 | difficile] impossibile 4 17 inpossibile cet. | ut non ueniant scandala] scandala non uenire 2 ut non ueniant scandalae 4* non uenire scandala 17 | uerumtamem uae] uerum uae 2 5 uae autem A | illi] om. 5 | ueniunt] uenient 4 ueniant 17 | **2** utilius est autem] 8 17 expedit 2 expediebat 5 utilius autem fuerat 4 utilius est A | illi] om. 2 | ne nasceretur] om. 2 5 A | aut lapis] 4 8 ut lapidem 2 si lapis (lapidem 5) cet.

lapis molaris inpositus fuisset collo illius et proiectus esset in marem, quam ut
scandalizet unum de pusillis istis. **3** Attendite uobis: si peccauerit frater tuus,
corripe illum. et si paenitentiam egerit, remitte illi. **4** et si septiens peccauerit in
die in te et septies conuersus fuerit at te dicens: ago paenitentiam, remitte illi. **5** Et
dixerunt apostoli domino: auge nobis fidem. **6** quibus ille dixit: si habueritis fidem
tanquam granum sinapis, dicetis muro huic: eradicare et plantare in mare, et
obaudisset uobis. **7** Quis autem uestrum habens seruum arantem aut pascentem
oues, qui regresso eo de agro statim dicet illi: transi et recumbe? **8** sed dicet illi:
praepara mihi, quod cenem, et succinctus ministra mihi, donec manducem et
bibam, et postea tu manducabis et bibet. **9** numquid aget gratias seruo, quoniam
fecit, quae praecepta sunt ei? **10** sic et uos, cum feceritis, quae praecepta sunt,
dicitis: serui inutiles sumus. facere, fecimus. **11** Et factum est, dum iret in

---

molaris] molae 5 8 | inpositus fuisset] circumiectus sit 2 circumdatus esset 5 imponatur 4 17 inponatur 8 A | collo] super collum 17 circa collum cet. | illius] 4 eius cet. | proiectus esset] 5 proiectus sit 2 proiciatur cet. | marem] mare cet. | quam] aut 5 | de] ex 2 | **3** Attendite] adtendite 2 5 antendite 8 | peccauerit] peccauerit in te 2 5 | corripe] 2 emenda 5 increpa cet. paenitentiam] penitentiam 8 | egerit] habuerit 4 8 17 | remitte] 2 dimitte cet. | **4** septiens] septies cet. | peccauerit in die] in die peccauerit cet. | et^{2}] et si si 4 | septies] septies in die 2 A conuersus] reuersus 2 5 | at te] ad te cet. om. 17 | ago paenitentiam] paenitentiam ago 2 paeniteor 5 4 paenitet me cet. | remitte] 2 4* dimitte (dimittes 17) cet. | **5** dixerunt] dixerunt illi 4 8 domino] om. 2 4 8 | auge] 17 domine adice 2 adde 5 domine adauge 4 domine auge 8 adauge A **6** quibus ille dixit] dixit autem illis 2 ad ille dixit illis 5 dixit autem dominus A et dixit illis cet. habueritis] haberetis 5 A | tanquam] 8 quasi 2 sicut (ut 17) cet. | dicetis] 17 dicitis 2 dicebatis 5 diceretis (diceritis 8) cet. | muro huic] utique monti huic 5 huic arbor moro (modo 2 4 morae 17 om. 8) cet. add. transi hinc ibide et transibat et moro 5 | eradicare et] om. 5 | plantare] 2 transfretare 8 transportare 17 transplatare (transplantari 5) cet. | mare] mari 2 | et^{2}] om. 4 | obaudisset uobis] 5 exaudiet uos 2 oboediret uobis A utique obaudisset uobis (uos 17) cet. | **7** uestrum] ex uestris 5 om. 4 | pascentem oues] pastorem 2 oues (om. A) pascentem cet. | qui regresso eo] et cum uenerit 2 qui ut intrauit 5 qui (cui 17) regresso (regredienti 4) cet. | statim dicet] non dicit 2 numquid dicit 5 dicet cet. | transi] continuo transi 2 5 statim transi A | et] om. cet. **8** sed] et non A | dicet] dicit 2 | illi] ei A om. 17 | praepara] para cet. | mihi^{1}] 5 4 om. cet. cenem] cene 2 | succinctus] accingere 2 cinge te 5 procinge te 17 praecinge te cet. | ministra] et ministra cet. | donec] usque dum 2 usque quo 5 | postea] 2 sic 4 post haec cet. | tu manducabis] manducauis 2 manducabis tu 5 | bibet] bibis 8 bibes cet. | **9** aget gratias] habet gratiam 2 5 gratiam aget 8^{c} gratiam habet cet. | seruo] seruo illi 2 A | quoniam] quia 2 5 A quod 4 8 17 praecepta sunt ei] 5 sibi inperauerat 8 sibi imperauerat A sibi (om. 2) imperata sunt cet. add. non puto cet. | **10** sic et uos] A sic itaque et uos 2 ita et uos 5 et uos cet. | feceritis] feceritis omnia A praecepta sunt] 4 17 uobis fuerint imperata 2 dico 5 praecepta sunt uobis 8 A | dicitis] 4 8 dicitis quoniam 5 dicite cet. | inutiles] superuacui 2 | facere] quod (quae 17) debuimus facere cet. **11** dum] cum 2 5 | iret in hierusalem] A iret hierusalem 2 iter faceret in hierusalem 5 hierusalem iret 4 uadit in iherusalem 8 uadit hierusalem 17

hierusalem, et ipse transiebat per mediam samariam et galilaeam et iericho. **12**
ingrediens autem in quendam uicum et ecce decem uiri leprosi steterunt a longe.
13 et leuauerunt uocem suam dicentes: iesu magister, miserere nobis. **14** et cum
audisset illos, dixit illis: euntes ostendite uos sacerdotibus. Et factum est, dum
irent, emundati sunt. **15** unus autem ex eis, cum uidisset, quia sanus est, reuersus
est cum uoce magna honorificans deum. **16** et procidit in faciem ad pedes illius
gratias agens. et ipse erat samarites. **17** Respondens autem iesus dixit: hi decem
mundati sunt? nouem ubi sunt? **18** ex his non est inuentus, qui reuersus honorem
daret deo, nisi hic alienigena? **19** et dixit illi: surge et uade, quoniam fides tua te
saluum fecit. **20** interrogatus autem a pharisaeis, quando uenturum esset regnum
dei, dixit eis: non uenit regnum dei obseruatione, **21** sed nec dicent: ecce hic aut
ecce illic. ecce enim regnum dei intra uos est. **22** Dixit autem ad discipulos suos:

---

et ipse] 2 5 om. cet. | transiebat] 8 A retransibat 2 praeteribat 5 transibat 4 17 | mediam samariam] medium samariae 2 5 | samariam] sammariam 8 | galilaeam] galileae 2 galiaeae 5 galilea 8 | iericho] 2 hiericho cet. om. 5 A | **12** ingrediens autem] et cum introiret 2 et introeunte eo 5 et ingredienti ei 4 et ingressus est 8 17 et cum ingrederetur A | in] om. A | quendam] 2 5 quodam 4 17 quondam 8 quoddam A | uicum] castello 4 castellum cet. | et ecce] ubi fuerunt 2 ubi erant 5 occurrerunt ei A | decem uiri leprosi] decem uiri illi leprosi 2 uiri leprosi decem 17 steterunt] et steterunt 5 qui steterunt A | a] de 2 5 | **13** leuauerunt uocem suam] clamauerunt uoce magna 2 5 leuauerunt uocem cet. | dicentes] om. 5 | iesu] iesum 2 17 | magister] 5 praeceptor (preceptor 8) cet. | nobis] nostri 2 A | **14** et cum audisset illos] et cum uidisset illos 2 et uidens eos 5 quos (quod 8) ut uidit cet. | illis] 5 om. cet. | euntes] curati estis ite 5 ite cet. ostendite] et ostendite 2 5 | Et factum est] factum est autem 5 | dum] cum 2 5 | irent] 5 A omnes simul irent 2 uadunt cet. | emundati] purgati 2 mundati cet. | **15** eis] 5 illis cet. | cum uidisset] cum uideret 2 uidens 5 ut uidit cet. | sanus] curatus 2 sanatus 8 17 mundatus cet. reuersus est] 5 rediuit 2 regressus est cet. | uoce magna] 2 magna uoce cet. | honorificans] clarificans 2 honorans 5 magnificauit 17 magnificans cet. | **16** procidit] cecidit (caecidit 2) cet. in faciem ad pedes illius] ad pedes eius in faciem 2 ante pedes eius 8 in faciem ante (ad 5) pedes eius cet. | gratias agens] gratias agens ei 4 magnificans 8 om. 5 | et ipse erat] et ipse fuit 2 erat autem 5 et hic erat cet. | samarites] 2 samaritanus (sammaritanus 8) cet. | **17** dixit] dixit illis 5 hi decem] hi x 4 nonne decem A | mundati] purgati 2 | nouem ubi sunt] nouem ubi 5 et nouem ubi sunt A | **18** ex his non est inuentus] et nemo ex eis reuersus est 2 ex his nemo inuentus est 5 non est inuentus A ex illis non est (erat 8) cet. | qui reuersus honorem daret] qui daret claritatem deo 2 reuertens qui dauit gloriam deo 5 qui rediret et daret gloriam A qui rediret (add. ex illis 17) et gratias ageret (agaret 4 agere 8) cet. | hic alienigena] alienigena iste 2 alienigena hic 5 **19** dixit] 5 dicit 2 ait cet. | surge] surgens 5 | et[2]] 2 8 om. cet. | quoniam] 5 quia cet. om. 17 | te saluum fecit] te saluabit 2 salbabit te 5 | **20** uenturum esset] ueniret 2 uenit cet. | dixit eis] at ille dixit eis 4 ait 8 respondit illis (eis A) et dixit cet. om. 17 | non uenit regnum dei] om. 17 obseruatione] cum obseruatione cet. | **21** sed nec] neque cet. | dicent] dicens 2 | aut] om. 8 17 illic] illi 5 | ecce[3]] nolite credere ecce 5 | **22** Dixit autem] 2 dixit ergo 5 et ait cet. | discipulos] discentes 2 | suos] om. 5 A uenient dies, ut concupiscatis uidere unum diem filii hominis, et non uidebitis. **23** et dicent uobis: ecce hic aut ecce illic. nolite ire nec sequi. **24** Sicut enim fulgul coruscans, sic erit filius hominis. **25** prius autem oportet illum multa pati et reprobari a generatione hac. **26** Et sicut factum est in diebus noe, sic erit et in diebus fili hominis. **27** edebant, bibebant, nubebant, nubebantur usque in diem, quo introiret noe in arcam. et uenit dilubium et perdidit omnes. **28** similiter et factum est et in diebus lot: edebant, bibebant, emebant, uendebant, plantabant, aedificabant. **29** qua die exiit lot a sodomis, pluit ignem de caelo et perdidit omnes. **30** similiter erit in die, qua filius hominis reuelabitur. **31** In illa hora qui erit super tectum et uasa illius in domo, non descendat tollere ea, et qui in agro, similiter non reuertatur retro. **32** memores estote uxoris lot. **33** Quicumque ergo quaesierit animam suam saluam facere, perdet illam, et qui perdiderit, saluam

---

uenient] ueniet 8 | ut] quando A | concupiscatis] 2 5 desideretis cet. | uidere unum diem filii hominis] A unum ex diebus filii hominis uidere 2 unum dierum horum fili hominis 5 uidere unum diem fili hominis 4 8 unum diem uidere filii hominis 17 | **23** aut] 5 et cet. om. 2 A | nolite ire] ne ieritis 2 5 | nec sequi] ne secuti fueritis 2 neque persequemini 5 neque sectemini cet. **24** Sicut enim] 5 quomodo enim 2 nam sicut cet. | fulgul] choruscatio 2 scoruscus 5 fulgur cet. coruscans] quae coruscat de caelo in patre quae sub caelum est 2 qui scoruscat de sub caelu scoruscat 5 fulgurans de caelo lucet in his quae sub caelo sunt 4 coruscans de sub celo 8 coruscans de sub caelo lucet in his quae sub caelo sunt 17 coruscans de sub caelo in ea quae sub caelo sunt fulget A | sic] 2 5 ita cet. | filius] et filius 5 4 17 add. in die sua A | **25** prius] primum cet. autem] enim 5 | illum multa pati] multa pati illum 2 eum multa pati 5 | generatione hac] saeculo isto 2 | **26** sicut] quomodo 2 | factum est] fuit 5 | sic] 2 5 ita cet. | et] om. 4 17 | fili] filii 2 4 A | **27** edebant] manducabant 2 sedebant 8 17 | bibebant] et bibebant 4 8 A | nubebant] uxores ducebant 4 A | nubebantur] uxores ducebant 8 17 dabantur ad nuptias A | diem] die 2 8 17 | quo] 5 8 in qua 2 qua cet. | introiret] introiuit 2 introiit 5 intrauit cet. | arcam] archa 2 uenit] factum est 2 fuit 5 | dilubium] diluuium cet. | omnes] omnia 2 | **28** et[1]] 2 sicut cet. om. 4 8 | factum est] fuit 5 om. 2 | diebus] om. 2 | lot] 2 5 loth cet. | edebant] manducabant 2 bibebant] 5 17 et bibebant cet. | uendebant] et uendebant 4 A | plantabant] nouellabant 2 **29** qua] quo 5 | die] 2 5 die autem cet. | exiit] exiuit 2 5 | lot] 5 8 loth cet. om. 2 | a sodomis] et tota sodomis 2 | ignem] sulfur et igne 2 ignem et sulphur A | perdidit omnes] 5 8 de eos perdidit 2 omnes perdidit cet. | **30** similiter] secundum haec cet. | erit] euenient 2 | in die] qua die 2 A dies 4 | qua] om. cet. | filius] 2 A fili cet. | reuelabitur] A uenerit 2 qua (qui 5 quia 4 que 8) reuelabitur cet. | **31** In illa hora] illo die 2 in illo die 5 | erit super tectum] 5 qui fuerit in tecto cet. | illius] eius cet. | non[1]] ne 4 17 A | ea] illa (illam 8) cet. | similiter] om. 4 | reuertatur] 2 conuertatur 5 redeat cet. | retro] similiter retro 4 | **32** memores estote] et mementote 5 | lot] 2 5 loth cet. | **33** Quicumque] qui 2 5 | ergo] autem 4 8 17 om. cet. | quaesierit] uoluerit 5 animam suam saluam facere] A biuicare animam suam 5 animam suam (anima sua 2) liberare (saluare 2 8) cet. | illam] eam 8 | qui] quicumque 4 8 A | perdiderit] 5 A perdiderit eam mei causa 2 perdiderit illam (eam 17) propter me cet. | saluam eam faciet] uiuificauit illam 2 5 uiuificabit eam A saluam faciet illam cet.

eam faciet. **34** dico enim uobis: hac noctu erint duo in lecto uno, unus adsumetur et alius relinquetur. **35** erint duae mollentes in unum, una relinquetur et alia adsumetur. duo in agro, unus adsumetur et alius relinquetur. **36** Et respondentes dixerunt illi: ubi, domine? **37** qui dixit illis: ubicumque fuerit corpus, illuc conueniunt aquilae.

18 Dicebat autem parabolam illis ob hoc, quod deberent semper orare et non deficere, **2** dicens: Iudex quidam erat in quadam ciuitate, qui deum non timebat, sed nec hominem reuerebatur. **3** uidua autem quaedam erat in eadem ciuitatem et ueniebat ad illum dicens: uindica me de aduersario meo. **4** et nolebat per tempus. Post haec autem dixit intra se: si deum non timeo nec hominem reor, **5** attamen quia molesta est mihi uidua haec, uindicabo illam, ne per tempore

---

34 enim] autem 2 om. cet. | hac noctu] quia illa nocte 2 hac nocte 5 in (om. A) illa nocte (noctu 8) cet. | erint] erunt cet. | duo in lecto uno] in lecto uno duo 5 duo in tecto uno A | unus] sed unus 2 | adsumetur] assumetur 17 A | alius] 8 unus 5 alter cet. | **35** erint duae mollentes in unum una relinquetur et alia adsumetur duo in agro unus adsumetur et alius relinquetur] duae molentes in uno sed una adsumetur et una relinquetur duo in agro unus adsumetur 2 duo molentes in uno una adsumetur et alia dimittetur duo in agro unus adsumetur et alius dimittetur 5 duae molentes in unum una adsumetur et una relinquetur duo in agro unus adsumetur et unus relinquetur 4 duae molentes in unum una adsumetur et una relinquetur duo in agro unus adsumetur et unus relinquetur 8 duo in agro unus assumetur et unus relinquetur duae molentes in unum una assumetur et una relinquetur 17 duae erunt molentes in unum una assumetur et altera relinquetur duo in agro unus assumetur et alter relinquetur A | **36** Et respondentes dixerunt illi] et responderunt et dixerunt illi 2 et respondentes dixerunt 5 respondentes autem dixerunt illi 4 et respondens dixerunt illi 8 respondentes dixerunt illi 17 respondentes dicunt illi A | ubi] quo fient 2 | **37** qui dixit illis] dixit 2 ad ille dixit illis 5 qui dixit eis A quibus ipse dixit cet. | ubicumque] ubi 2 5 | fuerit corpus] cadauer est corpus 5 | illuc] illo 2 ibi 5 illic 4 | conueniunt] colliguntur 2 congregabuntur cet. | aquilae] et aquilae 5 | **18:1** Dicebat] dicebant 2* | autem] om. 17 | parabolam] 4 et similitudinem 2 et parabolam 5 A etiam parabolam 8 etiam parabolam istam 17 | illis] 2 5 ad illos cet. | ob hoc] ad huc 2 om. cet. | quod] 5 quia 2 quoniam cet. deberent] oportet cet. | orare] operare 2 | deficere] deficiet 2 | **2** dicens] dicens hinc 2 om. 5 quadam ciuitate] ciuitate quadam 2 ciuitate 5 quadam ciuitatem 8 | qui] om. 2 | timebat] timens 2 5 | sed nec] nec 4 om. cet. | reuerebatur] non reuerens 5 non reuerebatur cet. **3** quaedam] om. 2 5 | eadem ciuitatem] illa ciuitate 2 ciuitate illa 5 A ciuitate cet. | et] quae 4 8 ueniebat] uenit 4 ueniens coepit 8 coepit 17 | illum] eum 2 5 A | dicens] dicere 8 17 | uindica] deuindica 5 | de] ab 2 5 | aduersario] abuersario 5 | **4** nolebat] noluit 4* | per tempus] longo tempore 2 in aliqod temporis 5 per tempore multo 4* per multum tempus cet. | Post haec] postea 2 | autem] ille 4* om. 5 | dixit] uenit 5 dicebat 4* | intra se] apud se 2 aput se et dicit 5 | si] etsi A | non] nonon 2 | nec] neque 2 et 5 | reor] non reuereor 5 reueor 8 reuereor cet. **5** attamen quia molesta est mihi uidua haec uindicabo illam] uel propter hoc quod mihi tedium facit uidua uindicabo eam 2 propter quod lauorem mihi praestat uidua haec uado et deuindico illam 5 tamen quia molesta est mihi haec uidua uindicabo illam cet. | ne] ut non 5 | per tempore] usque ad finem 2 in tempus 5 in nouissimo cet.

ueniens suggillet me. **6** Dixit autem dominus: audite, quid iudex iniquitatis dicet. **7**
deus autem non faciet uindicta electorum suorum clamantium die ac nocte
patientiam habens in illis? **8** dico uobis, quia facet uindic<tam> illorum celeriter.
attamen filius hominis ueniens, inueniet putas fidem super terram? **9** Dixit autem
et ad quosdam fidentes sibi, quasi sint iusti, et spernentes ceteros, parabolam
hanc: **10** Duo homines ascenderunt in templo orare, unus publicanus et alius
pharisaeus. **11** stans itaque pharisaeus intra se haec orabat: deus, gratias ago tibi,
quia non sum sicut ceteri hominum, raptores, iniusti, adulteri uelut hic
publicanus. **12** ieiuno bis in sabbato, decimas dono omnium, quaecumque
possideo. **13** Et publicanus a longe stans nolebat nec quidem oculos suos in caelum
adleuare, set percutiebat pectus suum dicens: deus, propitius esto mihi peccatori.
14 dico uobis, quia descendit hic iustificatus in domo sua prae illum pharisaeum,

---

ueniens] ueniendo 4 17 ueniat 8 | suggillet me] molestior sit mihi 2 constringat me 4 8 | **6** Dixit] 2 5 ait cet. | audite] audistis 2 | iniquitatis] iniustiae 2 | dicet] dixerit 4 dicit cet. | **7** deus] dominus 2 | faciet] facit 2 | uindicta] 2 uindictam cet. | clamantium] qui eum inclamant 2 qui clamant eum 5 clamantium ac se A | die ac nocte] die et nocte 2 nocte et die 5 | patientiam habens] et patiens est 2 5 et patientiam habebit A | in illis] super eos 5 | **8** quia] 2 A om. cet. facet] faciet 2 5 cito faciet A faciet cito cet. | uindictam] iudicium 2 uincdictam 8 | illorum] eorum 5 | celeriter] cito 2 confestim 5 om. cet. | attamen] uerum 2 uerum putat 5 uerumtamen A tamen cet. | ueniens] cum uenerit 2 ueniens ueniens 17 | inueniet putas] inueniet 5 numquid inueniet 4 17 putas inueniet cet. | super] 5 4 in cet. | terram] terra A | **9** et[1]] om. 2 4 | fidentes sibi] qui sibi placebant 2 qui confidens super se 5 qui sibi (in se A) confidebant cet. | quasi sint iusti] quia sunt iniusti 2 quoniam sunt iniusti 5 tamquam iniusti essent (om. A) cet. om. 17 spernentes ceteros] contemnunt ceteros 2 spernent reliquos hominum 5 aspernabantur ceteros A spernebant (spernebat 17) ceteros cet. | parabolam hanc] parabolam istam A similitudinem istam cet. om. 5 | **10** Duo homines] homines duo 2 | templo] 8 templum cet. | orare] 5 ut orarent cet. | publicanus et alius pharisaeus] 17 pharisaeus et unus publicanus 2 5 publicanus et alter farisaeus 4 publicanus et unus pharisaeus 8 pharisaeus et alter publicanus A | **11** stans itaque pharisaeus intra se haec orabat] pharisaeus cum stetisset talia intra se praecabatur 2 pharisaeus stans seorsum haec orabat 5 pharisaeus stans haec apud se orabat A stans itaque pharisaeus sic orabat cet. | ago tibi] tibi ago 2 | quia] quoniam 5 | sum] sunt 2 | sicut] quomodo 2 | hominum] 2 5 A homines cet. | raptores iniusti] iniusti raptores 2 | uelut] quomodo 2 sicut et 5 uelut etiam A uel (uelut 4) etiam sicut cet. | hic publicanus] publicanus iste 2 | **12** ieiuno] iaiuno 4* | decimas] decimo 5 | dono] do cet. om. 5 17 | omnium] omnibus 2 omnia 5 om. 17 | quaecumque] 8 17 quae cet. | possideo] adquiro 5 17 | **13** Et publicanus] publicanus autem 2 | a longe] de longinquo 2 | stans nolebat] stabat et 2 | nec] neque 2 | quidem] om. cet. oculos] oculus 8 | suos] 4 5 om. cet. | in caelum adleuare] in caelum uolebat leuare 2 sursum leuare ad caelum 4 leuare 17 in (ad A) caelum leuare cet. | set] sed tantum 4 sed cet. | percutiebat] percutebat 2 tundebat 5 | deus] domine deus 4 8 | propitius esto] miserere 5 repropitiare 4 propitiare 8 | **14** dico uobis] dico itaque uobis 4 | quia] om. 2 5 A | descendit] discendit 2 4 hic] hic publicanus 4 8 17 | iustificatus] iustificatus magis 4 | in domo sua] in domum suam cet. om. 5 | prae illum] praeter illum 5 ab illo A magis (om. 4) quam ille cet. | pharisaeum] pharisaeus cet. om. A

quoniam omnis, qui se exaltat, humiliabitur, et qui se humiliat, exaltabitur. **15**
offerebant autem ei infantes, ut illos tangeret. uidentes autem discipuli
obiurgabant eos. **16** Iesus autem imperauit eis dicens: sinite infantes uenire ad me
et nolite prohibere illos. talium est enim regnum caelorum. **17** Amen dico uobis,
quisque non acceperit regnum dei tamquam infans, non intrabit in illut. **18**
Interrogauit autem eum quidam dicens: magister bone, quid faciens uitam
aeternam possidebo? **19** Dixit autem illi iesus: quid me dicis bonum? nemo est
bonus nisi unus deus. **20** mandata nosti. ait: quae? non homicidium facies, non
adulterabis, non furtum facies, non falsum testimonium dices, honora patrem
tuum et matrem tuam. **21** qui dixit: haec omnia custodiui a iuuentute mea. **22**
Quod cum audisset iesus, dixit ei: adhuc unum tibi deest. omnia, quaecumquae
habes, uende et diuide ea pauperibus, et habebis thensaurum in caelis. et ueni,
sequere me. **23** qui cum audisset haec, tristes factus est. erat enim diues ualde. **24**

---

quoniam omnis] 5 17 qui se exaltabat quia omnis 2 quoniam 4* quia omnis 8 A | exaltat] exaltauerit 2 | humiliabitur] humiliauitur 2 | et qui se humiliat exaltabitur] 8 A et qui se humiliat exaltauitur 2 et qui humiliat se exaltabitur 5 et omnis qui se humiliat exaltabitur 4* om. 17 **15** offerebant] adferebant 8 afferebant 17 A | ei] illi 2 5 ad illum cet. | infantes] 4 5 et infantes cet. | illos] eos cet. | uidentes autem] 5 cum uidessent autem 2 quod cum uiderent (uiderunt 17) cet. | discipuli] discentes 2 | obiurgabant] corripuerunt 2 increpabant cet. | eos] 2 5 illos cet. **16** imperauit eis] ad se uocabat ea 5 conuocans illos (eos 2) cet. | dicens] 5 dixit cet. | sinite] dimittite 5 | infantes] 5 17 pueros cet. | et] om. 2 | nolite prohibere illos] nolite illos prohibere 2 nolite uetare eis 5 nolite eos uetare (prohibere 8) cet. | est enim] enim est 2 5 17 | caelorum] 4 dei cet. | **17** Amen] amen enim 5 | quisque] quicumque cet. | acceperit] receperit 2 | tamquam] quasi 2 sicut cet. | infans] infantem 5 puer (add. iste 17) cet. | intrabit] introiuit 2 intrauit 5 4 | illut] illum 2 8 illud cet. | **18** Interrogauit autem] 4 8 et interrogauit (interrogabit 17) cet. eum] illum 2 | quidam] quidam princeps 5 A | dicens] om. 5 | faciens] 5 A faciam 2 faciendo cet. | uitam aeternam possidebo] 17 A ut uitam aeternam consequar 2 uitam aeternam hereditabo 5 uitam in aeuo uenturo uidebo 4* uitam aeternam possideo 8 | **19** Dixit autem] ad ille dixit 5 et respondit 4* | illi] 2 5 ei 4 A om. 8 17 | dicis] dices 2 | est] 2 om. cet. | unus] solus 8 A deus] deus pater 5 | **20** mandata] manta 2 praecepta 5 | ait] ait illi 2 ad ille dixit 5 om. cet. quae] quae dicit illi 2 quae dixit autem iesus 5 om. cet. | non homicidium facies] non moechabis 5 non occides cet. om. 2 | non adulterabis] ne admiseris 2 non occides 5 non adulterium admittes 4 non adulterium comittes 8 non moechaueris 17 non moechaberis A | non^{3}] ne 2 | facies^{2}] feceris 2 | non^{4}] ne 2 | dices] dixeris 2 dicis 5 | honora] honorifica 2 | tuam] 4 om. cet **21** qui dixit] ille autem dixit 2 ad ille dixit 5 qui ait 4* A ait ille 4^{c} et ait illi 8 17 | haec omnia custodiui] omnia ista obseruaui 2 haec omnia ego custodiui 4* omnia custodiui haec 8 | mea] om. 5 | **22** Quod cum audisset] cum audisset autem illum (illam*) 2 audiens autem 5 quo (quod 4 8) audito cet. | dixit] 2 5 ait cet. | ei] A illi 2 5 om. cet. | tibi deest] deest tibi 8 | quaecumquae] quae 2 5 | diuide ea] da cet. | pauperibus] egenis 2 | thensaurum] thesạurum A | caelis] 2 5 caelo cet. | **23** qui cum audisset haec] ille autem cum audisset 2 ille autem audiens haec 5 his ille auditis cet. | tristes factus] ristis factus 5 contristatus cet. | erat enim diues] 5 fuit enim diues 2 quia diues erat cet. | ualde] multum 2

quem cum uidisset iesus contristatum, dixit: quam difficile, qui pecunias habent, in regno dei intrabunt. **25** facilius est enim camellum per foramem acus transire quam diuite in regnum dei. **26** Dixerunt autem, qui audiebant: et quis poterit saluus fieri? **27** dixit autem illis: quae inpossibilia sunt aput homines, possibilia uero aput deum sunt. **28** Dixit autem petrus: ecce nos relictis omnibus nostris secuti sumus te. **29** qui dixit eis: amen dico uobis, nemo est, qui reliquerit domum aut parentes aut fratres aut uxorem aut filios propter regnum dei, **30** qui non accipiet septies tantum in tempore isto et in futuro saeculo uitam aeternam possidebit. **31** Conuocatis autem duodecim discipulis dixit ad illos: ecce ascendimus in hierosolyma et consummabuntur omnia, quae scripta sunt per prophetas de filio hominis. **32** Tradetur enim gentibus et inludetur et conspuetur **33** et flagellatum occident illum et die tertia resurget. **34** et ipsi nihil horum

---

24 quem cum uidisset] cum uidisset autem illum 2 uidens autem illum (eum 5) cet. | iesus] A om. cet. | contristatum] 2 tristem factum cet. | dixit] A dixit illi (ill*) iesus 2 dixit iesus cet. quam] quomo 2 quomodo 5 | difficile] difficiliter 2 | pecunias] substantiam 2 | regno] regnum cet. | intrabunt] introibunt 2 5 | **25** enim] autem 5 17 om. 4 | camellum] 2 17 camelum cet. foramem] cauernam 2 | transire] introire 2 | diuite] diuitem cet. add. introire 5 intrare 4 A regnum] regno 4 8 17 | **26** Dixerunt autem] 2 dixerunt ergo 5 et dixerunt cet. | audiebant] audierunt 5 audiaebant 17 | poterit] potest cet. | saluus fieri] saluari 2 5 | **27** dixit autem illis] ille autem dixit 2 at ille dixit 5 ait illis A et (om. 4) ait illis iesus cet. | aput homines] in hominibus 5 apud homines cet. om. 8 | possibilia uero aput deum sunt] possibilia apud deum sunt 2 apud deum possibilia sunt 5 haec omnia possibilia sunt apud deum 4 omnia possibilia sunt apud deum 17 A om. 8 | **28** Dixit] 2 5 ait cet. | nos relictis omnibus nostris] remisimus omnia nostra 2 quae nostra sunt reliquimus 5 dimisimus omnia A relictis rebus nostris (om. 17) cet. | secuti sumus] et secuti sumus 2 5 A | **29** qui dixit eis] A ille autem dixit illis 2 ad ille dixit illis 5 quibus ipse dixit (ait 17) cet. | reliquerit] relinquet 2 17[c] dimisit 5 reliquit 4 A relinquat 8 17* | domum] domos 5 fratres] fratres aut sorores 5 | uxorem] uxore 2 add. aut fratres 17 | aut filios] aut filios in tempore hoc 5 | **30** qui non] 8 si non 5 et non A nisi ut cet. | accipiet] 5 recipias 2 recipiat cet. septies tantum] multo plura A | in tempore isto] in isto tempore 2 in tempore hoc 5 et in hoc tempore 4 in hoc tempore cet. | et] om. 8 | futuro saeculo] saeculo futuro 2* saeculum uenturum 5 saeculo (add. autem 8) uenturo cet. | uitam aeternam possidebit] uitam consequetur aeternam 2 uitam aeternam 5 A | **31** Conuocatis] sumpsit 2 adsumens 5 adsumpsit 4 8 assumpsit 17 A | autem] autem iesus 8 17 A | duodecim] xii 5 4 17 | discipulis] discipulos suos 4 discipulos 8 17 om. cet. | dixit] 5 et ait (dixit 2) cet. | ad illos] 2 4 illis cet. | in] 5 om. cet. | hierosolyma] 4 hierusalem 2 5 iherosolima 8 hierosolymam 17 A | per] de 8* | prophetas] profetas 2 5 **32** Tradetur enim gentibus] quia tradetur nationibus 2 quoniam tradetur gentibus 5 | inludetur] deridetur 2 iniuriabitur 5 add. et flagellabitur A | conspuetur] A sputis agitur 2 espuent in eum 5 inspuetur 4 expuent in eum 8 spuerunt 17 | **33** flagellatum] et flagellabunt et 2 et flagellis caesum 5 et postquam flagellauerint A | occident] occidunt 17 | illum] eum 5 A om. 2 | die tertia] A deteriores 2 tertia die cet. | resurget] urguent 2 | **34** et ipsi nihil horum] ille autem nihil horum 2 ipsi autem horum inihil 5 et ipse nihil horum 17

intellexerunt, sed erat uerbum absconsum ab eis, et non intellexerunt, quae dicebantur ad eos. **35** Factum est autem, dum adpropinquaret in iericho, quidam caecus sedebat secus uiam mendicans. **36** qui cum audisset turbam praetereuntem, interrogabat, quidnam hoc esset. **37** indicauerunt autem ei, quia iesus nazarenus transit. **38** et exclamauit dicens: Iesu, fili dauid, miserere mei. **39** et qui praeteribant, increpabant eum, ut taceret. ad ille multo magis clamabat: fili dauid, miserere mei. **40** Stans autem iesus iussit illum adduci. cumque adpropinquasset, interrogauit illum **41** dicens: quid tibi uis faciam? qui dixit: ut uideam. **42** Et respondens dixit illi iesus: respice, fides tua te saluum fecit. **43** et confestim uidere coepit et sequebatur eum honorificans deum. et omnis populus, cum uidisset, dederunt laudem deo.

---

sed erat] sed fuit 2 et erat 8 A | uerbum] uerbum istud A | absconsum] absconditum 8 17 A eis] ipsis 2 | et non intellexerunt] 4 17 et non cognoscebant 2 et nesciebant 5 ex his 8 et non intellegebant A | quae dicebantur] 5 A quod dicebatur 4 17 quae dicebat 8 om. 2 | ad eos] eum 2 ab eo 4 om. cet. | **35** Factum est autem] factum est autem in eo 5 | dum] 8 cum cet. | adpropinquaret] adpropiaret 5 8 appropinquaret 17 A | in] om. cet. | iericho] 2 5 iherico 8 hiericho cet. | quidam caecus sedebat secus uiam mendicans] caecus quidam mendicus sedebat circa uiam 2 caecus quidem mendicus sedebat secus uiam 5 et unus caecus sedebat secus uiam mendicans 8 caecus quidam sedebat secus uiam mendicans (mendicus 4) cet. | **36** qui cum audisset] cum audisset autem 2 audiens autem 5 et cum audiret cet. | turbam praetereuntem] turbas transeuntes 2 | interrogabat] interrogauit 2 | quidnam] 5 quid cet. | hoc esset] esset illud 2 esset hoc 5 | **37** indicauerunt] renuntiauerunt 2 dixerunt cet. | autem] om. 2 | ei] 8 A illi cet. quia] 2 5 quod cet. | nazarenus] A nazorenus 2 17 nazoreus cet. | transit] transiret A | **38** et] ille autem 2 at ille 5 | exclamauit] 2 5 clamauit cet. | Iesu] iesum 2 iesus 8 17 | fili] filii A mei] mihi 4 | **39** et qui praeteribant] qui praecedebant autem 2 at illi antecedebant 5 et (om. 17) qui praeibant cet. | increpabant] corripiebant 2 | eum] illum 5 om. 2 | ad ille] 5 ille autem 2 ipse uero cet. | multo] om. 5 | fili dauid miserere mei] 8 17 miserere mei fili dauid 2 filius dauid miserere mihi 5 fili dauid miserere mihi 4 filii dauid miserere mei A | **40** Stans] stetit 2 | iussit] et iussit 2 | illum[1]] eum 2 5 A | adduci] adduci ad se 4 A | cumque adpropinquasset] et cum accessisset 2 cum adpropiasset autem 5 et cum adpropinquasset 4 et cum adpropiasset 8 et cum appropiasset 17 et cum appropinquasset A | illum[2]] eum 5 | **41** dicens] om. 2 5 | tibi uis] uis tibi 5 | qui dixit] ille autem dixit 2 at ille dixit A ad ille dixit cet. | ut uideam] domine ut uideam 2 5 A ut uideam domine 4 8 17 | **42** respondens] om. A | dixit illi iesus] iesus 2 dixit ei 5 iesus dixit illi A | respice] uide 2 | fides] fide enim 2 | te saluum fecit] salbauit te 2 salbum te fecit 5 **43** confestim] continuo 2 | uidere coepit] respexit 5 uidit cet. | eum] illum 4 A | honorificans] clarificans 2 honorans 5 magnificans cet. | omnis] omnes 2 8 | populus] 2 5 plebs cet. | cum uidisset] 2 uidens 5 ut uidit cet. | dederunt] et dedit 2 dedit cet. | laudem deo] gloriam deo 5 deo laudem 8

19 Et ingressus circuibat hiericho. **2** et ecce uir nomine zaccheus, et hic erat princeps publicanorum et ipse erat locuples. **3** et quaerebat uidere iesum, qui esset, et non poterat prae turba, quoniam statura breui erat. **4** et procurrens ascendit in arborem sycomori, ut uideret illum, quoniam per illa parte transiturus erat. **5** Et factum est, dum transiret iesus, uidit illum et respiciens dixit ei: zacchaee, festinans descende, quoniam hodie in domo tua oportet me manere. **6** Et festinans descendit et excepit illum gaudens. **7** et cum uidissent, omnes murmurati sunt, quod aput uirum peccatorem introisset manere. **8** Stans autem zaccheus dixit ad dominum: ecce dimidiam partem bonorum meorum, domine, do pauperibus, et si cui quid fraudaui, quadruplum reddam. **9** Dixit autem iesus ad illos, quia hodie salus domui huic facta est, quoniam quidem et hic filius est abrahae. **10** uenit enim filius hominis saluum facere et quaerere perditum. **11**

19:1 Et ingressus] et cum introiret 2 et intrans 5 et habiit iesus et 4* | circuibat] pertransiebat 2 5 perambulabat cet. | hiericho] iericho 2 5 | **2** nomine] qui uocabatur nomine 2 | et[2]] om. 2 5 17 erat[1]] fuit 2 | et ipse] om. 2 5 | erat[2]] om. cet. | locuples] 5 diues cet. add. erat 8 | **3** uidere iesum] iesum uidere 8 | qui esset] quisset 5 quis esset cet. | prae] per 2 a 5 | turba] turbas 2 quoniam] quia cet. | statura] de statu 5 | breui] pusillus cet. | erat] fuit 2 | **4** et procurrens] praecessit autem in priore et 2 antecedens ab ante 5 et praecurrens cet. | arborem] arbore 2 sycomori] morum 5 sycomorum cet. om. 2 | illum] eum 5 | quoniam] quia cet. | per illa parte] illic 2 inde 5 A illa parte cet. | transiturus erat] 2 habebat transire 5 erat transiturus cet. **5** factum est] om. A | dum] 8 17 cum cet. | transiret iesus] illac transiret 5 uenisset ad locum A uidit illum et respiciens] respexit et uidit illum 2 uidit 5 uidit illum respicientem 4 uidit illum sursum aspiciens 8 uidit susum aspiciens 17 suspiciens iesus uidit illum A | dixit] et dixit cet. ei] 5 illi 2 ad eum cet. | zacchaee festinans] festina zacche 2 | descende] descendere 2 discende 4 | quoniam] quia cet. | hodie in domo tua oportet me manere] oportet hodie me in domo tua 2 in domo tua oportet me prandere hodie 8 | **6** excepit] suscepit 5 | illum] eum 5 | **7** et cum uidissent] 2 et uidentes 5 et cum uiderent (eum 8) cet. | murmurati sunt] murmurabant 2 5 murmurauerunt dicentes 4 murmurauerunt 8 17 murmurabant dicentes A | quod] quia 2 5 4 aput] apud 2 ad cet. | uirum peccatorem] peccatorem hominem 5 hominem peccatorem cet. introisset] introiuit 2 introibit 5 deuertit 4 17 diuertit 8 diuertisset A | manere] 5 8 hospitari 2 om. cet. | **8** Stans] stetit 2 | dixit] et dixit 2 | dominum] iesum 2 | dimidiam partem] dimidium cet. | bonorum meorum] ex substantia mea 2 de substantia mea 5 | domine] om. 2 4 17 | do pauperibus] do egenis 2 pauperibus do 5 add. domine 4 | cui quid] quid cui 2 cuius aliquid 5 quid aliquem A quid alicui cet. | fraudaui] 2 8 calumniaui 5 abstuli fraude 4 fraude abstuli 17 defraudaui A | quadruplum reddam] quadruplum reddo 2 restituo quadruplum 5 reddo quadruplum cet. | **9** Dixit] 2 5 ait cet. | autem] om. A | ad illos] om. 2 5 ad eum A | quia] 2 A quoniam 5 quod cet. | hodie salus domui huic] salus hodie domui huic 2 hodie salus in domo hac 5 hodie salus huic domui 8 | quoniam] 2 5 eo quod cet. | quidem] om. cet. | hic] 5 ipse cet. | filius est abrahae] 17 filius abrahae est 2 filius abraham est 5 sit filius abrahe 4 filius sit abrahae 8 A **10** uenit] ueniet 17* | enim] autem 17 | saluum facere et quaerere] salbare et quaerere 2 quaerere et saluum facere 4 8 quaerere et saluare cet. | perditum] quod perierat cet.

Audientibus autem haec illis addidit dicens parabolam, eo quod esset iuxta
hierusalem et quod putabant, quia confestim regnum dei manifestaretur. **12** Dixit
ergo: homo quidam paterfamilias profectus est in regionem longinquam accipere
regnum et reuerti. **13** uocatis autem decem seruis suis dedit illis decem mnas et
dixit ad eos: negotiamini, donec uenio. **14** ciues autem illius odiebant eum. Et
miserunt legationem post illum dicentes, quia nolumus hunc regnare super nos.
15 et factum est reuertente illo accepto regno, iussit uocari seruos suos, quibus
dederat pecuniam, ut sciret, quis quid negotiatus fuisset. **16** Uenit autem prior
dicens: domine, mna tua decem adquisiuit mnas. **17** et dixit illi: tanto melior, bone
serue, quia in minimo fidelis fuisti, eris potestatem habens supra decem ciuitates.
18 Et uenit alius dicens: domine, mna tua fecit alias quinque mnas. **19** dixit et huic:
et tu esto supra quinque ciuitates potestatem habens. **20** Et alius uenit dicens:
domine, ecce mna tua, quam habebam, repositam in sudario, **21** quoniam

---

11 Audientibus autem haec illis] et audientibus illis haec 2 audientium autem eorum haec 5 haec illis audientibus cet. | addidit dicens] aiecit et dixit 2 adiciens dixit cet. | parabolam] 5 A similitudinem cet. | eo quod] propter quod 5 | iuxta] 2 5 prope cet. | hierusalem] iherusalem 8 quod[2]] quia cet. om. 2 5 | putabant] putarent illi 2 putare d existimarent cet. | quia] 2 5 quod cet. | confestim] incipit 2 incipiet confestim 5 | manifestaretur] adparere 2 reuelari 5 | **12** ergo] autem 5 om. 2 | homo quidam] 5 A homo quidam (quidam homo 8) erat cet. | paterfamilias] generosus 2 nobilis 5 A diues cet. | profectus est] is abiit 4 abiit (habit 8) cet. | regionem] regione 2 | longinquam] longe 4 | accipere] accepere 2 accipere sibi 8 A | **13** uocatis autem decem seruis suis] A et uocitis autem decem seruis suis 2 uocans autem decem seruos suos 5 et uocauit decem seruos cet. | dedit] et dedit 4 8 17 | illis] eis 5 | mnas] minas 2 talenta 4 | dixit] 2 5 ait cet. | ad eos] 5 illis 2 ad illos cet. | donec] dum cet. | **14** illius] eius 2 17 A om. cet. | odiebant] oderant cet. | eum] 2 illum cet. om. 5 | miserunt] miserant 2 | legationem] legatos 5 | illum] eum 2 | quia] om. cet. | nolumus] nolimus 2 | regnare] hic regnare 17 | super nos] nobis 2 supra nos 5 | **15** reuertente illo] reuertenti illum 2 reuerti eum 5 ut (dum 8 17) rediret cet. accepto regno] accipientem regnum 5 | iussit] et dixit 5 et iussit cet. | uocari] uocari ad se 2 suos] 5 om. cet. | dederat] 2 5 dedit cet. | sciret] sciat 5 | quis quid negotiatus fuisset] quid egerint 2 quis negotati sunt 5 quis quantum negotiatus est 17 quantum quisque negotiatus esset cet. | **16** Uenit autem prior] et uenit primus 2 aduenit ergo primus 5 uenit autem primus cet. mna tua] mina tua 2 talentum tuum 4 | decem] x 4 | adquisiuit mnas] adquisiuit minas 2 mnas (talenta 4) adquisiuit (adquisiuis 5) cet. | **17** et dixit illi] ille autem dixit ad illum dicens 2 ad ille dixit illi 5 et ait illi cet. | tanto melior] euge cet. | bone serue] serue bone 8 17 | quia] quoniam 5 | minimo] modico cet. | fidelis fuisti] fuisti fidelis 2 17 | eris] esto 2 5 | habens] habiens 2 supra] super 2 5 | ciuitates] ciuitatis 2 | **18** Et uenit alius] 2 et alter uenit (ueniens 5) cet. dicens] et dixit 2 dixit 5 | domine] om. 8 | mna] mina 2 | fecit alias quinque mnas] fecit quinque minas 2 quinque adquisiuit mnas 5 fecit quinque mnas (talenta 4) cet. | **19** dixit et huic] dixit autem et huic 2 5 ait et huic 4 17 et ait et huic 8 et huic ait A | et tu esto] esto 2 esto et tu 5 supra] super 2 5 | ciuitates] ciuitatis 2 | potestatem habens] om. cet. | **20** Et alius uenit] 2 5 et alter uenit cet. | mna tua] mina tua 2 talentum tuum 4 | quam] quod 4 | habebam] 5 habui cet. repositam in sudario] 5 repositum in sudario 4 reposita in sudario 8 17 om. 2 | **21** quoniam timebam te] 5 quia timebam te 2 timui enim te A quia timui te cet.

timebam te, quia homo austerus es. tollis, quod non posuisti, et metes, quod non
seminasti. **22** ait illi: ex ore tuo iudicabo te, infidelis serue et male, sciebas me,
quia homo austeris sum, tollo, quod non posui, et meto, quod non seminaui. **23** et
quare non dedisti pecuniam meam ad mensam? et ego cum uenissem cum usuris,
exegissem eam? **24** Circumstantibus autem dixit: auferte ab illo et date ei, qui
decem mnas habet. **25** et dixerunt illi: domine, habet decem mnas. **26** dico uobis:
omni, qui habuerit, dabitur illi. ab eo autem, qui non habet, et quod habet,
auferetur ab eo. **27** Uerumtamen inimicos meos illos, qui noluerunt me regnare
super se, adducite hoc et iugulate in conspectu meo. **28** et his dictis ibat
hierosolymis ascendens. **29** Et factum est, cum adpropinquasset betphage et
bethania, ad montem, qui appellatur oliueti, misit duos ex discipulis suis **30**
dicens: Ite in uicum contra, in quo ingredientes inuenietis asinam cum pullum

---

quia homo austerus es] 17 A homo enim es austeris 2 homo es enim austeris 5 quod homo austeris es 4 quia homo austeris es 8 | tollis] tolles 5 tollens 8 | metes] 8 17 metis cet. | **22** ait illi] et dixit illi 2 ad ille dixit illi 5 et dixit ei 4 17 tunc dixit 8 dicit ei A | ex] 2 de cet. | iudicabo te] 5 te condemno 2 te iudico cet. | infidelis serue] serue inique 5 serue nequam A o infidelis serue 4 8 om. 2 | et male] om. cet. | sciebas me] sciebas cet. om. 2 | quia] 5 quoniam 2 quod cet. | homo austeris sum] ego austerus sum 2 ego homo sum austerus 5 ego austeris homo sum A ego (om. 8) homo austeris (austerus 17) sum cet. | tollo] tollens A | meto] metens A | **23** et quare] quare ergo 2 5 | ad mensam] nummulariis 2 super mensam 5 | cum uenissem] ueniens cet. | usuris] usura 5 | exegissem] 2 exigebam 5 utique exegissem cet. | eam] illud 2 5 A illum 4 illam 8 17 **24** Circumstantibus autem dixit] et dixit adsistentibus 2 dixit autem his qui astabant 5 et adstantibus dixit cet. | auferte] auferite 2 tollite 5 | ab illo] ab eo 5 ab illo talantum 4* mnam (mna 8) cet. | date] ferte 5 | ei] illi cet. om. 5 | decem mnas habet] 5 A decem minas habet 2 decem talanta habet 4* decem talenta habet 4^{c} habet decem mnas 8 habet x mnas 17 | **25** et dixerunt illi domine habet decem mnas] et dixerunt ei domine habet decem mnas 17 A om. cet. | **26** dico uobis] dico enim uobis 5 et ait illis dico autem uobis 17 dico autem uobis cet. | omni] quia omni 2 A quoniam omni 5 | qui habuerit] habenti cet. | dabitur] adicietur d | illi] om. cet. | et] etiam 17 | auferetur] tolletur 5 aufertur 17 | ab eo^{2}] illi 8 om. 17 | **27** Uerumtamen] uerum 2 uerumtamen dico uobis 8 | inimicos meos illos] illos inimicos meos 2 5 | noluerunt me regnare] me nolunt regnare 2 noluerunt regnare me 17 | se] eos 5 | hoc] huc 8 A | iugulate in conspectu meo] coram me interficite 2 occidite in conspecto meo 5 interficite ante me cet. add. et inutilem serbum eicite in tenebras exteriores ibi erit ploratus et stridor dentium 5 | **28** his dictis] et cum dixisset haec 2 et haec cum dixisset 5 | ibat] 5 ambulabat 2 praecedebat A abiit 8 17 | hierosolymis ascendens] cum ascenderet autem hierusalem 2 ascendens autem in hierusalem 5 ascendens in (om. 17 A) hierosolyma (iherosolima 8 hierosolymam 17) cet. | **29** Et factum est] om. 2 | cum] 5 A dum 8 17 om. 2 | adpropinquasset] 17 fuit 2 adpropiasset 5 adpropiaret 8 appropinquasset A betphage] in bethapagae 2 in betphage 5 ad bethphage A | bethania] bethaniae 8 17 | appellatur oliueti] oliueti 2 oliueti qui uocatur 5 qui uocatur oliueti (oliuetum 8) cet. | misit] et misit 2 duos] duo 2 8 | ex discipulis suis] ex discentibus 2 de discipulis suis 5 discipulos suos cet. **30** uicum contra] contra qui est castellus 5 castellum quod (om. 2) contra est cet. | in quo] et 5 in quod A | ingredientes] cum introieritis 2 introeuntes cet. | asinam cum pullum alligatum] asinae pullum alligatum 2 pullum 5 pullum asinae alligatum cet.

alligatum, super quem nullus sedit. soluite illam et adducite. **31** et si quis uos interrogauerit, quare soluitis, dicetis illi, quoniam dominus operam eius desiderat. **32** Abierunt autem, qui missi erant, sicut dixerat illis, inuenerunt asinam stantem. **33** et soluentibus eis asinam cum pullo dixerunt domini ipsius ad illos: Quid soluitis pullum? **34** qui dixerunt, quia domino suo necessarius est. **35** et adduxerunt illum ad iesum et substernentes uestimenta sua super pullum inposuerunt iesum. **36** Euntem autem illo substernebant ei uestimenta sua in uia. **37** adpropinquante autem eo ad discensum montis oliueti coepit omnis multitudo gaudens conlaudare deum uoce magna, de quibus uidebant omnibus uirtutibus, **38** dicentes: benedictus, qui uenit in nomine domini, benedictus rex, pax in caelo et gloria. **39** et quidam pharisaeorum de turba dixerunt ad illum: magister, obiurga illos. **40** qui dixit eis: dico uobis: si isti tacuerint, lapides clamabunt. **41** Et

super quem] 2 cui A in quo cet. | nullus] nemo hominum 2 5 nemo 8 17 nemo umquam hominum A | soluite illam] et soluentes 5 soluite illum (om. 2) cet. | et] om. 5 | adducite] adducite illum 2 **31** quis] qui 2 | uos interrogauerit] uobis dixerit 5 | quare soluitis] A ut quid soluitis 17 om. cet. dicetis] 8 sic dicetis cet. | illi] ei A om. cet. | quoniam] 5 quia cet. | operam eius desiderat] desiderat illum 2 eius opus habet 5 opera eius desiderat A | **32** Abierunt autem] et abierunt 2 et euntes 5 | qui missi erant] om. 2 | sicut dixerat illis inuenerunt] et sic inuenerunt stantem 2 et inuenerunt sicut dixit illis iesus (om. A) pullum (om. i) stantem (stantem pullum A) cet. | **33** et soluentibus eis] et cum soluerent 2 soluentibus autem illis A | asinam cum pullo dixerunt domini ipsius ad illos] pullum (om. 8 17) dixerunt domini eius ad illos cet. om. 2 | Quid soluitis pullum] om. 2 | **34** qui dixerunt] aiunt 2 sic dixerunt 5 at illi dixerunt cet. | quia] A quoniam 5 om. cet. | domino suo necessarius est] dominus opus est 2 dominus opera eius desiderat 8 dominus huius opus habet dominus operam eius desiderat 17 dominus eum necessarium habet A | **35** adduxerunt] 2 adducentes 5 duxerunt cet. | illum] pullum 2 5 | ad iesum] om. 2 5 | et[2]] om. 5 substernentes] superiecerunt 2 supermiserunt 5 iactauerunt 8 17 iactantes A | uestimenta sua] tunicas suas 5 | super] supra A | pullum] illum 2 eum 5 | inposuerunt] A et inposuerunt cet. **36** Euntem autem illo] 17 cum iret autem 2 eunte autem illo cet. | ei] illi 2 | in uia] in uiam 8 om. 5 | **37** adpropinquante autem eo] cum adpropinquaret autem 2 adpropiantibus autem illis 5 et cum adpropiaret iam 8 17 et cum appropinquaret iam A | discensum] 2 descensum cet. oliueti] oliuarum 2 5 | coepit] 2 5 coeperunt cet. | omnis multitudo] 5 omnis turba 2 omnes turbae cet. add. discipulorum 2 5 descendentium A | gaudens] gaudentes cet. | conlaudare] laudare cet. | magna] om. 5 | de quibus uidebant omnibus uirtutibus] de omnibus uirtutibus quas uiderant 2 de omnibus quibus uiderunt quae fiebant 5 super omnibus quas uiderant uirtutibus A om. 8 17 | **38** benedictus qui uenit in nomine domini benedictus rex] benedictus rex 2 benedictus qui uenit rex in nomine domini A | gloria] in excelsi 2 altissimis 5 in excelsis cet. **39** et quidam] quidam autem 2 5 | pharisaeorum] ex pharisaeis 2 de pharisaeis 5 | turba] 5 8 turbis cet. | ad illum] illi 2 ad eum 5 | obiurga] corripe 2 increpa cet. | illos] 8 17 discipulos 2 discipulos tuos 5 A | **40** qui dixit eis] et respondens dixit illis 2 respondes autem dixit illis 5 quibus ipse ait (dixit 8) cet. | dico uobis] om. 17 | si] quia si 5 A | isti] 2 5 hi cet. | tacuerint] tacebunt 5 17 | **41** Et cum adpropinquasset] et quomodo adpropinquauit 2 et cum adpropiasset 5 8 et ut adpropiauit 17 et ut appropinquauit A

cum adpropinquasset, uisa ciuitate fleuit super eam **42** dicens, quoniam si scires tu quamquam in hac tua die, quae ad pacem tuam absconsa essent, ab oculis, **43** quoniam uenient dies super te, et inicient inimici tui saepem et circundabunt te et continebunt te undique **44** et pauimentabunt te et natos tuos, qui in te sunt, et non relinquent lapidem supra lapidem in te, ob hoc, quod ignorasti tempus uisitationis tuae. **45** Et ingressus in templo coepit eicere uendentes in illo et ementes et mensas nummulariorum euertit et cathedras uendentium columbas **46** dicens eis: Scriptum est: domus mea domus orationis est, uos autem illam fecistis speluncam latronum. **47** Et erat docens cottidie in templo. pontifices autem et scribae et principes populi quaerebant illum perdere. **48** et non inueniebant, quid facerent. populus enim omnis suspensus erat audiens eum.

20 Et factum est autem, in una dierum docente illo populum in templo et adnuntiante, adstiterunt pontifices et scribae cum senioribus **2** dicentes: dic nobis,

---

uisa ciuitate] cum uidisset ciuitatem 2 uidens ciuitatem cet. | eam] 5 illum 8 illam cet. | **42** dicens] om. 17 | quoniam] 2 5 qua 8 quia 17 A | scires] scisses 5 cognouisses cet. | tu] et tu 5 A quamquam] equidem 17 et quidem 8 A om. 2 5 | hac tua die] ista die 2 diem hoc 5 hac die (om. 17) cet. | tuam] tibi cet. | absconsa essent] 2 nunc autem absconsum est 5 nunc uero abscondita sunt 8 abscondita sunt 17 nunc autem abscondita sunt A | ab oculis] ab oculis tuis cet. | **43** quoniam] 5 quia cet. | dies super te] 2 dies 5 dies in te cet. | inicient inimici tui saepem] circumfodient inimici tui fossam 2 mittent super te inimici saepem 5 circumdabunt te inimici tui uallo cet. circundabunt] circumdabunt 2 A circumcingent 5 circumibunt 8 17 | et continebunt te] et conpraehendent 5 et obsidebunt te uallo 8 et coangustabunt te A om. 2 17 | **44** pauimentabunt te] et ad solum te deponent 2 et ad nihilum deducent te 5 et (om. A) ad terram (add. et 17) prosternent te cet. | natos] filios cet. | tuos] 2 5 om. cet. | qui in te sunt] in te 2 om. 5 | relinquent] 17 A remittent 2 dimittent 5 relinquet 8 add. in te A | supra] 8 17 super cet. | in te[2]] in tota terra 2 in tota te 5 in te uniuersa 8 17 om. A | ob hoc] pro eo 2 propter 5 eo cet. | ignorasti] non cognouisti 5 non cognoueritis 17 non cognoueris cet. | tempus] in tempus 5 | **45** Et ingressus] cum uenisset autem 2 ueniens autem 5 | templo] templum cet. | eicere] expellere 2 | in illo] in eo 5 om. 2 et mensas nummulariorum] om. A | euertit] effundebat 2 et fudit 5 effudit 8 om. 17 A | et cathedras uendentium columbas] et catedras eorum qui uendebant columbas euertit 2 et cathedras uendentium columbas euertit 8 et cathedras uendentium et columbas 17 om. A | **46** eis] 5 illis 8 17 A om. 2 | Scriptum est] add. quoniam 5 quia A | est[2]] uocabitur 2 | illam fecistis] fecistis illam cet. | **47** erat] fuit 2 | pontifices autem] pontificis autem sacerdotum 2 principes autem sacerdotum cet. | scribae] tribae 5 | principes populi] 2 primi populi 5 principales (principes A) plebi cet. | illum] eum 2 5 | perdere] perdere eum 5 | **48** facerent] 2 facerent ei 5 facerent illi cet. | populus enim omnis] 2 5 omnis (omnes 8) enim populus cet. | suspensus erat] pendebat 2 5 | audiens] audire 5 | eum] 2 5 illum cet. | **20:1** Et factum est autem] factum est autem 2 5 | dierum] die 2 | illo] eo 5 8 | populum in templo] 17 A in templum populum 2 5 populo in templo 8 | et adnuntiante] benenuntiantem 2 et euangelizante cet. | adstiterunt] 2 5 conuenerunt cet. | pontifices] 2 principes sacerdotum cet. | senioribus] maioribus natu 2 praesbyteris 5 | **2** dicentes] et dixerunt 2 5 et aiunt dicentes cet. add. ad eum (illum 5) cet.

in qua potestatem haec facis et quis est, qui dedit tibi hanc potestatem? **3**
respondens autem dixit ad illos: interrogabo uos et ego et respondite mihi: **4**
baptismum iohannis de caelo erat an ex hominibus? **5** Ad illi cogitabant intra se
dicentes, quia si dixerimus de caelo, dicet nobis: quare ergo non credidistis illi? **6**
et si dixerimus ab hominibus, omnis populus lapidabit nos. sciunt enim iohanen
prophetam fuisse. **7** et responderunt se nescire unde. **8** et dixit illis iesus: nec ego
dico uobis, in qua potestate haec facio. **9** coepit autem dicere parabolam hanc:
uineam plantauit homo et locauit illam colonis, et ipse peregrinatus est
temporibus multis. **10** et tempore quodam misit ad illos colonos seruum, ut ex
fructuum uineae darent illi. et caesum illum dimiserunt uacuum. **11** et adposuit
alium mittere seruum quoque et illum caesum dimiserunt uacuum. **12** et adposuit
tertium mittere et illum uulneratum proiecerunt. **13** Dixit autem dominus uineae:

---

haec facis] facis ista 2 | et] 2 5 aut cet. | tibi] uobis 2 | hanc] istam 2 | **3** respondens] respondit 2 | dixit] et dixit 2 iesus dixit 8 iesus dicit 17 | illos] eos 2 5 | uos et ego] et uos ego 8 add. unum uerbum 5 A | et respondite] dicite 2 quod dicite 5 respondite 8 respondete 17 A | **4** baptismum] baptisma 2 baptismus 5 | de caelo erat] utrum de deo est 2 | an] aut 5 | ex] ab 2 5 **5** Ad illi cogitabant] illi autem cogitauerunt 2 at illi cogitabant cet. | intra se] apud se 2 ad semetipsos 5 inter se cet. | quia] 5 A om. cet. | dicet] dicit 2 | nobis] om. cet. | ergo] om. 8 17 | illi[2]] 8 17 in eum 2 ei 5 A | **6** et si] si autem 8 A | ab] ex 17 A | populus lapidabit nos] lapidauit nos populus 2 lapidabit nos populus omnes 5 plebs uniuersa lapidabit nos cet. | sciunt enim] persuasum est enim illis 2 scit 5 certum est enim 8 certi sunt enim 17 A | iohanen] iohannen 5 A iohannem cet. | prophetam] profetam 2 | fuisse] esse A | **7** se nescire] non scire se 2 nescire se 5 et iesus ait illis cet. | unde] unde esset A | **8** et dixit illis iesus] et iesus dixit eis 2 5 | nec] 5 neque cet. | uobis] om. 8 17 | haec] ista 2 hoc 8 | **9** coepit autem dicere] dicebat autem et 2 dicebat autem 5 coepit autem (add. iesus 8) dicere ad plebem cet. | parabolam hanc] 5 A similitudinem talem 2 hanc parabolam 8 17 | uineam plantauit homo] uineam nouellauit homo 2 homo plantauit uineam A | locauit] tradidit 5 | illam] 2 eam cet. | colonis] agricolis 2 5 | et ipse] ipse autem 2 5 | peregrinatus] 2 5 pelegre 8 peregre 17 A | est] 2 5 fuit cet. | temporibus multis] 2 tempora multa 5 multis temporibus cet. | **10** et tempore quodam] in tempore autem 2 quod autem tempore 5 et quodam tempore 8 17 et in tempore A | illos] om. cet. | colonos] agricolas 2 5 cultores cet. | seruum] seruum suum 8 17 | ut] om. 8 | ex] de cet. | fructuum] fructum 2 fructo 5 fructu cet. | illi] ei 5 | et[2]] 2 illi autem 5 coloni autem 8 cultores autem 17 qui A caesum illum] caeciderunt illum 2 caesum eum 5 illum caesum 8 caesum A | dimiserunt uacuum] 5 et dimiserunt inanem 2 dimiserunt inanem 8 17 dimiserunt eum inanem A | **11** et adposuit alium mittere seruum] misit alium seruum 2 5 addidit alterum mittere seruum (seruum mittere A) cet. | quoque] illi autem cet. | et illum] 2 5 et (om. A) hunc quoque cet. | caesum] ceciderunt et contumeliis egerunt et 2 caesum iniuriantes 5 caesum et sine honore 8 17 caedentes et afficientes contumelia A | uacuum] 5 inanem cet. om. 2 | **12** et adposuit tertium mittere] tertium misit 2 5 et addidit tertium mittere cet. | illum] hunc 5 | uulneratum] 8 uulnerauerunt et 2 17 uulnerantes 5 A | proiecerunt] expulerunt 2 dimiserunt uacuum 5 eiecerunt cet. | **13** Dixit autem dominus uineae] dominus autem uinea dixit 2 5 quid faciam? mittam filium meum carissimum, forsitam hunc reuerebuntur. **14** quem ut uiderunt coloni, cogitauerunt inter se dicentes: hic est heres, oc{ca}cidamus eum, ut nostra fiat hereditas. **15** et proiectum illum extra uineam occiderunt. quid ergo faciet dominus uineae? **16** ueniet et perdet colonos istos et tradet uineam aliis. qui com audissent dixerunt: absit. **17** Quique intuens eos dixit: quid ergo scriptum est? lapidem, quem reprobauerunt aedificantes hic factus est in capite anguli. **18** omnis, qui offendiderit super illum lapidem, conquassabitur. super quem ceciderit autem, comminuet illum. **19** et quaesierunt pontifices et scribae inicere illi manus eadem hora, et timuerunt populum. scierunt enim, quod ad illos dixisset parabolam hanc. **20** et cum discessissent, submiserunt subor<natos> fingentes se, ut caperent sermones illius, ut traderent eum potestati praesidis. **21** et interrogauerunt illum dicentes: magister, scimus, quoniam dicis uera et non accipes persona hominum, sed in ueritate uiam dei doces. **22** licet

---

carissimum] 8 unicum 2 dilectum 5 A dilectissimum 17 | forsitam] 5 8 fortasse 2 forsitan 17 A hunc] hunc cum uiderint 2 cum hunc uiderint A | reuerebuntur] uerebuntur 8 A | **14** quem ut uiderunt] et cum uidissent filium 2 uidentes autem illum 5 quem cum uiderunt 8 17 quem cum uidissent A | coloni] om. 5 | cogitauerunt] cogitabant 2 5 | inter se] 17 apud se 2 ad inuicem 5 et intra se 8 in se A | occacidamus] uenite occidamus 2 5 | eum] illum cet. | ut nostra fiat hereditas] 5 A et nostra fiat (sit 2 fiet 17) hereditas (add. eius 2) cet. | **15** proiectum] expulerunt 2 proicientes 5 eiectum 8 A eiecerunt 17 | illum] eum 2 5 | extra uineam] de uinea 2 | occiderunt] et occiderunt 2 17 | faciet] 2 5 faciet illis cet. | **16** colonos] agricolas 2 5 | istos] om. 2 5 tradet] dabit (dauit 2) cet. | qui com audissent] illi autem cum audissent 2 ad illi audientes 5 quo (quod 8) audito cet. | dixerunt] 2 5 dixerunt illi cet. | absit] absit domine 2 | **17** Quique intuens] ad ille inspiciens 5 ille (ipse 17) autem aspiciens (intuens 2) cet. | eos] illos 8 om. 2 | dixit] 2 5 ait cet. add. illis 2 8 17 | quid ergo] quid est ergo hoc (om. 5) cet. | scriptum est] quod scriptum est (add. hoc 5) cet. | factus est] est factus 17 | capite] caput (capud 2) cet. | **18** offendiderit] ceciderit (caeciderit 2) cet. | super[1]] 5 in 2 supra cet. | conquassabitur] confringetur 5 non conquassabitur 17 | super[2]] 2 5 supra cet. | quem ceciderit autem] 8 17 quem autem ceciderit 2 A autem quem ceciderit 5 | comminuet] commouet 2 | illum[2]] eum 5 | **19** quaesierunt] 2 quaerebant cet. add. illum 17 | pontifices et scribae] scribae et pontificis 2 principes sacerdotum et scribae cet. | inicere] inice 2 mittere cet. | illi] 2 super eum 5 in illum cet. | eadem hora] ipsa (illa A) hora cet. om. 2 | et timuerunt] timuerunt autem 2 5 | scierunt] 5 intellexerunt 2 cognouerunt cet. | quod] quoniam 2 5 | illos] 5 eos 2 ipsos cet. | dixisset] dixerit A dixit cet. | parabolam] 5 17 similitudinem cet. | hanc] 5 istam cet. | **20** cum discessissent] secesserunt 2 recedentes 5 cum recessissent 8 17 obseruantes A | submiserunt] et miserunt 2 miserunt 5 A subornatos] unum adque alterum 2 obsiduanos 5 insidiatores A om. 8 17 | fingentes se] qui simularent se iustos 2 in dolo loquentes esse se iustos 5 qui se iustos esse (om. A) simularent cet. caperent] A repraehenderent 2 adprehenderent cet. | sermones illius] uerba eius 2 uerborum eius 5 sermones eius 8 17 eum in sermone A | ut[2]] 5 et cet. | eum] 5 illum cet. | potestati praesidis] legato 2 praesidi 5 potestati et magistratui praesidis 8 principatui et potestati praesidis A om. 17 | **21** illum] eum 5 om. cet. | quoniam] quod 8 quia A | dicis uera] dices recte 2 5 recte dicis cet. add. et doces 2 5 A | non] nullius 5 | accipes] accipies 2 accipis cet. | persona] 2 personam cet. | hominum] om. cet. | doces] docens 8

nobis tributum dare caesari aut non? **23** Quorum uisa nequitia dixit ad illos: quid me temptatis? **24** ostendite mihi denarium: cuius habet imaginem et inscriptionem? respondentes dixerunt: caesaris. **25** qui dixit: reddite caesari, quae sunt caesaris {caesari}, et quae dei sunt, deo. **26** et non potuerunt sermonem eius capere coram populo et mirati in responso eius tacuerunt. **27** accedentes autem quidam sadduceorum, qui contradicunt resurrectionem non esse, interrogabant illum **28** dicentes: Magister, moises scripsit nobis: si unius frater mortuus fuerit habens uxorem et hic filios non habuerit, ut accipiat frater illius uxorem eius et resuscitet fratri suo semen. **29** Septem fratres erant, et prior {a} accepit uxorem et decessit sine filiis. **30** et sequens accepit eam et ipse decessit sine filiis. **31** tertius similiter autem et septem et non reliquerunt filium et defuncti sunt. **32** sed et mulier. **33** in resurrectione cuius eorum erit uxor? septem enim habuerunt illam

---

22 tributum dare caesari] dare caesari tributum 2 dare tributum caesari 8 A | aut] an A
23 Quorum uisa nequitia] cum cognouisset autem nequitiam illorum 2 cognoscens autem eorum iniquitatem 5 considerans autem (add. iesus 8) dolum illorum cet. | ad illos] 2 eis 8 ad (om. A) eos cet. | quid me temptatis] om. 2 | **24** denarium] figuram 5 | habet] habent 17* | inscriptionem] 17 A superscriptionem 2 superinscriptionem 5 scriptionem 8 | respondentes] responderunt et 2 | **25** qui dixit] ille autem dixit ad illos 2 ille autem dixit eis 5 et ait illis (add. iesus 8) cet. reddite] reddite ergo A | quae sunt caesaris] 5 quae caesaris sunt cet. | dei sunt] sunt dei 2
26 et non potuerunt] non potuerunt autem 5 | sermonem eius capere] repraehendere uerbum eius 2 eius uerbum adpraehendere 5 uerbum eius reprehendere cet. | coram] in conspectu 2 5 populo] populi 2 5 plebe (plebem 8) cet. | mirati] admirati 2 mirantes 5 | in] super 2 | responso] 8 A responsa 2 responsione 5 17 | **27** accedentes] 5 accesserunt cet. | sadduceorum] de saduceis 2 sadducaeorum cet. | contradicunt] dicunt 2 5 negant cet. | resurrectionem non esse] 2 5 esse ressurrectionem cet. | interrogabant] et (om. 5) interrogauerunt cet. | illum] 8 eum cet.
28 moises] moses A moyses cet. | unius frater] cuius frater 2 5 frater alicuis cet. | habens uxorem et hic filios non habuerit] sine liberis habens uxorem 2 sine filiis habens uxorem 5 habens uxorem et hic sine filiis (filius 8) cet. | accipiat] 2 5 accipiat eam cet. | illius] eius cet. uxorem[2]] uxorem illam 2 | eius] 5 om. cet. | resuscitet] 2 5 suscitet cet. | fratri suo semen] semen fratri suo cet. | **29** Septem fratres erant] septe autem erant fratres 2 erant aput nos septem (autem 8 ergo A) fratres 5 septem fratres (add. apud nos 8) cet. | prior] primus cet. accepit uxorem] accepta uxore 2 accipiens uxorem 5 | et[2]] om. 2 5 | decessit] 2 mortuus est cet. filiis] 5 A liberis 2 filio 8 17 | **30** et sequens] 17 A similiter et secundus 2 et secundus 5 om. 8 accepit eam et ipse decessit sine filiis] accepit eam et ipse mortuus est sine filiis 17 accepit illam et ipse mortuus est sine filio A om. 2 5 8 | **31** tertius] et tertius cet. add. accepit illam 8 17 A similiter autem] usque ad 2 similiter cet. | et septem] 5 septimum omnes 2 omnes (omnis 8) septem cet. | et[2]] A om. cet. | reliquerunt] A remiserunt 2 dimiserunt 5 relinquerunt 8 17 filium] 2 semen A filios cet. | defuncti sunt] mortui sunt 2 5 A om. 8 17 | **32** sed] nouissime 5 nouissime autem 8 nouissima A om. 2 17 | et mulier] et mulier mortua est 5 mortua est et mulier cet. om. 2 | **33** in resurrectione] 2 8 in resurrectione ergo cet. | eorum] om. 2 8 | septem enim habuerunt illam uxorem] septem enim habuerunt eam uxorem 5 de septem uxorem enim habuerunt illam 8 siquidem septem habuerunt eam uxorem A

uxorem. **34** Dixit illis iesus: fili huius saeculi generant et generantur, nubunt et nubuntur. **35** qui autem digni fuerint saeculum illum attingere in resurrectionem a mortuis, non nubunt nec nubuntur **36** nec enim iam morituri sunt. aequales enim angelis sunt dei, resurrectionis fili cum sint. **37** Quia autem surgunt mortui, moyses demonstrauit uobis dicit de rubo: deum abraham deum isac et deum iacob. **38** non est deus mortuorum, sed uiuentium. omnes enim illi uiuent. **39** Respondentes autem quidam de scribis dixerunt: magister, bene dixisti. **40** nec amplius audebant interrogare eum quicquam. **41** Dixit autem ad eos: quomodo dicunt christum filium dauid esse? **42** et ipse dauid dicit in libro salmorum: dicit dominus domino meo: sede ad dexteram meam, **43** donec ponam inimicos tuos

---

34 Dixit illis iesus] ille autem dixit ad illos 2 et dixit ad eos 5 et ait illis iesus (om. 17) cet. | fili] 17 filii cet. | huius saeculi] saeculi huius 2 A | generant et generantur] 2 pariuntur et pariunt 5 generantur et generant 8 17 om. A | nubunt et nubuntur] 5 nubunt et traduntur ad nuptias A om. cet. | **35** qui autem digni fuerint] 5 qui autem dignitationem fuerint 2 at hi qui digni habentur 8 hi autem qui digni habentur 17 ille uero qui digni habebuntur A | saeculum] saeculo A saeculi cet. | illum] huius 5 illo A illius cet. | attingere] habituri 2 obtinere 5 om. cet. | in resurrectionem] in resurrectione 2 et resurectione A et resurrectionis cet. | a] 2 ex cet. | non] 2 neque cet. nec nubuntur] neque nubentur 2 neque nubuntur 5 8 neque ducunt uxores 17 A | **36** nec] 5 neque cet. | iam morituri sunt] incipient mori 2 mori adhuc possunt 5 morientur 8 17 ultra mori poterunt (poterint*) A | aequales enim angelis sunt dei] aequalis enim sunt angelis dei 2 equales angelis enim sunt deo 5 nam sunt similis angelis dei 8 nam sunt similes angelis dei 17 aequales enim angelis sunt et filii sunt dei A | resurrectionis fili cum sint] cum sint filii resurrectionis 2 cum sint resurrectionis fili 5 quia resurrectionis filii sunt 8 17 cum sint filii resurrectionis A **37** Quia] quoniam 8 17 om. 2 | autem surgunt] resurgere autem 2 autem resurgunt 5 uero resurgunt 8 uero surgunt 17 uero resurgant A | mortui] mortuos 2 | moyses] et moses A | demonstrauit] significauit 2 5 ostendit cet. | uobis dicit] super rubum quando dixerit ei 2 in rubo quomodo dicit 5 sicut dixit 8 17 secus rubum sicut dicit A | de rubo] dominus deus dicens ego sum 2 uidi in rubo dominum 8 17 om. 5 A | deum abraham deum isac et deum iacob] deus abraham deus isac deus iacob 2 dominum deum abraham et deum isac (isaac A) et deum iacob cet. | **38** non est deus mortuorum] deus enim non est mortuorum 2 deus mortuorum non es 5 deus ergo mortuorum non est 8 17 deus autem non est mortuorum A | uiuentium] uiuorum cet. | illi uiuent] 5 illi uiuunt 2 illi uiuent ei 8 illi uiunt 17 uiuunt ei A | **39** Respondentes autem quidam] A responderunt autem quidam 2 respondens autem quidam cet. | de scribis] 2 5 scribarum cet. | dixerunt] et dixerunt 2 dixit 17 | magister] om. 2 | **40** nec amplius audebant] et iam non audebant 2 amplius autem non fuerunt ausi 5 et amplius non sunt ausi (audebant A) cet. | interrogare eum quicquam] interrogare illum quicquam 2 interrogare eum nihil 5 eum quicquam interrogare cet. **41** eos] 5 illos cet. add. iesus 8 17 add. quid uobis uidetur de christo cuius filius est 2 | quomodo] quomo 17 | dicunt] dicunt illi 2 | christum filium dauid esse] dauid dixit ad illos 2 christum filium dauid 5 | **42** et ipse] quomodo 2 | dicit[1]] dixit 8 17 | dicit[2]] 5 17 dixit cet. | ad dexteram meam] 2 a dexteram meam 5 a (ad 17) dextris meis cet. | **43** donec] quoadusque 2 usque dum 5

sub pedibus tuis. **44** Dauid dominum illum uocat et quomodo filius illius est? **45** audiente autem omni populo dixit ad discipulos suos: **46** cauete a scribis, qui uolunt ambulare in stolis et amant salutationes in foro et primos consessus in synagogis et primos discubitos in conuiuiis, **47** qui comedunt domos uiduarum fingentes longam orationem, hi accipient amplius poenae.

21 Rescipiens autem iesus uidit mittentes dona in altario diuites. **2** uidit etiam quendam uiduam pauperculam mittentem duos quadrantes **3** et dixit: uere dico uobis, quia uidua paupera haec plus omnium misit. **4** omnes enim isti, de quo super illis fuit, miserunt in dona dei, haec autem de exiguitate sua omnem facultatem suam, quam habebat, misit. **5** Et quibusdam dicentibus de templo, quod lapidibus optimis et bonis extructum esset, dixit: **6** haec uidetis, uenient dies, in quibus non relinquetur lapis super lapidem in pariete hic, qui non destruatur. 7

---

sub pedibus tuis] scabellum pedum tuorum A | **44** Dauid dominum illum uocat] 17 si dauid dominum illum uocat 2 si dauid in spiritu dominum illum uocat 8 dauid ergo dominum illum uocat A | et] A om. cet. | illius] 5 eius cet. | **45** audiente autem omni populo] 8 A et cum audiret omnis populus 2 audientes autem omni populo 5 audiente omnie populo 17 | dixit] dixit iesus 8 | ad discipulos suos] discipulis suis 2 A discipulis 5 | **46** cauete] 2 attendite uobis 8 attendite (adtendite A) cet. | a] ab 8 17 | amant] aman 2 amantium 5 | salutationes] salutationis 2 primos consessus] praesidere 2 primas cathedras cet. | synagogis] foro 8 | primos[2]] superiores 2 | discubitos] 8 recumbere 2 addubitos 5 discubitus 17 A | conuiuiis] cenis 2 5 conuiis 8 **47** comedunt domos uiduarum fingentes longam orationem] comedunt domus uiduarum et occansione longa adorantes 2 comedunt domos uiduarum occasione longa orantes 5 fingentes longam orationem (add. et 8) deuorant panes uiduarum 8 17 deuorant domos uiduarum simulantes longam orationem A | hi] ipsi 2 | amplius poenae] abuntius iudicium 2 amplius iudicium 5 damnationem maiorem cet. | **21:1** Rescipiens] aspexit 2 aspiciens 5 | iesus] 8 om. cet. | uidit] et uidit 2 | mittentes] qui mittebant 5 eos qui mittebant cet. | dona in altario] in gazophilacium dona sua 2 in gazophylacium munera sua 5 munera sua in gazophylacium (zaiophylacium 8) cet. **2** uidit etiam] et uidet 8 et uidit 17 uidit autem et cet. | quendam] 2 quandam cet. | uiduam] om. 17 | pauperculam] pauperem 2 pauperam 5 duos quadrantes] duo aera minuta 2 duo minus quod est codrantes 5 aera minuta (minutam 8) duo cet. | **3** quia] 5 A quoniam 2 om. 8 17 | uidua paupera haec] uidua ista 2 uidua haec paupera 5 paupera uidua haec paupercula 8 paupera haec paupercula 17 uidua haec pauper A | plus omnium] omnibus plus 2 plus omnibus 5 plus quam omnes cet. | misit] add. in dona dei 2 | **4** omnes enim] 2 5 nam omnes cet. | isti] hi 17 A om. 8 de[1]] 2 5 ex cet. | quo super illis fuit] eo quod superfuit illis 2 abundantia sua 5 abundanti sibi (om. 8) cet. | dona] 2 munera cet. | de[2]] 2 5 ex cet. | exiguitate sua] inopia sua 2 minimo suo 5 eo quod deest illi cet. | omnem facultatem suam] omne quemcumquem 2 omne substantiam suam 5 omnem uictum suum cet. | quam habebat] habuit uictum 2 quod habuit 5 quem habuit cet. | **5** Et quibusdam dicentibus] et cum quidam dicerent 2 et quorundam dicentium 5 | quod] quoniam 2 5 | optimis] bonis cet. | et bonis extructum] et donis exornatum 2 ornata est et depositionibus 5 et donis ornatum cet. | esset] A est cet. om. 5 | dixit] et dixit 17 | **6** haec uidetis] haec quae uidetis A | relinquetur] relinquetur hic 2 | super] supra 8 | in pariete hic] 5 hic in parietem 8 17 om. 2 A

Interrogauerunt autem eum dicentes: magister, quando haec erunt et quod
signum, cum haec incipient fieri? **8** ad ille dixit: uidete, ne seducamini. multi enim
uenient in nomine meo dicentes, quia ego sum et tempus adpropinquauit. nolite
sequi post illos. **9** Cum autem audieritis bella et separationes, nolite terreri.
oportet enim haec fieri primum, sed nundum erit finis in illis. **10** surget enim gens
super gentem et regnum super regnum. **11** terrimotus quoque magni per loca et
pestes et fames erunt formidinesquae de caelo et signa magna erunt et hiemes. **12**
ante haec autem omnia inmittent super uos manus suas, et persequentur et
tradent uos in synagogis et carceribus et ducemini ad reges causa nominis mei, **13**
ut sit in testimonio uobis. **14** Ponite ergo in cordibus uestris: non prius meletare,
quomodo rationem reddatis. **15** ego enim dabo uobis os et sapientiam, cui non
poterint resistere, qui aduersantur uobis. **16** trademini autem et a parentibus et

---

7 eum] discipuli 5 illum cet. | magister] 2 5 praeceptor cet. | haec^{1}] ista 2 | erunt] fient 2 fiunt 17 | cum haec incipient fieri] quando incipient fieri 2 aduentus tui 5 cum futura erunt 8 17 fieri incipient A | **8** ad ille dixit] 5 ille autem dixit 2 qui autem (om. A) dixit cet. | seducamini] erretis 2 5 | quia] 5 A quoniam 2 quod 8 17 | sum] 5 A sum christus cet. add. et multos seducent 2 adpropinquauit] 2 adpropiauit 5 8 appropinquauit 17 A | nolite sequi] ne abieritis 5 nolite ergo ire A nolite ire cet. | **9** Cum autem audieritis] cum coeperitis autem uidere 2 | bella] 2 pugnas 5 proelia cet. | separationes] turbationis 2 dissensiones 5 seditiones cet. | nolite terreri] nolite expauescere 2 ne timueritis 5 | enim] 2 5 om. 8 17 A | haec fieri primum] ista fieri primo 2 fieri hoc primum 5 haec primum fieri 8 17 primum haec fieri A | nundum] non continuo 2 5 non statim cet. | erit] om. cet. | in illis] 8 17 om. cet. | **10** surget enim] exsurget enim 5 nam surget 8 17 tunc dicebat illis surget A | super^{1}] 2 contra cet. | super^{2}] 2 contra 5 aduersus cet. | **11** terrimotus quoque] terrae motus 5 et terrimotus 8 et terremotus 17 et terrae motus A | per loca] 2 5 erunt per loca cet. | pestes et fames] fames et lues 2 fames et morbi 5 pestilentiae (pestilentia 8) et fames cet. | erunt^{1}] om. 2 A | formidinesquae] timores quoque 2 timores autem 5 terroresque (-quae 8) cet. | de] a 2 | et hiemes] et tempestates 8 17 om. cet. | **12** ante haec autem] 5 ante haec 2 sed ante haec cet. | inmittent] mittent 5 inicient cet. | super uos] 2 5 in uos 8 17 uobis A et tradent] tradentes cet. | uos^{2}] om. cet. | synagogis] synagogas 2^{c} 5 A | carceribus] carcares 5 custodias cet. | et ducemini] abducentes 2 ducentur 5 ducentes 8 17 trahentes A | reges] reges et potestates 2 reges et duces 5 reges et praesides cet. | causa nominis mei] propter nomen meum cet. | **13** ut sit in testimonio uobis] continget autem uobis in testimonium 2 continget (obtinget 5 contingent 17) enim (om. 5 autem A) uobis in testimonium (in testimonium uobis 17) cet. | **14** ergo] itaque 2 | prius meletare] promeletantes 5 praemeditari (prameditari 2) cet. | quomodo] quae 2 quemadmodum cet. om. 5 | rationem reddatis] respondere 5 respondeatis (respondatis 2) cet. | **15** dabo uobis] uobis dabo 5 | os] hos 8 | cui] ad quam 5 | poterint] 5 A poterit 2 possint 17 poterunt 8 | resistere] coresistere 2 om. 5 | qui aduersantur uobis] aut contradicere omnes aduersarii uestri 2 contradicere omnes aduersantes uobis 5 aduersarii uestri 8 17 et contradicere omnes aduersarii uestri A | **16** trademini] tradimini 2 8 | et^{1}] 2 5 om. cet. | a parentibus] om. 17 | et cognatis] om. 17 et (add. a 2) fratribus et cognatis cet.

cognatis et amicis, et morti adficient ex uobis, **17** et eritis odio omnibus causa nominis mei. **18** et capillus de capite uestro non periet. **19** in tolerantia uestra possidebitis animas uestras. **20** Cum autem uideritis circumdata{s}m ab exercitibus hierusalem, tunc scitote, quoniam adpropinquauit desolatio eius. **21** tunc qui sunt in iudaea, fugiant in montibus, et qui in medio eius, secedant, et qui in regionibus, ne intrent in eam, **22** quoniam dies iudicii hi sunt, ut inpleantur omnia, quae scripta sunt. **23** Uae praegnantibus et lactantibus in {in} illis diebus. erit necessitas magna super terram et ira populo huic. **24** et cadent in ore gladii et captiui ducentur in gentes uniuersa, et hierusalem erit in conculcationem nationum, donec repleantur tempora gentium. **25** et erint signa in sole et luna et stellis super terram, conpressio gentium in stupore sonus maris et undis, **26** arefrigescentibus hominibus a timore et expectatione superuenientium orbi

---

et amicis] om. 17 | et morti adficient] 8 et mortificabunt 2 et morti tradent 5 morte afficient 17 et morte adficient A | **17** odio] odibilis 2 odibiles ab 5 | omnibus] omnibus hominibus 8c 17 causa nominis mei] propter nomen meum cet. | **18** uestro] om. 8 | periet] 5 periuit 2 peribit cet. **19** tolerantia uestra] sufferentia uestra 5 patientia uestra A uestra patientia cet. | possidebitis] A possidetis 2 adquirite 5 17 adquiretis 8 | **20** Cum autem uideritis circumdatasm] cum uideritis autem circumdatam 2 cum autem uideritis circundare (circuiri 5) cet. | ab exercitibus hierusalem] ab excitu hierusalem 2 hierusalem ab exercitu 5 ab exercitu (exercitum 8) hierusalem (iherusalem 8) cet. | scitote] scietis 2 5 | quoniam] qui 8 quia A | adpropinquauit] adpropinuit 2 dpropiauit 8* adpropiauit 8c appropinquauit 17 A | **21** qui sunt in iudaea] qui in iudaea (iudea 2 17) sunt cet. | fugiant] fugiant a facie eius 8 | montibus] montes A | et[1]] om. 8 | in medio eius] in medio eius sunt 2 5 | secedant] 2 non exeant 5 discedant (discedat 8) cet. | in regionibus] in regionibus sunt 2 | ne] non cet. | intrent] introeant 2 intret 8 | eam] illam 2 | **22** quoniam] 5 quia cet. | iudicii hi sunt] uindictae isti sunt 2 uindictae sunt istae 5 ultionis hi (hii 8) sunt cet. inpleantur] 5 impleantur cet. | omnia quae scripta sunt] omnes scripturae 2 | **23** Uae] uae in 17 uae autem A | praegnantibus] 5 A eis quae in uentre habent 2 his quae in utero habent 8 his qui in utero habent 17 | lactantibus] quae mammant 2 quae lactant 5 quae ubera dant 8 17 nutrientibus A | erit] erit enim cet. | necessitas magna super terram] 2 necessitas magna super terra 5 supra terram pressura magna 8 praessura magna super terram 17 pressura magna supra terram A | populo huic] super populum istum 2 | **24** captiui] capti 8 | ducentur] erunt 2 | gentes uniuersa] omnibus gentis 8 17 omnes gentes cet. | erit in conculcationem nationum] erit inculcata a gentibus 2 erit calcata a gentibus 5 calcabitur a nationibus (gentibus A) cet. | donec] 17 A doneque 2 usque quo 5 dum 8 | repleantur] adimpleantur 2 inpleantur 5 8 impleantur 17 A gentium] nationum A om. 5 | **25** erint] erunt cet. | luna] in luna 2 | stellis] 8 17 in sideribus 2 5 in stellis A | super terram] et super terram 5 et in terris cet. | conpressio] conclusio 2 conflictio 5 pressura (praessura 17) cet. | in stupore] in confessione 2 et aporia 5 prae (pre 8) confusione cet. | sonus maris] sonante mare 5 sonitus maris (mares 2) cet. | undis] inundationes 2 salo 5 fluctuum (fluctum 8) cet. | **26** arefrigescentibus hominibus] deficientium hominum 5 arescentibus hominibus cet. | a] 5 prae (pre 8) cet. | et] om. 2 8 | expectatione] expectatione eorum 2 superuenientium] quae superueniunt 2 quae uentura sunt quae superuenient (superueniet 17) cet. | orbi terrarum] 5 orbi terrae 2 uniuerso orbi cet.

terrarum. uirtutes enim, quae sunt in caelo, mouebuntur. **27** Tunc uidebunt filium
hominis uenientem in nube cum potentia magna et gloria. **28** Incipientibus autem
his fieri respicite et leuate capita uestra, quoniam adpropinquat{e} liberatio
uestra. **29** Et dixit parabolam illis: uidete ficum et omnes arbores. **30** cum florient
a se, scitis in proximo esse aestatem. **31** sic et uos, cum uidebitis haec, scitote,
quoniam in proximo est regnum dei. **32** Amen dico uobis, quia non transiet gens
illa, donec omnia fiant. **33** caelum et terra transiet, uerba autem mea non
praeteribunt. **34** Attendite autem uobis, ne quando grauentur corda uestra
gratulatione et ebrietatibus et solligitudinibus saecularibus et instet super uos
repentaneus dies ille tanquam laqueus. **35** intrauit enim super omnes, qui sedent
super faciem totius terrae. **36** Uigilate autem in omni tempore orantes, ut digni
habeamini effugere omnia haec, quae futura, et stabitis ante filium hominis. **37**

---

uirtutes enim] 2 5 nam uirtutes cet. | quae sunt in caelo] 5 quae in caelo sunt 8 in caelo (caelorum A) cet. | **27** Tunc] et tunc cet. | nube] 5 A nubibus cet. | cum potentia] et potentatu 2 et uirtute 5 cum potestate cet. | magna] magno 2 multa 5 | gloria] 5 claritates 2 maiestate cet. **28** Incipientibus autem his] cum coeperint autem haec fieri 2 incipientium autem horum fieri 5 his autem fieri incipientibus (incipientibus fieri 8) cet. | respicite] A erigite uos 5 respirabitis 8 17 om. 2 | leuate] A leuauites 2 subleuate 5 leuabitis 8 17 | uestra[1]] om. 5 | adpropinquate] adpropinquat 2 5 adpropiat 8 appropiat 17 appropinquat A | liberatio uestra] 5 redemptio uestra cet. **29** parabolam illis] 5 illis similitudinem (similitudinem illis 2) cet. | ficum] ab arbore fici 2 ficulneam cet. | omnes arbores] omnibus arboribus 2 omnis arboris 8 | **30** florient] coeperint mittere 2 produxerint 5 producant 4 producunt cet. | a se] fructus suos 2 fructum suum 5 iam fructus 17 iam ex se fructum cet. | scitis] agnoscite 2 scitote iam 5 | in proximo esse aestatem] quoniam aestas est proxima 2 quia prope iam aestas est 5 quoniam (quia 8) prope (iam prope 4) est aestas cet. | **31** sic] 5 ita cet. | uos] om. 4 8 17 | cum uidebitis haec] cum uideritis omnia ista fieri 2 cum uideritis haec 5 cum uideritis haec fieri A haec cum uideritis fieri cet. | quoniam] quod 4 quia 8 | in proximo] 2 prope cet. | **32** quia] quoniam 2 5 17 | transiet] 2 praeteriet 4 preteriit 8 praeteribit (praeteriuit 17) cet. | gens illa] caelum istut 2 a generatione hac 17 generatio haec cet. | donec] doneque 2 usquae dum 5 | omnia] haec omnia 5 | fiant] perficiantur 2 **33** terra] tra 2 terram 8 | transiet] 2 4 praeteribunt 5 transibunt 8 A transient 17 | uerba] sermones 2 | mea] mei 2 | praeteribunt] 5 8 transient cet. | **34** autem] om. 5 | quando] 5 forte cet. | grauentur corda uestra] grauentur uestra corda 5 grauetur cor uestrum 17 | gratulatione] in crapula (crepula 5) cet. | ebrietatibus] ebrietate cet. | solligitudinibus] sollicitudinibus 2 soniis 5 curis A cogitationibus cet. | saecularibus] uitae 2 secularibus 8 huius uitae A | instet] adsistet 2 superueniat cet. | super] 2 5 in cet. | uos] nos 5 uobis 8 | repentaneus] subitaneus 2 subitanus 5 repentina cet. | dies ille] 2 5 dies illa cet. | tanquam] quasi 2 sicut 5 | laqueus] muscipula 2 | **35** intrauit enim] introiuit enim 2 introibit autem 5 enim superueniet A superueniet (superuenient 8) enim cet. | super[1]] 2 5 in cet. | omnes qui sedent] sedentes 5 | super[2]] supra 8 | totius terrae] 2 omnis (om. 8) terrae cet. | **36** autem] 2 5 itaque cet. | in] 2 5 om. cet. orantes] depraecantes 2 rogantes 5 | effugere] fugere 5 A | omnia haec] omnia ista 2 haec omnia 5 omnia ista 17 ista omnia cet. | futura] incipient fieri 5 futura sunt cet. | stabitis] stabatis 8 stare A | ante filium] in conspectu fili 5

erat autem per dies in templo docens, noctibus uero egrediebatur et demorabatur
in monte, qui dicitur oliuetum. **38** et omnis populus de luce uigilabant ad eum in
templo audire illum.

22 Adpropinquabat autem dies festus adzymorum qui dicitur pascha **2** et
quaerebant pontifices et scribae quomodo interficerent illum timebant enim
populum. **3** Intrauit autem satanas in iudam qui cognominatur iscarioth unum de
numero xii. **4** et abiit et conlocutus est pontificibus et scribis quemadmodum
traderet illum. **5** et gauisi sunt et polliciti sunt ei se pecuniam daturos. **6** et
quaerebat opportunitatem tradendi illum sine turba. **7** Uenit autem dies paschae.
8 et misit petrum et iohannem dicens: euntes parate nobis pascha manducare. **9**
qui dixerunt ei: ubi uis paremus? **10** dixit autem ad eos: ecce intrantibus uobis

---

37 per dies] interdies 2* per diem 5 diebus A interdie cet. | in templo docens] 5 docens in templo cet. | noctibus uero] noctibus autem 2 om. 5 | egrediebatur] exiebat 2 exiens cet. om. 5 | et demorabatur in monte] et manebat in montem 2 in monte habitabat 5 morabatur in monte A auocabatur in monte (montem 8) cet. | qui dicitur oliuetum] oliuarum 2 qui uocatur (uocabatur 4) oliueti cet. | **38** de luce] ante luce 2 om. cet. | uigilabant] ueniebat 2 uigilabat 5 manicabat cet. | ad eum] om. 4 17 | in templo audire illum] audire eum in templo 2 5 in templo audire eum cet. | **22:1** Adpropinquabat] adpropinquauit 2 5 adpropriauerunt 4* adpropriauit 4^{c} 8 appropiauit 17 appropinquabat A | festus] om. 5 4 | adzymorum] azymorum cet. | qui dicitur pascha] uocantur cena pura 4* quae 4^{c} phascha 8 | **2** et quaerebant pontifices] pontifices autem 2 principes autem sacerdotum 5 et quaerebant (querebant 8) principes (principis 8) sacerdotum cet. interficerent illum] perderent eum 5 eum interficerent (interficere 17) cet. | enim] 2 17 autem 5 uero cet. | populum] 2 5 plebem cet. | **3** Intrauit] introuit 2 | iudam] iudan 5 | cognominatur] 2 uocatur 5 cognominabatur cet. | iscarioth] 5 schariotes 2 scarloth 8 scarioth cet. | unum de numero xii] qui erat ex numero illorum duodecorum 2 qui erat de numero duodecim 5 unus de xii 4 unum de duodecim 8 A unum de xii 17 | **4** conlocutus] 2 5 locutus cet. | pontificibus] principibus sacerdotum 5 8 cum principibus (principes 17) sacerdotum cet. | et scribis] et magistratibus A om. 5 | quemadmodum] 4 A quemammodum 17 quomodo cet. | traderet illum] traderet eum 5 illum traderet cet. add. eis A | **5** et gauisi sunt] 5 A ille autem gauisi sunt 2 om. cet. | polliciti sunt] constituerunt 2 5 pacti sunt cet. | ei se pecuniam daturos] illi pecuniam dare 2 ei pecuniam dare 5 pecuniam illi dare (darent 8) cet. | **6** et quaerebat] 4 17 et sponpondit et quaerebat 2* et spopondit et quaerebat 2^{c} A et confessus est et quaerebat 5 et querebant 8 opportunitatem] oportunum tempus 2 opportunitatem temporis 8 | tradendi illum] ut eum traderet 2 ut traderet eum 5 ut traderet illum cet. | sine turba] 2 5 sine turba eis 4 17 eis sine turba 8 sine turbis A | **7** paschae] paschae in qua oportebat immolari pascha 2 5 paschae in qua necesse erat occidi pascha 4 pasche in qua necesse erat inmolari in pascha 8 paschae in quo necesse erat immolari pascha 17 azymorum in qua necesse erat occidi pascha A | **8** petrum] petru 17 | iohannem] iohannen 5 4 | dicens] dicentes 17* | euntes parate] ite et parate 2 manducare] ut manducemus cet. | **9** qui] illi autem 2 at illi cet. | ei] 5 illi 2 om. cet. | uis] om. 2 paremus] paramus tibi 2 paremus tibi 5 paremus tibi pasca 8 | **10** dixit autem] ille autem dixit 2 ad ille dixit 5 et dixit cet. | ad eos] A ad illos 4 8 17 om. 2 5 | intrantibus] introeuntibus cet.

ciuitatem, occurret uobis homo amporam aquae portans. sequimini illum in domo qua ingreditur. **11** et dicetis patrifamiliae domui: dicit tibi magister: ubi est refectio, ubi pascha cum discipulis meis edam. **12** et ille uobis ostendet maedianum stratum magnum: ibi parate. **13** Euntes autem inuenerunt sicut dixerat illis et parauerunt pascha. **14** Et cum facta est hora, discubuit et apostoli cum illo. **15** et dixit ad eos: desiderio cupiui hoc pascha manducare uobiscum antequam patiar. **16** dico enim uobis quoniam non edam illud donec inpleatur in regno dei. **17** Et accepto calice gratias egit dicens: sumite hoc et partimini in uobis. **18** dico enim uobis quoniam non bibam de fructu uineae donec regnum dei ueniat. **19** Et accepto pane gratias egit et confregit et dedit illis dicens: hoc est corpus meum. **20** *omissum* **21** attamen ecce manus proditoris mei mecum super mensam. **22** Filius quidem hominis secundum quod definitum est uadit. Uaerum

ciuitatem] ciuitate 4 | occurret] obuiabit 5 | homo] homo ferens 2 homo baiulans 5 | amporam] bascellum 5 amphoram cet. | sequimini] semini 5 | illum] 2 eum cet. | domo] domum cet. | qua] in qua 2 4 ubi 5 in quam cet. | ingreditur] introiit 2 introierit 5 intrant 8 intrat cet. **11** et dicetis] dicite 2 et dicitis 5 | patrifamiliae] patrifamilias 2 A paterfamilias 8 | domui] domus ipsius 2 domus 5 A om. 4 8 17 | dicit] icit 2* dicet 4 | tibi] om. 5 | refectio] hospitium 2 diuersorium cet. | pascha] phasca 8 | discipulis meis] discentibus meis 2 discipulos meos 5 edam] 5 manducem cet. | **12** et ille] ille 5 et ipse A | ostendet] ostendit 8 | maedianum] superiorem 5 pede plano 4 caenaculum A in superioribus cet. | stratum magnum] domum stratum 5 magnum stratum A locum stratum magnum cet. | ibi parate] et ibi parate A | **13** Euntes] abierunt 2 abientes 5 | autem] et 2 | sicut] quomodo 2 | dixerat] 5 dixit cet. | **14** est] fuit 5 esset cet. | discubuit] recubuit 2 5 | apostoli] duodecim apostoli A | illo] ipso 2 eo A | **15** et dixit] 5 dixit 2 et ait cet. | ad eos] 5 ad illos 2 illis cet. | desiderio cupiui] concupiscentiam concupi 2 concupiscentia concupiui 5 desiderio desideraui cet. | manducare] manducarae 2* | antequam] priusquam 2 5 | patiar] hoc patiar 8 | **16** quoniam] quia cet. om. 5 | non edam] iam non manducabo 2 5 ex hoc non manducabo cet. | illud] ab eo 5 | donec] usque 5 | inpleatur] adimplear 2 quo nobum edatur 5 impleatur cet. | v. 19 ante v. 17: et accepi panem et gratias egit et fregit et dedit eis dicens hoc est corpus meum 2 et accepto pane gratias egit et fregit et dedit illis dicens hoc est corpus meum 4 | **17** accepto calice] accepit calicem 2 accipiens calicem 5 gratias egit] et gratias egit 2 benedicens 5 | dicens] dixit 5 et dixit cet. | sumite] accipite cet. hoc] om. 2 A | et] om. 2 | partimini] 5 uiuite 2 diuidite cet. | in uobis] uobis 5 inter uos cet. **18** quoniam] amodo 2 5 quod cet. | non bibam] non uiuam amodo 2 | de fructu] de potione 2 a creatura 5 de generatione hac 4 de generatione cet. | uineae] 5 uitis huius 4 uitis cet. | donec] quoadusque 2 usque quo 5 | regnum dei ueniat] ueniat regnum dei 5 | **19** accepto] accipiens 5 pane] panem 5 panis 8 | gratias egit] benedixit 5 | et[1]] om. 5 | confregit] fregit cet. | illis] eis 5 A | hoc est corpus meum] add. quod pro uobis datur hoc facite in meam commemorationem A **21** attamen] uerum 2 uerumtamen cet. | proditoris mei] eius qui me tradat 2 qui tradet me 5 tradentes me 4 8 tradentis me cet. | mecum] mecum est A om. 5 | super] 2 5 in cet. | mensam] 2 8 mensa cet. | **22** Filius quidem] 5 et filius quidem 2 et quidem filius cet. | quod] om. 5 definitum est] A scripturam ante 2 praedefinitum 5 scriptum 4 perscriptum 8 praescriptum 17 Uaerum] uerum 2 uerumtamen cet.

uae homini illi per quem traditur. **23** et ipsi inquirebant inter se, quisnam esset,
qui hoc facturus esset. **24** Facta est autem contentio inter illos, quisnam esset
maior. **25** ad ille dixit eis: reges gentium dominantur eorum et qui potestatem in
eos exercunt beneficiorum largitores dicuntur. **26** Uos autem non ita, sed qui
maior est in uobis, fiat sicut minor, et qui praeest, ut qui ministrat. **27** quis enim
maior est? qui recumbit aut qui ministrat? in gentibus quidem qui recumbit, in
uobis autem non sic, sed qui ministrat. ego autem sum in medio uestrum sicut qui
ministrat. **28** Uos autem estis, qui permansistis mecum in temptationibus meis. **29**
et ego dispono uobis, sicut disposuit mihi pater meus regnum, **30** ut edatis et
bibatis super mensam meam in regno meo et sedeatis in xii sedibus iudicantes xii
tribus israel. **31** dixit autem dominus petro: simon, simon, ecce satanas postulauit
uos, ut {s}cribaret tamquam triticum. **32** ego autem rogaui pro te, ne deficeret

---

homini illi] 4 illi 2 5 illi homini cet. | traditur] 5 17 filius hominis traditur 4 tradetur cet. | **23** et ipsi] illi autem 2 ipsi autem 5 | inquirebant] coeperunt conquire 2 5 coeperunt quaerere A conquirebant cet. | inter se] ad inuicem 2 ad semetipsos 5 | quisnam] 2 quis cet. | esset[1]] esset ex eis A | qui] 5 A quod 2 om. cet. | hoc facturus esset] 2 A incipiet hoc agere 5 hoc facturus cet. **24** Facta est] erat 2 | contentio] et contentio 2 5 A | inter illos] in illis 2 in eis 5 inter eos cet. quisnam] quis 8 17 A | esset maior] 5 illorum uideretur maior esse 2 maior uideretur 4 eorum uideretur esse maior cet. | **25** ad ille dixit] 5 ille autem dixit 2 at ipse dixit 4 dixit autem cet. eis] illis 2 5 add. iesus 8 | eorum] illorum 2 | potestatem] potentatum 2 | in eos exercunt] habent bene agentes 2 habent eorum 5 in eos exercent 4* 17 habet bene gerentes eorum 8 habent super eos A | beneficiorum largitores] benefici 2 A ueniuoli 5 beneficiorum largiores 4 benigni 8 17 | dicuntur] 4* uocabuntur 2 uocantur cet. | **26** ita] 2 4 sic cet. | qui maior est in uobis] quis est maior in uobis 2 qui maior in uobis est 5 | fiat] efficiatur 4 | sicut] ut 2 4 | minor] 8 17 iunior 2 A minus 5 adulescentior 4 | praeest] 2 4 praesens est ducatum agit 5 praecessor est cet. ut] 4 quasi 2 sicut cet. | qui ministrat] 5 4 ministrans 2 ministrator cet. | **27** quis enim maior est] quis enim maior est magis 2 magis quam qui recumbit 5 nam quis maior est A | qui recumbit aut qui ministrat] qui ministrat aut qui recumbit 2 ego autem sum in medio uestrum 5 qui recumbit an qui ministrat A | in gentibus quidem] ueni non sicut 5 nonne 4 A | in uobis autem non sic] om. 5 4 A | sed] om. 4 A | qui ministrat[2]] sicut ministrans 5 om. 4 A | ego autem sum in medio uestrum] 4 17 ego autem cum in medio uestrum 2 et uos creuistris in ministerio meo 5 ego autem sum in uestro medio 8 ego autem in medio uestrum sum A | sicut] quasi 2 8 | qui[5]] 4 A om. cet. | ministrat[3]] 4 A ministrans 2 ministrat 5 minister 8 17 | **28** Uos autem estis] uos estis autem 2 uos estis 4 om. 5 | permansistis] permasistis 2 | **29** et ego dispono] ego autem disponam 2 et ego quidem dispono cet. | disposuit mihi] mihi disposuit 2 | meus] om. 2 5 | **30** super] in 4 | mensam meam] meam mensam 4 | in regno] et in regno 4 | meo] om. 2 5 | et[2]] om. 2 | sedeatis] sedentes 2 sedebitis 5 4 | in[2]] 4 super cet. | xii[1]] duodecim 8 om. 2 A | sedibus] 4 tronos 2 sedes 5 thronos cet. | xii[2]] 5 4 duodecim 2 17 (tribus iudicantes) 8 A | israel] isdrahel 2 israhel 5 A istrahel 4 8 add. in saecula saeculorum 2 | **31** dixit autem dominus] 5 ille autem dixit 2 ait autem dominus cet. | petro] simoni petro 17 | simon[1]] om. 2 | simon[2]] om. 2 17 ecce] quoniam 2 om. 4 | postulauit] 2 expetiuit cet. | uos ut] 5 A ut uos cet. | scribaret] cerneret 5 cribraret A uentilet cet. | tamquam] sicut cet. | **32** ego autem] om. 8 | rogaui] praecatus sum 5 | pro] de 5 | ne[1]] 4 ut non cet. | deficeret] deficiat cet.

fides tua. et tu tandem conuersus confirma fratres tuos. et rogate, ne intretis in temptatione. **33** dixit autem ei petrus: domine, tecum paratus sum et in carcerem et in mortem ire. **34** qui ait: dico tibi, petre, non cantabit hodie gallus, donec tu me ter abneges. **35** Et dixit eis: quando misi uos sine sacculo et pera et calciamentis, numquid aliquid defuit uobis. ad illi dixerunt: nihil. **36** dixit ergo: sed nunc, qui habet sacculum, tollat similiter et peram. et qui non habet, uendat tunicam suam et emat gladium. **37** Dico enim uobis, quoniam adhuc hoc, quod scribtum est, oportet inpleri in me: quod et cum iniustis deputatus est. Et de me quae sunt, finem habent. **38** ad ille dixit: domine, ecce gladii duo hic. qui dixit ei: sat est. **39** et egressus abiit secundum consuetudinem in montem olíueti. secuti sunt autem illum et discipuli eius. **40** et cum esset in eo loco, dixit illis: orate, ne intretis in temptationem. **41** Et ipse abolsus est ab illis tamquam lapidis ictus et positis

---

et tu] tu autem 2 5 | tandem] aliquando cet. om. 2 5 | conuersus] conuertere et fidere et 2 conuertere et 5 | confirma] conforta 2 | et rogate ne intretis in temptatione] et rogate ne intretis in temptanionem cet. om. 5 A | **33** dixit autem ei petrus] ille autem dixit illi 2 ad ille dixit illi 5 qui dixit ei A | tecum] et tecum 2 | carcerem] custodiam 2 carcere 4 | et[2]] om. 8 | mortem] morte 4 | **34** qui ait] dicit illi 2 at ille dixit 5 ad iesus dixit ei 8 et ille dixit cet. | non cantabit hodie gallus] nocte hac antequam gallus cantet 2 | cantabit] clamauit 5 cantauit 17 | donec] usque quo 5 om. 2 | tu] om. cet. | me ter abneges] ter me negabis 2 5 ter me adneges 4 ter abneges me 8 ter abneges 17 A add. nescire me 5 nosse me 17 A | **35** eis] illis 2 5 | misi uos] uos misi 2 | sacculo] saccello 2 8 sacellum 4 | et pera] et peram 4 om. 2 | numquid] ne 5 | aliquid] alicuius 2 4 cuius 5 | defuit uobis] 17 A indiguis 2 defecistis 5 eguistis 4 de uobis fuit 8 | ad] et 4 at cet. | dixerunt] dicunt 2 | nihil] nullius 2 5 4 | **36** dixit ergo] ille autem dixit 2 ad ille dixit 5 dixit ergo eis A | sacculum] saccellum 5 4 8 | tollat] tollet 5 | peram] chilotrum 2 | non] om. 8 uendat tunicam suam] uendat uestimentum suum 4 tunicat uendat eam 8 | emat] emet 5 **37** uobis] om. 5 4 | quoniam] quia 5 4 | adhuc] om. 5 4 | hoc] om. 4 17 | inpleri] conpleri 5 inplere 8 impleri cet. | quod et] et 4 quod ut 8 et quod A | iniustis] iniquis 5 8 incoelestibus 4* sceleratus 4[c] | deputatus est] computatus est 5 deportatus sum 4* deputatus sum 4[c] | Et de me quae sunt] et ea de me 5 quod etiam de me 4 etenim ea quae sunt de me A | habent] hauet 5 **38** ad ille dixit] 2 17 illi autem dixerunt 5 qui dixerunt ei 4 at illi dixerunt 8 A | domine ecce] ecce domine 5 ecce 17 | gladii duo hic] 2 A duo machaerae 5 gladia duo hic 4 duo gladii hic 8 gladi duo hic 17 | qui dixit] 4 17 ad ille dixit 2 at ille dixit 5 A at ille respondit 8 | ei] 17 illis 5 eis cet. om. 2 sat est] 17 est 2 sufficit 5 4 satis est 8 A | **39** egressus] exiens 5 egressus inde 8 | abiit] ibat cet. consuetudinem] 5 A consuetudinem suam cet. | montem] monte 4 17 | olíueti] oliuarum A illum] eum 5 8 | eius] om. 5 A | **40** et cum esset] cum fuisset autem 5 et cum peruenisset cet. in[1]] ad 8 17 A om. 2 5 4 | eo] om. cet. | loco] 5 locum cet. | temptationem] temtationem 2 A **41** Et ipse] ipse autem 5 | abolsus est] abulsus est 2 recessit 5 auolsus est 4 8 auulsus est 17 A illis] eis cet. | tamquam lapidis ictus] quasi lapides missionem 5 quantum iactus lapidis 17 quantum iactus est lapidis A quantum iactum lapidis cet. | positis genibus] ponens genua 5

genibus orabat **42** dicens: pater, non uoluntas mea, sed tua fiat. transfer{s} calicem hunc a me. **43** apparuit autem illi angelus de caelo confortians eum. **44** Et factus in agonia et prolixius orabat. et factus est sudor illius quasi guttae sanguinis decurrentis super terram. **45** et surgens ab oratione uenit ad discipulos suos et inuenit illos dormientes a maerore. **46** et dixit eis: quid dormitis? Surgite, orate, ne intretis in temptationem. **47** et adhuc eo loquente, ecce turba et qui uocabatur iudas, unus de duodecim, praecedebat illos. et accedens osculatus est iesum. **48** dixit autem iesus: iuda, osculo filium hominis tradis? **49** uidentes autem, qui erant circa illum quod futurum esset, dixerunt illi: domine, si percutiemus in gladio? **50** et percussit unus quidam ex illis seruum pontificis et abscidit aurem illius dextram. **51** dixit autem illi iesus: sine, usque hoc. et extendens manum

---

42 dicens] om. 4 | non uoluntas mea sed tua fiat transfers calicem hunc a me] non mea uoluntas sed tua fiat si uis transfert calicem istum a me 2 non uoluntas mea sed tua fiat si uis transferre hunc calicem a me 5 si uis transfer calicem hunc a me uerum non mea uoluntas sed tua fiat 4 17 non mea uoluntas sed tua fiat si uis transfer hunc calicem a me 8 si uis transfer calicem istum a me uerumtamen non mea uoluntas sed tua fiat A | **43** apparuit autem] uisus est autem 5 confortians] 5 conforstans 2 confortans cet. | eum] illum 4 | **44** factus[1]] factus est 2 4 17 | et[1]] 4 A om. cet. | prolixius] plolixius 2 uehementius 5 | et factus est] factus est autem 5 | illius] eius cet. | quasi] tamquam 8 sicut cet. | guttae] buccellae 5 | sanguinis] sanguisnis 2* | decurrentis] 17 A decurrentes 2 4 8 descendentes 5 | super] 5 in cet. | **45** et[1]] et factum est 4 | surgens] 5 cum surrexit cet. | oratione] orationem 8 | uenit] uenies 5 et uenisset cet. | suos] om. 5 | et[2]] om. cet. | illos dormientes] dormientes eos 5 eos dormientes 8 A | a] 5 prae cet. | maerore] tristitia cet. | **46** dixit] 5 ait cet. | eis] illis cet. om. 8 | quid] om. 5 | dormitis] dormites 2 Surgite] surgentes 5 | ne] ut non 5 | intretis in temptationem] in temptationem intretis 5 intretis in temtationem A | **47** et[1]] om. cet. | adhuc] A adhuc autem cet. | eo] illo 4 8 17 | loquente] loquentem 17 | turba] turba multa 5 turbae 4 17 | uocabatur] uocabtur 2 uocatur 5 | iudas] iudas iscariot 5 | de] ex 2 | duodecim] xii 5 4 17 | praecedebat] antecedebat cet. | illos] eos cet. | accedens] 5 adpropians 2 4 8 appropians 17 appropinquauit A | osculatus est iesum] iesu ut oscularetur eum A add. hoc enim signum dederat eis quem osculatus fuero ipse est 5 hoc enim signum dederat eis dicens quemcumque osculatus fuero hic est tenete eum 4 | **48** dixit autem iesus] 5 dixit autem illi 2 dixit autem illi iesus 4 8 17 iesus autem dixit d iesus autem dixit ei A **49** uidentes autem] 5 A quod cum uiderent eum 4 quod cum uiderent cet. | qui] 5 hi qui cet. erant circa illum] circa eum erant 5 circa ipsum erant cet. | quod futurum esset] quod factum est 5 quod fiebant 8 quod futurum erat A om. cet. | illi] domino 5 ei cet. | domine] om. 5 | si] uis 4 percutiemus] percutiemus eum 4 percutimus A | **50** quidam] om. cet. | ex] om. 5 | illis] eis 5 pontificis] principes sacerdotum 2 principis sacerdotum cet. | abscidit] abstulit 5 amputauit cet. aurem illius] eius auriculam 5 auriculam eius cet. | dextram] dexteram 17 | **51** dixit autem illi iesus] 17 ait autem iesus 2 8 respondens autem iesus dixit 5 4 respondens autem iesus ait A sine] sinite 5 A dimitte eum 4 | hoc] adhoc 17 huc A om. b | et extendens manum suam] 2 et extendens manum 5 et extendit manum suam iesus 8 om. cet.

suam tetigit eum et reintegrata est auris eius. **52** Dixit autem iesus ad eos, qui uenerant ad se, pontifices et antistites templi et seniores: tamquam ad latronem existis cum gladiis et fustibus. **53** cum cottidie essem uobiscum in templo, non extendebatis manus super me. sed haec est uestra hora et potestas a tenebrae. **54** Conprehensum autem eum adduxerunt et in domum pontificis. petrus autem sequebatur a longe. **55** incenso autem igne in medio atrio et consedentibus sedebat petrus in medio illorum. **56** Quem cum uidisset quaedam ancilla, intuens eum dixit: et hic ex illis est, qui cum eo erant. **57** ad ille negauit dicens: mulier, non noui eum. **58** et egressu{s}m illum ad ianuam uidit alia † et [...] ibi erant †: et hic fuit cum iesu nazareno. et rursus negauit cum iure iurando. **59** quem paulo post cum uidisset quidam, dixit: uere et hic cum iesu erat, nam et galilaeus est. **60**

---

tetigit] 5 iesus tetigit 2 et tetigit 4 et tetigit iesus 8 et cum tetigisset A om. 17 | eum] aurem eius 4 auriculam eius A om. 17 | reintegrata] redintegrata 2 8 restituta 5 sanauit 4 A om. 17 | est auris eius] 8 est aures eius 2 est auricula eius 5 eum 4 A add. p. 51 ait autem iesus sine usque hoc 4 **52** Dixit autem iesus ad eos qui uenerant ad se] A dixit autem ad eos qui aduenerant ad eum 5 et ad eos qui ad se uenerant (uerant 2) dixit cet. | pontifices] principes sacerdotum 5 A principibus sacerdotum cet. | antistites] praepositos 5 magistratus A magistratibus cet. | templi] populi 5 seniores] 5 A senioribus cet. | tamquam] sicut 5 quasi cet. | existis] uenistis 8 | fustibus] add. conprehendere me 8 | **53** cum cottidie essem uobiscum in templo] cottidie cum essem in templo uobiscum 5 cum (om. 8) cottidie uobiscum fuerim (fueram 8) in templo cet. | extendebatis] extendistis cet. | manus super me] manus in me 5 A in me manus (manum 2) cet. | est uestra hora] hora est uestra 4 erit hora uestra 8 est hora uestra cet. | a tenebrae] tenebrae 5 tenebrarum cet. | **54** Conprehensum autem eum] contenentes autem eum 5 conpraehendentes autem eum A et comprehensum (conpraehensum 2) illum cet. | adduxerunt] 5 duxerunt cet. | et] om. cet. | in] ad A | pontificis] principis sacerdotum cet. | autem²] 5 uero cet. | sequebatur] A add. eum 5 17 illum 2 4 8 | **55** incenso] incendentibus 5 accenso cet. | igne] ignem 5 igni cet. et] om. 17 | consedentibus] cum circumsedentibus 2 circumsedentium 5 circumsedentibus illis A circumsedentibus cet. | sedebat] sedixit 8 erat A om. 2 | petrus] A et petrus cet. | in medio illorum] cum eis calficiens 5 in medio eorum (sedebat 2) cet. | **56** Quem cum uidisset] A uidens autem eum 5 quem (om. 17) ut uidit (cum uidit 4) cet. | quaedam ancilla] puella quaedam 5 ancillam 8 ancilla quaedam A ancilla cet. add. sedentem (sedente 8) ad lumen cet. | intuens] et intendens in 5 et eum fuisset intuita A | eum] 5 illum cet. om. A | et hic ex illis est] et hic de eis 4 et hic de eis est cet. om. 5 A | qui] om. 5 A | eo] 5 illo A ipso cet. | erant] erat 5 A erat semper 2 erant semper cet. | **57** ad] 2 at cet. | negauit] add. eum 5 A | dicens] ei dicens 2 8 17 | mulier] om. 5 | non noui] nescio 5 | eum] illum cet. | **58** et egressusm illum ad ianuam] et iterum (om. 5 A) post pusillum cet. | uidit alia et] alius uidens eum 5 A uidens eum alius (alia 4) cet. | et hic fuit] uere homo et tu 2 id ipsum 5 et tu A homo et tu cet. | cum iesu nazareno] cum illo eras 2 de illis es A cum illo eras semper cet. | et rursus negauit] petrus autem dixit 2 ad ille dixit 5 petrus uero ait A qui respondit cet. | cum iure iurando] om. cet. add. o homo non sum A homo non sum ego (om. 5) cet. | **59** quem paulo post] et intercesso quasi horae unius 5 et interuallo facto quasi horae unius A et interuallo facto horae unius cet. | cum uidisset quidam] alius quis certabatur 5 alius quidam affirmabat A alius (add. quidam 8) contendens cet. | dixit] in ueritate dico 5 dicens A | uere] om. 5 | iesu] eo 5 illo cet. | iesu erat] etenim 5

Dixit autem petrus: homo, nescio quid dicis. et protinus adhuc loquente illo gallus cantauit. **61** et conuersus dominus, respexit petrum, et rememoratus est petrus uerbum domini, sicut dixit illi antequam gallus cantet, ter me negabis te scire. **62** *omissum* **63** Et uiri, qui continebant illum, deridebant eum. **64** et coperientes faciem illius, percutebant et interrogaba{m}<nt> illum dicentes: profetiza, quis est, qui percussit te. **65** Et alia multa blaspemantes dicebant ad eum. **66** et cum dies horta est, conuenerunt seniores populi pontifices et scribae et deduxerunt illum in concilium suum. **67** et interrogabant eum dicentes: si tu es christus, dic nobis. Dixit autem illis: si uobis dixero, non creditis. **68** si interrogauero, non respondebitis, sed nec dimittetis me. **69** amodo autem erit filius hominis sedens ad dextram uirtutis dei. **70** dixerunt autem ei omnes: tu es filius dei? dixit autem illis: uos dicitis, quia ego sum. **71** Qui dixerunt: quid adhuc egemus testimonio? audiuimus enim de ore illius.

---

60 Dixit autem] 5 et ait (at 2) cet. | quid] quod 8 | dicis] 5 A dicas cet. | protinus] continuo cet. adhuc] om. 8 | loquente illo] eo loquente 2 5 illo loquente cet. | gallus cantauit] 5 4 cantauit gallus cet. | **61** et[1] tunc 4* | et conuersus dominus] conuersus autem iesus 5 | rememoratus] remoratus 4 recordatus A | petrus] om. 5 | uerbum] uerborum 17 uerbi A | illi] om. A antequam] quia priusquam 5 A priusquam cet. | cantet] cantat 8 | me negabis] abnegabis me 5 add. hodie 4 8 | te scire] nosse 4 om. cet. | **63** Et uiri] uiri autem 5 | continebant] 5 tenebant cet. | illum] eum 5 4 A | deridebant] inludebant cet. om. 8 | eum] illum 2 ei A om. 8 | **64** et coperientes] 5 caedentes uelauerunt cet. om. 2 4 | faciem illius] eius faciem 5 eum cet. om. 2 4 percutebant] percutiebant eum 5 17 percutiebat eum et inludebant eum 8 percutiebant faciem eius A om. 2 4 | et[2]] om. 4 | interrogaba{m}<nt>]om. 5 4 | illum] eum cet. om. 5 4 | dicentes] dicebant 5 | profetiza] 2 propheta 5 profetiza nobis 17 prophetiza cet. add. dic nobis 4* | est] om. 8 | percussit te] percussit te cet. | **65** blaspemantes] 2 blasfemantes 5 blasphemiantes 8 blasphemantes cet. | ad] in 5 A | **66** et cum dies horta est] et ut (cum 5 om. 17) factus est dies cet. | conuenerunt] A congregati sunt 5 conuenit cet. | seniores] 5 A praesbiterium 2 presbyterium cet. | populi] 5 plebis cet. | pontifices] et principes (principis 8) sacerdotum cet. | deduxerunt] adduxerunt 5 duxerunt cet. | illum] eum 5 | **67** et interrogabant] om. 5 A | si[1]] om. 5 dic nobis] om. 5 | Dixit autem illis] et ait illis iesus 2 ad ille dixit illis 5 ait illis 4 et ait illis cet. creditis] credetis 5 creditis 4 credetis mihi A creditis mihi cet. | **68** si interrogauero] si interrogauero uos 8 si autem et interrogauero A om. 2 | respondebitis] respondebitis mihi A respondetis mihi cet. om. 2 | sed nec dimittetis me] neque demittitis 2 aut dimittetis 5 neque dimittetis 17 neque dimittetis cet. | **69** amodo] 5 4* ex hoc cet. | erit] om. 4* | sedens] sedebit 4* | ad dextram] 2 ad dexteram 5 ad dextris 8 17 a dextris 4 A | dei] om. 2 | **70** dixerunt autem] 5 A et dixerunt cet. | ei] om. cet. | tu es filius] 5 ergo tu es filius 8 tu ergo es filius cet. | dixit autem illis] ait autem illis 2 ad ille dixit illis 5 qui ait A ait autem illis cet. | dicitis] dicits 2* | quia] A quoniam 5 quod cet. | quia ego sum] om. 17 | **71** Qui dixerunt] ad illi dixerunt 2 at illi dixerunt cet. | egemus] opus habemus 5 desideramus cet. | testimonio] testium 5 testimonium cet. audiuimus enim] ipsi enim audiuimus 8 A | illius] eius 5 A ipsius cet.

23 et surgens uniuersa multitudo eorum, adduxerunt illum ad pilatum. **2**
coeperunt autem accusare illum dicentes: hunc inuenimus euertentem gentem
tributum dare caesari dicentem se christum regem esse{t}. **3** pilatus autem
interrogauit eum dicens: tu es rex iudaeorum? qui respondit illi: tu dicis. **4** pilatus
autem ait ad pontificis et turbam: nullam inuenio culpam in homine hoc. **5** Ad illi
inualescebant dicentes: commouet populum docens per totam iudaeam, inchoans
a galilaea usque hic. **6** pilatus autem, ut audiit galilaeam, interrogauit, an a
galilaea homo iste esset. **7** et cum cognouisset eum de herodis potestatem esse,
remisit illum ad herodem, qui erat et ipse hierosolymis in his diebus. **8** Herodes
autem uiso iesu gauisus est ualde. erat enim cupiens uidere illum propterea quod
audiret frequenter de illo, et sperabat aliquod signum uidere ab illo fieri. **9**
Interrogabat autem illum uerbis pluribus. ipse uero nihil respondebat illi. **10**
stabant autem pontifices uehementer accusantes eum. **11** spernens autem illum et

---

23:1 et surgens] et exsurgentes 5 et exsurgens 4 | uniuersa multitudo] omnes (omnis 2) multitudo cet. om. 5 | eorum] A illorum cet. om. 2 5 | adduxerunt] 5 duxerunt cet. | illum] eum 2 5 17 **2** illum] eum 5 | euertentem] subuertentem cet. | gentem] add. nostram et soluentem legem nostram et prophetas (profetas 2 om. 5 A) et prohibentem (prohiebentes 2 uetantem 5) cet. tributum] tributam 8 tributa cet. | dare] 5 8 dari cet. | dicentem] 8 dicentem autem 5 et dicentem cet. | regem esset] esse rege 8 | **3** interrogauit] 5 A audiens interrogauit (interrogabit 4) cet. | eum] autem 2 | qui respondit illi] ille autem respondit illi dicens 5 at (ad 2) ille respondens ait cet. | **4** pilatus autem ait] pilatus autem dixit 5 dixit autem pilatus 17 ait autem pilatus cet. | pontificis] principes (principis 2) sacerdotum cet. | turbam] turbas cet. | nullam] nihil cet. | culpam] causa 8 causae cet. | homine hoc] hoc homine (hominem 4) cet. | **5** Ad] at 2 inualescebant dicentes] inualiscebant dicentes 2 fortius dicebant 5 | commouet] seducit 5 docens] om. 4 17 | per] in 8 | totam] omnem 5 uniuersam (uniuersa 8) cet. | iudaeam] iudeam 2 iudea 8 | inchoans] et incipiens A incipiens cet. | galilaea] galilaeam 2 | hic] 5 huc 8 A hoc cet. add. et filios nostros et uxores auertit a nobis non enim baptizantur sicut et nos nec se mundant 2 | **6** pilatus autem ut audiit] audiens autem pilatus 5 pilatus autem audiens cet. | an] si cet. | a] de 5 | galilaea homo iste esset] homo galilaeus A a galilaea homo esset (essit 2 est 5) cet. **7** et cum cognouisset] et ut quod cognouisset 8 cognoscens autem 5 | eum de herodis potestatem esse] quia de potestate herodes est 5 quod de herodis potestate (potestatem 2 8 17) est (esset A) cet. remisit] A misit cet. | illum] eum 5 A | herodem] heroden 5 4 | qui erat et ipse hierosolymis] qui hierosolimis erat 2 cum esset hierosolymis 5 qui in (om. 17) hierosolymis erat 4 17 quia hierosolymis erat 8 qui et ipse hierosolymis erat A | in] 5 4 om. cet. | his] illis cet. | **8** Herodes] herodis 8 | uiso] uidens 5 | iesu] iesum 2 | cupiens uidere illum] uolens uidere eum de multis temporibus 5 cupiens ex multo tempore uidens eum A cupiens illum uidere ex multo tempore (temre 2*) cet. | propterea quod] propter quod 5 eo quod cet. | audiret] audirit 2 | frequenter] multa cet. om. 5 | illo¹] eo 5 | aliquod signum] quondam signum 5 | illo²] eo cet. | **9** illum] eum 5 4 | uerbis pluribus] in uerbis pluribus 5 multis sermonibus cet. | ipse uero] ille autem 5 ipse autem 17 at (ad 2) ipse cet. | respondebat illi] 5 respondebat 2 ei respondebat 4 illi respondebat cet. | **10** autem] 5 8 etiam cet. | pontifices] principes sacerdotum et scribae cet. | uehementer] fortiter 5 constanter cet. | eum] cum 5 | **11** spernens] speuit 2* exprobant 5 spreuit cet. illum] eum 5 | et¹] 5 om. cet.

herodes cum exercitu suo et delusum induens ueste candida remisit pilato. **12** facti sunt autem in amicitiam herodes et pilatus eadem hora. praeerant enim in inimicitiam. **13** Pilatus autem conuocans pontifices et principes populi **14** dixit ad illos: detulistis mihi hominem hunc tanquam aduertentem populum. et ecce ego coram uos interrogans nihil inueni dignum in hominem hoc de iis, quae accusatis eum. **15** sed nec herodes. remisi enim uos ad illum et ecce nihil dignum morte gestum est illi. **16** castigatum ergo illum dimittam. **17** *omissum* **18** Exclamabant autem totus populus dicentes: tolle hunc, dimitte autem nobis barabban{t}. **19** qui erat propter seditionem quandam factam in ciuitatem coniectus in carcerem, quia homicidium fecerat. **20** Rursus autem pilatus adlocutus est eis uolens dimittere iesum. **21** qui proclamabant dicentes: crucifige illum. **22** qui tertio dixit ad illos: quid enim mali fecit hic? nihil dignum mortis inueni in illo. castigatum ergo illum

---

exercitu suo] 5 A exercibus suis 2 exercitibus suis 4 8 | delusum] inludens 5 inlusit cet. | induens] coperiens eum 5 indutum illum (om. A) cet. | ueste candida] opertorium candidum 5 uestem albam 8 ueste alba 4 A | remisit] et remisit A | pilato] illum ad pilatum 2 4 eum pilato 5 ad pilatum 8 A | **12** facti sunt autem in amicitiam] cum essent autem in lite 5 et facti sunt amici A tunc amici facti sunt cet. | herodes et pilatus] pilatus et herodes facti sunt amici 5 | eadem hora] in ipso die 5 in ipsa die A ipsa die cet. | praeerant enim in inimicitiam] nam antea (ante 4) inimici fuerant (fuerunt 8 erant A) ad inuicem cet. om. 5 | **13** conuocans] 5 conuocatis cet. pontifices] principes sacerdotum 5 principibus sacerdotum cet. | principes] 5 senioribus 8 magistratibus cet. | populi] et omnem plebem 5 et plebe A plebis cet. | **14** illos] eos 5 | detulistis] obtulistis 2 adduxistis 5 optulistis cet. | mihi hominem hunc] 5 hunc hominem mihi 8 mihi hominem hunc cet. | tanquam] sicut 5 quasi cet. | aduertentem] auertentem cet. | populum] plebem 5 | ecce ego] ego autem 5 | coram uos interrogans] interrogans in conspectu uestro 5 coram uobis interrogans cet. | nihil] illum causam 2* nihil mali 5 nullam causam cet. | inueni] inuenio 2 4 8 | dignum] om. cet. | in hominem hoc] in hominem 2 in eo 5 in hoc homine 4 in hominem isto 8 in homine isto A | de iis] ex his cet. om. 5 | quae] quibus 2 4 de quibus 8 in quibus A om. 5 | accusatis eum] 8 eum accusatis cet. om. 5 | **15** nec] 5 neque cet. | remisi enim] misi enim 5 nam misi 4 nam remisi cet. | illum] eum 5 | et] om. 8 | ecce] om. 5 | dignum] regnum 2 | morte] mortem 2 mortis 5 | gestum] actum cet. | illi] in eo 5 ei A | **16** castigatum] emendans 5 emendabo 4 emendatum cet. | illum] eum 5 4 | dimittam] demittam 2 et dimittam 4 | **18** Exclamabant] exclamauerunt 5 exclamauit cet. | autem[1]] 5 8 autem simul cet. totus populus] uniuersi 5 uniuersa turba cet. | dicentes] 5 dicens cet. | tolle hunc] tolle hunc tolle hunc 5 | dimitte autem] 5 et dimitte (demitte 2) cet. | barabbant] barabban 2 A barabbam cet. | **19** seditionem] dissensionem 5 | ciuitatem] ciuitate 4 A add. et homicidium cet. | coniectus] missus cet. | quia homicidium fecerat] om. cet. | **20** Rursus] iterum cet. | adlocutus] aduocauit 5 locutus cet. | eis] eos 5 ad illos cet. | dimittere] demittere 2 | **21** qui] at (ad 2) illi cet. | proclamabant] clamauerunt 5 succlamabant cet. | dicentes] om. 5 | crucifige] crucifige crucifige 5 A | illum] eum 5 | **22** qui] ad ille 5 ille autem cet. | illos] eos 5 | mali] male 8 hic] 5 iste cet. | nihil] ullam 5 nullam cet. add. enim 2 4 | dignum] causam cet. | inueni] inuenio cet. | illo] 8 eum 5 eo cet. | castigatum] emendans 5 corripiam cet. | illum dimittam] dimittam eum 5 illum et dimittam (demittam 2) cet.

dimittam. **23** qui imminebant uocibus magnis postulantes: crucifige illum.
inualescebant uoces illorum. **24** Et pilatus decreuit fieri petitionem illorum. **25**
dimisit autem eum qui propter homicidium et seditionem coniectus erat in
carcerem. iesum autem tradidit uoluntati ipsorum. **26** Et cum deducerent eum,
simonem quendam cyreneum uenientem a uilla adprehendentes inposuerunt illi
crucem ferre post iesum. **27** sequebatur autem eum multitudo ingens populi et
mulierum quae plangebant se et lamentabant. **28** Ad quas conuersus iesus dixit:
filiae hierusalem, nolite flere me, uerum uos flete et natos uestros, **29** quoniam
uenient dies, in quibus dicent: felices steriles et uentres, qui non genuerunt, et
ubera, quae non educauerunt. **30** Tunc incipient dicere montibus: cadite super
nos, et collibus: tegite nos. **31** quoniam si in umido ligno haec faciunt, in arido
quid fiet? **32** Ducebantur autem et alii duo latrones cum illo interfici. **33** et cum
uenissent ad locum, qui appellatur caluariae, crucifixerunt eum et latrones, unum

---

23 qui] at illi (ad 2) cet. | imminebant] incumbebant 5 instabant cet. | postulantes] petentes 5 crucifige] crucifigi 5 ut crucifigeretur cet. | illum] eum 5 | inualescebant] et conualescebant 5 et inualescebant cet. | illorum] eorum cet. add. et principum sacerdotum 5 | **24** Et pilatus decreuit] iudicauit autem pilatus 5 et pilatus adiudicauit (adiutauit 2) cet. | illorum] eorum 5 A ipsorum cet. | **25** eum] illis eum cet. om. 5 | et seditionem] om. 5 | coniectus] missus cet. | erat] 5 fuerat cet. | in carcerem] add. quem petebant 5 A | autem[2]] 5 uero cet. | uoluntati] uoluntatem 2 | ipsorum] eorum cet. add. susceperunt ergo iesum et portans sibi crucem ducebatur 8 **26** Et cum] cum autem 5 | deducerent] duxerunt 5 ducerent cet. | simonem quendam] inuenerunt simonem quendam 2 adpraehendentes quendam simonem 5 adprehenderunt simonem quendam A | cyreneum] cyrenensem cet. | a] de cet. | uilla] agro 5 uillam 2 8 | adprehendentes] adprehenderunt (adpraehenderunt 2) cet. om. 5 A | inposuerunt] 5 eum et inposuerunt 2 8 et inposuerunt 4 A | illi] ei 5 | ferre] ut adferret 5 portare cet. | post] retro 5 | **27** sequebatur autem] et sequebatur etiam 2 | eum] illum cet. | multitudo ingens] multa turba A multitudo cet. mulierum] mulieres 5 | plangebant] plangebat 8 | se] eum 5 om. cet. | lamentabant] lamentabantur eum A | **28** Ad quas conuersus iesus dixit] iesus dixit ad eas 5 conuersus autem ad illas iesus dixit cet. | filiae] familiae 2 | hierusalem] 5 A isdrahelite 2 istrahelitae et 4 istrahel 8 flere me] plangere me neque lugete 5 flere super me A | uerum] sed cet. | uos] 5 super uos ipsas A uos ipsas cet. | flete] plorate 5 | natos] super filios A filios cet. | **29** quoniam] quoniam ecce A | dicent] dicenst 2* | felices] beata 2 beatae cet. | uentres] uteri 5 | qui] 2 A quae cet. genuerunt] peperunt 2 | educauerunt] enutrierunt 5 lactauerunt A nutrierunt cet. | **30** incipient dicere] incipere dicent 8 | cadite] cadete 2 | tegite] 5 operite cet. | **31** quoniam] 5 qua 2 quia cet. | umido] udo 2 4 humido 5 8 uiridi A | faciunt] fiunt 4 | **32** et] om. 4 | alii] om. 2 latrones] maligni 5 nequam A | illo] eo 5 A | interfici] 5 ut interficerentur A ut crucifigerentur cet. | **33** cum] 5 postquam cet. | uenissent] uenerunt cet. | ad[1]] 8 in cet. | appellatur] uocabatur 2 dicitur 8 uocatur cet. | caluariae] calbariae 2 | crucifixerunt] et ibi crucifixerunt 8 ibi crucifixerunt cet. | latrones] malignos simul 5 latrones cum eo 4* latrones duo 4[c] | unum] unus 2* 8 quidem ad dextram et alium ad sinistram. **34** Et diuidentes uestimemta ipsius, mittebant sortes. **35** et stabat populus exspectans. subsannabant autem eum principes intra se dicentes: alios saluos fecit, se saluum se faciat, si hic est christus dei electus. **36** Inridebant autem eum ei milites accedentes acetum offerentes ei. **37** et dicentes: tu es rex iudaeorum, salua te ipsum. **38** erat autem et inscriptio scripta super eum: rex iudaeorum hic. **39** Unus autem ex iis, qui suspensi erant malefici, blasphemabat illum dicens: nonne tu es christus? libera te et nos. **40** Respondens autem alius obiurgabat eum dicens: nec times deum, quoniam in eodem iudicio es? **41** et nos quidem iuste. digna enim, quorum gessimus, recepimus. Hic autem nihil mali fecit. **42** et dicebat ad iesum: memento mei, cum ueneris in regno tuo. **43** et dixit illi iesus: amen dico tibi, hodie mecum eris in

---

quidem] om. cet. | ad[2]] a 5 A | dextram] 2 8 dextra 4 dextris 5 A | alium] 2 4 alius 8 unum d alterum A | ad[3]] a 5 A | sinistram] 2 8 sinistris 5 A sinistra 4 add. iesus autem dicebat pater dimitte (demitte 2) illis non enim sciunt (nesciunt 4*) quid faciunt (faciant 4* faciam 8) cet. **34** Et diuidentes] partiebantur autem 5 diuidentes uero A diuidentes etiam cet. | Et diuidentes uestimemta ipsius mittebant sortes] om. 4* | ipsius] eius cet. | mittebant] mittentes 5 miserunt cet. | sortes] sortem 5 4[c] | **35** stabat] staba 2* | exspectans] uidens 5 spectans A expectans cet. subsannabant autem] 5 et deridebant cet. | eum] 5 8 illum cet. | principes] om. 5 | intra se] cum eis A om. cet. | dicentes] et dicebant illi 5 | fecit] fecisti 5 | se[2]] te ipsum 5 nunc se 4 8 saluum] salbum 2 5 | se[3]] om. cet. | faciat] fac 5 | hic est christus dei electus] filius es dei si christus es electus 5 hic est christus electus dei 8 | **36** Inridebant] dulebant 8 inludebant A deludebant cet. | eum] 5 4 illum 2 8 ei A | acetum] 5 et acetum cet. | offerentes] A offerebant cet. | ei[2]] 5 illi cet. | **37** et] om. cet. | tu es] habe 5 si tu es A | iudaeorum] iudaorum 2 | salua te ipsum] saluum te fac A libera te cet. om. 5 add. inponentes illi et de spinis coronam 5 | **38** erat autem] et erat 4 | et] 5 A om. cet. | inscriptio] 5 superscriptio cet. | scripta] 2 8 superscripta 5 inscripta 4 A | eum] 5 illum cet. add. graecis et (om. 5 4 8) latinis (om. 8) et (om. 5) hebreicis (habraicis 2 hebraicis 5 A) cet. | rex iudaeorum hic] hic est rex iudaeorum 4 A rex iudaeorum hic est cet. | **39** autem] 5 A etiam cet. | ex] de cet. | iis] his A om. cet. | qui suspensi erant] qui pendebant A pendentibus cet. | malefici] malignis 5 latronibus cet. | blasphemabat] blasphemabant 8 blasphemauit cet. | illum] 2 eum cet. om. 8 | dicens] om. 5 | nonne tu es] 4 8 si A om. 2 5 | libera te et nos] 8 salua temetipsum et nos 4 saluum fac et nos A om. 2 5 | **40** alius] 5 alter cet. | obiurgabat] increpabat cet. | eum] 5 illum cet. | nec times deum] 8 ne times dominum 2 quoniam non times tu dominum 5 neque times deum tu 4 neque tu times deum A | quoniam] 5 quid 2 quod 4 8 qui A | eodem iudicio] ea demnationem 2 ipso iudicio 5 eadem damnationem (damnatione A) cet. | es] est 8 et nos sumus 5 om. 2 | **41** iuste] add. haec patimur 4 | digna enim] digne enim 5 nam digna cet. | quorum gessimus] secundum quod egimus 5 factis nostris 4 factis cet. | recepimus] 2 4 recipimus cet. | autem] 5 uero cet. | mali fecit] inicum egit 5 mali gessit cet. | **42** et dicebat ad iesum] et conuersus ad dominum dixit illi 5 et dixit ad iesum 4 add. domine 2 8 A | memento] 5 A memor esto cet. | mei] me 5 add. domine 4 | cum ueneris in regno tuo] in die aduentus tui 5 quando uenies in regno tuo 4 cum ueneris in regnum tuum cet. **43** et dixit illi iesus] 8 A et dixit illi 2* respondens autem iesus dixit qui obiurgabat eum 5 et dixit ei iesus 4 | amen dico tibi] animequior esto 5 | hodie] quia hodie 4

paradiso. **44** et erat circiter hora sexta et tenebrae factae sunt super omnem terram et usque horam nonam. **45** intenebricatus est sol, et uelum templi scissum est medium. **46** et exclamans uoce magna iesus: Pater in manibus tuis commendo spiritum meum. et emisit spiritum. **47** quod cum uidisset centurio, honorificauit deum dicens: uere homo hic iustus erat. **48** et omnes, quae conuenerant turbae ad spectaculum hoc, uidentes ex ea, quae fiebant, percutentes pectora sua reuertebantur. **49** Stabant autem omnes noti illius a longe et mulieres, quae secutae fuerant illum a galilaea, uidentes haec. **50** Et ecce uir nomine ioseph, qui erat decurio bonus et iustus. **51** hic non consenserat consilio et opere illorum ab arimathia ciuitate iudaeorum, qui expectabat regnum dei. **52** hic accessit ad pilatum et petit corpus iesu. **53** et depositum inuoluit eum in sindonem et posuit illum in monumento sculptili, ubi nondum aliquis erat positus. **54** et dies erat cena

---

paradiso] paradiso patris 2 | **44** et erat] erat autem A | circiter] sicut 5 fere cet. | hora sexta] hora sexta diei 4 | super omnem terram] in totam terram 5 in uniuersa terra cet. | et[3]] om. cet. horam nonam] in nona hora 2 in hora nona 5 in nonam horam 4 in horam nonam 8 A | **45** intenebricatus] obscuratus autem 5 et obscuratus A obscuratus cet. | et uelum templi scissum est medium] et uelum templi scissum medium 2 p. v. 46 5 | **46** et[1]] om. 4 | exclamans] clamans cet. uoce magna iesus] 2 4 iesus uoce magna dixit 5 8 uoce magna iesus ait A | manibus tuis] manus tuas cet. | et[2]] et hoc cum dixisset 5 et hoc (haec 8 A) dicens cet. | emisit spiritum] 4 reddidit spiritum 2 exspirauit 5 A tradidit spiritum 8 | **47** quod cum uidisset centurio] et centurio clamans 5 uidens autem centurio cet. add. et qui cum eo erant 2 8 add. quod fiebat (factum fuerat A) cet. | honorificauit] magnificabant 2 8 honorificabat 5 magnificat 4 glorificauit A | dicens] dicentes 8 om. 2 | homo hic iustus erat] 4 iustus erat hic homo 5 hic homo iustus erat cet. **48** omnes] 5 omnis turba eorum A omnis turba cet. | quae[1]] 8 qui cet. | conuenerant turbae] simul erat 2 8 simul uenerant 5 simul aderant 4 A | spectaculum] spectaculum populi 5 | hoc] istud cet. om. 5 | uidentes] 5 et uidebant A qui uidebant cet. | ex ea] om. cet. | quae[2]] quod 2 fiebant] fiebat 2 facta sunt 5 | percutentes] pecutientes 2* percutientes cet. | pectora sua] pectora et frontes 5 | **49** illius] eius cet. | mulieres] add. qui ibi erant 8 | fuerant] 4 sunt 5 erant cet. | illum] eum 5 A | uidentes haec] 5 haec uidentes cet. | **50** qui erat decurio] decurio cum esset 5 | bonus et iustus] iustus et bonus 8 uir bonus et iustus A | **51** consenserat] erat consentiens 5 erat consensus 8 | consilio] concilio 4* 8 | opere illorum] actioni eorum 5 actibus eorum cet. | arimathia] arimatia 4 | ciuitate] ciuitates 4* 8 | iudaeorum] 5 iudeae cet. | qui] qui et ipse 8 | expectabat] expectabant 2 exspectabant cet. add. et ipse A | **52** hic accessit] et accedens 5 | et] om. 5 | petit] petiuit 5 petiit A | iesu] iesum 4* | **53** et depositum] et deponens 5 4* | inuoluit eum] inuoluit corpus iesu 5 illum inuoluit 4* illut inuoluit 4c inuoluit cet. in[1]] om. A | sindonem] 8 sendone nouam 4 sindone cet. | illum] eum cet. om. 2 | sculptili] sculpto 5 exciso cet. | ubi] 5 in quo cet. | nondum] adhuc 5 | aliquis] nemo 5 quisquam cet. erat positus] positus erat (fuerat 4 A) cet. add. et posito eo inposuit in monumento lapidem quem uix uiginti mouebant 5 | **54** et dies erat] erat autem dies 5 et dies erant 4* | cena purae] cena pura 8 parasceues A om. 5

purae et sabbatum inlucescebat. **55** consecutae duae mulieres, quae secutae
fuerant illum de galilaea, uiderunt monimentum et quomodo positum est corpus
illius. **56** reuersae autem parauerunt aromata et unguenta, et sabbato quidem
quieuerunt secundum mandatum.

24 Prima autem die sabbatorum uenerunt ante lucem ualde ad
monumentum adferentes, quae parauerunt. **2** inuenerunt autem lapidem
reuolutum a monumento. **3** ingressae autem non inuenerunt corpus. **4** Et factum
est, dum stuperent de hoc, ecce uiri duo adstiterunt iuxta illas in ueste fulgenti. **5**
timore autem adprehensae inclinantes faciem ad terram, dixerunt ad {ad} illas:
quid quaeritis uiuum cum mortuis? **6** Memoramini sicut locutus est uobis, dum
adhuc esset in galilaea **7** dicens, quoniam filium hominis oportet tradi et tertia die
resurgere. **8** et maemoratae sunt uerborum horum. **9** Et reuersae renuntiauerunt

---

et sabbatum inlucescebat] et sabbatum inluciscebat 2 ante sabbatum 5 | **55** consecutae] secutae sunt autem 5 subsecutae sunt autem 8 subsecutae (subsaecutae 2) autem cet. | duae] om. A secutae fuerant illum] erant simul uenientes 5 cum ipso uenerant cet. | de] a 5 | uiderunt] et uiderunt 5 | monimentum] monumentum eius 5 monumentum cet. | et quomodo positum est corpus illius] et quemadmodum (quaeadmodum 4) positum erat corpus eius cet. om. 5 | **56** reuersae autem] 5 et reuertentes cet. | aromata] aromatam 8 | et[2]] om. 8 | sabbato quidem] quidem sabbatum 5 | quieuerunt] requieuerunt 5 siluerunt cet. | secundum mandatum] om. 5 **24:1** Prima] una cet. | die sabbatorum] sabbati cet. | uenerunt ante lucem ualde] mane diluculo ueniebant 5 ualde diluculo uenerunt A uenerunt ualde tempore (deluculo 8) cet. | adferentes] 5 portantes cet. | parauerunt] parauerant 4 parauerant aromata A add. et quidam cum illis cogitabant autem intra se quis utique reuolueret lapidem 5 | **2** inuenerunt autem] uenientes autem inuenerunt 5 et inuenerunt cet. | a monumento] om. 4 | **3** ingressae autem] introeuntes autem 5 et ingressae A | corpus] add. domini iesu A | **4** stuperent] aporiarentur 5 contristarentur 8 mente consternatae essent (sunt 2) cet. | hoc] eo 5 facto 4 isto cet. | ecce] et ecce 4 | uiri duo] duo uiri cet. | adstiterunt] adsisterunt 5 steterunt cet. | iuxta] sicut 8 secus cet. om. 5 illas] eis 5 | ueste] amictu 5 | fulgenti] A fulgente 2 4 scoruscanti 5 splendida 8 | **5** timore autem adprehensae] in timore autem factae 5 cum timerent autem cet. | inclinantes] inclinauerunt 5 et declinarent cet. | faciem] uultos suos 5 uultum cet. | ad[1]] in cet. | terram] terra 5 dixerunt] ad illi dixerunt 5 | quaeritis] quaerites 2 | uiuum] 5 uiuentem cet. | **6** Memoramini] mementote autem 5 non est hic sed resurrexit recordamini A rememoramini cet. | sicut] quanta 5 qualiter cet. | uobis] uobiscum 4 | dum] cum cet. | esset in galilaea] 5 in galilaea esset cet. **7** dicens] om. 5 | quoniam] 5 quia cet. | filium hominis oportet] oportet filium hominis cet. tradi] tradi in manus hominum peccatorum A tradi in manus hominum cet. | et] add. crucifigi et cet. | tertia die] die tertia 4 A | resurgere] resurgi 8 | **8** maemoratae] memoratae 2* 5 rememoratae 2[c] 8 remoratae 4 recordatae A | horum] eius 5 A | **9** reuersae] 5 egresse 8 regressae cet. add. a monumento A | renuntiauerunt] 2 4 nuntiauerunt cet.

haec omnia illis undecim et ceteris omnibus. **10** erat autem magdalena et maria iacobi et iohanna et relique cum eis, que dicebant ad apostolos haec. **11** et uisa sunt illis tanquam delera uerba haec et non credebant eis. **12** *omissum* **13** Et ecce duo erant ex illis euntes in municipium stadios habentem lx ab hierusalem, cui nomen ammaus. **14** et ipsi tractabant de omnibus, quae his contegerant. **15** et factum est, dum tractarent ipsi, et iesus ascendens comitabatur cum illis. **16** oculi autem eorum tenebantur, ne agnoscerent illum. **17** Dixit autem ad eos: quae sunt uerba ista, quae tractatis ad alterutrum e{s}t estis tristes? **18** Respondens autem unus ex eis, cui nom{m}en est cleophas, dixit ad illum: Tu solus peregrinus es in hierusalem? nescis, quae gesta sunt in illa in diebus istis? **19** Qui ait illis: quae? et

haec omnia] omnia haec 5 | undecim] undecim discipulis 2 xi 4 | ceteris omnibus] omnibus reliquis 5 | **10** erat autem] om. 5 | magdalena] maria magdalena 5 maria magdalene cet. maria iacobi et iohanna] iohanna et maria iacobi cet. | relique] ceterae cet. | cum eis] 5 quae cum ipsis (eis A) fuerant (erant A) cet. | que] A om. 5 haec cet. | haec] 5 A om. cet. | **11** et uisa sunt illis] et paruerunt in conspectu eorum 5 et uisa sunt ante illos cet. | tanquam] quasi 5 sicut cet. | delera] derisus 5 delibramentum 4 deliramentum (deleramentum 2) cet. | haec] 5 ista cet. eis] 5 illis cet. add. lxxuiiii 2 | **13** Et ecce duo erant ex illis euntes] fuerunt autem duo ex illis euntes 2 erant autem duo abeuntes ex eis 5 et ecce duo ex illis ibant cet. add. in (om. 2) ipsa die cet. | municipium] castellum cet. | stadios habentem lx ab hierusalem] quod est ab hierosolymis stadia septem 2 iter habentis stadios sexaginta ab hierusalem 5 quod aberat stadia sexaginta ab hierusalem 4 quod aberat spatio stadiorum sexaginta ab hierusalem 8 quod erat in spatio stadiorum sexaginta ab hierusalem A | cui] om. cet. | ammaus] ammaus et cleopas 2 ulammaus 5 cleofas et ammaus 4 ammaus et cleophas 8 emmaus A | **14** et ipsi tractabant] fabulabantur autem ad inuicem 2 fabulabantur autem semetipsos 5 et ipsi fabulabantur 4 8 et ipsi loquebantur ad inuicem A | de] ex 4 | omnibus] 2 5 his omnibus cet. | his contegerant] contigerant horum 5 acciderant (accederant 2) cet. | **15** factum] factus 5 | dum tractarent ipsi] dum fabulantur et conquirerent ad inuicem 2 in eo fabulari eos et conquerere 5 dum fabulantur 4 dum fabularentur 8 dum fabularentur et secum quaererent A | et[2]] om. 2 | iesus] 2 5 ipse iesus cet. | ascendens] adpropinquauit 2 adpropians 5 superuenit 4 8 appropinquans A | comitabatur] et comitabatur 2 simul ibat 5 et ibat 4 8 ibat A | **16** eorum] illorum 8 | tenebantur] grauati erant 2 | ne agnoscerent illum] ut non cognoscerent eum 5 ne eum agnoscerent (cognoscerent 2) cet. | **17** Dixit autem ad eos] ille autem dixit ad illos (eos*) 2 ad ille dixit 5 et ait ad illos cet. | quae[1]] 5 qui cet. uerba ista] ista uerba 5 hi (hii 2 isti 8) sermones cet. | quae[2]] haec quae 5 quos cet. | tractatis] referitis 2 conferitis 5 confertis cet. | ad alterutrum] uos 5 ad inuicem cet. add. ambulantes 5 A estis tristes] steterunt tristes 2 tristes 5 | **18** Respondens autem unus ex eis] 5 respondit autem unus ad eum 2 respondit unus ex ipsis 4 et respondens unus ex ipsis 8 et respondens unus A cui nommen est] cui nomen erat 2 nomine 4 cui nomen cet. | cleophas] 8 cleofas 4 cleopas cet. dixit] et dixit 2 4 | ad illum] 2 ad eum 5 illi 4 ei 8 A | peregrinus es] A peregrinaris 2 aduena es 5 pelegrinus es 4 pelegrinus 8 | in[1]] ab 2 | nescis] nescisti 5 (et A) non cognouisti cet. | gesta] facta cet. | illa] ea 5 | in[3]] om. 2 A | diebus istis] 5 istis diebus 2 his diebus cet. | **19** Qui ait illis] ille autem dixit illis 2 ad ille dixit ei 5 quibus ille dixit 4 A ad ille dixit 8 | et ipsi dixerunt] illi autem dixerunt 2 et dixerunt (dicebant 4*) 4 A et illi dicebant 8 om. 5

ipsi dixerunt: de iesu nazareno, qui fuit propheta potens in opere et uerbo coram deo et omni populo. **20** quomodo hunc tradiderunt pontifices nostri in iudicio mortis et crucifixerunt illum. **21** nos uero sperauimus ipsum esse, qui redempturus esset istrahel, nunc tertia dies est hodie, ex quo facta sunt haec. **22** Et super his omnibus mulieres quaedam ex nobis exterruerunt hos, quae fuerunt mane ad monumentum. **23** et cum non inuenissent corpus eius, uenerunt dicentes Etiam uisionem angelorum se uidisse, qui dicunt eum uiuere. **24** Et abierunt quidam ex nobis ad monumentum. et inuenerunt ita, ut mulieres dixerunt, ipsum autem non uiderunt. **25** Et ipse dixit ad illos: insensati et graues corde in credendo omnibus, quibus locuti sunt prophaetae. **26** nonne haec oportebat pati christum et intrare in gloriam suam? **27** Et erat inchoans a moysen et omnibus prophetis interpraetans eis in omnibus scripturis de se. **28** et adpropinquauerunt in uicum,

---

iesu] iesum 2 | nazareno] 2 A nazoreo 5 nazareo 4 8 | qui] quid 8 | fuit propheta] 4 fuit propheta uir 8 fuit uir propheta (profeta 2) cet. | opere et uerbo] factis et dictis 2 uerbo et opera 5 opere et sermone cet. | coram] in conspectu 2 5 | deo] 8 A dei 2 5 deum 4 | et[3]] om. 5 | omni] uniuersi 2 | populo] A populi 2 5 plebe 4 8 | **20** quomodo] sicut 5 et quomodo A | hunc] eum A pontifices] sacerdotes 2 summi sacerdotes A principes sacerdotum cet. | nostri] et magistratus nostri 2 et potentes nostri 5 et omnes populus 4 et principes nostri A om. 8 | iudicio] iudicium 5 damnationem cet. | crucifixerunt illum] cruci eum fixerunt 2 4 crucifixerunt eum cet. | **21** uero] 4 autem cet. | sperauimus] 5 speramus 2 8 sperabamus 4 A | ipsum esse] 4 quia ipse fuit 2 quoniam ipse erat 5 quia ipse 8 A | qui redempturus esset istrahel] 4 qui redempturus erat isdrahel 2 qui incipebat saluare israhel 5 incipit liberare istrahel 8 esset redempturus israhel A nunc tertia dies est hodie] simul autem cum his tertium diem agit hodie 2 sed etiam et in omnibus istis tertium diem hodie agit 5 et nunc (add. super haec omnia A) tertia dies (add. est 4) hodie cet. ex quo] 2 5 quod 4 A ut 8 | facta sunt haec] haec (om. 2) facta sunt cet. | **22** Et] 4 8 sed 2 sed et 5 A | super] in 4 om. cet. | his omnibus] 4 8 om. cet. | quaedam] quedam 2 | ex nobis] 2 ex nostris cet. om. 5 | exterruerunt] commemorauerunt 2 seduxerunt 5 terruerunt cet. | hos] nos cet. | quae fuerunt mane] cum fuissent ante lucana 2 factae matutinae 5 quae ante lucem fuerant cet. | **23** et cum non inuenissent corpus eius] 2 5 et non inuento corpore eius cet. | dicentes] 2 5 se dicentes cet. | Etiam] om. 2 5 | se] 2 om. cet. | dicunt] dicebant 2 | eum] illum 2 **24** ex] de 2 5 | nobis] 2 his qui erant nobiscum 5 nostris cet. | ad] in 5 | inuenerunt ita] inuenerunt ista 2 inuenerunt sic 5 ita inuenerunt cet. | ut] sicut cet. | mulieres dixerunt] dixerunt mulieres 2 5 | ipsum] illum 5 | autem] 2 5 uero cet. | uiderunt] uidimus 2 5 | **25** Et ipse dixit ad illos] ille autem dixit ad illos 2 ad ille dixit ad eos 5 et ipse dixit ad eos (illos 8) cet. | insensati] o insensati 2 5 o stulti cet. | graues] tardi cet. | in credendo] ad credendum cet. om. 5 | omnibus] super omnia 2 in omnibus cet. | quibus] 5 quae cet. | prophaetae] profetae 2 5 | **26** nonne] quoniam 5 | haec] haec omnia 2 | oportebat] 2 5 oportuit cet. | pati christum] christum pati 8 | et] et ita 4 A | intrare] introire 2 5 | gloriam] claritatem 2 | suam] eius 5 | **27** erat] fuit 2 om. A | inchoans] incipiens cet. | moysen] mosen 5 mose A | omnibus[1]] omnium 5 prophetis] profetis 2 propheetarum 5 | interpraetans] 2[c] interpraetari 5 interpretabatur A (et 2) interpretans cet. | eis] illis cet. | omnibus[2]] om. 5 | de] 2 5 quae de cet. | se] eo 2 5 ipso cet. add. erant 4 8 A | **28** adpropinquauerunt] propinquauerunt 2 appropinquauerunt A adpropiauerunt cet. | in uicum] ad castellum 2 8 in castellum 5 castello 4 A

quem ibant, et ipse adfectabat se longius ire. **29** et coegerunt illum dicentes: mane nobiscum, quoniam ad uesperum iam declinauit dies. Et intrauit, ut cum eis maneret. **30** et factum est, cum discubuisset cum illis, acceptum panem benedixit et frangens porrigebat illis. **31** Et adaperti sunt oculi eorum et cognouerunt illum. et ipse nusquam conparuit ab illis. **32** et dixerunt ad alterutrum: nonne cor nostrum erat in nobis ardens in uia, cum adaperiebat nobis scripturas? **33** et surgentes eadem hora reuersi sunt in hierusalem. et inuenerunt collectos xi et eos, qui cum illis erant, **34** dicentes, quoniam uere resurrexit dominus et uisus est simoni. **35** Et ipsi enarrabant, quae in uia gesta erant et sicut agnitus est illis in fractione panis. **36** et dum haec loquuntur, ipse stetit in medio eorum. **37** exterriti autem et timore adprehensi putabant se spiritum uidere. **38** qui dixit illis: quid turbati estis et quare cogitationes ascendunt in corde uestro? **39** uidete manus

---

quem] ubi 5 quo cet. | et ipse] ipse autem 2 | adfectabat] similauit 2 fecit 5 finxit cet. | se] om. A | ire] abire 5 | **29** coegerunt] extorserunt 2 coxerunt 5 | illum] illi 2 eum 5 | mane] manete 8 | quoniam] quia 5 | ad uesperum iam declinauit dies] aduesperascit et inclinata est iam dies A | uesperum] uesperam 2 | iam] om. 5 | intrauit] introiuit 5 | ut cum eis maneret] ut maneret cum illis 2 manere cum illis 5 cum illis et mansit 4 cum illis 8 A | **30** cum discubuisset cum illis] in eo dum recumberet 2 cum recubuisset 5 dum recumbit cum illis 4 cum recumbit cum eis 8 dum recumberet cum illis A | acceptum] accipiens 5 accepit cet. | benedixit] 5 et benedixit cet. et[2]] ac 4 A | frangens] fregit et cet. om. 5 | porrigebat] tradidit 2 dabat 5 | **31** Et] cum accepissent autem panem ab eo 2 accipientium autem eorum panem ab eo 5 | adaperti] aperti cet. illum] 2 eum cet. | et ipse] et 4 ipse autem 8 | nusquam conparuit ab] 2 8 non conparuit ab 5 inuisus factus est 4 euanuit ex oculis A | illis] eorum A eis cet. | **32** et] ille autem 2 ad illi 5 alterutrum] semetipsos 5 inuicem cet. | nostrum] uestrum 8 | erat in nobis ardens] 4 8 fuit exterminatum 2 erat coopertum 5 ardens erat in nobis A | uia] uiam 4 8 om. cet. | cum] 4 8 quomodo in uia 2 quomodo loquebatur nobis in uia sicut 5 dum loqueretur in uia et A | adaperiebat] aperiebat 2 5 aperiret cet. | **33** surgentes] A surrexerunt tristes 2 surgestes contristati 5 surrexerunt cet. | eadem hora reuersi sunt] et reuersi sunt ipsa hora 2 ipsa (eadem A) hora et (om. 5 A) regressi (reuersi 5 egressi 8) sunt cet. | inuenerunt] add. undecim discipulos 2 collectos] 2 congregatos cet. add. illos 5 8 | xi] 5 in unum 2 undecim cet. | eos] om. 2 5 | illis] 4 eis 2 5 illos 8 ipsis A | **34** quoniam] 5 quia 2 quod cet. | uere] om. 4 A | resurrexit] 2 5 surrexerit 4 surrexit 8 A add. a mortuis 8 | dominus] add. uere A | uisus est] apparuit A | simoni] a simonem 4 8 | **35** ipsi] ipse 2 | enarrabant] exponebat ei 2 narrabant cet. | in uia gesta erant] in uia acta sunt 2 gesta erant (om. 5) in uia cet. | sicut] quoniam 2 quia 5 quomodo cet. | agnitus est illis] agnitus est illi 2 cognotus est eis 5 cognouerunt eum cet. | fractione panis] panis fractura 2 fractionem panis 8 | **36** et dum haec loquuntur] haec cum illi loquerentur 2 haec autem eorum loquentium 5 dum haec autem loquuntur (add. illi 4) cet. | ipse] iesus A | eorum] add. et dicit eis pax uobis ego sum nolite timere A | **37** exterriti autem] turbati autem 2 ipsi autem pauerunt 5 conturbatique 4 8 conturbati uero A | timore adprehensi] in timorem missi 2 timore tacti 5 conterriti cet. | putabant] 5 putauerunt 2 existimabant cet. | se] om. 5 | **38** qui dixit illis] ille autem dixit illis 2 ad ille dixit illis 5 dixit autem ad illos 4 8 et dixit eis A | quid] quare 5 | turbati] conturbati 5 | quare] ut quid 5 om. A | cogitationes] in cogitationes 5 | ascendunt] ascenderunt 4 8 | corde uestro] 4 8 cor uestrum 2 5 corda uestra A | **39** uidete[1]] uidete ecce 4 8

meas et pedes meos, quoniam ego sum ipsi. tractate et uidete, quoniam spiritus carnem et ossum non habet, sicut me uidetes habentem. **40** *omissum* **41** adhuc autem non credentibus illis et stupentibus prae gaudio dixit: habetis aliquid, quod edamus hic? **42** qui porrexerunt illi pisces assi partem et fauum. **43** et accipiens manducauit coram illis **44** et dixit eis: haec uerba, quae locutus sum aput uos, cum adhuc essem uobiscum, quoniam oportet inpleri omnia, quae scripta sunt in lege moysi et prophetis et psalmis de me. **45** tunc aperuit sensum illorum ad intellegendum scripturas. **46** et dixit eis, quoniam sic scriptum est christum pati et resurgere a mortuis tertia die. **47** et praedicari in nomine illius paenitentiam et remissionem peccatorum in omnibus gentibus incipiens ab hierusalem. **48** uos autem estis testes horum. **49** et ego mittam repromissionem patris super uos. uos autem sedete in ciuitatem, donec induamini uirtutem a summo. **50** eduxit autem illos usque ad bethaniam et extollens manus suas benedixit eos. **51** Et factum est,

---

meos] om. A | quoniam[1]] 2 quia cet. | ego sum] ego ipse sum 2 5 ego sum ipse 4 8 ipse ego sum A ipsi] ipse cet. | tractate] palpate cet. | quoniam[2]] 5 qua 8 quia cet. | carnem et ossum non habet] ossa non habet nec carnes 5 carnem et ossa non habet cet. | me] et me 5 | uidetes] uidetis cet. | habentem] 2 5 habere cet. | **41** adhuc autem non credentibus illis] 8 cum adhuc autem non credent illi 2 adhuc autem non credentibus eis 5 adhuc autem illis non credentibus 4 A et stupentibus prae gaudio] et cum admirarentur a gaudio 2 a gaudio et mirantium 5 et mirantibus prae gaudio cet. | dixit] dixit ad eos 2 | aliquid] 5 aliquid hic 4 hic aliquid cet. | quod] om. 2 8 | edamus] manducem 4 manducetur A manducare cet. | hic] 5 om. cet. | **42** qui] et 2 5 at illi cet. | porrexerunt] 2 5 optulerunt cet. | illi] 2 5 ei cet. | pisces assi partem] piscis assi partem 2 5 partem piscis assi (assam 4) cet. | et fauum] et de fauo 4 et fauum mellis 8 A om. 2 5 **43** accipiens] 5 accepit 2 om. cet. | manducauit coram illis] coram illis 2 in conspectu eorum manducauit 5 manducans coram ipsis 4 8 cum manducasset coram eis sumens reliquias dedit eis A | **44** et dixit eis] 5 et dixit illis 2 (add. et A) dixit ad eos cet. | haec uerba] isti sermones 2 isti sermones mei 5 haec sunt uerba cet. | quae[1]] quos 2 5 | aput] ad cet. | adhuc] om. 5 | oportet] 2 5 necesse est cet. | inpleri] adimpleri 2 suppleri 4 impleri cet. | moysi] moysei 5 mosi A prophetis] profetis 2 | **45** aperuit] adaperti sunt 5 | sensum illorum] eorum sensus 5 illis sensum cet. | ad intellegendum] ut intellegeant 5 ut intellegerent cet. | scripturas] ea quae scripta sunt 4 8 | **46** eis] illis 2 | quoniam] quia 2 5 | sic] si 8 om. 2 | est] erat 5 | christum] et sic oportebat christum A | a mortuis] om. 5 | tertia die] 2 die tertia 5 A om. 4 8 | **47** praedicari] praedicare 2 8 | illius] eius cet. | remissionem] remissa 4 | in[2]] usque in 2 super 5 | omnibus gentibus] omni gente 4 8 omnes gentes cet. | incipiens] 2 incipientium 5 incipientibus cet. hierusalem] 2 5 hierosolyma cet. | **48** uos autem] et uos 2 et uos autem 5 | estis testes] testes 5 testes estis 8 | horum] eorum 2 | **49** mittam] mitto cet. | repromissionem] promissionem 2 5 promissa 4 8 promissum A | patris] meam 2 5 patris mei cet. | super] 2 5 in cet. | uos[1]] uobis 4 uos[2]] illud 2 | in] hic in 8 | ciuitatem] 8 ciuitate cet. | donec] usque dum 5 quoadusque cet. induamini] induatis 2 | a summo] ex alto 2 A de alto 5 ab alto 4 8 | **50** eduxit] produxit 2 illos] illis 2 eum 8 eos cet. | usque] foras 5 A foris 4 8 om. 2 | ad] 5 quasi 2 in cet. | et extollens] et lebabit 2 lebans autem 5 et eleuatis cet. | manus suas] 2 manus 5 manibus suis (om. 8) cet. benedixit] et benedixit 2 | eos] illos 2 eis A

dum benediceret illos, discessit ab eis. **52** et ipsi reuersi sunt in hierusalem cum gaudio magno. **53** et erant semper in templo conlaudantes deum.

euangelium secundum
lucanum
explicit incipit
secundum
marcum

---

51 dum] cum 2 5 8 | benediceret] 5 A benedixisset 2 benedicit 4 8 | illos] eos 5 illis A | discessit] 2 5 recessit cet. | eis] illis 2 add. et ferebatur in caelum A | **52** reuersi] 2 5 adorantes regressi A regressi cet. | **53** semper in templo] in templo semper 2 | conlaudantes] laudantes cet. add. et benedicentes A | deum] deum amen A

Bibliography

Lexica and Grammars

ADRADOS, Francisco Rodriguez et al. (eds.), *Diccionario Griego-Español, vol. 1–* (Madrid: CSIC, 1980–).

BALZ, Horst et al. (eds.), *Exegetisches Wörterbuch zum Neuen Testament (EWNT)*, 3 vol. (3rd rev. ed.; Stuttgart: Kohlhammer, 2011).

BAUER, Walter, *Wörterbuch zum Neuen Testament Griechisch-Deutsches: Wörterbuch zu den Schriften des Neuen Testaments und der frühchristlichen Literatur* (6th rev. ed.; Institut für neutestamentliche Textforschung/Münster, with contributions of Viktor Reichmann; Kurt Aland and Barbara Aland eds.; Berlin: De Gruyter, 1988).

BLASS, Friedrich and DEBRUNNER, Albert (eds.), *Grammatik des neutestamentlichen Griechisch (BDR)* (17. ed.; Friedrich Rehkopf ed.; Göttingen: Vandenhoeck & Ruprecht, 1990).

BORNEMANN, Eduarda and RISCH, Ernst, *Griechische Grammatik* (2nd ed.; Göttingen: Diesterweg, 1978).

GEORGES, Karl Ernst, *Ausführliches Lateinisch-deutsch Handwörterbuch*, 2 vol. (repr. 8th rev. and enlarged ed.; Basel: WBG, 1959).

KITTEL, Gerhard and FRIEDRICH, Gerhard (eds.), *Theologisches Wörterbuch zum Neuen Testament (ThWNT)*, 10 vol. (Stuttgart: Kohlhammer, 1933–1976).

KÜHNER, Raphael et al., *Ausführliche Grammatik der griechischen Sprache: II/1–2* (3rd ed.; Hannover/Leipzig: Hahn, 1898/1904).

LAMPE, Geoffrey W. H. (ed.), *A Patristic Greek Lexicon* (Oxford: Oxford University Press, 1961–1996).

LEUMANN, Manu et al., *Lateinische Grammatik. Band 1: Lateinische Laut- und Formenlehre* (Munich: Beck, 1963).

LIDDELL, Henry George and SCOTT, Robert (eds.), *A Greek-English Lexicon. A New Edition, Revised and Augmented Throughout by Sir Henry Stuart Jones with the Assistance of Roderick McKenzie and with the Co-Operation of Many Scholars* (9th ed.; Oxford: Oxford University Press, 1996).

LUST, Johan et al. (eds.), *Greek-English Lexicon of the Septuagint* (revised ed.; Stuttgart: Hendrickson Publishers, 2003).

MONTANARI, Franco, *The Brill Dictionary of Ancient Greek* (Leiden: Brill, 2015).

MOULTON, James Hope at al., *A Grammar of New Testament Greek* (Edinburgh: T. & T. Clark, 1906).

MURAOKA, Takamitsu, *A Greek-English Lexicon of the Septuagint* (Louvain: Peeters, 2009).

NEUE, Friedrich and WAGENER, Carl, *Formenlehre der lateinischen Sprache* (Leipzig: Reisland, 1897).

NIEMEYER, Manfred, *Deutsches Ortsnamenbuch* (Berlin: De Gruyter, 2012).

PINKSTER, Harm, *The Oxford Latin Syntax: The Simple Clause* (Oxford: University Press, 2015).

RUBENBAUER, Hans and HOFMANN, Johannes B., *Lateinische Grammatik. Neu bearbeitet von Richard Heine* (12th ed.; Bamberg: Buchners).

SMYTH, Herbert Weir, *A Greek Grammar for Schools and Colleges* (New York: American Book Company, 1916).

Concordances

ALAND, Kurt (ed.), *Vollständige Konkordanz zum griechischen Neuen Testament: unter Zugrundelegung aller modernen kritischen Textausgaben und des Textus Receptus*, 2 vol. (Berlin: De Gruyter, 1978–1983).

BACHMANN, Horst et al. (eds.), *Computer-Konkordanz zum Novum Testamentum Graece: von Nestle Aland, 26. Aufl. und zum Greek New Testament* (3rd ed.; Institut für neutestamentliche Textforschung and Rechenzentrum der Universität Münster ed.; Berlin: De Gruyter, 1986).

https://doi.org/10.1515/9783111142531-009

FISCHER, Bonifatius, *Novae Concordantiae Bibliorum Sacrocum iuxta vulgatam versionem criticae editam*, 5 vol. (Stuttgart: Frommann-Holzboog, 1977).
HATCH, Edwin and REDPATH, Henry Adeney, *A Concordance to the Septuagint and the Other Greek Versions of the Old Testament (including the Apocryphal books)*, 3 vol. (Grand Rapids: Baker Academic, 1987).
MORGENTHALER, Robert, *Statistik des neutestamentlichen Wortschatzes* (2nd ed.; Zürich/ Stuttgart: Gotthelf, 1973).
MOULTON, William Fidian et al., *Concordance to the Greek Testament* (5th ed.; Edinburgh: Bloomsbury, 1993).
SCHMOLLER, Alfred, *Concordantiae Novi Testamenti Graeci: Handkonkordanz zum Neuen Testament* (8th ed.; Stuttgart: Deutsche Bibelgesellschaft, 1989).

Lexica

A Latin-Greek Index of the Vulgate New Testament Based on Alfred Schmoller's Handkonkordanz zum Griechischen Neuen Testament with an Index of Latin Equivalences Characteristic of 'African' and 'European' Old Latin Versions of the New Testament (Atlanta: Scholars Press, 1991).
Antike Medizin: Ein Lexikon (Karl-Heinz Leven ed., Munich: C.H. Beck, 2005).
Biblisch-historisches Handwörterbuch: Landeskunde, Geschichte, Religion, Kultur, Literatur (BHH), 4 vol. (Bo Reicke and Leonard Rost eds.; Göttingen: Vandenhoeck & Ruprecht, 1962–1979).
Der Kleine Pauly: Lexikon der Antike (KP), 5 vol. (Konrad Ziegler et al. eds.; Stuttgart: Druckenmüller, 1964–1975; paperback edition: dtv, 1979).
Der Neue Pauly. Enzyklopädie der Antike (DNP), 15 vol. (Hubert Cancik et al. eds.; Stuttgart/Weimar: J. B. Metzler, 1996–2003).
Etymological Dictionary of Latin and the Other Italic Languages (Michiel de Vaan ed.; Leiden/Boston: Brill, 2008).
Lexikon der alten Welt (LAW) (Carl Andresen ed.; Zürich: Artemis, 1965).
Lexikon der antiken christlichen Literatur (LACL) (Siegmar Döpp and Wilhelm Geerlings with the collaboration of Peter Bruns, Georg Röwekamp et al. eds.; 3rd ed.; Freiburg: Herder, 2002).
Lexikon des Hellenismus (Hatto H. Schmitt and Ernesto Vogt eds.; Wiesbaden: Harrasowitz, 2005).
Lexikon für Theologie und Kirche (LThK), 10 vol. (Joseph Höfer and Karl Rahner eds.; 2nd ed.; Freiburg: Herder, 1957–1968).
Neues Bibel-Lexikon (NBL), 3 vol. (Manfred Görg and Bernhard Lang eds.; Zürich: Patmos 1991–2001).
Paulys Real-Encyclopädie der classischen Altertumswissenschaft (PRE) (new ed. Georg Wissowa; Stuttgart: Metzler, 1. Reihe 1894–1963; 2. Reihe 1914–1972; Supplement 1 1903–1980).
Reallexikon für Antike und Christentum: Sachwörterbuch zur Auseinandersetzung des Christentums mit der antiken Welt (RAC) (Franz Joseph Dölger et al. eds.; Stuttgart: Hiersemann, 1950–).
Die Religion in Geschichte und Gegenwart: Handwörterbuch für Theologie und Religionswissenschaft (RGG), 8 vol. (Hans Dieter Betz ed.; 4th ed.; Tübingen: Mohr Siebeck, 1998–2005).
Theologische Realenzyklopädie (TRE) (Gerhard Krause and Gerhard Müller eds.; Berlin: De Gruyter, 1976–).

Electronic Ressources and Online Databasis

Advanced Papyrological Information System APIS
http://www.comubia.edu/cu/projects/digital/apis/

Biblia Hebraica Stuttgartensia (BHS)
https://www.bibelwissenschaft.de/online-bibeln/biblia-hebraica-stuttgartensia-bhs/lesen-im-bibeltext/

Brill's New Jacoby
http://referenceworks.brillonline.com/browse/.

Brill's New Pauly
http://referenceworks.brillonline.com/browse/

Checklist of Greek, Latin, Demotic, and Coptic Papyri, Ostraca and Tablets
http://scriptorium.lib.duke.edu/papyrus/texts/clist.html

Diccionario Griego – Español
http://dge.cchs.csic.es/xdge/

Duke Databank of Documentary Papyri (DDbDP)
http://papyri.infor/ddbdp/

Georges: Ausführliches lateinisch-deutsches Wörterbuch
http://www.zeno.org/Georges-1913

Novum Testamentum Graece (Nestle Aland) 28th edition
https://www.bibelwissenschaft.de/online-bibeln/novum-testamentum-graece-na-28/lesen-im-bibeltext/

Septuaginta (ed. Rahlfs and Hanhart)
https://www.bibelwissenschaft.de/online-bibeln/septuaginta-lxx/lesen-im-bibeltext/

Thesaurus Linguae Graecae
http://stephanus.tlg.uci.edu/

Thesaurus Linguae Latinae
http://emedia.bibliothek.uni-halle.de

Vetus Latina Brepol
http://www.brepols.net/Pages/BrowseBySeries.aspx?TreeSeries=VLD-O

Codices

ar (61); *Codex Ardmachanus*:
https://digitalcollections.tcd.ie/content/26/pdf/26.pdf

c (6): *Codex Colbertinus*
Bibl. nat. de France, Dép. des manuscrits, Lat. 254

d (5): *Codex Bezae Cantabrigiensis*
Cambridge University Library, MS Nn.2.41

*ff*² (8): *Codex Corbeiensis secundus*
Bibliothèque nationale de France, Lat. 17225

*g*¹ (7): *Codex Sangermanensis I*
Bibl. nat. de France, Dép. des manuscrits, Lat. 11553

*g*² (29): *Codex Sangermanensis II*
Bibl. nat. de France, Départ. des manuscrits, Lat. 13169

gat (30): *Codex Gatianus*
Bibl. nat. de France, Dép. des Manuscrits, NAL 1587

n, o (16): *Fragmenta Sangallensia*
https://www.e-codices.unifr.ch/en/list/one/csg/1394

p (54): *Codex Perpinianensis*
Bibl. nat. de France, Dép. des manuscrits, Lat. 321

q (*13*): *Codex Monacensis*
Evangeliar (Codex Valerianus) – BSB Clm 6224

*r*¹ *(14): Codex Usserianus primus*
Dublin, Trinity College – IE TCD MS 55

Editions

ABBOTT, Thomas Kingsmill, *Evangeliorum versio antehieronymiana ex codice Usseriano (Dublinensi) adiecta collatione codicis Usseriani alterius* (Dublin: Hodges, Figgis et So.: 1884).

ADRIAEN, Marc and BALLERINI, Paolo Angelo (eds.), *Expositio Evangelii secundum Lucam. Fragmenti in Esaiam* (CCSL 14; Turnhout: Brepols, 1957).

ALEXANDER, Jonathan J .G. and FOX, Peter, *The Book of Kells: MS 58 Trinity College Library Dublin. Facsimile edition*, 2 vol. (Luzern: Faksimile Verlag, 1990).

ALLENBACH, Jean et al. (eds.), *Biblia Patristica. Index des Citations et Allusions Biblique dans la Littérature Patristique* (Paris: CNRS, 1975–2000).

ANDRE, Jacques (ed.), *Pline L'ancien, Histoire naturelle, Livre xxv. Texte etabli, traduit et commenté* (Paris: Les Belles Lettres, 1974).

AYUSO MARAZUELA, Teófilo (ed.), *La Vetus Latina Hispana. Bd. 1: Prolegómenos: Introduccion General, Estudio y Análysis de las Fuentas* (Madrid: Instituto Francisco Suárez 1953–).

BACKHOUSE, Janet, *The Lindisfarne Gospels* (2nd ed.; London: Phaidon, 1994).

BAYARD, Louis, *St. Cyprien. Correspondance, texte établi et traduit* (Paris: Belles lettres, 1925).

BAZANT-HEGEMARK, Leo, *Aurelii Augustini Liber ad Orosium contra Priscillianistas et Origenistas Sermo adversus Judaeos, Liber de haeresibus ad Quodvultdeum. Text und textkritischer Apparat* (Diss. phil., Wien, 1969).

BEERMANN, Gustav and GREGORY, Caspar Rene, *Die Koridethi Evangelien* (Leipzig: Teubner, 1913).

BELSHEIM, Johannes, "Apostlarnes Gjerninger og Aabenbaringen i gammel latinsk Oversættelse efter det store Haandskrift ‚Gigas librorum' i det kgl. Bibliothek i Stockholm," in *Theologisk Tidskrift for den Evangelisk-Lutherske Kirke i Norge* (1879): 305–476.

BELSHEIM, Johannes, *Codex Aureus sive quattuor evangelia ante Hieronymum latine translata* (Christiania: Libraria Mallingiana, 1878).

BELSHEIM, Johannes, *Codex Colbertinus Parisiensis: Qvatuor Evangelia ante Hieronymum latine translata post editionem Petri Sabatier cum ipso codice collatam* (Christiania: Albert Cammermeyer, 1888).

BELSHEIM, Johannes, *Codex f² Corbeiensis siue quattuor euangelia ante Hieronymum latine translata* (Christiana: Aschehoug, 1887).

BELSHEIM, Johannes, *Codex Veronensis: Quattuor Euangelia ante Hieronymum latine translata eruta & codice scripto ut videtur saeculo quarto vel quinto in Bibliotheca episcopali veronensi asservatoet ex Josephi Blanchini editione principe* (Prag: Dr. Ed. Grégr a syn, 1904).

BELSHEIM, Johannes, *Codex Vindobonensis membraneus purpureus: literis argenteis aureisque scriptus: antiquissimae evangeliorum Lucae et Marci translationis latinae* (Leipzig: T. O. Weigel, 1885).

BELSHEIM, Johannes, *Evangelium secundum Matthaeum ante Hieronymum latine translatum e codice olim Claromontano nunc Vaticano* (Christiana: A. W. Brøggers Bogtrykkeri, 1892).

BELSHEIM, Johannes, *Quatuor Evangelia ante Hieronymum Latine Translata ex Reliquiis Codicis Vercellensis Saeculo ut videtur Quarto scripti et ex Editione Iriciana Principe* (Christiania: Libraria Mallingiana, 1897).

BÉVENOT, Maurice, *Sancti Cypriani episcopi opera 1: De ecclesiae* (CChr.SL 3; Turnhout: Brepols, 1972).

BIANCHINI, Giuseppe Maria, *Evangeliarium Quadruplex Latinae Versionis Antiquae seu Veteris Italicae* (Rome: De Rubeis, 1749).

BIANCHINI, Giuseppe Maria, *Vindiciae Canonicarum Scriptuarum. Vulgatae Latinae editionis I.* (Rome: Hieronymus Mainardus, 1740).

BICK, Josef, *Wiener Palimpseste, I. Teil: Cod. Palat. Vindobonensis 16, olim Bobbiensis* (Vienna: Akademie der Wissenschaften, 1908).

BOGAERT, Pierre-Maurice, "Fragment inédit de Didyme l' Aveugle en traduction latine ancienne," *RBen* 73 (1963): 9–16.

BROWN, Michelle P., *Das Buch von Lindisfarne. The Lindisfarne Gospels. Facsimile edition*, 2 vol. (Luzern: Faksimile Verlag, 2002).

BROX, Norbert (ed. and transl.), *Irenäus von Lyon: Epideixis, Adversus Haereses / Darlegung der apostolischen Verkündigung, Gegen die Häresien*, 5 vol. (Fontes Christiani 8; Freiburg: Herder, 1993–2001).

BRUYNE, Donatien de, "Deux feuillets d'un texte préhieronymien des Évangiles," *RBen* 35 (1923): 62–80.

BUCHANAN, Edgar Simmons, *The Four Gospels from the Codex Corbeiensis (ff²)* (Old Latin Biblical Texts 5; Oxford: Clarendon Press, 1907).

BUCHANAN, Edgar Simmons, *The Four Gospels from the Codex Veronensis (b)* (Old Latin Biblical Texts 6; Oxford: Clarendon Press, 1911).

CASSIODORUS, Flavius Magnus Aurelius, *In Psalterium Exposito* (BNF lat. 14491; Basel: Johannes Amerbach, 1491).

Corpus Christianorum Continuatio Medievalis (Turnhout: Brepols, 1966–).

Corpus Christianorum. Series Latina (Turnhout: Brepols, 1959–).

Corpus Scriptorum Ecclesiasticorum Latinorum (Universität Salzburg; Berlin: De Gruyter, 1866–).

ERASMUS, Desiderius, *In Nouum Testamentum Annotationes* (Basel, 1516).

Erzabtei Beuron (ed.), *Vetus Latina. Die Reste der altlateinischen Bibel* (Freiburg: Herder, 1949–).

EVANS, Ernest (ed. and trans.), *Tertullian. Adversus Marcionem*, 2 vol. (Oxford: Clarendon, 1972).

DEKKERS, Elegius and GAAR Aemilius, *Clavis Patrum Latinorum. Editio Tertia aucta et emendate* (Steenbrugge: Brepols, 1995).
DIERCKS, Gerardus Frederik, *Sancti Cypriani episcopi opera 3/1: Sancti Cypriani episcopi Epistularium. Ad fidem codicum summa cura selectorum necnon adhibitis* (CChr.SL 3B; Turnhout: Brepols,1994).
DIERCKS, Gerardus Frederik, *Sancti Cypriani episcopi opera 3/2: Sancti Cypriani episcopi Epistularium. Ad fidem codicum summa cura selectorum necnon adhibitis* (CChr.SL 3C; Turnhout: Brepols,1996).
FALLER, Otto (ed.), *Ambrosius. Opera: De fide livri V ad Gratianum Augustum* (CSEL 7; Vienna: 1962).
FALLER, Otto (ed.), *Ambrosius. De spiritu sancto. De incarnationis dominicae sacramento* (CSEL 79; Vienna: Akademie der Wissenschaften, 1964).
FEIERTAG, Jean-Louis, *S. Hieronymi Presbyteri Opera: Opera III, Opera Polemica 2: Contra Iohannem* (CCSL 79a; Turnhout: Brepols, 1999).
FERRERO, Giovanni Stephano, *Sancti Eusebii Vercellensis episcopi et martyris, eiusque in episcopatu successores vitae et res gestae* (Vercelli: Hieronymum Allarium et Michaelem Martam socios, 1609).
FREDE, Hermann Josef, *Epistula ad Ephesios. VL 24/1* (Freiburg: Herder, 1962–1964).
FREDE, Hermann Josef, *Epistulae ad Philippenses, Colossenses VL 24/2* (Freiburg: Herder 1966–1971).
FREDE, Hermann Josef, *Epistulae ad Thessalonicenses, Timotheum VL 25/1* (Freiburg: Herder 1975–1982).
FREDE, Hermann Josef, *Epistulae ad Titum, Philemonem, Hebraeos VL 25/2* (Freiburg: Herder 1983–1991).
GAMESON, Richard, *The Codex Aureus: An Eighth-Century Gospel Book, Stockholm, Kungliga Bibliotheket A. 135. Facsimile edition* (Copenhagen: Rosenkilde and Bagger, 2002).
GAMPER, Rudolph, LENZ, P., NIEVERGELT, A., ERHART, P, SCHULZ-FLÜGEL, E., *Die Vetus Latina-Fragmente aus dem Kloster St. Gallen* (Dietikon-Zürich: Urs Graf, 2012).
GASQUET, Francis Aidan, *Codex Vercellensis iamdudum ab Irico et Bianchino bis Edutus Denuo cum Manuscripto* (Rome: Pustet, 1914).
GILES, John A., *The Complete Works of Venerable Bede: In the Original Latin, Collated with the Manuscripts..., Accomp. by a New English Translation of the Historical Works and a Life of the Author = Opera Quae Supersunt Omnia : Nunc Primum in Anglia, Ope Codicum Manuscriptorum* (London: Whittaker, 1843).
GWYNN, Edward, *Book of Armagh: The Patrician Documents* (Facsimiles in Collotype of Irish manuscripts 3; Dublin: Stationery Office, 1937).
GWYNN, John, *Liber Ardmachanus: The Book of Armagh* (Dublin: Hodges, Figgis & Co. Ltd., 1913).
HAELEWYCK, Jean-Claude, *Evangelium secundum Marcum VL 17* (Freiburg: Herder, 2013–).
HEER, Joseph Michael, *Evangelium Gatianum: Quattuor evangelia latine translata ex codice Monasterii S. Gatiani Turomensis* (Freiburg: Herder, 1910).
HESBERT, René-Jean, *Corpus Antiphonalium Officii III. Invitoria et Antiphonae; IV. Responsoria, versus, hymni et varia* (Rerum ecclesisticarum documenta; Rome: Herder 1968; 1970).
HOLL, Karl, *Die griechischen christlichen Schriftsteller der ersten drei Jahrhunderte*, 3 vol. (25, 31, 37.; Leipzig: J. C. Hinrichs, 1915–1933; 2nd ed. vol. 2: Jürgen Dummer (ed.) Berlin: Akademie Verlag, 1980; 2nd ed. vol. 3: Jürgen Dummer (ed.) Berlin: Akademie Verlag, 1985).
HURST, David, *Beda Venerabilis. Opera exegetica. In Lucae Evangelium expositio* (CCSL 120; Turnhout: Brepolis, 1969).
HURST, David, *Beda Venerabilis. Opera exegetica. Homeliarum Evangelii libri 2* (CCSL 122; Turnhout: Brepolis, 1955).
HURST, David, *Beda Venerabilis. Opera exegetica. In librum beati patris Tobiae* (CCSL 119B; Turnhout: Brepolis, 1983): 3–19.
HURST, David and Adriaen, M. *Hieronymus, Commentatorium in Matheum libri 4* (CCSL 77; Turnhout: Brepolis, 1969) (with misprints).
HÜBNER, Emil (ed.), *Exempla Scripturae Epigraphicae Latinae: A Caesaris Dictatoris morte ad aetatem Iustiniani* (Berolini: Reimer, 1885).

IRICO, Giovanni Andrea, *Sacrosanctus Evangeliorum Codex Sancti Eusebii Vercellensis* (Mailand: Regia Curia, 1748).

JÜLICHER, Adolf et al. (ed.), *Itala: Das Neue Testament in altlateinischer Überlieferung – Lukas- Evangelium* (Berlin: De Gruyter, 1972–1976).

KOETSCHAU, Paul, *Origenes Werke: Zweiter Band: Buch V–VII Gegen Celsus, Die Schrift vom Gebet.* (Die griechischen christlichen Schriftsteller der ersten drei Jahrhunderte 3; Leipzig: J. C. Hinrichs, 1899).

KRAFT, Benedikt, *Die Evangelientexte des Hl. Irenaeus* (Freiburg: Herder, 1924).

LA BONNADIÈRE, Anne-Marie (ed.), *Biblia Augustianiana* (Paris: IEA, 1960–1975).

LAMBOT, Cyrillus, *Sancti Aurelii Augustini Hipponensis Episcopi. Sermones selecti duodeviginti* (Turnholt: Brepols, 1961).

LOMMATZSCH, Carol Henric Eduard (ed.), *Origenes opera omnia*, 25 vol. (Berlin: Haude & Spener, 1831–1848).

MARCOVICH, Miroslav (ed.), *Hippolytus. Refutation Omnium Haeresium* (Patristische Texte und Studien 25; Berlin: De Gruyter, 1986).

MARKSCHIES, Christoph (ed.), *Ambrosius von Mailand. De Fide (Ad Gratianum) – Über den Glauben* (Fontes Christiani, Turnhout: Brepols, 2005).

MERCATI, Giovanni, *Ambrosiaster. De tribus mensuris* (Studi e Testi 11; Rom: Tipografia Vaticana 1903).

MIGNE, Jacques Paul, *Patrologia Series Graeca* (Paris: D'Amboise, 1837–1866).

MIGNE, Jacques Paul, *Patrologia Series Latina* (Paris: D'Amboise, 1844–1864).

MÖLLER, L. and M. VOGEL (eds.), *Plinius. Die Naturgeschichte des Caius Plinius Secundus. Ins Deutsche übersetzt und mit Anmerkungen versehen von G.C. Wittstein*, 2 vol. (Wiesbaden: Marix Verlag, 2007).

OEHLER, Francis (ed.), *Tertullian, Quinti Septimi Florentis Tertulliani Quae Supersunt Omnia*, 3 vol. (Leipzig: T. O. Weigel, 1851–1854).

Nestle-Aland Novum Testamentum Graece (based on the work of Eberhard and Erwin Nestle; eds. Barbara and Kurt Aland, Johannes Karavidopoulos, Carlo M. Martini, Bruce M. Metzger; ed. by the Institute for New Testament Textual Research Münster/Westphalia under the direction of Holger Strutwolf; 28th rev. ed., Stuttgart: Deutsche Bibelgesellschaft, 2012).

Plutarch. Plutarchi Moralia, Vol. III. Recenserunt et emendaverunt (W.R. Paton and M. Pohlenz; Bibliotheca scriptorum Graecorum et Romanorum Teubneriana; Leipzig: Teubner, 1929).

RANKE, Ernst Constantin, *Curiensia evangelii Lucani fragmenta* (Vienna: Braumüller, 1873).

RANKE, Ernst Constantin, *Fragmenta antiquissimae evangelii Lucani versionis Latinae e membranis Curiensibus* (Marburg: Koch, 1872).

RAUER, Max, *Origenes Werke: Neunter Band: Die Homilien zu Lukas in der Übersetzung des Hieronymus und die griechischen Reste der Homilien und des Lukas Kommentars* (Die griechischen christlichen Schriftsteller der ersten Jahrhunderte 49; 2nd ed.; Berlin: Akademie-Verlag, 1959).

RETTIG, Heinrich Christian Michael, *Antiquissimus quatuor evangeliorum canonicorum Codex Sangallensis, Graeco-Latinus interlinearis* (Zürich: Friedrich Schulthess, 1836).

RUGGIERO, Fabio (ed.), *Atti dei martiri scilitani. Introduzione, testo, traduzione, testimonianze e commento* (Roma: Academia Nazionale dei Lincei, 1991).

SABATIER, Pierre, *Bibliorum Sacrorum Latinae Versiones Antiquae seu Vetus Italica et caeterae quaecunque in codicibus manuscriptis et antiquorum libris reperiri poterunt quae cum vulgata Latina, et cum textu Graeco comparator III* (Reims: Reginaldum Florentain, 1743).

SCHENKL, Caroli, *Ambrosius – Expositio evangelii secundum Lucam* (CSEL 32/4; Wien, 1902).

SCRIVENER, Frederick Henry Ambrose, *Bezae Codex Cantabrigiensis* (Cambridge: Deighton, Bell and Co., 1864).

SOUTER, Alexander, *Pseudo-Augustini. Quaestiones Veteris et Novi Testamenti* (CSEL 50; Wien: Verlag der österreichischen Akademie der Wissenschaften, 1908): 13–416.

STÄHLIN, Otto, FRÜCHTEL, Ludwig and TREU, Ursula (eds.), *Clement of Alexandria. Clemens Alexandrinus: Zweiter Band: Stromata Buch I–VI.* (Die griechischen christlichen Schriftsteller der ersten Jahrhunderte; 4th ed.; Berlin: Akademie-Verlag, 1985).

STONE, Michael E. and ERVINE, Roberta R. (eds.), *Epiphanius. The Armenian Texts of Epiphanius of Salamis De mensuris et ponderibus* (Corpus scriptorum christianorum orientalium, 583; Leuven: Peeters, 2000).

THIELE, Walter, *Epistulae Catholicae* VL 26/1 (Freiburg: Herder, 1956–1969).

TISCHENDORF, Constantin, *Evangelium Palatinum ineditum* (Leipzig: Brockhaus, 1847).

TISCHENDORF, Constantin, *Novum Testamentum Latine, interprete Hieronymo ex celeberrimo codice Amiatino* (Leipzig: Avernarius & Mendelssohn, 1850).

TISCHENDORF, Constantin, *Codex Laudianus* (Leipzig: Hinrichs, 1870).

TURNER, C. H., *The Oldest Manuscript of the Vulgate Gospels* (Oxford: Clarendon, 1931).

*Vetus Latina. Die Reste der altlateinischen Bibel. Nach Petrus Sabati*er (new coll. and publ., Archabbey of Beuron; Freiburg: Herder,1949–).

VOGELS, Heinrich Joseph, "Codex VII der Cathedralbibliothek von Verona (b^2)," in: *Colligere Fragmenta: Festschrift Alban Dold zum 70. Geburtstag am 7.7. 1952* (Texte und Arbeiten, 2nd supplement, Beuron: Kunstverlag, 1952): 1–12.

VOGELS, Heinrich Joseph, *Codex Rehdigeranus: Die vier Evangelien nach der lateinischen Handschrift R 169 der Stadtbibliothek Breslau* (Collectanea Biblica Latina 2; Rom: Pustet, 1913).

VOGELS, Heinrich Joseph, *Evangelium Colbertinum*, 2 vol. (Bonner Biblische Beiträge 4–5; Bonn: Peter Hanstein, 1953).

WEBER, Ruth, *Sancit Cypriani episcopi Opera I. Ad Quirinum, Ad fortunatum, De lapsis* (CCSL 3; Turnhout: Brepols, 1972): 3–179.

WEIHRICH, Franz, *Sancti Aureli Augustini. De consensu evangelistarum quaestiones* librl quattuor, (CSEL 43; Wien: Verlag der österreichischen Akademie der Wissenschaften, 1904): 63–80.

WEISSENRIEDER, Annette and VISINONI, André Luiz, *Fragmenta Curiensia. Ein Beitrag zur Sprache und Übersetzung des frühlateinischen Lukasevangeliums* (FoSub 10; Berlin: De Gruyter 2021).

WHITE, Henry Julian, *The Four Gospels from the Munich Ms. q, now numbered Lat. 6224 in the Royal Library at Munich* (Old Latin Biblical Texts 3; Oxford: Clarendon Press, 1888).

WORDSWORTH, John et al., *Portions of the Gospel according to St. Mark and St. Matthew* (Old Latin Biblical Texts 2; Oxford: Clarendon Press, 1886).

ZYCHA, Joseph, *Augustus: De fide et symbolo. De fide et operibus. De agone Christiano. De contenta. De bobo coniugali* (CSEL 41; repr.; Wien: Verlag der österreichischen Akademie der Wissenschaften,1900): 3–32.

Secondary Literature

AALDERS, Gerhard Jean Daniel, "Tertullian's quotations from St. Luke," *Mnemosyne* 5,4 (1937): 241–282.

ABEL, Fritz, "Die Ausbildung des bestimmten Artikels und der deiktischen Systeme der romanischen Sprachen, untersucht an der Sprache der lateinischen Bibel," *Glotta* 48,3 (1970): 229–259.

ADAMS, James N., *Social Variation and the Latin Language* (Cambridge: University Press, 2013).

ADAMS, James N., *The Regional Diversification of Latin 200BC-AD 600* (Cambridge: University Press, 2007).

ADAMS, James N., "The Latinity of C. Novius Eunus," *Zeitschrift für Papyrologie und Epigraphik* 82 (1990): 227–247.

AGHABABIAN, ANOUSH HANA, *Translating the Gospel of Matthew, with a Case Study of Latin and Armenian Deixis* (GEORGIA: UNIVERSITY OF GEORGIA, 2019).

ALAND, Kurt, *Die alten Übersetzungen des Neuen Testaments, die Kirchenväterzitate und Lektionare* (Berlin, New York: De Gruyter, 1972).

ALAND, Kurt and ALAND, Barbara, *Der Text des Neuen Testaments: Einführung in die wissenschaftlichen Ausgaben sowie in Theorie und Praxis der modernen Textkritik* (Grand Rapids: Eerdmans, 1982).

ALAND, Kurt et. al., *Text und Textwert der griechischen Handschriften des Neuen Testaments 4.1.1., Das Markusevangelium,* 2 vols. (ANTF 27. Berlin: De Gruyter, 1998).

ALLEN, W. Sidney, *Vox Latina. A Guide to the Pronunciation of Classical Latin* (Cambridge: University Press, 1965).

ANDRE, Aurélie, "La concurrence entre is et ille dans l'évolution de la langue latine: étude comparative, de Cicerón à saint Augustin," *Latomus* 69,2 (2010): 313–329.

ANDRE, Jaques, "Remarques sur la traduction des mots grecs dans le textes médicaux du Ve. Siècle," *Revue de philologie, de literature et d'histoire anciennes* 37 (1963): 47–67.

ANDRIST, Patrick, "Les testimonia de l'ad Quirinum de Cyprien et leur influence sur la polémique antijudaique posérieure," in: *Cristinesime nell'Antichità* (A. D'Anna and C. Zamagni; Hildesheim: Ohms, 2007): 175–198.

ARDUINI, Franca, and CAVALLO, Guglielmo, *The Shape of the Book, from Roll to Codex (3rd Century BC – 19th Century AD)* (Firenze: Mandragora, 2008).

ARTHUR, Paul, "From Vicus to Village: Italian Landscapes AD 400–1000," in: *Landscapes of Change* (Christie, Neil ed.; Milton Park: Routledge, 2004).

AUNE, David Edward, "Anthropological duality in the eschatology of 2 Corinthians 4:16–5:10," in: *Paul Beyond the Judaism/Hellenism Divide* (Troels Engberg-Pedersen ed.; Louisville: Westminster John Knox Press, 2001).

AUWERS, Jean-Marie, "Le texte latin des Évangiles dans le Codex de Bèze," in: *Codex Bezae: Studies from the Lunel Colloquium* (David Charles Parker and Christian-Bernard Amphoux eds., Leiden: Brill, 1996): 183–216.

BAKKER, Adophine H. A., *A Study of Codex Evang. Bobbiensis (k)* (Amsterdam: Noord-Hollandsche Vitgeversmaatschappij, 1933).

BALDI, Philip, "A Structural Ambiguity in Latin," *Classical Philology* 74,1 (1979): 49–52.

BALDI, Philip, "Latin *invicem*", *Zeitschrift für vergleichende Sprachforschung* 92,2 (1997): 300–303.

BALDI, Philip and CUZZOLIN, P., *New Perspectives on. Historical Latin Syntax* 4 vols. (Berlin: De Gruyter, 2009–2011).

BANNING, J. van, *Opus imperfectum in Matthaeum* (CCSL 87B; Turnhout: Brepols, 1988).

BARDENHEWER, Otto, *Ist Elisabeth eine Sängerin des Magnificat?* (Biblische StudienV.1; Kessinger, 1896).

BASTIAENSEN, Toon, "Exorcism: Tackling the Devil by Word and Mouth," in: *Demons and the Devil in Ancient and Early Christianity* (Nienke Vos and Willemien Otten eds., Leiden: Brill, 2011): 129–143.

BATIFFOL, Pierre, "Fragmenta Sangallensia," *RA* 4 (1885): 305–321.

BATIFFOL, Pierre, *Note sur un évangéliaire de Saint-Gall: Contribution à l'histoire de l'Itala* (Paris: Champion, 1884).

BAUER, Thomas Johann, "Vetus Latina – Lukasevangelium – Literatur" (unpublished paper).

BAUER, Thomas Johann, "Das Evangelium des Markion und die Vetus Latina," *ZAC* 21 (2017): 73–89.

BENGEL, Johann Albrecht, *Gnomon of the New Testament* (Philadelphia: Smith, English & Company, 1860).

BENKO, Stephen, "The Magnificat. History of the Controversy," *JBL* 86 (1967): 263–275.

BERGER, Samuel, *Histoire de la Vulgate Pendant les Premiers Siècles du Moyen Age* (New York: Burt Franklin, 1893).

BERNDT, Rainer et al., "Scientia" und "disciplina". Wissenstheorie und Wissenschaftspraxis im Wandel vom 12. zum 13. Jahrhundert (Berlin: De Gruyter, 2002).

BERTOCCHI, Alessandra et al., "Quantification," in: *Constituent Syntax: Quantification, Numerals, Possession, Anaphora* (Philip Baldi and Pierluigi Cuzzolin eds.; Berlin: De Gruyter, 2010): 19–174.

BILLEN, Albert Victor, *The Old Latin Texts of the Heptateuch* (Cambridge University Press: Cambridge, 1927).

BISCHOFF, Bernhard, *Paläographie des römischen Altertums und des abendländischen Mittelalters* Grundlagen der Germanistik, Bd. 24. (2nd rev. ed.; Berlin: Erich-Schmidt-Verlag, 1986).

BISCHOFF, Bernhard, "Zur Rekonstruktion des Sangallensis (Σ) und der Vorlage seiner Marginalien," *Biblica* 22 (1941): 147–158.

BISCHOFF, Bernhard, *Mittelalterliche Studien Bde. I-III* (Stuttgart: Hiersemann, 1966, 1967, 1984).

BISCHOFF, F. M., and MANIACI, M., "Pergament – Handschriftenformate – L Lagenkonstruktion," *Scrittura e Civiltà* 19 (1995): 277–319.

BLEICKEN, Jochen, "Kollisionen zwischen Sacrum und Publicum," *Hermes* 85 (Wiesbaden: F. Steiner, 1957).

BLUM, Matthias, "... denn sie wissen nicht, was sie tun.": zur Rezeption der Fürbitte Jesu am Kreuz (LK 23,34a) in der antiken jüdisch-christlichen Kontroverse (NF 46; Münster, Aschendorff 2004).

BLUMENTHAL, Peter and FESENMEIER, Ludwig, "Zur Erfolgsgeschichte von lat. *Sapere*," *RomGG* 13,1 (2007): 3–19.

BOGAERT, Pierre-Maurice, "Latin Versions," *The Anchor Bible Dictionary*, vol. 6 (1992): 33–47.

BOGAERT, Pierre-Maurice, "La Bible d'Augustin. Ètat des questions et application aux sermons Dolbeau," in: *Augustin Prédicateur (395–411)* (Goulöven Madec; Paris: IEA, 1998): 33–47.

BOUTON-TABOULOULIC, Anne-Isabelle, "Autorité et Tradition, La traduction latine de la Bible selon Saint Jérôme et Saint Augustine," *Augustinianum* 45 (2005): 185–229.

BOUSSET, Wilhelm, *Die Evangeliencitate Justins des Märtyrers in ihrem Wert für die Evangelienkritik* (Göttingen, 1891).

BOVON, François, *Das Evangelium nach Lukas, EKK III/2: Lk 9,51–14,35* (Neukirchen-Vluyn: Neukirchener Verlagsgesellschaft, 2020).

BOYCE, Bret, The Language of the Freedmen in Petronius' "Cena Trimalchionis" (Mnemosyne; Leiden: Brill, 1991).

BÖHM, Martina, *Samarien und die Samaritai bei Lukas. Eine Studie zum religionshistorischen und traditionsgeschichtlichen Hintergrund der lukanischen Samarientexte und zu deren topographischen Verhaftung* (WUNT 2, 111; Tübingen: Mohr Siebeck, 1999).

BREYTENBACH, Cilliers, "Galilee and Jerusalem: Text World and Historical World," in: *The Gospel According to Mark as Episodic Narrative* (Leiden: Brill, 2021): 106–118.

BRUYNE, Donatien de, "L'Itala de saint Augustin," *Rben* 30 (1913): 294–314.

BRUYNE, Donatien de, "Notes sur le manuscrit 6224 de Munich (Ms q des Évangiles)," *Rben* 28 (1911): 75–80.

BRUYNE, Donatien de, *Prefaces to the Latin Bible. With Introduction by Pierre-Maurice Bogart and Thomas O'Loughlin* (Turnhout: Brepols, 2015) = *Prefaces de la Bible latine* (Namur: Godenne, 1920; anonyme Publikation).

BRUYNE, Donatien de, *Summaries, Divisions and Rubrics of the Latin Bible. With Introduction by Pierre-Maurice Bogart and Thomas O'Loughlin* (Turnhout: Brepols, 2014) = *Sommaraires, divisions et rubriques de la Bible latine* (Namur: Godenne, 1914; anonyme Publikation).

BUCHANAN, Edward Simons, "The Codex Veronensis," *JThS* 37 (1908): 120–126.

BUHLMANN, Michael, "Die Klöster St. Gallen und Reichenau, das Königtum, die Baar und Trossingen im frühen Mittelalter," *VA* 74 (2014): 1–51.

BURKITT, Francis Crawford, "Itala Problems," in: *Scritti Varii di Letteratura* (FS Ambrogio Amelli O.S.B., Montecassino, 1920): 25–41.

BURKITT, Francis Crawford, "Saint Augustine's Bible and the ‚Itala'," *JThS* 42 (1910): 258–268, *Augustianianum* 45:1 (2006): 185–229.

BURKITT, Francis Crawford, *The Old Latin and the Itala, with an Appendix Containing the Text of the S. Gallen Palimpsest of Jeremiah* (Cambridge: University Press, 1896).

BURTON, Philip, "The Latin Version of the New Testament," in: *The Text of the New Testament in Contemporary Research: Essays on the Status Quaestionis* (Bart Denton Ehrman and Michael William Holmes eds.; Leiden: Brill, 2012): 167–200.

BURTON, Philip, *The Old Latin Gospels: A Study of their Texts and Language* (Oxford: University Press, 2002).

BUSER, Peter, *Die Bezeichnung für „Beten" und „Bitten" im christlichen Latein und im Altfranzösischen* (Ph.D., Bern, 1971).

BÜTTNER, Heinrich, "Die Bistümer während des frühen Mittelalters," in: *Frühes Christentum im schweizerischen Alpenraum* (Heinrich Büttner and Iso Müller eds.; Zürich: Benziger Verlag, 1967): 11–38.

BUSSE, Ulrich, *Die Wunder des Propheten Jesus: Die Rezeption, Komposition und Interpretation der Wundertradition im Evangelium des Lukas* (Stuttgart: Katholisches Bibelwerk, 1977).

CAPER, Flavius, De orthographia (H. Keil ed.; Grammatici Latini; vol. 7; Leipzig: Teubner, 1878), 105.17–18: y litteram nulla vox nostra adsciscit. ideo insultabis gylam dicentibus.

CASSIODORUS, Flavius Magnus Aurelius, In Psalterium Exposito, (BNF lat. 14491) (Basel: Johannes Amerbach, 1491).

CIMOSA, Mario, *Guida allo studio della Bibbia latina: Dalla Vetus Latina, alla Vulgata, alla Nova Vulgata* (Rom: Istituto patristico Augustinianum, 2008).

CHERUBINI, Paolo and PRATESI, Alessandro, *Paleografia latina: L'avventura grafica del mondo occidentale* (Vatikanstadt: Scuola Vaticana di Paleografia, 2010).

CLACKSON, James and HORROCKS, Geoffrey, The Blackwell History of the Latin language (Oxford: Blackwell Pub, 2007).

COLEMAN, Robert G. G, "Dialectal variation in republican Latin, with special reference to Praenestine," *Proceedings of the Cambridge Philological Society* 36,216 (1990): 1–25.

COLEMAN, Robert G. G., "The Formation of Specialized Vocabularies in Philosophy, Grammar, and Rhetoric: Winners and Losers," in: *Actes du Ve Colloque international sur le latin vulgaire et tardif* (Marius Lavency and Domenique Longrée eds., Louvain-la-Neuve: Peeteres, 1989): 77–89.

COLEMAN, Robert G. G., "Vulgar Latin and the Diversity of Christian Latin," in: *Actes du Ier Colloque international sur le latin vulgar et tardif* (József Herman ed.; Tübingen: Niemeyer, 1987): 37–52.

CORSSEN, Peter, WORDSWORTH, J. et al., "Portions of the Gospel according to St. Mark and St. Matthew," *GGA* 8 (1889): 299–319.

CROWN, Alan D., *Samaritan Scribes and Manuscripts* (Texts and Studies in Ancient Judamism 80; Tübingen: Mohr Siebeck, 2001).

CULLMANN, Oscar, *Das Gebet im Neuen Testament* (Tübingen: Mohr Siebeck, 1997).

DAVIES, Helen and ZAWACKI, Alexander, "Making Light Work: Manuscripts and Multispectral Imaging," *Journal of the Early Book Society for the Study of Manuscripts and Printing History* 22 (2019): 177–199.

DEIßMANN, Adolf, *Licht vom Osten: Das Neue Testament und die neuentdeckten Texte der hellenistisch-römischen Welt* (Tübingen: Mohr Siebeck, 1908).

DICKEY, Eleanor, *Latin Forms of Address: From Plautus to Apuleius* (Oxford: University Press, 2002).

DICKEY, Eleanor, "Art. Sanctus," *DNP* 10 (2011).

DIJKSTRA, Roald, "Epic Architecture: Architectural Terminology and the Cities of Bethlehem and Jerusalem in the Epics of Juvencus and Proba," in: *Monuments & Memory. Christian Cult Buildings and Constructions of the Past: Essays in Honour of Sible de Blaauw* (Verhoeven, M., Bosman, L. and van Asperen H. eds., Turnhout: Brepol, 2016).

DOMBART, B. and KALRB, A., *Augustinus. De civitate die libri 22* (CC 47–48 1955 = dies. Stuttgart: Teubner, 1981).

DOYLE, Peter, "The Text of Luke's Gospel in the Book of Mulling," *PRIA 73* (1972): 177–200.

DÖDERLEIN, Ludwig, *Lateinische Synonyme und Etymologien*, 7 vol. (Scientia, 1826).

DUPONT, Jacques, "Le couple parabolique du sénevé et du levain," in: *Études sur les évangiles synoptiques II* (Louvain: Presses universitaires, 1985): 609–623.

DURAND, Alain, "L'origine du Magnificat," *Revue Biblique* 7.1 (1898): 74–77.

DURST, Michael, *Geschichte der Kirche im Bistum Chur, Heft 1: Von den Anfängen bis zum Vertrag von Verdun (843)* (Straßburg: Editions du Signe, 2001).

EDWARDS, Sarah A., "P75 under the Magnifying Glass," *Novum Testamentum* 18,3 (1976): 190–212.

EGGER, Rita, *Josephus Flavius und die Samaritaner. Eine terminologische Untersuchung zur Identitätsklärung der Samaritaner* (Göttingen: Vandenhoeck & Ruprecht, 1986).

ELLIOTT, J. Keith, "Translations of the New Testament into Latin: The Old Latin and the Vulgate," in: *Aufstieg und Niedergang der Römischen Welt*, vol. II.26.1 (Wolfgang Haase and H. Temporini eds.; Berlin: De Gruyter,1992): 198–245.

EMMRICH, Martin, „Lucan Account of the Beelzebul Controversy," *Westminst. Theol. J.* 62 (2000): 267–279.

EVANS, Trevor Vivian, *Verbal Syntax in the Greek Pentateuch: Natural Greek Usage and Hebrew Interference* (Oxford: University Press, 2011).

EVERS, A. W., *Church, Cities, and People: A Study of the Plebs in the Church and Cities of Roman Africa in Late Antiquity* (Interdisciplinary Studies in Ancient Culture and Religion; Leuven: Peeters, 2010).

EVERSON, David, "An Examination of Synoptic Portions within the Vulgate," *VT* 58 (2008): 178–190.

FAHEY, Michael Andrew, *Cyprian and the Bible: A Study in the Third-Century Exegesis* (Tübingen: J.C.B. Mohr, 1971).

FEENEY, Denis, *Literature and Religion at Rome: Cultures, Contexts, and Beliefs* (Cambridge: University Press, 1998).

FELDMAN, Louis H., *Josephus's Interpretation of the Bible* (Hellenistic Culture and Society 2700; Berkeley: University of California Press, 1998).

FISCHER, Bonifatius, "Bibelausgaben des frühen Mittelalters," in: *Settimane di Studio del centro italiano di studi sull'alto Medioevo X: La Bibbia nell'alto medioevo* (Spoleto: CISAM, 1963): 519–600 = Fischer, *Lateinische Bibelhandschriften im frühen Mittelalter*: 35–100.

FISCHER, Bonifatius, *Lateinische Bibelhandschriften im frühen Mittelalter, Vetus Latina. Die Reste der altlateinischen Bibel* (Aus der Geschichte der lateinischen Bibel 11; Freiburg: Herder, 1985).

FISCHER, Bonifatius, "Das Neue Testament in lateinischer Sprache. Der gegenwärtige Stand seiner Erforschung und seine Bedeutung für die griechische Textgeschichte," in: *Die alten Übersetzungen des Neuen Testaments, die Kirchenväterzitate und Lektionare* (Kurt Aland ed.; Berlin: De Gruyter, 1972): 2–92.

FISCHER, Thomas, *Die römischen Provinzen: Eine Einführung in die Archäologie* (Stuttgart: Theiss, 2001).

FITZMYER, Joseph A., *The Gospel According to Luke*, 2 vol. (Anchor Bible 28, 28A.; Garden City: Doubleday, 1981–1985).

FREDE, Hermann Josef, "Die Zitate des Neuen Testaments bei den lateinischen Kirchenvätern," in: *Die alten Übersetzungen des Neuen Testaments, die Kirchenväterzitate und Lektionare* (Kurt Aland ed.; Berlin: De Gruyter, 1972): 455–478.

FREY-ANTHES, Henrike, "Art. Satan (AT)," in www.bibelwissenschaft.de/stichwort/26113.

FLEMMING, Rebecca, *Medicine and the Making of Roman Women: Gender, Nature, and Authority from Celsus to Galen* (Oxford: University Press, 2000).

FLEDDERMANN, Harry Taylor, *Mark and Q: A Study of the Overlap Texts* (Leuven: University Press, 1995).

GAENG, Paul Ami, "Is it Really the Accusative? A Century-Old Controversy Revisited," *ICS* 8,1 (1983): 155–164.

GALDI, Giovanbattista, "On coepi/incipio + infinitive: some new remarks," in: *Early and Late Latin. Continuity or Change* (James Adams and Nigel Vincent eds.; Cambridge: University Press, 2016), 246–265.

GAMBER, Klaus, „Die älteste abendländische Evangelien-Perikopenliste," *Münchener Theologische Zeitschrift* 13 (1962): 181–201.

GAMBER, Klaus, "Documenta Liturgiae Italiae," in: *Codices Liturgici Latini Antiquiores. Secunda edition aucta* (Fribourg: Universitätsverlag Fribourg, 1968).

GAMPER, Rudolf et al., Die Vetus Latina-Fragmente aus dem Kloster St. Gallen. Faksimile – Edition – Kommentar (Dietikon-Zürich: Urs Graf Verlag, 2012).

GARLANDA, A. Cerutti et al., "The Vercelli Gospels laid open: an investigation into the inks used to write the oldest Gospels in Latin," X-Ray Spectrometry (2008) 37: 286–292.

GARLANDA, A. Cerutti, "Evangeliario Eusebiano," in: *Verbum caro factum est... La Bibbia oggi e la sua trasmissione nei secoli, catalogo della mostra, a cura di S. Uggè e G. Ferraris,* (Vercelli, 2005).

GARLANDA, A. Cerutti, "Il restauro del Codex Vercellensis Evangeliorum nel primo Novecento," *Bolletino Storico Vercellense* 62,1 (2004): 131–151.

GATHERCOLE, Simon James, "The Titles of the Gospels in the Earliest New Testament Manuscripts," *ZNW* 104,1 (2013): 33–76.

GIGON, Olof Alfred, *Kommentar zum ersten Buch von Xenophons Memorabilien* (Basel: Reinhardt, 1953).

GIOANNI, Stéphane, "Apprendre à prier chez les Pères latins. La "personne" et la "communauté" des orants dans le christianisme ancien," in: *La prière en latin de l'Antiquité au XVIe siècle* (Turnhout: Brepols, 2006): 121–141.

GOLDBERGER, Walter, "Kraftausdrücke im Vulgärlatein," *Glotta* 18 (1929): 8–65.

GÓMEZ, L. U., La Petición Verbal en Latín. Estudio Léxico, semántico y pragmático (Madrid: Ediciones, 2009).

GORDON, R. "Art. Pontifex, Pontifices," *NP* 2006, online access July 2021.

GRANDGENT, Charles H., *An Introduction to Vulgar Latin* (Boston: Heath, 1907).

GRÄTZ, Sebastian, "Art. Himmelsrichtungen," in www.bibelwissenschaft.de/stichwort/21242.

GREEN, Joel B., "Jesus and the Daughter of Abraham (Luke 13:10–17) ," *CBQ* 51 (1989): 643–654.

GREEN, Joel B., *The Theology of the Gospel of Luke* (Cambridge: University Press, 1995).

GREVANDER, Sigfrid, *Untersuchungen zur Sprache der Mulomedicina Chironis* (Leipzig: Harrassowitz, 1926).

GRIBOMONT, J., "Les plus anciennes traductions latines," in: *Le monde latin antique et la Bible* (J. Fontaine and C. Pietri eds.; Bible de tous les temps 2; Paris, 1985): 43–65.

GRUNDMANN, Walter, *Das Evangelium nach Lukas* (Berlin: Evangelische Verlags-Anstalt, 1961).

GRYSON, Roger, *Altlateinische Handschriften/Manuscrits Vieux Latins. Première partie: Mss 1–275*. VL 1/2A. (Freiburg: Herder, 1999).

GRYSON, Roger, *Altlateinische Handschriften/Manuscrits Vieux Latins. Deuxième partie: Mss 300–485*. VL 1/2A. (Freiburg: Herder, 2004).

GRYSON, R. et al., *Répertoire général des auteurs ecclésiastiques latins de l'antiquité et du haut Moyen Âge* (Freiburg: Herder, 2007).

HAMERTON-KELLY, Robert Gerald, "A Note on Matthew XII.28par. Luke XI.20," *NTS* 11,2 (1965): 167–169.

HAMM, Michael Dennis, "The Freeing of the Bent Woman and the Restoration of Israel: Luke 13:10–17 as Narrative Theology," *NTS* 31 (1987): 23–44.

HARRIS, J. Rendel, *Codex Bezae: A Study of the So-Called Western Text of the New Testament* (Cambridge: University Press, 1861).

HARRIS, J. Rendel, *The Codex Sangallensis: A Study in the Text of the Old Latin Gospels* (reprint; Eugene: Wipf and Stock, 2015 = Clay & Sons, 1891).

HASELBERGER, Lothar, "Der Eustylos des Hermogenes," in: *Hermogenes und die hochhellenistische Architektur* (Wolfram Hoepfner et al. eds., Mainz: von Zabern, 1990): 81–83.

HAWKES, Jane and BOULTON, Meg (EDS.), *All Roads Lead to Rome. The Creation, Context and Transmission of the Codex Amiatinus* (Studia Traditionis Theologiae 31; Turnhout: Brepols, 2019).

HEINE, Gotthilf, *Bibliotheca Anecdotorum Seu Veterum Monumentorum Ecclesiasticorum: Collectio Novissima* (Leipzig: Lipsiae, 1848).

HERMAN, Jószef, *Vulgar Latin* (transl. Roger Wright; University Park: Pennsylvania State University Press, 2000).

HIGGINS, A. J. B., "The Latin Text of Luke in Marcion and Tertullian," *Vigiliae Christianae* 5,1 (1951): 1–42.

HJELM, Ingrid, *The Samaritans and Early Judaism: A Literary Analysis* (Bloomsbury, 2000).

HOFMANN, Johann Baptist and Szantyr, Anton, "Lateinische Syntax Und Stilistik," in: *Lateinische Grammatik* 2 (Munich: Beck, 1965).

HOFMANN, Johann B., Lateinische Umgangssprache (4th ed.; Heidelberg: Winter, 1978).

HOGETERP, Albert and Denaux, Adelbert, *Semitisms in Luke's Greek: A Descriptive Analysis of Lexical and Syntactical Domains of Semitic Language Influence in Luke's Gospel* (Tübingen: Mohr Siebeck, 2018).

HORTON, Charles, *The earliest Gospels: The Origins and Transmission of the Earliest Christian Gospels – The Contribution of the Chester Beatty Gospel P45* (London/New York: T&T Clark, 2004).

HOUGHTON, Hugh A. G., "Scripture and Latin Christian Manuscripts from North Africa," in: *The Bible in Christian North Africa. Part 1: Commencement to the "Confessiones" of Augustine (ca. 180 to 400 CE)* (Yates, Jonathan and Dupont, Anthony eds., Berlin: De Gruyter, 2020): 15–50.

HOUGHTON, Hugh A. G., "The Electronic Scriptorium: Markup for New Testament Manuscripts," in: *Digital Humanities in Biblical, early Jewish and Early Christian Studies* (Claire Clivaz, Andrew Gregory, and David Hamidovic eds., Leiden: Brill, 2014), 31–60.

HOUGHTON, Hugh A. G., *The Latin New Testament: A Guide to Its Early History, Texts, and Manuscripts* (Oxford: University Press, 2016).

HOUGHTON, Hugh A.G., "The Text of the Gospels in the Codex Amiatinus," in: *All Roads Lead to Rome. The Creation, Context and Transmission of the Codex Amiatinus* (Jane Hawkes et al. eds., Studia Traditionis Theologiae 31; Turnhout: Brepols, 2019), 77–88.

HOUGHTON, Hugh A. G., "The Use of the Latin Fathers for New Testament Textual Criticism," in: *The Text of the New Testament in Contemporary Research. Essays on the Status Quaestionis* (New Testament Tools, Studies, and Documents 42, 2nd ed., Ehrman, Bart D. and Holmes, Michael W. eds.; Leiden: Brill, 2012): 375–406.

HOUGHTON, Hugh A. G. and PARKER, D.C. (eds.), *Textual Variation: Theological and Social Tendencies* (Piscataway: Gorgias, 2008).

HOWARD, George, *The Gospel of Matthew According to a Primitive Hebrew Text* (Macon: Marcer, 1987).

HÜBNER, Ernst, *Exempla Scripturae Epigrapicae Latinae* (Berlin: 1885).

JEREMIAS, Joachim, *Die Gleichnisse Jesu* (Göttingen: Vandenhoeck & Ruprecht, 1998).

JEREMIAS, Joachim, *Die Sprache des Lukasevangeliums Sprache* (Göttingen: Vandenhoeck & Ruprecht, 1980).

JEREMIAS, Joachim, "Ἐν ἐκείνῃ τῇ ὥρᾳ, (ἐν) αὐτῇ τῇ ὥρᾳ," *ZNTW* 42,1 (1949): 214–217.

JEREMIAS, Joachim, "ΙΕΡΟΥΣΑΛΗΜ/ΙΕΡΟΣΟΛΥΜΑ," *ZNW* 56 (1974): 273–276.

JOST, Georg, "Die rätische Schreibstube vor 1200 Jahren," in: *Bündner Jahrbuch* (Chur: Bischofberger, 1974): 29–34.

JUCKEL, Andreas, "Die Bedeutung des Ms Vat. Syr. 268 für die Evangelien-Überlieferung der Harklensis," *OrChr* 83 (1999): 22–45.

JUDD, Frank F., "A Case for the Authenticity of Luke 23:17," *Bulletin for biblical research* 27,4 (2017): 527–537.

JÜLICHER, Adolf, *Die Gleichnisreden Jesu II* (Freiburg: Mohr Siebeck, 1888).

HARSH, Philip, "‚Angiportum', ‚Platea' and ‚Vicus'," *Classical Philology* 32 (1937): 44–58.

HENGEL, Martin, "Der Finger und die Herrschaft Gottes," in: *La main de Dieu, Die Hand Gottes* (René Kiefer und Jan Bergmann eds, Tübingen: Mohr Siebeck, 1997): 87–106.

KAHL, Brigitte W., "Armenevangelium und Heidenevangelium: ‚Sola scriptura' und die ökumenische Traditionsproblematik," *ThLZ* 110,10 (1985): 779–781.

KANNENGIESSER, Charles, *Handbook of Patristic Exegesis*, 2 vol. (Leiden: Brill, 2004).

KÄSEMANN, Ernst, "Lukas 11,14–28," in: *Exegetische Versuche und Besinnungen I* (Göttingen: Vandenhoeck & Ruprecht, 1964): 242–248.

KEEL, Othmar, "JHWH – der Gott aus dem Süden und sein Volk: Die Wurzeln der Religion Israels," *WUB* 49 (2008): 50–53.

KEDAR, B., "The Latin Translations," in: *Mikra: Text, Translation, Reading and Interpretation of the Hebrew Bible in Ancient Judaism and Early Christianity* (Compendia Rerum Iudaicarum ad Novum Testamentum 2,1, Mulder, Martin Jan ed.; Assen u. Maastricht, 1988): 299–338.

KHAN, Geoffrey, "The Tiberian Pronunciation Tradition of Biblical Hebrew," *Zeitschrift Für Althebraistik* 9,1 (1996): 1–23.

KILGALLEN, John J., "The Obligation to Heal. Luke 13:10–17," *Bib* 82 (2001): 402–409.

KLAUCK, Hans-Joseph, *Allegorie und Allegorese in synoptischen Gleichnistexten* (Münster: Aschendorff, 1978).

KLEIN, Hans, *Das Lukasevangelium* (Göttingen: Vandenhoeck & Ruprecht, 2006).

KLOPPENBORG, John Seargeant, "Q 11:14–26: Work Sheets for Reconstruction," *SBLASP* 24 (1985): 133–151.

KLOSTERMANN, Erich, *Das Lukasevangelium* (Tübingen: Mohr Siebeck, 1929).

KOCH, Robert, *Geist und Messias: Beitrag zur biblischen Theologie des Alten Testaments* (Freiburg: Herder, 1950).

KOESTER, Helmut, *Ancient Christian Gospels: Their History and Development* (Philadelphia: Trinity, 1990).

KLINGHARDT, Matthias, *Das älteste Evangelium und die Entstehung der kanonischen* Evangelien, 2 vol. (Tübingen: Francke, 2015).

KOLLMANN, Bernd, *Jesus und die Christen als Wundertäter: Studien zu Magie, Medizin und Schamanismus in Antike und Christentum* (Göttingen: Vandenhoeck & Ruprecht, 1996).

KREMER, Jacob, *Lukasevangelium* (Würzburg: Echter, 1988).

KROON, "A Framework for the Description of Latin Discourse markers," *Journal of Pragmatics* 30 (1998): 205–223.

KROON, Caroline, "Discourse markers, discourse structure and Functional Grammar," in: *Discourse and Pragmatics in Functional Grammar* (John H. Connolly et al. eds.; Berlin: De Gruyter, 1997): 17–32.

LABAHN, Michael, "Die Königin aus dem Süden und ihr Auftritt im Gericht: Q 11,31 oder zur (Wirkungs-)Geschichte einer Begegnungserzählung," in: *Rewriting and Reception in and of the Bible* (Jesper Høgenhaven et al. eds.; Tübingen: Mohr Siebeck 2018): 85–107.

LAES, Christian, *Disabilities and the Disabled in the Roman World. A Social and Cultural History* (Cambridge: Cambridge University Press, 2018).

LAKE, K. and BLAKE, R.P., "The Text of the Gospels and the Koridethi Codex," *The Harvard Theological Review* 16 (1923): 267–280.

LAGRANGE, Marie-Joseph, *Évangile Selon Saint Luc* (Paris: Victor Lecoffre, 1921).

LANGSLAW, D. R., *Medical Latin in the Roman Empire* (Oxford classical monographs; Oxford: Oxford University press, 2000).

LANGSLOW, David, "The Development of Latin Medical Terminology: Some Working Hypotheses," *PCPhS* 37 (1992): 106–130.

LANZONI, Francesco, *Le diocesi d'Italia dalle origini al principio del secolo VII (an. 604)* (Faenza: F. Lega, 1927).

LAPIDE, Pinchas, "Insights from Qumran into the Languages of Jesus," *Revue de Qumrân* 8 (1975): 483–501.

LAPIDGE, Michael, "Textual criticism and the literature of Anglo-Saxon England," *Bull. John Rylands Libr.* 73,1 (1991): 17–46.

LAUFEN, Rudolf, *Doppelüberlieferungen der Logienquelle und des Markusevangeliums* (Ph.D. Bonn, 1978).

LEUMANN et al., Lateinische Grammatik. Band 1: Lateinische Laut- und Formenlehre (Munich: Beck, 1963).

LORENZ, Peter E., *The History of Codex Bezae's Text in the Gospel of Mark* (Arbeiten zur Neutestamentlichen Textforschung 53; Berlin: De Gruyter, 2022).

LECLERCQ, Jean, "Scopis mundatam (Matth. 12,44; Lc. 11,25): Le balai dans la Bible et dans la Liturgie d'après la tradition latine," in: *Epektasis: Mélange J. Daniélou* (Paris: Beauchesne, 1972): 129–137.

LEGASSE, Simon, "L'Homme fort de Luc XI, 21–22," *NT* 5,1 (1962): 5–9.

LEVINE, Philip, "Historical Evidence for Calligraphic Activity in Vercelli from St. Eusebius to Atto," *Speculum* 30 (1955): 561–581.

LEVISON, John R., *The Spirit in First Century Judaism* (Leiden: Brill, 1997).

LONGENECKER, Richard N. (ed.), *Into God's Presence: Prayer in the New Testament* (Grand Rapids: Eerdmans, 2001).

LÖHR, Helmut, *Studien zum frühchristlichen und frühjüdischen Gebet* (Tübingen: Mohr Siebeck, 2003).

LOOS, Hendrik van der, *The Miracles of Jesus* (Leiden: Brill, 1965).

LORENZ, Peter E., *A History of Codex Bezae's Text in the Gospel of Mark* (Berlin: De Gruyter, 2022).

LORENZ, Peter E., "Ambrosiaster's Three Criteria of the True Text and a Possible Fourth-Century Background for Bezae's Bilingual Tradition," *Conversations with the Biblical World* 36 (2016): 126–147.

LORENZ, Peter E., "An examination of six objections to the theory of Latin influence on the Greek text of Codex Bezae," in: *At One Remove: The Text of the New Testament in Early Translations and Quotations* (H.A.G. Houghton and P. Montoro eds.; Piscataway, NJ: Gorgias, 2020): 173–187.

LOWE, Elias Avery, *Codieces Latini Antiquiores. A Palaeographical Guide to Latin Manuscripts prior to the ninth century, 11 vol. and Supplement* (Oxford: Clarendon, 1934–1971).

LOWE, Elias Avery, "The Oldest Omission Signs in Latin Manuscripts: Their Origin and Significance," in: *Miscellanea Giovanni Mercati, Studi e Testi, 126* (Vatican: Biblioteca Apostolica Vaticana, 1946), IV, 36–79.

LOWE, Elias Avery, "More Facts about Our Oldest Latin Manuscript," *Palaeographical Papers* 1 (1972): 251–74.

LÖFSTEDT, Einar, *Late Latin* (Oslo: H. Aschehoug & Co. W. Nygaard, 1959).

LÖFSTEDT, Einar, *Philologischer Kommentar zur Peregrinatio Aetheriae: Untersuchungen zur Geschichte der Lateinischen Sprache* (repr. 1st ed.; Uppsala, 1911; Darmstadt: Wissenschaft Buchgesellschaft, 1962).

LÜDTKE, Helmut, *Der Ursprung der romanischen Sprachen: Eine Geschichte der sprachlichen Kommunikation* (2nd ed.; Kiel: Westensee-Verlag, 2016).

LUNDSTRÖM, Sven, *Die Überlieferung der lateinischen Irenaeusübersetzung* (Uppsala: Acta Universitatis Upsaliensis, 1985).

LUNDSTRÖM, Sven, *Neue Studien zur lateinischen Irenäusübersetzung* (Lund: Gleerup, 1948).

LUNDSTRÖM, Sven, *Studien zur lateinischen Irenäusübersetzung* (Lund: Gleerup, 1943).

MASON, Steve, *Josephus. A History of the Jewish War: AD 66–74* (Cambridge: Cambridge University Press, 2016).

MCNAMARA, Martin, *The New Testament and the Palestinian Targum to the Pentateuch* (Rom: Pontifical Biblical Institute, 1966).

MERCATI, Giovanni, "Un paio di appunti sopra il codice purpureo veronese dei vangeli," *Revue biblique* 34 (1925): 396–400.

METZGER, Bruce M. and EHRMAN, Bart D., The Text of the New Testament: Its Transmission, Corruption, and Restoration (4. ed.; New York: Oxford University Press, 2005).

MACLAURIN, Evan C. B., "Beelzeboul," *NovT* 20,2 (1978): 156–160.

MALTBY, Robert, "Gerunds, Gerundives and their Greek Equivalents in Latin Bible Translations," in: Latin vulgaire – latin tardif 7 (Arias Abellán, Carmen ed., Sevilla, 2006): 425–442.

MANUWALD, Gesine, "Divine Messages and Human Actions in the Argonautica," in: *Ritual and Religion in Flavian Epic* (Antony Augoustakis ed., Oxford: University Press, 2013).

MARI, Tommaso, "Third person possessives from early Latin to late Latin and Romance," in: *Early and Late Latin. Continuity or Change?* (Adams, J. N. and Vincent, Nigel eds.; Cambridge: University Press, 2016).

MARTIMORT, Aimé-Georges, *Les lectures liturgiques et leurs livres* (Turnhout: Brepols, 1992).

MATTEI, Paul, "Recherches sur la Bible à Rome vers le milieu du IIIe siècle: Novatien et la Vetus Latina," *RBén* 105 (1995): 255–279.

MENKEN, Maarten J. J., "The Sources of the Old Testament Quotation in Matthew 2:23," *Journal of Biblical Literature* 120,3 (2001): 451–468.

METZGER, Bruce, *The Early Versions of the New Testament. Their Origins, Transmission and Limitations* (Oxford: Clarendon, 1977).

METZGER, Bruce, *A Textual Commentary on the Greek New Testament* (Peabody: Hendrickson Publishers, 2005).

MERX, Adalbert, *Die Evangelien des Markus und Lukas: Nach der Syrischen im Sinaikloster Gefundenen Palimpsesthandschrift* (Berlin: Georg Reimer, 1905).

MICHAELIS, Johann David, *Introduction to the New Testament* (London: Rivington, 1823).

MIKULOVÁ, Jana, "Verbs Introducing direct speech in late Latin Texts," *GLB* 20,2 (2015): 123–143.

MILL, J., *Prolegomena in Nouum Testamentum* (Oxford, 1707).

MILNE, C.H., *A Reconstruction of the Old-Latin Text or Texts of the Gospels Used by Saint Augustine* (Cambridge: UP, 1926).

MIZZI, Joseph, "The African Element in the Latin Text of Mt. XXIV of Cod. Cantabrigiensis," *Rbén* 78 (1968): 33–66.

MOHRMANN, Christine, *Collectanea Schrijnen. Verspreide opstellen van Dr. Jos. Schrijnen* (Nijmegen/Utrecht: Dekker van de Vegt, 1939).

MOHRMANN, Christine, *Die altchristliche Sondersprache in den Sermones des hl. Augustin* (Nijmegen/Utrecht: Dekker van de Vegt, 1932).

MOHRMANN, Christine, *Études sur latin des Chrétiens. Tome II: Latin chrétien et médiéval* (Roma: Edizioni di Storia e Letteratura, 1961).

MONTGOMERY, James A., *The Samaritans: The Earliest Jewish Sect; Their History and Literature* (Chicago: University of Chicago Press, 1908).
MOSS, Candida R., *The Other Christs: Imitating Jesus in Ancient Christian Ideologies of Martyrdom* (Oxford: Oxford University Press, 2010).
MÜLLER-LANCÉ, Johannes, *Latein für Romanisten*: *Ein Lehr- und Arbeitsbuch* (Tübingen: Narr Verlag, 2012).
MULLER, H. F., "A Chronology of Vulgar Latin," *Zeitschrift für romanische Philologie*, Supplements (Halle (Saale): Niemeyer, 1929).
MÜLLER, Paul-Gerhard, *Lukas-Evangelium* (Stuttgart: Katholisches Bibelwerk, 1986).
NESTLE, Wilhelm, "Wer nicht mit mir ist, der ist wider mich," *ZNW* 13 (1912): 84–87.
NEYREY, Jerome H., "Prayer in Other Words: A Social Science Model for Interpreting Prayers," in: *Social Scientific Models for Interpreting the Bible: Essays by the Context Group in Honor of Bruce J. Malina* (John J. Pilch ed., Leiden: Brill, 2001): 349–80.
NICKLAS, Tobias, "Eine Skizze zu Codex Coidethi (Θ 0,38)," *Novum Testamentum* 42 (2000): 316–327.
NONGBRI, Brent, "Reconsidering the Place of Papyrus Bodmer XIV–XV (P75) in the Textual Criticism of the New Testament," *Journal of Biblical Literature* 135,2 (2016): 405–437.
NORTH, J. Lionel, "Praying for a Good Spirit: Text, Context and Meaning of Luke 11.13," *JSNT* 28,2 (2005): 167–188.
O' DONNELL, James Joseph, *Augustine Confessions* (Oxford: University Press, 2012).
O'HARE, Daniel M., "Have You Seen, Son of Man?": A Study in the Translation and Vorlage of LXX Ezekiel 40–48 (Septuagint and Cognate Studies 57; Leiden: Brill, 2011).
OGDEN, Daniel, "Binding Spells: Curse Tablets and Voodoo Dolls in the Greek and Roman Worlds," in: *Witchcraft and Magic in Europe: Ancient Greece and Rome* (Bengt Ankarloo und Stuart Clark eds., Philadelphia: University Press, 1999): 1–90.
O'MALLEY, Thomas, *Tertullian and the Bible: Language – Imagery – Exegesis* (Utrecht: Dekker & Van De Vegt N.V. Nijmegen, 1967).
ONUKI, Takashi, "Tollwut in Q? Ein Versuch über Mt 12,43–5/Lk 11,24–6," *NTS* 46 (2000): 358–374.
OSTMEYER, Karl-Heinrich, *Kommunikation mit Gott und Christus* (Tübingen: Mohr Siebeck, 2006).
O'TOOLE, Robert F., "Some Exegetical Reflections on Luke 13:10–17," *Bib* 73 (1992): 84–107.
OTT, W., Gebet und Heil. Die Bedeutung der Gebetsparänese in der lukanischen Theologie (StANT 12; Munich: Kösel).
PALLÁS, José Mar Ia Romea, "La Biblia Cyprianea. Una muestra de su reconstrucción," in: *Actes del IXè simposi de la secció catalana de la SEEC*, vol. 2 (L. Ferres ed.; Barcelona: UP, 1991).
PALMER, Leonard Robert, *The Latin Language* (London: Farber and Farber, 1954) = (Norman, Oklahoma: University of Oklahoma Press, 1988).
PANAYOTAKIS, Stelios, "Expressions of Time in Early and Late Latin: the case of temporal *habet*," in: *Early and Late Latin: Continuity or Change?* (James Noel Adams and Nigel Vincent eds., Cambridge: University Press, 2016): 202–216.
PARKER, David C., *An Introduction to the New Testament Manuscripts and their Texts* (Cambridge: UP, 2008).
PARKER, David C., *Codex Bezae. An Early Manuscript and its Text* (Cambridge: UP, 1991).
PARKER, David, C., "The Translation of OYN in the Old Latin Gospels," *NTS* 31 (1985): 252–276.
PARKES, Malcolm Beckwith, *Pause and Effect: An Introduction to the History of Punctuation in the West* (Abingdon: Routledge, 2016).
PERRET, Franz A., *Fontes ad Historiam Regionis in Planis: Quellen zur Geschichte der Bezirke Gaster, Sargans und Werdenberg, als der rätischen Teile des Kantons St. Gallen* (Zürich: Im Selbstverlag, 1936).
PEROTTI, Pier Angelo, "La locuzione *quod si*, e altre simili," *Latomus* 59,1 (2000): 8–14.

PETITMENGIN, P., "Les plus anciens manuscrits de la Bible latine," in: Le monde antique et la Bible. Bible de touts les temps 2 (J. Fontaine und C. Pietri eds.; Paris, 1985): 89–127.

PINKSTER, Harm, "The use of 'quia' and 'quoniam' in Cicero, Seneca, and Tertullian," in: *Studies in classical linguistics in honor of Philip Baldi* (Leiden: Brill, 2010): 81–95.

PLATER, William E. and WHITE, Henry, *A Grammar of the Vulgate: Being an Introduction to the Study of the Latinity of the Vulgate Bible* (Oxford: Clarendon Press, 1926).

PLUMMER, Alfred, *A Critical and Exegetical on the Gospel According to S. Luke* (Edinburgh: T & T Clark, 1913).

PLUMMER, Reinhard, *Early Christian Authorson Samaritans and Samaritanism* (Texts and Studies in Ancient Judaism 92; Tübingen: Mohr Siebeck, 2022).

POLACHECK, Itzhak, SALKIN, Ira F., SCHENHAV, D. et al., "Damage to an ancient parchment document by Aspergillus," *Mycopathologia 106* (1989): 89–93.

POLETTO, Cecilia and SANFELICI, Emanuela, "22. Relative clauses," in: *Manual of Romance Morphosyntax and Syntax* (Dufter, Andreas and Stark, Elisabeth eds.; Berlin/ Boston: De Gruyter, 2017): 804–836.

PRIOR, J. Bruce, "The Use and Nonuse of Nomina Sacra in the Freer Gospel of Matthew," *The Freer Biblical Manuscripts. Fresh Studies of an American Treasure Trove* (2006): 147–166.

PRITCHARD, Roger Telfryn, "The ‚Ambrose' Text of Alexander and the Brahmans," *Classica et Mediaevalia* 44 (1993): 115–132.

QUAEGEBEUR, Jan, *Le dieu égyptien Shaï dans la religion et l'onomastique* (OLA 2; Leuven: Leuven University Press, 1975).

RADFORD, Robert S., "Contraction in the Case Forms of ‚Deus' and ‚Meus', ‚Is' and ‚Idem'. A Study of Contraction in Latin io- and eo-, ia- and ea- Stems," *AJPh* 29,3 (1908): 336–341.

RANKE, Ernst Constantin, "Ein kleiner Italafund," *ThStKr* 45 (1872): 505–520.

RAUK, John, "The Vocative of Deus and Its Problems," *Classical Philology* 92,2 (1997): 138–149.

RICCA, Davide, "Adverbs," in: *Constituent Syntax: Adverbial Phrases, Adverbs, Mood, Tense* (Philip Baldi and Pierluigi Cuzzolin eds., Berlin: De Gruyter, 2010): 109–192.

ROBBINS, Vernon K., "Beelzebul Controversy in Mark and Luke: Rhetorical and Social Analysis," *Forum* 7.3–4 (1991): 261–277.

ROTH, Dieter Thomas, "Did Tertullian possess a Greek Copy or a Latin Translation of Marcion's Gospel?," *VigC* 63 (2009): 429–67.

ROTH, Dieter Thomas, *The Text of Marcion's Gospel* (Leiden: Brill, 2015).

RÖNSCH, F., "Worauf beruht die Italaform Istrahel?," ZWTh 26 (1883): 497–499.

RUBIO, Gonzalo, "Semitic influence in the history of Latin syntax," in: Syntax of the Sentence vol. 1 (Baldi, Philip and Cuzzolin, Pierluigi eds., Berlin, New York: De Gruyter Mouton, 2009): 195–240.

RUNESSON, Anders, "Rethinking Early Jewish-Christian Relations: Matthean Community History as Pharisaic Intragroup Conflict," *Journal of Biblical Literature* 127,1 (2008): 95–132.

RÜCKER, Adolf, *Die Lukas-Homilien des Hl. Cyrill von Alexandrien* (Breslau: Goerlich & Coch, 1911).

RÜPKE, Jörg, RICHARDSON, David M. B. and GLOCK, Anne, Fasti Sacerdotum*: A Prosopography of Pagan, Jewish, and Christian Religious Officials in the City of Rome, 300 BC to AD 499* (Oxford: Oxford University Press, 2008).

SANDAY, W., TURNER, C. H. and SOUTER, A., *Nouum Testamentum S. Irenaei Episcopi Lugdunensis* (Oxford: Clarendon Press, 1923).

SANDNES, Karl Olav, *Early Christian Discourses on Jesus' Prayer at Gethsemane: Courageous, Committed, Cowardly?* (Leiden: Brill, 2015).

SAXER, V., "La Bible chez les Pères latins du IIIe siècle," in: *Le monde antique et la Bible. Bible de touts les temps 2* (J. Fontaine und C. Pietri eds., Paris 1985): 339–369.

SCHÄFER, Karl Theodor, *Die altlateinische Bibel: Rede zum Antritt des Rektorates der Rheinischen Friedrich-Wilhelms-Universität zu Bonn 1956* (Bonn: Peter Hanstein, 1957).
SCHELKENS, Karim, *Catholic Theology of Revelation on the Eve of Vatican II; A Redaction History of the Schema De fontibus revelationis* (1960–1962) (Brill's Series in Church History 41; Leiden: Brill, 2010).
SCHERRER, Gustav, *Verzeichnis der Handschriften der Stiftsbibliothek zu St. Gallen* (Halle: Olms, 1875).
SCHIRNER, R., *Inspice diligenter codices. Philologische Studien zu Augustins Umgang mit Bibelhandschriften und -übersetzungen* (Millennium-Studien 49, Berlin/ New York, 2015).
SCHMID, Ulrich B., *Marcion und sein Apostolos* (Berlin: De Gruyter, 1995).
SCHNEIDER, Gerhard, *Das Evangelium nach Lukas* (Gütersloh: Mohn, 1977).
SCHNELLE, Udo, *Die ersten 100 Jahre des Christentums 30–130 n. Chr.: Die Entstehungsgeschichte einer Weltreligion* (Göttingen: Vandenhoeck & Ruprecht, 2016).
SCHÖNTAG, Roger, "Il dibattito intorno al volgare antico tra Leonardo Bruni e Flavio Biondo suollo sfondo della cognizione linguistica di Dante," *Forum Italicum* 51 (2017): 553–572.
SCHÖNTAG, Roger, "Das Verständnis von Vulgärlatein in der Frühen Neuzeit vor dem Hintergrund der *questione della lingua*: Eine Untersuchung der Begriffsgeschichte im Rahmen einer varietätenlinguistischen Verortung," in: *Synchronie und Diachronie* (Barbara Sonnenhauser et al. eds.; Munich: Ibykos Verlag, 2017), 111–129.
SCHOTTROFF, Luise, "Lydia: Eine neue Qualität der Macht," in: *Zwischen Ohnmacht und Befreiung: Biblische Frauengestalten* (Karin Walter ed., Freiburg: Herder, 1988): 305–309.
SCHRIJNEN, Joseph, *Charakteristik des altchristlichen Latein* (Nijmegen/Utrecht: Dekker van de Vegt, 1932).
SCHUCHARDT, Hugo E. M., *Der Vokalismus des Vulgärlatein*, vol. 1–2 (reprint Hildesheim: Olms 1975 = Leipzig 1866–1868).
SCHULZ-FLÜGEL, E., "Bibelübersetzungen, 2. Übersetzungen ins Lateinische," in: *Religion in Geschichte und Gegenwart*, vol. 1 (1491–1494; H.D. Betz et al. eds.; Tübingen, 1998).
SCHULZE, Christian, *Celsus* (Studienbücher Antike 6; Darmstadt: WBG, 2001).
SCHÜRMANN, Heinz "Q Lk 11,14–36 kompositionsgeschichtlich befragt," in: *The Four Gospels I* (Frans van Segbroeck ed.; Leuven: University Press, 1992): 563–586.
SCHWARTZ, Günther, "λυθῆναι ἀπὸ τοῦ δεσμοῦ τούτου," *BibNot* 15 (1981): 47.
SCOTT, "Art. Regia," LTUR 4: 189–192.
SCRIVENER, Frederick Henry Ambrose, *A Plain Introduction to the Criticism of the New Testament* (London: Bell, 1894).
SEIM, Turid Karlsen, *The Double Message: Patterns of Gender in Luke-Acts* (Edinburgh: T.& T. Clark, 1994).
SEMLER, Johann Salomo, Jo. Sal. Semleri Apparatus Ad Liberalem Novi Testamenti Interpretationem: Illustrationis Exempla Multa E Epistola Ad Romanos Petita Sunt (Halae Magdeb: Tramp, 1767).
SHEERIN, Daniel, "Christian and Biblical Latin," in: *Medieval Latin: An Introduction and Bibliographical Guide* (Frank Anthony Carl Mantello and Arthur George Rigg eds., Washington: The Catholic University of American Press, 1996): 137–157.
SITTL, Karl, *Die lokalen Verschiedenheiten der lateinischen Sprache: mit besonderer Berücksichtigung des afrikanischen Lateins* (Erlangen: Andreas Deichert,1882).
SJÖRGEN, H., Zum Gebrauch des Futurums im Altlateinischen (Uppsala: Akademiska Bokhandeln, 1906).
SORENSEN, Eric, *Possession and Exorcism in the New Testament and Early Christianity* (Tübingen: Mohr Siebeck, 2002).
SOUTER, Alexander, *A Study of Ambrosiaster* (Cambridge: UP, 1905).
SPARKS, Hedley Frederick Davis, "The Latin Bible," in: *The Bible in its Ancient and English Versions* (Henry Wheeler Robinson ed.; Oxford: Clarendon, 1954): 100–110.
SPENCE, N.C. W., "Quantity and Quality in the Vowel-System of Vulgar Latin," *Word* 21 (1966): 1–18.

STADEL, Christian, *Hebraismen in den aramäischen Texten vom Toten Meer* (Heidelberg: Winter Verlag, 2008).

STEFFENS, Franz, *Lateinische Paläographie: 125 Tafeln in Lichtdruck mit gegenüberstehender Transkription nebst Erläuterungen und einer systematischen Darstellung der Entwicklung der lateinischen Schrift* (Trier: Schaar & Dathe, 1909).

STEINOVÁ, Evina, Notam Superponere Studui: The Use of Annotation Symbols in the Early Middle Ages (bibliogia 52; Turnhout: Brepols, 2019).

STERN, Karen, *Inscribing Devotion and Death: Archaeological Evidence for Jewish Populations of North Africa* (Leiden: Brill, 2008).

STINSON, Timothy, "Knowledge of the Flesh: Using DNA Analysis to Unlock Bibliographical Secrets of Medieval Parchment," *Papers of the Bibliographical Society of America* 103(4) (2008): 435–453.

STONE, Robert Conrad, *The Language of the Latin Text of Codex Bezae: With an Index Verborum* (Illinois Studies in Language and Literature 30,2/3; Illinois: University of Illinois Press, 1946).

SZEMLER, J., "Art. Pontifex," *RE Suppl.* 15:332–396.

ROBERT, C., *The Language of the Latin Text of Codex Bezae: With an Index Verborum* (Urbana: University of Illinois Press, 2009).

STOVER, Tim, *Epic and Empire in Vespasianic Rome: A New Reading of Valerius Flaccus' Argonautica* (Oxford: University Press, 2012).

STUMMER, Friedrich, *Einführung in die lateinische Bibel* (Paderborn: Schöningh, 1928).

SVENNUNG, Josef, *Syntaktische Semasiologische und Kritische Studien zu Orosius* (Uppsala: A.-B. Akademiska Bokhandeln, 1922).

TARRANT, R. J., "The Authenticity of the Letter of Sappho to Phaon (Heroides XV)," *Harvard studies in classical philology* 85 (1981): 133–153.

THIELMANN, P., "Der Ersatz des Reciprocums im Lateinischen," in: *Archiv für lateinische Lexikographie und Grammatik mit Einschluss des Älteren Mittelalters* 7 (Eduard Wölfflin ed., Leipzig: Teubner): 343–523.

THIELMANN, Philipp, "Die lateinische Übersetzung des Buches Sirach," *ALLG* 8 (1893): 501–561.

THIELMANN, Philipp, "Die lateinische Übersetzung des Buches der Weisheit," *ALLG* 8 (1893): 233–272.

THOMPSON, Edward M., Handbook of Greek and Latin Paleography (London: Paul, Trench, Trübner, 1894).

TJÄDER, Jan-Olof, "Der Ursprung der Unzialschrift," *BZGA* 74,1 (1974): 9–40.

TOMLINSON, Richard Alan, "Vitruvius and Hermogenes," in: *Munus non ingratum: Proceedings of the International Symposium on Vitruvius' De Architectura and the Hellenistic and Republican Architecture, Leiden, 20–23 January 1987* (Jong, Jan and Geertman, Herman eds.; Leiden: Stichting Bulletin Antieke Beschaving, 1989): 71–75.

TRAUBE, Ludwig, Nomina sacra: Versuch einer Geschichte der christlichen Kürzung (Munich: Beck, 1907).

TREMEL, Bernard, "A propos d'ac 20,7–12: puissance du thaumaturge ou du témoin?," *RThPh* 112 (1980): 359–369.

TSEDAKA, Benyamim, *Samaritans. Past and Present* (Studia Judaica; Forschungen zur Wissenschaft des Judentums 53; Berlin: De Gruyter, 2007).

Turner, Eric G., *The Typology of the Early Codex* (University of Pennsylvania Press, 1977; reprint, Wipf & Stock, 2010).

UGHELLI, F., "Vita antiqua," in: Italia sacra sive De Episcopis Italiae, et insularum adjacentium, rebusque ab iis praeclare gestis, deducta serie ad nostram usque aetatem, 2nd ed. (Venice: Sebastianum Coleti, 1717–1722): 754.

Ullman, Berthold L., Ancient Writing and its Influence (Our dept to Greece and Rome 38; London: Harrap, 1932).

Väänänen, Veikko, *Introduction au latin vulgaire* (Paris: Klincksieck, 1981).

Vagancy, L. and Amphoux, C.-B., *An Introduction to New Testament Textual Criticism* (transl. J. Read-Heimerdinger; Cambridge: CUP, 1991).

van der Horst, Pieter Willem, "Silent Prayer in Antiquity," *Numen* 41.1 (1994): 1–25.

van der Horst, Pieter Willem, "The Finger of God: Miscellaneous Notes on Luke 11:20 and its *Umwelt*," in: *Sayings of Jesus: Canonical and Non-Canonical: Essays in Honour of Tjitze Baarda* (William L. Petersen et al. eds., Leiden: Brill, 1997): 89–103.

Vincent, Nigel, "Continuity and Change from Latin to Romance," in: *Early and Late Latin. Continuity or Change* (James Adams and Nigel Vincent eds.; Cambridge: University Press, 2016), 1–13.

Verboomen, Alain, *L'imparfait périphrastique dans l'Évangile de Luc et dans la Septante: Contribution à l'étude du système verbal du grec néotestamentaire* (Leuven: Peeters, 1992).

Versteegh, Kees, "Dead or Alive: The Status of the Standard Language," in: *Bilingualism in Ancient Society: Language Contact and the Written Word* (James N. Adams et al. eds.; Oxford: Oxford University Press, 2002), 52–74.

Versteegh, Kees, "The Ghost of Vulgar Latin. History of a Misnomer," *Historiographica Linguistica* 48 (2021): 205–227.

Vetus Latina Arbeitsbericht. Vetus Latina. Gemeinnützige Stiftung zur Förderung der Herausgabe einer vollständigen Sammlung aller erhaltenen Reste der altlateinischen Bibelübersetzungen aus Handschriften und Zitaten bei alten Schriftstellern. Bericht der Stiftung und Forschungsbericht des Instituts (Beuron: Vetus Latina Institut, 1967–).

Vezin, Jean, "Les divisions du texte dans les Évangiles jusqu' à l'apparition de l'imprimerie," in: *Grafia e interpunzione del latino nel medioevo* (Maierù, Alfonso ed.; Rom: Dell'Ateneo, 1984): 53–68.

Vietmeier, Karl, *Beobachtungen über Caelius Aurelianus als Übersetzer medizinischer Fachausdrücke verlorener griechischer Schriften des methodischen Arztes Soranos von Ephesos* (Gütersloh: Thiele, 1937).

Vogels, Heinrich Joseph, *Evangelium Palatinum: Studien zur ältesten Geschichte der lateinischen Evangelienübersetzungen* (Münster: Aschendorff, 1926).

von Soden, Hans, *Das lateinische Neue Testament in Nordafrika zur Zeit Cyprians. Nach Bibelhandschriften und Väterzeugnissen* (Leipzig: J.C. Hinrichs'sche Buchhandlung, 1909).

Wackernagel, Jacob, Lectures on syntax: with special reference to Greek, Latin, and Germanic (D. Langslow ed.; Oxford:University Press, 2009).

Wall, Robert W., ",The Finger of God': Deuteronomy 9.10 and Luke 11.20," *NTS* 33 (1987): 144–150.

Wilkinson, John "The Case of the Bent Woman in Luke 13:10–17," *EQ* 49 (1977): 195–205.

Weder, Hans, *Die Gleichnisse Jesu als Metaphern: Traditions- und redaktionsgeschichtliche Analysen und Interpretationen* (Göttingen: Vandenhoeck & Ruprecht, 1990).

Weissenrieder, Annette, "Die Vater-Anrede des Lukasevangeliums, Vetus Latina: Eine Problemanzeige," in: *Im Gespräch mit C. F. Georg Heinrici: Beiträge zwischen Theologie und Religionswissenschaft* (Marco Frenchkowski and Lena Seehausen eds., Tübingen: Mohr Siebeck, 2021): 233–254.

Weissenrieder, Annette, "Pater sancte: The Father Appellation and the Imaginaires of Jerusalem in the Vetus Latina Luke 11:2," in: *Prayer and the Ancient City. Influences of Urban Space* (M. Patzelt, J. Rüpke, A. Weissenrieder eds.; Tübingen: Mohr Siebeck, 2021): 263–288.

Weissenrieder, Annette, *Images of Illness in the Gospel of Luke: Insights of Ancient Medical Texts* (Wissenschaftliche Untersuchungen Zum Neuen Testament 2,164; Tübingen: Mohr Siebeck, 2003).

WEISSENRIEDER, Annette, “Disease and Healing in a Changing World: ‚Medical‘ Vocabulary and Exorcism in the Vetus Latina Luke,” in: *Demons in Late Antiquity: Their Perception and Transformation in Different Literary Genres* (Eva Elm and Nicole Hartmann eds., Berlin/Boston: De Gruyter, 2020): 41–56.

WEISSENRIEDER, Annette, “Die Versuchung Jesu und die Übersetzungen von πτερύγιον in der Vetus Latina Lukasevangelium,” in: *Resonanztheologie* (H. Schwier et al.; FS G. Theißen, 2023), chap. 8, 42–53.

WEISSENRIEDER, Annette and André Luiz VISINONI, “Archi*text*ure: Sacred Spaces in the *Codex Vercellensis* (a, 3) Gospel of Luke,” in: *RRE* (2023): 119–141.

WEISSENRIEDER, Annette and VISINONI, André Luiz, “Illness, Suffering, and Treatment in a Changing World: Old Latin Gospels and »Medical« Vocabulary,” *Early Christianity* 13,3 (2022): 316–341.

WEISSENRIEDER, Annette and VISINONI, André Luiz, “The Codex Vercellensis (a) as Witness of the Gospel of Luke. Classification and Language in Light of Multispectral Images,” Early Christianity 16 (2022): 105–130.

WEISSENRIEDER, Annette and VISINONI, André Luiz, “The Fragmenta Curiensia (a^2) as Witnesses of the Gospel of Luke: Classification and Language,” in: *Early Christianity* 12 (2021): 135–156.

WEISSENRIEDER, Annette, “It Proceeded from Entrance of a Demon into the Man: Epileptic Seizures in Ancient Medical Texts and the New Testament,” in: *Embodiment in Evolution and Culture* (Gregor Etzelmüller and Christian Tewes eds.; Tübingen: Mohr Siebeck, 2016): 265–282.

WESENBERG, Burkhardt, “Zu den Schriften der griechischen Architekten,” *DiskAB* 4 (1983): 39–48.

WESTCOTT, Brooke F. and Fenton J. A. HORT, *The New Testament in the Original Greek. Introduction and Appendix to the Text* (New York: Harper, 1882).

WETTSTEIN, J. J., *Prolegomena ad Novi Testamenti Graeci editionem* (Amsterdam, 1751).

WIEFEL, Wolfgang, *Das Evangelium nach Lukas* (Leipzig: Evangelische Verlagsanstalt, 1988).

WHEELER, Arthur Leslie, “The Syntax of the Imperfect Indicative in Early Latin,” *CPh* 4,1 (1906): 357–390.

WÖLFFLIN, Eduard, *Archiv für lateinische Lexikographie und Grammatik mit Einschluss des älteren Mittellateins* (Leipzig: Teubner, 1900).

WOLTER, Michael, “Das Gebet der Jünger: Das Vaterunser im Lukasevangelium (Lk 11,2c–4),” in: *Das Vaterunser in seinen antiken Kontexten: Zum Gedenken an Eduard Lohse* (Florian Wilk ed.; Göttingen: Vandenhoeck & Ruprecht, 2016).

WOLTER, Michael, *Lukasevangelium* (Tübingen: Mohr Siebeck, 2008).

WOODS, Edward, *The ‚Finger of God‘ and Pneumatology in in Luke-Acts* (London: Bloomsbury Publishing, 2001).

WRIGHT, Roger, *A Sociophilological Study of Late Latin* (USML 10; Turnout: Brepols, 2002).

WRIGHT, Roger, *Latin vulgaire – latin tardif VIII* (Hildesheim: Olms, 2008).

YODER, James D., “The Language of the Greek Variants of Codex Bezae,” *Novum Testamentum* 3,4 (1959): 241–248.

ZANGENBERG, Jürgen, *Samareia: Antike Quellen zur Geschichte und Kultur der Samaritaner in deutscher Übersetzung* (Texte und Arbeiten zum neutestamentlichen Zeitalter 15; Tübingen/Basel: Francke, 1994).

ZIETHE, Carolin, *Auf seinen Namen werden die Völker hoffen: Die matthäische Rezeption der Schriften Israels zur Begründung des universalen Heils* (Berlin: De Gruyter, 2018).

ZIMMERMANN, Christiane, *Die Namen des Vaters: Studien zu Ausgewählten Neutestamentlichen Gottesbezeichnungen* (Leiden: Brill, 2007).

Index Locorum

Biblia Hebraica

Genesis 273 Fn. 220
1:11 239 Fn. 148

Exodus
16:7, 10 135
18:19 14 fn. 25
20:2 242 Fn.158
24:16–17 135

Leviticus 279 Fn. 240, Fn. 242

Numbers 182 Fn. 140
9:18 182
10:36 182

Deuteronomy
5:6 242 Fn. 158
26:13 104

Judges
6:8 171
21:19 105 Fn. 48

1 Kings
12 105 Fn. 48
18:4 171

2 Kings
10 105 Fn. 48

Nehemia
9:12–30 84
9:20 84
13:4–9.28 279 Fn. 238

Job 190

Psalms
48 148
142 84
142:10 84

Isaiah
4:2 77
11:1 77

Jeremiah
23:5 77
33:15 77
41:4–6 105 Fn. 48

Zechariah
3:8 77
6:12 77

Septuaginta

Genesis
3:16 227 Fn. 90

Leviticus
2:1 265 Fn. 206

Numbers
7:49 265 Fn. 206
22:32 198 Fn. 16

1Kingdoms (1Sam)
3:17–23b 140

3Kingdoms (1Kgs)
18:4 171

1Chronicles
21:1 198 Fn. 16

2Esra
19:20 84, 84 Fn. 58

https://doi.org/10.1515/9783111142531-010

Job
1:6–8 198 Fn. 16
2:2–4 198 Fn. 16
2:6–6 198 Fn. 16

Psalms
142:8c.10 84 Fn. 59
142:10 84
143:10 84

Sirach
18:16 85
18:16–17 85 Fn. 65

Isaiah
22:13 253 Fn. 186
61:2 80

Ezekiel
38:12 266 Fn. 207
40–48 262 Fn. 197

Zechariah
3:1–2 198 Fn. 16

Vulgata

Genesis
3:16 227 Fn. 90

Exodus
20:2 242

Leviticus
21:10 279, 279 Fn. 238

Numbers
35:25ff. 279 Fn. 238

Deuteronomy
5:6 242

4Regnum (2Kings)
12:9 279, Fn. 238
22:8 279, Fn. 238

2Paralipomenon
26:20 279 Fn. 238

Job
18:11 254 Fn.187

Psalmi
67:19 85
90:4 (b, 4) 182 Fn. 140
139:8 (b, 4) 182 Fn. 140

Sapientiae
19:7 182 Fn. 140

Biblia Graeca

Matthew 97, 253, 266
1:1–11 162
2:23 77
3:12 235
5:3 69
5:23–24 265
6:8 227 Fn. 93
6:32 227
7:11 85
8:31 69
9:32 126
10:12 74
11:12 119
12:22 126, 127
12:25 146
12:41 229
13:3 222
13:5 222
13:24 5
15:12–22 162

15:31 251
19:21 274 Fn. 225
23:18–27 162
24:12 259
24:33 75
24:47 274 Fn. 225
25:14 274 Fn. 225
25:30 5
27:15 66
27:46 226

Mark 105, 129, 253
1:1–5:30 72
1:7 239
5:12 69
5:30 77
7:2 235
7:32 126
8:38 147, 148 Fn. 110
9:43 249
10:47 171
12:37 78 Fn. 43
13:4 78 Fn. 43
13:27 5
14:61 78 Fn. 43
14:61–16:8 162
14:67 171
15:6 66
15:34 226 Fn. 69
16:18 227 Fn. 92

Luke
1:10 97 Fn. 20
1:13 98 Fn. 24
1:20 216
1:23 277
1:29 82
1:35 182
1:38 172
1:41 172
1:42–45 172
1:46 172
1:48 172
1:51 277
1:56 172
1:64 227 Fn. 91
1:71 32
1:75 68, 277
2:7 275
2:12 68
2:24 277
2:25 277
2:26 184, 235
2:28 227 Fn. 91, 249–250
2:34 181, 227 Fn. 91
2:37 98 Fn. 24
2:39 76–77, 86
2:51 74
3:12 79, 150
3:14 68
3:15 83, 100 Fn. 28
3:16 82
3:17 245, 248
3:18 277
3:21 97 Fn. 20
3:28 36
3:35 69
4:2 36, 198 Fn. 16, 246
4:3 231
4:4 226, 242
4:5–8 266
4:8 68
4:15 78 Fn. 43, 277
4:16 69, 79, 170, 212
4:19 79, 277
4:20 220
4:25 186
4:27 25, 268
4:31 135, 284
4:33 164
4:34 170
4:35 227 Fn. 92
4:36 164, 167
4:38 103
4:40 268
4:44 135 Fn. 89
5:2 63
5:3 214
5:5 25 Fn. 7, 80, 142, 148
5:7 214
5:12 98 Fn. 24, 99, 277
5:14 25 Fn. 7, 268
5:15 214, 268
5:16 97 Fn. 20, 135 Fn. 89

5:17	271–272
5:19	271
5:22	146–147
5:24	245
5:26	277, 285
5:29	270
5:31	251
5:33	98 Fn. 24
5:35	186
5:37	216, 221
6:1	246
6:4	246
6:8	146–147
6:10	143
6:12	97 Fn. 20, 135 Fn. 89, 280
6:20	68–69
6:22	246, 277
6:23	170
6:27	25 Fn. 7
6:28	97 Fn. 20
6:32	220
6:35	68, 277
6:43	79
6:44	25 Fn. 7, 82
6:45	5, 246, 277
6:49	79
7:7	25 Fn. 7
7:9	82
7:10	251
7:11	83, 183, 241
7:12	71
7:13	143–144, 148
7:15	140, 148
7:16	276
7:20	74
7:21	267–268
7:22	268
7:24	186 Fn. 145
7:26	76–77, 86
7:28	77
7:37	271
7:43	67, 287
7:45	244
8:1	271–272
8:2–3	175
8:3	274
8:6	255
8:10	75
8:12	198 Fn. 16
8:13	69
8:14	83, 168, 277
8:16	25 Fn. 7, 43, 222
8:17	80
8:22	183, 241
8:23	65, 250
8:27	68, 79
8:28	98 Fn. 24, 99, 277
8:29	69
8:37	183
8:38	98 Fn. 24
8:41	133, 236
8:45	76–77, 86, 142–143, 148
8:46	239
8:48	239
8:50	277
8:52	146
8:55	74, 142
9:1	245
9:2	268
9:6	271–272
9:10	64, 131
9:12	271–272
9:14	45
9:18	83, 97 Fn. 20
9:21	274 Fn. 224
9:22	277
9:23	75–76
9:25	80, 136, 148
9:26	147, 148 Fn. 110
9.28	97 Fn. 20
9:29	97 Fn. 20
9:30	140
9:38	98 Fn. 24, 99
9:38–40	99
9:39	268–269
9:40	98 Fn. 24, 99
9:41	248
9:42	268–269
9:43	277
9:44	133, 165
9:45	133
9:47	146, 246
9:52	183, 241
9:53	135 Fn. 89

9:55 82
9:55–56 81
9:56 25 Fn. 7
9:58 169
9:59 46
9:61 25 Fn. 7
10:2 98 Fn. 24, 99, 170
10:4 271
10:5 74–75
10:12 68, 79
10:19 84
10:21 66
10:25 244, 246
10:33 143–144, 148
10:38 271–272
11:1 97 Fn. 20
11:2 97 Fn. 20
11:2 66
11:4 25 Fn. 7
11:5 242
11:9–13 85
11:11 268
11:13 83–86
11:14 127
11:15 129
11:17 65, 146, 149
11:18 132
11:21 274
11:22 270
11:24 129
11:26 80, 85, 118, 148, 228
11:28 79
11:35 26
11:36 75 Fn. 39
11:41 67
11:42 68
11:43 262
11:44 255
11:45 246
11:46 246, 255, 271
11:47 252 Fn. 184
11:51 80, 265 Fn. 203
12:2 79
12:5 68, 245
12:7 25 Fn. 7
12:12 141
12:15 245, 271, 274
12:18 262
12:21 75 Fn. 39
12:27 80
12:29 246
12:30 277
12:31 79
12:33 274 Fn. 224
12:35 82
12:36 233
12:44 274 Fn. 224
13:2 5, 73
13:4 167–168
13:5 25 Fn. 7
13:11 268
13:13 276
13:16 133, 148
13:17 147–148, 277
13:18 77–78
13:20 76–77, 80, 86
13:22 47, 55, 271–272
13:24 104
13:31 252 Fn. 184
13:33 XV
13:34 252 Fn. 184
14:3 246
14:7 186
14:10 25 Fn. 7, 65
14:12 25 Fn. 7, 75 Fn. 40, 79, 255–256
14:14 256
14:28 241, 271
14:33 271, 274
15:2 186
15:8 270
15:13 244
15:15 272
15:17 164
15:20 143–144
15:23 214
15:27 214, 250–251, 293
15:30 25 Fn. 7, 104, 214, 272, 274
15:31 75, 269
15:32 74
16:1 269, 274 Fn. 224, 294
16:3 79, 148
16:6 272
16:7 272

16:8	76, 79
16:9	80
16:14	255
16:21	25 Fn. 7
16:28	246
17:8	25 Fn. 7
17:10	186
17:11	222
17:11–12	105
17:11–19	101
17:12	272
17:13	142–143, 148
17:14	268
17:15	268, 276 Fn. 229, 277
17:16	101
18:18	255
17:19	251 Fn. 183
17:20	27
18:1	97 Fn. 20
18:8	222
18:10	97 Fn. 20, 140
18:11	97 Fn. 20
18:13	25 Fn. 7
18:16	246
18:17	246
18:20	242, 246
18:30	82
18:31	82
18:33	186 Fn. 145
18:42	251 Fn. 183
18:43	247, 276 Fn. 229, 277
19:2	83, 232 Fn. 117
18:8	274 Fn. 224
19:9	133, 232 Fn. 117
19:10	251 Fn. 183
19:14	83, 255
19:17	246
19:24	79
19:26–21:29	162
19:27	250, 252
19:30	272–273
19:33	50
19:35	186 Fn. 145
19:37	277
19:42	68, 114
19:44	257
19:46	97 Fn. 20, 280
19:47	135 Fn. 89, 277
19:48	222
20:6	68
20:9	233
20:10	241, 272
20:16	230, 298
20:19	133
20:20	82
20:21	25 Fn. 7, 221
20:27	69
20:39	186 Fn. 145
20:44	78 Fn. 43
20:46	262
20:47	97 Fn. 20
21:1	83, 262, 264
21:2	76, 214
21:3	68, 228, 272
21:4	274
21:5	262–263
21:6	76
21:7	71, 78 Fn. 43
21:9	25 Fn. 7
21:11	150, 253
21:14	255, 259
21:18	222
21:19	277
21:26	255, 258
21:31	75
21:32	222
21:33	222
21:36	98 Fn. 24
22:2	252 Fn. 184
22:4	277
22:6	245
22:7	137
22:11	272, 275
22:12	263
22:18	248
22:19	75 Fn. 39
22:20	70, 75 Fn. 39
22:24	80
22:27	71
22:32	98 Fn. 24, 99
22:36	25 Fn. 7
22:40	97 Fn. 20
22:41	97 Fn. 20, 300
22:42	232

22:44	97 Fn. 20
22:45	97 Fn. 20, 249–250, 280
22:46	97 Fn. 20
22:49	214
22:50	277
22:52	186 Fn. 145, 277
22:53	255, 260
22:54	277
22:56	170
22:63	230
22:66	278
22:68	186
22:70	78 Fn. 43
23:2	68
23:3	80
23:4	278
23:8	135 Fn. 89
23:10	250, 278
23:13	278
23:14	71
23:17	65–67, 86
23:18	66
23:19	66
23:24	67
23:26–49	20
23:29	255
23:34	65–66, 86
23:36	71
23:37	82
23:40	71
23:43	71
23:45	250
23:47	164, 276
23:52	255
23:53	70
23:55	25 Fn. 7
24:3	75 Fn. 39
24:6	75 Fn. 39, 125, 134
24:10	175
24:11	250
24:12	75 Fn. 39
24:13	272–273
24:15	79
24:17	230
24:19	171
24:19c	170
24:20	278
24:21	167
24:22	25 Fn. 7
24:26	171
24:28	69, 272–273
24:31–32	71
24:36	75 Fn. 39
24:40	75 Fn. 39, 202
24:45	245
24:49	69, 278
24:51	75 Fn. 39
24:52	75 Fn. 39
24:53	278

John

1:1–8:38	72
7:30	246
7:31	229
7:36	242
7:44–8:12	162
10:29	229
16:23	227 Fn. 93
18:39	66

Acts	70 Fn. 14
1:16	84 Fn. 58
2:9b	84
4:34–35	265 Fn. 205
28:3–6	84

Romans

5:5	147 Fn. 105
6:9	227 Fn. 90
9:33	147 Fn. 105
10:11	147 Fn. 105

1 Corinthians

1:27	147 Fn. 105
11:4	147 Fn. 104
11:5	147 Fn. 104
11:22	147 Fn. 104

2 Corinthians

7:14	147 Fn. 104
9:4	147 Fn. 104

Ephesians

4:8	85 Fn. 66

6:11	270
6:13	270

1 Peter

2:6	147 Fn. 104
3:16	147 Fn. 104

Biblia Latina

Matthew	XIII–XXIII, 10, 12–13, 76, 163, 224, 238, 266, 273, 278 Fn. 232
1:1–11	162
1:18	XIX
1:21	232 Fn. 117
2:4	100
2:6	100
2:8	246 Fn. 170
2:21	100
3:6	233 Fn. 118
3:12	235
4:16	100, 233 Fn. 118
4:23	100
4:24	246
5:5–10	204
5:8	92 Fn. 11, 134 Fn. 87
5:25	233 Fn. 118
5:41	233 Fn. 118
6:8	227 Fn. 93
6:11	226
6:26	233 Fn. 118
6:32	227
7:10	92
7:13	119
8:4	233 Fn. 118
8:20	169
9:15	233 Fn. 118
9:18	226
9:30	233 Fn. 118
9:32	126
9:36	233 Fn. 118
10:16	18 Fn. 28
10:33	18 Fn. 28
11:5	94 Fn. 13
11:12	119
12:22	126–127
12:25	146–147
12:29	233 Fn. 118
12:32b	141
12:41	229
12:43	130
12:45	229
12:50	232 Fn. 117
13:3	18 Fn. 28, 222
13:5	222
13:7–8	132 Fn. 81
13:15	100
13:19	233 Fn. 118
13:24	5, 18 Fn. 28
13:44	233 Fn. 118
13:58	233 Fn. 118
14:2	232 Fn. 117
14:5	233 Fn. 118
14:14	233 Fn. 118
15:12–22	162
15:31	251
15:36	232
16:20	232 Fn. 117
18:2–5	246 Fn. 170
18:33	137 Fn. 96
19:21	274 Fn. 225
20:25	227
21:31	105
21:32	105
22:44	13
22:45	13
23:18–27	162
23:23	137
24:10	237 Fn. 140, 238 Fn. 142
24:12	259
24:47	274 Fn. 225
25:14	274 Fn. 225
25:30	5
25:32	237 Fn. 140
26:1	18 Fn. 28
26:29	248
27:15	66

27:46	226	11:33	226
27:61	175	12:15	233 Fn. 119
28:1	175	12:41	265 Fn. 204
		12:43	265 Fn. 204
Mark	XIII–XXIII, 10, 12, 50, 70, 273	13:8	223
		13:19	223
1:7	239	13:25	223
1:8	232 Fn. 117	13:27	5
1:26	269	14:11	233 Fn. 119
3:15	226	14:14	275–276
3:23	129	14:25	248
3:29	141	14:43	233 Fn. 119
4:41	237	14:47	278 Fn. 232
5:30	77	14:59	233 Fn. 119
7:2	235	14:61–16:8	162
7:32	126	14:67	233 Fn. 119
7:36	232 Fn. 117	15:6	66
8:16	237	15:10	278 Fn. 232
8:22	233	15:20	233 Fn. 119
8:23	233 Fn. 119	15:31	237, 278 Fn. 232
8:31	233 Fn. 119	15:47	173, 175
8:38	148	16:1	175
9:2	233 Fn. 119	16:18	227 Fn. 92
9:7	233 Fn. 119		
9:14	233 Fn. 119	Luke	XIII–XVI, 3–4, 10, 12–13, 21, 23 Fn. 2, 87, 123, 180, 196, 237
9:16	233 Fn. 119		
9:19	233 Fn. 119		
9:20	233 Fn. 119	1:1	XV
9:22	233 Fn. 119	1:1–8:29	XVII
9:25	233 Fn. 119	1:5	XIX
9:26	269	1:6	XV, 51, 216
9:34	233 Fn. 119	1:10	97 Fn. 20, 98
9:36	233 Fn. 119	1:13	98 Fn. 24, 107, 213
9:43	233 Fn. 119, 249	1:15	XV, 108, 141, 149
9:45	233 Fn. 119	1:16	212
9:47	233 Fn. 119	1:17	XV, 93, 108, 141, 149
10:14	233 Fn. 119	1:18	51
10:31	223	1:19	94 Fn. 13, 141, 149
10:35	233 Fn. 119	1:20	51, 141, 149, 209, 216–217
10:42	227, 233 Fn. 119	1:21	93, 108, 283
10:52	247–248	1:22	XV, 141, 149
11:2	233 Fn. 119	1:23	51, 277, 283
11:3	233 Fn. 119	1:24	108, 213
11:6	233 Fn. 119	1:27	XV, 201
11:7	233 Fn. 119	1:28	107, 190
11:18	233 Fn. 119	1:29	82
11:24	223, 224	1:32	131, 149, 190

1:33	149
1:35	108, 141, 182, 190
1:36	131, 149, 213
1:39	108, 149
1:41	172
1:42–45	172
1:45	51, 108
1:46	172–173, 176–177, 194
1:51	131, 149, 277, 283
1:54	212, 283
1:55	107
1:58	131, 149
1:59	246 Fn. 170
1:61	108
1:63	201
1:64	201, 227 Fn. 91
1:66	108, 246 Fn. 170
1:68	100 Fn. 28
1:71	32
1:72	XV
1:75	68, 277, 283
1:77	XV, 100 Fn. 28
1:79	146 Fn. 170
1:80	283
2:1	108
2:3	XV
2:4	51, 108, 212–213
2:7	275, 283
2:9	135, 149
2:10	51, 94 Fn. 13, 100 Fn. 28, 204
2:12	68, 216
2:13	184, 190
2:14	204
2:15	XV, 108, 149, 237 Fn. 140 – 141
2:16	35 Fn. 22
2:17	137–138, 246 Fn. 170
2:19	149
2:20	91, 92 Fn. 8, 94 Fn. 13, 108, 139, 149
2:21	18, 38, 51, 108, 177, 202, 209, 246 Fn. 170
2:22	51, 108, 131, 149, 202–203, 283
2:23	51
2:24	277, 283
2:25	107, 141, 212, 277, 283
2:26	XV, 141, 149, 184, 235
2:27	216 Fn. 66, 246 Fn. 170
2:28	227 Fn. 91, 249–250, 282–283
2:31	51, 100 Fn. 28, 149
2:32	100 Fn. 28, 212
2:33	141, 150
2:34	181, 190, 212, 227 Fn. 91
2:35	51
2:36	190
2:37	98 Fn. 24, 107
2:38	150, 212, 283
2:39	51, 76–77, 86, 283
2:40	108, 131, 150, 246 Fn. 170, 283
2:41	51, 204
2:42	51, 190, 283
2:43	108, 150
2:44	92 Fn. 8, 108
2:45	108
2:46	141, 150, 184–185, 190, 206, 283
2:47	107, 283
2:48	39, 51, 108, 201, 218
2:49	186, 190
2:50	232 Fn. 117
2:51	74, 108, 283
3:1	18, 213
3:3	166, 177, 283
3:4	204
3:8	40, 51, 283
3:9	213
3:10	100 Fn. 28, 185, 187, 190
3:12	79, 131
3:13	283
3:14	XV, 68, 150
3:15	51, 83, 283
3:16	82
3:17	51, 108, 245, 248
3:18	XV, 94 Fn. 13, 100 Fn. 28, 202, 277, 283
3:19	131, 150, 213
3:20	51
3:21	38, 51, 97 Fn. 20, 100 Fn. 28
3:22	131, 141, 150, 219
3:23	139, 150

3:23–38	36
3:28	36
3:28–31	36
3:31	36
3:35	69
4	134
4–9	XXII
4:1	18, 19, 202, 283
4:2	36, 246, 283
4:3	231
4:4	226, 242
4:5	131, 150, 267, 283
4:5–8	266
4:6	XV, 150
4:7	51, 223
4:8	51, 68, 150, 228
4:9	51, 125, 150, 229
4:9–11	266
4:10	150
4:13	51, 108, 166, 177
4:14	XV, 109, 150, 284
4:15	78 Fn. 43, 277, 284
4:16	69, 79, 150, 212, 284
4:17	51, 139, 150, 204
4:18	52, 94 Fn. 13, 284
4:18–19	94 Fn. 13
4:19	52, 79, 277, 284
4:20	139, 150, 220, 284
4:21	28, 52, 150, 219
4:22	284
4:23	40–41, 52, 91, 109, 150, 204
4:24	150, 284
4:25	109, 139, 150, 186–187, 190, 284
4:26	52, 131, 150
4:27	25, 52, 107, 212, 268, 284
4:28	41, 52, 209
4:29	52, 131, 139, 151
4:30	52, 284
4:31	135, 139, 151
4:32	52, 134, 141, 151
4:33	164–165, 177, 209
4:35	52, 227 Fn. 92, 284
4:36	52, 109, 164–165, 167, 177, 209, 237 Fn. 14 –141, 284
4:37	284
4:38	102–103, 109, 177, 190–191, 284
4:39	52, 104, 131, 151, 284
4:40	109, 139, 151, 268, 284
4:41	109, 284
4:42	94 Fn. 13, 131, 151, 284
4:43	52, 94 Fn. 13, 134, 141, 151, 208
4:44	135 Fn. 89
5:1	100 Fn. 28, 109, 284
5:2	63, 109, 216, 282, 284
5:3	52, 100 Fn. 28, 214, 284
5:4	151, 284
5:5	25 Fn. 7, 80, 142, 148, 151, 216, 282, 285
5:6	285
5:7	109, 214, 285
5:8	134, 151
5:9	285
5:10	52, 166, 177, 218
5:12	XV, 52, 98 Fn. 24, 99, 141, 151, 184, 191, 206, 220, 277, 285
5:13	285
5:14	25 Fn. 7, 107, 268, 285
5:15	52, 109, 268, 285
5:16	97 Fn. 20, 135 Fn. 89, 151
5:17	52, 204, 271–272, 285
5:18	XV, 132, 151
5:19	52, 109, 132, 141, 151, 214, 271, 285
5:20	168, 177
5:22	146, 219
5:24	245, 285
5:25	109, 151, 285
5:26	151, 277
5:27	210, 285
5:28	91, 109, 139, 151
5:29	151, 270, 285
5:31	251
5:33	XV, 42, 52, 91, 93, 98 Fn. 24, 99, 109, 285
5:34	218
5:35	186–187, 191
5:36	151, 285
5:37	52, 151, 216–217, 221, 282
6	233

6:1 233 Fn. 120, 246, 285
6:4 109, 246, 285
6:7 109
6:8 91, 109, 146–147, 233 Fn. 120
6:10 52, 139, 143, 151, 233 Fn. 120
6:11 184, 191, 232 Fn. 117, 237 Fn. 140, 285
6:12 52, 97 Fn. 20, 135 Fn. 89, 280
6:13 139, 151
6:15 285
6:16 52
6:17 100 Fn. 28, 109, 285
6:18 XV, 52, 91, 100 Fn. 28, 102, 107, 109, 209, 233 Fn. 120
6:19 52, 139, 152
6:20 30 Fn. 18, 39, 52, 68–69, 92–93, 96–97, 109, 134, 201, 285
6:21 52, 93, 109
6:22 52, 109, 139, 152, 168, 177, 218, 246, 277, 285
6:23 89, 110, 170, 177, 210, 233 Fn. 120
6:24 18–19, 52
6:27 25 Fn. 7
6:28 52, 97 Fn. 20
6:29 52, 188, 191, 201, 204–205
6:30 285
6:32 125, 152, 201, 220
6:33 142, 152
6:34 142, 152
6:35 52, 68, 93, 110, 218, 277, 286
6:36 177
6:37 53
6:38 168, 177, 219, 286
6:39 53, 152, 286
6:40 53, 233 Fn. 120, 286
6:42 53, 220
6:43 79, 152
6:44 25 Fn. 7, 82, 286
6:45 5, 35 Fn. 22, 53, 94, 110, 177, 186 Fn. 144, 187, 191, 211, 233 Fn. 120, 246, 277, 286
6:47 91, 110, 233 Fn. 120, 286
6:48 53, 125, 142, 152, 233 Fn. 120
6:49 37, 53, 79, 152, 286
7:1 100 Fn. 28, 209
7:2 110, 134, 139, 152, 242
7:3 91, 110
7:4 134, 142, 152
7:7 25 Fn. 7, 217
7:8 53, 100 Fn. 28, 286
7:9 82, 212
7:10 53, 251
7:11 18, 83, 110, 183, 241, 286
7:12 24, 53, 71, 100 Fn. 28, 110
7:13 144–145, 148, 219
7:14 53, 139, 152
7:15 140, 148, 152, 286
7:16 100 Fn. 28, 152, 276, 286
7:17 53, 110, 286
7:18 53, 94 Fn. 13, 286
7:20 53, 74
7:21 267–268, 286
7:22 94 Fn. 13, 107, 169 Fn. 115, 222, 268, 286
7:23 41, 53, 187, 191, 204
7:24 184, 186 Fn. 145, 191
7:26 53, 76–77, 86
7:27 152
7:28 77
7:29 100 Fn. 28, 110
7:31 125, 152, 286
7:32 39, 53, 110, 152, 201, 237 Fn. 140–141, 286
7:33 42, 53, 152, 246 Fn. 169
7:35 218
7:36 286
7:37 214 Fn. 60, 271, 286
7:38 53, 110, 286
7:39 92–93, 110, 214 Fn. 60, 286
7:40 286
7:41 152, 184, 191
7:42 187, 191, 286
7:43 24, 53, 67, 286
7:44 53
7:45 30–31, 53, 244, 286

7:46	18	8:39	206, 288
7:47	287	8:40	54, 153, 201, 288
7:48	53, 187–188, 191	8:41	133, 139, 153, 236, 288
7:49	287	8:42	100 Fn. 28, 153
8:1	39, 53, 94–96, 110, 152, 202, 271–272, 287	8:43	54, 288
8:2	53, 175, 287	8:44	139, 153, 202, 288
8:2–3	175	8:45	76–77, 86, 142, 143, 148, 153, 288
8:3	53, 213, 274, 287	8:46	94 Fn. 13, 125, 142, 153, 239, 240
8:4	100 Fn. 28, 152	8:47	54, 100 Fn. 28, 139, 153
8:5	18, 53, 287	8:48	54, 239, 288
8:6	53, 89, 110, 142, 152, 255, 287	8:49	110, 210
8:7	89, 110, 206, 287	8:49–11:3	XVII
8:8	110, 132, 142, 152, 287	8:50	277, 288
8:9	53, 287	8:51	54, 167, 177, 288
8:10	53, 75, 287	8:52	125, 131, 142, 146, 153
8:12	222	8:53	54
8:13	54, 69, 142, 152, 222, 287	8:54	54, 219, 288
8:14	83, 168, 177, 277, 287	8:55	74, 125, 142, 153, 288
8:15	188–189, 191, 287	8:56	54, 288
8:16	25 Fn. 7, 54, 100 Fn. 28, 207, 216, 222, 287	9:1	18, 20, 245, 288
		9:2	268
8:17	80, 110, 287	9:4	217
8:18	169, 177, 287	9:5	54, 219
8:19	142, 153, 287	9:6	271–272, 288
8:21	287	9:7	54, 288
8:22	183, 241, 287	9:6	94 Fn. 13, 153
8:23	44, 54, 65, 153, 250, 287	9:8	111
8:24	94, 110, 288	9:10	54, 64, 153, 191, 204, 288
8:25	91, 110, 237 Fn. 140, 238	9:11	111, 289
8:26	288	9:12	142, 153, 271–272, 289
8:27	54, 68, 79, 142, 153, 288	9:13	54, 100 Fn. 28, 153
8:28	54, 94, 98 Fn. 24, 99, 100, 110, 139, 153, 218, 277, 288	9:14	45, 54
		9:16	111, 153, 289
8:29	54, 69, 164 Fn. 113, 209, 288	9:17	289
		9:18	83, 97 Fn. 20, 131, 153, 289
8:30	164 Fn. 113	9:19	210
8:31	35 Fn. 22, 288	9:20	153, 289
8:32	166, 177, 288	9:21	274 Fn. 224, 289
8:33	54, 288	9:22	24, 54, 111, 206, 277, 289
8:34	153, 177	9:23	18, 75–76, 154
8:35	142, 153, 288	9:24	54, 289
8:36	94 Fn. 13, 153	9:25	38, 54, 80, 125, 136, 148, 154, 202, 289
8:37	110, 153, 183, 288		
8:38	98 Fn. 24, 100 Fn. 28, 125, 131, 153, 288	9:26	94, 111, 147, 148 Fn. 110
		9:28	97 Fn. 20, 154, 289

9:29 54, 97 Fn. 20, 289
9:30 139–140, 154
9:31 134 Fn. 88, 289
9:31–32 135
9:32 289
9:33 191
9:34 91, 111, 154
9:36 164 Fn. 113, 289
9:37 111, 202
9:38 94, 98 Fn. 24, 99, 107, 111, 289
9:38–40 99
9:39 268–269, 289
9:40 98–99, 154
9:41 111, 248, 289
9:42 54, 154, 268–269, 282, 289
9:43 111, 277, 289
9:44 133, 134 Fn. 88, 154, 165, 177
9:45 54, 131, 133, 154
9:47 146, 154, 246
9:48 111
9:48–10:20 XVIII
9:49 91, 111, 289
9:50 289
9:51 30, 54, 289
9:52 183, 241
9:53 92–93, 111, 135 Fn. 89, 289
9:54 54, 139, 154
9:55 82, 289
9:55–56 81
9:56 25 Fn. 7
9:57 206, 289
9:58 169–170, 178, 206
9:59 45, 54, 154, 289
9:61 25 Fn. 7, 54, 289
10:1 18, 20, 289
10:2 54, 98–99, 134, 170, 204, 218
10:3 111
10:4 271, 290
10:5 74–75
10:6 290
10:6–14:22 XXI
10:7 111, 290
10:8 111
10:11 290
10:12 68, 79, 154
10:13 154, 290
10:15 L 94, 111, 142, 154
10:16 125, 154
10:17 290
10:18 290
10:19 54, 84, 111, 290
10:20 XXI, 54, 111, 134 Fn. 85, 142, 154, 290
10:21 38, 54, 111, 202, 290
10:22 55, 205
10:23 55, 93, 111, 166, 178
10:25 244, 246
10:27 29–30, 55, 111
10:28 89, 111, 205
10:30 183, 191
10:31 XXI, 125, 154
10:32 91, 111
10:33 144–145, 148, 154
10:34 55, 131, 154, 206
10:35 290
10:36 111
10:37 155
10:38 111, 271–272, 290
10:39 91, 92 Fn. 8, 111, 290
10:40 55, 89, 111, 290
10:41 91, 112
10:44 92 Fn. 8
11 XXIII–XXIV, 33, 117, 125, 130, 194
11:1 18, 20, 94, 96–97, 112, 290
11:2 XVIII, 97 Fn. 20, 280–281
11:4 25 Fn. 7
11:5 125, 155, 242
11:6 155
11:9–13 85
11:11 XXII–XXIII, 55, 92, 138, 148, 268
11:11b 117
11:11–12 1
11:11–26 119
11:12 XIV, XVII–XIX, XXI–XXII, XXIV, 33, 138, 148
11:12–14 33
11:12–26 XIII
11:13 XIV, XVI, XVIII–XXIV, 33, 83, 86, 120, 124, 155, 218

11:14	XIV, XVI, XVIII–XXII, 33, 120, 126–129, 148	11:42	68, 89, 112
11:14–26	9	11:43	262, 291
11:15	XIV, XVIII, XX–XXIII, 128–129, 198 Fn. 16	11:44	55, 92–93, 112, 255, 291
11:16	XV, XVII–XX, XXII–XXIII	11:45	246, 291
11:17	XIV, XVII–XXIII, 65, 124, 129, 138, 142, 146, 148–149, 155	11:45–12:6	XVIII
11:18	XIV, XVIII, XX–XXIII, 120, 124, 129, 132, 138, 155, 198 Fn. 16	11:46	89–90, 112, 208, 246, 255–256, 271, 282, 291
11:19	XIV–XV, XVII–XXIII, 124–125, 139, 155, 232 Fn. 116	11:47	252 Fn. 184, 291
11:20	XVIII, XXI–XXII, XXIV, 120, 155, 290	11:48	232 Fn. 117
11:21	XIV–XVI, XIX, XXII, XXIV, 120, 155, 274, 290	11:49	232 Fn. 116
11:22	XIV, XX, XXIII, 120, 124, 127 Fn. 72, 132, 155, 270	11:50	55, 291
11:23	XV, XVII, XX, XXII–XXIII, 127 Fn. 72, 290	11:51	80, 265 Fn. 203
11:24	XV, XVIII, XX–XXIII, 120, 127 Fn. 72, 129, 155, 290	11:52	291
11:25	XVIII, XXII–XXIII, 120, 124, 127 Fn. 72, 155, 290	11:53	100 Fn. 28, 291
11:25–24:53	XVII	11:54	55
11:26	XVIII, XXI–XXIII, 80, 112, 117, 121, 124, 127 Fn. 72, 148, 155, 205, 228–229, 290	12:1	237 Fn. 140 –141, 238, 291
11:27	XV, XIX, 55, 117 Fn. 60, 118, 121, 127 Fn. 72	12:2	79, 112
11:28	XIV, XVII–XVIII, XXII–XXIII, 41, 46, 55, 79, 118, 121, 204, 232 Fn. 117, 290	12:3	291
11:28–37	XXII	12:4	18
11:29	55, 121, 155, 290	12:5	245, 291
11:31	290	12:6	202
11:32	55, 290	12:7	25 Fn. 7, 55
11:33	291	12:8	166, 178
11:35	26, 55, 112	12:10	XXI
11:36	75 Fn. 39	12:11	291
11:37	55, 204	12:12	141, 291
11:38	187, 191, 291	12:15	55, 112, 245, 271, 274, 291
11:39	94, 112, 291	12:16	55
11:40	30, 55, 291	12:17	291
11:41	67	12:18	210, 262, 291
		12:19	204
		12:20	55, 291
		12:21	75 Fn. 39
		12:22	155, 232 Fn. 116
		12:27	80, 183, 191
		12:28	XXI, 291
		12:29	246, 291
		12:30	93, 112, 277, 291
		12:31	79, 291
		12:32	XV, 291
		12:33	55, 210–211, 274 Fn. 224, 291
		12:34	211
		12:35	82, 291
		12:36	112, 233
		12:37	92–93, 112
		12:37–59	XIII

12:38–13:1 9
12:44 274 Fn. 224
13 XXIII, 117, 130, 134, 194
13:1 94 Fn. 13, 291
13:2 5, 73, 214 Fn. 59, 292
13:4 167–168, 178
13:5 25 Fn. 7, 112
13:7 55, 112, 292
13:8 210, 292
13:9 292
13:11 268, 292
13:12 292
13:13 155, 276, 292
13:14 100 Fn. 28
13:15 112
13:16 XIV–XV, 112, 118, 124, 133, 137, 139, 148, 155
13:17 XVII, XXI–XXIII, 100 Fn. 28, 118, 121, 124, 147–148, 155, 277, 292
13:18 XVII, XX, XXII, 112, 118
13:19 XVII, XX, 89, 118, 121, 124, 156, 208
13:20 XVII, 76–77, 80, 86, 118
13:21 XVII, 118–119
13:22 XIV, 47, 118–119, 121, 124, 156, 271–272, 292
13:23 XIV, XVII, 112, 118, 121, 230
13:24 XX–XXII, XXIV, 5, 55, 104, 119, 121, 133, 223
13:25 XIV, XVII, XXIII, 292
13:26 XVII, 118 Fn. 63
13:27 XVII–XVIII, 55, 124, 218
13:28 XIV, XVII, 55, 112, 118, 121, 213, 292
13:29 XXI, XXIV, 118 Fn. 61, 292
13:30 XIV, XX, XXII, 121, 292
13:31 121, 134, 252 Fn. 184, 292
13:32 XVII, 118, 122, 124, 133, 156, 292
13:33 XV, 92–93, 112, 122, 124, 134
13:34 252 Fn. 184
13:35 112
14:1 18, 20, 292
14:3 246
14:4 55, 107, 139, 156, 292
14:5 112
14:7 18, 55, 156, 186–187, 191, 292
14:8 55
14:9 156, 169, 178, 205, 292
14:10 25 Fn. 7, 55, 65, 113, 292
14:12 25 Fn. 7, 55, 75 Fn. 40, 79, 113, 156, 232 Fn. 117, 255–257, 282, 292
14:13 113
14:14 178, 191, 256
14:15 113, 139, 156
14:16 113, 292
14:17 189, 292
14:18 292
14:19 292
14:21 113, 293
14:22 156
14:23 55, 209, 293
14:24 92–93, 113, 293
14:25 113
14:26 293
14:27 293
14:28 55, 241, 271, 293
14:29 293
14:29–16:4 XXI
14:30 293
14:31 293
14:33 271, 274, 293
14:35 18, 56, 293
15 134
15:1 214 Fn. 59, 293
15:2 56, 113, 186–188, 192, 214 Fn. 59
15:4 113, 241 Fn. 153, 293
15:5 56, 91, 113
15:6 113
15:7 56, 113, 134, 156
15:8 56, 156, 202, 270
15:9 56, 214 Fn. 59, 293
15:10 113
15:11 18, 139, 156
15:11–32 179
15:12 56
15:13 244, 293
15:14 156, 232 Fn. 117
15:15 XXI, 56, 113, 272, 293

15:16	156, 202
15:17	56, 113, 164, 178
15:18	139, 156
15:19	56
15:20	56, 132, 144–145, 156, 293
15:21	293
15:22	293
15:23	214
15:24	134, 156, 204
15:25	113, 169, 178, 210, 293
15:26	113, 156
15:27	56, 156, 214, 250–252
15:28	178
15:29	204, 293
15:30	25 Fn. 7, 30, 56, 104–105, 113, 156, 214, 272, 274, 293
15:31	75, 156, 269
15:32	56, 74, 137 Fn. 95, 204, 294
16	134
16:1	18, 20, 113, 206, 269, 274 Fn. 224
16:2	156, 294
16:3	79, 148, 294
16:4	56, 156
16:5	294
16:6	188, 192, 272, 294
16:7	56, 272, 294
16:8	76, 79, 169, 178, 218, 294
16:9	80, 113, 156
16:10	294
16:11	169, 178, 181, 192
16:11–23:1	XXI
16:12	294
16:13	167, 178, 208, 294
16:14	56, 255, 294
16:15	157, 294
16:16	94 Fn. 13, 204, 294
16:17	56, 113, 294
16:18	31, 56, 294
16:19	18, 204, 294
16:20	157, 294
16:21	25 Fn. 7, 102, 113, 139, 157, 294
16:22	56, 157
16:23	29, 56, 167, 178, 294
16:24	56, 134, 142, 148 Fn. 111, 157
16:25	56, 218, 294
16:26	157, 294
16:27	294
16:28	246, 294
16:29	56, 157, 208, 213
16:30	295
16:31	157
16:48	208
17:1	295
17:2	XXI, 18, 139, 157, 166, 178, 295
17:3	114
17:4	206, 295
17:6	114, 157, 202, 295
17:7	295
17:8	25 Fn. 7, 56, 114, 295
17:9	157, 295
17:10	185–186, 192
17:11	106, 114, 222
17:11–12	107
17:11–19	101
17:12	56, 272, 295
17:13	56, 142–143, 148, 157
17:14	157, 268, 295
17:15	157, 268, 276 Fn. 229, 277, 295
17:16	29, 48, 56, 94, 101–102, 114, 232 Fn. 117, 233, 295
17:18	255, 295
17:19	134, 157, 251 Fn. 183
17:20	27, 56, 295
17:21	295
17:22	56, 114, 218
17:23	157, 295
17:24	29, 57, 157
17:25	57, 295
17:26	57, 218
17:27	57, 205
17:30	187, 192, 295
17:31	57, 114, 139, 157, 295
17:33	57, 192
17:34	57, 223–224
17:35	57
17:37	295
18:1	97 Fn. 20, 157, 295
18:2	57, 295
18:3	57, 219

18:4	57, 295
18:5	241, 295
18:6	222
18:7	89, 114
18:8	XVIII, 18, 20, 57, 222, 295
18:9	295
18:10	97 Fn. 20, 157
18:11	97 Fn. 20
18:12	295
18:13	XVIII, 25 Fn. 7, 295
18:14	296
18:15	140, 157, 296
18:16	57, 178, 246
18:17	157, 246, 296
18:19	114
18:20	242, 246, 282, 296
18:22	49, 57, 183, 192, 211, 296
18:23	158, 201
18:24	114, 185, 192, 296
18:25	57
18:26	114
18:27	57
18:30	57, 82, 140, 158
18:31	XVIII, 82, 158, 296
18:32	187, 192
18:33	186 Fn. 145, 192
18:34	232 Fn. 117
18:36	158
18:37	192, 296
18:38	218
18:39	158, 218, 232 Fn. 117, 296
18:41	296
18:42	251 Fn. 183
18:43	18, 28, 57, 100 Fn. 28, 114, 247–248, 276 Fn. 229, 277, 296
19:1	296
19:2	83, 158, 296
19:3	296
19:4	114, 241, 296
19:5	57, 131, 158, 296
19:6	XXI, 296
19:7	XXI, 114, 206
19:8	57, 274 Fn. 224, 296
19:9	57, 133, 158, 296
19:10	57, 251 Fn. 183, 296
19:11	296
19:12	296
19:13	131, 158, 185, 186 Fn. 145, 192, 296
19:14	83, 255, 296
19:15	158
19:16	296
19:17	XXI, 246, 282, 296
19:18	57, 114
19:19	297
19:20	140, 158
19:21	134, 158, 216
19:22	57, 114, 125, 158, 216, 297
19:23	114, 297
19:24	79, 297
19:25	297
19:26	297
19:26–21:9	XV
19:26–21:29	162
19:27	58, 250, 252–253, 297
19:28	158, 297
19:29	XVIII, 58, 297
19:30	114, 217, 240, 272–273, 297
19:31	58, 158, 192, 297
19:32	58
19:33	50, 58
19:34	183, 192, 297
19:35	114, 183, 185, 186 Fn. 145, 192, 297
19:37	89, 114, 158, 277, 297
19:38	58, 297
19:39	297
19:40	297
19:41	158
19:42	68, 297
19:43	58, 134, 158, 297
19:44	XVIII, 208, 257–258, 282, 297
19:45	58, 297
19:46	97 Fn. 20, 158, 280
19:47	94, 100 Fn. 28, 114, 135 Fn. 89, 277, 297
19:48	100 Fn. 28, 114, 222
20:1	58, 94–95, 100 Fn. 28, 114
20:2	58
20:3	58, 222
20:5	206, 297
20:6	58, 68, 100 Fn. 28

20:8 158
20:9 XXI, 28, 58, 115, 233
20:10 158, 241, 272, 297
20:11 158, 297
20:12 298
20:13 58
20:14 58, 298
20:16 38, 58, 202, 230
20:17 298
20:18 132, 158, 298
20:19 100 Fn. 28, 115, 133, 158, 298
20:20 58, 82, 158, 188, 192, 298
20:21 25 Fn. 7, 58, 89, 115, 221–222, 298
20:23 115
20:24 58
20:25 58, 125, 158, 298
20:26 XX, 100 Fn. 28, 298
20:27 69, 140, 158
20:28 58, 159, 298
20:29 58, 102, 115, 298
20:31 115, 159, 183, 192, 298
20:32 298
20:34 58, 115, 159, 218
20:35 58, 115, 298
20:36 159, 218, 223, 298
20:37 58, 213, 298
20:38 159, 222, 298
20:39 185, 186 Fn. 145, 192
20:41 131, 159, 202
20:44 159, 183, 192
20:45 100 Fn. 28
20:46 58, 115, 262, 298
20:47 58, 97 Fn. 20, 98, 298
20:64 222
21:1 83, 210, 262, 264, 266, 298
21:2 58, 76, 115, 214
21:3 68, 216, 228
21:4 58, 115, 272, 274, 298
21:5 30–31, 59, 187, 192, 262–264, 298
21:6 XXI, 76
21:7 XXI, 71, 242, 298
21:8 59, 159, 298
21:8–30 XIV
21:9 25 Fn. 7, 115, 298
21:10 115
21:12 159, 299
21:13 299
21:14 59, 255, 259–260, 282, 299
21:15 59, 223
21:17 299
21:18 159, 222
21:19 277, 299
21:20 59, 299
21:21 115
21:22 134, 159, 299
21:23 XX, 59, 100 Fn. 28
21:24 59, 299
21:25 59, 223, 299
21:26 125, 159, 255, 258–259, 282, 299
21:27 59, 159, 299
21:28 159
21:29 159, 299
21:30 XX, 299
21:31 59, 75, 115, 159, 222
21:32 115, 222, 299
21:33 222–223
21:34 XX, 59, 115, 159, 299
21:35 59, 115
21:36 59, 98
21:37 125, 159, 299
21:38 100 Fn. 28
22:1 210
22:2 XV, 94, 100 Fn. 28, 115, 252 Fn. 184
22:4 277, 299
22:5 59, 299
22:6 XVIII, XX, 245
22:7 XVIII, 137
22:8 XX
22:9 299
22:10 91, 115, 210, 299
22:11 XVIII, 159, 210, 272, 275–276, 300
22:12 204, 263, 300
22:13 140, 159
22:15 59, 131, 159
22:16 209, 300
22:17 159, 300
22:18 159, 248, 300
22:19 59, 75 Fn. 39, 300
22:20 XVIII, 75 Fn. 39

22:21	300
22:22	XX, 41, 59, 115, 204
22:23	XVIII, 115, 134 Fn. 88, 232 Fn. 117, 300
22:24	59, 80
22:25	XVIII, XXI, 206, 227
22:26	178
22:27	71
22:30	166, 178, 212
22:31	XX, 59, 115, 159, 188, 192, 300
22:32	98 Fn. 24, 99, 115, 300
22:34	59, 300
22:36	25 Fn. 7, 59
22:37	209
22:39	300
22:39–24:11	XVII
22:40	97 Fn. 20, 159, 300
22:41	38, 97 Fn. 20, 205
22:42	59, 232
22:43	59, 159
22:44	97 Fn. 20, 132, 160, 300
22:45	97 Fn. 20, 140, 160, 249, 250, 280, 282, 300
22:46	97 Fn. 20, 160, 300
22:47	XX, 59, 160, 178, 193, 300
22:49	160, 178, 214, 300
22:50	59, 277, 300
22:52	185, 186 Fn. 145, 193, 277, 300
22:53	59, 255, 260–261, 300
22:54	59, 160, 183, 193, 277, 300
22:55	160, 181, 183, 193, 301
22:56	60, 131, 160, 185, 193, 301
22:57	89, 115, 301
22:58	60
22:59	301
22:60	160, 301
22:61	301
22:63	160, 230, 301
22:64	60, 210, 301
22:65	60, 89–90, 116, 210
22:66	100 Fn. 28, 160, 187–188, 193, 208, 278, 301
22:68	186–187, 193
22:69	116
22:70	160, 183, 193, 301
22:71	301
23:1	160, 183, 193, 301
23:2	60, 68, 301
23:3	80, 301
23:4	60, 278, 301
23:5	100 Fn. 28, 133, 160, 206, 301
23:6	301
23:7	188, 193, 301
23:8	135 Fn. 89, 301
23:9	125, 160, 232 Fn. 117, 301
23:10	250, 278, 301
23:11	160, 301
23:12	237 Fn. 140, 301
23:13	100 Fn. 28, 140, 160, 278, 302
23:14	60, 71, 100 Fn. 28, 160, 302
23:15	160, 302
23:16	302
23:18	60, 100 Fn. 28, 140, 160, 302
23:19	302
23:20	60, 302
23:21	302
23:22	133, 160, 302
23:23	60, 137, 140, 160, 302
23:23–35	XXIII
23:24	302
23:25	140, 160, 302
23:26	160, 302
23:26–49	20
23:27	100 Fn. 28, 302
23:28	160, 302
23:29	255, 302
23:30	60, 160
23:31	60, 134, 161
23:32	140, 161
23:33	161, 302
23:34	302
23:35	60, 100 Fn. 28, 161, 303
23:36	71, 161, 185, 193, 303
23:37	82, 303
23:38	161
23:39	60, 91, 116, 303
23:40	71, 134, 161, 303
23:41	161, 303
23:43	71

23:44 303
23:45 250, 303
23:47 60, 161, 164, 276
23:48 60, 140, 161, 222, 303
23:49 30–31, 60, 161, 169, 303
23:51 161, 303
23:52 255, 303
23:53 60, 161
23:54 60
23:55 25 Fn. 7, 173–174, 202–303
23:56 140, 161, 303
24:1 161, 303
24:3 75 Fn. 39
24:4 303
24:5 60, 140, 161, 303
24:6 75 Fn. 39, 125, 134, 161, 304
24:7 161
24:8 60, 204
24:9 18, 161
24:10 60, 161, 173–176, 193, 204, 304
24:11 60, 133, 161, 175–176, 250, 304
24:11–39 XXIII
24:12 75 Fn. 39
24:13 60, 272–273, 304
24:14 202, 237 Fn. 140, 304
24:15 79, 304
24:16 60
24:17 60, 125, 161, 230, 237 Fn. 140–141, 304
24:18 61, 91, 116, 125, 161, 188, 193, 304
24:19 100 Fn. 28, 167, 171, 176, 178, 184, 188, 193, 304
24:19c 170
24:20 278, 304
24:21 134 Fn. 88, 140, 161, 166–167, 169, 178, 212
24:22 25 Fn. 7, 61, 116, 304
24:23 116
24:24 61, 116, 304
24:25 61, 161, 204, 232 Fn. 117, 304
24:26 171
24:27 89, 116, 304
24:28 69, 186, 188, 193, 272–273, 304
24:29 304
24:30 162, 202, 304
24:31 91, 116, 304
24:31–32 71
24:32 140, 237 Fn. 140–141, 304
24:33 61, 116, 162, 304
24:34 134, 162
24:35 304
24:36 18, 75 Fn. 39
24:37 162, 305
24:38 305
24:39 35, 61, 92–93, 116, 134, 162, 305
24:40 75 Fn. 39, 202
24:41 162, 305
24:42 226, 305
24:43 61, 140, 162
24:44 162
24:45 61, 245
24:46 116
24:47 61, 116, 305
24:49 69, 278, 305
24:50 61, 116, 162, 305
24:51 75 Fn. 39
24:52 75 Fn. 39
24:53 278, 305

John XIII–XXIII, 10, 12, 50, 65, 224, 238, 273
4:33 237 Fn. 140
5:36 227
5:44 237 Fn. 140
6:43 237 Fn. 140
6:53 237 Fn. 140
7:30 246
7:31 229
7:36 242
7:44–8:12 162
8:12 18 Fn. 28
8:20 265 Fn. 204
10:29 229
11:56 237 Fn. 140
11:57 278 Fn. 232
13:14 238 Fn. 142
13:22 237 Fn. 140
13:35 237 Fn. 140
15:3 226

15:12 237 Fn. 140
15:17 237 Fn. 140
15:21 278 Fn. 232
16:6 249 Fn. 176
16:17 237 Fn. 140
16:20 249 Fn. 176
16:21 249 Fn. 176
16:22 249 Fn. 176, 278 Fn. 232
16:23 227 Fn. 93
16:24 237 Fn. 140
17:8 232 Fn. 117
17:21 232 Fn. 117
18:3 278 Fn. 232
18:15 278 Fn. 232
18:39 66
19:6 278 Fn. 232
20:9 137 Fn. 96
21:7 13

Acts XIV, XXI
17:16 104
28:3–6 84

Romans
6:9 227 Fn. 90

1 Corinthians
1:27 147 Fn. 105
6:9 104

Ephesians 271
4:8 85

Revelation XXI

Pater ecclesiae

Ambrose
In psalmum enarrationes
36.12.2 132
102 182 fn. 140
Expositio Lucanum 130
8.60 143 fn. 102
320.703 143 fn. 102
De viduis
10.63 128 fn. 74

Ambrosiaster
In epistulam comm. Romanos CSEL
81.1.177 72 Fn. 28

Augustine of Hippo
confessiones
3.4.7 234 Fn. 122
De civitate dei
21.9 250 Fn. 179
De doctrina christiana 4, 197
2.15.22 4 Fn. 5
2.16.23 106 Fn. 53
2.22; PL 34.46 73 Fn. 32
In psalmos enarrationes
48.1.12.9 148
75.14 135
Epistulae
149.13.1.11–13 98
Quaestiones Numerorum
241.276 182 Fn. 140
242.309 182 Fn. 140
242.325 182 Fn. 140
Opere monachorum
16 (ed. Zycha) 148 Fn. 109
Psalmus contra partem Donati
97.1.17 140
138.20 234 Fn. 123
354.3 140
PL 1372
Sermones 172
4.265 148 Fn. 109
58.1 98, 98 Fn. 25
82.14 258 Fn. 192
105.4.6 92
105.6 85 Fn. 67
111.2 172 Fn. 121
232 172 Fn. 121
236 172 Fn. 121
332.4 258 Fn. 192
359A9 148 Fn. 109
De symbol sermo ad catechumenos
14 92

Cyprian of Carthage
Ad Fortunatum de exhortatione 196
Ad Quirinum 196
1.22 204 Fn. 34
2.6 204 Fn. 34
9.95 204 Fn. 34
Epistulae 100, 196
63.15 147 Fn. 108
Sermones 100

Cyprianus Gallus *see Pseudo-Cyprian*

Didymus
De spiritus sancto
PG 9, 1078A= 232 SC 386, 352–354 84 Fn. 61

Eusebius of Caesarea
Chronicon 179
Onomasticon
64.9–20 106–107
Praeparatio evangelica
8.14 84 Fn. 56

Hesychius of Jerusalem
PG 93.1058c–d 279 Fn. 239
PG 93.1059b 279 Fn. 239

Hieronymus *see Jerome*

Irenaeus
Adversus haeresis 137 Fn. 93
3.12.14 70 Fn. 13

Isidore of Sevilla
Etymologiarum 216
10.55 251 Fn. 181
15.2.11 273 Fn. 221
Quaestiones 135
30.24 135
Quaestiones Leviticus
12.1; PL 83.330a 279 Fn. 240
79; PL 34.170 279 Fn. 242

Jerome
Adversus Pelagianos
2.12 169 Fn. 116
1065 cc 305 127 Fn. 74
23.547 169 Fn. 116
26.233 172 Fn. 122
Chronicum praef.
2 179 Fn. 133–13, 180 Fn. 135–136
Commentarii in Esaiam
9:28, CC 73.360 169 Fn. 116
Epistulae
21.4f. 179
27 180 Fn. 137
72 73 Fn. 31
108.19.6 102 Fn. 32
Hom. Ps.
CC 78.275 169 Fn. 116
Praefatio in evangelistas ad Damasum
6–10.13–16 180 Fn. 138

Origen
In lucam homiliae
7 172 Fn. 122

Pseudo-Augustine
Speculum 92
27 83 Fn. 51

Pseudo-Cyprian
Heptateuchos
3.203–205 279 Fn. 241
Rebabtismate
9 172 fn. 121

Tertullian
Adversus Marcionem
3.18.8–10 101 Fn. 31
4.12 96 Fn. 17
4.14.13 92 Fn. 11, 134 Fn. 87
4.15 189 Fn. 147
4.19.1 275 Fn. 227
4.26.11 129 Fn. 79
4.27 256 Fn.189
4.27.3 67 Fn. 9
4.28.6 141 Fn. 101
4.28.7 141 Fn. 101
4.35.11 279 Fn. 24
Apologeticum
26.2 279 fn. 243

48 96 fn. 17
De carne Christi
12 96 fn. 17
De cultu feminarum
1.1 227 fn. 90
De exhortatione castitatis
13.1 279 fn. 243
De idolatria
185, CC 2.1119 169 fn. 117
4.39.3 253 fn. 187
De monogamia
17.3 279 fn. 243
De oratione
189 fn. 147
De praescriptione haereticorum
40.5 279 fn. 243
De pudicitia
227 fn. 90
De carnis resurrectione
22.5–6 258 fn. 194

Index scriptorum Graecorum et Romanorum

Alexander Aphrosidias
103 Fn. 35
De febris libellus 103 Fn. 35

Alexander of Tralles 103
Therapeutica
6.1.407.1–10 103 Fn. 39

Ammianus Marcellinus
104
24.7.3 104 Fn. 44

Apuleius
Herbarium
25.3 214 Fn. 58

Aristotle
Metaphysica
3.1000b (DK 31b109)
84

Beda
De orthographia I 208 Fn. 47

Bellum Hispanicum 244
36.2 244 Fn. 163

Boethius 199

Caesar 225, 241, 244, 280
Bellum civile
2.5 251 Fn. 182
3.39.1 230 Fn. 103
3.94.5 241 Fn. 156
Bellum gallicum
1.1.4 234 Fn. 125
1.3.7 236 Fn. 131
1.21.1 225 Fn. 85
1.48.1 225 Fn. 86
1.53 251 Fn. 180
2.18.6 236 Fn. 129
3.14 239 Fn. 149
5.44.14 236 Fn. 132
6.17.4 263 Fn. 199

Cassiodorus 19
Expositio in Psalterium
137
BNF lat. 14491 19 Fn. 32

Cassius Felix XV, 103 Fn. 41
142.15 103 Fn. 41
149.9 103 Fn. 35

Celsus 103–104
De medicina 103 Fn. 35
2.15.1 103 Fn. 41
3.3–17 103 Fn. 35
3.5.3 103 Fn. 40
3.8 104 Fn. 43
4.14 103 Fn. 35
5.28.18b 103, 103 Fn. 41

Cicero 14–15, 96, 179, 211 Fn. 53, 230–231, 234, 280
Atticus
9.6.3 230 Fn. 106
Brutus
132 230 Fn. 102
In Catilinam
3.10 251 Fn. 180
De Finibus
1.18 230 Fn. 104
Pro Murena
1.1 280
De Officiis
1.19.1 230 Fn. 105
De Optimo genere oratorum
14 179 Fn. 132
De Oratore
48.159 211 Fn. 53
De re publica (Cod.) 14
Sestius
68 235 Fn. 126

Consentius 30

Corpus Iuris Ciuilis 275
1.20.4 275 Fn. 228
4.6.37 275 Fn. 228

Dionysius of Halicarnassus 278

Donatus 199

Ennius 228–229
Tragoediae
41 R^{2-3} 229 Fn. 97

Epictetus
Dissertationes
1.24.1–2 119

Flavius Caper 209, 211
De orthographia
93.6 211 Fn. 53
105.17–18 209 Fn. 50

Florus 237
Vergilius orator an poeta
1.5 237 Fn. 137

Fronto
De differentiis vocabulorum
523 252 Fn. 185

Galen
Ad Glauconem de Methodo Medendi
11.57 269 Fn. 212

Herodotus
4.41 238 Fn. 147

Horace 226
Ars Poetica
108 250 Fn. 177
110 250

Inscriptionum Latinarum Collectio
2627 228 Fn. 95

Isidore
Etymologiae
10.55 251 Fn. 181
17.9.105 216
15.2.11 273 Fn. 221

Josephus 105–106, 105 Fn. 49–50, 279
Antiquitates Iudaicae 105 Fn. 49
6.11.359 279 Fn. 245
7.382 279 Fn. 245
7.393 279 Fn. 245
7.56 279, 279 Fn. 245
11.120 263 Fn. 200
18.1 264 Fn. 201
12.58 263 Fn. 200
12.78 264 Fn. 201
20.6 279 Fn. 245
20.118 105 Fn. 48
20.131 279 Fn. 245
20.162 279 Fn. 245
20.181 279 Fn. 245
20.194 279 Fn. 245
20.198 279 Fn. 245

20.205 279 Fn. 245
20.207 279 Fn. 245
20.208 279 Fn. 245
20.224 279 Fn. 245
20.227 279 Fn. 245
20.231 279 Fn. 245
Bellum Iudaicum 105 Fn. 49
1.26 279 Fn. 245
1.31 279 Fn. 245
1.33 279 Fn. 245
1.53 279 Fn. 245
1.68 279 Fn. 245
1.109 279 Fn. 245
1.152–153 279 Fn. 245
1.562 279 Fn. 245
1.573 279 Fn. 245
2.232 105 Fn. 48
2.413 264 Fn. 201
3.52 266 Fn. 208

Juvenal
1.4.66–67 231 Fn. 109

Juvencus 197
Euangeliorum libri 262

Lactantius 197

Livy
1.20.5–7 278 Fn. 233
2.10.9 236 Fn. 132
6.28.1 236 Fn. 129
8.17.1 244 Fn. 164
9.43.17 237 Fn. 134
34.50.1 148
38.55.11 269 Fn. 215

Lucan
7.177 237 Fn. 136

Mulomedicina Chironis
243
9.3 243 Fn. 161
10.10 243 Fn. 161
416 238 Fn. 146

Ovid
Tristia
3.1 148

Peregrinatio Aetheriae
244, 273
5.11 244 Fn. 165
7.7 273 Fn. 220

Petronius 98–99, 215
Satyricon 215
39.5–6 215 Fn. 63

Philo
De gigantibus
9 84 Fn. 57

Plato
Gorgias
526d–e 119
Phaedo
99b 239 Fn. 147

Plautus 225–228, 241, 243
Captivi
825 228 Fn. 96
1019 225 Fn. 84
Curculio
1.2.55 227 Fn. 94
Epidicus
728 280
Miles gloriosus 80
1269 280
Persa
4.3 225 Fn. 83
Rudens 241 Fn. 155
904 241 Fn. 155
Truculentus
4.14 225 Fn. 84
5.24 243 Fn. 162

Pliny the Younger 103
Naturalis historia
2.101 135
2.94 148
7.170 –172 103 Fn. 37
22.115 103 Fn. 37

26.17 103 Fn. 37

Priscian 199, 236
institutiones grammaticae
17.141 236 Fn. 130

Quintilian 206, 218
Institutio oratoria 256
1.7.5 206 Fn. 40
1.7.7–8 206 Fn. 44
8.3.77–80 256 Fn. 190
9.4.40 219 Fn. 76

Scribonius Largus 103
Compositiones
97.1 103 Fn. 38
Epistulae
7.19.2–3 103 Fn. 38

Sedulius
Paschale opus
4 143 Fn. 103
266.13 143 Fn. 103

Seneca 136, 136 Fn. 91
Ad Marcinam de consolatione
6.5.1 280
Epistulae morales ad Lucilium
14.6 103 Fn. 41

Strabo 84
11.8.4 84
15.3.15 84

Suetonius
Divus Augustus
30 273 Fn. 219

Tacitus
Annales
3.72 263 Fn. 199
Agricola
6.1 237 Fn. 135

Terence 225
Andria
2.1.10 230 Fn. 100
Heautontimorumenos
2.2 242
4.1.36–37 230 Fn. 101
4.1.39 225 Fn. 84

Varro 203, 207
De Lingua Latina
5.23–24 207 Fn. 45
5.83 278 Fn. 234
7.96 203 Fn. 31

Vegetius 243
Ars veterinaria sive mulomedicina
1.3–4 243 Fn. 160
49.19 243 Fn. 161

Velius Longus 217, 219
De orthographia
54.1–5 219 Fn. 76
61.16–62.2 208 Fn. 46
57.6–8 217 Fn. 69

Vergil
Aenaeis 85
1.278–279 85 Fn. 68
6.124 280
Georgica 85
2.498 85 Fn. 68

Vitruvius 257
1.6.1 273 Fn. 219
1.6.8 273 Fn. 219
1.6.12 273 Fn. 219
6.5.3 257 Fn. 191

Xenophon
De republica Lacedaemoniorum
10.4 238 Fn. 147

Corpus Inscriptionum Latinarum
1.168 218 Fn. 75
1.170 241 Fn. 152
1^2.3 74 Fn. 36
1^2.1012 231. Fn. 109
1^2.593 206 Fn. 39
2.2633 238 Fn. 143
4.202 218 Fn. 72

4.275	241 Fn. 152
4.960	218 Fn. 71
4.1173	220 Fn. 78
4.1824	206 Fn. 38
4.1860	205 Fn. 37
4.1860	206 Fn. 41
4.1880	205 Fn. 37, 206 Fn. 42
4.2013	206 Fn. 43
4.2400	206 Fn. 38
4.3129	215 Fn 64
4.3702	231 Fn. 107
4.7838	218 Fn. 70
6.641	215 Fn 64
6.975	273 Fn. 219
6.1287	218 Fn. 74
10.8249	218 Fn. 75
13.1668	223 Fn. 80
14.2977	228 Fn. 95
14.3679	211 Fn. 52

Index Rerum

Abbey 81
- Beuron VII, 195
- Chur 87, 116, 124, 129f., 194
- St. Gall VII, XVI
- Tech-Molling XXII
- Vercelli VII, XIII, 1f., 7, 9, 17, 27, 86–88, 117, 123, 163, 176, 190

ablative 13, 27, 43, 104, 165, 167, 183, 218f., 225–229, 240–244
- absolute 129
- instrumental 27
- graecism 260
- locative 167, 183
- of gerund 243–245

accusative 13, 146, 148, 165, 181–183, 219, 225–227, 231, 238 Fn. 144, 240f.

allograph, *see paelography*

allography (of dental occlusives) 205f.

Ambrose of Milan 98, 130, 132, 143 Fn. 102, 169, 196

aramaic 198 Fn. 16

architecture 261–267
- altar 265
- architectural terminology 262f., 266f.
- door 104
- house 4, 102, 190, 197, 236, 257
- pinnacle of the temple 266, 267 Fn. 209
- synagogue 78 Fn. 43, 262
- temple 107
- temple of Jerusalem 262, 263, 264, 266

aspirate sound 89, 90, 106, 204, 207, 210, 213f.

assimilation 66, 73, 75, 130, 167, 175, 208

Augustine of Hippo XVII, 4, 73, 83, 85, 92, 98, 100, 106 Fn. 53, 132, 135, 140, 148, 172, 182, 197, 233, 234, 258, 279

Augustus 200

bilingual XVI, 70–72, 127, 143, 229

Caelius Aurelianus XV, 176 Fn. 126

Caesar 81, 225, 239 Fn. 148, 241, 263 Fn. 199, 280

Caesarea 81, 106

Caesarean text 81

calques 94, 214, 254f., 261f., 276

capitula see paleography

cases 86, 88, 90, 92, 96, 98, 103, 105, 117, 119, 122f., 126, 132, 134, 136, 141, 143, 149, 162, 165, 181–184, 186, 195–187, 199f., 202, 204, 207f., 209, 212, 216, 220, 222, 225–229, 232–234, 239–241, 244, 246, 251, 257, 260, 262, 265, 270, 275, 278, 282

Christian Latin, *see translation*

Celsus 103, 104 Fn. 43, 148

(Special) Christian language 197f.

Christology 101, 170, 197

Church fathers 5, 83, 87, 92, 106f., 130, 134, 196, 250

Cicero 14, 15, 96, 179, 197, 211 Fn. 53, 230, 231, 234, 280

Claudius Aelianus 67

Clemens of Rome 195, 197

Codex
- bifolia 1, 9, 28
- *Alexandrinus* 63, 68, 70, 126, 129, 197
- *Amiatinus* XIII–XIV, XX, 15, 37, 88, 163, 179–194, 223, 249, 276
- *Ardmachanus* XIV, XIX, XX, XXII
- *Aureus* XIVf., XX, XXII, 83, 162
- *Bezae* VL5 XVI, XX, 67, 73, 75, 77, 92, 123, 130, 134, 140, 163, 164, 194, 195, 201, 203 Fn. 32, 206, 216, 217, 218, 221, 222, 225, 229, 232, 237, 244
- *Bezae* D, 05 26, 63, 66, 69–80, 82, 83, 123, 125, 127, 129, 136, 138, 140, 141, 142, 143, 173, 201, 278
- *Brixianus* XVIII, 5, 23, 32, 87, 127, 128, 147, 162, 196, 201
- *Claromontanus* XXI, 201
- *Colbertinus* XV, XVI, XVII, XIX, XXIII, 127, 162, 175
- *Corbeiensis secundus* XV, XVII, XVIII, XIX, XXI–XXIII, 23, 35 Fn. 22, 41, 87, 162f., 201, 232, 276, 280, 281
- *Fragmenta Curiensia* XIII, XVI, XVII, XX–XXIII, 3, 7, 9, 10, 11, 13, 15 Fn. 26, 17, 33, 46, 83, 86–87, 116–122, 125–130, 132–133, 137, 146–147, 149, 163, 194, 198, 229, 270, 276

https://doi.org/10.1515/9783111142531-011

- *Fragmenta Sangallensia* VII, 9, 163
- *Gatianus* XX, 230
- *Gigas* XX, XXI
- *Liber moliensis* XV, XXII
- *Monacensis* XV, XXII, XXIII, 5, 162, 196, 276
- *Palatinus* XVI, XVII, 4, 7, 19, 32, 34, 36, 41, 48, 63, 87–98, 100–127, 129, 130, 132f., 137, 140, 144, 163, 164, 167, 184, 188, 193, 194, 196, 201, 206, 212, 216 Fn. 66, 218, 221, 222, 224, 233, 238, 242, 244, 246, 253, 254, 263, 267, 270, 275f.
- *Perpinianensis* XXII
- *Rehdigeranus* XV, XXI–XXIII, 139, 162, 276
- *Sangallensis* XIII, XVI–XVII, 96, 117, 206
- *Sangermanensis primus* XIX
- *Sangermanensis secundus* XIX
- *Usserianus primus* XXIII, 129, 146, 162
- *Veronensis* XV, XVIII, 276
- *Vindobonensis* XXV, 36, 180, 202, 233, 235, Fn. 511 241

codicology XVII, 81
comperative
adverbs in a positive sense 141, 214, 228f.
compounds 3, 208, 222f., 282
Coniugatio periphrastica 138
Cyprian of Carthage XVII, 4f., 72, 98, 100, 136, 147, 170, 172, 182, 196f., 204, 231 Fn. 114, 238, 271
Cyprian Gallus 279

dative 13, 69, 127, 216, 218, 225f., 228
- instead of accusative 182
- predicative 73, 168
- reference 69

deponent 249
demon XVI, XXIIf., 52, 125–128, 153, 176, 204
- beelzebub XX–XXIII, 198 also Fn. 16
- unclean spirit 85

devoicing 175
diminutive 63, 214

education, Roman 199, 233
Entphonologisierung, see loss of aspirates
Entsonorisierung, see devoicing
Erasmus 83, 247
Eusebian
- Canon XXIII, XX, 17, 163
- section numbers XV, XVI, XVIII

Eusebius of Caesarea 106f., 179
Eusebius of Vercelli XIII, 7, 9, 17f., 21
exorcisms XVI, 103, 127, 129, 198 Fn. 16

future tense 67, 134f., 138, 186, 205 Fn. 36, 221–224, 241f., 257, 264, 282

genitive 27, 36, 135 Fn. 89, 217, 218, 228f., 241
- instead of ablative 225–228, 260
- of comparison 228
- replaced with de or ex 225, 227

gerund, *see ablative*
glossaries 71, 128, 129, 163, 170
God 20, 77, 84, 85, 97, 99, 101, 135, 146, 198 Fn. 16, 226, 235, 244, 248, 280
- deity 198 Fn. 19, 280
- god-fearing 20
- predication 66, 240–241, 244
- worship 4, 78 Fn. 43, 106, 197, 266

gods
- household gods 84

Graecism 175, 254f., 259f., 261

handwriting 2
haplography 24
Hebrew XIV, XXIII, 47, 85, 106, 138, 195, 209, 211–214, 238f., 242 Fn. 158, 262, 270 Fn. 217
healing 99, 102, 104f., 127, 247
Hilary of Poitiers 4f., 196f.
homoeoarcton 66
holy spirit 85, 172, 184, 235
hypercorrection 41, 184, 204, 209, 218–220, 282

Ignatius of Ephesus 195
illness 102f., 128, 267f.
imaging
- multi-spectral 1, 2, 9, 12, 23, 37, 38, 41, 42, 44, 46, 47, 49, 51–61, 163, 259, 260
- TX-Image 2, 25, 26, 27, 228
- VIS-Image 2

imperative 35, 119, 242f.
Imperial era 218, 226, 280
Imperial decree 280
indirect Speech 137 Fn. 96
infinitive 74, 119, 134, 136, 148, 184, 235, 242–245

inscription 74, 81, 202f., 205–207, 210, 218, 223, 228, 231, 238
insertion 11, 49, 66

Jerome XIV, XV, XVIII Fn. 14, 70, 72f., 107, 169, 172 Fn. 122, 179f., 182 Fn. 140, 189, 190, 208
Jerusalem XIV, 66, 81, 101, 106, 184, 229, 235, 257, 263, 266f., 279
Jesus Christ 20, 35f., 63, 66f., 81f., 96, 99, 101f., 104–106, 127, 129, 135, 170–172, 176, 188, 190, 198, 226, 229, 231f., 235f. 242, 248f., 257, 262, 263f., 266f., 269, 275
Justin Martyr 70, 195
Justinian 81

Lactantius 197
lacuna XIII–XV, XVIII, XXII, XXIII, 8, 27, 36, 37, 100, 147, 162
ligature 13, 15
loan-translation, *see calques*
loan-words 94, 198, 209, 210, 215, 246, 261f., 264, 282
– Christian terms 5, 93, 189
– cultural borrowings 270
– Jewish terms 264
loss of aspirates 89f., 201, 207, 214, 220, 226, 240
language
– rural 203
– literary register 99, 197, 228, 249, 282
– oral 167, 194
later hand XVI
Lucifer of Cagliari XV

measure 12, 28, 270
medicine 267–269
– folk 103
– rational 103
– Imperial 103f., 267
– veterinary 243
mixed-texts XIV, XIX, XX, XXII, 163, 195f.
mode 186, 219
monophthongization XXII, 26, 41, 203, 281
morphology 5, 108, 134, 214–224, 282
– word formation 214f., 255, 281
– declension 215–219, 225
– conjugation 135, 138, 139, 168, 186, 219, 220–224, 282

nasal consonats 13, 29, 204, 211 Fn. 53, 218
neuter 215–217, 231, 238, 282
– as neuter singular 43
nexus 13
Nomina sacra XXI, 13, 21, 24, 34, 37
North Africa 4, 15, 100f., 169f., 195, 197
Novatian 4, 197

orality 167, 194
orthography XIX, 30, 34, 88f., 103, 122, 197, 199–204, 207, 209–211, 213

paleography VII, 12–17, 20, 23f., 28, 30, 126
– allograph 13–15
– abbreviations XV, XVII, XIX, XX, 13, 19, 21, 24, 34
– *capitula* XIII–XIX, XXII, 17
– cauda 16f., 167
– cursive script XXIII, 16
– ekthesis 12, 24, 30
– hair stroke 16, 17
– initials 12
– letters (gold, silver, red, black) XIV–XXIII, 1
– letter (size) 10, 11, 12, 13, 24
– letters, cursive 11
– letters, capital 24
– ligatures 13, 15
– *litterae notabiliores* 12, 24, 30, 31
– ommission signs 11
– *rasura* 11
– rustic capitals 15, 16
– scriptio continua 16
– signature, quire 10, 11, 12
– shadow stroke 16, 17
– spatia 12, 13, 133
– superlines 29
– suspensions 29
– text block 8
– uncial XIV, XX, XXI, XXIII, 11, 12, 13, 15, 16, 23, 72, 86, 126, 163
– upper and lower bows 15, 17
palimpsest XXI, 14, 15
papyrus 19, 63–65, 67, 72, 86

paratext 3, 17–21, 24, 29, 37
- *Chresimon* 19
parchment XIV, XVI–XXIII, 3, 8f., 11, 23–25, 28f., 33, 42, 50, 117, 162
Pope Gregory II 179
Pope Damasus I 179f.
parallelism membrorum 84
participial construction 127, 129, 148
- Greek aorist 36, 137, 138, 143, 168, 186, 220, 221, 243, 244
- Latin imperfect 118, 127, 135, 137, 138, 148, 185, 186, 222, 241
- Latin perfect XVI, 31, 36, 138, 168, 185, 186, 220, 223, 241, 242, 282
- Latin present 138, 241
- Latin future 67, 134, 135, 138, 186, 221, 222–224, 241f., 282
- *See also deponent verbs*
passive voice 127, 138, 186, 219, 220, 280, 282
patristic citations 245
periphrastic constructions 135, 138, 226, 282
Philo of Alexandria 84
phonetic changes 88–91, 117, 197, 199, 200–203, 205–207, 209, 211, 213, 218, 240
phonetic
- diphthong XVI, XXII, 29, 203
- consonants 13, 29, 89, 167, 204–206, 210f.
- phoneme inventory 200, 203, 204, 221, 281
- spelling XIV, XV, 5, 29, 30, 35, 38, 39, 64, 81, 89, 167, 201, 203, 205, 207, 208, 209, 211f. 214, 220f., 270, 281
phraseology 247
poetic expression 182, 246, 249f., 282
Pompeii 205, 207, 218
prayer 66, 84f., 97–99, 106, 232, 280, 299
- *flere* 146
- *orare* 88, 97, 98 Fn. 24, 99, 107, 140, 157, 280
- *rogare* 97, 98, 178 Fn. 232
- *obsecratio* 93, 98–99, 107, 109
- *praecari* 98, 204
- *postulaui* 99, 115, 154
- *plorare* 146
- asking (for help) 66, 99, 280
- request 66, 85, 97, 99, 280
- plea-request 280, 299
- prayer instruction 85
present tense 42, 67, 75, 118, 133, 137f., 140, 168, 175, 179f., 186, 220, 221, 241–244, 246, 251
Priscian (grammarian) 199, 236
pronominal 167, 232, 235, 238

Quintilian 206, 218, 219 Fn. 76, 256
quire signature 12

reflexive constructions 184, 220, 234–237
religious groups
- Pharisees 127, 147, 235
- scribes 147
- crowd 66 Fn. 5

satan 120, 124, 127–129, 132, 155, 198
scribe 10, 24, 27, 29 Fn. 14, 31, 35 Fn. 22, 36, 38, 40, 42, 65, 66 Fn. 5, 75f., 81, 92, 101, 132, 141, 147f., 171, 175f., 181f., 190, 194, 211–213, 217, 230, 235, 258, 274, 282
science of translation, *see translation*
scribal error 11, 12, 24, 31, 40, 75, 175, 202
Scilitan Martyrs 195
semantics 88, 93, 107, 142, 164, 170, 188, 245, 247, 249, 251, 253, 255, 257, 259, 261, 263, 265, 267, 273, 277, 279
semantic extension 273, 275
semiticism 270
signature 12
social history 127 Fn. 74, 197, 199, 200, 281
- class 200, 211
- prestige 214
- reality 281
Sondersprache, see translation
Soranus of Ephesus 176 Fn. 126
Strabo 84
superlative 141, 280
syntax 5, 67, 68, 78, 79, 88, 90, 91, 108, 130, 134, 166, 182, 184, 190, 224–244
- cases 5, 117, 165, 181, 196, 200, 225, 227, 232, 233, 234, 239, 240
- Classical Latin syntax 67, 88, 108, 130, 184, 190, 227, 235, 238
- conflation of Syntax 166, 182, 184
- Greek Syntax 67, 68, 78,79, 181, 227, 239, 243
- morphosyntax 235, 236

– pronouns 13, 35, 50, 78, 79, 80, 90–92, 118, 125, 130, 132, 133, 149, 166, 182, 183, 184, 185, 205, 216, 217, 225, 229–239, 245
– verbal 241–244

Tacitus 88 Fn. 62, 237 Fn. 135, 263 Fn. 199
Tertullian 4, 67, 72, 92, 101, 134, 141, 141 Fn. 101, 169, 170, 189, 195 Fn. 1; 2, 238, 253, 254, 256, 258, 274, 279
text type XXIII, 146, 176, 218, 232, 233
– Afra XVI, XVII, 4f., 34, 50, 87, 92, 100, 107, 129, 134, 163, 194, 196
– European XIV, XVI–XVIII, XXI–XXIII, 4, 5, 50, 71, 87, 88, 94, 95, 100, 123, 126, 130, 148, 163, 164, 193, 196, 280
– Europeanisation 5, 181, 196
– Itala 4, 5, 34, 35, 36, 37, 43, 50, 71, 197
– Italian XV, XVIII, XIX, XX, XXI, XXII, 4, 5, 71, 87, 88, 108, 163, 176, 193
textual variant 5, 34, 37, 92, 126, 129, 134, 146, 148 Fn. 110, 271
titles
– running title 11, 29
– *capitula*, *see paleography*
translation
– Early Latin XX, 5, 107, 118, 122, 133, 198
– Late Latin 87, 89, 90, 91, 106, 107, 146, 149, 176, 183, 194, 197, 198, 199, 200, 201, 212, 215, 219, 225, 240, 241, 281
– Christian Latin 88, 198
– Classical Latin 43, 44, 87, 88, 90, 92, 98, 107, 130, 132, 133, 135, 141, 144, 146, 149, 176, 181, 182, 183, 184, 194, 197, 198, 199, 200, 201, 203, 204, 205, 209, 210, 212, 214, 215, 216, 217, 219, 220, 222, 224, 226, 227, 229, 230, 231, 232, 233, 234, 236, 238, 239, 240, 243, 244, 246, 250, 251, 254, 257, 269, 280, 282
– Pre-classical Latin 218
– Post-classical Latin 132, 281, 282, 283
– Silver Latin 281
– Special Christian language 197, 198
– Special readings XIII, XIV, XVI, XX, XXIII, 1, 106, 275, 278
– Vulgar Latin 118, 138, 148, 184, 186, 198, 199, 200, 201, 207, 212, 214
Trimalchio 215

variant readings 68, 82, 212, 226, 228, 231, 235, 243, 245, 246, 261, 276
Victor of Papua XIII
voiceless sound (*Sonorisierung*) 204, 205, 210, 212
Vulgar Latin, *see translation*
Vulgate XIII, XIV, XV, XVIII, XIX, XX, XXI, XXII, XXIV, 5, 23, 28, 33, 37, 43, 45, 70, 75, 81 Fn. 46, 82, 83, 87, 88, 92, 98, 104, 119, 123, 126, 130, 134, 144, 146, 163, 175, 179, 182, 190, 194, 196, 206, 212 Fn. 54, 227, 228, 229, 234, 237, 239, 242, 244, 249, 253 Fn. 186, 262, 270, 276, 278 Fn. 232, 279

underlying Greek text 63, 77, 78, 80, 260

Zoroastrism 84

Index Verborum Latinorum

abnegare 76
abolsus 38, 202, 205, 482
Abraham 213
accipes 58, 221f.
acrus 215
ad purgandam 245
adclaudere 208
addi 36
adferre 208, 269 Fn. 215, 302
adficere 208
adhorare 98
adnuntiare 53, 88, 94, 94 Fn. 13, 110, 114, 153, 208, 286, 294
adprehendere 139, 156, 167, 178, 188, 192, 209, 286
adpropinquare 59, 110, 155, 186, 188, 193, 209, 290, 293, 304
adstare 209, 284, 291, 297
adsumere 57, 209, 284, 296
aduersus 132, 290, 293, 390
adulterare 242, 246, 294
aedificabam 12, 262, 291
aegros 268, 284, 288
alis alium 236, 238
alium 45f., 54, 154, 238, 245, 294
alius 114, 161, 236, 238, 245
altarium 264–266, 298
alter 236
alteruter alterum 237
alterutrum 237f., 245, 284, 286, 304–305
amare 187, 189, 191, 220, 235f.
amicos 79, 156, 360
amplexus 249, 282
amplior 77, 364
ampora 210
apotheca 210
apparere 135, 208
aput 114, 206, 294
arbor 79, 299, 300
arefrigescere 255, 259, 282
arida 130, 155, 351
armaturam 124, 155, 270
atrium 290
attendite et uidete 242
audire 139, 149, 156f., 168–169, 177–178, 295
aula 290
auricula 214
austeris 57, 216

baeatus 40f., 53, 204, 364
baetus 204, 282
balneus 215
baptizare 5, 198, 215, 520
batus 270
beatus 41, 53, 118 Fn. 63, 204, 246, 282
bedsaida 63, 154, 558
benedicere aliquem 227
benenuntiare 88, 94, 114
bentilabrum 205
blaspemantes 89–90, 116, 613

caelum 203, 215, 222, 282, 299
caelus 215
capud 206
cathedras 262
cedere 82
celum 204, 282
cena 60, 151, 270
certamini 119
cessare 244
circumfulgere 135
circumire 242
circumspiciens 52, 139, 143, 151
ciuitates 39, 53, 121, 202, 271, 272
clausum 186, 187, 190
cognoscere 146
colligere 5, 121, 155, 290
columbam 219
comminuere 209
committere 149, 209, 291
commotus 143–144, 154
*communda*re 120, 124, 155, 209, 290
computare 209
concarpere 269, 282, 289
confirmare 242
confundere 147–149, 155, 289
congregare 5, 198, 574
conlaudare 209, 277, 297

https://doi.org/10.1515/9783111142531-012

conligare 55, 154, 209
conlocare 209, 283
conloqui 209, 287
conparere 209, 293
conplere 134 Fn. 88, 153, 209, 216
conplures 209, 287
conprimere 209
consessus 58, 262, 291, 298
contristatus 114, 143–144, 148, 158
conuersus 109, 164, 178
conuerticulum 262
conuiuium 113, 151, 270
copiosus 170
corus 270
creatura 248
cruciatus 246, 294
curare 102, 107, 288

daemone 69, 288, 290, 546–547
daemoniosus 126–127
data bona 33, 120
decor 179
delera 60, 175, 250, 304
denarius 270
deprecatio 98
diabulo 202
dicentes 39, 53, 140, 160, 201, 340
diligere 68, 187, 189, 191, 243
discarpere 269
discedere 82, 527
discens 95–96, 114, 246, 357
discipulus 95–96, 246, 428
disferre 208
disponsatam 201
dissipare 269
diuersiorium 275
dixerunt XX, 51, 53, 114, 202–203, 289, 296
DM̄E 13, 21
DM̄I 13, 21
DM̄S 13, 21
DŌM 13, 21
doctors legis 246
domum 74f., 111, 190f., 217, 236, 241, 290, 311
drachmas 270

edere 43, 246, 283, 285
eicere 129, 358
elaborate 119
elemosina 209
elemosyna 209
elisabel 172, 177, 213
elisabet 164, 171–174, 176, 177, 194, 213
epistylia 262
epulum 151, 270
Erodes 213
erubescere 147–148, 155
esse XVI, 59f., 223f., 284
euangelizare 93–94, 107, 114, 198, 215
euge 246, 282, 296
ex uestrum 241
ex(s)truere 263
exhortare 207
exortatio 107, 277, 283, 324
expellere 129, 598
expropari 206
expectare 243
extructus 262–263, 263 Fn. 199, 298

faciant 42, 52, 331
faciens 118, 119, 242, 244
factum 30, 54
facultates XVI, 155, 271, 274–275, 290–291, 293–294, 298
farina 118, 419
fatus 215
febre magna 102–104, 109
felix 204, 246
fideles 181, 192
fili XXII, 36, 57–58,156, 166, 177, 218–219, 244
filii 156, 218–219, 244
flere 146
formido 250, 253f., 299
fornicaria/-us 104–105, 113
fructus 248
fulgere 135
fulgul 29, 57, 588

gazophilacium 210, 262, 298

gens 68, 290
glorificare 155, 161, 276

Habraham 56, 208, 213
hallec 207

harena 89, 207, 538
Herodes 213
hiericho 106–107, 114, 454
hierosolymis 46–47, 55, 118, 297, 573, 596
holus 89, 112, 207
honeratis 89–90, 112, 208, 407
honorare 151–152, 155, 161, 255, 276–277, 284, 295–296
hospitium 275
hostiae 89
hyperbatorum amfractus 179, 180 Fn. 135

iericho 106f., 114
in superrando 245
incipere 134, 242
incolumis 250, 293
inextinctibilis 249
infans 158, 246
inmundus 52, 164, 167, 177, 208 Fn. 47, 209, 267, 286
inpendia 209, 271, 293
inpleti 41, 51, 151, 283, 323
inportabilis 209, 255-256, 282
inpossibilis 209, 295
inridere 56, 209, 303
intenebricatus 250, 303
interficere 252
interrogare 11 Fn. 13, 53, 54, 60, 69, 76, 184–185, 187, 190, 288
intrate 119
inuenibant 222
inuicem 236
inumbrare 182
ioannes 212
iohanen 58, 167, 177
iohannen 10, 51, 77, 167, 177, 184, 191
isac 212–213
isdrahel 134 Fn. 88, 167, 169, 178, 190, 212
israel 212, 244
israhel 102, 167, 169, 178, 190, 212, 244
istrahel 134 Fn. 88, 167, 169, 178, 190, 212, 283
iugulare 250–253, 297
iugulum 252
iustificationis 51, 216
iustus 113, 164–165, 178, 195, 298

labare 205
lebra 206
lectulo 271, 285
lepra 206
libet 202
lignari 218
locrari 38, 54, 80, 136, 148, 154, 202, 553
locutus 128, 226, 302
lubet 202
lucrare 136

macdalene 11 Fn. 14, 53 Fn. 45, 175, 287
machina 210
maeror 250, 300
magdalene 173, 176, 287, 304
magister 80, 94, 110, 142–143, 148, 151, 153, 157, 286
magnificare 151–152, 155, 161, 276f., 284, 289, 295
maior 77, 229, 294, 364
malus 5, 94, 110, 246, 277, 285
manducare 36f., 43, 113, 187, 191, 246
manus 249
maria 164, 172–177, 194, 304
mater 228
mendicare 148, 157
mereor 104
meretricibus 104, 113
misericordia 144, 154
misertus 143–144, 148, 154
monimentum 202
monumentum 202
morbus 102
mors 235
mortuus 140, 148, 152, 215
mulier 76–77, 173, 187–188, 191, 228
multus 170
mundus 136, 154
municipium 271f., 285
mutus 127f.
mysterium 73 Fn. 31, 75, 371, 544

nauicula 52, 63, 110, 153, 183, 214, 241, 284–285
nazaret 69, 82, 108, 212–213, 283–284, 336
nocere aliquem 227
Nonne 30, 55
nurus 215

oblibio 205
obscuratus 250
obsecratio 98f., 107, 109
obseruantes 82, 298, 575
occidere 252
offerre 127, 279 Fn. 244
ommutescere 209
operiet 222, 287
oportere 137, 139, 148, 155, 295
oraculum 262
oratio 88, 93, 97–99, 107, 109, 236 Fn. 131
ornatum 263
Osculum 30, 53, 368

palleum 188, 191, 201
parabola 150–153, 159, 245, 276, 282
paruolus 38, 202
pasche 51, 204
pater sancte 280–281
pauimentare 255, 257f., 282, 297
pauimentum 257
paupercula 214
pauperes 39, 52, 201, 425, 540
peccator 56, 73, 113, 142, 151, 166, 177, 214
peccatrix 214
peiora priorum 228
per illa parte 241, 296
percutetere 60, 222
perdere 80–81, 136, 148, 154, 184, 191
periclitabantur 44, 54, 546
periculari 44
peristylum 257 Fn. 191
peritus 246
persona 89, 115, 600
phasca 210
phascha 210
pinna templi 266
plebs 93, 100–101, 108, 509
plorare 146
plus omnium 228
pomari 218
pontifex 114, 278–279, 299
populus 68, 93, 100f., 100 Fn. 28, 108, 284, 302, 304, 332
porrigit 33, 138, 148
poterint XXII, 55, 59, 121, 223, 298
potestatem remittendi 245
praeceptor 93, 110, 142, 151, 153, 157
praedictus 231
praefatio XVIII, 179–180
praesepio 216
praessura 5, 299, 605
priusquam 141, 149, 187, 191, 301
profeta 76, 167, 171, 178, 210
profetis 89, 110, 358, 535, 552
profetizare 210
puer meum 217
pugillares 201
purgare 107, 245, 268, 28
purgation 107, 268, 285
purgatus 268, 284

quactiliari 218
quia 93, 109–113, 116, 120, 122, 133f., 141–142, 149, 151–153, 156–159, 161, 166f., 178, 183, 187, 191–193, 289, 291–297, 302, 305
quoniam 5, 35, 76, 93, 109–116, 120, 122, 133f., 141, 149, 151–154, 156–162, 166–167, 178, 183, 191–193, 290
quot 205

recipient 222, 287
reddere 54, 139, 150, 178, 256, 279 Fn. 244
refectio 272, 275f., 300
reliquid 89, 104, 111, 284, 400
requiescere 169–170, 178, 303
respicere 247
respondere 58, 67, 80, 125, 128–130, 160–161, 186–187, 192–193, 222, 226, 291, 299
resurgere 222
retia 151, 216, 282, 285
rogare 97f., 98 Fn. 26, 278 Fn. 232
rumpet 221

sabbatum 113

sacerdos 114, 278–279, 283
samaritanus 47–48, 56, 94, 101, 114, 398, 560
samarites 29, 48, 46, 94, 101f., 114
sanctus XVIII, 141, 280
sapientia 107, 223, 283, 327
satum 270
saturare 202
scandalizare 187, 191, 215

scitis 33, 124, 155
scribtus 206
secedere 82
sermon 133, 154, 161, 243, 258, 285
set nullus 25
siloa 167–168, 178
similitudo 150–152, 159, 246, 276, 282
simphonia 210
sinagoga 210
socrus 215
sola 112
sperare 162
spiritum bonum XIV, 83, 86, 120
spiritus 24, Fn. 6, 80, 141, 164, 216, 271 Fn. 218, 289
spiritus malus 289
sps *24 Fn. 6*
super 120, 124, 132, 141f., 144, 149–152, 155–158, 160, 166, 178, 263, 266, 284, 290–291, 293, 295, 298, 302–303
supradictus 231
suptus 54, 207
surdus 127–128

tanto melior 246, 282, 297
teloneum 270
temptatio 19, 54, 166, 177, 266
tenebrae 26, 55, 59, 255, 260–261, 310
tertia 118, 192, 289
theloneum 210
thensaurus 53, 211
tingere 5
tollet 222
tormentum 246, 295
tribulatio 5
tristitia 249–250, 282
tunica 151, 188, 191, 285
turba 100 Fn. 28, 111, 121, 142, 153, 155, 158, 161, 184, 191, 284, 302
turbo 65, 250, 287

uaso 43, 54, 216, 372
uasus 43
uenire 81, 109, 113, 139, 157, 164, 290, 295
uerbum 83, 133, 154, 216, 246, 285
uero XV, 98, 114, 158, 160f., 167, 178, 211 Fn. 53, 243, 301–302
uestibulum 262
uestimentum 188, 191, 250 Fn. 79, 285
uethleem 205
uibes 89, 111, 205, 397, 560
uidere 135, 146, 247
uidere coepit 247
uinea 248
uir 74, 141, 151, 153, 164, 167, 171, 176, 178, 218
uirtus 74, 76
uitium 103, 230
uitulus 214
uiuens 244, 294
ulna 249, 250, 283
umor 207
uniuersum 136, 154
uulnera 102, 114, 398

ypocrita 207